P9-DDB-255

WARMAN'S
Americana
& Collectibles

4TH EDITION

Edited by HARRY L. RINKER

A Price Guide Devoted to Today's
Collectibles, with Collecting Hints •
Histories • References • Clubs •
Museums • Completely Illustrated

Wallace-Homestead Book Company
Radnor, Pennsylvania

Copyright © 1990 by Wallace-Homestead Book Company,
Radnor, Pennsylvania 19089

All Rights Reserved
No portion of this book may be reproduced by any means—electronic, mechanical or
photographic—nor stored in an electronic storage and retrieval system, without prior
written permission from the publisher. Writers and reviewers may excerpt short portions
without written permission. All listings and prices have been checked for accuracy but
the publisher cannot be responsible for any errors that may have occurred.

ISBN: 0-87069-557-6
ISSN: 0739-6457
Library of Congress Catalog Card No.: 84-643834
Manufactured in the United States of America

2 3 4 5 6 7 8 9 0   9 8 7 6 5 4 3 2 1 0

Additional copies of this book may be obtained from your bookstore or directly from
the publisher, Wallace-Homestead Book Company, Radnor, PA 19089. Enclose $14.95
plus $2.00 for postage and handling for the 1st book, 50¢ for each additional book.
Pennsylvania residents please add 90¢ state sales tax per book.

EDITORIAL STAFF

HARRY L. RINKER
Editor

ELLEN L. SCHROY
Senior Editor

TERESE J. OSWALD
Associate Editor

**LOIS W. ANASTAS
JOCELYN C. BUTTERER**
Assistants

BOARD OF ADVISORS

Franklin Arnall
The Collector
P. O. Box 253
Claremont, CA 91711
(714) 621-2461
  Padlocks

Dick Bitterman
1701 West Chase Ave.
Chicago, IL 60626
(312) 743-3330
  Flag Collectibles; Pens and Pencils; Pin-Up Art; World War II Collectibles

Stanley A. Block
P. O. Box 222
Trumball, CT 06611
(203) 261-3223
  Marbles

Rick Botts
2545 SE 60th Ct.
Des Moines, IA 50317
(515) 265-8324
  Jukeboxes

Paul and Paula Brenner
1215 Grand Ave.
Spencer, IA 51301
(712) 262-4113
  Napkin Rings, Figural

Lissa L. Bryan-Smith and Richard M. Smith
Holiday Antiques
Box 208, R. D. 1
Danville, PA 17821
(717) 275-7796
  Christmas Items; Holiday Collectibles; Santa Claus

Jocelyn C. Butterer
137 South Main St.
Quakertown, PA 18951
(215) 536-9211
  Dog Collectibles

Lorie Cairns
Cairns Antiques
P. O. Box 445
Woodlake, CA 93286
(209) 564-2158
  Labels

Bob Cereghino
3E Torlina Ct.
Baltimore, MD 21207
(301) 944-7075
  Games; Lunch Boxes

Kathie Diehl
P. O. Box 5672
Baltimore, MD 21210
(301) 243-3747
  Little Golden Books

Craig Dinner
P. O. Box 455
Valley Stream, NY 11582
(516) 825-0145
  Figural, Bottle Openers

Marilyn Dipboye
31311 Blair Dr.
Warren, MI 48092
(313) 264-0285
  Cat Collectibles

Harvey Duke
115 Montague St.
Brooklyn, NY 11201
(718) 625-3536
  Autumn Leaf; Hall China

John Fetterman
Box 265, R. D. #1
Elysburg, PA 17824
(717) 672-3176
  Pinball Machines

Doug Flynn and Al Bolton
Holloway House
P. O. Box 210
Lititz, PA 17543
(717) 627-4567
  British Royalty Commemoratives

M. D. Fountain
201 Alvena
Wichita, KS 67203
(316) 943-1925
  Swankyswigs

Tom Gallagher, II
4 Ox Box Rd.
Westport, CT 06880
(203) 227-5244
Dairy Items; Milk Bottles

Roselyn Gerson
12 Alnwick Rd
Malverne, NY 11565
Compacts

Bob Greenbaum
Box 623
Beverly Hil Rd.
Coopersburg, PA 18036
(215) 282-4881
Fishing Collectibles

Ted Hake
Hake's Americana & Collecti-
bles
P. O. Box 1444
York, PA 17405
(717) 848-1333
Disneyana, Political Items

Doris & Burdell Hall
B & B Antiques
P. O. Box 1501
Fairfield Bay, AR 72088
(501) 884-6571
Morton Potteries

Mrs. Mary Hamburg
20 Cedar St.
Danville, IL 61832
(217) 446-2323
Pig Collectibles

Lois Holman
309 Walnut Lane
Branson, MO 65616
(417) 334-3273
Rose O'Neill

Tim Hughes
Hughes'
2410 North Hills Dr.
Williamsport, PA 17701
(717) 326-1045
*Newspapers, Headline Edi-
tions*

Joan Hull
1376 Nevada
Huron, SD 57350
(605) 352-1685
Hull Pottery

Abby Irons
Irons Antiques
R. D. #4, Box 101
Northampton, PA 18067
(215) 262-9335
Indian Souvenir Beadwork

David and Sue Irons
Irons Antiques
R. D. #4, Box 101
Northampton, PA 18067
(215) 262-9335
Irons

Judy Knauer
1224 Spring Valley Lane
West Chester, PA 19380
(215) 431-3477
Toothpicks

Tony Knipp
Horton Road
P. O. Box 105
Blooming Grove, NY 10914
Dairy Items; Milk Bottles

Ron Lieberman
The Family Album
R. D. #1, Box 42
Glen Rock, PA 17327
(717) 235-2134
*Books, Antiques and Collec-
tibles*

Elyce Litts
P. O. Box 394
Morris Plains, NJ 07950
(201) 361-4087
Geisha Girl

Wray Martin
221 Upper Paradise
Hamilton, Ontario
Canada, L9C 5C1
(416) 383-0454
Matchcovers

Richard W. Massiglia
380 Medford St.
Somerville, MA 02145
(617) 625-4067
Elephant Collectibles

Nancy McMichael
2205 California St., N. W.
Washington, D. C., 20008
(202) 234-7484
Snowdomes

Gary L. Miller and K. M. Scotty
Mitchell
Millchell
2112 Lipscomb
Ft. Worth, TX 76110
(817) 923-3274
Electrical Appliances

Michael R. Moyer
324 North 16th St.
Allentown, PA 18102
(215) 434-0892
Football Cards

Joseph Murdoch
Golf Collector's Society
638 Wagner Rd.
Lafayette Hill, PA 19444
(215) 828-4492
Golf Collectibles

Susan Brown Nicholson
P. O. Box 595
Lislie, IL 60532
(312) 964-5240
*Magazines; Magazine Cov-
ers and Tear Sheets; Post
Cards*

Joan Collett Oates
5912 Kingsfield Dr.
W. Bloomfield, MI 48322
(313) 661-2335
Phoenix Bird Pattern

Clark Phelps
Amusement Sales
127 North Main
Midvale, UT 84047
(801) 255-4731
Punchboards

Lois Pool
The National Button Society
2733 Juno Place
Akron, OH 44313
(216) 533-9186
  Buttons

Frank N. Potter
Route 375, Box 164
Woodstock, NY 12498
(914) 679-5596
  Moxie

Ken Prag
Grand Central Station Antiques
1676 Market St.
San Francisco, CA 94102
(415) 566-6400
  Stocks and Bond Certificates

Evalene Pulati
National Valentine Collectors
Association
P. O. Box 1404
Santa Ana, CA 92702
  Valentines

Jim and Nancy Schaut
Box 4764 New River Stage II
Phoenix, AZ 85027
(602) 465-9610
  Horse Collectibles

Virginia R. Scott
275 Milledge Terrace
Athens, GA 30606
(404) 548-5966
  Candlewick

Jack Seiderman
1050 N. E. 120 St.
Miami, FL 33161
(305) 893-6847
  Cigarette Lighters

John Selsam
R. D. #1, Box 240A
Lewisburg, PA 17837
(717) 326-1921
  Baseball Collectibles

Henry and Doris Sigourney
Sigourney's Antiques
P. O. Box 447
Cavendish, VT 05142
(802) 226-7713
  Golliwogs and Dutch Dolls

The Stevensons
316 Sage Lane
Euless, TX 76039
(817) 354-8903
  Scouting

David Stone
"For Here Or To Go"
5000 "Y"
Sacramento, CA 95817
(916) 451-0243
  Fast Food Collectibles

Mark Supnick
8524 NW 2nd St.
Coral Springs, FL 33071
(305) 755-3449
  Shawnee Pottery

George Theofiles
Miscellaneous Man
Box 1776
New Freedom, PA. 17349
(717) 235-4766
  Posters

Greg Tunks
150 Hohldale
Houston, TX 77022
(713) 691-1387
  Credit Coins and Cards

Margaret L. Tyrell
117 North 40th St.
Allentown, PA 18104
(215) 395-9364
  Children's Books

John Waldsmith
Antique Graphics
P. O. Box 191
Sycamore, OH 44882
(419) 927-2930
  Stereo   Viewers;   Stereographs; Viewmasters

Fred L. Wilhelm
828 Hermes Ave.
Leucadia, CA 92024
(619) 753-8264
  Soldiers, Dimestore

Anne D. Williams
49 Brooks Ave.
Lewiston, ME 04240
(207) 783-8732
  Puzzles

Kathy Wojciechowski
P. O. Box 230
Peotone, IL 60468
  Nippon

Estelle Zalkin
7524 West Treasure Dr.
Miami Beach, FL 33141
(305) 864-3012
  Thimbles

INTRODUCTION

Collectibles are fun because they are the things with which your grandparents, your parents, and you have played and lived. This book is a nostalgic trip down memory lane. You may be angry about the things you or your parents discarded and thrilled by the value of the things that were saved. Most important, this book reaffirms the joy of collecting because it clearly demonstrates that it is acceptable to collect anything you wish. Finally, remember one simple fact. All of today's antiques were collectibles in the past.

WHAT IS A COLLECTIBLE?

Of the several books in the collectibles field, none offers a strong definition of the word, "collectible." The result is confusion, blurring the distinction between antiques and collectibles.

For the purpose of this book, four criteria were established to define the word "collectible." The item must have been (1) mass produced and (2) made in the twentieth century. The majority of the items in each category (3) must sell between a few pennies and two hundred dollars, and (4) they must have been made in America or collected heavily in America. The ideal collectible should fit all four qualifications. But if an item fits two of the four, we considered it a collectible.

There is a fifth factor: attitude. I collect things relating to the American canal movement. As a result, I own a number of pieces of dark blue English Staffordshire which were made when the Erie Canal was completed in the mid-1820s. Staffordshire of this type is considered a blue chip antique, but I collect it primarily for its "canal related" value. Does this make it a collectible rather than an antique? In my eyes and mind it does.

Since collecting antiques became fashionable in the early twentieth century, there have been attempts to define certain groups of objects as "true" antiques, worthy of sophisticated collectors, and to ignore the remaining items. Most museums clearly demonstrate this attitude. Where do early twentieth century tin toys, toy soldiers, or dolls fit? We designate them as "prestige" collectibles, objects making the transition in people's minds from collectible to antique.

In reality these divisions are artificial and deserve to be broken down. Today's Star Wars items, if properly preserved, will someday be over one hundred years old. They may be a much better key to interpreting life in the twentieth century than the Knoll furniture now found on pedestals in leading museums in the United States.

Collectors of the categories found in this book deserve credit for their attention to scholarship and skill by which they have assembled their collections. This book attests to how strong and encompassing the collectibles market has become through their efforts.

PRICE NOTES

Prices in the collectibles field are not as firmly established as in the antiques area. Nevertheless, we do not use ranges unless we feel they were absolutely necessary.

Our pricing is based on an object being in very good condition. If otherwise, we note this in our description. It would be ideal to suggest that mint, or unused, examples of all objects do exist. Objects from the past were used, whether they be glass, china, dolls, or toys. Because of this use, some normal wear must be expected. Furthermore, if the original box is important in establishing a price, it is assumed that the box is present with the article.

The biggest problem in the collectibles field is that an object may have more than one price. A George Eastman bubble gum card may be worth one dollar to a bubble gum card collector, but thirty-five dollars to a collector of photographic memorabilia. I saw the same card marked both ways. In preparing prices for this guide we have looked at the object within the category being considered. Hence, a "girly" matchcover sells for twenty-five to fifty cents to a matchcover collector and two to five dollars to a pin-up art collector. However, if all you can find are matchcover collectors, you'd best take the quarter and move on.

Some collectibles do have regional interest. However, a national price consensus is slowly forming through publication of specialized price guides, collectors' club newsletters, and magazines and newspapers. This guide also has contributed to breaking down regional pricing.

ORGANIZATION OF THE BOOK

Listings: We have attempted to make the listings descriptive enough so the specific object can be identified. Most guides limit their descriptions to one line, but not *Warman's*. We have placed emphasis on those items which are being sold actively in the marketplace. Nevertheless, some harder-to-find objects are included in order to demonstrate the market spread. A few categories in this book also appear in *Warman's Antiques and Their Prices*. The individual listings, however, seldom overlap except for a few minor instances. It is our intention to show the low to middle price range of a category in *Warman's Americana & Collectibles*, and the middle to upper range in our main antiques guide, thus creating two true companion volumes for the general dealer or collector.

Collecting Hints: This section calls attention to specific hints as they relate to the category. We note where cross category collecting and nostalgia are critical in pricing. Clues are given to spotting reproductions. In most cases, we just scratch the surface. We encourage collectors to consult specialized publications.

History: Here we discuss the category, describe how the object was made, who are or were the leading manufacturers, and the variations of form and style. In many instances a chronology for the objects is established. Finally, we place the object in a social context— how it was used, for what purposes, etc.

References: A few general references are listed to encourage collectors to learn more about their objects. Included are author, title, most recent edition, publisher (if published by a small firm or individual, we have indicated "published by author"), and a date of publication.

Finding these books may present a problem. The antiques and collectibles field is blessed with a dedicated core of book dealers who stock these specialized publications. You may find them at flea markets, antiques shows, and through their advertisements in leading publications in the field. Many dealers publish annual or semi-annual catalogs. Ask to be put on their mailing lists. Books go out-of-print quickly, yet many books printed over twenty-five years ago remain the standard work in their field. Also, haunt used-book dealers for collectibles reference material.

Collectors' Clubs: The large number of collectors' clubs adds vitality to the collectibles field. Their publications and conventions produce knowledge which often cannot be found anywhere else. Many of these clubs are short lived; others are so strong that they have regional and local chapters.

Periodicals: In respect to the collectibles field, there are certain general monthly periodicals to which the general collector should subscribe:

Antiques & Collecting Hobbies, 1006 South Michigan Avenue, Chicago, IL 60605.

Collectors' Showcase, P.O. Box 6929, San Diego, CA 92106.

There are also a number of specialized collectibles periodicals, e.g., *Antique Toy World* (P. O. Box 34509, Chicago, IL 60634). Special attention is directed toward the publications of Krause Publications, Inc., (700 East State Street, Iola, WI 54945).

Although no weekly publication is devoted exclusively to collectibles, *The Antique Trader Weekly* (Box 1050, Dubuque, IA 52001) and *Antique Week* (P. O. Box 90, Knightstown, IN 46148) extensively cover the range of items listed in this book. Specialized auctions of prestige collectibles are regularly reported in depth in the *Maine Antique Digest* (Box 358, Waldoboro, ME 04572).

Museums: The best way to study a specific field is to see as many documented examples as possible. For this reason, we have listed museums where significant collections of collectibles are on display. Special attention must be directed to the Margaret Woodbury Strong Museum in Rochester, New York, and the Smithsonian Institution's Museum of American History in Washington, D.C.

Reproductions: Reproductions are a major concern, especially with any item related to advertising. Most reproductions are unmarked; the newness of their appearance is often the best clue to uncovering them. Where "Reproduction Alert" appears, a watchful eye should be kept within the entire category. Specific objects known to be reproduced are marked within the listings with an asterisk (*).

Reproductions are only one aspect of the problem; outright fakes are another. Unscrupulous manufacturers make fantasy items which never existed, e.g., Hopalong Cassidy guitar from the non-existent Jefferson Musical Toys.

RESEARCH

We obtain our prices from many key sources—dealers, publications, auctions, collectors, and field work. The generosity with which dealers have given advice is a credit to the field. Everyone recognizes the need for a guide that is specific and has accurate prices. We study newspapers, magazines, newsletters, and other publications in the collectibles and antiques field. All of them are critical in understanding what is available in the market. Special recognition must be given to those collectors' club newsletters and magazines which discuss prices.

Our staff is constantly in the field—from Massachusetts to Florida, Pennsylvania to California. Our Board of Advisors provides regional as well as specialized information. Over one hundred specialized auctions are held annually, and their results are provided to our office. Finally, private collectors have worked closely with us, sharing their knowledge of price trends and developments unique to their specialties.

BUYER'S GUIDE, NOT SELLER'S GUIDE

Warman's Americana & Collectibles is designed to be a buyer's guide, a guide to what you would have to pay to purchase an object on the open market from a dealer or collector. **It is not a seller's guide to prices.** People frequently make this mistake and are deceiving themselves by doing so.

If you have an object mentioned in this book and wish to sell it, you should expect to receive approximately 35% to 40% of the values listed. If the object cannot be resold quickly, expect to receive even less. The truth is simple. Knowing to whom to sell an object is worth 50% or more of its value. Buyers are very specialized; dealers work for years to assemble a list of collectors who will pay top dollar for an item.

Examine your piece as objectively as possible. If it is something from your childhood, try to step back from the personal memories in evaluating its condition. As an antiques appraiser, I spend a great deal of my time telling people their treasures are not "gold," but items readily available in the marketplace.

With respect to buying and selling, a simple philosophy is that a good purchase occurs when both the buyer and seller are happy with the price. Don't look back. Hindsight has little value in the collectibles field. Given time, things tend to balance out.

WHERE TO BUY COLLECTIBLES

The collectible has become standard auction house fare in the 1980s. Christie's (502 Park Avenue, New York, NY 10002) and Sotheby's (1334 York Avenue, New York, NY 10021) conduct collectibles sales several times each year. Specialized auction firms, e.g., Lloyd Ralston Toys (447 Stratfield Road, Fairfield, CT 06432) in toys and Greenberg's (7566 Main Street, Sykesville, MD 21784) in trains, have proven the viability of the collectible as a focal point.

The major collectibles marketing thrust continues to be the mail auction, either with material on consignment or directly owned. Hake's Americana & Collectibles (P.O. Box 1444, York, PA 17405) is the leading mail auction. Hake's is being challenged by Debby and Marty Krim's New England Auction Gallery (P. O. Box 2273, Peabody, MA 01960), Smith House Toy Sales (P. O. Box 336, Eliot, ME 03903), and a host of others.

Direct sale catalogs abound. Most major categories have one or more. These dealers and many more advertise in periodicals and collectors' clubs' newsletters. Most require an annual fee to receive their catalogs.

Of course, there is an unlimited number of flea markets, house and country auctions, church bazaars, and garage sales. However, if you are a specialized collector, you may spend days looking for something to add to your collection. If you add in your time to the cost of the object, its real cost will be much higher than the purchase price.

All of which brings us to the final source, the specialized dealer. The collectibles field is so broad that dealers do specialize. Find the dealers who handle your material and work with them to build your collection.

BOARD OF ADVISORS

Our Board of Advisors are dealers, authors, collectors and leaders of collectors' clubs throughout the United States. All are dedicated to accuracy in description and pricing. If you wish to buy or sell an object in their field of expertise, drop them a note. Please include a stamped, self-addressed envelope with all correspondence. If time or interest permits, they will respond.

We now list the names of our advisors at the end of their respective categories. Their full mailing address and often their phone numbers are in the front of this book.

COMMENTS INVITED

Warman's Americana & Collectibles is a major effort to deal with a complex field. Our readers are encouraged to send their comments and suggestions to Rinker Enterprises, P. O. Box 248, Zionsville, PA 18092.

ACKNOWLEDGMENTS

For the past eight years Stanley and Katherine Greene have provided the leadership for Warman Publishing Company, continuing a tradition of excellence that began with Edwin G. Warman over forty years ago. It is time to say goodbye and wish them well in their future endeavors.

Warman Publishing is now an imprint of Wallace-Homestead Book Company. There are exciting times ahead. The editorial staff welcomes our new owner and pledges to continue the quality and usefulness of our past publications.

Although my name appears on the front cover, this book is a product of the work of a dedicated staff, Board of Advisors, and hundreds of individuals who have shared their price lists, research data, letters, and personal observations. I also receive support and encouragement from Connie A. Moore, my wife, whose patience I continually try and whose sense of order is shattered by my many new acquisitions that add to the burden of already cluttered closets, halls, and portions of rooms in our home.

Thanks to Chris Allen, my staff is now known as the "Rinkettes." Ellen L. Schroy, Terese J. Oswald, Lois W. Anastas, and Jocelyn C. Butterer deserve as much credit for this book as I do. They are more than just staff, they are family.

Two of the critical elements in the preparation of this book are the photography and typesetting. VIP Color Lab of Bethlehem, Pennsylvania, is responsible for the high quality of the photographs used for reproduction. Ruttle, Shaw & Wetherill of Fort Washington, Pennsylvania, performed the typesetting and layout. A special thanks to Frank Righter and Bruce Nesbitt who never once told us that something could not be done the way we wanted it.

Finally, our thanks to you—our users. You demand only excellence from a Warman product. You will accept nothing less. By meeting your demands, *Warman's Americana & Collectibles* continues unchallenged as the nation's leading general price guide to twentieth century collectibles.

P. O. Box 248   Harry L. Rinker
Zionsville, PA 18092   Editor
                                                                              October 1989

ADVERTISING

Collecting Hints: Many factors affect the price of an advertising collectible - the product and its manufacturer, the objects or persons used in the advertisement, the period and aesthetics of design, the designer and illustrator of the piece, and the form the advertisement takes. Add to this the continued use of advertising material as decorative elements in bars, restaurants, and other public places. The interior decorator purchases at a very different price level than the collector.

In truth, almost every advertising item is sought by a specialized collector in one or more collectible areas. The result is a divergence in pricing, with the price quoted to an advertising collector usually lower than that quoted to a specialized collector.

Most collectors seem to concentrate on the period prior to 1940, with special emphasis on the decades from 1880 to 1910. New collectors should examine the advertising material from the post-1940 period. Much of this material still is very inexpensive and likely to rise in value as the decorator trends associated with the 1950s through the 1970s gain in importance.

History: The earliest advertising in America is found in colonial newspapers and printed broadsides. By the mid-19th century manufacturers began to examine how a product was packaged. The box could convey a message and help identify and sell more of the product. The advent of the high speed, lithograph printing press led to regional and national magazines, resulting in new advertising markets. The lithograph press also brought the element of vivid colors into the advertising spectrum.

Simultaneously the general store branched out into specialized departments or individual stores. By 1880 advertising premiums, such as mirrors, paperweights, trade cards, etc., arrived on the scene. Premiums remained popular through the early 1960s, especially with children.

Advertising continues to respond to changing opportunities and times. The advertising character developed in the early 1900s. By the 1950s the star endorser was established firmly as an advertising vehicle. Advertising became a big business as specialized firms, many headquartered in New York City, developed to meet manufacturers' needs.

References: Kit Barry, *The Advertising Trade Card: Information And Prices, Book I*, privately printed, 1981; Al Bergevin, *Food Drink Containers And Their Prices*, Wallace-Homestead, 1978; Jim Cope, *Old Advertising*, Great American Publishing Co., 1980; M. J. Franklin, *British Biscuit Tins 1868-1939: An Aspect of Decorative Packaging*, Schiffer Publishing, 1979; Robert Joy, *The Trade Card In Nineteenth-Century American*, University of Missouri Press, 1987; Ray Klug,

Antique Advertising Encyclopedia, Schiffer Publishing, Ltd, 1978, updated price guide; Ray Klug, *Antique Advertising Encyclopedia, First Edition*, , Schiffer Publishing, Ltd, 1985; Ralph and Terry Kovel, *Kovels' Advertising Collectibles Price List*, Crown Publishers, Inc., 1986; Murray Card (International) Ltd, *Cigarette Card Values: Murray's 1988 Guide to Cigarette & Other Trade Cards* published by authors, 1988; Joleen Robison and Kay Sellers, *Advertising Dolls: Identification and Value Guide*, Collector Books, 1980; Robert W. and Harriet Swedberg, *Vintage Advertising Series, Tins' N' Bins*, Wallace-Homestead, 1985.

Collectors' Clubs: The Ephemera Society of America, P. O. Box 224, Ravena, NY 12143; Tin Container Collectors Association, P. O. Box 440101, Aurora, CA 80014. *Tin Type* (monthly).

Periodical: National Association of Paper and Advertising Collectibles, P. O. Box 500, Mt Joye, PA 17552, *P.A.C.*, monthly newspaper.

REPRODUCTION ALERT

ASHTRAY

Alabama Marble & Tile Co.	23.00
Ames Heating Pumps, metal, figural pump	10.00
Baker's Cocoa	85.00
Bengal Gin, ceramic, tiger	35.00
Blue Diamond Coal Co, 6", metal	15.00
CBS Hytron Tubes, 1921–52	18.00
Chesterfield, boxed	18.00
Coors Beer, ceramic	4.00
Crook Paper Box Co, Kansas City, MO, cast iron, cowboy hat shape	45.00
Dobbs Hats, glass, black amethyst, hat shape	22.00
Dr. Pepper, tin	35.00
Firestone, tire, copper	10.00
GE Transformers	18.00
Gehl Farm Equipment	75.00
General Motors, 4", brass, relief, grille design, "Who Serves Progress Serves America" and "Designed And Produced By Terstedt Div./General Motors Crop" inscription	40.00
Goodrich Tire, glass, green	45.00
Grants Scotch Whiskey, cobalt blue	10.00
Grapette Soda, milk glass	35.00
H. Fendrick Cigar Co, brass	15.00
John Deere, 3¼", galvanized metal, deer jumping over log	25.00
Levy's Jewish Rye Bread, Art Deco, milk glass, black boy eating bread	65.00
KMO Radio Station, 5 x 6½", brass, c1930	15.00
Michelin Tires, 5½" d, plastic brown, seated off-white trademark figure, England, c1950	50.00

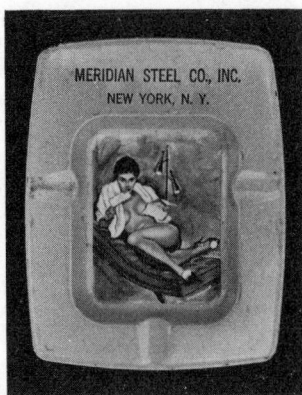

Ashtray, Meridan Steel Co. Inc., NY, pin-up girl illus, 3¾ x 4¾", $7.50.

Molson Porter Ale, enamel ware, cobalt blue	20.00
Nash Depot Stove	28.00
National Foundry, Brooklyn, NY, cast iron	24.00
Pyrene Fire Extinguisher, figural, bakelite	40.00
Rhino Flex Tires	12.00
S & S Saddlery and Co, Springfield, MO, horseshoe shape	45.00
Security National Bank, Trenton, NJ, brown glaze, c1927	15.00
Suntory Whiskey, stoneware	12.00
Truman's Ale	15.00
Twin Bears Store, 4½", chalkware, dated 1931	40.00
Universal Studios, metal, emb, cameras and crew	15.00
Walter E. Schatt Willys Distributor, Rookwood	90.00

BOXES

Argo Starch, unopened, 1930s	10.00
Armour's Washing Powder, shipping box	4.00
Baker's Chocolate, 12 lb, wooden	15.00
Bliss Native Herbs, includes contents and directions	6.00
Bossie's Best Brand Butter, pound	2.00
Boston Wafers 5¢ Candy, children and wafers	20.00
Candy's Faultless Powdered Dance Floor Wax, 3¼", cardboard	8.00
Capitol Scouring Soap, wooden	15.00
Churn Baking Soda, woman churning butter, unused, 1920s	10.00
Daylight Soap, wood	20.00
Dr. Johnson's Educator Crackers	38.00
Eagle Asbestors Stove Lining, 2¾ x 3¾", cardboard	8.00
Edgemont Crackers	12.00

Fairies Bath Perfume, unopened, 1920s	6.00
Father John's Medicine, 9¾ x 11 x 11⅜", wood	35.00
Gold Dust Twins, 5 oz, washing powder, full, 1930	12.50
Honor Bright Soap, 2½ x 3¾", cardboard	5.00
Houston's Biscuits, Auburn, ME, 10 x 21", wood, hinged	25.00
Jessop's Cough Drops	4.00

Box, Ideal Raisins, white ground, green grapes, red and black letters, 6⅛ x 3¾ x 1¾", $10.00.

Johnson & Johnson, wood, drawers, paper label	75.00
Ladies Favorite Polish, 4", paper label .	5.00
Linita Cigars, 1920	45.00
Metropolitan Life Insurance, black, wood lid	35.00
National Lead Co, paint chip sample box	15.00
Near's Stock & Poultry Mixture, 9 x 16¾", cov, wood	45.00
Old Plug Tobacco, Irvin & Leedys, Henry Country, VA, 4 x 7 x 12", walnut	20.00
Quaker Puffed Rice, 5 oz, 1919	17.50
Prat's Veterinary Clic Cure, 6", blue, red, and yellow	15.00
Regal Underwear, cardboard	15.00
Reynold's Rat Driver Poison, 3½ x 7", cardboard, c1900	5.00
Royal Baking Powder, wood, 1800s	125.00
Soapine, Kendall Mfg Co, 5 x 11½"	25.00
Stickney & Poore's Mustard, 18 x 10", green, red label	45.00
Ward Baking Co, wooden	18.00
White Swan, oatmeal, 4 oz	27.50
Whitehead & Hoag, dovetailed, 8 x 10"	28.00

BROCHURE

American Range	5.00
Bon Ami, The Chick That Never Grew Up	10.00
Burlington Railroad Route, Chicago, 1934, 18 pgs	8.00

Burma Shave, Vol. X, 44 jingles, 1942 **6.00**
Crescent Bicycles, 1899 . . . . **20.00**
Enterprising Mfg Co, IL, kitchen utensils, 1898 . . . . **30.00**
Gillispie Hydraulic Governor for Water Wheels **15.00**
Grandpa's Wonder Soap, 3 x 5" **4.00**
Hire's Merry Rhymes **12.00**
Hood's Parlor Games **12.00**
Imperial Furniture, early 1920s **5.00**
International Harvester, 3 x 5½", 1910 **15.00**
Junket's Flibbity Jibbit **8.50**
Kelvinator, 1944 . . . . **8.00**
Larkin Soap, 1885 . . . . **15.00**
Leffel's Double Turbine Water Wheel, 1881 . . . . **20.00**

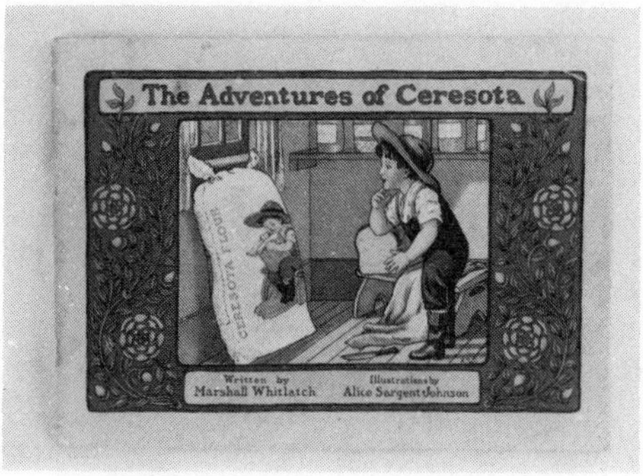

Brochure, "The Adventures of Ceresota," Marshal Whitlach, copyright 1912, Northwestern Consolidated Milling Co, 8 x 6", $20.00.

Magic Yeast, 3 x 5" **4.00**
Oldsmobile, 8 pgs, 1948 . . . . **8.00**
Parks Air College, St Louis, 64 pgs . . . **12.00**
Pasadena Tournament of Roses, 1947 . **25.00**
Philco Radio, fold out, 1936 . . . . **5.00**
Queen of Bermuda, 8 x 10", opens to poster, ship on cov, c1935 . . . . **35.00**
Smith & Wesson Revolvers **38.00**
Studebaker, 1934 . . . . **48.00**
Western Pines, Buildings, Rooms & Furnishings, 1960, 20 pgs **5.00**

BUTTONS

Ann Arbor, The Baler For Business **30.00**
Banner Lumber Co, 1¼", yellow, blue, and red, c1907–20 . . . . **15.00**
Bear Brand Hosiery, ⅞", multicolored, red rim, white lettering, bear, c1910 **18.00**
Buster Brown Hose Supporters, ⅞", multicolored, black and white rim inscription **35.00**
Ceresota Flour, 1¼", trademark figure, early 1900s **20.00**

Cinderella Rubberettes, 1", two girls, red, white, blue, black, and flesh-tones, 1930s **20.00**
Derby Refining Co Petroleum Products, celluloid, star, red, white, and blue, c1930 . . . . **8.00**
Dutch Boy Paints, ⅞" **10.00**
Famous Biscuit Co, 1¼", blue and white text, 1921 company outing in Pittsburgh **10.00**
Gilletts Lye, 1¼" **45.00**
Grain Belt Beer, 1", "I'm Friendly," 1930 **5.00**
Kar-A-Van Coffee, ⅞", camel, multicolored, red and white rim, 1901–10 . . **25.00**
Karma Biscuits, 1¼", multicolored, portrait of young lady holding bright red, white, and yellow box, Ontario Biscuit Co, c1900 . . . . **50.00**
Kis-Me Gum, ⅞", red, white, and purple, 1896–1900 . . . . **25.00**
Leby's Bros Dairy **8.00**
Liberty Flour, 1¼", multicolored, 1903 copyright **35.00**
Miller's Cocoa, ⅞", multicolored, metal button hook attachment, c1896–1900 **25.00**
Nabisco, boy wearing yellow raincoat **10.00**
Oliver Typewriter **20.00**
Peerless Biscuit Co, 1¾", black and white logo, bright red ground, light blue tulips, c1912 . . . . **20.00**
Peru Plow, 1¼", multicolored, white ground, c1900 . . . . **15.00**
Prisco Lanterns, 2" **20.00**
Racine–Sattley Co, 1¼", multicolored, huge bright red wheel pushing plowshare through clouds, gold and white rim, black lettering **48.00**
Red Cross Macaroni, 1¼", red, white, and blue "Long Mac" cartoon, 1930s **30.00**
Rex Vienna Sausage, 1", multicolored, issued Cudahy Packing and Canning Co, early 1900s **25.00**
Rouge Rex Shoes, Grand Rapids, MI, 1½" **15.00**
Samson Wind Mills **15.00**
Sherwood Spring Coaster, 1¼", multicolored, little boy and girl riding toy wagon, light green shaded ground, back paper label with text for coaster wagon made by Sherwood Bros Mfg Co, Canastota, NY, c1900 **80.00**
Studebaker, star **25.00**
Sunshine Biscuits **8.00**
The Hanover Shoe, 1¾" d, black and white illus of high button shoe, red and black inscription "Old Home Week, Harrisburg, PA, 1905" **35.00**
Van Camp's Pork & Beans **8.00**
Wiemann's Java Tea, ⅞", multicolored, container on white background, 1911–20 . . . . **20.00**
Worcester Salt, 1¼", black, white, and

Buttons, pinback, left, Chevrolet, litho tin, mfg by Geraghty & Co, ⅞″ d, $8.00; right, Winchester, Junior Rifle Corps, celluloid, ⅞″ d, $35.00.

blue, gold rim, steam engine background, 1900–12	15.00
Yum Yum Bread, 1″, multicolored, Oriental lady, simulated Oriental lettering inscription, 1911–20	40.00

MIRRORS

Adams Chiclets	52.00
American Line	35.00
Angelus Marshmallows, cherub	45.00
B & G Sandwich Shop	45.00
Beehive Overalls, woman in overalls	75.00
Better Made Ice Cream	30.00
Brotherhood Overalls, Victorian nude	60.00
Buckwheat Flour, 1⅞″, red and white paper under glass, text "For Best Cakes," metal rim, c1900	20.00
Calox Oxygen Toothpowder	20.00
Central Plumbing, Worcester	20.00
Ceresota Flour, boy	30.00
Clothiers & Hatters, 2¾″, oval, rounded, celluloid, tinted pastel tones, deep brown shading to black ground, depicts men's clothing items	40.00
Coast Fir Lumber Co, Portland, OR	28.00
Dr. Daniel's, woman and horse	75.00
Dr. Hebras Viola Cream	65.00

Mirror, Dingman Soap, red ground, white letters, printed, emb, 1⅞″ d, $30.00.

Duffy's Whiskey Makes the Weak Strong, oval	30.00
Globe A1 Flour	15.00
Grinnell Bros, Michigan's leading music house, Detroit, litho	45.00
Haines Shoe Wizard	20.00
H. L. Price & Co. Clothing	68.00
Holeproof Hosiery, Hanover	20.00
Horlick's Dairy Maid	45.00
International Shirt & Collar Co, 2¼″, celluloid, multicolored, white ground, camel wearing Shriner fez, blindfolded gentleman dressed in long shirt and boots, c1900	48.00
J P Coat's Thread, baby with powder puff	25.00
Kaufman Bros Family Liquor Store, beer keg shape	25.00
Kleinert's Dress Shields	47.50
Lady Laurel Stoves, wall, oval, woman and bread	155.00
Lowry & Goebles Furniture	55.00
Maryland Casualty Ins, Oklahoma, 1959	45.00
Mascot Tobacco	30.00
Merrian & Millard Grain Co, Omaha	25.00
Milling and Cattle Feeding, 1¾ x 2¾″, celluloid, black and white grain mill, Abingdon, IL, Burlington route railroad box car on rail, c1900	45.00
Morton's Salt, 1¾″, blue and white, "Morton's Salt/When It Rains-It Pours," c1930	40.00
Nature's Remedies	25.00
Oliver Plow, James Oliver picture	75.00
Quality Shoes, 2¾″, oval, celluloid, multicolored, auburn haired woman, small gold crown, dark red-brown ground, early 1900s	50.00
Parisian Novelty Company, Chicago, 3½″	35.00
Rock Island Stove Co	30.00
San Francisco Call Carriers Assn	30.00
Schaeffer Piano, yellow	48.00
Schrank Undergarments	28.00
Scranton Life Insurance Co, 1¾″, black and white, early 1900	10.00

Silberzahn Ensilage Cutter, Gehl Bros, West Bend, Wis, silage cutter, red and black on cream **60.00**
Sondheim's Clothes, 1¾", red, white, and blue paper insert, bright tin rim, early 1900s **20.00**
Stacy's Chocolates, Rochester, NY **20.00**
The Elite Petticoat, 2¼", celluloid, lady modeling green underskirt and white adjustable top, bright red lettering, dealer's name in black, early 1900s **60.00**

Gillette, mfg by Whitehead & Hoag, Newark, NJ, 2⅛", $30.00.

The Maccabees Ins Co, celluloid, baby **45.00**
Traveler's Insurance, oval **35.00**
Trunkdome Trunk Co, Spring St, LA, red and gold **28.00**
Union Standard Shoes **22.00**
Whirlpool Washer **20.00**
Workman's Friend, 2½", black and white, celluloid, design of worker and magnifying glass, sold by H H Debolt, c1900 .... **75.00**

MISCELLANEOUS

Anvil, Anvil Overalls, Hard To Beat, High Point, NC **35.00**
Bank
  Calumet Baking Powder, tin, 4" **75.00**
  Fidelity National Bank & Trust Co, bronze, pictures bank **12.00**
  Fulton County Trust, Gloversville, NY, clock **75.00**
  Gulf Gas, pump, cardboard **15.00**
  Mellow Cup Coffee **22.00**
  Rival Dog Food, tin **12.00**
  Sohio Premex Oil, tin **10.00**
Baseball Bat, Quaker State and Sports Illus., wood, 16" **20.00**
Bear, A & W Root Beer **42.00**
Billhook
  Red Goose Shoe, 1949 .... **3.50**
  Ceresota Flour **45.00**

Blotter
  Goodrich Rubber Tennis Shoe, kids playing ball **9.00**
  Morton Salt **5.00**
Book, Morton Salt Co, *Home Meat Curing Made Easy*, 1941 .... **12.00**
Bookmark
  Heintz's Shoes, children, 1910 ..... **4.00**
  Heinz Pickle **12.50**
Bowl, Planter's Peanut **45.00**
Broom Holder, J. F. Owens, Fairbury, NE, 1930s **9.00**
Calendar
  Bell-Cap Plasters, 1908, children playing with dog **45.00**
  Belmont Park, Lawrence, Methuen, 1910, woman and horse head, 10" **25.00**
  Hood's Sarsaparilla, 1894 .... **45.00**
  New York Life Insurance, 1930-31 calendar **2.00**
  RC Cola, 1949 .... **40.00**
Canister, Bowey's Hot Chocolate Cream, orange, aluminum lid, black man serving hot chocolate **110.00**
Charm Bracelet, Planters Peanuts **14.00**
Clip, ⅞", "Lehman's Clothes," brass spring clip, dealer's name in red, black lettering, white ground, c1904 **20.00**
Clock
  Monarch Fine Foods, electric, lions head **185.00**
  Quaker State Motor Oil, round **100.00**
  Star Brand Shoes, sq **85.00**
Coat Hanger, San Francisco Cleaning & Drying Works, wood **10.00**
Cookie Jar, National Biscuit Co, stacking, orig lid and tag **200.00**
Crate
  L.C. Smith Typewriter, lid **55.00**
  Old Dutch Cleanser, wood, Dutch lady **35.00**
Crayons, Red Goose Shoes, boxed, unused **12.00**
Cup, Heinz Pickle **15.00**
Cup and Saucer, Bowey's Chocolate .. **28.00**
Dish, Clark's Teaberry Gum, 4¾ x 7", 2¾" h pedestal base with inscription on both sides, c1930 .... **30.00**
Display
  Clarks Teaberry Gum, holder, amethyst **150.00**
  Whitman's Candy, man, 1920s **350.00**
Doll, Eskimo Pie **8.00**
Door Push
  Junge's Bread, porcelain **35.00**
  Montreal Pure Malt Rye, The Uri Co **55.00**
  Salada Tea, porcelain, yellow and red **65.00**
Fan
  Campbell Soup, tomato **75.00**
  Hormel Dairy Brand Ham, diecut, farm girl **25.00**

Levering Coffee, paper **11.00**
Millar's Coffee, colorful Indian **25.00**
Foam Scraper, Num Nyr Pretzels **35.00**
Funnel
   Lash's Bitters, copper **85.00**
   Rippey's Extract of Vanilla, tin **22.50**
Jar
   Schapps Coconut, coconut finial . . . **225.00**
   Squirell Peanut, raised design, paper
     label **65.00**
   Wan-Eta cocoa, Boston, amber, 1 qt **35.00**
Key Chain, Little Princess Telephone . . **2.00**
Knife, Star Brand Shoe, figural **68.00**
Lemon Squeezer, Sunkist logo on han-
   dles **18.00**
Lollipop Holder, Morses Pure Pops,
   bulldog **75.00**
Magic Set, Franco-American Novelty Co **48.00**
Match Holder
   Buckwalter Stoves, celluloid **12.00**
   Kool Cigarettes **25.00**
   Zephyr Flour, wall type **50.00**
Match Safe
   DeLaval **115.00**
   First National Bank of Blairsville,
     metal and celluloid **40.00**
   International Tailoring Co **28.00**
   Val Blatz Brewing Co **65.00**
Mending Kit, Real Silk Hosiery **2.00**
Money Clip, 7/8", black and white cel-
   luloid, brass spring clip, detailed
   black dress show, inscribed "Fine
   Shoes," Petersburg, VA dealer's name
   and address, 1896 . . . . **40.00**
Mug
   Carter Carburetor, stoneware **15.00**
   Oliver Typewriter Co, Annual Confer-
     ence, December 30, 1905 . . . . **375.00**
   Whitetower Restaurant **22.00**
Oilstone, Bagley's Tobacco, 2¾", cel-
   luloid, multicolored tobacco can, red
   ground, mounted on back of emery
   whetstone, c1900 . . . . **75.00**
Pail
   After Glow Coffee **42.00**
   Empress Coffee **40.00**
   Miles Lard, Indian pictured **37.50**
   Raco Lard **42.50**
   Toyland Peanut Butter **95.00**
   Veribest Mince Meat **67.50**
Paint Book, Ceresota Flour, *The Adven-
   tures of Ceresota*, 1912, unused **45.00**
Paper Clip, Lane Mfg Co, Montpelier,
   VT, 2½", spring metal clip, 1¾" black
   and white celluloid with illus of saw-
   mill, c1900 . . . . **25.00**
Pencil Clip
   Diamond Crystal Salt **7.50**
   Morton's Salt **4.00**
   Ritz Crackers, 7/8", litho tin, yellow,
     blue, and red, tiny Nabisco logo,
     c1930 . . . . **6.00**

White House Coffee, ¾", celluloid,
   detailed illus of White House, dark
   blue ground, white lettering, c1920 **10.00**
Pencil Sharpener, Baker's Cocoa Girl,
   figural **25.00**
Pennant, McFadden's Electric Brand
   Coffee, 37" l **135.00**
Pin Holder, Prudential, mother and
   baby **10.00**
Pitcher, G. W. Seven Star Whiskey, alu-
   minum **5.00**
Plate, General Telephone, 9¾", china **25.00**
Playing Cards, Bluebird Bus System,
   1947 . . . . **22.00**
Pocket Knife, Star Brand Shoes, case . . **58.00**
Postcard, Greyhound **5.00**
Pouch, Tiger Chewing Tobacco, black
   and white, linen, stitched edge, tiger
   illus on each side, early 1900s **20.00**
Puzzle, Campfire Marshmallows, enve-
   lope **15.00**
Razor Dispenser, Listerine, elephant . . **9.00**
Recipe Cards, Towle's Log Cabin Syrup,
   set of 24 . . . . **35.00**
Ring, Hartford Insurance, Junior Fire
   Marshal, brass, red enamel **35.00**
Ruler
   Clark Bars, wood **6.00**
   G Felsenthal & Sons, Chicago, 1 x 6",
     celluloid, inch and metric rules,
     listing of celluloid novelties offered **20.00**
   Glory Soap Chips, 5½", folding, cel-
     luloid, blue and orange trademark
     of Swift & Co, and logo for Key-
     stone Laundry Soap, monthly cal-
     endars for first six months of 1919 **18.00**
   Hartford, tin, painted, ornate, 1906 . **12.50**
   Northwestern Terra Cotta Co, Chi-
     cago, 1¾ x 12", black and white,
     celluloid, dark orange logo, black
     and white illus of factory, Chicago
     skyline on reverse, c1900 . . . . **40.00**
   Western Union, 7¼", diecut, silver
     and blue logo, telegraph and cable
     rates, 1905 patent date **20.00**
Soap, Sinclair Heating Oils, figural, oil
   truck, perfumed, 1940 . . . . **8.00**
Sheet Music, Bromo Seltzer adv **12.00**
Spoon
   Hot Dan's French's Mustard, figural
     handle, Beetleware **6.00**
   Soronitz Chocolates **20.00**
Stickpin, Staute Blend High Grade Cof-
   fee, ¾", oval, brass, Orr Mizell & Co
   on back, early 1900 . . . . **10.00**
Tape Measure
   Abbotts Ice Cream, black, white, and
     red picture **15.00**
   Fab **30.00**
   Lewis Lye & Piano Co **20.00**
Teapot, Salada **10.00**
Tie Tack, Harley Davidson **4.00**

Tile, McCormick Spices, ceramic, 1955 **10.00**
Tobacco Humidor, Union Leader, tin . **45.00**
Trivet, The Cleveland Foundry Co, cast
iron **35.00**
Tumbler, Small Grain Distilling, Louis-
ville, 4", etched, paneled sides **50.00**
Watch Fob
Abraham Fur Co, triangle shape **225.00**
Biston's Golden Grain Coffee, coffee
bean shape **135.00**
Gooch's Macaroni **30.00**
Window Decal, Koesters Bread, brightly
colored litho, twin baby girls, unused **15.00**
Yardstick, Kaiser Automobile **15.00**

PAPERWEIGHTS

Aetna Insurance, mirror **30.00**
American Glass & Construction Co.,
Rochester, NY, glass reinforced with
wire, rect, 3 x 4½" **15.00**
Auto Owner's Insurance, 1955 .... **15.00**
Bell System, bell shape, glass, blue ... **95.00**
Best Pig Forceps, compliments J. Rei-
mers, Davenport, Iowa, pig shape,
glass, 6" **100.00**
Columbia National Bank, glass **10.00**
Compliments of American Card Cloth-
ing Co, Worcester, MA, glass, 1882 **25.00**
Crane Co, Chicago, 75th Anniversary,
brass, round, 2⅜" d **30.00**

**Paperweight, J R Leeson & Co, Boston,
Linen Thread Importers, black and white,
2⅝ x 4⅛", $50.00.**

El Roco Gas, iron, figural **25.00**
Elgin Watches **25.00**
Fidel Ganahl Lumber Co, St Louis, 4",
lumber truck **75.00**
Hanover Safe Deposit Co **20.00**
Holt Motors, iron, figural **25.00**
Independent Press Room, Los Angles,
rect, glass **15.00**
Kellogg's, Vitrolite, girl holding box,
c1905 .... **450.00**

Lehigh Sewer Pipe & Tile Co, Ft Dodge,
IA, glass, rect, 4 x 2½" **12.00**
Lindeke Warner & Schurmeier Dry
Goods & Notions, 3 x 4", rect, dome
shape, black and orange lettering ... **15.00**
Macbeth–Evans Glass Co, Pittsburgh,
rect **15.00**
Matthew's Decorative Glass Co, New
York City, 3" d, domed hemisphere,
decorative trademark logo, early
1900s **50.00**
National Surety Co, bronze, spread ea-
gle on world globe **45.00**
NCR Co., paper currency weight **65.00**
New York Telephone Bell System, bell
shape, glass, blue **50.00**
North River Insurance Co, 3¾" d, brass,
round, 100th Anniversary, 1822–
1922 .... **50.00**
Osborne Co Harvesting Machinery, Au-
burn, NY, glass **24.00**
P.H. Hanes & Co, Mammoth Tobacco
Works, Winston, NC, round, glass,
embedded factory picture **125.00**
Parke-Davis, pewter, baby in womb .. **25.00**
Prudential Insurance Co of America
50th Anniversary, 1875–1925, brass,
round, 2⅞" d **37.50**
Purdue Foundry, cast iron, Kewpie ... **35.00**
Quick Service Express, 4 x 2½", mirror
bottom **30.00**
Read Radio News, cast iron, radio dial
shape **80.00**
Renown Stoves, cast iron, alligator,
brown **22.00**
Scottish Union Insurance Co, Hartford,
CT, brass, rect, 2½ x 3⅞" **75.00**
Smith Bros Cough Drop, cast iron, emb **35.00**
Texaco Station, brass, anvil shape **12.00**
Wright Manufacturer and Dealer in
Drain Tools, Fairmount, IN, duck in
weeds **65.00**
Wurtz Auto Garage, Degenhart **55.00**

POSTERS

Arm & Hammer, boy laughing at hunter,
1910 .... **250.00**
Aviation Cadet Training, 26 x 20", 1943 **50.00**
Bickmore Shave Cream, 30 x 21", man
putting cream on brush, 1930 ...... **20.00**
Bull Durham, 17 x 7", 1940 .... **25.00**
Chesterfield Cigarettes, c1940 .... **12.00**
Crusader Tobacco, 13 x 7", c1900 ... **25.00**
Du Pont Gun Powder, game birds, 1920 **165.00**
Eberhardt & Ober Brewery, 1890s **650.00**
Ferry's Seeds, 20½ x 27½", blonde lady
wearing military covered bib overalls,
1910 copyright **60.00**
Golden Eagle Tobacco, 13 x 7", c1900 **30.00**
Humming Hosiery, girl sitting on buggy
seat **65.00**

Poster, The Hambletonian Stallion, Oswego Prince, breeding broadside, c1881, 14⅛ x 20½", $100.00.

K. M. Krone's Sample Room, Walcott, IA 35.00
Lion Coffee, 11 x 14", brass reinforcement top and bottom, c1890 ...... 40.00
Metropolitan Opera House, c1918 ... 60.00
National Biscuit Co, 22 x 12", c1925 . 32.00
Old Dutch Cleanser, 15 x 20", fabric, can illus, blue and white background, red border, French inscriptions, 1930s 75.00
Overhauls Paper, 1920 .... 6.00
Packer's Tar Soap, 9 x 12", barber shaving, 1900 .... 30.00
Raleigh Cigarettes, 15 x 10", 1940 .... 25.00
Satin Skin Powder, 42 x 26", 1903 ... 35.00
Van Camps, 1959 .... 10.00
Wings Cigarettes, 15 x 10", 1940 ..... 25.00

SIGNS

Abbey Imbrie Fishing Tackle, tin, logo and dolphin, 1906 .... 225.00

Sign, Imperial Tobacco Co, Wills White Star, multicolored, cardboard back, Great Britain, 7½ x 10", $50.00.

Admiration Coffee Co, 23 x 33", cardboard 30.00
Bavarian Beer, 10 x 5", tin 20.00
Berkley Knit, 8 x 10", stand-up, man with tie, 1925 .... 30.00
Blue Jay Corn Plasters, 13½ x 7", man whittling, sitting in rocking chair ... 125.00
Borax Dry Soap, metal, red and white 45.00
Botl'O Grape, 16 x 20", tin, emb 30.00
Bowles Livestock Commission Co, woman on ladder, animals eating picked apples 225.00
Brown's Mule Tobacco, mule reaching in window pulling cover off man ... 175.00
Burma Shave, wooden 70.00
Butternut Bread, tin 25.00
Carhartt Overalls, 10 x 24", tin, emb, c1920 .... 30.00
Chi-Namel Varnish, 20 x 13", metal, diecut, 1920 .... 200.00
Cloverdale, 12 x 10", tin emb, 1930s . 25.00
Comstock's Liniment, diecut, golfer rubbing liniment on elbow 85.00
Continental Trailways Bus Depot, porcelain, map of United States 190.00
Copenhagen Beer, Viking 40.00
Cork Distilleries Co, hp, framed 165.00
Cramer's Fertilizer 40.00
Crescent Beverages, 19½ x 13", tin, emb 55.00
Crest Flour, 5 x 8", cardboard, c1920 . 5.00
Davis Carriage M'F'G Co, Petersburg, VA, "Headquarters For Everything To Ride In Or Work With", tin, 7 x 20", orange and black lettering, yellow background 155.00
Diamond Dyes, 10 x 14", diamond shape, cloth swatches under glass .. 125.00
Dixon's Stove Polish, 6 x 8", paper ... 65.00
Don Murano Cigars, 19" d, tin, girl in pink dress, self framed 330.00
Dutchess Trousers, tin, emb, shows turn of century trousers 150.00
Eastside Lager, celluloid 30.00
Eckhart & Becker, celluloid 45.00
Eddy's Bread, 3 x 29", tin, emb, 1940s 25.00
Electro Batteries, 18 x 9", tin 20.00
Fisk Tire, 36 x 28", porcelain 40.00
Frazer Axle Grease, 10 x 13", litho, two farmers on country road, wheel of wagon, c1890 .... 70.00
Frostie, 12 x 23", tin 25.00
Goody Headache Powder, cardboard, girl, 1940s 10.00
Grape Nuts, tin, girl and St Bernard, 1905 .... 620.00
Green River Whiskey, 18 x 22", cardboard, framed 140.00
Hanna Paints, 3 x 12", tin, emb, c1940 10.00
Hickey-Freeman, 3D type, hand holding needle and thread 75.00
Hommel Wine, Sandusky, OH, 19 x

26", stone litho, factory, grapes, and
bottles, 1896 .... **150.00**
Hump Hairpins, 16 x 14", tin, diecut . **150.00**
Huseman Soda, Clear and Sparkling,
100% Pure, 13 x 19", tin, emb **30.00**
Iceman's Snow Scraper, 6 x 16", brass,
painted, 1928 .... **30.00**
Ismert-Hincke Flour Co, emb **95.00**
Jersey Ice Cream, 16 x 34", tin, c1940 **40.00**

**Sign, Republic Casualty Co, Pittsburgh,
PA, tin and cardboard, printed, 19¼ x
13¼", $85.00.**

K. C. Baking Powder, 12 x 28", tin, two
sided, 1930s **45.00**
Kibber's Candies, 9 c 8", brass **50.00**
Kremo Rootbeer, 13 x 19", tin, emb .. **45.00**
Lash Bitters, 14 x 21", litho on wood,
Victorian lady **400.00**
Low-Shoes, Baur-Mullarky Co, Keokuk,
IA, 37 x 12", c1920 .... **90.00**
Lutz Funeral Home, 10 x 15", cast brass
cornerstone **55.00**
Lux Fire Extinguishing Equipment, 13 x
28", porcelain, two sided, motorboat **70.00**
Ma's Rootbeer, grandma and six pack . **75.00**
McNess Products, 13 x 16", metal, side
mount **20.00**
Mikado Pencils, 20", sq, paper, 1930 . **75.00**
Miller M. Fogg, House and Sign Painter,
27¼ x 23¾", wood, gray ground,
black and yellow frame **190.00**
Mother Dexter's Bread, blackboard type **35.00**
Munsingwear, 24 x 36", cardboard,
woman **90.00**
Mutual Insurance, indian logo **65.00**
Nehi Soda, 15 x 4", "Gas Today," chalk-
board **425.00**
New York Daily News, paper litho,
newsboy, delivery wagon, and NY
skyline, 1890 .... **270.00**
Northern Beer, Superior, WI, 6 x 13",
tin, c1930 .... **25.00**
Norwich Suntan Oil, 10 x 16", tin, litho,
c1930 .... **75.00**

Oh Boy Gum, 17 x 10", tin, 1930s ... **85.00**
Orange Crush, 29 x40", cardboard, little
girl with bottle, framed **125.00**
Otto Stahl's, 12 x 16", tin, "Ready To
Eat Meats," c1910 .... **90.00**
Overland Motors, 24 x 36", porcelain,
whippet **175.00**
Parker's Cold Cream, 7½ x 11½", stan-
dup, Victorian woman, 1905 ...... **90.00**
Pennsylvania Tires, yellow and blue,
round, 36" **50.00**
Perry's Beverages, 14 x 20", tin, emb,
picture of bottle, 1940s **35.00**
Pfeffer Bros. Pianos, Seneca, IL, 8 x 24",
tin **25.00**
Pierce Paints, porcelain **75.00**
Piff's Beverages, 20 x 28", tin, bottle,
c1940 .... **25.00**
Portland Cement, Middle Branch, OH,
round porcelain **75.00**
Purity Flour, 36 x 24", porcelain, white,
yellow, and dark blue **70.00**
Rawleigh's Talcum Powder, nursery
scenes **30.00**
Red Jacket Tobacco, cardboard, base-
ball scene, 22 x 28" **125.00**
Rice's Seeds, 24 x 12", paper, man with
cabbage **75.00**
Rhinelander Butter, tin, two packages of
butter **75.00**
S & H Fro-Joy Ice Cream, 17½ x 24",
metal, c1930 .... **70.00**
Schuler's Chip, tin **55.00**
Sealship Oysters, two sided, porcelain,
flanged **125.00**
Simplex Typewriter, tin, 1905 .... **35.00**
Sinclair Diesel **30.00**
Steven's Pharmacy Inc, 11½ x 24", tin,
black on white **15.00**
Stickney Poor Spice Co, orig wood
frame **250.00**
Stroh's Beer, 14 x 20", tin, cherubic man
in hat **250.00**
Sunbeam Bread **60.00**
Sweet Maris Gum, diecut **45.00**
Texaco Marine White Gasoline, Cargrey
Gold, 12", winged wheel **30.00**
Threshermen & Farmers Ins, 8 x 15" .. **25.00**
Time Plug Tobacco, 12" sq, cardboard **25.00**
United Service Motors, porcelain, arrow
shape **145.00**
Vernors Gingerale, 25 x 17½", tin, slate-
board, 1959 .... **20.00**
White Rose Bread, baker boy carrying
bread **295.00**
Wolf's Head Motor Oil, metal **40.00**

THERMOMETER

Atlas Perma-Guard Anti-Freeze, 39" .. **35.00**
B-1 Lemon Lime, tin, c1950 .... **20.00**
B-Q-R Pills, 16", yellow and black ... **25.00**

Bire-Leys, 12", tin 30.00
Borden Feed, boxed, 1952 .... 25.00
Buffalo rock, 26", red bottle and letter-
  ing, yellow background 35.00
Carolina Burlap Bag Co, 24", wood,
  black letters, red border, yellow back-
  ground, 1915 .... 100.00
Cash Value Tobacco, tin 22.50
Champion Spark Plugs 20.00
Dr. Pierce's Chemical Co, bakelite,
  1931 .... 18.00
Endicott Johnson & Co, 21", wood,
  black letters, 1915 .... 180.00
Ex-Lax, porcelain 75.00
F. E. Crymbe Fine Confectionary and Ice
  Cream, 21", wood, black letters,
  1915 .... 90.00
First National Bank, Fremont, Ohio,
  wood, boxed 30.00
Folgers Coffee, 9", can shape 75.00

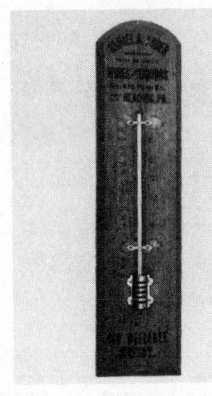

Thermometer, Old Reliable Whiskey, Daniel A Yoder Wines & Liquors, wood, $40.00.

Frank's Pale Dry Ginger Ale, 27", por-
  celain, green bottle, red background,
  1915 .... 125.00
Frog, Switch and Manufacturing Co,
  Carlisle, PA, 36", dark blue trim,
  white background 45.00
Georgia Real Estate Co, 21", wood,
  1915 .... 70.00
Golden Acres Hybrid Seeds 35.00
Happy Jim Chewing Tobacco, 35" 75.00
Hickory Harness Co, 21", wood, black
  lettering, white background, 1925 .. 65.00
Jests Antacid, porcelain, 36" 110.00
King Plows & Farm Tools, 12", wood,
  red and black trim, white back-
  ground, 1940 .... 65.00
Lash's Bitters, 21", wood, natural finish 130.00
Luminall, 39", 1950 .... 60.00
Naco Fertilizer Co, Charleston, SC ... 22.00
Nyal Drugstore Service, 38" 28.00

Old Dutch Rootbeer, 27", 1940 ...... 65.00
Pal Orange Ade, 26" 40.00
Red Comb Poultry Feeds, 4 x 6", diecut,
  tin, eggshell color egg design with
  red, white, and blue logo, white
  background with blue lettering 40.00
Rislone 55.00
Rochester American Insurance Co, NY,
  porcelain 27.00
Sauer's Vanilla, 1919, wooden 68.00
Snow Goose Flour, 39", blue trim, white
  background 50.00
Standard Fruit & Steamship Co, New
  Orleans 15.00
Standard Oil, tin, boxed 20.00
Stegmaier Beer, round, glass 43.00
Taylor's Pride Chewing Tobacco, 6 x
  16" 10.00
Wards Vitomin Bread, porcelain 275.00

TIN

A.D.S. Rose Talc 18.00
American Lady, coffee, #3 size 65.00
Apollo Marshmallows, 2 x 4", round .. 55.00
Atlas Blasting Caps 15.00
Bagley's Sweet Tips Tobacco, pocket . 45.00
Bee Brand Insect Powder 12.00
Bell Tower Phonograph Needles, red . 10.00
Blackstone's Laxative, multicolored ... 10.00
Blue Bonnet, coffee, #2 size 85.00
Blue Heaven Tobacco, beige and blue 5.00
Boyol Salve For Drawing 4.00
Buffalo Brand Peanut Butter, 1 lb 85.00
Calvert Oysters 14.00
Calumet, indian 10.00

Tin, cigar, Train Master, blue ground, gold dec, 5½ x 3¾ x ¼", $35.00.

Campfire Marshmallow 20.00
Caruso Peanut 15.00
Colgate Toothpowder, 1906 .... 45.00
Cuticura Talcum, lady on one side,
  baby on other 25.00
Dilling Marshmallows 20.00
Dr. Hobson's Arnica Salve, includes
  contents and directions 6.00

Dr. R. S. Parker's Sure Kidney Pills, 3½"	2.00
Dream Girl Talc	35.00
Drostes Cocoa	13.00
Edgeworth Tobacco, 3¼ x 4½"	12.00
Educator Cracker	95.00
Eggo Baking Powder	20.00
Ex-Cel-Siss Talcum	15.00
Fireside Gems Candy, 8", round, girl sitting on bench	10.00
Flaroma Coffee, #1 size	17.50
Folgers, #1 size, 1931	12.00
Frishmuth's Whittle Cut Tobacco	15.00
Gardenia Talcum	5.00
Golden Bear Cookies, 5½ x 5¾", black and orange	20.00
Golden Wedding Coffee, 2½ oz size	110.00
Half & Half Tobacco, 1926	6.00
Huyler's Candy, 8 x 11½", rect	12.00
Jewel Tea Baking Powder	6.00
Johnson & Johnson Baby Powder	18.00
Johnston's Chocolates	6.00
Jolly Time Popcorn	35.00
Jumbo Popcorn, elephant	28.00
Kellogg's Drinket, sample	37.50
Kelly-Springfield, tire repair	35.00
Kohrs Crown Lard, red	15.00
Lander's Lilacs and Roses, talc	17.50
Latona Coffee, 5 lb	75.00
Maxim's Talcum Powder	95.00
McCormick Tea	12.00
Merkel's Toothpowder	8.00

Tin, nutmeg, Van Curler Brand, Schenectady, NY, 8 oz, yellow ground, red base, 3⅝ x 1⅞ x 5", $15.00.

Milligun's Coffee, 1 lb	15.00
Mojo Perfect, coffee, #1 size, 1923	37.50
Morris Fine Confectionery, 8½ x 7"	15.00
Nature's Remedy Tablet	3.00
Old Andy, coffee, #1 size, cardboard	22.50
Old Griffin Sterling Paste Shoe Polish	12.00
Ovaltine, 1921	20.00
Panama Typewriter, airplane and map	25.00
Parke-Davis Botanic Herb	25.00

Pepsi Syrup, drum	65.00
Pickmore Gall Salve, directions	10.00
Piper Heidsieck Chewing tobacco, litho, hinged lid, c1910	8.00
Planters Blanched Almonds, unopened	65.00
Raptco Wafers, flat, emb	25.00
Reichard's Cadet Cigar	65.00
Rich's Crystallized Canton Ginger, 4½ x 7½ x 8", yellow and black	15.00
Sauer's Selected Spices, cream, red, and dark blue	5.00
Snowdrift Coconut, 12" d, 6¼" h, red and yellow, Hoboken, NJ	40.00
Sozodont Tooth Powder	35.00
Star Maid Peanut, 10 lbs, girl	80.00
Sunshine Biscuit, iron sides	15.00
Sunshine Fruit Cake, Egyptian woman dec	10.00
Sweet Burley, yellow	75.00
Tetley Tea, 3¾ x 6 x 5¾" oval	42.00
Towle Molasses	30.00
Tuskeegee Belle Hair Cream, black girl in cap and gown	40.00
Underwood Typewriter	7.00
Union Blacking, Union Jack, paper label	25.00
Union Leader Tobacco, red, gold eagle	25.00
Vanta Powder, baby	15.00
Vantine's Canton Crystallized Ginger	5.00
White Witch, talc	12.50
William's Baby Talc, 1911	15.00
Wise Potato Chips, 12 x 8", blue, pink, and tan, owl and flowers, 1951	10.00
Wizard Carpet Clean, 1901	37.50
Y & S Licorice Lozenges, glass front	65.00
Yardley's, Old English, talc	10.00

TRADE CARDS

Collecting Hints: Most advertising trade cards sell in the range from $1.00 to $10.00. A few command higher prices because of subject matter, artist, or scarcity. The advertised product being shown is among the most desirable features of a card. Many were made in sets, and collectors still seek to complete them today.

Cards taken from old albums should be handled with care, as there is often valuable information on the reverse side. Kit Barry's *The Advertising Trade Card* (privately printed, 1981) contains excellent information for the removal of cards from album pages.

History: These cards are small, thin cardboard pieces extolling the merits of a product and bearing the name and address of a merchant.

With the invention of lithography, colorful trade cards became a popular advertising medium in the late 19th and early 20th centuries. They were made to appeal to children, especially. Young and old alike collected and treasured them in albums and scrapbooks. Very few are dated; 1880 to 1893 were the prime years for trade cards; 1810 to 1850 cards can be found, but rarely. By 1900 trade cards were rapidly losing their popularity, perhaps due to the influx of the household magazine. By 1910 they had vanished from the American scene, except in rare instances.

Notes: The listing for trade cards is as follows: product name, description of card, copyright date if known, printer if known, and size. We have tried to focus on cards which show the product. All cards are in full color unless otherwise specified. There are thousands of cards in several hundred categories. We have tried to give a sampling to show the market range.

Bitters, Drugs, and Medicines

Acorn Salve, diecut, acorn shape	3.00
Bell's Cocktail Bitters, puzzle, black on white	5.00
Brown's Dentifrice	12.00
Burdock Blood Bitters, three kittens in basket	2.00
Coderre's Infants' Syrup, Elliott	5.00
Colton's Nervine Strengthening Bitters .	7.00
Cushman's Menthol Inhaler Will Cure It, child smoking	3.00
Dr. P. T. Baron, black on pink	5.00
Extract Of Roots Cures Dyspepsia	15.00
Globe Cocktail Bitters, black on white	5.00
Graves Balsam of Wild Cherry & Tar ..	2.00
Hand's Remedies, Rochester, children and chickens, dated 1886	6.00
Hoen, gentleman and lady, brown on white	4.00
Judson's Mountain Herb Pills	6.00
Knapp's Throat Cure, 1880–90	4.00
Lothrops & Pinkham Pharmacists	3.00
M. K. Paine Druggist & Pharmacist, Forbes	6.00

Quaker Bitters, girl in barrel	4.00
Rubifoam For the Teeth	3.00
Schenck's Pulmonic Syrup, Harris, hold to light type, two children and cat sleeping	6.00
W & S Cough Drops, Gast	2.00
Wheat Bitters, man and women in boat, lake scene, black on white	4.00
Wild Indian Lung Balsam, Bufford, dated 1889	4.00

Clothing

F. Mayer Boot & Shoe Co, Milwaukee, three boys playing hopscotch, poem by Ella Wheeler	2.00
Koch Bros, Allentown's Leading Clothing Makers, girl holding fan, boy in sailor suit, Maud Humphrey, 1902 ..	10.00
Quakermaid Stockings, Young, Knight, Field & Co, Phila, PA, c1930	2.00
Todtman Clothier, diecut, black child in wash tub	10.00
Warner Bros Coraline Corsets, 3 x 5" .	15.00
Wolff & Grunauer Tailors, 3 x 4½", 1880s	7.00

Cosmetics and Perfumes

A Kaercher's Persian Balm, Donaldson	5.00
Bazin & Sargent's Face Powder	3.00
Bowker's Odeur Du Bois Perfume	1.00
Espey's Fragrant Cream	4.00
Hagan's Magnolia balm	5.00
Howard's Lotus Flower cologne	3.00
Hoyt's German Cologne, 1892	12.00
Mennen's Borated Talcum Baby Powder	3.00
Mikado Cologne	8.00
Solon Palmer, diecut, flowers in bowl .	3.00

Trade Cards, left, clothing, Eureka Health Corset, adv on back, 3¹⁄₁₆ x 5³⁄₁₆", $3.00; center, clothing retailer, Koch Bros, Maud Humphrey illus, 3 x 5", $10.00; right, food, I Like Crown Prince Coffee, 3 x 5", $5.00.

Trade Cards, left, manufacturing, Howe Scale, Page, Fargo & Co, Pittsburgh–Philadelphia, multicolored, marked "Hatch Litho Co, NY," $7.50; center, organ, Estey Phonorium, litho of factory on back, marked "Forbes," 3⅛ x 5¹⁄₁₆", $6.00; right, thread, Clark's O. N. T. Spool Cotton, young black, multicolored, $8.00.

Food

A&P Tea Co	15.00
Alden's Vinegar, pictures blacks	7.00
Hire's Rootbeer	4.00
James Vick, Seed Man, Rochester, NY, diecut, potato shape	2.00
Mack's Milk Chocolate	2.00
Muzzy's Corn Starch, 1870, black serving couple in cafe	10.00
Northern Pacific Railroad Baked Potato, dated 1909	8.00
Pillsbury's Best, pictures blacks	7.00
Pratt Food Company	3.00
Red Rose Tea, Rockwell, 1958	6.00

Household

Acme White Lead & Color Works, Granite Floor Paint	5.00
Allan's Fly Brick	4.00
Berry Bros Hard Oil Finish, 7 x 4", emb, Uncle Sam	45.00
Briddell Cutlery Factory, 1930s	2.00
Conqueror Clothes Wringer, fold up	12.00
Luca's Co, Paints and Varnishes, factory scenes both sides	6.00
Webb's Superior Stove Polish, green on gold	2.00

Retail

Buckeye Force Pumps, Mast, Fous & C, Springfield, OH, boy pumping water	8.00
Clark Bicycle Co, magic, Christmas, Santa on high wheeler, 1880s	20.00
Emerson Piano Co, black on green	2.00
Gypsy Queen Cigarettes, 1896	2.00
Malcolm Love & Co, woman holding violin	7.00

Moline Wagon Co, Moline, IL, couple in wagon	3.00
U.S. Cartridge Co	75.00

Sewing Machines

Davis Sewing Machine, lady sitting on bench	3.00
Domestic Sewing Machine Co, boy and girl under sewing machine	3.00
Household Sewing Machine	3.00
National Wax Thread Sewing machine, diecut, horse, black on yellow	4.00
New Home Sewing Machine Co, diecut, butterfly	2.00
R. I. Braiding Machine Co, black on white	3.00
Remington Sewing Machine	4.00
Singer Sewing Machine, American Song Bird series, set of 16, 1926–33	28.00
Standard Sewing Machine Co, Nature's Kindergarten	5.00
Wanzer & Co, Oriental figures	4.00
Wilson Sewing Machine Co, lady sewing	5.00

Soap

Cashmere Bouquet Toilet Soap, Colgate & Co	3.00
Higgins Laundry Soap, 3⅛ x 4¼", sailor and captain	4.00
Pears' Soap, baby	10.00
Pyle's Pearline, Pearline Soap Co, court jester	2.00
Sapolio, Enoch Morgan & Sons, boy and fancy clothes	2.00
Soapine, girl and doll	7.00
Swan Soap, 5 x 7½", Victorian	12.00

Stoves and Ranges

Garland Stoves & Ranges 8.00

Thread

Clark's
  Mile End, girl with kitten, c1887 ...   2.00
  ONT Thread, diecut, spool of thread
    shape 4.00
J & P Coats
  Girl holding two dogs 1.00
  Frog, lake scene 2.00
  Lady standing by chair 1.00
  Rabbits with musical instruments,
    c1887 ....   2.00
Merrick Thread Co, woman and child at
  beach 2.00
Willimantic Thread, cupid tying thread
  around world 3.00

TRAY

American Brewery & Malting Co, Great
  Falls, MT, 12", roses 40.00
Art Butts Sporting Goods, Oneonta, NY,
  hunting dog in field, scalloped
  crimped border, 3 x 5" 35.00
Bailey's Whiskey, tip 60.00
Beamer Shoes, Victorian woman, c1900   60.00
Bevo Beverage, team horses and wagon,
  wood grain border, 1900s 125.00
Big Jo Flour, tip 50.00

Tray, Cottolene Shortening, black
ground, multicolored illus, mfg by N K
Fairbank Co, 4¼" d, $40.00.

Buffalo Brewing, Sacramento, CA, Ha-
  waiian girl playing ukelele, c1910 ..   275.00
C. D. Kenny Coffee Co, 9½", round,
  Santa Claus 50.00
Carnation Milk, 3½ x 5½", tip, oval,
  cows in pasture 20.00
Cilley & Bennetch, Lebanon, PA, Our

Shoes Wear Well, 3½ x 4⅞", tip,
  1904 St. Louis World's Fair Electric
  Building 10.00
Cold Spring Moeschlin, Sunbury, PA,
  nickel plated 75.00
Continental Insurance Co, St. Louis, 4",
  tip, 1920s 14.00
Croft Ale, round, red and white on black   40.00
Diamond Wedding Rye, woman wear-
  ing large hat, c1900 ....   200.00
Dobler Brewing Co, Albany, NY, Amer-
  ican Can Co, 13" d, pretty lady 40.00
Donaldson's Dept. Store, tip 38.00
Douglas Ice Cream, girl eating ice
  cream, wearing yellow dress, 1913 .   140.00
Eureka Flour, tip, Annabell portrait ...   30.00
Evinrude Motor Co, Milwaukee, 4", tip,
  woman in boat 50.00
Fairy Soap, 13" 110.00
Folmers Ice Cream 80.00
F. P. Home Lighting, tip, woman by
  stove 50.00
Franklin Life Insurance Co, 4", tip, Ben
  Franklin 30.00
Germania Brewing, stag 130.00
Gettelman Beer, Milwaukee, round,
  hand holding glass 30.00
Green River Whiskey, 12" d, black man
  and horse 75.00
Hanley's Peerless Ale, enamelware ...   65.00
Havana Superfina Cigars, 3", indian ..   125.00
Heck's Capudine Medicine 200.00
Hinckel Brewery, Albany, round, elk
  scene, red rim 130.00
Hunt Shoe Co, tip, tin, stag 50.00
I. & G. N. Wood and Coal Yard, 14 x
  17", oval, vase with roses 40.00
James Meeds Furniture, 4", tip 65.00
Kaiser Wilhelm Magen Bitters 195.00
Kemp Burpee Success Manure Spreader,
  3½ x 5", tip 60.00
Kenny's Coffee Co, 5", tip, round,
  American flag 40.00
Lomax's Celery Tonic, 10 x 13", oval,
  black, gold letters 80.00
Lover Brand Shoes, tip, dog 15.00
McSorley's beer, solitaire player 125.00
Mirinda Soda 20.00
Mount Vernon Milk, 3 x 5", tip, oval .   20.00
Narragansett Lager Ale, Providence, RI,
  round, red 20.00
Ogdens St. Julien Tobacco Cool & Fra-
  grant, 13", round 20.00
Old Reliable Coffee, 4", tip, round, girl   40.00
Ortiebs Beer and Ale, round, red, black,
  and yellow 20.00
Peter Doelger Bottled Beer, tip, center
  logo 90.00
Pittsburgh Butchers and Packers, tip, lady   70.00
Prudential Life Insurance, tip, 1920s ..   20.00
Pure Milk Co, ice cream and milk, 1900   110.00
Red Earl Cigars, 3½", tip 50.00

Resinal Soap For Skin Diseases, 4½", tip, round, girl with roses **40.00**

Rockford Watches, 3 x 5", tip, oval, 1910 .... **30.00**

Schmauss Garden and Cafe, Milwaukee, 6" **70.00**

Seitz Beer, Easton, PA, tip, eagle **90.00**

Simon Pure Ale and Beer, Buffalo, round, green **40.00**

Staley's Flour, horse and girl, 1905 ... **40.00**

Stollwerck Chocolates and Cocoa, tip . **50.00**

Sweet Caporal—Compliments Kinney Brothers, 11 x 19", oval, pressed cardboard, tobacco **25.00**

Teaberry Gum, glass, amber **95.00**

Universal Stoves, 4", tip, round, c1910 **35.00**

Valley Forge Beer, Washington's headquarters **40.00**

Welsbach Mantels, tip, eagle **35.00**

Wolverine Toy Co, 4 x 6", c1920 .... **90.00**

Wrigley's Mineral Scouring Soap, tip, cat standing on boxes **65.00**

WHISTLE

Note: Whistles are assumed to be made of tin, unless designated otherwise. Many whistles have matching clickers. It is not unusual to see whistles marked 100 to 500% above these prices. Dealers attempt to appeal to the special interest collector. All prices have been noted at flea markets during the past year. See Clickers.

Atwater Kent Radios **13.00**

Butter-Nut Bread, yellow and black ... **4.00**

Endicott Johnson Shoes, 1½ x 2", green litho tin, bi–plane shape, red lettering, marked "Made In Germany," c1930 .... **20.00**

Whistle, Freihofer's Bread, litho tin, $5.00.

Erna's Portraits, 2½", orange and black **2.00**

Golden Royal Milk, yellow and black . **2.00**

Haines the Shoe Wizard, trapezoid shaped, plastic, "Blow And Talk Of Haines The Shoe Wizard/Shoes For All" inscription, late 1940s **18.00**

Leo R Cox Insurance, 2½", red and white **2.00**

Old Reliable Coffee **4.00**

Oscar Mayer Weiner, hot dog shape, red, c1950 .... **12.00**

Planters Peanut, plastic, blue and yellow, 1950–60 .... **8.00**

Purity Ice Cream, trapezoid, plastic, 3½ x 2¼", black top, orange lettering, Penn Dairies, Inc., light blue base, c1940 .... **20.00**

Triangle Brand Shows, 1 x 2½", litho, orange top, black inscriptions, c1930 **18.00**

Tydol Gas, plastic **12.00**

Wermuth Furs, aluminum, "Toot for Wermuth Furs" **8.00**

ADVERTISING CHARACTERS

Collecting Hints: Concentrate on one advertising character. Three dimensional objects are more eagerly sought than two dimensional objects. Some local dairies, restaurants and other businesses developed advertising characters. This area has received little focus from collectors.

History: Advertising characters represent a sampling of those characters used in advertising from the early 20th century to the present.

Americans learned to recognize specific products by their particular advertising characters. During the first half of the 1900s, many immigrants could not read but could identify with the colorful characters. The advertising character helped to sell the product.

Some manufacturers developed similar names for products of lesser quality, like Fariee Soap versus the popular Fairy Soap. Later when trade laws were enacted, this practice was stopped. Use of trademarks had become popular by this time. The advertising character often was part of the trademark.

Trademarks and advertising characters are found on product labels, in magazines, as premiums, and on other types of advertising. Popular cartoon characters also were used to advertise products.

Some advertising characters were designed especially to promote a specific product like Mr. Peanut and the Campbell Kids. The first time the popular Campbell Kids appeared, it was on streetcar advertising in 1906. The illustrations of Grace G. Drayton were aimed at housewives. The Campbell Kids were gradually dropped from Campbell's advertising until the television industry expanded the advertising market. In 1951, Campbell redesigned the kids and successfully reissued them. The kids were redesigned again in 1966. Other advertising characters also have enjoyed a long life, e.g., Aunt Jemima. Others, like Kayo and the Yellow Kid, have disappeared from modern advertising.

References: David Longest, *Character Toys and Collectibles,* Collector Books, 1984; David Longest, *Character Toys and Collectibles, Second Series* Collector Books, 1987; Richard D. and Barbara Reddock, *Planters Peanuts, Advertising & Collectibles,* Wallace-Homestead, 1978; Joleen Robison and Kay Sellers, *Advertising Dolls, Identification and Value Guide,* Collector Books, 1980; Dave Stivers, *The Nabisco Brands Collection of Cream of Wheat Advertising Art,* Collectors' Showcase, 1986.

Periodical: *Kids Illustrated Drayton Supplement* (K.I.D.S), 649 Bayview Drive, Akron, OH 44319, bimonthly.

REPRODUCTION ALERT

See: All advertising categories; Black Memorabilia; Cartoon Characters; Fast Food; Planter's Peanuts.

Aunt Jemima
  Bell, 1940s 85.00
  Doll, 13", cloth 125.00
  Pinback Button, ⅞", portrait, c1896–
    1900 .... 35.00
  Placemat, "Aunt Jemima's Kitchen," 15.00
  Syrup Pitcher 35.00
  Salt and Pepper Shaker, 3½", pr 35.00

Buster Brown and Tige, sign, plastic, decal, 7¼ x 6½", $20.00.

Buster Brown
  Book
    Book of Travels, 1912 .... 45.00
    Buster Brown's Latest, 5 x 7¼", 16 pgs, premium issued by Buster Brown Hosiery Mills, Chattanooga, TN, 1909 copyright, R F Outcault signature on cov art, three different stories 85.00
  Calendar Plate, 1909, 7", Buster and Tige 48.00
  Compact, 2" d, brass, emb logo "Buster Brown Shoes, First Because

Of The Last," Buster holding shoe along Tige, reverse with hinged door and small mirror, c1930 .... 65.00
Cup and Saucer, Buster and Tige, sgd 45.00
Fan, framed 85.00
Gyroscope, Buster Brown Shoes, MIB 25.00
Lapel Stud, 1¼", white metal, silver finish, Buster with hand on Tige's head, c1900 .... 40.00
Mirror, pocket, 1946 .... 22.00
Pinback Button
  ⅞"
    Brownbilt Club, multicolored, white ground, black lettering, c1924 .... 15.00
    Buster Brown Blue Ribbon Shoes, brown, gray ground, back adv paper 40.00
    Buster Brown Gang, multicolored, litho, c1920 .... 20.00
    Buster Brown Hose Supporter, multicolored, Buster holding paint brush and pair of supporters, light green ground shading to white edges, c1900 35.00
  1", Buster Brown Blue Ribbon Shoes, sepia, photo-like portrait of Buster and Tige, paper text on back, c1902–10 .... 18.00
Pitcher, 3¼" 30.00
Plate, 6" 30.00
Premium Comic and Mobile Card, Smilin Ed Radio Show, 7 x 10" comic book, full color, 16 pgs, 1959 copyright, 8 x 12" uncut full color card, Christmas motif 35.00
Shoe Box, Buster Brown Shoes 15.00
Stickpin, diecut, emb, name on hat, c1900 .... 50.00
Wallet, 1946 .... 22.00
Whistle, 1 x 2⅝", litho tin, multicolored, brown ground, Buster and Tige, c1920 .... 35.00
Campbell Kids
  ABC Bowl 16.00
  Book, *Campbell Kids At Home* 15.00
  Doll, cloth, straw filled, painted features, movable limbs, 1909 ...... 250.00
  Fork and Spoon, 4" l, engraved Campbell Kids handle, inscription "M-M-M Good," William Rogers SP, 1950s 25.00
  Garden Set, display card with five metal toy tools, wood handles, c1950 .... 40.00
  Mirror, pocket 100.00
  Mug, girl 8.00
  Spoon 8.00
  Toy
    Boxcar 10.00
    Truck, pull type, wood, Fisher Price 80.00

Charlie The Tuna

Bathroom Scale, 13", oval, 1972 copyright **25.00**

Clock, 4" d, 6" h, brass, windup, Charlie on dial in blue, orange, and red, 1969 copyright, marked "Lux Time Div Of Robertshaw Controls Co" **50.00**

Doll, 7½", vinyl **20.00**

Lamp, 10" h, plaster, painted **70.00**

Chiquita Banana

Doll, Kellogg's, uncut, 1944 .... **27.00**

Sheet Music, Chiquita and Calypso musicians front, 1947 copyright .. **12.00**

Doe-Wah-Jack

Catalog, Furnaces and Ranges, 1935 **28.00**

Spoon, figural, round oak stoves ... **65.00**

Dutch Boy Paint

Hand Puppet, 11", vinyl head, fabric body, orig cellophane bag, 1960s **40.00**

Match Holder **75.00**

Paint Book, Dutch Boy illus, unused, 1907–20 .... **25.00**

Paperweight, lead, figural **18.00**

Elsie the Cow

Bank, 3½ x 5 x 7", white metal, painted, Master Casater Mfg Co, c1950 .... **75.00**

Cartoon Book, 3¼ x 4", 16 pgs, early 1940s **20.00**

Charm, plastic **15.00**

Cookbook, hardback, 1952 .... **15.00**

Cookie Jar, barrel base, Elsie climbing out top lid **100.00**

Doll

12½", stuffed, plush, colored soft vinyl plastic head, chest tag with Borden Co copyright and maker's label My-Toy, c1950 .... **50.00**

15", stuffed, vinyl plastic head, orig Elsie with Borden Co copyright tag, 1950–60 .... **40.00**

22", stuffed, felt, blue and white fabric dress, white apron, soft vinyl head, yellow felt slippers .. **30.00**

Key Chain, fob, figural, 1950 ...... **3.00**

Milk Bottle, gallon, marked "Borden's" **12.00**

Pinback Button, 1½", plastic, diecut, yellow, gold raised head center, 1950s **8.00**

Puzzle, palm, illus of Elsie **15.00**

Rattle, 4½" **18.00**

Soap, 2½ x 5 x 5", cardboard baby room scene box, 3½" h figural castille soap figure of Beauregard, c1940, orig box **20.00**

Toy, pull, wooden **150.00**

Gold Dust Twins Washing Powder

Calendar, 1933 .... **20.00**

Fan, 7½" d, diecut, cardboard, litho,

multicolored, Twins at 1904 World's Fair, wood handle **150.00**

Pinback Button, ⅞", pair of black boys in washtub, 1898 .... **55.00**

Sign, 20 x 13", paper, orange and black, "Let The Gold Dust Twins Do Your Work" **90.00**

Jolly Green Giant, doll, 16", cloth, leaf tunic and hat, 1966 .... **10.00**

Kool Cigarette Penguin

Match Holder, tin, wall, penguin smoking **15.00**

Pinback Button, 1", Willie between donkey and elephant, 1930s **20.00**

Salt and Pepper Shakers, pr, 3½" h, plastic, Willie and Millie **25.00**

Nipper, RCA Victor

Charm

Brass, 1½", disk, "His Master's Voice," on front with image of phonograph and Nipper, back with "RCA Victor, Div of Radio Corp of America" **25.00**

Celluloid, small brass loop, Japanese, c1930 .... **15.00**

Coffee Mug, plastic **5.00**

Pin, 1¼", celluloid, diecut, red, white, and blue, dealer's name on back, c1900 .... **28.00**

Salt and Pepper Shakers, pr, plastic, Victrola and Nipper dog, 1950s .. **25.00**

Snowdome **35.00**

Statue, 4", chalkware **25.00**

Purple Cow, Pick–Ohio Hotel, Youngstown, OH, cov sugar bowl, marked "Shenango China, New Castle, PA," $10.00.

Philip Morris

Cigarette Sample Pack, 1½ x 3", "Guest Package," Johnny on each side, orig cellophane seal, unopened, 1930–40 .... **25.00**

Placecard, Johnny **15.00**

Pillsbury Dough Boy
Bank **20.00**
Clock **18.00**
Cookie Jar **40.00**
Doll **8.00**
Salt and Pepper Shaker, pr **20.00**
Telephone **75.00**
Watch **30.00**
Poll Parrot
Toy, spinner top, 1¾", metal, diecut,
yellow, red, green, spins when
blown, c1940s **25.00**
Whistle, 2", tin, red, yellow, and
green **12.00**
Red Goose
Bank **125.00**
Figure, 12", ceramic, counter display **45.00**
Reddy Kilowatt
Ashtray
Glass, clear, red and white picture
in bowl, 1960s **15.00**
China, white, red illus, 1957 .... **10.00**
Butter Dish, pottery **18.00**
Figure
3" h, rubber, c1940s **50.00**
6" h, diecut, red and ivory, plastic,
glow in the dark type, 1961
copyright **40.00**
Hand Care Kit, contains lotion pillow
packets, red, white, and blue glossy
folder, Washington Water Power
Co, c1950 .... **15.00**
Matchbook Cover, 1½ x 4½", red,
black, white, and silver, cardboard,
Reddy and electric range, Niagara
Hudson Power Co, c1930 .... **18.00**
Pinback Button
¾", Reddy Kilowatt, The Mighty
Atom, red, white and blue,
c1950 .... **15.00**
⅞", Reddy dressed in red, white
ground, c1930 .... **20.00**

**Wrigley's Mother Goose, booklet, 4 x
5⅞", $20.00.**

1", red, white, and blue, white
ground, listening pose **5.00**
Sign, 4¾ x 10½", litho tin, silver
ground, blue lettering, red figure,
adv electric bill payments, hanging
chain, c1950 .... **60.00**
Stick Pin, 1", diecut brass, brass col-
ored figure, red body, c1940 ..... **10.00**
Tile **15.00**
Schmoo
Bank, 1948 .... **25.00**
Belt, leather **45.00**
Snap, Crackle & Pop, Kellogg's Rice
Krispies
Ink Blotter, 3½ x 5½", colorful, c1940 **5.00**
Puppet, hand, set of 3 .... **30.00**
Speedy Alka Seltzer
Bank, figural, 4¾" h, plastic **60.00**
Figure, 5½" h, plastic, 1960s **15.00**
Teddy Snow Crop, puppet, 8" h, white
plush fabric, vinyl face, name and
"CF" label, c1950s **50.00**
Tony the Tiger, Kellogg's, spoon, SP .. **5.00**

AERONAUTICA

Collecting Hints: This is a very new field. The
majority of collectors have focused on personalities, especially Charles Lindbergh and Amelia
Earhart. However, new collectors are urged to
look to the products of airlines, especially those
items related to the pre-jet era.

History: The first airlines in the United States
depended on subsidies from the government for
carrying mail for most of their income. The first
non-Post Office Department flight for mail carrying was in 1926 between Detroit and Chicago.
By 1930 there were 38 domestic and 5 international airlines operating in the United States. A
typical passenger load was ten. After World War
II, four engine planes with a capacity of 100 or
more passengers were introduced.

The jet age was launched in the 1950s. In 1955
Capitol Airlines used British made turboprop air-
liners in domestic service. In 1958 National Airlines began domestic jet passenger service. The
giant Boeing 747 went into operation in 1970 as
part of the Pan American fleet. The Civil Aero-
nautics Board, which regulates the airline industry, ended control of routes in 1982 and fares in
1983.

Major American airlines include American Airlines, Delta Air Lines, Northwest Airlines, Pan
American World Airways, Trans World Airlines,
and United Airlines. There are many regional
lines as well; new airlines are forming as a result
of deregulation.

References: Aeronautica & Air Label Collectors
Club of Aerophilatelic Federation of America, *Air*

Transport Label Catalog, published by club; Stan Baumwald, *Junior Crew Member Wings,* published by author; Trev Davis and Fred Chan, *Airline Playing Cards: Illustrated Reference Guide, 2nd Edition,* published by authors, 1987.

Collectors' Club: The World Airline Historical Society, 3381 Apple Tree Lane, Erlanger, KY 41018.

AIRLINES

Baggage Sticker, Pan American, blue and white, wing over globe emblem, "The System of The Flying Clippers"   **4.00**

Breakfast Set, American Airlines, butter pat, cup and saucer, 6" plate, marked "Mayer China" **35.00**

Cup and Saucer
  American Airlines, marked "Mayer China" **20.00**
  TWA, white, gold emblem, marked "Rosenthal, Germany" **25.00**

Fan
  Air India, litho, blue and orange, cream ground, route map, four stylized figures, c1960 ....   **8.00**
  BOAC, litho, six ethnic figures, multicolored, Japan, c1960 ......   **5.00**

Lapel Stud, ½", TWA, brass, red enamel   **18.00**

Lighter, Pan Am **15.00**

Plate, Convair Corp, marked "Vernon Kilns" **25.00**

Postcard, Flying Hostesses of Eastern Air, c1940 ....   **5.00**

Poster, Air France Nordafrika, 25 x 40", airliner swooping over North African setting, c1946 ....   **250.00**

Puzzle, American Airlines, 707 jet in flight, frame tray, Milton Bradley, 1960 copyright **15.00**

Schedule, Air France, 4 x 9" paper folder, opens to 9 x 20" sheet, air route map of Europe, three major routes, int. black and white photo of Golden Clipper 10-seater, c1930 ...   **20.00**

Soup Bowl, cream, handles, Trans-World Airlines, white, red banner, gold star with RA (Royal Ambassador) in center, marked "Rosenthal China"   **15.00**

Tableware
  Pan American, silverplated knife and fork, propeller passenger plane, inscribed "Flagship," marked "Insico," c1940 ....   **28.00**
  United Airlines, fork **6.00**

Toy
  American Airlines Flagship, orig propellers, Fisher Price **175.00**
  Capital Airlines Viscount, airplane, 14" wingspan, Linemar, c1950 ...   **85.00**

GENERAL

Advertising
  Sign, tin, White Flyer Armour Laundry Soap Makes Dirt Fly, white Bleriot plane, 1912 ....   **250.00**
  Trade Cards, Goudey Sky Birds, complete set of 24 ....   **100.00**

Book
  Booth, Harold H, author and illus, *Book of Modern Warplanes,* 1942, 9½ x 12", hard cover, 28 pgs, orig dust jacket **30.00**
  Jordanoff, *Through the Overcast,* 1941 ....   **15.00**

Calendar Plate, 6½", biplane, 1912 ...   **35.00**

Cigarette Lighter, 6", chrome plated metal, desk type, propeller opens lighter compartment in wing, c1937   **75.00**

Coloring Book, *Airplanes To Color,* 10 x 14", 24 pgs, Saalfield, 1930, 24 pgs, premium for Silver Wings bars **55.00**

Fan, 18", multicolored litho, airplane, Hotel Sherman, Chicago, 1910 ....   **28.00**

Guide Book, *American Airplanes Picture Guide Book,* Whitman, 1940, 3½ x 6", full color illus and text **15.00**

Magazine
  Aero Digest, June 1935, 9 x 12", 88 pgs, black and white photos and articles **8.00**
  Air Trails, Dec 1937, 8½ x 11½", 96 pgs, full color cov **10.00**
  Battle Planes, 1941, Dell Publication, 40 pgs, full color cov art by Charles Rosner, illus of war aircraft **25.00**
  Flying Aces, February, 1939, 8½ x 11½", 82 pgs, full color cov art by August Schomburg **10.00**
  Popular Aviation, March, 1936, 8½ x 11½", 70 pgs, full color cov art by Herman R. Bollin **15.00**

Patch, 7½ x 9", yellow, blue, and red, Boeing, Wichita Division, c1940 ...   **18.00**

Pin
  ¾", brass, two shades of blue, gold, white, "Pratt and Whitney, USA Dependable Engines," eagle head dec, c1930 ....   **12.00**
  1", brass, Boeing, c1940 ....   **15.00**

Pinback Button
  ⅞"
    Megow Contest, red, white, and blue member button **10.00**
    Teamsters Airline Division, black and white, jet, c1960 ....   **12.00**
  ¹¹⁄₁₆", black and white litho, twin engine propeller plane, issued by David C Cook Publishing Co, 1930s **10.00**
  ¹³⁄₁₆", Planes and Pilots series, set of 70, 1930s

Bleriot's Monoplane, black, white, and peach, #29 .... 12.00

China Clipper, black and gray litho, #20 .... 10.00

Douglas DC-2, black, white, and peach litho, #19 .... 12.00

1", black and tan, Wayne Aero Club, c1930 .... 20.00

1½"

Curtiss, multicolored, biplane, rear propeller, flags of four nations, red script inscription "Curtiss," c1911 .... 100.00

LLLL, red, white, and blue, celluloid, "Loyalty League of Lumberman and Loggers," biplane, warship, spruce trees, WWI era ... 30.00

2¾", oval, celluloid, red, white, blue, and green, International Aviation Day, El Paso, TX, Dec 1945, fabric ribbons in patriotic colors for America and Mexico 42.00

Planter, 7", hot air balloon shape, ceramic, German 30.00

Plate, 10½", white, china, brown illus of five aircraft with titles, made for Martin Aviation by Vernon Kilns, c1940 .... 50.00

Postcard

Claremont NH, plane and hanger, 1928 .... 28.00

International Pan Am Airport, Miami FL, linen 3.50

Print

7½ x 9½", full color illus of North American B-25 bomber, artist George Sheppard, Quaker Oats premium, orig brown mailing envelope 40.00

14 x 16½", set of four commissioned by Thompson Products, Cleveland, artist Charles H Hubbell, transport planes, multicolored 30.00

Propeller, 32", wood, marked "Kroehler" 50.00

Pulp Magazine, *Dare Devil Aces*, 7 x 9½", May 1943, 98 pgs 18.00

Puzzle, 1⅞", palm, metal rim, multicolored paper under glass, yellow hot air balloon rising above village house and church steeple, diecut passenger in basket, red inscription "Carriages, Implements, Harness, Chas H Childs & Co, Utica, NY," c1900 .... 90.00

Sign, Hi Plane Tobacco, 11 x 36" self framed emb tin, multicolored 115.00

Sheet Music, "A Modern Honeymoon," Wright Bros type plane 15.00

Watch Fob, 1¼ x 1½", silvered white metal, raised illus of single wing passenger plane, c1920 .... 18.00

PERSONALITIES

Byrd, Richard

Autograph, 8 x 10", black and white semi-glossy photo, Admiral Byrd embarking 1940s transport plane, browned ink signature 25.00

Book, *Alone*, account of stay in Antarctica, 1934, autographed 115.00

Watch and Fob, 2" silvered brass pocketwatch, 1½ x 2" diecut silvered metal fob, commemorating 1929 flight 200.00

Corrigan, Douglas

Book, autobiography, *That's My Story*, published by E P Dutton & Co, 1938, 5½ x 8¼", hard cov, 221 pages, 56 sepia photos 15.00

Photograph, 3 x 4", waving from cabin of airplane, autographed, 1938 .... 80.00

Earhart, Amelia

Book, *20 Hours 40 Min, Our Flight In The Friendship*, publisher G P Putman & Sons, NY, 1928, 1st ed, autographed 350.00

Pinback Button, 1¼"

Atlantic, Newfoundland to Wales, black and white, gray photo of Earhart and passengers Lou Gordon and William Stultz, 1928 .. 300.00

Bond Bread, Friendship, black, white, and orange, button #5 from 1930 series 38.00

Plate, 8½" sq, Lindbergh commemorative, yellow ground, multicolored transfer, marked "Limoges China, Sterling, Golden Glow," $30.00.

Fitzmaurice, Col, pinback button, 1¼", black and white photo of Fitzmaurice and aircraft Breman, attached striped green, white, and orange ribbon and white metal airplane, c1928 .... 40.00

Hughes, Howard

Game, "The Howard Hughes Game,"

11 x 17 x 3", Family Games Inc, thick brown plastic box designed as attache case, orig cardboard label and shrink wrap, copyright 1972 . **100.00**
Pinback Button, 1¼", red, white, and blue rim, black and white photo, white ground, July 1938 flight around the world **40.00**
Lindbergh, Charles
  Bookends, pr, 5 x 5½", cast iron, raised images of Lindbergh in flight uniform, eagle at shoulder, Art Deco style inscription "The Aviator," 1929 copyright **100.00**
  Christmas Light Bulb, 3" h, electric, ½" socket thread, aviation uniform **40.00**
  Fabric, 33 x 35", drapery type, repeated designs of Lindbergh and plane in flight, maroon, white ground **115.00**
  Mirror, pocket, 2¼ x 3½", celluloid, black and white photo, plane illus, red, white, and blue patriotic border **60.00**
  Pillow Cover, silk like fabric, blue stitched border and trim, black and white illus of Lindbergh, plane, American flag, central banner "New York to Paris," solid blue backing, 18½ x 17½" **70.00**
  Pinback Button
  1¼"
    Bond Bread, Spirit of St Louis, dark red, black, and white, button #1, 1930 series **35.00**
    Captain Lindbergh, black and white photo **20.00**
    New York to Paris, bright red, white, and blue design, blue photo of Lindy, white ground, white metal replica of plane attached to red, white, and blue fabric ribbon **225.00**
    1⅜", red, white, and blue litho, photo of Lindy, eagle, Spirit of St Louis, Statue of Liberty, and Eiffel Tower in blue, American flags . **100.00**
  Postcard, 3¼ x 5½", air mail, black and white, issued to welcome Lindbergh, Milwaukee, August 1927, back text endorses air mail **25.00**
  Poster, 8 x 9½", Spirit of St Louis Cigars, dark blue, light blue, and white **35.00**
  Sheet Music, "Lindy, Lindy," 9¼ x 12¼", Wolfe Gilbert and Abel Baer, 1927 copyright, black, white, and orange cov **20.00**
Wright Bros
  Magazine Article, Youth's Companion, Oct 1, 1908, black and white cov, 11 x 16½", 16 pgs **25.00**

Photograph, 31 x 41", 1st flight, 1903, framed **150.00**
Tape Measure, 1¾", black and white, celluloid, 1910 Trenton, NJ, Fair . **90.00**
Watch Fob, Dayton, OH, celebration, 1909 . . . . **35.00**

AKRO AGATE GLASS

Collecting Hints: Akro Agate is marked "Made in USA" and often includes a mold number. Some pieces also include a small crow in the mark. It is a thick type of glass; therefore, collectors should buy only mint pieces. The marbleized types of Akro Agate were made in many color combinations. The serious collector should be looking for unusual combinations.

History: The Akro Agate Co. was formed in 1911. Their major product was marbles. In 1914 the owners moved from near Akron, Ohio, to Clarksburg, West Virginia, where they opened a large factory. They continued to produce marbles profitably until after the Depression. In 1930, the competition in the marble business became too great, and Akro Agate Co. decided to diversify into other products.

Two of their most successful products were the floral ware lines and children's dishes, first made in 1935. The children's dishes were very popular until after World War II when metal dishes captured the market.

The Akro Agate Co. also made special containers for cosmetics firms including the Mexicali cigarette jar, which was originally filled with Pick Wick bath salts, and a special line made for the Jean Vivaudou Co., Inc. Operations continued successfully until 1948. The factory, a victim of imports, metals, and increased use of plastics, was sold to the Clarksburg Glass Co. in 1951.

Reference: Gene Florence, *The Collectors Encyclopedia of Akro Agate Glassware*, Collector Books, 1975.

Collectors' Club: Akro Agate Art Association, P.O. Box, 758, Salem, NH 03079.

REPRODUCTION ALERT: Pieces currently reproduced are not marked "Made In USA" and are missing the mold number and crow.

Ashtray
  Ellipsoid, dark jade **5.00**
  Rectangular, turquoise **5.00**
  Square
    Green and white marbleized **6.00**
    Red and white marbleized **6.00**
Basket, orange and white marbleized, two handles **28.50**
Bell, 5¼", pumpkin **50.00**
Bowl
  3⅜" d, Concentric Ring, light blue . **25.00**

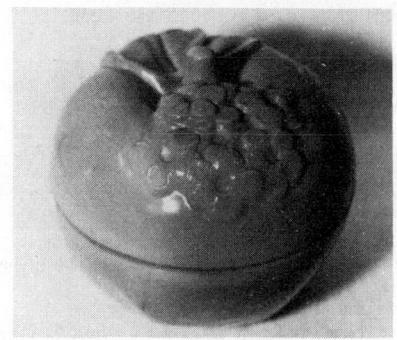

Powder Jar, cov, apple shape, pumpkin, $165.00.

5", emb leaves, orange and white marbleized	**35.00**
6", Westite, brown and white marbleized	**18.00**
Candlesticks, pr, 3½" h, green and white marbleized	**28.00**
Children's Dishes	
Bowl	
Octagonal Open, large, white ...	**8.00**
Stacked Disc and Panel, large, green	**14.50**
Creamer	
Interior Stacked Disc and Panel, cobalt, 1⅜"	**45.00**
Stacked Disc and Panel, pumpkin, 1¼"	**22.50**
Cup	
Chiquita, green, 1½"	**8.00**
Concentric Ring, pumpkin, clear handle, 1¼"	**22.50**
Octagonal	
Orange and white	**7.00**
Pumpkin, 1½"	**15.00**
Plain Jane	**12.50**
Stippled Band, topaz trans optic, 1¼"	**15.00**
Cup and Saucer, Concentric Ring, azure trans optic, 1¼"	**25.00**
Pitcher	
Interior Stacked Disc and Panel, transparent green	**9.00**
Octagonal, light blue, 2⅞"	**20.00**
Stacked Disc, green	**5.00**
Plate	
Concentric Ring, azure trans optic, 3¼"	**15.00**
Octagonal, green, 4¼"	**7.00**
Stippled Band, topaz trans optic, 3¼"	**9.50**
Saucer	
Chiquita Green, 3⅛"	**4.00**
Octagonal, lemonade and oxblood	**9.00**
Sugar, Octagonal, orange and white	**6.50**

Teapot, cov	
Interior Stacked Disc and Panel, azure trans optic, 2⅜"	**45.00**
Stacked Disc and Panel, blue, 2⅜"	**25.00**
Tumbler	
Interior Stacked Disc and Panel, transparent green	**7.00**
Octagonal	
Green	**5.00**
Yellow, 2"	**20.00**
Stacked Disc, white	**3.00**
Stacked Disc and Panel, pink, 2" .	**15.00**

Children's Tea Set, octagonal, three opaque colors, orig box, $125.00.

Children's Play Dish Set	
7 pcs, Stippled Band, lemonade set, jade trans optic, pitcher and six tumblers	**75.00**
11 pcs, Stippled Band, azure	**100.00**
12 pcs, Chiquita, green, MIB	**85.00**
17 pcs, Concentric Ring, small size, pink, aqua, and white	**140.00**
23 pcs, Octagonal, opaque green and white	**125.00**
Cigarette Box, Mexicali	**28.00**
Cigarette Holder, green and white marbleized	**10.00**
Demitasse Cup and Saucer, orange and white	**12.50**
Flower Pot	
1½", orange and white	**6.00**
1¾", yellow, ribbed top	**6.50**
3½", dark blue, ribbed top	**9.50**
4", Stacked Disc, blue and white marbleized	**15.00**
5¼", Westite, brown and white marbleized	**15.00**
Jardiniere, 4½", Westite, green and white marbleized	**17.50**
Lamp, brown and white marbleized, orig Akro shade	**90.00**
Match Holder, gun shape, marbleized, 3"	**10.00**

Mexicali Jar, cov
  Blue and white **20.00**
  Orange and white **20.00**
Powder Jar
  Apple, pumpkin **165.00**
  Scottie, blue **48.00**
Tumbler, 2⅝", Octagonal, green and
  white **6.00**
Urn, ftd, 3¼", orange and white **6.50**
Vase
  4⅜", Jean Vivaudou Co, emb han-
    dles, blue and white **8.50**
  8", Ribs and Flutes, cobalt **38.00**

ALUMINUM, HAND WROUGHT

Collecting Hints: Some manufacturers' marks are synonymous with quality, e.g., Continental Hand Wrought Silverlook. However, some quality pieces are not marked and should not be overlooked. Check carefully for pitting, deep scratches, and missing pieces of glassware.

History: During the late 1920s the use of aluminum for purely utilitarian purposes resulted in a variety of decorative household accessories. Although manufactured by a variety of methods, the hammered aluminum with repousse patterns appears to have been the most popular and certainly was more demanding of the skill of the craftsman producing the articles.

At one time many companies were competing for the aluminum giftware market with numerous silver companies adding aluminum articles as promotional items or as a more competitive and affordable product during the depression years. Many well known and highly esteemed metalsmiths contributed their skills to the production of hammered aluminum. With the advent of mass production methods and the accompanying wider distribution of aluminum giftware, the demand began to decline, leaving only a few producers who have continued to turn out quality work by the age old and time-tested methods of metal crafting.

Reference: Dannie Woodard and Billie Wood, *Hammered Aluminum: Wrought Collectibles*, privately printed, 1983.

Ashtray
  Hand Forged/Everlast Metal, 6", berry,
    straight sides **6.00**
  Wendell August Forge, 4 x 6", adv,
    Quaker State Motor Oil, dogwood
    dec **7.50**
Basket
  Continental Silver Co. Inc, 7¾", Chry-
    santhemum pattern, #1088 ...... **15.00**

Hand Forged, 12", flared sides, Har-
  vest pattern, scalloped handle **8.00**
Milcraft, 13", flat, Intaglio Wheat pat-
  tern, double strand handle **10.00**
Bowl
  Arthur Armour, 8", gold anodized,
    pine and mountains **12.00**
  Continental Silverlook, 11¼", chry-
    santhemum pattern, applied leaves,
    marked "No. 715" **14.00**
  Rodney Kent, 10", tulip, flower rib-
    bon handles, marked "No. 450" . **20.00**
  West Bend, 14", grapes, hammered
    ground **15.00**
Butter Dish
  Buenilum, round, domed cov, double
    loop finial, glass insert **17.50**
  Unmarked, rect,¼ lb size, stamped
    paisley pattern, rosette on cov ... **8.00**

Tray, flying geese dec, unknown manufacturer, 9¼ x 16½", $18.00.

Candleholder
  Buenilum, 6" h, beaded edge base,
    aluminum stem with wooden ball **5.00**
  Everlast Forged Aluminum
    2½" sq base, arrow shape, corners
      form feet, handle, "marked No.
      1020" **3.50**
    5½" saucer, lily **5.00**
Candy Dish, cov, 4½", dogwood dec on
  aluminum cov, glass base **5.00**
Casserole Holder, cov
  Everlast Forged Metal, 7½", rose,
    beaded knob **12.00**
  Unmarked, 10", footed ring, wheat
    and vegetables, fan shape handles
    and knob, baking dish **15.00**
Coaster, Wendell August Forge
  3¼", Edison Institute Museum En-
    trance **3.25**
  4¼", State of Texas, various symbols **3.50**
  5", turtle **3.00**
Cocktail Shaker, Buenilum, straight
  sides, grooved Art Deco top, clear
  plastic knob lid **12.00**
Compote, Continental Hand Wrought
  Silverlook, 5" h, wild rose, #1083 .. **12.00**

Creamer and Sugar Set, matching tray
  Continental Hand Wrought Silver-
    look, chyrsanthemum, grooved
    handles, applied leaves, tray
    marked **18.00**
  World Hand Forged, cupped shape,
    tray marked **8.00**
Crumb Tray, Farberware, hammered
  shiny finish **6.50**
Desk Set, Everlast Forge three pc, grad-
  uated sizes, Bali bamboo pattern,
  marked "B 24" **20.00**
Gravy Boat, Hand Forged/Everlast
  Metal, 7", curled handle, underplate,
  and ladle, ... **10.00**
Ice Bucket, cov, Lehman, 11½" h, dou-
  ble twisted handles, plastic knob on
  lid **12.00**
Ladle, Argental Cellini Craft, 14½",
  overall, small hammer marks **18.00**
Lazy Susan
  Rodney Kent, 16", cov glass dish, rib-
    bon and flower trim **10.00**
  Continental Silverlook, 18", leaf and
    acorns **15.00**
Match Box Holder, Wendell August
  Forge, kitchen box size, pine **8.00**
Napkin Holder, trefoil shape, ftd, fruit
  dec **4.00**
Pitcher
  Buenilum, ovoid, slender neck,
    twisted handle, finial **24.00**
  Keystone, thick band handle **8.00**
Punch Ladle, twisted handle, looped fi-
  nial, unmarked Buenilum style **12.00**
Salad Set, Buenilum Hand Wrought, 13"
  bowl, tulip dec, matching serving
  utensils **15.00**
Samovar, I gal container with spigot,
  double loop finial cov, stand and cov
  candle holder, unmarked Buenilum
  style **35.00**
Serving Dish, Continental Hand
  Wrought, Silverlook, 7¾", wild rose
  pattern, hammered ground **10.00**
Silent Butler, Henry & Miller, 6 x 8",
  oval, floral bouquet **8.00**
Tray
  Arthur Armour, 10 x 16", gold anod-
    ized, chessmen **15.00**
  Buenilum, 12 x 18", leaf and flower,
    fluted edge **18.00**
  Farber & Shlevin, 7½ x 14½", zinnia
    panel, spiral handle **18.00**
  National Silver Co, 11 x 16", bird on
    flowering limb **15.00**
  Rodney Kent, 14 x 20", tulip, handles,
    marked "No. 425" **25.00**
Water Set, World Hand Forged,
  pitcher, eight 20 oz tumblers, ap-
  plied flowers, sq knot handle on
  pitcher **45.00**

AMERICAN DINNERWARE

Collecting Hints: The companies who manufactured American Dinnerware made different
shapes, sizes, and hundreds of patterns. Most of
these dinnerware pieces are backstamped. A
backstamp usually includes the company name,
logo, pattern name or shape, and production
numbers. Many companies changed the backstamp to promote a new line or pattern, thus
creating many confusing backstamps. A collector
should learn all the marks and backstamps associated with their particular area of collecting.

The majority of American dinnerware is collected by pattern or company. Remember that
some companies kept the same pattern in production for several decades. Condition is the key
element. Since production runs were large, do
not settle for damaged pieces.

Prices for individual pieces are generally
higher than when they are sold in sets. This is a
phenomenon common to all dinnerware china,
European or American. The reason is that many
people have a basic set and are looking for filler
pieces. After all, only the most avid collector will
own more than a half dozen sets of china.

History: The origins of the American Dinnerware
industry were in East Liverpool, Ohio, an area
rich in natural clay deposits. James Bennett
started a factory there in 1839. Benjamin Harker
assisted with financial backing and supplied raw
materials. The first salesman was Issac Knowles.

By 1844, Bennett left the area and Benjamin
Harker had founded the Harker Pottery Co. Many
other potteries also were established. Their first
products were yellow ware, named for the color
assumed by the clay when fired. In 1879, white
ware was developed by Harker, Knowles, and
Laughlin, further establishing the dinnerware industry in the area. The development of white
ware necessitated decoration and skilled people
to do it.

The American dinnerware industry thrived in
the 1940s, a period that saw Americans buying
American made products. By the 1950s, the
number of potteries decreased. The increased use
of plastics and imports greatly hurt the industry.
The few companies that remain have included
institutional wares in their production.

References: Jo Cunningham, *The Collector's En-
cyclopedia of American Dinnerware,* Collector
Books, 1982; Pat Dole, *Purinton Pottery,* pri-
vately printed, 1985; Delleen Enge, *Franciscan
Ware,* Collector Books, 1981; Winnie Keillor,
Dishes, What Else? Blue Ridge of Course!, pri-
vately printed, 1983; Lois Lehner, *Lehner's En-
cyclopedia of US Marks on Pottery, Porcelain &
Clay,* Collector Books, 1988; Jim Martin and
Bette Cooper, *Monmouth-Western Stoneware,*

Wallace-Homestead, 1983; Betty Newbound, *The Gunshot Guide To Values of American Made China & Pottery*, Book 2, privately printed, 1983; Betty Newbound, *Southern Potteries, Inc. Blue Ridge Dinnerware, 3rd Edition*, Collector Books, 1989; Robert H. Schneider, *Coors Rosebud Pottery*, Busche-Waugh-Henry Publications, 1984.

Periodicals: *The Daze*, 12135 North State Road, Otisville, MI 48463; *The New Glaze*, P. O. Box 4782, Birmingham, AL 35206; *National Blue Ridge Newsletter*, P. O. Box 298, Blountville, TN 37617.

BLUE RIDGE

Blue Ridge dinnerware was produced by Southern Potteries of Erwin, Tennessee, from the late 1930s until 1956. The company used eight shapes and over 400 different patterns.

Blue Ridge, Dogwood pattern, vegetable dish, yellow and brown, 9¼ x 7", $5.00.

Beaded Apple
Bowl, 5"	1.50
Cup	1.50
Plate, 10½"	3.50
Saucer	1.00

Bluebell Bouquet
Bowl, 9", oval	12.00
Carafe, cov	25.00
Cup	3.50

Plate
6", bread and butter	1.75
7", luncheon	3.00
9¼", dinner	4.25

Colonial Style
Cake Knife	8.50
Cake Plate	10.00
Cereal Bowl	3.00
Coaster	7.50
Demitasse Cup and Saucer	12.00
Fruit Bowl	2.75
Gravy Boat	12.00

Plate
6", bread and butter	3.75

7", luncheon	4.50
9¼", dinner	8.25
Relish, divided	15.00
Salt and Pepper Shakers, pr	12.00
Saucer	1.50
Vegetable Bowl	8.00

Mardi Gras
Creamer	2.00
Cup	5.00
Fruit Bowl	3.25
Gravy Boat, underplate	18.00

Plate
6½", bread and butter	1.00
7", luncheon	2.00
9½", dinner	3.00
Saucer	.50
Vegetable Bowl, 9"	7.50

Nocturne, Colonial Blank

Bowl
5¼"	2.50
6"	3.00
Creamer and Sugar	7.00
Cup and Saucer	4.00

Plate
6¼", bread and butter	2.50
6½", sq	3.00
10", dinner	4.00
Platter, 11½", oval	8.00
Vegetable Bowl, 9½", round	8.00

Poinsettia
Creamer	8.00
Cup	6.00

Plate
6", bread and butter	3.00
9½", dinner	8.00
Saucer	1.00
Sugar, cov	12.00

COORS

Coors Pottery was manufactured in Golden, Colorado, from 1920 to 1939.

Rosebud
Baking Pan, 12¼ x 8¼ x 2¼"	20.00
Bean Pot, cov, yellow	18.00
Cake Knife, 10" l, maroon, yellow rosebud, three green leaves	20.00
Cake Plate	18.00
Casserole, cov, 3½ pint, green	35.00
Cereal Bowl, 6", yellow	10.00
Cookie Jar, cov, yellow	24.00
Cream Soup Bowl, 4", blue	12.00
Custard Cup, blue	9.00
Fruit Bowl, 5", maroon	12.00
Honey Pot, cov	20.00
Mixing Bowl, handle, orange	24.00
Pie Baker	12.75

Plate
6", bread and butter, rose	9.00
7", salad, yellow	9.75
9", dinner, green	10.00

Soup Plate, 8", green	15.00
Teapot, large, rose	48.00
Utility Jar, cov, yellow	24.00

CROOKSVILLE

The Crooksville China Company, Crooksville, Ohio, was founded in 1902 for the manufacture of artware "such as vases, flowerpots, and novelties." Dinnerware soon became its stock and trade. Crooksville's Pantry "Bak In" line was an extremely popular addition to their existing 1930s lines. Silhouette was one of the most popular patterns that Crooksville made. The Silhouette decal is in black on a yellow glaze ground and shows two men sitting at a table with a dog looking up at them, waiting for food.

Apple Blossom
Bowl, 5"	2.00
Creamer	4.00
Cup	1.50
Plate	
6", bread and butter	1.75
8", luncheon	2.50
9", dinner	3.50
Saucer	.75
Sugar, cov	5.00

Country Home
Cup	3.00
Plate	
6", bread and butter	2.00
8", luncheon	3.50
9", diner	5.00
Saucer	1.00

Petit Point House
Cup	4.50
Fruit Bowl, 5"	2.50
Mixing Bowl, 8¼"	5.75
Pie Baker	15.00
Plate	
6", bread and butter, emb border	3.00
9", dinner	8.00
Platter, 13¼"	7.00
Salt and Pepper Shakers, pr	12.00
Saucer	2.00
Soup Plate, 7¼"	3.50
Teapot	25.00
Vegetable Bowl, 9"	6.00

Silhouette
Batter Jug, cov	45.00
Candy Dish, metal trim	18.00
Casserole, cov	25.00
Creamer	6.50
Cup	6.00
Pie Baker	16.50
Pitcher, ice lip	50.00
Plate	
7", salad	3.50
9", dinner	7.50
Saucer	2.00

Tumbler	12.00
Vegetable Bowl, 9"	15.00

EDWIN M. KNOWLES CHINA COMPANY

This dinnerware was manufactured in East Liverpool, Ohio, from 1900 to 1963.

E. Knowles, Yorktown shape, maroon, 11¾" plate, $4.00.

Fruits
Batter Jug, cov	18.00
Casserole, cov, 8½"	7.00
Mixing Bowl, 8½"	6.50
Pitcher	12.00
Plate	
6", bread and butter	1.75
9¼", dinner	3.50
11", utility	8.50
Salt and Pepper Shakers, pr	15.00

Tia Juana
Bowl, 5"	8.00
Creamer	6.50
Cup	8.00
Plate	
7", salad	5.00
10, dinner	8.25
Platter	10.00
Salt and Pepper Shakers, pr	12.00
Saucer	2.00

Yorktown
Bowl, 5½"	
Wine	3.50
Yellow	3.50
Casserole, cov	15.00
Creamer, rust	4.00
Cup	3.00
Plate	
7", salad	2.50
8", luncheon	2.25
10", dinner	3.75
Salt and Pepper Shakers, pr, blue	8.00
Saucer	1.25

Soup, flat
Rust	**5.00**
Wine	**5.00**

FRANCISCAN

Made by Gladding McBean and Co, California, 1934 to the present. Over fifteen patterns were produced before 1940. The hand decorated patterns began with Apple Pattern in 1940, Desert Rose in 1941, and Ivy in 1948. Other patterns were made by using decals and some hand decorating. Coronado pattern, introduced in 1936 was made with both a satin and glossy finish. Over forty different marks were used before 1940. The firm merged with Lock Joint Pipe Company in 1963. In July, 1979, it was merged with Wegdwood Limited of England. The Glendale, California, plant closed in 1984.

Apple
Ashtray	**10.00**
Bowl	
5¼"	**7.00**
7½"	**16.00**
8½"	**16.00**
9"	**20.00**
Butter Dish, cov	**16.00**
Cream Soup	**10.00**
Creamer, 2¾"	**8.00**
Cup	**10.00**
Demitasse Cup and Saucer	**15.00**
Egg Cup	**12.50**
Gravy Boat	**15.00**
Pitcher, 9", one liter	**40.00**
Plate	
6", bread and butter	**3.00**
8", luncheon	**12.00**
9½", dinner	**12.00**
10½", dinner	**16.00**
Platter, 14"	**24.00**
Relish, 10"	**20.00**
Salad Bowl	**25.00**
Salt and Pepper Shakers, pr	**12.00**
Saucer	**2.00**
Sherbet, glass, hp	**5.00**
Soup Plate, flat, 8½"	**14.00**
Spoon Rest	**10.00**
Sugar, cov	**10.00**
Tumbler, glass, hp	**5.00**
Vegetable, divided	**35.00**
Coronado	
Bowl, 7½", coral, satin	**7.00**
Candlesticks, pr, coral, satin	**25.00**
Cereal Bowl	**12.00**
Chop Plate, 12", turquoise, satin	**7.00**
Cream Soup, underplate	**15.50**
Cup and Saucer, coral, satin	**3.50**
Demitasse Cup and Saucer, yellow	**15.00**
Demitasse Pot, rose	**35.00**
Gravy Boat, underplate	**25.00**

Plate	
6", bread and butter, yellow glossy	**4.50**
7½", salad	**8.50**
8½", luncheon	**9.50**
9", dinner	
Coral, satin	**4.50**
Turquoise, satin	**4.00**
Yellow, satin	**4.00**
Platter, 13", ivory satin	**27.50**
Sherbet	**8.50**
Teapot	**35.00**
Desert Rose	
Butter Dish, cov, ¼ lb	**25.00**
Cereal Bowl, 6"	**8.00**
Creamer	**15.00**
Cup	**8.00**
Egg Box, cov	**30.00**
Egg Cup	**12.50**
Fruit Bowl	**6.00**
Goblet, glass	**15.00**
Gravy Boat, attached underplate	**25.00**
Juice Tumbler, glass, 4"	**10.00**
Plate	
6", bread and butter	**4.50**
8", luncheon	**7.00**
10½", dinner	**12.00**
Platter, 14"	**25.00**
Salad Bowl, 9"	**28.00**
Saucer	**3.00**
Soup, 7", rim	**14.00**
Teapot	**30.00**
Tumbler, 5³⁄₁₆", china	**15.00**
Ivy	
Butter, cov, ¼ lb	**38.00**
Casserole, cov	**40.00**
Cereal Bowl, 6"	**6.50**
Creamer	**12.00**
Cup and Saucer	**7.00**
Pitcher, water	**40.00**
Plate	
6½", bread and butter	**4.50**
8⅜", luncheon	**7.00**
10", dinner	**8.00**
Platter	
11", oval	**22.50**
14", oval	**36.00**
Relish, 10", oval	**20.00**
Saucer	**2.75**
Soup	**10.00**
Sugar, cov	**15.00**
Teapot, cov	**40.00**
Vegetable Bowl	
8", round	**27.00**
12", divided, oval	**30.00**
Starburst	
Bowl	
5"	**6.00**
10½"	**12.00**
Creamer	**15.00**
Cup	**5.50**
Gravy Boat, liner	**35.00**
Nut Bowl, brass	**7.50**

Plate
6", bread and butter	....	**2.50**
8", luncheon	....	**4.50**
9½", dinner	....	**7.50**
Platter, 13"	....	**13.00**
Saucer	....	**1.50**
Sugar	....	**27.00**
Tea Cup and Saucer	....	**20.00**

PURINTON

Bernard Purinton founded Purinton Pottery in 1936 in Wellsville, Ohio. In 1941 the pottery was relocated to Shippenville, Pennsylvania. The plant ceased operations around 1959. Purinton Pottery used no decals; all wares were hand painted. William H. Blair and Dorothy Purinton were the chief designers.

Purinton, Apple pattern, 6⅛" plate, $5.00.

Apple
Bowl, berry	....	**6.25**
Cereal Bowl	....	**6.75**
Cookie Jar, cov	....	**28.00**
Creamer	....	**8.00**
Cruet	....	**20.00**
Cup	....	**4.00**
Honey Pot, 7"	....	**8.00**
Jar, cov, 6¾"	....	**28.00**
Jug, 2 pints	....	**15.00**
Mug	....	**25.00**

Plate
6", bread and butter	....	**5.00**
9", dinner	....	**5.00**
Relish, divided	....	**18.00**
Salt and Pepper Shakers, pr	....	**12.00**
Sugar, cov	....	**15.00**
Vegetable Bowl, 11½"	....	**18.00**
Fruits, lazy susan, triangular can set	..	**75.00**

ROYAL CHINA COMPANY

This dinnerware has been manufactured in Sebring, Ohio, from 1934 to the present.

Colonial Homestead
Cup, green and white	....	**1.50**
Plate		
6", bread and butter, green and white	....	**1.50**
9", dinner, green and white	......	**12.00**
Saucer, green and white	....	**1.00**

Currier and Ives
Bowl, 5½", blue	....	**1.50**
Cake Plate, 10½", handles, blue	...	**6.00**
Calendar Plate, 1973, blue	....	**3.50**
Cereal Bowl, 6½"	....	**5.00**
Chop Plate, blue	....	**10.00**
Creamer, blue	....	**2.00**
Cup and Saucer, blue	....	**2.00**
Gravy Boat, underplate, blue	......	**12.00**
Pie Baker, 10"	....	**10.00**
Plate		
6", bread and butter, blue	....	**1.25**
7½", salad	....	**2.00**
10", dinner, green	....	**2.00**
Salt and Pepper Shakers, pr, blue	...	**10.00**
Soup, flat, blue	....	**4.00**
Sugar, cov, blue	....	**4.00**
Teapot, blue	....	**25.00**

Memory Lane, pink and white
Bowl		
5½"	....	**2.00**
10"	....	**8.00**
Butter Dish, cov	....	**18.00**
Cake Plate	....	**8.00**
Casserole, cov	....	**25.00**
Chop Plate	....	**12.00**
Plate		
7", bread and butter	....	**2.50**
9", dinner	....	**4.00**
Soup Plate	....	**5.00**
Teapot	....	**18.50**

Old Curiosity Shop
Bowl, 10"	....	**5.00**
Cake Plate	....	**8.00**
Creamer	....	**3.00**
Cup and Saucer	....	**1.50**
Plate		
6", bread and butter	....	**1.50**
10", dinner	....	**2.00**
Platter, tab handle	....	**8.00**
Soup, flat	....	**3.00**
Tray, metal, round, green	....	**7.00**

STANGL

This dinnerware was manufactured in Trenton, New Jersey, from 1930 to 1978.

Country Garden
Condiment Set, two cruets, salt and pepper shakers, matching tray	...	**30.00**
Creamer	....	**4.00**
Pitcher	....	**8.00**
Sandwich Plate, 10", center handle	.	**15.00**

Prelude
Creamer 3.00
Cup and Saucer 5.00
Plate
6", bread and butter 2.00
8", luncheon 3.00
10", dinner 4.00
Provincial
Bowl, 10" 15.00
Chop Plate 15.00
Cup 2.00
Plate, 10", dinner 12.00
Platter, 13" 15.00
Vegetable Dish, divided 18.00
Thistle
Cereal Bowl 4.00
Chop Plate, 14" 10.00
Coaster 5.00
Coffeepot, cov 25.00
Creamer 6.00
Cup and Saucer 8.00
Fruit Bowl 5.00
Pitcher 12.00
Plate
6", bread and butter 6.00
9", dinner 8.00
Sherbet 12.00
Soup, flat 6.50
Sugar, cov 10.00
Teapot 25.00

TAYLOR, SMITH, AND TAYLOR

Founded in Chester, WV, in 1903 and remained in the family's control until purchased by Anchor Hocking in 1973. The tableware division was closed in 1981. Five pastel glazes were used: Windsor Blue, Persian Cream, Sharon Pink, Surf Green, and Chatham Gray.

Luray
Bowl
5½", Windsor Blue 3.50
9", Persian Cream 7.50
Cream Soup, Windsor Blue, orig liner 33.00
Creamer
Persian Cream 2.75
Sharon Pink 2.75
Windsor Blue 2.75
Cup and Saucer
Persian Cream 4.25
Sharon Pink 5.25
Surf Green 5.50
Windsor Blue 4.25
Egg Cup, double
Persian Cream 12.00
Sharon Pink 12.00
Windsor Blue 13.00
Gravy Boat, attached underplate, Surf
Green 16.50
Plate
6", bread and butter

Sharon Pink 1.75
Surf Green 1.50
Windsor Blue 1.50
7", salad
Surf Green 3.00
Windsor Blue 3.00
9¼", dinner
Persian Cream 4.50
Sharon Pink 3.50
Surf Green 3.25
Windsor Blue 3.25
10", dinner
Persian Cream 9.50
Sharon Pink 9.50
Surf Green 9.25
Windsor Blue 9.75
Platter
11¾", Surf Green 8.00
13½"
Chatham Gray 9.00
Sharon Pink 8.00
Salt Shaker
Persian Cream 5.00
Sharon Pink 5.00
Windsor Blue 6.00
Saucer, Persian Cream 1.50
Soup Bowl
Persian Cream 6.50
Sharon Pink 8.00
Surf Green 6.50
Sugar, cov, Windsor Blue 6.00
Vegetable Bowl, 10", oval, Chatham
Gray 7.00

WATTS POTTERY

Apple
Bean Pot 75.00
Cereal Bowl 20.00
Mixing Bowl, large 45.00
Mug 65.00
Pie Plate, adv 85.00
Pitcher
Ice lip, #17 .... 65.00
Sq, #69 .... 90.00
Salad Bowl 38.00
Salt Shaker, hourglass shape 45.00
Vegetable Bowl, cov, large knob ... 45.00
Bleeding Heart, bean pot 45.00
Morning Glory, creamer 55.00
Rooster
Bowl, adv 50.00
Pitcher, adv 45.00
Salt Shaker, adv 50.00
Tulips, pitcher, #16 .... 55.00

AUTOGRAPHS

Collecting Hints: The condition and content of letters and documents bears significantly on value. Signatures should be crisp, clear, and located so that they do not detract from the rest of the item. Whenever possible, obtain a notarized statement of authenticity, especially for pieces over $100.

Forgeries abound. Copying machines compound the problem. Further, many signatures of political figures, especially presidents, movie stars, and sports heroes are machine or secretary signed rather than by the individual themselves. Photographic reproduction can produce a signature resembling an original. Check all signatures using a good magnifying glass or microscope.

Presentation material, something marked "To _____," is of less value than a non-presentation item. The presentation personalizes the piece and often restricts interest, except to someone with the same name.

There are autograph mills throughout the country run by people who write to noteworthy individuals requesting their signatures on large groups of material. They in turn sell this material on the autograph market. Buy an autograph of a living person only after the most careful consideration and examination.

Autograph items are sold using standard abbreviations denoting type and size. They are:

ADS	Autograph Document Signed
ALS	Autograph Letter Signed
AQS	Autograph Quotation Signed
CS	Card Signed
DS	Document (printed) Signed
LS	Letter Signed
PS	Photograph Signed
TLS	Typed Letter Signed
Folio	12 x 16"
4to	8 x 10"
8vo	5 x 7"
12mo	3 x 5"

History: Autograph collecting is an old established tradition, perhaps dating back to the first signed documents and letters. Early letters were few, hence, treasured by individuals in private archives. Municipalities, churches, and other institutions maintained extensive archives to document past actions.

Autograph collecting became fashionable during the 19th century. However, early collectors focused on the signatures alone, clipping off the signed portion of a letter or document. Eventually collectors realized that the entire document was valuable.

The advent of movie stars, followed by sports, rock 'n roll, and television personalities, brought autograph collecting to the popular level. Fans pursued these individuals with autograph books, programs and photographs. Everything imaginable was offered for signatures. Realizing the value of their signatures and the speculation that oc-

curs, modern stars and heroes are less willing to sign material than in the past.

References: Mary A. Benjamin, *Autographs: A Key To Collecting*, Dover Publications, 1946/1988; Bob Bennett, *A Collector's Guide to Autographs with Prices*, Wallace-Homestead, 1987; Charles Hamilton, *American Autographs*, University of Oklahoma Press, 1983; George Sanders, Helen Sanders, and Ralph Roberts, *The Price Guide to Autographs*, Wallace-Homestead, 1988.

Collectors' Clubs: Manuscript Society, 350 Niagara Street, Burbank, CA 91505; Universal Autograph Collectors Club, P. O. Box 6181, Washington, DC 20044-6181.

Autograph Letters Signed (ALS)
Beebe, Charles W, American naturalist, 8vo	25.00
Benet, William R, poet and editor, Saturday Review stationery, 8vo	25.00
Bouck, Wm C, NY canal commissioner, 1847, NY	65.00
Dolbear, Amos E, American physicist and inventor, lined stationery, 1894, 4to, 2 full pgs	225.00
Drew, John, actor, Hotel Ponchartrain stationery, early 1900s, 4 single pages, 6 x 9"	150.00
Hale, Edward E, author, April, 1908, 10 x 6", laid down on heavy board, waterstained borders	75.00
Lowell, James Russell, American poet, plain stationery, 4 x 6"	50.00
McNair, C, Civil War Confederate general, lined stationery, 1875, 4to	150.00
O'Beirne, James R, Civil War Union officer, Grand View Hotel stationery, 1885, 6 x 8"	75.00
Porter, Gene Stratton, author and poet, 1919, 4to	200.00
Proctor, Thomas, Revolutionary War, sheriff of Philadelphia, 1786, 4to	75.00
Rubinstein, Helene, holograph address, Paris picture postcard	90.00
Sopwith, Thomas, aviator, personal stationery, 1973, 8vo	250.00
White Eagle, Sioux Indian Chief, WY, written from Buffalo, NY, 1921, 4to, lined paper	275.00

Cards Signed (CS)
Beatles, 1964 fan club card, signed boldly by all four	20.00
Bush, Barbara, Blair House stationery, 3 x 2"	55.00
Cornell, Katherine, American author, calling card, bold signature	20.00
Dorsey, Tommy, American band leader, c1940	25.00
Harding, Florence Kling, First Lady,	

black ink signature, engraving of White House, 6 x 4" card **60.00**

Mancini, Henry, musician and composer, inscribed, full signature, one bar of music penned, 5 x 3" white card **25.00**

Roosevelt, Eleanor, White House card **75.00**

Sousa, John Philip, card mounted to album page **125.00**

Stotz, Carl E, Little League Founder, 1956, ink signature, 5 x 3" card with 1956 Little League player pocket calendar **35.00**

Takei, George, Star Trek, 3 x 2" white card, dark blue "Star Trek" imprinted at top, blue image of *Enterprise* **50.00**

Document Signed (DS)

Beaver, James A, Civil War Union General, supply requisition, partly printed, c1861, 4to **75.00**

Caruso, Enrico, tenor, bank check, Feb 15, 1913 .... **400.00**

Edison, Thomas A., minutes from Board of Directors meeting, folio, 2 pgs, c1920 .... **275.00**

Ellenshaw, Peter, Disney Art Director, color brochure, sgd on cov, 11 x 8" **50.00**

Jackson, Andrew, President, land grant to Palmer Eliot, IL, Jan 3, 1832 .... **50.00**

Key, D M, Postmaster at West Point, 1880, folio **45.00**

Pickering, Timothy, Secretary of War, 1796, Philadelphia, partly printed passport, waterstained, 4to **75.00**

Serling, Rod, writer and producer, bank check, June, 1968 .... **275.00**

Tubb, Ernest, bank check, canceled, 1977 .... **10.00**

First Day Covers (FDS)

Anderson, Maxie, Larry Newman, and Ben Abruzzo, hot air balloonists, honoring their Atlantic Ocean crossing, canceled Washington, DC, Sept 1978 .... **175.00**

Astaire, Fred and Ginger Rogers, honoring the 50th Anniversary of Talking Pictures, canceled Hollywood, 1977 .... **185.00**

DeBakey, Michael E and Denton A Cooley, MD, honoring Charles R Drew, MD, canceled Washington, DC, 1981 .... **35.00**

Griebling, Otto, hand painted watercolor cachet of clown, sgd on blank **35.00**

Hillary, E P and Vivian Fuchs, honoring Antartic Treaty, canceled Washington, DC, 1971 .... **45.00**

Monaco, Prince Rainier, honoring "Great American Presidents: Washington, Lincoln, FDR, and Eisenhower," canceled 1966, blue ink signature **45.00**

Rogers, Richard, honoring W C Handy, canceled Memphis, 1969 . **75.00**

Sopwith, Thomas, UN Airmail, canceled 1963 .... **100.00**

Soyer, Raphael, artist, honoring Winslow Homer, canceled Gloucester, MA, 1962 .... **85.00**

Yeager, Chuck and Scott Crossfield, honoring Glenn Curtiss, canceled NY, 1980 .... **45.00**

Letters Signed (LS)

Sherman, John, Secretary of State, lined personal stationery, 1886, OH, 5 x 8" **45.00**

Vinton, D. H., Chief Q. M. in Mexican War, light blue stationery, aged, 4to **45.00**

Photograph Signed (PS)

Abruzzo, Ben, hot air balloonist, color, 4to **160.00**

Alda, Allen, black and white glossy, portrait pose, inscribed, white borders trimmed, 7 x 9" **15.00**

Allen, Woody, black and white glossy, portrait pose, inscribed, white borders trimmed, 7 x 9" ... **15.00**

Beatty, Warren, black and white glossy, photographer credits on verso, white borders trimmed, 7 x 9" **60.00**

Carter, J, President, black and white glossy, bust pose, 4to **45.00**

Clarke, Arthur C, author, black and white glossy, bust pose, 9 x 8" ... **30.00**

Crosby, Bing, black and white glossy, golf club, old hat, 4to **125.00**

Crabbe, Buster, black and white glossy, inscribed, signed as Buster Crabbe and Flash Gordon, 4to ... **75.00**

Dangerfield, Rodney, black and white glossy, portrait pose, white borders trimmed, 7 x 9" **10.00**

DeLuise, Dom, black and white glossy, portrait pose, inscribed, white borders trimmed, 7 x 9" ... **10.00**

Field, Marshall, president of Chicago Sun, black and white glossy, bust pose, 4to **30.00**

Fontaine, Joan, wearing big hat and flowers, black and white glossy, photographer credits on verso, 1937, 7 x 9" **30.00**

Griebling, Otto and Freddie Freeman, clowns, black and white glossy, bust pose, inscribed "Polack Bros Circus Season 1950," 4to **50.00**

Hamilton, Margaret, beginning of Wizard of Oz costume, black and

white glossy, white borders trimmed, 7 x 9" **150.00**
Keel, Howard, black and white glossy, portrait pose, inscribed, white borders trimmed, 7 x 9" ... **10.00**
Lancaster, Burt, black and white glossy, portrait pose, white borders trimmed, 7 x 9" **15.00**
Montana, Joe, football player, uniform, color, glossy, 4to **25.00**
Novak, Kim, black and white glossy, portrait pose, inscribed, white borders trimmed, 7 x 9" **15.00**
Peck, Gregory, casual pose, black and white glossy, photographer credits on verso, white borders trimmed, 7 x 9" **35.00**
Penny, J C, founder of dept store, sepia, bust pose, seated, 3 x 4" **50.00**
Peters, Bernadette, black and white glossy, portrait pose, inscribed, white borders trimmed, 7 x 9" ... **10.00**
Reynolds, Debby, black and white glossy, portrait pose, inscribed, white borders trimmed, 7 x 9" ... **15.00**
Robards, Jason, black and white glossy, portrait pose, inscribed, white borders trimmed, 7 x 9" ... **10.00**
Shatner, William, black and white glossy, Star Trek, 4to **25.00**
Shore, Dinah, black and white glossy, portrait pose, inscribed, white borders trimmed, 7 x 9" **10.00**
Staubach, Roger, football player, uniform, color, glossy, 4to **20.00**
Stewart, James, black and white glossy, from "The Stratton Story," 4to **55.00**
Tierney, Gene, black and white glossy, portrait pose, inscribed, white borders trimmed, 7 x 9" ... **10.00**
Williams, Esther, black and white glossy, portrait pose, inscribed, white borders trimmed, 7 x 9" ... **15.00**
Williams, Tennessee, author, black and white glossy, bust pose, casual dress, 8vo **300.00**
Wynn, Keenan, from 1953 "Tennessee Champ," MGM, black and white glossy, photographer credits on verso, white borders trimmed, 7 x 9" **60.00**
Typed Letters Signed (TLS)
Black, Hugo L, Associate Supreme Court Justice, thank you note, Supreme Court stationery, 1965 .... **65.00**
Coolidge, Calvin, President, MA Governor stationery, 1918, 4to **200.00**
Fiske, Minnie Madden, American actress, 1900, Stratford Hotel, Philadelphia, 4to **25.00**
Ford, Edsel B, fund raising letter, 4to **75.00**

Ford, Jerry, President, US Congress stationery, 1969, 4to **75.00**
Godfrey, Arthur, TV personality, personalized CBS business stationery, 1947 .... **60.00**
Grace, E G, President of Bethlehem Steel, business stationery, to son, 1932, 4to **75.00**
Hoover, Herbert, President, personal stationery, 1950 .... **100.00**
Hughes, Charles E, Supreme Court Chief Justice, Supreme Court stationery, 1911 .... **75.00**
O'Connor, Sandra D, Supreme Court Justice, Supreme Court stationery, orig envelope, 4to, 2 pcs **60.00**
Putnam, George Haven, publisher, National Association of Book Publishers stationery, 1929, 4to **40.00**
Rogers, Will C, III, Capt., *USS Vincenness*, official stationery, Aug 24, 1988, 7 x 8½", orig envelope, 2 pcs **100.00**

AUTOMATA, MODERN

BATTERY OPERATED AND WINDUP

Collecting Hints: Prices fluctuate greatly. Many of the collectors are in Japan and dealers must allow enough margin for shipment of pieces overseas. Operating condition is a key factor. Many pieces had accessory parts; these must be present to have full value. The original box, especially if it has a label, adds 10 to 20% to the price. Also, the more elaborate the action of the automata, the higher the value.

History: Automata began as "cheap" Japanese import goods in the 1950s. They were meant for amusement only, many finding themselves located on the shelves of bars in the recreation rooms of private homes. They were marketed through 5 and 10 cent stores and outlets.

The subjects were animal—bears being favored—and humans. Most were battery operated; but some were wind-up or had remote control. Quality of pieces varies greatly, with Linemar being among the best made.

The collecting craze started in the late 1970s. In 1981 Lloyd Ralston Toys, Fairfield, Connecticut, held the first auction featuring automata. Its success established the market nationally.

References: Don Hultzman, "Battery Operated Toys," in Richard O'Brien, *Collecting Toys*, Books Americana, 1985, 4th ed.; Brian Moran, *Battery Toys*, Schiffer Publishing Ltd, 1984.

Army Tank Gunner, 10 x 4 x 6", litho tin, wind-up, dark olive green, bright red, yellow, black, and white details, sparks in front as soldier pops up firing gun, Marx, c1950 .... **175.00**

Balloon Vendor, 4½ x 7 x 12", tin, fabric, vinyl, battery, clown type face, body moves, hand shakes metal bell, holds four plastic balls on wire rods, Yone, Japan **90.00**

Burger Chef, 6 x 6½ x 9", litho tin, fabric, and plush, battery, dog cooking hamburger, brick grill litho base, red plastic burner which lights, one hand cooks and flips hamburger, other holds salt shaker, tin eyes move up and down, brown plush ears move, Yone, Japan **100.00**

Coogan, Jackie, 2 x 3 x 7", litho tin, wind-up, dressed as "The Kid," blue-green overalls, light pink shirt with red stripes, bright yellow suspenders, upper part of body moves to right, eyes to left, back marked "Made in Germany," c1920 .... **500.00**

Happy Santa, lighted eyes, orig box, marked "RF" in diamond/Alps/Made In Japan, $85.00.

Dancer, 3½ x 4½ x 8½", litho tin and celluloid, wind-up man standing by black and white tin sign "Hollywood" and "Vine," red fabric jacket, black and white checked pants, red and white tie, tin hands and cane, feet tap out rhythm, Occupied Japan **165.00**

Elephant, Moving Elephant, 2 x 5 x 4¼", celluloid, wind-up, gray and white, bright yellow blanket trimmed in purple, blue celluloid cap, brass bell in trunk, tail spins, head moves, ears flop, bell rings, orig key, beige cardboard box with multicolored paper label, Occupied Japan **150.00**

Fireman, 4½ x 6½" multicolored litho base, three metal ladder sections extend to 25", four metal wheels, center

with bright red and orange scene of eight firemen fighting fire, 7" litho tin fireman climbs up and down ladder, Sonsco, Japan, c1950 .... **150.00**

Gypsy Fortune Teller, 6 x 7 x 11", battery, fabric cov, black outfit, red trim, pearls, molded vinyl face and hands, hold sheet of red fabric, white plastic ball, black and red printed fortunes, dark red tin base, coin inserted, gypsy nods her head, eyes light, arm moves and delivers card, multicolored orig box, Ichida, Japan **850.00**

Haunted House Mystery Bank, 7 x 9 x 8", multicolored house, gray plastic base and roof, tin litho sides, coin goes in doorstep, light goes on above door, door opens, ghostly figure appears and retrieves coin, Brumberger, Brooklyn, c1960 .... **350.00**

Horse Racing, 6½ x 19½ x 3", plastic, six small brown horses ridden by multicolored tin jockeys, tin and cardboard "Horse Racing" sign post, orig box, Shinsei, Japan, c1970 .... **35.00**

Lincoln-Continental Mark V With Retractable Top, 4 x 11 x 13", litho tin, multicolored detailed int., black, white, and red wheels, tin grills and bumpers, red plastic cov wire to remote control battery box, multicolored orig box, Cragston Toys, Japan **450.00**

Magic Snowman, 5 x 7 x 11½", white fabric, bright red facial accents and gloves, light brown scarf, holding tin handled broom and brass bell, stream of air blows out top of hat and keeps small stryofoam ball in air, eyes light, broom waves, orig instruction sheet, gold colored box with cellophane window, black lettering, foil sticker, Modern Toys, Japan, c1960 .... **200.00**

Miss Friday, 5½ x 8½ x 7½", litho tin, vinyl, fabric, battery, secretary seated at tin desk, vinyl hands move up and down on tin typewriter, roller moves to left and right with bell sound, tin upper body, vinyl head and arms, blonde rooted ponytail, black, white, and pink plaid fabric skirt, Japan ... **90.00**

Musical Rabbit, litho metal, beats drum, orig box, Japan **30.00**

Poodle, 4 x 11 x 10", white plush, bright red, gray, and yellow plaid body, pink neck bow, walks and wags tail as eyes light up, c1950 .... **75.00**

Santa, 4 x 7 x 12", bright red velvet like suit, white plus trim, arm moves to shake bell, other arm moves large brass edged star on pole, entire body rocks back and forth, c1960 .... **135.00**

Santa on Sled, 9 x 2½ x 4½", litho tin

wind-up, built-in key, large colorful reindeer with brown plastic feet and yellow antlers, three dimensional Santa, red fabric hat, white cotton beard, reindeer bucks, multicolored orig box, Mikuni, Japan, c1960 .... **55.00**
Squirrel, 3 x 5 x 6", litho tin, brown and yellow, blue and white apron, moves forward to bring metal walnut to mouth, mouth opens, large black, white, and brown eyes move, brown rubber ears, brown plush tail, Stone Mountain, Japan, distributed by Cragston, multicolored orig box, c1950 .... **65.00**
Teacup Ride, 7 x 7 x 6½", litho tin, multicolored, passenger train, roller coaster, carousel, and ride with eight moving arms, three vinyl teacups and saucers with litho tin insert of child, Kanto Toys, Japan, c1960 .... **65.00**
Telephone Bear, 3 x 4 x 6½", litho tin, fabric, and plush, wind-up, built-in key, tin blue pants, red shoes, red and white striped fabric shirt, beige rubber hands, gray plus body, bell rings, lifts receiver to head to answer tin telephone, multiclored orig box, Alps, Japan **90.00**

AUTUMN LEAF PATTERN

Collecting Hints: Most Autumn Leaf pieces are backstamped with two marks. Both contain the words "Halls Superior Quality" and "Mary Dunbar," the latter a Jewel Tea trademark.

History: Hall China first made Autumn Leaf pattern china in 1933 as a premium for the Jewel Tea Company. Large orders for Autumn Leaf are credited with carrying The Hall China Company through the latter years of the Depression, thus saving the company from going out of business.

Autumn Leaf remained in production until 1978. Over the years, many different pieces were added and dropped from the line. Generally, pieces with short production lives are more desirable. Other companies made matching accessories in metal, glass, and plastic and are very collectible. Also look for Jewel Tea toy trucks.

References: Harvey Duke, *Superior Quality Hall China*, ELO Books, 1977; Harvey Duke, *Hall 2*, ELO Books, 1985; Harvey Duke, *The Official Price Guide to Pottery and Porcelain*, House of Collectibles, 1989; Margaret and Kenn Whitmyer, *The Collector's Encyclopedia of Hall China*, Collector Books, 1989.

Collectors' Club: National Autumn Leaf Collec-

tor's Society, 120 West Dowell Road, McHenry, IL 60050.

Berry Bowl, 5½" d, $5.00.

Baker, oval	**65.00**
Bean Pot, two handles	**90.00**
Bowl	
5½", fruit	**4.00**
6½", cereal	**8.50**
8½", soup	**10.00**
Butter Dish, 1 lb	**175.00**
Cake Plate	**14.00**
Cake Safe, metal	**20.00**
Canister Set, sq, 4 pcs	**125.00**
Casserole	**25.00**
Coaster	**4.00**
Coffeepot	
China Dripper	**175.00**
Electrical	**240.00**
Cookie Jar	**90.00**
Cream Soup	**16.50**
Creamer	**8.00**
Cup	**7.00**
Custard Cup	**5.00**
Drip Jar, cov	**14.00**
Fruitcake Tin	**5.00**
Gravy Boat	**18.00**
Marmalade, 3 pcs	**45.00**
Mixing Bowl Set, nesting, 3 pcs	**40.00**
Mug, ftd	**75.00**
Mustard, 3 pcs	**45.00**
Pickle Dish	**20.00**
Pie Baker	**19.00**
Pitcher	
Ball shape	**25.00**
Ear shaped handle	**14.00**
Plate	
6", bread and butter	**4.00**
7¼", pie	**4.00**
8", salad	**8.50**
9", dinner	**7.50**
10", dinner	**9.00**
Platter, oval	
11½"	**15.00**
13½"	**15.00**
Salad Bowl	**14.00**

Salt and Pepper Shakers, pr
    Large 20.00
    Small 14.00
Saucer 3.00
Souffle Dish
    Large 14.00
    Small 8.00

Salt and Pepper Shakers, range size, $15.00.

Stack Set 55.00
Sugar, vertical lines 20.00
Tablecloth, sailcloth, sq 65.00
Tea Towel 20.00
Teapot, Aladdin 35.00
Tidbit Tray, three tiers 40.00
Toaster Cover, plastic 20.00
Toy, truck, orange 35.00
Tray
    Oval, metal 50.00
    Rect, glass, wood handles 70.00
Tumbler, frosted
    9 oz 18.00
    14 oz 11.00
Vase, bud 150.00
Vegetable Dish
    Divided 55.00
    Oval
        Covered 36.00
        Open 15.00
    Round 65.00

AVON

Collecting Hints: Avon collectibles cover a wide range of objects, including California Perfume Company bottles, decanters, soaps, children items, jewelry, plates, catalogs, etc. Another phase of collecting focuses on Avon Representatives and Managers' awards.

Avon products are well marked. Four main marks exist. The name of the California Perfume Company appears from 1930 to 1936. The words "Avon Products, Inc." have been used since 1937 on the trademark.

Due to the vast number of Avon collectibles, a collector should buy only items of interest. Do not ignore foreign Avon material, although it is hard to find. New items take longer to increase in value than older items. Do not change the object in any way that destroys the value.

History: David H. McConnell founded the California Perfume Co. in 1886. He hired saleswomen, a radical concept for that time. They used a door-to-door technique to sell their first product, "Little Dot," a set of five perfumes; thus was born the "Avon Lady." By 1979 there were more than one million.

In 1929, California Perfume Co. became the Avon Company. The tiny perfume company grew into a giant corporation. Avon bottles attracted collector interest in the 1960s.

References: Bud Hastin, *Bud Hastin's Avon Bottles Collectors Encyclopedia, 10th Edition,* privately printed, 1984; Joe Weiss, *Avon 8 - Western World Handbook & Price Guide to Avon Bottles,* Western World Publishers, 1987.

Collectors' Clubs: Bud Hastin's National Avon Collector's Club, P. O. Box 9868, Kansas City, MO 64134; Western World Avon Collectors Club, 23785, Pleasant Hills, CA 93535.

Museums: Nicholas Avon Museum, MTD Rt. Box 71, Clifton, VA 24422.

REPRODUCTION ALERT

Note: Prices quoted are for full, mint and boxed condition.

Awards and Representatives Gifts
    Charm Bracelet, silver, six charms, 1959 .... 190.00
    Key Ring, gold lucite, green box, 1973 .... 8.00
    Necklace, sterling silver, acorn, velvet pouch, Tiffany box and card, 1980 .... 80.00
    Order Book, 1968, Charisma, red pen 5.00
    Paperweight, clear lucite, silvertone design and oak tree, 1980 .... 20.00
    Pin, Manager's, diamond crown guard, 1961 .... 145.00
    Stick Pin, butterfly, gold tone, enameled, 1981 .... 3.50
    Tie Tac, telephone, gold tone, 1981 12.00
California Perfume Company
    Almond Meal, Violet, 8 oz, glass jar, 1893 .... 130.00
    Bath Salts, Ariel, glass, ribbed, 1903 68.00
    Perfume
        Carnation, 1 oz, glass, ribbed, 1923 .... 125.00
        White Rose, clear glass, orig neck ribbon, 1918 .... 135.00
    Soap
        Almond, buttermilk, and cucumber, yellow, pink, and green box and wrappers, three bars, 1906 85.00

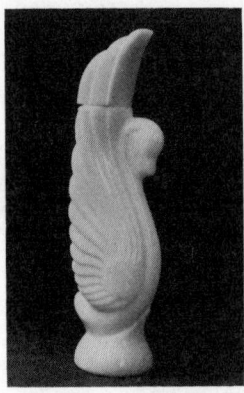  

Left: Women's Item, cologne, Swan Lake Charisma, 3 oz, 1972–76, 8″ h, $5.00; center: Men's Item, Stage Coach, Wild Country After Shave, glass, brown, $7.50; right: Women's Item, hand lotion, Country Jug, 10 oz, $5.00.

Dr Zabriskie's, 1915, brown, emb,
orig blue box **48.00**
Vegetable Oil, set of three, light or-
ange, turquoise and white paper
wrapping, 1936 . . . . **35.00**
Talcum
California Perfume Company, tin . **12.00**
California Rose, 3½ oz, 1921 . . . . **100.00**
Toilet Water, Lily Of The Valley, 2 oz,
glass, ribbed, 1923 . . . . **90.00**
Children's Items
Baby Lotion
Bear, 10 oz, pink, matching pump
dispenser, 1981 . . . . **6.00**
Lamb, 6 oz, white plastic, 1975 . . **3.00**
Bank, Humpty Dumpty, 5″, ceramic,
1982 . . . . **15.00**
Bubble Bath
Freddy The Frog, mug, 5 oz, white
glass, red top, 1970 . . . . **6.50**
Linus, plastic, 1970 . . . . **5.00**
Mickey Mouse, plastic, 1969 . . . . **5.00**
Snoopy, snow flyer, plastic, 1973 . **6.50**
Comb and Brush Set
Bear, red, white, and blue, 1976 . **2.00**
Hot Dog, yellow and red plastic,
1975 . . . . **2.50**
Nail Brush
Alligator, green plastic, 1975 . . . . **2.50**
Happy Hippo, 3″ l, pink, 1973 . . . **2.00**
Set
Cowboy Set, white box, two red
leatherette cowboy cuffs, cream
hair dressing, toothpaste, and
toothbrush, 1950 . . . . **50.00**
Hair Trainer, 6 oz bottle, blue cap,
red and white label, plastic
comb, 1957 . . . . **20.00**
Rough N' Ready, white, red, and
green box, 4 oz hair cream, chap
check, and soap, 1953 . . . . **40.00**

Shampoo
Charlie Brown, 4 oz, plastic, 1969 **6.50**
Jet Plane, red, white, and blue plastic tube, white plastic wings,
1965 . . . . **1.75**
Soap
Easter Bonnet, soap on a rope, yel-
low, 1970 . . . . **6.50**
Football Helmet, soap on a rope,
yellow, white cord, 1974 . . . . . . **3.50**
Tub Racer, three speed boats, red,
blue, and yellow, 1970 . . . . **5.00**
Wilbur The Whale, soap on a rope,
blue soap, white cord, 5 oz,
1975 . . . . **4.00**
Toothpaste, Toofie, 3½ oz, white
tube, raccoon, pink cap, pink
toothbrush, 1968 . . . . **4.00**
Men's Items
After Shave, figural
Cable Car, green painted glass,
plastic green and white top, 1975 **7.50**
Corncob Pipe, decanter, 3 oz, am-
ber glass, black plastic stem, MIB **3.50**
Covered Wagon, glass, 1970 . . . . **7.50**
Eight Ball, decanter, 3 oz, black
and white, black cap **2.50**
Fire Truck, decanter, 4 pcs, clear
red glass, plastic hook and ladder
section, decals **12.00**
Gavel, amber glass, brown plastic
handle, 1967 . . . . **12.00**
Golf Cart, green glass, 5½″ l, 1973 **4.50**
Hard Hat, 4 oz, yellow plastic,
clear glass, 1977 . . . . **4.25**
Indian Head Penny, 4 oz, 4″,
bronze painted glass, 1970 . . . . **3.00**
Pheasant, brown glass, green plas-
tic head, 1972 . . . . **7.50**
Pony Express, brown glass, copper
man, 1971 . . . . **6.00**

Rainbow Trout, plastic head over
cap, 1973 .... 5.00
Spirit of St Louis, glass, silver paint,
1970 .... 12.00
US Mail Truck, plastic and glass,
red, white, and blue 6.50
Body Splash, tennis ball, 3 oz, light
green flocking, clear glass, green
cap base, 1977 .... 3.50
Chess Piece, 3 oz, amber glass, silver
colored top
King, 1972 .... 5.00
Pawn, 1975 .... 4.00
Queen, 1973 .... 5.00
Rook, 1974 .... 4.75
Hair Lotion, figural
Bowling Pin, 4 oz, white plastic,
red trim, 1960 .... 20.00
Mini Bike, 4 oz, light amber glass,
1972 .... 5.00
Tractor, amber glass, amber plastic
front, 1974 .... 8.00
Set
Commodore, maroon and white
box, 4 oz after shave, two white
handkerchiefs, maroon paper
talc box, 1943 .... 75.00
Esquire, maroon box, 4 oz bottle of
Bay Rum, shaving cream tube,
talc can, 1940, MIB 80.00
Valet, maroon and ivory box, 4 oz
after shave, shaving cream tube,
talc can, smoker's tooth powder,
1945 .... 90.00
Miscellaneous
Bowl, 6" d, American Heirloom, In-
dependence Day, 1981, black plastic base stand, MIB 18.00
Hostess Bell, silver plated, 5½" h,
1978 .... 18.00
Plate, 8½" d, Premium Set, set of
eight, Country Fair pattern, Blue
Ridge 48.00
Women's Items
Bubble Bath, Christmas Sparkler, red,
1969 .... 9.00
Candle
Fostoria, clear glass holder, per-
fumed, 1973 .... 6.00
Gingerbread House, brown and
white, 1977 .... 7.50
Mt Vernon, sauce pitcher, blue
glass, 1977, MIB 12.00
Plum Pudding, 4" h, brown, green,
and white, 1978 .... 5.00
Snowman, 5½" h, white, green
trim, 1981 .... 6.00
Turtle, white glass, green glass
shell, 1972 .... 5.00
Christmas Ornament, decanter, fi-
gural
Angel, 2 oz, white top, 1974 .... 4.00

Rocking Horse, clear glass, 1979 . 5.00
Cologne
Betsy Ross, glass, white, 1976 ... 12.00
Calculator, 4 oz, black glass, 1979 5.00
Catch A Fish, decanter, 3 oz, dark
tan, light tan plastic top, yellow
hat, brown plastic pole, 1976 .. 8.00
Church Mouse Bride, plastic top,
white veil, milk glass base, 1978 5.00
Flower Maiden, glass, yellow paint,
1974 .... 7.50
Library Lamp, 4 oz, gold plated
base, gold cap, 1976 .... 5.00
Looking Glass, hand mirror shape,
clear glass, 6½" h, 1970 ...... 3.00
Oops, decanter, white glass, brown
spots, ice cream cone shape,
1981 .... 5.00
Santa, figural, MIB 35.00
Foaming Bath Oil
Aladdin's Lamp, green glass, gold
cap, 1971 .... 8.50
Cruet, amber, ribbed, 1973 ...... 5.00
Golden Flamingo, decanter, clear
glass, gold dec, 6 oz 3.00
Victorian Washstand, buff, plastic
simulated marble top, blue
pitcher and bowl cap, 4 oz, 1973 4.00
Hand Lotion
Coffeepot, country style, glass,
blue, 1979 .... 8.00
Rooster, 6 oz, milk glass, red plastic
head, 1973 .... 5.00
Lip Gloss, compact, Lucky Penny, 2",
1978 .... 2.00
Mouthwash, decanter, Bermuda
Fresh, plastic, purple, green top, 6
oz 1.50
Perfume Glace
Cameo Ring, 1970, MIB 18.00
Heart Compact, pink plastic, 1982 2.00
Owl Pin, gold metal, green eyes,
gold and green box, 1968 ..... 7.50
Pill Box, black and gold, red rose,
1967 .... 5.00
Pomander
Frog, 3" h, ceramic, white, yellow
and green trim, 1980 .... 10.00
Heart, Wedgwood blue and white,
plastic, white tassel, 1973 ..... 2.75
Parasol, lavender, 1974 .... 3.00
Picture Hat, yellow and pink, plas-
tic, yellow cord and tassel, 1975 4.00
Sachet, cream type
Heart, white glass base, white plas-
tic top, gold dove dec, 1977 ... 3.00
Petit Point, purple glass base, cloth
insert on lid, 1 oz 2.00
Salt Shaker, milk glass, yellow and
white buttercups, yellow plastic
cap, 1974 .... 3.00

Set
   Brocade, brown and white box,
      white lining, beauty dust, per-
      fume rollette, and cream sachet,
      1967 .... **25.00**
   Fragrance Notes, writing paper,
      sealing wax, goldtone seal, 1977   **6.50**
   Perfume Handkerchief, two small
      bottles of perfume, four handker-
      chiefs with red and green flower
      cutouts, 1933 .... **75.00**
   Spectator, turquoise and white box,
      two dram perfume bottle, lip-
      stick, and rouge compact, 1939   **60.00**
   Sunny Hours, white umbrella, 1
      dram perfume, deluxe lipstick,
      1952 .... **40.00**

BAKELITE

Collecting Hints: Bakelite often is confused with
plastic. There are three key questions to help
identify bakelite: 1) is it thick and in a bright,
primary color [black, green, red, or yellow]; 2)
is the object from the 1920 to 1940 period; and,
3) is the object normally associated with a synthetic material?

   The collecting of bakelite has reached matu-
rity. Prices are stable. Art Deco bakelite items
remain especially strong in the current market.

History: Bakelite, a substitute for hard rubber,
celluloid, and similar materials, is a synthetic
resinous material made from formaldehyde and
phenol. It was invented by L. H. Baekeland in
1913. Bakelite was easily dyed and molded into
many brightly colored objects during the Art
Deco period.

   Bakelite has been used as the secondary element in many household and kitchen items (especially handles), as ornamentation on clothing,
and in jewelry of the Art Deco and later periods.
Bakelite often imitated natural materials such as
amber, tortoise shell, onyx, jet, and wood.

References: Corinne Davidov and Ginny Re-
dington Dawes, *The Bakelite Jewelry Book*,
Abbeville Press, 1988; Lyngerde Kelley and
Nancy Schiffer, *Plastic Jewelry*, Schiffer Publish-
ing, 1987; Lyndi Stewart McNulty, *Wallace-
Homestead Price Guide To Plastic Collectibles*,
Wallace-Homestead, 1987.

HOUSEHOLD ITEMS

Bank, jukebox shape, musical **50.00**
Bookends, pr, Art Deco, geometric
   shape, green and yellow **60.00**
Cigarette Case, hand shaped closure,
   French **155.00**
Cigarette Holder, 12", chrome **10.00**
Clock, Telechron, electric **48.00**

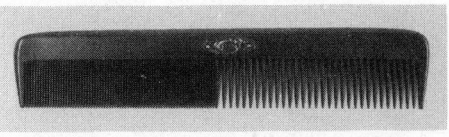

Comb, gold emb floral dec, 9" l, $4.00.

Cocktail Set, bakelite and chrome
   shaker, six cocktails, chrome tray ...   **30.00**
Dresser Set, mirror, comb, brush, man-
   icure accessories, yellow and orange,
   enameled Art Deco design **80.00**
Inkwell, streamlined, black, lid **20.00**
Pencil Sharpener, figural
   Clock **25.00**
   Dog, Scottie **35.00**
Poker Chip Set, multicolored chips, yel-
   low holder **45.00**
Roulette Wheel, multicolored Catalin
   chips, wood rack, orig box, 1930s . **300.00**
Telephone, Kelloggs Series 1000,
   brown, Art Deco style, chrome dial .   **85.00**
Vase, bud, red and yellow swirl, chrome
   base **8.00**

JEWELRY

Beads, large green marbleized beads,
   12" l **55.00**
Bracelet
   Bangle, bright yellow, red, black, and
      green enamel dec **25.00**
   Link, jade green **35.00**
Buckle, 3", green, rhinestone dec, 2 pcs   **20.00**
Earrings, Art Deco, yellow and black
   circles **12.00**
Pendant, rose, yellow **20.00**
Pin
   Bambi **15.00**
   Cluster of Fruit, multicolored **18.00**
   Penguin **15.00**
Ring, red, Art Deco dome style **10.00**

KITCHEN ITEMS

Bottle Opener, 8½", red handle **5.00**
Cake Server, green handle **4.00**
Corkscrew, steel, yellow handle **5.00**
Flatware, red handle
   Knife **1.25**
   Fork **1.00**
   Spoon **1.00**
Mortar and Pestle, yellow and orange
   swirl **25.00**
Salt and Pepper Shakers, pr, yellow and
   green half moons, matching tray ...   **12.00**

BANKS, STILL

Collecting Hints: The rarity of a still bank has
much to do with determining its value. Common
banks, such as tin advertising banks, have limited

value. The Statue of Liberty cast iron bank by A. C. Williams sells in the hundreds of dollars. See Long and Pitman's book for a rarity scale for banks.

Banks are collected by maker, material, or subject. Subject is the most prominent, focusing on with categories such as animals, food, mailboxes, safes, transportation, world's fair, etc. There is a heavy crossover in buyers from other collectible fields.

Banks are graded by condition. They should be in very good to mint condition and retain all original paint or decorative motif. Few banks are truly rare; hence, the collector should wait until he finds a bank in the condition he seeks.

History: Banks with no mechanical action are known as still banks. The first banks were made of wood, pottery, or from gourds. Redware and stoneware banks, made by America's early potters, are prized possessions of today's collector.

Still banks reached a "golden age" with the arrival of the cast iron bank. Leading manufacturing companies include Arcade Mfg. Co., J. Chein & Co., Hubley, J. & E. Stevens, and A. C. Williams. The banks often were ornately painted to enhance their appeal. During the cast iron era, some banks and other businesses used the still bank as a form of advertising.

The tin lithograph advertising bank reached its zenith between 1930 and 1955. The tin bank was an important premium, whether it be a Pabst Blue Ribbon beer can bank or a Gerber's Orange Juice bank. Most tin advertising banks resembled the packaging shape of the product.

Almost every substance has been used to make a still bank—die cast white metal, aluminum, brass, plastic, glass, etc. Many of the early glass candy containers also converted to banksonce the candy was eaten. Thousands of varieties of still banks were made and hundreds of new varieties appear on the market each year.

References: Earnest and Ida Long and Jane Pitman, *Dictionary of Still Banks*, Long's Americana, 1980; Andy and Susan Moore, *Penny Bank Book, Collecting Still Banks*, Schiffer Publishing, Ltd., 1984; Hubert B. Whiting, *Old Iron Still Banks*, Forward's Color Productions, Inc., 1968, out of print.

Collectors' Club: Still Bank Collectors Club of America, Carl White, J & W Seligman & Co, 1 Banker's Trust Plaza, 24th Floor, New York, NY 10006, *Penny Bank Post,* publication.

REPRODUCTION ALERT

Advertising
Atlas Storage, tin	**18.00**
Bremen, IN, bank, rock shape, cast metal	**15.00**
Budweiser Barley Malt Syrup	**15.00**
Citizens Federal Savings, cable car, key, metal	**20.00**

Advertising, Boscul Coffee, mfg by W S Scull Co, 2½ x 2¼", $15.00.

Franklin Savings Institution, Greenfield, MA, book, cast iron, 4½ x 3½"	**65.00**
Gulf Oil, figural, oil tank	**24.00**
Hamm's Beer, 16", bear with calendar	**35.00**
Harris Trust and Savings, Chicago, lion, pot metal	**25.00**
Howard Johnson, 3½", plastic, c1950	**20.00**
Imperial Life Insurance Co, Ashville, NC, Ben Franklin, pot metal	**32.00**
Kool Cigarettes, cigarette pack shape, tin	**20.00**
Lucas Paint	**8.50**
Ocean Spray Cranberry Juice, tin	**12.50**
Old Dutch Cleanser, litho tin	**25.00**
Phillips 66 Motor Oil, 3½", tin	**15.00**
Rival Dog Food, tin	**12.00**
Singer Sewing Machine, 3½", figural, book, red cov, plastic base, c1930	**18.00**
So. Central Bell, mouse shape	**12.00**
Triangle Shoes	**12.00**
Wolf's Head Motor Oil, tin	**12.00**

Cast Iron
Baseball Player, c1900	**85.00**
Bear, 7" h, stealing honey from beehive, c1908	**175.00**
Billiken, emb "Billiken Shoes Bring Luck," c1909	**65.00**
Boy Scout, 6"	**100.00**
Buffalo, 4½" l, Arcade	**90.00**
Building	
Bank, domed, 4¾" h, AC Williams	**35.00**
Garage, 2½" h, two car, c1930	**135.00**
House, 3" h, small front porch, c1910	**75.00**
Log Cabin, 2½" h, c1882	**185.00**
US Treasury Bank, NY, sheet metal base, Grey Iron, 1925	**80.00**
Buster Brown and Tige, 5½" h, c1910	**140.00**
Camel	**85.00**
Cat, 2½" h, with ball	**165.00**
Circus Dog, tub	**48.00**
Clock, emb "A Money Saver," Arcade, c1910	**50.00**

Clown, 6¼", gold, red trim **48.00**
Deer **40.00**
Elephant, 4", red blanket, wheels ... **75.00**
Indian, head, 5" h **65.00**
Horse, black, emb "Beauty" **60.00**
Humpty Dumpty, 5½", sitting on
   brick wall, c1930 .... **150.00**
Pig
   Hitler type, "Make Him Squeal" . **75.00**
   Sitting **85.00**
Refrigerator, marked "Electrolux" ... **45.00**
Safe, combination, black, emb "Se-
   curity Safe Deposit" **90.00**
St Bernard, standing, pack **72.00**
Top Hat, marked "Pass Around The
   Hat" **85.00**
Turkey **48.00**
US Mail, green, 3½" h **65.00**
Ceramic
   Batman, 7", glazed, 1966 .... **15.00**
   Mammy, 7" **35.00**
   St Bernard, leaning on keg **15.00**
Chalkware, owl, 7", figural **60.00**
Character
   Bugs Bunny, pot metal **47.00**
   Campbell Kids, cast iron, c1915 ... **165.00**
   Fred Flintstone, 12½" h **15.00**
   Little Max's Lunch, plastic **10.00**
Composition, Scottie dog in barrel, 5½" **18.00**
Die Cast
   Alligator, 5", climbing on rocks, gilt
      paint **35.00**
   Car, Cadillac, 1958 .... **18.00**
   Horse, 5½", standing, saddle, bronze
      finish **20.00**
   Jack and Jill, 5", holding pail, dark
      bronze finish **25.00**
   Pig, 4½", screw trap, mfd by AA
      Brooks **7.50**
   Rocking Horse, 4½", bronze finish . **20.00**
Dime Register
   Captain Marvel, litho tin, opens at

**Dime Register, Snow White, litho tin,
$85.00.**

$5.00, 1948 copyright, Fawcett
   Publications **65.00**
Cash Register, litho tin
   3½", Get Rich Quick Bank, Marx **30.00**
   5", Universal 3 Coin Bank **60.00**
Clock, 7", domed shape, pressed
   steel, marked "Kingsbury" **95.00**
Eagle Pencil Co, tin, round **25.00**
Prudential Insurance, 7", cast iron,
   nickel plated, book shape **100.00**
Superman, litho tin, opens at $5.00,
   copyright, DC Publications **70.00**
Uncle Sam, 1941 .... **38.00**
World's Fair, NY, 1964, orig card ... **20.00**
Glass
   Esso, clear, emb "Watch Savings
      Grow" **12.00**
   Grapette, clown **25.00**
   Liberty Bell, emb "1919" **20.00**
   Lincoln Bank, bottle shape, orig top
      hat cap, paper label, 9" **45.00**
   Pig, blue **25.00**
   Pittsburgh Paints, log cabin shape, pa-
      per label **25.00**
Metal
   Elephant, emb "GAR-RU," metallic
      green, 9 x 5" **45.00**
   Savings For Baby, book shape, toys
      and stork holding baby **55.00**
Plastic, figural
   Colonel Sanders **15.00**
   Laurel and Hardy, 14" **40.00**
   Moose, antlers **25.00**
Pottery
   Bear, seated **24.00**
   Humpty Dumpty, Philco adv **18.00**
   Pig, white, brown spots **20.00**
   Rabbit, 5", white **20.00**
Tin
   Barrel, Happy Days, Chein **18.00**
   Building
      Bank, cupola, blue, red roof,
         c1870 .... **60.00**
      Church, hand stenciled "Savings
         Bank," gold lettering, ivory
         ground, blue roof, c1860 ...... **50.00**
   Drum, 3", litho dec, trap with key .. **18.00**
   Round
      Fern Bissell Peat dec **18.00**
      Mexican dec **18.00**
   Suitcase, litho, printed labels, key
      lock, marked "Marx" **25.00**
   World, globe **12.00**
Wood
   Barrel, 3½", green paint, chrome
      bands, decaled "Sunny Future
      Bank" **7.50**
   Chest, rect, hinged, metal dec,
      marked "Germany" **12.00**
   Swiss Chalet, 5 x 2½ x 4", emb metal
      dec, key lock **20.00**

BARBER SHOP COLLECTIBLES

Collecting Hints: Many barber shop collectibles have a porcelain finish. If chipped or cracked, the porcelain is difficult, if not impossible, to repair. Buy barber poles and chairs in very good or better condition. A good display appearance is a key consideration.

Many old barber shops are still in business. Their back rooms often contain excellent display pieces.

History: The neighborhood barber shop was an important social and cultural institution in the 19th and first half of the 20th centuries. Men and boys gathered to gossip, exchange business news, and check current fashions. "Girlie" magazines and comic books, usually forbidden at home, were among the reading literature, as were adventure and police gazettes and magazines.

In the 1960s the number of barber shops dropped by half in the United States. "Unisex" shops broke the traditional men-only barriers. In the 1980s several chains run barber and hair dressing shops on a regional and national basis.

Reference: Richard Holiner, *Collecting Barber Bottles*, Collector Books, 1986; Phillip L. Krumholz, *Value Guide For Barberiana & Shaving Collectibles*, Ad-Lib Publishing Co, 1988.

Collectors' Clubs: National Shaving Mug Collectors' Association, 11 Walton Avenue, White Plains, NY 10606; Safety Razor Collectors' Guild, P. O. Box 885, Crescent City, CA 95531.

Antiseptic Container, 8" h, plated brass	40.00
Ashtray, 5" d, Wm Marvy Supply giveaway	10.00
Basin, white, flowers and insects dec, red, blue, and green trim, scalloped edge, marked "68.005"	175.00

Blade Bank
China

Barber	25.00
Shaving Brush, 6" h	20.00

Tin

Ever-Ready, treasure chest	15.00
Gem, safe with combination	20.00

Blade Tin

Challenge, c1898	20.00
Yankee, c1900	55.00
Book, Melvin L Senery, *Gillette's Social Redemption*, 1907, 783 pgs	60.00

Bottle
Advertising

Le Varns Hair Tonic, glass, labeled	68.00
T Noonan Barber Supply, cobalt blue	50.00
Tricopherous, aqua, handblown	35.00
Amber, floral, dot pattern	75.00

Barber Bottle, Opalescent Swirl pattern, blue, 6⅞" h, $95.00.

Amethyst, pr	400.00
Bristol, bell, hp, cherubs, scene, gold trim	150.00
Clambroth, Witch Hazel, 8"	45.00
Milk Glass, sq, fern pattern	60.00
Ruby, floral	120.00

Bowl

Brass, c1820	200.00
China, 14" d, floral and insect pattern, scalloped edge, gold trim	250.00
Business Card, 6 x 3¼", man cutting hair, "The Newest and Most Sanitary Shop in Providence"	10.00

Cabinet

Sterilizer, 12" h, wood, glass door, United Beauty Co	50.00
Storage, woodgrain tin, shelves and racks, Safetee Brand	20.00

Catalog

Biedermeier, German barber supply, 48 pgs, German text, c1910	20.00
Cattaraugus Cutlery Co, 81 pgs, 1925	70.00
Simms & Co, T S, shaving brushes, 31 pgs, c1910	15.00

Chair
Adult

Oak, without head rest, 1890	500.00
Pedestal base, round set, Theo Kochs Manufacturer	325.00
Walnut, replaced velvet, 1870s	1,500.00
Child's, porcelainized, nickel plated trim, leather upholstery, c1920	350.00
Clippers, Andis, c1940	20.00
Counter Mat, 9 x 8", Wardonia Razor Blades, rubber	15.00

Display Case

Gillette, 4" h, store, wood and glass, c1940	40.00
Remington Cutlery, holds 20 razors	175.00
Hair Net, blonde, orig envelope	3.00
Lamp, 9" h, barber pole	35.00
License, framed, c1930	40.00

Mug Rack

Pine, 38" h, holds 24 mugs	150.00

Revolving, 41" h, wood, holds barber
 tools **140.00**
Neck Duster, cherry wood handle **25.00**
Newspaper, Barber's Journal, 1881 ... **10.00**
Painting, 8 x 10", oil, man being shaved **200.00**
Paperweight, Norvell-Shapleigh Hdwe
 Co **20.00**
Plate, 7", barber pole, mugs, and barber
 dec, Jockey Hitching Post, 1881 ... **12.00**
Playing Cards, Gillette, 1905, unused . **150.00**
Pool
 Porcelain and Glass, 84", rotating top,
  floor mount, electric motor **750.00**
 Stained Glass and Porcelain, 42", wall
  mount, Theo Kochs, Manufacturer **875.00**
 Wood, 28" h, red, white, and blue,
  round top with stars **120.00**
Postcard, Unsafe Safety Razor, c1910 . **10.00**
Razor Hone
 Bracher, Karl, Jr Mfg Co, c1920 .... **5.00**
 Keen Kutter, E C Simmons, cardboard
  box **25.00**
Safety Razor, Gillette, SS blade **125.00**
Sharpener
 Allegro, cardboard box, unused **15.00**
 Twinplex **5.00**
Shaving Brush, aluminum handle, emb
 design, c1910 .... **8.00**

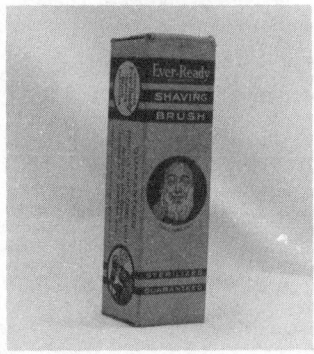

**Shaving Brush, Ever Ready, blue box,
black celluloid handle, dark bristles,
$15.00.**

Shaving Mirror
 Celluloid, 7" h, folding, German sil-
  ver trim, milk glass insert **15.00**
 Porcelain, brass plated trim, barber
  pole **50.00**
 Silver Plated, 14" h, Colonial silver,
  beveled mirror, c1920 .... **20.00**
Shaving Mug
 Advertising, Tonique Delux **90.00**
 Fraternal
  Ancient Order of United Workers,
   gold, monogrammed **150.00**
  Astra Castra Numen Lumen **100.00**

JROUAM, gold, monogrammed .. **55.00**
 Woodmen of America, gold, mon-
  ogrammed **60.00**
 Occupational, monogrammed
  Banker **150.00**
  Carpenter, man working on bench,
   John Shipee, marked "D & C" . **300.00**
  Deliveryman, bakery delivery
   scene, gold **200.00**
  Farmer, driving hay wagon, gold . **175.00**
  Milk man, milk wagon **350.00**
  Plumber, bathroom scene **400.00**
  Tinsmith, tools **175.00**
 Scuttle, men, women, girl, and
  cherub oval reserve, royal blue
  ground, gold trim **50.00**
Sign
 10 x 14", Leukroth's Oriental Hair
  tonic, cardboard, color litho, morning grace woman **200.00**
 13¼ x 39½", pressed steel, Wildroot,
  white ground, red, white, and blue
  barber pole, name in red letters,
  other inscription in blue, c1950 .. **50.00**
 19" l, Andis Clippers, plastic, lights
  up **25.00**
Sink, oval, porcelain, brass faucets ... **300.00**
Sterilizer, green glass, brass top, two
 mesh shelves **60.00**
Strop, 9 x 2½ x 2", leather, two sided,
 marked "Horse Hide Burl Finish" in
 gold **15.00**
Stropper
 Flemington, wood handle, c1920 .. **12.00**
 Rundel, metal, c1920 .... **20.00**
Thermometer, Schick adv, 1950s **75.00**
Towel Steamer, nickel plated copper,
 porcelain over steel base **300.00**
Trimmer
 Quick Trimmer Inc, plastic **4.00**
 Saftrim, metal, fits in razor **2.00**

BARBIE

Collecting Hints: Barbie and related material are
manufactured in tremendously large quantities.
Consequently, the real value rests only in material that is in excellent to mint condition and
which has its original packaging in very good or
better condition. If items show signs of heavy
use, their value is probably minimal.

Collectors prefer items from the first decade of
production. Learn how to distinguish a Barbie
#1 doll from its successors. The Barbie market
is one of many subtleties, which you should be
aware of.

Recently collectors have shifted their focus
from the dolls themselves to the accessories.
There have been rapid price increases in early
clothing and accessories, with some of the prices
bordering on speculation.

History: In 1945 Harold Matson (MATT) and Ruth and Elliott (EL) Handler founded Mattel. Initially the company made picture frames. The company became involved in the toy market when Elliott Handler began to make doll furniture from scrap material. When Harold Matson left the firm, Elliott Handler became chief designer and Ruth Handler principal marketer. In 1955 Mattel advertised its products on "The Mickey Mouse Club" television show. From then, the company prospered.

In 1958 Mattel patented a fashion doll. The doll was named "Barbie" and reached the toy shelves in 1959. By 1960 Barbie's popularity was assured.

Development of a boy friend for Barbie, named Ken after the Handler's son, began in 1960. Over the years many other dolls were added to the line. Clothing, vehicles, room settings, and other accessories became an integral part of the line.

From September 1961 through July 1972 Mattel published a Barbie magazine. At its peak the Barbie Fan Club was the second largest girls' organization, next to the Girl Scouts, in the United States.

Barbie sales are approaching the 100 million mark. Annual sales exceed five million units. Barbie is one of the most successful dolls in history.

References: Billyboy, *Barbie: Her Life and Times,* Crown Publishers, Inc., 1987; Sibyl DeWein and Joan Ashabraner, *The Collectors Encyclopedia of Barbie Dolls and Collectibles,* Collector Books, 1977 (1988 value update); Paris and Susan Manos, *The Wonder of Barbie: Dolls and Accessories 1976-1986,* Collector Books, 1987; Paris and Susan Manos, *The World of Barbie Dolls: An Illustrated Value Guide,* Collector Books, 1983 (1988 value update).

Ballerina Stage, 1976	**35.00**
Beach Bus, 1974	**25.00**
Beauty Kit, 1961, MIB	**24.00**
Bracelet, essay contest	**50.00**
Car	
Corvette, 1968, MIB	**55.00**
Dune Buggy, Irwin, MIB	**75.00**
Case, pink, space for doll and clothes, 1977	**15.00**
Clothes	
American Airlines Stewardess, #984, 1961	**25.00**
Arabian Nights, #0874, 1963	**35.00**
Ballerina, #989, 1961	**20.00**
Busy Gal, #981, 1958	**35.00**
Candlelight Capers, Julia, #1753, 1969	**15.00**
Career Girl, #954, 1963	**20.00**
Check The Suit, #1794, 1970	**10.00**
Disco Date, #1633, 1963	**25.00**

Evening Gala, #1660, 1965	**40.00**
Fur Stole, 1960s	**20.00**
Garden Tea Party, #1606, 1964	**25.00**
Hurray For Leather, #1477, 1969	**20.00**
Icebreaker, #942, 1962	**20.00**
It's Cold Outside, #0819, 1969	**15.00**
Light N Lazy, #3339, 1972	**5.00**
Lunch Date, #1600, 1964	**25.00**
Orange Blossom, #987, 1962	**20.00**
Party Date, #958, 1963	**18.00**
Picnic Set, #976, 1958	**50.00**
Reception Line, #1654, 1965	**30.00**
Ship Ahoy, #1918, 1964	**20.00**
Silver Serenade, #3419, 1971	**10.00**
Summer Job, #1422, 1965	**45.00**
Tangerine Scene, #1451, 1970	**18.00**
Tennis Anyone, #941 1962	**18.00**
Victorian Velvet, #3431, 1971	**15.00**
Winter Wow, #1486, 1970	**12.00**
Yellow-Mellop, #1484, 1969	**12.00**
Colorforms Set	**7.50**
Country Camper, 18 x 9½ x 8"	**7.50**
Diary, 1963, unused	**20.00**

Mattel, 11½", Barbie #2, 1960, brown ponytail, pearl earrings, orig stand, $350.00.

Doll	
Barbie	
American Girl	**65.00**
Bendable legs, wedding dress, two other outfits, 1965	**100.00**
Bubble Cut Fashion, orig box, stand, and clothing, 1962 copyright	**65.00**
Fashion Queen, MIB	**225.00**
Gold Medal Skater, 1975, MIB	**55.00**
Happy Holidays, MIB	**60.00**
Quick Curl, 1973, painted eyelashes	**15.00**
Talking, 1972, MIB	**75.00**
Titian Hair, 1961	**170.00**
Cara, ballerina, MIB	**50.00**

Christie, Malibu, 1973	20.00
Francie, Growing Pretty Hair, 1970 .	65.00
Julia, Twist 'n Turn, 2 pc uniform, 1969	25.00
Ken	
Flocked hair, orig box, extra clothes, 1961	45.00
Gold Medal Skier, 1975, MIB	60.00
Walk Lively, 1972	35.00
Midge, bendable legs, 1965, brunette, MIB	285.00
P. J., Gold Medal Gymnast, 1975, MIB	50.00
Skipper	
Living, 1970, MIB	20.00
Malibu, 1971, MIB	18.00
Straight legs, 1964, sun tanned skin, MIB	50.00
Dream House, 1962, minor wear	65.00
Furniture	
Bed, marked "Regal"	30.00
Bedroom Suite, "Francie Mod a Go-Go," marked "Susy Goose," MIB .	175.00
Chifforobe, Barbie & Midge, queen size, MIB	50.00
Chaise Lounge	30.00
Sofa, bed, and coffee table	30.00
Game	
Prom Game	18.00
Skipper, 16 x 16" playing board, orig 9½ x 19½ x 2" box, 1964 Mattel copyright	20.00
Hangers, doll size, plastic, orig package, 1968	5.00
Magazine, "Mattel Barbie Magazine," Jan-Feb 1969, 8½ x 10½", 22 pgs ..	12.00
Make-Up Case, 1963, unused	20.00
Nurse Kit, Pressman	17.50
Paper Doll, Whitman, #1967:59, cardboard folder, two 11½" diecut dolls, neatly cut, 1967 Mattel copyright ..	30.00
Record Case, 1961, MIB	18.00
Sewing Machine, Sew Magic, includes accessories, 1972, Mattel	30.00
Sewing Pattern	
Advance Pattern Co, six patterns for trousseau wardrobe, used, orig worn envelope, 1962	12.00
Simplicity, doll clothing, blouse, pants, shorts, dresses, jackets, used, orig worn envelope, c1965 .	10.00
Store Display	
Barbie & Stacey Fashion Boutique ..	200.00
Wonderful World of Barbie	250.00
Suitcase, Ken, 1962	15.00
Wrist Watch, 1963	45.00

BASEBALL CARDS

Collecting Hints: Condition is a key factor. The list below is priced for cards in excellent condition, and collectors should strive only for cards in excellent to mint condition.

Concentrate on the superstars; these cards are most likely to increase in value. Buy full sets of modern cards. In this way you have the superstars of tomorrow on hand. When a player becomes a member of the Baseball Hall of Fame, his cards and other memorabilia will increase significantly.

The price of cards fluctuates rapidly; it changes on a weekly basis. Spend time studying the market before investing heavily. Finally, reproduced cards and sets have become a fact of life in this category. Novice collectors should not buy cards until they can tell the difference between the originals and reproductions.

The latest trend is the collection of rookie cards, i.e., the first year of issue for a player. This is a highly speculative category at the moment.

History: Baseball cards date from the late 19th century. By 1900 the most common cards, known as "T" cards, were those produced by tobacco companies such as American Tobacco Co., with the majority of the tobacco-related cards being produced between 1909 and 1915. By far the most popular set was "T206" issued between 1909 and 1911. During the 1920s American Caramel, National Caramel, and York Caramel candy companies, issued cards identified in lists as "E" cards.

From 1933 to 1941 Goudey Gum Co. of Boston and, in 1939, Gum, Inc., were the big producers of baseball cards. Following World War II, Bowman Gum of Philadelphia (B.G.H.L.I.), the successor to Gum, Inc., lead the way. Topps, Inc. (T.C.G.) of Brooklyn, New York, followed. Topps bought Bowman in 1956 and enjoyed almost a monopoly in card production until 1981.

In 1981 Topps was challenged by Fleer of Philadelphia and Donruss of Memphis. All three companies annually produce sets of cards numbering 600 cards or more.

References: Dan Albaugh, *Standard Catalog of Baseball Cards, First Edition,* Krause Publications, Inc., 1988; James Beckett, *The Official 1990 Price Guide to Baseball Cards, Ninth Edition,* House of Collectibles, 1989; James Beckett, *Sports Americana Baseball Card Price Guide, No. 10,* Edgewater Book Co., Inc., 1988; Gene Florence, *The Standard Baseball Card Price Guide,* Collector Books, 1989; Bob Lemke and Dan Albaugh, *Sports Collectors Digest Baseball Card Price Guide, Third Edition,* Krause Publications, Inc., 1989.

Periodicals: The following appear on a monthly or semi-monthly basis: *Baseball Card News,* 700 E. State Street, Iola, WI 54990; *Baseball Cards,* 700 E. State Street, Iola, WI 54990; *Baseball Hobby News,* 9528 Miramar Road, San Diego, CA 92126; Beckett Baseball Monthly, 3410 Mid

Court, Suite 110, Carrolton, TX 75006; *Sports Collectors Digest*, 700 E. State Street, Iola, WI 54990; *The Trader Speaks*, 3 Pleasant Drive, Lake Ronkonkoma, NY 11779.

Collectors' Clubs: There are many local card collecting clubs throughout the United States. However, there is no national organization at the present time.

REPRODUCTION ALERT: The 1952 Topps set, except for 5 cards, was reproduced in 1983 and clearly marked by Topps. In addition, a number of cards have been illegally reprinted including the following Topps cards:

1963 Peter Rose, rookie card, #537
1971 Pete Rose, #100
1971 Steve Garvey, #341
1972 Pete Rose, #559
1972 Steve Garvey, #686
1972 Rod Carew, #695
1973 Willie Mays, #100
1973 Hank Aaron, #305
1973 Mike Schmidt, rookie card, #615

Note: The listing for the cards beginning in 1948 shows the price for a complete set, common player price, and superstars. The number of cards in each set is indicated in parentheses.

American Carmel Co, Tom Griffith, out-field, Brooklyn Nationals, $5.00.

PRE-BOWMAN/TOPPS PERIOD

Tobacco Insert
  T-206, white border, color
    Complete set (523) **10,000.00**
    Major League players (1-389) **15.00**
    Minor League players (390-475) .. **16.00**
    Southern League players (476-523) **37.00**
Candy Companies
  E-120, American Caramels, color, 1922
    Complete set (240) **1,350.00**
    Common player (1-240) **5.00**

Goudey and Gum, Inc.
  1933, Goudey Gum, color
    Complete set (240) **7,200.00**
    Common player (1-40) **17.50**
    Common player (41-44) **15.00**
    Common player (45-52) **17.50**
    Common player (53-240) **15.00**
  1941, Goudey Gum, black and white
    Complete set (33) **1,100.00**
    Common player (1-33) **16.00**

BOWMAN ERA

1948 Bowman (black and white)
  Complete set (48) **525.00**
  Common player (1-36) **5.00**
  Common player (37-48) **7.50**
  2 Ewell Blackwell **6.00**
  5 Bob Feller **30.00**
  12 John Sain **8.00**
  17 Enos Slaughter **17.50**
  29 Joe Page **15.00**
  32 Bill Rigney **6.00**
  43 Bruce Edwards **7.50**
1949 Bowman
  Complete set (240) **2,975.00**
  Common player (1-36) **5.00**
  Common player (37-73) **6.00**
  Common player (74-144) **5.00**
  Common player (145-240) **20.00**
  2 Whitey Lockman **5.00**
  19 Bobby Brown **10.00**
  43 Dale Mitchell **6.00**
  65 Enos Slaughter **15.00**
  100 Gil Hodges **30.00**
  157 Walt Masterson **20.00**
  214 Richie Ashburn **87.00**
1950 Bowman
  Complete set (252) **1,825.00**
  Common player (1-72) **10.00**
  Common player (72-252) **5.00**
  4 Gus Zemial **10.00**
  18 Eddie Robinson **10.00**
  46 Yogi Berra **80.00**
  84 Richie Ashburn **12.50**
  217 Casey Stengel **32.00**
  244 Dale Coogan **5.00**
  248 Sam Jethroe **6.00**
1951 Bowman (color)
  Complete set (324) **3,850.00**
  Common player (1-36) **5.00**
  Common player (37-252) **5.00**
  Common player (253-324) **15.00**
  26 Phil Rizzuto **20.00**
  53 Bob Lemon **15.00**
  122 Joe Garagiola **20.00**
  233 Leo Durocher **12.50**
  314 Johnny Sain **18.00**
1952 Bowman (color)
  Complete set (252) **475.00**
  Common player (1-216) **1.00**
  Common player (217-252) **2.00**

1 Yogi Berra	18.00
44 Roy Campanella	16.00
101 Mickey Mantle	100.00
196 Stan Musial	30.00
218 Willie Mays	85.00

1953 Bowman (black and white)

Complete set (64)	850.00
Common player (1-64)	10.00
15 Johnny Mize	40.00
25 Johnny Sain	20.00
39 Casey Stengel	100.00
50 Dutch Leonard	10.00
64 Andy Hansen	15.00

1953 Bowman (color)

Complete set (160)	1,200.00
Common player (1-112)	10.00
Common player (113-128)	16.00
Common player (129-160)	12.00
8 Al Rosen	12.00
46 Roy Campanella	70.00
59 Mickey Mantle	500.00
81 Enos Slaughter	20.00
118 Billy Martin	70.00
130 Cass Michaels	12.00
148 Billy Goodman	14.00
160 Cal Abrams	15.00

1954 Bowman

Complete set (224)	450.00
Common player (1-128)	2.00
Common player (129-224)	2.40
34 Sammy White	2.00
89 Willie Mays	100.00
132 Bob Feller	20.00
161 Yogi Berra	40.00
177 Whitey Ford	18.00
218 Preacher Roe	4.00

1955 Bowman (color)

Complete set (320)	1,150.00
Common player (1-224)	2.50
Common player (225-320)	4.00
1 Hoyt Wilhelm	12.00
22 Roy Campanella	22.00
23 Al Kaline	20.00
179 Hank Aaron	45.00
202 Mickey Mantle	120.00
242 Ernie Banks	80.00

TOPPS ERA

1951 Topps, blue backs

Complete set (52)	625.00
Common player (1-52)	10.00
3 Richie Ashburn	20.00
37 Bobby Doerr	20.00
39 Ed Lopat	15.00
50 Johnny Mize	25.00

1951 Topps, red backs

Complete set (52)	250.00
Common player (1-52)	3.00
1 Yogi Berra	25.00
5 Phil Rizzuto	10.00

31 Gil Hodges	10.00
38 Duke Snider	20.00

1952 Topps

Complete set (407)	2,600.00
Common player (1-80)	11.00
Common player (81-250)	6.00
Common player (251-280)	12.00
Common player (281-300)	15.00
Common player (301-310)	12.00
Common player (311-407)	70.00
1 Andy Pafko	16.00
10 Al Rosen	16.00
26 Monte Irvin	18.00
33 Warren Spahn	25.00
37 Duke Snider	35.00
48 Joe Page (correct)	16.00
48 Joe Page (error)	40.00
59 Robin Roberts	20.00
65 Enos Slaughter	20.00
88 Bob Feller	30.00
175 Billy Martin	53.00
191 Yogi Berra	60.00
216 Richie Ashburn	12.00
312 Jackie Robinson	300.00
400 Bill Dickey	225.00
407 Eddie Mathews	250.00

1953 Topps

Complete set (280)	2,800.00
Common player (1-165)	4.50
Common player (166-220)	3.50
Common player (221-280)	16.00
10 Smokey Burgess	10.00
27 Roy Campanella	44.00
37 Eddie Mathews	20.00
76 Pee Wee Reese	30.00
77 Johnny Mize	6.75
82 Mickey Mantle	420.00
114 Phil Rizzuto	22.00
147 Warren Spahn	25.00
191 Ralph Kiner	12.50
207 Whitey Ford	20.00
220 Satchell Paige	80.00
258 Jim Gilliam	70.00
263 John Podres	70.00
280 Milt Bolling	25.00

1954 Topps

Complete set (250)	1,675.00
Common player (1-50)	3.50
Common player (51-75)	3.00
Common player (76-250)	3.50
1 Ted Williams	63.00
3 Monte Irvin	8.75
10 Jackie Robinson	40.00
17 Phil Rizzuto	17.50
32 Duke Snider	30.00
70 Larry Doby	12.50
94 Ernie Banks	110.00
102 Gil Hodges	15.00
128 Henry Aaron	200.00
132 Tom Lasorda	36.00
201 Al Kaline	110.00
250 Ted Williams	63.00

1955 Topps
  Complete set (210) 1,225.00
  Common player (1-160) 2.50
  Common player (151-160) 3.50
  Common player (161-210) 4.50
  1 Dusty Rhodes 6.00
  28 Ernie Banks 20.00
  50 Jackie Robinson 35.00
  100 Monte Irvin 8.75
  123 Sandy Koufax 100.00
  124 Harmon Killebrew 36.00
  155 Ed Mathews 23.00
  164 Roberto Clemente 130.00
  187 Gil Hodges 45.00
  194 Willie Mays 110.00
  198 Yogi Berra 63.00
  210 Duke Snider 88.00
1956 Topps
  Complete set (340) 1,260.00
  Common player (1-100) 1.50
  Common player (101-180) 2.50
  Common player (181-260) 3.00
  Common player (261-340) 2.50
  10 Warren Spahn 10.00
  15 Ernie Banks 12.50
  30 Jackie Robinson 35.00
  31 Hank Aaron 40.00
  33 Roberto Clemente 40.00
  109 Enos Slaughter 9.00
  110 Yogi Berra 27.00
  130 Willie Mays 40.00
  135 Mickey Mantle 200.00
  164 Harmon Killebrew 20.00
  251 New York Yankees 30.00
  292 Luis Aparicio 17.50
1957 Topps
  Complete set (407) 1,575.00
  Common player (1-264) 1.25
  Common player (265-352) 5.00
  Common player (353-407) 1.25
  2 Yogi Berra 25.00
  10 Willie Mays 40.00
  18 Don Drysdale 32.00
  25 Whitey Ford 15.00
  76 Roberto Clemente 37.00
  95 Mickey Mantle 200.00
  170 Duke Snider 25.00
  277 Johnny Podres 15.00
  302 Sandy Koufax 200.00
  328 Brooks Robinson 80.00
  338 Jim Bunning 25.00
1958 Topps
  Complete set (495) 975.00
  Common player (1-110) 1.25
  Common player (111-440) 1.00
  Common player (441-495) .... .60
  1 Ted Williams 35.00
  5 Willie Mays 10.00
  47 Roger Maris 70.00
  52 Roberto Clemente 20.00
  150 Mickey Mantle 130.00
  187 Sandy Koufax 28.00

1959 Topps
  Complete set (572) 975.00
  Common player (1-110) 1.00
  Common player (111-506) .... .70
  Common player (507-572) 2.50
  10 Mickey Mantle 110.00
  50 Willie Mays 27.00
  150 Stan Musial 20.00
  163 Sandy Koufax 17.50
  202 Roger Maris 20.00
  380 Hank Aaron 25.00
  514 Bob Gibson 40.00
  550 Roy Campanella 25.00
1960 Topps
  Complete set (572) 875.00
  Common player (1-286) .... .50
  Common player (287-440) .... .60
  Common player (441-506) .... .90
  Common player (507-572) 2.25
  28 Brooks Robinson 10.00
  136 Jim Kaat 10.00
  148 Carl Yastrzemski 75.00
  200 Willie Mays 22.00
  250 Stan Musial 20.00
  300 Hank Aaron 25.00
  316 Willie McCovey 32.00
  350 Mickey Mantle 110.00
  564 Willie Mays, AS 20.00
  566 Hank Aaron, AS 20.00
1961 Topps
  Complete set (589) 1,260.00
  Common player (1-370) .... .45
  Common player (371-522) .... .60
  Common player (523-589) 7.50
  2 Roger Maris 15.00
  10 Brooks Robinson 9.00
  150 Willie Mays 20.00
  287 Carl Yastrzemski 42.00
  300 Mickey Mantle 80.00
  360 Frank Robinson 9.00
  417 Juan Marichal 30.00
  545 Hoyt Wilhelm 20.00
  578 Mickey Mantle AS 100.00
  579 Willie Mays AS 50.00
1963 Topps
  Complete set (576) 950.00
  Common player (1-283) .... .25
  Common player (284-446) .... .45
  Common player (447-506) 2.25
  Common player (507-576) 1.25
  25 Al Kaline 5.00
  54 Rookie Stars 3.25
  108 Hoyt Wilhelm 3.00
  115 Carl Yastrzemski 25.00
  120 Roger Maris 10.00
  126 Bob Uecker 9.00
  242 Power Plus 5.00
  275 Ed Mathews 4.00
  345 Brooks Robinson 10.00
  360 Don Drysdale 6.00
  412 Dodger Big Three 7.50
  472 Lou Brock 32.00

490 Willie McCovey	**22.00**
550 Duke Snider	**20.00**

1964 Topps
Complete set (587)	**600.00**
Common player (1-370)	**.25**
Common player (371-522)	**.40**
Common player (523-587)	**1.25**
13 Hoyt Williams	**3.00**
21 Yogi Berra	**10.00**
50 Mickey Mantle	**70.00**
125 Pete Rose	**65.00**
167 Senators Rookies	**6.00**
210 Carl Yastrzemski	**20.00**
225 Roger Maris	**10.00**
250 Al Kaline	**5.00**
280 Juan Marichal	**4.00**
324 Casey Stengel	**4.00**
342 Willie Stargell	**9.00**
460 Bob Gibson	**6.00**
468 Gaylord Perry	**7.50**
541 Braves Rookies	**27.00**
543 Bob Uecker	**15.00**

1965 Topps
Complete set (598)	**700.00**
Common player (1-198)	**.25**
Common player (199-446)	**.35**
Common player (447-522)	**.45**
Common player (523-598)	**1.25**
16 Astros Rookies	**15.00**
160 Bob Clemente	**15.00**
207 Pete Rose	**70.00**
250 Willie Mays	**20.00**
300 Sandy Koufax	**20.00**
330 Whitey Ford	**6.00**
350 Mickey Mantle	**120.00**
385 Carl Yastrzemski	**25.00**
477 Cardinals Rookies	**45.00**
540 Lou Brock	**12.50**
581 N.L. Rookies	**17.50**

1966 Topps
Complete set (598)	**750.00**
Common player (1-110)	**.20**
Common player (111-446)	**.25**
Common player (447-522)	**.75**
Common player (523-598)	**3.00**
1 Willie Mays	**15.00**
30 Pete Rose	**30.00**
36 Jim Hunter	**6.00**
50 Mickey Mantle	**70.00**
70 Carl Yastrzemski	**20.00**
126 Jim Palmer	**22.00**
288 Dodgers Rookies	**20.00**
500 Hank Aaron	**20.00**
550 Willie McCovey	**30.00**
598 Gaylord Perry	**30.00**

1967 Topps
Complete set (609)	**825.00**
Common player (1-110)	**.20**
Common player (111-370)	**.25**
Common player (371-457)	**.30**
Common player (458-533)	**.70**
Common player (534-609)	**2.00**

5 Whitey Ford	**4.00**
45 Roger Maris	**6.00**
146 Steve Carlton	**20.00**
150 Mickey Mantle	**70.00**
200 Willie Mays	**15.00**
355 Carl Yastrzemski	**27.00**
430 Pete Rose	**32.00**
569 A.L. Rookies	**62.00**
570 Maury Wills	**22.00**
581 Mets Rookies	**200.00**
600 Brooks Robinson	**62.00**

1968 Topps
Complete set (598)	**450.00**
Common player (1-456)	**.20**
Common player (457-598)	**.40**
45 Tom Seaver	**22.00**
72 Tommy John	**1.75**
150 Bob Clemente	**9.00**
177 Mets Rookies	**62.00**
230 Pete Rose	**22.00**
247 Reds Rookies	**25.00**
257 Phil Niekro	**2.00**
365 Brooks Robinson AS	**2.50**
490 Super Stars	**11.50**
530 Bird Belters	**2.25**

1969 Topps
Complete set (664)	**425.00**
Common player (1-218)	**.20**
Common player (219-327)	**.30**
Common player (328-512)	**.20**
Common player (513-664)	**.25**
50 Bob Clemente	**9.00**
82 Pirates Rookies	**5.00**
95 Johnny Bench	**20.00**
120 Pete Rose	**15.00**
190 Willie Mays	**10.00**
200 Bob Gibson	**3.50**
260 Reggie Jackson	**80.00**
480 Tom Seaver	**15.00**
533 Nolan Ryan	**20.00**
573 Jim Palmer	**5.00**
597 A.L. Rookies	**6.00**

1970 Topps
Complete set (720)	**325.00**
Common player (1-546)	**.15**
Common player (547-633)	**.25**
Common player (634-720)	**.60**
10 Carl Yastrzemski	**9.00**
140 Reggie Jackson	**15.00**
150 Harmon Killebrew	**2.50**
189 Yankees Rookies	**15.00**
210 Juan Marichal	**2.25**
220 Steve Carlton	**6.00**
290 Rod Carew	**6.00**
300 Tom Seaver	**10.00**
537 Joe Morgan	**2.00**
539 Phillies Rookies	**1.50**
580 Pete Rose	**35.00**
660 Johnny Bench	**37.00**
712 Nolan Ryan	**20.00**

1971 Topps
Complete set (752)	**350.00**

Topps, 1971 American League Playoffs, Orioles, $5.00.

Common player (1-523)	.20
Common player (524-643)	.35
Common player (644-752)	.70
5 Thurman Munson	7.50
20 Reggie Jackson	10.00
26 Bert Blyleven	5.00
30 Phil Niekro	1.75
100 Pete Rose	22.00
160 Tom Seaver	7.50
250 Johnny Bench	7.50
264 Joe Morgan	1.75
341 Steve Garvey	27.00
525 Ernie Banks	5.00
570 Jim Palmer	4.50
740 Luis Aparicio	5.00

1972 Topps

Complete set (787)	325.00
Common player (1-394)	.13
Common player (395-525)	.15
Common player (526-656)	.25
Common player (657-787)	.60
49 Willie Mays	6.00
79 Red Sox Rookies	7.50
100 Frank Robinson	2.00
130 Bob Gibson	2.00
299 Hank Aaron	6.00
420 Steve Carlton	7.50
433 Johnny Bench	7.50
559 Pete Rose	27.00
686 Steve Garvey	32.00
761 Major League Rookies	5.00

1973 Topps

Complete set (660)	184.00
Common player (1-396)	.13
Common player (397-528)	.20
Common player (529-660)	.50
31 Buddy Bell	1.75
50 Roberto Clemente	5.00
130 Pete Rose	10.00
160 Jim Palmer	2.00
193 Carlton Fisk	1.75
245 Carl Yastrzemski	5.00
350 Tom Seaver	4.00

380 Johnny Bench	4.00
615 Rookie Third Basemen	75.00

1974 Topps

Complete set (660)	150.00
Common player	.10
10 Johnny Bench	3.25
50 Rod Carew	2.75
80 Tom Seaver	3.00
130 Reggie Jackson	4.00
252 Dave Parker	7.50
283 Mike Schmidt	17.50
300 Pete Rose	7.50
456 Dave Winfield	12.50
575 Steve Garvey	4.00

1975 Topps

Complete set (660)	225.00
Common player (1-132)	.13
Common player (133-660)	1.10
20 Thurman Munson	2.00
70 Mike Schmidt	9.00
233 Robin Yount	15.00
228 George Brett	25.00
300 Reggie Jackson	3.50
320 Pete Rose	7.50
370 Tom Seaver	3.00
616 Rookies Outfielders	20.00

1976 Topps

Complete set (660)	110.00
Common player	.08
19 George Brett	6.00
230 Carl Yastrzemski	2.00
240 Pete Rose	7.50
316 Robin Yount	3.00
340 Jim Rice	6.00
441 Gary Carter	6.00
480 Mike Schmidt	6.00
542 Keith Hernandez	3.00

1977 Topps

Complete set (660)	110.00
Common player	.08
10 Reggie Jackson	3.50
60 Jim Rice	3.25
110 Steve Carlton	2.25
140 Mike Schmidt	4.25
295 Gary Carter	3.25
400 Steve Garvey	1.75
450 Pete Rose	4.50
473 Rookies Outfielders	9.00

1978 Topps

Complete set (726)	90.00
Common player	.06
20 Pete Rose	1.75
36 Eddie Murray	17.50
72 Andre Dawson	2.00
120 Gary Carter	1.75
143 Keith Hernandez	1.25
200 Reggie Jackson	1.75
350 Steve Garvey	1.00
360 Mike Schmidt	2.50
708 Rookie Catchers	15.00

1979 Topps

Complete set (726)	60.00

Common player	.06
25 Steve Carlton	1.25
39 Dale Murphy	4.00
116 Ozzie Smith	3.50
469 Lance Parrish	1.75
640 Eddie Murray	2.50
650 Pete Rose	2.25
700 Reggie Jackson	.70

1980 Topps

Complete set (726)	60.00
Common player	.06
70 Gary Carter	1.25
77 Dave Stieb	.90
270 Mike Schmidt	.70
482 Rickey Henderson	14.00
540 Pete Rose	2.00
681 Mets Future Stars	3.00

1981 Topps

Complete set (726)	60.00
Common player	.06
110 Carl Yastrzemski	1.25
261 Rickey Henderson	2.75
315 Kirk Gibson	2.50
479 Expos Future Stars	6.50
504 Dale Murphy	2.00
600 Johnny Bench	.90
700 George Brett	1.75

Topps, 1982, #247, Pedro Guerrero, $.06.

1982 Topps

Complete set (792)	56.00
Common player	.06
21 Orioles Future Stars	7.50
70 Tim Raines	1.25
100 Mike Schmidt	.90
191 Tim Wallach	1.50
254 Jorge Bell	9.00
439 Dave Righetti	1.50
510 Fernando Valenzuela	1.25
668 Dale Murphy	1.50
780 Pete Rose	1.75

1983 Topps

Complete set (792)	60.00

Common player	.06
49 Willie McGee	.2.00
60 Johnny Bench	.45
70 Steve Carlton	.35
83 Ryne Sandberg	4.50
163 Cal Ripken	1.50
238 Bud Black	.40
251 Alan Wiggins	.35
268 Storm Davis	.50
350 Robin Yount	.25
431 Gary Gaetti	2.00
482 Tony Gwynn	11.00
498 Wade Boggs	22.00
586 Frank Viola	1.25
760 Dale Murphy	1.25

1984 Topps

Complete set (792)	56.00
Common player	.06
8 Don Mattingly	20.00
30 Wade Boggs	5.25
100 Reggie Jackson	.45
182 Darryl Strawberry	6.75
251 Tony Gwynn	1.25
300 Pete Rose	1.25
380 Steve Garvey	.40
596 Ryne Sandberg	.90

BASEBALL COLLECTIBLES

Collecting Hints: Baseball memorabilia spans a wide range of items that have been produced since baseball became the national pastime over 100 years ago. This variety has made it more difficult to establish reliable values, leaving it to the collector himself to identify and determine what price to pay for any particular item he uncovers. This "value in the eye of the beholder" approach works well with the veteran collector. The novice collector should solicit the advice of a reliable dealer or advanced collector above values before investing heavily. This is compounded by the emerging interest in unique pieces, especially items associated with superstars such as Cobb, Ruth, and Mantle that now command inordinately high prices.

Because of the unlimited variety of items available, it is virtually impossible to collect everything. Develop a collecting strategy, concentrating on particular player(s), team(s), or type of collectibles, such as Hartland Statues or Perez-Steele autographed postcards. This special emphasis allows the collector to become more familiar with the key elements effecting pricing within their area of interest, such as condition and availability, and permits him to build his collection within a prescribed budget.

History: Baseball has its beginnings in the mid-19th century and by 1900 had become the national pastime. Whether sandlot or big league, baseball was part of most every male's life until the 1950s, when leisure activities expanded in a myriad of directions.

The superstar has always been the key element in the game. Baseball greats were popular visitors at banquets, parades, and more recently at baseball autograph shows. They were subjects of extensive newspaper coverage and, with heightened radio and TV exposure, achieved true celebrity status. The impact of baseball on American life has been enormous.

References: James Beckett and Dennis W. Eckes, *The Sport Americana Baseball Memorabilia and Autograph Price Guide,* Edgewater Book Co, Inc., 1982; James Beckett, *The Sport Americana Price Guide To Baseball Collectibles,* Edgewater Book Co, Inc., 1988; Don Raycraft and Stew Salowitz, *Collector's Guide to Baseball Memorabilia,* Collector Books, 1987; Bert Randolph Sugar, *The Sports Collector Bible,* Bobbs-Merrill Co, Inc, 1983.

Collectors' Club: Society for Baseball Research, P. O. Box 323, Cooperstown, NY 13326. Members receive *Baseball Research Journal, The SABR Bulletin* and *The National Pastime.*

Museum: Baseball Hall of Fame and Museum, Cooperstown, NY.

Advisor: John Selsam.

REPRODUCTION ALERT: Autographs and equipment.

AUTOGRAPHS

Collecting autographs of baseball players, both past and present, has emerged as the most popular aspect of the hobby. Autographs may be obtained in a wide variety of formats - 3 x 5 cards, photographs, baseballs, and Perez-Steele postcards, etc. Values assigned to autographs fluctuate widely due to the fact so many variables enter into price determination - type and condition of the item signed, popularity of the player involved and their willingness to sign, and the authenticity of the signature.

Baseballs

Individuals
Aaron, Hank	21.00
Bench, Johnny	18.00
Canseco, Jose	25.00
Cobb, Ty	200.00
DiMaggio, Joe	75.00
Gooden, Dwight	25.00
Mantle, Mickey	30.00
Mattingly, Don	35.00
Robinson, Jackie	125.00
Schmidt, Mike	15.00
Ruth, Babe	500.00

Baseball, autographed by Joe DiMaggio, $75.00.

Teams
1927 Yankees	1,200.00
1951 Yankees	280.00
1960 Pirates	120.00
1970 Orioles	75.00
1970 Reds	100.00
1986 Mets	90.00
1988 Dodgers	60.00

3 X 5", Cards

Boggs, Wade	4.00
Campanella, Roy	75.00
Mathewson, Christy	300.00
Musial, Stan	4.00
Robinson, Brooks	4.00
Ruth, Babe	250.00
Williams, Ted	8.00

Photographs

Berra, Yogi	12.00
Brett, George	9.00
Carlton, Steve	12.00
Cobb, Ty	180.00
Davis, Eric	10.00
Koufax, Sandy	18.00
Gehrig, Lou	400.00
Hershiser, Orel	10.00
Seaver, Tom	15.00
Stengel, Casey	50.00

Perez-Steele Postcards

The fastest growing area of autograph collecting is this beautiful set of Hall of Fame postcards, created by renowned baseball artist Dick Perez. They are a perfect autograph medium—either signed directly on the card or matted with signatures of deceased hall of Famers. Values increase significantly for older Hall of Fame members depending on their ability and willingness to sign or the limited number of cards signed before a player died.

Perez–Steele Card, autographed by Ted Williams, $125.00.

Banks, Ernie	20.00
Feller, Bob	15.00
Kaline, Al	20.00
Mantle, Mickey	150.00
Mays, Willie	45.00
Musial, Stan	35.00
Paige, Satchel	1,200.00
Snider, Duke	25.00
Williams, Ted	125.00

EQUIPMENT

This area has expanded at a consistent rate in the past several years with the introduction of many new articles. However, the growth has been tempered by the dramatic increase in the number of reproductions that have appeared on the market. It is extremely difficult to detect the difference between legitimate items and good imitations, causing many collectors to limit their purchases in this area. The key to purchasing is to know the source of the article, such as a letter of authenticity from the player or team. If this is not available, or if you are not completely confident of an object's authenticity, the best course of action is to pass on it. Prices continue to fluctuate widely with no defined structure developing to date.

Bats
  Common Major Leaguer

Cracked	12.00
Uncracked	25.00
Garvey, Steve, cracked	60.00
Jackson, Reggie	125.00
Ruth, Babe	1,200.00
Smalley, Roy, cracked	16.00
Winfield, Dave	90.00

Jerseys
  Individuals

Clemens, Roger, 1985 Home	900.00
Kaline, Al, 1972 Home	1,250.00
Ripkin, Cal, 1988 Road	600.00
Murphy, Dale, 1985 Home	1,000.00

  Teams, Home Common Players

Astros, 1980	300.00
Dodgers, 1986	200.00
Pirates, 1982	125.00
Twins, 1988	150.00

HARTLAND STATUES

Hartland statues continue to be one of the most popular baseball collectibles. Originally produced by the Hartland Plastics Company, Hartland, Wisconsin, from 1960 to 1963, these six to eight inch colorfully handpainted plastic figures are easily identified as they exhibit a remarkable resemblance to the players they depict. Interest in these statues heightened greatly when Hartland announced in July of 1988 they would reproduce the set from re-tooled original molds as a 25th Anniversary Commemorative Edition. They are clearly marked on the back of the statue and the box so they cannot be confused with the originals.

Hartland Statue, Mickey Mantle, $185.00.

Aaron, Henry	135.00
Aparicio, Luis	190.00
Banks, Ernie	175.00
Berra, Yogi	160.00
Colavito, Rocky	400.00
Drysdale, Don	250.00
Fox, Nellie	160.00
Groat, Dick	480.00
Killebrew, Harmon	325.00
Mantle, Mickey	185.00
Maris, Roger	260.00
Mathews, Ed	90.00
Mays, Willie	145.00

Musial, Stan 150.00
Ruth, Babe 125.00
Snider, Duke 225.00
Spahn, Warren 90.00
Williams, Ted 170.00

PRESS PINS

The newest collecting area centers on world Series and All-Star Press Pins. Issued by World Series participants beginning in 1911 and by Major League Baseball at All-Star games since 1938, these imaginatively designed and colorfully decorated pieces of jewelry are among the most attractive of baseball collectibles. Due to their limited production and closely controlled distribution to the press and guests, these items are difficult to locate and command high prices.

Press Pin, 1952 Yankee World Series, $300.00.

1939, Yankees 600.00
1956, All-Star, Washington 500.00
1963, Dodgers 225.00
1972, Oakland 300.00
1976, Cincinnati 175.00
1984, Tigers and San Diego 60.00
1986, Mets 200.00

YEARBOOKS AND PROGRAMS

A time honored tradition since the late 1800s is the souvenir program sold at ball parks. Since thousands are sold daily during the season, values for regular season programs are minimal with the exception of key games in baseball history, e.g., no-hitters, Babe Ruth's 60th home run, etc. More valuable programs include those issued for All-Star and World Series games since they are in limited supply and the demand naturally is much greater. In contrast to programs, yearbooks are a more recent innovation. First issued in the late 1940s, they have remained a popular collectors time over the years. As expected, collecting of programs and yearbooks usually focuses on the collector's favorite team(s); values primarily are determined by age, condition and availability.

Program, 1927 World Series, $650.00.

1927, program, World Series, Yankees
vs. Pirates 650.00
1946, program, World Series, Cardinals
vs. Red Sox 100.00
1950, yearbook, Phillies 50.00
1951, program, World Series, Yankees
vs. Giants 70.00
1954, yearbook, Brooklyn Dodgers ... 50.00
1955, program, All-Star Game, Milwaukee 80.00
1962, yearbook, New York Mets 50.00
1964, program, All-Star Game, New
York 30.00
1965, yearbook, Los Angeles Dodgers 20.00
1967, program, World Series, Cardinals
vs. Red Sox 35.00
1972, yearbook, Boston Red Sox 12.00
1977, program, World Series, Yankees
vs. Dodgers 12.00

BEATLES

Collecting Hints: Beatles' collectibles date from 1964 to the present. The majority of memorabilia items were produced from 1964-68. The most valuable items are marked "NEMS." Most collectors are interested in mint or near mint items only. Some items in very good condition, especially if scarce, have considerable value as well.

Each year Sotheby's holds one or two auctions which include Beatles' memorabilia, primarily one of a kind items such as guitars and stage costumes. These items command high prices. The "average" collector generally does not participate.

History: The fascination with the Beatles began in 1964. Soon the whole country was caught up in Beatlemania. The members of the group included John Lennon, Paul McCartney, George Harrison and Ringo Starr. The group broke up in 1970. After this date, the members pursued their individual musical careers. Beatlemania took on new life after the death of John Lennon.

References: Jeff Augsburger, Marty Eck, and Rick Rann, *The Beatles Memorabilia Price Guide*, Branyan Press, 1988; Barbara Fenick, *Collecting The Beatles, An Introduction and Price Guide to Fab Four Collectibles, Records and Memorabilia, Volume 1* (1984) and *Volume 2* (1988), Pierian Press.

Collectors' Club: Beatles Fan Club of Great Britain, Superstore Productions, 123 Marina, St Leonards on Sea, East Sussex, England TN 38 OBN.

Periodicals: Beatlefan, P. O. Box 33515, Decatur, GA 30033; Good Day Sunshine, Liverpool Productions, 397 Edgewood Avenue, New Haven, CT 06511.

REPRODUCTION ALERT: Records, picture sleeves, and album jackets have been counterfeited. Sound quality may be inferior. Printing on labels and picture jackets usually is inferior to the original. Many pieces of memorabilia also have been reproduced, often with some change in size, color, design, etc.

Apron, paper, white, black pictures, names and song titles	**75.00**
Bag, 9½ x 10", textured vinyl, red, portraits, inscription and signatures in black, cord carrying strap, 1964	**150.00**
Bank, 8", papier mache, rubber plug, mfg by Pride Creations	**100.00**
Beach Towel, 34 x 57", terrycloth, Beatles in bathing suits, 1960s	**100.00**
Belt Buckle, 2 x 3", metal, gold, black and white group picture	**20.00**
Blanket, 62 x 80", wool, tan, printed black and red bust figures and instruments, "The Beatles" center, mfg by Whitney	**150.00**

Record Case, olive green ground, black figures, white handle, copyright 1966 by NEMS Enterprises, Ltd, plastic, 8¼" h, $75.00.

Bongos, 5¼" h, plastic, red, white skin tops, croup sticker, Mastro decal, mfg by Mastro	**225.00**
Book, *Yellow Submarine*, paperback, 128 pgs, Signet book, Oct. 1968	**15.00**
Bowl, 6" d, pottery, blue and black fired decal, mfg by Washington Pottery	**50.00**
Bubble Gum Cards, set of 100	**60.00**
Calendar, 12 x 12", spiral bound, 1969, Golden Press, orig brown paper envelope	**50.00**
Cake Decorations	**7.50**
Candy Dish, 4½" d, scalloped edges	**50.00**
Clothes Hanger, George, Yellow Submarine	**85.00**
Clothing	
Nightshirt, cotton, white, black and white posed picture, "The Beatles"	**60.00**
Socks, crew, white, patch on ankle	**50.00**
Stockings, nylon, Holland	**40.00**
Sweatshirt, cotton, white, posed picture, "The Beatles"	**30.00**
Coaster, Yellow Submarine, cardboard, 4" sq, set of 12	**60.00**
Coin Holder, 3 x 2", plastic, red, faces and names on front, squeeze to open	**10.00**
Coloring book, 8¼ x 11", Saalfield, 1964 Nems copyright, includes 8 black and white photos, unused	**50.00**
Comb, 3¼ x 15", plastic, Beatles and signature label, "Jumbo Comb" inscription, Lido Toys, 1964	**100.00**
Costume, Paul, molded plastic face mask, full length outfit, child's 12-14, Nems copyright, 1964	**175.00**
Doll	
Plastic, Ringo, 4½" h, drum around neck, black suit, marked "1964"	**35.00**
Set of four	
Inflatable	**80.00**
Remco, orig instruments	**275.00**
Vinyl, Paul McCartney	**40.00**
Drum, 14" d, red sparkle finish, "The Beatles Drum" on skin, metal stand, mfg by Mastro	**300.00**
Figure, 6½" h, plaster, painted, glazed, set of 4, Greenware, 1960s	**100.00**
Game, Flip Your Wig, 16 x 18½" board, Milton Bradley, 1964 copyright	**80.00**
Glass, 6½" h, tapered, plastic, white, photo scene around side, gold signatures, Nems copyright	**25.00**
Handkerchief, 8½" sq	**15.00**
Headband, orig package	**40.00**
Keychain, 3", John Lennon, mfg by Anabus	**5.00**
Lunch Box, Yellow Submarine, thermos, King-Seeley Thermos co, 1968 King Features and Subafilms Ltd. copyright	**100.00**
Magazine Cover, Post, August 1964	**10.00**
Mug, 4" h, pottery, white, group fired decal,	**50.00**

Nodder
    Paul McCartney, 4", plastic, gold base   **45.00**
    Ringo, 7" **50.00**
    Set of four, 8", MIB **425.00**
Notebook, 8½ x 11", Paul **20.00**
Ornament, 6½", blown glass, figural,
    mid 1960 .... **100.00**
Pencil Case, 8 x 3½", vinyl, blue, group
    picture and autographs, zipper top,
    Standard Plastic Products **30.00**
Pennant, 23" l, felt, white, red, black,
    and white design, printed illus and
    signatures, red trim and streamers,
    "Official Licensee" copyright, c1964   **75.00**
Pinback Button, 2½", "I Like Beatles,"
    black, white, and blue, changes im-
    ages from text to group photo, mid
    1960s **20.00**
Playing Cards, single deck, boxed **50.00**
Portrait, 19 x 30", linen, black and white
    figures, lavender background, black
    and white guitars, drums, and cym-
    bals border design, "Made In Ireland"
    and "Ulster" copyright inscriptions,
    mid-1960 .... **125.00**
Poster
    London Palladium Royal Command
      Performance, Beatles posed at
      doorway with black signatures,
      1964 Nems copyright **20.00**
    Wings Over America, Paul Mc-
      Cartney, 19 x 28", June 13-14,
      1976 ....   **15.00**
Program, Sept. 5, 1964 concert, Inter-
    national Amphitheater, Chicago, 8
    pgs **75.00**
Purse, clutch, 9½ x 5½", cloth, white,
    black faces and autographs, zipper
    top, 5½" black strap handle **40.00**
Puzzle, Yellow Submarine, 650 pcs, un-
    opened, Jaymar, 1968 copyright **75.00**
Ring, flasher, plastic, adjustable, set of
    4, mid 1960s **40.00**
Scarf, 26" sq, white, faces, records, and
    instruments design on one corner ...   **10.00**
School Bag, 12 x 9 x 3½", tan, "The
    Beatles" printed on flap, handle and
    shoulder strap **200.00**
Scrapbook, with articles **65.00**
Sheet Music, She Loves You, red tone
    and white photo and design, 1963
    copyright **15.00**
Soap Container, Ringo, 10", removable
    head, plastic, Colgate-Palmolive Co,
    1965 Nems Copyright **75.00**
Stage, cardboard, drum set, used with
    Applause Beatles' dolls, MIB **20.00**
Stationery, twenty 8½ x 10½" sheets and
    envelopes, Yellow Submarine char-
    acters, boxed **12.00**
Sunglasses, plastic, black, green lenses,
    Solarex **20.00**

Tile, 6", sq, ceramic, group picture,
    "The Beatles", mfg by Carter Tiles ..   **75.00**
Vase, 14" h, ceramic **350.00**
Water Color Set, Yellow Submarine,
    contains 4 pictures and 6 colors, un-
    opened, Craft Master, 1968 copyright   **75.00**
Wig, black, tag includes black and
    white diecut Beatles photos, uno-
    pened, Lowell Toy, mid-1960s **40.00**

BEER BOTTLES

Collecting Hints: Beer bottles often are found by
digging in old dumps or wells. When found,
these bottles may have discolored and flaked.
However, the key is whether the bottle remains
unbroken or not. Damage to the bottle is of
greater concern in pricing than the discoloration.

Concentrate on the bottles from one brewery
or area. When an example is brought back to an
area of its origin, it is likely to command more
money then when sold outside the local region.
A brewery is likely to change its bottle style several times in the course of its history. This also is
true for the paper label designs found on later
bottles.

The early bottles had special closures. The bottle is worth more if the closure is intact. The
metal caps are not critical to the value of later
bottles. However, an active collecting interest in
metal caps is growing, as witnessed by dealer
displays at several recent beer collector shows.

History: Breweries began in America shortly after
the arrival of the first settlers. By the mid-19th
century most farmsteads had a small brewery on
them. Local breweries dominated the market until the arrival of Prohibition. A few larger breweries were able to adjust, but the majority closed.

When Prohibition ended, a much smaller
number of local breweries renewed production.
The advertising, distribution, and production
costs of the 1950s and 1960s led to the closing
of most local breweries and the merger of many
other breweries into a few nationally oriented
companies.

In the 1960s imported beers from Europe entered the American market. Some companies
signed licensing agreements to produce these foreign labels in the United States. The 1980s have
witnessed the growing popularity of beers
brewed in Canada and Mexico.

References: Ralph and Terry Kovel, *The Kovels'
Bottle List, 8th Edition,* Crown Publishers, 1987;
*The Official Price Guide to Bottles Old & New,
Tenth Edition,* House of Collectibles, 1986; Carlo
and Dorothy Sellari, *The Standard Old Bottle
Price Guide,* Collector Books, 1989.

Collectors' Club: American Breweriana Association, Inc., P. O. Box 6082, Colorado Springs,
CO 80934.

Embossed

Buffalo Brewing Co, Sacramento, CA, emb buffalo jumping through horseshoe, 12", amber, blob top **18.00**

Callie & Co Limited, emb dog's head, St Helens below center, 8¼", dark green, ring type blob top **15.00**

Chattachoochee Brewing Co, Brownsville, AL 9½", aqua **8.00**

Cumberland Brew Co, Cumberland, MD, amber **8.00**

Excelsior, 9¼", aqua **15.00**

Germania Brewing Co, 7½", aqua ..   **12.00**

Hand Brew Co, Pawtucket, RI, aqua   **12.00**

Hinckel Brew Co, Albany, Boston, Manchester, fancy, amber, blob top   **15.00**

Iroquois, Buffalo, Indian head, amber   **10.00**

McCormick Brewery, 1897, Boston, clear **10.00**

National Brewing Co, Baltimore, eagle, amber, blob top **17.50**

Piel Bros, East New York Brewery, fancy logo, aqua **15.00**

Royal Ruby, ABM, 9½" **18.00**

Trommer's Evergreen Brewery, 9¼", aqua **7.50**

Esquire Premium Pale Beer, Jones Brewing Co, Smithton, PA, 7 oz, painted label, $5.00.

Painted Label

Augusta Brewing Co, Augusta, CA, 7", aqua **12.00**

Camden City Brewery, 9", amber ...   **9.00**

Cock n' Bull Ginger Beer, 7", crown top **4.00**

Gutsch Brew, 8½", red **15.00**

Rolling Rock Extra Pale, blue and white label, green bottle, unopened   **15.00**

Schlitz Brewing Co, 9½", amber ...   **8.00**

Paper Label

Central Brand Extra Lager Beer, 9¼", aqua **5.00**

Cooks 500 Ale, 9½", aqua **3.50**

Diamond Jim's Beer, 9¼", aqua **5.00**

Grand Prize Beer, Gulf Brewing Co, Houston, 9", clear, crown top **7.50**

Mineral Spring Beer, 9", aqua **5.00**

Pabst Extract, amber, two labels **8.00**

Schells Beer, Schells Brewing Co, 9½", amber **3.50**

Southern Brewing Co, machine made, 9½", green **2.50**

Stoneware

Biscombe's, 8½, brown and tan **9.00**

Ginger Beer, c1915 ....   **35.00**

Pink's Ltd, Chichester, Ginger Beer, 7", c1920 ....   **5.00**

BEER CANS

Collecting Hints: Rusted and dented cans have little value unless they are rare. Most collectors remove the beer from the cans. Cans should be opened from the bottom to preserve the top unopened.

As beer can collecting became popular, companies issued special collectors' cans which never contained beer. Many were bought on speculation; value has been shaky.

History: Before Prohibition, beer was stored and shipped in kegs and dispensed in returnable bottles. When the Prohibition Act was repealed in 1933, only 700 of 1700 breweries resumed operation. Expanding distribution created the need for an inexpensive container that would permit beer to be stored longer and shipped safely. Cans were the answer.

The first patent for a lined can was issued to the American Can Co. on Sept. 25, 1934, for their "Keglined" process. Gotfried Kruger Brewing Co., Newark, New Jersey, was the first brewery to use the can. Pabst was the first major company to join the canned beer movement.

Continental Can Co. introduced the conetop beer can in 1935. Schlitz was the first brewery to use this type of can. The next major change in beer can design was the aluminum pop-top in 1962.

Reference: Thomas Toepfer, *American Beer Can Encyclopedia,* Collector Books, 1983-84 edition.

Collectors' Club: Beer Can Collectors of America, 747 Merus Court, Fenton, MO 63026.

Note: The listings are the name, type of beer, brewery location, top identification, price. The following abbreviations are used in the listings:

CR - Crowntainer type cone top
CT - cone type
FT - flat top
PT - pull top
ML - malt liquor.

7 oz.

Ace Hi M.L., Ace, Chicago, IL, FT . **100.00**

Lucky Lager, Lucky Lager, San Francisco, CA, FT **9.00**
Olympia Light, Olympia, Olympia, WA, PT **5.00**
Rolling Rock, Latrobe, Latrobe, PA, PT **1.00**
Ruppert Knickerbocker, Ruppert, 2 cities, PT **3.00**

8 oz.

Bantam, Goebel, Detroit, MI, FT ... **25.00**
Colt 45 M.L., National, 4 cities, PT . **1.00**
Country Club, Pearl, 2 cities, PT ... **4.00**
French 76 M.L., National, Baltimore, MD, PT **45.00**
Goebel Ale, Goebel, Detroit, MI, FT **30.00**
Neuweiler, Neuweiler's, Allentown, PA, FT **15.00**
Pikes Pike M.L., Walter, Pueblo, CO, FT **40.00**
Tech Premium, Pittsburgh, Pittsburgh, PA, FT **50.00**

Muhlheim Draft, 12 oz, $10.00.

10 oz.

Budweiser, Anheuser-Busch, 7 cities, PT **4.00**
Fabacher Brau, Jackson, New Orleans, LA, PT **10.00**
Lite, Miller, 3 cities, PT .... **.50**
Schaefer, Schaefer, 3 cities, PT **2.50**

11 and 12 oz.

ABC Ale, Wagner, Columbus, OH, PT **2.00**
Acme, Acme, Los Angeles, CA, FT . **15.00**
Adler Brau, Walter, Appleton, WI, FT **12.00**
Altes, National, Detroit, MI, FT **35.00**
Balboa, Southern, Los Angeles, CA, FT **125.00**
Ballantine, P. Ballantine, Newark, NJ, PT **2.00**
Berghoff, Berghoff, Ft. Wayne, IN, FT **65.00**
Black Label, Carling, 4 cities, FT ... **4.00**
Breunig's, Rice Lake, Rice Lake, WI, FT **5.00**
Burgermeister, Burgermeister, San Francisco, CA, FT **10.00**
Butte Special, Butte, Butte, MT, FT . **20.00**
Champale M.L., Champale, Norfolk, VA, PT **7.00**

Chief Oshkosh, Oshkosh, Oshkosh, WI, FT **9.00**
Cook's, Associated, 3 cities, PT **4.00**
Crown Darby, Westminister, Chicago, IL, FT **200.00**
Dawson Lager, Dawson, Hammonton, NJ, PT **1.00**
Drewry's Oldstock Ale, Drewrys, South Bend, IN, FT **30.00**
Dutch Treat, Dutch Treat, Phoenix, AZ, PT **1.00**
Eastside Old Tap, Pabst, Los Angeles, CA, FT **10.00**
Esslinger, Ruppert, New York, NY, PT **30.00**
Falls City, Falls City, Louisville, KY, FT **8.00**
Fehr's Draft, Fehr, Louisville, KY, FT **15.00**
Fisher Light, General, 2 cities, PT .. **1.00**
Frankenmuth Old English Ale, Frankenmuth, Frankenmuth, MI, FT .. **50.00**
Gablinger's, Forrest, New Bedford, MA, PT **4.00**
Gettelman, Gettleman, Milwaukee, WI, FT **20.00**
Great Falls Select, Great Falls, Great Falls, MT, FT **15.00**
Hamm's, Hamm, St. Paul, MN, PT . **2.00**
Heidelbrau, Heileman, LaCrosse, WI, PT **1.00**
Horlacher Pilsner, Horlacher, Allentown, PA, FT **8.00**
Iroquois Draft, Iroquois, Buffalo, NY, PT **2.00**
Karlsbrau, Duluth, Duluth, MN, FT . **10.00**
Kentucky M.L., Fehr, Louisville, KY, FT **38.00**
Leinenkugel's, Heinenkugel, Chippewa Falls, WI, FT **6.00**
Manheim, Reading, Reading, PA, FT **10.00**
Meister Brau, Peter Hand, Chicago, IL, FT **25.00**
Milwaukee's Best, Miller, Milwaukee, WI, PT **4.00**
National Bohemian, National, Detroit, MI, FT **10.00**
North Star, Associated, 3 cities, PT . **2.00**
Oertels '92, Oertel, Louisville, KY, PT **10.00**
Old Crown Ale, Centlivre, Ft. Wayne, IN, FT **40.00**
Old Reading, Old Reading, Reading, PA, FT **100.00**
Pearl Draft, Pearl, 2 cities, PT **15.00**
Piels Draft Ale, Piel, Willimansett, MA, PT **50.00**
Queens Brau, Queen City, Cumberland, MD, FT **45.00**
Red Top, Drewrys, South Bend, IN, PT **6.00**
Royal Amber, Heileman, 4 cities, PT **1.00**
Schaefer, Schaefer, Albany, NY, PT : **4.00**
Schlitz Light (1975), Schlitz, 6 cities, PT .... **.75**

Schoenling, Schoenling, Cincinnati, OH, PT 1.00

Stein Haus, Schell, New Ulm, MN, PT 3.00

Tavern Pale, Atlantic, Chicago, IL, FT 25.00

Topper, Eastern, Hammonton, NJ, PT 1.00

Tudor Ale, Cumberland, Cumberland, MD, PT 1.50

Utica Club Pale Ale, West End, Utica, NY, FT 40.00

Valley Forge, Valley Forge, Norristown, PA, FT 15.00

Walter's Light, Walter, Pueblo, Co, PT 2.00

West Virginia Pilsner, Little Switzerland, Huntington, WV, PT 3.00

Wunderbrau, Wunderbrau, Cincinnati, Oh, FT 60.00

Yuengling, Yuengling, Pottsville, PA, PT 2.00

12 oz., Cone Top

Aero Club Pale Select, East Idaho, Pocatello, ID, CT 100.00

Breunig's Lager, Rice Lake, Rice Lake, WI, Ct 50.00

Dawson's Pale Ale, Dawson, New Bedford, MA, CT 40.00

Falstaff, Falstaff, 3 cities, CT 25.00

Grain Belt Golden Premium, Minneapolis, Minneapolis, MN, CT 30.00

Haas Pilsner, Haas, Houghton, MI, CC 70.00

Menominee Champion, Menominee-Marinette, Menominee, MI, CT .. 50.00

Rahr's, Rahr's Green Bay, Green Bay, WI, CR 45.00

Stag Premium Dry, Griesedieck-Western, 2 cities, CT 25.00

Ye Tavern, Lafayette, Lafayette, IN, CT 90.00

15 and 16 oz.

Altes, National, Detroit, MI, PT 4.00

Blatz, Pabst, Los Angeles, CA, PT .. 6.00

Burger, Burger, Cincinnati, OH, PT . 25.00

Champagne Velvet, Associated, 3 cities, PT 10.00

Eastside Old Tap, Pabst, Los Angeles, CA, FT 15.00

Grace Bros. Bavarian, Maier, Los Angeles, CA, PT 35.00

Hamm's Draft, Hamm, 3 cities, PT . 3.00

Krueger Ale, Krueger, Cranston, RI, PT 10.00

Mustang Malt Lager, Pittsburgh, Pittsburgh, PA, PT 25.00

Old German, Eastern, Hammonton, NJ, PT 2.00

Piels Light, Piels, Brooklyn, NY, FT . 20.00

Spur Stout M.L., Sick's Rainier, Seattle, WA, PT 40.00

Sterling Draft, Sterling, Evansville, IN, PT 15.00

Whale's White Ale, National, 4 cities, PT 25.00

BELLS

Collecting Hints: The bell category is very large. Collectors should focus on a single topic (door bells, school bells, sleigh bells, etc.), on bells from a single country or geographic area, or on bells made from a single substance. Once a bell style becomes popular, its production may last for many decades. Only the most experienced dealer and collector can determine age accurately.

Collecting glass bells has become very popular. Collectors should be alert for wine or cordial glasses which have had their base removed, been reversed, and then been converted to a bell by the addition of a clapper. These conversions are worth substantially less than glass forms designed and originally made as bells.

There is an active market in limited edition collectors' bells. Some occasionally are copies of older models, so collectors should become familiar with the patterns.

Develop an eye for quality. The bells of the late 19th century show a high degree of workmanship and artistic style. Most of all, buy a bell because you find enjoyment in it—both visually and through its ring.

History: Bells have been used for centuries for many different purposes. They have been traced as far back as 2697 B.C., though at that time they did not have any true tone. One of the oldest bells is the "crotal," a tiny sphere with small holes and a ball of stone or metal inside. This type now appears as the sleigh bell, the Christmas bell or the bells on Indian dancers.

True bell making began when bronze, the mixing of tin and copper, was discovered. There are now many types of materials of which bells are made—almost as many materials as there are uses for them.

Collectors' Club: American Bell Association, Rt 1, Box 286, Natronia Heights, PA 15065.

See: Limited Editions or Collector Items.

REPRODUCTION ALERT

Animal

Horse, 3", brass 15.00

Sheep, brass, leather strap, three graduated sizes 40.00

Brass

Indian head, 3¼" d, 7½" h, Lansaery 100.00

Kewpie 25.00

Lady

5" h, 3¼" d, wearing full dress and bonnet 65.00

7" h, 5¾" d, wearing hoop skirt, holding fan 95.00

Brass, Disciples, Matthew, Luke, and John, $45.00.

Lucy Locket, 4¾" h, 2⅛" d, fancy outfit and hat	65.00
Napoleon, 3⅜" d, 7" h	75.00
Neville Chamberlain, figural handle, 2½" d, 5¼" h	65.00
Owl, 4", emb feathers	40.00
Pilgrim Lady, 5" h, 3⅛" d	55.00
Queen Elizabeth I, 5½" h, 2⅝" d, crown on head	65.00
Welsh Woman, 3¼", spinning wheel clapper	65.00
Carriage, nickel plated brass, floor mount	135.00
Church, 30" d, saddle and wheel	900.00
Commerative, Queen Elizabeth II Silver Jubilee, 4½" h, marked "Aynsley" . .	25.00
Fire, 12", brass	75.00

Glass, Daisy and Button pattern, amber, 6⅝", $20.00.

Glass
Amber, floral etching, clear handle, 5"	25.00
Art Glass, 6 x 13", mint green	375.00

Burmese, clear handle and clapper, glossy finish, 5⅜" d, 9½" h	450.00
Carnival, marigold, hobnail, Imperial	125.00
Cranberry, gold edge, acid leaves . .	30.00
Crystal, hand blown, satin angel figural handle, France	20.00
Cut, 4½", cornflowers and leaves . .	160.00
Green, hp flowers	15.00
Ruby	
Clear handle, 12"	50.00
Etched deer and castle pattern, Bohemian	100.00
Satin, white, hp flowers, clear handle	30.00
Porcelain	
Art Deco, woman, Japan	75.00
Hummel, Let's Sing, #700, 1978 . . .	60.00
Nippon, hp roses, cobalt blue and gold ground	135.00
Pottery, 3", chef holding glass and wine bottle, marked "Occupied Japan" . .	25.00
Railroad, bronze	
12" d, mount and clapper	250.00
17", yoke and cradle	875.00
School	
9½", hand, metal, turned wood handle	50.00
24", cast iron, marked "O S Bell Co, Hillsboro, Ohio"	550.00
Ship, 8", includes mount	65.00
Sleigh, brass, graduated	200.00
Yacht, 5¾", brass	40.00

BICYCLES

Collecting Hints: Collectors divide bicycles into two groups - antique and classic. The antique category covers early high wheelers through safety bikes made into the 1920s and 1930s. Highly stylized bicycles from the 1930s and 1940s represent the transitional step to the classic period, beginning in the late 1940s and running through the end of the balloon tire era.

Unfortunately there are no reliable guide books for the beginning collector. A good rule is that any older bike in good condition is worth collecting.

Never pay much for a bicycle that is rusted, incomplete, or repaired with non-original parts. Replacement of leather seats or rubber handle bars does not effect value since these have a short life time.

Restoration is an accepted practice. Make certain to store an old bicycle high (hung by its frame to protect the tires) and dry (no more than 50% humidity).

Do not forget all the secondary material, e.g., advertising premiums, brochures, catalogs, posters, etc., that featured the bicycle. This material provides important historical data for research, especially for restoration.

History: In 1818 Baron Karl von Drais, a German, invented the Draisienne, a push scooter, that is viewed as the "first" bicycle. In 1839 Patrick MacMillan, a Scot, added a treadle system; a few years later Pierre Michaux, a Frenchman, revolutionized the design by adding a pedal system. The bicycle was introduced in America at the 1876 Centennial.

Early bicycles were high wheelers with a heavy iron frame and two disportionately sized wheels with wooden rims and tires. The exaggerated front wheel was for speed, the small rear wheel for balance.

James Starley, an Englishman, is responsible for developing a bicycle with two wheels of equal size. Pedals drove the rear wheels by means of a chain and sprocket. By 1892 the wooden rim wheel was replaced by pneumatic air-filled tires to be followed by the standard rubber tire with inner tube.

1898 witnessed the development of the coaster brake. This important milestone made cycling a true family sport. Bicycling became a cult among the urban middle class. As the new century dawned, over four million Americans owned bicycles.

The automobile challenged the popularity of bicycling beginning in the 1920s. Since that time, interest in bicycling has been cyclical. Technical advances continued. The 1970s was the decade of the ten speed.

The success of American Olympiads in cycling and cycle racing, especially the Tour d'France, have kept the public's attention focused on the bicycle. However, the tremendous resurgence enjoyed by bicycling in the 1970s appears to have ended. The next craze is probably some distance in the future.

References: Frederick Alderson, *Bicycling: A History*, Praeger, 1972; A. Ritchie, *King of the Road*, Ten Speed Press.

Periodicals: *Antique/Classic Bicycle News*, P.O. Box 1049, Ann Arbor, MI 48106; *Bicycle Trader*, P. O. Box 5600, Pittsburgh, PA 15207.

Collectors' Club: Wheelmen, Henry Ford Museum, Dearborn, MI 48121.

Museum: Antique and Classic Bicycle Museum of America, Ann Arbor, MI.

Advertising
  Folder, Schwinn-Built Bicycles, 3¼ x
    6", illus of nine bicycles, c1948 ..   **50.00**
  Trade Card, Clark Bicycle Co, Christmas, Santa on high wheeler, 1880s   **20.00**
Badge
  1¼ x 2½", brass link, "Philadelphia
    to Wilmington," Sept 5, 1896,
    worn orig silver finish **65.00**
  1¼ x 3", brass link, "First Prize

Award," Springfield Meet, May 30,
    1896 ....   **80.00**
  1½ x 4", copper finished brass link,
    "Half Century Meet," Oct 29,
    1905, sponsored by Patterson
    Wheelmen **85.00**
  2 x 2", diecut, brass, club name
    "Highland Cyclists," c1890, English **20.00**
Bicycle
  B. F. Goodrich, boy's, 26 x 2.125
    tires, new paint, orig light, carrier,
    locking fork, bendix auto 2-speed   **150.00**
  Columbia, Three Star Deluxe
    Boy's, orig condition **425.00**
    Men's, 26", good condition **300.00**
  Comet, men's, worn orig paint,
    coaster brake, aluminum fenders .   **75.00**
  Dayton, boy's, 26", worn orig paint,
    carrier, 1937 ....   **500.00**
  Elgin, Skylark, lady's, worn orig paint,
    headlight, carrier, white sidewalls,
    1936 ....   **650.00**
  Higgins, lady's, worn orig paint, carrier, skirt guards, truss rod, rusty
    rims **85.00**
  Monarch, Silver King, lady's, worn
    orig paint, headlight, 1936 ......   **250.00**
  Remington Arms Co, tandem, wood
    rims, fixed drive, block chain, center frame drive, good condition ..   **575.00**
  Roadmaster, girl's, cream and blue,
    red pinstripe, horn tank, headlight,
    luggage carrier, chrome rims, orig
    condition **125.00**
  Rollfast, boy's, 24", orig blue and
    white paint, carrier, headlight,
    white sidewalls, 1954 ....   **125.00**
  Schwinn
    Boy's, 26", horn tank, 1941 .....   **350.00**
    Tandem, Town and Country, triple,
      red, chrome fenders, chain
      guard, orig paint and striping ..   **850.00**
  Seneca, Model 97, lady's, wood handlebars, orig grips, rat trap pedals,
    wood rear fenders, wood rims,
    fixed drive, block chain, orig seat,
    orig decals **175.00**
  Shelby, Supreme, boy's, 24", spring
    front fork, horn tank, headlight,
    chrome rear carrier, orig green and
    cream two tone paint, orig green
    tires, white sidewalls, 1949 ......   **450.00**
  Walton, tandem, wood rim, block
    chain fixed drive, rat trap pedals,
    new cork grips, new polymer tires   **450.00**
  Western Flyer, X-53, boy's, 26" **100.00**
Brakes, coaster
  Corbin Duplex **12.00**
  Musselman, mounted on early metal
    adv display stand **15.00**
  New Departure Duplex **10.00**

Catalog
  Crawford Bicycles, American Bicycle
    Co, Hagerstown, MD, 1901, black
    and white, illus, 12 pgs, 5½ x 6¾"   30.00
  Mead Cycle, Chicago, 1914, 62 pgs,
    9 x 12" 50.00
  J Strauss, Buffalo, NY, 1914, 157 pgs,
    7 x 10" 15.00

Container, 2¾" d, 1½" h, silvered brass,
  porcelain lid, black and white center
  illus of male and female cyclists,
  Union Cycle Mfg Co, Boston, issued
  by O'Hara Waltham Dial Co, c1896   80.00

Lapel Stud
  ⅝"
  Eagle Bicycle, white enamel on
    brass, globe and eagle design ..   48.00
  League of American Wheelmen,
    blue enamel, threaded post back,
    League symbol, c1890 ....   40.00
  ⅞", celluloid, silvered brass stud
    back, c1890
  Alert Bicycle, blue and white 15.00
  Chief Bicycle, blue and white, In-
    dian head and wheel spokes illus   20.00
  Globe and Mascot Bicycles, pur-
    ple, white letters 18.00
  Waverlys Half Nickel Forks, blue
    and white 18.00

Light
  Battery operated, Schwinn Phantom,
    chrome 60.00
  Carbide, nickel plated brass, red and
    green side lenses, crystal front lens,
    marked "20th Century Mfg Co" ..   40.00
  Pedals, Schwinn, girl's, glass reflectors   60.00

Pin, 1 x 1¾", mechanical, brass, flanged
  wheels, red enameled center, 1887
  Tennessee Centennial, Nashville, 2½
  x 4½" orig card 65.00

Pinback Button
  ⅞"
  Flint Bicycle, light green arrow-
    head, bright yellow ground 18.00
  Gadke/Moffett Bearings, sepia
    photo of Faithful Gadke, rim in-
    scription "Moffett Ball Roller
    Bearings," c1896 ....   35.00
  Hunter Bicycles, black and white
    photo of hunting dog with game
    bird in mouth, late 1890s 40.00
  LAW/Good Roads, multicolored,
    purple rim around League sym-
    bol, c1896 ....   20.00
  Morrow Coaster Brakes, gold bicy-
    cle brake, green ground, gold
    rim, white lettering, early 1900s   18.00
  Sherman Bicycles, black and white
    photo portrait of General Sher-
    man 38.00

Seat
  DeLuxe Messenger, leather, balloon
    tire type bicycle 15.00
  Monarch, twin 25.00
Stickpin
  Columbia Pneumatic, ⅞", diecut rep-
    lica of bicycle tire with inscription
    on tire wall, center band with blue
    name 40.00
  Lovell Diamond Cycles, ⅞", black
    and white, diamond logo design,
    c1896 ....   25.00
Tire
  Balloon, 26 x 2.125
    Gum Wall Sidewalls 6.00
    White Sidewalls 8.00
  Schwinn, wide, white sidewalls,
    knobbys 15.00

BIG LITTLE BOOKS

Collecting Hints: As more research is done and
published on Big Little Books, the factors determining value shift. Condition always has been a
key. Few examples are in pristine mint condition
since the books were used heavily by the children who owned them. Each collector strives to
obtain copies free from as many defects (bent
edges on cover, missing spine, torn pages, mu-
tilation with crayon or pencil, missing pages,
etc.) as possible.

The main character in a book will determine
price since it is a collector from another field
who will vie with the Big Little Book collector
for the same work. Dick Tracy, Disney characters, Buck Rogers, Flash Gordon, Charlie Chan,
The Green Hornet and Tom Mix are examples.
Other cowboy heroes are experiencing renewed
popularity.

Until recently little attention has been directed
to the artists who produced the books. Now examples by Alex Raymond and Henry Vallely
command top dollar. Other desirable artists are
Al Capp, Allen Dean, Alfred Andriola, and Will
Gould. Personal taste still is a critical factor at
this time.

Little is known as to how many copies of each
book were printed. Scarcity charts have been
prepared, but constantly are being revised. Books
tend to hit the market in hoards, with prices
fluctuating accordingly. However, the last decade has witnessed a stabilization of prices.

Larry Lowery, in the introduction to his book,
has prepared an excellent section on the care
and storage of Big Little Books. He also deserves
credit for the detailed research which he has
brought to each listing.

History: Big Little Books, although a trademark
of the Whitman Publishing Co., is a term used
to describe a wealth of children's books pub-

lished during the 1930s and continuing to the present day. The origin of Big Little Books dates to a number of 1920s series by Whitman among which were Fairy Tales, Forest Friends and Boy Adventure.

The first Big Little Book appeared in 1933. Ten different page lengths and eight different sizes were tried by Whitman prior to the 1940s. Whitman and Saalfied Publishing Company dominated the field. However, other publishers did enter the market. Among them were Engel-Van Wiseman, Lynn Publishing Co., Goldsmith Publishing Co. and Dell Publishing Co.

Whitman also deserves attention for the various remarketing efforts it undertook with many of its titles. It contracted to provide Big Little Book premiums for Cocomalt, Kool Aid, Pan-Am Gas, Macy's, Lily-Tulip's Tarzan Ice Cream and others. Among its series names are Wee Little Books, Big Big Books, Nickel Books, Penny Books and Famous Comics.

In the 1950s television characters were introduced into Big Little Book format. Whitman Publishing became part of Western Publishing, owned by Mattel. Waldman and Son Publishing Co. under its subsidiary, Moby Books, issued their first Big Little Book- style book in 1977.

References: Larry Lowery, *Lowery's The Collector's Guide To Big Little Books and Similar Books*, privately printed, 1981; James Stuart Thomas, *The Big Little Book Price Guide*, Wallace-Homestead, 1983.

Collectors' Club: Big Little Book Collector's Club of America, P.O. Box 732, Danville, CA 94526.

Note: Books are priced in very fine condition. Cover and spine are intact with only slight bending at the corners. All pages are present; only slightest discoloration of pages. Book has a crispness from cover color to inside.

No effort has been made to list the variations and premiums published by Whitman.

Abbreviations:
WBLB = Whitman Big Little Book
WBELB = Whitman Better Little Book
hc = hard cover
ms = Movie size, 4⅝ x 5¼ x ⅞"
sc = soft cover
ss = standard size, 3⅝ x 4½ x 1½"

See: Cartoon Characters, Cowboy Heroes, Disneyana and Space Adventurers.

AERONAUTICS

Adventures of Tiny Tim, WBLB, #767, 1935, Stanley Link, artist and author, ss, 384 pgs, hc **18.00**
Ceiling Zero, Lynn Publishing Co, L20, 1935, Warner Bros Pictures, artist and author, 5 x 7½ x 5⅛", 128 pgs, hc . **25.00**

Don Winslow And The Great War Plot, WBELB, #1489, 1940, Lt Frank V Martinek, artist and author, ss, 432 pgs, hc **25.00**
Don Winslow, Navy Intelligence Ace, WBELB, #1418, 1942, Lt Frank V Martinek, artist and author, ss, 432 pgs, hc, flip-it feature **28.00**
Hall of Fame of the Air, WBLB, #1159, 1936, Clayton Knight, artist, Capt Eddie Rickenbacher, author, ss, 432 pgs, hc **12.00**
Skyroads with Clipper Williams of the Flying Legion, WBELB, #1439, 1938, Russell Kenton, artist, Lt Dick Calkins, author, ss, 432 pgs, hc **12.00**
Speed Douglas And The Mole Gang, WBELB, #1455, 1941, Erwin L Hess, artist, Charles Arthur, author, ss, 432 pgs, hc, flip-it feature **30.00**
Tailspin Tommy, Air Racer, Saalfield, #1183, 1940, Hal Forrest, artist and author, ss, 400 pgs, hc **35.00**
Tailspin Tommy And The Lost Transport, WBELB, #1413, 1938, Hal Forrest, artist and author, ss, 432 pgs, hc **35.00**
Wings of the USA, WBELB, #1407, 1940, Thomas Hickey, artist, Peter A Wyckoff, author, ss, 432 pgs, h c .. **12.00**

CARTOON CHARACTERS, MOVIE

Adventures of Andy Panda, Dell, #15, 1943, Walter Lantz Productions, artist and author, 4 x 5½", 192 pgs, sc ... **25.00**
Betty Boop in Snow White, WBLB, #1119, 1934, Max Fleischer, Paramount Talkartoon, artist, Wallace West, author, 4⅝ x 5¼ x 1", 160 pgs, hc, softcover spine **35.00**
Felix The Cat, WBLB, #1129, 1936, adapted from Pat Sullivan, ss, 432 pgs, hc **32.50**
Mickey Mouse Runs His Own Newspaper, WBLB, #1409, 1937, Floyd Gottfredson, artist and author, ss, 432 pgs, hc **40.00**
Mickey Mouse The Detective, WBLB, #1139, 1934, Floyd Gottfredson, artist and author, ss, 432 pgs, hc **35.00**
Porky Pig and Petunia, WBLB, #1408, 1942, Leon Schlesinger Productions, artist and author, ss, 432 pgs, hc ... **25.00**

CARTOON CHARACTERS, NEWSPAPER

Ghost Avenger, WBELB, #1462, 1943, Henry E Vallely, artist, Russell R Win-

Reg'lar Fellers, Gene Byrnes, artist and author, Whitman Publishing Co, # 754, 1933, standard size, hardcover, 320 pgs, Cocomalt premium, $30.00.

terbotham, author, ss, 432 pgs, hc, flip-it feature 35.00

Katzenjammer Kids in the Mountains, Saalfield Little Big Book, #1055, 1934, H H Knerr, artist and author, 7¾ x 3⅝ x ⅞", 160 pgs 35.00

Little Annie Rooney On The Highway To Adventure, WBLB, #1406, 1938, Darrell McClure, artist, Brandon Walsh, author, ss, 432 pgs, hc 40.00

Little Lulu, Alvin, and Tubby, WBELB, #1429, 1947, Marjorie H Buell, artist and author, ss, 288 pgs, hc 30.00

Moon Mullins and The Plushbottom Twins, WBLB, #1134, 1935, Frank Willard, artist and author, ss, 432 pgs 20.00

Popeye's Ark, Saalfield Little Big Book, #1117, 1936, Elzie C. Segar, artist and author, 4¾ x 5¼ x ⅞", 160 pgs, hc 38.50

Smitty Golden Gloves Tournament, WBLB, #745, 1933, Walter Berndt, artist and author, ss, 320 pgs, hc ... 12.00

Wimpy, the Hamburger Eater, WBLB, #1458, 1938, Elzie Cresler Segar, ss, 432 pgs, hc 25.00

DETECTIVE

A G–Man In Action, Saalfield Publishing Co, #1173, 1940, J R White, artist, Dick Adair, author, ss, 400 pgs 10.00

Dan Dunn, Secret Operative 48 And The Crime Master, WBLB, #1171, 1937, Norman Marsh, artist and author, ss, 432 pgs 18.00

Denny The Ace Detective, Saalfield Publishing Co, #1156, 1938, Henry Muhmeim artist, Dick Adair, author, ss 12.00

Ellery Queen, Adventure Of Last Man

Club, WBELB, #1406, 1940, adapted from *Ellery Queen*, ss, 432 pgs 35.00

G–Man Allen, Saalfield Publishing Co, #1162, 1939, J R White, artist, James McNeal, author, ss, 432 pgs, hc ... 10.00

Inspector Charlie Chan, Villainy On The High Seas, WBELB, #1424, 1942, Alfred Andriola, artist, adapted from Earl Deer Biggers, ss, 432 pgs, hc .. 45.00

Inspector Wade And The Feathered Serpent, Saalfield Publishing Co, #1194, 1940, adapted from Edgar Wallace, ss, 400 pgs, hc, sewn binding 12.00

Inspector Wade of Scotland Yard, Saalfield Publishing Co, #1186, 1940, ss, adapted from Edgar Wallace, 400 pgs, hc 12.00

Red Barry Undercover Man, Will Gould, author, Whitman Publishing Co, #1426, Better Little Book, 1937, standard size, hardcover, 432 pgs, $10.00.

King of Crime, Saalfield Publishing Co, #1134, 1938, Paton Edwards, artist, Joe Carson, author, ss, 400 pgs, hc, sewn binding, varnished 28.00

Secret Agent X–9, WBLB, #1144, 1936, Alex Raymond, artist, Charles Flanders, author, ss, 432 pgs, hc 15.00

JUNGLE

Danger Trails In Africa, WBLB, #1151, Martin Johnson, artist and author, 432 pgs, hc 15.00

Og, Son of Fire, WBLB, #1115, 1936, Irving Crump, artist and author, ss, 432 pgs, hc 30.00

Smilin' Jack And The Jungle Pipe Line, WBELB, #1419, 1947, Zack Mosley, artist, Helen Berke, author, ss, 352 pgs, hc 25.00

Tarzan Escapes, WBLB, #1182, 1936, MGM Pictures, adapted from Edgar Rice Burroughs, ss, 240 pgs, hc 15.00

LITERATURE

Black Beauty, Saalfield Little Big Book, #1057, 1934, Park Sumner, artist, adapted from Anna Sewell by Althea L Clinton, 4¾ x 5¼ x ⅞", 160 pgs, hc **15.00**
Little Miss Muffett, WBLB, #1120, 1936, Fanny Y Cory, artist and author, ss, 432 pgs, hc **14.00**
The Spy, WBLB, #768, 1936, ss, 300 pgs, hc **15.00**

MOVIE

An Hour With You, WBLB, #774, 1934, ms, 160 pgs, hc, softcover spine **18.00**
David Copperfield, WBLB, #1148, 1934, MGM Pictures, ms, 160 pgs, hc, softcover spine **30.00**
It Happened One Night, Saalfield Little Big Book, #1098, 1935, Columbia Pictures, adapted by Robert Riskin, 4¾ x 5¼ x ⅞", 160 pgs, hc **24.50**
Mickey Rooney Himself, WBELB, #1427, 1939, MGM Picture, Eleanor Packer, author, ms, 240 pgs, hc **40.00**
The Buccaneer, WBLB, #1470, 1938, Paramount Pictures, ms, 240 pgs, hc **42.00**
The Lost Patrol, WBLB, #753, 1934, RKO Pictures, ms, 160 pgs, hc, softcover spine **40.00**
The Story of Charlie McCarthy and Edgar Bergen, WBLB, #1456, 1938, Henry E Vallely, artist, Eleanor Packer, author, ss, 288 pgs, hc **20.00**
Treasure Island, WBLB, #1141, 1934, MGM Pictures, adapted by Eleanor Packer, ms, 160 pgs, hc, softcover spine **35.00**
Westward Ho, John Wayne, Engel-Van Wiseman, WBLB, #18, 1935, Republic Pictures, adapted by Edward Finlay, 4¼ x 5½ x ¾", 160 pgs, hc **36.00**

RADIO

Believe It Or Not, WBLB, #760, 1933, Robert Ripley, author, ms, 160 pgs, hc, softcover spine **25.00**
Jack Armstrong And The Ivory Treasure, WBLB, #1435, 1937, Henry E Vallely, artist, Leslie N Daniels, Jr, author, ss, 432 pgs, hc **30.00**
Jack Armstrong And The Mystery Of The Iron Key, WBELB, #1432, 1939, Henry E Vallely, artist, ss, 432 pgs, hc **32.00**
Maximo The Amazing Super-Man, WBELB, #1436, 1940, Henry E Vallely, artist, Russell R Winterbotham, author, ss, 432 pgs, hc **40.00**
Radio Patrol And Big Dan's Mobsters,

Gene Autry and the Bandits of Silver Tip, Whitman Publishing Co, #700-10, Better Little Book, 1948, tall size, 3⅛ x 5½ x ⅝", hardcover, 200 pgs, $12.00.

WBELB, #1498, 1941, Eddie Sullivan, artist, Charlie Schmidt, author, ss, 432 pgs, hc **30.00**
The Green Hornet Returns, WBELB, #1496, 1941, adapted from Fran Striker, ss, 432 pgs, hc **20.00**
The Shadow and the Living Death, WBELB, #1430, 1940, Erwin L Hess, artist, Maxwell Grant, author, ss, 432 pgs, hc **20.00**

WESTERN

Big Chief Wahoo And The Lost Pioneers, WBELB, #1432, 1942, Elmer Woggon, artist, Allen Saunders, author, ss, hc, 432 pgs, flip-it feature **35.00**
Flame Boy and the Indian's Secret, WBELB, #1464, 1938, Sekakuku, artist, Goren Arnold, author, ss, 300 pgs, hc **12.00**
Pioneers of the Wild West, World Syndicate Publishing Co, 1933, J Carroll Mansfield, artist and author, ss, 186 pgs, clothbound **20.00**
Shooting Sheriffs, WBLB, #1195, 1936, Leon Morgan, author, ss, 432 pgs, hc **12.00**

BLACK MEMORABILIA

Collecting Hints: Black memorabilia was produced in vast quantities and variations. As a result, collectors have a large field from which to choose and should concentrate on one or a combination of limited categories.

Outstanding examples or extremely derogatory designs in any given area of the field command higher prices. Certain categories, e.g., cookie jars, draw a higher concentration of collector interest resulting in higher prices. Regional pricing also is a factor.

New collectors frequently overpay for common items of little worth because they mistakenly assume all Black collectibles are rare or of great value. As in any other collecting field, misinformation and a lack of knowledge leads to these exaggerated values. The Black memorabilia collector is particularly vulnerable to this practice since so little documentation exists on the subject.

New collectors should familiarize themselves with the field by first studying the market, price trends, and existing reference material. Again, because of the limited reference material and the relative newness of the field, seeking out other collectors is especially valuable for the novice.

Black memorabilia has developed into an established collecting field primarily within the past few years and continues to grow with increased public attention and interest.

History: The term "Black memorabilia" refers to a broad range of collectibles that often overlap other collecting fields, e.g., toys, postcards, etc. It also encompasses African artifacts, items created by slaves or related to the slavery era, modern Black cultural contributions to literature, art, etc., and material associated with the Civil Rights Movement and the Black experience throughout history.

The earliest known examples of Black memorabilia include primitive African designs and tribal artifacts. Black American dates back to the arrival of African natives upon American shores.

The advent of the 1900s launched an incredible amount and variety of material depicting Blacks, most often in a derogatory and dehumanizing manner that clearly reflected the stereotypical attitude held toward the Black race during this period. The popularity of Black portrayals in this unflattering fashion flourished as the century wore on.

As the growth of the Civil Rights Movement escalated and aroused public awareness to the Black plight, attitudes changed. Public outrage and pressure eventually put a halt to the offensive practice during the early 1950s.

Black representations still are being produced today in many forms, but no longer in the demoralizing designs of the past. These modern objects, while not as historically significant as earlier examples, will become the Black memorabilia of tomorrow.

References: Patiki Gibbs, *Black Collectibles Sold In America,* Collector Books, 1987; Patiki Gibbs and Tyson Gibbs, *The Collector's Encyclopedia of Black Dolls,* Collector Books, 1987; Dawn Reno, *Collecting Black Americana,* Crown Publishing Co, 1986; Darrell A Smith, *Black Amer-*

icana: A Personal Collection, Black Relics, Inc., 1988.

Periodicals: *Black Ethnic Collectibles,* 1401 Asbury Court, Hyattsville, MD 20782.

Museums: Black American West Museum, Denver, CO; Black Archives Research Center and Museum, Florida A&M University, Tallahassee, FL; National Baseball Hall of Fame, Cooperstown, NY; Studio Museum, Harlem, NY; Center for African Art, New York, NY; The Jazz Hall of Fame, New York, NY; Schomburg Center for Research in Black Culture, New York, NY; John Brown Wax Museum, Harper's Ferry, WV; The Museum of African Art, Smithsonian Institution, Washington, D.C.; Robeson Archives, Howard University, Washington, D.C.

REPRODUCTION ALERT: Very few reproductions are found in the Black memorabilia market at this time. Those that do exist tend to be made of easily reproducible materials which generally show signs of "newness." Collectors should beware of any given item offered in large or unlimited quantities.

Note: The following price listing is based upon items in excellent to mint condition. Major paint loss, chips, cracks, fading, tears, or other extreme signs of age warrant a considerable reduction in value, except in very rare or limited production items. Collectors should expect a certain amount of wear on susceptible surfaces.

Advertising Trade Card, Sanford's Ginger, Potter Drug and Chemical Co, Boston, black girl with child in watermelon cradle, multicolored litho, mfg by Forbes, Boston, $7.50.

Advertising
  Box, 11½" w, Masons Challenge
    Blacking, paper label, wood box . **75.00**
  Doll, Cream of Wheat, 18" h, stuffed,
    chef, 1960s **50.00**

Hat, Aunt Jemima Breakfast Club, paper, fold-out style, 11" l **15.00**
Magazine Ad, Cream of Wheat, 1916–24 .... **10.00**
Pail, Yum Yum Tobacco, black boy, 8" **310.00**
Photograph, Joe Louis, Fletchers Castoria, 9½ x 11½", framed **50.00**
Poster
  Mil-Kay Vitamin Drink, 22½ x 33", matted and framed **75.00**
  O'Baby Chocolate Dairy Drink, cardboard, multicolored, 14½ x 22½" **135.00**
Puzzle, Amos and Andy, Pepsodent Co, 1932, 8 x 10" **85.00**
Tin
  3¾" h, Delites Cocoa, paper label **45.00**
  7¾" h, Sunny South Peanuts **65.00**
  11" h, C D Kenney, Mammy's Favorite Brand Coffee, Mammy carrying coffeepot and cup **120.00**
Tip Tray, 4" d, Cottolene Shortening, litho tin **55.00**
Trade Card
  Globe Shoe & Clothing Co, 6 x 3¾", Negro boy **8.00**
  Sapolio Soap **8.00**
Ashtray
  3", boy in outhouse while other boy waits, bisque, marked "Japan" ... **20.00**
  3¼"
    Boy, seated, eating melon slice, empty rind is tray, plaster **50.00**
    Skillet, painted cast iron, black man's face in center, marked "Virginia Beach, VA" **20.00**
  3½"
    Boy, head, ceramic, marked "Japan" **25.00**
    Boy and Crow, beside match holder shaped like tree stump, bisque, marked "Japan" **30.00**
  4¾", nodder, boy in yellow hat, smoking cigar, painted metal, marked "Occupied Japan" **45.00**
Autograph, Booker T Washington, Oct 6, 1908 letter, 11 x 12", matted and framed **150.00**
Bank
  Aluminum, Sharkie's Tao Burnley, patent #32537, movable eyes, ears, tongue, arm, and hand, worn paint **150.00**
  Cast Iron
    Sharecropper, 5½" **155.00**
    Two faced boy, 4" h **225.00**
  Glass, Uncle Joe, Nash's Mustard, figural, applied lips, 4½" h **25.00**
Baseball Pennant, NY Black Yankees, felt, 25" l **125.00**
Beer Cap, 1¼", Boggles, Katzenjammer

character, "Goldenrod Beer Comicaps Tastes Better," 1935 copyright . **25.00**
Bell, 4" h, Mammy, silvered metal bell, painted wood and cloth **25.00**
Bill of Sale, Louisiana, slave, 1841 ... **110.00**

Children's Book, *The Story of Little Black Sambo,* McLaughlin Brothers, Inc, Springfield, MA, 1931, 16 pgs, $15.00.

Book
  Little Black Sambo, 1932 .... **65.00**
  Minstrel Joke Book, 1898 .... **20.00**
  Topsy Turvey's Pigtails, 1938 ...... **45.00**
  Turkey Trot and The Black Santa, 1940s **70.00**
Bottle Opener, minstrel, painted wood, 7" h **30.00**
Bust, Martin Luther King **75.00**
Carnival Chalkware, grim faced boy on toilet, 9½" h **15.00**
Cigar Box
  Old Plantation Brand, emb, 11" l ... **50.00**
  Sir Jonathon Brand, wood, 6¼" l ... **20.00**
Cigarette Holder
  3½" l, bisque, youth on clothesline, slots for ashes, marked "Japan" .. **15.00**
  5½" l, ceramic, boy with melon, melon bowl for ashes **25.00**
Comics Page, Kemple Duke of Dahomey, 1911 .... **30.00**
Cookie Jar
  Chef, marked "Pearl China" **250.00**
  Mammy, 11" h, marked "McCoy" .. **100.00**
Creamer and Sugar, F & F **90.00**
Crumb Brush, 7" h, figural, painted wood, bristle skirt, blue **55.00**
Dish Towel, Mammy **20.00**
Doll
  Bisque Head, painted face, glass eyes, copyright and Shackman sticker on back **70.00**
  Cloth, handmade
    7" h, girl, embroidered features, braided hair **50.00**

13" h, Topsy Turvey, painted features, black girl with skirt turns
to reveal white girl with braids . **55.00**
14" h, cloth body, hard face, hands,
and feet, gingham dress, apron
and kerchief **85.00**
Plastic, Talking Chatty Baby, Mattel,
orig box **100.00**
Door Stop, 13½" h, cast iron, mammy,
painted, Littco label **250.00**
Fan, adv
Coon Chicken Inn **20.00**
Jamup & Honey, 14" h, cardboard,
black and white **30.00**
Figure
Accordion Player, 6½" h, bisque, hp,
marked "Japan" **25.00**
Bongo players, pr **20.00**
Boxers, pr **45.00**
Boy playing guitar, girl dancing, felt
tree, marked "Souvenir Niagara
Falls" **22.00**
Boy with chicken, astride alligator,
6½" l, ceramic **70.00**
Dancer, female, ring earrings, fur skirt **22.00**
Man, carrying cane, celluloid, triangular tin base, marked "Germany"
and "W" in circle, 1920–30, 3½"
h **50.00**
Porter, carrying suitcase, bird cage,
golf clubs and bag, metal, diecut,
painted, 2" h, 1930s **60.00**
Warrior with shield and spear **22.00**
Woman, 4½" h, native clothing, bisque, hp, marked "Occupied Ja-
pan" **15.00**
Game
Chocolate Splash, 7 x 10 x 1½", cardboard box, paper label, target
game, Willis G Young Mfg, Chi-
cago, 1916 copyright **100.00**
Little Black Sambo, orig box **38.00**
The Game Of Hitch Hiker, 13 x 13 x
1½", Whitman, copyright 1937 .. **50.00**
Three Black Crows, bean bag, painted
wooden standing frame, swing out
targets, sgd, 24" l **125.00**
Zoo Hoo, cardboard, Lubbers & Bell
Mfg Co, boxed **90.00**
Greeting Card, "Birfday," 1900s **5.00**
Hook, pot holder, chalkware, man, bow
tie **15.00**
Lunch Box, Dixie Kid Tobacco, tin,
black child **150.00**
Map, Cream of Wheat premium, Jolly
Bill and Jane Moon Map, 21 x 28",
black and white cartoon illus, center
illus of Rastus, 1933 .... **80.00**
Match Holder, 5¾" h, ceramic, woman,
scalloped collar and sleeves **30.00**
Memo Pad, Mammy, 10", Hampden
Novelty Co, patent **65.00**

Menu, Coon Chicken Inn, small **35.00**
Minstrel Program, Penn Wheelmen
Frolic of 1927, Orpheum Theater, 64
pgs **25.00**
Mug, 5" h, ceramic, black butler with
food tray, titled "Junior Feed 1915" . **75.00**
Party Favor, diecut, expandable colored
paper ovals, boy eating watermelon,
3½" d **25.00**
Pie Bird
Chef **50.00**
Mammy **45.00**
Pencil Holder, 5½" l, celluloid, alligator
with black's head in mouth, c1930 . **15.00**
Pillow, 18 x 19", embroidered, man
walking with chicken, "If the Man in
the Moon were a Coon," faded **375.00**
Pin, 1⅛" h, diecut silvered brass, black
Kewpie, dark blue hair bow and dress **15.00**
Pin Cushion, black baby, movable
limbs, sitting, tape measure **75.00**
Pinback Button
⅞"
Famous Jockey Series, multicolored, titled "Hamilton, Celebrated American Jockey," light
blue and white racing silks,
c1898 .... **10.00**
Hassan Cigarettes, multicolored,
cartoon illus, "Who Said
Chicken," black man, artist Hal
Hoffman, back paper text, c1910 **7.50**
Whitehead & Hoag Co, celluloid,
black and white, photo of three
black youngsters, inscription
"Here Comes De Parade, Jus
Look At Dem Badges," c1896 .. **60.00**
1¼", Parsons Feeder, multicolored,
cartoon illus of pair of irate os-
triches squawking at black young-
ster, inscription "You Are The
Sucker We've Been Laying For,
Why Don't You Get A Parsons
Feeder," c1910 .... **115.00**
1¾", Duluth Flour, multicolored,
black chef, c1902 .... **80.00**
Pipe Rack, 12" l, figural, male head with
large hat, brass **210.00**
Planter
Boy sitting under palm tree **22.00**
Boy with watermelon, black and gold **20.00**
Girl beside ear of corn **30.00**
Playing Cards, 3¼" d, tin container, cir-
cular playing cards, titled "Suther-
land's Circular Coon Cards," Hartley
Bros Pty Ltd, Australia, early 1900s . **150.00**
Post Card
Humorous, "There's Something
Doing," 1911 .... **15.00**
New Year Greetings, 1914 .... **15.00**
Pickaninnies photo, 1912 .... **12.00**
Potholder Plaque, 5", wood, mammy

portrait center, two brass hooks, c1940 .... **15.00**
Puzzle, jigsaw, titled "Woozy Jig," cardboard, orig box **35.00**
Recipe Book
    Aunt Jemima, 1928 .... **8.00**
    Knox Gelatin, black child, 1915 .... **5.00**
Ring Holder, wall, negro **28.00**
Salt and Pepper Shakers, pr
    Boys seated on green peas **35.00**
    Man and Woman, exaggerated features, marked "USA No 877" **75.00**
    Native and palm tree **55.00**
Sheet Music
    A Warmin' Up in Dixie, 1899 ..... **30.00**
    At an Ole Virginia Wedding, 1899 . **45.00**
    Aunt Jemima's Picnic Day, 1914 ... **20.00**

    Banjo Song, 6 pgs, red, white, and blue black strumming banjo and circus side show illus, 1934 copyright **8.00**
    Little Alabama Coon, 1893 .... **24.00**
    Mammy's Lullaby, 4 pgs, 1919 ..... **15.00**
    My Sugar Coated Chocolate Boy, 1919 .... **10.00**

    Sam the Accordion Man **12.00**
    Short'nin' Bread, 6 pgs, red, white, and blue cov, 1928 .... **10.00**
    When The Coons Are On The Move, 1901 copyright, 13½ x 17", matted and framed **55.00**

Smoking Stand, 25" h, figural, butler holding green ashtray, painted wood **100.00**
Soda Bottle, emb "Mammy" **65.00**

Souvenir Spoon, 4½", 1895 Cotton States and International Exposition, sterling silver, child's, porcelain enamel of black youngster, sliced watermelon illus in bowl, "Atlanta" on handle, reverse marked "Charles W Crankshaw, copyright '95" **75.00**

String Holder
    Boy, bending aside watermelon, plaster **28.00**
    Mammy **55.00**

Stove Pipe Vent Cov, 9½" d , multicolored, black youngster with straw hat, holding banjo, looking at two others driving vehicle made of corn ear, watermelon wheels, passenger with pink plumed hat, brass frame and hanging chain, asbestos backing, c1900 .... **100.00**

Tea Set, teapot, creamer, and sugar, Sambo, English **255.00**
Teapot, large black fireman **55.00**
Toaster Cover, Mammy, marked "Souvenir of New Orleans" **30.00**
Toothpick Holder, metal, cotton bale, two blacks **125.00**

Toy
    Alabama Corn Jigger, litho, tin, windup, 10" h, Strauss, minor paint touch up **175.00**
    Boxing, Wakouwa Champs, painted wood, 5" h **50.00**
    Squeeze, Trapeze Artist, painted wood, 8" h **30.00**
    Stick, painted wood
        Dancin Dan, board, orig instructions, 11" h **45.00**
        Tap Dancer, tuxedo, 16" h **40.00**
Wall Plaque
    Man and Woman, 2½ x 3½", painted plaster, black face, bright red lips, red bandanna, and yellow bow tie, c1950, pr **25.00**
    Youngster, 5 x 8", pigtails, bright red parasol, gray dress, yellow accents, c1950 .... **18.00**
Wall Pocket, man, Blackamoor, marked "Royal Copley" **25.00**
Water Sprinkler, Mammy **150.00**
Whiskey Flask, adv, Green River, "The Whiskey Without a Headache," leather cov glass, 6½" h **150.00**
World War I
    Photograph, soldier, oval frame with convex glass, 25 x 18" **75.00**
    Print, "Our Colored Hero," Renesch, 1918, 11 x 16", multicolored, framed **100.00**

BOOKS—ANTIQUES AND COLLECTIBLES

Collecting Hints: Many books were published in several printings and editions. Since most collectors' primary reason for acquiring these books is for the information that they contain, it is best to acquire the last, not the first edition, since it most likely contains the most complete information.

Many books about antiques and collectibles prior to 1950 had dust jackets. The book should not be considered complete if the jacket has been lost. Also check to make certain that all illustrations are present.

Many popular editions were issued. These were printed on lesser quality paper and have poorer bindings. Avoid them whenever possible.

There are a number of dealers who specialize in out-of-print books about antiques and collectibles. You will find their advertisements in the trade magazines and newspapers. Do not hesitate to contact them with your needs. It may take from a few months to several years, but eventually they will find the book or books you are seeking.

Abbreviations denoting sizes:
Folio 12 × 16"
4to 8 × 10"
8vo 5 × 7"
12mo 3 × 5"

History: The first books about antiques appeared at the end of the nineteenth century. By the 1920s books about antiques were standard fare among publishers. Topics ranged from books on antique furniture and English Staffordshire to "how-to" books on collecting and going to auctions. Many of the books from this period, e.g., George and Helen McKearin's *Two Hundred Years of American Blown Glass*, have become classics.

In the 1960s the antiques and collectibles field witnessed the birth of a publishing explosion. The number of books issued yearly increased many fold. Today there are few topics not covered by a specialized book.

Because of the specialized nature of many books about antiques and collectibles, titles tend to go out-of-print very rapidly. Many are privately published by the authors or small firms.

Advisor: Ron Lieberman

Note: Pre–1945 titles should be checked in the current edition of *American Book Prices Current*. However, do not be surprised if you do not find a title listed. Many of the books are in the $10.00 to $50.00 range, too low a figure to find their way into *American Book Prices Current*.

CERAMICS

Buten, *Wedgwood Rarities*, 1969, 4to, 320 pgs	85.00
Earle, *China Collecting in America*, 1892, 8vo, 429 pgs	20.00
Fisher, *The Decoration of English Porcelain - A Description of the Painting and Printing on English Porcelain, 1750–1850*, London, 1954, 4to, 213 pgs, dj	60.00
Godden, Geoffrey, *The Illustrated Guide to Lowestoft Porcelain*, 1964, 4to, 765 pgs, dj	35.00
Klamkin, *White House China*, 1972, 8vo, 184 pgs, dj	35.00
Mew, *Battersea Enamels*, Medici Society, London, 1926, 8vo, 27 pgs	90.00
Moore, *Delftware, Dutch and English*, New York, 1908, 12mo, 78 pgs	12.50
Powell, *Antique Shaving Mugs of the United States*, Hearst, 1972, 8vo, 272 pgs	25.00
Roseville Pottery, *Pottery*, 1930, 12mo, 24 pgs, soft cover	25.00
Savage, *Eighteenth Century English Porcelain* London, 1962, 8vo, 243 pgs, dj	35.00
Ware, *Occupational Shaving Mugs*, 1949, 8vo, 96 pgs, dj	35.00

FURNITURE

Bishop, *Centuries and Styles of the American Chair, 1640–1970*, 1972, 4to, 516 pgs, dj	65.00
Cornelius, *Early American Furniture*, 1926, 8vo, 278 pgs	25.00
Fales, *American Painted Furniture, 1660–1880*, New York, 1972, 4to, 299 pgs, dj	75.00
Greenlaw, *New England Furniture at Williamsburg*, 1974, 4to, 195 pgs, dj	150.00
Hummel, *A Winterthur Guide to American Chippendale Furniture, Middle Atlantic and Southern Colonies*, 1976, small 8vo, 142 pgs, soft cover	15.00
Iverson, *The American Chair, 1630–1890*, 1957, 8vo, 241 pgs, line drawings by E. Donnelly, dj	45.00
Lyon, *Colonial Furniture of New England - A Study of the Domestic Furniture in Use in the Seventeenth and Eighteenth Centuries*, 1924, 4to, 285 pgs, new edition limited to 515 copies	150.00
Montgomery, *American Furniture, The Federal Period*, 1966, 4to, 497 pgs, dj	150.00
Nutting, Wallace, *Furniture of the Pilgrim Century, 1620–1720*, 1921, 4to, 587 pgs, first edition	100.00
Ormsbee, *The Windsor Chair*, 1962, 8vo, 233 pgs, dj	40.00
Poesch, *Early Furniture of Louisiana, 1750–1830*, 1972, 4to, 85 pgs, soft cover	65.00
Strange, T. A. *English Furniture*, London, 1986, Studio Edition, 376 pgs, dj	35.00
Wills, *Craftsmen and Cabinetmakers of Classic English Furniture*, Furniture, 1974, 8vo, 136 pgs, dj	30.00

GLASS

Barrett, Noel, *Blown and Pressed American Glass*, 1966, 8vo, 15 pgs, spiral bound	12.50
Belknap, E. McCamley, *Milk Glass*, 1959, 8vo, 327 pgs, torn dj	45.00
Kamm, Minnie Watson	
A Sixth Pitcher Book, Second Edition, 1954, 8vo, 97 pgs, soft cover, spiral bound	7.50
The Kamm-Wood Encyclopedia of Antique Pattern Glass, 1961, 8vo, 656 pgs, editor: Wood, 2 volumes	40.00
Two Hundred Pattern Glass Pitchers, Fifth Edition, 1952, 8vo, 138 pgs, soft cover, spiral bound	7.50
Lee, Ruth Webb	
Early American Pressed Glass, Third Edition, 1933, 8vo, 683 pgs	20.00
Victorian Glass–Specialties of the	

19th Century, Eighth Edition, 1944,
8vo, 608 pgs, worn dj **20.00**
Pearson, *American Cut Glass For The
Discriminating Collector, Third Edi-
tion*, 1965, 4to, 204 pgs, dj **40.00**
Revi, Albert, *Nineteenth Century Glass,
First Edition*, 1959, 4to, 270 pgs,
worn dj **25.00**

METALS

Frank, *Old French Ironwork*, 1950, 8vo,
221 pgs, dj **50.00**
Hankenson, *Trivets*, 1963, 8vo, 107
pgs, spiral bound, soft cover **20.00**
Kauffman, H. J., *Early American Copper, Tin, and Brass*, 1950, 4to, 112
pgs, dj, inscribed **50.00**
Powers and Floyd, *Early American Decorated Tinware*, 1957, 4to, 267 pgs,
worn dj **75.00**
Sonn, *Early American Wrought Iron*,
1928, 3 volumes, 629 pgs, green
binding, gold lettering **450.00**

MISCELLANEOUS

Albert, *A Button Collector's Second
Journal*, 1941, 8vo, 333 pgs, in-
scribed **25.00**
Cole, A, *Antiques, How To Identify, Buy,
Sell, Refinish and Care*, 1958 ...... **10.00**
Comstock, *Concise Encyclopedia of
American Antiques*, 1969, 848 pgs . **15.00**
Elisseef, D. and V., K. Shoten, editor, *A
Pictorial Encyclopedia of the Oriental
Arts-Japan*, Crown, 1968, 4to, 4 vol-
umes, brown cloth boards, plastic dj **48.00**
Flowers, *Victorian Jewelry*, 1967, 8vo,
271 pgs, dj **75.00**
Haffner, Sylvia, *Judaic Tokens and Med-
als*, American Israel Numismatic As-
sociation, 1978, 4to, 402 pgs **25.00**
Sack, Israel, *The Israel Sack Collections
of American Antiques*, 1928, 8vo, soft
cover **35.00**
Stoudt, *Early Pennsylvania Arts and
Crafts*, 1964, 4to, 364 pgs, dj **50.00**
Warman, Edwin G., *Antiques and Their
Current Prices*, 1st ed., 1949 .... **35.00**
Younghusband and Davenport, *The
Crown Jewels of England*, 1919, 4to,
84 pgs, 18 tipped in color plates with
tissue guards, black and white frontis,
decorated cloth, limited to 1,400
numbered copies **125.00**

PEWTER

Cotterell, *Old Pewter, Its Makers and
Marks in England, Scotland, and Ireland*, 1974, 4to, 432 pgs, dj **70.00**

Myers, *Some Notes on American Pew-
terers*, 1926, 8vo, 96 pgs, soiled,
hinges loose, limited to 1,000 copies **50.00**

SILVER

Bigelow, *Historic Silver of the Colonies
and Its Makers*, 1948, small 8vo, 476
pgs, worn dj **25.00**
Fales, *Early American Silver for the Cautious Collector*, 1970, 8vo, 329 pgs,
dj **35.00**
Green, *Coin Silver Spoonmakers*, 1968,
8vo, 13 pgs, soft cover, first edition
of 500 copies **12.50**
Harris, *The Price Guide to Antique Silver*, Woodbridge, 1969, 12 mo, 532
pgs, dj **25.00**
Markham, C. A., editor, *Chaffers Handbook To Hall Marks On Gold and Silver Plate, Sixth Edition*, London,
1932, 12mo, 151 pgs **25.00**
Pleasants and Sill, *Maryland Silversmiths, 1715–1830*, 1930, 4to, 324
pgs, limited to 300 copies **375.00**
Unitt, Peter, *Canadian Silver, Silverplate, and Related Glass*, Ontario,
1970, 4to, 256 pgs, dj **125.00**
Williams, *Silversmiths of New Jersey,
1700–1825*, 1949, 8vo, 164 pgs ... **225.00**

TEXTILES

Hall, *A Book of Handwoven Coverlets*,
Rutland, 1966, 8vo, 411 pgs, dj, reprint of 1912 edition **40.00**
Percival, *The Chintz Book*, London,
1923, 8vo, 103 pgs **125.00**
Robertson, *American Quilts*, New York,
1948, 8vo, 152 pgs, dj **40.00**

BOTTLE OPENERS, FIGURAL

Collecting Hints: Condition is most important.
Worn or missing paint and repainted surfaces
lower value. Damaged or rusty pieces have
greatly diminished value.

History: Figural bottle openers were produced
expressly for removing a bottle cap from a bottle.
They were made in a variety of metals, including
cast iron, brass, bronze, and white metal. Cast
iron, brass, and bronze openers are generally
solid castings; white metal openers are usually
cast in hollow blown molds.
   The vast majority of figural bottle openers date
from the 1950s and 1960s. Paint variation on a
figure is very common.

References: Donald Bull, *A Price Guide to Beer*

Advertising, Openers and Corkscrews, Donald Bull, 1981; Michael Jordan, *Figural Bottle Openers,* available from Figural Bottle Opener Collectors.

Collectors' Clubs: Figural Bottle Opener Collectors, 13018 Clarion Road, Fort Washington, MD, 20744; Just For Openers, 63 October Lane, Trumbull, CT 06611.

Advisor: Craig Dinner.

REPRODUCTION ALERT

Donkey, painted white metal, 3⅝" h, $25.00.

Bear, 3⅞ x 3¹⁄₁₆", brass, wall mount, head, black highlights, John Wright Co **65.00**
Black Boy with alligator
    2⅝" h, hands down, green alligator, Wilton Products **135.00**
    3" h, hand in air, green alligator and base, John Wright Co **165.00**
Black Man, 4⅜ x 3¾", wall mount, smiling, red bow tie, Wilton Products **85.00**
Cathy Coed, 4⅛" h, cast iron, preppy girl holding stack of books, green base with white front, sgd "L & L Favors" **310.00**
Clown, 4⅛ x 4", brass, wall mount, white bow tie with red polka dots, bald head, sgd "495" on back, John Wright Co **70.00**
Cockatoo, 3¼" h, cast iron, orange and yellow chest, red and orange comb, green base with black background, John Wright Co **95.00**
Cowboy with Guitar, 4⅞" h, cast iron, yellow, brown, and gray guitar, green cactus, black shoes, red bandanna, John Wright Co **100.00**
Dinky Dan, 3¹³⁄₁₆" h, cast iron, preppy boy with hands in pockets, green base, sgd "Gadzik Phila" on back **245.00**
Do Do Bird, 2¾" h, cast iron, cream, black highlights, red beak **165.00**
Drunk
    Lamp Post, 4⁵⁄₁₆", green lamp post,

black tux, hat, shoes, and base, John Wright Co **10.00**
Sign Post, 3⅞" h, man holding post, white sign, black post, tux, and hat **15.00**
Elephant, 3¹⁄₁₆" h
    John Wright Co, sitting on four legs, white highlights on mouth and trunk, trunk in circle, red mouth and nostrils **30.00**
    Wilton Products, sitting, trunk in circle, gray, pink nostrils, white toe nails **30.00**
Four Eyes, two sets of eyes
    Bald Man, 3¾ x 3⅜", blue eyes, large black mustache, Wilton Products . **30.00**
    Man, 4 x 3⅞", black hair and mustache, John Wright Co **30.00**
    Women, brass, blue eyes, marked "Wilton Products" on back **30.00**
Freddie Frosh, 4" h, cast iron, preppy boy standing with hands in pockets, legs crossed, green base with white front, sgd "L & L Favors" on back .. **275.00**
Grass Skirt Greek, 5" h, cast iron, black native girl, white sign and post, green base, sgd "Gadzik Phila" on back .. **265.00**
Madamoiselle, 4½" h, cast iron, streetwalker by lamp post, black, flesh face, hands, and legs, yellow light, John Wright Co **15.00**
Paddy the Pledgemaster, 4" h, cast iron, preppy boy, green base with white front, sgd "Gadzik Phila" **245.00**
Pelican, cast iron
    3¼" h, white, black and red highlights, yellow beak, orange feet, ruffled black comb, green base ... **155.00**
    3⅜", red and black, yellow beak, orange feet, green base, Wilton Products **45.00**
    3¾" h, cream, orange beak and feet, head up, green base, John Wright Co **145.00**
Rooster
    3³⁄₁₆" h, bronze, yellow, orange, black, and white body, orange-yellow feet, green base, tail opener, Wilton Products **35.00**
    3⅞" h, metal, black body, red comb, orange-yellow beak and feet, green base, opener under tail, John Wright Co **45.00**
Sailor, 3¾" h, hitchhiking, white uniform, black tie and shoes, white sign with black trim, John Wright Co **30.00**
Sea Gull, 3³⁄₁₆" h, cast iron, cream, black and gray highlights, red beak, orange feet, gray and black stump, John Wright Co **35.00**
Seahorse, 4¼ h, brass, green, white highlights, green base with blue and black highlights **65.00**

BREWERIANA

Collecting Hints: Many collectors concentrate on items from one specific brewery or region. An item will bring slightly more when it is sold in its locality. Regional Collector clubs and shows abound.

History: Collecting material associated with the brewing industry developed in the 1960s when many local breweries ceased production. Three areas occupy the collectors' interest—pre-Prohibition material, advertising items for use in taverns and premiums designed for individual use.

References: Donald Bull, *A Price Guide To Beer Advertising Openers And Corkscrews*, privately printed, 1981; Donald Bull, Manfred Friedrich, and Robert Gottschalk, *American Breweries*, Bullworks, 1984; Keith Osborne and Brian Pipe, *The International Book of Beer Labels, Mats, & Coasters*, Chartwell Books, 1979.

Collectors' Clubs: American Breweriana Association, P. O. Box 6082, Colorado Springs, CO 80934; Eastern Coast Breweriana Association, 312 Hamilton Blvd, Piscataway, NJ 08850; National Association of Breweriana, Advertising, 2343 Mat–tu–Wee Lane, Wauwatoca, WI 53226.

REPRODUCTION ALERT, especially in advertising trays.

Menu, Anheuser–Busch Budweiser, multicolored, 7¼ x 11¼", $5.00.

Advertising
  Pinback Button
    Bass Ale, Columbus, OH, 1899 .. | 27.50
    Dubuque Malting Co, 1¼", multicolored, green hop leaves between red and yellow circles, white outer rim, black lettering, c1898 .... | 35.00
    National Premium Pilsner, 1¼", blue and white, National Bohe-

mian Brewery, Baltimore, cartoon image of Mr. Pilsner, c1930 | 15.00
    Old Dutch Beer, 1¼", multicolored scene of elderly couple enjoying beer with dinner, black ground, c1906 .... | 30.00
    Terre Haute Brewing Co, 1¼", brewery building, c1897 ...... | 18.00
    Tezor Manhattan Cocktail, ⅞", multicolored, young lady sampling product, holding fan in other hand, c1907 .... | 50.00
Badge, 1899 American Brewers Association Convention, "ABA" inscription, enamel and brass plated ...... | 15.00
Bank, Pabst, beer can .... | 15.00
Blotter, Bergdoll Brewing Co, 3 x 7½", black and white Louis Bergdoll portrait and Christmas holly design, 60th Anniversary, 1909, unused .... | 45.00
Book, 32nd Annual Convention of Master Brewers Association Of America 1935, 116 pgs .... | 20.00
Bottle
    Leisen Henes Beer, squat, aqua .... | 38.00
    Sunshine Beer, green, smiling boy .. | 10.00
Bottle Opener
    Miller Beer, 1955 .... | 35.00
    Schlitz .... | 8.00
Calendar, Rheingold Beer, 1943 ...... | 12.00
Cigarette Dispenser, Lager Beer, aluminum .... | 70.00
Clock
    Dakota Beer, light-up .... | 25.00
    Duquesne Beer, Art Deco, reverse painting .... | 350.00
    Hornung Beer, glass and metal, lights up, 1934 .... | 345.00
    Lowenbrau, electric .... | 35.00
Coaster
    Black Forest Beer .... | 15.00
    Schmidt Brewery, St. Paul, 4", round, 1930s .... | 3.00
    Smith Bros, tin .... | 6.50
Corkscrew
    Anheuser-Busch, encased .... | 75.00
    D.H. Russel Rye .... | 20.00
Cribbage Board, "Drink Rhinelander Beer" .... | 20.00
Display, Pabst Beer, old car, wheels turn | 150.00
Door Stop, Hanley's Ale, cast iron, bulldog .... | 550.00
Figure
    Heineken Beer, 12", composition, bottle and pipe-smoking Dutchman on base, 1950s .... | 75.00
Fishing Lure, Schlitz, bottle shape .... | 7.00
Foam Scraper
    Goetz Brewery, celluloid .... | 15.00
    Meister Brau, celluloid .... | 18.00
    Rubsams & Hormann Brewing ..... | 16.00

Glass
  Dayton Breweries **100.00**
Goblet
  Lion Brewery, emb **45.00**
  Wm. Pfeifer Weiss Beer **115.00**
Ice Pick, Empire Lager, Black Horse Ale **27.00**
Knife, boot shape, West End Brewing . **65.00**
Lapel Pin
  Bert and Harry Fan Club, ¾ x ⅞",
    diecut brass, blue paint, cartoon
    figures, National Bohemian Brew-
    ery Co, Baltimore, c1950 ...... **18.00**
  Schlitz, 1¼", diecut, enameled brass,
    red logo, light blue hot air balloon,
    white cloud, c1970 .... **10.00**
Light, Bohemian Beer, wall, cartoon an-
  imals **30.00**
Match Holder, American Brewing Co.,
  3", stoneware, blue and gray, Roch-
  ester & Westcott & Parker, Dealers in
  Coal & Wood, Utica **125.00**
Mug
  Ebling Brewing Co, factory scene ... **15.00**
  Minneapolis Brewing Co Grain Belt
    Beer **60.00**
  Stang Brewery, Sandusky, factory
    scene **100.00**
Opener, Anheuser-Busch, silvered
  brass, corkscrew, early 1900 .... **40.00**
Peanut Dispenser, Miller Beer **15.00**
Pinback button, Miller brewery, girl on
  moon **18.00**
Postcard, Budweiser, fold-out, 8 Clydes-
  dale horses, 1960s, unused **10.00**
Poster, Atlantic Ale Beers, 1930s **75.00**
Sign
  Berghoff Brewing Corp, Ft. Wayne,
    Indians, 13 x 21", tin **250.00**
  Chihuahua Beer, train **18.00**
  Dubois Brewery, 42 x 60", factory
    scene **1,200.00**
  Heileman's Old Style, light-up **27.50**
  National Bohemian Beer, light-up,
    cartoon animals **50.00**
  Neuweiler Beer & Ale, 18 x 26", litho,
    metal, c1950 .... **60.00**
  Schiltz, lighted **85.00**
  Stag Beer, light-up, cash register **27.50**
  Wagner's Augustiner Beer, tin **48.00**
Shot Glass, etched
  Fulton Whiskey, Covington, Kentucky **15.00**
  Henry Schnelten's Whiskeys, Quincy,
    IL **15.00**
  Peoria Co. Club Whiskey, Peoria, IL **22.50**
  Shawhan Whiskey, Weston, Missouri **22.50**
Statue, Pfeiffer's Beer, 8" h, little man
  playing flute **35.00**
Thermometer, Rueter & Co, Highland
  Spring Brewery, Boston, patented
  1885, 9", brass **175.00**
Token, Hamms Beer **20.00**

Tray, Hornung Beer, Jacob Hornung Brewing Co, Philadelphia, silver ground, gold French horn, 12" d, $65.00.

Tip Tray
  Bartels Lager, Ale & Porter **80.00**
  Old Export, black and gold, logo ... **50.00**
  The West End Brewing Co **90.00**
Tray
  Berghoff Beer **65.00**
  Cold Spring Brewing, 13", oval **425.00**
  Falstaff, 24", round, metal, maiden
    pouring beer **110.00**
  Goetz, 1950s **15.00**
  Muehlebach Beer **17.50**
  Schaefer **7.50**
  Silver Bar Ale, Tampa, round **65.00**
Watch Fob, Anheuser-Busch, 1½", die-
  cut, silvered brass, enameled red,
  white, and blue trademark **50.00**

BRITISH ROYALTY COMMEMORATIVES

Collecting Hints: Some collectors choose one monarch around whom to build their collections. Others choose only pieces for special occasions, such as coronations, jubilees, marriages, investitures, births, or memorials. Another approach is to specialize in only one form, e.g., thimbles, mugs, beakers, teapots, spoons, etc.

Since most early pieces were used in the home for eating and drinking, it is especially difficult to find older commemoratives in good condition. Wear from use and age often shows through fading and loss of colors and transfers. Porous pottery pieces lend themselves to crazing inside and out from age and shrinkage.

Serious collectors seek the older and rarer pieces, while keeping up-to-date with examples from the modern events. Crown shaped teapots, etched and cut crystal, hand and machine woven tapestries, and jewelry are just a few of the things that link old and new collecting.

History: British commemorative china was first produced rather crudely in design and form.

These were basically cheaper and more available pieces of Delft, stoneware, and slipware. With John Brook's invention of transfer printing in the mid-18th century, British commemorative wares bore a closer likeness to the reigning monarch.

King George IV's coronation was the first royal occasion for which children received municipal gifts. Some towns presented medals, while others gave plates with commemorative inscriptions. China commemorative pieces were produced by the thousands for Queen Victoria's 1887 and 1897 jubilees. It was not until 1902 that the presentation of municipal gifts became widespread; the practice is continued today. Thousands of children received mugs with the official coronation design of Queen Elizabeth II in celebration of her 1953 coronation.

Through the years, improved production techniques combined with finer artistic design have enhanced the overall appearance of British Royalty commemoratives. Aynsley, Minton, Paragon, Royal Doulton, Shelley, Wedgwood, and other leading manufacturers have produced outstanding limited and unlimited edition items. Artists such as Clarice Cliff, Dame Laura Knight, and Professor Richard Guyatt have designed special pieces.

Some British Royalty commemoratives are easily recognized by the portraits of the monarchs they honor. Often these portraits are surrounded by decorations such as flags, the national flowers (roses, thistles, daffodils, and shamrocks), ribbons with commemorative messages or lions and unicorns. Cyphers and crowns also are popular decorations. Royal residences such as Windsor Castle, Balmoral and Highgrove House may also appear. Town mottos or crests were added to individualize municipal gifts for earlier coronations. Advertisers often linked their products to royal events.

Other British Royalty commemoratives are not easy to recognize. Many do not have portraits of monarchs on them, although there might be a silhouette profile. Other characteristics include crowns, dragons, royal coats of arms, national flowers, swords, sceptres, dates, messages and cyphers of the monarch. Earlier pieces sometimes bear crude likenesses of early monarchs. Timely verses or couplets may be inscribed, e.g., "God Save The King," "Long Live The Queen."

A listing of outstanding achievements or inventions during a monarch's reign may appear on jubilee or memorial pieces. Some newer items list the order of succession to the throne, previous holders of a title, and family trees.

References: M. H. Davey and D. J. Mannion, *Fifty Years Of Royal Commemorative China 1887–1937*, Dayman Publications, 1988; Peter Johnson, *Royal Memorabilia; A Phillips Collectors Guide*, Dunestyle Publishing, Ltd., 1988; John May, *Victoria Remembered, A Royal History 1817–1861*, Heinemann, London, 1983; John and Jennifer May, *Commemorative Pottery 1780–1900, A Guide for Collectors*, Charles Scribner's Sons, 1972; Josephine Jackson, *Fired For Royalty*, Heaton Moor, 1977; David Rogers, *Coronation Souvenirs and Commemoratives*, Latimer New Dimensions, Ltd., 1975; Sussex Commemorative Ware Centre, *200 Commemoratives*, Metra Print Enterprises, 1979; Geoffrey Warren, *Royal Souvenirs*, Orbis, 1977; Audrey B. Zeder, *British Royal Commemoratives*, Wallace-Homestead, 1986.

Advisors: Doug Flynn and Al Bolton.

Queen Elizabeth II, February 6, 1952, to present

Coronation, June 2, 1953

Cup and Saucer

Color coat of arms and dec, Stanley	95.00
Sepia portrait	
Gold trim, Washington Pottery Ltd	20.00
Inside cup, Royal Albert	40.00

Dish

4" d, color portrait, Royal Winton	12.00
4¼" d, sepia profile portrait, Rosina	16.00

Jam Pot, 5" h, orb shape, color and gold dec, Wedgwood & Co Ltd 90.00

Mug

3¼" h, sepia portrait, color dec, Royal Doulton	57.00
3½" h, emb profile portrait and commemoration, Beswick	20.00
4¼" h, sepia portrait, color dec, gold trim, Royal Albert	35.00

Pin Tray, 4¾" d, color coat of arms, gold trim, Paragon 31.00

Plate

6½" d, sepia portrait with Prince Charles and Princess Anne, color dec, gold trim, Salisbury	50.00
8" d, crown, cypher, and date, Poole Pottery	55.00
8¾" d, color portrait and dec, gold trim, Royal Winton	20.00

Tin

1¼ x 6¼ x 4½", color portrait, W D Wills	16.00
2¾ x 5¾ x 3¾", color portrait with Prince Philip, John Derbyshire & Son	25.00

Silver Jubilee, 1977

Bell, 5½" h, applied roses, silver trim, Crown Staffordshire	30.00
Box, cov, 1½ x 2½", silver cypher on lid, Crown Staffordshire	20.00
Loving Cup, 3½" h, black and white portrait, color dec	40.00

Mug

3¼" h, red profile portrait, red
and blue dec, Adams **25.00**

4" h, gold coat of arms and trim,
Royal Doulton **55.00**

4¾" h, black and white portrait
by Snowdon, Wedgwood **50.00**

Plate

7½" d, color portrait black background, limited edition of
10,000, Crown Staffordshire . **60.00**

8¼" d, light blue profile, white
Jasperware, Wedgwood **70.00**

10½" d, color coat of arms, blue
border with gold overlay, Aynsley **75.00**

40th Wedding Anniversary, November 20, 1987

Mug, 3¼" h, gold profile portraits,
color dec, Caverswall **40.00**

Plate, 8½" d, gold profile portraits,
color dec, Caverswall **50.00**

Prince Charles' Investiture as Prince of
Wales, July 1, 1969

Dish, 1½" h, 5½" d, color coat of
arms and dec, ftd, Aynsley **50.00**

Mug

3" h, gold and bronze profile portrait, color dec, Weatherby **60.00**

3¾" h, orange commemoration,
yellow background **20.00**

Plate

6½" d, Prince of Wales feathers
center, Rye Pottery **55.00**

8¼" d, sepia portrait, color dec,
Coronet **60.00**

Prince Charles and Lady Diana Spencer,
Royal Wedding, July 29, 1981

Bell, 5" h, color portraits and dec,
Crown Staffordshire **50.00**

Chalice, 5" h, gold and color coat of
arms, Royal Worcester **75.00**

Mug

3⅛" h, color coat of arms, Wood
and Sons **20.00**

3½" h, sepia portraits, color dec,
Pall Mall Ware **35.00**

Plate

9¾" d, gold profile portraits, color
dec, Weatherby **45.00**

10" d, St Paul's Cathedral center,
color dec, Denby **50.00**

10½" d, black and white portraits,
color and gold dec **40.00**

Playing Cards, double dec, color portraits, British Monarchs, Grimaud . **30.00**

Teapot, 4½" h, sepia portraits, color
dec **55.00**

Tea Towel, 29 x 18½", Irish linen,
color portraits, Ulster **15.00**

Tin

3" h, 6¼" d, color portraits, red and
gold dec, Lyons **30.00**

4½" h, 2½" d, color portraits and
dec, money box, Bowler **18.00**

Prince William of Wales, born June 21,
1982

Bowl, 1¾" h, 6" d, color portraits of
Prince and Princess of Wales, color
nursery scenes, Coalport **35.00**

Cradle, 2¼ x 2½ x 1¼", color and
gold dec, Caverswall **30.00**

Loving Cup, 3¾" h, color family portrait, limited edition of 250, Coronet **60.00**

Mug

2¼" h, color picture of Windsor
Castle, Aynsley **25.00**

2¾" h, gold dec, Wedgwood **65.00**

3½" h

Color cherubs, birds, and flowers, Royal Worcester **45.00**

Pram on front, J & J May **65.00**

Prince Charles and Lady Diana Spencer, playing cards, double deck, British Monarchs, color portraits, to commemorate royal wedding, Grimaud, $30.00.

Prince Henry of Wales, born September 15, 1984
Bell, 3½" h, color picture of Balmoral Castle, Aynsley **30.00**
Mug, 3" h, gold dec, Wedgwood ... **65.00**
Prince Andrew and Miss Sarah Ferguson, Royal Wedding, July 23, 1986
Box, cov, 1¾" h, heart shape, color portraits and dec **25.00**
Cup and Saucer, color portraits and dec, Coalport **45.00**
Mug
3½" h, corgis and wedding bells, Kiln Kraft **30.00**
3¾" h
Color portraits, Colclough **25.00**
Color portraits and dec, musical, unmarked **25.00**
Plate
7¾" d, color portrait in wedding attire, Coronet **45.00**
8" d, color portraits and flowers, Royal Albert **45.00**
8⅛" d, color portraits and dec, Johnson Ceramics **25.00**
Princess Beatrice's Birth, August 8, 1988, mug, 3½" h, Duke and Duchess of York profiles, Caverswall **45.00**
King George VI and Queen Elizabeth, December 11, 1936 to February 6, 1952
Coronation, May 12, 1937
Ashtray, 4" sq, sepia profile portraits, color dec **20.00**
Dish, 3¾" d, sepia portraits, color dec **25.00**
Mug
3" h, sepia portraits, Princess Margaret on reverse, Ideal ... **45.00**
4¼" h, raised portraits, glass, amber **45.00**
4½" h, crown and cypher, blue and green **45.00**
Plate
6¼" d, color flags and crown dec, Paragon **45.00**
6¾" d, sepia profile portraits, color dec **25.00**
7" d, sepia portraits, Princess Elizabeth at bottom, Hanley . **35.00**
Queen Elizabeth, The Queen Mother, 80th Birthday, August 4, 1980
Mug
3¾" h, sepia portrait, Coronet ... **50.00**
4¾" h, color portrait and dec, Crown Staffordshire **70.00**
Plate
8¼" d, brown tone profile portrait, color dec, Royal Doulton **70.00**
10½" d, color coat of arms and dec, Aynsley **65.00**
King Edward VIII, January 20, 1936, ab-

dicated December 11, 1936, died May 28, 1972. Coronation scheduled for May 12, 1937. Coronation items are not rare since most were in stores prior to the abdication.
Coronation
Mug
3⅞" h, shaving, sepia portrait, color dec **85.00**
4" h, crystal, etched crown, cypher, and date, Stuart **75.00**
4¼" h, sepia portrait, color dec, Aynsley **80.00**
Plate
6¼" d, sepia profile portrait, color dec, Tuscan **45.00**
8½" sq, sepia portrait, color dec, J & C Meakin **45.00**
Tin
2" h, 5¾" d, blue tone portrait, color dec, Watler's Palm Toffee **55.00**
3½" h, 9¼" d, sepia portrait in Army uniform, J Bottomley .. **45.00**
In Memoriam, plate, 10½" d, gold dec, puce border with gold overlay, limited edition of 1,000, Coalport **185.00**
King George V and Queen Mary, May 6, 1910 to January 20, 1936
Coronation, June 26, 1911
Bust, pr, 7" h, color dec, black plinths **150.00**
Egg Cup, pr, 2½" h, color portraits, Germany **70.00**
Mug
3" h, color coat of arms, Britannia, Foley **75.00**
3½" h, color portraits and dec . **65.00**
Plate, 7" d, color portraits **40.00**
Tin, ¾" x 6 x 4¼", color portraits and dec, Fry & Sons **45.00**
Vase, 5½" h, color portrait of Queen Mary, sgd "Russell & Sons" **75.00**
Silver Jubilee, 1935
Egg Cup, 2½" h, sepia portraits, color dec **35.00**
Mug
4" h
Color coat of arms and dec, Shelley **55.00**
Sepia portraits, color dec, Grafton **65.00**
4¼" h, sepia portraits, color dec, Diamond China **50.00**
Tin
1⅝" x 4¼ x 2¾", sepia portraits, Windsor Castle **35.00**
2¼ x 6¾ x 5", purple tone emb portraits and dec **35.00**
King Edward VII and Queen Alexandra, January 22, 1901 to May 6, 1910.

King Edward VII and Queen Alexandra, 8¼" h clock with sepia scene titled "Windsor Castle From The Thames," pair of 6¾" h matching vases with sepia portraits of King Edward VII and Queen Alexandra, cobalt blue ground, unmarked, $380.00.

Coronation originally scheduled for June 26, 1902, but postponed because of the King's appendicitis attack. It took place on August 9, 1902. Items with the earlier date are far more common.

Coronation
  Cup and Saucer, color portraits and dec, enamel on tin **95.00**
  Mug
    3¼" h, sepia portraits, color dec, W Lowe **115.00**
    4" h, emb portraits and flowers, color dec, Doulton Lambeth .   **270.00**
  Plate
    7" d, color portraits and dec, Foley **65.00**
    8¾" d, color portraits, Made in Austria **70.00**
  Vase, pr, 6¾" h and clock, 8¼" h, sepia portraits, cobalt blue background **380.00**
Queen Victoria and Prince Albert, June 20, 1837 to January 22, 1901

Prince Albert In Memoriam (died December 14, 1861)
  Book Mark, 9 x 2½", silk, black and white portrait **60.00**
Golden Jubilee, 1887
  Beaker, 4" h, sepia young and mature portraits, Doulton Burslem .   **95.00**
  Mug
    3" h, color shield and dec **60.00**
    3¼" h, color crown and ribbons, William Whiteley **90.00**
Diamond Jubilee, 1897
  Cup and Saucer, black and white portraits of four generations, color dec, Made in France **125.00**
  Plate
    7" d, blue tone portrait and dec, R H Plant **85.00**
    10⅜" d, sepia portrait and dec, Sampson Bridgwood & Son . .   **220.00**
In Memoriam
  Book Mark, 6 x 1¾", black on white commemoration **95.00**
  Plaque, 6½" d, color portrait, black border, Grimwade Brothers **290.00**

Queen Victoria, plate, sepia portrait and dec, Sampson Bridgwood & Son, 10⅜" d, $220.00.

BROWNIES

Collecting Hints: Brownie items appear across the collectibles spectrum and are reasonably plentiful. Buy pieces in very good or better condition.

Most collectors begin by focusing on the books. Because of their popularity, they went through many printings and editions. Strive to obtain first editions whenever possible.

Brownie material is most often found at specialized toy shows and paper shows. The flat, two dimensional items, e.g., advertising trade cards, are nice, but make acquiring three dimensional objects, e.g., a Brownie bowling set, your top priority.

History: Palmer Cox (1840–1924) created *The Brownies*, comical elf-like creatures, for *St. Nicholas* magazine. The inspiration for the cartoon characters came from the legends Cox heard in his boyhood home of Granby, Province Quebec, Canada. After stays in California (1863–78) and New York, Cox eventually retired to Brownie Castle, Granby.

Dozens of little cartoon Brownies, each having triangular faces, wide eyed expressions, and spindly legs, appeared in poems, stories, and panels to the delight of children from the late 1880s through the early 1920s. Each Brownie had a distinct personality and name, e.g., Uncle Sam, The London Bobby, The Chairman, and Bellhop. Thirteen separate Brownie books appeared, beginning with *The Brownies, Their Book* in 1887.

Brownies were one of the first successful cartoon advertising merchandisers. Beginning in the 1890s the Brownie image appeared on a wealth of products from children's china dish sets to sheet music. The famous Eastman Brownie Camera No. 2A achieved its name because of the Brownies used on the box and in advertising.

Reference: David Longest, *Character Toys and Collectibles, Second Series*, Collector Books, 1987.

Game, Brownie Kick-In Top, 8½ x 8¾ x 1⅜" metal bowl, five wood balls, two piece spinning top, M. H. Miller Co, c1910, $50.00.

Advertising
Box, Little Buster Popcorn, Brownies
   illus 12.00
Ruler, Mrs Winslow's Soothing Syrup 25.00
Trade Card, American Machine Co,
   ice cream freezers 15.00
Book, Palmer Cox author and illustrator
   Bomba, The Merry Old King 30.00
   Brownie Primer, Century Co 40.00

Brownies In Fairyland, Century Co .. 35.00
Brownies In The Phillippines, Century
   Co 75.00
Busy Brownies, 1897, Vol 1, No 1 . 25.00
Palmer Cox Brownie Yearbook, Mc-
   Loughlin Bros, 1895 .... 175.00
The Brownies Abroad, 1941, 18th
   printing, dust jacket 30.00
The Brownies Their Book, 1887 .... 110.00
The Jolly Chinee, 6¼ x 9", 36 pgs, full
   color cov, supplement to Philadel-
   phia Inquirer, Jan 3, 1897 .... 25.00
Candlestick, Brownies and Uncle Sam,
   majolica 175.00
Charm, 1", white metal, black finish,
   Brownie wearing vest and cap, c1900 35.00
Creamer, 2½" h, china, Brownies smok-
   ing pipe, verse on back 50.00
Cup and Saucer, child size 100.00
Demitasse Spoon, enameled dec 25.00
Desk Accessory, basket, 2 x 2½ x 4",
   brass, Brownie at base 75.00
Mold, ice cream, figural 185.00
Napkin Ring, silverplated, figural 75.00
Paper Doll, Lion Coffee adv 18.00
Plate, marked "Cook & Hancock, Tren-
   ton" 60.00
Puzzle, Brownie Puzzle Blocks, c1900 350.00
Salt and Pepper Shakers, pr, Mt Wash-
   ington glass, Brownie Sailor and
   Brownie Indian 245.00
Sewing, needle book, Columbian Expo,
   Brownie Policeman, 1893 .... 48.00
Sheet Music, *Frolic of the Brownies,*
   1896 .... 30.00
Soda Bottle, emb figures, 1926 .... 25.00
Stamp Set, rubber stamps, complete .. 35.00
Stickpin, Brownie Policeman 20.00
Tea Set, MIB 500.00
Tobacco Humidor, majolica, glazed,
   cap lid, 3½ x 4 x 6" Defender figure,
   dark pinks and white, blue and white
   glazed tassel on cap, c1890 .... 150.00
Toby Jug, 3½", majolica 35.00
Towel Set and Transfers, set of six linen
   dish towels, 17 x 34", embroidered
   design of Brownies performing house-
   hold chores, iron–on transfer kit by
   Butterick Publishing Co, c1930 .... 165.00

BUBBLE GUM CARDS, NON-SPORT

Collecting Hints: Don't buy individual cards; buy full sets. The price of a set is below the sum of individual cards. By collecting sets you do lose some of the fun of trading cards, nevertheless, cards from this vintage are sold by sets. Any set should contain a sample of the wrapper plus any stickers that belong to the set.

Because of the availability of these cards, make certain the sets you buy are in mint condition. You can buy boxes of gum packages. With Topps you are 100% certain you will get at least one full set from a box. Donruss and Fleer average 85%.

Collectors should store cards in plastic sleeves. Place the wrapper first and then the cards in numerical order.

History: The birthplace of the modern bubble gum (trading) card is the tobacco insert cards of the late 19th century. From 1885 to 1894 there were over 500 sets issued, with only about 25 devoted to sports. Trading cards lost their popularity in the decade following World War I. However, in 1933 "Indian Gum" issued a product containing a stick of bubble gum and a card in a waxed paper package. A revolution had begun.

Goudey Gum and National Chicle controlled the market until the arrival of Gum, Inc., in 1936. Gum, Inc., issued The Lone Ranger and Superman sets in 1940. From 1943 to 1947 the market in cards was again quiet. In 1948 Bowman entered the picture. A year later Topps Chewing Gum produced some non-sports cards. A war between Bowman and Topps ensued until 1956 when Topps bought Bowman.

Although Topps enjoyed a dominant position in the baseball card market, it had continual rivals in the non-sports field. Frank Fleer Company, Leaf Brands, and Philadelphia Chewing Gum provided competition in the 1960s. Fleer and Donruss Chewing Gum provide the modern day assault.

References: Christopher Benjamin and Dennis W. Eckes, *The Sport Americana Price Guide To The Non-Sport Cards, Number 2,* (1983) and *Number 3, Part Two,* (1988) Edgewater Book Company.

Bowman, Jets, Rockets, Spaceman, (R701, 108 cards, Philadelphia, 1951), 2¹⁄₁₆ x 3⅛", top, Card 4, Final Check Before Blastoff, $2.50; bottom, Card 33, Battling Space Cell, $2.50.

BOWMAN

1948, Movie Stars, 2¹⁄₁₆ x 2½", 36 cards
Set	75.00
Wrapper	50.00

1950, Wild Man, 2¹⁄₁₆ x 2½", 72 cards
Cards #1-36, set	75.00
Cards #37-72, set	125.00
Wrapper	35.00

1953, Antique Autos, 2½ x 3¾", 48 cards
Set	50.00
Three D Glasses	5.00
Wrapper	5.00

1954, US Navy Victories, 2½ x 3¾", 48 cards
Set	50.00
Wrapper	25.00

DONRUSS

1964
Addams Family, 66 cards	60.00
Combat, Series I, 66 cards	55.00

1965
Disneyland, 66 cards, puzzle back	45.00
Freddie & The Dreamers, 66 cards	40.00
1966, Monkees, 44 cards	38.00
1968, Flying Nun, 66 cards	55.00
1973, Osmonds, 66 cards	30.00
1976, Bionic Woman, 44 cards	3.50

1978
All-Pro Skateboard, 44 sticker cards	6.00
Elvis Presley, 66 cards	3.50
1979, Rock Stars, 66 cards	2.50
1980, Dukes Of Hazzard, 66 cards	3.50
1983, Magnum PI, 66 cards	3.50

FLEER

1963, Goofy Gags, 55 cards	15.00
1965, Gomer Pyle, 66 cards	10.00
1966, Three Stooges, 66 cards	80.00
1968, My Kookie Klassmates, 20 cards, 9 autograph stamp sheets	15.00
1972, Drag Nationals, 70 cards	16.00
1979, Gong Show, 66 cards, 10 stickers	5.00
1981, Here's Bo, 72 cards, 12 posters	5.00
1983, Mad, 128 stickers	15.00
1984, Dragon's Lair, 63 stickers, 30 rub-off games	10.00

LEAF

1966, Good Guys & Bad Guys, 72 cards	50.00

1967
Garrisons' Gorillas, 72 cards	50.00
Star Trek, 72 cards	550.00

Topps, Davy Crockett, (R712-11, 80 cards), 2⅝ x 3¾", orange, Card 1, King of the Wild Frontier, $.50.

PHILADELPHIA CHEWING GUM CO

1953, Blackstone's Magic Tricks, 24
  folders **60.00**
1965, James Bond, 66 cards **55.00**
1966
  Green Berets, 66 cards **40.00**
  James Bond, Thunderball, 66 cards . **60.00**
  Tarzan, 66 cards **40.00**
1967, Daktari, 66 cards **20.00**
1969, Dark Shadows, Series II, 66
  cards, green **80.00**
1972, Happy Horoscopes, 72 cards .. **20.00**

Topps, Freedom's War, (R709-2, 203 cards), 2¹⁄₁₆ x 2⅝", Card 65, Korea, How-itzer, $.50.

TOPPS

1961, Crazy Cards, 66 cards **60.00**
1962
  Casey & Kildare, 110 cards **95.00**
  Civil War News, 88 cards **175.00**
1963
  Astronauts, 55 cards **50.00**

Beverly HIllbillies, 66 cards **80.00**
Famous Americans, 80 cards **260.00**
Flag Midgee, 99 cards **40.00**
1964, Johnson vs. Goldwater, 66 cards **45.00**
1965
  Daniel Boone, 55 cards **25.00**
  King Kong, 55 cards **20.00**
  Kookie Plaks, 88 cards **60.00**
1966
  Batman, Riddler back series, 38 cards **50.00**
  Flipper, 30 cards **400.00**
  Lost In Space, 55 cards **160.00**
1967, Angry Stickers, 88 .... **150.00**
1970
  Brady Bunch, 88 cards **150.00**
  Comic Cover, 44 stickers **75.00**
1971, Bobby Sherman "Getting To-
  gether," 55 cards **450.00**
1974, Evel Knievel, 60 cards **35.00**
1975
  Bay City Rollers, 66 cards **20.00**
  Good Times, 55 cards, 21 stickers .. **8.00**
1976, Happy Days, 44 cards, 11 stickers **4.00**
1977, Charlie's Angels, Series I, 55
  cards **6.00**
1978
  Battlestar Galactica, 132 cards, 22
    stickers **10.00**
  Close Encounters, 66 cards, 11 stick-
    ers **3.50**
  Grease, Series I, 66 cards, 11 stickers **3.00**
1979, Buck Rogers, 88 cards, 22 stickers **5.00**
1980, Empire Strikes Back, Series I ... **5.00**
1983, A-Team, 66 cards, 12 stickers .. **3.50**
1985
  Cyndi Lauper, 66 cards **3.00**
  Rambo, 66 cards, 22 stickers **8.00**
1987, Alf, 69 cards, 18 stickers **8.00**

BUTTONS

Collecting Hints: Buttons are collected according to age, material, and subject matter. The National Button Society, founded in 1939, has designated 1918 as the dividing line between old and modern buttons. Shanks and backmarks are important keys in determining the age of buttons. Older buttons attract the most attention of collectors.

Buttons generally are mounted on trays or cards in artistic designs. A uniform series of circles helps outline the buttons presented. The majority of the collectors mount their buttons by the material of which the button is made, e.g., fabric, metals, glass, enamels, pearl, ceramic, etc. All buttons are classified into four divisions: General (old buttons), Uniform, Modern, and Specialized. The old buttons have 15 sections, further divided into 289 categories. The National

Button Society maintains a Classification Committee which constantly reviews previous designations.

It is difficult to determine which area of button collecting is most popular. Dealers abound. Metal detectors play an important part in locating old buttons on battlefields.

History: Buttons are objects used to hold articles of clothing in a desired place. In the 18th century buttons were worn basically by men as status symbols and a sign of wealth. During the peak of this period it was not unusual to find complete sets of 24 buttons on one coat.

Americans always have been fashion conscious and used buttons as a form of decoration. Brass buttons were made as early as 1750 by Casper Wister of Philadelphia. The Shaker colony at New Lebanon, New York, has records of button production in 1789.

Buttons, like many other objects, became ornate and very decorative during the Victorian era. Some Victorian buttons included subject matter taken from fairy tales, heroes, nursery rhymes, literature, and nature. Buttons of the late 19th century tend to feature two piece construction. Today brass, steel, and copper of the early buttons has been replaced by wood, leather, plastic, and glass.

References: There are a large number of button books; most are privately printed. Some examples are: Viviane Ertell, *The Colorful World of Buttons*; Elizabeth Hughes and Marion Lester, *The Big Book of Buttons*, 1983; Don Van Court, *The Railroad Button Book, Transportation Buttons, Volume One - Railroads*, published by author, 1987.

Collectors' Club: National Button Society, 2733 Juno Place, Akron, OH 44313.

Museum: Copper Union Museum for the Art of Decoration, New York, NY.

Advisor: Lois Pool.

REPRODUCTION ALERT Reproductions of buttons, e.g., the White House button made from the original die, do exist. Be careful.

Brass, metal shank, "The Good Samaritan," prior to 1918, $7.50.

Brass
¾", owl head, steel eyes, steel back		**12.00**
⅞"		
Chyrsanthemum, pierced, blue-green trim		**1.50**
Utah State Seal, beehive design, convex		**1.50**
1"		
Acorn		**3.00**
Heart, lacy		**4.50**
1⅛", Halley's Comet, engraved stars, black sky		**5.00**
1¼", Little Colonel, silvered design, lacquered		**20.00**
1½"		
Buffalo, high relief, gilt		**20.00**
Cat, climbing over wall, lizard, openwork top		**20.00**
Flowers, urn, steel stud, brass back		**7.50**
Tulips, etched edge, attached steel back		**5.00**
1¾"		
Gay Nineties, stamped filigree, engraved border, cobalt glass center		**5.00**
Phoenix, diecut, brass back		**7.50**

Celluloid, 1½", tennis player, 1 pc, c1930 .... **3.00**

China
1", calico		**1.75**
1¼", stencil dec		**3.00**

Cinnabar, 1¼", Oriental, carved flowers ... **12.00**

Enamel, 1", Nut Tree Boy, late 19th C ... **25.00**

Glass
⅜", cranberry, faceted ball		**1.00**
5/16", jeweled, narrow brass rim, black glass center, spiral cone		**1.25**
⅝", black irid luster		
Animal		**3.00**
Building		**2.50**
¾", silver luster, lacy design		**.50**
⅞", convex, black, purple, red, and gray swirl, brass shank		**4.00**
1", Czechoslovakia, Realistics, vegetables, c1945		**.50**
1⅛"		
Camphor, bar, hp rose dec		**5.00**
Milk Glass, hp, brass border		**2.00**
1½", black, grapes and leaves, brass shank, pat 1899		**2.00**
2", purple swirl center, cut steel border, brass trim encased in dark blue plastic		**7.50**

Metal
½", Girl at Gate, amethyst		**4.50**
¾", Cupid, torch		**2.50**
2¼", Elizabeth II		**15.00**

Military, brass, assorted sizes, 1 pc
American
Excelsior National Guard, NYSA, eagle above shield, convex		**6.50**
NY State, relief		**7.50**

Horn, clock face, dyed black, prior to 1918, $4.00.

NJ National Guard, convex	**6.50**
Ohio, convex	**5.50**

English
Devonshire Regiment	**6.50**
Royal Army Ordnance Corp	**6.00**

Paperweight, ¾"
Floral, blue petals, green leaves	**20.00**
Signed "J," John Gooderham	**25.00**

Passementerie, ⅝", red glass, riveted to metal **25.00**

Pearl
¼", round, metal shank, card of 6	**5.00**
½", rose carving	**1.00**
¾", bird carving	**1.25**
1", heart shape	**1.25**

Pewter
⅝", daisy, bright cut trim, pearl flower head	**1.75**
¾", Bandmaster Uniform, emb lyre, 2 pcs	**3.00**
1½", Ugly Duckling, swan, bull rushes, hand tinted	**8.50**

Plastic, assorted sizes
Bulldogs, white, red collars, set of 6, orig card	**3.50**
Donald Duck, white	**2.50**
Teddy Bears, brown, red bow ties	**1.00**

Porcelain, ½", 19th C, transfer design, self shank **7.50**

Satsuma, 1⅛", chyrsanthemum, polychrome, white ground, gold rim **15.00**

Silver
½", Thailand, engraved design, Niello, c1940	**8.50**
1", Navajo Indian, turquoise center, 20th C	**12.00**

Steel, ¾", blue irid, inverted bowl shape, brass filigree **5.00**

CALENDARS

Collecting Hints: Value increases if all monthly pages are attached. Most calendars are bought by collectors interested in the subject on the calendar as opposed to the calendar itself.

History: Calendars were a popular advertising giveaway in the late 19th century and first five decades of the 20th. Recently, a calendar craze has swept bookstores throughout America. These topic-oriented calendars contain little or no advertising.

Additional Listing: Pin-up Art.

REPRODUCTION ALERT

1898, Youth Companion Magazine, fold out type, 8 x 11" closed, $40.00.

1888, Hood's Sarsaparilla	**42.00**
1889, Buckeye Fire Insurance, color illus of Victorian woman, 28 x 20"	**275.00**
1890, Success Horse Collars, 14 x 24"	**350.00**
1894, Halfield and Kerney, children, folding, 12½ x 7½"	**80.00**
1897, Boston Rubber Shoe Co, 7 x 8½", 6 pgs	**30.00**
1898, Fairbands Fairy Floral Calendar, 12 x 8½", 6 pgs, orig string holder	**80.00**
1899, Youth's Companion	**40.00**
1901, Grand Union Tea, 12 x 8½", 4 pgs	**25.00**
1904, Blatz Beer, dark haired woman	**375.00**
1905, Rock Crystal Salt, Chicago, celluloid, memo pad	**25.00**
1907, Scranton Tobacco Co, 19½ x 15"	**250.00**
1913, Gross Druggist, Harrisburg, PA, multicolored, celluloid	**30.00**
1914, Ashland Brewery, WI	**65.00**
1916, Metropolitan Insurance	**15.00**
1918, American Glass Co, Cincinnati, celluloid, ruler and blotter, black and white	**12.00**
1921, DeLaval, little boy fishing	**65.00**
1922, Sacred Art, color illus, 9 x 17"	**5.00**
1926, Mary Pickford, Pompeian	**48.00**
1927, Wrigley's Double Mint Gum, 3½ x 6"	**28.00**
1930, Peter's Cartridge	**250.00**
1931, DeLaval, illus by Norman Priss	**150.00**
1934, Seiberling Tire, illus by Rolf Armstrong	**32.00**
1936, Oliver Tractors	**75.00**

1937, Traveller's, Currier and Ives illus **35.00**
1939, Johnson Winged Gasoline **17.50**
1942, Dionne Quints, Springtime, 12 x 15" **15.00**
1943, Esquire, illus by Varga, orig envelope **45.00**
1946, Bathing Beauty, titled "I'll Say So," illus by Rolf Armstrong **75.00**
1947, Esquire, pin-up illus by Varga .. **40.00**
1948, First Dates, 8 x 11" **20.00**
1950, Sweet Sixteen, 8 x 11" **25.00**
1951, Four Seasons, illus by Norman Rockwell **35.00**
1952, Smooth Sailing, 12 x 15", orig envelope **30.00**
1954, Elvgren, "Some Help!," pin-up girl painting Scottie **75.00**
1963, Pasadena Tournament of Roses . **15.00**
1966, Union Pacific RR **8.00**
1969, Union Pacific RR Centennial ... **20.00**
1978, Fantasies of Women **35.00**
Perpetual, advertising type, revolving wheel cov
   1950–1977, Massachusetts Mutual, 1½" diecut aluminum, 100th anniversary text in dark red letters **8.50**
   1952–1979, Texaco, 1¾", diecut, gold colored tin, revolving disk, keychain tab, black logo inscription and 50th anniversary dates **10.00**
   1953–1980, Ford Motors, 1½", diecut, revolving brass wheel, Ford logo and Brooklyn agency address on front **20.00**
   1963–1990, IBM, 1½", diecut, aluminum, red, white, and blue design promoting US savings bonds **5.00**
   1965–1992, Bell System, 1½", gold colored aluminum, blue and white logo **8.00**

CAMERAS

Collecting Hints: The camera market seems to fluctuate weekly. However, the long range average price for any camera is steady. The Leica market no longer is in an upward movement, but interest in unusual cameras, e. g., subminiatures and stereo cameras, is growing.

Leather covered cameras should have all the leather. Some wear does not detract from the value.

Folding cameras should have the bellows in good condition. Black bellows should be light tight. Colored bellows matching colored cameras need not be light tight. Having a matching bellow adds to the value of a colored camera.

History: A German monk, Johann Zahn, is credited with creating in the early 1800s the first fully portable wood box camera with a movable lens, an adjustable aperture, and a mirror to project the image. Zahn could view his image, but had no film on which to record it. In 1826 Joseph Nicephore Niepce produced the first photographic plate. Louise Jacques Mande Daguerre joined Niepce in his efforts. Peter Von Voigtlander of Vienna developed the quality lens needed. The photography industry was born.

The Germans were the initial leaders in camera manufacture. By the late 19th century the English and French had a strong market position. American strength would begin around 1900. America's strongest contributions have come in the development of films and the Polaroid camera, invented by Dr. Land and marketed in late 1948.

George Eastman revolutionized the photography industry in 1888 when his simple box camera was introduced. It was small, 3¼ x 3¾ x 6½", and was modeled after earlier European examples. The camera had a magazine and could take 100 pictures without being reloaded. The pictures were 2½" in diameter. Many later models built upon the success of Kodak No. 1. Kodak's first folding camera was Model No. 4; the Brownie arrived in 1900.

Prior to World War II Japan made the Konica and Minolta. After the war Japan made a strong commitment to the camera market. The Japanese have introduced many technical changes into the camera, including solar power.

References: Jim and Joan McKeown, *Price Guide To Antique And Classic Still Cameras, 1987–1988*, published by authors, 1988; Myron Wolf, *Blue Book Illustrated Price Guide To Collectible & Useable Cameras*, 2nd Master Edition; published by author, 1985; Jason Schneider, *Jason Schneider On Camera Collecting*, Wallace-Homestead, 1985.

Periodical: *Photique*, One Magnolia Hill, West Hartford, CT 06117.

Collectors' Clubs: National Stereoscopic Association, P.O. Box 14801, Columbus, OH 43214; Photographic Historical Society, P. O. Box 9563, Rochester, NY 14604.

Museums: International Museum of Photography, George Eastman House, 900 East Avenue, Rochester, NY 14607.

Agfa Kamerawerke (Munich, Germany), merged with Ansco 1928
   Agfaflex, SLR, Prontor 1–300, c1959 **50.00**
   Karat 36, 35mm, c1952 .... **42.00**
   Isolette III, c1952 .... **30.00**
   Preis-Box, Meniscus lens, c1932 ... **10.00**
Ansco (Binghamton, NY), merged with Agfa 1928
   Buster Brown, MIB **38.00**
   Dollar Box Camera, 4 x 3½ x 2½", 127 film, green, c1910 .... **12.00**
   Readyset Royal, folding **20.00**

Perfex, One-O-One, Camera Corp of America, Wollensak lens, Alphax shutter, F4, 5/50 mm, 1947–1950, $30.00.

Argus, Inc (Ann Arbor, MI)
A2B, 35mm, 1939–50 .... 18.00
Lady Carefree, 126 cartridge, tan, white brocade cov 5.00
Blair Camera Co (Boston, MA), became part of Eastman Kodak in 1908
Baby Hawk Eye, 7 oz, box, c1896 . 125.00
Tourist Hawk Eye, folding rollfilm, 3½ x 3½", wooden standard conceals lens and shutter, c1900 .... 120.00
Bosley Corp of America (New York, NY), B2, 35mm, 1949–56 .... 25.00
Camera Corp of America (Chicago, IL), Perfex Fifty-Five, 35mm, c1940 .... 32.00
Conley Camera Co (Rochester, NY), Kewpie No. 2A, box 15.00
Detrola Corp (Detroit, MI), Model KW, 127 film 20.00
Eastman Kodak Co (Rochester, NY)
Bantam RF, 828 film ....: 30.00
Brownie, No. 2, box 12.00
Bullet Camera, plastic, 127 film 10.00
Duaflex, twin lens reflex 5.00
Kodak 35, Rangefinder, 35mm 20.00
Kodak Stereo, 35mm 90.00
Signet 35, 35mm 25.00
Franke & Heidecke (Braunschweig, Germany), Rolleicord V, twin lens relfex 80.00
Graflex, Inc (Rochester, NY), RB Graflex Series B, single lens relfex, 3¼ x 4¼" 75.00
Minolta (Chiyoda Kogaku Seiko Co, Ltd, Osaka, Japan)
Minolta Hi-Matic 7, 35mm, built-in meter, 1963 .... 40.00
Minolta SR–1S, 1964 .... 80.00
Minolta 24 Rapid, 24 x 24mm, 35mm rangefinder, built-in meter 80.00
Norton Laboratories, Norton, black plastic, stamped metal viewfinder, c1934 .... 20.00
Olympic Camera Works (Japan)
Olympic, bakelite half frame, Olympic shutter, c1934 .... 75.00

Super Olympic, bakelite body, first Japanese 35mm, c1935 .... 85.00
Pentacon (Dresden, Germany)
Contax F, 35mm SLR, semi automatic cocking diaphragm, c1957 ..... 85.00
Pentacon FB, built-in exposure meter, Tessar lens, 1959 .... 80.00
Taxona, 24 x 24mm exposures on 35mm film, Novonar lens, Tempor 1–300 shutter, 1950 .... 30.00
Polaroid 95, orig model 20.00
Rolls Camera Mfg Co (Chicago, IL)
Rolls Twin 620, cast aluminum box, 620 film, c1939 .... 10.00
Super Rolls 35mm, cast metal, retractable front, helical focusing 15.00
Spartus Press Flash, box, built-in flash reflector 12.00
Top Camera Works, (Occupied Japan), cast metal, subminiature, fixed focus lens, 1948 .... 80.00
Voigtlander & Sohn (Braunschweig, Germany), Avus, folding plate 42.00
Zeiss (Jeno, Stuttgart, and Dresden, Germany)
Aerial, 13 x 18cm, cast metal, two hand grips, folding frame finder, c1930 .... 250.00
Box Tengor 56/2, chrome trim, Frontar f9 lens, 1948 .... 30.00
Nettar, 6 x 6cm, folding 35.00
Tessco, double extension 9 x 12cm, folding plate, 1927 .... 60.00
Victrix, folding plate, "Zeiss Ikon" on lens, 1927 .... 90.00
Zenith Camera Corp
Comet, plastic, 4 x 6cm, 127 film, c1947 .... 10.00
Sharpshooter, black and silver metal box, c1948 .... 7.50

CANAL COLLECTIBLES

Collecting Hints: Concentrate on one state or one specific canal. Look not only for canal material, but for the canal motif on non-canal items.

Beware of people trying to pass off tools and lanterns as having a canal origin. Ship boatyards used exactly the same tools as the canal boatyards. Insist on a good provenance for any canal item and check out the family name in the canal records.

Canal buffs are extremely well organized. Try to make contact early in your collecting interest with individuals working on the same topics as you. Many collectors own more than one example of an item and will gladly sell the duplicate to a new collector.

History: The American canal era has its origins in the 18th century with projects in New England, along the Potomac, and Louisiana. George Washington was intensely interested in canals and was a shareholder in several canal companies.

The building of the Erie and Champlain canals in New York launched canal mania. From 1825 to 1840 hundreds of canal projects were begun. States such as Pennsylvania and Ohio actually had more miles of canals than New York.

While the railroads contributed in the demise of the canals, it was the high maintenance costs, repair due to floods, and economic depressions which finally closed many of the canals.

A number of canals continued into the twentieth century. Modern canals include the Chesapeake and Delaware Canal and the Erie Barge Canal.

References: James Lee, *Tales The Boatmen Told*, Canal Press, 1977; William J. McKelvey, *Champlain To Chesapeake: A Canal Era Pictorial Cruise*, Canal Press, 1978; Harry L. Rinker, *"The Old Raging Erie . . . There Have Been Several Changes": A Postcard History Of The Erie And Other New York State Canals (1895 to 1915)*, Canal Captain's Press, 1984.

Collectors' Clubs: American Canal Society, 809 Rathton Road, York, PA 17403. *American Canals* (quarterly); Canal Society of Ohio, 120 E. Mill Street, Suite 402, Akron, OH 44308. *Towpaths* (quarterly); Pennsylvania Canal Society, c/o Canal Museum, P. O. Box 877, Easton, PA 18042. *Canal Currents* (quarterly).

Museums: Canal Museum, Hugh Moore Park, Easton, PA; Chesapeake and Delaware Canal Museum, Chesapeake City, DE; Erie Canal Museum, Syracuse, NY.

Advertising Trade Card, Burdett Organ Co., Erie, PA, dated 1883, front features the Lehigh River and Lehigh Canal at the bend of Bear Mountain in Mauch Chunk, PA 6.00
Ashtray, 5" d, Pennsbury Pottery, shows Lehigh Canal boat at dock, camelback bridge in background, advertising premium from "The Solebury National Bank of New Hope Pa.", green, gray, and brown, light brown ground 15.00
Bank Note, broken
Chemung Canal Bank, $10 note, No. 1896, September 1, 1846, Elmira, NY, vignette of Greek god reclining in front of flight of canal locks, engraved by Rawdon, Wright, Hatch & Co. 30.00
Sanford Bank, Georgia, $10 note, No. 10 A, January 17, 1861, issued in Sanford, center vignette of Rockville bridge in Harrisburg, PA, showing train in foreground with

eastern division of Pennsylvania Main Line Canal between railroad and river, engraved by Toppan, Carpenter, Caslier & Co. 15.00
Tide Water Canal, $1 note, No. 10782C, May 1, 1840, issued in Baltimore, MD, two vignettes, first with oval showing mule pulling canalboat, second of New York scene, engraved by Draper, Toppen & Co 50.00
Book
Doran, Edith M., *High-Water Cargo*, New Brunswick, NJ: Rutgers University Press: 1950 and 1965, 224 pgs, hardcover, orig dj, illus. by Forrest Orr, novel about life along the Delaware and Raritan Canal in the 1850s 20.00
Gard, R. Max and William H. Vodrey, Jr., *The Sandy And Beaver Canal*, East Liverpool, OH: East Liverpool Historical Society: 1952, 210 pgs, softcover, map insert 40.00
Robert J. McClellan, *The Delaware Canal: A Picture Story*, New Brunswick, NJ: Rutgers University Press: 1967, 112 pgs, hardcover, orig dj 15.00
Whitford, Noble E., *History Of The Canal System Of New York Together With Brief Histories Of The Canals Of The United States and Canada, Volume 1 and Volume 2*, issued as a *Supplement To The Annual Report Of The State Engineer And Surveyor Of The State Of New York*, Albany: Brandow Printing Company: 1906, Volume 1 - 1025 pgs, hardcover, Volume 2 - 522 pgs, hardcover, and foldout charts, price for set 100.00
Check
Albany City Bank, No. 82871, March 27, 1857, $10,116 deposited by H H. Martin to the credit of The Treasurer of the State of New York on a/c of the Canal Fund 15.00
The First National Bank of Liverpool, Pennsylvania, yellow ground, features a square photograph in upper left corner marked "Old Canal Boat Days, Liverpool, Pennsylvania, 1906," photograph actually of boats on Chesapeake and Ohio Canal near Williamsport, MD, check unissued 5.00
Document
Pay Order, Ohio Canal, No. 2007, April 5, 1828, $100 for work done under the contract of Wilcox & Dill for section 115 of the Ohio Canal south of Portage Summit 10.00

Towing receipt, "B." and "S." Towing Line, Bernard & Samsel, Steam Tug *"William Cramp"*, towing from Bristol to Bridesburg for Lehigh Coal and Navigation Co. canalboat, Philadelphia, June 5, 1916 .   **5.00**

Manuscript

ALS, Abner Lacock, Office of Western Division of Penna. Canal, February 11, 1828, to Alexander Mahon, Treasurer of the Board of Canal Commissioners, letter informing Mahon that Lacock has issued a check for $35,000 . . . .   **40.00**

ALS, R. & G. D. Coleman, Lebanon Furnaces, May 31, 1849, to Eckert & Stone, concerning passage of boats on Susquehanna and Tidewater Canal near Safe Harbor, PA   **25.00**

Book, Walter D. Edmonds, *Chad Hanna*, Little, Brown, & Co, Boston, 1940, $12.00.

Medal, commemorative, 100th Anniversary of Hamburg Savings And Trust Company, 1872–1972, bronze, obv. shows bank bldg, rev. shows mules pulling canalboat, bronze, 1½" d, orig packaging **10.00**

Patent Model

#154,978, William Baxter and William Baxter, Jr., September 15, 1874, wooden boat model, introduction of steam propulsion, the Baxters won a special prize awarded by New York for the best method of introducing steam propulsion to canals **300.00**

#218,363, Bernard Bird, Buffalo, NY, August 12, 1879, coupling devices for lines, white metal working model, spring powered whiffletree that snaps open when a lever is thrown **150.00**

Photograph, Minetto Shade Cloth Co., Minetto, NY, black and white, 8⅞" x 6⅛", shows canal and lock in lower left quadrant, river through center, and town in background **20.00**

Pinback Button

1¾", Power House And Locks, Sault St. Marie, MI, black and white photograph, attached red ribbon **10.00**

3⅛" x 2⅛", Canal Days Badge, Manayunk, PA, May 17, 1980, blue ground, photo of canal passing under railroad bridge **4.00**

Post Card

Canada, "On the Canal, Lachine," multicolored, marked "Valentine' Series," shows pleasure boats and work scows tied up along bank . .   **2.50**

Delaware Canal, photo postcard of aqueduct at Point Pleasant, PA, sepia tone **7.50**

Erie Canal, "American Locomotive Works, Schenectady, NY," full view, multicolored, shows plant bldgs, railroad lines, and canal (to left) **5.00**

James River and Kanawha Canal, "Old Libby Prison, Richmond, Va", multicolored, made by Hugh C. Leighton Company, Portland, ME, #25682, printed in Germany, ca. 1910, shows canal horizontally across center, Libby Prison building in background, sailing vessels to right **4.00**

Soo Locks, "Birds' Eye View Of Locks, Soo, Mich.," multicolored, published by Young, Lord & Rhoades, Sault Ste. Marie, MI, shows boat ready to enter lock on left and boat exiting lock on right   **3.00**

Puzzle, wooden, jigsaw, Joseph K. Straus, No. P-201, "Great Falls Tavern" (Chesapeake and Ohio Canal), 9" x 12", 200 pieces, orig box **25.00**

Staffordshire, American Historical

Jackson, Job and John, View of Canal, Little Falls, Mohawk River, soup, 10½", light pink transfer, long stem roses border **80.00**

William Ridgway, Harper's Ferry From The Potomac Side, plate, 9", black transfer, shows Chesapeake and Ohio Canal at base of mountain in background **50.00**

Unknown Maker, Canal View Series, pitcher, 7", featuring three transfers (View of Lake George, View of Aqueduct Bridge at Rochester, and Lafayette), yellowish cream ground, carmine line at top, "v" floral motif on handle, cracked **1,500.00**

Wedgwood, plate, 9¼", Poe Lock, Sault Ste. Marie, MI, shows boats exiting lock, dark blue, first quarter of 20th C, made for Rudell Drug Co. in Sault Ste. Marie **50.00**

Enoch Wood & Sons, Erie Canal, View Of The Aqueduct Bridge At Little Falls, chamber pot lid, 8⅜" d, dark blue, oval handle held in place with support piece screwed into top **250.00**

Stereograph

Chesapeake and Ohio Canal, "No. 327 Harper's Ferry," photographed and published by Kilburn Brothers, Littleton, NH, shows railroad bridge across Potomac, C & O canal in foreground **7.50**

Lehigh Canal, "View in the Gap - Early Morning," Klechner's Stereoscopic Views of the Lehigh and Wyoming Valleys On The Line of the Central Railroad of New Jersey (L. & S. Div), shows canal aqueduct at Lehigh Gap, yellow ground **10.00**

Pennsylvania Main Line Canal, "#217. Jack's Narrows", part of The Scenery Of The Pennsylvania Railroad series, Purviance, Philadelphia, yellow card, shows canal with bridge across river in background **5.00**

Stock Certificate or Mortgage Bond

Black River Canal, New York, No. 109, issued November 9, 1837, center vignette of goddesses flanking oval shield featuring sunrise scene with spread-winged eagle on top, three vignettes on left of which two are oval New York State Stock cuts, a small railroad and a small steamship vignette on right, signed by Robert White, cancelled with large oval cuts, engraved by Rawdon, Wright & Hatch **75.00**

Chesapeake & Delaware Canal, No. 2427, 15 shares, issued June 15, 1913, vignette of wooden summit bridge built in 1826, light yellow tone, cancelled **15.00**

New York State 5 per cent Stock on behalf of the Delaware and Hudson Canal, No. 70, March 16, 1827, side identification vignettes only, hand cancelled, engraved by J. H. Hill **45.00**

Pennsylvania Canal Company, Six Percent Mortgage Bond, Principal Payable July 1st, 1910, No. 4, center vignette of canalboat about to cross under a stone arch railroad

bridge, stamp cancelled, coupons clipped, folded **50.00**

Ticket, C. M. Reed's Passage Ticket, 10⅜" x 4¼", unissued, ca. 1840s, features a small vignette of a steamship and a small vignette of a canalboat at top **20.00**

CANDLEWICK

Collecting Hints: Select pieces without chips, cracks, or scratches. Learn the characteristics, shapes, and types of Imperial pieces made. Many items have been made that are similar to Candlewick and are often mixed with Candlewick at shops and sales. Beware!

History: Candlewick, Imperial Glass Corp.'s No. 400 pattern, was introduced in 1936 and was made continuously until October 1982 when Imperial declared bankruptcy. In 1984 Imperial was sold to Lancaster–Colony Corp and Consolidated Stores International, Inc. Imperial's assets including inventory, molds, buildings, and equipment were liquidated in 1985.

The buildings and site were purchased by Anna Maroon of Maroon Enterprises, Bridgeport, Ohio. At present, the site is being developed as a tourist attraction with sales shops, a glass–making shop, and plans for a museum.

Imperial's Candlewick molds were bought by groups, companies, and individuals. Approximately 200 molds were purchased by Mirror Images, Lansing, Michigan. Eighteen small molds were bought by Boyd Crystal Art Glass, Cambridge, Ohio. The disposition of many Candlewick molds has not been disclosed.

Candlewick is characterized by the crystal–drop beading used around the edge of many pieces; around the foot of tumblers, shakers, and other items; in the stems of glasses, compotes, cake and cheese stands; on the handles of cups, pitchers, bowls, and serving pieces; on stoppers and finials; and on the handles of ladles, forks, and spoons. The beading is small on some pieces, while on others it is larger and heavier.

A large variety of pieces were produced in the Candlewick pattern. Over 650 items and sets are known. Shapes include round, oval, oblong, heart, and square. Imperial added or discontinued items according to popularity and demand. The largest assortment of pieces and sets were made during the late 1940s and early 1950s.

Candlewick was produced mostly in crystal. Viennese Blue (pale blue, 1937–38), Ritz Blue (cobalt, 1938–41), and Ruby Red (red, 1937–41) were made. Other colors that have been found include amber, black, emerald green, lavender, pink, and light yellow. From 1977 to 1980, four items of 3400 Candlewick stemware were made in solid Ultra Blue, Nut Brown, Verde Green, and Sunshine Yellow. Solid black stemware was made on an experimental basis at the same time.

Other decorations on Candlewick include silver overlay, gold encrustations, cuttings, etchings, and hand–painted designs. Pieces have been found with fired–on gold, red, blue, and green beading. Other companies encased Candlewick pieces in silver, chrome, brass, and wood.

References: Virginia R. Scott, *The Collector's Guide to Imperial Candlewick, 2nd Edition,* privately printed, (available from the author), 1987; Mary M. Wetzel, *Candlewick, The Jewel of Imperial,* 2nd Edition, 1986.

Periodical: The National Candlewick Collector Newsletter, 275 Milledge Terrace, Athens, GA 30606.

Museum: Bellaire Museum, Bellaire, OH 43906.

Advisor: Virginia R. Scott

REPRODUCTION ALERT: Six inch baskets in pink and Alexandrite and a pink four piece child's set (consisting of a demitasse cup and saucer, 6" plate, and 5" nappy) have been made by Viking Glass Co. for Mirror Images, Lansing, Michigan. In 1987 Viking made clear plates, bowls, cups, saucers, large and small flat–base sugars and creamers (400/30 and 400/122), and 6½" trays (400/29) for Mirror Images. These pieces have ground bottoms and are somewhat heavier than original Candlewick pieces. They are not marked. Light green Candlewick items have recently appeared. The origin of these items is not presently known.

Boyd Crystal Art Glass, Cambridge, Ohio, has used Candlewick molds to make items in various slag and clear colors. All Boyd molds have been marked with a B in a diamond trademark.

Ashtray, beaded edge
2¾" round, large beads, 400/19	**5.00**
4", round, cigarette rest at side, 400/118	**8.00**
6", round, small beads, 400/60	
Advertising	**15.00**
Center holder for match book	**25.00**
Nested set, round large beads, 3 pcs	
4", 5", 6", crystal set, 400/450 ...	**20.00**
4" blue with stars, 5" yellow with shield, 6" pink with eagle, patriotic designs, 400/550	**35.00**
4" red, 5" white, 6" blue	**75.00**
Banana Stand, 10" plate, two sides turned up, 4-bead stem, 400/03E ...	**150.00**
Basket, 11", applied handle, 400/73/0	**75.00**
Bell, 5" h, 4 bead handle, 400/108 ...	**30.00**
Bon Bon Dish, 6", heart shape, applied round handle, 400/51H	**117.50**
Bowl, beaded edge	
5", fruit, 400/1F	**8.00**

6", sq, 400/232	**35.00**
9", sq, fancy crimped, four round toes, 400/74 SC	
Black	**95.00**
Crystal	**30.00**
Light blue	**45.00**
Red	**95.00**
10", two handles, 400/145B	**20.00**
12", flat, curved up rim, 400/92F ...	**35.00**
13", mushroom, 400/92L	**45.00**
Buffet Set, 4 pcs, 6½" divided bowl, 400/84; 14" plate, 400/92D; two 3-bead ladles, 400/165; set 400/94 ...	**45.00**
Butter Dish, cov, beaded edge, rect California, 6¾" l, 4" w, 400/276	
Beaded top	**45.00**
No bead top	**35.00**
One Quarter Pound, beaded top, 400/161	**20.00**
Cake Plate and Stand, beaded edge	
10"	
Belled foot, wedge shaped markings, early style, 400/67D	**55.00**
Flat foot, 400/67D	**35.00**
11", 4-bead stem, 400/103D	**50.00**
14", round, flat, birthday cake plate, 72 holes for candles, 400/160 ...	**185.00**
Candleholder	
2" h, 5½" w, mushroom, 400/86 ...	**17.00**
5½", ftd, beaded bowl, three section of arched beads on stem, 400/224	**25.00**
6", urn, rolled over, beaded top, 1-bead stem, 400/129R	**35.00**
9", 3-light, oval beaded base, 400/115	**35.00**
Candy Dish, 5½", box, beaded edge, 2-bead finial cov, 400/59	**25.00**
Candy Jar, domed beaded foot, 1 bead stem, partitioned bowl, 400/140	
Early style	**75.00**
2-bead lid	**50.00**
Celery Tray, 13½", oval, curved handles, 400/105	**25.00**
Centerpiece Set	
7¾" lily vase insert, beaded top, 2-bead bottom, peg, 400/196 set ...	**75.00**
9" flower candle centerpiece, crimped bowl, ftd, 400/196FC ...	**45.00**
Cheese and Cracker Set, 14" plate, 400/92D, 5½" ftd compote, flat top, 1-bead stem, 400/88, set	
Crystal	**35.00**
Light Blue	**55.00**
Cigarette Box, 5", oblong, large beads, domed beaded cov, 400/134	**20.00**
Cigarette Set, 6 pcs, 3" jar, domed foot, small beads, 400/44; four 2¾" round ashtrays, 400/164; kidney shaped tray, 400/29, 400/129/6 set	**45.00**
Coaster, 4", round	
Five rays in bottom, 400/78, early style	**6.00**

Ten rays in bottom, 400/78 . . . . **4.00**
Cocktail Set, 2 pcs, 6" plate, off center
large indent, 400/39, 3400 Line oys-
ter cocktail glass, 400/91 set **22.50**
Compote
  5", 3-bead arched handle,plain base,
    400/220 . . . . **30.00**
  5½", 4-bead steam, 400/45 . . . . **17.50**
Condiment Set
  3 pcs, two cone shaped oil and vinegar cruets, flat base, 3-bead stoppers, 7" kidney shape tray, 400/29;
  400/2911 set **45.00**
  5 pcs, two pear shaped cruets, 4 oz
  oil, 400/274; 6 oz vinegar, 400/
  275; two bulbous beaded base
  shakers, 400/96; oval beaded tray,
  400/159; 400/2796 set **55.00**
Console Set, 4 pcs
  12" d float bowl, 400/92F; two 2-light
  candleholders, bead center circle,
  400/100; 400/920F set **60.00**
  13" mushroom bowl, 400/92L; two
  mushroom candleholders, 400/86;
  400/8692L **65.00**
Cordial Bottle, 38 oz
  Domed beaded foot, 3 bead stopper,
  400/18 . . . . **65.00**
  Domed foot, handled, crystal body,
  red foot and stopper, 400/82 . . . . . **100.00**
Creamer and Sugar
  3 pcs, individual size, flat bottoms,
  beaded handle, 400/30; kidney
  shape tray, 400/29; 400/29/30 set **22.50**
  Beaded foot, plain handle, c1937–
  40, 400/31 set Crystal **30.00**
  Light blue **50.00**
Cup and Saucer
  After Dinner, slender small cup, 5"
  beaded saucer, 400/77 . . . . **15.00**
  Coffee, slender cup, beaded handle,
  5½" saucer, 400/37 . . . . **8.50**
  Tea, round cup, beaded handle, 5½"
  saucer, 400/35 . . . . **7.50**
Decanter Set, 8 pcs, 26 oz bottle,
beaded foot, round stopper, 400/163;
six trumpet stem, beaded foot cocktail
glasses, 400/190; 400/1630 set **135.00**
Deviled Egg Tray, 11½", twelve indents,
heart shape center handle, 400/154 . **75.00**
Dressing Set, 9" oval beaded tray, 400/
159; beaded foot marmalade jar with
ladle, 400/1989; mustard jar, beaded
foot, 3" spoon, 400/156 . . . . **55.00**
Egg Cup, 6 oz
  Large beads, flat base, 400/19 . . . . . **12.00**
  Small beads, domed foot, 400/19,
  early style **15.00**
Lamp, hurricane, 3 pcs
  Bohemian, 3½" candleholder, rolled
  edge, flashed red, 400/79R; globe
  flashed with cranberry dec, bird

and leaves, gold tracings, 400/79
set **75.00**
Crystal, 3½" candleholder, rolled
edge, 400/79R; peg adapter with
beaded flange, 400/152; chimney,
crimped or plain; 400/152R set . . **50.00**
Lemon Tray, 5½" plate, center handle,
three sections of arched beads, large
top ball, 400/221 . . . . **22.50**
Marmalade Set, 3 pcs, rounded jar, flat
beaded foot, 2-bead finial, notched
beaded edge lid, 3-bead ladle, 400/
8918 set **25.00**
Mayonnaise Set, 3 pcs, 7" beaded un-
derplate, 400/23D; 5½" bowl, 400/
23; 3-bead ladle, 400/23 . . . . **20.00**
Mint Tray, 9", heart shape center han-
dle, 400/149D **20.00**
Mirror, 4½" d, round, beaded edge, two
ball feet, question mark handle on
back for stand, made for I. Rice Co . **65.00**
Mustard Jar, 2 pcs, beaded foot, beaded
edge, notched cov, 3" spoon with
shell bowl, 400/156 . . . . **20.00**
Pastry Tray, 11½", beaded plate, heart
shape center handle, 400/68D **30.00**

Salad Plate, crescent shaped, $48.00.

Pitcher
  16 oz, Lilliputian, beaded foot, plain
  handle, 400/19 . . . . **125.00**
  80 oz, beaded foot, beaded handle,
  plain handle, 400/18 . . . . **110.00**
  80 oz, beaded handle, ice lip, 400/
  24 . . . . **75.00**
Plate, beaded edge
  4", butter or coaster, 400/34 . . . . **4.00**
  6", bread and butter, 400/1D **5.00**
  8", salad, 400/5D **8.00**
  8½", salad, 400/5D **8.00**
  9", luncheon, 400/7D **12.00**
  10", handles, 400/72D **18.50**
  10", dinner, 400 /10D **19.50**
  10½", dinner, 400/10D **19.50**
  12", crimped, handles, 400/145C . . **27.50**
  17", torte, 400/17D **35.00**

Punch Set, 15 pcs, six quart 13″ bowl, 400/20B; 17″ torte plate, cupped edge, 400/20V; twelve cups, beaded handle, 400/37; ladle, 400/91; 400/20 set **200.00**

Relish Dish, beaded edge
  6½″, two parts, two tab handles, 400/54 .... **10.00**
  8″, two parts, two tab handles, 400/268 .... **15.00**
  8½″, round, 4 parts, four tab handles, 400/55 .... **12.50**
  10½″, three parts, two curved dividers, 400/56, early style **27.50**

Salad Set, 4 pcs, 10½″ bowl, 400/75B; 13″ cupped plate, 400/75V; fork and spoon, 5 large bead handles, 400/75; 400/75B set **60.00**

Salt and Pepper Shakers, pr
  Individual Size, beaded foot, chrome tops, 400/109 .... **12.00**
  Round, beaded foot, 8-beads, chrome tops, 400/96 .... **10.00**
  Round, flat beaded foot, 9-beads, plastic tops, 400/96, early style .. **15.00**
  Round, hollow trumpet foot, beaded, chrome tops, 400/190 .... **20.00**

Sauce Boat, 2 pcs, oval pitcher, plain handle, no beads, 9″ oval plate, indent, 400/169D, 400/169 set **80.00**

Stemware
  Bell stems, hollow, beaded, trumpet shaped bowl, 400/190 line
    Cocktail, 4 oz **16.50**
    Goblet, 10 oz **15.00**
    Seafood Icer, 1 pc **30.00**
    Sherbet, 5 oz **12.50**
    Wine, 5 oz **15.00**
  Flared bell tops
    1 bead stem
      Parfait, 6 oz **30.00**
      Sherbet, 5 oz, low **11.50**
      Tumbler, 12 oz, iced tea **15.00**
    4 graduated beads in stem, 3400 Line
      Champagne, 6 oz **12.50**
      Cordial, 1 oz **22.50**
      Goblet, 9 oz **17.50**
      Sherbet, 6 oz **12.50**
      Wine, 5 oz **17.50**

Tid-Bit Server, 3 pcs, nested, heart shaped, 4½″, 5½″, 6¼″, beaded edges, 400/750 .... **25.00**

Tid-Bit Tray, two tier, 7½″ and 10½″ plates joined with metal rod, round handle at top, 400/2701 .... **50.00**

Tumbler
  Beaded base, straight sides, 400/19
    Iced Tea, 12 oz **12.00**
    Juice, 5 oz **8.00**
    Old Fashioned, 7 oz **12.50**
    Sherbet, 5 oz, low **7.50**

    Water, 10 oz **10.00**
    Wine, 3 oz **12.50**
  Domed beaded foot, rounded top, 400/18
    Dessert, 6 oz **18.50**
    Iced Tea, 12 oz **20.00**
    Water, 9 oz **20.00**

Vase
  5¾″, bud, miniature, beaded foot, small beads, fluted top, 400/107 . **25.00**
  7″, rolled top edge, small beads on solid glass arch for handles, 400/87R **30.00**
  8″
    Crimped, beaded top, arched bead handle, 400/87C **22.50**
    Fan, graduated beads joined to sides, 400/87F **22.50**
  8½″
    Bud, ball, narrowed top section slants, handle, 400/227 .... **35.00**
    Bud, trumpet, fluted, 400/28 ..... **20.00**
    Flared top, beaded foot, resembles 3400 stemware, 400/21 .... **35.00**
  10″, straight sides like 400/19 tumblers, 400/22 .... **30.00**

CANDY CONTAINERS

Collecting Hints: Candy containers with original paint, candy and closures command a high premium, but be aware of reproduced parts and repainting. The closure is a critical part of each container; its loss detracts significantly from the value.

Small figural perfumes and other miniatures often are sold as candy containers. Study all reference books available and talk with other collectors before entering the market. Be aware of reproductions.

History: One of the first candy containers was manufactured in 1876 by Croft, Wilbur and Co., confectioners. They filled a small glass Liberty Bell with candy and sold it at the 1876 Centennial Exposition in Philadelphia.

Jeannette, Pennsylvania, was a center for the packaging of candy in containers. Principal firms included Victory Glass, J. H. Millstein, T. H. Stough, and J. C. Crosetti. Earlier manufacturers were West Bros. of Grapeville, Pennsylvania, L. E. Smith of Mt. Pleasant, Pennsylvania, and Cambridge Glass of Cambridge, Ohio.

Containers were produced in shapes that would appeal to children and usually sold for ten cents. Candy containers remained popular until the 1960s when they became too expensive to mass produce.

References: Eikelberner and Agadjanian, *American Glass Candy Containers* (out-of-print); Jennie Long, *An Album of Candy Containers,* privately printed, 1978; Robert Matthews, *Antiquers of Glass Candy Containers,* privately printed, 1970; Mary Louise Stanley, *A Century of Glass Toys,* privately printed, n.d.

Collectors' Club: Candy Containers Collectors of America, Box 184, Lucerne Mines, PA 15754. The organization has a newsletter, *The Candy Gram,* and holds an annual convention with show and sale.

REPRODUCTION ALERT

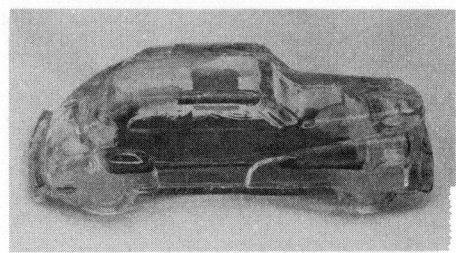

Automobile, streamlined, clear glass, Victory Glass Co, Jeannette, PA, $35.00.

Art Glass, basket, cobalt, ruby and white spatter, clear handled, applied acorn finial **70.00**
Bisque
  Pumpkin, 3" h, man **35.00**
  Witch, 5½" h, holding vegetables . . **35.00**
Cardboard, duck, nodding head **10.00**
Chalk, turkey, metal feet, Germany . . . **25.00**
Cotton, bunny **55.00**
Cotton Batting
  Birds in nest, Japan **60.00**
  Owl, 4", glass eyes **190.00**
Glass
  Airplane
    *Passenger, 4⅜" l, emb, three windows on each side, metal screw cap, tin propeller **175.00**
    Spirit of St Louis, glass body, tin wings and carriage, wheels attached, name lithoed on wings . **385.00**
  Ambulance, Red Cross, 3⅞" l, paper label printed with Red Cross symbol, gold screw cap, printed "T. H. Stough" **80.00**
  Automobile
    Model T **12.00**
    Sedan **35.00**
    *Streamlined, 5" l, pebbled roof, cardboard closure, printed "Victory Glass Inc., Toy Division, Jeannette, PA" **25.00**
  Barney Google **325.00**
  *Basket, hanging, attached chain, emb grape and vine dec, clear glass, gold paint **28.50**

*Bath Tub, 4¾" l, emb "Dolly's Bath Tub," open top, painted white . . . **300.00**
Battleship, 5⅛" l, four guns, cardboard closure, printed "Victory Glass Inc." **25.00**
Bear **35.00**
Bulldog, 4¼" h, sitting, orig paint . . **75.00**
*Chick, 3⅝" h, standing, painted yellow, tin closure **90.00**
Chicken on nest, Millstein **10.00**
Dog **15.00**
Duck on nest **60.00**
Fire Engine, "Little Boiler No 1" **50.00**
Flapper, 10¹³⁄₁₆" h, 3" d round base, paper mask **20.00**
Gun
  *Indian Head revolver, 5⅜" l, emb "Indian Chief" on one side of grip, running horse emb on other side, screw cap closure **75.00**
  Pistol **30.00**
  *Whistling Jim, 3⅝" l, emb "JR 22" on grip, attached whistle, red and white swirl cardboard tube, tin whistle, marked "T. H. Stough" **18.00**
Hen on nest, Millstein **14.00**
Horn **22.00**
Horse and wagon **17.00**
Lantern
  Large **30.00**
  Small **28.00**
Locomotive
  *3½" l, blown bottle, cardboard tube, tin whistle, emb single window on each side, emb "#4" above cowcatcher **18.00**
  *3¾" l, blown bottle, cardboard tube, tin whistle, emb "E3," Stough **25.00**
  *4⁷⁄₁₆" l, emb "999," man in window, screw cap closure **100.00**
Owl, 4⅜" h, stylized feathers, gold tin screw cap **80.00**
Pipe, 10¼" l, Bavarian type style, wicker bowl, amber mouth piece with cork closure **35.00**
*Powder Horn, 4⅞" l, emb "Pat Appd For," metal screw cap **50.00**
Rabbit
  Holding carrot, Stough Co, 1947 . **27.00**
  Seated on egg **125.00**
*Rooster, 5" h, crowing, gold screw cap closure **120.00**
Scottie, Crosetti Co, tin closure, 1962 **3.00**
Ship **30.00**
Spark Plug **125.00**
Swan Boat, 4¼" l, glass rabbit and chick riding in swan boat, tin closure, emb "V. G. Co, Jeannette, PA" **625.00**
Telephone **50.00**
*Trumpet, 5" l, tin mouthpiece, three

raised emb valves, screw cap closure **135.00**
Uncle Sam, hat, milk glass, painted
red, white, and blue, slotted push
in tin closure **65.00**
Vase **7.00**

Battleship, clear glass, 5½" l, $25.00.

Papier Mache
Apple, 3¾" h, singing **190.00**
Black Cat, 4¼" h, sitting on pumpkin,
marked "Germany" **70.00**
Chicken, 4½", red comb, Germany . **60.00**
Duck, 6¾" h, dressed **35.00**
Hen **55.00**
Irishman, 2", top hat and pipe **4.00**
Rabbit
6", beside tub **27.00**
7", standing, glass eyes **35.00**
7½" h, wearing hat and scarf,
painted, glass eyes **20.00**
Reindeer, 8" h, metal antlers, glass
eyes, marked "Germany" **190.00**
Santa's Boot **15.00**
Santa Claus, 8¾" h, red paint, marked
"Pat Appl For" **30.00**
Skull, 2¼" h, marked "Germany" .. **75.00**
Snow White, 5½", 1938 .... **90.00**
Turkey, 7" **45.00**
Plaster, 4" h, turkey, painted, marked
"Germany" **25.00**
Ruby Stained, Royal Crystal, Barret ... **125.00**
Tin
Building, 2¾ x 2", 4 pcs, West Bros,
c1914 .... **40.00**
Football, Germany **12.00**
Snow White & Seven Dwarfs, Walt
Disney Productions **15.00**

CANDY MOLDS

Collecting Hints: Insist on molds in very good or mint condition. The candy shop had to carefully clean molds to insure good impressions each time. Molds with rust or signs of wear rapidly lose value.

History: The chocolate or candy shops of Europe and America used molds to make elaborate

chocolate candy items for holiday and other festive occasions. The heyday for these items was 1880 to 1940. Mass production, competition, and the high cost of labor and supplies brought an end to local candy shops.

The makers of chocolate molds are often difficult to determine. Unlike pewter ice cream molds, makers marks were not always on the mold or were covered by frames. Eppelsheimer & Co. of New York marked many of their molds, either with their name or a design resembling a child's toy shop with "Trade Mark" and "NY."

Many chocolate molds were imported from Germany and Holland and are marked with the country of origin and, in some cases, the mold maker's name.

References: Ray Broekel, *The Chocolate Chronicles*, Wallace-Homestead, 1985; Eleanore Bunn, *Metal Molds*, Collector Books, 1981, out of print; Judene Divone, *Anton Reiche Chocolate Mould Reprint Catalog*, Oakton Hills Publications, 1983.

Museum: Wilbur's Americana Candy Museum, Lititz, PA.

REPRODUCTION ALERT

Clown and Dancer, pewter, clown marked "#17515/#5/Anton/Reichet/Dresden," dancer marked "17514/#2/Anton/Richet/Dresden," 6¾" h, each $30.00.

CHOCOLATE MOLD

Clamp Type, no hinge, two pieces
Basket, 1½ x 4", tin **35.00**
Bulldog, 3" h, tin, seated **40.00**
Cigar, 9¾", tin **20.00**
Dancer, 6¾", pewter, marked "Anton/
Richet/ Dresden" **30.00**
Felix The Cat, tin, arm raised, bowtie **45.00**
Indian, 7½", copper, marked "Germany" **30.00**

Rabbit, 6¼", tin, standing, marked "Made in Germany"	15.00
Rooster, 6¼" h, tin	45.00
Teddy Bear, 11" h, tin, marked "2644"	150.00
Turtle, tin	20.00
Witch, tin	35.00

Frame or Book Type, hinged

Chicks, 5" h, tin, baby in bonnets, two cavities, marked "Made in Germany"	30.00
Cowboy, holding lasso	45.00
Heart, tin, emb cupid, double hinges	60.00
Jenny Lind, 3 parts	75.00
Lamb, tin, small	50.00
Lion, tin	45.00
Rabbit, 8", eyeglasses, paint brushes, and pail, 3 parts	90.00
Rooster, 10" h, tin	135.00
Squirrel, 15" h, tin, bushy tail, acorn	175.00

Tray Type

Car, 3 x 5", four door sedan	12.00
Egg, 15" l, 9 cavities	10.00
Leaf, 2½ x 1½", 30 rect bars	40.00
Santa, 4½" h, 9¼" l, tin, 4 cavities, marked "Dresden/U S Distributor/T C Weyland, NY"	70.00

HARD CANDY

Clamp type, 2 pieces

Chicken on nest, 2 x 7", pewter	50.00
Rooster, 2 x 5", 3 cavities	20.00
Rose, tin, 6 cavities, lollipop	45.00

MAPLE SUGAR

Clamp type, 2 pieces

Dog's head, 3⅞", tin	60.00
Elephant	10.00
Fern	8.00
Girl and dog, 4¼" w, 4½" h, buff clay	15.00
Rabbit, 1¾" w, 2" h, wood, marked "Germany"	35.00

CARNIVAL CHALKWARE

Collecting Hints: Most chalkware pieces appear worn, either because of age or inexpensive production techniques. These factors do not affect the value, provided the piece is whole and has no repairs. Some pieces are decorated with sparkley silver. This adds nothing to the authenticity of the piece nor its value. Carnival chalkware in bank form is considered part of this category.

History: Carnival chalkware, cheerfully painted plaster of paris figures, was manufactured as a cheap decorative, art form. Doll and novelty companies mass produced and sold chalkware for as little as a dollar a dozen. Many independents, mostly immigrants, molded chalkware figures in their garages. They sold directly to carnival booth owners.

Some pieces are marked and dated; most are not. The soft nature of chalkware means it is easily chipped or broken.

Carnival chalkware was marketed for a nominal price at dime stores. However, its prime popularity was as a prize at games of chance located along carnival midways. Concessionaires, e.g., breaking a balloon with a dart, awarded small prizes, called a "build up." As you won, you accumulated the smaller prizes and finally traded them for a larger prize, often a piece of chalkware.

Chalkware ranges in size from three to twenty-four inches. Most pieces were three dimensional. However, some had flat backs, ranging from a plaque format to a half thick figure. Colors depended upon the taste of each individual decorator.

A wide variety of animal, character, and personality figures were made in chalkware. You can find Betty Boop, Sally Rand, Mae West, Shirley Temple, Charlie McCarthy, W. C. Fields, Mickey Mouse, etc. However, you will not find these names on the figures or in the advertising literature of the company who made them. Shirley Temple was the "Smile Doll"; Mae West was the "Mae Doll." Most character dolls were bootlegged, made without permission.

Although some carnival chalkware was made before the 1920s, its peak popularity was in the 1930s and 40s. The use of chalkware prizes declined in the late 1950s and reached its demise in the 1960s.

References: Thomas G. Morris, *The Carnival Chalk Prize*, Prize Publishers, 1985; Ted Sroufer, *Midway Mania*, L-W, Inc., 1985.

Alice The Goon, 10", King Features Syndicate, c1945	60.00
Buddy Lee, 13½", hand painted, cotton cap, c1930	65.00
Captain Marvel, 14½", c1940	50.00
Cat, 10", bank, c1940	10.00
Circus Horse, 10", c1930	18.00

Dog

Bull Dog, 6", Bonzo, English, cap, bottle in mouth, c1930	75.00
Collie, 18", c1940	15.00
Terrier, 8", black and white, rhinestone eyes, c1940	10.00
Donald Duck, long bill	60.00
Dopey, 6", c1937	42.00
Elephant, bank, c1930	12.00
Fan Dancer, 16", marked "Portland Statuary Co," c1935	50.00

Maggie, 9¾" h, fleshtones, maroon dress, blue stockings, black shoes, black hair, blue base, stamp marked "Geo McManus, Manufactured by Ye Towne Gossip, San Francisco," $165.00.

Felix The Cat, 12½"	**65.00**
Ferdinand The Bull, 8½", c1940	**20.00**
Fields, W. C., 6", plaque, top hat and cigar, c1937	**20.00**
Flapper, 10", reclining girl, painted bobbed air, red pants and top, 1920	**100.00**
Gigolo, string holder	**28.00**
Hula Girl, 17", grass skirt, c1940	**20.00**
Johnny, 12", Phillip Morris, marked "Jenkins, 1934"	**60.00**
Lady and Dog, 11¼", full ruffled skirt, floral trim, c1935	**12.00**
Lamb, 7", flat back, marked "Rosemead Novelty Co," c1940	**5.00**
Lamp Doll, 15", movable arms, long marcelled hair, c1920	**125.00**
Lone Ranger	**70.00**
Majorette, 12", marked "El Segundo Novelty Co," 1949	**24.00**
McCarthy, Charlie	**40.00**
Mickey Mouse	**65.00**
Miss America, 15", bathing suit, c1940	**20.00**
Pig, 10", standing, carrying tray, wearing jacket and hat, marked "J. Y. Jenkins, 1937"	**20.00**
Pirate, Captain Kiddo, 1929	**60.00**
Popeye, 18", King Features Syndicate, c1930	**90.00**
Ship, 10", flat back, c1940	**5.00**
Snow White	**45.00**
Squirrel, 12", eating corn, c1940	**7.50**
Stripper, 13½", heart shaped medallion, c1935	**35.00**
Sweater Girl, 11½", c1930	**24.00**
Temple, Shirley, 12", 1935	**60.00**
Valentino, Rudolph, 15", dressed as sheik, c1925	**100.00**
Washington, George, 12", marked "A Incrocci, Pittsburgh, PA," c1940	**60.00**
West, Mae, 14", white dress, c1937 ..	**65.00**
Wimpy, 18", c1940	**32.00**
World War II GI, 6", face in center of victory sign, c1945	**15.00**

CARTES DE VISITE AND CABINET CARDS

Collecting Hints: The vast majority of card photographs were personal portraits and have little collecting value. Most collectors prefer photographs of uncommon subjects, e.g., animals, famous people, circus performers, military, occupational, sports, etc.

The earlier Cartes de Visite are more desirable. The photographer's imprint or logo on a card does add some value. Photographs in excellent condition with no fading, spotting, soiling, or tears bring the highest prices.

History: Cartes de Visite, or calling card, photographs were patented in France in 1854, flourished from 1857 to 1910, and survived into the 1920s. The most common Cartes de Visite was a 2¼ x 3¾", head and shoulder portrait printed on albumen paper and mounted on a card 2½ x 4". Multi-lens cameras were used by the photographer to produce four to eight exposures on a single glass negative plate. A contact print was made from this which would yield four to eight identical photographs on one piece of photographic paper. The photographs would be cut apart and mounted on cards. These cards were put in albums or simply handed out when visiting, similar to today's business cards.

In 1866 the Cabinet Card was introduced in England and shortly thereafter in the United States. It was produced similar to Cartes de Visite, but could have utilized several styles of photographic processes. A Cabinet Card measured 4 x 5" and was mounted on a card 4½ x 6½". Portraits in cabinet size were more appealing because of the larger facial detail and the fact that images could be retouched. By the 1880s the Cabinet Card was as popular as the Cartes de Visite and by the 1890s was produced almost exclusively. Cabinet Cards flourished until shortly after the turn of the century.

References: William C. Darrah, *Cartes de Visite in Nineteenth Century Photography,* William C. Darrah, 1981; George Gilbert, *Collecting Photographica,* Hawthorne Books, Inc., 1976; B. E. C. Howarth-Loomes, *Victorian Photography: An Introduction for Collectors and Connoisseurs,* St. Martin's Press, Inc., 1974; William Welling, *Collectors Guide To Nineteenth Century Photographs,* Collier Books, 1976.

Periodical: *The Photographic Historian,* Box B, Granby, MA 01033.

Collectors' Clubs: American Photographic Historical Society, P. O. Box 9563, Rochester, NY 14604; Photographic Historical Society of New England, Inc., P. O. Box M, West Newton Station, Boston, MA 02165; Western Photographic Collectors Association, P. O. Box 4294, Whittier, CA 90607.

Periodical: *Photograph Collector,* 127 East 59th Street, New York, NY 10022.

Museums: International Museum of Photography, George Eastman House, Rochester, NY; Smithsonian Institution, Washington, D.C.; University of Texas at Austin, Austin, TX

Advisors: Robin and Dave Wheeler.

REPRODUCTION ALERT: Excellent reproductions of Lincoln as well as other Civil War era figures on Cartes de Visite and Cabinet Cards have been made.

Note: Prices listed are for cards in excellent condition. Cards with soiling, staining, tears, or copy photographs are worth about half the prices listed. The categories on the list are for the most common or collectible types; other collecting categories do exist. CDV = Cartes de Visite. CC = Cabinet Card.

Cartes de Visite, Governor Andrew, MA, 3¹⁵⁄₁₆ x 2⅜", $10.00

	CDV	CC
Animals		
Cat	9.00	8.00
Chicken	15.00	12.50
Dog	5.00	5.00
Horse	5.00	5.00
Wild Animal	10.00	8.00
Autographs on CDV or CC (add)		
Actor or Actress	100%	100%

	CDV	CC
Famous People	100%	100%
Lincoln	500.00+	500.00+
Presidents	50.00+	50.00+
Blacks	10.00	10.00
Boats		
Canoe	4.00	3.00
Paddle Wheeler	25.00	20.00
Rowboat	4.00	3.00
US Navy, identified	20.00	25.00
Children		
Cute portraits	1.00	1.00
Twins with doll	18.00	25.00
With animal	7.00	6.00
With doll, must show doll's detail	10.00	10.00
With toy—drum, boat, gun, wagon, etc.	8.00	6.00
Circus Performers and Freaks		
Dwarfs	12.00	12.00
Fat people	12.00	12.00
Giants	12.00	12.00
Midgets	12.00	12.00
Siamese Twins	15.00	15.00
Snake Lady	15.00	15.00
Strongmen	20.00	20.00
Tattooed People	15.00	25.00
Tom Thumb		
Anthony	10.00	10.00
Brady	10.00	10.00
Others	12.00	12.00
Costumes, Native Dress		
Chinese or Japanese	7.00	5.00
Egyptian or Indian	6.00	4.00
Other	5.00	3.00
Engravings, Copies		
Anthony or Brady		
Paintings, famous	1.00	1.00
Religious	1.00	1.00
Statues	1.00	1.00
Unknown photographers		
Paintings, famous	.50	.50
Religious	.50	.50
Statues	.50	.50
World's Fairs and Expositions	8.00	8.00
Gambling, Drinking, Smoking		
Drinkers, glasses and bottles	1.00	1.00
Gamblers, with cards	12.00	12.00
Smokers, with cigars or cigarettes	1.00	1.00
Locomotive, clear, close view	35.00	30.00
Medical/Dental		
Doctor with instruments	15.00	15.00
Operating on patent	25.00	25.00

	CDV	CC
Military Civil War, battle ground scene	35.00	—
Civil War Soldiers, Union (Confederate add 30%)		
Armed, carbine ...	25.00	—
Armed, pistol or knife in belt	35.00	—
Armed, sword.....	15.00	—
Brady, Gardner or Gurney	10.00	—
Holding knife or pistol in front ...	45.00	—
Unarmed portrait ..	6.00	—
Civil War Officer or General, Union (Confederate add 30%)		
Brady, Gardner or Gurney	18.00	—

Cabinet Photo, trick photograph, five images of same person, Bosworth, Springfield, MA, 6½ x 4¼", $8.00.

	CDV	CC
Custer by Brady or Gardner........	175.00	175.00
Grant, by Brady or Gurney	35.00	35.00
Sherman or Sheridan by Brady ...	25.00	25.00
Foreign Soldiers		
Armed, carbine ...	10.00	8.00
Armed, sword.....	5.00	4.00
In uniform........	8.00	3.00
Indian Wars		
Armed, carbine ...	18.00	15.00
Armed, sword.....	8.00	6.00
Soldier..........	4.00	3.00
Nudes, Risque		
Female, bare breasted.........	15.00	15.00
Female, frontal view .	25.00	25.00
Male..............	35.00	35.00
Objects		
Clocks	7.00	6.00
Flowers	2.00	2.00
Furniture	7.00	6.00
Still Life...........	3.00	2.00
Occupational		
Factories		
Exterior	8.00	6.00
Interior..........	12.00	12.00
Workers, interior ..	15.00	13.00
Firemen, Policemen in uniform........	8.00	7.00
Musician, instrument.	7.00	6.00
Workers		
In work clothes ...	1.00	1.00
With tools........	10.00	10.00
Outdoor, U.S. Subjects		
Building, single	7.00	6.00
Church............	2.00	2.00
Disaster or flood damage	10.00	10.00

	CDV	CC
House	3.00	3.00
Scenic view	5.00	4.00
School	2.00	2.00
Streets		
Busy with people..	12.00	10.00
Quiet	9.00	8.00
Western, people...	18.00	15.00
Town	9.00	8.00
People, Famous		
Actresses, Actors		
Anthony, Brady, Falk, Gutekunst, Mora or Sarony ...	6.00	6.00
Unknown Photographers........	4.00	4.00
Artists..............	15.00	12.00
Bernhardt, Sarah	20.00	24.00
Composers	15.00	12.00
Grant, by Anthony or Brady............	35.00	30.00
Greely, Horace......	30.00	40.00
Langtry, Lillie	20.00	20.00
Lincoln, by Anthony, Brady or Gardner..	150.00	150.00
Lincoln, engraving or copy...........	10.00	10.00
Painters	15.00	12.00
Presidents, by Anthony, Brady or Gurney	25.00	20.00
Political Figures	10.00	8.00
State Political Figures	5.00	5.00
Walt Whitman	30.00	40.00
Writers.............	15.00	12.00
Photographers, Famous		
Anthony............	3.00	3.00
Bierstadt	1.00	1.00
Bogardus...........	1.00	1.00
Brady..............	6.00	6.00
Fredericks	1.00	1.00

	CDV	CC		CDV	CC
Gardner............	3.00	3.00	Sports		
Gurney	3.00	3.00	Baseball		
Gutekunst	1.00	1.00	Amateur, player or		
Hawes, J. J.........	6.00	6.00	team...........	20.00	15.00
Sarony	1.00	1.00	Professional, player		
Whipple	1.00	1.00	or team		
Wing	1.00	1.00	Individuals	30.00	25.00
Photographers, Women,			With Equipment...	45.00	40.00
cards stamped with			Bikers		
name or studio......	1.00	1.00	High wheel bike ..	15.00	24.00
Photographic			Portrait..........	8.00	8.00
Cards, interesting ad			Boxer.............	20.00	25.00
on back..........	1.00	1.00	Fisherman, rod.....	7.00	6.00
Person, camera as			Gymnast	25.00	30.00
prop.............	15.00	12.00	Hunter, rifle	8.00	7.00
Person, stereoscope..	8.00	8.00	Mountain Climber ...	3.00	3.00
Photographer with			Skaters		
camera..........	150.00	150.00	Ice skater, portrait .	5.00	4.00
Photograph Gallery			Roller skater,		
Exterior	30.00	25.00	portrait........	5.00	4.00
Interior, cameras ..	50.00	50.00	Wedding, bride &		
Traveling Photograph			groom	3.00	3.00
Studio	60.00	60.00	Western, west of Missis-		
			sippi River		
			Cowboys		
			Armed	35.00	35.00
			Dude, Kansas City,		
			c1860	50.00	65.00
			Typical western		
			wear..........	20.00	15.00
			Indians		
			Armed	50.00	45.00
			Full dress........	35.00	30.00
			Geronimo	65.00	65.00
			Group	45.00	40.00
			Sitting Bull	65.00	65.00

Cartes de Visite, group portrait, eleven people, F J Weber photographer, Erie, PA, 4⅛ x 2½", $3.00.

	CDV	CC
Portraits		
1 person	.10	.10
2 or 3 people	.15	.15
4 or 5 people	.50	.50
6 or more people....	1.00	1.00
Foreign portraits.....	.10	.10
Hand tinted portraits.	3.00	3.00
Twins..............	1.00	1.00
Triplets.............	1.00	1.00
Uglies	1.00	1.00
Post Mortem		
Memorial card, photo............	6.00	5.00
Memorial card, no photo............	—	1.00
Revenue Stamp On Back, common subject only	1.00	1.00

CARTOON CHARACTERS

Collecting Hints: A vast majority of collectible categories yield an object related to a cartoon character. Cartoon characters appeared in advertising, books, comics, movies, television, and as a theme in thousands of products designed for children.

Concentrate on one character or the characters from a single strip. Most collectors tend to focus on a cartoon character that was part of their childhood. Another method is to focus on the work of a single artist. Several artists produced more than one cartoon character.

The most popular cartoon characters of the early period are Barney Google, Betty Boop, Dick Tracy, Gasoline Alley, Li'l Abner, Little Orphan Annie, and Popeye. The movie cartoons produced Bugs Bunny, Felix the Cat, Mighty

Mouse, Porky Pig, and a wealth of Disney characters. The popular modern cartoon characters include Garfield, Peanuts and Snoopy.

History: The first daily comic strip was Bud Fisher's Mutt and Jeff which appeared in 1907. By the 1920s the Sunday comics became an American institution. One of the leading syndicators was Captain Joseph Patterson of the News-Tribune. Patterson, who partially conceived and named "Moon Mullins" and "Little Orphan Annie," worked with Chester Gould to develop "Dick Tracy" in the early 1930s.

Walt Disney and others pioneered the movie cartoon, both in short and full length form. Disney and Warner Brothers characters dominated the 1940 to 1960 period. With the advent of television the cartoon characters of Hanna-Barbera, e.g., the Flintstones, added a third major force. Independent studios produced cartoon characters for the television and characters multiplied rapidly. By the 1970s the trend was to produce strips with human characters, rather than the animated animals of the earlier period.

A successful cartoon character created many spin-offs. Comic books and paperback books, earlier Big Little Books, followed quickly. Games, dolls, room furnishings, and other materials which appealed to children are marketed. The secondary market products may produce more income for the cartoonist than the drawings themselves.

References: Bob Bennett, *Collecting Original Cartoon Art,* Wallace-Homestead, 1987; Maurice Horn and Richard Marshall (eds.), *World Encyclopedia of Comics,* Chelsea House Publications; David Longest, *Character Toys and Collectibles, First Series,* (1984) and *Second Series,* (1987), Collector Books.

Museum: The Museum of Cartoon Art, Port Chester, NY.

See: Disneyana and index for specific character.

Andy Panda, Walter Lantz artist
  Big Little Book, *Andy Panda And The Mad Dog Mystery,* Whitman, #1431 . . . . **40.00**
  Pinback Button, 1¼", black, white, and red, bright yellow ground, slogan "New Funnies/Andy Panda" . **20.00**
  Plaque, 7", ceramic, figural, multicolored, marked "Napco Ceramics," 1958 . . . . **55.00**
Archie, Bob Montana artist
  Doll, cloth, 18" h **15.00**
  Figure, 5", Syrocco, painted, brown military uniform and hat, 1944 . . . **12.00**
  Pinback Button, 1½", Member Archie Club, blue, white, and orange, 1950s **15.00**

Barney Google, Billy DeBeck artist
  Book, *Barney Google and Spark Plug,* Cupples & Leon, 1925, Billy De-Beck artist, 10 x 10", cardboard cov, black and white comic strips **75.00**
  Doll, 17", Snuffy Smith, stuffed, felt, movable head, black floppy hat, orange shirt, green trousers, green felt suspender, amber and black eyes, 1930s **150.00**
  Game, Barney Google An' Snuffy Smith, Milton Bradley, 1963, 16" sq board, full color, boxed **35.00**
  Pinback Button, 13⁄16", litho, Kellogg's Pep Button
    Barney Google **12.00**
    Snuffy Smith **12.00**
  Toy, 4" h, 5" l, Spark Plug, jigsawed wood figure, identical design on each side, 1925 copyright, DeBeck signature **165.00**
Betty Boop, Max Fleischer artist
  Charm, 1", celluloid, tinted, 1930s, Japanese **35.00**
  Figure
    3", celluloid, movable arms, holding diecut celluloid violin and bow, short red dress, 1930s . . . **165.00**
    3¾", bisque, red cap, soft blue coat, purple belt, red shoes, white body, black and white eyes, red eyebrows, name stamped on back, marked "Made In Japan," and Fleischer Studios copyright, 1930s **300.00**
  Pin, 1½", silvered brass, Betty, small link chain attached to silver Scotty dog, 1930s **60.00**
  Playing Cards **70.00**
  Valentine, mechanical, 3½ x 4½", diecut round eyes, 1940 . . . . **35.00**
Blondie, Murat (Chic) Young artist
  Book, *25 Years With Blondie,* 1958, Chic Young artist, 8 x 11", soft cover, 96 pgs, black and white comic strip reprints **18.00**
  Coloring Book, 8½ x 11", 1954, Dell Publishing, unused **20.00**
  Greeting Card, 5 x 6", birthday for wife, full color, Dagwood illus, Hallmark, 1939 copyright **15.00**
  Pinback Button, 13⁄16", litho, Kellogg's Pep Button
    Blondie **12.00**
    Dagwood **12.00**
  Valentine, 3 x 4", diecut, unauthorized illus of Alexander and Daisy, 1940s **12.00**
Bringing Up Father, George McManus
  Figure, 5" h, Jiggs, wood, jointed, black outfit, white bib, brown shoes, fleshtone, red peg wood

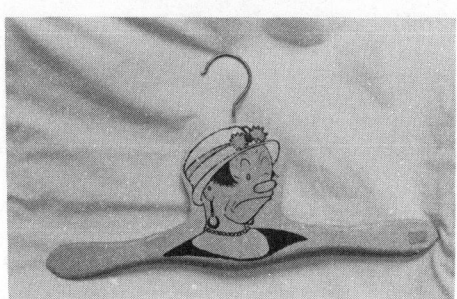

Maggie, wooden hanger, pink ground, multicolored illus, 15 x 8¾", $25.00.

nose, brown wood peg cigar, orange wood cane, name and copyright symbol stamped on front, 1930s **85.00**
Figure Set, Bringing Up Father, three 4" painted bisque figures, each marked "King Features copyright," "Made In Japan," and mold number, 4½ x 5 x ½" multicolored orig litho paper box with 1934 copyright **150.00**
Movie Poster, 40½ x 80", three sheet, Monogram Pictures, Morgan Litho Corp, 1940s **75.00**
Pinback Button
¾", black, white, and red, Joplin Globe, 1930s **18.00**
1", black, white, and red, Detroit Times, back paper adv contest . **20.00**
Salt and Pepper Shakers, pr, 2½", figural, Maggie and Jiggs, orange china set holder, marked "Made In Japan," 1930s **65.00**
Bugs Bunny, Leon Schlesinger, Warner Bros
Animation Cel, 10½ x 12½", acetate sheet, full color 6 x 7½" art, gray and white body, Warner Bros, 1970s **65.00**
Bank, pot metal **47.00**
Doll, cloth, 18" h **15.00**
Game, "Bugs Bunny Adventure Game," 9½ x 19 x 1½", Milton Bradley, 1961 copyright, 16 x 18½" game board, unused **18.00**
Paint Book, 8½ x 11", Whitman, 1944, unused **12.00**
Casper The Friendly Ghost, Harvey Comics
Pinback Button
1³⁄₁₆", litho, Kellogg's Pep Button . **12.00**
1⅜", black, green litho, Los Angeles Evening Herald & Express, serial number, c1930 .... **20.00**
Puppet, 8", hand, white cloth body,

vinyl head, eyes and tongue move, 1950s **25.00**
Dan Dunn, Norman Marsh artist
Big Little Book, *Dan Dunn, Secret Operative 48 and the Border Smugglers,* Whitman Better Little Book, 1938, 432 pgs **20.00**
Pinback Button
1³⁄₁₆", litho, black and white, slogan "Saturday Daily News" in red, 1940s **15.00**
1¼", litho, Philadelphia Evening Ledger, black jacket, purple tie and hat, bright orange ground, "I'm Operative 48," orig back paper, 1930s **65.00**
Dennis The Menace, Hank Ketcham artist
Book, Hank Ketcham, *Dennis The Menace,* Holt & Co, 1952 copyright, first edition, single black and white panel cartoons, 6¼ x 9¼", full color hard cover, 62 pgs **20.00**
Creamer, marked "F & F Mold & Die Works" **15.00**
Puzzle, frame, Whitman, 1960 ..... **18.00**
Dick Tracy, Chester Gould
Big Little Book, *Dick Tracy Encounters Facey,* Whitman, #2001, Paul S Newman, 1967 .... **8.50**
Candy Bar Wrapper, color picture, premium offer, 1950s **10.00**
Figure
Bonnie Braids, plastic, orig store card, 1951 .... **15.00**
Dick Tracy, rubber, 1969 .... **10.00**
Game, Dick Tracy Master Detective Board Game, Selright, 1961 ..... **18.00**
Playing Cards, 1934, MIB **35.00**
Toy, two way radio set, MIB, 1950 . **32.00**
Felix The Cat, Pat Sullivan artist
Advertising Brochure, 10½ x 16½", glossy paper, color ad, text for Kodatoy Film Projector and Theater, Eastman Kodak Co, late 1920s ... **60.00**
Clicker, tin litho, Germany, 1929 ... **25.00**
Figure
2", painted white metal, wire spring mounted head, holds tin red parasol, black and white, name on chest, late 1920s **100.00**
4", wood, stiff cardboard ears, jointed, label on tummy, foot with 75% of orig patent label of June 23, 1925, Schoenhut **125.00**
Pencil Box, 2½ x 4¾ x ⅜", cardboard, American Pencil Co, black and white Felix, full color ground, Pat Sullivan copyright, full color scene of children doing artwork of peacock near Washington Monument on reverse, early 1930s **45.00**

Foxy Grandpa, papier mache and wood, Grandpa on horse, blue suit, red tie, flesh tone head, white shirt, 7", $125.00.

Foxy Grandpa, C. E. Schultze, artist
Bookmark, aluminum, heart shape .   **30.00**
Cartoon Book, *The Latest Larks of Foxy Grandpa*, M. A. Donohue & Co, 1905, 9½ x 15½", cardboard cov, 24 pgs, full color comic strips   **50.00**
Valentine, 6 x 10", diecut, Tuck, c1905 ....   **18.00**
Whistle, clay, figural **40.00**
Gasoline Alley, Frank King artist
Nodder, 2¾", bisque, Skeezix, Germany **48.00**
Pinback Button, ¹³⁄₁₆", litho, Uncle Walt, Kellogg's Pep Button **12.00**
Toothbrush Holder, 5" h, Uncle Walt, glossy brown hair, yellow shirt, red bow tie, blue pants, name, "Feature Artists Syndicate," and "Made In Japan" on back, 1930s **100.00**
Gumps, The, Sidney Smith artist
Figure, 4", bisque, Andy Gump **48.00**

Andy Gump, pinback button, Schutter's Old Gold Candy, Gump Charities, litho tin, mfg by Parisian Novelty Co, 1", $8.00.

Mirror and Brush, combination, 3¼" d, Andy Gump **45.00**
Pinback Button
¹³⁄₁₆", "Uncle Bim," litho, Kellogg's Pep Button **15.00**
1¼", "Andy Gump For President," black and white Andy, red bow tie, dark blue rim inscribed "Andy Gump Nite, Wed 27th Midway Gardens," orig paper back text **30.00**
Planter, 2½ x 3 x 5", painted bisque, Andy and Min, brown derby, light blue coat, brown trousers, light green dress, names and "Feature Artists Syndicate" on back, 1930s   **80.00**
Happy Hooligan, Fred Opper, artist
Ashtray, 5½", porcelain, multicolored, shoe beside Happy holds matches, striker on base **70.00**
Lapel Stud, 1", diecut, white metal, silvered, dark blue trim, early 1900s **35.00**
Nodder, 7½", composition **25.00**
Pinback Button, 1¼", multicolored
Are You Goin' Or Comin' To The Shoemakers Fair Fitzhugh Hall, gray pants, green jacket, red ground **30.00**
New York Sunday American Newspaper, black, white, and dark pink, back paper relating to contest **28.00**
Harold Teen, Carl Ed artist
Book, *The Adventures of Harold Teen*, Cupples & Leon, 1931, Carl Ed artist, 7 x 8½", 32 pgs, full color cov, comic strip reprints **50.00**
Game, 7½ x 13½" box, spinner and orig tokens, 1930s **15.00**
Pinback Button, ¹³⁄₁₆", litho, Kellogg's Pep Button **12.00**
Ukulele, 20" h, painted pressed wood, metal tuning keys, gut strings, Teen characters around opening and bridge, art by Carl Ed, orig carrying case, 1930s **350.00**
Henry, Carl Anderson artist
Pinback Button, 1⅜", black, green litho, Los Angeles Evening Herald & Express, serial number, c1930 .   **20.00**
Toy, squeeze, 9¾", vinyl **24.00**
Joe Palooka, Ham Fisher
Air Pump, 8", litho, aluminum, marked "Joe Palooka Athletic Pump" **30.00**
Lunch Box, tin, litho, 1948 ....   **45.00**
Pinback Button, ¹³⁄₁₆", litho, multicolored, marked "Comic Togs," **15.00**
Puppet, hand **18.00**
Krazy Kat, George Harriman artist
Doll, 18" h, stuffed, felt, blue, diecut

white felt face, white felt feet, tail missing, orig tag marked "Manufactured Under Special Arrangement With Geo. Harriman," patent application Averill Mfg, Co, NY, c1920 .... **450.00**

Mask, paper, Einson-Freeman Co, 1930s **75.00**

Pin

1", brass, enamel, black and white, holding sign "So's Your Old Man" **65.00**

1½", brass, enamel, black and white, green eyes, walking, playing banjo **80.00**

Pinback Button

⅞"

Charles Mintz's Krazy Kat–Columbia Pictures, black, white, and red litho, 1930s **30.00**

Hit Him With A Brick, white illus, dark blue ground, back paper adv for Perfection Cigarettes **20.00**

1⅜", black, green litho, Los Angeles Evening Herald & Express, serial number, c1930 .... **20.00**

Li'l Abner, Al Capp artist

Charm, Shmoo, 1", bright silver plastic, 1940s **15.00**

Hair Barrette, 2⅛", oval, brass, diecut, 1940s **18.00**

Pinback Button, 1³⁄₁₆", litho, black and white, slogan "Saturday Daily News" in red, 1940s

Li'l Abner **15.00**

Mammy Yochum **15.00**

Planter, china, manuf by Pearce, 1952 Al Capp copyright

Mammy Yochum, 2½ x 4 x 3½", white face, black eyes, glossy black cap **50.00**

Pappy Yochum, 3 x 5 x 3", fleshtone face, brown eyes, white hair **50.00**

Ring, Lucky, Shmoo, brass, adjustable, mint luster, 1940s **40.00**

Tumbler, 5", clear glass, Li'l Abner running with two Shmoos, 1949 . **8.50**

Little Lulu, Marjorie Henderson Buell artist

Big Little Book, Little Lulu, Alvin, and Tubby, Whitman, #1429, 1947 .. **30.00**

Doll, 15" h, stuffed cloth, stuffed fabric head, black felt and yarn hair, western outfit, 1940s **80.00**

Mask, 11 x 12", diecut, stiff paper, Lulu and Tubby, Kleenex Tissues premium, 1950s, pr **40.00**

Picture, 8 x 10", full color, Lulu and surprised dog leaping through paper hoop into its bath water, 1944

Marjorie H Buell copyright, 10 x 12" white wood frame **80.00**

Puzzle, 11½ x 15", frame tray, multicolored, Lulu and Tubby on her tricycle, Whitman, 1954 Marjorie Henderson Buell copyright .. **30.00**

Tumbler, 4¾", clear, bright red and black Lulu skipping rope, elephant "Baldy" on reverse, Buell copyright **60.00**

Mutt and Jeff, Bud Fisher

Bank, cast iron **125.00**

Blotter, 4 x 9", black, white, and red, cardboard, adv silent film cartoons, 1920s **18.00**

Book, Mutt & Jeff, Cupples & Leon, 1922, Bud Fisher artist, Famous Comic Book series #8, 10 x 10", 48 pgs, black and white comic strip reprints **35.00**

Pinback Button, 1³⁄₁₆", litho, black and white, slogan "Saturday Daily News" in red, 1940s

Jeff **15.00**

Mutt **15.00**

Moon Mullins, Frank Willard artist

Advertising, transfer picture, Kayo Chocolate, 5 x 7", full color diecut of Kayo, 1930s **35.00**

Marble, ⅝" d, glass, Kayo portrait center, white, dark green spot, name in black, 1930s **90.00**

Nodder, 3⅞", bisque, Moon Mullins, Germany **60.00**

Pinback Button, 1³⁄₁₆", litho, Kayo, Kellogg's Pep Button **12.00**

Toothbrush Holder, 5", bisque, Moon Mullins **55.00**

Peanuts, Charles Schulz artist

Pen Holder, Snoopy **65.00**

Pinback Button, 1¾"

Charlie Brown and Snoopy, black lettering, bright yellow ground, issued by Simon Simple, 1960s **12.00**

Snoopy, black lettering, light green ground, issued by Simon Simple, 1960s **10.00**

Snoopy For President, red, white, and blue, 1966 copyright **18.00**

Popeye, E. C. Segar artist

Bank, 3 x 4 x 4½", metal, litho, multicolored, marked "Popeye Daily Quarter Bank," Kalon Co, 1950s **100.00**

Charm, 1¼", celluloid, small brass loop, bright tinted orange, pink, black, and green, Japanese, 1930s **20.00**

Game, card, 5 x 6½ x 1", Whitman, 1937 .... **40.00**

Magazine, Children's Playmate, Dec 1958, 2 pgs comic strip by Sims & Saboly, 6 x 9", 62 pgs **20.00**

Pin, 1½", silvered brass, enameled,

blue, black, and red outfit, white
cap, 1930s **65.00**
Pinback Button
1¼", black, white, red, and fleshtone, New York Evening Journal,
back paper with adv text for contest **20.00**
1⅜", black, green litho, Los Angeles Evening Herald & Express, serial number, c1930 .... **20.00**
Valentine, 1943 .... **5.00**
Wallpaper, 10 foot roll, 1940 ...... **125.00**
Porky Pig, Leon Schlesinger, Warner
Bros
Animation Cel, 8 x 10¼", Porky in
Robin Hood outfit, holding ball
over head, 1940s **50.00**
Big Little Book, *Porky Pig And His
Gang*, Whitman, #1404 .... **35.00**
Container, 9½" h, liquid soap,
molded vinyl plastic body, hard
plastic removable head, 1960s ... **18.00**
Toy, 5½", rubber, marked "Sun Rub-
ber Co" **45.00**
Skippy, Percy Crosby artist
Mug, whistle handle, silver plated,
drawings and dialogue on sides .. **48.00**
Pinback Button, 1", black, white, and
red, Detroit Times, back paper adv
contest **20.00**
Smitty, Walter Berndt artist
Book, *Smitty*, Cupples & Leon, 1928,
Walter Berndt, artist, 7 x 8½", 32
pgs, full color cov, comic strip re-
prints **50.00**
Marble, ⅝" d, glass, portrait center,
yellow, light green streak, name in
black, 1930s **90.00**
Nodder, bisque **85.00**
Pinback Button, 1³⁄₁₆", litho, Kellogg's
Pep Button **12.00**
Wrist Watch, gray aged dial, black,
white, red, and green figure, Ne-
whaven Clock Co, 1935, over-
wound, band missing, orig case .. **175.00**
Winnie Winkle, Martin Branner artist
Book, *Winnie Winkle and the Dia-
mond Heirlooms*, Whitman, 1946,
hard cov, dust jacket **12.00**
Cigar Box, 3½ x 5½ x 9¼", Winnie,
picture on lid, artist M. M. Branner
signature, 1930s **40.00**
Key Chain, ¾", cube, characters on
each side, 1940s **15.00**
Pinback Button, 1³⁄₁₆", litho, Kellogg's
Pep Button
Ma **12.00**
Rip **12.00**
Woody Woodpecker, Walter Lantz artist
Book, *Woody Woodpecker's Peck of
Trouble*, Whitman, 1951, 6 x 6½",
hard cov **5.00**

Doll, 24", stuffed, cloth, 1¼"
multicolored celluloid button inscribed "My Pal!" on chest, red
body, white corduroy feet and
hands, white vinyl bib, felt face accents, bright yellow beak, 1950s . **90.00**
Kazoo, 7", plastic, red, orig instructions, MIB, 1950s **5.00**
Night Lamp, 20", hard plastic, figural,
electrical, vivid colors, 1974 Walter Lantz copyright **40.00**
Wall Plaque, 5½ x 7½", plaster,
glossy, multicolored, holding yellow glazed hat in one hand, white
suitcase in other, 1956 Walter Lantz
copyright **55.00**
Yellow Kid, R. F. Outcault artist
Cigar Box, 5½ x 9 x 4", wood, hinged
lid with lightly engraved portrait of
Kid, similar picture and title int.,
orig red label "Smoke Yellow Kid
Cigars, Manuf'd by D R Fleming,
Curwensville, PA," early 1900s ... **300.00**
Ice Cream Mold, 4¾", hinged, full
figure **185.00**
Pinback Button, issued by High Ad-
miral Cigarettes, c1896
No. 3, Kid standing in barrel, Mrs.
Murphy mends clothes **15.00**
No. 4, Kid with mandolin **20.00**
No. 7, Kid with goat **22.00**
No. 14, Kid with large white collar,
dressed to go to ball **25.00**
No. 24, Kid as accountant, pencil
behind ear, large strip of adding
machine tape **22.00**
No. 84, Kid hanging out wash, "Say-
Monday Iz De Tooghest Day Ob
De Week" **35.00**
No. 138, Kid with US flag **25.00**

CASINO COLLECTIBLES

Collecting Hints: A collection of modern casino
collectibles can be assembled very modestly.
This is one reason why there has been a growing
interest in this field.

Many collectors display poker chips of the various casinos in albums similar to those used by
coin collectors. Matchcovers can be assembled
in the same manner. Often, just the Ace of
Spades from a casino deck is mounted in an
album, as they are the most ornate and contain
pertinent information. The back of the casino
cards generally are plain, unless a souvenir deck
is purchased from the casino gift shop.

History: Most American and European casinos
offered souvenirs to gambling tourists. In addi-

tion, many gamblers were able to sneak out a few items not normally offered as souvenirs.

The earliest casinos in America were privately owned clubs known as gambling dens. The better ones were beautifully decorated and were referred to as "Splendid Hells" by reformers. These clubs often featured free meals, drinks and cigars to all players.

The European casinos such as those at Monaco and Monte Carlo were the summer stomping ground for the wealthy. Fortunes were won or lost at the turn of a card.

Collectors seek and display items from these early casinos, as well as collectibles from the modern casinos of America. Poker chips, decks of cards, dice, and marked souvenirs (gambling games, ashtrays, matchcovers, etc.) are just some of the items which are available.

Deck of Cards, Harrah's Reno and Lake Tahoe, diamond back, US Playing Card Co, $15.00.

Cards, Decks
  Monte Carlo, c1915, MIB 15.00
  Sierra Sids, Sparks Winnemucca,
    Mesquite, Nevada, MIB 15.00
Dice
  C. T. Club, ½", ivory, c1880 ....   75.00
  Flamingo Club, ¾", magenta, white
    pips 20.00
  Loew's Monte Carlo, ¾", emb, ma-
    genta, plastic case 15.00
  Sahara Casino, Las Vegas, magenta,
    modern 6.00
  Sands Hotel, Las Vegas 12.00
Poker Chip
  Duff & Co, ivory , emb "D" on both
    sides, c1880 ....   25.00
  Long's Club, square edged roulette
    chip, composition 5.00
  S.S. Rex Oceanliner Casino, white
    with black letters, 5 in center, or-
    ange border, 1½" d, c1930, pr ..   42.00
  Tango, $100, Long Beach, CA, 1½"
    d, dark blue, inlay of gambling
    ship, c1930 ....   40.00

Miscellaneous
  Apron, The Southern Club, Hot
    Springs, Ark, black, yellow writing,
    elastic strap 25.00
  Book, *Pioneer Nevada,* published by
    Harolds Club, Reno, 1951, 204 pgs   60.00
  Calendar, Clicquot Club, 1953 .....   25.00
  Crap Layout, Horseshoe Club, printed
    with three colors, c1930 ....   75.00
  Magazine, Casino & Cabaret Maga-
    zine, August, 1981 ....   5.00
  Postcard
    American Casino, slot machines,
      pre-1940 ....   10.00
    Reno Casino, int. scene, unused .   25.00
  Roulette Watch, Souvenir of Monte
    Carlo, tin case, slow spinning in-
    dicator, light weight 75.00
  Roulette Wheel, 8" d, wood and
    metal, four prong spinner, cloth
    layout, maker stamped on bottom   35.00
  Slot Machine, floor model
    Bally 10¢ Super Bars, 64 x 24", four
      reel, reverse painted glass 175.00
    Jennings 10¢ Standard Chief, wood
      and chrome case, three reel, pay-
      out card 775.00
    Manhattan 25/30¢ Dual Play, three
      reels 100.00

CAT COLLECTIBLES

Collecting Hints: Cat related material can be found in almost all collecting categories. Advertising items, dolls, figurines, folk art, jewelry, needlework, plates, postcards, and stamps are just a few of them. Because of the popularity of cats, modern objects d'feline constantly are appearing on the market. However, as cat collectors becomes more experienced, their interests are more with antique, rather than newer items.

The cat collector competes with collectors from other areas. Chessie, the C & O Railroad cat, is collected by railroad and advertising buffs. Felix is a favorite of toy and cartoon character enthusiasts.

Because cat collectors are attracted to all cat items, all breeds, and realistic or abstract depictions, they tend to buy too many items. It is best to specialize. Money and display space extend only so far; time for research is limited. Three of the most popular new areas of cat collecting are cat cards, calendars, and stickers.

Throughout the 1980s cats have grown in popularity as the pet of choice and along with this has grown the love of collecting cat items. The new and newer (secondary) market, tomorrow's collectibles, has grown by leaps and bounds. Some cat pieces bought ten years ago are showing considerable price increases. As true antique cats become rare and costly buy what you can, but also concentrate on quality, limited editions, and original pieces in the current market.

History: Cats always have been on a roller coaster ride between peaks of favoritism and valleys of superstition. In ancient Egypt cats were deified. Cats were feared by Europeans in the Middle Ages. Customs and rituals bore down brutally on felines. Cats became associated with witchcraft, resulting in tales and superstitions which linger to the present. This lack of popularity is why antique cat items are scarce.

Cats appear in TV programs, movies, cartoons, and many advertising ads in addition to those for cat food. Garfield remains popular; Felix has made a come back; and, a new feline, Motley, is emerging. Objects associated with these modern cartoon cats are tomorrow's collectibles.

References: Bruce Johnson, *American Catalogue: The Cat in American Folk Art*, Avon Books, 1976; Alice Muncaster and Ellen Yanow; *The Cat Made Me Buy It*, Crown, 1984; Alice L. Muncaster and Ellen Yanow Sawyer, *The Cat Sold It!*, Crown, 1986; Silvester and Mobbs, *The Cat Fancier: A Guide To Catland Postcards*, Longman Group, 1982.

Collectors' Club: Cat Collectors, 31311 Blair Drive, Warren, MI 48092. *CATTALK* (bimonthly).

Museum: The Metropolitan Museum of Art, New York, NY; British Museum, London, England; The Cat Museum, Basel, Switzerland.

Advisor: Marilyn Dipboye.

REPRODUCTION ALERT

Painting on porcelain, girl with cat, 10 x 8", $1,400.00.

Art

   Chromolithograph, 21 x 25", "Mixing the colors" unsigned, "Anxious Moments" sgd Brunhilde, framed, c1898–90, pr **425.00**

   Drawing, 9 x 9", "Fat Cat," pen and ink, double matted, textured frame, under glass, sgd George Engle ... **30.00**

   Etching, 13 x 17", "Sweet Tooth," colored, framed under glass, Meta Pluckebaum, c1930 .... **50.00**

   Photograph, 12 x 18", black and white, cat face close up, B. Doyle Peterson, dated 1969 .... **20.00**

   Portfolio, four prints, James Lockhart, Walden Press, USA, 1960 copyright **25.00**

   Poster, 16 x 22", adv, "Puss 'N' Boots" (Le Chat Botte), mounted on canvas, Jules Cheret, c1890 ..... **450.00**

   Print, 16 x 16", light wood frame with reddish inner frame, c1940

     Chessie **50.00**

     Chessie with family **50.00**

Ashtray

   4½" l, cat and dog in black shoe, "Souvenir Lemington, Canada," marked "Made in Japan" **25.00**

   5" l, ceramic, crouching cat, front paws extended, brown, marked "Made in China" **20.00**

   8" l, crystal, dish set into back, Velmeir **44.00**

Book

   Felix The Cat, Saalfield, 1910 ...... **25.00**

   Kittens and Cats, Eulalie Osgood Grover, Houghton Mifflin Co, 1911 **20.00**

   Puss 'N' Boots, Louis Wain illus, c1908 .... **30.00**

   Pussy Paint Book, figural, 15 pgs, Saalfield, 1915 .... **35.00**

Children's Dishes

   Creamer, 3" h, transfer of two cats and children's toys, German, c1900 .. **30.00**

   Cup and Saucer, cat and dog **60.00**

   Plate, bone china, three black cats, gold border, marked "Allerton," c1920 .... **65.00**

   Tea Set, 15 pcs, marked "Warwick" **30.00**

Creamer

   Orange and white, black cat handle, 5¼" h, marked "Erphila Fayence Germany" **24.00**

   Siamese, figural, red bow, tail handle, 5" h **12.00**

   Sapphire blue and light cinnamon, gray cat handle, marked "Royal Bayreuth" **215.00**

Fairy Lamp, 4 x 4", cat, owl, and dog, bisque, glass eyes **250.00**

Figurine

   2½" h

     Black cat on gold tassel pillow, Dresden mark **140.00**

     White and brown cat on green and gold pillow, Chelsea type, anchor mark **120.00**

3" h, cat on green pillow with gold tassel, bisque, white, marked "Cappe, Italy" **110.00**

5¼" h, 6½" l, two attached tabby cats, playing, striped, red bows, Japan paper label, marked "Deebee" ... **30.00**

5½", Holly Hobby with two kittens at milk bowl, titled "Life is More Fun When It's Shared" on base, Japan paper label **10.00**

7" h, blue bow, marked "Made in Spain" and "Vista Allegra D'Art" . **32.00**

8½" h, white cat, pink ribbon and flowers on neck, impressed "Cordey" **600.00**

Folk Art, fabric, stuffed with aromatic pine needles, orig paper tag "Paines Fir Balsam Products, Lewiston, Maine," 7½" h, $10.00.

Folkart

Ashtray, 27" h, wood, black cat, c1930 .... **85.00**

Basket, woven, brown and red, cat face lid

16¼" d **15.00**

19½" d **18.00**

22½" d **22.00**

Rack, 11" h, wood, black cat, paper label, marked "Made in Norway" **22.00**

Wall hanging, 15 x 17", velour, white and black cat sitting up, orange and black background **36.00**

Game, Black Cat Fortune Telling Game, Parker Brothers **20.00**

Lamp, TV type, two Siamese cats, 13½" h mother, 8½" h kitten, ceramic, hollow eyes, c1950 .... **75.00**

Limited Edition Plate

Bing and Grondahl, Mother's Day, 1971, "Cat with Kitten" **20.00**

Royal Copenhagen, 1970, "Christmas Rose and Cat" **30.00**

Schmid, 1980, "Surprise in the Cellar," Lowell Davis **75.00**

Match Holder, cat scene, ftd, marked "Wavecrest" **225.00**

Pillow

18" sq, velvet, maroon, gray hooked yarn cat, lying down, blue ribbon, white whiskers, red claws, c1920 **130.00**

24", oval, needlepoint, two-toned gray cat, sitting on two-toned purple pillow, orange bow, orange gathered satin sides, Germany, c1920 .... **175.00**

Planter

3 x 3½", ceramic, Figaro, marked "Occupied Japan" **28.00**

4¼" h, 6" l, horseshoe shape kitten, curled up tail, creamy white, flowers, pink trim and bow **12.00**

6¾" h, 7½" l, kitten with basket, cream, incised "Hull Art USA 61" **14.00**

9" h, Siamese cat sitting up, unmarked **24.00**

Plate, 1902 St. Louis World's Fair, three kittens in gold leaf, emb **35.00**

Postcard

Calendar, 1965, 8¼ x 4", West Germany **10.00**

Squeak type

Black and white glossy **8.00**

Hand colored **12.00**

Salt and Pepper Shakers, pr

Cat

Black

Sitting cross legged, Rosemeade Pottery **36.00**

Sitting up, red bow, 4" h, Shafford label **22.00**

Blue and white, pink bows, 7½" h, Japan paper label **12.00**

Siamese, comical, 4" h, paper label marked "Norcrest Japan" **8.00**

Spotted, white baskets, 3½" d, 2½" h, paper label marked "Ron Gordon Designs Taiwan" **10.00**

Tiger, hugging, 3½" h, marked "Occupied Japan" **25.00**

Kitten in watering pail, floral pattern, one cat gray, other yellow, 3" h, Japan paper label **12.00**

Stuffed Toy

Felix, 14" h, stuffed, mohair, button on ear, Chad Valley **195.00**

Kitten, plush, black and white, green eyes, pink bow and nose, c1950 . **18.00**

Teapot, black cat

1½ cup, unmarked **24.00**

2 cup, #RD1951, marked "Shafford" **28.00**

Toothpick Holder

Cat in floral and leaves wreath, dotted rim, marked "Wavecrest" **245.00**

Cat on pillow, glass

Amber, Daisy and Button pattern, 3½" h **65.00**

Blue, daisy pattern, 3½" h **85.00**

Teapot, gray, black trim, aqua bow, marked "Tony Wood Studio, England," 9½" h, $40.00.

Toy
Bubble pipe, celluloid, cat face **15.00**
Spinning Top, tin, litho, yellow prowling cats, blue ground, red trim, red wood handle, marked "Ohio Art Co" **18.00**

CATALOGS

Collecting Hints: The price of an old catalog is affected by the condition, data, type of material advertised, and location of advertiser.

History: Catalogs are used as excellent research sources. The complete manufacturing line of a given item is often described, along with prices, styles, colors, etc. Old catalogs provide a good way to date objects.

Many old catalogs are reprinted for use by collectors as an aid to identification of their specialities, such as Imperial and The Cambridge Glass Co.

Reference: Don Fredgant, *American Trade Catalogs,* Collector Books, 1984.

AUCTION

Christies, London, Ralph Berval Collection, 1855 .... **125.00**
Cloverdell Farm, horses, 1898 .... **15.00**
Lexington Horse Auction, 1936 ...... **20.00**
Old Glory Horse Auction, 1907 ...... **20.00**

MAIL ORDER

Bellas Hess, 1917 .... **45.00**
Chicago Mail Order, 1939 .... **10.00**
Lane Bryant, 1929 .... **17.00**
Larkin Plan, Factory To Family, Fall and Winter, 1917–18, 188 pgs, 8 x 11", fully illus **35.00**

Montgomery Ward
1912, No. 80 .... **85.00**
1934, Seed **5.00**
1942, Spring and Summer **30.00**
1950, Christmas **45.00**
Sears Roebuck
1917, July and August, 120 pgs **10.00**
1932, Fall and Winter, 1035 pgs ... **40.00**
1951, Christmas **35.00**
Spiegel, 1937, Spring & Summer **38.00**

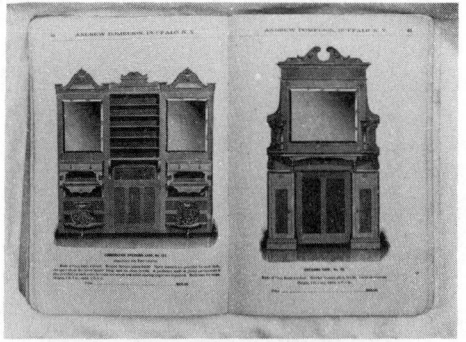

Barber Supplies, Andrew Domedion, Buffalo, NY, paper cov, 7 x 10¼", 140 pgs, $8.00

TRADE

Aermotor Co, Chicago, Water Supply Bulletin No. 35, 40 pgs, 4½ x 8¼" . **24.00**
Aladdin Lamps, 1933, 46 pgs, 9 x 11" **65.00**
Art Colony's, c1930, 48 pgs **25.00**
Baldwin Steel Co, NY, c1919, 79 pgs, 6 x 9¼", Hudson High Speed Tools .. **7.00**
Baltimore Salvage Co, MD, Spring Hardware News, 1936, 32 pgs, 10 x 7¼" **10.00**
Birdsell Wagons, early 1900 .... **35.00**
Blue Book Jewelers, 1932 .... **100.00**
Brown-Sharpe Tool, 1929 .... **30.00**
Buegeleisen and Jacobson Musical Instruments, NY, 1906, 128 pgs, 8½ x 12" **75.00**
Burpee Seeds, 1915 .... **17.50**
C & E Marshall Jewelers, 1933 .... **34.00**
Cashman's Seed, 1916 .... **8.00**
Chase Nursery Co, Chase, AL, Fall and Spring, 1922, 32 pgs, 7 x 10" **16.00**
Chicago House Wrecking Co, IL, 1908, 216 pgs, 6 x 9" **28.00**
Coates and Rainear, Inc, Philadelphia, PA, 393 pgs, 7¾ x 10¾", hardcover, hardware, tool, and machinery **20.00**
Coulton Optical, 1899 .... **135.00**
Crouse Hinds Traffic Signal Systems, 1926, 8 x 10½" **35.00**
Dave Cook Tackle, 1940 .... **6.00**

Drake Hardware, 1943	**38.00**
Dunham Brothers Co, Brattleboro, Vt, fall and winter, 1912, 64 pgs	**20.00**
Ellwood Woven Wire Fences and Gates, 1900, 31 pgs, 3½ x 6¼"	**12.50**
Evinrude Motors, 1915	**90.00**
Excelsior Mantle, WV, 1924, 288 pgs, 17 color illus	**46.00**
Farquahar's Garden Annual Seed Catalog, 1908-09	**20.00**
Fairbanks Scales, 1914, 236 pgs, 4½ x 7"	**55.00**
Frank H. Stewart, Electric Household Supplies, Phila., 72 pgs, c1905	**65.00**
Gilbert, The New Erector, 1938, 25 pgs	**30.00**
Globe Optical Co, Boston, 1904, 176 pgs, 8 x 10"	**65.00**
Great Western Gun Works, Pittsburgh, 1888, 64 pgs	**50.00**
Greenfield Tool, 1939	**18.00**
Henry Paulson Jewelers, 1941	**28.00**
Houses of Stucco, 1926	**15.00**
International Textbook Co, Scranton, PA, 1909, 6 x 9"	**28.00**
James and Holmstrom, NY, pianos, c1911, six plates	**36.00**
Kelly-How-Thomson Hardware, 1913 .	**125.00**
King Mantle Co, Knoxville, TN, 1900, 64 pgs, 6 x 9¼"	**30.00**
Kohler Plumbing Fixtures, 1929, 72 pgs	**22.00**
Libbey Cut Glass, 1896	**20.00**
Lufkin Rule Co, Saginaw, MI, c1928, 128 pgs, 8 x 5¼", precision tools ..	**10.00**
McCall's Pattern, 1911	**18.00**
McKinley Music Co, Chicago and NY, 1906, 64 pgs, 6 x 9½"	**7.00**
McMaster-Carr Tool, 1948	**60.00**
Miller's Hardware, Christmas-Toys, 1935, 24 pgs	**25.00**
Montgomery Ward, Chicago, 1919, 44 pgs, 11 x 14", sewing machines	**55.00**
Murphy's Chair, 1940–41	**12.00**
New England Butt Co, Providence, RI, 1923, 34 pgs, braiding machinery ..	**13.00**
Packard, Lindermann & Oliver Organ, 1909, 22 pgs	**75.00**
Peaslee–Gaulbert Co, Inc, Louisville, KY, "Homes and How to Paint Them," c1913, 32 pgs, 8 x 10", color illus	**20.00**
Public Service Electrical Supply Co, Baltimore, 1920	**75.00**
Putnam and Co, NY, c1916, 24 pgs, 6¾ x 4½", rolling ladders	**15.00**
Rubelmann-Lucas Hardware, St. Louis, 1909, no covers	**20.00**
Russell, Burdsall & Ward Bolt and Nut Co, Port Chester, NY, 1926, 154 pgs, 8 x 5¼"	**10.00**
Schell's Seed, 1931	**10.00**
Smith Bros Seed Co, Auburn, NY, 1910, 32 pgs, 8½ x 10¼", two color plates	**18.00**

Spaulding Catalog of Athletic Goods, 1910, 112 pgs	**35.00**
Standard Sanitary Manufacturing Co, Pittsburgh, PA, 1919, 64 pgs, 5 x 7¾", plumbing fixtures	**16.00**
Steel City Electric Co, Pittsburgh, PA, 1918, 105 pgs, 6 x 9"	**5.00**
Thayer Manufacturing Co, Los Angeles, CA, 1921, 176 pgs, 6 x 9", magic tricks and accessories	**32.00**
Vermont Marble Co, Proctor, VT, c1913, 46 pgs, 10½ x 8¼", int. and ext. illus of banks	**45.00**
W. & C. Tools, early 1900	**20.00**
W. Water Closets, T. Kelly Bros., Chicago, 40 pgs, 1919	**40.00**
Walworth Mfg. Co, Boston, 1897, 320 pgs, 7½ x 5¼", hardcover, brass and wrought iron hardware and architectural details	**20.00**
Western Sash and Door, house trim and stained windows, 1899	**25.00**
Western Telephone Co, Chicago, 1898, 136 pgs, 6 x 9"	**75.00**
Wheeler Industrial Reflector Co, Boston, MA, Jan 1929, 68 pgs, 8½ x 10" ...	**18.00**
Wilcox Mfg. Co., Garage Door Hardware, Aurora, Ill., 160 pgs, 1928 ...	**24.00**
Winsor and Newton, Inc, NY, 1936, 91 pgs, artists supplies, 64 brilliant color patches, 6 x 9"	**18.00**
Wm Deering Co. Mfg. Harvesting Machinery, early 1900	**45.00**
Wood Homes Bureau, Cleveland, OH, 1926, 174 pgs, 12 x 9", dedication by Cleveland Board of Lumber Dealers, illus of 101 homes and scale plans	**40.00**

CELLULOID ITEMS

Collecting Hints: There are few collectors of celluloid per se. Most celluloid is sought because it relates to another collecting field.

It was possible to place a printed message on a celluloid surface. For this reason celluloid was a popular medium for the advertising giveaways of the 1880 to 1900 period. Old celluloid is quite brittle and can be easily broken. It must be handled carefully. Collectors should be aware of celluloid's flammable tendencies.

History: Celluloid is the trade name for a thin, tough, flammable material made of cellulose nitrate and camphor. It was invented just prior to 1870, and was used mainly in making toilet articles. It also was an inexpensive material for jewelry, figurines, vases, etc. Celluloid frequently was made to simulate more expensive materials, e.g., amber, bone, ivory, and tortoise shell.

Celluloid became a popular medium for the toy industry of the 1920s and 30s. Character toys included Charlie Chaplin and Charlie McCarthy. The advent of bakelite and plastic brought an end to celluloid items.

Animal
Cat, 10", black and white **40.00**
Elephant, 3½", gray **25.00**
Pig, 2" l **6.00**
Ram, 2" l **6.00**
Reindeer, 3½" **15.00**
Rhino, 2" l **6.00**
Swan, white **5.00**
Tiger, 2" l **6.50**
Band-Aid Case, 1½ x 2¼", red, white, and blue, railroad engine design, inscribed "Hamilton Watch," text on back, c1900 .... **25.00**

Counter, Compliments of Kennedy Furniture Co, Chicago, IL, merchandise listed on back, 3 x 1⅜", $8.00.

Blotter Pad
3 x 7½", Kingan Meat Co, multicolored mariner trademark, c1829 .. **25.00**
3 x 8", Bryan-Marsh Mazda, multicolored illus, blue and white celluloid cotter pin, c1920 .... **30.00**
Bracelet
Bangle, mottled brown, tortoiseshell imitation, rhinestones **25.00**
Chain, red, hanging berries **30.00**
Cake Top Figure
Bride, 4" **5.00**
Groom, 4½" **5.00**
Calendar, Buffalo Distilling Co, 5 x 5½", perpetual, multicolored, tin filigree corners, cardboard easel back, Whitehead and Hoag Co, 1904 patent date **80.00**
Carving Set, fork and knife, ivory colored handle, engraved steel blade .. **30.00**
Dresser Set
5 pcs, pearlized ivory **35.00**
9 pcs, ivory, minor wear on clock .. **30.00**
12 pcs, pearlized green, orig black case **115.00**

Figure
Baby, 4", movable arms and legs ... **4.00**
Boy, 2", pink jacket, multicolored shorts **5.00**
Girl, 2", blonde braids and short pink dress **5.00**
Foam Scraper, Grain Belt Beer adv ... **15.00**
Lapel Stud, ⅞"
Waverly Bicycles, black and white portrait of lady cyclist, c1895 .... **30.00**
Zenith Saddle, metal lapel stud back, white inscription, blue ground, c1895 .... **10.00**
Manicure Set, ivory colored handles, folding leather case, 10 pcs **30.00**
Mirror, Berry Brothers Varnish, multicolored, brass rim, red and blue slogan "The Largest Varnish Factory In The World" **50.00**
Nail File Case, ½ x 3½", Chevrolet, white case, swing out metal nail file, blue inscription and logo, c1920 ... **15.00**
Necklace, Art Deco dangling disks, cellulose acetate chain **28.00**
Note Pad, 2½ x 3¼", self adv, issued by Whitehead & Hoag Co, multicolored cov, blue and white illus of Newark NJ home office and 1918 calendar on back **65.00**
Pen Wiper, 1½ x 3½", diecut, "Sergeants' Dog Remedies," multicolored, hunter dog, pointer position, adv on reverse, c1900 .... **35.00**
Pencil Clip
Bakers Chocolate, ¾", blue, white, and light yellow, metal clip, c1920 **15.00**
Chi-Namel, ¾", multicolored, Oriental figure, silvered tin clip, c1920 **25.00**
Diamond Edge, ⅞", black, white, and red, silvered tin clip, early 1900s . **10.00**
Pillsbury's Best Feeds, ⅞", red, white, and blue, silvered tin clip, c1920 **12.00**
Tuxedo Feeds, ⅞", black, white, and red, silvered tin clip, c1930 ..... **12.00**
Picture, 3⅝ x 5", oval, Chopin, easel back **10.00**
Place Card Holder, snowman, angels, and elves, set of eight, MIB **17.50**
Rattle, 4½", cupid in wreath **15.00**
Ruler, 1 x 6", G Felsenthal & Sons, Chicago, inch and metric rules, adv on back for celluloid novelties, c1900 . **20.00**
Sewing Kit, red stripes **8.00**
Stamp Case
1½ x 2¼", multicolored products, inscribed "Parke's Tea," small supply of early band-aids **20.00**
1½ x 2½", multicolored postage stamps, black and white 1904 calendar, inscribed "The Daily News," text of Chicago Daily News **22.00**
1¾ x 2⅛", multicolored postage

stamps, black and white text, inscribed "Gluck's Cleaning Works," 1909 calendar **20.00**
Toy
  Roly Poly
    Boy, 1¼", holding flag, beanie cap, ¾" tin wheels **7.50**
    Cat, 1½", waving hello **8.50**
    Duck, 3½", umbrella, c1930 .... **25.00**
    Rabbit, 1½", pink, colored ball base **8.50**
  Windup, Ma Bunny wheeling baby in carriage **100.00**
Watch Fob
  1¾", multicolored female cyclist, red ground, gold wings, green banner, inscribed "New Departure," black reverse with company name and address in gold, c1900 .... **125.00**
  2⅛", multicolored, purple rim, inscribed "Meet Me At Webster City Street Fair 1899," woman with mask and hat **50.00**
Whistle, 1½", Evening Star Safety, Circus Whistlin' For Safety, blue letters, bright orange ground, c1930 .... **25.00**

CHILDREN'S BOOKS

Collecting Hints: Most collectors look for books by a certain author or illustrator. Others are interested in books from a certain time period such as the 19th century. Accumulating the complete run of a series such as Tom Swift, Nancy Drew, or the Hardy Boys is of interest to some collectors. Subject categories are popular too, and include ethnic books, mechanical books, first editions, award winning books, certain kinds of animals, rag books, Big Little Books, and those with photographic illustrations.

A good way to learn about children's books is to go to libraries and museums where special children's collections have been developed. Books on various aspects of children's literature are a necessity. You also should read a general book on book collecting to provide you with background information. Significant bits of information can be found on the title page and verso of the title page of a book. This information is especially important in determining the edition of a book. You eventually will want to own a few reference books most closely associated with your collection.

Although children's books can be found at all the usual places where antiques and collectibles are for sale, also seek out book and paper shows. Get to know dealers who specialize in children's books; ask to receive their lists or catalogs. Some dealers offer to locate certain books for you. Most used and out-of-print book stores have a section

with children's books . If your author or illustrator is still actively writing or illustrating, a regular book store may carry his most recent book.

Things to be considered when purchasing books are the presence of a dust jacket or box, condition of the book, the edition, quality of illustrations and binding, and the prominence of the author or illustrator. Books should be examined very carefully to make sure that all pages and illustrations are present. Missing pages will reduce the value of the book. Try to buy books in the best condition you can afford. Even if your budget is limited, you can still find very nice inexpensive children's books if you keep looking.

History: William Caxton, a printer in England, is considered to have been the first publisher of children's books. Among his early publications was *Aesop's Fables* printed in 1484. Other very early books include John Cotton's *Spiritual Milk for Boston Babes* in 1646, *Orbis Pictis* translated from the Latin about 1657, and *The New England Primer* in 1691.

Children's classics had their beginning with *Robinson Crusoe* in 1719, *Gulliver's Travels* in 1726, and Perrault's *Tales of Mother Goose* translated into English in 1729. The well known *A Visit from St. Nicholas* by Clement C. Moore appeared in 1823. Some of the best known children's works were published between 1840 and 1900. A few Lear's *Book of Nonsense, Andersen's* and Grimm's *Fairy Tales, Alice in Wonderland, Hans Brinker, Little Women, Tom Sawyer, Treasure Island, Heidi, A Child's Garden of Verses,* and *Little Black Sambo.*

Series books for boys and girls began around the turn of the century. The Stratemeyer Syndicate, established about 1906, became especially well known for their series, such as Tom Swift, The Bobbsey Twins, Nancy Drew, Hardy Boys, and many others.

Following the turn of the century, informational books such as Van Loon's *The Story of Mankind* were published. This book received the first Newbery Medal in 1922. This award, given for the year's most distinguished literature for children, was established to honor John Newbery, an English publisher of children's books. Biographies and poetry also became popular.

The most extensive development, however, has been with picture books. Photography and new technologies for reproducing illustrations have made picture book publishing a major part of the children's book field. The Caldecott Medal, given for the most distinguished picture book published in the United States, was established in 1938. The award, which honors Randolph Caldecott, an English illustrator from the 1800's, was first given in 1938 to Dorothy Lathrop for *Animals of the Bible.*

During the late 1800s, novelty children's books appeared. Lothar Meggendorfer, Ernest

Nister, and Raphael Tuck were the most well known publishers of these fascinating pop-up, and mechanical or movable books. The popularity of this type of book has continued to the present. Some of the early movable books are being reproduced especially by Intervisual Communication, Inc., of California.

Books that tie in with children's television programs, e.g., Sesame Street, and toys, e.g., Cabbage Patch dolls, have become prominent. Modern merchandising methods include multimedia packaging of various combinations of books, toys, puzzles, cassette tapes, videos, etc. There are even books which unfold and become a costume to be worn by children.

References: Barbara Bader, *American Picture Books From Noah's Ark To The Beast Within,* Macmillan, 1976; Virginia Haviland, *Children's Literature, A Guide To Reference Sources,* Library of Congress, 1966, first supplement 1972, second supplement 1977, third supplement 1982; Bettina Hurlimann, *Three Centuries Of Children's Books In Europe,* tr. and ed. by Brian W. Alderson, World, 1968; Cornelia L. Meigs, ed., *A Critical History of Children's Literature,* Macmillan, 1969, 2nd ed.

Collectors' Clubs: Louisa May Alcott Memorial Assoc., P. O. Box 343, Concord, MA 01742; Horatio Alger Society, 4907 Allison Drive, Lansing, MI 48910; International Wizard of Oz Club (L. Frank Baum), Box 95, Kinderhook, IL 62345; Thorton W. Burgess Society, Inc., P. O. Box 45, Dept. B, East Sandwich, MA 02537; Burroughs Bibliophiles (Edgar Rice Burroughs), P. O. Box 588, Wytheville, VA 24382; Lewis Carroll Society of North America, 617 Rockford Road, Silver Spring, MD 20902; Dickens Society, Dept. of English, University of Southern California, Los Angeles, CA 90089; Fantasy Association, P. O. Box 24560, Los Angeles, CA 90024; Kate Greenaway Society, 10 Felton Avenue, Ridley Park, PA 19078; Happyhours Brotherhood, 87 School Street, Fall River, MA 02770; Uncle Remus Museum (Joel Chandler Harris), P. O. Box 184, Eatonton, GA 31024; Kipling Society (Rudyard Kipling), c/o Dr. Enamul Karim, Dept. of English, Rockford College; Rockford, IL 61108; Melville Society (Herman Melville), c/oDonald Yannella, Dept. of English, Glassboro State College, Glassboro, NJ 08028; Mystery and Detective Series Review, P. O. Box 3488, Tucson, AZ 85722; Mythopoeil Society, P. O. Box 4671, Whittier, CA 90607; National Fantasy Fan Federation, c/o Sally A. Syrjala, P. O. Box 149, Centerville, MA 02632; New York C. S. Lewis Society, c/o Jerry L. Daniel, 419 Springfield Ave., Westfield NJ 07092; Series Book Collector Society, c/o Jack Brahce, 5270 Moceri Ln, Grand Blanc, MI 48439; Stowe-Day Foundation (Harriet Beecher Stowe), 77 Forest St., Hartford, CT 06105; American Hobbit Association (J. R. R. Tolkien), 2436 Meadow Drive, N., Wilmette, IL 60091; American Tolkien Society, P. O. Box 277, Union Lake, MI 48085; Tolkien Fellowships, c/o Bill Spicer, 329 N. Avenue 66, Los Angeles, CA 90042; Mark Twain Boyhood Home Association, 208 Hill Street, Hannibal, MO 63401; Mark Twain Memorial, Nook Farm, 351 Farmington Ave., Hartford, CT 06105; Mark Twain Research Foundation, Perry, MO 63462; Mark Twain Society, c/o George Daneluk, Jersey City State College, 2039 Kennedy Memorial Blvd., Jersey City, NJ 07035; Yellowback Library, 811 Boulder Ave., Des Moines, IA 50315.

Libraries and Museums: Many of the clubs maintain museums. *Subject Collections* by Lee Ash (ed.) contains a list of public and academic libraries which have children's book collections. A number of large collections can be found at: Florida State University, Tallahassee, FL; Free Library of Philadelphia, PA; Library of Congress, Washington, DC; Pierpont Morgan Library, New York, NY; Toronto Public Library, Toronto, Ontario, Canada; University of Minnesota, Walter Library, Minneapolis, MN; University of South Florida, Tampa, FL

Advisor: Margaret L. Tyrrell.

Notes: Prices are based on first editions with a dust jacket (dj) and in very good condition. The absence of a dust jacket, later printings and a condition less than "very good" are all factors that lessen the value of a book.

Autographed copies and those that come in a special box are additional factors that will increase the value. Books that have been award winners, e.g., Newbery, Caldecott, etc., generally are higher in value. Unp=unpaged.

Reprints: A number of replicas of antique originals are now appearing on the market, with most being done by Evergreen Press and Merrimack. A new "Children's Classics" series offers reprints of books illustrated by Jessie Willcox Smith, Edmund Dulac, Frederick Richardson and possibly others.

Adams, Eustace L., *Pirates of the Air,* Grossett & Dunlap, 1929, 212 pgs, dj, Candy Lane Series **4.00**
Alcott, Louisa M., *An Old Fashioned Girl,* Clara Burd, illus, Winston, 1928, 342, pgs, dj, 1st ed **30.00**
Alexander, Lloyd, *The Castle of Llyr,* Evaline Ness, illus, Holt, Rinehart & Winston, 1966, 201 pgs, dj, 1st ed, sgd by Alexander, (Drydain Cycle) . .   **35.00**
Allen, Betsy, *The Riddle in Red,* Grossett & Dunlap, 1948, 212 pgs, dj, Connie Blair Series **3.00**
Anglund, Joan, Walsh, *A Year Is Round,* Harcourt, Brace, World, 1966, unp, dj, 1st ed **10.00**

Kellogg's Story Book of Games, Kellogg Co, 1931, #190, eight pages, cover, spinner separate, $12.00.

Appleton, Victor, *Don Sturdy in the Land of Giants,* Grossett & Dunlap, 1930, 244 pgs, dj 6.00

Appleton, Victor, *Tom Swift Among the Fire Fighters,* Grossett & Dunlap, 1921, 214 pgs 9.00

Ardizzone, Edward, *Tim's Last Voyage,* Bodley Head, 1972, unp, dj, 1st ed 35.00

Austin, Margot, *Peter Churchmouse,* E. P. Dutton, 1941, unp, dj, 1st ed 50.00

Bailey, Arthur Scott, *The Tale of Cuffy Bear,* Harry L. Smith, illus, Grossett & Dunlap, 1915, 112 pgs, dj 10.00

Bannerman, Helen, *Little Black Sambo,* Violet Lamont, illus, Whitman, 1959, unp 15.00

Barbour, Ralph Henry, *Behind The Line,* Appleton, 1906, 258 pgs 7.00

Barnyard Babies, Milo Winter, illus, Merrill, 1936, unp, wraps 18.00

Baum, L. Frank, *The Road To Oz,* Harry McNaught, illus, Simon & Schuster, 1951, unp, 1st ed, Golden Book ... 15.00

Bee, Clair, *Hoop Crazy,* Grosset & Dunlap, 1950, 215 pgs, dj, Chip Hilton Sports Story 6.00

Borden, Marion, *Hooray for Lassie,* Carol Marshall, illus, Whitman, 1964, unp, Tell-A-Tale Book 5.00

Brandeis, Madeline, *Mitz and Fritz of Germany,* Grossett & Dunlap, 1933, 160 pgs 4.00

Burd, Clara, illus, *Animals on the Farm,* Saalfield, 1936, unp, wraps 28.00

Burgess, Thornton W., *Blacky the Cow,* Harrison Cady, illus, Grossett & Dunlap, 1922, 206 pgs, dj 8.00

Burgess, Thornton W., *Lightfoot the Deer,* Harrison Cady, illus, Little Brown, 1921, 205 pgs, 1st ed 95.00

Burgess, Thornton W., *Milk and Honey,* Nina R. Jordan, illus, Whitman, 1927, unp 6.00

Burtis, Thomson, *Rex Lee Trailing Air Bandits,* Grossett & Dunlap, 1931, 248 pgs, dj 4.00

Byj, Charlotte, *Christmas on Stage,* Polygraph Co of America, 1950, unp, 5 pop ups 25.00

Chadwick, Lester, *Baseball Joe, Champion of the League,* Cupples & Leon, 1925, 246 pgs, dj 9.00

Chapman, Allen, *Fred Fenton the Pitcher,* Cupples & Leon, 1913, 206 pgs, dj 7.00

Chapman, Allen, *Ralph on the Midnight Flyer,* Grossett & Dunlap, 1923, 248 pgs, dj 9.00

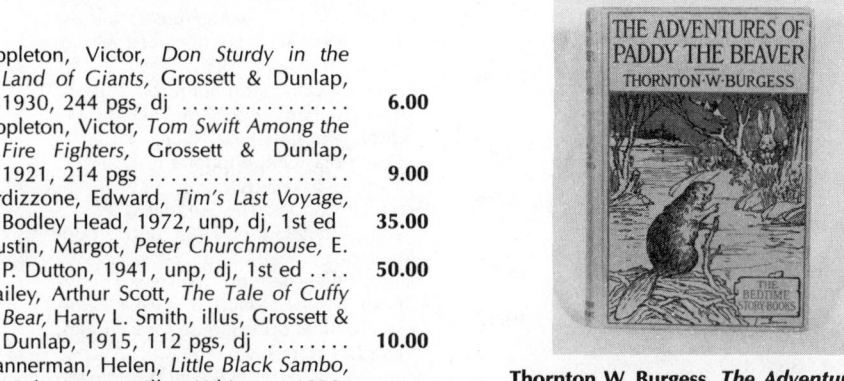

Thornton W. Burgess, *The Adventures of Paddy The Beaver,* Bedtime Story Books, Boston, Little, Brown & Co, 1917, 4¾ x 7 x½", $8.00.

Chatterbox, J. Erskine Clarde, editor, Esxes & Lauriat, 1896, 412 pgs 16.00

Clifton, Oliver Lee, *The Camp Fire Boys At Silver Fox Farm,* Barse & Hopkins, 1924, 246 pgs 6.00

Cyr, Ellen M., *The Children's Second Reader,* Ginn, 1894, 197 pgs 12.00

Curtis, Alice Turner, *Little Maid of Quebec,* Penn Pub Co, 1936, 224 pgs, dj 8.00

Dawson, Lucy, *Lucy Dawson's Dogs,* Whitman, 1938, unp, wraps 25.00

Disney, Walt, *Pinocchio and His Puppet Show Adventure,* Random House, 1973, unp, 1st ed, Disney's Wonderful World of Reading 8.00

Dixon, Franklin W., *Footprints Under the Window,* Grossett & Dunlap, 1933, 214 pgs, Hardy Boys 4.00

Dixon, Franklin W., *The Yellow Feather Mystery,* Grossett & Dunlap, 1971, 181 pgs, Hardy Boys 3.00

Dodge, Mary Mapes, *Hans Brinker or, The Silver Skates*, Hilda Van Stockum, illus, World, 1946, 335 pgs **10.00**

Drake, Robert L., *The Boy Allies At Jutland*, A. L. Burt, 1917, 255 pgs, dj, Navy series **6.00**

Elson, William H & William S. Gray, *Elson-Gray Basic Readers-Book Two*, Scott, Foresman, 1936, 240 pgs **5.00**

Edwards, Leo, *Poppy Ott's Pedigreed Pickles*, Grossett & Dunlap **7.00**

Farley, Walter, *The Black Stallion Races*, Random House, 1955, 256 pgs, dj, 1st ed **18.00**

Fassett, James H., *The Beacon First Reader*, Ginn, 1913, 160 pgs **10.00**

Finley, Martha, *Elsie Dinsmore*, Donohue, nd, c1920, 395 pgs **10.00**

Fryer, Jane Eayre, *The Mary Frances Storybook*, Edwin John Prittie, illus, Winston, 1921, 328 pgs **45.00**

Gag, Wanda, *Snow White and the Seven Dwarfs*, Coward-McCann, 1938, 43 pgs, dj **20.00**

Garis, Howard R., *The Curly Tops and Their Playmates*, Cupples & Leon, 1922, 246 pgs **3.00**

Garis, Howard R., *Uncle Wiggily's Airship*, Platt & Munk, 1939, 185 pgs . **10.00**

Gruelle, Johnny, *Raggedy Ann and Andy and the Camel with the Wrinkled Knees*, Bobbs-Merrill, 1951, 95 pgs . **15.00**

Gruelle, Johnny, *Raggedy Ann's Alphabet Book*, Donohue, 1925, 40 pgs, dj **40.00**

Hayes, Clair W., *The Boy Troopers on Duty*, A.L. Burt, 1922, 221 pgs, Army series **3.00**

Hazlett, Edward E., *He's Jake, The Story of a Submarine Dog*, Paul Brown, illus, Dodd Mead, 1947, 154 pgs, dj **6.00**

Holling, Holling C, *The Book of Cowboys*, H C & Lucille Holling, illus, Platt & Munk, 1936, 126 pgs, dj, 1st ed **25.00**

Hoover, Latharo, *The Campfire Boys in the Brazilian Wilderness*, A. L. Burt, 1929, 255 pgs **4.00**

Hope, Laura Lee, *Bobbsey Twins at Indian Hollow*, Marie Schubert, illus, Grossett & Dunlap, 1940, 214 pgs . **4.00**

Hughes, Thomas, *Tom Brown's School Days*, Dodd Mead, 1900, 339 pgs .. **10.00**

Inchfawn, Fay, *Who goes to the Wood*, Diana Thorne, illus, Winston, 1942, 229 pgs **12.00**

Irwin, Inez Haynes, *Marda's Little Houseboat*, Grossett & Dunlap, 1943, 207 pgs **13.00**

Jackson, Leroy F., *The Peter Patter Book*, Blanche Fisher Wright, illus, Rand McNally, 1915, 110 pgs **30.00**

James, Will, *Sun Up, Tales of the Cow Camps*, Junior Literary Guild, 1931, 342 pgs **40.00**

Keene, Carolyn, *Mystery of the Brass Bound Trunk*, Russell H. Tandy, illus, Grossett & Dunlap, 1940, 220 pgs, dj **10.00**

Keene, Carolyn, *Secret at the Gatehouse*, F. Warren, illus, Grossett & Dunlap, 1940, 216 pgs, dj, Dana Girls **5.00**

Keene, Carolyn, *The Spider Sapphire Mystery*, Grossett & Dunlap, 1968, 176 pgs, dj **3.00**

King, Frank, *Skeezix and Pal*, Reilly & Lee, 1925, unp **16.00**

Kubasta, V., *Ricky the Rabbit*, Bancroft, 1961, 8 pgs, pop-up **20.00**

Lenski, Lois, *The Little Farm*, Oxford Univ Press, 1942, unp, dj, 1st ed .. **18.00**

Lobel, Arnold, *Frog and Toad Together*, Harper & Row, 1972, 64 pgs **8.00**

Mariana, *Miss Flora McFlimsey and the Baby New Year*, Lothrop, Lee & Shepard, 1951, unp, dj **22.00**

Mayhew, Ralph and Johnston Burges, *The Pie Party Book, the 5th Bubble Book*, Rhoda Chase, illus, Harper & Columbia Graphophone Co, 1919, 15 pgs, 3 records **30.00**

Merrill, Marion, *The Animated Pinocchio*, Citadel Press, 1945, unp, 3 pop-ups **25.00**

Miller, Olive Beaupre, *Nursery Friends from France*, Maud & Miska Petersham, illus, Book House for Children, 1927, 191 pgs **35.00**

Milne, A. A., *Winnie Ille Pu (Winnie the Pooh in Latin)*, Dutton, 1961, 121 pgs, dj **6.00**

Montgomery, Frances Trego, *Billy Wiskers' Kids*, W. H. Fry, illus, Saalfield, 1903, 134 pgs, dj **25.00**

Mother Goose, Pelagie Doane, illus, Random House, 1940, unp, dj **15.00**

Mother Goose, Mary Lafetya Russell, illus, Sam Gabriel, 1911, unp **15.00**

Nesbit, Wilbur D., *The Tumbledown Town*, John Gee, illus, Volland, 1926, unp, Sunny Book **25.00**

Newberry, Clare Turlay, *Mittens*, Harper, 1936, unp, dj, 1st ed **50.00**

Packer, Eleanor, Lewis, *A Day with Our Gang*, Whitman, 1929, unp **18.00**

Perkins, Lucy Fitch, *The Puritan Twins*, Houghton Mifflin, 1921, 178 pgs ... **16.00**

Petersham, Maud & Miska, *The Story Book of Food*, Winston, 1947, unp . **7.00**

Pyle, Howard, *Otto of the Silver Hand*, Scribner, 1906, 173 pgs **30.00**

Pyle, Katherine, *The Christmas Angel*, Little, Brown, 1900, 136 pgs, 1st ed **40.00**

Schulz, Charles M., *He's Your Dog,*

Charlie Brown!, World, 1968, unp, 1st ed **8.00**

Sendak, Maurice, *The Sign On Rosie's Door,*Harper & Row, 1960, 46 pgs, dj, 1st ed **45.00**

Sidney, Margaret, *Five Little Peppers Grown Up,* Mente, illus, D. Lathrop, 1892, 527 pgs, 1st ed **75.00**

Spyri, Johanna, *Heidi,* Frances Brundage, illus, Saalfield, 1924, 307 pgs **18.00**

Stockton, Frank R., *The Bee-man of Orb,* Maurice Sendak, illus, Holt, Rinehart & Winston, 1964, 46 pgs, dj, 1st ed, sgd by illus **100.00**

Sutton, Margaret, *The Name on the Bracelet,* Pelagie Doane, illus, Grossett & Dunlap, 1940, 216 pgs, dj ... **10.00**

Sutton, Margaret, *Who Will Play With Me?,* Corinne Dillon, illus, Wonder books, 1951, unp **12.00**

Tatham, Julie C., *Cherry Ames Mountaineer Nurse,* Grossett & Dunlap, dj **3.50**

Thorndyke, Helen Louise, *Honey Bunch: Her First Summer on an Island,* Grossett & Dunlap, 1929, 184 pgs **3.00**

Thorne-Thomsen, Gudrun, *East O' the Sun and West O' the Moon,* Frederick Richardson, illus, Row, Peterson, 1912, 218 pgs **20.00**

Tudor, Tasha, *First Poems of Childhood,* Platt & Munk, 1967, 45 pgs, dj, 1st ed **35.00**

Ungerer, Tomi, *The Mellops Strike Oil,* Harper, 1958, 32 pgs, 1st ed, dj ... **23.00**

Uttley, Alison, *Little Grey Rabbit's Pancake Day,* Margaret Tempest, illus, Collins, 1967, 63 pgs **25.00**

Watson, Jane Werner, *The True Story of Smokey the Bear,*Feodor Rojankovsky, illus, Golden Press, 1955, unp, 1st ed **10.00**

Wells, Helen, *Vicki Finds the Answer,* Grossett & Dunlap, 1947, dj, Vicki Barr series **5.00**

White, Stewart Edward, *Daniel Boone: Wilderness Scout,* James Daugherty, illus, Garden City, 1922, 274 pgs .. **15.00**

Wiggin, Kate Douglas, *The New Chronicles of Rebecca,* F. C. Yohn, illus, Houghton Mifflin, 1907, 278 pgs, 1st ed **22.00**

Winfield, Arthur M., *The Rover Boys Down East,* Grossett & Dunlap, 1911, 288 pgs, 1st ed, dj **10.00**

CHILDREN'S DISHES

Collecting Hints: Children's dishes were played with, so a bit of wear is to be expected. Avoid rusty metal dishes. Also avoid broken glass dishes.

History: Dishes for children to play with have been popular from Victorian times to the present. Many glass companies made small child-size sets in the same patterns as large table sets. Many young girls delighted in using a set just like mother's.

During the period when Depression glass was popular, the manufacturers also made child-size pieces to complement the full size lines. These child-size dishes were used for tea parties, doll parties, and many other happy occasions.

Child-size dishes are found in aluminum, tin, china, and glass.

References: Doris Anderson Lechler, *Children's Glass Dishes, China and Furniture,* Collector Books, 1983; Doris Anderson Lechler, *Children's Glass Dishes, China, Furniture, Volume II* Collector Books, 1986; Lorraine May Punchard, *Child's Play,* privately printed, 1982; Margaret and Kenn Whitmyer, *Children's Dishes,* Collector Books, 1984.

See: Akro Agate

Wood, Dainty Maid Tea Set, Newton & Thompson Mfg Co, Brandon, VT, orig box 5⅜ x 4 x 1½", $65.00.

Akro Agate
  Creamer
    Interior Panel, opaque, blue **25.00**
    Concentric Ring, opaque, light blue, small **9.00**
  Cup
    Chiquita, lavender **25.00**
    Concentric Ring, pumpkin, closed handle, 1⅜" **45.00**
  Dinner Set, 11 pcs, Stippled Band, azure **100.00**
  Pitcher, Octagonal, dark blue, open handle, 2⅞" **20.00**
  Plate, Concentric Rib Opaque, dark blue **6.00**
  Saucer
    Interior Panel, opaque, blue, large **4.75**
    Octagonal, closed handle, white, large **2.75**
  Tea Set, 23 pcs, Octagonal, opaque green and white **125.00**

Teapot, Concentric Rib Opaque, cobalt, white lid **30.00**
Tumbler, Octagonal, cream **10.00**
Aluminum, silverware set, four spoons, two forks, knife, and pie server **4.50**
Celluloid, 21 pc dinnerware and silverware, Lacy Edge, light blue **30.00**
China
Canister Set, 22 pcs, flour, tea, coffee, oatmeal, and spices, orange luster, three red flowers, wooden lids .. **135.00**
Cereal Bowl, Blue Willow, large size, Japanese **30.00**
Creamer and Sugar, Blue Willow, Japanese **15.00**
Cup and Saucer
Blue Willow, 2¼", Occupied Japan **12.50**
Moss Rose **4.50**
Gravy Boat, attached underplate, Blue Willow, Occupied Japan **65.00**
Plate
Blue Willow, 3¾", Occupied Japan **5.75**
Moss Rose, 4½" **2.00**
Platter, Moss Rose, oval **7.50**
Tea Set
5 pcs, Little Mae, cylinder shape, Staffordshire **85.00**
18 pcs, Blue Willow, large size, Japanese **225.00**
21 pcs, six cups and saucers, four 3¾" plates, cov teapot, cov sugar, and creamer, hp flowers and green band, Japanese **35.00**
23 pcs, six cups and saucers, plates, creamer, sugar, teapot, blue and white, clippership dec, Japanese **175.00**
24 pcs, six cups and saucers, plates, creamer, sugar, teapot, platter, Brown Willow, pastels, Staffordshire **300.00**
Teapot, cov, Blue Willow, Occupied Japan **30.00**
Depression Glass
Creamer
Cherry Blossom, pink **25.00**
Doric and Pansy, pink **25.00**
Cup and Saucer, Cherry Blossom, pink **28.00**
Place Setting, cup, saucer, and plate, Cherry Blossom, delphite **35.00**
Plate, dinner
Cherry Blossom, delphite **6.50**
Moderntone, pastel, yellow **5.00**
Saucer, Cherry Blossom, pink **6.00**
Sugar, Cherry Blossom, pink **25.00**
Table Set, Sweetheart, 4 pcs, ... **85.00**
Tea Set
12 pcs, Homespun, pink, MIB ... **225.00**
14 pcs
Doric and Pansy, teal **250.00**
Laurel Ivory, green band, McKee **225.00**

15 pcs, Houze, blue **475.00**
Teapot, Moderntone, beige, lemon lid **75.00**
Milk Glass
Butter, cov
Pennsylvania, gold trim **45.00**
Wild Rose **50.00**
Pattern Glass
Berry Bowl, individual, Fine Cut X . **18.00**
Berry Bowl, master, Fine Cut X **30.00**
Butter, cov
Doyle's 500, amber **100.00**
Wee Branches, alphabet base **110.00**
Creamer
Fernland **15.00**
Hawaiian Lei **10.00**
Hobnail with Thumbprint base, amber **40.00**
Nursery Rhyme **30.00**

Pattern Glass, Tulip & Honeycomb pattern, creamer and sugar, $45.00.

Creamer and Sugar
Tappan, amber **25.00**
Tulip and Honeycomb **45.00**
Cup and Saucer, Lion **40.00**
Mug
Fighting Cats **25.00**
Heron **10.00**
Old Butterfly **30.00**
Pitcher, Nursery Rhyme **100.00**
Punch Bowl, Nursery Rhyme **35.00**
Punch Bowl Set, punch bowl, six cups
Flattened Diamond and Sunburst . **68.00**
Nursery Rhyme **150.00**
Tulip and Honeycomb **75.00**
Spooner
Hawaiian Lei **20.00**
Menagerie Fish, amber **145.00**
Sugar, cov
Fernland **18.00**
Hawaiian Lei **30.00**
Nursery Rhyme **45.00**
Table Set, 4 pcs
Arrowhead in Oval **75.00**
Beaded Swirl **110.00**

Oval Star **65.00**
Pennsylvania, excellent gold **285.00**
Tumbler
Nursery Rhyme **15.00**
Sandwich Ten Panel, sapphire blue **135.00**
Plastic
Chocolate Set, Banner, service for
four, napkin holder, silverware ... **75.00**
Dinnerware Set
9 pcs, Tinkerbelle, Walt Disney,
service for two **18.00**
17 pcs, Alice in Wonderland,
Plasco, service for four, beige .. **40.00**
Silverware Set
6 pcs, two knives, forks, and
spoons, Plasco, pink, orig cardboard **3.25**
8 pcs, serving set, two knives,
forks, and spoons, Bestmaid, red,
orig cardboard **3.75**

CHRISTMAS ITEMS

Collecting Hints: Beware of reproduction ornaments. New reproductions are usually brighter in
color and have shiny paint. Older ornaments
should show some signs of handling. It is common to find tops replaced on ornaments.

History: Early Christmas decorations and ornaments were handmade. In 1865 the Pennsylvania
Dutch brought the first glass ornaments to America. By 1870, glass ornaments were being sold
in major cities. By the turn of the century, the
demand created a cottage industry in European
countries. Several towns in Germany and Czechoslovakia produced lovely ornaments, which
were imported by F. W. Woolworth, Sears, etc.,
who found a ready market.

References: Robert Brenner, *Christmas Past,* Shif-
fer Publishing, Inc., 1986; Maggie Rogers and
Peter Hallinan, *The Santa Claus Picture Book,* E.
P. Dutton, Inc., 1984; Maggie Rogers and Judith
Hawkins, *The Glass Christmas Ornament, Old &
New,* Timber Press, 1977; Nancy Schiffer, *Christ-
mas Ornaments: A Festive Study,* Schiffer Pub-
lishing, Ltd, 1984.

Museums: Many museums prepare special
Christmas exhibits.

Advisor: Lissa L. Bryan-Smith.

Additional Listings: Santa Claus.

REPRODUCTION ALERT

CHRISTMAS VILLAGE/GARDEN

Animal
1" h
Chicken, white, rubber, USA **5.00**

Dog, celluloid, brown, marked "Japan" **5.00**
Pig, celluloid, pink, marked "Japan" **5.00**
1½" h, bisque, chicken, marked "Japan" **6.50**
1¾" h, sheep, composition, wool
coat, wood legs, marked "Germany" **20.00**
2" h
Calf, black and white, rubber, USA **6.00**
Chicken, composition, metal feet,
marked "Germany" **15.00**
3" h
Cow, celluloid, brown, USA **7.00**
Horse, celluloid, gray, marked "Japan" **7.00**
Sheep, composition, wool coat,
wood legs, marked "Germany"
on paper collar **35.00**
3½", horse, brown and tan, rubber,
USA **7.00**
4¼" h, donkey, composition, gray,
wood legs, marked "Germany" .. **40.00**
5" h
Camel, celluloid, brown, USA ... **12.00**
Cow, composition, brown, wood
legs, marked "Germany" **45.00**
Fence
2½" h
Red and green, wooden, eight 6"
folding sections **30.00**
White, two rail fence, green wood
base, six 14" sections, home
made **55.00**
6" h, green wood, three rail fence,
three 12" sections, home made,
two gates **30.00**
8" h, blue four rail wood fence, six
18" sections, home made **70.00**
Set, metal, green and red, orig box
marked "Toy Fence, S & G Novelties" **150.00**
House
2½", cardboard, frosting on roof,
marked "Japan" **4.50**
3"
Chalk, bank, corner building,
white, marked "Made In Japan" **10.00**
Log House, frosting on roof, red
wood chimney, marked "Ger-
many" **10.00**
3½"
Cardboard, litho, USA **6.00**
Chalk, theater, yellow, marked
"Made in Japan" **10.00**
4½", cardboard, foil finish, frosting
on roof, marked "Japan" **5.00**
6", cardboard, litho, church, frosting
on roof, USA **8.00**

NON TREE-RELATED ITEMS

Book
Douglas, Lloyd C, *Home for Christmas,* Grosset and Dunlap Pub, NY, 1937 .... **3.00**
Kent, Rockwell, *A Northern Christmas,* American Artists Group Inc, 1941 .... **7.00**
Sawyer, Ruth, *This Way To Christmas,* Harper & Bros, NY, 1916, frontpiece by Norman Rockwell **7.50**
Stevenson, Robert Louis, *A Christmas Sermon,* Charles Scribner & Sons, NY, 1919 .... **3.50**
Williamson, C N and A M, *Rosemary, A Christmas Story,"* A L Burt Co, NY, 1906 .... **4.50**
Candy Box, 3 x 5 x 1½", cardboard, various painted Christmas scenes, 1930s **5.00**

Post Card, Santa Claus, Oilette Series, Card #1822, Tuck, England, 1907, $20.00.

Candy Cane, 5" l, chenille, red and white, Japan **5.50**
Candy Container, 4" l, airship, silver, removable nose, three dimensional, Dresden **250.00**
Children's Books
Brown, Abbie Farwell, *The Christmas Angel,* Mifflin Co, NY, 1910 ..... **5.00**
Price, Margaret Evans, illus, *The Manger Babe,* Stecher Litho Co, 1916 . **15.00**
Shearon, Lillian Nicholson, *The Little Miser,* Bobbs-Merrill Pub, NY, 1945 **3.50**
Greeting Card
"A Joyous Christmas," caroler with Art Deco background, flat card, verse on front, USA **1.50**
"A Merry Christmas," three children in winter clothes, huddled beneath an umbrella, Wolf & Co, NY **2.50**

"Christmas Blessing," leather type, church surrounded by holly, flat card, S Hildersheimer & Co **5.00**
"Christmas Greetings," emb holly, silver background, three pages of verse, The Art Lithographic Co ... **6.00**
"Christmas Thoughts," Marry E. Miller, International Art Pub Co, NY, Berlin **3.50**
"Hearty Greetings," cut out emb border, holly on front, verse inside .. **3.50**
"Merry Christmas From Our House," dogs in a little Christmas house, USA, 1930s **2.50**
"Sincere Good Wishes," greetings inside, Raphael Tuck & Sons, London **5.00**
"Wishing You A Happy Christmas," two birds on branches, sepia tones, Raphael Tuck & Sons, London ... **3.00**
"Wishing You A Very Happy Christmas," dog with riding crop in mouth, standing beside wooden pull toy horse **5.00**
Music Box, church, cardboard, frosting, paper stained glass windows, removable roof, wind-up, plays Silent Night, marked "Japan," orig box ... **25.00**
Nativity
Germany
Angel, 4½" l, composition, wax covering, spun glass wings, human hair, net and lace robe ... **40.00**
Crib, composition, 1½" l wax Baby Jesus **7.50**
Manger, composition and wood .. **25.00**
Mary, 5" h, composition, kneeling, green base **9.00**
Joseph, 5½" h, composition, kneeling, green base **9.00**
Shepherd, 5¼" h, composition, kneeling **9.00**
Wise Man, 6" h, composition, standing **9.00**
Japan
Joseph, 2" h, composition, kneeling **1.50**
Mary, 2" h, composition, kneeling **1.50**
Set
Bisque figures, sheep, and cow, orig box, all marked "Occupied Japan" **75.00**
Chalk figures glued inside cardboard manger **16.00**

TREE-RELATED ITEMS

Angel
4" h, hard plastic, white and silver, USA, 1950s **5.00**
9" h, Nurenberg style, gold, paper foil pleated skirt, gold emb paper wings, composition head, tree top ornament, Germany, 1930s **25.00**

Icicles
  4" h, glass, twisted, annealed hook,
    clear 3.00
  4½" h, plastic, clear, hook, set of 20 5.00
  5" h, metal, lacquer of various colors,
    twisted 5.00
Light Bulb
  Figural
    Bear, clear glass, early, marked
      "Germany" 100.00
    Chinese Lantern, milk glass, festive
      colors, Japan 10.00
    Clown, clear glass, red and green,
      marked "Germany" 55.00
    House, milk glass, pink and white,
      Japan 10.00
    Street Lantern, milk glass, snow
      cap, green, white, and black, Ja-
      pan 12.00
    Zeppelin, milk glass, red, white,
      and blue, Japan 20.00
  Set
    Bubblelights, orig box, working .. 35.00
    Celluloid bulbs, figural, people,
      orig box, working 200.00
    Milk Glass, figural, orig box, Japan 85.00

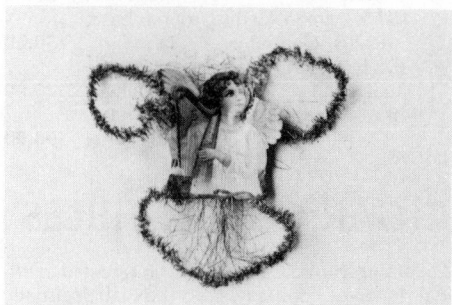

**Ornament, diecut paper, angel, multicol-
ored, tinsel and wire wings and base,
$15.00.**

Ornament
  Chromolithograph
    Angel, crescent moon, cellophane
      background, Germany, 1880–
      1910 .... 12.00
    Father Christmas, litho upper torso,
      cotton batting skirt, Germany,
      1890–1910 .... 100.00
    Girl, dancing, tinsel trim, Germany,
      1890 .... 12.00
    Woman, reading book, litho upper
      torso, crepe paper skirt 14.00
  Dresden
    2" h, emb gold star, tinsel trim, flat 30.00
    2½" h
      Camel, brown, one hump, three
        dimensional 95.00

Reindeer, gold, three dimensional 95.00
3" h, English setter, silver, copper,
  and green, flat 50.00
3" l
  Reindeer, pulling red cart, three
    dimensional 110.00
  Star, gold emb, flat, spun gold
    wire 30.00
3½" h, heart, gold, diecut flowers
  in center, flat 35.00
4" l, eagle, gold, copper and green,
  olive branch, flat 45.00
5" h
  Fish, silver, emb, two sided 60.00
  Stag, gold, copper trees at base,
    green lawn, flat 55.00
6" l
  Fish, gold emb, two sided, semi-
    flat 75.00
  Slipper, gold, netting and tinsel
    at toe, chromolithograph trim
    on heel, flat 40.00
6½" h, rooster, gold, copper, and
  green trim, flat 55.00
6½ x 8" l, swan, swimming in
  pond, semi-concealed in rushes,
  gold, green and copper trim, flat 55.00
Foil, Japan
  Cornucopia, bright colors 2.00
  Geometric shapes, fold-out 1.50

**Ornament, glass, Santa Claus, red suit,
green tree, yellow base, 3⅝" h, $75.00.**

Glass, figural, Germany
  Basket, cloth flowers, silvered,
    1930s 35.00
  Bell, 3" h, wire clapper, silvered,
    red, white, and blue stripe,
    1930s 12.00
  Carrot, 3½" h, silvered, orange
    matte finish, green tucksheer
    leaf, 1910–1920 .... 50.00

Clown, 3½" h, silvered, pink suit and hat, marked "My Darling" on chest, 1920s **60.00**

Crown, 1½" h, silvered, gold, blue trim, 1920–1930s **15.00**

Doll Head, 2¼" h, silvered, bisque tint face, fine detailed facial features, yellow hair, red ribbon, 1920s **120.00**

Fish, 3" l, unsilvered, gold paint, red trim, 1900–10 .... **60.00**

Heart, 2¼" h, silvered, gold, white and red trim, 1930s **15.00**

House, 3" h, silvered, blue and white trim, 1920–1930s **25.00**

Icicle

12" h, silvered, green, white snow top, 1930s **38.00**

3½" h, silvered, diamond shape, pink, 1930–42 .... **10.00**

Parasol, 8" h, unsilvered, pink lacquer, lametta trim, Victorian, 1890–1910 .... **45.00**

Purse, 2¼" h, clutch style, silvered, 1930s **30.00**

Sail Boat, 3¾" h, unsilvered, pink, wire and litho trim, 1910 ...... **50.00**

Snowman, 2¾" h, silvered, playing accordion, 1930s **42.00**

Songbird, on clip, silvered, red and black trim, 1920s **18.00**

Wine Keg, unsilvered, wire trim, gold painted highlights, Victorian, 1900 .... **80.00**

Vase, 3½" h, litho flowers, wire trim, unsilvered, 1910 .... **40.00**

Hard Plastic

Carousel, metal fan, twirls from heat of light bulbs **5.00**

Rudolf, 3¼" h, marked "Rudolpf, Red Nosed Reindeer" **7.00**

Santa Claus, 3" h, red and white, plastic hook on top of head **6.00**

Kugel

2" d, round, silver, brass hook ... **25.00**

4" d, round, blue, brass hook **40.00**

5" l, grapes, purple **80.00**

6" d, round, green, brass hook ... **65.00**

Metal, various geometric shapes, tin and lead alloy, colored lacquer highlights **10.00**

Pressed Cotton, Japan

Apple, 2½" h, red, white, and pink **12.00**

Peach, 3" h, yellow, white, and pink **15.00**

Pear, 2½" h, yellow and red **12.00**

Strawberry, 1¼", red **10.00**

Reindeer

1" h, metal, brown, standing, marked "Germany" **20.00**

3" h

Art Glass, brown and white, paper and rhinestone collars **35.00**

Celluloid, brown, standing, marked "Irwin" **7.00**

Composition, brown, wooden legs, marked "Germany" **30.00**

Metal, brown, lying down **35.00**

4" h, metal, brown, standing, marked "Germany" **35.00**

5" h, blown glass, silvered, doe and fawn, annealed together, Germany **75.00**

6" h, celluloid, white, red glass eyes, standing, Japan **15.00**

8" h, celluloid, elk type, red, Japan . **20.00**

Tree

Brush

1½" h, green, red base **2.00**

5" h

Green, red base **6.50**

White, red base **7.50**

9" h, green, decorated with glass beads, red base **15.00**

12" h, green, red base **18.00**

Feather

9" h, white, red sq base with gold stencil trim, 1950s, West Germany **85.00**

18" h, green, white round base, 1920s, Germany **150.00**

36" h, green, red berries, candle clips, sq white base, Germany . **325.00**

48" h, green, white round base, Germany **400.00**

CIGAR COLLECTIBLES

Collecting Hints: Concentrate on one geographical region or company. Cigar box labels usually are found in large concentrations. Check on availability before paying high prices.

History: Tobacco was one of the first export products of the American colonies. By 1750 smoking began to become socially acceptable for males. The cigar reached its zenith from 1880 to 1930 when it was the boardroom and after dinner symbol for the withdrawal of males to privacy and conversation.

Cigar companies were quick to recognize national political, sports and popular heroes. They encouraged them to use cigars and placed their faces on promotional material.

The lithograph printing press brought color and popularity to labels, seals and bands. Many have memories of a cigar band ring given by a grandfather or family friend. The popularity of the cigarette in the 1940s reduced the cigar to second place in the tobacco field. Today, cigar related material is minimal due to the smaller number of companies making cigars.

Reference: Tony Hyman, *Handbook of American Cigar Boxes,* Arnet Art Museum, 1979.

Collectors' Club: International Seal, Label and Cigar Band Society, 8915 E. Bellevue Street, Tucson, AZ 85715.

Museum: Arnet Collection, New York Public Library, New York, NY

Dish, dec with multicolored cigar bands, green felt back, 7⅛" d, $28.00.

Box, oak, zinc liner	25.00
Cigar Cutter, figural, cast iron, pelican on tray, match holder on tail, Roth	65.00
Cigar Holder	
Amber, solid gold band	55.00
Tortoiseshell	3.00
Cigar Piercer, 3" l, silvered brass, celluloid wrapper band inscribed "Westchester County Bar Association, Annual Dinner, 1915," sharp metal point	45.00
Counter, 1½ x 3", celluloid, Bloomer Club Cigar adv, movable disk wheels, two ladies in bloomers sipping champagne, c1900	18.00
Display Cigar Box, 2½ x 5½ x 8½", wood, Certified Primo Cigar Box, full color litho paper designs, c1930	35.00
Lighter, counter type, cast iron, bulldog, 4½" h	85.00
Match Safe, Union Made Cigars, 21¼ x 2¾", bright silvered brass, celluloid cov with light blue Union Cigar label, black inscriptions and artwork, issued by Cigar Makers Union #97, Boston	80.00
Matchbook Holder	
Muriel Cigars, blued metal, 1⅛ x 1⅝" multicolored celluloid insert, woman in multicolored portrait, small gold frame, dark red ground, c1920	60.00
San Felice, 1½ x 2¼", blued metal, 1½" oval celluloid, multicolored insert inscribed "For Gentlemen Of Good Taste," well dressed gentle-	

man seated in wicker chair smoking cigar, c1920	65.00
Mirror, pocket, Union Made Cigars adv, 2⅛", celluloid, detailed union label, light blue, black lettering, c1900	50.00
Notepad	
Hemmeter Cigar Co, floral and cigar design cover, calendar, unused	15.00
Union Cigar, 2 x 3", celluloid cov, black and white union anti-trust text, blue facsimile Union cigar label on each side, c1901	35.00
Pinback Button	
1¼", Union Made Cigars, red, white, blue, and black, light green cigar label, c1890	20.00
2⅛" d, "American's Favorite, The People's Choice Cigar," black and white portraits of Tom Moore, Henry George, bright red text, blue design representing baseball stitching, back paper text, c1898	65.00
Sign	
Admiration Cigars, 5½ x 7½", tin, litho, multicolor	90.00
Fame & Fortune 3 Cent Cigars, 8 x 14", tin	55.00
Tin	
Club House Cigars, 3 x 5"	25.00
Los Ramos cigars, 5 x 3¾"	8.00
Mohawk Chief, oval	550.00
Old Abe Cigars, round, paper label	60.00
Ology Cigars, 3¼ x 5¼"	4.00
Possum, red, "Am Good & Sweet"	70.00
Reichard's Cadet Cigar	65.00
Webster, 3½ x 5¼ x 1¼", litho, multicolored lid illus, c1930	20.00
Tobacco Humidor, Don Porto Cigar, tin	17.50
Watch Fob, United Cigar Makers League, 1¾", black and white, mirror back, metal strap loop, c1900	50.00

CIGARETTE ITEMS

Collecting Hints: Don't overlook the advertising which appeared in the national magazines of the 1940s to 1960s. The number of star and public heroes endorsing cigarettes is large. Modern promotional material for brands such as Marlboro and Salem has been issued in large numbers, and much has been put aside by collectors. Most collectors tend to concentrate on the pre-1950 period.

History: Although the cigarette industry dates back to the late 19th century, it was the decades of the 1930s and 1940s that saw cigarettes become the dominant tobacco product. The cigarette industry launched massive advertising and promotional campaigns. Radio was one of the principal advertising vehicles. In the 1950s, television became the dominant advertising medium.

The Surgeon General's Report, which warned of the danger of cigarette smoking, led to restrictions on advertising and limited the places where cigarettes could be smoked. The industry reacted with a new advertising approach aimed at females and people in the 20 to 40 year age bracket. The need to continue the strong positive public image for cigarette smoking still leads to more and more cigarette related items entering the collectibles marketplace.

Reference: Murray Cards International, Ltd., *Cigarette Card Values: Murray's 1988 Guide To Cigarette & Other Trade Cards*, 1988.

Collectors' Clubs: Cigarette Pack Collectors Association, 61 Searle Street, Georgetown, MA 01833; International Seal, Label & Cigar Band Society, 8915 East Bellevue St, Tuscon, AZ 85715.

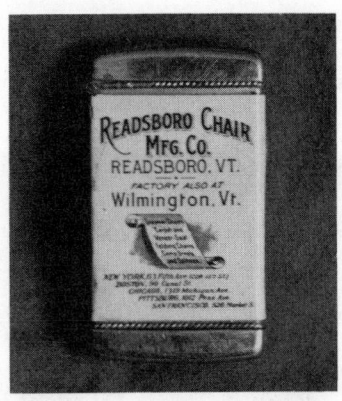

Match Holder, Readsboro Chair Mfg Co, office locations on front, examples of folding chairs and tables on back, plated tin base, striker on bottom, 1½ x 2¾ x½", $40.00.

Ashtray, Fatima Cigarettes, matchbox holder, marked "Nippon"	**100.00**
Banner, Old Gold Cigarettes, "Not A Cough In A Car Load," 42 x 120"	**75.00**
Cigarette Card, American	
Allen & Ginter, Pirates of the Spanish Main, 1888	**10.00**
Kinney Tobacco Co., Military and Naval Uniforms, 1887	**2.00**
Wings Cigarettes	
First series of 50	**40.00**
Series B, set of 50	**40.00**
Cigarette Card Album, 1889	
Allen & Ginter	
Fish From American Waters	**50.00**
Napoleon	**40.00**
Quadrupeds	**50.00**
W Duck & Sons, Terrors of America	**50.00**
Cigarette Case	
2½ x 3", tan leather, cardboard, Fatima, veiled lady in gold, "Ninth Annual Convention/A.A.C. of A./ Baltimore June 1913" on reverse	**20.00**
3 x 4", enameled, woman's	
Black, envelope style, red stone dec	**15.00**
Peacock design	**45.00**
Cigarette Case and Lighter, Evans, 1940	**29.00**
Clock, adv, Vantage Cigarettes, battery operated	**20.00**
Lighter, adv	
Hastings Piston Ring, 3" l tin metal tube, removable black cap, red, yellow, and black trademark, yellow ground, c1940	**15.00**
Pan Am	**15.00**
Skelly, 3" l brass tube, removable red cap, red logo and inscription, pearl white ground, c1940	**10.00**
United Lacquer, oil drum shape	**9.00**

Match Box Holder, 6" base, ceramic, Fatima Turkish Cigarettes	**85.00**
Pinback Button	
⅞", Perfection Cigarettes, brown haired woman, light blue dress, daisies on bow, shaded blue ground, back paper text	**15.00**
1", Phillip Morris, celluloid, Johnny, c1930	**18.00**
1¼", Pick Pug Cut Tobacco, blonde woman, black ground, back paper text, c1900	**20.00**
Playing Cards, Camel Cigarettes	**18.00**
Poster	
Kool Cigarettes, 12 x 18", smoking penguin points to pack, c1933	**35.00**
Natural Cigarettes, 26 x 18", Arab with horse and rifle, 1910, framed	**300.00**
Wings, The New Deal Cigarette, 12 x 18", multicolored	**30.00**
Silk	
1", Wm Randolph Hearst For Governor	**7.50**
3¼", William McKinley	**20.00**
Sign, Spud Cigarettes, 24 x 30", girl and puppy	**38.00**
Store Display, Chesterfield, Christmas, 1940s	**5.00**
Thermometer	
Salem Cigarettes	**12.00**
Winston Cigarettes, tin	**36.00**
Tin	
Black Cat Cigarettes	**10.00**
Camel Cigarettes, 4½ x 5½ x ½", camel and desert scene, 1930s	**18.00**
Chesterfield, dec	**25.00**
Edgeworth Pipe Tobacco, blue	**6.00**
Lucky Strike, 1950s	**15.00**

Melachrino, 3 x 10 x 1¼", hinged, litho, assortment of Egyptian cigarettes, c1920 .... **18.00**
Murad, fifty cigarettes, 5½ x 3 x 1¼", oblong, Canadian, 1897 stamp ... **38.00**
Omar Cigarettes, 9 x 6 x 1" **10.00**
Pall Mall, 7 x 8", Christmas dec **12.50**

CIRCUS ITEMS

Collecting Hints: Circus programs are one of the most popular items in this category. Individuals have collected them since the 1920s. Programs prior to the 1930s are hard to find; post 1930 material is readily available.

Model building plays an active part in collecting. Some kits are available. However, most collectors like to build their models from scratch. Great attention is placed on accuracy of detail.

There is a wealth of books published about the circus. These are sought by collectors both for intrinsic as well as research value.

History: The 18th century circus was a small traveling company of acrobats and jugglers, and the first record of an American troupe was at that time. Washington is known to have attended a circus performance.

By the mid-19th century the tent circus with accompanying side shows and menagerie became popular throughout America. P. T. Barnum was one of the early circus promoters. His American Museum in New York in 1841 featured live animal acts. Other successful Barnum promotions included Jenny Lind in 1850, Tom Thumb from 1843 to 1883, and the purchase of Jumbo from the London Zoo in 1883.

The Ringlings and Barnum and Bailey brought a magical quality to the circus. The golden age of the tent circus was the 1920s to the 1940s when a large circus would consist of over 100 railroad cars.

As television challenged live entertainment, the tent circus fell on hard times. Expenses for travel, food, staff, etc., mounted. A number of mergers took place, and many smaller companies simply went out of business. There are a few tent circuses remaining. However, most modern circuses now perform inside large convention centers.

Collectors' Clubs: Circus Fans of America, Four Center Drive, Camp Hill, PA 17011; The Circus Historical Society, 743 Beverly Park Place, Jackson, MI 49203; The Circus Model Builders International, 347 Lonsdale Avenue, Dayton, OH 45419.

Museums: The Barnum Museum, Bridgeport, CT; Circus World Museum, Baraboo, WI; Ringling Circus Museum, Sarasota, FL.

Book
August, Dean, *When Circus Comes To Town,* contemporary **2.00**
Beatty, Clyde, *Jungle Performers,* 1941, FE, dj, autographed by author **90.00**
Desmond, Alice, *Barnum Presents General Tom Thumb,* 1954 ...... **15.00**
Freedman, Jill, *Circus Days,* 100 pgs **8.00**
Jensen, Dean, *The Biggest, The Smallest, The Longest, The Shortest, A History of Wisconsin Circuses,* 8½ x 11", 230 pgs **15.00**
Miller, Art "Doc," *Little Old Show,* paperback **8.00**
Plowden, Gene, *Maestro of the Circus, The Story of Merle Evans,* 1971 **12.50**
Calendar, Circus World Museum, 1974 **5.00**
Letterhead, Ringling Bros, multicolored, five brothers with crest, 1909 ...... **18.00**
Lithographs
Cristiani Bros, Big Wild Animal Circus, 22 x 28", litho, polar bear, lion, giraffe, rhino, tiger, and hippo drawing, yellow lettering, black trim, plastic cov, F.D. Freeland ... **26.00**
Dailey Bros Big 5 Ring Railroad Wild Animal Circus, full color blond woman riding pair of tigers, purple and green banner, white and green lettering, Central Show Printing Co Inc **25.00**
Magazine, Ringling Brothers & Barnum & Bailey, 1936 .... **8.00**
Menu, Greatest Show on Earth, Nov 12, 1898, full color **100.00**
Model, 1" scale
Bareback riders, man and woman, two horses **800.00**
Clarke Bros Circus, two wheel hitch **50.00**
Hay Wagon and harness, blue and red **300.00**
Railroad Flat Car **200.00**
Side Show paraphernalia, fourteen set ups **1,120.00**
Pass, Annual, 1953, cardboard, emb animals **2.00**
Playing Cards,
Old Maid, Circus Edition **5.00**
Ringling Bros and Barnum & Bailey Circus, miniature size **12.00**
Poster
Arthur Bros
1940
Big Railroad Show, arrival parade with showgirls on horses and elephants **90.00**
Second Largest Circus On Earth, red and yellow **60.00**
1943, Amusing Wire Display, navy, orange, and red, tightrope walker in top hat **170.00**

Barnum & Bailey
  1894, The Grand Equestrian Tour-
    nament, rough riders, inset Civil
    and Military horsemanship illus,
    Strobridge Litho 725.00
  1913, Lion and Tiger, reclining jun-
    gle cats, circus logo, Strobridge
    Litho 275.00
Clyde Beatty Circus
  1935, Clyde Beatty Circus, holds
    reign over field of wild jungle
    cats, date tag "July 4, Glendale
    Speedway" bottom 50.00
Cole Bros
  1930, Champion, champion rider
    astride prancing horse 80.00
  All The Marvels, animals in cages,
    Erie Litho 210.00
Hagenbeck-Wallace
  1925, Capt Clyde Beatty, World's
    Most Daring Trainer, posing with
    lions, tigers, and leopards pyra-
    mid 270.00
King Bros, 1946, clown face, red and
    yellow, advertising arrival 210.00

Poster, Ringling Bros, 20 x 28", $100.00.

Ringling Bros and Barnum & Bailey
  1935, jolly clown portrait, blue
    ground, Erie Litho 270.00
  1938, The Greatest Wild Animal
    Display, presents Terrell Jacobs,
    World's Foremost Trainer, Strob-
    ridge Litho 625.00
  1940, The Great Alzanax, high
    wire act, red ground, reverse im-
    printed "The Incredible Unus"
    for magenta test run 150.00
Program
  Barnum & Bailey, 1953 .... 10.00
  Cole Bros Clyde Beatty, 1969, 24 pgs,
    40 photos 5.00
  Gentry Bros & James Patterson, 1924   15.00
  Hamid-Morgan, 1948 .... 7.00
  Ringling Bros Barnum & Bailey, 1962,
    53 pgs, 10 articles, 90 photos 6.00

Puzzle, circus, framed, Milton Bradley   30.00
Record, Old Time Circus Calliope, Wur-
    litzer Calliola, Paul Eakin's Gay 90's
    Village 5.00
Routebook
  Barnum & Bailey, 1906 .... 225.00
  Cristiani Bros Circus, 1958 .... 25.00
  Forepaugh, Adam, shows, 1891 .... 225.00
Sign, 43 x 65", Aqua Circus, wood,
    painted, scallop border, woman in
    1890s garb with parachute 140.00
Souvenir book, Ringling Bros and
    Barnum & Bailey Circus, 1939 .....   15.00
Ticket Stub Book, Hagenbeck Wallace
    Circus, 1935 .... 10.00
Toy, wood, Schoenhut
  Horse, painted eyes, brown saddle . 130.00
  Tiger, glass eyes 200.00
  Ringmaster, 8½" h, painted eyes ... 155.00
Wagon Wheel, wood, metal rim, red,
    white, and blue painted spokes 250.00

CLICKERS

Collecting Hints: Clickers with pictures are more desirable than clickers with just printing. Value is reduced by scratches in the paint and rust. Some companies issued several variations of a single design—be alert for them in your collecting.

History: Clickers were a popular advertising medium for products and services ranging from plumbing supplies, political aspirants, soft drinks, hotels, to beer and whiskey. The most commonly found clickers are those which were given to children in shoe stores. Brands include Buster Brown, Poll Parrot, and Red Goose. Many shoe store clickers have advertising whistle mates.

Clickers were not confined to advertising. They were a popular holiday item, especially at Halloween. Impressed animal forms also provided a style for clickers.

The vast majority of clickers were made of tin. The older and rarer clickers were made of celluloid.

ADVERTISING

Acker's Candy Shop, Atlantic City,
    metal, early 1900 .... 20.00
Barton's Dyan Shine Shoe Polish, yel-
    low, black, and white, checkerboard
    trim 10.00
Buster Brown Hosiery, red, white, and
    blue, 1930–40 .... 22.00
Calvert Whiskey, red and white, 1950s   8.00
El Captain Coffee, yellow, red, and
    black, 1930s 18.00
Ellis Chile, chile, red, yellow, and green   8.00

**Fort Pitt Brewing Co/Sharpsburg, PA,
litho tin, yellow ground, green and red
dec, $15.00.**

Fort Pitt Lager Brews, beer bottle, green background, 1930s	15.00
Gold E Slide binder, silver and blue, 1940–50	8.00
Mayer Shoes, 1¼", round, celluloid, white, black print, "It's Mayer Shoes I chirp about, they are the best without a doubt"	35.00
New and True Coffee, c1930	15.00
Nu Icy Soft Drink, yellow and blue, 1930s	15.00
Octagon Soap, soap package illus, "The Noisy Snapper Jack" on back	10.00
Olympic Park, female in bathing suit, 1930s	18.00
Real-Kill Bug Killer	18.00
Red Goose Shoes, red and yellow, tin, c1930	12.00
Sunbeam Bread, Stroehman, 4½ x 2¾", white, red, and yellow	5.00
USA Today, black and white, early 1980s	5.00

NON-ADVERTISING

Banjo, 2½ x 1", puppet, multicolored, Japan	2.00
Birds and Nest, birds move to feed babies when clicked	10.00
Black Man, blue and white striped pants, marked "Germany", c1930	18.00
Clown, 1½ x 2¼", multicolored, Japan	2.00
Cowboy, shooting	75.00
Dog, 3 x 1¾", white, blue, red, and yellow, "DOG," Japan	2.00
Felix, sitting on bench with arm around girlfriend, c1930	30.00
Frog, 1½ x 3 x 1", yellow, green, and red	2.00
Halloween	
Black cat and pumpkin, c1930–40	10.00
Witch and pumpkin, orange, black, and white	15.00
Witch on broomstick, black, white, red, and orange, c1940	12.00
Ice Cream, multi illus, 1930s	15.00
Jiminy Crickett, yellow and green, 1940 copyright	20.00
Jockey on horse, figural	75.00
Machine Gunner	40.00
Mickey Mouse, playing drum	35.00
Owl, 1¾ x 3⅛", clock with "Owl" in middle, blue, yellow, red, and white, Japan	2.00
Police Dept. Badge, 1½ x 2½", gold, silver, and red	2.00
Political, "Click with Dick," 1¾", litho, red letters on white	5.00

CLOCKS

Collecting Hints: Many clocks of the twentieth century were reproductions of earlier styles. Therefore, dating should be checked by patent dates on the mechanism, maker's label, and construction techniques.

The principal buyers for the advertising and figural clocks are not the clock collectors, but the specialist with whose area of interest the clock overlaps. For example, the Pluto alarm clock is of far greater importance to a Disneyana collector, then to most clock collectors.

Condition is critical. Rust and non-working condition detract heavily from the price.

History: The clock always has served a dual function: decorative and utilitarian. Beginning in the late 19th century the clock became an important advertising vehicle, a tradition still continuing today. As character and personality became part of the American scene, the clock was a logical target, whether an alarm or wall model. The novelty clock, especially figural, was common in the 1930 to the 1960 period.

In the 1970s the popularity of digital wrist watches and clocks has led to less emphasis on the clock as a promotional item.

Collectors' Club: National Association of Watch and Clock Collectors, Inc., P.O. Box 33, Columbia, PA 17512. *Bulletin* (bimonthly).

Museum: Museum of National Association of Watch and Clock Collectors, Columbia, PA.

Additional Listings: See *Warman's Antiques and Their Prices.*

Advertising	
Breyer's Ice Cream, wood, sailboat, chrome sails	50.00
Budweiser, 5½ x 4½ x 14", revolving, duck in flight on reverse, marble base with emblem	85.00
Bulova, wall	48.00

Charlie the Tuna, alarm, copyright 1969, Star-Kist Foods, Inc., Robertshaw Controls Co, Lux Time Division, Lebanon, TN, USA, $15.00.

Cincinnati Reds, logo, wood frame, electric, 1940s	60.00
Coca-Cola, "Drink Coca-Cola In Bottles," sq, wood case, electric, Selected Devices Co, NY	215.00
Frostie Root Beer, metal, fluorescent bulb	150.00
Jefferson "Golden Hour," electric ...	85.00
John Deere, 14" d, round, electric ..	65.00
Kodak, "Pictures Are Priceless—Use Kodak Film," 15½", sq, lights up .	35.00
Sauers Extract, New Haven Clock Co, wall	975.00
7–Up, oak frame, c1950	100.00
Sprite, wood frame, quartz, c1980 .	30.00
St Joseph's Aspirin, neon	300.00
Tetley Tea Time, 13", blue and gray, tin, Art Deco	85.00
Warren Telephone Co, Ashland, MA, oak	80.00

Alarm

Bradley, brass, double bells, Germany	35.00
Mickey Mouse	45.00
Peter's Shoes, New Haven Clock Co, 4 x 4", Art Deco, c1930	50.00
Purina Poultry Chows, electric, three dials, red, white, and blue checkerboard bag	40.00
Star Wars, talking	25.00
Trix The Rabbit, c1960	15.00
War, Gilbert, orig box	60.00

Character

Donald Duck, 9" h, wall, glazed china, 2¼" d case inscribed "Blessings," blue outfit, green glazed ground, orig gold sticker marked "Waechtersbach," inscription "Walt Disney Productions, J. A. Sural Hanua/Main—Made In Germany," c1950	175.00
Howdy Doody, talking	65.00

Mickey Mouse, Bradley, animated hands	25.00
Pluto, 4 x 5 x 9", electric, black, white, and red plastic, bone hands, moving eyes and tongue, c1940 ..	100.00
Sesame Street, school	25.00

Figural

Artist's Palette, bakelite	35.00
Davy Crockett, wall, pendulum	75.00
Doghouse, 11" h, iron, dog looking out, flowers	80.00
Owl, Wise Potato Chip, electric	75.00
Refrigerator, 8½" h, metal, painted white, GE label, Warren Telechron Co, Ashland, MA	185.00
Spinning Wheel, Lux, animated	80.00
Tape Measure, tan, Lux	45.00

Kitchen

Chef, 10½" h, electric, wall, white, Sessions Clock Co, Forestville	24.00
Donut, 8¾" h, dark herbal green glaze, Clifton Art Pottery	85.00

CLOTHING

Collecting Hints: Vintage clothing should be clean and in good repair. Designer labels and original boxes can add to the value.

Collecting vintage clothing appears to have reached a plateau. Although there are still dedicated collectors, the category is no longer attracting a rash of new collectors annually.

History: Clothing is collected and studied as a reference source in learning about fashion, construction and types of materials used.

References: Maryanne Dolan, *Vintage Clothing, 1880-1960, Second Edition,* Books Americana, 1988; Tina Irick-Nauer, *The First Price Guide to Antique and Vintage Clothes,* E. P. Dutton, 1983; Sheila Malouff, *Collectible Clothing With Prices,* Wallace Homestead, 1983; Terry McCormick, *The Consumer's Guide To Vintage Clothing,* Dembner Books, 1987; Diane McGee, *A Passion For Fashion,* Simmons-Boardman Books, Inc, 1987.

Periodical: *Vintage Clothing Newsletter,* P.O. Box 1422, Corvallis, OR 97339.

Collectors' Club: The Costume Society of America, P. O. Box 761, Englishtown, NJ 07726.

Museums: Metropolitan Museum of Art, New York, NY; the Costume and Textile Department of the Los Angeles County Museum of Art, Los Angeles, CA; Philadelphia Museum of Art, Philadelphia, PA.

Bathing Suit

Black, stretchy fabric, back buttons, flared skirt, c1930	**45.00**

Black and white, matching slippers
and hat, c1890 . . . .   **50.00**
Bloomers
Crepe Satin, peach, silk embroidery,
lace trim, 1920s **18.00**
Wool, cream **25.00**
Blouse
Chiffon, green, child's, multiple rows
of ruffles **15.00**
Cotton, white, cutwork, Victorian . .   **20.00**
Lace, ecru, evening style, gathered
waist, 1950s **18.00**
Poplin, white, middy style, c1910 . .   **15.00**
Silk, cream, embroidered, 1900s . . .   **65.00**
Cape
Mohair, black, ankle length, c1930 .   **75.00**
Velvet, red, white satin lining **70.00**
Wool, dark blue, quilted lining, 18" l,
c1920 . . . .   **65.00**
Capelet
Beaded, all over design, beaded
fringe, c1850s **100.00**
Feathers, ostrich, gray satin ribbon .   **50.00**
Fur, black beaver **25.00**
Christening Gown, cotton, white
Cutwork embroidery collar, tuck
pleats around ruffled skirt **65.00**
Machine sewn, lace, hand embroi-
dery, 42" l **50.00**
Coat
Cashmere, red, silver fox collar, full
length, c1940 . . . .   **50.00**
Cotton, baby's, gathered yoke and ca-
pelet, embroidery, flannel lining . .   **25.00**
Fur
Alaskan Seal, black, mink trim,
padded shoulders, c1940 . . . . . .   **100.00**
Muskrat, bell shaped sleeves,
c1940 . . . .   **90.00**
Persian Lamb, black, matching hat   **75.00**
Squirrel, gray, wide cuffs, padded
shoulders, c1940 . . . .   **80.00**
Linen, boy's, hand stitched, dec cuffs   **35.00**
Plush, lady's, black, Flapper style, bat
wing sleeves **125.00**
Silk
Baby's, pink, label "Paris Best" . .   **45.00**
Lady's, black, evening, three quar-
ter length, c1915 . . . .   **36.00**
Velvet, lady's, navy blue, beaded
dec, black fox collar and cuffs, red
satin lining, 1920s **250.00**
Wool, blue, beaver collar and cuffs,
blouson, drop waist style, c1920 .   **100.00**
Dress
Batiste, white, lace, high neck, full
skirt, long sleeves, c1900 . . . .   **150.00**
Calico, blue, 2 pc, matching bonnet,
c1900 . . . .   **165.00**
Chiffon, blue, edges trimmed with
braided fabric, 1925 . . . .   **40.00**

Dress, child's, matching cape, white cotton, $85.00.

Child's
Gingham, blue and white, hand
and machine sewn, white em-
broidery trim, 25" h **50.00**
Lawn, white, lace, drop waist,
c1910 . . . .   **60.00**
Rayon, raspberry, accordion pleats,
c1930 . . . .   **15.00**
Silk
Peach, embroidered collar and
skirt, short sleeves, c1920 . . .   **35.00**
Red, drop waist, black trim,
bowed sash, c1910 . . . .   **75.00**
Velvet, red, white nylon, Shirley
Temple style, Cinderella tag . . .   **15.00**
Wool, dark green, Amish, c1930 .   **45.00**
Cotton, day type, gold, net trim,
c1900 . . . .   **20.00**
Crepe, pink, beading, Flapper style .   **125.00**
Georgette, pink, many layers of geor-
gette and chiffon, c1920 . . . .   **75.00**
Knit, 2 pc, 1930 . . . .   **25.00**
Linen, embroidered wisteria inserts,
Irish lace trim **150.00**
Satin, black, padded shoulders, waist
swag, 1940s **75.00**
Silk
Black, chiffon sleeves, embroidery,
1923 . . . .   **48.00**
Black, lace, ecru beaded bodice,
c1920 . . . .   **75.00**
Blue, floral print, lace trim, Victo-
rian **150.00**
Brown, black accents, c1910 . . . .   **50.00**
Silk Faille, mourning, black, c1890 .   **100.00**
Silk Taffeta, purple, marcasite but-
tons, late 1800s **35.00**
Wool, pink, lace trim, c1890 . . . . . .   **125.00**
Dressing Gown, satin, ruby red, fagoted
ruffled edges, 1930 . . . .   **28.00**
Duster, linen, shawl collar, 1900s **100.00**
Evening Gown
Chiffon and velvet, black, Empire
waist, shirred bodice, 1930 . . . . . .   **45.00**
Crepe, brown, matching velvet ca-
pelet with feather trim, c1930 . . . .   **40.00**

Net and Taffeta, black, lace flowers, c1940	**48.00**
Organza, white, shirred, rhinestones, c1940	**45.00**
Evening Jacket, crepe, pink, floral patterned sequins, lined, 1940	**58.00**
Petticoat, white cotton, crocheted insert, wide crocheted hem	**45.00**

Prom Gown

Georgette, yellow, embroidered bodice, strapless, c1960	**25.00**
Net and Taffeta, pink, layered skirt, bow trim, c1950	**35.00**

Skirt

Cotton, white, Victorian, walking	**40.00**
Linen, gore style, Edwardian type	**40.00**
Polished Cotton, floral print, full, c1950	**24.00**
Wool, black, Victorian	**40.00**

Suit

Boy's, wool, herringbone, lined, Amish, c1920	**40.00**
Lady's, wool, navy, pintucks, silk lining, 1921	**55.00**
Sweater, cashmere, white pearl trim	**35.00**

Wedding Gown

Net and Lace, cream, high neck, two pc style, c1900	**165.00**
Satin, ivory, padded shoulders, sweetheart neckline, waist swag, self train, c1940	**125.00**
Silk Faille, lace, ribbon, and pearl trim, train	**170.00**

CLOTHING ACCESSORIES

Collecting Hint: Vintage clothing accessories are quite stylish with many of today's fashions.

History: Clothing accessories are items used to complete a fashionable outfit. Collecting clothing accessories is a more recent hobby and is growing rapidly.

References: Maryanne Dolan, *Vintage Clothing, 1880-1960, Second Edition,* Books Americana, 1988; Evelyn Haertig, *Antique Combs & Purses,* Gallery Graphics Press, 1983; Richard Holiner, Revised Second Edition, *Antique Purses,* Collector Books, 1987; Tina Irick-Nauer, *The First Price Guide to Antique and Vintage Clothes,* E. P. Dutton, 1983; Sheila Malouff, *Collectible Clothing With Prices,* Wallace Homestead, 1983; Terry McCormick, *The Consumer's Guide To Vintage Clothing,* Dembner Books, 1987; Diane McGee, *A Passion For Fashion,* Simmons-Boardman Books, Inc, 1987.

Periodical: *Vintage Clothing Newsletter,* P.O. Box 1422, Corvallis, OR 97339.

Collectors' Club: The Costume Society of America, 330 West 42nd Street, Suite 1702, New York, NY 10036.

Museums: Metropolitan Museum of Art, New York, NY; The Costume and Textile Department of the Los Angeles County Museum of Art, Los Angeles, CA; Philadelphia Museum of Art, Philadelphia, PA.

Apron, calico, red and white	**25.00**
Baby Bonnet, cotton, tatted, ribbon rosettes	**15.00**
Bed Jacket, satin, pink, lavish ecru lace, labeled "B Altman & Co, NY," 1930s	**30.00**
Boudoir Cap, crocheted, pink rosettes	**12.00**

Bonnet

Silk, hand crocheted lace	**36.00**
Straw, finely woven, worn silk lining	**135.00**
Boots, work type, leather, early, 11" h, pr	**25.00**
Bustle, canvas and woven wire	**30.00**
Change Purse, cut steel beads, ecru crochet, push bottom clasp, fringe, leaf dec, 2½ x 3½", inscribed "B Cottle, 1847"	**65.00**

Collar

Beaded, white, 1930s	**12.00**
Cotton, white, embroidered, wide, scalloped	**20.00**
Cosmetic Case, gold mesh, Whiting Davis, 3 x 4"	**15.00**
Costume, Matador, heavily embroidered, sequins and gold metallic thread, minor wear	**120.00**
Corset, sateen, orig Sears Roebuck box	**15.00**
Fan, ostrich feathers, black carved wood sticks, 11 x 23"	**100.00**

Gloves

Lady's, kid, white, long	**20.00**
Men's, driving, leather, black, c1910	**25.00**

Handbag, mesh, enamel floral design, white and silver metal frame, $25.00.

Handbag
  Alligator, suede lining **18.00**
  Beaded
    Abstract design, white and gray,
    milk glass beads, beaded handle,
    zipper, 5", marked "Czechoslo-
    vakia" **20.00**
    Florals, pink and blue, shiny beads,
    gold frame **45.00**
    Lucite, pearlized, round lid, lunch
    box clasp, twisted handle, seashell
    dec **17.50**
    Mesh, enameled, white ground, black
    leaf spray, Mandalian **55.00**
    Patchwork, Seminole, drawstring,
    grass bottom, blue, c1960 . . . . **25.00**
    Pearl, envelope, label "Hong Kong" **15.00**
    Plastic, child, red, imitation leather,
    three Scotties dec, silver frame and
    chain, int. mirror **20.00**
    Sequins, irid multicolored, silver and
    seed pearl dec, rhinestone clasp,
    fancy frame, Belgium **30.00**
    Silk, clutch, black, cut steel beads,
    label marked "France," c1930 . . . **42.00**
    Wool, handwoven, New Mexico, Na-
    vajo rug design, white ground, Fred
    Harvey, c1940 . . . . **35.00**

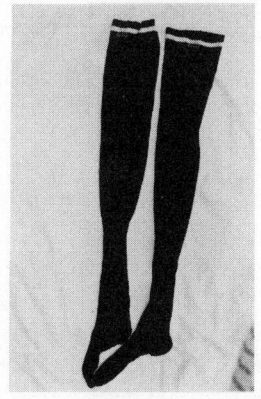

Stockings, lady's, black, $16.00.

Handkerchief
  10¾ x 18", printed, child's, white cotton, red design, "Old Mother Hub-
  bard," framed **50.00**
  11" sq, printed, child's, white cotton,
  red and black design, scene of children in goat coat, minor stains and
  small hole **30.00**
  14¾" sq, printed, white cotton, red
  design, birds and wild beasts,
  framed, pr **130.00**
  17¾ x 18½", printed, white cotton,

    multicolored Indian heads, blue
    border **85.00**
Hat, lady's
  Felt, cloche, black **15.00**
  Satin, pillbox, black, netting **18.00**
  Straw, wide brim, multicolored chif-
  fon flowers, c1940 . . . . **20.00**
Hat and Purse Set, pillbox hat, leopard
  skin, matching purse **100.00**
Lap Robe, wool, embroidered, leather
  binding **50.00**
Muff
  Marabou, white **45.00**
  Sable, brown, tails **100.00**
Sash, purple, beaded, c1850 . . . . **100.00**
Scarf
  Cotton, dog print, marked "Occupied
  Japan" **18.00**
  Silk, man's, fringed **15.00**
Shawl
  Cotton, mint green, fully embroi-
  dered, fringed edges, 1925 . . . . . . **35.00**
  Paisley
    Printed design, 66 x 128", minor
    wear and stains **60.00**
    Woven design
      59 x 118", black center medal-
      lion **215.00**
      68 x 69" **165.00**
Shoes
  Boy's, leather, Oxford style, two tone
  brown **35.00**
  Lady's
    Leather, brown, high button top . . **40.00**
    Suede, gray, c1920 . . . . **25.00**
  Men's, tennis, high top, c1920 . . . . . **20.00**
Spats, wool, gray, c1900 . . . . **24.00**
Travel Kit, gentleman's, alligator, seven
  accessories, c1940 . . . . **18.00**
Yoke, crocheted, ribbon trim **15.00**

COCA-COLA ITEMS

Collecting Hints: Most Coca-Cola items were produced in large quantity; the company was a leader in sales and promotional materials. Don't ignore the large amount of Coca-Cola material in languages other than English. Remember, "Coke" has a world-wide market.

History: The originator of Coca-Cola was John Pemberton, a pharmacist from Atlanta, Georgia. In 1886, Dr. Pemberton introduced a patent medicine to relieve headaches, stomach disorders, and other minor maladies. Unfortunately, his failing health and meager finances forced him to sell his interest.

In 1888, Asa G. Candler became the sole owner of Coca-Cola. Candler improved the formula, increased the advertising budget, and widened the distribution. Accidentally, a patient was given a dose of the syrup mixed with carbonated water instead of the usual still water. The result was a tastier, more refreshing drink.

As sales increased in the 1890s, Candler recognized that the product was more suitable for the soft drink market and began advertising it as such. From these beginnings a myriad of advertising items have been issued to invite all to "Drink Coca-Cola."

Dates of interest: "Coke" was first used in advertising in 1941. The distinctive shaped bottle was registered as a trademark on April 12, 1960.

References: Shelly and Helen Goldstein, *Coca-Cola Collectibles,* (four volumes, plus index), privately printed, 1970s; Deborah Goldstein Hill, Wallace-Homestead *Price Guide To Coca-Cola Collectibles,* Wallace-Homestead, 1984; Allan Petretti, *Petretti's Coca-Cola Collectibles Price Guide, 4th Edition* Nostalgia Publications, Inc., 1989; Al Wilson, *Collectors Guide to Coca-Cola Items, Volume I, Revised* L-W Book Sales, 1985; Al Wilson, *Collectors Guide To Coca-Cola Items, Volume II,* L–W Book Sales, 1987.

Collectors' Club: The Coca-Cola Collectors Club International, P. O. Box 546, Holmdel, NJ 07733; The Cola Clan, 2084 Continental Drive, N. E., Atlanta, GA 30345.

Museum: Schmidt's Coca-Cola Museum, Elizabethtown, KY.

REPRODUCTION ALERT, especially in the area of Coca-Cola trays.

Advertisement	
1910, magazine, "The Housewife," colorful	72.00
1913, newspaper, White Sox manager Callahan, white and black	8.00
1938, newspaper, color, 15 x 21", girl at cooler	12.00
Apron, white, green stripe, Lee tag and button	40.00
Arcade Card, bathing beauty	8.00
Ashtray, glass, spade	20.00
Bank, dispensing machine shape, plastic, red, 1960s, C & G Toys	30.00
Banner, 11 x 22", paper, c1951	14.00
Baseball, 1950s	35.00
Billfold, pigskin, 1950s	20.00
Blotter	
1923	22.50
1953	3.00
Book Cover, boy in grass, 1930–31	6.00
Bookmark, green artwork, Nordica, 1905	500.00
Bottle	
Amber, Columbus, OH	35.00
Brass	10.00
Bottle Opener, copper	2.00
Box, wooden	55.00

Bridge Score Pad	10.00
Button, metal, 1950	325.00
Calendar	
1959, birds	12.00
1967	20.00
1972, Victorian lady	10.00
Camera, 2¼ x 5¼", metal, red and white design, 110 film, orig box, late 1970s	35.00
Carrier, metal	15.00
Chalkboard, diner menu	38.00
Change Purse, c1915	45.00
Checker Set, orig box	25.00
Cigarette Lighter	
Bottle shape, metal cap	15.00
Chrome, with flashlight	100.00
Clock	
Electric, 15", sq, metal	95.00
Pendulum, battery, 1970s	350.00
Coaster, German	10.00
Cooler, 24 x 36"	180.00
Compact, ladies	10.00
Coupon, Free Bottle of Coke, 1920s	10.00
Creamer, lid, amber	20.00
Cuff Links, bottle shape, pr	40.00
Dart Board, 1950s	40.00
Dish, 7¼" d, round, glass, etched world dec, 1967	30.00
Dispenser, 1950s	75.00
Dominoes	7.50
Door Lock	70.00
Door Push, porcelain, 11 x 4", French, 1930s	100.00
Fan, 1930, St. Louis, MO, Bottling Co	45.00
Fly Swatter, wood handle, 1942	6.00
Glass	
6 oz, set of 12, orig box	55.00
10 oz, gold, 1950s	50.00
Ice Pick, 9", wood handle, box, 1940s	15.00
Key Chain, Golden Anniversary	2.00
Knife with bottle opener	5.00
Map, History of US 1492-1942 with Coke logo on top, 1943	35.00
Marbles, c1950	20.00
Menu Board, 26 x 36"	150.00
Mirror, pocket, 2¾", oval, World War I Girl of 1917	200.00
Necktie, c1950	30.00
Needle Case, 1924	30.00
Notebook, 3½ x 6", red, white lettering, 1943 calendar inside, unused	25.00
Notepad, WWII	10.00
Paperweight, calendar, mid-Atlantic	20.00
Pencil, mechanical, 1930	30.00
Pencil Box, includes contents	35.00
Pencil Case, cardboard, snap lid inscribed "Drink Coca-Cola/Delicious...Refreshing," includes, 2 ink blotters with 1937 copyright, pencils, ink pen, wood ruler, eraser, unused	20.00
Perfume Bottle	48.00
Ping Pong Paddle, set of 4	25.00

Pitcher, Midsouth Cola Clan September-
  fest 15.00
Plate, Knowles China 140.00
Playing Card, It's The Real Thing, 1971   5.00
Pocket Knife, Chicago World's Fair,
  1933 .... 30.00
Pretzel Dish, aluminum, c1938 ...... 40.00
Punchboard, 7 x 8", unused, 1940s ...   5.00
Radio, bottle shape, 8" h, light green
  plastic, aluminum cap 15.00
Ruler, 12" 12.50
Sign
  Plastic, 10 x 17", light-up, c1950 ... 60.00
  Porcelain over tin, 52", pictures bottle 85.00
  Tin, "Ice Cold," shows straight sided
    paper label bottle 250.00
Sheet Music, "The Coca-Cola Girl,"
  1927 .... 125.00
Straw Holder 22.00
Syrup Jug, gallon, 1930 .... 28.00

Playing Cards, 1943, $45.00.

Thermometer, bottle shape, gold, orig
  box, 1950s 20.00
Thimble, aluminum 25.00
Tin, 1939 .... 85.00
Toy, delivery truck, Matchbox No. 37,
  1958 .... 55.00
Tray
  1914, Betty, tip 65.00
  1917, Elaine 250.00
  1931, boy eating sandwich, Rockwell 200.00
  1934, Weissmuller & Sullivan 185.00
  1936, multi illus, red trimmed gold
    edge 100.00
  1939 .... 65.00
  1948 .... 45.00
  1950, Menu Girl 27.00
  1973 .... 5.00
Uniform Patch, "Enjoy Coke" 2.00
Visor, cardboard, c1960 ....   5.00
Wallet, gold stamped logo, emb bottle 30.00
Watch Fob, brass, 1912 .... 295.00
Whistle, litho, tin, red, yellow, and
  black, "The Pause That Refreshes" on
  side, 1930s 100.00
Yo Yo, Edwards Bo-Lo 85.00

COMIC BOOKS

Collecting Hints: Remember, age does *not* determine value! Prices fluctuate according to supply and demand in the marketplace. Collectors should always buy comic books in the best possible condition. While archival restoration is available, it's frequently costly and may involve a certain amount of risk.

Comic books should be stored in an upright position away from sunlight, dampness, and insect infestations. Avoid stacking comic books because the weight of the uppermost books may cause acid and oils to migrate. This results in stains on the covers of books near the bottom of the stack which are difficult or impossible to remove.

Golden Age (1939–1950s) Marvel and D.C. first issues and key appearances continue to gain in popularity as do more current favorites like Marvel's "X-Men" and D.C.'s "The New Teen Titans."

History: Who would ever believe that a cheap, disposable product sold in the 1890s would be responsible for the multi-million dollar industry composed of comic books and their spin-offs today? That 2¢ item was none other than the Sunday newspaper. Improved printing techniques helped 1890s newspaper publishers change from a weekly format to a daily one that included a full page of comics. The rotary printing press allowed the use of color in the "funnies." Comics were soon reprinted as advertising promotions by companies such as Proctor & Gamble products and movie theatres.

It wasn't long until reprint books like these promotional giveaways were selling in candy and stationery stores for 10¢ each. They appeared in various formats and sizes, many with odd shapes and cardboard covers. Others were printed on newsprint and resembled comic books sold today.

Comics printed prior to 1938 have value today only as historical artifacts or intellectual curiosities.

From 1939 to 1950 comic book publishers regaled readers with humor, adventure, western, and mystery tales. Super-heroes such as "Batman," "Superman," and "Captain America" first appeared in books during this era. This was the "Golden Age" of comics, a time for expansion and growth.

Unfortunately, the bubble burst in the spring of 1954 when Fredric Wertham published his book, *Seduction of the Innocent.* That book pointed a guilt-laden finger at the comic industry for corrupting youth, causing juvenile delinquency, and undermining American values. This book forced many publishers out of business, while others fought to establish a "comics code" to assure parents that their comics were compliant with morality and decency censures upheld by the code authority.

Thus, the Silver Age of comics is marked by a declining number of publishers due to the public uproar surrounding Wertham's book and the increased production costs of an inflationary economy.

The period starting with 1960 and continuing to the present has been marked by a revitalizing surge of interest in comic books. Starting with Marvel's introduction of "The Fantastic Four" and "The Amazing Spiderman," the market has increased to the extent that many new publishers are now rubbing elbows with the giants and the competition is keen!

Part of the reason for this upswing must be credited to that same inflationary economy that spelled disaster for publishers in the 50s. This time, however, people are buying valuable comics as a hedge against inflation. Even young people are aware of the market potential. Today's piggy bank investors may well be tomorrow's Wall Street tycoons.

References: Stephen Becker, *Comic Art in America,* Simon and Schuster, Inc., 1959; Pierre Couperie and Maurice C. Horn, *A History of the Comic Strip,* Crown Publishers, Inc. 1968; Hubert H. Crawford, *Crawford's Encyclopedia of Comic Books,* Jonathan David Publisher's, Inc., 1978; Les Daniels, *COMIX, A History of Comic Books in America,* Bonanza Books, 1971; Jules Feiffer, *The Great Comic Book Heroes,* The Dial Press, 1965, first paperback edition, 1977; Harry A. Hopkins, *Fandom Directory,* Fandom Computer Services, 1983; Maurice Horn (ed.), *World Encyclopedia of Comics,* Chelsea House; Robert M. Overstreet, *The Official Comic Book Price Guide,* House of Collectibles, 1989; Reinhold Reitberger-Wolfgang Fuchs, *Comics, Anatomy of a Mass Medium,* Little, Brown and Company, 1971; Jerry Robinson, *The Comics, An Illustrated History of Comic Strip Art,* G. P. Putnam's Sons, 1974.

Periodicals: *Comic Buyers Guide,* 700 State Street, Iola, WI 54990; *Nemo: Classic Comics Library,* 4359 Cornell Road, Agoura, CA 91301.

Museum: Museum of Cartoon Art, Rye, NY.

REPRODUCTION ALERT: Publishers frequently reprint popular stories, even complete books, so the buyer must pay strict attention to the title, not just the portion printed in outsized letters on the front cover. If there's ever any doubt, look inside at the fine print on the bottom of the inside cover or first page. The correct title will be printed there in capital letters.

Buyers also should pay attention to the size of the comic they purchase. Many customers have been misled by unscrupulous dealers recently. The comics offered are exact replicas of expensive Golden Age D.C. titles, which would nor-

mally sell for thousands of dollars. The seller offers the large, 10 by 13½", copy of Superman #1 in mint condition for ten to a hundred dollars. The novice collector jumps at the chance since he knows this book sells for thousands on the open market. When the buyer gets his "find" home and checks the value, he discovers that he's paid way too much for the treasury sized "Famous First Edition" comic printed in the mid-seventies by D.C. These comics originally sold for one dollar each and are exact reprints except for the size. Several came with outer covers which announced the fact that they were reprints, but it didn't take long for dishonest dealers to remove these and sell the remaining portion for greatly inflated prices.

Notes: Just like advertising, comic books affect and reflect the culture which nurtures them. Large letters, bright colors, and "pulse-pounding" action seem to hype this product. Many would say comics are as American as mom's apple pie since good almost always triumphs over evil. Yet there's truly something for every taste in the vast array of comics available today. There are underground (adult situation) comics, foreign comics, educational comics, and comics intended to promote the sale of products or services.

The following listing concentrates on "mainstream" American comics published between 1938 and 1985. Prices may vary from region to region due to excessive demand in some areas. Prices given are for comic books in fine condition; that is, these comics are like new in most respects, but may show a little wear. Comics should be complete; no pages or chunks cut out.

Classic Comics

Classics Illustrated started with #35. All first editions carry an advertisement for the next issue

Marvel Comics Group, *2001, A Space Odyssey,* **Premiere Issue, #1, Dec, 02672, 6⅝ x 10⅛", $3.00.**

(except #168 and #169) on the inside covers. All titles have been reprinted and reprints are worth only 10–25% of first edition values. Prices listed here are for first edition titles only.

Benjamin Franklin, #1	35.00
Black Beauty, #1	20.00
Dr Jekyll and Mr Hyde, #1	250.00
Frankenstein, #1	275.00
Gulliver's Travels, #1	75.00
Kidnaped, #1	40.00
Rip Van Winkle and the Headless Horseman, #1	120.00
The Adventures of Marco Polo, #1	100.00
The Pathfinder, #1	125.00
The Prince and the Pauper, #1	200.00
Twenty Thousand Leagues Under The Sea, #1	56.00
Westward Ho!, #1	250.00

Crime

Authentic Police Cases, #15	20.00
Crime and Punishment, #40	16.00
Crime Mysteries, #14	20.00
Famous Crimes, #3	25.00
Keen Detective Funnies, #5	75.00
Kerry Drake Detective Cases, #6	10.00
Mr District Attorney, #15	15.00
Parole Breakers, #3	30.00
True Crime Comics, #5	65.00

Funny Animals

Animal Adventures, #3	2.50
Animal Comics, #6	40.00
Bugs Bunny, #300	5.00
Daffy, #50	1.00
Huckleberry Hound Chuckleberry Tales, #19	.50
Mighty Mouse, #10	8.00
Porky Pig, #180	10.00
Scooby Doo, #5	1.00
Tom and Jerry, #80	2.50
Woody Woodpecker, #200	4.50

Horror

Amazing Detective Cases, #12	7.50
Chilling Tales of Horror, #4	1.25
Dark Mysteries, #20	15.00
Eerie, #14	15.00
House of Secrets, #48	2.00
House of Terror, #226	1.75
Mister Mystery, #12	75.00
Tales of Horror, #7	8.50
Vault of Horror, #14	125.00
Worlds of Fear, #7	8.75

Jungle

All Top, #18	35.00
Evangeline, #6	1.00
Jo Jo, #7	75.00
Jungle Action, #13	.75
Jungle Jim, #5	2.00
Jungle Twins, #3	.75
Nyoka, The Jungle Girl 14	30.00
Ramar of the Jungle, #5	8.50
Tarzan, #25	35.00

Wambi Jungle Boy, #9	12.00
Zoot, #11	50.00

Juvenile

Archie Comics, #65	7.50
Casper, #3	5.00
Henry, 1946, #3	1.75
Hug A Bunch#3	.75
Katy Keene, #11	30.00
Josie, #22	2.25
Little Lulu, #146	60.00
Nutty Comics, #6	4.50
Patsy Walker, #20	15.00
Pebbles & Bam Bam, #10	2.00
Richie Rich, #80	5.00
Wendy the Witch, #6	24.00

Fawcett, *Dennis The Menace in London,* $4.00.

Newspaper Reprints

Comics On Parade, #36	17.50
Dick Tracy, #25	35.00
Feature Book, #10	75.00
Foxy Grandpa, #1900	60.00
Gasoline Alley, #1	24.00
Joe Palooka, #2	25.00
Mutt & Jeff, #10	25.00
Penny, #6	8.00
Sparkler, #53	20.00
Tip Top, #2	75.00

Number 1's

Avengers, original	350.00
Batman	3,600.00
Daring Mystery Comics	1,285.00
Exciting Comics	165.00
Fantastic Four	600.00
Journey Into Mystery	300.00
Justice League of America	325.00
Superman	9,500.00
X-Men	160.00

Radio/TV/Movie Related

Augie Doogie, #1	7.50
Big Town, #35	4.50

Fury, #1218	10.00	Human Torch, #12	95.00
Gang Busters, #15	50.00	Plastic Man, #64	20.00
Lucy Show, #2	20.00	The Dazzler, #21	1.00
McHale's Navy, #2	3.25	The Eagle, #2	75.00
Space Ghost, #3	2.25	Wonder Woman, #145	3.00
Star Wars, #4	2.50		
Uncle Milty, #2	12.00		

Three Dimensional

3-D Action, #1	35.00
3-D Bozo The Clown	2.50
3-D Funny Movies, #1	40.00
3-D Love, #1	35.00
3-D Sheena, Jungle Queen, #1	58.00
3-D Superman, 1953	115.00
3-D Tales of the West, #1	45.00

Fawcett, *Sweethearts*, October, 1949, Vol 14, No. 80, $2.50.

Walt Disney

Beagle Boys, #10	1.00
Chip 'n Dale, #17	2.25
Dynabrite, Donald Duck, #4	.80
Huey, Dewey, and Louie Junior Woodchucks, #23	2.50
Ludwig Von Drake, #4	3.50
Pinocchio Learns About Kites, 1954	60.00
Super Goof, #11	1.00
Walt Disney Presents, #6	2.50
Walt Disney's Comics & Stories, #3	5.00
Zorro, #3	2.75

Romance

Boy Meets Girl, #8	4.00
Date with Debbi, #15	3.00
Dream of Love, #2	1.50
Exciting Romances, #30	11.00
Falling In Love, #20	3.00
Love Letters, #49	8.00
Love Mystery, #3	17.50
Love Stories, #2	8.00
Romantic Secrets, #23	4.00

Science Fiction

Amazing Adventures, #2	18.00
Magus, Robot Fighter, #3	12.00
Micronauts, #30	.75
Planet Comics, #20	120.00
Strange Adventures, #18	25.00
Strange Mysteries, #3	12.00
Strange Worlds, #5	28.00
Weird Mysteries, #7	50.00
Weird Science Fantasy, #25	60.00

Sports

All Sports Comics, #4	8.00
Babe Ruth Sports Comics, #5	5.00
Football Thrills, #2	7.00
Joe Louis, #2	20.00
Sport Comics, #3	10.00
Sport Stars, #4	7.25
True Sport Picture Stories, #5	12.00

Super Heroes

Amazing Spiderman, #30	15.00
Batman, #78	30.00
Captain America, #112	12.50
Detective, #80	50.00

War

All American Men of War, #30	5.75
Attack, #16	.75
Attack At Sea, #5	.50
Black Cat Mystery, #30	15.00
Black Diamond Western, #18	12.00
Boys' Ranch, #4	55.00
G. I. Joe, #14	4.50
How The Boys and Girls Can Help Win The War, #1	60.00
Jet Heroes, #1	10.00
Judy Joins The Waves, 1951	4.50
Navy War Heroes, #3	1.00
War Comics, #45	5.00
War Heroes, #8	1.00

Western

Annie Oakley and Tagg, #4	10.00
Bill Boyd Western, #7	20.00
Cheyenne Kid, #12	16.50
Dale Evans, #3	20.00
Gabby Hayes Western, #50	10.00
Gene Autry Comics, #25	5.00
Ken Maynard Western, #2	20.00
Luke Short's Western Stories, #848	18.00
Rawhide Kid, #60	1.00
Roy Rogers Comics, #12	18.50
Tom Mix Western, #35	12.00
Western Gunfighters, #12	3.75

COMPACTS

Collecting Hints: Only mirrors that are broken should be removed and replaced in a vintage compact. Do not replace a mirror that is discolored, flawed, or in need of resilvering. The original mirror enhances the value of the compact.

Never apply a sticker directly to the surface of a compact. The acids from the glue may discolor or irreparably damage the finish, especially an enamel finish.

If a compact comes in the original box or pouch, do not destroy or discard it. The value of the compact is increased if it has its original presentation box.

History: In the first quarter of the 20th century attitudes regarding cosmetics changed drastically. The use of make-up during the day was no longer looked upon with disdain. As women became "liberated" and as more and more of them entered the business world the use of cosmetics became a routine and necessary part of a woman's grooming. Portable containers for cosmetics became a necessity.

Compacts were made in a myriad of shapes, styles, combinations and motifs, all reflecting the mood of the times. Every conceivable natural or man–made medium was used in the manufacture of compacts. Commemorative, premium, souvenir, patriotic, figural, combination compacts, Art Deco, and enamel compacts are a few examples of the compacts that were made in the United States and abroad. Compacts combined with cigarette cases, music boxes, watches, hatpins, canes, lighters, etc. also were very popular.

Compacts were made and used until the late 1950s when women opted for the "Au Natural" look. Compacts manufactured prior to that time are considered vintage compacts.

Some vintage compacts were exquisitely crafted, often enameled or encrusted with precious or synthetic jewels. These compacts were considered a form of jewelry or fashion accessory. The intricate and exacting workmanship of some vintage compacts would be virtually impossible to duplicate today.

Reference: Roselyn Gerson, *Ladies' Compacts of the 19th and 20th Centuries,* Wallace-Homestead, Book Co, 1989.

Collectors' Club: The Compact Collectors Club, P. O. Box Letter S, Lynbrook, NY 11563.

Periodical: The Powder Puff Newsletter, P. O. Box Letter S, Lynbrook, NY 11563.

Advisor: Roselyn Gerson.

Amita, Damascene, black matte finish, inlaid with gold and silver view of Mt Fuji, capped in silver, Japan **125.00**
Arden, Elizabeth, light blue enamel, harlequin mask dec **80.00**
Avon, oval, lid dec with blue and green checkerboard pattern **25.00**
E. A. M., Art Deco, blue enameled tango-chain compact, red and yellow abstract design, powder sifter and at-

Weltzunder blue marbleized enamel Kamra-Pak style vanity case and matching cigarette lighter, silvered metal cut out map of U. S. Zone on lid, front opens to reveal powder compartment, reverse side reveals cigarette compartment, slide out lipstick, orig presentation box, Germany, $165.00.

tached lipstick, finger ring carrying chain **175.00**
Evans, goldtone and mother-of-pearl, compact and lipstick combination .. **35.00**
Hudnut, Richard, Deauville, blue cloisonne tango-chain vanity, metal mirror, compartments for powder and rouge, lipstick attached to finger ring chain **175.00**
K & K, brass colored engine tooled dec basket compact, multicolored silk flowers enclosed in plastic domed lid, emb swinging handle **90.00**
Kamra-Pak style, multicolored tooled leather cov Persian design **65.00**
Rowenta, brown enamel, oval, petit point compact **40.00**
Unknown Maker
   Enamel, ebony, "eight ball" style ... **90.00**
   Enamel and goldtone, roll top style, Germany **115.00**
   German Silver, fluted, vanity, chatelaine, orig compact, coin holder, memo book, locket, pin container, and stamp holder, complete **450.00**
   Goldtone
      Heart shape, brocade lid **40.00**
      Triangle shape, raised elephants dec **35.00**
   Lucite, blue, Sterling repousse medallion of two doves **100.00**
   Plastic, red, white, and blue, Naval Officer's cap shape **65.00**
   Silver Plated, antique, triangular, hand mirror shape, lipstick concealed in handle, int. and ext. mirrors, turquoise cabochon thumbpiece **135.00**

Sterling Silver, antique, enamel painted lid scene, gilded int., Italy **300.00**
Volupte
  Goldtone, hand shaped **85.00**
  Watchcase Compact, picture locket on flower dec lid **60.00**
Whiting & Davis Co, Piccadilly, gilded mesh, vanity bag, compact incorporated in front lid, carrying chain **200.00**
Woodworth, Karess, polished goldtone, corset shaped, vanity case, powder and rouge compartments **25.00**
Yardley, goldtone, vanity case
  Red, white, and blue emb design on lid, powder and rouge compartments **50.00**
  White enamel feather dec on lid, powder and rouge compartments, tandem lipstick **50.00**

COOKBOOKS

Collecting Hints: Look for books in good, clean condition. Watch for special interesting notes in margins.

History: Among the earliest Americana cookbooks are *The Frugal Housewife; or, Complete Woman Cook* by Susanna Carter, published in Philadelphia in 1796 and *American Cookery* by Amelia Simmons, published in Hartford, Connecticut in 1796. Cookbooks of this era are crudely written, for most cooks could not read well and measuring devices were not yet refined.

Other types of collectible cookbooks include those used as premiums or advertisements. This type is much less expensive than the rare 18th century books.

Reference: Linda Campbell Franklin, *300 Years of Kitchen Collectibles, 2nd Edition,* Books Americana, 1984.

All About Home Baking, General Foods Corp, 144 pgs, yellow and black plaid cov, 1935 .... **7.50**
Better Homes & Gardens, 414 pgs, 1953 **12.00**
Blueberry Hill Menu Cookbook, Masterson, NY, 1963, 363 pgs **8.50**
Calumet Baking Co., *Reliable Recipes,* 11th edition **10.00**
Campbell Kids Junior, 1954 .... **5.00**
Chafing Dish Suggestions, Rochester Stamping Co **5.00**
Chicken Of The Sea Recipe Booklet, Hopalong Cassidy, 1951 .... **25.00**
Cox's Manual of Gelatin Cookery, 1914 **5.00**
Cross Creek Cookery, Rawlings, NY, 1942, first edition **22.00**
Economy Administration Cookbook, 1913, 696 pgs **45.00**

Famous Star's Favorite Foods, 245 pgs, includes Jack Benny, Bogart, Crawford, Shirley Temple, Gable, Muni, Raft, Weissmuller, 1938 .... **30.00**
Fifty-Two Sunday Dinners By Elizabeth O. Hiller, 1915 .... **15.00**
Fleischman Co., *Delicious Dishes,* 1919 **10.00**
General Foods, *All About Home Baking,* multicolored kitchen photos, hardbound, 1933 .... **8.00**
Gold Medal Flour Cookbook, 1904 ... **15.00**

Hershey's Index Recipe Book, cov illus by Frances Tipton, Hunter Litho, USA, written by Mrs Christine Frederick, copyright and published by Hershey, 1934, 5½ x 7½", $10.00.

Hershey Chocolate Recipe Book, 1930 **8.50**
Housekeeping in Old Virginia, John Morton & Co, hardbound, 1879, 528 pgs **90.00**
Imperial Cookbook, Townsend, 1890, 527 pgs **50.00**
Jolly Times, Juvenille Recipes, 1934 .. **8.50**
Ladies' Home Journal Cookbook, first edition, 1960 .... **9.50**
Maytag Dutch Oven Gas Range, 1949 **5.00**
Methacol, Mammy on cov, 1921 ..... **15.00**
Pennsylvania Dutch Cook Book of Fine Old Recipes, Sunbonnet Girl on cov, 48 pgs, 1936 .... **12.00**
Pillsbury Family Cookbook, 1963 ..... **9.50**
Prudence Penny Cookbook, color illus, 1940, 815 pgs **8.50**
Royal Baking Powder, *Any One Can Bake,* 100 pgs, 1929 .... **6.00**
Rumford's Baking Powder Recipe Book, 1911 .... **25.00**
Science of Food and Cookery, H S Anderson, Pacific Press, 1921 .... **18.00**
Shumway's Canning Recipes, booklet . **4.00**
St Louis Stamping Co, 1877, 63 pgs, graniteware manuf **30.00**

Stillmeadow Cookbook, Gladys Taber,
first edition, dust jacket **18.00**
Universal Cookbooks, Jeanie L. Taylor,
185 pgs, 1888 . . . . **12.00**
Virginia Housewife Cookbook,, 1838 . **250.00**
Walter Baker Chocolate Cookbook,
1925 . . . . **8.50**
Weight Watchers, first edition, 1978 . . **6.00**
White House, Zieman & Gillette, 619
pgs, copyright 1887–1915 . . . . **30.00**

COOKIE CUTTERS

Collecting Hints: Cookie cutters exist in abundance throughout the United States. The early cutters were handmade, and the tradition and skill survives to the present time. By the late 19th century, cutters also were manufactured and sold for a few pennies through mail order houses and in general stores.

A collector should develop a collection theme—shape, broad general approach, or cutters for use. In buying old or used cutters, carefully examine the cutters which now are available new. Many cutters identical with "old" cutters still are made. Learn which old cutters were handcrafted and which were machine made. When uncertain about whether a cutter is old and valued for its age, ask "What would I pay for it new?" This method helps to eliminate wild purchases and disappointments when a cutter is misjudged.

There are many tinsmiths working today who will duplicate any cutter, often using old techniques to make it. Cutters can be aged. Sellers often misrepresent the age of cutters out of ignorance, rather than an obvious attempt to deceive.

History: Late in the 19th century, factories began producing cookie cutters resembling the handcrafted cutters of an earlier period. It was soon obvious that making uniform backs of relatively thin material speeded up the process and cut costs. Many unusual cutters were patented during this period; advertising cutters also were made.

The 1869 Dover Stamping Company catalog is the first documented record of a manufactured cookie cutter. The cutter pictured in the catalog is well developed, far beyond a "beginning" status. Manufactured cutters probably were made before the 1869 date.

Two innovations in the 1925–1950 period were the use of aluminum and plastic. Since 1965, two events occurred which influenced the cookie collecting field. The first is an influx of younger people into the collecting field through the interest in crafts. The second is the Hallmark cutters in their varied plastic tones which renewed interest in cutter use.

Reference: Phyllis S. Wetherill, *Art in the Kitchen: Cookie Cutters and Cookie Molds,* Schiffer Publishing, Ltd, 1985.

Collectors' Club: Cookie Collector's Club, 1167 Teal Road, S. W., Dellroy, OH 44620.

ADVERTISING AND PREMIUM CUTTERS

Betty Crocker, premium, gingerbread
boy, plastic, blue, flatback, handle . **1.50**
Egg Baking Powder Co, adv, 1½" d,
metal, egg handle, 1902 . . . . **40.00**
Fanchon Flour, adv, "USE FANCHON
THE FLOUR OF QUALITY," round,
fold down handle **10.00**
Garland Stoves, "Garland Stoves and
Ranges," fire shape, flames across top **22.00**
Hills Brothers Co, Dromedary Coconut
premium, metal, camel outline,
rounded handle, 1916 . . . . **25.00**
Quaker Oats, premium, standing bear,
flatback, handle, plastic, yellow **3.00**
Swans Down Cake Flour, premium, aluminum, card party shapes, riveted
handles, (three different sets exist;
each has different styles of printing on
box) **22.00**
Wrigley, premium, Troll, aluminum, self
handle, Mirro **12.00**

FOREIGN CUTTERS

Chinese, sold as "Authenic Old Chinese
Cookie Mold," 2 pcs fit together,
wood mold, one flat with four geometric designs marked in wood, other
with cut out geometric shapes, independent appraisal is difficult **15.00**
France
Fish, metal, outline, brace, Matfer . . **8.00**
Punch, 5 x 2½", outline, unusual border making handle, sgd "France" . . . **25.00**
Scalloped, 2" d, 2" h, round, plunger
mechanism to make hole in center,
sgd "Lenard made in France Brevet
No. 825442" **15.00**
German
Santa with tree, flatback, metal, to be
used with printed picture **12.00**
Three round, metal, scalloped cutters,
graduated sizes, two larger with
braces sgd "Faka Christel," instruction sheet, c1950 . . . . **6.00**
Three Scallop, card party club shape,
long stem and pointed ends (device
for cutting cookie and by squeezing
long stem, moving it to the baking
sheet), fair condition **4.00**
Mexico, violin, outline, metal, arched
handle . . . . **.50**

HANDCRAFTED CUTTERS

Antique

Animal, dog or cow, four legged, flatback, handle **15.00**

Bear, 2½ x 3", irregular back, handle
missing, narrow cutting edge, one
corner slightly bent **10.00**

Man, 3 x 5½", high hat, frock coat,
handle removed **85.00**

Pitcher, 4 x 6", irregular back, handle **70.00**

Rabbit, 4 x 6", irregular back, short
ears, missing handle **100.00**

Reindeer, 5 x 6", irregular back, strut-
ting position, four legs and grouped
antlers, handle **115.00**

Woman, 3 x 9", flat back, front view,
large head, small body, fuzzy hair **120.00**

Modern

Tinsmiths stopped making handcrafted cutters
because of change of circumstances, retirement,
or death. The following cutters are no longer
available new.

Dautrich, 6 x 7", heart, inner tulip
design, sgd "Dautrich, 1976" **25.00**

Hastings, 2½ x 5", rabbit, flatback,
sgd "H" **10.00**

John Holochwest, coal oil lamp, 1" w
handle identifies cutter **7.00**

Wib Lauter, 5 x 7", US map, flatback,
handle, humorous saying, sgd ... **12.00**

W. Roberts, anvil, flatback, handle,
sgd "W Roberts" **8.00**

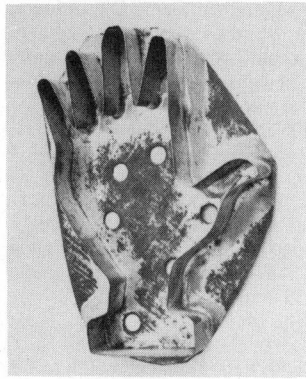

**Hand, galvanized tin, six air holes, 3¼ x
4½", $35.00.**

METAL

Identified

A & J

Children's Set, gingerbread boy and
rabbit, backs, wood handles, sgd
"A & J" in diamond

Gingerbread Boy **15.00**

Rabbit **15.00**

Outline cutters, A & J handles or
handles with faces

Gingerbread Boy **15.00**

Rabbit **15.00**

Dixon Specialities, Inc., Wonder
Bridge Cutters, cardboard box
showing woman making cookies,
blue and orange colors, four large
cutters, card party shapes, c1940 . **25.00**

Fox Run, pr, 6½ x 10½", colonial
man and woman, backs painted in
mottled brown-gray design, inner
designs, c1965 .... **50.00**

Lenore Deskow, round, SS cube, cuts
heart, triangle, 3 part design, sgd
"1972 Sterling Lenore Deskow,
Inc." **35.00**

J. W. Shull, round, slightly domed
top, sgd **10.00**

Unidentified

Children's Set, outline with brace,
woman's face drawn on yellow
wood handles

Chicken **10.00**

Gingerbread Boy **10.00**

German or Italian, 16 round outline
cutters, plain, graduated sizes, rust,
bending, or other wear, (Similar
cutters available new, design interest and present availability do not
override condition) **10.00**

PLASTIC

Some plastic cookie cutters have a value based
partly on the fact that reproduction is difficult.
(The many examples of reproduction of plastic
cutters without permission ordinarily occur
within a few years after the original cutters are
made.)

Education Products, marbleized,
multicolored, sgd "Kleeware, England"

Burro, Camel, Elephant, Horse, each **3.50**

Set, 4 pcs **20.00**

Hallmark, large, orange, Snoopy and
the Great Pumpkin **25.00**

Life Like, cherry red, handles, cutters
now made with Educational Products
signature **1.00**

McB's, red, back, handle, cutters are
not sgd but can be identified because
they have no corners

Angel, profile view **3.50**

Cowboy, hands at waist, knees bent **3.50**

Miller Cookie Cutter Co, gingerbread
boy, back and handle, orig card

Green **10.00**

Red **6.00**

Nord Cutters, circular handles

Angel **2.50**

Cat	3.00
Cherry Tree or leaf tree	2.50
Clock	2.50
Man in the moon	3.00

Northwestern Products Co, Little Deb cutters, pastel colors, yellow and aqua, 1" cutters with two parallel handles, currently available in red plastic from Arthur Douglas Company, England

Elephant	.60
Horse	.50
Santa	.75
Set of 6	5.00

Ohio Art Co Pastry and Canister Set, originally 23 items, c1953

Cowboy	2.00
Indian	2.00
Set, 23 items	25.00

Southwest Indian Foundation, outline, hanger, orig card

Star, red	5.00
Tree, green	5.00

SPECIAL TYPES

Cookie Mold, Lamb of God, clay, sgd "EE, Switzerland" 10.00
Cookie Pan
    Ladyfinger, made in England 4.00
    Twelve animals, cast iron 12.00
Cookie Press, Ateco, bag, design mechanism 25.00
Doughnut Cutter, rolling, wood and brass, sgd "D. D. Hetherinton, Birmingham, Patent No 16798" 12.00
Rolling Cutter, 10" l, five attached cutters, handle, metal and plastic, made in Italy or Hong Kong, sold by many companies for decades and still available new 4.00
Springerle
    Board, 4 x 5", six sections, orig sticker "Nayco", c1940 .... 6.00
    Rolling Pin, twelve machine carved squares, available new 4.00

STORYBOOK CUTTERS

More and more different sets of cutters illustrating famous children's stories are being located. They are of great interest to collectors; many are scarce.

Blondie and Dagwood Set, six cutters, plastic, yellow, Dagwood, Blondie, Daisy, two children, and puppies, orig box (Reissued recently in red plastic) 35.00
Goldilocks and the Three Bears, four outline cutters, plastic, red, orig box 35.00
Little Red Riding Hood Set, metal outline cutters, braces, Little Red Riding Hood, house, wolf, and grandmother, may be stamped "Made in Germany for S. J. Company" or S. Joseph Company," orig box 45.00
Tom and Jerry, six plastic cutters, backs and handles, set of 6
    Ivory 20.00
    Red 10.00

COOKIE JARS

Collecting Hints: Cookie jars are subject to chips and paint flaking. Collectors should concentrate on jars which have their original lid and are in very good or better condition.

Learn to identify makers' marks and codes. Do not fail to include some of the contemporary manufacturers in your collection.

Above all, ignore the prices and hype associated with the cookie jars sold at the Andy Warhol sale in 1988. Neither is realistic.

History: Cookie jars, colorful and often whimsical, areone of the fastest growing categories in the collectibles field. Many cookie jars have been made by more than one company and as a result can be found with different marks. This resulted from mergers or splits by manufacturers, e.g., Brush-McCoy which is now Nelson McCoy. Molds also were traded and sold among companies.

Cookie jars often were redesigned to reflect newer tastes. Hence, the same jar may be found in several different style variations.

Reference: Harold Nichols, *McCoy Cookie Jars: From The First To The Latest,* Nichols Publishing, 1987; Ermagene Westfall, *An Illustrated Value Guide To Cookie Jars,* Collector Books, 1983.

Abingdon Pottery Company
    Hobby Horse, marked "Abingdon USA" 75.00
    Hippopotamus, sitting, incised mark "549" 90.00
    Humpty Dumpty, yellow brick wall, incised mark "663" 100.00
    Jack-in-Box, A B C on front, incised mark "611" 120.00
    Little Miss Muffet, marked "662" ... 110.00
American Bisque Company
    Chef 25.00
    Churn Boy 95.00
    Coffeepot, black, marked "USA" ... 15.00
    Ernie 65.00
    Poodle 40.00
Brush-McCoy
    Bobby Baker 25.00
    Brown Cow 75.00
    Cinderella Pumpkin 100.00
    Clock 135.00

Clown **135.00**
Davy Crockett **75.00**
Humpty Dumpty **40.00**
Keebler Tree House **50.00**
Lantern **40.00**
Night Owl **50.00**
Raggedy Ann **45.00**
Red Riding Hood **175.00**
Squirrel on Log **40.00**
California Originals
Cookie Monster, marked "Muppets
  Inc 970" **38.00**
Pelican, brown **35.00**
Cardinal
Cookie Safe, marked "Cardinal 309
  USA" **24.00**
Soldier, marked "312 USA Cardinal" **50.00**
Doranne of California
Cow with Milk Can, marked "C J 106
  USA Doranne" **30.00**
Shoe House **25.00**
Frankoma, barrel, black, marked "97 V
  Frankoma" **30.00**
Fredricksburg Art Pottery, Dove, pink,
  marked "FAPCO" **40.00**
Gilner, rooster, marked "Gilner G 622" **28.00**
Harvey Productions Inc, Casper, marked
  "Harvey Productions INc USA" **250.00**
Hull Pottery, Big Apple **25.00**
McCoy Pottery
Barn, cow in door **120.00**
Basket of Potatoes **20.00**
Bear, sleeping **50.00**
Black Stove **20.00**
Chipmunk **60.00**
Chef **45.00**
Cook Stove, white **40.00**
Duck, yellow **50.00**
Dutch Treat Barn **45.00**
Friendship 7 Spaceship **175.00**
Happy Face **30.00**
Indian Head **160.00**
Kitten, black and pink, black painted
  "Cookies" **45.00**
Pelican **60.00**
Pig **20.00**
Popeye **75.00**
Star Wars, C3PO **85.00**
Tea Kettle **20.00**
Train **50.00**
W. C. Fields **60.00**
World Globe **100.00**
Pottery Guild, Dutch Girl **50.00**

Red Wing Pottery Company
Bob White **55.00**
Chef, blue **60.00**
Pineapple, blue, incised mark "Red
  Wing" **40.00**
Regal China
Goldilocks **125.00**
Peek-A-Boo **425.00**

Quaker Oats, cookie recipe on back,
  marked "Regal China" **80.00**
Robinson Ransbottom Pottery
Cow Jumped Over Moon, gold trim **56.00**
Rooster, brown, marked " R R P Co
  Roseville O. USA" **30.00**
Sheriff Pig, yellow hat, marked "R R
  P Co Roseville Ohio 3634" **32.00**

**Puss 'N' Boots, ivory, red bow, yellow
bird, blue trim, Shawnee, $35.00.**

Shawnee Pottery Company
Cloverleaf Pig **65.00**
Drummer Boy **65.00**
Dutch Boy **55.00**
Ear of Corn **75.00**
Puss 'N' Boots, gold, flowers, maroon
  bow **35.00**
Sesame Street, Ernie **85.00**
Sitting Elephant **45.00**
Smiling Pig, flowers, red scarf **65.00**
Sierra Vista
Old Fashioned Telephone, marked
  "Pat 44859 Sierra Vista Ceramics
  Pasadena Calif USA" **35.00**
Treasure Chest, marked "Sierra Vista
  Calif 50" **25.00**
Treasure Craft, cat, mouse on back ... **30.00**
Twin Winton
Collegiate Owl, marked "Twin Win-
  ton Calif USA" **25.00**
Raccoon **35.00**
Unknown Maker
Cinderella, hp, 22K gold trim, orig tag **100.00**
Clown Head **30.00**
Cookie House **30.00**
Cow, purple **45.00**
Cow Jumped Over the Moon, with
  gold **85.00**
Hobby Horse **30.00**
Witch **30.00**
Walt Disney
Dumbo, marked "Patented Turnabout
  4 in 1 Dumbo Walt Disney" **68.00**

Thumper, marked "Reg US Pat Off
Celebrate Made in USA" and "Walt
Disney Productions" **75.00**
Tigger, marked "Walt Disney Produc-
tions" **85.00**

COWBOY HEROES

Collecting Hints: Cowboy hero material was collected and saved in great numbers. Don't get
fooled into thinking an object is rare until you
have checked carefully. Tom Mix material remains the most desirable, followed closely by
Hopalong Cassidy, Roy Rogers, and Gene Autry
memorabilia. Material associated with the western stars of the silent era and early talking films
still has not achieved its full potential as a collectible.

History: The era when the cowboy and longhorn
cattle dominated the Great Western Plains was
short, lasting only from the end of the Civil War
to the late 1880s. Dime novelists romanticized
this period and created a love affair in America's
heart for the Golden West.

Motion pictures saw the cowboy as a prime
entertainment feature. William S. Hart developed
the character of the cowboy hero—often in love
with his horse more than the girl. He was followed by Tom Mix, Ken Maynard, Tim McCoy,
and Buck Jones. The "B" movie, the second
feature of a double bill, was often of the cowboy
genre.

In 1935 William Boyd starred in the first of the
Hopalong Cassidy films. Gene Autry, "a singing
cowboy," gained popularity over the airwaves of
the West and Midwest. By the late 1930s, Autry's
Melody Ranch was a national institution on the
air as well as the screen. Roy Rogers replaced
Autry as the featured cowboy at Republic Pictures in the mid-1940s. Although the Lone
Ranger first appeared on the airwaves in 1933,
he did not enter the movie medium until 1938.

The early years of television enhanced the careers of the big three—Autry, Boyd, and Rogers.
The appearance of the Lone Ranger in shows
made specifically for television strengthened the
key role held by the cowboy hero. "Gunsmoke,"
"Wagon Train," "Rawhide," "The Rifleman,"
"Paladin," and "Bonanza" were just a few of the
shows that followed.

By the early 1970s the cowboy hero had fallen
from grace, relegated to reruns or specials. In
early 1983 The Library of Congress in Washington conducted a major show on the "Cowboy
Hero," perhaps a true indication that he is now
a part of past history.

References: Theodore L. Hake and Robert D.
Cauler, *Six Gun Heroes: A Price Guide To Movie
Cowboy Collectibles,* Wallace Homestead,
1976; Robert Heide and John Gilman, *Cowboy*

Collectibles, Harper & Row, 1982; Lee J. Felbin-
ger, *The Lone Ranger Pictorial Scrapbook,* pub-
lished by author, 1988; David Rothel, *The Gene
Autry Book,* Empire Publishing Co, 1988; David
Rothel, *The Roy Rogers Book,* Empire Publishing
Company, 1987.

Museums: Gene Autry Western Heritage Museum, Los Angeles, CA; National Cowboy Hall
of Fame and Western Heroes, Oklahoma City,
OK; Roy Rogers Museum, Victorville, CA.

GENE AUTRY

Arcade Card, c1950 .... **2.00**
Belt, size 28, leather, brown, tooled,
floral design, silvered metal buckle,
diecut circular silvered metal belt
loop, engraved red depiction of Autry
and signature, name inscribed inner
side, c1940 .... **100.00**
Belt Buckle, brass, name and figure out-
lined in red, c1950 .... **35.00**
Book
Better Little Book
*Gene Autry and the Bandits of Sil-
ver Tip,* Whitman, 1940 .... **15.00**
Gene Autry/Cowboy Detective,
Whitman, 1940, full color illus **25.00**
Tell-A-Tale Book, *Gene Autry Makes
A New Friend,* Whitman, 28 pgs,
1952 .... **20.00**
Cap Pistol, 8", silvered metal, simulated
pearl handle, c1950 .... **35.00**
Comic Book, Vol. 1, No. 12, February
1948, Gene Autry Comics **8.00**
Decal, 5 x 7", iron on, Autry and Champ
Junior, black, white, and red, c1950 **8.00**
Galoshes, rubber, cowboy boot shape,
red and white **45.00**
Guitar, orig box, Emenee **55.00**
Holster, 11", "Gene Autry Flying A
Ranch," leather, black, rigid silvered
metal with floral pattern and oval
blank center, white inscription on belt
strip, c1950 .... **75.00**
Lobby Card, 11 x 14"
Gene Autry And The Mounties, Co-
lumbia, 1950 .... **10.00**
Silver Canyon, Columbia, 1951 .... **8.00**
Sioux City Sue, multicolored, 1950 . **15.00**
Whirlwind, set of eight, red, white,
blue, and yellow design **100.00**
Lunch Box **70.00**
Magazine
Look, August 1, 1950, "Gene Autry
Millionaire Cowboy" **10.00**
Screen Stories, May, 1948, "The
Strawberry Roan," story and photos **5.00**
Magic Slate, Lowe **65.00**
Movie Serial, VHS, Phantom Empire .. **35.00**
Paper Doll Book, 10½ x 13", Whitman,

four punchout figures, six uncut cloth-
ing pgs, 1950 .... **150.00**
Pinback Button, 1¼", flesh tones, red,
white, and blue **15.00**
Pistol, cap **50.00**
Plaque, 4½ x 5½", masonite, full color
photo, beveled edges, metal hanging
loop on back, c1950 .... **40.00**
Plate, 9½", china, white, Gene with
Champion center, brands border ... **25.00**
Post Card, 3½ x 5", "Home of Gene
Autry," full color, c1940 .... **10.00**
Poster, 27 x 41", Rim of the Canyon,
Columbia Pictures, Morgan Litho,
1949 .... **35.00**
Program, "Gene Autry Championship
Rodeo," April 11–16, 1941, 18 pgs,
8½ x 10½", blue photo of Autry and
Champion on front cover **50.00**
Puzzle, frametray, Autry and Champion,
Whitman, #2981, c1950 .... **8.50**
Record
My Alabama Home, banner **14.00**
The Yellow Rose of Texas, Oriole .. **10.00**
Scarf, 18 x 21", silk, purple, green, dark
blue, and white illus and design,
Gene with guitar in horseshoe in cor-
ner and western motifs, 1940s **75.00**
School Bag, 10 x 14", vinyl, dark tan
pebble grained design, fabric int.,
carrying strap, Autry on Champion on
front, 1940–50 .... **100.00**
Sheet Music
Goodbye, Little Darlin', Goodbye, 9 x
12", 6 pgs, blue tone photo, 1940
copyright **20.00**
You're The Only Star in My Blue
Heaven, 9 x 12", small picture of
Gene, large picture of Enoch Light,
1938 .... **8.00**
Song Book, #2, 1934, cov illus **25.00**
Tablet, 5½ x 9", full color cover photo,
black signature, 1940–50 .... **20.00**
Thermos **25.00**
Tie Bar, brass, portrait of Gene, small
western symbols, 2¾" l, c1950 .... **35.00**
View Master Reel, "Gene Autry and His
Wonder Horse "Champion," #950,
1950 .... **10.00**
Wall Plaque **25.00**
Waste Can, 6 x 7 x 12", oval, white
ground, decal inscribed "Gene Autry,
America's No. 1 Cowboy and Cham-
pion, His Wonder Horse" **40.00**
Wrist Watch **125.00**

HOPALONG CASSIDY

Badge, metal, six point star, raised figure, c1950 .... **15.00**
Bank, 2 x 2 x 4½" h, bronze colored
plastic, Savings Rodeo program pre-

mium, New Hampshire Savings Bank,
Concord on back, early 1950s **40.00**
Banner, black and white felt, 28" l,
Hoppy on horse, 1950 .... **12.50**

**Hopalong Cassidy, *Life* magazine, June
12, 1950, $18.00.**

Bedspread, 72 x 90", Hoppy riding Topper over fence, beige ground **50.00**
Binoculars, color picture decals on silvered metal hand grips, red plastic
eye viewers, early 1950s **50.00**
Book, *Hopalong Cassidy Lends A Helping Hand*, 6½ x 8", Bonnie Book,
Samuel Lowe Co, 1950, 24 pgs **25.00**
Bowl, cereal **25.00**
Cap Gun, metal trigger, leather holster,
marked "Hopalong Cassidy, Wyandotte" **650.00**
Chinese Checkers, 12½ x 14½" board,
marbles, orig box, Milton Bradley,
1950 .... **35.00**
Clothing
Bowtie, 4" w, wine colored, name in
yellow, red, and white letters, brass
dot accents top and bottom edge,
metal snap-on clips **50.00**
Cowgirl outfit, four pcs, Iskin, orig
box, 1950 .... **120.00**
Necktie, 32", two colorful pictures,
white ground **18.00**
Coaster, set of 4, 4" d, black, white, and
yellow, "Spun Honey Spreads like
Butter" **10.00**
Coloring Book **50.00**
Compass Hat Ring **185.00**
Crayon and Stencil Set, MIB **95.00**
Decals, set of 3, color water Hoppy and
Topper transfers, unused, c1950 ... **25.00**
Dental Kit, toothbrush and toothpaste . **40.00**
Display, Butternut Bread **100.00**
Dominoes, MIB **65.00**

Figure, Hoppy and Topper, plastic, Ideal **100.00**

Game

    Canasta, orig box **125.00**

    Hopalong Cassidy Pony Express Toss Game, 12 x 18" masonite board, black, white, and red painted glossy surface, diecut target hole openings, two wood pegs, missing beanbags, 12 x 18 x 1" flattened box, Transogram, 1950 copyright **50.00**

Glass **20.00**

Greeting Card, 6½ x 7½" diecut card with slot, 3 x 7" diecut pistol, inscriptions "Shoot The Works! It's Your Birthday!," and "Put Your Belt Through The Slits and Wear The Gun And Holster Just Like Hoppy," Buzza Cardozo, Hollywood, early 1950s .. **40.00**

Handkerchief, 11½ x 12", fabric, white, brown, blue, red, and black needlework Hoppy and Topper, red Hoppy and blue Topper names in needlepoint **25.00**

Ice Cream Bag, 5¼ x 12", silver foil, insulated, blue, silver background, blue photo, inscription "Enjoy Hoppy's Favorite Brand," unused, early 1950s **40.00**

Knife **40.00**

Lamp

    Aladdin, holster, night light **145.00**

    "Roto-Vue," 10" h, Hopalong Cassidy Bar-20 Ranch and Topper, marked "Econolity Corp, CA" **265.00**

Lobby Card, 11 x 14", full color scene, 1947 United Artists film "Unexpected Guest," Hopalong holding fainted woman **20.00**

Lunch Box and Thermos, 1954 .... **70.00**

Magazine, Life, 1950 .... **18.00**

Milk Carton, 1 qt, wax coating, multicolored picture on one side, tan ground, c1950 .... **20.00**

Mug, 3" h, white glass, red picture and signature **15.00**

Neckerchief, red, Hoppy riding Topper, border dec **10.00**

Night Light, holster shape, Alladin **200.00**

Notebook, 9½ x 11", cardboard, full color picture on front and back, two rings, 1950s **50.00**

Paint Set, large, MIB, 1950 .... **65.00**

Paper Plate, 6", set of 8, orig package, c1950 .... **10.00**

Photo Album **50.00**

Plate, 9", white, Hoppy and Topper in blue **22.00**

Pocketknife, 3½" l, steel, black plastic insert panels, two steel and one utility blades, metal loop, Hammer Brand, USA, early 1950s **75.00**

Post Card, 3½ x 5½", #5720, full color

illus, Valentine & Sons, Great Britain, unused, early 1950s **30.00**

Potato Chip Can **200.00**

Puppet, 10½" h, printed fabric body, molded vinyl head and black hat, inscribed name, 1951 copyright **100.00**

Record Album, Hopalong and Singing Bandit, book, two records **37.50**

Ring, club, metal **50.00**

School Bag, 10 x 14", vinyl, black, pebble grain design, white plastic handle, leather straps with silvered metal buckles, white trim, unused, early 1950s **100.00**

Sign, 11 x 41½", cardboard, red and white Hoppy picture, painted litho, simulated wood grain background, "Hoppy's Favorite," and Melville Milk **100.00**

Sheet Music, Lazy Rolls The Rio Grande, blue and white, Hoppy riding Topper, cattle herd background, 1939 .... **15.00**

Stationery, orig folder and stationery .. **65.00**

Tablet, 8 x 10", full color cover photo and signature, unused, 1950s **15.00**

Token, metal, c1950 .... **5.00**

Toy, rocking horse, wind-up, marked "Marx" **350.00**

View Master Reel, No. 955, Hopalong Cassidy and Topper, c1950 .... **12.00**

Wallet **20.00**

Wrist Watch, boxed **150.00**

LONE RANGER

Adventure Set, The Carson City Bank Robbery, orig box, Hubley, 1972 ... **22.00**

Badge, secret compartment **45.00**

Better Little Book

    The Lone Ranger and Dead Men's Mine, Whitman, 1939 .... **50.00**

    The Lone Ranger and the Black Shirt Highwayman, Whitman, 1939 ... **40.00**

Big Little Book

    The Lone Ranger and His Horse Silver, Whitman, 1935 .... **50.00**

    The Lone Ranger and The Menace of Murder Valley, Whitman, 1938 ... **40.00**

Binoculars, orig decals **75.00**

Book Bag, 10 x 12", Lone Ranger and Tonto riding across desert, 1950s ... **40.00**

Calendar, 1939 .... **75.00**

Cereal Box, Cheerios, Frontiertown ... **75.00**

Clothing

    Cowboy Outfit, five pcs, Yankiboy, orig box, 1947 .... **150.00**

    Skirt **30.00**

Coloring Book, "Lone Ranger Ranch Fun Book," 8½ x 11", Whitman, 1956, 64 pgs, Cheerios premium ... **75.00**

Comic Book, 2½ x 7", *The Lone Ranger*

and the Story of Silver, Cherrios premium, 1954 .... **8.00**

Flashlight, 7" l, red plastic head, litho scene around side, diecut bullet shape 4 page instruction sheet, boxed, early 1950s **75.00**

Game

   Card, Parker Bros, Lone Ranger, Tonto, and western motifs pictured on cards, 3½ x 5", 1938 .... **65.00**

   Round-Up, c1950 .... **40.00**

   The Lone Ranger & Tonto Board Game, unopened, Warren, 1978 . **15.00**

Gun and Holster set, MIB **130.00**

Hairbrush, late 1930s **45.00**

Harmonica, orig package **45.00**

Hat, 11½ x 13 x 3", felt, brown, molded and starched, red label attachment, adjustable drawstring, orig label stitched on brim, Arlington Co, 1966 copyright **50.00**

Manual, *Cramer's Lone Ranger Safety Club,* 5¼ x 8¼", 32 pgs, issued by Cramer's Butter-Cream Sliced Bread, 1939 copyright **150.00**

Mask, 3¼ x 14", diecut paper, black, inscribed "Hi Yo Silver," 1938 Lone Ranger copyright, Schultz Butter-Nut Bread, and Dolly Madison Cakes on back **60.00**

Model, Aurora, 1967, MIB **125.00**

Movie and lobby card set, 1956 ..... **400.00**

Noisemaker, horn, 5" l, litho metal, white plastic mouthpiece, "Ichi," Japan, 1960s **15.00**

Paint Set, Bradley, c1940, MIB **55.00**

Pedometer, boxed **60.00**

Pencil, silver, bullet shape **14.00**

Pencil Box, 4 x 8½", cardboard, dark brown, Lone Ranger on Silver image, silver signature, late 1930s **35.00**

Photo, Silver Cup premium, 1936 .... **25.00**

Pinback Button, 1", Lone Ranger Safety Scout, silver, blue enamel, c1930 .. **20.00**

Record, "He Saves Booneville Gold," 78 rpm, 10 x 10" jacket, Decca No 6, 1952 .... **15.00**

Record Player, wood **185.00**

Ring, filmstrip, orig box and instructions **175.00**

Snow Dome, Lone Ranger roping calf . **65.00**

Spoon, 6", silvered brass, "The Lone Ranger Hi-Yo Silver" on handle, 1938 copyright **35.00**

Suspenders, child's, Lone Ranger, Tonto, silver guns, and other illus, 1938 patent date **450.00**

Target, tin **95.00**

Toothbrush Holder, 4" h, plaster, painted, 1938 .... **75.00**

Toy, 7" h, wind-up, litho tin, Marx, copyright 1938 .... **100.00**

Wrist Watch, metal case, clear plexiglas

crystal, Lone Ranger on galloping Silver, black numerals, orig tan leather straps, c1940 .... **150.00**

TOM MIX

Bandanna, mulitcolored, Tom on horseback, "Best Wishes—Tom Mix" **50.00**

Belt, 26" l, glows in the dark, secret compartment, brass buckle, 1945 .. **90.00**

Big Little Book

   Tom Mix and The Hoard of Montezuma, Whitman, 1937, 424 pgs .. **30.00**

   Tom Mix and The Stranger From The South, Whitman, 1936, 424 pgs .. **25.00**

Coloring Book, 11 x 14", 96 pgs, full color portrait on cov, Whitman, 1935 **50.00**

Comic book, #23, *Return of the Past,* Tom Mix Western Comic, 1949 .... **12.00**

Decoder Button, set of five, 3½ x 5" folder explaining use **50.00**

Lariat, orig mailing envelope **40.00**

Letterhead, 8 x 11", black and white photo, red with blue outline "Tom Mix Circus" title, bamboo frame under glass, late 1930s **75.00**

Magazine, *Motion Picture Classic,* "Just Him and Tony" story, 1929 .... **20.00**

Make-up Kit, black diecut cardboard eyeglasses and eye patch, pink fabric nose, two mustaches, two tin containers, instruction sheet with ten example disguises, orig mailing envelope, 1940 Ralston premium **125.00**

Paint Book, 8½ x 11½", Whitman, 1940 copyright, unused **40.00**

Pennant, 22½" l, felt, "Tom Mix Circus and Wild West," Tom on horseback, burnt orange background, streamers on end **120.00**

Periscope, 9" l, cardboard, blue, inscribed "Ralston Straight Shooters" . **65.00**

Premium Catalog, 2½ x 3½", opens to 9 x 14", brown, dark green, and white, 1938 .... **35.00**

Puppet, 9", hand, fabric body, molded vinyl head, 1950–60 .... **60.00**

Rocking Horse **200.00**

Sign, 6 x 24", paper, "Round Up The Boys And Bring 'Em In," orange, yellow, black, and white print, Imperial Knife Co, Providence, RI, 1930s ... **150.00**

Spurs, pr, aluminum, stamped "TM Bar Brand," orig mailing box, Ralston premium, c1949 .... **50.00**

Target, 12 x 15", Indian Blow Gun Target, paper mounted on cardboard, red, white, and blue, Ralston Cereal premium, 1940 .... **60.00**

Telegraph Set, metal telegraph key, blue and white cardboard box with Tom and Ralston photo, 5 x 7½" **40.00**

Telescope Set, 3½" l, gold plastic bullet shape telescope, magnifying glass, secret code signaler, and birdcall, 9 x 12" instruction sheet, orig mailing box, Ralston premium, 1950 .... **150.00**

Watch Fob, 1½ x 2", metal, gold finish, shovel and pick design, clear plastic dome inset holds gold ore sample, "Ralston Straight Shooters Genuine Gold Ore From America's Richest Gold District" and Tom Mix bar brand on reverse, Ralston premium, c1940 .... **75.00**

Roy Rogers, sheet music, Along the Navajo Trail, Larry Markes, Dick Charles, and Eddie de Lange, lyrics and music, 1942–45, Leeds Music Co, NYC, $15.00.

ROY ROGERS

Advertising Display, 9 x 12½", "Roy Rogers Cub Hunter Pocket Knives," cardboard, c1950 .... **90.00**

Bank, still
  Metal, boot and spur **30.00**
  Tin litho, Trigger **55.00**

Bedspread, 66 x 92", woven, tan, repeated band design, rope inscription "Roy Rogers and Trigger," 1940–50 **125.00**

Belt and Holster Set, leather, dark brown, white accent trims, 7½" l holster with silvered tin decorative piece with red glass stone in center, four metal bullets, 1940-50 .... **60.00**

Billfold **35.00**

Binoculars, 5 x 6", plastic, black, two color decals **30.00**

Book
  Gopher Creek Gunman **15.00**
  Roy Rogers and The Sure 'nough Cowpoke, Tell-A-Tale, Whitman, 1950 .... **5.00**

Camera, box, MIB **45.00**

Cap Gun **35.00**

Clock
  Alarm, color dial, c1970 .... **25.00**
  Motion, Roy and Trigger, marked "Ingraham" **225.00**

Clothing
  Chaps, vinyl **30.00**
  Gloves, 9" l, leather, yellow silhouette of Roy on Trigger, western motifs, fringe sides **40.00**
  Outfit, girl's, Dale Evans, 2 pcs ... **80.00**
  Shirt, boy's size small, cotton, light blue, dark blue collar and shoulder, red, green, and blue plaid collar, raised stitched design on front, green stitched lettering, slash pocket, mid 1950s **50.00**
  Vest and Chaps, boy's, cowhide **60.00**

Coin, copper, emb Roy Rogers on front, Trigger on back, c1950 .... **7.50**

Coloring Book, 15 x 11", Roy Rogers and Dale Evans, color cov, 1952 ... **20.00**

Figure, Hartland **110.00**

Game, Roy Rogers Rodeo Game, 1949 **125.00**

Guitar, wood, full size, orig case, instruction book **250.00**

Gun, marked "Roy Rogers Tuck-Away" **17.50**

Gun and Holster Set **85.00**

Harmonica, 1¼ x 4¼", white plastic and silvered metal, engraved "Good Luck" and "King Of The Cowboys" on top, orig unopened plastic blister retail card **50.00**

Horseshoe Set, four rubber horseshoes, wood stakes with rubber bases, two black, other two brown, Roy and Trigger signatures, boxed, unused, Knox-Rees, 1940–50 .... **200.00**

Knife, horseshoe, two blades, pearl insert **10.00**

Lantern, missing insert **30.00**

Lobby Card, 11 x 14"
  In Old Amarillo, 1951 .... **10.00**
  North of the Great Divide, 1950 ... **8.00**

Magazine
  Movie Life Magazine, "Life Story in Pix of Roy's Bride-Dale Evans," story and black and white photos, March, 1948 .... **25.00**
  Saturday Evening Post, Roy and Dale on cov, full page photo inside, April, 1980 .... **8.50**

Magazine Ad, Life, July 12, 1943 .... **10.00**

Mug, plastic, Quaker Oats premium, c1940 .... **10.00**

Nodder, 6½" h, square green base, Japan marking, 1962 copyright **125.00**

Notebook, 10½ x 13", two ring, brown, tan and maroon picture on white background, dark brown vinyl trim, zippered, late 1940s **150.00**

Paint book, 1944 .... **12.00**

Paper Dolls
  1953, Roy and Dale, cut out, orig
    folder **65.00**
  1954, Whitman **55.00**
Pen, 5" l, retractable ballpoint, silvered
  metal top with "RR" initials, light
  blue plastic bottom with black Roy
  and Trigger and inscription, 1950s .. **30.00**
Pinback Button, 1¼", celluloid, black,
  yellow, and white, c1950 .... **5.00**
Pocket Knife **45.00**
Pocket Watch **260.00**
Program, World Championship Rodeo,
  featuring Roy Rogers and Trigger,
  25th year, stories and photos, 1955 . **15.00**
Puzzle, Trigger and Bullet **10.00**
Statue, Hartland, Roy and Trigger **350.00**
Tent, canvas **125.00**
Thermos, Double R bar Ranch, c1950 **12.50**
Toy
  Pull, 7 x 9 x 12", covered wagon with
    canvas top and blue metal wheels,
    horse, paper labels, N H Hill Brass
    Company **45.00**
  Roy Rogers Mineral City, litho tin,
    post office, bank, hotel, Bar-M
    house, Marx **350.00**
Wrist Watch, Dale Evans with Butter-
  milk, orig straps, 1950s **50.00**
Yo-Yo, promotion, Roy and Trigger, orig
  wrapper **40.00**

CHARACTERS, OTHER

Annie Oakley
  Book, *Annie Oakley,* Shannon Garst,
    Julian Messner, 1968, 186 pgs ... **10.00**
  Cabinet Photo, 4 x 6½", holding rifle **95.00**
  Craft Set, two cloth full color pictures,
    diecut cardboard frames, unopened
    sequins and beads, Gabriel, 1955
    copyright, 12 x 17 x 1½" box, un-
    used **75.00**
  Game, 16 x 16" board of adventure
    map, Annie on horseback center,
    includes markers, disks, spinner,
    and play money, 8½ × 16½ ×
    1½" box, Milton Bradley **20.00**
  Lunch box, Aladdin, 1955 .... **25.00**
  Pinback Button, ⅞" w, black and
    white portrait surrounded by gray
    horseshoe, green four leaf clover,
    red slogan "I Use U.M.C. Ammu-
    nition To Obtain The Best Results,"
    back paper text "Compliments Of
    Annie Oakley," brass pin **90.00**
Better Little Book, Whitman
  *Desert Eagle And The Hidden For-
    tress,* #1431, J.R. White, artist,
    James O. Parson, author, 1941,
    standard size, 432 pgs, hardcover **15.00**

*The Range Busters in Saddle Moun-
  tain Roundup,* #1441, Henry E.
  Vallely, artist, Eleanor Packer, au-
  thor, 1942, standard size, 432 pgs,
  hardcover, flip-it feature **15.00**
Big Little Book, Whitman
  Guns In The Roaring West, #1426,
    Steve Saxton, author, 1937, stan-
    dard size, 300 pgs, hardcover **12.00**
  Riders of Lone Trails, #1425, Steve
    Saxton, author, 1937, standard
    size, 300 pgs, hardcover **15.00**
  The Texas Kid, #1429, Milt Youn-
    gren, artist, Steve Saxton, author,
    1936, standard size, 432 pgs, hard-
    cover **18.00**
Cisco Kid
  Premium
    Gun, red, white, and blue card-
     board, Cisco's picture on handle,
     clicker mounted inside, adver-
     tises TV show and Tip-Top Bread **40.00**
    Label Sheet, 8 x 8¼" folded, holds
     16 adventure pictures from
     Ward's Tip-top Bread end labels,
     titled "Bolder & Bullets Story,"
     black and white photo front
     panel **75.00**
    Tablet, 8 x 10", color picture on pink
     ground, inscribed "From Your
     Good Amigo, Duncan Renaldo—
     Cisco Kid" **20.00**
    Tie Clasp **15.00**
    View Master Reel, *Cisco Kid, Duncan
     Renaldo,* 1950 .... **10.00**
Davy Crockett
  Badge, orig card **15.00**
  Bank
    2½ x 2½ x ⅝", dime register type,
     litho metal, full color scenes, mid
     1950s **75.00**
    5", metal **25.00**
  Belt, size 24, leather, diecut brass
    buckle with red accents, "Davy
    Crockett," three repeated long rifles
    and tooled designs, mid 1950s ... **40.00**
  Bow Tie **15.00**
  Cookie Jar, 7 x 8 x 10", china, raised
    gold letter name on front, C Miller
    copyright and "55" on bottom, no
    lid **75.00**
  Game, Davy Crockett's Alamo Game,
    sixteen playing cards, 94 paper
    marker playing pieces, 8 pgs in-
    struction leaflet, 13¼ x 17 x 1½"
    box, Lowell Toy Corp, mid 1950s **50.00**
  Glass, 3" h, Crockett on horseback in
    brown and yellow, mid 1950s ... **15.00**
  Horseshoe Set, four rubber horsesh-
    oes with name and western sym-
    bols, two rubber bases with wood
    pegs, Auburn Toys, mid 1950s ... **40.00**

Lamp, 7½" h, china, glazed, 4½ x 6½" green base, felt bottom, 1950s ... **75.00**

Ruler, 6", paper, adv Atlas Soap **5.00**

School Bag, 11 x 12", fabric, brown, tan vinyl fringe, vinyl cover with Crockett scene, brown shoulder strap, brass buckle, unused, 1950s **75.00**

Teepee, full size **65.00**

Wallet, 3 x 3½", vinyl, brown, gold foil-like picture sticker, molded clear plastic cov, blue accents, name in red **25.00**

Wyatt Earp

Badge, Marshall, metal, orig card .. **10.00**

Gun and Holster set, 8½" l silvered white metal gun with grained white plastic grips, uses roll caps, leather holster brown and tan design and Wyatt Earp name, emb floral design around belt slots **75.00**

Puzzle, frame tray, 11½ x 14½", full color photo portrait, Whitman, 1958 copyright **25.00**

Statue, Hartland **150.00**

Sunglasses, 12½ x 19" display card holding twelve plastic sunglasses with green lenses, 1" flasher picture in center of each, Merit Mfg Co, 1950–60 .... **75.00**

Hartland Figures, plastic, removable parts (saddle, hats, guns, etc)

Jim Hardie, Tales of Wells Fargo, 8" h **75.00**

Tom Jeffords, Broken Arrow, full size **100.00**

Jumbo Book Series, Saalfield

Boss Of The Chisholm Trail, #1153, Ralph C. Hitchcock, artist, Guy L. Maynard, author, 1939, standard size, 400 pgs, hardcover **12.00**

The Ranger And The Cowboy, #1163, Albert Wick, artist, Ward M. Stevens, author, 1939, standard size, 400 pgs, hardcover **14.00**

Paladin

Business Card, 2 x 3½", black and white **5.00**

Game, checkers, 12" sq board with pictures of Paladin on side, plastic playing pieces, plastic bag with label, 1960 .... **18.00**

Lunch Box, Aladdin, 1960 .... **25.00**

Ranger Joe

Gun, 6½" l, wood, painted black, white cardboard grips, yellow lettering, red insignia, fires rubber bands, c1950 .... **75.00**

Mug, 3" h, glass, white, blue portrait illus, c1950 .... **15.00**

Red Ryder

Better Little Book, Whitman

Red Ryder, The Fighting Westerner, 1940 .... **20.00**

Red Ryder, *Red Ryder and the Thunder Trail,* **Whitman, Jerry McGill author, Fred Harman artist, 8 x 5¾ x 1¼", 1956, $25.00.**

Red Ryder and the Secret Canyon, 1948, standard size, 288 pgs, hardcover **18.00**

Red Ryder in War on the Range, #1473, 1945, standard size, 352 pgs, hardcover **15.00**

Coin, metal, gold, JC Penney premium, 1942–45 .... **5.00**

Gloves, pr, leather, black, white suede fringe, silver Red Ryder depiction, tag with premium offer on reverse, Wells Lamont Corp, sized for 8-10 years **50.00**

Handkerchief, 11 x 13", white, red, green, and tan print design, c1940 **15.00**

Pocketknife, 3½" l, steel, light yellow marbled plastic inserts, portrait and name in red on one side, two blades, Camco USA, c1940 ..... **75.00**

Rifleman

Game, Rifleman, Milton Bradley, 1959 .... **20.00**

Hat, 11 x 13 x 3", red felt, diecut fabric label on front with silvery black and white photo on yellow and red background, gold dec crown cord with adjustable chin strap, orig label "Official Western Hat As Seen On TV," Tex-Felt, 1958 copyright **75.00**

Lunch Box, Aladdin, 1961 .... **25.00**

Rifle, 32" l, metal and plastic, Hubley New Flip Special, orig box, 1958 **70.00**

Rin-Tin-Tin

Book, Rin-Tin-Tin Book of Dog Care, 7 x 10", 182 pgs, Lee Duncan ... **40.00**

Game, Adventures of Rin-Tin-Tin, 17 x 17" board, playing pieces, cards,

Rin-Tin-Tin, Rusty, marble game, Nabisco Shredded Wheat, $7.00.

and unopened plastic coins, Transogram, 1955 .... 25.00

Little Golden Book, *Rin-Tin-Tin and Rusty,* 1955 .... 8.00

Puzzle, 14 x 18½" assembled, full color photo, 7½ x 10 x 2½" box, Jaymar, 1957 copyright 40.00

Record, "Rinty Breaks Through," 78 rpm, 10 x 10" cardboard cover, Columbia label, 1955 copyright 35.00

Statue, Hartland, c1950 .... 35.00

View Master Reel, set of three reels with orig envelopes, 1955 copyright 25.00

Straight Arrow

Bandanna, 16¹⁄₁₂ x 18", red, white, and blue portrait, Straight Arrow on racing horse, and Indian motifs, red background, inscribed "Kaneewah Fury," 1949 copyright, Nabisco premium 60.00

Bracelet, "Mystic Wrist Kit," plastic, gold, Straight Arrow profile on lid, gold colored metal arrowhead inscribed "Straight Arrow," removable secret compartment, keychain, and gold plastic cowry shell charm, Nabisco premium, 1950 .... 150.00

Game, Target Game, 10½ x 14" litho tin board, three magnetic feather tipped arrows, spring steel crossgun bow, orig box, National Biscuit Co, c1950 .... 70.00

Wild Bill Hickok

Game

Cavalry and Indians, 14 x 14" board, punched cardboard disks, 7½ x 14 x 1½" box with Hickok on horse talking to Indian Chief 40.00

Wild Bill Hickok, Bilt-Rite, 1956 . 15.00

Map, 24 x 36", paper, "Wild Bill Hickok Treasure Map," Hickok drawing and jingles in lower left corner, western illus throughout, and shows over 300 treasure sites, Rand McNally, 1950s 60.00

Poster, 27 x 41", full color, red sky background, "The Ghost Of Crossbone Canyon" in red and blue on yellow background 50.00

Wagon Train

Coloring Book, full color photo of Ward Bond and Robert Horton front and back, 8 colored pages, Whitman, 1959 .... 25.00

Cowboy Outfit, leather gun and holster, repeater rifle, metal spurs, 27 x 8 x 12" box with Ward Bond and Robert Horton picture, Leslie Henry 60.00

Jack Ingram, arcade card, green, $12.00.

PERSONALITIES

Arcade Cards, 3¼ x 5¼", inscribed

Buster Crabbe, green 4.00

Monte Hale, Monte and horse, black 3.00

George Montgomery, bust, black ... 2.50

Wild Bill Elliott, ¾ length, pink 3.00

Benson, Bobby

Big Little Book, *Bobby Benson on the H-Bar-O Ranch,* Whitman, 1934 . 40.00

Hobby Kit, diecut leather parts, assembles to gun belt and double holster, grained western motifs, plastic stitching cords and rivets, orig packaging and box, 1954 copyright, Street & Smith Publications 50.00

Brown, Johnny Mack

Lobby Card, 11 x 14", titled "Rustlers of Red Dog," blue and white, Universal 8.00

Photograph, 8 x 10", full color, yellow margin band on top, 1950s movie titled "Border Renegades" 15.00

Buffalo Bill

Cabinet Photo, 4¼ x 6½", black and white close-up portrait, c1890 ... 75.00

Figurine, 2⅛", metal, Blenheim 20.00

Hart, William S.
  Exhibit Card, 3½ x 5½", yellowtone photo, 1931 .... **15.00**
  Tablet, 6 x 9", brown and white portrait, Picture Land Stars series, c1920 .... **40.00**
Hayes, Gabby
  Coloring Book, 8 x 10½", *Magic Dial Funny Coloring Book,* diecut television screen opening in front with disk wheel, Samuel Lowe Co, c1950 .... **50.00**
  Dixie Lid, 2¼", brown photo, rim inscription titled "Wyoming," 1947 **25.00**
  Puzzle, 10¼ x 14½", frame tray, full color illus, Hayes and Kagran copyrights, early 1950s **25.00**
  Rocking horse **200.00**
Jones, Buck
  BB Gun, 36", wood stock with printed sundial, metal side with name, metal compass insert, Daisy **90.00**
  Better Little Book, *Buck Jones and The Two-Gun Kid,*" #1404, 1937, Whitman **30.00**
  Big Little Book, *The Fighting Code,* #1104, Columbia Pictures, artists, Pat Patterson, author, 1934, 160 pgs, hardcover, soft spine **35.00**
  Book, *Songs of the Western Trails,* 60 pgs, words and music, 9 x 12", 1940 copyright **40.00**
  Five Star Library Series, *Rocky Rhodes,* #15, Engel-Van Wiseman, Universal Pictures, artist, adapted by Harry Ormiston, 1935, 160 pgs, hardcover **35.00**
  Magazine, Remember When Magazine, 8½ x 11", Jones on cov, story and black and white photos inside, 1974 .... **7.50**
  Pinback Button, "Buck Jones Club," enamel on brass, horseshoe, picture in center, 1930s **15.00**
Masterson, Bat
  Arcade Card, c1950 .... **2.00**
  Costume, orig box **125.00**
  Game, Bat Masterson Board Game, Lowell Toy Mfg Co, 1958 .... **15.00**
Maynard, Ken
  Autograph, 8 x 10" black and white glossy photo, black inked signature "Ken Maynard 1941" **125.00**
  Big Little Book, *Ken Maynard in Western Justice,* #1430, Whitman, Irwin Myers, artist, Rex Loomis, author, 1938, standard size, 432 pgs, hardcover **22.00**
  Little Big Book, Saalfield, *Strawberry Roan,* Universal Pictures, artist, Grace Mack, author, 1934, 4¾ x 5¼", 160 pgs, hardcover **22.00**

  Premium, photo, 9 x 11", color, black and white "In Old Santa Fe" scenes on back, Dixie **30.00**
McCoy, Tim
  Autograph, 8 x 10" glossy black and white photo, purple inked signature "Best Wishes Tim McCoy," c1940 **75.00**
  Better Little Book, *Tim McCoy And The Sandy Gulch Stampede,* #1490, Whitman, 1939 .... **40.00**
  Big Little Book, Whitman, *The Prescott Kid,* #1152, Columbia Pictures, artist, adapted by Eleanor Packer, 1935, 4⅝ x 5¼", 160 pgs, hardcover, soft spine **25.00**
  Lobby Poster, 11 x 14", set of 8, 1930s
    Fighting Renegade **100.00**
    Straight Shooter **125.00**
  Premium, photo, 9 x 11", color, black and white movie scenes on back, Dixie **15.00**
Robertson, Dale, platter, 12½" oval, china, western scene includes "Star Hotel," "Dale Robertson" on top, Wellsville China Co signature on bottom **75.00**
Rogers, Will, figure, 5⅞" h, wood, wearing brown suit, name on front, 1940s copyright **50.00**
Walker, Clint
  Autograph, 8 x 10" glossy photo, blue inked signature **100.00**
  Tablet, 8 x 10", "Cheyenne" **8.00**
Wayne, John
  Arcade Card, c1950 .... **2.00**
  Coin, metal, gold, c1979 .... **7.50**
  Coloring Book, 11 x 15", 32 pgs, ten colored pages, Saalfield, #2354-15, 1951 copyright **50.00**
  Holster Set, leather belt, two holsters with name on side, orig box, early 1950s **45.00**
  Knife, memorial, metal and plastic, "The Duke—John Wayne (1907–1979)" **10.00**
  Movie Still, 8 x 10", black and white **4.00**
  Pinback button, 2½", "In Memory of a Great American" **5.00**
  Sheet Music, "Put Your Arms Around Me, Honey," 9 x 12", 4 pgs, black and white photo, of Wayne, Martha Scott and Dale Evans, 1937 copyright **15.00**
  Stationery, black and white drawing, includes envelope **2.50**

CRACKER JACK

Collecting Hints: Most collectors concentrate on the pre-plastic era. Toys in the original packaging are very rare. One possibility for specializing is toys from a given decade, for example in World War II soldiers, tanks, artillery pieces and other war related items.

Many prizes are marked "Cracker Jack" or carry a picture of the Sailor Boy and Bingo, his dog. Unmarked prizes can be confused with gumball machine novelties or prizes from Checkers, a rival firm.

History: F. W. Rueckheim, a popcorn store owner in Chicago, introduced a mixture of popcorn, peanuts, and molasses at the World's Columbian Exposition in 1893. Three years later the name "Cracker Jack" was applied to it. It gained popularity quickly and by 1908 appeared in the lyrics of *Take Me Out To The Ball Game*.

In 1910 Rueckheim included coupons on the box which could be redeemed for prizes. In 1912 prizes appeared in the box itself. The early prizes were made of paper, tin, lead, wood and porcelain. Plastic was introduced in 1948.

The Borden Company's Cracker Jack prize collection numbers over 10,000 examples; but this is not all of them. Knowledge continues to expand as more examples are found in bottoms of drawers, old jewelry boxes and attics.

Today's items are largely paper, the plastic magnifying glass being one exception. The company buys toys in lots of 25 million and keeps hundreds of prizes in circulation at one time. Borden's annual production is about 400 million boxes.

Reference: Alex Jaramillo, *Cracker Jack Prizes*, Abbeville Press, 1989.

Stationery, envelope, red and blue box, 6¾ x 3⅝", $6.00.

Advertising Trade Card, riddles 4.00
Booklet
  Cracker Jack Riddles, 2¾ x 5", published by Rueckheim Bros & Eckstein, 40 pgs, black and white illus, red, white, blue, and black cov . .   35.00
  National Songs, 2½ x 3½", 16 pgs, patriotic songs, c1918–20 . . . .   30.00
Bookmark, 2½" l, diecut, litho tin, brown Spaniel, c1930 . . . .   20.00

Cap, paper, red white and blue, "Me For Cracker Jack" **50.00**
Clicker, aluminum **15.00**
Cookbook, *One Taste Invites Another*, 4 x 6", 16 pgs **15.00**
Doll, 15", rag, Sailor boy **100.00**
Easel, 2¼", litho tin, Herby **50.00**
Flip Book, Charlie Chaplin, 1¼ x 2", paper, 20 pgs, black and white photos, adv Cracker Jack and for "Moving Picture Of Charlie Chaplin In The Champion" **65.00**
Lapel Stud
  1", oval, dark finished white metal, raised illus of Sailor Jack and dog Bingo, inscribed "Me For Cracker Jack," c1930 . . . .   **35.00**
  2", silvered white metal, wing design, center inscribed "Cracker Jack Air Corps," c1930 . . . .   **38.00**
Magnifying Glass, ¾ x 1¼", green plastic case, swing-out clear plastic loop lens, c1960 . . . .   **7.50**
Mask, 8½ x 10", "Cracker Jack" on front, c1960 . . . .   **15.00**
Mirror, pocket, 2", celluloid, red, white, and blue box, dark blue ground, inscribed "Cracker Jack It's Good To Eat And Can't Be Beat," and "Look At The Cracker Jack On The Other Side" . .   **60.00**
Palm Puzzle, 1½", silvered tin rim, mirror back, early 1900s **40.00**
Pencil, wood **15.00**
Pocket Watch, tin **15.00**
Postcard, Cracker Jack Bears, number 1-16 . . . .   **15.00**
Prize
  Coin, aluminum, emb, "Honest Old Abe," "The Great Emancipator," and "Join Cracker Jack Mystery Club" on reverse **5.00**
  Wagon, ¼ x 2 x 1", red, white, and blue, litho tin, fold-over wagon and horse, c1930 . . . .   **45.00**
Radio, plastic, glossy paper Cracker Jack box design, Borden co, c1970 . . . . .   **45.00**
Sign, 6 x 12", porcelain, enameled, boy and dog **10.00**
Tab, 2", h, tin, diecut, lightly emb, red, white, and blue **50.00**
Top, 1½", red, white, and blue, litho tin, wooden peg, c1940 . . . .   **18.00**
Toy
  Freight car, 3" l, bright orange, Jack and slogan, white orig tires, Tootsietoy **50.00**
  Jumping Frog, cardboard **10.00**
  Lion in Cage, litho tin, diecut, "Cracker Jack Shows" inscription on roof, late 1930s **60.00**
  Spinner, rainbow, marked, c1940 . .   **8.00**
  Truck, litho tin, Cracker Jack adv on

Top, litho tin, 1930s, $18.00.

one side, other Angelus Marshmallows, "The More You Eat-The More You Want" on roof **40.00**
Whistle, tin, marked "Cracker Jack," c1930 . . . . **25.00**

CREDIT COINS AND CARDS

Collecting Hints: Specialization is the key to successful collecting. Plan a collection that can be completed. Completeness tends to increase a collection's value.

When collecting charge coins, stay away from rusted or damaged pieces. Inferior pieces attract little interest unless rare.

Metal charge plates have little collector interest. They should remain affordable for years which means they'll probably not advance in value.

Most interest is in credit cards. Scarce and rare cards, when they can be located, are still affordable. National credit cards are eagerly sought. American Express is the most popular.

Paper and laminated paper credit cards are highly desirable. When it comes to collecting these, don't concern yourself with condition. Go ahead and acquire any you find. They're so difficult to locate that it could take years to find another specimen. Some are so rare that they might be unique!

Plastic credit cards issued before 1970 are scarce. Occasionally, you'll find a mint condition card. Generally, you'll have to settle for used. Plastic cards issued after 1980 should be collected in mint condition.

The best collecting hint is, collect what you like. You'll provide yourself with years of enjoyment and that's the best investment you'll ever make!

History: Charge coins, the first credit pieces, started being issued in the 1890s. Charge coins are approximately the size of a quarter or half dollar. Because of their size, they were often carried with change. This is why they were commonly referred to as coins.

Charge coins come in various shapes, sizes and materials. Most are square, round or oval. Some are in the shapes of shirts, socks or hats. They're made from various materials such as fiber, German silver, celluloid, steel and copper. The issuing stores has its name, monogram or initials on the coin., Each coin has a customer identification number. Charge coins were still in use as late as 1959.

Metal charge plates were in use from the 1930s to the 1950s. These plates look like military dog tags. The front of the plate contains the customer's name, address and account number. The back has a piece of cardboard that carries the store's name and customer's signature space.

Paper credit cards were in use in the early 1930s. They were easily damaged, so some companies began laminating them with clear plastic in the 1940s. Laminated cards were issued until the 1950s. The plastic cards, we know today, replaced the laminated cards in the late 1950s.

References: Greg Tunks, *Credit Card Collecting Bonanza,* privately printed, 1986.

Periodical: *Credit Card Collector,* 150 Hohldale, Houston, TX 77022.

Advisor: Greg Tunks.

Token, E Keller & Sons, Allentown, PA, $7.50.

CHARGE COINS

Abraham & Straus, A & S, hat shape . .	**15.00**
L Bamberger & Company, celluloid . . .	**250.00**
Boggs & Buhl, B & B, oval, white metal	**10.00**
Conrad's, picture of store, round	**18.00**
Gimbel Bros, lion holding shield, rect .	**10.00**
Horace Partridge, round, copper	**12.00**
Lit Bros, scalloped, oval, 1921	**18.00**
Jordan Marsh Co, JMCo, irregular oval	**20.00**
R. A. McWhirr, oval, white metal, 3-digit account number	**15.00**
Nathan Snellenberg, NS&Co, irregular round, white metal	**10.00**

Pocohontas Pioneer Garage, oval, white
metal **12.00**
Strawbridge & Clothier, arrowhead
shape **20.00**
R. H. White Co, RHWCo, irregular pear
shape **20.00**

CREDIT CARDS

Air Travel Card, 1981 .... **5.00**
American Express
  1959, paperboard, April 30 .... **400.00**
  1969, violet, centurion upper left cor-
    ner **80.00**
  1971, green, large centurion profile **25.00**
  1972, green, The Money Card to right **20.00**
  1974
    Gold, The Executive Money Card **45.00**
    Green, The Money Card centered **20.00**
  1975, gold, Executive Card **30.00**
  Current
    Gold **5.00**
    Green **4.00**
Arco
  Lifetime Credit Card, gold top **20.00**
  White, 1977 .... **4.00**
BankAmericard, 1968, 12-digit account
number **12.00**
Bloomingdale's, white with tan border **7.00**
Carte Blanche
  1965 .... **35.00**
  1968, First National City Bank **25.00**
  1974, gold **40.00**
  1977, Avco **18.00**
Central Card, Central National Bank of
Cleveland, late 1960s **15.00**
Champlin, gas island drawing **12.00**
Chevron, two attendants servicing car,
1967 .... **15.00**
Choice **3.00**
Citgo, Lifetime Credit Card **15.00**
Diners Club
  1955, booklet, paperboard **350.00**
  1966, colored blocks, blue top **45.00**
  1979, colored blocks, white top with
    blue border **15.00**
DX, Preferred Credit Card, 1962 ..... **15.00**
Frederick's of Hollywood, Fabulous
Filmland Fashions, red top **12.00**
Gimbels, gold card **6.00**
Gulf, car, boat, and plane **8.00**
Humble, 1962, waving attendant **18.00**
Illinois Bankcharge, 1968, red, white,
and blue shield **12.00**
International Credit Card, International
Charge Inc, 1961 .... **25.00**
Lit Brothers
  Blue and white striped **7.00**
  Metal charge plate
    Leather carrying case **18.00**
    Plastic carrying case **12.00**

Longchamps Restaurants, two women
kissing **55.00**
Macy's, red star on front **5.00**
MasterCard
  Pre-hologram **3.00**
  Pre-hologram, design **4.00**
  Hologram, design **4.00**
Midwest Bank Card, late 1960s **12.00**
Mobil, 1960, full color drawing of gas
station **20.00**
Mobilgas, 1951, paperboard **60.00**
Montgomery Ward
  Punched data charg-all card **8.00**
  Yellow and white, small size **6.00**
National Car Rental, 1978, V.I.P. Club **4.00**
Pan Am Take Off Card, 1971 .... **10.00**
Phillips Executive Courtesy Card **15.00**
Saks Fifth Avenue, paperboard **25.00**
Sears, drawing of store, customer, cat-
alog, and telephone on back **8.00**
Sinclair, 1970, red top, waving dinosaur **12.00**
Skelly, Ladies Credit Card, gloved hands
holding Skelly symbol **15.00**
Speedwell-Marathon Credit Card, Dec
31, 1962 .... **20.00**
Standard Oil
  1936, paperboard **80.00**
  1965, emb customer's full address .. **18.00**
  1973, map of US **12.00**
Sunoco, 1975, custom blended gas
pump drawing **5.00**
The Texas Company, paperboard, 1957 **50.00**
Tresler Comet, photo of Cincinnati ... **8.00**
TWA, swim suited couple
  1970, large profile **10.00**
  1980, small profile **5.00**
Uni-Card
  1969, incised emb **25.00**
  1971 .... **12.00**
Union 76, 1973 .... **8.00**
Vickers, Lifetime Courtesy Card **15.00**
Visa
  Pre-hologram **2.50**
  Pre-hologram, design **4.00**
  Hologram, design **4.00**
White Flint, Citizens Bank of Maryland,
1981 .... **4.00**

DAIRY ITEMS

Collecting Hints: Concentrate on the material associated with one specific dairy, region or national firm. Much of the material available relates to advertising such as blotters, brochures, postcards, and trade cards.

Collectors of dairy items compete with many other groups. Milk bottle collectors try to supplement their collection with these "go-withs." Farm item collectors concentrate on cream separator materials and other farm related items. Ice cream collectors seek cartons and other material. Finally, home decorators like the milk cans and other large, showy objects.

History: There were hundreds of small dairies and creameries scattered throughout the United States during the late 19th and mid-20th centuries. Many issued a variety of material to promote their products.

Eventually regional cooperatives expanded the marketing regions, and many smaller dairies closed. Companies such as Borden distributed products on a national level. Borden created the advertising character of "Elsie, the Borden Cow" to help sell its products. Additional consolidation of firms has occurred, encouraged in part by state milk marketing boards and Federal subsidies.

Reference: John Tutton, *Udder Delight*, published by author.

Periodical: *The Milk Route*, 4 Ox Bow Road, Westport, CT 06880.

Museums: The Farmers Museum, Cooperstown, NY; Southwest Dairy Museum, Arlington, TX; Billings Farm Museum, Woodstock, VT.

Advisors: Tom Gallagher and Tony Knipp.

Notes: A milk bottle cap refers to a plug type cap placed on a bottle by the dairy in a bottling room. A milk bottle cover was made of either metal or glass and often contained dairy advertising. It was used to cover the bottle after the paper cap was removed. A milk bottle cap pick was used to remove the plug type milk bottle caps. A milk bottle cap opener had the same function but was used to remove a different style cap found on more modern bottles, known as the DACRO type.

See: Milk Bottles.

Advertising
   Booklet, picture of Windsor Farm

Creamer, porcelain, 2½" h, maroon lettering, Navy Commissary, marked "Sterling, East Liverpool, OH," $10.00.

Dairy, Denver, CO, on front, picture of horses, "We Pull for Windsor," on back, inside with pictures of plant and workers, 18 pgs, early 1930s **15.00**
Fan, girl in highchair who has spilled milk from her cup on front, "Compliments of Lebel's Dairy, 145 E. Hollis Street, Nashua, NH" on back **10.00**
Tradecard
   Borden's, three children hugging each other and holding a can of Borden's Condensed Milk, directions for use, New York city address (71 Hudson St.) on back, copyright 1889 .... **10.00**
   T.W. Decker & Sons, little girl swinging on the moon, discussion of Decker's new plant at Pawling, NY, and listing of New York city depots on back **12.00**
Bank, Rutter Bros. Dairy Products, dairy truck, plastic, white, red decal, c1960 **40.00**
Blotter
   Union Grove Dairy, display **32.00**
   Universal Super Strength Milk Bottles, picture of plant in Parkersburg, WV, address of NE representative in Hartford, CT, white and orange lettering, white ground **7.00**
Butter Box, Bossie's Best Brand Butter, four color picture of a Jersey cow, Aberdeen Creamery Co., folded **5.00**
Calendar, Broad View Farm, pure milk from our accredited herd, Rochester, NH, little girl climbs steps of house and reaches for a giant bottle of Broad View Farm's milk, tear sheet for each month with saying about milk, dated 1927 .... **12.00**
Cream Siphon, Marvel, aluminum, fits in bottle and siphons cream into a cream pitcher or other vessel **6.00**
Cream Top Spoon, used with cream top bottle
   Fritchett Bros. Dairy, Pat. Applied For **12.00**
   Pat. Sept. 2, 1924, aluminum **10.00**
Creamer
   American Dairy Foods **12.00**
   Anthony's Cream **13.00**
   Casey's Dairy **12.00**
   Prairie Farms **9.00**
   Rosebud Dairy **9.00**
   Swaner's, orig cap **16.00**
   Tastemark Cream **9.00**
   Velvet, Owensboro, KY **17.50**
Crock, Model Dairy **30.00**
Hanger, 9¾" h, Gridley Dairy, assorted colors, Little Miss Curleylocks pictured in various outfits, set of 5 .... **45.00**

Hot Pad Holder, 4¼ x 4¼", Kriebel's Dairies, Hereford, PA, muslin, hemp backing **1.50**

Measuring Cup, Pyrex, 8 oz., Lenkerbrook Farms, Inc, glass, red markings **5.00**

Measuring Cup, Lenkerbrook Farms, Inc, glass red markings, 8 oz, Pyrex **5.00**

Milk Book, Fairfield Dairy, multicolored Hoen illus, c1900 .... **15.00**

Milk Bottle

Grasslands Dairy, qt **10.00**

Te Croney Dairy, Clymer, NY, qt, baby reaching for bottle **4.00**

Bottle Caps, left: red, green letters, 1⅝" d, $.25; right: green, cream ground, 1⅝" d, $.20.

Milk Bottle Cap

Christmas Seal Cap of 1939, pictures 1939 Christmas seal **3.00**

Davol Anti Germ, rubber, fits over lip of milk bottle to keep out dirt, orig container **7.00**

Grade A Raw Milk, red and white .. **.25**

Heber Springs Dairy, Heber Springs, AR .... **.10**

I.O.O.F. Independent Order of Odd Fellows, Home Pasteurized Milk, Greensburg, IN .... **.20**

Kents Dairy Farms, Vitamin D, Olean, NY .... **.10**

Parker Goat Dairy, Raw Milk, picture of goat **1.25**

Set, U.S. Presidents, 35 in set, price for set **10.00**

War Cap, "Milk wouldn't be here if (swastika) were (large swastika) ... **5.00**

Milk Bottle Cap Opener, DACRO

Brock Hall Dairy Products on front, Purity Protected Dacro Sealed Milk on back **5.00**

Deerfoot Farms, Southborough, MA **5.00**

Milk Bottle Cap Pick

Borden Select Milk **5.00**

Sheffield Farms Company, Inc **5.00**

Milk Bottle Cap Pick and Bottle Opener, Forest Glen Creamery Co **6.00**

Milk Bottle Carrier, metal, wire handle, holds 6 round quarts **10.00**

Milk Bottle Cover

Dorsey, aluminum, clamps on milk

bottle and has a movable cover with pouring spout underneath ... **5.00**

Frigidare, green glass, fits over bottle lip to keep out dirt **8.00**

Milk Box, wood, dairy name, holds 4 to 6 quarts **7.00**

Milk Can, 10 gallons

Brass nameplate showing name of shipper **18.00**

Plain or with dairy's name **10.00**

Mug

Dairy Dell **16.00**

Isaly Buttermilk, barrel shape, ironstone **75.00**

Pencil, Rutters Dairy, York and Hanover, PA, wood, unused **4.00**

Pickle Fork, 8", Dayton, OH, Finest Dairy Products Co **6.00**

Playing Cards, Quality Dairy, Q motif on each, complete deck **8.00**

Post Card

Borden's Condensed Milk Plant No. 1, Brewster, NY, side view of plant, signed on front by plant manager, addressed to Borden's office at 108 Hudson Street, NYC **10.00**

Ebert Ice Cream Company, factory pictured **5.00**

Elsie, Elmer, and Beauregard, traveling representatives of Borden's family of fine foods, shows characters in traveling bedroom, explanation of bedroom furnishings on back, color **4.00**

Premium List, Mohawk Condensed Milk Co., 17 Hudson Street, NYC, can of Sweet Clover Brand Condensed Milk on front, can of Gold Cross Brand Condensed Milk on back, 40 pgs 1927 .... **5.00**

Printer's Dies, to print milk bottle caps, dairy name, town, and state **5.00**

Puzzle, jigsaw, cardboard, 18 x 11", Borden's milk wagon and milkman, middle piece shaped like milk bottle, 1928 .... **100.00**

Ruler, 6", Bryant & Champman Dairy, Hartford, CT, wood **4.00**

Sewing Item

Measuring Tape, "Cass Dairy Farm, Inc., Jersey & Ayshire Milk, For Service Call 820 W Athol, MA" on front, reverse "You Can Whip Our Cream But You Can't Beat Our Milk, Try Our Cream," celluloid container **30.00**

Sewing Kit, Borden's Mitchell Dairy, Elsie pictured on cov, "Milk's Good Anytime, Better still Make It Borden's" slogan **8.00**

Stamp Case, Evans Dairy, 1⅜ x 2¼",

black and white horse-drawn dairy
wagon photo, red inscription **20.00**
Stickpin
  Empire Cream Separator **20.00**
  National Cream Separator, Quaker . **10.00**
  Sharples Separator **25.00**
Table Mat, asbestos, Dengler Dairies,
  Telford, PA, "When Baking Use This
  Mat, When Cooking Use our Milk,
  There's Health in Every Drop, Den-
  gler Dairies, Telford, Pa., Phone 370 **5.00**
Tip Tray, DeLaval **85.00**
Token, Muskalonge View Dairy, Fre-
  mont, OH, plastic, good for one quart
  of homogenized milk **5.00**
Toy, milk tanker, Lesney, England, plas-
  tic, blue and white, "Milk's The One"
  on side **6.00**

DEGENHART GLASS

Collecting Hints: Degenhart pressed glass novelties are collected by mold (Forget-Me-Not
toothpick holders or all Degenhart toothpick
holders), by individual colors (Rubina or Bloody
Mary), or by group colors (opaque, iridescent,
crystal, or slag).

Correct color identification is the key to full
enjoyment of collecting Degenhart glass. Because of the slight variations in the hundreds of
colors produced at the Degenhart Crystal Art
Glass factory from 1947 to 1978, it is important
for beginning collectors to acquire the eye for
distinguishing Degenhart colors, particularly the
green and blue variations. A knowledgeable collector or dealer should be sought for guidance.
Side by side color comparison is extremely helpful.

Later glass produced by the factory can be
distinguished by the trademark of a "D" in a
heart or only a "D" on certain molds where
space prohibited the full mark. Use of this mark
began around 1972 and by late 1977 most of the
molds had been marked. Prior to this time,
c1947–1972, no glass was marked with the exception of the owl, and occasionally other pieces
that were identified by hand stamping a block
letter "D" to the object as it came out of the
mold. This hand stamping was started and continued during the period 1967 to 1972.

Collecting unmarked Degenhart glass made
from 1947 to c1970 poses no problem once a
collector becomes familiar with molds and colors
being worked during that period. Some of the
most sought after colors such as Amethyst &
White Slag, Amethyst Carnival, and Custard Slag
are unmarked, yet are the most desirable. Keep
in mind that some colors such as Custard (opaque
yellow), Heliotrope (opaque purple), and Tomato
(opaque orange red) were repeated and can be

found marked and unmarked depending on production date.

History: John (1884–1964) and Elizabeth (1889–
1978) Degenhart operated the Crystal Art Glass
factory of Cambridge, Ohio, from 1947 to 1978.
The factory specialized in reproduction pressed
glass novelties and paperweights. Over 50 molds
were worked by this factory including ten toothpick holders, five salts, and six animal covered
dishes of various sizes.

When the factory ceased operation, many of
the molds were purchased by Boyd Crystal Art
Glass, Cambridge, OH. Boyd has issued pieces
in many new colors. All are marked with a "B"
in a diamond.

Reference: Gene Florence, *Degenhart Glass and
Paperweights: A Collector's Guide To Colors And
Values*, Degenhart Paperweight and Glass Mu-
seum, 1982.

Collectors' Club: "The Friends of Degenhart,"
Degenhart Paperweight and Glass Museum, Inc.,
P. O. Box 186, Cambridge, OH 43725.

Museum: The Degenhart Paperweight and Glass
Museum, Inc., Cambridge, OH. The museum
covers all types of Ohio valley glass.

REPRODUCTION ALERT: Although most of the
Degenhart molds were reproductions themselves, there are contemporary pieces that can
be confusing such as Kanawha's bird salt and
bow slipper; L. G. Wright's mini-slipper, daisy &
button salt, and 5" robin covered dish; and many
other contemporary American pieces. The 3" bird
salt and mini-pitcher also are made by an unknown glassmaker in Taiwan.

**Shoe, Daisy and Button, pink, cat's face,
$45.00**

Animal Covered Dish
  Hen, 3", introduced 1968, marked
    1973
      Champagne **35.00**
      Dark green **25.00**
      Pigeon Blood **48.00**
      Sapphire Blue **20.00**
      Slag, Brown Sparrow **48.00**

Robin, introduced 1960, marked 1972

Bloody Mary	**90.00**
Taffeta	**50.00**

Turkey, introduced 1971, marked 1972

Amethyst	**50.00**
Crown Tuscan	**50.00**
Custard	**60.00**
Slag, gray	**80.00**
Basket, cobalt blue	**18.00**

Bicentennial Bell, introduced 1974, marked 1974

Amethyst	**3.50**
Canary	**15.00**
Elizabeth's Lime Ice	**12.00**
Heatherbloom	**4.00**
Peach	**8.50**
Seafoam	**8.50**

Candy Dish, cov, Wildflower pattern, introduced 1971, marked 1972

Crystal	**15.00**
Pink	**25.00**
Twilight Blue	**37.50**

Chick, 2"

Crown Tuscan	**30.00**
Vaseline	**18.00**

Creamer and Sugar, Texas, introduced 1962, marked 1972

Emerald Green	**50.00**
Pink	**45.00**

Cup Plate

Heart and Lyre, introduced 1965, marked c1977

Cobalt Blue	**11.00**
Gold	**8.50**
Sapphire Blue	**12.50**

Seal of Ohio, introduced 1971, marked c1977

Amethyst	**15.00**
Cobalt Blue	**17.50**
Sunset	**10.00**

Gypsy Pot, introduced 1962, marked 1972

Blue Jay	**20.00**
Canary	**20.00**
Cobalt Blue	**22.50**
Pigeon Blood	**25.00**
Tomato	**30.00**

Hand, introduced 1949, marked c1975

Amethyst	**8.50**
Blue and White	**20.00**
Crown Tuscan	**18.00**
Frosty Jade	**15.00**
Persimmon	**8.00**

Hat, Daisy and Button, introduced 1974, marked 1972

Amethyst	**8.00**
Custard	**20.00**
Opalescent	**12.00**
Vaseline	**15.00**

Jewelry Box, Heart, introduced 1964, marked 1972

Baby Green	**25.00**
Crown Tuscan	**48.00**
Fawn	**18.00**
Light Chocolate Creme	**35.00**
Old Lavender	**25.00**

Owl, introduced 1967, marked 1967, over 200 colors made

Amberina	**35.00**
Amethyst	**30.00**
Bluebell	**30.00**
Charcoal	**40.00**
Crown Tuscan	**30.00**
Frosty Jade	**45.00**
Ivorina	**30.00**
Lavender Blue	**50.00**
Midnight Sun	**30.00**
Seafoam	**37.50**
Sunset	**25.00**
Willow Blue	**48.00**

Paperweight

Crystal Art Glass Paperweight, Zack and Bernard Boyd, Rollin Braden, Gus Theret, and William Degenhart

Ceramic animal encased in air traps	**135.00**
Decal Weight	**50.00**
Five Bubble	**50.00**
Name Weight	**50.00**
Peacock Feather	**50.00**

Paperweight by John or Charles Degenhart

Cartoon Characters	**175.00**
Double Tree	**80.00**
Flower Pot	**85.00**
Gear Shift Knob, patented 1929 ..	**125.00**
Name Weight	**50.00**
Rose, red and white	**300.00**
Window Weight, overlay	**400.00**

Pooch, introduced 1976, marked 1976, approximately 110 colors made

April Green	**15.00**
Bernard Boyd's Ebony	**18.00**
Fawn	**20.00**
Royal Violet	**17.50**

Slag

Caramel Custard	**22.00**
Ivory	**20.00**
Marble, blue	**20.00**

Priscilla, introduced 1976, marked 1976, 40 colors made

Amethyst	**85.00**
Blue and White	**88.00**
Crown Tuscan	**75.00**
Crystal	**40.00**
Delft	**90.00**
Ivory	**85.00**
Jade Green	**100.00**
Peach	**60.00**

Salt

Daisy and Button, introduced 1970, marked 1972

Amethyst	**15.00**
Bittersweet	**15.00**
Cobalt	**12.00**
Lime Ice	**15.00**
Star and Dewdrop, introduced 1952, marked 1972	
Aqua	**15.00**
Henry's Blue	**16.50**
Opalescent	**15.00**
Sapphire Blue	**16.50**
Topaz	**18.00**

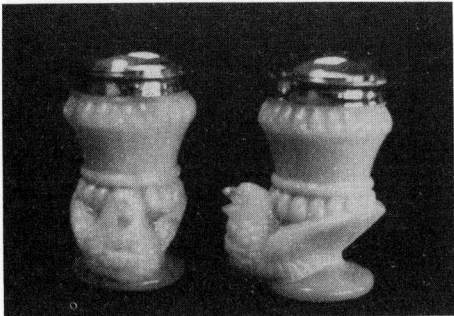

Salt and Pepper Shakers, pr, birds, baby green, $30.00.

Salt and Pepper Shakers, pr, Birds, introduced 1958, marked 1973	
Amberina	**25.00**
Antique Blue	**20.00**
Gun Metal	**18.00**
Taffeta	**22.00**
Shoe, figural	
Baby Shoe, milk glass	**15.00**
High Button Boot, light blue	**25.00**
Slipper, bow, caramel	**30.00**
Skate, green, orig decal	**30.00**
Smoky Bear, jade green	**30.00**
Tiger, lavender blue	**30.00**
Tomahawk, introduced 1947, marked c1975	
Blue Green	**20.00**
Persimmon	**30.00**
Toothpick Holder	
Baby or Tramp Shoe, introduced 1962, marked 1972	
Bluebell	**15.00**
Chocolate Creme	**16.75**
Opaque Blue	**18.00**
Pearl Gray	**15.00**
Beaded Oval, introduced 1967, marked 1972	
Fog	**14.00**
Old Lavender	**20.00**
Sapphire Blue	**20.00**
Teal	**18.00**
Colonial Drape and Heart, introduced 1961, marked 1974	
Amber	**15.00**

Clear	**15.00**
Custard	**20.00**
Daisy and Button, introduced 1970, marked 1972	
Dichromatic	**24.00**
Light Blue Slag	**25.00**
Pink	**17.50**
Forget-Me-Not, introduced 1965, marked 1972, made in over 150 colors	
Caramel	**8.50**
Dogwood	**24.00**
Heatherbloom	**20.00**
Misty Green	**12.00**
Persimmon	**15.00**
Toffee	**20.00**
Heart	
Amethyst	**15.00**
Crystal	**7.50**
Opaque Glass, blue	**35.00**

DEPRESSION GLASS

Collecting Hint: Many collectors specialize in one pattern; others collect by a particular color. Prices listed are for pieces in mint condition—no chips, scratches, etc.

History: Depression glass is glassware made during the period 1920–1940. It was an inexpensive machine-made glass, produced by several different glass companies.

The colors varied from company to company. The number of items made for each pattern also varied. Like pattern glass, depression glass pattern names are sometimes confusing; therefore, a collector should learn all names for their particular pattern.

References: Gene Florence, *The Collector's Encyclopedia of Depression Glass, Eighth Edition*, Collector Books, 1988; Gene Florence, *Elegant Glassware of the Depression Era, Third Edition*, Collector Books, 1988; Gene Florence, *Very Rare Glassware of the Depression Years*, Collector Books, 1987; Carl F. Luckey and Mary Burris, *An Identification & Value Guide To Depression Era Glassware, Second Edition*, Books Americana, 1984; Mark Schliesmann, *Price Survey, Second Edition*, Park Avenue Publications, Ltd, 1984; Hazel Marie Weatherman, *1984 Supplement & Price Trends for Colored Glassware of the Depression Era, Book 1*, published by author, 1984.

Periodical: *The Daze*, Box 57, Ottisville, MI 48463.

Collectors' Club: National Depression Glass Association, Inc., P. O. Box 1128, Springfield, MO 65808.

REPRODUCTION ALERT: Because of recent interest in collecting depression glass, many reproductions are surfacing. Most reproductions are made in colors not originally made. They are sometimes made in the original molds and often marked. However, several patterns have been reproduced in original colors but the molds are slightly different. Thorough knowledge of patterns, colors and markings is very important.

Send a self addressed stamped business envelope to *The Daze* and request a copy of their glass reproduction list. It is one of the best bargains in the collectibles field.

ADAM

Jeannette Glass Company, 1932 through 1934. Made in crystal, delphite blue, green, pink, and yellow. The price for crystal is low because of low demand. Delphite blue and yellow pieces are rare.

	Green	Pink		Green	Pink
Ashtray, 4¼"..............	18.50	24.00	Plate		
Bowl			6", sherbet............	8.00	7.50
4¾", dessert...........	10.00	9.50	7¾", sq, salad.........	8.00	7.50
5¾", cereal............	30.00	30.00	9", sq, dinner..........	16.00	16.00
7¾".................	15.00	16.00	9", grill..............	13.25	12.50
9"..................	30.00	20.00	Platter, 11¾".............	15.00	15.00
10", oval.............	17.50	15.00	Relish Dish, 8", divided...	12.00	10.00
Butter Dish............	225.00	60.00	Salt and Pepper Shakers, pr	75.00	45.00
Cake Plate, 10", ftd......	17.50	14.00	Saucer..................	4.00	3.50
Candlesticks, pr, 4"......	72.00	50.00	Sherbet, 3"..............	25.00	15.00
Candy Jar, cov, 2½"......	80.00	60.00	Sugar, cov...............	40.00	30.00
Coaster, 3¼"..........	12.00	14.50	Tumbler		
Creamer................	14.00	12.00	4½".................	16.00	16.00
Cup..................	16.00	18.00	5½".................	30.00	28.00
Lamp.................	200.00	200.00	Vase, 7½"..............	35.00	95.00
Pitcher, 32 oz...........	30.00	24.50			

AMERICAN SWEETHEART

MacBeth Evans Glass Company, 1930 to 1936. Made in blue, Cremax, Monax, pink, red, and color rimmed Monax.

	Blue	Cremax	Monax	Pink	Red
Bowl					
3¾", flat, berry.............	—	—	—	25.00	—
6", cereal.................	—	8.00	12.00	9.00	—
9", berry.................	—	30.00	45.00	25.00	—
11", oval, vegetable.........	—	—	48.00	38.00	—
Console Bowl, 18"............	725.00	—	250.00	—	665.00
Cream Soup, 4½".............	—	—	40.00	30.00	—
Creamer....................	85.00	—	6.50	6.00	75.00
Cup........................	75.00	—	9.25	10.00	62.00
Lamp Shade.................	—	400.00	385.00	—	—
Pitcher					
7½", 60 oz................	—	—	—	400.00	—
8", 80 oz.................	—	—	—	375.00	—
Plate					
6", bread and butter.........	—	—	3.00	2.00	—
8", salad..................	60.00	—	5.75	5.00	40.00
9", luncheon...............	—	—	8.75	—	—
9¾", dinner...............	—	—	14.00	15.00	—
10¼", dinner..............	—	—	15.00	—	—
11", chop.................	—	—	10.00	—	—
15½", server..............	275.00	—	165.00	—	225.00
Platter, 13".................	—	—	40.00	24.00	—
Salt and Pepper Shakers, pr, ftd.	—	—	200.00	225.00	—
Saucer.....................	22.00	—	4.00	2.00	20.00

	Blue	Cremax	Monax	Pink	Red
Sherbet	—	—	15.00	10.00	—
Sugar.	72.00	60.00	5.00	7.00	65.00
Tidbit Server, 3 tiers	525.00	—	160.00	—	425.00
Tumbler					
3½", 5 oz.	—	—	—	40.00	—
4¼", 9 oz.	—	—	—	42.50	—
4¾", 10 oz	—	—	—	45.00	—

BEADED BLOCK

Imperial Glass Company, 1927 through 1930s. Made in amber, crystal, green, ice blue, iridescent, milk white, pink, red, opalescent, and vaseline. Production was limited in iridescent, milk white, opalescent, and red.

	Amber	Crystal	Green	Other Colors	Pink
Bowl					
4½", lily	8.00	6.00	7.50	15.00	8.00
5½", sq.	6.00	4.00	6.00	9.00	6.50
6", deep	8.00	6.50	8.00	15.00	7.50
6½"	8.00	6.00	8.50	15.00	8.00
7¼", round, flared	8.00	8.25	6.00	12.00	8.00
7½", round, fluted	19.50	17.50	12.00	20.00	17.50
Celery, 8¼"	10.00	10.00	8.50	18.00	10.00
Creamer	36.00	30.00	10.00	40.00	30.00
Jelly, 4½"					
Flared, stemmed	25.00	20.00	15.00	30.00	25.00
Round, two handles	35.00	25.00	20.00	35.00	28.00
Stemmed	25.00	20.00	15.00	30.00	25.00
Pickle, 6½", two handles	12.00	10.00	8.00	15.00	12.00
Pitcher, 5¼".	85.00	85.00	50.00	—	85.00
Plate					
7¾", sq.	7.50	7.50	7.50	8.50	7.50
8¾"	10.00	10.00	9.00	15.00	10.00
Sugar.	38.00	30.00	20.00	40.00	30.00
Vase, 6"	15.00	15.00	10.00	20.00	15.00

CHERRY BLOSSOM

Jeannette Glass Company, 1930 through 1939. Made in delphite (opaque blue), green, and pink. Limited production in crystal, jadite (opaque green), and red. Reproductions abound in this pattern. Because reproductions have been made by several companies, the variations are many. Be cautious of patterns off center, crude leaves, and even fewer cherries. The reproductions exist in the original colors and also several shades that were not made by Jeannette. AOP means all over pattern. PAT means pattern only at top.

	Delphite	Green	Pink
Bowl			
4¾", berry	10.00	12.00	9.00
5¾", cereal	—	26.00	22.00
8½", berry	35.00	16.00	14.00
10½", fruit	—	42.50	40.00
Butter Dish, cov	—	67.50	55.00
Cake Plate, 10¼"	—	18.00	15.00
Coaster	—	8.50	10.00
Creamer	15.00	12.50	11.00
Cup	14.00	18.00	12.00
Mug	—	145.00	165.00

	Delphite	Green	Pink
Pitcher			
6¾", AOP	—	40.00	30.00
8", PAT, ftd	65.00	45.00	40.00
Plate			
6", sherbet	8.50	5.00	5.00
7", salad	—	15.00	12.00
9", dinner	12.00	14.00	12.00
9", grill	12.00	16.00	18.00
10", grill	—	40.00	—
Platter, oval			
11"	30.00	24.00	20.00
13"	—	30.00	23.00
Sandwich Tray, 10½"	14.00	12.00	11.00
Saucer	3.00	3.25	2.25
Sherbet	11.00	12.00	9.50
Sugar	15.00	12.00	10.00
Tumbler			
3½", 4 oz, flat, PAT	—	20.00	15.00
4¼", 9 oz, flat, PAT	—	18.00	15.00
3¾", 4 oz, ftd, AOP	15.00	14.00	12.00
4½", 8 oz, ftd, AOP	—	25.00	20.00
4½", 9 oz, ftd, AOP	15.00	25.00	20.00
5", 12 oz, flat, PAT	—	50.00	40.00

CLOVERLEAF

Hazel Atlas Glass Company, 1930 through 1936. Made in black, crystal, green, pink, and yellow.

	Black	Crystal	Green	Pink	Yellow
Ashtray, 4"	60.00	—	—	—	—
Bowl					
4", dessert	—	8.50	20.00	12.00	18.00
5", cereal	—	10.00	20.00	20.00	—
7", salad	—	12.00	30.00	35.00	—
8"	—	—	48.00	—	—
Candy Dish, cov	—	—	40.00	85.00	—
Creamer	15.00	5.00	8.00	—	12.50
Cup	10.75	3.00	6.00	5.00	8.00
Plate					
6", sherbet	20.00	—	4.00	—	5.00
8", luncheon	22.00	3.00	6.00	5.00	10.00
10¼", grill	—	—	15.00	18.00	—
Salt and Pepper Shakers, pr,	60.00	—	24.00	—	85.00

Adam, candlesticks, 3¾" h, pink, $50.00.

Cloverleaf, cup and saucer, pink, $7.00.

	Black	Crystal	Green	Pink	Yellow
Saucer.....................	3.50	1.25	2.25	2.00	3.00
Sherbet, ftd	12.75	3.00	4.00	4.50	8.75
Sugar, ftd	15.00	7.50	7.75	—	12.50
Tumbler					
3¾", 10oz	—	—	30.00	—	—
4", 9 oz	—	—	25.00	15.00	—
5¾", 10 oz, ftd	—	—	16.50	—	18.50

COLUMBIA

Federal Glass Company, 1938-1942. Made in crystal and pink.

	Crystal	Pink		Crystal	Pink
Bowl			Plate		
5", cereal..............	10.00	—	6", bread and butter	1.50	5.00
8", low soup...........	12.00	—	9½", luncheon.........	3.75	14.75
8½", salad.............	12.00	—	11", chop	6.00	—
10½", ruffled	12.50	—	Saucer	1.50	5.00
Butter Dish, cov..........	12.00	14.00	Snack Plate..............	20.00	—
Cup	3.50	10.00	Tumbler................	10.00	—

CUPID

Paden City Glass Company, 1930s. Made in black, canary yellow, green, light blue, and pink. All colors currently have the same values.

	All Colors		All Colors
Bowl		Ice Tub, 4¾"	60.00
8½", oval, ftd..................	40.00	Lamp, silver overlay	145.00
9¼", center handle	45.00	Mayonnaise, 6" d.................	40.00
Cake Plate, 11¾"..................	45.00	Plate	
Cake Stand, 2" h, ftd.............	40.00	8", luncheon...................	20.00
Candlesticks, pr, 5" w.............	50.00	10½", dinner	30.00
Candy, cov, ftd, 4¾" h	72.00	Samovar	185.00
Compote, 6¼"	30.00	Sugar, 5", ftd.................	36.00
Console Bowl, 11".................	48.50	Tray, 10¾", center handle	40.00
Creamer, 5", ftd	36.00	Vase, fan shape	75.00
Ice Bucket, 6"....................	65.00		

DAISY

(Number 620) Indiana Glass Company. Crystal was made in 1933, followed by amber in 1940. Dark green was made in the 1960s and has the same values as crystal.

	Amber	Crystal		Amber	Crystal
Bowl			Plate		
4½", berry.............	6.00	3.75	6", sherbet.............	2.00	9.50
6", cereal..............	19.00	10.00	7⅜", salad.............	9.50	6.50
7⅜", berry.............	8.00	4.00	8⅜", luncheon	2.50	7.50
9⅜", berry.............	18.00	10.00	9⅜", dinner	6.75	3.75
10", oval, vegetable	14.00	10.00	10⅜, grill	18.00	3.50
Cream Soup, 4½"	6.00	3.75	Platter, 10¾".............	15.00	10.00
Cake Plate, 11½".........	5.00	8.50	Relish, three part	20.00	10.00
Creamer.................	7.00	5.00	Sandwich Plate, 11½".....	5.00	8.50
Cup	5.00	2.00	Saucer	2.00	1.50

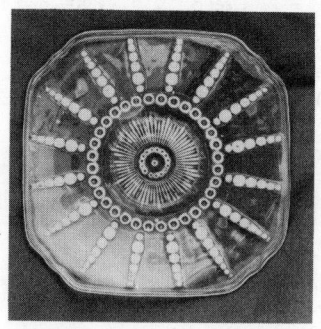

Columbia, saucer, crystal, $1.50.

Floral, butter dish, cov, pink, $72.00.

	Amber	Crystal			Amber	Crystal
Sherbet	8.00	3.00	Tumbler, ftd			
Sugar, ftd.	7.00	4.00	9 oz	14.00	7.00
			12 oz	35.00	18.50

FLORAL

"Poinsetta," Jeannette Glass Company, 1931–1935. Made in Delphite, green, and pink. Some pieces are found in amber, crystal, jadite, red, rose, yellow, and even caramel. As research continues into Depression Glass, more pieces are identified in these unusual colors. Several of the rarer pieces and colors are found in Canada and England.

	Delphite	Green	Pink
Bowl			
4", berry.	28.00	18.00	15.00
7½", salad	40.00	10.00	8.00
8", vegetable, cov.	45.00	22.50	20.00
9", vegetable	—	18.00	14.00
Butter Dish, cov	—	75.00	72.00
Candlesticks, pr	—	60.00	55.00
Candy Jar, cov.	—	32.50	60.00
Coaster.	—	7.50	7.50
Creamer	60.00	15.00	12.00
Cup.	—	6.00	8.00
Lamp.	—	225.00	225.00
Pitcher			
8", 32 oz	—	25.00	20.00
10¼", 48 oz	—	175.00	150.00
Plate			
6", sherbet	—	6.00	3.00
8", salad.	—	8.00	7.00
9", dinner.	100.00	15.00	11.00
Platter, 10¾"	100.00	12.50	9.00
Refrigerator Dish, cov, 5" sq.	—	50.00	—
Relish, 2 part.	—	10.00	8.00
Salt and Pepper Shakers, pr, 4"	—	40.00	35.00
Saucer.	—	6.00	4.00
Sherbet.	72.00	11.00	10.00
Sugar.	50.00	18.00	15.00
Tray, 6", sq	—	12.00	10.00
Tumbler			
3½", 3 oz, ftd	—	13.00	—

	Delphite	Green	Pink
4″, 5 oz, ftd..............................	—	15.00	12.00
4¾″, 7 oz, ftd.............................	90.00	15.00	12.00
5¼″, 9 oz, ftd.............................	—	32.00	30.00

FLORENTINE NO. 1

"Old Florentine, Poppy No. 1," Hazel Atlas Glass Company, 1932–35. Made in cobalt blue, crystal, green, pink, and yellow.

	Cobalt Blue	Crystal	Green	Pink	Yellow
Ashtray, 5½″	—	17.50	17.50	22.00	24.00
Bowl					
5″, berry...................	15.00	3.00	3.00	8.50	12.00
6″, cereal	—	15.00	17.50	12.50	16.00
8½″, berry	—	12.00	15.00	22.00	24.00
9½″, oval, vegetable	—	35.00	35.00	37.50	37.50
Butter Dish, cov	—	100.00	100.00	115.00	125.00
Creamer....................	45.00	4.00	6.00	12.00	15.00
Cup........................	65.00	6.00	6.00	12.00	10.00
Pitcher					
6½″, 36 oz, ftd.............	600.00	35.00	35.00	38.00	40.00
7½″, 48 oz, ice lip..........	—	42.00	45.00	90.00	110.00
Plate					
6″, sherbet.................	—	3.00	3.00	3.50	4.00
8½″, salad	—	4.00	4.25	9.00	9.75
10″, dinner.................	—	7.00	7.50	9.00	12.00
10″, grill...................	—	7.50	9.00	12.00	12.00
Platter, 11½″	—	9.00	10.00	15.00	18.00
Salt and Pepper Shakers, pr, ftd .	—	28.00	31.00	45.00	45.00
Saucer......................	—	2.00	2.00	2.50	3.00
Sherbet.....................	—	4.00	6.50	5.50	7.50
Sugar, cov	42.00	5.25	8.00	6.00	10.00
Tumbler					
3¾″, 5 oz..................	—	10.00	12.00	18.00	15.00
4¾″, 10 oz	—	18.00	18.00	15.00	15.00
5¼″, 12 oz, ftd	—	20.00	20.00	20.00	20.00

JANE-RAY

Anchor Hocking Glass Corp, 1940s through the 1960s. This later period depression type glass was made in a light green opaque glass, known as Jadite. Pieces found with the original paper label will command a slightly higher price.

	Jadite		Jadite
Bowl		Plate	
4⅞″, dessert	1.75	7¾″, salad.....................	1.50
5⅞″, oatmeal	2.00	9⅛″, dinner	2.50
7⅝″, soup.....................	3.50	Platter	6.00
8¼″, vegetable.................	4.50	Saucer	.75
Creamer.........................	2.00	Sugar, cov.......................	4.50
Cup	1.50		

MISS AMERICA

"Diamond Pattern," Hocking Glass Company, 1935–1937. Made in crytal, green, pink, and red. Limited pieces of this pattern have also been found in cobalt blue, ice blue, and even jadite. This pattern has been reproduced.

	Crystal	Green	Pink	Red
Bowl				
4½", berry	—	7.50	—	—
6¼", berry	5.75	10.00	12.00	—
8¾"	24.00	—	40.00	—
10", vegetable, oval	10.00	—	15.00	—
Butter Dish, cov	185.00	—	375.00	—
Cake Plate, 12", ftd	15.00	—	25.00	—
Candy Jar, cov	50.00	—	100.00	—
Celery Dish, 10½"	7.50	—	15.00	—
Coaster	12.00	—	17.50	—
Compote	12.00	—	18.00	—
Creamer, ftd	7.50	—	12.00	130.00
Cup	7.50	8.00	15.00	—
Goblet, 5½"	17.50	—	35.00	165.00
Pitcher				
8"	40.00	—	85.00	—
8½", ice lip	60.00	—	95.00	—
Plate				
5¾", sherbet	3.00	5.00	5.00	—
8½", luncheon	5.00	8.00	15.00	60.00
10¼", dinner	10.00	—	18.00	—
10¼", grill	10.00	—	15.00	—
Platter, 12¼"	10.00	—	15.00	—
Relish, 8¾"	7.00	—	12.75	—
Salt and Pepper Shakers, pr	24.00	275.00	45.00	—
Saucer	2.75	—	4.25	—
Sherbet	6.75	—	10.00	—
Sugar	6.00	—	12.75	125.00
Tumbler				
4", juice	12.00	—	35.00	—
4½", 10 oz, water	12.00	13.50	20.00	—
5¾", 14 oz, ice tea	20.00	—	42.00	—
Wine, 3¾"	17.50	—	50.00	165.00

OYSTER AND PEARL

Anchor Hocking Glass Corp, 1938–1940. Made in crystal, pink, ruby red, and white with fired on pink or green. Crystal and pink have the same values. The fired on white pieces usually have the same value whether the color is pink or green.

	Crystal	Royal Ruby	White
Bowl			
5½"	5.00	9.00	—
6½"	8.00	15.00	—
10½"	15.00	30.00	12.00
Candlesticks, pr, 3½"	15.00	30.00	—
Nappy, 5¼", heart shape	—	—	14.00
Relish, 10¼"	6.00	—	—
Sandwich Plate, 13½"	10.00	25.00	—

PARROT

"Sylvan," Federal Glass Company, 1931–1932. Made in amber, and green, with limited production in crystal and blue.

	Amber	Green		Amber	Green
Bowl			9", dinner	25.00	30.00
5", berry	10.00	12.00	10½", grill.	18.00	20.00
7", soup.	25.00	28.00	Platter	48.00	30.00
8", berry	60.00	50.00	Salt and Pepper Shakers, pr	—	175.00
10", oval, vegetable	45.00	35.00	Saucer	8.00	8.75
Butter Dish, cov.	600.00	200.00	Sherbet, cone.	15.00	18.00
Creamer, ftd	30.00	20.00	Sugar, cov.	325.00	150.00
Cup	20.00	25.00	Trivet	—	500.00
Pitcher, 8½"	—	850.00	Tumbler		
Plate			4¼"	90.00	90.00
5¾", sherbet.	12.00	17.50	5½"	95.00	95.00
7½", salad.	—	17.50	5¾"	90.00	95.00

ROULETTE

"Many Windows," Hocking Glass Co, 1935—1939. Made in crystal, green, and pink.

	Crystal	Green	Pink
Bowl, 9".	8.00	10.00	8.50
Cup.	3.50	4.50	3.50
Pitcher, 8"	22.50	24.00	22.50
Plate			
6", sherbet.	2.00	2.25	2.00
8½", luncheon	4.00	4.25	4.00
Sandwich Plate, 12".	7.50	8.00	7.50
Saucer.	1.25	2.00	1.25
Sherbet	3.00	4.00	3.00
Tumbler			
3¼", juice	4.50	8.50	4.50
3¼", old fashioned.	8.50	18.00	8.50
4⅛", water.	10.00	12.00	10.00
5⅛", iced tea.	10.00	17.50	10.00
5½", water.	10.00	15.00	10.00
Whiskey, 2½"	7.00	9.00	7.00

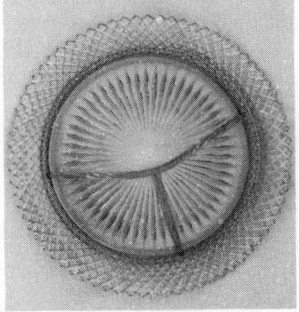

Miss America, grill plate, 10¼", crystal, $10.00.

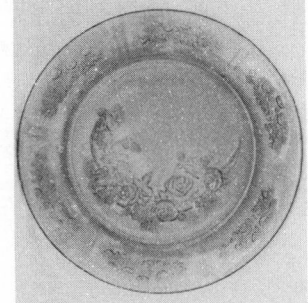

Sharon, plate, 9", dinner, pink, $10.00.

SHARON

"Cabbage Rose," Federal Glass Co, 1935–1939. Made in amber, some crystal, green, and pink. Covered butter and cheese dishes have been reproduced in the original colors and several new colors.

	Amber	Green	Pink
Bowl			
5", berry	6.00	8.00	7.50
6", cereal	11.00	17.25	15.00
7½", flat soup	25.00	—	25.00
8½", berry	5.00	20.00	15.00
9½", oval, vegetable	10.00	18.00	16.50
10½", fruit	15.00	25.00	22.00
Butter Dish, cov	40.00	65.00	35.00
Cake Plate	16.00	45.00	25.00
Candy Jar, cov	35.00	130.00	38.00
Cheese Dish, cov	150.00	—	575.00
Cream Soup, 5"	15.50	32.50	30.00
Creamer, ftd	10.00	14.00	12.00
Cup	8.00	12.00	10.00
Jam Dish, 7½"	25.00	35.00	95.00
Plate			
6", bread and butter	3.00	4.50	3.00
7½", salad	10.00	15.00	12.00
9½", dinner	9.75	12.00	10.00
Platter	12.00	16.00	14.00
Salt and Pepper Shakers, pr	35.00	55.00	35.00
Saucer	4.00	6.00	5.00
Sherbet	9.00	20.00	10.00
Sugar, cov	25.00	75.00	50.00
Tumbler			
4⅛", 9 oz, thick	21.00	42.50	20.00
4⅛", 9 oz, thin	21.00	50.00	20.00
5¼", 12 oz, thick	28.00	80.00	35.00
5¼", 12 oz, thin	37.50	75.00	55.00
6½", 15 oz, ftd	60.00	—	32.50

TWISTED OPTIC

Imperial Glass Co, 1927–1930. Made in amber, some blue, canary yellow, green, and pink. Amber, green, and pink have the same values. Values of blue and canary yellow pieces would be 50% more.

	Amber/Green/Pink			Amber/Green/Pink
Bowl			7½", oval, indent	4.00
5", cereal	3.00		8", luncheon	2.00
7", salad	6.00		Preserve, slotted lid	20.00
Candlesticks, 3", pr	10.00		Sandwich Server	
Candy Jar, cov	18.00		Center handle	18.00
Cream Soup, 4¾"	8.00		Two handles	10.00
Creamer	6.50		Saucer	1.00
Cup	3.00		Sherbet	5.00
Pitcher	18.00		Sugar	6.50
Plate			Tumbler	
6", sherbet	1.50		4½", 9 oz	5.00
7", salad	2.00		5¼", 12 oz	6.00

VICTORY

Diamond Glassware Co, 1929–1932. Made in amber, black, cobalt blue, green, and pink.

	Amber/ Green/ Pink	Black/ Cobalt Blue		Amber/ Green/ Pink	Black/ Cobalt Blue
Bon Bon, 7"	10.00	15.00	Gravy Boat, underplate....	120.00	250.00
Bowl			Mayonnaise, 3 pcs	35.00	65.00
6½"	8.00	18.00	Plate		
8½"	12.00	20.00	6", bread and butter	3.50	7.50
9"	25.00	45.00	7", salad	5.00	10.00
12½"	24.00	50.00	8", luncheon...........	5.75	12.00
Candlesticks, 3", pr.......	25.00	65.00	9", dinner	15.00	24.00
Cheese and Cracker Set ...	35.00	—	Platter	18.00	40.00
Compote, 6".............	10.00	—	Sandwich Server	20.00	42.50
Console Bowl, 12"........	25.00	—	Saucer	2.50	6.00
Creamer.................	10.00	28.00	Sherbet	10.00	18.00
Cup	7.00	18.00	Sugar	10.00	30.00
Goblet	15.00	—			

VITROCK

(Flower Rim) Anchor Hocking Glass Co, 1934-1937. This pattern has an emb floral rim and was made with a white body. Fired on colors such as blue, green, red, and yellow were also made. Pieces with fired on colors have the same value as all white pieces.

	White		White
Bowl		Plate	
4", berry	3.00	7¼", salad....................	1.50
6", fruit	4.00	8¾", luncheon.................	2.50
7½", cereal...................	3.00	9", soup......................	6.50
9½", vegetable...............	7.00	10", dinner	5.00
Cream Soup, 5½"	8.00	Platter	15.00
Creamer.....................	3.00	Saucer	1.00
Cup	2.50	Sugar	3.50

DIONNE QUINTUPLETS

Collecting Hints: Almost all the doll companies in the 1930s released dolls resembling the Quints. The only "genuine" Dionne Quintuplet dolls are the Madame Alexander dolls dating from 1935 to 1939. They realized the highest prices.

History: The Dionne Quintuplets were born on May 28, 1934, on a small farm between Corbeil and Callander, Ontario, Canada. The five baby girls weighed a total of 10 lbs, 1¼ ozs. They were delivered by Dr. Dafoe and two midwives. They were named Yvonne, Annette, Cecile, Emilie, and Marie.

When they were just two days old, their father, Oliva Dionne, and the parish priest signed a contract to exhibit the babies at the Chicago World's Fair. The Canadian government passed "An Act For the Protection Of the Dionne Quintuplets" to prevent this. The girls became special wards of King George V.

A special house, the Dafoe Hospital, was built for them across the road from their place of birth. It had one-way glass through which visitors could view the children. People came by the thousands during the mid to late 30s. In this nursery they were attended by Dr. Dafoe and a staff of professionals. Newspapers gave daily reports and photographs of their progress. Souvenirs of every type were sold including rocks, called "Fertility Stones," from the farm which brought between 50¢ and $1.00.

Emilie died in a convent August 1954 and Marie died February 27, 1970. Yvonne, Annette, and Cecile remain alive today.

Reference: John Axe, *The Collectible Dionne Quintuplets*, Hobby House Press, 1977.

Collectors' Club: Dionne Quint Collectors, P.O. Box 2527, Woburn, MA 01888. *Quint News* (quarterly).

Baby Feeding Dish, china, Quints illus Book **30.00**

> *Dionne Quintuplets Picture Album, The Complete Story of Their First Two Years,* Dell, 1936 .... **25.00**
> *Dionne Quintuplets Play Mother Goose,* Dell, 1938 .... **20.00**
> *Now We're Two Years Old,* Whitman, 1936 .... **25.00**
> *Soon We'll Be Three Years Old: The Five Dionne Quintuplets Book,* Whitman, 1936 .... **20.00**

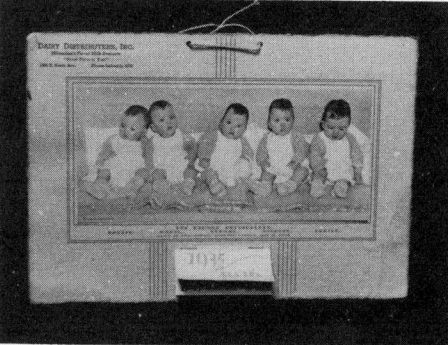

Calendar, 1935–36, Dairy Distributors, Inc., Milwaukee, WI, multicolored picture, 11¼ x 8", $20.00.

Calendar
> 1936, Watch Us Grow, quints, mother, and father, 9 x 4" **25.00**
> 1937, Robotman & Sons Dairy, quints wearing pink dresses **15.00**
> 1939, full pad **15.00**
> 1942, Springtime, 12 x 15" **15.00**
> 1943, Sunny Day, ocean scene **25.00**

Cake Plate, 11½" d, china, white, gold maple leaf at top, red rim, center color portraits titled "Dionne Quintuplets, Born May 28, 1934, Callander, Ontario, Canada" **135.00**

Candy Bar Display Box, 2 x 8 x 11", "Baby Ruth–First and Only Candy Served the Dionne Quints," cardboard **60.00**

Cereal Bowl, 6" d, silvered brass, engraved first names, raised figure of Quints in base **35.00**

Doll
> 7¾", set of five, composition heads and jointed bodies, blonde painted and molded hair, brown painted eyes, painted open mouth, orig

clothes and suitcase, "Alexander" marked on back, c1935 ....**1,500.00**

11½", composition, fully jointed, mohair wig over molded straight hair, closed mouth, brown sleep eyes with real lashes, marked "Dionne/ Alexander, 1936" **250.00**

Fan, 14", wood handle, titled "Quints At The Beach," adv on back, 1936 . **18.00**

Game, pinball, "Place The Quintuplets In The Carriage," 3½ x 5", green tin frame **17.50**

Handkerchief, 9" sq, portraits of Quints, rabbits **15.00**

Key Chain, 3" l, celluloid, dark green, gold lettering, "Souvenir of Quint Land, Callander, Canada" **28.00**

Lobby Card, 11 x 14", "Five Of A Kind," color, girls playing piano, 1938 .... **65.00**

Magazine Article, First Communion, Sept. 2, 1940, Life, 102 pgs **25.00**

Miniature, doll set, bisque, jointed arms and legs, orig dresses, rocking cradle **375.00**

Paper Dolls, uncut book, *The Dionne Babies,* Merrill, 1935 .... **225.00**

Photograph, 10 x 14", 1935, parents signature on reverse, framed **65.00**

Playing Cards, pink and white checkered box, illus of Quints gathering flowers **36.00**

Poster, 14½ x 31½", full color, illus color photo portraits premiums of Quints, Quaker Oats, NEA Service, 1935 copyright **85.00**

Program, theater, promotion for "The Country Doctor," 1936 .... **20.00**

Sheet Music, "Quintuplets' Lullaby," words and music, tinted photo front cov, 6 pgs **10.00**

Spoon, Cecile **25.00**

Teaspoon, set of 5 .... **75.00**

Thermometer, 4 x 6", cardboard, brown and white, glass thermometer, Quints in chairs **30.00**

DIRIGIBLES AND ZEPPELINS

Collecting Hints: All areas of dirigible and zeppelin material remain stable. Focus on one specific topic, e.g., material about one airship, models and toys, postcards, etc. The field is very broad, and a collector might exhaust his funds trying to be comprehensive. The most common collecting focus is material relating to specific flights.

History: An airship, also known as a dirigible or zeppelin, is any self-propelled aircraft that is lighter than air and can be steered. The Germans, under the leadership of Count Ferdinand von Zeppelin (1838–1917), developed the dirigible airship into a transoceanic transportation vehicle.

Both the United States and Germany built airships for commercial use in the 1930s. The *Graf Zeppelin* made an historic trip around the world. The era came to an end on May 6, 1937, when the seven million cubic foot Zeppelin *Hindenburg* burst into flames while anchoring at the mast in Lakehurst, New Jersey.

Airships continued to be used by the military for shore patrol. The Lakehurst Naval Air Station remained open until the 1970s. Today, the Goodyear Company blimps play a key role in the televising of national sporting events and at special celebrations.

References: Walter Curley, *The Graf Zeppelin's Flights to South America,* Spellman Museum, 1970; Arthur Falk, *Hindenburg Crash Mail,* Clear Color Litho, 1976; Sieger, *Zeppelin Post Katalog,* Wurttemberg, 1981, in German.

Collectors' Club: Zepplin Collectors Club, P.O. Box A3843, Chicago, IL 60690.

Museum: Jody's Stamp Studio, 6001 Riverdale Avenue, Riverdale, Bronx, NY, 10471.

REPRODUCTION ALERT

Bank, 6½" l, *Graf Zeppelin,* silver painted cast iron, c1920 .... 45.00
Big Little Book, Russell R. Winterbotham, *Captain Robb of Dirigible ZR-90 and the Disappearing Zeppelin,* Whitman Better Little Book, 1941, Al Lewin, artist, 3⅝ x 4½ x 1½" 18.00
Book, Hugh Allen, *The Story of the Airship, Goodyear,* Goodyear Tire and Rubber Co, 1932, hardcover, 96 pgs 15.00
Bookmark, heart shape, marked "Duralumin Used In The Airship *Akron,* Made by Goodyear Zeppelin Corp, Akron, OH," illus of zeppelin 25.00
Bottle, *Graf Zep,* 9½" h, clear, issued by John Graf Co, Milwaukee, raised airship and name, c1920 .... 70.00
Brochure, 5½ x 8", adv "Al–Cariod, The Ideal Antacid," illus of *Los Angeles* . 20.00
Candy Mold, 10" l, 3½" h, tin, *Los Angeles* 115.00
Comb, 4", marked "Duralumin Used In The Airship *Akron,* Made by Goodyear Zeppelin Corp, Akron, OH," illus of zeppelin 25.00
Employee Badge, 2⅛", black and white, Lakehurst, NJ, 1939 .... 18.00
Game
  Graf Zeppelin, card, 3½ x 5 x 1½" orig box, 48 cards, instruction leaflet, printed in German, 1928 .... 115.00
  Graf Zeppelin World Flight Game, 11

x 15 x 1½" orig box, 14 x 21½" board, 1928 flight, German instructions 200.00
Mirror, pocket, 2½", *Graf Zeppelin,* celluloid, photo and illus of aerial view of North and South America 115.00
Nail File, 3", stamped metal, zeppelin shape 60.00
Needle Book, China Clipper brand ... 10.00
Newspaper, New York Times, "Hindenburg Crashes In Flames, May 6, 1937" 40.00
Patch, Zeppelin *Eckener Spende,* cloth, brass rim, Germany, 1930s 48.00
Pennant, *Graf Zeppelin,* 29" l, brown felt, white airship and inscription ... 100.00
Pill Box, 2", metal and glass, emb picture of *Graf Zeppelin* and Magellan's fleet 60.00
Pin
  ½ x 1⅞", diecut aluminum, detailed airship, inset black and white glossy photo of Count Ferdinand Von Zeppelin, c1920 .... 150.00
  1⅝", diecut, rolled silvered brass, swastika on each tail fin, c1936
  D-LZ 130 .... 60.00
  D-LZ 129, Hindenburg, Olympic ring symbol on side 70.00
Pinback Button
  1¼", red, white, and blue, "Lakehurst," zeppelin in hangar at Naval Air Station, 1930s 60.00
  1¾", celluloid, "Honorary Pilot," Tydol Flying A Airship 17.50
Pipe, 5½" l, zeppelin shape, bakelite stem, briarwood bowl 125.00
Post Card, eagle over zeppelin and bust of Count Zeppelin, Imperial German colors, 1918 .... 50.00
Poster, 20 x 30", "Join The Air Services, Give Er The Gun, Learn–Earn," litho, Forbes 375.00
Schedule, *Hindenburg, Graf Zep,* 1937, 4 x 9" glossy paper folds to 9 x 24" sheet, int. black and white photos, plans, menu, text on flights, published March, 1937 by German Zeppelin Transport Co and American Zeppelin Transport Inc 60.00
Souvenir, *Airship Akron,* 4¼" d disk, emb "Duralumin," black illus of airship, c1930 .... 80.00
Timetable, *Hindenburg,* French, 3 fold, 3⅞ x 8⅜" folded 20.00
Toy
  4¾", cast iron, painted green, marked "Navy" 85.00
  10½", litho, tin, wind-up, Trans-Atlantic, silver ground, red and blue lettering, US flag and stars 150.00
Watch Fob, 1¼ x 1¾", diecut, enameled and painted brass, emb "Ameri-

ca's Greatest Airship Port," silvered landing field, center Knights of Columbus design, red, white, and blue enameled lower part emb "Belleville, IL," 1924 .... **55.00**
Whistle, tin, figural, multicolored **18.00**

DISNEYANA

Collecting Hints: The products from the 1930s command the most attention. Animated celluloids range in value from $75 into the tens of thousands of dollars depending on subject and complexity of scene. Disneyana is a popular subject, and items tend to be priced on the high side.

Make condition a key element in your purchase. An incomplete toy or game should sell for 40 to 50% less than one in mint condition.

History: Walt Disney and the creations of the famous Disney studio hold a place of fondness and enchantment in the hearts of Americans and people throughout the world. The release of "Steamboat Willie" in 1928 heralded an entertainment empire.

Walt and his brother, Roy, showed shrewd business acumen. From the beginning they licensed the reproduction of Disney characters in products ranging from wrist watches to clothing.

The market in Disneyana has been established by a few determined dealers and auction houses. Hake's Americana and Collectibles has specialized in Disney material for over a decade. Sotheby's Collector Carousel auctions and Lloyd Ralston Toys auctions have continued the trend.

Walt Disney characters are popular throughout the world. Belgium is a leading producer of Disneyana along with England, France, and Japan. The Disney characters often take on the regional characteristics of the host country; don't be surprised to find a strange looking Mickey Mouse or Donald Duck. Disney has opened a new theme park in Japan; it will produce a wealth of new Disney collectibles.

References: Marcia Blitz, *Donald Duck,* Harmony Books, 1979; Robert Heide and John Gilman, *Cartoon Collectibles,* Doubleday & Co., Inc., 1984; Leonard Maltin, *The Disney Films,* Crown Publishers, 1973; Richard Schickel, *The Disney Version: The Life, Times, Art and Commerce of Walt Disney,* Avon Books, 1968; Michael Stern, *Stern's Guide to Disney Collectibles,* Collector Books, 1989; Tom Tumbusch, *Tomart's Illustrated Disneyana Catalog and Price Guide, Volume 1* (1985), *Volume 2* (1985), *Volume 3* (1985), *Volume 4* (1987), Tomart Publications; Tom Tumbusch, *Tomart's Illustrated Disneyana Catalog and Price Guide, Condensed Edition,* Tomart Publications, 1989.

Archives: Walt Disney Archives, 500 South Buena Vista Street, Burbank, CA 91521.

Collectors' Club: Mouse Club, 2056 Cirone Way, San Jose, CA 95124.

Advisor: Ted Hake.

Bambi
  Alarm clock, 2 x 3½ x 5", metal, blue, color dial of Bambi, flower and Thumper, unused, orig box, Bayard, 1970 copyright **125.00**
  Figure, 9½" h, plush, velvet, orig tags, c1950 .... **75.00**
  Lamp, orig shade **25.00**
  Movie Poster, 27 x 41", 1948 ...... **125.00**
  Planter, 2 x 5 x 5", ceramic, glazed, light blue, white streaks and splatters, Bambi mounted on front edge, marked "USA-UP2" **40.00**
  Toy, stuffed, Dakin **12.00**
Cinderella
  Bank, 6½", ceramic, white, pastel coloring, "Cinderella" pressed on back, 1950 copyright **50.00**
  Sand Pail, 4" h, plastic, dark blue, red litho tin handle, oval head decal on side, Marx Toys copyright **20.00**

Davy Crocket, pen knife, Walt Disney, Fess Parker, $20.00.

Davy Crockett
  Bank, 5½" h, metal, bronze finish, mid 1950s **40.00**
  Belt, size 28, leather, black, diecut white metal buckle, mid 1950s .. **15.00**
  Doll, 29" h, stuffed, cloth, molded plastic face, c1955 .... **150.00**
  Drinking Glass, 4¾" h, frosted, brown text and illus, Ritchey's Milk premium, mid 1950s **15.00**
  Lunchbox, 4 x 8½ x 6½", marked "King Of The Wild Frontier" on one side, marked "Walt Disney's Frontierland/Kit Carson/Cowboy, Plainsman, Indian Fighter" and "An Official Disneyland Product," no thermos, c1956 .... **30.00**
  Pencil Case, 5 x 11 x 2", cardboard, red, tray and one drawer, Fess Parker label on top, Hassenfeld Bros . **30.00**
  Raccoon Cap, unused **25.00**

Rifle, 32" l, metal and plastic, tan and black, blue impressed logo, cardboard carrying case, c1955 ...... **60.00**

Tie Slide, metal **8.00**

Wallet, 3½ x 4", plastic, Davy image with fabric hat **25.00**

Donald Duck

Book, *Walt Disney's Donald Duck,* 9½ x 13", 12 pgs, Whitman, 1935 **200.00**

Charm, ⅞" h, three dimensional, blue, yellow, and pink, brass loop at top, c1935 .... **15.00**

Donald Duck, figure, bisque, riding tricycle, marked "Japan," 3¼" h, $35.00.

Coloring book, 7½ x 8½", 16 pgs, orange and white cov, Whitman, 1946, unused **20.00**

Greeting Card, Easter, 5 x 5", front and inside illus, Disney Enterprises copyright, marked "WW721A" and dated 1938 .... **30.00**

Handkerchief, 8½", sq, red, white, blue, yellow, and green, Donald about to run into tree stump, "How To Ski" manual flies out of hands, 1950s **10.00**

Mask, rubber **15.00**

Nodder, 6" h, composition, orig black on gold tag, Disney Productions/Japan sticker on base edge **25.00**

Pocket Watch, red, white, blue, and yellow image, Ingersoll, 1939 .... **400.00**

Puppet, 9½" h, blue and white checkered body, vinyl head, diecut white felt hands, orig tag, Gund, c1950 **25.00**

Sand Pail, 8" h, 8" d, Donald as traffic policeman with three nephews on tricycles, blue int., movable handle, Ohio Art, 1938 Enterprises copyright **50.00**

Statue, 3½ x 4½ x 13½", plaster, painted, dark green base, 1950s .. **40.00**

Toothbrush Holder, 4¼" h, double,

bisque, pair of Donalds arm-in-arm, painted, white, blue, and orange **200.00**

Toy, squeeze, rubber, blue and yellow, Dell, 1950s **15.00**

Ferdinand The Bull

Figure, 3", bisque **20.00**

Pillow, 16" sq, velvet, maroon, seated in bull ring smelling flowers, exasperated matador, c1930 .... **65.00**

Portrait, 10 x 12", lead and red pencil image, 1938 Disney copyright ink stamp **100.00**

Goofy

Bank, 11" h, vinyl, head, missing rubber trap, marked "Play Pal Plastics," 1971 Disney copyright **12.00**

Figurine, 2", bisque, c1930 .... **30.00**

Pencil Sharpener, 1⅛" d, plastic, colorful decal, late 1930s **20.00**

Pin, ⅞", brass, enamel paint, tie tac back, 1964 LA Olympics issue, orig pink plastic holder **15.00**

Ludwig Von Drake

Figurine, 6", plastic, cloth jacket, 1961 copyright **5.00**

Game, Professor Ludwig Von Drake Presents Walt Disney's Wonderful World of Color–A Game Based on the TV Program, 9 x 17", Parker Bros, 1962 .... **20.00**

Mickey Mouse

Alarm clock, 2 x 4¼ x 4½", red case, Bayard, made in France, late 1960s **150.00**

Book

Mickey Mouse's Summer Vacation, 1948 .... **15.00**

Mickey Never Fails, DC. Heath, Boston, 104 pgs, 1939 copyright **35.00**

The Miracle Maker, 1948 .... **20.00**

Bracelet, 2" d, silvered brass, black and white porcelain insert, c1930 **50.00**

Coaster, cork back, MIB, set of 6 ... **8.00**

Figure

Mickey and Minnie, holding cane and umbrella, bisque, 4½", marked "Walt E. Disney," pr ... **150.00**

Mickey on firetruck, Auburn Rubber **45.00**

Night Light, 2½" h, plastic, three dimensional head figure, black, red, and beige, c1950 .... **20.00**

Nodder, 1940s **40.00**

Paint Set, boxed, 1939 .... **70.00**

Planter, Mickey in cowboy outfit ... **35.00**

Playing Cards, red and white Mickey juggling deck of cards scene, orig box, marked "W.D. Ent" **40.00**

Puppet, hand, Mickey and Minnie, pr **30.00**

Purse, 2½ x 4", metal mesh, Mickey and Minnie walking along roadway, chain link handle **100.00**

Mickey Mouse, toy, fire truck, painted rubber, red, yellow, black, and silver, Sun Rubber Co, 6¼", $40.00.

Ring, SS 60.00
Rug, 22 x 40", Mickey launching rocket, Thumper watching, white fringe, c1950 .... 50.00
Sheet Music, "What! No Mickey Mouse," 9 x 12", includes movie and German version, Irving Caesar, 1932 copyright, "Published By License Arrangement By Walt Disney" 25.00
Toothbrush Holder, 5¼" h, bisque, movable arm 250.00
Toy
　Squeaker, 5", marked "Made in Italy" 4.00
　Stuffed, velvet, musical, Mickey Mouse Club 60.00
Trivet, 5½" d, cast iron, cut out figure, black finish, three metal legs 125.00
Wrist Watch, brass finish case, black, white, red, yellow, and fleshtone image, red gloved hands point to numbers, black leather straps, Bradley, c1970 .... 25.00
Mickey Mouse Club
　Club Card, 2¼ x 2¾", light blue card, red and dark blue printing, "Member Mickey Mouse club—Warner Bros, Chief Mickey Mouse," club creed printed on back, c1930 .... 60.00
　Music Box, cardboard, wind-up, club logo, mirror and blue fabric inside, plastic Mickey figure pops up, plays official club song, Jaymar, late 1960s 40.00
　Picture Gun, metal, battery operated, four films, boxed, c1950s 50.00
　Pinback Button, Mickey Mouse Club 14.00
　Record, 78 rpm, extra play, 10 x 10" album cov with black and white Jimmy Dodd and Mouseketeers photo, Simon and Schuster, 1955 copyright 20.00
　Train Set, wood, "Mickey Mouse Club Train," 3 pcs, Strombecker, late 1950s 50.00

Vest Kit, Mouseketeer, MIB 45.00
Minnie Mouse
　Ashtray, 3 x 5 x 2", oval, green and orange dec, black, white, and orange figure perched on back, marked "Made In Japan," c1930 . 100.00
　Cup, 3", Minnie waving hanky, SP .. 75.00
　Figure, 4" h, bisque, holding tennis racket, c1980 .... 5.00
　Pocket Watch, abstract sunburst design on back, orange dress and shoes, yellow diecut gloves 100.00
　Puppet, hand, 10" h, vinyl head, fabric body, diecut white felt hands, orig tag, 1950s 25.00
　Toy, 5 x 8", wind-up, trapeze, 5½" celluloid figure flips over wire frame, c1930 .... 200.00
Miscellaneous
Disneyland
　Doll, 13" h, Tinkerbell, rubber, diecut translucent plastic wings, olive green dress, c1955 .... 40.00
　Game
　　20,000 Leagues Under the Sea, Jaymar Games, Walt Disney Productions, MIB 50.00
　　Walt Disney's Score Around, Ideal, 1969, box 25.00
　Guidebook, Walt Disney's Guide to Disneyland," 8 x 11½", 28 pgs, 1964 edition 15.00
　Lunch Box, Disney school bus, domed 20.00
　Puzzle, 20,000 Leagues Under the Sea, 11 x 14", full color, Jaymar, c1954 .... 10.00
　Souvenir Plate, 6" d, china, stylized brown, orange, and yellow castle logo, gold edge, "Japan" sticker, 1950–60 .... 15.00

Fantasia, water color, 3 x 4", night time village scene, black, gray, white, and blue shades, mounted on 7½ x 9" white poster board, Disney Studio ink stamp on back, Phil Dike, dated 10-26-39 .... 250.00
Jungle Book, record, 33⅓ rpm, includes The Bare Necessities, I Wa'na Be Like You, Trust In Me, and Colonel Hathi's March, envelope, Disneyland label, 1972 copyright 8.00
Ugly Duckling, drinking glass, 4¾" h, green and illus, dark blue band, "1939 Walt Disney All Star Parade" 25.00
Peter Pan
　Doll, 9½" h, squeeze, rubber, green outfit, red shoes, Sun Rubber, c1953 .... 30.00
　Sheet Music, 9 x 12", "Your Mother

And Mine," white, green, and
brown cov, 1951 copyright **12.00**

Pinnochio

Figure, 7½" h, wood, jointed, composition head, decal on chest, Ideal **200.00**

Game, Walt Disney's Pinnochio
Game, 15 x 22" board, spinner, 10
cards, three plastic playing pieces,
orig box, Whitman copyright 1962 **25.00**

Lunchbox, 4 x 8 x 7", emb side
scenes, orig name sticker, Aladdin,
c1960–70 .... **20.00**

Post Card, three dimensional, full col-
or, 6 x 7" white plastic frame, W.C.
Jones Publishing, Los Angeles **12.00**

Sheet Music, "When You Wish Upon
A Star," 1939 .... **20.00**

Tray, 8 x 10", tin, litho, Pinocchio and
Gepetto, 1940 copyright **20.00**

Wrist Watch, white dial, image in
light purple circle, diecut hands, replaced black plastic bands, Ingersoll, 1948 .... **120.00**

Pluto

Bank, 9" h, Pluto behind dog house,
one movable arm, "Animal Toys
Plus Inc" and Disney copyright,
c1970 .... **8.00**

Figure, 3½" h, rubber, black and tan,
Lakeside, c1970 .... **5.00**

Light, wall, 5½ x 6½ x 1", ceramic,
molded, Pluto in doorway of dog
house, Railley Corp, 1947 .... **100.00**

Nodder, 5½" h, composition, black
felt ears, light green base, marked
"Walt Disney Productions/Made In
Japan" **30.00**

Puppet, 5½" h, wood, push type, yellow, black oilcloth ears, red collar,
Kohner, c1950 .... **15.00**

Tile, 4", sq, ceramic, Pluto holding
bone, Kemper-Thomas company,
late 1940s **20.00**

Wall Plaque, 10½ x 14", cardboard,
diecut, Pluto, dog house, and bone
dish, linen hanger with brass eyelet, Youngstown Pressed Steel Company, 1940s **25.00**

Sleeping Beauty

Glass, 5" h, yellow blue, and dark red
dec, Sleeping Beauty touching
spindle, 1958 copyright **12.00**

Original Art Cel, 8 x 10", Prince in
black and gray uniform, deep pink
cape, Disneyland Art Corner label **125.00**

Puzzle, 11 x 14", purple border, Jaymar, c1959 .... **12.00**

Snow White and the Seven Dwarfs

Book, *Snow White and the Seven
Dwarfs*, Whitman #925, 16 pgs .. **15.00**

Box, 5 x 5 x 2¼", tin, red edge, silver

dwarfs marching to work illus,
Snow White waving on top, c1939 **100.00**

Handkerchief, 8½" sq, red white,
blue, and brown, Snow White, rabbits, raccoons, and bluebirds
scene, "W.D. Ent" copyright **25.00**

Paint Book, 7 x 10½", Whitman,
1938 copyright, 80 pgs, half neatly
colored **25.00**

Perfume, Sneezy, Russian **14.00**

Planter, ceramic, glazed, pastel
shades, late 1940s
Dopey, 3½ x 7 x 6½" **30.00**
Snow White, 3 x 6 x 6½" **40.00**

Recipe Booklet, 6 x 7", 12 pgs, Snow
White and Dwarfs illus on every
page, "Presented By The American
Dairy Association," 1955 copyright **20.00**

Sewing Card, 6 x 8", Snow White images, green, pink, and blue yarn,
set of 3, c1939 .... **25.00**

Soap, detailed 5" h, Snow White and
3½" h Seven Dwarfs figures, character's name and Disney Enterprises copyright of 1938 on back of
each, white book design box, Lightfoot Schultz Co **200.00**

Tea Set, teapot, creamer and sugar,
six cups and saucers, and 8 x 10"
serving tray pink background, color
designs, boxed, Ohio Art, 1937 Enterprises copyright **350.00**

Three Pigs

Ashtray, 3 x 3½ x 3¼", glazed china,
dark blue luster, pigs perched on
edge playing musical instrument,
early 1930s **75.00**

Mug, 3", white, enameled, pigs playing instruments and dancing on
wolf as rug **25.00**

Pencil Set, 2½ x 5½ x¼" box, wolf
on chimney of pigs brick house,
tray pictures wolf falling into boil-
ing water kettle, pigs and wolf
scenes on back, includes six used
pencils, c1930 .... **15.00**

Sheet Music, "Who's Afraid Of The
Big Bad Wolf?," blue, white, and
orange cov, 1933 .... **15.00**

Zorro

Flashlight, 3" l, plastic, yellow, brass
chain, c1960 .... **20.00**

Game, Zorro Game, Whitman, 1965
copyright **25.00**

Stickpin, 2¼" h, brass, black and
white emb plastic portrait, 1964
Disney Productions copyright **15.00**

Target, Zorro Spring Action Target,
diecut cardboard, brown plastic
dart gun, three darts, boxed, unused, Knickerbocker Toy, c1960 . **60.00**

DOG COLLECTIBLES

Collecting Hints: A collection of dog related items may be based on one particular breed. Another way to collect dog items is by items picturing a dog or even dog-shaped objects. With millions of dog owners in the United States, dog collectibles are very popular.

History: Dogs, long recognized as "Man's Best Friend," have been a part of human life since the early cavemen. The first dogs probably were used for hunting and protection against the wilder animals. After man learned that dogs could be trained to provide useful services, many types of dogs were bred and trained for specific purposes. Over 100 breeds of dogs have evolved from the first dog which roamed the earth over 15 million years ago. Today, dogs are still hunters, protectors, herders, and are trained to see and hear for people.

Man has continued to domesticate the dog, developing today's popular breeds. The American Kennel Club has divided the breeds into seven classifications: herding, hounds, sporting, non-sporting, terriers, toy breeds, and working dogs.

In 1859 in Newcastle, England, the first modern dog show was held. People enjoyed this show and many others were started. The breeding of prize dogs became important. The bloodlines of important dogs were established and recorded. Today, the dogs with the largest pedigrees command the highest prices.

As the dog's popularity grew, so did its appearance on objects. They became popular in literature, in paintings and other art forms.

Periodical: The Canine Collector's Companion, P. O. box 2948, Portland, OR 97208-2948.

Museum: The Dog Museum of America, Jarville House, (1721 South Mason Road), St. Louis, MO.

Advisor: Jocelyn C. Butterer.

Advertising Trade Card, furniture, Pittsburgh, PA, $4.00.

Advertising
Bank, Dr Ross Dog Food, tin can shape, c1950	4.00
Needle Case, RCA, Nipper, gramophone, tin	5.00
Pinback Button, 1¼"	
Chew Bull Dog Twist, multicolored, blue ground, c1896	20.00
Kenmore Motor Co, "Get A Scottie Free With A Blue Ribbon Car," black and white, two Scotties, c1930	15.00
P B Ale, multicolored, bull dog, back paper text adv Van Nostrand's Ale, Bunker Hill Breweries, c1910	35.00
Salt and Pepper Shakers, pr	
His Master's Voice, marked "Lenox"	110.00
Kennel Ration, plastic	7.00
RCA Nipper, phonograph, plastic, c1950	15.00
Ashtray, metal, Scottie, emb "Hollywood Hotel"	75.00
Bank	
Mechanical, Trick Dog, plastic	50.00
Still, figural	
Dog with pack, Whiting #113	225.00
Scottie in barrel, composition, 5½" h	18.00
Spaniel, cast iron, 9½"	70.00
Bell, brass, Bull Dog handle	60.00
Bookends, pr	
German Shepherd, cast iron	30.00
Scotties, red and black, double crown mark, Goebel	125.00
Book, Dr N Rowe, *Field Dog Stud Books*, copyright 1901–23, set of 16	600.00
Calendar Plate, 1912, Harry Scott, Hartford, CT	32.00
Candy Container, Bull Dog, seated	85.00
Cheroot Holder, carved ivory, figural, dog, orig case, Meerschaum	55.00
Chimney Plate, 11" d, Collie, orig hanging chain	30.00
Cigarette Lighter, Westie, metal, head twists off for lighter	45.00
Coasters, Scotties, plastic, orig case, set of 4	8.00
Cookie Jar, Dalmatians, marked "McCoy"	90.00
Creamer, figural, Poodle, marked "Royal Bayreuth"	170.00
Doorstop, cast iron	
Bull Dog	80.00
English Setter, standing on point, old black and white paint, 10" l	125.00
German Shepherd	100.00
Scotties, two dogs	65.00
Terrier, Bradley and Hubbard	500.00
Figure	
Boxer, marked "Morton Studios"	35.00

Figure, Bulldog, china, white, black high-lights, marked "Made in Japan," 3" h, 6" l, $5.00.

Bull Dog
Bronzed white metal, 3 x 5" 20.00
Celluloid 10.00
Cocker Spaniel, marked "Goldschei-
der" 65.00
Dachshund, 5½" l, marked "Rosen-
thal" 45.00
Foo Dog, 8", marked "China" 50.00
Hound Dog, marked "Morton Stu-
dios" 40.00
Poodle, 3", marked "Hummel" 25.00
Scottie, glass eyes, composition 125.00
Spaniel
5½", flat back, chalkware 20.00
5½ x 8 x 11", mottled brown and
yellow, seated on shell cornered
vase, Rockingham, c1850 ..... 570.00
10", white ground, rust colored
spots, Staffordshire 130.00
St Bernard, 9", carrying Princess
Royal, Staffordshire, c1845 ...... 250.00
Foot Scraper, Dachshund, cast iron ... 75.00
Hood Ornament, Ford, leaping grey-
hounds 100.00
Humidor, Pug Dog, silver plated,
hinged box lid, 6 x 5" 225.00
Inkwell, Greyhound, Staffordshire,
c1850 .... 155.00
Lamp, TV type, Afgan Hound, dark cop-
per luster, ceramic 35.00
Lap Rope, wool, hunting dog with bird
in mouth 65.00
Mug, 6" h, tan glaze, brown St Bernard
head, marked "China" 18.00
Napkin Ring, Scottie, bakelite 35.00
Nodder, Dachshund, 12", papier mache 20.00
Nutcracker, 13" l, cast iron 75.00
Paperweight
Glass, shaggy frosted head, reverse
molded in dome, Iowa City 35.00
Terra Cotta, reclining setter, rect base,
marked "NY Architectural Terra
Cotta Co, 1886," 3½ x 5" 75.00
Pencil Sharpener
Scottie, bakelite 35.00
Terrier, white plastic, Germany 25.00

Pipe, carved, "Dog & Deer" **135.00**
Pitcher, 8½", Bull Dog, open mouth,
marked "Majolica" **300.00**
Planter, hunting dog, bisque, marked
"Germany" **18.00**
Print, framed
8½ x 11", Morrel Circus Calendar,
1949, Collie, Wolfhound, Poodle,
and Terrier jumping over circus
stool **15.00**
12 x 24", Hound, Spaniel, and Setter,
matted **30.00**
Rug, hooked, Scottie and Terrier, c1920 **220.00**
Stuffed Toy
Airdale, 4" h, glass eyes, bell on neck
ribbon **25.00**
Cocker Spaniel, 4½", Steiff **75.00**
Schnauzer type, long haired, 10",
Steiff **125.00**
Westie, white, jointed, glass eyes, 12" **40.00**
Tape Measure, 3", Poodle, figural, gray,
tape in tail **18.00**
Tobacco Set, Boxer, pink hat, standing
by gate, tree stump match holder, stri-
ker on side, majolica **95.00**
Toy
Scottie, squeeze toy, 6", glass eyes,
playful barking stance **85.00**
Terrier, pull toy, brown ears and tail,
metal frame, wheels **65.00**
Tin Container, 12 x 7 x 5", red and
cream, two Scotties **18.00**
Whistle, dog head, pewter, 1¼", c1850 **85.00**

DOLL HOUSE FURNISHINGS

Collecting Hints: Doll house furnishings are chil-dren's toys. Some wear may be expected. It is possible to find entire room sets in original boxes. These sets will command a higher price.

History: Doll house furnishings are the tiny ar-ticles of furniture and accessories used to outfit a doll house. They may be made of many types of materials, from fine handmade wooden pieces to molded plastic. Furnishings were played with by children to decorate and redecorate their fa-vorite dollhouse. Several toy manufacturers, such as Tootsietoy, Petite Princess, and Renwal, made doll house furnishings.

Doll houses and doll house furnishings have undergone a current craze and are highly collec-tible. Many artists and craftsmen devote hours to making scale furniture and accessories. This type of artist-oriented doll house furnishings is not included in this listing. It does, however, affect the market by offering the buyer a choice of an old piece versus a present day handmade piece.

References: Flora Gill Jacobs, *Dolls Houses in America: Historic Preservation in Miniature*, Charles Schribner's Sons; Constance Eileen King, *Dolls and Dolls Houses*, Hamlyn; Von Wilckens, *Mansions in Miniature*, Tuttle.

Periodicals: Miniature Collector, 12 Queen Anne Place, Marion, OH 43306; Nutshell News, Clifton House, Clifton, VA 22024.

Collectors' Clubs: International Guild Miniature Artisans, P. O. Box 842, Summit, NJ 07901. Newsletter (biannual); National Association of Miniature Enthusiasts, 351 Oak Place, Suite E, Brea, CA 92621. *Miniature Gazette* (quarterly).

Museums: Kansas City Doll House Museum, Kansas City, MO; Margaret Woodbury Strong Museum, Rochester, NY; Mildred Mahoney Jubilee Doll House Museum, Fort Erie, Canada; Toy Museum of Atlanta, Atlanta, GA; Washington Dolls' House and Toy Museum, Washington, DC.

Bathinette, Renwal	**12.00**
Bathroom Set	
Renwal, 3 pcs	**10.00**
Tootsietoy, 10 pcs, orig box	**75.00**
Bed	
Petite Princess	**18.00**
Renwal, twin size	**5.00**
Bedroom Suite	
Biedermier, bed, marble topped stand, armoire	**350.00**
Ideal, plastic, c1940, MIB	**25.00**
Tootsietoy, 6 pcs, orig box	**60.00**
Buffet, Petite Princess, MIB	**15.00**
Candelabra, Petite Princess	**20.00**
Chair	
Arm	
Petite Princess, matching ottoman	**20.00**
Tootsietoy	**12.00**
Side, Petite Princess, red satin, MIB	**14.00**
Wing Back, Petite Princess, MIB	**12.00**
Chaise Lounge, Petite Princess, MIB, c1964	**20.00**
Chest of Drawers	
Hand Made, walnut, 4 x 6 x 7"	**48.00**
Petite Princess, plastic, MIB, 1964	**15.00**
Cradle, wood	**25.00**
Cup and Saucer, ironstone, 5/8"	**5.00**
Desk, maple, hinged front, royal blue and black int., 3½ x 6"	**100.00**
Dining Room	
Suite	
Arcade, Curtis, cast iron, white laquer finish, two high backed benches, matching 4¾" l table, openwork legs, 1936	**50.00**
Tootsietoy, Daisy, circular pedestal table, four chairs, buffet, sideboard, and tea cart, orig box, 8 pcs	**65.00**

Table, Petite Princess, MIB	**20.00**
Table and Chairs, Renwal, four chairs	**20.00**
Doll, bisque, shoulderhead, molded hair, painted facial features, muslin body	
4½", girl, blonde hair, Kate Greenaway style cape and muff	**100.00**
5"	
Chauffer, molded brown cap, brown felt suit	**70.00**
Maid, bobbed hair, short blue dress, lace trimmed apron	**60.00**
6¼", mother, molded upswept chignon, high collar dress, leg o'mutton sleeves, lace apron	**75.00**
7", father, brown hair and mustache, orig wool tweed suit, white shirt, tie	**60.00**
Fernery, 4¼" h, tin, painted red and gold, two circular trays, fancy scrolled legs	**175.00**
Foot Warmer, brass, working drawer, ¾"	**35.00**
Ice Cream Set, 3½" circular table, twisted metal legs, four matching chairs, heart shaped backs, four blue lemonade glasses, matching blown pitcher, 10 pcs	**100.00**
Ironing Board, folding, Kilgore, cast iron, c1930	**20.00**

Set, Little Homemaker Plastic Kitchen, 8 pieces, marked "Plastic Art Toy Corporation, Rutherford, NJ, Plasco Toy," $40.00.

Kitchen	
Cupboard, Petite Princess, MIB	**40.00**
Sink, Petite Princess, accessories, MIB	**50.00**
Suite	
German, finished hardwood, painted bright salmon, PA Dutch style dec of hearts and flowers in red, yellow, and brown, 4¼" hutch, 4" l domed trunk, sq table,	

three chairs, cradle, bench, oven, box marked "Seit 1912, Kuhn Operboyeriche Heima-thust," MIB **50.00**

Ideal, plastic, MIB, 7 pcs, c1940 . **30.00**

Tootsietoy, green, cupboard, table, chair, and stove, green, orig litho box, 4 pcs **40.00**

Refrigerator, Arcade, cast iron, white laquer, gray trim, 5¾" h, marked "Leonard" **35.00**

Lamp

Floor, 4", black, soft metal, gilded frame, glass beaded shade **100.00**

Table, 3", blue painted base, bulbous milk glass shade **42.00**

Living Room Suite

Arcade, cast iron, sofa, chair, deep pink, maroon trim, removable cushion, 2 pcs **165.00**

Tootsietoy, Daisy Doll House Furniture, gold, sofa, two chairs, library table, floor lamp, table lamp, and phonograph stand, 7 pcs **60.00**

Patio Set, litho tin, round table, four chairs, floral design, 5 pcs **35.00**

Piano

Ideal, plastic, litho, mirror **25.00**

Petite Princess, grand, MIB **20.00**

Renwal, matching bench **12.00**

Potty Chair, 3", gilt soft metal, spindled back, floral dec chamber pot, wheels, c1900 .... **24.00**

Radio, Renwal **30.00**

Rocking Chair, carved arms, fabric seat and back **25.00**

Rug, polar bear, white, royal purple velvet lining, glass bead eyes **25.00**

Set, Nancy Forbes, wooden, general household furnishings, MIB **65.00**

Settee, Arcade, cast iron **80.00**

Sofa

Petite Princess, green, MIB **18.00**

Tootsietoy, metal **35.00**

Stool, Tootsietoy, metal **12.00**

Tea Cart, Petite Princess **20.00**

Tea Set, porcelain, teapot, creamer, sugar, and tray, 6 pcs **50.00**

Television, Petite Princess, MIB **60.00**

Vanity, Renwal **8.00**

Washing Machine, Sally Ann, cast iron, working rubber wringers, c1920 .... **48.00**

DOLLS

Collecting Hints: The most important criteria in buying dolls are sentiment and condition. The value of a particular doll increases if it is a childhood favorite or family heirloom.

When pricing a doll, condition is the most important aspect. Excellent condition means that the doll has all original parts.

The wig should not be soiled or restyled. The surface of the skin must be free of marks and blemishes. Original sleep eyes must be free moving. All mechanical parts should be operational. Original clothing means original dress, underclothes, shoes, and socks in excellent and clean condition, preferably with original tags and labels.

A doll that is mint in the original box is listed as "MIB." Many modern collectible doll prices depend on the original box. Mattel's original Barbie doll, for example, is valued over $1,000. MIB. However, without the original box, the doll is worth much less. Another pricing consideration is appeal. Only a collector knows how important and valuable a particular doll is to her collection.

Modern and 20th century dolls are highly collectible. They offer many appealing features to collectors, one of which is price. A collector of modern dolls need not spend thousands of dollars. This type of doll collecting fits into the average person's budget.

Another feature is the sizes of dolls which enables collectors to artfully display them. Many dolls are made of materials easily cleaned and maintained. An attractive appeal of modern dolls is that they are easily available at flea markets, garage sales, swap meets, etc.

History: The history of modern doll manufacturers is long and varied. While competitors, these companies used similar procedures, molds, and ideas. When Effanbee was successful with the Patsy dolls, Horsman soon followed with a Patsy look–alike named Dorothy. Vogue's Ginny doll was imitated by Cosmopolitan's Ginger. Some manufacturers reused molds, changed sizes, and names to produce dolls which were similar for many years.

Dolls have always been popular with Americans. The early Patsy dolls with their own wardrobes were a success in the 1930s and 1940s. During the 1950s Vogue's Ginny Doll was very successful generating the sales of dolls, clothes, and accessories. The next decade of children enjoyed Mattel's Barbie. Collectors will determine what the collectible dolls of the 1970s and 1980s will be. Doll collecting has become a major hobby.

References: Johana Gast Anderton, *More Twentieth Century Dolls From Bisque to Vinyl, Volume A–H, Volume I–Z, Revised Edition,* Wallace-Homestead, 1974; John Axe, *The Encyclopedia of Celebrity Dolls,* Hobbie House Press, Inc. 1983; Julie Collier, *Official Identification and Price Guide to Antique and Modern Dolls, Fourth Edition,* House of Collectibles, 1989; Jan Foulke, *9th Blue Book Dolls & Values,* Hobby House Press, Inc., 1989; R. Lane Herron, *Herron's Price*

Guide to Dolls, Wallace-Homestead, 1989; Jeanne Du Chateau Niswonger, *That Doll, Ginny,* Cody Publications, 1978; Susan Paris and Carol Manos, *Barbie Dolls,* Collector Books, 1982; Susan Paris and Carol Manos, *The World of Barbie Dolls,* Collector Books, 1983; Patricia R. Smith, *Modern Collector's Dolls, Editions 1, 2, 3, 4, 5,* Collector Books, 1973, 1975, 1976, 1979, 1984; Marjorie Victoria Sturges Uhl, *Madame Alexander, Ladies of Fashion,* Collector Books, 1982.

Periodicals: *Celebrity Doll Journal,* 6 Court Place, Puyallup, WA 98372; *Costume Quarterly for Doll Collectors,* 38 Middlesex Drive, St Louis, MO 63144; *Doll Artisan,* Doll Artisan Guild, 35 Main Street, Oneonta, NY 13820; *Doll Reader,* Hobby House Press, Inc, 900 Frederick St, Cumberland, MD 21502; *Doll Times,* 218 West Woodin, Dallas, TX 75224; *Dolls, The Collector's Magazine,* 1910 Bisque Lane, P. O. Box 1972, Marion, OH 43305; *National Doll World,* 306 East Parr Road, Bernie, IN 46711; *United Collectors,* Master Key To The World of Dolls, P. O, Box 1160, Chatsworth, GA 30705;

Collectors' Clubs: Ginny Doll Club, 305 West Beacon Road, Lakeland, FL 33803; United Federation of Doll Clubs, P. O. Box 14146, Parkville, MO 64152.

Museums: Margaret Woodbury Strong Museum, Rochester, NY; Museum of Collectible Dolls, Lakeland, FL; Yesteryears Museum, Sandwich, MA.

Note: All prices listed here are for dolls in excellent condition and original clothes, unless otherwise noted.

AMERICAN ARTISTS

Americans have been making dolls for children for centuries. During the past several decades, several artists began to make dolls on a limited edition basis, emphasizing exquisite detailing and uniqueness. Today's doll artists offer a varied range of collectible dolls.

The listing below is a sampling of artist dolls which have been sold during the past year. Many artists currently producing dolls are not included because their works have not yet begun to appear in the secondary market. Speculation runs high in this area of doll collecting.

Appalachian Artworks, Inc., Xavier Roberts, orig Cabbage Patch
1980, TV Celebrity Girl **625.00**
1981, Sailor **275.00**
1984, Christmas Boy, all cloth **375.00**
Cochran, Dewees, 15", Cindy, latex, jointed neck, shoulders, and hips, human hair wig, painted eyes, character face, c1948 .... **600.00**

DeHetre, Terre, Punkin, 1988 DOTY award **155.00**
Sullivan, Elsie, 13", Trudy, composition head, flanged neck, muslin body, three painted faces, blonde mohair wisps, painted baby facial features, mohair flannel hooded pajamas, MIB; mark: An Elsie Sullivan Creation, Trudy 3 in 1 Doll, New York, c1940 **265.00**
Wellings, Norah
14½", Royal Canadian Mountie, velvet **165.00**
15", girl, felt, blonde braids, wrist label **200.00**
19", Pajama Bag Doll, velvet head, dark skin tone, pajama bag body, painted features, mohair wig, felt shoes, orig sticker on foot, c1928 **85.00**
39", Mexican Boy, pressed felt face, velvet body, inset brown glass eyes, yellow felt hat, c1935 **85.00**
Zeller, Fawn, 17½", Jackie Kennedy, porcelain shoulderhead, slender neck, muslin body, bisque forearm, painted side parted bouffant hair, painted facial features, pink satin dress, applied seed pearls, c1962 .. **425.00**

AMERICAN CHARACTER DOLL COMPANY

The American Character Doll Company was founded in 1918 and made high quality dolls. When the company was liquidated in 1968, many molds were purchased by the Ideal Toy Co. American Character Dolls are marked with the full company name, "Amer. Char." or "Amer. Char" in a circle. Early composition dolls were marked "Petite."

8"
Betsy McCall, hard plastic, jointed knees, brunette rooted hair, sleep eyes, orig red and white striped skirt, white organdy top, red shoes, c1960 .... **45.00**
Michael Landon, "Little Joe, Bonanza," vinyl, fully jointed body, painted brown hair and eyes, molded clothing, c1965 .... **42.00**
10", Toni, collegiate outfit, orig booklet **70.00**
10½", Tiny Toodles, vinyl, molded, painted hair, 1958 .... **25.00**
11", Tiny Tears, hard plastic head, vinyl body, curly rooted hair, sunsuit, wood and plastic bathinette, c1955 ...... **100.00**
13", Bottle Tot, composition head, body mark, orig tagged clothes **175.00**
16", Baby, composition head, stuffed cloth body and limbs, molded, painted brown hair, brown sleep

eyes, c1925; mark: A. M. Char. Doll,
c1925 . . . . **125.00**
18"
Sally, composition head, cloth body,
orig clothes **200.00**
Sweet Sue, plastic head, vinyl jointed
body **150.00**
Toodle-Loo, fully jointed, magic foam
plastic body, rooted blonde synthetic hair, painted brown eyes,
closed mouth; mark: American
Doll & Toy Co, 1961 . . . . **175.00**
23", Chuckles, all vinyl, rooted blonde
saran hair, painted, brown eyes,
closed mouth, elastic strung legs;
mark: Amer. Doll & Toy Co/1961/
copyright **150.00**
25", Clown, molded, painted white
head and hair, excelsior–stuffed cloth
body, decal eyes, orig clown suit,
c1918; mark: AM Doll **200.00**

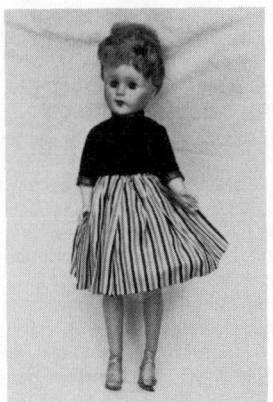

Arranbee, 19", Nancy Lee, vinyl head, hard plastic body, arms, legs, rooted dark blonde hair, high heel shoes, orig dress, $85.00.

ARRANBEE

This company was founded in 1922. Arranbee's finest dolls were made in hard plastic. One
of Arranbee's most popular dolls was Nancy, and
later Nanette. The company was sold to Vogue
Dolls, Inc. in 1959. Marks used by this company
include "Arranbee," "R&B," and "Made In
USA."

8", Little Dear, stuffed vinyl body, rooted
hair, blue sleep eyes, c1956 . . . . **80.00**
11", Littlest Angel, vinyl head, hard
plastic body, jointed, rooted dark
brown hair; mark: R & B on head,
1959 . . . . **40.00**
13", Angel Skin, stuffed soft vinyl head,

stuffed magic skin body and limbs,
molded, painted hair, inset stationary
blue eyes, closed mouth; mark: R &
B on head, orig tag: The R & B Family/
Rock Me, Nanette/Little Angel, Angel
Face/Littlest Angel, Dream Baby/Baby
Bunting, Angel Skin/Taffy, MIB,
c1954 . . . . **80.00**
14", Nancy Lee, vinyl, blonde wig, blue
sleep eyes, closed mouth, orig red
and white taffeta dress; mark: R & B/
Quality/Doll/Nancy Lee, c1947 . . . . **115.00**
15"
Baby Bunting, vinylite plastic head,
stuffed magic skin body, molded,
painted hair, pink fleece bunting;
mark: 17BBS/R & B/D6 on head,
orig tag reads: Head is of Vinylite
Plastic by Bakelite Company **60.00**
Nanette, all hard plastic, glued on
wig, sleep eyes, walker, cotton pinafore, straw hat, MIB, 1952 . . . . . **250.00**
17½", child, all composition, jointed
body, blue sleep eyes, brown wig,
closed mouth; mark: R & B, c1940 . **70.00**
19"
Judy, hard plastic, nylon blonde wig,
braids, metal knob to wind hair
back into head, open mouth; mark:
210 on head, body, Pat.
2,537,598, c1951 . . . . **75.00**
Rosie, composition, swivel head,
cloth body, molded hair, 1935 . . . **85.00**
20", Dream Baby, composition shoulderhead, cloth body, painted hair, re-
dressed, c1925 . . . . **110.00**
21", Nanette, hard plastic fully jointed
body, saran braided wig, blue sleep
eyes, closed mouth, orig clothes,
1953 . . . . **125.00**
23", Taffy, plastic, socket head, blue
eyes, brunette saran wig, straight
walker legs, blue striped satin skirt,
white organdy blouse, ruffled sleeves,
straw hat, 1954 . . . . **175.00**

COSMOPOLITAN DOLL COMPANY

Little recorded history is available about this
company. Dolls dating from the late 1940s
through the 1960s are found with the mark of
CDC. It is believed that the company made many
unmarked dolls. One of their most popular dolls
was Ginger, made in 1955–1956, which was a
takeoff of Vogue Doll's Ginny. Many of these
Ginger dolls are found with original clothes made
by the Terri Lee Doll Company.

7½"
Ginger, hard plastic, glued on wig,
walker, head turns, 1955
Bedtime Outfit **35.00**

Bride's Outfit	40.00
Ice Skating Outfit	40.00
Mousketeer Outfit	45.00

Ginger, vinyl head, hard plastic body, arms, and legs, rooted medium blonde hair, closed mouth; mark: Ginger on head, 1956 .... **35.00**

8½", Little Miss Ginger, vinyl head, hard plastic body, rooted ash blonde hair, closed mouth, high heel feet; mark: Little Miss Ginger, 1956 .... **20.00**

14", Merri, plastic, rooted blonde hair, high heel feet, red gown, white fur trim; mark: AE1406/41, backward AE on lower back, 1960 .... **20.00**

25", Emily, hard plastic swivel head shoulderplate, cloth body, composition arms and legs, glued on blonde wig, open mouth, two teeth, 1949 . **60.00**

DELUXE READING, DELUXE TOPPER, TOPPER CORPORATION, TOPPER TOYS

Deluxe Toy Creations are all names used by Deluxe Toys. This company specialized in dolls that can do things. The company went out of business in 1972.

6", Dawn and Friends, series, vinyl, jointed at neck, shoulders, waist, hips, posable legs, rooted hair; mark: Copyright 1970/Topper Corp/Hong Kong on lower back, additional mark on head

Angie, black hair, brown eyes; mark: 51/D10 .... **10.00**

Dale, negro, black hair, brown eyes; mark: 4/H86 .... **12.00**

Dawn, blonde hair, blue eyes; mark: 343/S11A **15.00**

7", Susie Cutie, vinyl, rooted blonde hair, stationary blue eyes, battery operated; mark: Deluxe Reading/1967/ GX on head, Pat. Pending/1 on back **20.00**

10", Baby Party, vinyl head and arms, hard plastic body and legs, rooted blonde hair, painted eyes, blows whistle and balloon, redressed **35.00**

18", Luv-N-Care, vinyl head, hard plastic body, rooted blonde hair, blue sleep eyes, open mouth, battery operated; mark: Deluxe Topper, 1969 . **48.00**

23", Sweet Amy School Girl, vinyl head, one pc latex body; mark: A-1 on head, MIB **50.00**

EEGEE DOLL MFG COMPANY

The owner and founder of this company was E. G. Goldberger. He began his company in 1917, marking his dolls "E. G." Other marks used by the company include "E. Goldberger" and "Eegee."

11", Dimples, vinyl head, cloth bean bag type body, rooted blonde hair, painted eyes, dimples, music box, key wind on back; mark: 148D/Eegee Co **24.00**

12", Andy, vinyl head, arms, plastic body, legs, molded blonde hair, painted side glancing eyes, dressed as airline pilot; mark: EG-1961 on head and lower back **18.00**

14"

Granny, vinyl head, plastic body, long white hair in bun, hair grows, mature face; mark: Eegee/3 .... **65.00**

Layette Baby, hard plastic head, latex body, molded, painted head, glassine sleep eyes, orig layette, MIB, c1948 .... **65.00**

19"

Bundle of Joy, vinyl head, arms, plastic legs, stuffed cloth body, light brown rooted hair, open mouth, 2 curled fingers; mark: 19-4 Eegee Co, 1964 .... **18.00**

Miss Charming, composition, jointed, blonde mohair wig, green sleep eyes, Shirley Temple copy; mark: E. G., 1936 .... **75.00**

My Fair Lady, vinyl head and body, blonde hair, black net, orig costume, c1958 .... **55.00**

21", Karena Ballerina, hard plastic and vinyl, rooted hair, sleep eyes, jointed at knees, ankles, neck, shoulders, and hips, ballet shoes, satin and net ballet dress, c1958, MIB **45.00**

23", Susan Stroller, vinyl head, hard plastic walker, cries, c1958 .... **50.00**

EFFANBEE DOLL CORPORATION

The Effanbee Doll Corporation was founded in 1912 by Bernard E. Fleischaker and Hugo Baum. Its most successful line was the Pasty Doll and its many variations. Patsy was such a success that a whole wardrobe was designed and it also sold well. This was the first marketing of a doll and her wardrobe.

Effanbee experimented with materials as well as molds. Rubber was first used in 1930; the use of hard plastic began in 1949. Today vinyl has replaced composition. Effanbee is still making dolls and last year's catalog contained over 170 specimens.

8"

Baby Tinyette, 1932	**165.00**
Button Nose, Betty, 1943	**165.00**
Fluffy, 1954	**40.00**

9", Fairy Princess, 1935 .... **185.00**
10", Wolf, 1934 .... **185.00**
11", Billy Boy, 1915 .... **100.00**
11½", Babyette, composition head and
hands, stuffed pink cloth body,
molded painted brown hair, closed
eyes and mouth, orig tags and box,
c1945 .... **100.00**
12"
Butterball, all vinyl, molded blonde
hair, orig box, 1969 .... **60.00**
Cupcake, 1963 .... **40.00**
Dy Dee Baby, caracal wig, orig ward-
robe and trunk **185.00**
Miss Coquette, 1916 .... **125.00**
Newborn Baby, 1925 .... **125.00**
Red Cross Nurse, 1918 .... **125.00**
14"
My Fair Baby, 1968 .... **45.00**
Patricia Walker, 1952 .... **125.00**
15"
Alice, 1958 .... **145.00**
Baby Blanche, 1918 .... **150.00**
Mickey Baby, 1938 .... **135.00**
16"
Beach Baby, 1923 .... **145.00**
Cookie, 1968 .... **50.00**
Dorothy Dainty, 1916 .... **125.00**
Honey Walker, 1953 .... **145.00**
Li'l Darlin, 1947 .... **75.00**
18"
Anne Shirley, composition, orig
clothes **175.00**
Cinderella, 1952 .... **200.00**
Prince Charming, 1952 .... **225.00**
School Girl Writing, 1963 .... **80.00**
Snowsuit Susan, 1967 .... **85.00**
Today's Girl, 1943 .... **140.00**
20", Sugar Plum, 1980 .... **65.00**
21", Rootie Kazootie, 1954 .... **125.00**
24", Boudoir Doll, 1938 .... **125.00**
29", Elizabeth, 1938 .... **175.00**

HASBRO

Hasbro is primarily a toy manufacturer. One
of their most popular dolls was GI Joe and his
friends. The detailed accessories made for GI Joe
include military sets and numerous adventure
type (camping, mountain climbing, etc.). Hasbro
is also noted for their advertising and personality
dolls.

7½", Junior Miss Sewing Kit, jointed
arms, orig box contains doll patterns,
material, dresses to sew, sewing implements, orig 11½ x 15½" box,
c1948 .... **25.00**
9", Choo Choo Charlie, soft vinyl head,
stuffed cotton bean bag body, rooted
hair, painted eyes; mark: Copyright

1973 Quaker City Chocolate & Conf'y
Co, Inc **20.00**
12", GI Joe, vinyl, flocked hair, beard,
orig clothes, c1794 .... **18.00**
17", Amanda, Sweet Dreams, stuffed
gingham head and body, yarn hair,
black felt eyes, button nose, embroidered smile, eyelet lace trimmed
night cap, orchid print dress, 1974 . **12.00**

**Horsman, 11", Cupcake, plastic head and
hands, bean bag body, molded painted
features, rooted curly hair, orig clothes,
$20.00.**

HORSMAN DOLLS COMPANY INC.

The Horsman Dolls Company Inc. was
founded in 1865 by E. I. Horsman, who began
by importing dolls. Soon after the founding,
Horsman produced bisque dolls. It was the first
company to produce the Campbell Kids. They
invented Fairy Skin in 1946, Miracle Hair in
1952, and Super Flex in 1954. The Horsman
process for synthetic rubber and early vinyl has
always been of high quality.

11", Peterkin, composition, character
face, molded hair, painted side glancing eyes, watermelon smile, c1915 . **215.00**
12"
Baby Bumps, negro, cloth body,
arms, legs, painted hair, eyes, large
well molded ears, orig romper,
c1912 .... **250.00**
Mary Poppins, all vinyl, 5 pc body,
black rooted hair, painted blue
eyes, extra clothes, c1965 .... **40.00**
12½", Ruthie, all vinyl rooted black
hair, Oriental hair style, long straight
legs, dimpled knees; mark: 12–6aa
on upper legs, B–1 on upper arms .. **30.00**
13", Campbell Kid, composition head,

painted at neck, shoulders, and hips, light brown hair, painted side glancing googly eyes, 2 pc brown knicker suit, c1940 .... **185.00**

14", Bye–Lo, vinyl head, arms, and legs, cloth body, molded straight hair, painted eyes, christening outfit; mark: Horsman Doll/1972 on head, MIB .. **50.00**

15"

Dimples Toddler, redressed **150.00**

Tynie Baby, composition head, cloth body, composition arms, sleep eyes, closed mouth **250.00**

16", Baby Dimples, composition, orig clothes **185.00**

18"

Ella Cinders, composition head, cloth body, composition arms and lower legs, molded black hair, painted facial features, orig dress, c1925 ... **225.00**

Joyce, composition shoulderhead head, arms, and legs, cloth body, glued on bright red mohair hair .. **50.00**

19", Pram Baby, vinyl, jointed head, glass sleep eyes, closed mouth, coos **65.00**

20", Rosebud, composition head, arms, and legs, cloth body, painted eyes, human hair wig **100.00**

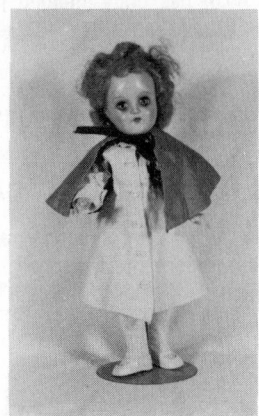

Ideal, 14½", Miss Curity, all hard plastic, posable legs and arms, orig nurse uniform and cape, $125.00.

IDEAL TOY CORPORATION

The Ideal Toy Corp. was formed in 1902 by Morris Michtom to produce his teddy bear. By 1915 the company had become a leader in the industry by introducing the first sleep eyes. In 1939, Ideal developed magic skin. It was the first company to use plastic. Some of their most popular lines include Shirley Temple, Betsy Wetsy, and Toni dolls.

10", Little Miss Revlon, vinyl, rooted saran hair, sleep eyes, orig clothes, c1957 .... **80.00**

12"

Baby Snooks, composition head and hands, wooden torso, wire limbs, redressed **200.00**

Betsy Wetsy, composition head, rubber body, jointed at neck, shoulders, and hips, drinks, wets, and cries; mark: Ideal **50.00**

Fanny Brice, composition head, flexible wire body, composition hands, wooden feet, molded brown hair, painted features, orig clothes, c1938 .... **185.00**

Liberty Boy, World War I soldier, composition head, jointed at neck, shoulders, and hips, molded khaki uniform, c1917 .... **120.00**

Shirley Temple, vinyl five pc body, rooted hair, sleep eyes, c1957 ... **75.00**

14"

Betsy McCall, vinyl head, hard plastic body, dark brown curly saran wig, round brown sleep eyes; mark: P-90 on head, orig clothes, c1953 . **100.00**

Mary Hartline, hard plastic, jointed neck, shoulders, and hips, nylon wig, sleep eyes, closed mouth; mark: Ideal Doll **175.00**

16", Baby Giggles, vinyl head, arms, and legs, plastic body, rooted hair, blue eyes, MIB, 1965 .... **45.00**

17", Bonnie Walker, hard plastic, walker, blue sleep eyes, open mouth, two upper teeth, cryer, redressed ... **85.00**

18"

Baby, composition head, lower arms, and legs, cloth body, molded hair, flirty eyes, closed mouth; mark: Ideal Doll, c1938 .... **175.00**

Betty Jane, composition, jointed neck, shoulders, and hips, lashed sleep eyes, open mouth, teeth, orig clothes; mark: Ideal 18, 1943 .... **200.00**

Judy Garland, composition, five pc body, red-brown mohair braids, brown sleep eyes, orig Wizard of Oz blue checked dress, c1939 ... **650.00**

Shirley Temple, composition head and body, jointed at shoulders and hips, blonde mohair wig, blue sleep eyes, open mouth, c1935 .. **265.00**

20", Thumbelina, vinyl head, arms, and legs, cloth body, rooted dark blond hair, painted blue eyes, music box; mark: Ideal Toy Corp, 1962 .... **45.00**

21", Princess Mary, vinyl head, plastic body, orig ball gown and wrist tags, 1952 .... **150.00**

22"
Kissy, soft vinyl head, rigid vinyl body, rooted hair, MIB, c1962 ... **48.00**
Saucy Walker, vinyl head, hard plastic body, orig wig, flirty eyes, orig dress, c1955 .... **75.00**
27", Sister–Coos, composition head and shoulderplate, cloth stuffed body, composition arms and legs, brown mohair wig, brown sleep eyes, redressed, c1935 .... **175.00**
36", Patty Playpal, vinyl head and arms, plastic body, rooted brown hair, blue sleep eyes, closed mouth, orig clothes, 1960 .... **125.00**

Madame Alexander, 8", composition, orig costumes and wicker basket, $1,200.00.

MADAME ALEXANDER DOLL COMPANY

The Madame Alexander Doll Co was started in 1923 by Bertha Alexander. The dolls made by this company are beautifully done with exquisite costumes. They have made hundreds of dolls including several series such as the International Dolls and the Americana Dolls. Marks used by this company include "Madame Alexander," "Alexander," "Alex," and many are unmarked on the body but can be identified by clothing tags. Today, Madame Alexander continues to make dolls which are very collectible. Many dolls are made in a limited time period of one year. Others are offered for several years before being discontinued.

8", Americana Series
Amish Boy, orig clothes, c1965 .... **450.00**
Colonial Girl, orig clothes, c1962 .. **350.00**
8", International Series
China, 1973 .... **235.00**
Greek Boy, jointed knees, 1968 .... **275.00**
Morocco **225.00**
Spanish Boy, 1964 .... **375.00**
Thailand, 1970 .... **135.00**
9", Wendy–Ann, composition, jointed at neck, shoulders, and hips, human hair wig, painted eyes, orig clothes; mark: Wendy–Ann Mme Alexander" **265.00**
9½", Cissette Renoir, hard plastic, jointed knees, high heel shoes, brown hair, blue sleep eyes, red taffeta hat, navy blue dress, orig MA Renoir dress tag **100.00**
12"
Brenda Starr, vinyl head and arms, hard plastic body and legs, jointed hips and knees, rooted red hair, orig clothes, 1964 .... **800.00**
Little Genius, baby, hard plastic head, arms, and legs, cloth body, blonde mohair wig, blue sleep eyes, organdy baby dress, petticoat, and bloomers **100.00**
13", Princess Elizabeth, composition, jointed at neck, shoulders, and hips, mohair wig, Betty face, sleep eyes; mark: Princess Elizabeth, Alexander Doll Co **275.00**
14"
Alice In Wonderland, hard plastic, blonde hair, blue eyes, blue taffeta dress, 1950 .... **700.00**
Binnie Walker, hard plastic, blonde hair, black stripped dress, yellow pinafore, and straw hat, MIB, c1950 .... **500.00**
Goldilocks, vinyl head and arms, hard plastic torso and legs, blonde synthetic wig, sleep eyes, orig clothes; mark: Alexander, copyright 1978 .... **100.00**
Jenny Lind and Cat, vinyl head and arms, hard plastic torso and legs, synthetic wig, sleep eyes, orig clothes; mark: Alexander, copyright 1969 .... **300.00**
Kathy, hard rubber, five pc jointed baby body, molded hair, blue sleep eyes, open mouth, nurser, long white organdy gown, lace trim, matching cap, c1954 .... **75.00**
Madelaine, composition, jointed at neck, arms, and legs, blonde wig, brown sleep eyes, orig clothes, orig MA Madelaine dress tag, gold octagonal wrist tag **200.00**
Maggie, hard plastic, walker, blonde mohair wig, brown sleep eyes, peach colored taffeta dress, rhinestone buttons, name on dress tag . **125.00**
Mary Ann, vinyl head and arms, hard plastic torso and legs, synthetic wig, sleep eyes, orig clothes; mark: Alexander, copyright 1965 ...... **270.00**
Nina Ballerina, hard plastic, jointed at neck, shoulders, and hips, brown wig, sleep eyes, closed mouth, orig clothes; mark: Alexander **300.00**

15"

Elise, hard plastic, jointed elbow, knee, and ankle, blonde wig, blue sleep eyes, pink taffeta dress, blue dress coat, matching straw bonnet, orig MA Elise cloth dress tag, orig box **125.00**

Kelly, vinyl and hard plastic, blonde hair, brown sleep eyes, blue gingham dress, rose pinafore, orig MA dress tag, part of orig box ... **100.00**

16"

Amy, cloth doll, dressed mask face, blonde hair, painted blue eyes, flowered print dress, replaced shoes and socks, cloth dress tag .. **80.00**

Marybel, vinyl head, rigid vinyl body and limbs, jointed waist, blonde rooted hair, brown sleep eyes, open/closed mouth, orig clothes and case, c1959 .... **160.00**

18", Baby, hard plastic head, vinyl arms and legs, cloth body, orig pink organdy dress, smocked coat, matching bonnet, orig MA dress tag **85.00**

20", Cissy, brown hair, blue sleep eyes, orig bridal gown and accessories, cloth dress tag **150.00**

MATTEL, INC.

Mattel, Inc. was started in 1945. The most celebrated doll they make is Barbie, which was designed by one of the company's founders, Ruth Handler, in 1958. Barbie Dolls were dressed in bathing suits and sold in boxes. Her many outfits and accessories were also marketed successfully. Skipper, Ken, Midge, Skooter, and Francie are part of Barbie's extended circle of family and friends. Mattel has sponsored two trade-in programs for Barbie Dolls, the first in 1967. The purpose was to introduce the new bendable Barbie. This trade-in drew more than 1,250,000 dolls. In 1970, Mattel introduced Living Skipper with a trade-in deal.

10½"

Buffy and Mrs Beasley, vinyl head, plastic body, blonde ponytails, painted blue eyes, painted upper teeth, pull talk string, holding Mrs Beasley, MIB, c1969 .... **125.00**

Donny and Marie Osmond, vinyl heads, plastic bodies, painted eyes, orig clothes, sold as pair, MIB, c1977 .... **40.00**

11½"

Barbie

1959, #1, vinyl, brunette hair, MIB **950.00**

1960, #3, vinyl, blonde hair, MIB **200.00**

1962, #4, vinyl, bubble cut, orig box, stand, and clothing **65.00**

1975, Olympic Gold Medalist, MIB **55.00**

Ken, orig doctor's uniform, orig stand, 1961 .... **60.00**

Truly Scrumptious, Chitty Chitty Bang Bang, vinyl, straight legs, blonde hair, pink and white gown, matching hat; mark: Mattel, #1108, c1969 .... **90.00**

12", Cheerful Tearful, vinyl head and body, orig clothes, 1966 .... **35.00**

16", Bozo The Clown, vinyl head, cloth body, pull talk string, c1962 .... **65.00**

18", Chatty Cathy, soft vinyl head, hard plastic body, rooted blonde dynel hair, blue sleep eyes, open mouth, two teeth, voice box, MIB, c1965 .. **60.00**

25", Charmin Cathy, vinyl head and arms, plastic body and legs, rooted blonde hair, blue side glancing sleep eyes, closed mouth, orig clothes and metal trunk, 1961 .... **100.00**

NANCY ANN STORYBOOK DOLLS

Nancy Ann Storybook Dolls were started in 1941 by Nancy Ann Abbott. The first dolls used doll bodies from Europe and Japan. The bodies were repainted and then dressed in Nancy Ann Storybook Doll Costumes. However, the bodies were not suitable and production soon began in California using imported English clays to make bisque bodies. The company used hard plastics and vinyls in 1952 through 1959. The Nancy Ann Storybook Dolls have been reintroduced and are being packed in polka dot boxes by Nancy Ann Storybook Dolls, Division of Giant Consolidated Industries of Salt Lake City, Utah.

3½", Christening Baby, all hard plastic, molded painted yellow hair, closed mouth, straight baby legs, jointed shoulders, hips; mark: Storybook Dolls/USA/Trademark/Reg 1952 .... **25.00**

5", all bisque, one piece body, head, painted eyes; mark: Story/Book/Doll/USA on back, wrist tag with name, 1941–47

Autumn **28.00**

Little Joan **25.00**

Lucy Locket, blue hat **25.00**

5½"

All bisque, one piece, painted features

Bridesmaid Teen **30.00**

Southern Belle **28.00**

Valentine **20.00**

All hard plastic, fully jointed, painted features, black sleep eyes

Daffidown Dilly **30.00**

First Communion **25.00**

School Days **20.00**

6", Jeannie, Moonlight and Roses, hard

plastic, black sleep eyes; mark: Storybook Dolls/USA/Trademark/Reg 1952 .... **25.00**
10", Lori Ann Walker, all hard plastic, head turns, glued on brown wig; mark: Nancy Ann on head, dress tag: Styled by Nancy Ann Storybook Dolls, Inc/San Francisco/Calif, 1953 **35.00**
11", Debbie, all hard plastic, orig clothes ...,..................... **60.00**

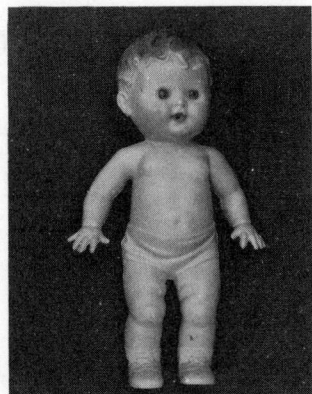

Sun Rubber, 10½", Tod-L-Dee, one piece body, head, molded, painted hair, open nurser mouth, molded diaper, shoes, and socks, $25.00.

SUN RUBBER COMPANY

The Sun Rubber Company produced all rubber or lasiloid vinyl dolls. Many have molded features and clothes.

7", Happy Kappy, one piece rubber body, molded painted hair, painted blue eyes, open/closed mouth, yellow hat; mark: The Sun Rubber Co/Barberton, OH/Made in USA/Ruth E. Newton/New York/NY **25.00**
10", So Wee, bottle, booties, jacket, towel, soap, MIB **35.00**
10½", Tod–L–Dee, one piece rubber body, molded painted hair, open nurser mouth, molded diaper, shoes, and socks **25.00**
11"
  Betty Bows, rubber, fully jointed, molded hair, blue sleep eyes, drinks and wets; mark: Betty Bows/ Copyright The Sun Rubber Co/Barberton, OH USA/34A, c1953 .... **35.00**
  Gerber Baby, all rubber, molded, painted hair, open mouth, nurser, dimples, crossed baby legs; mark:

Gerber Baby/Gerber Products Co on head **45.00**

TERRI LEE DOLLS

The founder and designer of the Terri Lee family was Mrs. Violet Lee Gradwohl of Lincoln, Nebraska. She made the first Terri Lee doll in 1948. Jerri Lee, a brother, was trademarked in 1948. Connie Lee joined the family in 1955. Mrs. Gradwohl issued lifetime guarantees for each doll, which were honored until the demise of the company in the 1960s.

8", Ginger Girl Scout, orig clothes **100.00**
9", Baby Linda, all vinyl, molded painted hair, black eyes, c1951 .... **90.00**
10"
  Tiny Jerri Lee, hard plastic, fully jointed, blonde curly wig, brown sleep eyes, closed mouth **175.00**
  Tiny Terri Lee, hard plastic, fully jointed, blonde wig, inset eyes, closed mouth **130.00**
16"
  Benji, hard plastic, swivel head, jointed hard plastic body, black wig, painted features; mark: Terri Lee/Pat Pending, c1946 .... **450.00**
  Jerri Lee, hard plastic, jointed at neck, shoulders, and hips, orig curly wig, painted eyes, orig clothing and accessories; mark: Jerri Lee **225.00**
  Terri Lee, hard plastic, jointed at neck, shoulders, and hips, orig curly wig, painted eyes, orig clothing and accessories; mark: Terri Lee **200.00**
17", Patty Jo, hard plastic, swivel head, jointed hard plastic body, black styled wig, painted brown eyes, closed mouth, orig dress, c1946 .... **450.00**

VOGUE DOLLS

Vogue Dolls was founded by Mrs. Jennie H. Graves. She began a small doll shop which specialized in well made costumes. The original business of doll clothing lead to a cottage industry which employed over 500 home sewers in 1950. This branch of the industry peaked in the late 1950s with over 800 home workers plus several hundred more at the factory. During World War II, the shortages created a market for an American doll source. Mrs. Graves created the Ginny doll and promoted her heavily. The Ginny Doll was the first doll created with a separate wardrobe and accessories. For many years Vogue issued one hundred new outfits for Ginny alone. They continued to produce their own dolls and clothing for others. Ginny Dolls reached their heyday in the 1950s and are still being made today.

Note: The Ginny doll was reproduced in 1985.

7"

Hansel and Gretel, hard plastic, jointed at neck, shoulders, and hips, blonde mohair wigs, blue sleep eyes, orig clothes and booklet "The Vogue Doll Family," copyright 1958; mark: Ginny/Vogue Dolls, and Hansel/Vogue Dolls, pr **325.00**

Toddles, composition, jointed neck, shoulders, and hips, molded hair, painted side glancing eyes, orig clothes; mark: Vogue on head, Doll Co on back, Toddles stamped on sole of shoe, MIB **265.00**

7½", Crib Crowd Baby, all hard plastic, curved baby legs, painted eyes, blonde synthetic ringlets wig, orig tagged dress, rubber pants, c1949 .. **425.00**

8", Ginny

1948–1950, all hard plastic, painted eyes, molded hair, mohair wig; mark: Vogue on head, Vogue Doll on back

Cinderella **150.00**
Clown **225.00**
Coronation Queen, MIB **1,100.00**
Springtime **115.00**
Valentine **125.00**

1950–1953, moving eyes; mark: Vogue on head, Vogue Doll on back

Catholic Nun **165.00**
Christmas **125.00**
Mistress Mary **135.00**
Roller Skating **200.00**

1954, walking mechanism; mark: Ginny on back, Vogue Dolls, Inc. Pat. Pend., Made in USA

Ballerina, poodle cut wig **100.00**
Rainy Day **75.00**
School Dress **75.00**
Springtime **70.00**

1957, bending knees

Beach outfit **75.00**
Davy Crockett **80.00**
Southern Belle **90.00**

1963, soft vinyl head, rooted hair

Bridesmaid **45.00**
Faraway Places, France **50.00**
Mary Had A Little Lamb **75.00**

10"

Jeff, orig clothes **35.00**
Jill, hand painted, bride's dress **50.00**

12"

Baby Dear, all composition, bent baby limbs, 1961 .... **40.00**
Betty Jane, all composition, bent right arm, braided pigtails, red plaid woven cotton dress, white eyelet trim; tag: Vogue Dolls Inc., 1947 . **85.00**

20", Welcome Home Baby **50.00**
22", Hug A Bye Baby, pink pajamas, MIB **40.00**

ELECTRICAL APPLIANCES

Collecting Hints: Small electric appliances are still readily available and can be found at estate and garage sales, flea markets, auctions, and best of all, Grandma's attic. They generally cost very little, making them attractive to collectors on a limited budget.

Most old toasters, waffle irons, and other appliances still work. Construction was simple with basic, 2-wire connections. If repairs are necessary, it usually is simple to return an appliance to good working order.

Whenever possible ask to plug in the appliance to see if it heats. On "flip-flop" type toasters (the most numerous type), check to see if elements are intact around mica and not broken.

Most appliances used a standard size cord, still available at hardware stores. Some early companies did have strange plugs and their appliances will only accept cords made for that company. In such an instance, buy the appliance only if the cord accompanies it.

Do not buy an appliance that is in non-working order, in poor or rusted condition, or with missing parts unless you plan to strip it for parts. Dirt does not count. With a little care and time, most of the old appliances will clean up to a sparkling appearance. Aluminum mag wheel polish, available at auto parts stores, used with a soft rag will produce wonderful results. Also, a non-abrasive kitchen cleanser can be of great help.

As with most collectibles, the original box or instructions for any item can enhance the value and add up to 25%. Also beware of chrome, silver, and other plated articles stripped to their base metal, usually brass or copper. Devalue these by 50%.

History: The first all electric kitchen appeared at the 1893 Chicago World's Fair and included a dish washer, that looked like a torture device, and range. Electrical appliances for the home began gaining popularity just after 1900 in the major eastern and western cosmopolitan cities. Appliances were sold door to door by their inventors. Small appliances did not gain favor in the rural areas until the late 1910s and early 1920s. However, the majority of the populace did not trust electricity.

By the 1920s, competition among electrical companies was keen; innovations in electrical appliances were many. Changes were rapid. The electric servants were here to stay. Most small appliance companies were bought by bigger companies. These, in turn, have been swallowed up by the huge conglomerates of today.

Some Firsts in electrical appliances are:

1882 Patent for electric iron (H. W. Seeley [Hot-point])
1903 Detachable cord (G. E. Iron)
1905 G. E. Toaster (Model X-2)
1905 Westinghouse toaster (Toaster Stove)
1909 Travel iron (G. E.)
1911 Electric frying pay (Westinghouse)
1912 Electric waffle iron (Westinghouse)
1917 Table Stove (Armstrong)
1918 Toaster/Percolator (Armstrong "Perc-O-Toaster")
1920 Heat indicator on waffle iron (Armstrong)
1920 Flip-flop toasters appear (everyone)
1920 Mixer on permanent base (Hobart Kitchen Aid)
1920 Electric egg cooker (Hankscraft)
1923 Portable mixer (Air-O-Mix "Whip-All")
1924 Automatic iron (Westinghouse)
1924 Home malt mixer (Hamilton Beach #1)
1926 Automatic pop-up toaster (Toastmaster #1-A-1)
1926 Steam iron (Eldec)
1937 Home coffee mill (Hobart Kitchen Aid)
1937 Automatic coffee maker (Farberware "Coffee Robot")
1937 Conveyance device toaster ("Toast-O-Lator")

References: Linda Campbell Franklin, *300 Years of Kitchen Collectibles, Second Edition*, Books Americana, 1984; Don Fredgant, *Electrical Collectibles, Relics of the Electrical Age*, Padre Productions, 1981; Howard Hazelcorn, *Hazelcorn's Price Guide To Old Electrical Toasters, 1908–1940*, H. J. H. Publications, no date, 1988–89 revised price list available; Greg Ivy (compiler), *Early Fans*, Kurt House, 1983.

Collectors' Club: American Fan Collector Association, 4606 Travis, Dallas, TX 75205.

Advisors: Gary L. Miller, K. M. Scotty Mitchell.

All Rite Co., IN
Sandwich Toaster, "Hostess," 1930, 5 x 5 x 4½" h, sq, ftd, heavy aluminum body with screw-off black wooden handle, orig Art Deco orange and black box with "Suggestions" book **40.00**
Angelus
Campfire Bar-B-Q Marshmallow Toaster, 3" sq, lightweight metal body, includes 2 pcs: sq base and dot pierced, flattened pyramid top; base on two loop wire legs with rubber encased cushion feet; three small metal 2-prong forks **55.00**

Armstrong Mfg. Co.
Percolator and Toaster, "Perc-O-Toaster," Model PT, 1918, nickel, two plug, combination percolator and toaster, sq base, cabriolle legs, slip-out toast rack in base **60.00**
Table Top Stove, 1917, porcelain and nickel body with toaster rack, broiler pan and liner, waffle iron, skillet, four egg poacher, and lid, black wooden handles, orig cord . **95.00**
Waffle Iron, early 1920s, Pat. Pend. Model "W," 7" round plates, metal tag, black wooden handles (first heat indicator) **25.00**
Brannon, Inc., Detroit, Michigan
Iron, Cordless, "Cord-Less-Matic," 1930s, Pat. Pend., plug-in detachable base and contacts in sole plate, black painted metal, bakelite handles **25.00**

Toaster, Challenge, Art Deco design, two slice, chrome plated, $18.00.

Calkins Appliance Co., Niles, Michigan
Hot Plate/Toaster, "Breakfaster," 1930s, Model #T-2, Art Deco design, louvered, round corner sq aluminum body, bakelite base and handles, small rect door in side opens and brings out toast tray, top has hot plate **35.00**
Chronmaster, NY, Chicago
Drink Master, "Mixall," Pat. 1934, 14", Art Deco design, black metal stand holds chrome motor housing, chrome knob on top, front switch, single shaft, clear glass with silver bands, mixes drinks, whips cream, etc. **30.00**
Coleman Lamp & Stove Co., Wichita, Kansas
Waffle Iron, Model 17, Pat. App. For., 7½" round plates in round chrome body, 14" oval base, high style Art Deco, small china insert on lid,

black and white gazelle motif, black bakelite handles **30.00**

Dominion
Popcorn Popper, 1920s, Model #75, cylindrical, pierced nickel body, cabriolle legs, hand crank, red wooden handles and knob **24.00**

Dover Mfg. Co., Dover, Ohio
Iron, Child's, "Dover Co-Ed," #27-1/2, 5" plate, two and one half pound nickel body, green wooden handle **20.00**

Mary Dunbar (Chicago Elect. Mfg. Co.)
Mixer, "Handymix," late 1930s, #D-121124, 11½" mixer on stand, push switch, two beaters **16.00**

Edison (See General Electric)

Estate Stove Co, Hamilton, OH
Toaster, Model 177, 1922, nickel, sq body, canted, pierced door rack on four sides, all turn simultaneously with one button movement **75.00**

Eureka Vacuum Cleaner Co., Detroit, Michigan
Electric Range, 1930s, 15 x 13 x 19" h, high style Art Deco, cream painted body, black porcelainized trim, chamfered shape top, emb design with "Eureka" across at angle, black bakelite handle, int. racks, sides fold down with chrome surfaces and round hot plates; lower front has panel with large red indicator light, black bakelite controls for oven temp, hi–med–lo for hotplates and pre–warm and hi–med–lo control for oven; stands on short feet made into sides of body; top carrying handle, restored **80.00**

Everhot
Cooker, Pat. 1925, Cat. #EC-JR-10, 13" h, 9½" cylindrical body, chrome middle Art Deco design with large "Everhot" emb, black base and top, aluminum lock-on lid, fitted int. with three pans and lids **50.00**

Farberware
Broiler/Grill, "Broiler Robot," 1938, 11" round nickel body, two part with internal rack, domed lid with element and three top feet to reverse and turn from broiler to grill, heat indicated **30.00**
Coffee Maker, late 1930s, Model #208, 12½", chrome with garland drape, black wooden handles **15.00**
Coffee Robot, 1937, chrome body with glass top bowl, thermostat keeps coffee and stirs **35.00**

General Electric
Dining Room Set, 1918–19, all with nickel bodies, wooden handles, and paw feet
  Chafing Dish **50.00**
  Hot Plate **25.00**
  Percolator, glass top **45.00**
  Water Kettle **50.00**
Hot Plate, "Disk Stove," 1920s, Cat. #40101, 6" heavy round iron top on chrome, three tall triangular pierced legs, bun wooden feet, lower shelf **30.00**
Mixer, 1938, Cat. #149 M8, Ser. #10-A, removable top on stand, cream metal and black, bakelite handle, work light in top, three beaters in row, white bowls, head folds down **30.00**
Table Top Stove, late 1910s, 7" sq nickel pierced base and frame holds elements, slots for poacher, broiler, griddle pan, marked "Hotpoint" **75.00**
Toaster
  1908, Model D-12, white china base, open wire frame, lift-off warming rack, china screw-in plug, first marketed toaster **125.00**
  1910–14, Cat. #125 T22, Edison Electric App. Co, flip-flop type, pierced geometric warming top and doors, large black wooden knobs **35.00**
  1910, Cat. #214 T-5, nickel base, open sides, separate warming rack, top "tab" holders **45.00**
  1933, Radio Toggle, two slice flip over type, pierced nickel body, doors, and top, large radio knob on side to reverse toast **95.00**
Waffle Iron, 1900, solid iron, three short legs, coiled wire, heat dissipating handles, separate screw-in plugs for top and bottom **95.00**

General Mills (Betty Crocker)
Deep Fryer, late 1940s, Model 9-A, 11 x 7" chrome body, rounded corners, black bakelite base with red control, chrome lid, aluminum basket **25.00**
Iron, "Tru-Heat" Iron and Steam Attachment, late 1940s, Model GM-1-B and GM-4-A, chrome body, side rest, black handles, red knob, MIB **35.00**

A. C. Gilbert
Home Malt Mixer, 1930s, 13" h, chrome, domed motor housing, "crinkle green" painted base **65.00**
Mixer, "Polar Club" Electric Hand Mixer, 1929, #B-89, 9½", gray paint, blue wooden handle, single shaft, orig box, unused appearance **75.00**

Hamilton Beach

Mixer, 1930–40s, Model "G" Ser. #366839, cream metal painted body, slip-off base, beaters in one unit, bakelite handle, white bowls ... **25.00**

Home Motor, 1910s, #29650192, attachments for various household functions, (motor only) **30.00**

Handy Hannah

Knife Sharpener, electric, 1930s, Cat. #4950, 4½" round, red and cream body, low flat base **10.00**

Mixer, late 1930s, Cat. #495, natural wooden handle, single shaft, quart jar base **22.00**

Hankscraft

Egg Cooker, 1930s, Model 599, yellow ceramic, chrome lid, large yellow ceramic knob, instructions on base and cord tag **15.00**

Hotpoint (see General Electric)

Kenmore (Sears)

Mixer, "Portable Hand Mixer," early 1940s, Model 322-8220, 5", cream plastic body, single shaft (4½") orig box and booklet **25.00**

Toaster, early 1940s, Model #307-6323-1, two slice automatic pop-up, mechanical clock timing mechanism, rounded chrome body and base, bakelite handles and knobs . **15.00**

Kitchen Aid (Hobart)

Coffee Mill, 1936, Model A-9, 13½" overall, cream metal motor base, sloped sides and adjustment ring at top, clear glass top, open at both ends, black metal screw-on lid, first home coffee grinder **60.00**

Mixer, "Kitchen Aid," 1939, 14 x 12", rounded cream body with heavy aluminum trim and handle, includes screw-down aluminum bowl, wire whisk beater, aluminum meat grinder, and dough hook, looks nearly identical to recent models **50.00**

Knapp-Monarch

Iron, Travel, "Gad-A-Bout," late 1930s, Cat. #403-R, folding chrome and brown handle, flat chrome body, heat indicator, brown zippered bag **12.00**

Mixer, mid 1930s, Cat. #6-501, 9½", white metal motor housing, louvered sides, red plastic open handle, three cup white glass measuring base **20.00**

Popcorn Popper, 1930–40, Cat. #12A-500B, oil type, aluminum body, wire base, domed glass lid with vented sides, walnut handles, measuring cup **20.00**

Toaster, mid 1930s, Cat. #21-501, rounded chrome Art Deco body, flip-flop type, bakelite handles, mechanical opening device **20.00**

Waffle Iron, 1930s, 6" round plates, dessert size. low body, black wooden knobs, dec top **15.00**

Majestic Electric Appliance Corp, San Francisco

Hotcake/Waffle Iron, 1923, reversible 8" round plated, knob on top acts as foot for open two part grill, makes two cakes at once, nickel body, black wood knobs **45.00**

Manning Bowman

Chafing Dish, 1925, Cat. #601, Ser. #K-601, high style Art Deco design, chrome, round tray/hot plate, hot water dish, bowl, and lid, black bakelite handles, three prong hi–lo plug **45.00**

Coffee Percolator, 1920s, Cat. #381/9, 12" chrome Art Deco body, reeded band at neck and above stepped base, part of dining room set consisting of chafing dish and waffle maker **35.00**

Coffee Urn Set (1910–1925) Cat. #C474-8, Ser. #10-30, 15" urn, creamer, sugar, and tray, nickel chrome tapered faceted body, ivory bakelite swing handles, short cabriolle legs **60.00**

Toaster

1926, #1225, nickel body, double wire mechanical turnover doors, bakelite knobs, pierced top, flat prongs **35.00**

1930s, Ser. #11-27, "Meriden Homelectrics," flip-flop type, thin pierced doors and top, tab feet, flat prongs **25.00**

Waffle Iron

1920s, early, Ser. #24, Art. 1605, 7" round plates, nickel body, domed faceted lid, cabriolle legs and attached tray **25.00**

1924–40, Ser. #6060, "Twin-O-Matic," double, high style Art Deco, chrome, round flip-over, (waffle top and bottom) on chrome and bakelite "cradle," heat indicator in middle top, orig booklet **65.00**

1930s, Cat. #1646, Ser. #11-55, 7" round plates, 9½" sq base, high style Art Deco, chrome, stepped bakelite feet, drop handles, reeded edges, top, booklet **30.00**

Merit Made Inc., Buffalo, NY

Toaster, 1930s, Ser. #024146, unusual rounded design, Art Deco flip-flop type, solid body painted silver gray on black metal base, plunger opener on top, both sides open simultaneously, never used . **30.00**

Miracle Electric Co., Chicago
Flour Sifter, electric, 1930s, ivory metal body, push button above blue wooden handle, decal label, unused **35.00**

Mirro
Tea Kettle, 1930–40s, domed shape, flat bottom, polished aluminum, four quart, whistle cover and bakelite handle **20.00**

Montgomery Ward & Company (manufactured for)
Clock Timer, 1940s, cream body, flat swivel base, wind-up with electric plug in back, silver and red (also made in other combinations) **15.00**
Toaster, mid 1930s, Model 9-4KW 2298-B, flip-flop type, sq body, rounded corners, chrome, bakelite handles, mechanical open, dec sides **18.00**

Porcelier Mfg. Co., Greensburg, PA
Breakfast Service, dining room type, 1930s–early 1940s, all items have total porcelain bodies, including handles; bodies are cream colored, basketweave texture, multicolored floral transfer designs, service includes:
Coffee Percolator #5007 .... **55.00**
Creamer and Sugar (two lids), unmarked **30.00**
Sandwich Grill, #5004 .... **45.00**
Toaster, #5002 .... **75.00**
Waffle Iron, # unknown **45.00**
Complete five piece set **250.00**

Royal Rochester (Robeson Rochester, NY)
Coffee Percolator, 1920s, #366 B-29, 10", nickel body over copper, black wooden handles **15.00**
Egg Cooker, "The Rochester," 1912, egg shaped nickel body, flared base, flat prongs, domed lid, int. fitted skillet/pan, sealed element in base, 4 pcs **35.00**

Silex (& Proctor Silex) Philadelphia
Blender, early 1940s, #D2606, cream sq metal base housing one speed motor, push button switch, four cup sq tapered glass top, Art Deco center vertical design and measure, soft black plastic lid **12.00**
Coffee Dripolator, mid 1930s, #550 EC-8, 13" rounded chrome and bakelite hot plate, two piece all glass pot and top, bakelite handle

and stand, glass center, rubber connection center, 3 pcs **18.00**
Iron, "Never Lift," 1935–37, #966-B, high style Art Deco, pop-up mechanical on back of sole plate, work light in handle, attached cord, heat indicator, Proctor **25.00**

Sunbeam (Chicago Flexible Shaft Co.)
Coffee Dripolator, "Coffee Master," 1935–44, 12½", chrome, Art Design on side, bakelite, 2 pcs **20.00**
Iron
Late 1920s–early 1930s, dark green painted metal box with bail handle, fold down front and lift top, cord compartment, decal (Chicago Flexible Shaft Co, 34 Years of Quality), stand, first all-over heat element **40.00**
1940s, "Iron Master," Model #52, 2¾ lb chrome body, steam attachment #52-A, orig boxes, papers, and tags, unused **40.00**
Mixer, "Mixmaster," 1930, Model "K," cream metal body, folding handle on stand, green glass bowl/juicer **40.00**
Toaster
1924, #4, Chicago Flexible Shaft Co., rect bed 5 x 9" on flat "L" Art Deco feet, chrome body, flat horizontal, horizontal flip-flop cage, black handles (also came with round reeded legs) **45.00**
1930s, Model #T-1E, Chicago Flexible Shaft Co., high style Art Deco design, two slice top loader automatic, chrome body, concentric lines, indicated light, bakelite base and handles, includes large rect glass divided relish tray with toaster compartment **65.00**
1932–40, #T-9, high style Art Deco design, two slice top load automatic, rounded chrome body, bakelite handles, round glass tray and liner, rect liner and four glass trays **65.00**

Toastmaster (Waters Center Co., Minneapolis)
Toaster
1927, Model 1-A-1, single slice, mechanical clock mechanism, chrome, Art Deco, thin sq body, one top rounded corner, louvered sides, slightly large base, bakelite controls, first automatic pop-up **80.00**
1929, Model 1-A-3, high style Art Deco, chrome, sq body, one chamfered top end, vertically

fluted design on sides, third pop-up model **35.00**

Toast-O-Lator (Long Island, NY)

Toast-O-Lator, 1938, Model "J" Ser. #49, Art Deco, chrome, tall rectangle with flat sides and top, rounded vertical ends, bakelite base, slot in each end, toast "walks" through past small round window, double mechanical track, off-on switch .. **40.00**

Union Die Casting, Whittier, CA

Can Opener, "Kitchen Pal," 1956, Mod. #58, Ser. #7-2031, bright yellow metal body, chrome trim, orig booklet, first electric can opener, unused **25.00**

United Metal Goods Mfg. Inc.

Coffee Percolator, 1940s, Cat #760, tilting frame, 17" wide, urn shaped body and pierced frame, dec mid body band, emb spout base, ornate handle, indicator light **65.00**

U. S. Manufacturing Co.

Popcorn Popper

Dry popper, 1920–30s, #1, two pc heater in base, lid, hand crank, silver painted metal body with red lid, three red wood vertical dowel legs attached to side **18.00**

Oil, 1920–30s, Model #10, 3 pcs separate heater, pad, and lid, bakelite handles, knobs, hand crank (came in various color combinations) **36.00**

Universal (Landers, Frary & Clark)

Baby Bottle Warmer, 1912–14, #E-9930, 4¾" cylindrical open can like body, nickel, but feet, side wood handle, lid **8.00**

Breakfast Set, porcelain, early 1920–30s, set with cream china bodies, vertical facets, blue and orange floral transfer designs, coffeepot and syrup are chrome mounted, waffle is chrome with pierced stand, drop handle, and china lid insert

Coffee Percolator #E-6927 ...... **60.00**

Creamer and Sugar, cov (LF&C) .. **25.00**

Syrup (LF&C) **20.00**

Waffle Iron, #E-6324 .... **60.00**

Complete set **200.00**

Chafing Dish, 1908–14, #E-940, two quart copper body, hot water pan and lid, faceted base and lid, probably nickel plated originally (add 25% for orig finish,) flat prongs, black wooden handles and knob . **50.00**

Coffee Service, 4 pcs

1912–12, #E-9189, nickel chrome, 14" urn on flattened base, tri-form applied legs, drop reverse bail handles, creamer

and cov sugar, rect tray with rounded corners, applied leaf banding on all parts as well as etched in to glass insert **50.00**

1912–24 #E-9119, nickel chrome, 16½" h classical urn on flared base, creamer, cov sugar, and tray, open handles with flat tops, large glass insert in leg, black wooden handles on spigot **125.00**

1912–24, #E9239, 11" h unusual shape classical but squatty urn, nickel, upturned open scrolled handles, tall flared base on short feet, smaller top flared with wide opening and green depression glass insert, footed creamer, cov sugar, large oval tray **195.00**

Coffee Urn, 15½" h, classical design, nickel, cabriolle legs, tall curved handles, flat tops, lid has large swirled glass insert **35.00**

Sandwich Grill/Waffle Iron, 1940s, #EA-8601, 10 x 5½" plates, two waffles, attached tray with bakelite handles, wheat dec on top, reusable plates **25.00**

Table Top Stove, 1924, (LF&C), Model #E-988, 7" sq, large control with white china selector, chrome and aluminum frame, pierced holder, broiler and rack, four egg poacher, skillet, and lid, black wooden handles **150.00**

Tea Kettle, 1910–20, #E-973, low teapot shape, flared base, flattened top with tall handle and shaped, black wooden holder, top knob .. **45.00**

Toaster

1912–20, flat, pierced top, concave sides, vertically hinged mechanical reversible wire doors, flat base, small wooden handle **60.00**

1913–15, trademark "LMP" in diamond, pat. 1905, no model #, pierced design on spring doors, slender chrome body, flat base, attached tab feet, attached curved warming rack **40.00**

Late 1920s–early 1930s, #E-7542, single slice automatic with mechanical clock mechanism, end opening with pop-out rack, slender chrome sq body, circle dec on sides, good design, Landers

Double Slice **75.00**

Single Slice **50.00**

Waffle Iron, pat. 1916, (LF&C) horizontal type, rect 8 x 4¼" top, nickel, round tapered legs and attached tray, black wooden handles, important two headed cord **75.00**

United Metal Goods Mfg, Inc
  Coffee Maker/Server, 1930s, Model 750, 11½" chrome pot with pierced tulip design surrounding clear glass liner that lights up when coffee is made, black wooden handle and feet **45.00**
Unmarked Appliances. These appliances are totally unmarked and give no clue to manufacturer.
  Bun Warmer, 1930s, 10" round bowl, high style Art Deco, chrome, domed cov, three equally spaced feet and top knob are large red, yellow, and green painted wood balls, removable fitted wire basket **25.00**
  Mixer, small, mid 1930s, 8", green metal encased motor, metal handle, green depression glass measured Vidrio cup **25.00**
  Popcorn Popper, early, close mesh wire basket set in tin, hand crank, black wooden handle and knob, sets atop tin "can" which holds element, attached cord **25.00**
  Sandwich Grill, 1920s, 6 x 17", triple, nickel body, angled legs, tab feet, black wooden handles **25.00**
  Waffle Iron, child's, 1930s, 4" sq, green handle, slender, tall legs ... **25.00**
Waverly Products, Inc., Sandusky, OH
  Iron, "Steam-O-Matic," 1931–44, Model B-300, hammered aluminum body, temperature control, 9 hole plate, black bakelite handle, orig box, paper, and funnel, unused **35.00**
Westinghouse, Mansfield, OH
  Coffee Dripolator, 1940s, Cat. #CM-81, 14" h, black bakelite handles, 2 pcs **20.00**
  Frying Pan, 1911, steel, cord in wooden handle, sits on six legged iron detachable base, 6" d, inverts to make hot plate, first electric frying pan **150.00**
  Hot Plate, 1920s, Cat. #PH-103, 7" round plate, round green porcelainized metal top, hexagonal nickel base, three faceted legs **20.00**
  Iron, "Adjust-O-Matic," 1924, Cat. #LJG 4, early control, heat indicator, black wooden handle, detached cord **25.00**
  Roaster Oven, late 1940s, white metal painted body, aluminum top with window top and gray plastic handle, includes lift-out gray graniteware pan, griddle, three cov and marked glass baking dishes, matching stand with clock timer and storage **50.00**
  Toaster, 1910s, Style #231570, flip-

flop type, nickel body, wire doors, pierced warmer top, cord with china plug **35.00**
  Toaster Stove, June 1904 and 1914, Type "O" Set. #198158-B, 9 x 5" low rect nickel body, removable cabriolle legs, dark metal length-wise strip top surface, serving tray and rack, coiled wire handles, orig box, paper guarantee, first Westinghouse toaster, unused **125.00**
  Waffle Iron, 1905–1921, 9 x 5¼" plates, heavy nickel body, straight legs, mechanical opening front handle, first electric waffle iron found to date **75.00**

ELEPHANTS

Collecting Hints: There is a vast number of elephant shaped or elephant related items. Concentrate on one type of object (toys, vases, bookends, etc.), one substance (china, wood, paper), one chronological period, or one type of elephant—African or Indian. The elephants of Africa and India do differ, a fact not widely recognized by the lay reader.

Perhaps the most popular elephant collectibles center around Jumbo and Dumbo, the Disney character who was a circus outcast and the first flying elephant. The "GOP" material is usually left to the political collector.

Because of the large number of items available, stress quality. Study the market carefully before buying. Elephant collecting is subject to phases of popularity, with its level being modest at the current time.

History: The elephant held a unique fascination to early Americans. Early specimens were shown in barns and moved at night to avoid a free look. The arrival of Jumbo in England, his subsequent purchase by P. T. Barnum, and his removal to America brought elephant mania to new heights.

American zoological parks always have had an elephant as one of their main attractions. The popularity of the circus in the early 20th century also helped draw continual attention to the elephant, through posters, setup, the parade, and center ring.

Hunting elephants was considered "big game" sport; participants included President Theodore Roosevelt. The search always was for the largest known example. It is not unexpected that it is an elephant that dominates the entrance to the Museum of Natural History of the Smithsonian Institution in Washington, D.C.

Television, through shows such as "Wild Kingdom," has destroyed some of the fascination of a first encounter with all real wild animals, the elephant included. The elephant has become so well known that it is, alas, now considered quite commonplace.

Collectors' Club: The National Elephant Collector's Society, 89 Massachusetts Avenue, Box 7, Boston, MA 02115.

Advisor: Richard W. Massiglia.

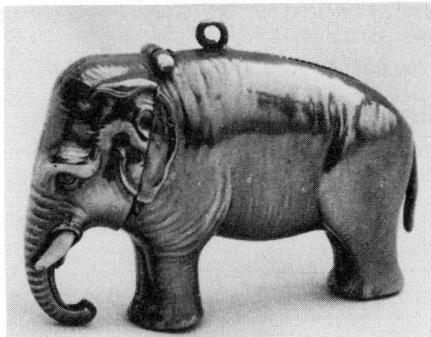

Match Safe, brass, silver plated, ivory tusk, English, unmarked, 2¼", $175.00

Adv, sign, Brown's Jumbo Bread, 15 x 13", tin, diecut, elephant with trunk curled down, blanket on back, c1930 **135.00**
Automata, 3¼ x 4 x 6", cymbal and drum, c1960, made by M & M, Japan **30.00**
Bank, mechanical, cast iron
  Elephant with clown, 5¾" **800.00**
  Jumbo The Elephant **650.00**
Bank, still
  Bisque, 3 x 3½ x 5", Elmer The Elephant, movable trunk, gray, yellow, and red **275.00**
  Ceramic, 5 x 6 x 6", Dumbo, red, gray, and pink, marked "Hagen Renaker Potteries" **200.00**
Book
  Allen, Edward, *Fun By The Ton* **15.00**
  Cobb, Mabel, *Old Phoebe* **12.00**
Bottle Opener, cast iron, elephant sitting on rear legs, curled up trunk **30.00**
Candy Container, GOP Elephant, glass, clear **120.00**
Cartoon Art, Dumbo, Disney Original Animation Art, pastel sketch, 1941 film **700.00**
Charm, ¾", Dumbo, plastic, green, 1940 .... **8.00**
Christmas Ornament
  Blown Glass, 3½", gray elephant, red blanket **80.00**
  Dresden, 3", silver, emb cardboard, Dresden, Germany **130.00**
Figure
  Ceramic
    2" l, 1½" h, shaded gray glaze ... **5.00**

    3½" l, 2¾" h, irid brown–orange, gold applied to ears, marked "Japan" **7.50**
  3 x 3½ x 4", Dumbo, gray, pink ears, yellow hat, Shaw, c1949 . **125.00**
  3½ x 5½ x 5½", Dumbo, sitting, yellow and pink, Shaw **60.00**
  4 x 6 x 5", Dumbo, glazed, seated, marked "Ceramic Kiln," made by Vernon Kiln **125.00**
  Plastic, 1" h, Dumbo, blue and black, Disneykin, Marx, 1960s **12.00**
  Rubber, 5" h, Elmer Elephant, gray, bow tie, and hat, Sieberling **120.00**
  Sterling Silver, sgd "Faberge" **1,650.00**
Jar, 2" d, 3½" h, Jumbo Peanuts, litho tin lid with picture of elephant, elephant on side, Frank Tea & Spice Co, c1930 .... **35.00**
Letter Opener, 7½" l, hollow celluloid, marked "Depose–Germany," c1900 **30.00**
Nodder, 3½" l, 1¾" h, hollow celluloid, gray back and head, pink ears, white belly, silver painted tusks **30.00**
Paperweight, 3½" d, glass, limited edition of 100, Max Erlacher, sgd **250.00**
Pie Bird, figural elephant, c1930 ..... **35.00**
Pinback Button, 1¼", Dumbo, 1941 .. **30.00**
Pitcher, ceramic, Dumbo
  4 x 5 x 6", white and blue, Disney copyright, 1940s **55.00**
  6½ x 8 x 8", marked "Leeds China," 1947, white and pink base marked "Disney/Dumbo" **80.00**
Plate, 4", elephant and baby elephant, Dedham Pottery **350.00**

Bookends, metal base, syrocowood, white elephant standing under palm trees, made in USA, 6½" h, $25.00.

Pole Screen Base, painted black and gilt, surmounted by castles, pr **8,000.00**
Poster, adv, 47 x 58", Lil Nil Cigarette Papers, litho, trumpeting elephant, linen backing **200.00**
Puppet, marionette, 39", plastic and fur,

Bill Baird, used for *Carnival of the Animals,* and *Ed Sullivan Show,* ... **5,500.00**
Record Album, *Dumbo Soundtrack,* three records, 10 x 12" **90.00**
Salt and Pepper Shakers, pr, Noah's Ark, porcelain, hp, gray, pink ears, elephants cuddle, issued by Franklin Mint, Jonathan Goode design **20.00**
Souvenir, celluloid, elephant on top of ball on black base, trunk raised, "Old Orchard, Maine" sticker, marked "Japan" on base **50.00**
Stuffed Animal, 21 x 23", white, red back cov, wood handle, wheels, Steiff, Germany **575.00**
Tobacco Tin Tag, elephant shaped
Jumbo **7.50**
Red Elephant **4.00**
Toy
Pull Toy, 11" h, elephant on wheels, tan mohair, red felt trappings, head moves from side to side when tail is turned, Schuco, Germany **200.00**
Walker
Baby Jumbo, 5" l, 3" h, wood, litho elephant on both sides, hard plastic, movable legs **40.00**
Rider on back, rider carries parasol, spins when elephant walks, W Britain & Sons, 1890 .... **2,250.00**
Umbrella Stand, foot **385.00**
Vase, 15" h, cloisonne, enameled with stylized animals and flowers, turquoise ground, ovoid vase and cov on reverse, pr **2,200.00**
Watch, Republican Campaign type
Bush, '88 .... **30.00**
Limited Edition, red, white, and blue face and strap, black and gold watch design **50.00**

FARM COLLECTIBLES

Collecting Hints: The country look makes farm implements and other items very popular with interior decorators. Often items are varnished or refinished to make them more appealing, but in fact this lowers their value to the serious collector.

Farm items were used heavily; collectors should look for signs of use to add individuality and authenticity to the pieces.

History: Initially farm products were made by local craftsmen—the blacksmith, wheelwright, or the farmer himself. Product designs varied greatly.

The industrial age and the "golden age" of American agriculture go hand in hand. By 1880–1900 manufacturers saw the farm market as an

important source of sales. Farmers demanded quality products, capable of withstanding hard use. In the 1940s urban growth began to draw attention away from the rural areas and consolidation of farms took place. Bigger machinery was developed. Farm collectibles after 1940 have not yet achieved great popularity.

Reference: Lar Hothem, *Collecting Farm Antiques: Identification and Values,* Books Americana, 1982.

Collectors' Club: Cast Iron Seat Collectors Association, RFD #2, Box 40, Le Center, MN 56057.

Museum: Pennsylvania Farm Museum, Landis Valley, PA.

Advertising Mirror, Empire Cream Separator Co, 2¾", oval, celluloid, multicolored, blonde girl, ethnic costume, pink bonnet, white apron, dark green ground, c1900 .... **65.00**
Axe, broad, 8½ x 9⅜", wood handle . **65.00**
Book, *1857 Practical Farrier for Farmers,* 288 pgs **42.50**
Branding Iron, wrought iron, "LazyB" **30.00**
Catalog
McCormick Deering Tractor Model W-30 Parts, 1940 .... **35.00**
Port Huron Threshing Machinery, 1903 .... **30.00**

Egg Shipping Crate, wood, marked "Gardiner Egg Carrier, made by New England Box Co, Boston, Mass," 13¾ x 10¼", $200.00.

Chick Feeder, tin **15.00**
Corn Dryer, wrought iron **15.00**
Corn Planter, marked "Acme" **30.00**
Egg Box, 10 x 13 x 15", pine, forged metal bands on cov and sides **75.00**
Egg Candler, 8" h, tin, kerosene burner, mica window **20.00**
Feed Bag, cotton, black illus of sheep . **7.50**
Flax Comb, 17½" l, wrought iron, ram's horn finials **120.00**

Grain Shovel, wood, carved dec **285.00**
Hay Rake, varnished, 48½" **50.00**
Hinge, barn, wrought iron, strap, 27" . **60.00**
Implement Seat, cast iron
  Bradley's Mower **100.00**
  Hoover & Co **65.00**
Lapel Stud, 1935 International Livestock
  Exposition, 1", enameled brass, agri-
  cultural exhibit building **20.00**
Match Safe, Hudson & Thurber Co,
  Minneapolis, celluloid cov silvered
  brass, multicolored illus of nude
  woman, titled "Love's Repose," prod-
  ucts listed, 1905 copyright **90.00**
Milking Stool, wooden, three short legs **50.00**
Pinback Button
  Brinkler Ranch, 1", multicolored,
    woman in western outfit, feeding
    chickens, c1930 .... **8.00**
  Buerkens Mfg Co, Pella, IA, 1¼", red
    and white, farm wagon within out-
    line of Dutch wooden shoe, c1900 **22.50**
  Imperial Plow, ⅞", multicolored,
    white ground, illus of farmer and
    gentleman discussing the plow, top
    rim inscription "The Imperial Is The
    Best Plow In The World," name
    Bucher & Gibbs Plow Co in red,
    c1898 .... **30.00**
  Increscent Brand Fertilizer, ⅞",
    muilticolored, moon crescent, gold
    shield motif, light green ground,
    c1907 .... **18.00**
  New Idea Manure Spreader, 1",
    multicolored, horsedrawn spreader
    in field, country scene, top rim in-
    scription "At Work In The Field,"
    c1900 .... **75.00**
  Quick-Lite Electric Lantern, 1", gold
    lantern, black ground, pink glow,
    c1920 .... **20.00**
Ruler, folding, International Harvester
  Co, ½ x 4½", celluloid, printed
  monthly calendars for 1909 and
  1910, lists of farm products, black in-
  scriptions on one side, red on reverse **20.00**
Sap Spout, wood, carved **5.00**
Seed Dryer, chestnut frame, pine spin-
  dles, 21 x 43" **75.00**
Sheep Shears, 13¾" l, steel, marked
  "Cast Steel, W P Ward" **20.00**
Shovel, cast iron, wood handle **25.00**
Slide Rule, American Hame and Bit Co,
  ¾ x 6½", celluloid, used to determine
  mouth bits and halter pieces, c1900. **20.00**
Tobacco Drying Basket, 38" sq, woven
  splint, old red paint **150.00**
Wagon Seat, wood, wrought iron trim,
  hinged compartment, 42" **200.00**
Winnow Sieve, wood, punched tin
  sieve **100.00**

FARM TOYS

Collecting Hints: It is best to specialize in a single type of model, e.g., cast iron; models by one specific company; models of one type of farm machinery; or models in one size—1/16 scale being the most popular.

The tractor is the most popular vehicle. Accessories include wagons and trailers, manure spreaders, plows, disks, planters, and cultivators. Harvesting equipment also comes in model form.

History: The vast majority of farm models date from the early 1920s to the present. Manufacturers of farm equipment such as John Deere, International Harvester, Massey-Ferguson, Ford, and White Motors issued models to correspond to their full sized products. These firms contracted with America's leading toy manufacturers, such as Arcade Company, Dent, Ertl, Hubley, Killgore, and Vindex, to make the models.

The early models were cast iron, being replaced later by diecast, aluminum, and plastic. As production models were changed, so too were the toy models. Although most models are made in a scale of 1/16, other scales were used, e.g., 1/12, 1/20, 1/25, 1/32, and 1/50.

Toy manufacturers outside the United States have entered the picture. Firms such as Dinky, Corgi and Lesney produce models of American equipment as well as those of foreign manufacturers, among which are Deutz, Fiat, Leyland, and Porsche.

Limited edition models are being produced today to respond to the growing collector market. Controlled production is keeping their value high.

References: Raymond E. Crilley and Charles E. Burkholder, *Collecting Model Farm Toys of the World, Revised Edition,*Aztex Corporation, 1984; Raymond E. Crilley and Charles E. Burkholder, *International Directory of Model Farm Tractors,* Schiffer Publishing, Ltd, 1985; Dave Nolt, *Farm Toy Price Guide, 1988 Edition,* published by author, 1988; Richard Sonnek, *Dick's Farm Toy Price Guide & Checklist: Tractors and Machinery, 1886–1988,* published by author, 1988.

Periodicals: *Miniature Tractor & Implement,* 1881 Eagley Road, East Springfield, PA 16411; *The Toy Farmer,* R. R. 2, Box 5, LaMoure, ND 58458; *The Toy Tractor Times,* P. O. Box 156, Osage, IA 50461.

Collectors' Club: Ertl Replica Collectors' Club, Highways 136 and 20, Dyersville, IA 52040.

Baler
  International Harvester, diecast, 1/16
    scale, four bales, Ertl, 1967 ...... **18.00**
  John Deere, pressed steel, 1/16 scale,
    plastic teeth, Carter, 1952 .... **80.00**
  Oliver **50.00**

Tru-Scale, pressed steel, 1/16 scale, red, Carter, 1952 .... **45.00**
Bulldozer
  Caterpillar, driver, yellow, Matchbox, 1963 .... **20.00**
  International Harvester, yellow, head-lights, radiator, Ertl, 1960 .... **38.00**
Combine
  Case, diecast, 1/16 scale, plastic reel, Ertl, 1974 .... **75.00**
  Massey Ferguson, diecast, 1/16 scale, yellow wheels, Ertl, 1973 .... **50.00**
  Marx, tin, friction, MIB **25.00**
  White, plastic, 1/24 scale, red and white **80.00**
Combine Gleaner, International Harvester, diecast, 1/32 scale, open reel supports, Ertl, 1966 .... **45.00**
Corn Picker
  John Deere, pressed steel, 1/16 scale, Carter, 1952 .... **100.00**
  Tru-Scale, pressed steel, 1/16 scale, Carter, 1971 .... **70.00**
Corn Sheller, Minneapolis Moline
  Pull Type, decaled, 1/16 scale, rubber tires **95.00**
  Truck Mounted, International Truck chassis, blower tube sock, shovels, corn rake **200.00**
Cream Separator, International Harvester, cast iron, 1/12 scale, black plated bowl and pail, Arcade, 1930 **250.00**
Dirt Scraper, John Deere, diecast, 1/16 scale, hitch, Ertl, 1960 .... **80.00**
Disc
  International Harvester
    Diecast, 1/16 scale, sure-lock hitch blades, Ertl, 1965 .... **20.00**
    Pressed Steel, 1/16 scale, four gang, red, Carter, 1950 .... **65.00**
  Tru-Scale, pressed steel, 1/16, Carter, 1952 .... **30.00**
Elevator, John Deere, pressed steel, 1/16 scale, Carter, 1960 .... **85.00**
Grain Drill
  John Deere, pressed steel, 1/16 scale, Carter, 1960 .... **125.00**
  Tru-Scale, pressed steel, 1/16 scale, Carter, 1972 .... **65.00**
Harrow, tandem disc, Corgi, 1967, MIB **12.00**
Hay Mower, John Deere, diecast, 1/16 scale, Ertl, 1961 .... **35.00**
Horse Trailer, Rice's Beaufort Double Horse Box, Corgi **20.00**
Industrial Crawler
  Caterpillar
    Cast Iron, 7½", closed engine, yellow, Arcade, 1932 .... **800.00**
    Diecast, 1/24 scale, name in casting, Reuhl, 1950 .... **400.00**
  International Harvester
    Cast Iron, 1/16 scale, Arcade, 1940 **450.00**

Diecast, 1/16 scale, blade, orig decal, Ertl, 1960 .... **75.00**
John Deere 440, 95% orig paint, orig box **400.00**
Lionel, plastic, 1/43 scale, 1950 ... **35.00**
Manure Spreader
  Case, plastic, 1/16 scale, MP, 1950 . **75.00**
  John Deere, diecast, 1/16 scale, tin wheels, Ertl, 1960 .... **40.00**
  Minneapolis Moline, aluminum, 1/32, Slik, 1950 .... **60.00**
  New Holland, high sides, Ertl **40.00**
Mower, Tru-Scale, pressed steel, 1/16 scale, Carter, 1970 .... **30.00**
Planter, White **15.00**
Plow
  John Deere
    Diecast, 1/16 scale, Ertl, 1960 ... **40.00**
    Pressed Steel, 1/16 scale, Carter, 1950 .... **75.00**
  McCormick-Deering, cast iron, 7¼", red, yellow wheels, Arcade, 1932 **65.00**
  Tru-Scale, pressed steel, 1/16 scale, Carter, 1970 .... **25.00**
Threshing Machine
  John Deere, cast iron, Arcade, 1930 **125.00**
  McCormick-Deering, cast iron, Arcade, orig decal **100.00**

Tractor, International, made by Ertl Co, metal and plastic, red body, rubber tires, 1/32 scale, $55.00.

Tractor
  Allis Chalmers
    Cast Iron
      6¼", emb name on rear wheels, Arcade, 1940 .... **175.00**
      7", painted driver, Dent, 1940 . **250.00**
    Diecast, 1/16 scale, bar grill, Ertl, 1965 .... **200.00**
    Plastic, 1/25 scale, Beaver Falls Show insert, Yoder **75.00**
  Case
    Diecast, 1/16 scale, Agri King, white, Ertl, 1974 .... **150.00**
    Plastic, 1/16 scale, Casomatic, Johan, 1956 .... **400.00**
  Ford, red, rubber tires, Tootsietoy .. **25.00**

International Harvester, spun cast zinc, 1/16 scale, steerable, AT & T	70.00

John Deere

Cast Iron, 1/16 scale, nickel plated man, rubber wheels, Arcade, 1940 .... **300.00**

Diecast, 1/16 scale, three part hitch, Ertl, 1956 .... **250.00**

Lincoln Massey, 44 .... **95.00**

Massey Ferguson, diecast

1/16 scale, metal wheels, Ertl, 1965 **90.00**

1/32 scale, Britians, 1978 .... **12.00**

Minneapolis Moline

Diecast, 1/25 scale, yellow, Ertl, 1965 .... **85.00**

Rubber, 1/16 scale, red, Auburn, 1950 .... **20.00**

Tru-Scale, diecast, 1/16 scale, Carter, 1975 .... **60.00**

White, diecast, 1/16 scale, red decal **20.00**

Truck

Dodge Farm Truck, Dinky, 1950s .. **25.00**

Ford, Model T Pickup, Tootsietoy, c1916 .... **30.00**

Mack, Farm Hauler, B-Line, Tootsietoy, c1955 .... **28.00**

Stake, diecast, 4¼" l, blue, high sides, open cab, Hubley, c1936 .... **75.00**

Wagon

John Deere

Diecast, 1/16 scale, metal wheels, Ertl, 1960 .... **80.00**

Wood, cast iron gears, 1/16 scale, Arcade, 1940 .... **275.00**

Minneapolis Moline, pressed steel, 1/32 scale, rubber wheels, Slik, 1950 **20.00**

FAST FOOD MEMORABILIA

Collecting Hints: Premiums, made primarily of cardboard or plastic and of recent vintage, are the mainstay of today's fast food collector. Other items sought are advertising signs and posters, character dolls, promotional glasses and trayliners. In fact, anything associated with a restaurant chain is collectible. The most sought after material is from McDonald's.

Collectors should concentrate only on mint items. Premiums should be unassembled or sealed in an unopened plastic bag.

Collecting fast food memorabilia has grown rapidly during the last half of the 1980s. Efforts are underway for a national convention of fast food collectors in 1990. More than ever before, the fast food chains continue to churn out an amazing array of collectibles.

History: During the period just after World War II, the only convenience restaurants were the coffee shops and diners located along America's highways or in the towns and cities. As suburbia grew, its young families created a demand for a faster and less expensive type of food service.

Ray A. Kroc responded by opening his first McDonald's drive-in restaurant in Des Plaines, Illinois, in 1955. By offering a limited menu of hamburgers, french fries, and drinks, Kroc kept his costs and prices down. This successful concept of assembly line food preparation soon was imitated, but never surpassed by a myriad of competitors.

By the mid-1960s the race was on with franchising seen as the new economic frontier. As the competition increased, the need to develop advertising promotions was imperative. A plethora of promotional give-aways entered the scene.

Periodical: *For Here or to Go,* P.O. Box 162281, Sacramento, CA 95816.

Advisor: David Stone.

Note: Prices are for mint condition items sealed in their original wrappers or packages and unassembled.

A & W

Decals, sheet, iron-on, Root Beer Bear and A & W logo, 1977 .... **2.50**

Doll, Root Beer Bear, plush **10.00**

Meal Box, A & W Playtown, folds into A & W Root Beer stand, 1984 ..... **2.00**

Puppet, hand, Root Beer Bear, cloth .. **6.50**

Record, 45 rpm, promotional, "Vic Damone Swings With A & W," 1960s . **17.00**

Straw, The Great Root Beer Bear

Paper Wrapper, 1977 .... **4.00**

Plastic Wrapper, 1982 .... **2.50**

BURGER KING

Three Dimensional

Airplane, "Yumbo Yet," Styrofoam, 1976 .... **4.50**

Clip, "Spokey," for bicycle wheel spokes, colorful, 1981 .... **2.50**

Doll, rag, newer Burger King character **6.50**

Frisbee, plastic

3¾", emb with Burger King character torso **3.00**

9½", features R2D2, C3PO, and Darth Vadar from "Empire Strikes Back," 1981 .... **6.00**

Glider, "King Glider," Styrofoam, 1978 .... **4.00**

Pinback, ¾" d, metal, "Happy Face," eyes made of the Burger King corporate logo **3.50**

Puppet, hand, plastic, full figure
  New King character 1.50
  Old King character 8.00
Ring, plastic, old King character 6.00
Whistle, pickle, green plastic 5.00
Two Dimensional (paper)
  Bookmark, strip of 5, cardboard,
    characters, 1979 . . . .   4.00
  Calendar, 1980 Burger King Calendar,
    "The Year Of The Olympic games,"
    the year the United States did not
    compete in the Soviet Union 6.00
  Card Game, Burger King Rummy, orig
    box, 1978 . . . .   3.50
  Coupon Calendar, 1976 Burger King
    Bicentennial 5.00
  Crown, paper
    Gold metallic finish 1.00
    Jewel-like design, "Have It Your
      Way" slogan 7.00
  Game
    "King Checker Chess Game," 1978   3.50
    "The King Fun Game," board and
      plastic spinner, 1976 . . . .   5.00
  Game Card, "Everybody Wins," 1981   1.50
  Magic Frame Trick, 1982 . . . .   2.00
  Meal Box
    "Burger King Magic Meal," magic
      tricks printed on side, 1981 . . . .   2.50
    "Burger King Restaurant," 1986 . .   2.50
    "Burger King Town Apartments,"
      1986 . . . .   2.00
    "Thundercats," 1986 . . . .   2.50
  Periscope, cardboard, "King Eye
    Spy," 1980 . . . .   2.50
  Pocket, iron-on, King's face, 1978 . .   1.50
  Trading Cards, set of 36, "The Empire
    Strikes Back" scenes, 1981 . . . . . .   16.00
  Transfer Picture, rub-off "King Picture
    Story," 1979 . . . .   2.50
  Valentine, sheet of 6, features Burger
    King "King," 1977 . . . .   4.00

CARL'S JR.

Bookmark, plastic, Happy Star charac-
  ter, 1985 . . . .   2.50
Eraser/pencil top, plastic, standing
  Happy Star character 2.00
Meal Box
  Magnet School, 1988 . . . .   1.50
  Star Flyer, flying saucer, cardboard,
    1985 . . . .   2.50
Puppet, hand, plastic, "Count on Carl's
  Jr.," 1983 . . . .   1.00
Ring, plastic, Happy Star
  Character in center of circle 2.75
  Full Figure of character 2.00
Sticker, puffy, Happy Star, wiggly eyes,
  1984 . . . .   1.50
Sticker Puzzle, Carl's Jr., 1984 . . . .   2.00

Sunglasses, cardboard, star shape, no
  lenses, 1983 . . . .   2.50

DAIRY QUEEN

Meal Box, Hot Doggity, features Dennis
  the Menace 1.50
Puppet, hand, plastic, Dennis the Men-
  ace 1.00
Salt and Pepper Shaker, ceramic, ice
  cream cone shape 5.00
Whistle, plastic, ice cream cone shape   3.50

DOMINOS PIZZA

Figure, set of 3, Noid as boxer, construction worker, and wizard, plastic,
  1988 . . . .   4.50
Toy, 5", Noid, plastic, poseable and
  bendable, 1987 . . . .   5.00

KENTUCKY FRIED CHICKEN

Mask, Colonel Sanders, plastic, early
  1970s 15.00
Meal Box, "Colonel's Kids," featured
  Fog Horn Leghorn, 1987 . . . .   2.00
Menu, Harmen Cafe, "Home of the fa-
  mous Kentucky Fried Chicken," die-
  cut Colonel image on side, mid 1950s   30.00
Nodder, Colonel Sanders, plastic, early
  1970s 10.00

**Doll, Ronald McDonald, cloth, printed,
red, yellow, black, and white, 16½" h,
$6.50.**

McDONALD'S

Three Dimensional
  Bank
    Ceramic, 12", mid 1980s 12.00
    Plastic, McDonaldland, wastebas-
      ket, 1975 . . . .   7.50

Comb, plastic
  Ronald McDonald, 1980 .... **4.00**
  Vroomer Groomer, 1985 .... **2.00**
Cup, "Who Framed Roger Rabbit"
  movie, plastic, 1988 .... **1.00**
Plate, set of 4, melmac, colorful, one
  for each season of the year, 1977 **25.00**
Premium
  "Collector Can," plastic sardine
    can, McDonaldland character in-
    side, 1982 .... **3.00**
  "Tic Tac Mac," plastic, tic tac toe
    game, 1981 .... **5.00**
  Walking Grimace Toy, plastic,
    1974 .... **8.00**
  McDonald's game top, plastic,
    1985 .... **2.00**
  McDonald's "Hello Copter," plas-
    tic, 1986 .... **1.50**
  Ronald McDonald scissors, plastic,
    1982 .... **3.50**
  Ronald McDonald Parachute, plas-
    tic Ronald, paper tube, para-
    chute inside, early 1970s **7.50**
  Grimace Whistle, plastic, 1981 .. **3.50**
Radio, french fry
  1st version, AM, 1977 .... **25.00**
  2nd version, AM/FM, 1977 copy-
    right, released mid 1980s **15.00**
Ring, Ronald McDonald & McBoo
  Halloween, flasher, plastic, 1979 . **5.00**
Ruler
  "Ronald McDonald Ruler," card-
    board, early 1970s **7.50**
  "McMetrics"
    Metal, mid 1970s **5.50**
    Plastic, 1980 .... **3.50**
Toothbrush, Hamburglar, 1985 ..... **4.50**
Two Dimensional
  Book
    Fievel's Boat Trip, features "An
     American Tail" scenes, 1986 .. **2.00**
    Fun in a Bun, activity, hamburger
     shape, 1978 .... **5.00**
  Calendar
    1977, "Ronald McDonald Coloring
     Calendar" **7.50**
    1984, "Ronald McDonald Coloring
     Calendar of the 1984 Olympic
     Games" **4.50**
  Comic
    McDonaldland Comics #101,
     1976 .... **6.50**
    McDonaldland Fun Times, mystery
     issue, 1983 .... **3.00**
  Folder, "Back to School Mc-
    Sportsquiz," 1974 .... **5.00**
  Fun Club Kit, Ronald McDonald,
    membership card, certificate, sta-
    tionary, secret message decoder,
    iron-on decal, puzzle page, and 9
    x 12" printed envelope, 1977 .... **20.00**

Game
  Card, McDonald's Funny Rummy,
    1983 .... **5.00**
  Ring Toss, Ring Around Ronald,
    1978 .... **3.50**
Happy Meal Box
  Giggles & Games, 1982 .... **3.00**
  Lego Building Set, 1984 .... **2.50**
  Mac Tonight, 1988 .... **1.00**
  Star Trek, set of 6, based on first
    movie, 1979 .... **30.00**
Map, Ronald McDonald Map of the
  Moon, US landing on the Moon
  commemoration, 1969 .... **15.00**
Puzzle
  McDonald's Big Mac, folding, 1985 **1.50**
  McDonaldland, 14 x 9", 1978 ... **6.00**
Song Sheet Trayliner, "McFavorite
  Clown," 1974 .... **10.00**
Trading Card, set of 24, San Francisco
  49ers football team, 1986 .... **10.00**
Toy
  McDonald's Colorforms, playset
    premium, 1986 .... **2.00**
  McDonald's Time Machine Col-
    oring Board, 1986 .... **2.00**
  Ronald McDonald's Fossil Photos
    Magic Slate, 1986 .... **1.50**
  Ronald McDonald Magic Pad,
    1976 .... **2.50**
Valentine, strip of 6, McDonaldland
  characters, 1978 .... **4.00**

WENDY'S

Meal Box, "The Good Stuff Gang,"
  1988 .... **1.50**
Puppet, hand, Wendy girl character .. **1.00**

FIESTA WARE

Collecting Hints: Buy pieces without any cracks, chips, or scratches whenever possible. Fiesta ware can be identified by bands of concentric circles.

History: Fiesta ware is colorful pottery dinnerware made by the Homer Laughlin China Company. It was designed by Frederick Read. Production started in 1936. Fiesta ware was redesigned in 1969 and discontinued in 1972. In 1986 it was reintroduced.

References: Linda D. Farmer, *The Farmer's Wife's Fiesta Inventory & Price Guide*, privately printed, 1984; Sharon and Bob Huxford, *The Collectors Encyclopedia of Fiesta with Harlequin and Riviera, Sixth Edition,*Collector Books, 1987.

Ashtray, yellow **25.00**

Bowl, fruit, cobalt blue, 11⅝"d, 2¾"h, $90.00.

Bowl
 4¾"
  Cobalt Blue **12.00**
  Ivory **10.00**
  Red **12.00**
  Rose **20.00**
 5½"
  Red **22.00**
  Rose **28.00**
 6"
  Cobalt Blue **20.00**
  Forest Green **25.00**
  Turquoise **16.00**
 8½", Forest Green **30.00**
 9½", Turquoise **18.00**
 11¾", fruit
  Ivory **90.00**
  Light Green **90.00**
Candlesticks, pr, bulbous
 Light Green **32.00**
 Red **44.00**
Canister, medium, yellow, green lid .. **135.00**
Carafe, turquoise **95.00**
Casserole, cov, ivory **50.00**
Chop Plate, 16"
 Forest Green **16.00**
 Ivory **18.00**
Compote, 12"
 Cobalt Blue **40.00**
 Ivory **60.00**
Cream Soup, charcoal gray **24.00**
Creamer
 Cobalt Blue **7.50**
 Forest Green **15.00**
 Turquoise **10.00**
Creamer and Sugar, individual size, yel-
 low **80.00**
Cup and Saucer
 Chartreuse **17.50**
 Charcoal Gray **22.00**
 Cobalt Blue **18.00**
 Light Green **16.00**
 Red **22.00**
Demitasse Cup and Saucer, cobalt blue **28.00**

Egg Cup
 Cobalt Blue **40.00**
 Ivory **30.00**
 Light Green **24.00**
 Turquoise **35.00**
 Yellow **35.00**
Gravy Boat
 Charcoal Gray **40.00**
 Forest Green **42.50**
 Ivory **20.00**
 Rose **40.00**
 Yellow **20.00**
Jug, two pint
 Chartreuse **55.00**
 Red **35.00**
 Turquoise **40.00**
Mug, Tom & Jerry
 Forest Green **42.00**
 Ivory **35.00**
 Rose **55.00**
 Turquoise **25.00**
 Yellow **30.00**
Mustard, cov, cobalt blue **80.00**
Pitcher
 Disc, juice
  Red **65.00**
  Yellow **32.00**
 Disc, water
  Light Green **50.00**
  Ivory **55.00**
  Red **70.00**
Plate
 6", dessert
  Charcoal Gray **25.00**
  Ivory **5.00**
 7½", bread and butter
  Forest Green **8.00**
  Red **6.50**
 8", salad
  Charcoal Gray **7.50**
  Cobalt Blue **8.00**
 9", luncheon
  Cobalt Blue **7.50**
  Forest Green **9.00**
  Ivory **5.00**
  Red **9.00**
  Turquoise **5.00**
 10", dinner
  Cobalt Blue **9.00**
  Forest Green **10.00**
  Ivory **13.00**
  Red **12.00**
  Yellow **9.00**
 10½", grill, ivory **9.00**
Platter, oval
 Rose **30.00**
 Yellow **16.00**
Relish Tray
 Light Green **90.00**
 Yellow **85.00**
Salt and Pepper Shakers, pr
 Light Green **12.00**

Forest Green	35.00
Red	16.00
Turquoise	12.00
Saucer	
Light Green	3.00
Red	3.50
Rose	2.75
Turquoise	3.00
Soup Bowl, deep	
Turquoise	16.00
Yellow	16.00
Stack Set, cov, yellow, green, navy, and	
red	175.00
Sugar, cov, yellow	20.00
Syrup, green	135.00
Teapot	
Forest Green	130.00
Rose	125.00
Tumbler	
Juice	
Ivory	15.00
Red	40.00
Rose	35.00
Water, 10 oz	
Light Green	23.00
Yellow	22.00
Utility Tray, ivory	20.00

FIREHOUSE COLLECTIBLES

Collecting Hints: It was fashionable for a period of time to put a date on the back of a fireman's helmet. This date is usually the date the fire company was organized, not the date the helmet was made.

Firehouse collectibles is a very broad area of collecting. The older, scarcer collectibles, such as helmets and firemarks, command high prices. The newer collectibles, e.g., cards and badges, are more reasonably priced. This area of collecting is continually growing and expanding.

History: The volunteer fire company has played a vital role in the protection and social growth of many towns and rural areas. Paid professional firemen are usually found in large metropolitan areas. Each fire company has prided itself on equipment and uniforms. Annual conventions and parades give the individual fire companies a chance to show off their equipment. These conventions and parades have produced a wealth of firehouse related collectibles.

Reference: Mary Jane and James Piatti, *Firehouse Collectibles*, The Engine House, 1979.

Museums: There are many museums devoted to firehouse collectibles. Large collections are housed at: Insurance Company of North America (I.N.A.) Museum, 1600 Arch St., Philadelphia,

PA; Oklahoma State Fireman's Association Museum, Inc., 2716 NE 50th St., Oklahoma City, OK; and San Francisco Fire Dept. Pioneer Memorial Museum, 655 Presidio Ave., San Francisco, CA.

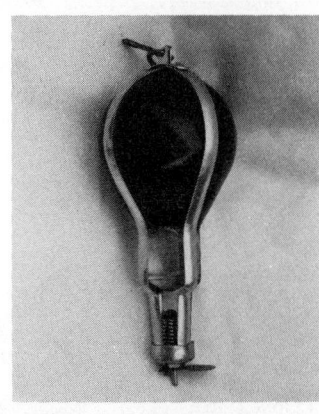

Fire Extinguisher, Red Comet, marked "Red Comet Inc, Littleton, Colorado," $30.00.

Advertising	
Booklet, American Fire Extinquisher Co, Boston, 60 pgs, 1967	45.00
Poster, Hydropult–Most Efficient Fire Engine in the World, scene of fire at Palace Garden, Oct, 1860, 11 x 14", framed	175.00
Sign, 13 x 28", Lux Fire Extinguishing Equipment, porcelain, double sided, multicolored illus of motorboat	75.00
Trade Card, Buckeye Force Pumps, negro pumping water to put out house fire, Springfield, OH	24.00
Alarm Box, cast iron, pedestal, emb "City of Chicago," restored	275.00
Badge	
1½", diecut, silver plate, "Vigilance," spear on shield	40.00
2¾", celluloid, red helmet, Kearny & Trecker District 7	20.00
Bell, 12", brass	75.00
Belt, black leather, white lettering "Rescue No 1"	65.00
Book	
Ahrens–Fox: The Rolls–Royce of Fire Engines, Haas, 1982, paperback, 159 pgs	25.00
Brief History of the Massachusetts Charitable Fire Society, Sprague, 1893	36.00
1917 New York Fire Dept History, hardcover, 218 pgs, 8 x 10"	5.00
Bucket, galvanized tin, red lettering, "Fire Only"	35.00

Children's Book, *The Mickey Mouse Fire Brigade,* Whitman, 1936, hard cover, 7 x 10", color cov, black and white illus 80.00

Daguerreotype, fireman, hat, horn, and uniform, tinted 500.00

Engine House Gong, Gamewell
6", key wind, chrome 100.00
10", pull chain, aluminum 125.00

Engine Name Plate
Ahrens–Fox 10.00
LaFrance 15.00
Mack Trucks, bulldog 20.00

Extinguisher, glass
Bottle type, orig label, holder, and box, Larkin 75.00
Hand grenade type, Harden, blue glass, patent August 8, 1871 ..... 90.00

Fire Engine, pumper
Dodge, 1932 ....3,500.00
Mack, 1936, Hale pump 4,000.00

Lantern, Goodwill Fire Co, brass, etched globe, King 450.00

Lapel Stud, ⅞", red, white, and blue, celluloid, "Woolf's Best Made Clothing," 1890 .... 15.00

Paperweight, 4", cast iron, hat shape, insurance co adv 37.50

Photograph, negative, glass, Chicago Fire Dept #6 pumper 40.00

Pinback Button
⅞"
Fire Department Ambulance, white, red lettering, red cross, c1920 .... 15.00
Fire Prevention Week, red and white, paper back with funeral home text, c1940 .... 12.00
Junior Fire Prevention League, red and white, c1940 .... 15.00
1"
Firemen's Booster, black and white pumper, red inscription, c1900   20.00
Grinnel Automatic Sprinkler, celluloid, brass frame, early 1900s   18.00
Harrisburg Firemen's Soldiers' Monument, June 21, 1924 dedication 10.00
1¼", celluloid
Eastern Association of Fire Chiefs, gold and brown, crossed hose nozzles, c1940 .... 12.00
Fire Dept Day, multicolored portrait, blue and white rim, 1915 .   24.00
Fire Scene, silver horse drawn pumper, black ground, early 1900s .   24.00
Good Will Ambulance, black and white, 1900s horse drawn ambulance 15.00
Greensburg V.F.D., black picture, bright gold ground, 1940s PA celebration 10.00

Hose Co #2, white, red, blue, and fleshtones, black lettering, 1904   20.00
Iowa Firemen's Assn, red, white, and blue, c1940 .... 10.00
Park Extension, black and white photo of 1938 ambulance 7.50
Portrait, fireman, multicolored, white ground 18.00
Rainbow Fire Company, multicolored, white ground, 1928 department outing 10.00
Rescue Scene, multicolored, firemen rescuing baby, early 1900s   28.00

Postcard, Chemical and Hose Co No 2, Johnstown, PA, photograph of horse drawn wagon in front of fire house .   12.00

Puzzle, slice type, Milton Bradley Co, orig 8 x 9" box, c1913–35 .... 75.00

Stevensgraph, titled "For Life or Death," fire engine rushing to burning house, orig mat and frame 325.00

Toy
10½", metal, emb "Fire Engine No. 526," Hubley, c1936 .... 65.00
13½", rubber tires, removable hose reel, bell, six firemen, steam boiler, 1936, Arcade 110.00
17½", red and yellow, sharply streamlined skirted fenders, white ladders, open cargo back, Buddy L, 1940 .   38.00
35", extension ladder, red body, silver painted ladders, yellow removable saddle, leatherette seat, crank, orig decals, Buddy L, 1945 .... 65.00

FISHING COLLECTIBLES

Collecting Hints: The fishing collectibles category is rapidly expanding as the rare items are becoming more expensive and harder to locate. New categories include landing nets, minnow traps, bait boxes, advertising signs, catalogs, and fish decoys used in ice spearing. Items in original containers and in mint condition command top prices. Lures that have been painted over the original decoration or rods that have been refinished or broken have little collector value.

Early wooden plugs (before 1920), split bamboo fly rods made by the master craftsmen of that era, and reels constructed of German silver with special detail or unique mechanical features are the items most sought by advanced collectors.

The number of serious collectors is steadily increasing as indicated by the membership in the "National Fishing Lure Collectors Club" which has approximately 2,000 active members.

History: Early man caught fish with crude spears

and hooks made of bone, horn, and flint. By the middle 1800s metal lures with hooks attached were produced in New York State. Later, the metal was curved and glass beads added for greater attraction. Spinners with wood-painted bodies and glass eyes appeared around 1890. Soon after, wood plugs with glass eyes were being produced by many different makers. A large number of patents were issued in this time period covering developments of hook hangers, body styles, and devices to add movement of the plug as it was drawn through the water. The wood plug era lasted up to the mid-1930s when plugs constructed of plastic were introduced.

With the development of casting plugs, it became necessary to produce fishing reels capable of accomplishing that task with ease. Reels first appeared as a simple device to hold a fishing line. Improvements included multiplying gears, retrieving line levelers, drags, clicks, and a variety of construction materials. The range of quality in reel manufacture varied considerably. Collectors are mainly interested in reels made with quality materials and workmanship, or those exhibiting unusual features.

Early fishing rods were made of solid wood which were heavy and prone to break easily. By gluing together strips of tapered pieces of split bamboo a rod was fashioned which was light in weight and had greatly improved strength. The early split bamboo rods were round with silk wrappings to hold the bamboo strips together. With improvements in glue, fewer wrappings were needed, and rods became slim and lightweight. Rods were built in various lengths and thicknesses depending upon the type of fishing and bait used. Rod makers' names and models can usually be found on the metal parts of the handle or on the rod near the handle.

References: Jim Brown, *Fishing Reel Patents of The US, 1838–1940;* published by author; Clyde A Harbin, *James Heddon's Sons Catalogues,* CAH Enterprises, 1977; Art and Scott Kimball, *Collecting Old Fishing Tackle,* Aardvark Publications, Inc., 1980; Art and Scott Kimball, *Early Fishing Plugs of the U. S. A.,* Aardvark Publications, Inc., 1985; Art and Scott Kimball, *The Fish Decoy,* Aardvark Publications, Inc.; Carl F. Luckey, *Old Fishing Lures and Tackle: Identification and Value Guide, Volume I and II,* Books Americana; Albert J. Munger, *Those Old Fishing Reels,* privately printed, 1982; J. L. Smith, *Antique Rods and Reels,* Gowe Printing, 1986; Richard L. Streater, *Streater's Reference Catalog of Old Fishing Lures, Volume I and II*; Steven K. Vernon, *Antique Fishing Reels,* Stackpole Books, 1984.

Collectors' Club: National Fishing Lure Collectors Club, P. O. Box 1791, Dearborn, MI 48121.

Museums: National Fishing Tackle Museum, Ar-

cadia, OK; American Fishing Tackle Mfg. Assn. Museum, Arlington Heights, IL; Sayner Museum, Sayner, WI.

Advisor: Bob Greenbaum

REPRODUCTION ALERT: Lures and fish decoys.

Advertising
Calendar, 14 x 18", Bristol Steel Rod Co, color, 1935	**55.00**
Catalog, Heddon Co, color illus, 1934	**45.00**
Sign, 30 x 50", from old store, wood, carved fish, handmade, painted, black and white	**235.00**
Sign, South Bend Co, boy holding stringer of fish	**65.00**

Bobber
Hand carved and painted float, 8" l, tapered ends, orange, green, white, and red stripes	**65.00**
Panfish float, 5" l, hp, black, red, and white stripes	**10.00**
Pike float, 12" l, hp, yellow, green, and red stripes	**24.00**

Creel, wicker, ribbed bow front, straight back, 12" l, 8" h, 6" d, $18.00.

Creel
Crushed willow, 14 x 9 x 7", leather bound, form fit	**24.00**
Wicker, center lid hole, early 1900	**55.00**

Decoy
Ice King, 7" l, perch, wood, painted, Bear Creek Co	**65.00**
Leroy Howell, 6½" l, fish, gray body, black metal fins	**110.00**
Randall, 6" l, cast aluminum, green painted scale	**20.00**

Lure, plug, wood
Creek Chub Co
Baby beetle, yellow and green wings	**35.00**
Jointed Pikie, perch finish, glass eyes, orig box, #700	**18.00**

Mouse, black, short fat body, pressed eyes 12.00

Heddon Co
Minnow, rainbow color, fat body, glass eyes, L-rig, #150 .... 25.00
Musky Crazy Crawler, yellow and red, pressed eyes 38.00
King Bassor, red, gold spot, glass eyes 30.00
Spin diver, white, red head and tail, glass eyes, L-Rig 120.00
Zig Wag, shiner scale finish, glass eyes, L-Rig, two hooks 15.00

Shakespeare Co
Baby Frog, pop eye 15.00
Mouse, 3⅝″ l, white and red, thin body, glass eyes 27.00
Strike-It Lure, green, yellow, and red spots, glass eyes 40.00

South Bend Co
Bass Oreno, 3½″ l, frog spot color 15.00
Panatella, green crackleback finish, glass eyes, boxed 45.00

Miscellaneous
Al Foss Oriental Wiggler, white, glass eyes, molded hook, #3 .. 25.00
Carters Bestever, 3″ l, white and red, pressed eyes 8.00
Keeling Little Tom, red, green, and black spotted 12.00

Paw Paw
Sucker, perch finish, tack eyes . 27.00
Underwater Minnow, green and black, tack eyes, three hook . 15.00

Minnow Trap
Checotah Okla Pat, glass, camp type, tinted blue and green 45.00
Hand made, 12 x 10 x 10″, metal and mesh, hinged door 32.00
Shakespeare, glass, pale green, metal lid, emb name, l gal 85.00

Reel
H L Leonard, Pat #191813, 4″ d, salmon, German silver and hard rubber, marked 475.00
Hardy Perfect Fly Reel, 3⅜ x 1¼″, English 145.00
Hendryx, raised pillar type multiply-ing, nickel over brass, fancy han-dle, horn knob, two buttons on back plate drag/click 25.00
Horton Mfg Co, #25, Blue Grass Sim-plex 165.00
Meisselbach Co, tripart #580, cast-ing, nickel plated brass 25.00
Pflueger Summit, Model 1993, level wind casting, boxed 20.00
South Bend, #1131A, casting, shiny finish, orig box 15.00
Union Hardware co, raised pillar type, nickel and brass 20.00
Winchester, Model #1135, fly, black finish 60.00

Rod, Split Bamboo Fly
Hardy, 7′ l, 2 pc, one tip, English .. 200.00
Heddon Co, 5½′ l, casting, nickel sil-ver fittings, fish decal brown wraps, bag and tube 35.00
Horrocks & Ibbotson, 9′ l, 3 pc, two tips, maroon wraps 40.00
Orvis Impregnated Battenkill, 8½′ l, two tips, cloth bag, aluminum tube 235.00
Shakespeare Co, Premier Model, 9′ l, 3 pcs, two tips, red silk wrappings, cloth bag, metal tube 55.00
Union Hardware, Kingfisher, 90″ l, salt water boat rod, dark brown wraps 25.00

FLAG COLLECTIBLES

Collecting Hints: Public Law 829, 77th Con-gress, approved December 22, 1942, describes a detailed set of rules for flag etiquette. Collectors should become familiar with this law.

The amount of material on which the Ameri-can flag is portrayed is limitless. Collectors tend to focus on those items on which the flag enjoys a prominent position.

History: The Continental or Grand Union flag, consisting of 13 alternate red and white stripes with a British Union Jack in the upper left corner, was first used on January 1, 1776, on Prospect Hill near Boston. On June 14, 1777, the Conti-nental Congress adopted a flag design similar to the Continental flag, but with the Union Jack replaced by a blue field with thirteen stars. The stars could be arranged in any fashion. Historical documentation to support the claim that Betsy Ross made the first Stars and Stripes is lacking.

Reel, casting, Pennell Reel Co, Phila, 40 yard line capacity, all brass, 1½″ d, $15.00.

On January 13, 1794, Congress voted to add two stars and two stripes to the flag in recognition of Vermont and Kentucky joining the Union. On April 18, 1818, when there were 20 states, Congress adopted a law returning to the original 13 stripes and adding a new star for each state admitted. The star would be added on the July 4th following admission. The 49th star, for Alaska, was added July 4, 1959; the 50th star, for Hawaii, was added July 4, 1960.

Reference: Boleslow and Marie-Louis D'Otrange Mastai, *The Stars and Stripes: The American Flag As Art And As History From The Birth Of The Republic To The Present,* Alfred Knopf, 1973.

Collectors' Clubs: Flag Research Center, 3 Edgehill Road, Winchester, MA 01890; North American Vexillological Association, 3 Edgehill Road, Winchester, MA 01890.

Museums: State capitals in northern states; Hardisty Flag Museum, Hardisty, Alberta, Canada; Tumbling Waters Museum of Flags, Prattville, AL.

Advisor: Richard Bitterman.

FLAGS

29 star, 7 x 10″, parade flag, coarse cotton material, Great Star pattern, used during Mexican–American War, discoloted **125.00**
36 star
  21½ x 36″, parade flag, mounted on stick, five point star design, star pattern of 6,6,6,6,6,6 .... **85.00**
  25 x 22″, parade flag, printed muslin **85.00**
37 star, 16 x 24″, parade flag, 1867–1877, muslin, all printed **40.00**
38 star, 12½ x 22″, coarse muslin, mounted on stick, star pattern of 6,7,6,6,7,6 .... **12.00**
42 star, four flags on swatch, direct from flag manufacturer, uncut, were to be 11½ x 16¾″ when cut up and mounted on a stick, flag makers prepared banners with 42 stars during the winter of 1889 for adoption on July 4, 1890; however, a last minute addition on July 3 of Idaho as a state made 43 stars necessary, so these banners never made it; $20 per flag on fabric swatch **100.00**
44 star, 3½ x 2¼″, child's parade type, pattern of 8,7,7,7,7,8 and five point star **15.00**
45 star, 32 x 47″, 1896–1908, printed on silk, bright colors, black heading and no grommets **75.00**
46 star, 4 x 5′, 1908–1912, stars sewn on, Oklahoma **35.00**
48 star, 5¾ x 4½″, 1912–1959, printed

on heavy canvas-type material, used on D-Day in Infantry invasion, men wore them under the camouflage net on their helmets **47.00**
49 star, 4 x 5¾″, 1959–1960, child's parade flag, silk, wood stick, Alaska **18.00**

Certificate, Francis Scott Key Memorial Association, framed, 1908, 14½ x 11½″, $25.00.

FLAG RELATED

Catalog, Detra Flag Company, Catalog #24, 6½ x 9″, 1941, NY and Los Angeles **40.00**
China and Glass
  Button
    ½″ d, glass dome, flag printed inside, 6 mounted on card **12.00**
    1¾″ d, horse button, glass dome with eagle and flag **18.00**
  Magic Lantern Slide, 42 star flag, c1889, hand tinted, mounted in wood **30.00**
  Magnifying Glass, pocket, ¾ x 1¼″, oval, Voorhees Rubber Mfg Co adv, American flag artwork **37.00**
  Plate
    10″ d, ''Washington's Headquarters, Newburg, NY, 1783–1883,'' crossed flags under house, brown printing on cream plate **25.00**
    1904, St. Louis World's Fair, Washington, Jefferson, Lafayette and Napoleon's faces, very colorful . **120.00**
Fabric
  Advertising Ribbon, Leonards Spool Silk, Northampton, MA, silk **20.00**
  Armand, WWII, 48 star flag, worn by paratrooper on D-Day invasion, two safety pins **45.00**
  Bandanna, 22 x 25″, silk, flag inside wreath of 36 stars **110.00**

Handkerchief, WWI, flags of US and France, embroidered
  "A Kiss from France" **5.00**
  "Souvenir France 1919" **5.00**
  "To My Dear Sweetheart" **5.00**
Scarf, 17 x 15", silk, Chicago 1893 Expo, panorama of Expo overlaying American flag **45.00**

Plate, 1904, St Louis Fair, commemorating Washington, Jefferson, Lafayette, and Napoleon, $55.00.

Metal
  Badge, Foresters of America, with red, white and blue ribbon **4.00**
  Clock, God Bless America, mantel, WWII vintage, small American flag waves back and forth as second hand, Howard Miller Mfg, very colorful and hokey **90.00**
  Match Box, 1½ x 2¾", Civil War period, emb, picture of Stars and Stripes on one side, Miss Columbia on reverse **65.00**
  Pin Back, "Our Flag" **3.00**
  Stickpin
    Celluloid, American flag, 48 stars, advertising, S A Cook for US Senator **4.00**
    Metal, ⅜ x⅝", 13 stars, c1925, 2" long pin **4.00**
  Token, 3¾" d, "The Dix Token Coin," Civil War, commemorates the order of General John Adams Dix, Jan 29, 1861, "If anyone attempts to haul down the American flag, shoot him on the spot," copper-colored coin, picture of "The flag of our Union" on one side and quote on the other **10.00**
Paper
  Advertising Trade Card
    Hub Gore, 3½ x 6¼", Uncle Sam holding shoe, saying "Hub Gore Makers of Elastic For Shoes, It Was Honored at the World's Fair of 1893" **9.00**
    Major's Cement, 3 x 4¼", two

American flags decorating display of 125 lb weights holding suspended object, full color, adv "Major's Leather Cement—For Sale By Druggists and Crockery Dealers" **9.00**
Merrick's Thread, 2¾ x 4½", two infant children, one beating Civil War type drum, other waving flag, titled "Young America" . . . **4.00**
Certificate, Betsy Ross Flag Association, 1917, serial #38181, Series N, 12 x 16", C H Weisgerber painting **38.00**
Envelope
  Civil War, angry eagle with shield hanging from his mouth and ribbon that reads "Liberty or Death," 34 large stars going around all four edges; each state has its name within its own star **28.00**
  Printed semblances of Stars and Stripes with 45 stars covering address side **20.00**
Postcard
  Printed semblances of Stars and Stripes covering address side, picture of Wm H Taft for President **15.00**
  Printed semblances of Stars and Stripes covering address side, picture of Wm H Taft for President, July 4, 1908, 46 stars, used **18.00**
Poster, 14 x 29", lithograph, "History of Old Glory," Babbitt soap giveaway **145.00**
Print, Currier and Ives, "The Star Spangled Banner," #481, 11¼ x 15½" **165.00**
Sheet Music
  "America Forever March," E T Paull Music Co, Columbia draped in flag, shield, and eagle **30.00**
  "Miss America," two step by J Edmund Barnum, lady with stars, red and white striped dress, large flowing flag **20.00**
  "Stars & Stripes Forever March," John Phillip Sousa portrait in upper left hand corner, Old Glory in center, published by John Church Co **20.00**
  "The Triumphant Banner," E T Paull **25.00**
Song Sheet, published by Chas Magnus, NY, 5 x 8"
  "The Female Auctioneer," lady dressed in costume, waving flag **30.00**
  "The Flag with The 34 Stars," six verses and chorus, illus of soldiers marching with hand colored flag **35.00**

"Traitor Spare That Flag," four verses by Rev J P Lundy, illus of Columbia and her shield, waving flag **35.00**
Thread Box, cov, black lacquer finish, decal, picture of spool of white thread and American flag, marked "Use Merricks Six Cord Thread For Hand and Machine Sewing"
2½ x 1½" **14.00**
3 x 1¾" **18.00**

FOOTBALL CARDS

Collecting Hints: Condition is a key factor. Buy cards that are in very good condition, i.e., free from any creases and damaged corners. When possible strive to acquire cards in excellent to mint condition. Rob Erbe's *The American Premium Guide To Baseball Cards* (Books Americana, 1982) photographically illustrates in the introduction how to determine the condition of a card. What applies to a baseball card is equally true for a football card.

The football card market is just beginning to develop. Prices still are modest. Develop a collecting strategy, such as cards related to one year, one player, Heisman trophy winners, or one team. There are large numbers of cards available; a novice collector can be easily overwhelmed.

History: Football cards have been produced since the 1890s. However, it was not until 1933 that the first bubble gum football card appeared in the Goudey Sport Kings set. In 1935 National Chicle of Cambridge, Massachusetts, produced the first full set of gum cards devoted exclusively to football.

Both Leaf Gum of Chicago and Bowman Gum of Philadelphia produced sets of football cards in 1948. Leaf discontinued production after their 1949 issue. Bowman Gum continued until 1955. Topps Chewing Gum entered the market in 1950 with its college stars set. Topps became a fixture in the football card market with its 1955 All-American set. From 1956 through 1963 Topps printed a card set of National Football League players, combining them with the American Football League players in 1961.

Topps produced sets with only American Football League players from 1964 to 1967. The Philadelphia Gum Company made National Football League card sets during this period. Beginning in 1968 and continuing to the present, Topps has produced sets of National Football League cards, the name adopted by the merger of the two leagues. Topps' only competition during this time came in 1970 and 1971 from Kellogg's Cereal who issued sets of football related cards.

Reference: Dr. James Beckett and Dennis W.

Eckes, *The Sport Americana Football, Hockey, Basketball and Boxing Card Price Guide #5*, Edgewater Books, 1987.

Periodicals: *Current Card Prices*, P. O. Box 480, East Islip, NY 11730; *Sports Collectors Digest*, 700 E. State Street, Iola, WI 54990.

Advisor: Michael R. Moyer.

Topps, NFL Leaders, 1978, Frank Corral and Pat Leahy, $.10.

Bell Brand
1959
    Common card **4.00**
    Sid Gilman **5.00**
1960
    Common card **5.00**
    Gene Selawski **120.00**
Bowman Gum Company
1948
    Common card **2.25**
    Sid Luckman **18.00**
1950
    Common card **1.75**
    Y.A. Tittle **20.00**
1951
    Common card **1.50**
    Norm Van Brocklin **12.00**
1952
    Common card
      Large **2.50**
      Small **1.25**
    Tom Landry
      Large **50.00**
      Small **30.00**
1955
    Common card **1.00**
    Doak Walker **5.00**
Fleer Gum Company
1960
    Common card .... **.35**
    Ron Mix **2.00**
1961
    Common card .... **.30**
    Jim Brown **11.00**

1962
  Common card .... .35
  Don Maynard 3.00
Kellogg's Cereal
1970
  Common card .... .25
  Gale Sayers 1.50
1971
  Common card 1.00
  Bob Griese 3.50
Leaf Gum
1948
  Common card 3.00
  Bobby Layne 2.00
1949
  Common card 2.00
  John Lujack 10.00
National Chicle Company
1935
  Common card 12.50
  Bronco Nagurski 400.00
Philadelphia Gum Company
1964
  Common card .... .25
  Merlin Olsen 12.00
  Don Meredith 5.00
1965
  Common card .... .25
  Paul Warfield 6.00
1966
  Common card .... .20
  Fran Tarkenton 3.75
1967
  Common card .... .20
  Bart Starr 2.50
Topps Chewing Gum Inc
1950
  Common card 1.25
  Darryl Royal 12.00
1951
  Common card .... .40
  Bill Wade 2.00
1955
  Common card .... .75
  Four Horsemen 20.00
  Jim Thorpe 15.00
1956
  Common card .... .50
  Lenny Moore 5.00
1957
  Common card .... .50
  John Unitas 15.00
1958
  Common card .... .30
  George Blanda 3.50
1959
  Common card .... .30
  Jim Brown 12.00
1960
  Common card .... .25
  Chuck Bednarik 2.00

1961
  Common card .... .25
  John Brodie 7.00
1962
  Common card .... .20
  Mike Ditka 6.50
1963
  Common card .... .20
  Willie Wood 3.00
1964
  Common card .... .25
  Len Dawson 4.50
1965
  Common card .... .75
  Jack Kemp 18.00
1966
  Common card .... .20
  George Blanda 3.50
1967
  Common card .... .20
  Ben Davidson 1.50
1968
  Common card .... .15
  Joe Namath 9.00
1969
  Common card .... .15
  Brian Piccolo 14.00
1970
  Common card .... .15
  O. J. Simpson 13.00
1971
  Common card .... .15
  Willie Lanier 2.50
1972
  Common card .... .10
  Terry Bradshaw 3.00
  Lyle Alzado 4.00
1973
  Common card .... .10
  Jack Ham 2.00
  Roger Staubach 3.25
1974
  Common card .... .05
  Roger Staubach 2.50
  Ken Stabler 1.10
1975
  Common card .... .05
  Dan Fouts 3.50
  Lynn Swann 2.00
1976
  Common card .... .05
  O. J. Simpson 2.00
  Randy White 1.50
1977
  Common card .... .05
  Steve Largent 5.00
  Fran Tarkenton 2.00
1978
  Common card .... .05
  Tony Dorsett 3.00
1979
  Common card .... .05

Doug Williams	**1.00**

1980
Common card	.03
Phil Simms	1.00
Dan Pastorini	.20

1981
Common card	.02
Joe Montana	2.00
Walter Payton	.65

1982
Common card	.02
Lawrence Taylor	2.00

FRANKOMA POTTERY

Collecting Hints: Prior to 1954 all Frankoma pottery was made with a honey-tan colored clay from Ada, Oklahoma. Since 1954 Frankoma has used a brick red clay from Sapulpa. During the early 1970s the clay became lighter and is now pink in color.

There were a number of early marks. One most eagerly sought is the leopard pacing on the FRANKOMA name. Since the 1938 fire, all pieces have carried only the name FRANKOMA.

History: John N. Frank founded a ceramic art department at Oklahoma University in Norman and taught there for several years. In 1933 Frank established his own business and began making Oklahoma's first commercial pottery. Frankoma moved from Norman to Sapulpa, Oklahoma, in 1938.

A fire completely destroyed the new plant later the same year, but rebuilding began almost immediately. The company remained in Sapulpa and continued to grow. Frankoma is the only American pottery to be permanently exhibited at the International Ceramic Museum of Italy.

In 1983 Frankoma celebrated its fiftieth anniversary. In September 1983 a disastrous fire struck once again, destroying 97% of Frankoma's facilities. The rebuilt Frankoma Pottery reopened in July 1984. Production has been limited to 1983 production molds only. All other molds were lost in the fire.

References: Phyllis and Tom Bess, *Frankoma Treasures*, published by author, 1983; Susan N. Cox, *Collectors Guide To Frankoma Pottery, Book I* (1979), *Book II* (1982), published by author.

Ashtray
Fish, 7"	**7.00**
Horseshoe, green	**10.00**
Texas, state shape, gold	**10.00**
Bean Pot, cov, Plainsman, green and brown	**9.00**
Bird Feeder	**20.00**

Bookends, pr
Boots, #433	**24.00**

Vase, wheel, mottled green, imp "Frankoma 94," 6¾" h, $18.00.

Leopard	**115.00**
Women with long hair, green and brown glaze	**125.00**

Bottle
11½", morning glory blue, white int., 1979	**28.00**
13", flame, white int., black base, signed "Grace Lee Frank," 1973 .	**30.00**

Bowl
Chip and Dip	**20.00**
Lazybones, 25 oz	**7.50**
Shell, 12"	**20.00**
Carafe, cov, Plainsman, green and brown	**5.00**
Casserole, cov, Wagon Wheel, tan glaze	**15.00**

Christmas Card
1952	**65.00**
1958	**50.00**
1965	**48.00**
1968	**35.00**
1975	**30.00**
1980	**18.00**
Corn Tray	**5.00**
Cowboy Hat, 4½", green and brown ..	**5.00**

Figure
English Setter, 5"	**48.00**
Fan Dancer, 8½", green and bronze glaze	**125.00**
Gardener Boy	**95.00**
Gardener Girl	**90.00**
Harlem Hoofer, 13", black semi-nude dancer	**200.00**
Puma, seated, Ada clay	**75.00**
Swan, 9", open tail, brown glaze ...	**20.00**
Flower Frog, mermaid	**350.00**
Jar, carved, #70, green	**25.00**

Mug
Donkey, red, 1976	**19.00**
GOP, blue, 1970	**50.00**
Mustache	**8.00**

Planter
Drill Bit	**5.50**
Elephant	**6.00**

Mallard, 9½"	**9.00**
Turtle	**6.50**
Wagon Wheel, 6½", Prairie Green glaze, incised mark	**25.00**

Plate

Battle for Independence, Bicentennial Series, 1974, 8½"	**20.00**
Birth of Eternal Life, 1977	**20.00**
Christmas, 1968	**15.00**
Conestoga Wagon	**75.00**
Daniel the Courageous, Teenagers of the Bible Series, 1979, 7"	**24.00**
Jesus the Carpenter, Teenagers of the Bible Series, 1972, 7"	**8.00**
Largemouth Bass, Wildlife Series, 1975, 7"	**20.00**
Oklahoma Diamond Jubilee, 1907–82, 8½"	**35.00**
Patriots-Leaders, Bicentennial Series, 1973, 8½"	**90.00**
Peter the Fisherman, Teenagers of the Bible Series, 1977, 7"	**20.00**
Prairie Chicken, Wildlife Series, 1974, 7"	**28.00**
Symbols of Freedom, Bicentennial Series, 1976, 8½"	**25.00**
Souvenir Plate, Oklahoma	**18.00**
Teapot, Wagon Wheel, 1½ cup, green and brown	**7.50**

Trivet

Horseshoes, green	**10.00**
Lazybones	**30.00**
Luigi's Showboat	**18.00**
Unicorn	**5.00**

Vase

2⅝"	**25.00**
6½", marked "Frank Potteries"	**175.00**
6¾", Wagon Wheel, mottled green	**18.00**
9", peacock blue glaze, 1934–42	**25.00**
9½, octagonal, red	**10.00**

Wall Pocket

Boot, Woodland moss	**15.00**
Indian Chief, Ada clay	**35.00**

FRATERNAL ORGANIZATIONS

Collecting Hints: Fraternal items break down into three groups. The first focuses on the literature, pins and badges, and costume paraphernalia which belonged to individual members of each organization. This material can be found easily. The second group is the ornamentation and furniture used in lodge halls for ceremonial purposes. Many of these items were made locally and are highly symbolic. Folk art collectors have latched on to them and have driven prices artificially high.

The third group relates to the regional and national conventions of the fraternal organizations. Each meeting generally produces a number of specialized souvenir items. These conventions are one of the few times when public visibility is drawn to a fraternal group; hence, convention souvenirs are the most commonly found items.

Concentrate on one fraternal group. Since so much emphasis has been placed on Masonic and Shriner material, new collectors are urged to focus on one of the other organizations.

History: Benevolent and secret societies played an important part in American society from the late 18th century to the mid-20th century. Groups ranged from Eagles, Elks, Moose, and Orioles to Odd Fellows, Redmen, and Woodmen. These secret societies had lodges or meeting halls, secret ceremonies, ritualistic materials, and souvenir items from conventions and regional meetings.

Initially the societies were organized to aid members or their families in times of distress or death. They evolved from this purpose into important social clubs by the late 19th century. Women's auxiliaries were organized. In the 1950s, with the arrival of civil rights, an attack occurred on the secretiveness and often discriminatory practices of these societies. Americans had greater outlets for leisure and social life, and less need for the benevolent aspects of the groups. The fraternal movement, with the exception of the Masonic order, suffered serious membership loss. Many local chapters closed and sold their lodge halls. This has resulted in many items arriving in the antique market.

Note: This category does not include the souvenir and other items related to the many service clubs of the 20th century, such as the Lions, Rotary, etc., who replaced the focus of many of the fraternal group members. Items from these service groups are not yet viewed as collectible by the general marketplace.

Benevolent & Protective Order of Elks, B.P.O.E.

Ashtray, bronze	**30.00**
Book, Ellis, Charles, *Elk's Authentic History of Elk's*, 1910, purple cov, 700 pgs	**35.00**
Bookmark, emb, elk's head, SS	**18.00**
Calendar Plate, 1907, 9½", Order of Elks center	**50.00**
Collar Box, leather, drawer, Elk emblem	**40.00**
Container, 2 x 1½", brass, presented to Bert Cook, Norwalk, Ohio	**25.00**
Fountain Pen, 10K gold	**20.00**
Mug, pottery, Roseville	**70.00**
Paperweight, round, glass, elk	**20.00**
Pinback Button, BPOE, 1910	**10.00**
Plate, Grand Lodge Reunion, Philadelphia, July 15–20, 1907, tin	**50.00**

Masonic, apron, silk, applied border, creased, minor fabric loss, designed by T Kensett, Cheshire, CT, 1812, 13 x 16¼", $350.00.

Shaving Mug, full color elk, gold letters 30.00
Stein, stoneware, green and brown glaze, Elks slogan and "Detroit Michigan" on front, pewter lid, marked "Germany" 75.00
Tie Rack, 7 x 8", wall type, plated brass 15.00
Watch Fob, elk's head, two teeth ... 150.00
Fraternal Order of Eagles, F.O.E.
  Ashtray 12.00
  Pinback Button, 1¾", celluloid, multicolored, Great Lakes excursion steamship, "Cleveland 1912" in blue border with multi floral design, red, white, and blue fabric flag ribbon, 1¼ x 1½" red, white, and blue enameled brass pendant with entwined initials "FOE" 75.00
  Watch Fob, bronze, F.O.E., Liberty, Truth, Justice, Equality, 1918 .... 8.00
Foresters of America, axe, 34" l, wood, painted folk art dec, red, white, and blue, gilt flags, elk, curved handles, Melford, MA, 1911 .... 265.00
Improved Order of Red Man
  Grave Marker, brass, Indian on top . 50.00
  Pinback Button, gold and red ribbon, 1904 .... 45.00
Independent Order of Odd Fellows, I.O.O.F.
  Automobile Tail Light Lens, glass, red, emb IOOF, three link chain, c1910 .... 18.00
  Badge, hanging, 1893 World's Columbian Exposition, Chicago souvenir, brass, inlaid black enamel . 60.00
  Coin, nickel/silver, detailed graphics 40.00
  Letterhead, 7½ x 9¾", Canal Lodge No 48, Searsmont, ME, 1840s ... 8.00

Plate, 8", Royal Copenhagen, Frigate, 1905 .... 100.00
Shaving Mug, multishaded, green transfer, F.L.T. in chain link, marked "C T Atlwasser Silesia" .. 50.00
Teaspoon, IOOF, SS, 1915 .... 25.00
Trivet, 8¼" l, insignia and heart in hand in laurel wreath 30.00
Knights of Columbus
  Paperweight, glass, clear, milk glass insert, black logo, floral border .. 30.00
  Plate, Vienna Art, 1905 .... 38.00
  Shaving Mug, name and emblem ... 100.00
  Sword and Scabbard, brass hilt, black painted grips, raised eagle dec, metal scabbard 55.00
Knights of Pythias
  Goblet, green, 1900 .... 28.00
  Medal, metal 15.00
  Ribbon, 1903 .... 8.00
  Shaving Mug, armor center, gold lettering and trim, marked "T & V France" and artist initials 105.00
  Sword 68.00
Knights Templar
  Letter Opener, bronze 15.00
  Mug, blue, symbols, 1910 .... 35.00
  Plate, 10", Grand Knights Templar Commandery, 54 Annual Conclave, Harrisburg, PA, 1909 ..... 90.00
Loyal Order of Moose
  Shaving Mug, black, gold trim, brown moose, "Vic Chamar," marked T & V Limoges 68.00
  Watch Fob, double tooth 75.00

Masonic, glass, Syria, Pittsburgh, PA, 1909, amber and white, 4½" h, $20.00.

Masonic
  Belt Buckle, SP 22.00
  Bible, 1200 pgs, 9½ x 11½ x 2½", leather binding, 22 kt gold stamping, illus, c1931 .... 65.00
  Book, *Encyclopedia of Free Masonry*, published by Masonic History Co,

1919, two volumes, 943 pgs, black cov, gold trim **50.00**
Bookends, bronzed, relief symbols, pr **20.00**
Catalog, Henderson-Ames Co, Masonic Lodge Supplies, 1924, 104 pgs **50.00**
Chart, 19 x 24", Masonic motif scenes and symbols, Hatch & Co, Trinity Bldg, Broadway, NY, 1865 ...... **40.00**
Coin, SS **10.00**
Creamer, 4¾", Gloversville, German **20.00**
Cup Plate, 3¼", Beth Horon Lodge, Brookline, Mass, Inst. Sept, 1870, light blue transfer, gilt rim **80.00**
Jug, 5¼", pink transfer symbols, Liverpool **90.00**
Magazine, *Masonic World,* War Unity issue, Sept, 1942 .... **10.00**
Matchsafe, symbols, SP, 1905 ...... **60.00**
Mirror, hand **35.00**
Nodder, 7", papier mache, Mystic Shrine decal on fez, string tassel, orig paint **30.00**
Penny, 1916, Norfolk, VA **18.00**
Pitcher, custard glass, Chicago, IL .. **75.00**
Plate
8", Pittsburgh, PA, Oct, 1912 .... **20.00**
10¼", portrait, Benton, cobalt border, Rosenthal **50.00**
Ring, man's, gold, 19th C **145.00**
Shaving Mug, Masonic symbol and flowers, gold and blue details, "JM Abell," marked "Vienna Austria" . **25.00**
Sign, convex, reverse painted, mother-of-pearl and silver foil dec, red, white, and blue shield, yellow stars, gold and black trim, framed **85.00**
Spoon, Klitzner, Providence, RI **10.00**
Tape Measure, round, celluloid, symbols, c1920 .... **15.00**
Trivet **10.00**
Order of Eastern Star, O.E.S.
Cup and Saucer, emblem **15.00**
Hatpin, long shank **30.00**
Pin, star shape, 14 karat gold, three diamond chips **60.00**
Ring, white gold, jeweled star, diamond center **90.00**
Shrine
Candlesticks, crystal, cut, 1900, pr . **100.00**
Cup, glass, Cleveland, 1896 .... **45.00**
Glass, Detroit, 1897 .... **45.00**
Hat, fez, brass scarab **22.00**
Loving Cup, three handles, Niagara Falls, 1905 .... **40.00**
Mug, Saratoga, Indian, 1903 .... **35.00**
Nodder, 7", composition, man wearing tuxedo and maroon shrine hat, c1960 .... **20.00**
Pin, lapel, 32nd emblem, SS **12.00**
Tumbler, 4½", milk glass, gold emblems, c1910 .... **60.00**

Wine Glass, commemorative, Washington, DC, 1900 .... **30.00**

FROGS

Collecting Hints: The frog is a popular theme in art work, but often enjoys a secondary rather than a primary position. As with other animal collectibles, the frog collector competes with collectors from other subject areas for the same object.

The frog has lent its name to several items from flower frog to railroad frog switches to the attachment device holding a sword scabbard to a belt. True collectors usually include an example of these in their collection.

History: A frog is a small, tailless animal with bulging eyes and long back legs. The first frogs appeared about 180 million years ago; today there are more than 2,000 species.

Throughout history frogs have been a source of superstition. One myth says frogs fall from the sky during rain.

The frog in character form has appeared in cartoons, on television and in movies. Flip the Frog is one example. The Buster Brown show featured Froggy the Gremlin. Kermit the Frog is the star of the Muppets, both on television and in the movies.

Periodical: *Flower Frog Gazette,* P. O. Box 106, Trumbull, CT 06611.

Collectors' Club: The Frog Pond, P. O. Box 193, Beech Grove, IN 46107.

Toy, windup, litho tin and felt, green, yellow butterfly, marked "Made in Japan," 4¾" l, $35.00.

Advertising Trade Card, Pond's Extract, black, light green, and buff **6.00**
Bank
4⅛" l, cast iron, Iron Art, 1973 .... **55.00**
6", pottery, seated, green glaze **30.00**
Basket, figural **30.00**
Candleholder, 5", glass, black, R Tiffin, OH **65.00**

Candy Mold, 5", tin, chocolate **25.00**

Christmas Ornament, blown glass, crouching position, c1930 .... **18.00**

Clicker, 3", Life of Party Products, Kirchhof, Newark, NJ **6.00**

Cookie Jar, 11 x 7", china, figural, holding flower bouquet, wearing dark green jacket, red bow tie, black top hat, c1950 .... **40.00**

Doorstop, 7¼" l, cast iron, orig green and yellow paint **135.00**

Figure

Ceramic, brown frog beating blue drum, Occupied Japan **12.00**

Pewter, 1", cast **10.00**

Redware, 4¾" l, green glaze **85.00**

Soapstone **35.00**

Flower Frog, figural, Van Briggle, 1915 **90.00**

Garden Ornament, 5 x 6", bronze **45.00**

Key Chain, 1", metal disc, frog riding bicycle, c1940 .... **8.00**

Mug

4", garden scene, transfer print, molded black frog inside, Staffordshire, 19th C **160.00**

4½", molded frog inside, Pratt Ware **125.00**

5½", molded frog inside, mottled brown, glazed **135.00**

Paperweight, celluloid and iron, advertising **35.00**

Planter

2½ x 3½ x 4", china, glazed, Flip the frog playing leap frog with a horse, c1930 .... **35.00**

7½", frog and lily pad, McCoy **32.00**

Salt and Pepper Set, figural on tray, 3 pcs, Occupied Japan **12.50**

Toothpick Holder, frog pulling snail shell, SP **55.00**

Toy

Croaker the Frog, 10½" h, rubber, Rempel Man, boxed **45.00**

Flip the Frog, 3", wood, jointed, green, beige hands and feet, raised eyeballs, c1930 .... **75.00**

Froggy, 5", felt **45.00**

Vase, 6", figural, seated, floral top, Occupied Japan **12.00**

Whimsy, 2¾ x 3¼", bisque, two frogs sitting in front of two eggs **75.00**

FRUIT JARS

Collecting Hints: Old canning jars can be found at flea markets, household sales, and antique shows. Interest in fruit jars is stable.

Some collectors base their collections on a specific geographical area, others on one manufacturer or one color. Another possible way to collect fruit jars is by patent date. Over 50 different types bear a patent date of 1858. Note: The patent date does not mean the jar was made in that year.

History: An innovative Philadelphia glass maker, Thomas W. Dyott, began promoting his glass canning jars in 1829. John Landis Mason patented the screw type canning jar on November 30, 1858. The progress of the American glass industry and manufacturing processes can be studied through fruit jars. Early handmade jars show bits of local history.

Many ways were devised to close the jars securely. Lids of fruit jars can be a separate collectible, but most collectors feel it is more desirous to have a complete fruit jar. Closures can be as simple as cork or wax seal. Other closures include zinc lids, glass, wire bails, metal screw bands, and today's rubber sealed metal lids.

References: Alice M. Creswick, *The Fruit Jar Works, Volume I* and *Volume 2*, published by author; Alice M. Creswick, *Red Book No. 5: The Collector's Guide To Old Fruit Jars*, published by author, 1986; Bill Schroeder, *1000 Fruit Jars: Priced And Illustrated*, 5th Edition, Collector Books, 1987.

Periodical: *Fruit Jar Newsletter*, 364 Gregory Avenue, West Orange, NJ 07052.

Note: Fruit Jars listed below are machine made unless otherwise noted.

All Right, aqua, qt, metal disc, wire clamp **75.00**

Anderson Preserving Co., clear, qt, metal lid **12.00**

Atlas Mason, aqua, qt, zinc lid **25.00**

Mason's, 1½ quart, aqua, patent November 30th, 1858, $6.50.

Ball

Eclipse, Wide Mouth, clear, qt, glass lid, wire bail **2.50**

Ideal, aqua, pt, glass lid, wire bail .. **2.00**

Mason, aqua, qt, emb backwards "s,"
zinc lid **4.00**
Perfection, aqua, qt, glass lid, zinc
band, handmade **18.50**
Bamberger's Mason Jar, blue, qt, glass
lid, wire bail **10.00**
Brockway Clear-Vu Mason, clear ½ pt,
metal lid **2.50**
Calcutt's, clear, qt, glass screw lid,
handmade **35.00**
Clarks Peerless, aqua, pt, glass lid **8.00**
Crown Mason, clear, qt, zinc lid **1.50**
Cunningham & Ihmsen, aqua, qt, wax
seal **15.00**
Dillon, aqua, qt, wax seal **12.00**
Dunkley, clear, qt, hinged glass lid ... **5.00**
Easy Vacuum Jar, clear, qt, glass lid,
wire clamp **25.00**
Everlasting Jar, Improved, clear, qt, glass
lid, toggles **15.00**
Franklin Fruit Jar, aqua, qt, glass lid .. **35.0**
Gem, Wallaceburg, clear, pt, glass lid,
screw band **5.00**
Globe, green, pt, glass lid, lever bail . **30.00**
Hansee's Palace Home Jar, clear, qt,
glass lid **50.00**
Hazel Preserve Jar, clear, qt, glass lid . **8.50**
I G Co, aqua, qt, wax seal **25.00**
Independent Jar, clear, qt, glass lid ... **35.00**
Jewell Jar, clear, ½ gallon, glass lid,
screw band **8.00**
Johnson & Johnson, NJ, amber, qt, glass
lid **20.00**
Keystone, clear, pt, zinc lid **10.00**
Knox Mason, clear, qt, zinc lid **4.00**
Leotric, aqua, ½ gallon, glass lid, wire
bail **10.00**
Lustre, aqua, pt, glass lid, wire bail ... **8.00**
Mallinger, clear, qt, zinc lid **4.00**
Mason
  Improved, green, qt, glass lid, screw
  band **2.00**
  Keystone in circle, Patent Nov 30,
  1858, green, qt, zinc lid **8.00**
  Root, aqua, qt, zinc lid **4.00**
Mid West, Canadian Made, clear, qt,
glass lid, screw band **5.00**
Norge, clear, qt, glass lid, metal band **10.00**
Opler Brothers, clear, qt, glass lid, wire
bail **5.00**
Peoria Pottery, gray pottery, brown
glaze, pt **20.00**
Perfect Seal, clear, qt, rubber seal **3.00**
Presto Wide Mouth, clear, ½ pt, glass
lid, wire bail **2.50**
Rhodes, Kalamazoo, MI, aqua, pt, zinc
lid **6.00**
Samco Genuine Mason, clear, 3 gallon,
zinc lid **15.00**
Standard, aqua, qt, wax seal **20.00**
Tropical Canners, clear, pt, zinc lid ... **4.00**
Universal, clear, qt, zinc lid **5.00**

White Crown Mason, aqua, qt, zinc lid **10.00**
Woodbury, aqua, glass lid, metal clip . **25.00**
Young's Pat May 27, 1902, stoneware,
brown neck, metal clamp lid **20.00**

GAMBLING COLLECTIBLES

Collecting Hints: All the equipment used in the various banking games such as Chuck-A-Luck, Faro, Hazard, Keno, and Roulette are collected today. Cheating devices used by professional sharpers are highly sought.

A well rounded gambling collectibles display also includes old books, prints, postcards, photographs, and articles relating to the field.

History: American history reveals that gambling always has been a popular pastime for the general public, as well as a sure way to make a "quick buck" for the professional *sharper*.

In the late 18th and early 19th centuries, governmental agencies and other entities used lotteries to supplant taxes as a means to raise funds needed to construct schools, libraries, and other civic developments. Many of the state and city lotteries proved to be crooked and fixed, a fact which adds to the collecting appeal. Lottery tickets, broadsides, ads, and brochures are very ornate and display well, mounted and framed.

Most of the gambling paraphernalia was manufactured by "gambling supply houses" that were located throughout the country. They sold their equipment via catalogs. As the majority of the equipment offered was "gaffed," the catalogs never were meant to be viewed by the general public. The catalogs are sought by collectors for their information and are difficult to find.

Perhaps the most significant gambling collectibles are those relating to the American West. Many collectors of saloon and western "cowboy" items seek gambling paraphernalia traceable to the West. Equipment marked with a western manufacturer's name generally will fetch a higher price than a comparable eastern made piece.

References: *Old West Collectibles*, Great American Publishing Co.; Dale Seymour, *Antique Gambling Chips*, Past Pleasures, 1985.

CHEATING DEVICES

Book, *Tricks with Cards Complete Manual of Card Conjuring*, Professor Hoffman, 250 pgs, hardcover, gold lettering, 1st ed, 1889 .... **15.00**
Corner Rounder, lever style, solid brass,
complete **600.00**
Dice, weighted, black with white, always totals 12, set of three **35.00**

Holdout
  Franks, Pat Nov 22, 1887 .... **110.00**
  Wizard, 2½" l, nickel plated brass,
    pat Feb 5, 1888 .... **70.00**
Wheel, 14", double Roulette type,
  carved cherry wood upper wheel with
  six holes, 20" lower wood wheel,
  controlled underneath, 1870 .... **950.00**

CHUCK-A-LUCK EQUIPMENT

Dice, ⅝", celluloid, used in cage, set of
  three **10.00**
Dice Cage, nickel plated brass
  11" h, 6" w, two celluloid dice **150.00**
  18½" h, 13" w, calfskin ends, 16 lbs,
    Mason & Co, Newark, NJ **390.00**
Layout, 30½ x 9½ x ¾", vinyl, black,
  yellow painted numbers, pr **55.00**

DICE

Celluloid, 1", red, white spots, round
  corners, set of five, MIB **40.00**
Ivory, ⅝", pr **50.00**
Sterling Silver, ½", sq, marked "Sterling
  925" **35.00**

FARO

Cards, sq corners, Samuel Hart & Co,
  New York, complete **110.00**
Casekeeper
  Geo Mason & Co, Denver, Colo,
    spade suit, walnut, composition
    beads, ace with crossed American
    flags **325.00**
  George W Williams, New York, heart
    suit, walnut, closed box style, ivory
    blue and natural colored beads,
    cribbage board **425.00**
Chip Rack, 18" l, 10" w, blue-green bil-
  liard cloth lined bottom **75.00**
Dealing box, German silver, straight,
  unmarked **175.00**
Layout, felt, walnut trim, George Mason
  & Co, 1910 Laurence St, Denver ... **550.00**

HORSE RACE COLLECTIBLES

Bookmaker's Supply Catalog, 19 pgs,
  1895, illus **25.00**
Game, Derby Day With Hurdles, Parker
  Bros, boxed **8.00**
Score Card, Grand Circuit Meet, Providence, RI, 1902 .... **10.00**
Stop Watch, 2" d, long chain, Meylan **65.00**
Trade Stimulator, 3 x 10 x 8½", wood
  and metal case, glass top, two
  through twelve horses around outside, silver and black scenes, side lever spin dice **250.00**

KENO EQUIPMENT

Cards, 136, wood, covered material and
  paper, H C Evans & Co, Chicago,
  Keno Cards **225.00**
Hopper, walnut, blue-green billiard
  cloth lined bowl, plated metal mouth,
  acorn finial, three carved feet **425.00**

Catalog Supplements, Hunt & Company, left: Catalog Supplement, 32 pages, 3¾ x 6¹⁄₁₆", $20.00; center: Master Key Systems, 40 pgs, 3½ x 6¼", $18.00; right: Run-Up Systems, 40 pgs, 3½ x 6¼", $15.00.

MISCELLANEOUS

Bingo Cage, 9" h, metal, red celluloid
  handle, eleven wood balls, 9 cards,
  1941 copyright **12.00**
Book
  Card Games and How to Play Them,
    123 pgs, soft cov, 1900 copyright **18.00**
  Gambler's Don't Gamble, Michael
    MacDougall & JC Furnas, 167 pgs,
    illus, 1939 .... **28.00**
Bottle, figural, slot machine shape
  8 x 5", Liberty Bell, gray, 24 karat gold
    dec, Ezra Brooks **20.00**
  9 x 9", Barney's, red **15.00**
Card Press, 9½ x 4½ x 3", dovetailed,
  holds ten decks, handle **140.00**
Catalog
  H C Evans & Co, Secret Blue Book,
    Gambling Supply, 1936, 72 pgs .. **50.00**
  K C Card Co, Blue Book No 520
    Gambling Equipment, 68 pgs **40.00**
Chromolithograph, 16 x 24", men play-
  ing poker in hunting lodge, titled
  "Respecters of Limits," framed, sgd
  "William Eaton" **100.00**
Card Counter, plated, imitation ivory
  face, black lettering **18.00**
Gambling Dirk, 9" l, mother of pearl,
  marked "Pookes Clarke" **100.00**
Shot Glass, ribbed dec, porcelain dice
  in bottom **24.00**
Sign, 11 x 30", Carlisle Whiskey adv,
  titled "A Bold Bluff," dogs gambling,

silver and black background, orig
frame impressed "Carlisle Rye" **70.00**
Tintype, 2¼ x 4", two men playing cards **12.00**
Tray, 11" d, tin, red, black, and white,
martini center, card border **50.00**

POKER

Arcade Game, 10 x 15 x 6", 1¢ draw,
five play, counter top type, wood and
metal case, orig graphics, c1930 ... **370.00**
Book, *The Game of Draw Poker,* John
Keller, NY 84, pgs, 1887, 4½ x 4¼" **25.00**
Chip Set
Bone, 37 rect and 39 round, geometric design, wood box **125.00**
Composition, set of 24, emb horse
and jockey pattern, red, white, and
blue, double sided **40.00**
Chip Holder, bakelite, pink and black,
Art Deco, pressed red, white, and
blue composition chips, holds four
sets of 50 chips, card rack **75.00**
Chip Rack, 11½ x 4" h, revolving,
wood, German silver handle, holds
400 chips and four decks of cards .. **35.00**
Lighter, 2", poker dice set shape,
marked "Old Crow The Greatest
Name In Bourbon" **30.00**

ROULETTE

Ball, set of three, one metal, two composition **15.00**
Chip Rack, walnut, holds 1,500 chips **100.00**
Game, Spear's Co, lithographed **15.00**
Layout, 40 x 19", hp, oilcloth, black and
red betting areas, wood trim **135.00**
Tray, 13" d, metal, roulette wheel rim . **30.00**
Wheel, 8" d, wood and metal, single
and double zero decal, four prong
spinner, cloth layout, makers stamp
on bottom **35.00**

WHEEL OF FORTUNE

9½" d, table top style, yellow, black,
and red numbers and designs, 12" h,
black wood stand **55.00**
20", 30 numbers, hp, cutout painted
center, yellow and white, red ground,
unmarked **145.00**
60", complete wheel, glass faced
"Dice," mounting hardware, G Ma-
son, Chicago **1,000.00**

GAMES

Collecting Hints: Make certain a game has all its
parts. The box lid or instruction booklet usually

contains a full list of all pieces. Collectors tend
to specialize by theme, e.g., western, science
fiction, Disney, etc. Most television games fall
into the ten to twenty-five dollar range, offering
the beginning collector a chance to acquire a
large number of games without a big capital outlay.

Don't stack game boxes more than five deep
or mix sizes. Place a piece of acid free paper
between each game to prevent bleeding from
inks and to minimize wear. Keep the games
stored in a dry location. Extreme dryness and
extreme moisture are both undesirable.

History: A board game dating from 4,000 B.C.
was discovered in ruins in Upper Egypt. Board
games were used throughout recorded history,
but reached popularity during the Victorian era.
Most board games combine skill (from chess),
luck and ability (from cards), and pure chance
(from dice). By 1900 Milton Bradley, Parker
Brothers, C. H. Joslin and McLoughlin were the
leading manufacturers.

Monopoly was invented in 1933 and first issued by Parker Brothers in 1935. Before the advent of television, the board game was a staple
in evening entertainment. Many board games
from the 1930s and 1940s focused on radio personalities, e.g., Fibber McGee or The Quiz Kids.

In the late 1940s television became popular.
The game industry responded. The golden age of
the TV board game was from 1955 to 1968. The
movies, e.g., James Bond, also led to the creation
of games, but never to the extent of the television
programs.

References: Avedon and Sutton-Smith, *The Study
of Games,* Wiley & Son, 1971; Lee Dennis, *Warman's Antique American Games, 1840-1940,*
Warman Publishing, 1983; Walter Gibson, *Family Games America Plays,* Doubleday & Co.,
1970; Jefferson Graham, *Come on Down!!!, The
TV Game Show Book,* Abbeville Press, 1988.

Collectors' Club: American Game Collectors Association, 4628 Barlow Drive, Bartlesville, OK
74006.

Advisor: Bob Cereghino.

Note: Prices are for game that are complete and
whose boxes are in very good or better condition.

**Milton Bradley, The Flying Nun, 1968,
$20.00.**

Allison
  1961, Car 54 .... **65.00**
American Publishing Corp.
  1977, Gong Show **5.00**
Athletic Products co, Inc.
  1950s, Today With Dave Garroway **20.00**
Frederich H. Beach
  1941, Take It And Double, 2nd series **10.00**
Betty-B
  1955, Break The Bank, 1st ed **10.00**
  1956, Robin Hood **20.00**
Bilt-Rite
  1956, Wild Bill Hickok **30.00**
Milton Bradley
  1930s, Prisoner of Zenda **15.00**
  1941–45, Bataan: The Battle Of The
    Philippines **25.00**
  1941–45, Bizertie Gertie **20.00**
  1944, Ella Cinders, 4483 .... **20.00**
  1944, Nancy and Sluggo, 4484 .... **17.50**
  1946, Li'l Abner: His Game, 4166 . **22.50**
  1950
    Captain Video **40.00**
    Hopalong Cassidy **25.00**
    Howdy Doody's T.V. Game **30.00**
  1955, Annie Oakley **2.00**
  1955, Winchell & Mahoney Chug-
    gedy Chug Game **30.00**
  1956, Sgt. Preston **15.00**
  1957, Name That Tune **10.00**
  1958, Alfred Hitchcock Presents
    Why? **10.00**
  1958, Cheyenne **35.00**
  1959, Rifleman **40.00**
  1959, Tales of Wells Fargo **25.00**
  1960, Deputy **25.00**
  1960, Men Into Space **30.00**
  1960, Video Village **20.00**
  1960, Wagon Train **20.00**
  1961, Margie **20.00**
  1961, Soupy Sales Go Go Go **30.00**
  1963, Patty Duke **15.00**
  1964, Outer Limits **75.00**
  1964, Voyage To The Bottom Of The
    Sea **20.00**
  1965, Eye Guess **8.00**
  1965, I Dream of Jeannie **30.00**
  1965, Lost In Sapce **60.00**
  1965, PDQ **8.00**
  1966, Batman **25.00**
  1966, Branded **20.00**
  1966, Goldfinger **20.00**
  1966, Green Hornet **50.00**
  1966, Ipcress File, movie **10.00**
  1966, James Bond **20.00**
  1966, Secret Agent **50.00**
  1967, Captain America **15.00**
  1967, Personality **8.00**
  1968, Barnabas Collins (with fangs) . **20.00**
  1968, Flying Nun **20.00**
  1968, Twiggy **25.00**
  1969, Official Baseball Game **40.00**

  1971, Partridge Family **5.00**
  1974, Apple's Way **4.00**
  1974, Emergency **1.00**
  1974, Planet Of The Apes **1.00**
  1974, Walton's **1.00**
  1975, Baretta **1.00**
  1975, Space 1999 .... **6.00**
  1975, SWAT **1.00**
  1977, Charlie's Angels **1.00**
  1977, Family Feud, 1st ed **1.00**
  1977, Starsky & Hutch **1.00**
  1982, Fall Guy **1.00**
  Miscellaneous
    Candy Land **1.00**
    Chutes and Ladders **1.00**
    Easy Money **1.00**
    Game Of The States **1.00**
    Go To The Head Of The Class ... **1.00**
    Intrigue **3.00**
    Park and Shop **3.00**
    Pirate And Traveler **6.00**
    Rack-O **1.00**
    Treasure Hunt **3.00**
    Uncle Wiggly **2.00**
Cardinal
  1982, General Hospital **1.00**
Club Aluminum Products Company
  1942, Whirling Words, wood version **30.00**
Corey Game Company
  1941, You're Out, baseball game ... **20.00**
Embossing Company
  1940s, Jack-Be-Nimble **8.00**
Ewing
  1955, Davy Crockett **25.00**
Gardner
  1956, You'll Never Get Rich (Sgt.
    Bilko) **50.00**
  1958, Boots and Saddles **40.00**
Gem
  1965, Bewitched **25.00**
  1965, Gilligan's Island **40.00**
H-G
  1956, Circus Boy **40.00**
Hasbro
  1959, Leave It To Beaver, three vari-
    eties, each **30.00**
  1965, Munsters, three varieties, each **100.00**
  1968, Dating Game, 1st ed **7.00**
  1968, Laugh In **15.00**
Highlander
  1955, George Goebel **20.00**
Ideal
  1961, Rebel **25.00**
  1962, Dr. Kildare **20.00**
  1963, Combat **35.00**
  1963, Nurses **20.00**
  1963, PT 109 .... **12.00**
  1964, Addams Family **60.00**
  1964, Fugitive **50.00**
  1964, Twilight Zone **100.00**
  1965, F Troop **60.00**
  1965, Get Smart **40.00**

1965, I Spy	25.00
1965, Man From UNCLE	20.00
1965, 12 O'Clock High	20.00
1966, Mission Impossible	60.00
1966, T.H.E. Cat	25.00
1966, Time Tunnel	60.00
1967, Star Trek	75.00
1975, Welcome Back Kotter	2.00
1978, Fantasy Island	1.00
1981, Dukes Of Hazzard	1.00

Leister Game Company

1945, Autographs	15.00

Lido Toy Company

1950s, Air Race Around The World	8.00

E. S. Lowe Co., Inc.

1940s, Fox Hunt	12.50

Samuel Lowe Company

1941, Airplane Speedway Game, No. 581-11	25.00
1941, Cross Country, No. 581-12, railroad train	20.00

Lowell

1954, Beat The Clock, 1st ed	10.00
1956, I've Got A Secret	12.00
1956, $64,000 Question	15.00
1956, This Is Your Life	20.00
1958, Bat Masterson	30.00
1958, Concentration, 1st ed	10.00
1958, Gunsmoke	25.00
1959, Steve Canyon	12.00
1959, Laramie	35.00
1959, 3 Stooges	150.00
1959, Rawhide	50.00
1959, Surfside Six	50.00
1960, Peter Gunn	30.00
1960, 77 Sunset Strip	30.00
1960, Wanted: Dead Or Alive	100.00
1961, Charge Account	7.00
1961, Sea Hunt	25.00
1962, College Bowl	12.00
1963, Candid Camera	20.00
1963, Hawaiian Eye	25.00

Mattel

1963, Word For Word	6.00
1967, Gentle Ben	15.00

Memphis Plastic Enterprises, Inc.

1955, Baseball Game	30.00

Parker Brothers

1940s, Camelot	6.00
1949/50, Clue, detective game	8.00
1959, Have Gun Will Travel	35.00
1961, Number Please	9.00
1962, Mr. Ed	25.00
1966, As the World Turns	10.00
1968, Thunderbirds	45.00
1968, Under Sea World Of Jacques Cousteau	10.00
1969, The Blondie Game	7.00
1969, Goodbye Mr. Chips, movie	10.00
1970, Tiny Tim	15.00
1975, Happy Days	1.00
1977, Barney Miller	1.00

Parker Brothers, Bonanza, $14.00.

1977, Laverne & Shirley	1.00
1983, Wicket The Ewok	1.00
Miscellaneous (modern production)	
Children's Hour	1.00
Dig	1.00
Monopoly	
Pre-1940	35.00
Modern	1.00
Pit	1.00
Pollyana	2.00
Rich Uncle	1.00
Rook	1.00
Sorry	1.00
Touring	1.00
Walt Disney's Uncle Remus Game	25.00

Play Rite

1960, Johnny Unitas	40.00

Pressman

1954, Groucho TV Quiz Game	50.00

Reiss

1977, Mary Hartmann	20.00

Remco

1965, Shindig	20.00
1968, Family Affair	40.00
1968, Mod Squad	30.00
1968, That Girl	20.00

Rosebud Art company

1940s, Jungle Hunt	20.00

Selchow & Righter

1940s, Snake Eyes, black theme	25.00
1948, Huggin' The Rail	30.00
1953, The Game of Assembly Line, No. 61	20.00
1961, Straightaway	12.00
Miscellaneous (modern production)	
Meet The Presidents	2.00
Mr. Ree	4.00
Parcheesi	1.00
Scrabble	2.00

Standard Toycraft

1960, Dennis The Menace	25.00
1963, Beverly Hillbillies	20.00
1963, Petticoat Junction	25.00
1964, Dick Van Dyke	35.00

1966, Gidget **25.00**
Teenage Publishing company
1957, Elvis Presley Game Of Love .. **500.00**
Transogram
1955, Captain Gallant **20.00**
1955, Dragnet **20.00**
1955, Rin-Tin-Tin **25.00**
1956, Jackie Gleason, Away We Go **25.00**
1957, Buccaneers **20.00**
1957, Tic Tac Dough, 1st ed **10.00**
1958, Gray Ghost **35.00**
1958, Life And Legend of Wyatt Earp **40.00**
1959, Perry Mason **20.00**
1960, It's A Mad, Mad, Mad World,
    Mad Magazine **10.00**
1960, Johnny Ringo **30.00**
1960, Philip Marlow **20.00**
1961, Aquanauts **15.00**
1961, Ben Casey **15.00**
1961, Detectives **15.00**
1961, Untouchables **80.00**
1962, Game Of The Kennedys **15.00**
1962, Lucy Show **20.00**
1962, Route 66 .... **50.00**
1962, Virginian **35.00**
1963, Burke's Law **25.00**
1963, Mr. Novak **20.00**
1966, Hogan's Heroes **30.00**
1967, Gomer Pyle **20.00**
1967, Monkees **100.00**
1975, M.A.S.H. **12.00**
Unknown Manufacturers
1962, Chet Huntley NBC News **12.00**
1970, Spiro Agnew's American His-
    tory Challenge Game **10.00**
1973, Watergate Caper **10.00**
Dexter Wayne
1953, Ramar Of The Jungle **15.00**
Whiting
1954, Pinky Lee Runaway Frankfurt-
    ers **15.00**
1955, Lassie **15.00**
1956, Lone Ranger **35.00**
Whitman Publishing Company
1958, Zorro **15.00**
1968, Dark Shadows **25.00**
1981, Clash Of The Titans **7.00**

GASOLINE COLLECTIBLES

Collecting Hints: There still is plenty of material in the storage area of old garages; try to find a cooperative owner. If your budget is modest, concentrate on paper ephemera, such as maps. Regionally related items will bring slightly more in their area of origin.

History: The selling of gasoline has come full circle. The general store, livery stable, and black-

smith were the first people to sell gasoline. Today the mini-market is a viable factor in gasoline sales. The gas crisis of 1973 brought the circle to a close. The gas station, whose golden era was from the 1930s to the 1960s, is beginning to disappear. The loss of the independently owned station is doubly felt because it also was the center of automobile repair.

The abolition of credit cards by ARCO marked another shift. Reduction in price for paying cash is a new marketing device. Elimination of free maps, promotional trinkets, and other advertising material already is a fact. As more and more stores in shopping centers sell oil, parts, and other related automobile products, it is doubtful whether the gasoline station will ever recover its past position.

Collectors' Clubs: Automobile License Plate Collectors Association, Box 712, Weston, WV 26452; International Petroliana Collectors Association, 2151 East Dublin–Granville Road, Suite G292, Columbus, OH 43229.

References: Scott Anderson, *Check The Oil*, Wallace-Homestead, 1986.

PERIODICAL: *Hemmings Motor News*, Box 100, Bennington, VT 05201.

REPRODUCTION ALERT: Small advertising signs and pump globes have been extensively reproduced.

Oil Can, Penn-Glenn Oil Works, 1,000 Mile Motor Oil, 8 quarts, red and yellow ground, blue letters, $15.00.

Anti-Freeze Tin, Eveready Prestone, 1
    gal, 1929 .... **17.50**
Ashtray, Goodyear, tire shape, amber
    glass center **32.00**
Bank, still
    En-Ar-Co Motor Oil **22.50**
    Humble Tiger, 8½", hard plastic, fi-
    gural, orange and tan, Humble Oil
    and Refining Co 1962 copyright .. **15.00**

Texaco, 2 x 3 x 7½", china, gasoline pump, red star, green and white lettering, small plastic gas hose, c1940 .... **30.00**

Calendar

Crown Gasoline, 1968, tin over cardboard, dial thermometer, gold, orange letters, 19½ x 8½" **45.00**

Johnson Winged Gasoline, 1939 ... **17.50**

Fish Hook, Mobilgas Flying Red Horse **35.00**

Gas Globe, Pemco **110.00**

Key Chain, 1½ x 1½", Mobilgas, diecut, white plastic, flying red horse, blue title, Iowa service station adv on back, c1940 .... **12.50**

License Plate Tag, ¾ x 2"

Goodrich Tires and Batteries, PA tag, orange and blue, 1940 .... **12.00**

Mobil, flying red horse **12.50**

Lubricant Tin, Texaco **17.50**

Manual, Pontiac, 1937 .... **20.00**

Oil Can

Archer, Indian shooting bow and arrow, airplane **12.00**

Phillips, c1950 .... **6.00**

Texaco, spout, 1927 .... **36.00**

Universal **5.00**

Paperweight, Exide Battery, figural **30.00**

Pillow, Esso Tiger, figural, smiling tiger head **15.00**

Pinback Button

1", Shell Safety Button, orange, red, and white, litho, c1930 .... **8.00**

1¼"

Esso, multicolored, Santa, light blue ground, red inscription, red and blue logo, c1912 .... **60.00**

Veedol, black and orange, white ground, oil can, Tyde Water Oil Co, early 1900s **10.00**

1¾", Texaco Scottie Contest, brown and white, two Scotties, c1930 .. **10.00**

Pocket Knife, miniature, 1½" l, silvered steel, white plastic cov, single blade, marked "USA," c1940

Alluwe Gasoline Co **7.50**

Frank's Auto Supply **7.50**

Houghton Inc, Chemicals and Anti-Freeze **7.50**

Salt and Pepper Shakers, pr, Texaco gas pumps **15.00**

Sewing Kit, Rio Grande Gasoline, 2" l, brass cylinder, celluloid cov with red, white, and blue logos, removable brass thimble, c1930 .... **20.00**

Sign

Conoco, porcelain, V shaped **45.00**

Firestone's Supreme Tires, steel **27.50**

Olizum "America's Finest Oil," two sided, 19½ x 27½", heavy porcelain, multicolored **175.00**

Stickpin, Texaco, ⅝", silvered brass, red star, green enameled "T," c1940 ... **12.00**

Tire Pressure Gauge, Schrader, patent 1909, Firestone Tires **15.00**

GEISHA GIRL PORCELAIN

Collecting Hints: Check for enamel and gold wear as well as porcelain flakes, hairlines, etc. Buy only items in good to mint condition. Become familiar with the type of items produced so you are not fooled by a "pitcher" that actually is a lidless cocoa pot or a lidless sugar bowl which may appear to be a planter.

Check the designs on all items within a set. Be aware that a "set" contains items complementary in size and with the same pattern executed in the same manner on all pieces. Value depends upon condition, quality, pattern, border color, and type of piece. Teapots, cups and saucers, and red bordered items are the most common.

History: Geisha Girl porcelain is a Japanese export ware whose production commenced during the last quarter of the 19th century and continued heavily until WW II. Limited quantities were produced after WW II and are called "modern" Geisha ware.

Geisha Girl porcelain features over 150 different patterns focusing on the flora, fauna, animal life, both real and mythical, and people of premodern Japan. The name is derived from the fact that all the wares contain lovely kimono-clad Japanese ladies as part of the pattern. It was manufactured and decorated by over 100 different establishments.

Colors and design methods vary greatly. The most common examples bear a red–orange stencil design over which artists hand painted enamels. Other examples have a different color stencil, may be wholly hand painted, or decaled. In the majority of instances, items bear a border color of red, light green, pine green, cobalt blue, greenish blue, turquoise, brown, black, or a lovely combination of several colors. Borders themselves are often further embellished with lacing, flowers, diapering, dots, or stripings of gold or contrastingly colored enamels.

Although Geisha Girl was produced in an Oriental pattern, it was meant for export to the Western market. Therefore, most shapes represent those used in the West during the early days of the twentieth century. These forms include tea items, cocoa sets, luncheon sets, dresser sets, (powder jars, hair receivers, ring trees, etc.), and vases. Examples of children's and doll house size also exist.

Maker marks found on Geisha Girl porcelain include many of the famous Nippon trademarks,

Japanese signatures (including Kutani), and post-Nippon indicators.

Reference: Elyce Litts, *The Collector's Encyclopedia of Geisha Girl Porcelain,* Collector Books, 1988.

Periodical: *The Geisha Girl Porcelain Newsletter,* P. O. Box 394, Morris Plains, NJ 07950.

Collectors' Club: The subscribers to *The Geisha Girl Porcelain Newsletter* also are a club of collectors who exchange experiences, ideas, photos, and collectibles via the newsletter.

Advisor: Elyce Litts.

REPRODUCTION ALERT: "Modern" Geisha ware was sold in Oriental import shops until the early 1980s. Reproduced forms, all having a red border, include bail handled tea sets, five piece dresser sets, sake sets, toothbrush holders, and ginger jars. Also produced was a children's set of demitasse cups, each having a different border color.

The chief characteristics of reproduction are very white porcelain, minimal background washes, sparse detail coloring, and no gold or occasionally very bright gold enameling. Old gold should show tarnish.

Also watch for Czechoslovakian reproductions made in the 1920s. Some will be marked with the country of origin, but others bear only a faux-Oriental mark. Generally these items are decaled or very simply hand painted. Faces of the geisha will be distinctively different than those on Japanese Geisha ware.

BY LAND AND BY SEA

This is an example of diminutive Geisha ware, in that the geisha figures are very tiny when compared to the overall designed space. At the forefront of this pattern is a lady in a sampan. On a bridge above her rides a samurai on horseback, accompanied by a retainer. The underlying stencil is black. The border, also stenciled, is composed of alternating sections of stylized bamboo and diapering overlaid by floral vines. Tan and dark green colors predominate, accented by pinks and reds.

Cocoa Set, cov chocolate pot, five cups and saucers	**85.00**
Luncheon Set, hexagonal demitasse pot, six hexagonal cups, round saucers, six 7" plates	**165.00**
Plate, 7"	**12.00**
Tea Cup and Saucer	**12.00**

CHILD REACHING FOR BUTTERFLY

There are several variations of this pattern which feature two geisha chatting while a child attempts to catch a butterfly alighting on a nearby

Child Reaching for Butterfly, tea cup and saucer, Variation B, $12.00.

plant. Another constant is a porch placed to the rear right of the scene. Variation A is the most common, displaying the child to the left of the geisha and a dark green porch of two sides. Variation B shows an uncolored bamboo porch with stairway access. Variation C shows the child between the two foremost geisha. The porch is overflowing with flowers and upper quadrant features a display of billowing fabric and dangling lanterns, all highly ornamented.

Egg Cup, red, Variation A	**12.00**
Mustard Jar, red, Variation A	**18.00**
Plate, 7", red	
Variation A	**12.00**
Variation C	**15.00**
Salt and Pepper Shakers, pr, red, Variation A	**15.00**
Tea Cup and Saucer	
Variation A	**10.00**
Variation B	**12.00**
Variation C	**18.00**

GARDEN BENCH

There seems to be endless varieties of this pattern series, the focal point of which are geisha seated around a bench in some lovely flower adorned garden. Variant letters refer to those described either in the *Collector's Encyclopedia of Geisha Girl Porcelain* or *The Geisha Girl Porcelain Newsletter.*

Box, 6", hexagonal, red, Variant B	**26.00**
Cocoa Pot, blue, Variant B	**55.00**
Condiment Set, salt and pepper shakers, mustard pot, and tray, multicolored border, Variant Q, marked "Royal Kaga Nippon"	**45.00**
Dresser Tray, clover shape, red and green geometrics, Variant F, marked "Plum Blossom, Hand Painted, Japan"	**75.00**
Pitcher, 2½", child's, red, Variant N	**15.00**
Plate	
7¼", red, Variant B	**16.00**
8½", green, Variant C	**25.00**

Garden Bench, box, Variant B, hexagonal, red, 6", $26.00.

Ring Tree, gold hand shaped stem, multicolored border, Variant Q, marked "Kutani" **65.00**
Tea Cup and Saucer, red and green geometrics, Variant S **24.00**
Teapot, cov, melon ribbed, blue with red spout, Variant C, marked "Japan" **30.00**

Garden Bench, condiment set, Variant Q, multicolored border, $45.00.

MEETING B

This variant of the Meeting series features two ladies who have stopped to chat. At least one child is present, often pulling at the hand of one of the women. This pattern is often found in reserves on beautifully decorated backgrounds of floral decor or completely covered with richly colored carp in a stream.

Cracker Jar, blue border, carp background **95.00**
Creamer, green banded border, floral background **24.00**
Demitasse Cup and Saucer, subject pattern, Shishi pattern and scenic reserves, border of alternating red and green semi-circles with gold, floral background, sgd "Tashiro" **25.00**
Demitasse Pot, pedestal, red border, carp background **65.00**
Ginger Jar, dark green border, carp background **85.00**

Sake Cup, red border, carp background   **14.00**
Tea Cup and Saucer, green banded border, floral background **28.00**

VARIOUS PATTERNS

Bon Bon Dish, Courtesy in reserve on floral ground, red **20.00**
Candlesticks, pr, Parasol D, red **100.00**
Cheese and Cracker Dish, Boat Festival, blue, marked "Plum Blossom, Japan"   **50.00**
Condiment Set, salt and pepper shakers, mustard pot, toothpick holder, and cherry blossom shape tray, Duck Watching B, pine green **48.00**
Cookie Jar, green pepper shape, Battledore, green **70.00**
Creamer and Sugar, shaped like miniature cocoa pot and cracker jar, River's Edge, red with green geometrics **65.00**
Demitasse Place Setting, cup, saucer, and plate, Fan A and Garden Bench A in reserves on crane and floral background, blue marked "Japan" **27.00**
Ice Cream Set, master bowl, plus five individual serving bowls, Fan A, red   **95.00**
Jar, cylindrical, cov, Temple A, green M in wreath mark **65.00**
Powder Jar, Lantern Gateway, red **26.00**
Roll Tray, Chinese Coin, floret–shape, green leaf handles **45.00**
Sugar Shaker, hexagonal, handled, Prayer Ribbon, red, marked "Japan"   **55.00**
Toothpick Holder, River's Edge, red, int. washed with blue, dec with fauna and birds, marked "Kutani" **65.00**
Vase, 3½", bulbous, Cloud B, red, trifooted **25.00**

GLASS COLLECTIBLES, MODERN

Collecting Hints: For the past several years, modern glass collectibles have been a source of speculation among collectors. Some new glass now is selling below initial retail as overstocked dealers are trying to unload. All this actually has resulted in a stabilization of prices. Prices now are constant from dealer to dealer as can be seen in the advertising in the *Glass Review*, a magazine for collectors of both old and new glass.

The first issue in a series often brings the highest price. Collectors are urged to concentrate on assembling full sets of one figure. Focusing on a single color is difficult because of the large variances in color and different companies' interpretation of the same color.

Several series have been left off the price list since the companies did not press their promised amount. They stopped midway or just barely into the series. This practice, while cost effective, is deceptive to the collector.

History: The popularity of limited edition plates, the success of Degenhart Crystal Art Glass and a renewed interest in old glass forms in the 1960s and 1970s led several companies into producing modern glass collectibles. Leading firms include Boyd's Crystal Art Glass Company, Fenton, Vi Hunter, Mosser, Pisello Art Glass, and Summit Art Glass Company.

The modern glass collectible is organized into four categories—limited edition series, limited edition single items, collectible company colors, and series.

The limited edition series usually has between 12 and 18 colors issued of a single pattern. The new colors appear monthly or bimonthly. The form generally is new.

The limited edition single item, often utilizing an early mold from an existing company, is issued in a color not previously used and in limited numbers from 100 to 1,000.

Collectible company colors are open stock. However, many smaller companies may make a limited amount of a color, e.g., shadings and slags. Once the color is used, it is not prepared again. Hence, some of these figurines have become collectible.

The recent closing of several glass factories, e.g., Imperial, Seneca, Tiffin, and Westmoreland, has resulted in the sale of their molds and a new collectible category within modern glass collectibles: reissues.

In the 1950s the Imperial Glass Company acquired over 10,000 molds when the Heisey and Cambridge glass factories closed. They used very few of these molds in production over the next thirty years. When Imperial Glass Company closed in early 1985, these molds, as well as their own, were sold. The Heisey Collectors of America, Inc., purchased 4,000 original Heisey molds, all except for sixty Old Williamsburg pattern. The Cambridge and Imperial molds were scattered to Michigan, Ohio, Pennsylvania, Texas, West Virginia, and Germany.

In late 1984 the Westmoreland Glass Company started selling their 20,000 molds, many from the mid-1880s. Collectors are concerned about repressings. *The Glass Review* issues a monthly update of who is acquiring the molds and what reissues are being made.

The big trend is miniatures. Several glass producers are offering miniature versions of their larger items or beginning a new item in miniature size.

Periodical: *Glass Review,* P. O. Box 7188, Redlands, CA 92373.

LIMITED EDITION SERIES

Items produced in limited amounts in a series. Usually not more than 1,000 per color for 12 to 16 variations. To distinguish between each collectible figurine a name is given each color. In some instances a name actually is molded into each figurine and changed each time the new color is issued.

Edna Barnes
   5", orange juice reamer. Made at Mosser from original Imperial Glass mold. A 2½" miniature version of the same in a series of 12. Each marked with Barnes's logo: "B".
   Cranberry Ice

2½"	5.50
5"	8.50
Depression Green	
2½"	6.00
5"	10.00
Red Glow	
2½"	7.75
5"	10.00

Boyd Crystal Art
   Balloon Bear, Patrick, limited to 30 colors, 2" h, solid glass

Alexandrite	6.00
Country Red	6.50
Colonial Doll, introduced October 1984, limited to 26 different names and colors	18.00
Hobo Clown, Freddie, limited to 30 colors, 3" h, solid glass	
Cobalt	8.50
Alexandrite	8.00

Guernsey Glass
   Rocky, rocking horse. A reproduction of a 1915 Cambridge candy container, 4¼" l, 3" h, 12 issues. Each marked "B" in a triangle.

Blue Boy	12.00
Carousel Slag	12.00
Hi-O-Silver	12.00
Holly Berry	10.00
Royal Prince	14.00

Vi Hunter
   Carousel Horse, 4½" h, six issues per year, beginning 1985, gold frost first issue 15.00
   Jenny, 4¼", doll, 12 per year plus bell. First issued January 1979, in Cornflower Blue Slag. Beginning in 1983 only 4 per year will be issued as a series and marked "1983." All dolls in 1979, 1980, 1981, and 1982, are marked with an "H." Also beginning in 1983 these dolls will be marketed in an open edition and not a part of the limited edition series; they will be marked "Open Edition."

1979, set of 12, plus bell	500.00
1980, set of 12, plus bell	200.00
1981, set of 12	150.00

Jenny Bell. Each Christmas a bell is issued.

1979, No. 1, Cobalt Carnival	**30.00**
1980, N0. 2, Pearl Carnival	**25.00**
1981, No. 3, Samurai Red	**20.00**
1982, No. 4, Mistletoe Slag	**18.00**

Josh, 4½", boy doll. Pairs with Jenny. Introduced 1981 in colors to match Jenny.

First issue	**18.00**
1981, set of 12, plus bell	**400.00**
1982, set of 12, plus bell	**300.00**

Mirror Images

Bear, ruby

Baby	**40.00**
Mama	**40.00**

Venus Rising, 6½", Cambridge mold of a lady flower frog (reworked for solid base). Series of 12, each color available solid or frosted, each marked "IG-81." First issued in Midnight Magic in early 1981.

Empress Jade	**24.00**
Irish Lass	**24.00**
Midnight Magic	**42.00**
Pink Pixie	**24.00**
Sunmaid Frosted	**24.00**

Mosser. This company has produced three limited edition clown figurines. The third clown will be released in 1983. Other collectible color items from this company listed under the "Collectible Company Colors."

Balloon Clown, 3½", sitting, holding balloons, 16 issues. Each individually named on back of clown. Introduced January 1981, with Arty. Note that the names begin with the first letter of the alphabet and continue through the letter O. A special "dealer clown" with handpainted balloons was made and sent to selected dealers prior to the series start. These are highly sought after.

Arty	**100.00**
Bags	**20.00**
Cleo	**20.00**
Daisy	**20.00**
Dealer Clown	**225.00**
Eros	**20.00**
Flip	**10.00**
Gabby–Maxi	**10.00**
McGoo	**10.00**
Niki	**10.00**
Orie	**10.00**
Set of 16	**300.00**

Barrel Clown, 3½", sitting on a barrel. Issued January 1982, with "Poko," 12 issues in a continuation of the alphabet P through Z, the last one marked "The End."

Poko	**12.00**

Quinn	**10.00**
Rufus	**10.00**

Pisello Art Glass

Chief Thundercloud Toothpick, 2½", each dated and sgd "P" in a circle, less than 1,000 of each, introduced 1983

Color 1, cobalt blue carnival	**15.00**
Color 2, chocolate slag	**15.00**
Color 3, milk white	**15.00**

Flipper, 3½ x 2½", miniature, covered dolphin. Based on Greentown dolphin. Introduced late 1982.

Chocolate	**12.00**
Marigold Carnival	**12.00**
Red Carnival	**14.00**
Vaseline Canary	**12.00**

John and Sarah, The Amish Couple, 2½", sgd "P" in a circle, cobalt blue carnival, pr **20.00**

Summit Art Glass Company

Clown Elephant, 4¾", elephant figurine. Reproduction of Cambridge candy container. 12 issues, each with a name on the back. Introduced December 1982, in Jimmy.

Jimmy, Ringling Red	**16.00**
Tommy, Calliope	**16.00**

Melanie, 5¼", doll. Copied from Cambridge figurine, two 12 doll series plus a Mother's Day bell. First issued August 1980, in "Tom's Surprise." Mold destroyed June 10, 1983, after 24 dolls and 2 bells were pressed.

Autumn Glow	**15.00**
Canyon Whisper	**15.00**
Dream Spinners	**15.00**
Green Swirl	**15.00**
Set of 24 dolls, plus 2 bells	**300.00**

Oscar, 4½" l, 2½" h, sitting lion. First issued June 1981, in Seastorm Rainbow. Mold will be destroyed after 12 issues.

Golden Goddess	**12.00**
Harvest Gold	**12.00**
Paradise Orchid	**12.00**
Snowsparkle	**12.00**

LIMITED SINGLE ITEM

A single item, often from an old original mold, is made in a color not previously issued and in a limited number from 100 to 1,000. In this category also would be a mold used from a company or a custom-made mold used for a one-time special color run.

Cherished Editions

Love Bouquet, series of six items from Fenton. Burmese with handpainted flowers, artist signed and dated, 350 sets only.

Basket, 5"	42.50
Bud Vase, 6"	32.50

Jack-In-The-Pulpit Vase

6½"	32.50
10"	48.00
Rose Bowl, 4½"	28.00
Rose Bowl, 4½", ruffled	30.00

Doris Lechler. A series of children's collectibles designed by Doris Lechler and made by Fenton Art Glass, limited to 500 sets per color, 3 colors per style.

Elizabeth Series, 6" ruffled lemonade set with six 2" tumblers

Amethyst, hp lilies of the valley	55.00
Amethyst, undecorated	45.00
Burmese, hp roses	60.00
Custard, hp violets	50.00

Elizabeth Series, Tumble-Up, a water carafe with matching glass turned over the decanter top, 5" h

Custard, hp violets	50.00
Ruby Overlay	50.00

Grace Series, 8 pcs, lemonade set,

cobalt overlay	85.00

COLLECTIBLE COMPANY COLORS

Large glass companies have many molds and the amount of glass made is not limited. Smaller companies don't actually limit the amount of glass run, but, certain items become "limited" because a given color will not be repeated.

Boyd's Crystal Art Glass Company. Trademark on all items "B" in a diamond.

Debbie Duck, introduced July 21, 1981

Cobalt	6.00
Furr Green	6.00
Mardi Gras	6.00
Snow	5.00

Ducklings, introduced Sept 15, 1981

Crown Tuscan	2.50
Furr Green	3.00
Golden Delight	2.50
Light Rose	2.50
Mardi Gras	3.00

Joey, leaping pony, introduced March, 1980

Chocolate	30.00
Furr Green	10.00
Lavender	12.00
Persimmon	25.00
Sand piper	8.00
Zack Slag	12.00

Louise, doll, introduced Sept 1979

Apricot	20.00
Firefly	15.00
Flame	15.00
Golden Delight	10.00
Lemon Ice	100.00

Skippy, sitting dog

Crown Tuscan	10.00
Golden Delight	8.00
Light Rose	8.00
Pippin Green	8.00

Mosser Glass Company. Trademark is the letter "M."

Bear, solid, sitting, Violet D'Orr	24.00
Candlestick, child's, opaque blue, Dutch boy and dog	5.00

Children's Dishes

Berry Set, Cherry Thumbprint, master berry, four serving bowls	35.00
Butter Dish, cov, Cherry Thumbprint	15.00
Cereal Set, Jennifer, pink, four cereal bowls, milk pitcher	18.00
Cracker Jar, cov, Cherry Thumbprint	18.00
Creamer and Sugar, Cherry Thumbprint	17.00
Dessert Set, Jennifer, yellow, four plates, round divided relish dish	18.00
Juice Set, Jennifer, green, pitcher, four tumblers	18.00
Spooner, Cherry Thumbprint	9.00
Table Set, Jennifer, pink, cov butter, creamer, cov sugar	16.50

GOLF COLLECTIBLES

Collecting Hints: Condition is very important as collectors grow in sophistication and knowledge. The more modern the item, the better the condition should be.

It is extremely rare to find a club or ball made before 1800, and any equipment made before 1850 is scarce. There were few books, with a couple of very rare exceptions, published before 1857. Few pieces of equipment made after 1895 are rare.

Some items, such as scorecards, ball markers, golf pencils, and bag tags are so common that their value is negligible.

Most American clubs and other items manufactured after 1895 are rather common. Some modern equipment, 1950–65, is in demand, but primarily for actual play rather than collection or display.

The very old material is found in Scotland and England, unless brought to this country early in this century. Christie's, Sotheby's, and Phillips' hold several major auctions of golf collectibles each year in London, Edinburgh, and Chester. Golf collectible sales often coincide with the British Open Championship each July. The English market is more established, but the American market is growing rapidly. Auctions of golf items and memorabilia now are held in the United States. 1988 sales by R. W. Murray (Kennebunk, ME) and Phillips' established a number of record prices.

The prices of golf clubs escalated tremendously in the 1970s, but have stabilized in more recent years. The prices of golf books, which for many years remained static, have risen dramatically in the 1980s. Art prints, drawings, etchings, etc. have remained static, but pottery, china, glass, and other secondary items, especially Royal Doulton, have attracted premium prices.

History: Golf has been played in Scotland since the 15th century. Until 1850 it was a game played by gentry, with a few exceptions. With the introduction of the cheaper and more durable "guttie" ball in 1848, the game became more popular and spread to England and other countries, especially where Scottish emigrants settled.

There are documents indicating golf was played in America before the Revolution. The great popularity of golf began about 1890 in both England and the United States.

References: Henderson & Stark, *Golf In The Making*; Pat Kennedy, *Golf Club Trademarks*, privately printed; John M. and Morton W. Olman, *Encyclopedia of Golf Collectibles: A Collector's Identification and Value Guide*, Books Americana, 1985; Janet Seagle, *The Club Makers*, United States Golf Association; Tom Wishon, *Golf Club Identification and Price Guide*.

Collectors' Club: Golf Collectors' Society, P. O. Box 491, Shawnee Mission, KS 66202.

Museums: Ralph Miller Memorial Library, City of Industry, CA; United States Golf Association, "Golf House," Far Hills, NJ; World Golf Hall of Fame, Pinehurst, NC.

BOOK

Adams, R. U., *John Henry Smith, A Humorous Romance of Outdoor Life,* 1905 .... **75.00**
Anderson, John, *The American Annual Golf Guide,* 1924 .... **40.00**
Baeert, Raymond, *The Adventures of Monsieur Depont: Golf Champion,* . **225.00**
Batchelor, Gerald, *Golf Stories,* 1914 . **40.00**
Bauchope, C. Robertson (ed.), *The Golfing Annual,* Vol. 1 .... **335.00**
Baxter, Peter, *Golf in Perth and Perthshire: Traditional, Historical and Modern,* 1899 .... **400.00**
Beldam, George W., *World's Champion Golfers: Their Art Disclosed by the Ultra-Rapid Camera,* 1924 .... **40.00**
Boomer, Percy, *On Learning Golf,* 1942 **12.00**
Browning, Robert H. K., *Golf in the Sun All Year Round,* 1931 .... **30.00**

Campbell, Patrick, *How to Become a Scratch Golfer,* 1963 .... **12.50**
Clark, Robert, *Royal and Ancient Game,* 3rd ed, 1899 .... **210.00**
Collett, Glenna, *Ladies in the Rough* .. **50.00**
Chronicles, Joe, *Uncle Jed, Caddie Master,* 1934 .... **80.00**
Darwin, B., *Green Memories,* 1928 .. **280.00**
Duncan, G., *Golf for Women* **25.00**
E. M. B. & G. R. T., *Humours and Emotions of Golf,* 1905 .... **40.00**
Golfers Gallery by Old Masters, A, portfolio of colored illus **425.00**
Gordon, John, *Understanding Golf,* 1926 .... **25.00**
Guldahl, Ralph, *Groove Your Golf* **15.00**
Harris, Robert, *Sixty Years of Golf* **50.00**
Haultain, *The Mystery of Golf,* 2nd ed, 1912 .... **70.00**
Helme, Eleanor E., *Lady Golfer's Tip Book,* 1923 .... **30.00**
Hilton, Harold H., *My Golfing Remembrances,* 1891 .... **300.00**
Hoyle's Games, 1790 ed **165.00**
Hutchinson, H. G., *The Badminton Library: Golf,* 1st ed, 1890 .... **90.00**
Irwin, J. F., *Golf Sketches,* 1892 ...... **125.00**
Jerome, *The Golf Club Mystery* **10.00**
Kahn, Liz, *Tony Jacklin: The Price of Success* **10.00**
Martin, H. B., *Pictorial Golf* **10.00**
Mayer, Richard, *How to Think and Sing Like A Golf Champion* **12.50**
Mortimer, Charles G. & Pignon, Fred, *The Story of the Open Championship 1860–1950,* 1952 .... **40.00**
Nelson, Byron, *Winning Golf,* 1947 .. **7.50**
Park, Willie, *The Game of Golf,* 1896 **125.00**
Ray, Edward, *Driving, Approaching and Putting,* 1922 .... **30.00**
Sapper, *Uncle James' Golf Match,* 1950 **40.00**
Smith, Robert Howie, *The Golfer's Year Book for 1866,* **400.00**
Travis, W. J., *Practical Golf,* NY, 1902 **35.00**
USGA Yearbook, 1931 .... **25.00**
Vaile, P. A., *The Soul of Golf* **20.00**
Wodehouse, P. G.
    Golf Without Tears **25.00**
    The Heart of a Goof **17.50**

EQUIPMENT

Bag
    Busey Patent Caddy, mahogany, ash pipod, birch handle, canvas and leather ball pocket, club tube **280.00**
    Leather, Tony Lema, 1964 British Open Champion **50.00**
Ball
    Bramble ball
        Spring Vale Hawk **22.00**
        The Crown **15.00**

The Pneumatic 60.00
Chemico Bob, yellow dot 35.00
Feather Ball
  J. Gourlay, early 19th C, maker's
    name 1,000.00
  Tom Morris 2,500.00
Gutty
  Hand hammered 180.00
  Mitchell, Manchester 35.00
  Ocobo 130.00
Halley's, parachute ball "for garden
  practice," orig box 135.00
Sq Dimple
  DSO Colonel, 29 weight 60.00
  North British, practice, box of 12 . 110.00

Tee, rubber, Manhattan, marked "The Reddy Tee Co., Inc., Patent 1915," $60.00.

Club (Note: w/s—wood shaft; s/s—steel
  shaft)
Iron
  Burke juvenile mashie, w/s 22.00
  Hagen concave wedge, 1930, w/s 115.00
  Hagen Iron-man sand wedge, w/s. 120.00
  George Nicol niblic, anti-shank,
    w/s 40.00
  Spalding F-4, c1922, w/s 10.00
  Tom Stewart lofter, smooth face,
    w/s 45.00
  Urquehart patent adjustable club,
    w/s 260.00
  Wilson wedge, Staff model, c1959,
    s/s 36.00
  6 smooth face, w/s 25.00
Putter
  Tommy Armour IMG Ironmaster,
    s/s 85.00
  Forgan, scared-head, long-nose,
    shaft stamped 100.00
  R. T. Jones "Calamity Jane," s/s .. 60.00
  Mills, "L" model, aluminum head 37.50
  A. Patrick, long nose, scared head,
    w/s 140.00
  Schenectady, w/s 50.00
  R. Simpson, socket head, c1900,
    w/s 85.00
  Spalding Cash-in, s/s 45.00
Wood
  Davie Anderson scared-head
    driver, w/s 65.00

Auchterlonie scared-head brassie,
  w/s 30.00
C.S. Butchart, scared-head driver,
  shaft stamped 35.00
Dunn's patent one-piece driver ...1,000.00
McGregor Tourney 693W driver,
  c1953, s/s 115.00
Tom Morris, scared head, bulger
  and brassie, horn insert, stamped
  "T. Morris, St. Andrews" 120.00
Ben Sayers spoon, scared-head,
  w/s 40.00

PRINTS, DRAWINGS, ETC.

Cartoon
  "Fore" and "After," pr, John Hassall 175.00
  "Golf Amenities," A T Smith, orig
    Punch, India ink 225.00
  "Spy," H. H. Hilton, Vanity Fair 55.00
Painting
  "Golfer Playing Long Shot from
    Bunker," Tom Peddie, oil on board,
    sgd 400.00
  "The Golfing Lassie," unknown, oil
    on board 175.00
  Winter scene showing golfers playing
    to the mark, 17th C Dutch School,
    oil on relaid canvas 2,750.00
Photograph, Harry Vardon, sgd, 1929 . 200.00
Print
  "In the Sand, St Andrews," after Mi-
    chael Brown 35.00
  "North Berwick: Perfection and the
    Redan," Cecil Aldin, sgd by artist 1,000.00
  "Royal and Ancient, St. Andrews,
    1798," Frank Paton, etching, vi-
    gnettes in margin, sgd by artist ... 225.00
  "The First Tee," Dendy Sadler, etch-
    ing, colored 30.00
Sketches, Gene Sarazen, black chalk,
  Ridgewell 35.00

SECONDARY ITEMS

Autograph, ALS, sgd by Harry Vardon,
  1931, framed and glazed 125.00
Bookends, 4 x 6", golfer in relief 55.00
Cigarette
  Box, hammered pewter, surmounted
    by mesh gutty ball and two clubs . 35.00
  Card
    Player Cigarettes, 25 in set 40.00
    Wills, "Famous Golfers" 50.00
  Case, silver, cov, enameled Edwar-
    dian golfer scene 280.00
Decanter
  Jim Beam Bottle, 53rd PGA Champi-
    onship, 1971 .... 35.00
  Limited Edition Whiskey, Hawaiian
    Open, 1972 .... 17.50

Doorstop, cast iron, green grass, red coat, gray pants, black highlights, 10" h, $450.00.

Figurine, Harry Vardon, bronze, by
  Henry Pegram, 1908 ....1,430.00
Game
  Golf-o-matics, Royal London 18.00
  Spin-Golf, Chad Valley, boxed 45.00
Golf Digest, magazine, 12 issues, 1963   15.00
Hatpin, golf club shape head 25.00
Medal
  Amateur Championship, British 910.00
  Royal Aberdeen, weekly handicap,
    1937 ....   125.00
Paperweight, glass, U.S. Open, 1980 .   25.00
Plate
  Golfing rabbits, Royal Doulton Bun-
    nykins 40.00
  Transfer after Reynolds, pottery 80.00
Post Card
  Gibson, set of 5, c1905 ....   20.00
  Rules of Golf, 9 in set, Crombie 30.00
  St. Andrews, 24 sepia views, c1900   145.00
Scorecard, 5,300, all different 420.00
Spoon, set of 6, case 60.00
Teaspoons, silver, set of six 45.00
Toast Rack, electro-plate, four divisions
  created by crossed clubs 80.00
Towel, bag, 1980 U.S. Open 7.00
Vase, blue and white pottery, printed
  golfing scenes, Mitchell, 1910, pr ..   200.00
Watch, mesh golf ball shape, Swiss ...   110.00

GOLLIWOGG AND DUTCH DOLLS

Collecting Hints: Study the Upton books to learn to identify the Golliwogg figure and the Dutch dolls. England is a prime source for Golliwogg material. Black collectors often will acquire Golliwogg material for their collections.

The illustrations in the Upton books have value

separately. Often books are destroyed so that individual prints can be sold for framing.

History: The first volume featuring the Golliwogg and the five Dutch Dolls (Meg, Weg, Peg, Sarah Jane, and Midget) was published in 1898 by Longman, Green Co., of London, New York, and Bombay. The text and illustration were by Florence K. Upton; Bertha Upton wrote the verses. The first book contained 31 color illustrations.

The Golliwogg was adopted as an advertising character by Robertson's, a manufacturer of jams and jellies. The Golliwogg's popularity also led to a number of toy related items being issued.

Advisor: Henry and Doris Sigourney.

Perfume Bottle, "Le Golliwogg/de Vigney/Paris," painted glass, black puff hair, 3½" h, $75.00.

Balloon, 5", golliwogg face, marked
  "Castle Howard York 1977 World Hot
  Air Balloon Championship" 35.00
Band, 3" h, plaster, E. E. Robertson's
  Jam adv, 8 pcs 125.00
Bank, still
  Aluminum 100.00
  Cast Iron 200.00
Biscuit Tin, Jacob's Biscuits, 3¾" d, oc-
  tagonal shape, golliwogg with toy sol-
  diers 60.00
Book-Titles (13 in series): *Adventures Of
  Two Dutch Dolls And A Golliwogg,
  Golliwogg At The Sea-Side, Golli-
  wogg In Holland, Golliwogg In War,
  Golliwogg's Air-Ship, Golliwogg's
  "Auto-Go-Cart," Golliwogg's Bicycle
  club, Golliwogg's Circus, Golliwogg's
  Desert Island, Golliwogg's Fox-Hunt,
  Golliwogg's Polar Adventures, Golli-
  wogg In The African Jungle, and Gol-
  liwogg's Christmas;* books measure
  11⅜ x 8⅝", 64 pgs
  Mint Condition 200.00
  Excellent Condition 140.00

Very Good Condition	**100.00**
Fair Condition	**50.00**
Book, *The Three Golliwoggs*, Enid Blyton, 1969	**15.00**
Bookmark, celluloid, Robertson's Jams	**20.00**
Candy Container, 3⅛" h, tin, figural, Rowntree's Cachous	**200.00**
Cookbook, *Good Golly Recipe Book*, Robertson's	**20.00**

Doll
Paper, 2" h, Robertson's Golden Shred Marmalade adv, same themes as pins **1.00**
Rag, 10, 16, and 18" **20.00**
Figure, 2½' h, plaster, electrified, Robertson's Jam adv **500.00**
Greeting Card, birthday, golliwogg pushing rabbit in wheelbarrow **8.00**
Mug, Easter Bunny and egg **12.00**
Perfume Bottle, figural, golliwogg **550.00**
Pin, 1⅜", enamel on brass, promotion for Robertson's Golden Shred Marmalade, themes include: Accordion Player, Bag Piper, Boy Scout, Boxer, Cricket Player, Field Hockey Player, Golfer, Guitarist, Ice Skater, Lacrosse Player, Rugby Player, Saxophonist, Soccer Player, Tennis Player, Trainman with stop sign, Trombonist and Violinist **12.00**
Plate
China, Robertson & Son, Made by Barratts, Staffordshire, c1904
7" **75.00**
9" **75.00**
White enamel, 10", "The Golliwogg's Joy Ride" **40.00**
Playing Card, each with illus from various Upton Books, Thomas DeLaRue & Co, Ltd, London **85.00**
Sugar Bowl, 3" d, china **60.00**
Thermometer, 19", plastic, Robertson's Jam adv **45.00**
Toy
Dinky Toy, "Guy" van, 5¼", red, "Robertson's Golden Shred" **260.00**
Squeak, rubber, 6¼" h, black face, jacket and shoes, white shirt and gloves, red tie and pants, marked "Combey, Made in England, 1546" **35.00**

GONDER POTTERY

Collecting Hints: Learn to identify the Gonder glazes and forms. Once you do, you will have no trouble identifying the pieces. Since production is recent, many examples still can be found in basements and at garage sales. Dealers have been buying Gonder pieces and placing them in storage in anticipation of a future rise in prices.

History: Lawton Gonder purchased the Zane Pottery of Zanesville, Ohio, in 1941. Previously Gonder had worked for the Ohio Pottery, American Encaustic Tiling, Cherry Art Tile, and Florence Pottery. He was a consultant for Fraunfelter China and Standard Tile. Gonder renamed the Zane Pottery the Gonder Ceramic Arts, Inc.

Gonder's pottery was high priced for its time. Besides a mingled color glaze, the pottery made a flambe glaze, a gold crackle glaze, and a line of old Chinese crackle reproduction pottery. Many shapes followed the Rum Rill patterns from the Florence Pottery.

Almost all Gonder Pottery is marked. Some had paper labels, but the majority had one of the following impressed marks: "GONDER CERAMIC ART," "Gonder/Original" in script, "Gonder" in script, "GONDER/U.S.A.," "Gonder (script)/U.S.A.," and "GONDER" in a semicircle.

The company expanded in 1946, opening the Elgee pottery which made lamp bases. The plant burned in 1954. A brief expansion occurred at the main plant, but production ceased in 1957.

Reference: Ralph and Terry Kovel, *The Kovel's Collector's Guide To American Art Pottery*, Crown Publishers, 1974.

Periodical: *The New Glaze*, P. O. Box 4782, Birmingham, AL 35206.

Collectors' Club: American Art Pottery Association, 9825 Upton Circle, Bloomington, MN 55431.

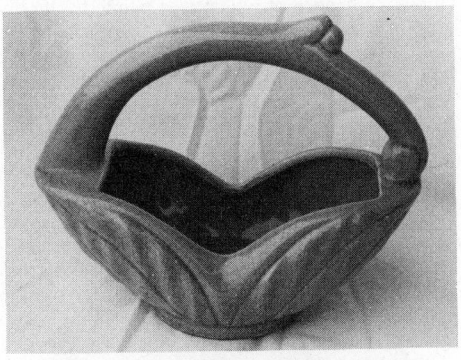

Basket, leaf pattern, turquoise exterior, pink–coral interior, marked "H-39 Gonder, USA" 8" w, 6½" h, $30.00.

Bowl, 7", swirl, blue and brown glossy glaze, flower frog	**20.00**
Candlesticks, pr, 4¾", turquoise ext., pink int., imp mark "E-12/Gonder/USA"	**15.00**

Cornucopia
6", gray, pink int. **10.00**
7½", leafy, scrolled, brown and pink **12.00**

Creamer and Sugar, dark brown drip,
brown spatter ground **25.00**
Ewer
   7½", bulbous, mottled maroon **25.00**
   8", light green, matte finish **25.00**
   13", Shell and Star, green **50.00**
Planter, Madonna, mottled pink and
   gray **15.00**
Swan, 7", shaded blue, pink int. **10.00**
Vase
   6", twisted, mottled green **10.00**
   6½", greenish blue glaze, handles . .   **10.00**
   7", aqua and brown mottled, pink int.   **12.00**
   8", lavender and brown glaze, swans
   on base, marked "1-147, USA" . .   **30.00**
   9", fan, mottled gray, pink int., han-
   dles **18.00**
   11", petal and leaf dec, blue **20.00**
   12", glossy yellow, mottled red glaze,
   emb leaves **35.00**

GOOFUS GLASS

Collecting Hints: Original paint is important. If
a piece is peeling, the price is lowered by 50%.
   Although Goofus glass does not respond well
to cleaning with detergents, it can be restored by
using a fine metal polish. Test a small area with
a cotton swab before starting.

History: Goofus glass also is known as Mexican
Ware, Hooligan glass, and Pickle glass. It is a
pressed glass with relief or impressed designs,
the back or face of which was painted. The design areas often are in red and green with the
ground in metallic gold or bronze. The favorite
design motif is some form of flower. The period
of popularity of Goofus glass was from 1890 to
1920.
   Goofus glass was used as a premium at carnivals, similar to carnival glass. It also was sold
in local general and department stores. Goofus
glass came in many forms—bowls, compotes,
jars, jewel boxes, lamps, pickle jars, plates, powder jars, and vases. Several carnival patterns and
forms have been found with Goofus decoration
including Nasturtium plates, bowls, and lamp
bases, Peacock Fantail lamp and vase, Beaded
Oval bowl, and Grape Wheel plate. Goofus decoration also appeared on some pieces of opalescent glass.
   Several companies made Goofus glass: Crescent Glass Company, Wellsburg, West Virginia;
Imperial Glass Corporation, Bellaire, Ohio;
LaBelle Glass Works, Bridgeport, Ohio; and
Northwood Glass Co., Indiana, Pennsylvania,
Wheeling, West Virginia, and Bridgeport, Ohio.
Northwood marks include "N," "N" in one cir-
cle, "N" in two circles, and one or two circles
without the "N."
   Goofus glass lost its popularity when people

found the paint tarnished or scaled off after repeated washings and wear. No record of its manufacture has been found after 1920.

Reference: Carolyn McKinley, *Goofus Glass*,
Collector Books, 1984.

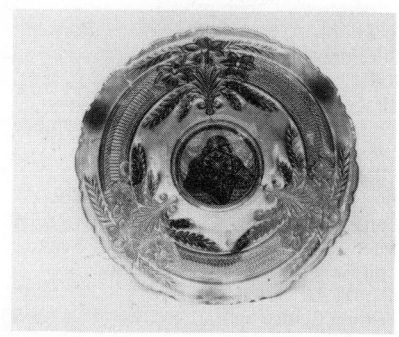

**Plate, gold ground, red flowers, 10¾" d,
$15.00.**

Ashtray, red rose dec, emb adv **8.00**
Basket, 5", strawberry dec **45.00**
Bowl
   6½", Grape and Lattice, red grapes,
   gold ground, ruffled rim **35.00**
   7", thistle and scrolling leaves, red
   dec, gold ground, ruffled rim **20.00**
   8½", floral, red dec, gold ground . . .   **20.00**
   9", cherries, red dec, gold ground . .   **20.00**
   10", pears and apples dec **30.00**
Bread Plate, 7 x 11", The Last Supper,
   red and gold, grapes and foliage bor-
   der **60.00**
Cake Plate, 12", red roses, gold ground   **15.00**
Coaster, 3", floral, red dec, gold ground   **10.00**
Compote
   6", jelly, strawberries and foliage, ruf-
   fled **28.00**
   6½", poppy, red flowers, gold foliage,
   green ground, sgd "Northwood" .   **32.00**
   9½", floral and foliage dec, red and
   gold dec, green ground, crimped
   and fluted rim, pedestal foot, sgd
   "Northwood" **30.00**
Dresser Tray, 6", Cabbage Rose, red
   roses, gold foliage, clear ground . . .   **28.00**
Jewel Box, 4 x 2", basketweave, rose
   dec **40.00**
Miniature Lamp, 12" h, Cabbage Rose   **42.00**
Mug, Cabbage Rose dec, gold ground   **30.00**
Nappy, 6½", Cherry, red cherries, gold
   foliage, clear ground **35.00**
Pin Dish, 6½", oval, red and black flo-
   rals **15.00**
Pitcher, red rose bud, gold leaves **48.00**
Plate
   7¾", red carnations, gold ground . . .   **18.00**
   8", red poppies, gold ground **25.00**

10½", grapes dec, gold ground, irid
pink edge **25.00**
Platter, 18", red rose dec, gold ground **65.00**
Rose Bowl, 4" d, red roses, gold ground **20.00**
Salt and Pepper Shakers, pr, poppy ... **32.50**
Toothpick Holder, red rose and foliage,
gold ground **20.00**
Tray, 8¼ x 11", red chrysanthemum
dec, gold ground **35.00**
Tumbler, 6", red rose dec, gold ground **25.00**
Vase
6", Cabbage Rose, red dec, gold
ground **40.00**
7¼", grapes dec **25.00**
9", poppies, blue and red dec, gold
ground **25.00**

GRANITEWARE

Collecting Hints: Old graniteware is heavier than
new graniteware. Pieces with cast iron handles
date from 1870 to 1890; wood handles date from
1900 to 1910. Other dating clues are seams,
wood knobs, and tin lids.

History: Graniteware is the name commonly
given to iron or steel kitchenware covered with
enamel coating.

The first graniteware was made in Germany in
the 1830s. It was not produced in the United
States until the 1860s. At the start of World War
I, when European manufacturers turned to the
making of war weapons, American producers
took over the market.

Colors commonly marketed were white and
gray. Each company made their own special col-
or, including shades of blue, green, brown, violet, cream, and red. Graniteware still is manufactured with the earliest pieces in greatest
demand among collectors.

Reference: Vernagene Vogelzang and Evelyn
Welch, *Graniteware, Collectors' Guide With
Prices, Volume 1* (1981), and *Volume 2* (1986),
Wallace-Homestead.

Collectors' Club: National Graniteware Society,
4818 Reamer Road, Center Point, IA 52213.

Angel Food Pan, gray **20.00**
Baking Pan, cobalt swirl, long **100.00**
Bedpan, hospital, blue swirl **90.00**
Bowl, 7½" d, 3¼" h, Onyxware, dark
brown, white mottling **20.00**
Bread Riser
Blue swirl, old tin lid **175.00**
Gray mottled, small, matching lid .. **80.00**
Bucket, matching strainer, Majestic,
brown swirl **60.00**
Children's Dishes
Cup and Saucer, blue **50.00**
Dinner Set, blue, 7 pcs **210.00**
Funnel, blue **45.00**

**Berry Pail, gray and black, 7" d, 4¾" h,
$45.00.**

Chamber Pot
6" h, 7½" d, child's, gray **10.00**
8" h, 9½" d, gray **15.00**
Coffeepot
Blue Swirl, eight cup **80.00**
Brown Swirl, large **250.00**
Gray **25.00**
Red Swirl, gooseneck **300.00**
White **20.00**
Colander, gray, pedestal, 12" d **20.00**
Cream Pail, blue swirl, one qt **100.00**
Creamer, turquoise swirl, 5" h **12.00**
Cup, blue swirl **30.00**
Cuspidor, blue swirl **30.00**
Dipper
Dark brown, small white mottling,
Onyxware **40.00**
Gray, mottled, Windsor **8.00**
Dishpan, 5" h, 16" d, gray **10.00**
Double Boiler, 3 pcs
Blue Swirl **60.00**
Gray, mottled **35.00**
Frying Pan, 8" d, medium dark blue,
white flecks **45.00**
Funnel, large, cobalt swirl **45.00**
Grater, azure blue **50.00**
Hot Plate, electric, spattered green ... **150.00**
Jelly Roll Pan, round, medium blue swirl **65.00**
Ladle, lavender swirl ext., white int. .. **35.00**
Measuring Cup, one cup, gray mottled **85.00**
Milk Kettle, blue swirl **25.00**
Mixing Bowl
Medium, blue mottled **48.00**
Small, red and white swirl **90.00**
Mold, fluted, white **40.00**
Muffin Pan, eight cups, cobalt swirl .. **170.00**
Mug
Cobalt swirl **40.00**
Cream, green trim **6.50**
Pail, 7½ x 6½", gray mottled, tin lid .. **45.00**
Pan, heart shape, gray mottled, set of
three, old tin lid **145.00**

Percolator, blue, mottled, bulbous, glass lid	50.00
Pie Plate, blue swirl	20.00
Pitcher	
6", green, shaded	20.00
8½", gray	40.00
Plate	
Turquoise, divided	45.00
Yellow and green	60.00
Potty, cobalt swirl	180.00
Preserving Kettle, blue, shaded, 4 qt	30.00
Pudding Pan, cobalt and white swirl, 8" d	40.00
Roaster	
Large, emerald green swirl	250.00
Round, gray	40.00
Turkey, large, gray	45.00
Salt Box, white, German	55.00
Scoop, grocery, large, gray, mottled, wooden handle	35.00
Soap Dish, dark brown, white mottling, Onyxware, wall mounted, insert	30.00
Spatula, gray	24.00
Spoon, sky blue, 11"	18.00
Sugar, cov, white	45.00
Table and Chairs, child's, ABC top	150.00
Teapot	
Blue, gooseneck	190.00
Turquoise	95.00
Tumbler	
Azure Blue, orig label	35.00
White, nesting, set of 4, German	55.00
Wash Board, blue speckled	75.00
Wash Bowl and Pitcher, gray	115.00
Wash Pan, 3¼" h, 12" d, gray	8.00

HALL CHINA

Collecting Hints: Hall China Company named many of their patterns, but some of these pattern names are being gradually changed by dealers to other names. A good example of this is the Silhouette pattern; the common name is Taverne. Dealers have also devised nicknames for shapes like J-sunshine and sani-grid.

Due to its high quality, most Hall China pieces are still in wonderful condition. There is no reason to pay full price for imperfect pieces.

History: Hall China Company was born out of the dissolution of the East Liverpool Potteries Company. Robert Hall, a partner in the merger, died within months of forming the new company. Robert T. Hall, his son, took over.

At first, the company produced the same semiporcelain dinnerware and toiletware that was being made at the other potteries in East Liverpool, Ohio. Robert T. Hall began to experiment in an attempt to duplicate an ancient Chinese one-fire process that would produce a non-crazing vitrified china, with body and glaze being

fired at the same time. He succeeded in 1911. Hall has been made that way ever since.

Hall's basic products are institutional ware (hotel and restaurant) to the trade only. However, they also have produced many retail and premium lines, e.g. Autumn Leaf for Jewel Tea and Blue Bouquet for the Standard Coffee Co. of New Orleans. A popular line is the gold-decorated teapots that were introduced for retail sale in 1920. In 1931 kitchenware was introduced, soon followed by dinnerware. These lines were decorated in both solid colors and decals for retail and premium sales.

Hall is still producing china at its plant in East Liverpool, Ohio.

References: Harvey Duke, *Superior Quality Hall China*, ELO Books, 1977; Harvey Duke, *Hall 2*, ELO Books, 1985; Harvey Duke, *The Official Price Guide to Pottery and Porcelain*, House of Collectibles, 1989; Margaret and Kenn Whitmyer, *The Collector's Encyclopedia of Hall China*, Collector Books, 1989.

Advisor: Harvey Duke.

Note: Hall has been reissuing many of its products in its new Americana retail line for several years now. They are all decorated in solid colors. If you are a new collector and are unsure if an item is new or old, you may want to buy only the items with decal or gold decorations, as these pieces have not been reissued and there is no intention of doing so. Because of this reissue, prices have dropped slightly on a few solid-colored items.

See: Autumn Leaf.

Pitcher, Wildfire pattern, pink roses, blue ribbon, white ground, $30.00.

PATTERNS

BLUE BLOSSOM. Silk screened floral decal on cobalt blue glaze. This kitchenware line was retailed in the 1930s and 1940s.

Bean Pot	70.00
Casserole	
Oval, handle	45.00
Saf-handle (Sundial)	25.00
Coffee Server, Saf-handle (Sundial)	175.00
Creamer, New York shape	40.00
Custard Cup	16.00
Drip, open, tab handles	25.00
Leftover, loop handle	50.00
Pitcher	
Ball shape	35.00
Loop handle	55.00
1½ pint	25.00
Salt and Pepper Shakers, pr, handles	40.00
Sugar, New York shape	45.00
Syrup, Saf-handle (Sundial)	80.00
Teapot, Streamline	140.00

BLUE BOUQUET. A premium line made for Standard Coffee from the 1950s to 1960s.

Creamer, Boston	10.00
Cup	9.00
Fruit Bowl, 5½"	6.00
Pie Baker	22.00
Plate	
6", bread and butter	6.00
9", dinner	9.00
Platter, 11¼", oval	13.00
Salad Bowl, 9"	14.00
Salt and Pepper Shakers, pr, egg shape	20.00
Saucer	3.00
Sugar, Boston	12.00
Teapot, Aladdin	55.00
Vegetable Bowl, 9¼", round	15.00

CROCUS. Produced in the 1930s and 1940s as a premium line for Best Tea and other companies.

Bean Pot	65.00
Casserole, Sunshine (Radiance)	35.00
Coffeepot, without drip	45.00
Creamer, Art Deco	15.00
Cup	8.00
Fruit Bowl, 5⅝"	5.00
Gravy	19.00
Jug, bell shape	45.00
Leftover, sq	40.00
Mug	40.00
Pie Baker	22.00
Plate	
6⅛", bread and butter	8.00
7¼", pie	7.00
8¼", salad	7.00
10¼", dinner	14.00
Platter, 13¼", oval	18.00
Pretzel Jar	75.00
Salad Bowl	20.00
Salt and Pepper Shakers, pr, handles	28.00
Saucer	3.00
Soup Bowl, 8½"	15.00
Soup Tureen	150.00

Sugar, Art Deco	18.00
Teapot, New York, six cup	50.00
Tidbit Server	30.00
Vegetable Bowl, 9⅛", round	20.00
Water Bottle	200.00

POPPY. (Orange Poppy) A premium line made for the Great American Tea Company. Available from 1933 through the 1950s.

Cake Server	65.00
Casserole, Sunshine (Radiance)	32.00
Cereal Bowl 6"	7.00
Cup	9.00
Custard Cup	4.00
Jug, ball shape	32.00
Leftover, loop handle	45.00
Mustard, 3 pcs	45.00
Pie Baker	19.00
Plate	
6⅛", bread and butter	6.00
7¼", pie	7.00
9⅛", dinner	10.00
Platter, oval, 11¼"	13.00
Salt and Pepper Shakers, pr, handles	22.00
Saucer	4.00
Souffle Dish	14.00
Soup Bowl, 8½"	14.00
Teapot	
Boston	55.00
Doughnut	165.00
Vegetable Bowl, 9⅛", round	14.00

RED POPPY. A premium line made for Grand Union Tea Company. Produced from mid-1930s until mid-1950s.

Cake Plate	16.00
Casserole	25.00
Creamer	7.00
Cup	5.00
Custard Cup	4.00
Drip, open, tab handles	22.00
Fruit Bowl, 5⅝"	3.50
Gravy	18.00
Jug, ball shape	32.00
Mixing Bowl, set of 3	35.00
Plate	
7¼", pie	5.00
8¼", salad	6.00
9⅛", dinner	5.00
Platter, 13¼", oval	16.00
Saucer	1.50
Salt and Pepper Shakers, pr, handles	12.00
Soup Bowl, 8½"	9.00
Sugar	8.00
Teapot	
Aladdin	50.00
New York	40.00
Vegetable Bowl, 10½", oval	11.00

ROSE PARADE. A retail line brought out in the early forties.

Bean Pot	35.00
Bowl Set, 3 pcs	60.00
Casserole	25.00
Creamer	9.00
Custard Cup	10.00
Drip, cov	16.00
Pitcher, large	22.00
Salad Bowl	16.00
Salt and Pepper Shakers, pr	25.00
Souffle Dish	22.00
Sugar, open	9.00
Teapot	32.00

TAVERNE. (Silhouette) A premium line made for several companies including Cook Coffee, Helicks, and Standard Coffee.

Bean Pot	85.00
Casserole	35.00
Cereal Bowl, 6"	7.00
Coffeepot, china drip	110.00
Creamer	10.00
Cup	9.00
Drip, cov, Colonial (Medallion)	16.00
Fruit Bowl, 5⅝"	6.00
Jug, tall	60.00
Leftover, rect	20.00
Mixing Bowl, set of 3	60.00
Mug	30.00
Pie Baker	20.00
Plate	
7¼", pie	7.00
9⅛", dinner	9.00
10", dinner	11.00
Platter	
11¼"	13.00
13¼"	16.00
Salad Bowl	14.00
Salt and Pepper Shakers, pr, round	20.00
Saucer	3.00
Soup Bowl, 8½"	13.00
Sugar	12.00
Teapot, New York	80.00
Tea Tile, 6", round	90.00
Vegetable Bowl, 10½", oval	15.00

REFRIGERATOR WARE

The first refrigerators were made with the motor sitting on top of the body. In the 1930s, designs were streamlined and the motor was incorporated in the body. Accessories (water servers, butters, and leftovers) were often included with the refrigerator as a promotion. Many of these pieces match the design of the refrigerators they originally came with.

ARISTOCRAT. (Hercules) A promotional line for Westinghouse.

Butter	17.00
Leftover	12.00
Water Server, lid, cobalt	70.00

BINGO. (Zephyr) Hall's retail line. Most often found in Chinese Red.

Butter	70.00
Leftover	55.00
Water Bottle, cork tip	
7" h	60.00
7⅝" h	55.00

EMPEROR. (General) A promotional line for Westinghouse.

Butter	14.00
Leftover	10.00
Water Server, lid, Delphinium	35.00

HOTPOINT.

Leftover	
Rectangular	22.00
Round	
6⅝"	16.00
7⅝"	18.00
8⅞"	22.00
Square	
4"	13.00
4⅞"	15.00
5⅞"	18.00
6⅞"	22.00
8½"	22.00
Water Server, cork tip	45.00

PATRICIAN. (Phoenix) A promotional line for Westinghouse.

Butter	12.00
Leftover	10.00
Water Server, cov	
Cobalt	110.00
Delphinium	35.00

TEAPOT

All prices below are for gold decorated teapots, except Chinese Red. As a general rule, the common colors are cadet blue, canary, cobalt, emerald, maroon, and turquoise. For undecorated teapots, deduct 10%.

Airflow, Chinese Red	45.00
Aladdin, black	40.00
Albany, turquoise	25.00
Automobile, Chinese Red	375.00
Baltimore, emerald	35.00
French, cadet blue	25.00
Hollywood, maroon	25.00
Los Angeles, cobalt	25.00
Moderne, canary	15.00
Nautilus, turquoise	65.00
New York, delphinium	30.00
Parade, canary	18.00
Streamline, cadet blue	40.00
Surfside, emerald	55.00

Windshield, camellia	**20.00**
World's Fair	**250.00**

HARKER POTTERY

Collecting Hints: In 1965 Harker China had the capacity to produce 25 million pieces of dinnerware each year. Hence, there is a great deal of Harker material available at garage sales and flea markets. Many patterns also were kept in production for decades.

Between 1935 and 1955 the Harker Company organized Columbia Chinaware, a sales organization used to market Harker products in small towns across the country. The line included enamel ware, glass and aluminum products. One pattern of Columbia Chinaware was "Autumn Leaf," eagerly sought by Autumn Leaf collectors.

Collectors should focus on Harker patterns by famous designers. Among these are Russel Wright's White Clover and George Bauer's Cameoware. Many patterns will be found with different color grounds. Other patterns were designed to have mass appeal. Colonial Lady was popular at "dish nites" at the movies or other businesses.

Shapes and forms did change through the decades. An interesting collection might focus on one object, e.g., a sugar or creamer, collected in a variety of patterns from different historical periods. Watch for unusual pieces. The Countryside pattern features a rolling pin, scoop and cake server.

History: The Harker Company began in 1840 when Benjamin Harker, an English slater turned farmer in East Liverpool, Ohio, built a kiln and began making yellow ware products from clay deposits on his land. The business was managed by members of the Harker family until the Civil War when David Boyce, a brother-in-law, took over the operation. Although a Harker resumed management after the war, members of the Boyce family assumed key roles within the firm; David G. Boyce, a grandson of David, served as president.

In 1879 the first whiteware products were introduced. A disastrous flood in 1884 caused severe financial problems which the company overcame. In 1931 the company moved to Chester, West Virginia, to escape the flooding problems. In 1945 Harker introduced Cameoware made by the engobe process. The engobe or layered effect was achieved by placing a copper mask over the bisque and sand blasting to leave the design imprint. The white rose pattern on blue ground was marketed as "White Rose Carv-Kraft" in Montgomery Ward stores.

The Harker Company used a large variety of backstamps and names. Hotoven cookingware featured a scroll, draped over pots, with a kiln design at top. Columbia Chinaware had a circular stamp with the Statue of Liberty.

Harker made a Rockingham ware line in the 1960s. The hound handled pitcher and mugs were included. The Jeannette Glass Company purchased the Harker Company and the plant was closed in March, 1972. Ohio Stoneware, Inc., utilized the plant building until it was destroyed by fire in 1975.

References: Jo Cunningham, *The Collector's Encyclopedia Of American Dinnerware,* Collector Books, 1982; Betty Newbound, *The Gunshot Guide To Values Of American Made China & Pottery,* Book 2, privately printed, 1983.

Periodical: *The Daze,* 12135 North State Road, Otisville, MI 48463; *The New Glaze,* P.O. Box 4782, Birmingham, AL 35206.

See: Russel Wright

Berry Dish, floral decal, gray border, $2.50.

Amy	
Bean Pot, individual	**6.00**
Casserole, cov, individual	**6.50**
Creamer and Sugar	**7.00**
Plate	
6", bread and butter	**3.75**
7½", salad	**4.00**
8", luncheon	**4.50**
9", dinner	**6.00**
12", serving	**8.00**
Platter, 11½"	**8.00**
Rolling Pin	**55.00**
Soup Bowl, tab handle	**6.00**
Teapot	**30.00**
Cameoware	
Bowl, 7", pink	**9.50**
Casserole, cov, blue and white, 8½"	**18.00**
Child's Feeding Dish	**30.00**
Creamer	**4.50**
Cup and Saucer	**8.75**
Drip Jar, cov, teal	**15.00**
Mixing Bowl, blue, large	**15.00**
Mug, child's, blue and white	**8.00**
Pitcher, cov	**15.00**

Plate
6½", bread and butter 3.00
10", dinner, blue and white 5.00
Range Set 20.00
Rolling Pin, pink and white 50.00
Sugar, cov 5.50
Teapot 28.00
Modern Tulip
Bowl
6" 3.00
9½" 7.00
Cake Server, brown 12.00
Casserole, cov, 8½" 20.00
Cup and Saucer 3.50
Mixing Bowl, 9" 10.00
Pie Baker 8.00
Plate
6¾", sq, snack 2.75
9", dinner 4.00
11⅜", serving 6.00
Platter, 14" 7.00
Salad Fork 12.00
Pate Sur Pate
Creamer, green 2.50
Plate, 6¾" sq, green 2.50
Platter, 13", gray 5.75
Salt and Pepper Shakers, pr, gray ... 6.00
Sugar, cov, green 4.00
Red Apple
Batter Jug, cov 25.00
Bowl, 9", berry 15.00
Cake Server 12.50
Casserole, cov, individual 6.00
Creamer 8.00
Mixing Bowl, 10" 15.00
Plate, 6" 2.50
Salt and Pepper Shakers, pr 10.00
Spoon 12.00
Sugar, cov 10.00
Tea Tile 20.00
Teapot 28.00
Utility Bowl, 9" 10.00

HATPINS

Collecting Hints: Shanks of hatpins come in
varying lengths. A group of hatpins in a decorative hatpin holder makes a nice decorative accent. Purchase hatpins with straight shanks and
solid mountings. Hatpins should be free of rust
or tarnish and chips or flakes.

History: Hatpins were popular from 1850
through the 1920s. The main purpose of a hatpin
was to hold a lady's hat to her head. When the
style of fashion included large brimmed hats and
long, thick hair, the hatpin was a necessity. As
with other necessities, designers soon began to
decorate and embellish hatpins with stylish designs, semi-precious stones and metals. Subjects
of commonly found hatpins range from com-

memorative, insects and sporting events to florals.
Some hatpins were used as extensions of a
lady's costume and had ends coordinated to the
lady's outfit. Other hatpins were designed by the
milliner to become an integral part of the hat
design. Hatpins also served another purpose for
well dressed ladies. These long shafted pins were
valuable weapons when threatened and often
were used to keep an overzealous suitor in his
proper place.

Reference: Lillian Baker, *Hatpins & Hatpin Holders*, Collector Books, 1983 (1988 Value Update).

Collectors' Club: International Club For Collectors of Hatpins and Hatpin Holders, 15237 Cha-
nera Avenue, Gardena, California, 90249.

Museum: Los Angeles Art Museum, Costume Department, Los Angeles, CA.

**Left: Dartmouth College, $25.00; right:
Bunker Hill Monument, Sterling, $20.00.**

Amethyst, bulldog, carved 275.00
Brass, 1¼", triangular, Art Nouveau,
amethyst bezel set accent, c1905 ... 40.00
Carnival Glass, Flying Bat, purple 35.00
Cloisonne, 1¼", round, flower and but-
terfly, blue ground, button sleeve me-
tallic mounting, foil back, steel shank,
marked with Japanese letters 75.00
Enamel
Art Nouveau style, calla lily, translu-
cent, white and green, c1910 .... 120.00
Bow shape, pearl center 45.00
Gold, 14K
Ball, cutout motif, American, c1896   75.00
Shamrock, seed pearls 100.00
Ivory
Chrysanthemum and floral motif, 1",
hollow, carved, head unscrews .. 75.00
Elephant on ball, 1½", figural, hand
carved 110.00
Mosaic, 1½", round, white and rose
flowers, green leaves, yellow centers,
blue ground, gold beaded edge, brass
shank 65.00
Mother of Pearl
Baroque, 1½", faceted ruby color ac-
cent, rolled gold strap type mount-
ing, 6" steel shank, c1890 .... 60.00
Snake motif, ruby head gold top,
American 175.00

Porcelain
  Ball, ceramic transfer, hp accents,
    gold overlay, c1895 . . . . **110.00**
  Romantic scene, rhinestone border,
    9½" shank **55.00**
Rhinestone
  Butterfly, figural, blue body **30.00**
  Circular, large center stone, three
    other rows **40.00**
  Flower cluster, 8½" shank **15.00**
Satsuma
  Geisha girl, 14" shank **25.00**
  Iris blooms, 1¾", hp, 7¼" steel shank **100.00**
Sterling Silver
  Arts and Crafts design, 2¾", steel
    shank, marked "Sterling," c1885 . **45.00**
  Clover, three leaf, pearl center **60.00**
  Head, man in turban, repousse and
    detailed etching, steel shank,
    marked "sterling" and "sterling
    top," c1890 . . . . **85.00**
  Shield motif, American, c1896 . . . . . **55.00**
  Sweet pea, 1¼", figural, 8" steel
    shank, stamped "Delamothe,"
    c1900 . . . . **65.00**
Tortoise Shell
  Ball, ½", overall gold dotted pique
    work **65.00**
  Pear shape, 1¼", ribboned pique
    work **120.00**

HOLIDAY COLLECTIBLES

Collecting Hints: The most common holiday item is the postcard. Collectors tend to specialize in one holiday. Christmas, Halloween, and Easter are the most desirable. New collectors still can find bargains especially in the Thanksgiving and Valentine's Day collectibles.

Holiday items change annually. Manufacturers constantly must appeal to the same buyer.

History: Holidays are an important part of American life. Many have both religious and secular overtones such as Christmas, St. Patrick's Day, Easter, and Halloween. National holidays such as the Fourth of July and Thanksgiving are part of one's yearly planning. There are regional holidays. Fastnacht day in Pennsylvania–German country is just one example.

Some holidays are the creation of the merchandising industry, e.g., Valentine's Day, Mother's Day, Father's Day, etc. The two leading forces in the perpetuation of holiday gift giving are the card industry and the floral industry. Through slick promotional campaigns they constantly create new occasions to give their products. Other marketing aspects follow quickly.

Holiday collectibles also keep pace with pop-ular trends. Peanuts is now being challenged by Strawberry Shortcake, the Smurfs, and Star Wars.

References: L-W Book Sales (pub.), *Favors & Novelties: Wholesale Trade List No. 26, 1924–1925*, price list available; Margaret Schiffer, *Holidays Toys and Decorations*, Schiffer Publishing Ltd., 1985.

Newsletters: *Hearts to Holly: The Holiday Collectors Newsletter,* P. O. Box 105, Amherst, NH 03031; *Trick or Treat Trader,* P. O. Box 1058, Derry, NH 03038.

Advisors: Dick Smith and Lissa L. Bryan-Smith.

New Year, post card, Raphael Kirchner, Paris, artist, $60.00.

EASTER

Basket
  3 x 5", printed cardboard, pastel colors, trimmed with colored eggs,
    USA, 1930s **7.00**
  6" d, 10" handle, brown, wood,
    painted flowers, paper label
    marked on base "Made In Germany" **18.00**
  8" d, yellow metal, metal handle, rabbits and chicks painted on outside,
    Chein Toy Co **15.00**
Candy Container
  Chick and Egg, 6" h, papier mache,
    yellow chick, black glass eyes,
    standing next to egg candy container, USA **55.00**
  Duck, 4" h, yellow composition, ribbon around neck, standing on 3" d
    round cardboard box, opens at
    base, Germany **35.00**
  Egg, 4" l, papier mache, litho of boy
    golfer on front, separates in middle,
    marked "Germany" **15.00**
  Farm House, 3½" h, bright colors,
    surrounded by brown wooden

fence, composition chicks and rabbit in yard, roof comes off for candy, Germany **48.00**

Hen on Nest, 6" h, sepia tones, egg crate papier mache, separates at nest, USA **65.00**

Rabbit

  4" h, on all fours, brown composition, removable cotton tail for candy **55.00**

  8" h, pot belly, white, head and ears on wire spring, white glass beading trim, separates at belt line, marked "US Zone, Germany" . **15.00**

  9" h, begging, composition, gold color, glass eyes, removable head, marked "Germany" **50.00**

Rooster, 5" h, composition, bright colors, fine detail, metal feet, removable head, marked "Germany" .. **60.00**

Centerpiece, tissue paper fold-out basket, tissue paper fold-out eggs, cardboard rabbit in center, USA **13.00**

Chickens

  1" h, rubber, chicken, white, marked "Auburn Rubber Co, USA" **3.50**

  1½" h, black composition hen on brood of yellow chicks, marked "Japan" **5.00**

  2" h

    Bisque, bright colors, marked "Japan" **5.50**

    Composition, rooster, metal feet, marked "Germany" **10.00**

    Cotton Batting, chick, wire legs, paper beak, marked "Japan" ... **18.00**

  4" h

    Composition

      Hen, metal feet, marked "Germany" **28.00**

      Hen on Nest, straw nest, marked "Germany" **35.00**

    Cotton Batting, wire legs, glass eyes, chenille beak, marked "Japan" **40.00**

  5" h

    Celluloid, felt clothing and feet, standing, marked "Japan" **25.00**

    Plastic, hard, red, rattles when moved, USA **7.00**

Egg

  3" l, sugar, wrapped in cellophane, scrap scene of children playing, marked "Czech" **6.00**

  5" l, white opaque glass, painted spring scene, "Happy Easter" painted in gold trim **25.00**

Postcard

  "A Happy Easter," yellow chicks dancing around the Maypole while mother hen watches from side, Germany, 1913 .... **1.25**

"A Joyous Easter," two small children sitting by a large basket full of chicks and colored eggs **1.00**

"Bright and Happy Easter for You," Gibson Girl kissing chick in garden **1.25**

"Easter Greetings," boy holding colored eggs in lap, marked "Made in USA" **1.00**

Rabbit

  1½" h, diecut, multicolored, marked "Germany" **1.50**

  5" h

    Chalk, brown flocking, nodder, marked "USA," 1950s **11.00**

    Plastic, hard, mother rabbit dressed in yellow, brown glasses **7.00**

  5½" h, composition, white, pink golfing clothes, swinging golf club, marked "Germany" **38.00**

  7" h, hard plastic, rabbit pushing baby buggy, pink, blue details **12.00**

  10" h, comic, comic face, paper ears, pink, rocking green base **68.00**

Toy, 5" h, rabbit, wind-up, metal cov rabbit fur, hops, marked "Japan" ... **55.00**

FOURTH OF JULY

Postcard, "4th of July Greeting," red, white, and blue, gold ground, Germany, 1910 .... **2.00**

GEORGE WASHINGTON'S BIRTHDAY

Candy Container

  Axe, 5" h, fabric over cardboard, plug in handle for candy, Germany ... **25.00**

  Stump, 3" h, papier mache, surrounded by cherries, marked "Germany" **45.00**

Diecut, 2½" h, George Washington, hatchet with cherry, flanked by stump with hatchet, set of 3 .... **8.00**

HALLOWEEN

Candy Container

  Cat

    3" h, crepe paper, nut or candy cup type, braided handle, black diecut cat on front, USA **10.00**

    4" h, hard plastic, orange and black, arched back, open area in back for candy, USA, 1950s ... **7.50**

    5½", papier mache, black, metal spring tail, removable head, Germany, 1930s **110.00**

  Owl, 8" h, papier mache, orange, opening in bottom for candy, USA **40.00**

  Pumpkin Man, 3" h, orange head,

green suit, standing on round box,
marked "Germany" **85.00**
Scarecrow, 8" h, hard plastic, pumpkin head, orange and black, open
area in back for lollipops, USA,
1950s **15.00**

**Halloween, lantern, cardboard and pa-
per, black silk, orange background, four
panels, witch with cat, singing cat, owl,
and screeching cat, each panel 10 x 5¼",
$35.00.**

Witch
  5" h, papier mache, red painted
  dress, straw broom, flax hair, removable head, Germany **250.00**
  8" h, papier mache, black and orange, sack on back for candy,
  Germany **95.00**
Centerpiece, emb flat cardboard,
marked "Beistle, USA," 1950s
  10" h, cat on moon **10.00**
  14" h, Jack O'Lantern **10.00**
Costume
  Clown, home made, baggy, yellow
  and black, trimmed in bells, matching pointed clown hat with bells,
  1940s **8.00**
  Porky Pig, child's, large, plastic mask,
  cloth suit and cap, Warner Bros,
  orig box, 1950s **10.00**
  Robin Hood, child's, medium, yellow
  and green suit, black silk screened
  Robin Hood on front, felt hat with
  feather and badges, plastic mask,
  orig box, 1950s **7.50**
  Skeleton, adult's, medium, black
  cloth jumpsuit, white painted
  bones, black pull over mask–cap,
  white painted skull face, 1930s .. **10.00**
Diecut, 2½" h, witches on broom, set
of forty on sheet, marked "Germany" **20.00**
Fan, 9" h, orange and black, Halloween
figures, Germany **35.00**
Game, "I Am A Dumb Skull," cardboard, mechanical, 1930s, USA **30.00**

Lantern
  3" h, glass, pumpkin head, painted
  orange, brightly colored face, wire
  handle, candle holder in base, USA **40.00**
  5" h
    Egg Crate Papier Mache, pumpkin
    head, orange, paper insert be-
    hind cut out eyes, wire bail, USA
    "O" shaped mouth **40.00**
    Smiling mouth **45.00**
    Tin, pumpkin on wooden pole,
    candleholder in base, faced or-
    ange and green, smiling face,
    marked "Germany" **125.00**
  6" h, papier mache, cat's head, black,
  orig paper insert behind eyes and
  mouth, wire bail, marked "Germany" **150.00**
  7" h
    Cardboard, black, four sided, cut
    in witch silhouette, orange tissue
    paper background, wire bail,
    USA **42.00**
    Egg Crate Papier Mache, cat's head
    on fence, orange, paper insert
    behind eyes and mouth **60.00**
    Papier Mache, devil head, two tone
    red, paper insert behind cut out
    eyes and mouth, wire bail, Ger-
    many **100.00**
Mask
  Duck, cloth, starched beak, blue hat,
  elastic tie **25.00**
  Half Mask
    Cloth, various colors, elastic tie .. **3.50**
    Papier Mache, black, gold trim,
    string tie **5.00**
  Happy Woman, painted cloth, string
  ties, marked "Japan" **6.00**
  Pirate, papier mache, string ties,
  marked "Germany" **10.00**
  Princess, papier mache, yellow human hair, string tie, marked "Germany" **15.00**
  Somber Face, wire mesh, painted
  face, long gray horsehair beard,
  string ties **55.00**
Noisemaker
  2½", clicker, metal, orange and
  black, frog shape, USA **10.00**
  3" d, round
    Rattle, tin, wooden handle, orange,
    white, and green, pumpkin and
    cats litho, USA **7.50**
    Squeakers, orange pumpkin face,
    cardboard and cloth, marked
    "Germany" **20.00**
  3½" d, round, cardboard cov with orange and black tissue paper,
  wooden handle **10.00**
  6½", tin, orange and black, picture of
  costumed girl, marked "Germany" **15.00**

10" l, 2" d, rattle, home made, tin can type, cov with orange and black Halloween designs, small stones inside, wooden stick handle **15.00**

Pitcher, 1½" h, bisque, Halloween face **14.00**

ST PATRICK'S DAY

Corkscrew, Irish blackthorn handle, marked "Happy St Patrick's Day," green cloth ribbon attached to handle **10.00**

Diecut
Set of 40, shamrock with Irish girl in center, marked "Germany" **20.00**
Set of 42, Irish boy in green top hat, clay pipe in mouth, marked "Germany" **15.00**
Single, 3" h, gold harp entwined with shamrocks and green ribbon, marked "Germany" **1.50**

Doll, 4½" h, boy, composition, green and white felt clothing, white felt hat with shamrock trim, marked "Japan" **35.00**

Pin, "Erin Go Bragh" across face, Irish flag, American flag, shamrock, and harp, green satin ribbon attached to pin, paper on back of pin marked "12th St Badge and Novelty House, Phila, PA" **6.50**

Postcard
"Erin Go Bragh," white top hat, clay pipe, and shillelagh, marked "New York" **1.00**
"Ireland Forever," shamrock with view of Ireland in each leaf, marked "Germany" **1.00**
"Saint Patrick of Ireland," religious card, Saint Patrick portrayed above a church, printed in Italy **2.00**
"To My Little Coleen," girl dressed in green, large shamrock for hair bow, marked "London" **1.50**

THANKSGIVING

Candy Container, turkey
5" h, composition, fan tail, opening at base, marked "Japan" **35.00**
6" h, composition, folded tail, glass eyes, metal feet, removable head, marked "Germany" **45.00**
6½" h, composition, fan tail, horsehair beard, metal feet, marked "Germany" **40.00**
8" h, egg crate papier mache, pale orange, opening in base, marked "Alco Co, USA" **30.00**
12" h, composition, fan tail, horsehair beard, metal feet, marked "Germany" **85.00**

Figurine, 4" h, composition, man and woman Pilgrims, marked "Germany" **45.00**

Thanksgiving, candy container, turkey, painted papier mache body, lead feet, 3¾" h, $12.00.

Place Card, 3" h, emb cardboard turkey, stand-up type, USA **5.00**

Postcard
"A Thanksgiving Greeting," large harvest pumpkin in background, three turkeys eating from dish outside a home, 1910 .... **1.00**
"Hearty Good Cheer For Thanksgiving Day," autumn arrangement with turkey, marked "Saxony, 1914" .. **1.00**
"Thanksgiving Greetings," two small boys dressed as chefs, carrying huge dressed turkey on platter, marked "Saxony, 1908" **1.50**

Turkey
1¼" h, pot metal, molded feet, marked "England" **10.00**
1½" h, rubber, black, red and green trim, USA **7.50**
2" h, composition, fan tail, metal feet, marked "Germany" **15.00**
4" h, celluloid, white, pink, and blue, weighted bottom, marked "Irwin, USA" **25.00**
6" h, composition, folded tail, green base, marked "Japan" **35.00**

VALENTINE'S DAY

Greeting Card
3" h, "To My Valentine," heart shape, girl on front, bordered by hearts, verse inside, marked "Whitney, USA" **2.50**
3 x 4", Valentine poem about kitten, little girl on front having tea party with kitten, marked "Ernest Nister, London, #839" **9.00**
4" h, "A Valentine Specially For You," delivery boy on motorbike holding

red hearts, stand-up, marked "Germany" **7.00**

4½" h, "Best Wishes," shades of blue, picture of bird in center, poem beneath, no greeting inside **5.00**

5" h

Flat, "With Love's Greetings," boy dressed in blue on garden bench, greeting on back of card **7.50**

Fold-Out, "With Best Wishes," two cupids embracing, bordered by birds, marked "Germany" **11.00**

Mechanical, "To My Love," gray cat, movable eyes and mouth, stand-up, marked "Germany" .. **7.50**

5½" h, "To My Valentine," boy serenading girl with mandolin, bordered by white doves and red roses, fold-out with red tissue paper, marked "Germany," 1930s **11.00**

6" h, "To My Sweetheart," white dog, envelope in mouth, stand-up, marked "Germany" **3.50**

6 x 10", mechanical, steamroller filled with children holding hearts, wheels turn and children move up and down, tab operated, marked "Germany" **18.00**

6½" h

Boy with girl covering his eyes, trimmed with white emb paper lace, greeting inside, marked "Whitney, USA" **7.00**

"St Valentine's Greetings," three small children dressed in winter clothing playing in white birch forest, heart shaped greeting with falling snow border, easel stand-up, letter E in circle mark **10.00**

"To My Sweetheart," card style, small girl in green dress and hat, red wild rose border, verse inside **10.00**

9" h, mechanical

Chicken carrying a baby wrapped in blanket, blanket in beak, baby holds valentine, as baby swings, chicken's eyes move, stand-up, marked "Germany" **15.00**

"Tell You Who Is My Valentine," ferris wheel, two children in each car, string operation makes ferris wheel turn, stand-up, marked "Germany" **15.00**

Postcard

"Be My Valentine," small girl in purple dress holding bouquet of roses, large gold heart and verse in background, marked "Whitney, USA," 1930s **1.00**

Cupid on swing of roses, bordered by red hearts and gold scroll work, small verse, marked "E Nash" ... **1.25**

"February 14th," trimmed in green ivy, cupids shooting hearts and arrows at two lovers enclosed in heart, marked "Germany, 1910" .. **1.50**

"To My Valentine," two cupids holding garland of hearts, verse, and two gold hearts at base of card, marked "London, 1910" **1.50**

HOMER LAUGHLIN

Collecting Hints: The original trademark from 1871 to 1890 merely identified the products as "Laughlin Brothers." The next trademark featured the American eagle astride the prostrate British lion. The third marking featured a monogram of "HLC" which has appeared, with slight variations, on all dinnerware since about 1900. The 1900 trademark contained a number which identified month, year and plant at which the product was made. Letter codes were used in later periods.

So much attention has been placed on Fiesta that other interesting patterns have not achieved the popularity which they deserve. Prices still are moderate. Some of the patterns from the 1930 to 1940 period have contemporary designs that are highly artistic.

Virginia Rose is a shape, not a pattern name. Several different decals can be found, with delicate pink flowers the most common.

History: Homer Laughlin and his brother, Shakespeare, built two pottery kilns in East Liverpool, Ohio, in 1871. Shakespeare withdrew in 1879, leaving Homer to operate the business alone. Laughlin became one of the first firms to produce American-made whiteware. In 1896, William Wills and a Pittsburgh group led by Marcus Aaron bought the Laughlin firm.

Expansion followed. Two new plants were built in Laughlin Station, Ohio. In 1906, the first plant (#4) was built in Newall, West Virginia. In 1923 plant #6 was built at Newall and featured a continuous tunnel kiln. Similar kilns were added at the other plants. Other advances included spray glazing and mechanical jiggering.

In the 1930 to 1960 period several new dinnerware lines were added, including the Wells Art Glaze line. Ovenserve and Kitchen Kraft were the cooking ware lines. The colored glaze lines of Fiesta, Harlequin and Rhythm captured major market shares. In 1959 a translucent table china line was introduced. Today, the annual manufacturing capacity is over 45 million pieces.

References: Jo Cunningham, *The Collector's Encyclopedia of American Dinnerware*, Collector Books, 1982; Betty Newbound, *The Gunshot Guide To Values Of American Made China & Pottery*, Book 2, privately printed, 1983.

Periodicals: *The Daze,* 12135 North State Road, Otisville, MI 48463; *The New Glaze,* P.O. Box 4782, Birmingham, AL 35206.

REPRODUCTION ALERT. Harlequin and Fiesta lines were reissued in 1978 and marked accordingly.

See: Fiesta

Pie Plate, Kitchen Kraft Oven Serve pattern, 9¾" d, $8.50.

Amberstone
Bowl, 5½", fruit	5.50
Butter, cov,¼ lb	28.00
Coffee Server	20.00
Cup	4.00
Gravy Boat	12.00

Plate
6", bread and butter	3.50
9", dinner	5.75
Saucer	2.50
Tray, center handle	18.00

Hacienda
Bowl
9", oval	13.00
9½", round	18.00
Casserole, cov	98.00
Creamer	5.00
Fruit Bowl, 5"	6.00

Plate
6", bread and butter	3.50
7", dessert	6.00
9", dinner	10.00

Platter
11"	15.00
11¾"	12.00
Sugar, cov	6.00
Vegetable Bowl, oval	15.00

Harlequin
Ashtray, basketweave, turquoise	25.00
Bowl, 5½", rose	4.00
Chop Plate, rose	12.00
Creamer and Sugar, cov, spruce green	22.50

Cup and Saucer
Green	6.00
Turquoise	4.00
Yellow	5.00
Egg Cup, double, yellow	8.00

Nut Dish
Blue	5.00
Red	5.00
Wine	5.00

Pitcher
Ball
Rose	45.00
Yellow	25.00
Water, red	33.00

Plate
7", salad
Rose	4.00
Yellow	2.50

9", dinner
Dark Green	7.00
Turquoise	4.00
Yellow	4.00

10", dinner
Turquoise	6.00
Wine	15.00
Salad Bowl, individual, yellow	10.00
Soup, chartreuse	10.00

Tumbler
Red	25.00
Spring Green	25.00

Mexicana
Cake Plate, red trim	24.00
Casserole, cov, 8½", red trim	40.00
Creamer and Sugar, cov	20.00
Cup	8.00
Fruit Bowl, 5"	6.00
Pie Plate	28.00

Plate
6", bread and butter	3.50
10", dinner	22.00
Platter, 13"	15.00
Salt and Pepper Shakers, pr	40.00
Saucer	2.00

Serving Pieces
Fork	50.00
Pie Server	55.00
Soup, flat	12.00

Riviera Ivy, gold trim
Bowl, 5"	3.00
Creamer	3.50
Cup and Saucer	5.00
Gravy Boat, attached underplate	45.00

Plate
6", bread and butter	1.50
8", luncheon	4.00
9", dinner	10.00
Platter, 14"	9.00
Soup, flat	5.00
Sugar, cov	4.50
Vegetable Bowl, oval	8.00

Virginia Rose
Bowl
5½"	3.00
8½"	8.00
Creamer	7.00
Cup and Saucer	7.50
Gravy Boat	15.00

Mixing Bowl	**30.00**
Plate	
6", bread and butter	**2.00**
7", luncheon	**3.00**
9½", dinner	**5.50**
Soup, flat, 8½"	**12.00**
Sugar, cov	**10.00**
Tureen, cov, oval	**30.00**

HORSE COLLECTIBLES

Collecting Hints: Equine memorabilia encompass a wide range of collectibles, from the tack and equipment used by the horse to advertising items featuring horses and specific horse related material such as old quarter horse stud books.

Although the figurine is the most common type of equine collectible, horse theme material can be found in almost every other collecting category. Most hobbyists choose to concentrate on one form, e.g., board games, figurines, plates, or advertising tins. Some collectors limit their memorabilia to their favorite breed or even to one particular horse, for example, Roy Roger's beautiful palomino, Trigger.

Hunting, horse racing, rodeo, state fairs, and Olympic equestrian events have fostered a wealth of ribbons, trophies, programs, certificates, and other memorabilia. Such miscellany is valuable only to a handful of collectors specializing in that area. An exception would be the highly unusual, such as a handmade quilt stitched by a wheelchair-bound cowboy that incorporates all the ribbons he had been awarded in his long and successful rodeo career.

History: Since the introduction of the mustang to North America by the Spanish explorers and its subsequent capture and taming by the American Indians, the horse has been an integral part of life in the United States. Horses helped to chart the course of American history — from the horse ridden by Paul Revere on his famous "midnight ride" to the tough little burros and mules that opened the West to ranching and mining; from the rugged mounts of the Pony Express to Traveler, the horse ridden by General Robert E. Lee to Appomattox where he surrendered the Confederacy, and Black Jack, the riderless horse who figured so dramatically in the funeral procession of President John F. Kennedy.

For centuries, the horse was a necessity, the main form of transportation. Horses delivered our mail and groceries, brought the doctor, police, or firemen to our home when needed, plowed our fields, and provided entertainment — whether simply as transportation to social gatherings or as the event itself through racing, rodeo, circus, movies, and television appearances.

Today, the horse is a pampered family pet.

According to a 1988 study by a Yale social ecologist, the horse has a strong hold on second place as the most beloved animal companion. Only dogs were regarded more highly.

This resurgence in equine popularity, coupled with the continuing infatuation of little girls with horses, has spawned a whole new generation of equine collectibles for the future—My Little Pony, Cabbage Patch Ponies, etc.

Collectors' Club: Equine Collectors Club, Box 4764 New River Stage II, Phoenix, AZ 85027. *Horsin' Around* (monthly).

Museums: Harness Racing Hall of Fame, Goshen, NY; Pony Express Museum, St. Joseph, MO.

Advisors: Jim and Nancy Schaut.

REPRODUCTION ALERT: Many cast iron, horse drawn vehicles are being imported from the Far East.

EQUIPMENT AND RELATED ITEMS

Bridle, braided leather strips, 1930s	**45.00**
Bridle Rosettes, Masonic emblem under convex glass, pr	**40.00**
Buggy Whip, 84" overall, carved wood horsehead handle	**40.00**
Chaps, leather, custom made metal studs ranch brand, early 1900s	**350.00**
Draft Horse Merit, 3 x 3", brass, standing harnessed work horse, fancy border	**30.00**
Hearse, glass enclosed, ornate, built 1845, St Louis Casket Co	**6,000.00**
Mochila, leather, four mail pockets, Western saddle horn slot, used by Pony Express riders	**400.00**
Plow, iron and oak, 2 or 3 horse team, Richland Farm Implements, 1880s	**300.00**
Riding Crop, ornate silver handle	**60.00**
Road Grader, metal and wood, horse drawn	**900.00**
Robe, buggy, woven with horse picture	**85.00**
Saddle	
Army McClelland type, 1870s	**450.00**
Side, elaborate tooled leather dec, made by Jacobs, patented 1890	**600.00**
Sleigh Bells, leather strap with buckle, 29 graduated bells	**235.00**
Spurs, wrought iron dec, rowels, Mexican craftsman, early 1900s	**175.00**
Stirrup, wood, rounded bottom, worn leather cover	**15.00**
Surrey, two seater, kerosene lamps, harness, and leather seats	**2,700.00**
Veterinary Tool, ecrazier	**35.00**
Wagon Jack, 30" high, iron and wood, manufactured in Boston, MA, dated 1863	**90.00**

Wagon Seat, leather cov, springs and
steel frame **150.00**
Watering Trough, 24 x 48", cast iron .. **175.00**

**Ashtray, Art Deco style, pink glass base,
black horse, $35.00.**

THEME ITEMS

Advertising
Ashtray, White Horse Whiskey, white
china, figural horse head, painted   **10.00**
Box, "Baum's Horse and Stock Food"
label, wood, 1910 .... **125.00**
Calendar, Iroquois Brewing Co, In-
dian on Paint Pony, 1897 .... **75.00**
Sign, 14 x 22", tin, Mobil flying red
horse **50.00**
Tin, Newton's Heave Cough Horse
Cure, pocket, trotting horse with
driver **45.00**
Trade Card, Galena Axle Grease Co   **5.00**
Tray, Falls City Brewing Co, 13" d,
topless girl on horse **250.00**
Bank, 10" l, cast iron, mechanical, "Al-
ways did despise a mule," black
jockey on kicking mule, late 1800s . **600.00**
Book, *National Velvet*, Enid Bagnold, dj,
1st ed **50.00**
Bookend, 7" h, horsehead, glass,
Heisey, c1937–55, pr **185.00**
Candy Mold, 7" l, donkey, #15919,
Vormenfabrien, Holland **30.00**
Carousel Horse, 48" h, prancing, carved
by Herschell-Spillman, 1880 ......**2,000.00**
Catalog
Janesville Buggies, 98 pgs, 1914 ... **100.00**
Oaklawn Percheron Horses, 134 pgs,
draft horse sale, 1884 .... **125.00**
Christmas Ornament, Hobby Horse,
Dresden **80.00**
Cookie Jar, Hobby Horse figural, McCoy
Pottery, 1948–51 .... **60.00**
Decanter, Man-O-War, Ezra Brooks,
1969 .... **18.00**
Doorstop, 5" l, cast iron, horse figure,
Hubley **175.00**

Figure
Barclay, rearing horse, mounted In-
dian **25.00**
Breyer #166, Buckskin foal, laying . **40.00**
Fostoria Glass, 3 x 2½", clear, colt,
sitting, 1938–44 .... **40.00**
Hartland, Dale Evans on horse, But-
termilk **15.00**
Jade, 6" h, carved, wood stand **195.00**
Royal Doulton, Chestnut mare and
foal, HN2522 .... **450.00**
Fruit Crate Label, Bronco, Redlands,
CA, orange, cowboy on bucking
horse, stone litho **5.00**
Game, Derby Day, board folds out to
72", six wooden horses and hurdles,
Parker Brothers, copyright 1959 .... **40.00**
Glass, Kentucky Derby, 100th running,
1974 .... **8.00**

**Cup and Saucer, hunt scene, marked
"Gray & Sons, England," $15.00.**

Lapel Pin, figural, donkey, "Vote Democratic," 1960s **10.00**
Lunchpail, tin, Gene Autry and Champion, 1950s **50.00**
Magazine, Western Horseman, Vol VII,
Jan 1942, Pony Express feature article **10.00**
Mustache Cup, "The Life of a Fireman,"
horsedrawn pumper racing to burning
building **40.00**
Olympic Pin, stylized horse with Olym-
pic Ring, Labatt's Beer sponsor of
1984 Equestrian Team **12.00**
Pillow, 13" d, needlepoint, gray pranc-
ing horse, green and brown ground . **15.00**
Pin Cushion, metal, horseshoe shape . **10.00**
Plate, "Nearing Finish," Kentucky
Derby Series, Reed and Barton, 1972 **100.00**
Poster, Clydesdales, 50th Anniversary of
Anheuser Busch, 1933–83 .... **2.00**
Print, Celebrated trotting Horse Henry,
Currier and Ives **195.00**
Puzzle, Tom Mix and horse, Tony Jr.,
1930s Rexall Drug Store giveaway .. **40.00**

Rocking Horse, hand carved, horsehair
  mane and tail **700.00**
Sheet Music, Donkey Serenade **3.00**
Snowdome, man, mule,and mountain
  scene, Souvenir of Missouri, 1950s . **10.00**
Stamp, Pony Express, canceled Aug. 21,
  1860, San Francisco **25.00**
Tobacco Tin, Dan Patch **50.00**
Toy
  Pull, 16" h, horsehair mane and tail,
    glass eyes, wood base, red wood
    wheels, late 19th C **600.00**
  Truck, three horses, driver, hook, and
    ladder, Hubley, 1910 .... **320.00**
Weathervane, full bodied, prancing
  horse, molded copper, mounted on
  cast iron, 1880s **900.00**
Windmill Weight, 20" l, cast iron, run-
  ning horse, Donforth, Batavia, IL, late
  1880s **400.00**
Whirligig, 14" l, man chasing runaway
  mule, 1920s **225.00**

HULL POTTERY

Collecting Hints: Hull Pottery has distinctive
markings on the bottom of its vases that help the
collector identify them immediately. Early stoneware pottery has an "H." The famous matte
pieces, a favorite of most collectors, contain pattern numbers. For example, Camelia pieces are
marked with numbers in the 100's, Iris pieces
have 400 numbers, and Wildflower numbers
with a W– preceding their number. Most of
Hull's vases are also marked with their height in
inches, making determining their value much
easier. Items made after 1950 are marked with
"hull" or "Hull" in large script writing and are
usually glossy.

History: In 1905 Addis E. Hull purchased the
Acme Pottery Co. in Crooksville, Ohio. In 1917
A. E. Hull Pottery Co. began to make a line of
art pottery for florists and gift shops. The company also made novelties, kitchenware, and stoneware. During the Depression, the company's
largest production was tiles.

In 1950 the factory was destroyed by a flood
and fire. By 1952 it was back in production,
operating with the Hull Pottery Company name.
At this time Hull added its newer glossy finish
pottery plus developed Regal and Floraline as
trade names for pieces sold in flower shops.
Hull's brown House 'n Garden line of kitchen
and dinnerware achieved great popularity and
was the main line of pottery being produced prior
to the plant closing its doors in 1986. Hull's
Little Red Riding Hood kitchenware was manufactured between 1943 and 1957 and is a favorite
of collectors, including many who do not collect
other Hull items.

Hull collectors are beginning to seriously collect the glossy ware and kitchen items. Since the
plant has closed, all Hull pieces have become
desirable.

References: Brenda Roberts, *The Collectors Encyclopedia of Hull Pottery*, Collector Books,
1980; Mark E. Supnick, *Collecting Hull Pottery's
"Little Red Riding Hood": A Pictorial Reference
And Price Guide*, L–W Book Sales, 1989.

Advisor: Joan Hull.

Note: Unless otherwise marked, all objects listed
are vases.

**Orchid, jardiniere, marked "317–4¾,"
$40.00.**

PRE-1950 PATTERNS

Bowknot
  B-2-5" **45.00**
  B-8-8" **7.00**
  B-18-5¾", jardiniere **65.00**
  B-21-10½", basket **350.00**
Camelia (Open Rose)
  116-12", console bowl, bird handles **125.00**
  117-6½", candleholders, bird shape,
    pr **125.00**
  128-4¾', pitcher **35.00**
  136-6½" **85.00**
Dogwood (Wild Rose)
  502-6½", vase, suspended **75.00**
  509-6½" **50.00**
  522, cornucopia, small **35.00**
Iris (Narcissus)
  402-7" **55.00**
  409-12", bowl, oval **95.00**
  412-4", basket, hanging **50.00**
Jack-in-the-Pulpit (Calla Lily)
  520-33-6½" **50.00**
  530-33-9" **110.00**
  570-33-5", cornucopia **45.00**
Little Red Riding Hood
  Cookie Jar 135889 .... **100.00**
  Creamer, side pour **75.00**
  Sugar, side pour **75.00**
  Teapot **150.00**

Little Red Riding Hood, cookie jar, 13″, $100.00.

Magnolia
    5-7″, ewer 50.00
    9-10½″ 65.00
    10-10½″, basket 175.00
    20-15″, vase, floor type 225.00
Orchid
    320-10½″ 145.00
    303-8″ 85.00
    304-6″ 50.00
Pinecone
    55 .... 45.00
Pink Magnolia (glossy)
    H-20-21-22, tea set 125.00
Poppy
    603-4¾″, jardiniere 50.00
    604-8″, bowl, boat shape 75.00
    611-6½″ 65.00
Rosella
    R-7-6¼″ 35.00
    R-6½″, pitcher 45.00
    R-10-6½″, wall pocket, heart shape . 50.00
Stoneware
    #492, stein, Alpine scene 35.00
    26 H-8″ 45.00
Thistle, #53-6½″ 45.00
Tulip
    107-33-6″ 55.00
    115-33-7″, jardiniere 150.00
    116-33-6″, flower pot 75.00
Waterlily
    L-6-6½″ 40.00
    L-13-10½″ 85.00
    L-21-13½″, console bowl 85.00
    L-22, candleholder, pr 50.00
Wildflower
    W-5-6½″ 35.00
    W-12-9½″ 55.00
    W-19-13½″, ewer 250.00
    69-4″, candleholder, double 75.00
    71-12″ 100.00
    78-8½″ 75.00
Woodland (Matte)
    W-6-6½″, ewer 50.00

W-14-10″, planter 55.00
W-15-8½″, bud vase, double 50.00

POST-1950 PATTERNS (glossy)

Blossom Flite
    T-1-6″, honey jug 35.00
    T-6-10½″, cornucopia 50.00
    T-9-10″, bowl basket 65.00
Butterfly
    B-3-7″, ashtray 45.00
    B-17, basket, large 85.00
    B-18-19-20, tea set 115.00
Ebbtide
    E-6-9½″, Angel Fish 55.00
    E-9-11¾″ 65.00
Figural Planters
    93-6″, love birds 30.00
    114-8″, poodle 40.00
    115-8″, giraffe 40.00
Parchment & Pine
    S-1 .... 25.00
    S-7, pitcher, large 115.00
Serende (birds)
    S-12-14″ 70.00
    S-22, mug 35.00
Sunglow (kitchenware)
    50-9½″, mixing bowl 30.00
    82-8½″, whiskbroom wall pocket .. 45.00
    98-7½″, flower pot 25.00
Tokay (grapes)
    2-6″ 30.00
    9-7½″, candy dish, lid 55.00
    11-10½″, basket, moon 75.00
Woodland
    W-4-6½″ 30.00
    W-16-8½″ 45.00
    W-29 & 30, console set 95.00

HUMMEL ITEMS

Collecting Hints: A key to Hummel figures is the mark. Collectors are advised to get the early marks whenever possible. Since production runs were large, almost all figurines, no matter what the mark, exist in large numbers.

Prices fluctuate a great deal. Antique newspapers, such as *The Antique Trader,* and dealers often run ads showing discounts on the modern pieces. The slightest damage to a piece lowers the value significantly.

Before World War II and for a few years after, the Goebel Company made objects, such as vases, for export. These often had the early mark. Prices are modest for these items because few collectors concentrate on them. The Hummel books do not list them. This aspect of the Goebel Company offers the chance for an excellent research project.

History: Hummel items are the original creations

of the German artist, Berta Hummel. Born in 1909 in Massing, Bavaria, into a family where the arts were a part of everyday living, her talents were encouraged by her parents and formal educators from early childhood. At the age of 18, she was enrolled in the Academy of Fine Arts in Munich to further her mastery of drawing and the palette.

She entered the Convent of Siessen and became Sister Maria Innocentia in 1934. In this Franciscan cloister, she continued drawing and painting images of her childhood friends.

In 1935, W. Goebel Co. in Rodental, Germany, conceived the idea of reproducing Sister Berta's sketches into 3-dimensional bisque figurines. John Schmid discovered the German-made figurines. The Schmid Brothers of Randolph, Massachusetts, introduced the figurines to America and became Goebel's U.S. distributor.

In 1967, Goebel began distributing Hummel items in the U.S. and a controversy developed between the two companies involving the Hummel family and the convent. Law suits and counter suits ensued. The German courts finally effected a compromise. The convent held legal rights to all works produced by Sister Berta from 1934 until her death in 1964 and licensed Goebel to reproduce these works. Schmid was to deal directly with the Hummel family for permission to reproduce any pre-convent art work.

All authentic Hummels bear both the signature, M.I. Hummel, and a Goebel trademark. Various trademarks were used to identify the year of production. The Crown Mark (CM) was used in 1935, Full Bee (FB) 1940–1959; Small Stylized Bee (SSB) 1960–1972; Large Stylized Bee (LSB) 1960–1963; Three Line Mark (3L) 1964–1972; Last Bee Mark (LB) 1972–1980, Missing Bee Mark (MB) 1979–Present.

References: John F. Hotchkiss, *Hummel Art II,* Wallace-Homestead, 1981; John F. Hotchkiss, *Hotchkiss' Handbook To Hummel Art with Current Prices,* Wallace-Homestead, 1982; Carl F. Luckey, *Luckey's Hummel Figurines & Plates, 7th Edition,* Books Americana, 1987; Lawrence L. Wonsch, *Hummel Copycats with Values,* Wallace-Homestead, 1987.

Collectors' Club: Goebel Collectors' Club, 105 White Plains Road, Tarrytown, NY 10591.

Museum: Goebel Museum, Tarrytown, NY.

Anniversary Plate
    1975, Stormy Weather, #280, FE ... **165.00**
    1980, Spring Dance, #281 .... **135.00**
    1985, Auf Wiedersehen **160.00**
Ashtray
    Boy With Bird, #166 .... **80.00**
    Joyful, #33 .... **75.00**
    Let's Sing, #114 .... **75.00**
Bank, Little Thrifty, c1972 .... **50.00**

Bell
    Knit One **85.00**
    Let's Sing **140.00**
    Mountaineer **85.00**
    Sing Along **80.00**
    Thoughtful **80.00**
Calendar, 1955, 12 illus **15.00**
Candlestick, Girl With Fir Tree, 1956 . **35.00**

Christmas Ornament, 1974, The Guardian Angel, 3¾" d, $15.00.

Christmas Plate
    1971, Heavenly Angel, #264 ...... **725.00**
    1972, Hear Ye, Hear Ye, #265 .... **125.00**
    1973, Globe Trotter, #266 .... **70.00**
    1974, Goose Girl, #267 .... **100.00**
    1975, Ride Into Christmas, #268 ... **90.00**
    1976, Apple Tree Girl, #269 ...... **80.00**
    1977, Apple Tree Boy, #270 ...... **95.00**
    1978, Happy Pastime, #271 .... **75.00**
    1979, Singing Lesson, #272 .... **85.00**
    1980, School Girl, #273 .... **100.00**
    1981, Umbrella Boy, #274 .... **100.00**
    1982, Umbrella Girl, #275 .... **110.00**
    1983, Postman, #276 .... **110.00**
    1984, A Gift From Heaven, #277 .. **105.00**
    1985, Chick Girl, #278 .... **110.00**
    1986, Playmates, #279 .... **125.00**
    1987, Feeding Time, #283 .... **135.00**
    1988, Little Goat Herder, #284 .... **135.00**
    1989, Farm Boy **115.00**
Doll
    Carnival, porcelain **190.00**
    Chimney Sweep **50.00**
    Easter Greetings, porcelain **200.00**
    Gretel **50.00**
    Hansel **50.00**
    Little Knitter **50.00**
    Postman, porcelain **200.00**
    Rosa, pink **40.00**
Figure
    Adoration, #23/111, 7⅛", LB **375.00**
    Angelic Song, #144, MB **65.00**
    Apple Tree Boy, #142/3/0, SSB **85.00**
    Apple Tree Girl, #141/1, LB **145.00**
    Artist, #304, MB **90.00**
    Baker, #128, SSB **85.00**

Barnyard Hero, #195/2/0, FB **115.00**
Be Patient, 6", SSB **145.00**
Bird Duet, #169, MB **115.00**
Bookworm, #8, LB **75.00**
Boots, #143/I, SSB **175.00**
Brother, #95, FB **100.00**
Builder, #305, 3L **82.00**
Carnival, #328, MB **80.00**
Chick Girl, #57/0, FB **100.00**
Cinderella, #337, MB **110.00**
Culprits, #56, SSB **200.00**
Doctor, #127, FB **120.00**
Doll Bath, #319, LB **75.00**
Duet, #130, CM **300.00**
Easter Time, #378, SSB **100.00**
Eventide, SSB **135.00**
Farewell, FB **275.00**
Farm Boy, #66, CM **400.00**
Feeding Time, #199/1, FB **215.00**
Follow The Leader, LB **425.00**
Friends, #136/1, 5", 3L **85.00**

Figure, Kiss Me, #311, three line mark, 6⅛" h, $145.00

Gay Adventure, #356, MB **75.00**
Girl with Doll, #239B, MB **25.00**
Globe Trotter, #79, SSB **60.00**
Good Hunting, #307, 3L **130.00**
Goose Girl, #47/0, FB, 4¼" **200.00**
Happy Traveler, #109/0, SSB **50.00**
Hear Ye, #15/0, CM **300.00**
Herald Angels, #37, FB **80.00**
Joyful, #53, FB **100.00**
Just Resting, #112/I, CM **300.00**
Kiss Me, #311, 3L **145.00**
Little Band, #392, FB **125.00**
Little Fiddler, #4, CM **250.00**
Little Gardener, #72, FB **60.00**
Little Hiker, #16/2/0, FB **80.00**
Little Scholar, #80, SSB **55.00**
Lost Sheep, #68/0, SSB **72.00**
March Winds, #43, CM **200.00**

Merry Wanderer, #7/II, CM **500.00**
Mountaineer, #315, 3L **145.00**
Not For You, #317, 3L **85.00**
Out of Danger, #56/B, SSB **110.00**
Photographer, FB **225.00**
Postman, #119, MB **80.00**
Puppy Love, #1, SSB **75.00**
Retreat to Safety, #201/2/0, 3L **90.00**
School Boy, #82/0, MB **70.00**
School Girl, #81/2/0, SSB **60.00**
Sensitive Hunter, #6/0, CM **275.00**
Serenade, #85/0, SSB **70.00**
Signs of Spring, 4", both shoes, LB . **400.00**
Sister, #98/0, MB **65.00**
Skier, #59, FB **175.00**
Soloist, #135, FB **80.00**
Spring Cheer, #72, SSB **80.00**
Stormy Weather, #71, FB **425.00**
Sweet Music, #186, CM **125.00**
Telling Her Secret, #196/0, FB **235.00**
To Market, #49/3/0, MB **75.00**
Tuneful Angel, #359, MB **40.00**
Village Boy, #51/2/0, CM **115.00**
Volunteers, #50/2/0,FB **200.00**
Waiter, #154/0, FB **1309.00**
Wash Day, #321, 3L **80.00**
Wayside Devotion, #28/2, 7½", FB . **300.00**
Weary Wanderer, #204, MB **80.00**
Worship, #84/0, CM **250.00**
Font
  Angel Cloud, #206, 3L **25.00**
  Angel Sitting, #167, 3L **40.00**
  Angel With Birds, #22/0, MB **18.00**
  Angels At Prayer, #91B, SSB **70.00**
  Child With Flowers, #36/0, FB **48.00**
  Good Shepherd, #35/0, MB **25.00**
  Madonna and Child, #243, MB **25.00**
  Worship, #164, FB **120.00**
Inkwell, With Loving Greetings, blue . **135.00**
Lamp
  Apple Tree Boy, #M/230, LB **165.00**
  Birthday Serenade, #M/231/1FB, re-
    verse mold **900.00**
  Good Friends, #M/228, LB **165.00**
  Just Resting, #M/225/11, LB **175.00**
  Loves Me, Loves Me Not, #M/227,
    FB, c1970 .... **180.00**
  Out of Danger, FB **275.00**
Music Box
  Chick Girl **235.00**
  Ride Into Christmas **240.00**
Nativity Figures
  Angel Serenade, #214/D/11 .... **40.00**
  Donkey, #214/J/11 .... **35.00**
  Infant Jesus, #260 .... **80.00**
  King, kneeling on one knee, #214/M/
    11 .... **100.00**
  Lamb, #214/0/11 .... **15.00**
  Little Tooter, #214/H/11 .... **65.00**
  Madonna, #214/A/M/11 .... **110.00**
  Stable, 3 pc, #214/S11 .... **35.00**
Print, Moonlight Return, litho, FE **500.00**

Wall Plaque

Ba Bee Ring, #30 A, #30 B, set, MB   **100.00**
Child in Bed, #137, 3L **40.00**
Fitting Butterfly, #139, FB **125.00**
Little Fiddler, #93, FB **120.00**
Quartet, #134, SSB **150.00**
Retreat to Safety, #126, LB **80.00**
Searching Angel, LB **70.00**
Swaying Lullaby, #165, LB **85.00**
Vacation Time, #123, 3L **140.00**

INDIAN SOUVENIR BEADWORK

Collecting Hints: Colored beaded items are much more desirable than clear beaded work. A general rule is that the larger a piece, the more valuable it is. Pieces with large animals and flags seem to be the most popular among collectors.

Probably the most important aspect of the value of these beaded items is the condition of the beads and fabric. If the fabric is badly faded, value diminishes quickly.

History: In the late 19th and early 20th centuries, the Indian tribes of Northwest America made beadwork items for the souvenir trade. The vast majority were sold in the Niagara Falls area, a tourist mecca of that period. The extent of their work included pincushions, match holders, picture frames, and other useful pieces.

The best of the Indian beadwork occurred in the early 1900s, but later examples were made. Further, production was not limited to the Indian tribes; non-Indian products were identical in style and format. Since the vast majority was Indian in origin, all examples are included in this section.

Advisors: Abby Irons.

Bird

5", tan fabric, clear beads, dangling
cherries on branch **65.00**
7", yellow cotton fabric, clear and
multicolored beads, beaded collar,
cherries in mouth and stick, dated
under tail 1910 ....   **130.00**
9", green cotton fabric, clear beads,
cherries in mouth, two dangling
cherries on stick, dated 1913 ....   **140.00**

Boat

3 x 9", gold cotton fabric, clear and
multicolored beads, marked "FAST
BOAT 1901" **55.00**
4 x 7½", maroon velvet fabric,
multicolored beaded flowers, dated
1929 ....   **45.00**

Boot

4 x 7"
Green velvet fabric, multicolored
beads, birds and flowers **40.00**
Red cotton velvet, multicolored
beads, flower and leaves **35.00**
9 x 12", polished cotton, heavy flower
and leaves dec, scalloped edge ..   **75.00**

Frame

6 x 8", blue fabric, clear beads, flowers and leaves **60.00**
8 x 10", cotton fabric, rabbits, flowers, and leaves dec **95.00**
Match Holder, 4 x 5", cotton fabric, geometric design, two partitions, dated
1908 ....   **45.00**

Pincushion, heart, black velvet ground, yellow bird, red letters, orange dates, trimmed in red, 4¼" h, $30.00.

Pincushion

4 x 4", heart shape, leaves and vines,
"Niagara Falls" **30.00**
5 x 5", sq, geometric design, "1910"
in center **32.00**
6 x 6½", velvet fabric, "Toronto Exhibition 1924" **50.00**
8 x 8", multicolored beads, diamond
shape, "Allentown Fair 1940" **45.00**
10 x 10", velvet and cotton satin fabric, clear and multicolored beads,
six pointed star, birds, and beaver   **95.00**

Pocketbook, hinged lid

2 x 7 x 9", pink cotton satin, clear
beads, cat design, pink and white
bead edge **115.00**
3½ x 4 x 4", wool fabric, geometric
design, dated 1901 ....   **50.00**
5 x 5 x 7", pink cotton fabric, flowers
and leaves, dangling drops bottom   **85.00**
6 x 6 x 9", heavy bead layers, crossed
flags, maple leaf, dog, and running
deer **165.00**

INSULATORS

Collecting Hints: Learn the shapes of the insulators and the abbreviations which appear on them. Some commonly found abbreviations are: "B" (Brookfield), "B & O" (Baltimore and Ohio), "EC&M Co SF" (Electrical Construction and Maintenance Company of San Francisco), "ER" (Erie Railroad), "WGM Co" (Western Glass Manufacturing Company), and "WUT Co" (Western Union Telegraph Company).

The majority of the insulators are priced below $50.00. However, there are examples of threaded and threadless insulators which have exceeded $2,000. There has been little movement in the price of glass insulators for the past years. The top insulators in each category are:

Threaded
```
CD 139, Combination Safety/Pat. Ap-
   plied for, aqua  ............ 2,500.00
CD 180, Liquid Insulator/blank, ice
   aqua  .................... 2,500.00
CD 138-9, Patent Applied for/blank,
   aqua  .................... 2,400.00
CD 176, Lower wire ridge, Whitall
   Tatum Co. No. 12 made in U.S.A./
   lower  wire  ridge,  Patent  No.
   1708038, straw  ............ 2,300.00
CD 181, no name and no embossing 2,200.00
```
Threadless
```
CD 731, no name and no embossing,
   white milk glass  ........... 3,000.00
CD 739, no name and no embossing,
   similar   to   jade   green   milk
   glass  .................... 3,000.00
CD 737, Leffert's/blank, green  .... 2,500.00
CD 790, no name and no embossing,
   known as Tea Pot, aqua  ..... 2,200.00
CD 788, no name and no embossing,
   known as slash top  ......... 2,200.00
```

The six Fry Glass insulators are not counted in this survey. They are not common threadless insulators because they were made only between 1844 and 1865.

There has been virtually no movement in the price of glass insulators for the past two years.

History: The invention of the telegraph in 1832 created the need for a glass or ceramic insulator. The first patent was given to Ezra Cornell in 1844. The principal manufacturing era was from 1850 to the mid–1900s. Leading companies include Armstrong (1938–69), Brookfield (1865–1922), California (1912–16), Gayner (1920–22), Hemingray (1871–1919), Lynchburg (1923–25), Maydwell (1935–40), McLaughlin (1923–25), and Whitall Tatum (1920–38).

Initially, insulators were threadless. Shortly after the Civil War, L. A. Cauvet received a patent for a threaded insulator. Drip points prevented water from laying on the insulator and causing a short. The double skirt kept moisture from the peg or pin.

There are about five hundred different styles of glass insulators. Each different style insulator has been given a "CD" (consolidated design) number which are found in N. R. Woodward's *The Glass Insulator In America*. Colors and names of the makers and all lettering found on the same style insulator have nothing to do with the CD number. Only the style of the insulator is the key to the numbering.

References: Gary G. Cranfill and Greg A. Kareofelas, *The Glass Insulator: A Comprehensive Reference*, published by author, 1973, separate price list; N. R. Woodward, *The Glass Insulator In America*, published by author, 1973.

Collectors' Club: National Insulator Association, 5 Brownstone Road, East Granby, CT 06026.

Museums: Big Thicket Museum, Saratoga, TX; Edison Plaza Museum, Beaumont, TX.

Note: The information on the front of the insulator is first, followed by a slash, followed by the information on the back of the insulator.

Hemingray, No. 40, aqua, 3¾" d, 4¼" h, $2.00.

THREADED INSULATORS

```
CD 102
   BGM Co, smooth base, purple  .....   18.00
   California/blank, blue  ............   15.00
CD 102.2, Westinghouse, smooth base,
   blue  ..........................  130.00
CD 112,  New  England  Telegraph  &
   Telephone, smooth base, green  ....   80.00
CD 122, McLaughlin, round drip points,
   apple green  ...................    7.50
CD 145
   W. Brookfield/New York
      Aqua  .......................    5.00
```

Light Green	7.00

California/blank

Burgundy	25.00
Green-Light Purple	15.00
Purple	20.00
Sage Green	5.00

CD 155, Armstrong's DPL, smooth

base, clear	1.00

CD 160

Hemingray 14/Made in USA

Aqua	5.00
Clear	6.00
Dark Smoke	10.00

CD 162, SS & Co, smooth base, lime

green	150.00

CD 168

Hemingray Made in USA/D510

Carnival	25.00
Clear	4.00
Green	7.00
Ice Blue	6.00

Whitall Tatum Co. No. 11/Made in USA

Ice Blue	15.00
Light Aqua	20.00
Light Green	30.00

CD 317, Chambers, smooth base, lime

green	150.00
CD 320, Pyrex, smooth base, clear	10.00

THREADLESS INSULATORS

CD 718, no name and no embossing

Aqua	200.00
Black Glass	350.00
Emerald Green	300.00
Olive Green	300.00

CD 724, Chester, smooth base, dark co-

balt	600.00

CD 728, Boston Bottle Works, smooth

base, light aqua	60.00
CD 731, McKee, smooth base, aqua	150.00

IRONS

Collecting Hints: Heavy rusting, pitting, and missing parts detract from an iron's value. As a collector becomes more advanced, he may accept some of these defects on a rare and unusual iron. However, the beginning collector is urged to concentrate on irons in very good to excellent condition.

European, Oriental, and other foreign irons are desirable, since many unusual types come from these areas and some models were prototypes for later American-made irons.

History: Ironing devices have been in use for many centuries, with early references dating from 1100. Irons from the Medieval, Renaissance, and early industrial era can be found in Europe, but

are rare. Fine brass engraved irons and hand-wrought irons dominated the period prior to 1850.

After 1850 the iron began a series of rapid evolutionary changes. New models were patented monthly. The housewife and tailor sought the latest improvement to keep "up-to-date."

The irons of the 1850 to 1910 period were heated in four ways—(1) a hot metal slug was inserted into the body, (2) a burning solid, such as coal or charcoal, was placed in the body, (3) a liquid or gas, such as alcohol, gasoline, or natural gas, was fed from an external tank and burned in the body, and (4) conduction heating, usually by drawing heat from a stove top.

Irons from the 1850 to 1910 period are plentiful and varied. Many models and novelty irons still have not been documented by collectors. Electric irons have not yet found favor among most iron collectors.

References: Esther S. Berney, *A Collectors Guide To Pressing Irons And Trivets,* Crown Publishers, Inc., 1977; A. H. Glissman, *The Evolution Of The Sad Iron,* privately printed, 1970; Brian Jewell, *Smoothing Irons: A History And Collectors Guide,* Wallace-Homestead, 1977; Judy (author) and Frank (illustrator) Politzer, *Early Tuesday Morning: More Little Irons and Trivets,* published by author, 1986; Judy and Frank Politzer, *Tuesday's Children,* published by author, 1977; Ted and V. Swanson, *The Swanson Collection,* privately printed.

Collectors' Clubs: *Friends of Ancient Smoothing Irons,* Box 215, Carlsbad CA 92008; Midwest Sad Iron Collectors Club, 500 Adventureland Drive, Altoona, IA 50009.

Museums: Henry Ford Museum, Dearborn, MI; Shelburne Museum, Shelburne, VT; Sturbridge Village, Sturbridge, MA.

Advisors: David and Sue Irons.

REPRODUCTION ALERT: The most often reproduced irons are the miniatures, especially the swan's neck and flat irons. Reproductions of some large European varieties are available, but poor construction, use of thin metals, and the unusually fine condition easily identifies them as new.

Note: The irons listed are American made unless otherwise noted.

Alcohol, Gasoline and Natural Gas
Alcohol/Gas

Bugolette, Austria, travel, 5½ x 2", inverted, tin shield	8.00
Drammel, Akron Lamp & Mfg Co, rear spherical tank, crescent shape base, c1918	45.00

Revolving alcohol, 8" l, crimper, three ironing surfaces, rear fluid

Soapstone, marked "Hood's Patent/Pat'd Jan 15, 1867," $75.00.

tank, made by John Yarger, Jan 1884 .... **250.00**

"The Improved Easy Iron," 7⅛" l, ribbing on sides, rear cylindrical fluid tank, mfg by Foote Co, Dayton, OH **45.00**

Natural Gas

Imperial, G Humphrey, 7" l, five vent holes, crescent shape **45.00**

Schreiber & Goldberg, New York, NY, front gas pipe, rear vent, 1910 .... **60.00**

Charcoal

German/Austrian, various lengths, latch includes man's head, rooster, etc, lift lid, 1880s **70.00**

Ideal, 6½", snub chimney, lift-off lid, rear vent, early 1900s **70.00**

Ne Plus Ultra, two pointed, adjustable top vent holes, two side dampers, 1910–20 .... **95.00**

Standard, goose neck spout, shield handle, removable spout and handle, 1890s **45.00**

Flat and Sad Irons

Colebrookdale, cast iron, "C" in shield **14.00**

Dover Mfg co, detachable tin cov, sgd "Asbestos" base

Double pointed **25.00**

Sleeve style **35.00**

Triangular base **30.00**

English/French, 3½" l, oval base cap, 1860s **65.00**

French, low profile base, small lip .. **20.00**

Mrs. Potts, detachable rainbow handle, two pointed base **15.00**

Sensible, Stueter, single point base, side latch mechanism **25.00**

Sweeney Sleeve, cast iron, 1899 ... **45.00**

Tailor, twisted handle, #20 .... **25.00**

Triangular soapstone base, 6" l, Hood's Patent, Jan 15, 1867 ..... **85.00**

Unknown Maker

Cast Iron, 18900–1910 .... **10.00**

Wrought iron, 6" **35.00**

Fluters

Hand

American Machine, roller style, 1920s **50.00**

Bless and Drake, charcoal rim and fluter combination **65.00**

Howell's Wave Fluter, wave pattern top and base, brass base overlay **150.00**

New Geneva, rocker style **40.00**

Scissor, 2¾ x 1½", wrought, fluter head **85.00**

Streeter, T style roller, 1878 ...... **85.00**

The Best, rocker style **45.00**

Machine

American Machine Co, Star, orig paint **150.00**

Knox, 4", orig paint, mfg by Saubier & Sons **140.00**

Miniatures

Cast iron, 3" l **35.00**

Dover type, 3½" l **40.00**

Enterprise Mfg Co, 3½" l, rainbow handle with holes **45.00**

French, 2¾", decorative, low profile **50.00**

Hollow grip, 3" l, English **45.00**

Sleeve, 2" l, cast iron **50.00**

Slug, brass, rear lift trap, triangular base, English **135.00**

Swan, 2 to 3"

No paint **40.00**

Orig paint **95.00**

Slug

Austrian, 8" l, ox tongue bullet nose, wood saw grip handle **75.00**

English, 3 to 9", brass, turned posts, triangular base, wood handle and knife gate **120.00**

Specialty Irons and Accessories

Ball iron, long handle, English **60.00**

Billiard Table Iron, 5 x 10", #20, English **175.00**

Goffering

Brass, 5" l barrel, tripod feet, English **185.00**

Kenrich, 6" l barrel, S shape stand **75.00**

Wrought iron, 6" l barrel, European, 1800s **600.00**

Laundry stove, flat belly surface supports six to eight irons **300.00**

Pyramid shape, cast iron, iron heater, three irons **110.00**

Slickenstove, 3" d, dark green, black glass **200.00**

Tolliker, 6", wood, crown or hat polish **115.00**

Kerich, box, 5 to 6" l, rear lift trap door, high profile base **110.00**

Scandinavia, 6" l, brass, ornate posts and grooved top surface, rear hinged door, 1800s **190.00**

JEWELRY, COSTUME

Collecting Hints: Two diverse factors influence price—artistic merit and personal appeal. The result is that there is a wide fluctuation in market prices. Also, the changing values of gold and silver cause prices to vary.

Jewelry prices vary regionally, depending on what is popular in a given area. Costume jewelry, since it was mass produced, should be bought in very good or mint condition. Most stones in costume jewelry are not real. Advanced collectors generally can distinguish stones and metals; novice collectors should study carefully before trusting their eyes and a ten power loop.

History: The design of jewelry closely followed costume design. Early inventions which influenced jewelry design were the pin making machine in 1832, the development of the electroplating process by the English firm of Elkington in the 1860s, and die stamping machinery.

The Art Deco and Art Nouveau eras made inexpensive costume jewelry acceptable. Mass production of tin-like pins, bracelets, rings, etc., followed. Newark (New Jersey), New York, and Philadelphia became centers for jewelry manufacturing, challenging Providence, Rhode Island, which had held the position in 1800. Coro Incorporated of Providence employed over 2,000 people in 1946.

Gold was removed from circulation in 1933, reducing the amount of gold related jewelry items. Scarcity of materials during World War II further aided the move to plastic and lesser metals. Precious stones were replaced by "gemstones" and glass imitations.

Mass produced jewelry employed the talents of many famous designers. Rapid communication of style changes through magazines and newspapers led to fads which quickly swept across the country. By the 1950s fine costume jewelry appeared on the market and received acceptance, even among the more sophisticated buyers.

References: Lillian Baker, *100 Years of Collectible Jewelry*, Collector Books, 1978 (1989 value update); Corinne Davidov and Ginny Redington Dawes, *The Bakelite Jewelry Book*, Abbeville Press, 1988; Maryanne Dolan, *Collecting Rhinestone Jewelry, Second Edition*, Books Americana, 1989; S. Sylvia Henzel, *Collectible Costume Jewelry, Second Edition*, Wallace Homestead, 1987; Lyngerde Kelley and Nancy Schiffer, *Plastic Jewelry*, Schiffer Publishing Ltd., 1987; J. L. Lynnlee, *All That Glitters*, Schiffer Publishing, Ltd., 1986; Nancy N. Schiffer, *Costume Jewelry: The Fun of Collecting*, Schiffer Publishing Ltd., 1988.

Note: The following abbreviations are used:

GF—Gold filled
SS—Sterling silver
YG—Yellow gold
YGF—Yellow gold filled

Bar Pin
   Bakelite, red bar, red cherries with green leaves suspended from red bakelite chain **75.00**
   Silver, sterling, black Scottie paperweight type center **20.00**

Scatter Pins, man and woman, yarn motif, gold plated, 1½" h, pr, $4.50.

Beads
   Bakelite, brown faceted beads, 6½ to 20 mm, c1920 .... **80.00**
   Bohemian, black and amber, Art Deco, 54" **60.00**
   Coral, ¼" d beads, cylindrical 10K YG clasp, 16" l **35.00**
   Mother of Pearl, graduated elongated beads, 24" l **45.00**
   Plastic
      Amber, transparent, 28" l **65.00**
      Pearls, gray, c1920 .... **65.00**
Belt Buckle
   Bakelite, two pears, green leaves ... **85.00**
   Mother of Pearl, swastika shape **12.00**
Bracelet
   Bakelite
      Bangle, ivory color, carved floral dec, c1920 .... **50.00**
      Charm, gold colored chain, dark figural strawberries and leaves, c1930 .... **65.00**
   Catalin, hinged, orange, double goldfish, white eyes **45.00**
   Gold, cuff, crab, shell and pearl dec, marked "Joseff of Hollywood," 1960s **250.00**
   Plastic, bangle, lemon yellow, marked "Monet," c1980 .... **25.00**

Rhinestone, six links, pierced work,
1920s style, marked "Lido," c1950   **50.00**
Silver, link, marked "Monet," c1960   **25.00**
Silverplated, cuff, hinged, pierced
band, cameo center, marked
"M.M.C.C.O," c1960 ....   **50.00**

Bracelet and Earrings Set
  Gold Filled, lapis-like cabochons,
    marked "Schaparelli" **75.00**
  Rhinestones, marked "Joseph Mazer"   **65.00**
  Silver, mesh wire link, safety chain,
    marked "Hobe" **35.00**
Bracelet and Ring Set, snake bracelet
  and ring, marked "Whiting Davis" .   **95.00**

Brooch
  Lucite, propeller, wood, hand carved,
    1950s **28.00**
  Plastic, propeller, bright, 1950s **28.00**
  Rhinestone
    Crystal, hand cut, marked "Weiss"   **50.00**
    Ice blue, #G-427, marked "Eisen-
      berg" **135.00**
    Pale pink, #2145, marked "Eisen-
      berg" **140.00**

Brooch and Earrings Set
  Coral and pearl, marked "Haskell" .   **75.00**
  Rhinestones, multicolored stones,
    large, oversized stones, marked
    "Kramer" **55.00**

Chain
  Brass, double strand, chased bar
    links, 11" l **35.00**
  Yellow Gold Filled, double link, 24" l   **40.00**

Charm
  Sterling Silver ·
    Baby Shoe, ¾" l **25.00**
    Bell, moving clapper **20.00**
    Carousel, moving horses **25.00**
    Sweet Sixteen, disc, engraved dates   **20.00**
    Typewriter, moving carriage **25.00**
  Yellow Gold
    Anniversary, diamond chip **50.00**
    Cat, enamel eyes **25.00**
    Spinning Wheel **35.00**
    Thimble **30.00**
    Wishbone **30.00**
    Yacht **35.00**

Choker
  Crystal and rhinestones, gold setting,
    tassel drop, marked "Kenneth
    Lane" **150.00**
  Gold mesh, floral design, marked
    "Napier" **20.00**
  Rhinestones and gilt, marked "Tri-
    fari," c1950 ....   **60.00**
Choker and Earrings Set
  Gold Filled, sea shells, marked "Kre-
    mentz" **50.00**
  Rhinestones, crystal, fringed design,
    marked "Sarah Coventry" **30.00**

Clip
  Gold Filled, marked "Eisenberg Orig-
    inal," 3 x 4" orig box **165.00**
  Carnelian, Art Deco style, rect,
    marked "RAJ" **25.00**
  Moonstones and enamel, marked
    "Trifari" **38.00**
  Rhinestones, marquisette center,
    oval, 2½" **12.50**
Cuff Links
  Celluloid, monogrammed, black trim   **25.00**
  Gold Filled, ovals, monogrammed ..   **40.00**
  Silver, yachts **35.00**

**Pin and Earrings Set, rhinestones, yellow
and brown colored stones, gold colored
base metal, $8.00.**

Earrings
  Enamel, black flower petals, rhine-
    stone cluster center, marked
    "Coro," c1950 ....   **40.00**
  Paste and rhinestone, simulated em-
    eralds, dangle, marked "Weiss" ..   **25.00**
  Pave Hoop Dangle, daisy shaped gold
    toned stud, marked "Miriam Has-
    kell" **275.00**
  Pearl, paste, and gold, metal drop,
    marked "Joseff of Hollywood" ...   **150.00**
  Plastic, burnt orange button and
    beads, clear rhinestones, clip type,
    marked "Trifari" **25.00**
  Rhinestone
    Cluster, ice blue, descending rhine-
      stone ribbons, marked "Eisen-
      berg" **48.00**
  Sterling Silver
    Dragonflies, gold wash, enamel
      dec **65.00**
    Leaves, 1", marked "Heeber" **18.00**
    Teardrops, fish scale dec, blue and
      silver, marked "Monet" **10.00**
Hairpin, plastic, imitation tortoiseshell,
  rhinestone dec, c1956 ....   **15.00**
Locket
  Gold Filled, heart, engraved center .   **35.00**
  Gold Plated, rect, red rose enamel

center, light green ground, push
button opening, marked "Coro" .. **38.00**
Lorgnette, plastic, pink, rhinestone stud-
ded frame and design, twisted handle   **50.00**
Necklace
Bakelite, clear link chain, amber and
brown sq beads, c1930 .... **50.00**
Gold mesh chain, ropes of green and
brown rhinestones, front tassel,
marked "Hobe" **160.00**
Indian style, green oval cabochon
drop, jeweled chain, marked "Hat-
tie Carnegie" **200.00**
Pearl, eight strand, 1970s, marked
"Trifari" **65.00**
Rhinestones, marked "Trifari" **55.00**
Necklace Set
Aurora Borealis, necklace and earrings, cluster type **140.00**
Faux Pearl, twisted multi–strand
necklace with plastic coral colored
rose, rhinestone accents, necklace,
earrings, and stick pin, marked
"Kenneth J Lane" **185.00**
Glass, necklace, bracelet, and ear-
rings, green, pink, and irid glass
beads, orig paper tag, marked "Eu-
gene" **145.00**
Paste emeralds and rhinestones, pendant necklace, oval clip earrings,
marked "Kramer" **135.00**
Rhinestones, light blue and pale lavender, necklace and bracelet,
marked "Eisenberg" **200.00**
Pendant
Gold
Lion mask and ring pendant,
marked "Kenneth Lane" **35.00**
Loops, varying wire widths, jade
cabochon center, marked "Van
Dell" **20.00**
Opalescent Stones, double oval pen-
dant, marked "Hollycraft," c1950 **75.00**
Pearls and Coral, gold chain, baroque
pearls, carved coral beads and pen-
dant, marked "Miriam Haskell" .. **175.00**
Pin
Catalin, floral and leaves, pink, ivory,
green leaves, openwork and carv-
ing **25.00**
Celluloid, seven yellow, amber, and
red leaves, clear stems **40.00**
Glass, cherry, marked "Austria" **10.00**
Gold Filled, baroque pearl, Capri-
corn, marked "KJL" **100.00**
Lucite, humorous dog, clear body,
colored trim **35.00**
Plastic, parrot, yellow, blue rhine-
stone eyes, marked "Buch and
Deichmann, Copenhagen" **35.00**
Rhinestones and enamel, wishing
well **15.00**

Sterling Silver, bull, marked "Cini" . **55.00**
Ring
Gold Filled
Child's, oval center, small hearts on
either side, orig box **75.00**
Man's, tiger's eye, oval mounting **100.00**
Yellow Gold, 14K, engagement and
wedding set, three faceted diamonds, 14K white gold open back
settings, 3.01 carat diamonds in
wedding ring, grooved shoulders,
plain shank, size 7¾, c1935 ..... **125.00**
Tie Clasp
Enamel, Masonic emblem, 14K YG
bar **90.00**
Rhinestone, initial "T", white gold
setting **25.00**
Wrist Watch, lady's, camouflage type,
hinged bracelet, gold leaf cov face,
marked "Emerson" **45.00**

JUKEBOXES

Collecting Hints: Jukebox chronology falls into
four distinct periods:

In the pre-1938 period jukeboxes were constructed mainly of wood and resembled a radio
or phonograph cabinet. In this period Wurlitzer
jukeboxes are the most collectible, but their
value usually is under $600.00.

From 1938 to 1948 the addition of plastics and
animation units gave the jukebox a more gaudy
appearance. These jukeboxes played 78 RPM
records. Wurlitzer jukeboxes are king, with
Rock-Ola the second most popular. This era contains the most valuable models, e.g., Wurlitzer
models 750, 850, 950, 1015, and 1080, plus
others.

The 1940-1960 era jukeboxes are collected for
the "Happy Days" (named for the TV show) feel-
ing: drive-in food, long skirts, sweater girls, and
good times. These jukeboxes play 45 RPM records. They rate in value second to those of the
1938-48 period. The period is referred to as the
Seeburg era. Prices usually are under $1,500.00.

The 1961 and newer jukeboxes often are not
considered collectible because the record mechanism is not visible, thus removing one of a boxes
alluring qualities.

There are exceptions to these generalizations.
Collectors should have a price and identification
guide to help make choices. Many original and
reproduction parts are available for Seeburg and
Wurlitzer jukeboxes. In many cases incomplete
jukeboxes can be restored. Jukeboxes that are in
working order and can be maintained in that
condition are the best machines to own.

Wait about three to four months after becoming interested in jukeboxes before buying a machine. Use this time to educate yourself about a

machine's desirability and learn how missing components will effect its value.

History: First came the phonograph; the coin-operated phonograph followed. When electrical amplification became possible, the amplified coin-operated phonograph, known as a jukebox, evolved.

The heyday of the jukebox was the 1940s. Between 1946 and 1947 Wurlitzer produced 56,000 model 1015 jukeboxes, the largest production run of all time. The jukebox was the center of every teenage "hangout" from drug stores and restaurants to pool halls and dance parlors. They even invaded select private homes. Jukeboxes were cheaper than a live band, and, unlike radio, one could hear his or her favorite song when and as often as one wished.

Styles changed in the 1960s. Portable radios coupled with "Top 40" radio stations fulfilled the need for daily repetition of songs. Television changed evening entertainment patterns. The need for the jukebox vanished.

References: Frank Adams, *Wurlitzer Jukeboxes, 1934-1974*, AMR Publishing, 1983; Frank Adams, *Wurlitzer Jukeboxes: Volume II*, AMR Publishing, 1984; Rick Botts, *A Complete Identification Guide To The Wurlitzer Jukebox*, privately printed, 1984; Rick Botts, *1985 Jukebox Collectors Directory & Yellow Pages*, published by author, 1985; Rick Botts, *Jukebox Restoration Guide*, published by author, 1985; Stephan K. Loots, *The Official Victory Glass Price Guide To Antique Jukeboxes 1984-85*, published by author, 1985; Vincent Lynch, *Jukebox: The Golden Age*, published by author, 1980.

Periodicals: *Jukebox Collector Newsletter*, 2545 SE 60th St., Des Moines, IA 50317; *Loose Change*, 21176 South Alameda Street, Long Beach, CA 90810.

Museums: Jukeboxes have not reached the status of museum pieces. The best places to see approximately 100 or more jukeboxes in one place is at a coin-op show.

Advisor: Rick Botts.

AMI, model
A	900.00
B	750.00
C	500.00
D	400.00
E	500.00

Mills, model
Empress	950.00
Throne of Music	750.00

Packard, Manhattan 1,600.00

Rock-Ola, model
1422	1,500.00
1426	1,600.00
1428	1,500.00
1432	700.00
1434	750.00
1436	750.00
1438	700.00

Seeburg, model
147	600.00
M100B	750.00
M100W	650.00
HF100G	810.00
HF100R	860.00
V-200	810.00

Wurlitzer, model
412	750.00
600	850.00
616	625.00
700	1,620.00
750	1,800.00
780	2,500.00
800	1,800.00
850	5,500.00
950	8,000.00
1015	3,500.00
1050	4.500.00

KEYS

Collecting Hints: The modern hobby of key collecting began with the publication of *Standard Guide To Key Collecting* which illustrates keys by function and describes keys by style and metal content. Most key collectors focus on a special type of key, e.g., folding keys, railroad keys, car keys, etc.

Very few, if any, American-manufactured keys can be called truly rare, although some may be currently in the very difficult stage to find. Little is know as to the quantity that was manufactured, how popular they were when first produced and marketed, or how many survived.

Some keys are abundant in certain areas of the country and scarce in others. Do not spend heavily just because you have never heard or seen an example before. The best advice is to seek out other collectors and join a national organization.

History: The key as a symbol has held a mystical charm since Biblical times. The Catholic Church has keys in its coat of arms. During the Middle Ages, noblemen and women carried a large collection of keys hanging from their girdles to denote their status, the more keys the higher the status.

Many kings and other royal members practiced the art of key making. Presentation keys began during the earliest years when cities were walled enclaves. When a visitor was held in high esteem by the townspeople, he would be presented with a key to the city gate. Thus, we now have the honorary "Key To The City."

When it was popular to go on a Grand Tour of Europe in the 17th to 19th centuries, keys were among the most acquired objects. Unfortunately, many of these keys were fantasies created by the inventive local hustlers. Examples are King Tut's Tomb key, the key to the house where Mary stayed in Egypt, Bastille keys, Newgate Prison keys, and Tower of London keys.

References: Don Stewart, *The Charles J. Mc-Queen Collection, Railroad Switch Keys, United States-Canada-World,* published by author; Don Stewart, *Collectors Guide, Antique Classic Marque Car Keys, United States 1915–1970,* published by author; Don Stewart, *Collectors Guide, Yale Jail/Prison Locks & Keys, 1884–1957,* published by author; Don Stewart, *Standard Guide To Key Collecting, United States-Canada 1850–1975, Second Edition* published by author.

Collectors' Club: Key Collectors International, P. O. Box 9397, Phoenix, AZ 85068.

Museums: Lock Museum of America, Terryville, CT; Mechanics Institute, New York, NY.

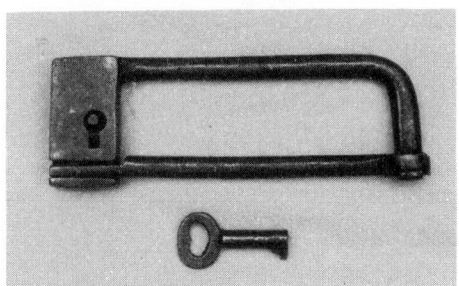

Money Bag Lock, brass, 3″, $35.00.

Cabinet, Barrel Type	
Brass, decorative bow	
1½″	3.00
2″	4.50
2½″	5.50
3″	8.00
Brass, standard bow and bit	
1½″	1.00
2″	1.50
2½″	2.50
3″	3.50
Bronze, gold plated bow	
1½″, decorative	8.50
2″, Art Deco design	12.00
2″, decorative	9.00
2″, dolphin design	8.50
2½″, decorative	10.00
2½″, dolphin design	12.00
Iron, painted, 3″, plastic bow, Art Deco design	9.50
Nickel plated	
2¼″, lyre design bow	5.50
2½″, Art Deco design bow	5.00

Steel	
1½″, standard bow and bit	.50
2″, Art Deco design	6.00
2″, standard bow and bit	.50
3″, standard bow and bit	.75
Car	
Auburn, logo, Yale, Jr	2.00
Basco	
Early, flat steel	1.50
Set, #31-54, total of 24 keys	25.00
Chrysler "Omega" keys, brass, five piece set	
1933, Yale	15.00
1934, Yale	12.00
CLUM, #DB76-DB99, set of 24 keys	35.00
Dodge	
Any metal, no name	.50
Brass, reverse "Caskey-Dupree"	1.25
Nickel-Silver, reverse "Caskey-Dupree"	1.00
Dodge/Chevrolet, rear deck key	2.00
Edsel, two keys, any maker	5.00
Ford, Model "T"	
Any Metal, no logo	.75
Brass, Ford logo	
"B" in circle mark	2.00
C-D mark	2.00
Crown mark	8.00
Diamond mark	2.00
No mark	1.50
"V" in circle mark	12.00
Coil Switch Lever Key	2.50
Dealers Keys, set of 4	12.50
Nickel-Silver, Ford Logo	
"B" in circle mark	1.75
C-D mark	1.75
Diamond mark	1.75
No mark	1.50
Ford, rear deck key	2.00
Nash logo key, Ilco #132	5.00
Omega, nickel-silver, 5 piece set, 1933 or 1934, Yale	6.50
Omega type, nickel-silver, any maker besides Yale	.75
Packard logo key, gold plated, 50th anniversary	8.00
Studebaker	
Eagle Lock Co., logo key	1.50
Yale, aluminum	1.00
Yale, Jr., logo key	1.50
Car, Special	
Auto Dealer Presentation Keys	
Diamond, Continental, gold	75.00
Gold Plated	1.50
Sterling Silver	12.00
Crest Key	
Common Cars	1.00
Hudson, Frazer, Nash and Packard	3.00
Gas Companies, Premium type	
Aluminum	.75
Key Metal	1.00
OSCO Colt 45 Key, orig box	25.00

Pocket Knife, one blade, one key
    Mother Of Pearl Handle **15.00**
    Plastic Handle **10.00**
Casting Plate, bronze
    2½" **15.00**
    3" **18.00**
    4" **22.00**
    6" **28.00**
Door
    Brass, standard bow and bit
        3" **3.00**
        4" **5.00**
        5" **8.00**
        6" **12.00**
    Bronze
        4", Keen Kutter bow **5.50**
        6", special logo bow **15.00**
    Steel
        3", decorative bow **3.00**
        3", Keen Kutter bow **3.50**
        3", standard bow and bit . . . .   **.75**
        5", standard bow and bit **3.50**
Folding, Jackknife
    Bronze and Steel, bit cuts, 5"
        Maker's name · **18.00**
        No maker's name **15.00**
    Steel bit cuts
        5½", maker's name—Branford,
           MW&CO., nc **8.00**
        5½", maker's name—Ilco, Graham,
           etc **6.50**
        5½", no maker's name **5.00**
    Steel, uncut, 5½"
        Maker's name **6.00**
        No maker's name **4.00**
Gate
    Bronze, bit type
        4" **6.00**
        6" **12.00**
    Iron, bit type
        6" **4.00**
        8" **6.00**
Hotel
    Bit Type, Bronze
        3", Hotel name and room number
           on bow **4.50**
        3", Tag silhouette of hotel, bronze   **8.00**
        4", Standard tag, room number,
           etc., white metal **3.50**
        4", Tag silhouette of hotel, white
           metal **10.00**
    Bit Type, Steel, 3"
        Bronze Tag **3.00**
        Fiber Tag, room number and name   **2.25**
        Hotel name and room number on
           bow **3.75**
        Large Tag, oval, silhouette, bronze   **8.00**
        Standard Tag, room number, etc.,
           bronze **4.00**
    Bit Type, Steel, 4"
        Bronze Tag **3.50**

Hotel, left: Hotel Northland, Green Bay, Wis, $4.50; right: The Charlotte, Charlotte, N.C., $6.50.

    Large Tag, oval, hotel founder,
        bronze **12.00**
    Large Tag, rectangle, hotel name,
        white metal **6.50**
    Pin Tumbler
        Large bow, hotel name and room
           number on bow **1.25**
        Plastic or Fiber tag **1.00**
Jail (reproduction alert)
    Bronze, bit type with cuts
        4¼", open oval bow, Newell **35.00**
        4½", barrel type **28.00**
    Bronze, lever tumbler cut, 4½", Fol-
        ger-Adams, oval bow with "A" . .   **18.00**
    Nickel-Silver, pin tumbler, Yale Mo-
    gul
        Cut **15.00**
        Uncut blank **12.00**
    Spike Key, 5½"
        Bronze bow, steel bit, serial no., no
           maker's name **35.00**
        Nickel plated steel, open oval bow,
           no maker's name, no serial no.,
           bit cuts **30.00**
        Steel plated bow, serial no., Yale,
           marked **40.00**
    Steel, flat, lever tumbler, Folger-Ad-
    ams
        Cut **18.00**
        Uncut blank **12.00**
    Steel, large oval open bow, 4¼",
        S&G, lever type, uncut **30.00**
Keys To The City, Presentation
    1½", gold plated, small jewel, city
        and/or recipient's name **8.00**
    2", iron, brass plated, Master Lock
        Co., 1933 World's Fair **7.50**

2½", gold plated, pin back, "City of
Boise, Idaho" **18.00**
2½", white metal, "Be A Golden Key
For Happiness" **1.00**
4", 22K gold plated, Salt Lake City, **12.00**
6", antique bronze, any city **14.00**
6 to 10", gold plated, name engraved
Famous Person **32.00**
Historical Person **75.00**
Obscure Person **25.00**
7", gold plated, presentation leather-
ette type folder **40.00**
8", copper plated, 1933 Chicago
World's Fair, Hall of Science **15.00**
8", 22K gold plated, Cumberland ... **24.00**
10", Chicago World's Fair, copper,
thermometer **8.50**
Pocket Door, bow folds sideways
Bronze
Art Deco, triangular bow **15.00**
"T" bow, cut, knurled nut **8.00**
Nickel Plated
Art Deco, square bow **18.00**
Art Nouveau, oval bow **15.00**
Pocket Door, slide stem
Bronze, "T" bow
Knurled nut **8.00**
Screw **8.00**
Steel, "T" bow, screw **10.00**
Railroad (reproduction alert)
A&S Abilene & Southern **25.00**
ARR Alaska Railroad **20.00**
AT&SF Atchison Topeka & Santa Fe . **15.00**
B&M RR Boston & Maine **20.00**
C&O Chesapeake & Ohio **12.50**
CM&ST P SIGNAL Chicago Milwau-
kee & St. Paul **10.00**
CRI & P RR Chicago Rock Island &
Pacific **12.50**
D&RGW RR Denver & Rio Grande
Western **18.50**
DT RR Detroit Terminal **18.50**
ESS CO Eastern/Erie Steamship Co. . **18.00**
FC NG RR Fulton County Narrow
Gauge **85.00**
GTW Grand Trunk Western **18.00**
IC RR Illinois Central **10.00**
LS&MS Lake Shore & Michigan South
Steel **15.00**
LM RR Little Miami Railroad **55.00**
MC RR Michigan Central **18.00**
MN RY Milwaukee Northern **45.00**
NP RY Northern Pacific Railway ... **18.00**
O&W RR Oregon & Washington ... **35.00**
PENN RR Pennsylvania Railroad ... **18.00**
FRISCO St. Louis San Francisco **18.00**
SPCO&CS Southern Pacific **8.00**
SPTCO Southern Pacific **6.00**
TT RR Toledo Terminal Railroad ... **18.00**
UPRR Union Pacific **14.00**
VGN Virginian **30.00**
WPRR Western Pacific Railroad **12.50**

Ship, bit type
Bronze, bit type
Foreign ship tags **6.00**
Ship name on bow **10.00**
Bronze, tag, bit type, factory type tags
2" **6.00**
3" **8.00**
Bronze, ship made tags, bit type, fac-
tory type tags
2 to 3" **4.50**
4" **5.00**
Iron/steel, bronze tags, 3 to 4" **3.00**
Pin Tumbler Type
Passenger Liner Tags **8.00**
US Army Ship Tags **8.50**
US Coast Guard Tags **3.00**
USN Tag **2.00**
Watch
Brass, 1"
Advertising type, ½ x ¾" **6.00**
Advertising type, shield **10.00**
Art Nouveau, loop bow **8.00**
Plain, swivel **2.00**
Brass/gold plated, 1", large number . **4.00**
Brass and Steel, 1"
Loop bow, folds **4.00**
Swivel **2.00**
Gold, 14K, 1", engraved **75.00**
Gold Plated, 1"
Advertising type **12.00**
Decorated bow **8.00**
Gold Plated and Silver, 1"
Cigar Cutter accessory **25.00**
Plain **18.00**
Jeweler's Key
Brass, 6 point **18.00**
Steel and Brass
5 Point **12.00**
6 Point **15.00**
Set, #2 to #11, brass/gold plated,
large numbers, 10 total **75.00**
Sterling Silver 1", rose on bow, etc. . **35.00**

KITCHEN COLLECTIBLES

Collecting Hints: Bargins still can be found, especially at flea markets and garage sales. Look
to the design of appliances for statements about
a given age, e.g., the Art Deco design on toasters
and coffee pots of the 1910–1920 period.

The country decorating craze has caused most
collectors to concentrate on the 1860–1900 period. Kitchen products of the 1900–1940 period
with their enamel glazes and dependability are
just coming into vogue.

History: The kitchen was a central focal point in
a family's environment until frozen food, TV dinners, and microwaves freed the family to con-

centrate on other parts of the house during meal time. Initially, food preparation involved both the long and short term. Home canning remained popular through the early 1950s.

Many early kitchen utensils were handmade and prized by their owners. Next came a period of utilitarian products of tin and other metals. However, the housewife did not wish to work in a sterile environment, so color was added through enamel and plastic while design began to serve both an aesthetic and functional purpose.

The advent of home electricity changed the type and style of kitchen products. Many products went through fads such as the toaster, electric knife, and now the food processor. The high technology field already has made inroads into the kitchen and another revolution seems at hand.

References: Jane H. Celehar, *Kitchens and Gadgets, 1920 To 1950,* Wallace-Homestead, 1982; Linda Campbell Franklin, *300 Years Of Kitchen Collectibles, 2nd Edition,* Books Americana, 1984; Bill and Denise Harned, *Griswold Cast Collectibles: History & Values,* privately printed, 1988; Mary Lou Mathews, *American Kitchen And Country Collectibles,* L-W Promotions, 1984; Glydon Shirley, *The Miracle in Grandmother's Kitchen,* privately printed, 1983; Frances Thompson, *Antiques from the Country Kitchen,* Wallace-Homestead, 1985.

See: Advertising, Cookbooks, Kitchen Glassware, Reamers.

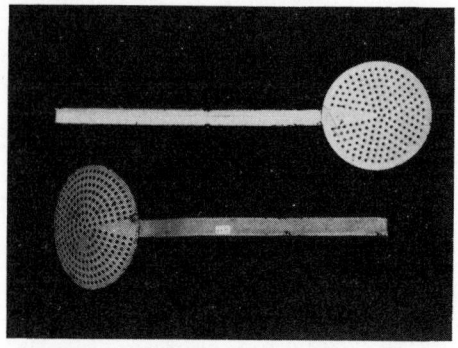

Skimmers, enamel, top: white, 16" l, $24.00; bottom: tan, 13½" l, deeply turned base, $14.00.

Apple Corer, White Mountain, orig box	24.00
Apple Peeler, Turntable No 98	75.00
Basket, 4½" d, 5½" h, wire, folding, tulip form	40.00
Basting Spoon, granite, cobalt handle .	12.00
Beater Jar, electric, red top	14.00
Biscuit Cutter, 1½", tin, bail	6.00

Bowl	
10" w, 11" l, 3" h, walnut	55.00
10½" d, mocha, brown bands	75.00
Bread Board, 12" d, 7½" pine handle, American	90.00
Bread Box, tin, 12" l, white, red top . .	12.00
Breadstick Pan, nickled cast iron, Wagner Ware	30.00
Bundt Pan, iron, scalloped, 4½ x 10½", 18th C	90.00
Butter Churn	
Dazey, No 40, wood paddles	85.00
McDade Pottery, 3 gal, stoneware, McDade, Texas, missing lid	70.00
Butter Fork, 7 x 2½", maple, hand carved	20.00
Butter Mold, 1¾ x 3½", turned maple, stylized star	35.00
Butter Paddle, 10 x 5", maple, carved .	65.00
Butter Stamp, 4¾ x 5", pine, octagonal, starflower, c1840	140.00
Button Hook, Miller's Cocoa, ⅞" multicolored celluloid oval, metal hook, c1896	30.00
Cake Pan, tin	
8", Swans Down Cake Flour	12.00
10", tube, handle, Vanity Co	15.00
12", black, wire loop handle, Fries .	10.00
Catalog, Sunray Kitchen and Parlor Stoves, 48 pgs, 7 x 10½"	25.00
Chafing Dish, Art Deco, Manning Bowman	40.00
Can Opener, cast iron, fish figure, c1865	130.00
Cheese Box, 15 x 10", shaker style . . .	75.00
Cheese Grater, hanging, china, white, gold trim, enameled blue forget-me-nots	55.00
Cheese Slicer, enameled wood handle, marked "Unsco-Germany"	7.00
Cherry Pitter, Rollman	35.00
Cleanser, Guardian Service, unopened, black and silver Art Deco design . . .	30.00
Clothes Sprinkler, ceramic, elephant . .	25.00
Coffee Bin, tin, painted and stenciled, roll top, gold designs, cartouche winter scene	225.00
Coffee Boiler, graniteware, turquoise, cobalt handle	40.00
Coffee Grinder	
Lap type, drawer with porcelain knob, crank handle, brass cup, sgd "D.D. Post, Lahaska, Pa, Maker"	220.00
Table Top type, Enterprise Model 10, clamp-on, orig stenciling	60.00
Wall, Arcade, crystal	65.00
Cookbook	
Dr. Price's Baking Powder Billy In Bunbury, 1925	16.00
Fire King Casserole Recipes, 30 pgs, Anchor Hocking Glass illus, 1944	6.00
Cornbread Pan, iron, Griswold, mini .	40.00

Corn Stick Pan, cast iron, Griswold ... **30.00**
Dipper, 7", copper, tin lined, forged brass handle, impressed "M M" on side **65.00**
Dish Pan, enamel, gray **12.00**
Dough Bowl, 12½", round, wood **35.00**
Egg Basket, 14 x 14", splint, handled, Ohio **75.00**
Egg Cup, wood, pedestal, yellow smoke grained, 1830, pr **120.00**
Egg Whip
  Cream, handle, dated 1906 .... **12.00**
  Spring whip, enameled wood handle **8.00**
Flour Sifter, Bromweld's, side crank, red wood knob **10.00**
Food Chopper, Universal **6.00**
Food Mill, Foley, 2 pcs **15.00**
Fruit Press, Griswold #2 .... **60.00**
Funnel
  Black, white granite, 2¾" **28.00**
  Gray, Elliptical **38.00**
Griddle, cast iron, Griswold **25.00**
Jelly Mold, 3½" d, 3½" h, tin, Madelinie, stamped "Of 539" **20.00**
Knife, chopping, 6½", curved steel blade, wood handle, Henry Disston & Sons **15.00**
Lemon Squeezer
  6½", tin plated iron **18.00**
  11", maple, hinged **55.00**
Liquid Measure, copper, haystack shape, swing bail, side handle **175.00**
Loaf Pan, gray granite **24.00**

Meat Grinder, Sargent & Co, Pat. March 8, 1892 .... **35.00**
Meat Tenderizer, 2 x 2½ x 3", rect, iron, heavy handle **35.00**
Meat Thermometer, 6", hanging, Taylor **8.50**
Milk Jug, enamelware, gray, cov **25.00**
Mixing Bowl, 7", graniteware, red and white swirl **75.00**
Mixing Spoon, wood handle, slotted bowl, Androck, Made in USA **15.00**
Mold
  Charles Field, No 4, lead, hammer . **55.00**
  Griswold
    Lamb, orig box **105.00**
    Rabbit **225.00**
Oven Broom, 10½" l, birch, splint, attributed to hewn handle, New York State, 1830 .... **30.00**
Oyster Ladle, tin **25.00**
Pan, 5¼" d, graniteware, blue-gray, rolled edge **20.00**
Pantry Box, 6½ x 12½", dry red paint, 4 fingers **350.00**
Pea Sheller, 12" h, screw clamp, black wood handle, bean slicer, Vaughans **35.00**
Pie Bird
  4½", bird, blue and yellow **18.00**
  4¾", duck, blue **22.00**

5"
  Duck, yellow **22.00**
  Pixie, turquoise, white mushroom **35.00**
Pinback Button
  1¼", Rabbit's Foot Baking Powder, good luck symbols, red, white, and blue ribbon dec, blue lettering, white ground, c1900 .... **15.00**
  1½", Fleischmann's Yeast, John Dough, multicolored, dark blue ground, c1910 .... **30.00**
  1¾"
    Anti-Yellow Oleomargarine, yellow, black, and white, dairy industry protest, c1891 .... **50.00**
    Boston Beans, brown and white, Pilgrim boy
      c1901 .... **28.00**
      c1910 .... **20.00**
  2⅛"
    Ceresota Flour, brown rim, sepia illus, Northwestern Consolidated Milling Co of Minnesota, c1901 **28.00**
    Star Brand Butter, multicolored, butter container, First Premium National Butter Exhibit 1896, back text for MN dairy, c1897 . **25.00**
Popover Pan, six popovers, Griswold, marked "Erie PA, USA 6141 No 18" **45.00**
Potato Masher, 9", zig zag wire end, wood handle **25.00**
Pudding Mold, stoneware, English **35.00**

Rolling Pin, porcelain body, white ground, blue floral dec, turned wooden handles, 13¾" l, $18.00.

Rolling Pin
  19", turned tiger and bird's eye maple **45.00**
  20", maple **35.00**
Salt Box, 8 x 17½", rect, pine, hinged lid **95.00**
Scoop, 8" l, 2" w, wood, hand carved **50.00**
Sifter
  Sift-Chine, marked **10.00**
  Three screens, colorful **15.00**
Skillet, cast iron
  Griswold
    No 7 .... **25.00**
    No 14 .... **125.00**
  Wagner, MiPet, No. 3 .... **10.00**
  Wapak Indian Head, No 9 .... **150.00**
Skimmer Ladle, cobalt handle **15.00**
Spoon Holder, butternut, 1800s **225.00**

Strainer, wire mesh bowl, twisted wire
and wood handle 6.00
String Holder
    Cathedral pattern, iron, round 22.00
    Dutch Boy 22.50
    Scottie Dog 37.50
Sugar Scoop, wood, hand carved,
    curved handle, c1820 . . . . 110.00
Tea Caddy, 8½" h, tin, painted, red fruit,
    yellow leaves, cap 240.00
Tea Kettle, copper, gooseneck, dove-
    tailed, sgd "JMWE" and hallmark .. 150.00
Toaster, Speed Master, electric, flip
    open sides, Son Chief Electric Co,
    Winsted, Co, MIB 30.00
Tomato Slicer, enameled wood handle,
    orig litho sleeve 10.00
Trivet, punched tin 18.00
Vegetable Basket, 7" d, 5" h, wire, ta-
    pered, bale handle, 1870 . . . .   35.00
Vegetable Chopper, glass jar, red
    painted steel lid 20.00
Waffle Iron
    Griswold #8 . . . .   40.00
    Wagner, 3" d 45.00
Wash Pan, gray granite, sgd 45.00
Whisk, 10", snow shoe shape, twisted
    wire handle 12.00

KITCHEN GLASSWARE

Collecting Hints: Kitchen Glassware was made
in large numbers. Although collectors do tolerate
signs of use, they will not accept pieces with
heavy damage. Many of the products contain
applied decals; these should be in good condition. A collection can be built inexpensively by
concentrating on one form such as canister sets,
measuring cups, reamers, etc.

History: The Depression era brought inexpensive
kitchen and table products to center stage. Hocking, Hazel Atlas, McKee, U. S. Glass, and Westmoreland were companies which led in the production of these items.

Kitchen Glassware complemented Depression
Glass. Many items were produced in the same
color and style. Because the glass was molded,
added decorative elements included ribs, fluting,
arches and thumbprint patterns. Kitchen Glassware was thick to achieve durability. The result
were forms which were difficult to handle at
times and often awkward aesthetically. After
World War II, aluminum products began to replace Kitchen Glassware.

References: Gene Florence, *Kitchen Glassware
of the Depression Years, Third Edition*, Collector
Books, 1987; Glyndon, Shirley, *The Miracle in
Grandmother's Kitchen*, privately printed, 1983.

See: Reamers.

**Beater, green measuring cup, marked
"Vidro Prod. Company, Chicago, IL, Patent No. 1,935,851," $15.00.**

Ashtray, jadite 6.00
Bowl
    6", Federal Glass Co, amber 3.50
    6½", Federal Glass Co
        Amber 3.00
        Pink 6.50
    7½"
        Federal Glass Co, pink 9.00
        Hocking, Tulips 7.00
    8½", Federal Glass Co, amber 4.50
    9½"
        Federal Glass Co, pink 13.50
        Hocking, Tulips 10.00
    11", white 8.00
Butter Box, green, 2 lb 125.00
Butter Dish, cobalt blue, Hazel Atlas
    Crisscross, 1 lb 60.00
Canister Set, amber, sugar, flour, and tea
    canister, salt box, three spice contain-
    ers 425.00
Casserole, cov
    Fire-King, 1 pt, Ovenware, blue 9.00
    Pyrex, white 25.00
Cereal Bowl, Fire-King, Ovenware, blue   9.50
Crock, Jeannette, jadite, 40 oz, knob
    finial 30.00
Custard Cup, Fire-King, Ovenware,
    blue, 4" 2.50
Drippings Bowl, Delphite 55.00
Egg Cup
    Fire-King, jadite 4.50
    Jadite, ftd 6.00
Funnel, green 30.00
Grease Jar, Hocking, Tulips, cov 10.00
Iced Tea Spoon, colored handles, set of
    12 . . . .   50.00
Loaf Pan
    Fire-King, Ovenware, blue 13.00
    Glassbake, 5 x 8", cov, clear, knob
        finial 25.00

Match Holder, Delphite **45.00**
Mayonnaise Ladle, amber **14.00**
Measuring Bowl, Fire-King, sapphire
blue **15.00**
Mixing Bowl, Jadite
6½", pouring spout **8.00**
9" **12.00**
Mug, Fire-King, sapphire blue **12.00**
Napkin Holder, crystal, scalloped,
frosted flowers **25.00**
Pie Pan, Fire-King, Ovenware, blue,
8½" **4.00**
Pitcher, jadite, sunflower base **32.00**
Punch Ladle, amber **28.00**
Reamer, Sunkist, caramel **225.00**
Refrigerator Bowl, cov, round, vertical
ribs
6" **6.50**
9" **12.00**
Refrigerator Dish, cov
4 x 4", crystal **4.00**
4½ x 9", Jennyware Ultra **12.00**
8 x 8"
Amber, Federal Glass Co **15.00**
Crystal **8.00**
Salad Utensil Set, green handles **25.00**
Salt and Pepper Shakers, pr
5¼", bulbous base, fired on blue,
black tops **6.50**
6", bulbous, delphite **12.75**
Sugar Canister, Jeannette, delphite,
metal lid, 40 oz **110.00**
Sugar Shaker, jadite **35.00**
Towel Holder, green **10.00**
Tray, 10½" d, Concentric Ring, green
transparent **10.00**
Vase, bud, jadite **5.00**

LABELS

Collecting Hint: Damaged, trimmed or torn labels are less valuable than labels in mint condition.

History: The first fruit crate art was created by California fruit growers about 1880. The labels became very colorful and covered many subjects. Most depict the type of fruit held in the box. With the advent of cardboard boxes in the 1940s, fruit crate art ended and their labels became collectible.

References: Jerry Chicone, Jr., *Florida's Classic Crates,* privately printed, 1985; Gordon T. McClelland and Jay T. Last, *Fruit Box Labels, A Collector's Guide,* Hillcrest Press, Inc., 1983; John Salkin and Laurie Gordon, *Orange Crate Art, The Story of Labels That Launched a Golden Era,* Warner Books, 1976.

Collectors' Club: Citrus Label Society, 16633 Ventura Blvd, No. 1011, Encino, CA 91436. *Citrus Peal* (monthly).

Advisor: Lorie Cairns

Vegetables, Cousin Elmer Brand, multicolored, $1.00.

Apples
Blewett Pass, autos on mountain
road, 1940s **1.00**
Circle G, red and yellow apples, red
background **1.00**
Hula, topless hula girl seated under
palm tree, blue background **1.00**
Jack's, playing card hand, four jacks,
blue background **1.00**
Majestic, tassels and royal crown,
blue background **1.00**
Sebastopol Queen, apple headed
queen, red apples, black background .... **.50**
Wenoka, Indian profile on white arrowhead, blue background **3.00**
Broom
Capitol, capitol building, Washington
DC .... **.50**
Giant, man flexing biceps .... **.50**
Indian Queen, indian lady in forest,
tepees .... **.50**
Monarch, king holding scepter ..... **.50**
Winner, lady holding torch .... **.50**
Cherry
California Cherries, California poppies and cherries .... **.25**
Camel, camel and master on desert,
sphinx, pyramids, and palms .... **.25**
High Hand, hand holding aces ..... **.25**
Mountain, snowy Mt Hood, red cherries, red border .... **.50**
San Ardo, cherry cluster, farm scene,
blue background .... **.25**
Strangio & Massaro, red and yellow
cherries, hills and orchard .... **.15**
Cigar
Big B Brand, honey bee, yellow background .... **.25**
Crane's Imported, gilt, crane, scenic **1.00**

Jewelo, romantic, gentleman and lady **1.00**
Peg, black high top shoe **1.00**
Silver Prince, white bearded scholar **1.00**
Cosmetic
Boyson's Velvet Cream, purple and
green, gilt, 3¼ x 2" . . . . **.50**
Fairy Cream, emb, gilt, florals, 3 x
3¼" . . . . **.75**
Violet Toilet Water, violets, gilt, oval **.75**
Cranberry, approx 7 x 10"
Arbutus, pink arbutus flower spray,
green leaves **2.00**
Gem, diamond sunburst **1.00**
Jersey Belle, brunette lady in blue .. **2.00**
Grape, approx 13 x 4"
American Beauty, red rose, dark green
background **2.00**
Baby Turtle, nude blonde baby on tur-
tles back, blue grapes, red back-
ground . . . . **.50**
Brandt, Brant goose at seashore . . . . **.75**
C D Pruner, red bunch of grapes,
vineyard scene background . . . . . . **.50**
Famiglia, family of four picking
grapes . . . . **.75**
Lucerne, four pink, red, and white
carnations, black background . . . . **.50**
Northern Eagle, red bunch of grapes,
flying eagle . . . . **.50**
Rayo, sunrise scene over planted
field, yellow grapes . . . . **.25**
Sierra Sue, smiling cowgirl, snowy
mountains, country scene back-
ground . . . . **.75**
Thorobreds, brown boxer dog . . . . . . **.50**
Valley Queen, regal young lady wear-
ing crown, red grapes, c1926 . . . . **.50**
WOW, bug-eyed brown bear, swing-
ing from tree branch . . . . **.75**

**Lemons, La Patera, black ground, green,
red, and blue letters, $1.00.**

Lemon, approx 12½ x 8¾"
Arboleda, scenic, Goleta **1.00**
Channel, seacoast scene, blue back-
ground, Santa Barbara **1.00**
Evening Star, shining star over Spanish
Mission, San Fernando **2.00**

Fallbrook, mountain, stream, pine
tress, lemons, leaves, and blos-
soms, black background, Fallbrook **1.00**
Golden State, four lemons, California
map, Lemon Cove **1.00**
La Patera, blue pond, grove scene,
Goleta **1.00**
Morning Smile, lemon on opened
Sunkist wrapper, blue background **1.00**
Oxnard, man and oxen team tilling
soil, Spanish dwelling and country
scene, Oxnard **1.00**
Pacific, Hawaiian Islands on lemon,
trade routes on Asia, Australia, and
Pacific coast maps, blue ocean
background, 1917, Santa Barbara **2.00**
Ramona Memories, romantic Spanish
senorita, roses in hair, San Fernan-
ado **2.00**
Santa Rosa, ranch scene, lemon
groves, two men, burro, and Span-
ish dwelling, Oxnard **1.00**
Silver Moon, Spanish mission, palms,
groves, mountains, and city lights,
yellow moon in background, San
Fernando **2.00**
Wave, two lemons, blossoms, and
leaves, red background, Santa
Paula **1.00**
Melon
Foothigh, sexy girl, black back-
ground, 9 x 4" . . . . **.50**
Miss Giffen, two little girls, blue back-
ground, 6 x 14" . . . . **.50**
Orange, approx 10 x 11"
Altissimo, pink, aqua and blue moun-
tains, blue sky, Placentia, dated
1918 . . . . **1.00**
Brownies, Brownies preparing orange
juice, blue background, Lemon
Cove **2.00**
Caledonia, thistle spray, tartan plaid
background, Placentia **1.00**
Cycle, four seasons scenes, Fillmore **2.00**
Dash, orange in blue diamond, green
background, Santa Paula **1.00**
Fillmore Crest, three oranges, green
leaves, turquoise background, blue
border, Fillmore **1.00**
Full O'Juice, partial peeled orange,
glass of orange juice, lavender
background, Redlands **2.00**
Green Mill, avocado green Dutch
windmill, yellow skies, white
clouds, Placentia **2.00**
Hill Beauty, orchard scene, purple
mountains, yellow and blue sky,
aqua background, Porterville **1.00**
Idyllwild, two oranges, scenic, snowy
mountains, black background, Riv-
erside **1.00**

John & Martha, oranges, white background, Reedley 1.00

Kaweah River Belle, country scene, Spanish mission, bunch of oranges, Lemon Cove 5.00

Linen, embroidered "Linen", black background, dated 1929, Irvine .. 1.00

Madras, orange, blossoms, and leaves, black background, Irvine . 1.00

Navajo, Indian brave, stitched leather like background, Riverside 10.00

Orbit, orange shape meteor, starry evening sky, royal blue background, Exeter 2.00

Pala Brave, Indian Chief wearing headdress, maroon background, Placentia 3.00

Red Bird, red eagles, black background, Porterville 1.00

Rocky Hill, Indian chief on horseback, blue background, Exeter ... 1.00

Satin, Sunkist orange, pink draped satin, Irvine 1.00

Shamrock, shamrock in sky over orange groves, Placentia 1.00

Talisman, three talisman roses, blue and black background, Redlands . 2.00

Una Good, large orange with blossoms and leaves, gilt, white background, Woodlake 1.00

Victoria, Queen Victoria portrait, jewels with oranges and leaves, Riverside 2.00

Pears, approx 10¾ x 7¼"
Covered Wagon, pioneer scene 2.00
El Rio Orchards, pair of yellow pears, blue background .... .50
Far West, blue frontiersman silhouette standing by lake 1.00
High Land, hand holding four aces, blue background 1.00
Lake Co Diamond, pear in diamond .50
Life, fisherman hooking trout, mountain background 2.00
Maryka, blond girl portrait .... .50
Oh Yes—We Grow The Best, two yellow pears, blue background ..... .50
Yuba Orchard, pair of yellow pears, blue background .... .50

Vegetables
Artichoke
Bronco, cowboy riding bronco, blue background, 9 x 10" 2.00
Ocean Mist, artichoke, sea wave, and mist, 9¼ x 8½" 1.00
San Luis, farm scene in diamond, navy background 1.00
Asparagus
Caligras, men harvesting scene, horse drawn wagon 2.00
King O'Hearts, playing card, king of hearts, black background ... 1.00

Red Rooster, crowing rooster, yellow, red, and navy background 1.00
Spring Time Magic, elves celebrating harvest 1.00
Broccoli, Ocean Mist, shore scene, blue background .... .25
Celery, Blue Goose, blue goose, orange background .... .25
Lettuce, Twins, girl and boy holding head of lettuce, blue background . 1.00
Peas, Elkhorn, elks head, peas in pods, brown background .... .50
Tomato
Big Chief, Indian chief and tomatoes, strip label .... .25
Front Page, "Extra" newspaper and red tomato, black background . 1.00
Green feather, feather, black background .... .25
Sun Prince, allover tomato background .... .25
Yam
Coon, raccoon holding yam, 9" sq 2.00
Ports, designs and yams in corners .50
Sho-Am-Sweet, smiling black chef holding platter, 7 x 4" 1.00
Sunset Packers, two yams, Art Deco design .... .50

LETTER OPENERS

Collecting Hints: The advertising and celluloid letter openers are the most eagerly sought. Most letter openers dating from 1940 to the present have little collector interest and value.

New collectors might focus on the openers issued from within a specific geographic region. Blanks were available that could be used to carry a local message.

History: The letter opener reflects the attributes of the period in which it was created. In the Colonial period elegant silver letter openers graced the desks of the middle and upper class. As letters became inexpensive to mail and a popular form of communication, the need for letter openers grew.

The late 19th century witnessed the popularity of the lithographed tin, advertising letter opener. They usually were given away. By the 1920s brass and other metals captured the flowing lines of the Art Nouveau and Art Deco periods. The handcraft movements, e.g., Roycroft, produced some distinctively styled letter openers during the 1910 to 1930 period.

By the early 1950s letter openers lost their individuality. Americans phoned, rather than wrote. Plastic openers of uniform design became standard. Letter openers were relegated from the desk top to the desk drawer.

Silver, English, impressed shell and ring at top, incised Phoenix bird, two hallmarks, 11⅞" l, $20.00.

Advertising
Armstrong Cork Co, 6½", celluloid, 5" rule on one side, printed cork gauge for measuring bottle neck sizes on reverse **15.00**
Bastian Bros, 9", steel blade, silvered brass handle inscribed "Compliments of Bastian Bros Co, Metal and Celluloid Adv Specialities, Rochester, NY," single pocketknife blade in handle, c1900 .... **40.00**
Coes Wrench Co, 7½", celluloid, die-cut, wrench shape, black printing of wrench holding nut and adv slogans on back, c1910 .... **25.00**
Hoskins, Wm H, Office Supply Co, Philadelphia, PA, celluloid, white, blue printing on one side, red on reverse, c1900 .... **18.00**
Humphrey Inverted, 7½", celluloid, solid white blade, black and white handle shaped as gas operated ceiling lighting fixture, gold stripes ... **30.00**
Kellogg's Cereal, 9", celluloid, figural, rooster's head, white, gray feathering, amber eye, bright red comb, inscribed "We Can't Help Crowing Once In A While - W K Kellogg," back reads "Distributed Through The Jobbing Trade Only," "Made In Germany" **100.00**
National Cash Register, 5½", white metal, diecut, detailed illus in black of cash register, adv text, c1900 .. **45.00**
Whitehead and Hoag, 5" l, flat silvered brass opener, two celluloid inserts on handle, Art Nouveau drawing of Dutch girl with yellow tulip on one, other reads "Compliments of Whitehead & Hoag Co, Advertising Novelties with Merit, Branches In All Large Cities," c1900 .... **50.00**
Wilson, Jas G, New York City, celluloid, blinds and shutters adv, 8¾", white, 6" ruler printed on one side, black and white illus, c1895 ..... **35.00**
Yellow Pages, celluloid, figural **25.00**
Celluloid, figural
Alligator, 7", hollow beige alligator, small black and white eyes, 2½" l

black lead pencil with celluloid head of black man held in mouth, tail marked "St Augustine, FL," underneath marked "Germany," c1900 .... **75.00**
Elephant, 7½", white and shaded brown, black ink inscription "Kingston, Canada," marked "Depose—Germany," c1900 .... **35.00**
Fraternal, Knights Templar, 1½ x 6", die-cut, white, souvenir of Grand Commandery of West Virginia 1910 Chicago conclave, multicolored masonic symbols **40.00**
Indian, 7", beige, black accents, seated, smoking pipe, red, white, and blue headpiece, 4"l thin black lead pencil **60.00**
Mother of Pearl, figural, Napoleon ... **75.00**
Owl, 9", white, owl's head handle, black textured feathers, blue tint eyes, metal tape measure attached to back, c1900 .... **75.00**

LIGHTERS

Collecting Hints: It is important to understand the condition terms used by collectors: (1) new—without any sign of use and often having the original box, (2) excellent—like new although used but with marks that are only visible with a magnifying glass, (3) very good—perfect finish with slight wear, (4) average—signs of moderate use. Collectors shy away from lighters in less than average condition.

It is important that the sparking or lighting mechanism works whether it be flint, liquid fuel, or gas. Repairing a lighter to working order is accepted among collectors.

New collectors are best advised to focus on lighters from a single manufacturer (Dunhill), time period (World War II), or type (e.g., table lighters). Among the advanced collecting approaches are advertising lighters, figural lighters, and pen lighters.

History: Although lighters for fire and firearms date back to the seventeenth century and earlier, the cigarette lighter (the focus of this category) did not become established until the first quarter of the twentieth century. By the 1920s it enjoyed a prominent place in most American homes, even those of non-smokers who kept a lighter handy for those who did.

Major manufacturers included Bowers, Dunhill, Evans, Marathon, Parker, Ronson, and Zippo. Well over a thousand different manufacturers produced lighters. The principal manufacturing centers were the United States and Japan. Australia, England, France, Germany, Siam, and Switzerland also produced lighters. In fact, there was at least one lighter manufacturer in every industrialized country in the mid-twentieth century.

Periodical: *On The Lighter Side*, Route 3, 136 Circle Drive, Quitman, TX 75783.

Collectors' Club: Lighter Collectors International Society, 829 Rockaway Street, Grove City, CA 93433; Zippy Collectors Club, Inc., 118 West Sixth Avenue, York, PA 17404.

Chrome, golf score keeper motif, Japan, 2¾ x 1½", $20.00.

Advertising
AMF, rhodium plated, Minix, Japan .	8.50
Camel Cigarettes, chrome, Crown, Japan	5.00
Chesterfield Cigarettes, Continental, Japan	3.00
Florida Radiator Co, chrome, Balboa, Japan	3.50
Marlboro Cigarettes, gold plated, red and white, gas, Unilite, Korea . . .	5.00
Salem Cigarettes, chrome, Penguin, Japan	5.00
Winston Cigarettes, chrome, Zenith, Japan	5.00

Figural
Airplane, "Spirit of St. Louis," gold plated, wood base, automatic spring action, Swank, Japan	150.00
Beer Can, "Pabst," chrome, Elgin . .	12.50
Bowling Ball, gold plated, black ceramic ball and pins, Tilso, Japan .	10.00
Car, "1903 Packard," chrome, black ceramic, Amico, Japan	15.00
Horse, chrome, brown ceramic, gold trim, 7", Japan	20.00
Knight, chrome, musical base plays "No Can Do," automatic spring action, Hamilton	45.00
Piano, chrome, white plastic, automatic spring action, Prince, Japan	15.00
Space Needle, "Seattle Worlds Fair," chrome, 10" h, Needlelight	27.50
Top Hat, gold plated, gray ceramic, Evans	17.50

Penciliter
Ronson, 14K gold filled	15.00
Stewart, gold plated	10.00

Pipeliter
Flamex, chrome, gas, Japan	12.50
Nimrod, alum, orig box and instructions	15.00
Pipe Mate, chrome, E S Kelly, Akron, OH adv, Japan	6.00

Pocket
Brown & Bigelow, chrome, blue, fish on front	2.00
Corona, matted black, gas, Japan . . .	12.00
Dorsey, aluminum, screwdriver on filler	7.00
Evr-Lite, aluminum	5.00
Heit, chrome, blue bottom, gas, Japan	10.00
Dreisler, gold plated, gas, engraved "Monica" reverse	3.50
Lido, chrome, side opens for two hidden pictures, Japan	17.50
Penguin, pearls and red stones, Japan	1.00
Perky, silver and gold, engraved Japanese scene	10.00
Sanford, plastic reservoir, adjustable wick	4.50
Starlite, gold plated, colored stones on front, Japan	5.00
Stratoflame, gold plated, butane cartridge	4.00
Studio 53, chrome, gas, Japan	11.50
Thorens, Vedette Model, nickel plated, automatic spring action . . .	20.00
Tres Bon, gold plated and tortoise lacquer, gas, Japan	4.50
Striker, Match King, chrome	10.00

Table Type
ASR, rhodium plated, automatic spring action	10.00
Chase, chrome, automatic spring action	22.50
Colibri, chrome and light oak, gas, Japan	10.00

Evans
Gold plated, red plaid body	6.00
Gold plated and green enamel, gas	8.50
Executive, chrome, brown leather base	17.50
Franklin M. Whiting, sterling silver, crystal base	10.00
Giv-a-gift, gold plated, green glass base, full reservoir	12.50
PAC, ceramic and gold plated, hp flowers, black base, Japan	8.50
Ronson, Varaflame, gold plated, England	15.00
Rowenta, nickel plated over brass, engraved, automatic spring action, Germany	20.00
Strikalite, crystal, cut glass	3.50

United, gold plated, copper plated
base **5.50**
Tank type
Ambassador, chrome, marked "US
Pat #1,022,140" **45.00**
Continental, snake skin covering, Ja-
pan **8.00**
Empress, chrome, round body, Japan **7.00**
Wales, chrome **17.50**

LIMITED EDITIONS OR COLLECTOR ITEMS

Collecting Hints: The first edition of a series usually commands a higher price. When buying a
limited edition collectible be aware that the original box and/or certificates increase the value of
the piece. Be alert to special discounts and sales.

History: Limited edition plate collecting began
with the advent of Christmas plates issued by
Bing and Grondahl in 1895. Royal Copenhagen
soon followed. During the late 1960s and early
1970s, several potteries, glass factories, and
mints began to issue plates, bells, eggs, mugs,
etc. which commemorated special events, people, places, holidays. For a period of time these
items increased in popularity and value. But in
the late 1970s, the market became flooded with
many collectibles and the market declined.

There are many new issues of collector items
annually. Some of these collectibles can be found
listed under specific headings, such as Hummel,
Norman Rockwell, etc.

References: *The Bradford Book of Collector
Plates, 12th Edition,* published by Bradford Ex-
change, 1987; Diane Carnevale, *Collectibles
Market Guide & Price Index to Limited Edition
Plates, Figurines, Bells, Graphics, Steins, and
Dolls, Fifth Edition,* Collectors' Information Bu-
reau, 1988; Gene Ehlert, *The Official Price
Guide To Collector Plates, Fifth Edition,* House
of Collectibles, 1988; Paul Stark, *Limited Edition
Collectibles, Everything You May Ever Need To
Know,* New Gallery Press, 1988.

Periodicals: *Collector Editions,* 170 Fifth Ave,
New York, NY 10010. *Collectors Mart,* 15100
W. Kellogg, Wichita, KS 67235; *Plate World,*
9200 North Maryland Avenue, Niles, IL 60648;
Precious Moments Collector, P. O. Box 410707,
Kansas City, MO 64141.

Collectors' Clubs: Foxfire Farm (Lowell Davis)
Club, 55 Pacella Park Drive, Randolph, MA
02368; Goebel Collectors' Club, 105 White
Plains Road, Tarrytown, NY 10591; Gorham
Collectors Club, P. O. Box 6472, Providence, RI

02940; Precious Moments Collectors' Club, 1
Enesco Plaza, Elk Grove Village, IL 60009.

Museum: Bradford Museum, Niles, IL.

BELLS

Anri, J. Ferrandiz, artist, wooden
1976, Christmas, FE **50.00**
1977, Christmas **40.00**
1978, Christmas **40.00**
1979, Christmas **30.00**
1980, The Christmas King **18.50**
1981, Lighting the Way **18.50**
1982, Caring **18.50**
1983, Behold **18.50**
1985, Nature's Dream **18.50**
Berlin, 1978, Christmas **25.00**
Bing & Grondahl, Christmas
1974 .... **180.00**
1975 .... **70.00**
1980 .... **70.00**
1981 .... **15.00**
1982 .... **35.00**
Danbury Mint, Norman Rockwell artist
1975, Doctor and Doll **50.00**
1976, No Swimming **40.00**
1977, Santa's Mail **40.00**
DeGrazia
1980, Los Ninos **55.00**
1981, Festival of Lights **45.00**
1982, Little Prayer **40.00**
Franklin Mint, 1979, Unicorn, porcelain **35.00**
Goebel
Angels
1976, color, FE **28.00**
1978, white **6.00**
1979
Green **12.00**
Lavender **12.50**
Yellow **12.00**
White **10.00**
1980
Blue **12.00**
Pink **12.00**
Red **12.00**
White **10.00**
1981
Green **12.00**
Lavender **12.00**
White **10.00**
Yellow **12.00**
1982
Green **14.00**
Red **14.00**
White **14.00**
Yellow **14.00**
Crystal, 1978, FE **10.00**
Mother's Day, FE, Crystal **37.50**
Noel
1978, Ruby **60.00**
1979, Cobalt **50.00**

Gorham
1975, Sweet Song So Young	**50.00**
1976, Tavern Sign Painter	**30.00**
1977, Chilling Chore	**30.00**
1978, Currier & Ives	**20.00**

1979
Beguilling Buttercup	**25.00**
Christmas	**25.00**

1980
Christmas	**25.00**
Love	**25.00**
1981, Ski Skills	**27.00**

1982
Young Man's Fancy	**25.00**
Coal Season's Coming	**25.00**

1983
Christmas Medley	**30.00**
The Milkmaid	**25.00**

1984
Tiny Tim	**28.00**
Young Love	**28.00**
1985, Yuletide Reflections	**32.50**
1986, Home For The Holidays	**32.50**
1987, Merry Christmas Grandma ...	**30.00**

Hummel, see HUMMEL
Hutschenreuther, 1978, Christmas	**8.00**
Leyendecker, 1977, Christmas	**6.00**
Llardo, 1987, Christmas	**30.00**

Noritake
1975, Christmas	**10.00**
1978, Christmas	**8.00**
1981, Christmas	**20.00**
1982, Christmas	**35.00**

Pickard
1977, The First Noel, FE	**75.00**
1978, O Little Town of Bethlehem ..	**70.00**
1979, Silent Night	**80.00**
1980, Hark! The Herald Angels Sing	**80.00**

Reco
1980, I Love You, FE	**20.00**
1981, Sea Echoes	**20.00**
1982, Talk to Me	**20.00**

River Shore
1979, Allison	**48.00**
1980, Katrina	**45.00**
1981, Spring Flowers	**175.00**
1982, American Gothic	**50.00**

Schmid
Peanuts
1976, Christmas	**25.00**
1977, Christmas	**18.00**
1978, Mother's Day	**15.00**
1979, A Special Letter	**25.00**
1980, Waiting for Santa	**25.00**
1981, Mission for Mom	**20.00**
1982, Perfect Performance	**18.00**
1983, Peanuts in Concert	**12.00**
1984, Snoopy and the Beagle Scouts	**12.00**

Raggedy Ann
1976, Christmas	**15.00**
1977, Christmas	**10.00**

1978, Christmas	**10.00**
Walt Disney, 1981, Christmas	**18.00**

Zemsky
1978, Christmas	**20.00**
1979, Christmas, pewter	**25.00**

Vague Shadows
1985, Hail to the Chief	**18.00**
1986, Westward Ho!	**18.00**
1987, Small Talk	**18.00**

Wedgwood
1979, Penguins, FE	**48.00**
1981, Polar Bears	**40.00**
1982, Moose	**35.00**
1983, Fur Seals	**32.00**
1984, Ibex	**50.00**
1985, Puffin	**60.00**
1986, Ermine	**60.00**

Doll, Bing and Grondahl, 1984, Else, 12¼" h, $250.00.

DOLLS

Enesco Imports
1983, Katie Lynne, 16" h	**175.00**
1984, Kristy, 12"	**150.00**
1985, Bethany, 12"	**125.00**
1986, Bong Bong, 13"	**145.00**

Gorham
1981
Alexandria, 19" h	**350.00**
Christina, 16"	**250.00**
Melinda, 14"	**250.00**
Ellice, 18"	**275.00**

1982
Jeremy, 23"	**450.00**
Mlle. Monique, 12"	**250.00**
Mlle. Yvonne, 12"	**275.00**
Mr. Anton, 12"	**165.00**
1983, Ashley	**875.00**

1984
Holly, Christmas	**750.00**
Nicole	**450.00**
Summer Holly Hobbie, 12"	**65.00**

1985
Amanda, 19"	**365.00**

Ariel, 16"	175.00
Best Friends	40.00
Lydia, 19"	1,000.00
1986	
Jessica	150.00
Meredith	225.00
Veronica, 19"	300.00
1987	
Silver Bell, 17"	175.00
Valentine Lady, Jane	145.00
Hamilton Collection	
American Fashion Doll Collection, 1985	
Heather	125.00
Melanie	120.00
Roxanne	120.00
Victoria	125.00
Hakata	
1981, Peony Maiden	150.00
1982, The Marionette	75.00
1985, Autumn Song Maiden	75.00
Royal Doulton by Nisbet	
Big Sister	225.00
First Born	175.00
Little Model	185.00
Little Sister	165.00
Pink Ribbon	160.00
Pink Sash	145.00
Royal Baby	350.00
The Muffs	175.00
Vera	185.00
Waiting, Swans Down, Series II	175.00
Winter	180.00
Winter's Sister	150.00

EGGS

Anri, 1979, Beatrix Potter	5.00
Cybis Studios, 1983, FE, 5" h, Faberge style	300.00
Ferrandiz	
1978, FE	15.00
1979	12.00
1980	9.50
1981	9.00
1982	8.00
1983	18.00
Franklin Mint, 1979, porcelain	35.00
Goebel	
1978, Easter	10.00
1979, Easter	8.00
1980	
Crystal	6.00
Easter	9.75
1981, Easter	12.00
1982, Easter	8.00
1983, Easter	28.00
Gorham, bone china, pink rose, 4¼"	18.00
Noritake	
1971, Easter, FE	75.00
1972, Easter	35.00
1973, Easter	18.00

1974, Easter	8.00
1975, Easter	10.00
1976, Easter	10.00
1977, Easter	12.50
1978, Easter	14.00
1979, Easter	14.00
1980, Easter	14.00
1981, Easter	15.00
1982, Easter	15.00
1983, Easter	28.50
1984, Easter	20.00
Royal Bayreuth	
1975	8.50
1976	6.50
1977	5.50
1979	16.00
1980	15.00
Veneto Flair	
1975	14.50
1976	14.50
1977	15.00
1983, FE, luster finish, new series	20.00
Wedgwood	
1977	35.00
1978	25.00
1979	18.00
1983	40.00

FIGURINES

Anri, Sarah Kay artist	
1983	
From The Garden	200.00
Morning Chores, FE	300.00
Playtime	225.00
Sweeping	250.00
Waiting for Mother	185.00
Wake Up Kiss, 4"	100.00
1984	
Daydreaming, 4"	125.00
Flowers for You, 6"	220.00
Special Delivery, mini	50.00
Tag Along, 6"	200.00
1985	
Afternoon Tea, 6"	250.00
Giddyap!, 4"	85.00
Tis The Season, 6"	235.00
Yuletide Cheer, 4"	115.00
1986	
Finishing Touch, 4"	85.00
Our Puppy, 1½"	40.00
Sweet Treat, 6"	175.00
With This Ring, 4"	90.00
1987	
Afternoon Tea, 11"	575.00
All Mine, 6"	240.00
Cuddles, 6"	240.00
Little Nanny, 4"	150.00
Burgues	
1972, Canon Wren	800.00
1976	
Anniversary Orchid	125.00

Bay Breasted Warbler **250.00**
Piliated Woodpecker **350.00**
Red Squirrel **225.00**
1978, Young Cottontail **325.00**
1981, Joy **85.00**
1982, Frosty **75.00**
1983, Oscar, cat **100.00**
1984, Cymbidium, Pink Blush **80.00**
Cybis
1963, Magnolia **400.00**
1964, Rebecca **345.00**
1967, Kitten, blue ribbon **500.00**
1968, Narcissus **500.00**
1969, Clematis with House Wren .. **315.00**
1970, Dutch Crocus **750.00**
1971, Appaloosa Colt **285.00**
1973, Goldilocks **325.00**
1974, Mary, Mary **750.00**
1975
   Barnaby Bear **300.00**
   George Washington Bust **300.00**
1976
   Bunny, Muffet **125.00**
   Melissa **400.00**
1977, Marigold **375.00**
1978, Edith **300.00**
1985, Nativity Lamb **125.00**
1986, Dapple Gray Foal **185.00**

Goebel
1971, Fritz the Happy Boozer **50.00**
1972, Bob the Bookworm **50.00**
1973, Maid of the Mist, 14″ **750.00**
1978, Smiling Through, 5½″ **75.00**
1982, The Garden Fancier **40.00**
1984, On The Fairway **45.00**
1985, Gentle Breezes **45.00**
1987, Chick on a Pig **65.00**

Hummel, see HUMMEL

Llardo
1971, Elephants **475.00**
1973, Going Fishing **90.00**
1974, Passionate Dance **2,500.00**
1975, Wedding **100.00**
1977, My Baby **1,115.00**
1978
   Butterfly **200.00**
   Chrysanthemum **225.00**
1980, Reading **175.00**
1983
   California Poppy **100.00**
   White Peony **90.00**
1985, Youthful Beauty **800.00**
1986
   Little Traveler **90.00**
   Ragamuffin **125.00**
1987, Spring Bouquets **125.00**

River Shore
1978
   Akiku, Baby Seal, FE **145.00**
   Fannie, fawn **80.00**
   Roosevelt, bear **60.00**

1979
   Rosecoe, red fox kit **50.00**
   Scooter **48.00**
1980
   Colt **50.00**
   Lamb **48.00**
1981, Zuela, elephant **60.00**
1982, Kay's Doll **90.00**
Rockwell, Norman, see NORMAN
ROCKWELL
Royal Doulton
1969, HRH Prince Charles, bust ... **400.00**
1974, Lady Musicians, cymbals **475.00**
1976, Fledging Bluebird **450.00**
1977
   Soldiers, Private, Delaware Reg,
     1777 .... **850.00**
   Winter Wren **375.00**
1982, Sweet and Twenties, Monte
   Carlo **175.00**
Series
   Beatrix Potter
     Benjamin Bunny **25.00**
     Lady Mouse **20.00**
     Mrs. Rabbit & Bunnies **25.00**
     Old Mr. Brown **20.00**
     Peter Rabbit **25.00**
     Rebecca Puddle-duck **20.00**
   Bunnykins
     Artist **15.00**
     Autumn Days **17.00**
     Clean Sweep **14.00**
     Family Photograph **24.00**
     Grandpa's Story **17.00**
     Sleepy Time **12.00**
     Springtime **18.00**
     Tally Ho **15.00**
   Dickens
     Bumble **20.00**
     Mrs. Bardell **24.00**
     Scrooge **25.00**
   Lord of Rings, Tolkien
     Aragorn **45.00**
     Bilbo **35.00**
     Gandalf **50.00**
     Gimli **45.00**
     Gollum **35.00**
     Legolas **45.00**
Royal Orleans Porcelain, Marilyn Mon-
   roe **80.00**
Schmid
   Lowell Davis, artist
     1979, Country Road **275.00**
     1980, Two's Company **45.00**
     1981, Plum Tuckered Out **225.00**
     1982, Right Church, Wrong Pew . **80.00**
     1983, Stirring Up Trouble **165.00**
     1984, Catnapping Too **72.00**
     1985, Out of Step **45.00**
   Raggedy Ann
     1980, Christmas **7.00**
     1981, Christmas **8.00**

Vague Shadows
  1982
    Blue Spruce **50.00**
    Major Leaguer **95.00**
  1983
    Hockey Player **60.00**
    Siesta **60.00**
  1984
    Arapaho **60.00**
    Sweet Dreams **65.00**
  1985, Lovers **50.00**
  1986, Christmas Cactus **15.00**

MUGS

Bing & Grondahl
  1978, FE **50.00**
  1980 .... **25.00**
Franklin Mint, 1979, Father's Day **40.00**
Gorham
  1981, Bugs Bunny **8.00**
  1981, Tom & Jerry, 4 × 4" h **9.00**
Lynell Studios, 1983, FE, Gnome Series
  Gnomelyweds **8.00**
  Mama Gnome **7.00**
  Gnome Sweet Gnome **6.50**
Royal Copenhagen
  1967, large **200.00**
  1968, large **24.00**
  1972, large **24.00**
  1976, large **25.00**
  1979, small **28.00**
  1980
    Large **65.00**
    Small **25.00**
  1981
    Large **70.00**
    Small **35.00**
  1983, small **30.00**
Royal Doulton, Santa, second edition . **75.00**
Schmid, Zemsky, musical, 1981, Paddington Bear **25.00**
Wedgwood
  1971, Christmas **35.00**
  1972, Christmas **30.00**
  1973, Christmas **40.00**
  1974, Christmas **30.00**
  1975, Christmas **30.00**
  1976, Christmas **30.00**
  1977, Father's Day **25.00**
  1978, Father's Day **25.00**
  1979, Christmas **25.00**
  1980, Christmas **25.00**
  1981, Christmas **35.00**
  1982, Christmas **40.00**

MUSIC BOXES

Anri
  Jemima **100.00**
  Peter Rabbit **100.00**
  Pigling **100.00**

Ferrandiz
  Angel **140.00**
  Chorale **125.00**
  Drummer **185.00**
  Flower Girl **150.00**
  Going Home **275.00**
  Letter, The **150.00**
  Proud Mother **140.00**
  Spring Arrivals **120.00**
  Wanderlust **110.00**
Gorham
  Cardinal, double, 6" h, hp, sculp-
    tured, porcelain **30.00**
  Happy Birthday, animals **35.00**
  Santa & Sleigh, 6" h **20.00**
  Sesame Street, Big Bird & Snowman,
    7" h **24.00**
Schmid
  Paddington Bear
    1981, Christmas **35.00**
    1982 .... **22.00**
  Peanuts
    30th Anniversary **18.00**
    1981
      Christmas **28.00**
      Mother's Day **18.00**
    1982
      Christmas **30.00**
      Mother's Day **20.00**
  Raggedy Ann
    1980 .... **15.00**
    1981 .... **15.00**
    1982, Flying High **20.00**
Walt Disney
  1980, Christmas, FE **42.00**
  1981, Christmas **30.00**
  1982, Christmas **25.00**

ORNAMENTS

Anri
  Beatrix Potter Series
    Amiable Guinea **12.00**
    Hunca Munca **12.00**
    Jeremy Fisher **12.50**
    Mrs. Rigby **10.00**
    Pigling Bland **12.00**
    Tom Kitten **12.75**
  1982, Alpine Mother, pastel pink ... **14.00**
Danbury Mint, angel, 4" **45.00**
Davis, Lowell, R.F.D. Series, FE **15.00**
Ferrandiz
  1978, FE **22.00**
  1979 .... **15.00**
  1980 .... **15.00**
  1981 .... **18.00**
Goebel
  1978
    Santa, colorful, FE **12.00**
    Santa, white, FE **10.00**
  1982, Santa **18.00**

Gorham
  1972, Snowflake **25.00**
  1973, Snowflake **35.00**
  1979, Tiny Tim, FE **8.00**
  1980
    Santa, FE, miniature series **8.00**
    Snowflake, SP **8.00**
  1981
    Doll, Rosebud, china, 8" h **12.00**
    Santa, miniature **10.00**
    Snowflake **30.00**
    Toy Soldier, wooden, red jacket,
      blue hat **4.50**
Hallmark
  1974, Mary Hamilton, orig Charmer
    Design **7.50**
  1975, Betsy Clark **7.50**
  1979, Special Teacher, satin **4.50**
  1980, Baby's First Christmas **15.00**
  1981
    Candyville Express **25.00**
    Friendly Fiddler **15.00**
    St. Nicholas, tin **10.00**
  1982
    Cookie Mouse **17.50**
    Cowboy Snowman **10.00**
    Jingling Teddy **12.00**
    Peeking Elf **6.50**
    Soldier, clothespin, FE **25.00**
Haviland
  1972 .... **8.00**
  1973 .... **8.00**
  1974 .... **12.00**
  1975 .... **6.00**
  1976 .... **6.00**
  1977 .... **8.00**
  1978 .... **7.50**
  1979 .... **7.25**
  1980 .... **18.00**
  1981 .... **20.00**
  1982 .... **22.00**
International Silver, Twelve Days of
  Christmas, SS, each **25.00**
Lenox, 1982, FE, snowflake emb porcelain, 24K gold finials, date, 6" h .. **40.00**
Lunt
  1974, Trefoil **20.00**
  1980, Medallion **18.00**
Reed & Barton
  1980, Christmas Castle **28.00**
  1981
    Bringing Home The Tree, SP **15.00**
    Cross **18.00**
  1982, Little Shepherd Yuletide, SS .. **15.00**
Schmid
  Paddington Bear, 1982
    Ball **5.00**
    Figural **10.00**
  Raggedy Ann
    1976, FE **6.00**
    1977 .... **3.50**
    1978 .... **3.00**

  1979 .... **3.25**
  1980 .... **3.00**
  1982, Figural **10.00**
Walt Disney
  1974, FE **15.00**
  1975 .... **5.00**
  1976 .... **10.00**
  1977 .... **4.50**
  1978 .... **4.00**
  1979 .... **4.00**
  1980 .... **3.50**
  1981 .... **3.00**
  1982 Figural **10.00**
Towle
  1971, Twelve Days of Christmas, SP
    medallion **250.00**
  1982, SP **15.00**
Wallace Silversmiths
  1971, Bell **225.00**
  1978, Bell **30.00**

PLATES

Anri (Italy)

Christmas Plates, J Ferrandiz, 12" d
  1972 Christ in the Manger **225.00**
  1973 Christmas **220.00**
  1974 Holy Night **90.00**
  1975 Flight Into Egypt **80.00**
  1976 Tree of Life **60.00**
  1977 Girl with Flowers **175.00**
  1978 Leading the Way **165.00**
  1979 The Drummer **170.00**
  1980 Rejoice **150.00**
  1981 Spreading the Word **150.00**
  1982 The Shepherd Family **150.00**
  1983 Peace Attend Thee **150.00**

Bareuther (Germany)

Christmas Plates, Hans Mueller artist,
  8" d
  1967 Stiftskirche, FE **100.00**
  1968 Kapplkirche **35.00**
  1969 Christkindlemarkt **20.00**
  1970 Chapel in Oberndorf **18.00**
  1971 Toys for Sale **20.00**
  1972 Christmas in Munich **35.00**
  1973 Christmas Sleigh Ride **20.00**
  1974 Church In The Black Forest ... **20.00**
  1975 Snowman **25.00**
  1976 Chapel in the Hills **25.00**
  1977 Story Time (Christmas Story) .. **30.00**
  1978 Mittenwald **30.00**
  1979 Winter Day **40.00**
  1980 Miltenberg **38.00**
  1981 Walk in the Forest **40.00**
  1982 Bad Wimpfen **40.00**
  1983 The Night Before Christmas ... **45.00**
  1984 Zeil on the River Main **42.50**
  1985 Winter Wonderland **42.50**

1986 Christmas in Forchhe **42.50**
1987 Decorating the Tree **46.50**

Bareuther

Father's Day Series, Hans Mueller artist, 8" d
1969 Castle Neuschwanstein **48.00**
1970 Castle Pfalz **15.00**
1971 Castle Heidelberg **24.00**
1972 Castle Hohenschwangau **30.00**
1973 Castle Katz **30.00**
1974 Wurzburg Castle **45.00**
1975 Castle Lichtenstein **32.50**
1976 Castle Hohenzollern **25.00**
1977 Castle Eltz **30.00**
1978 Castle Falkenstein **30.00**
1979 Castle Rheinstein **30.00**
1980 Castle Cochum **35.00**
1981 Castle Gutenfels **40.00**
1982 Castle Zwingenberg **40.00**
1983 Castle Lauenstein **40.00**
1984 Castle Neuenstein **42.50**
Mother's Day
1969 Mother & Children, FE **75.00**
1970 Mother & Children **30.00**
1971 Mother & Children **20.00**
1972 Mother & Children **22.00**
1973 Mother & Children **22.00**
1974 Musical Children **35.00**
1975 Spring Outing **25.00**
1976 Rocking The Cradle **28.00**
1977 Noon Feeding **28.00**
1978 Blind Man's Bluff **28.00**
1979 Mother's Love **38.00**
1980 The First Cherries **35.00**
1981 Playtime **40.00**
1982 Suppertime **40.00**
1984 Village Children **42.50**

Berlin (Germany)

Christmas Plates, various artists, 7¾" d
1970 Christmas In Bernkastel **130.00**
1971 Christmas In Rothenburg On Tauber **30.00**
1972 Christmas In Michelstadt **50.00**
1973 Christmas In Wendelstein **42.00**
1974 Christmas In Bremen **25.00**
1975 Christmas In Dortland **60.00**
1976 Christmas Eve In Augsburg ... **30.00**
1977 Christmas Eve In Hamburg ... **32.00**
1978 Christmas Market At The Berlin Cathedral **55.00**
1978 Christmas Eve In Greetsiel **55.00**
1980 Christmas Eve In Miltenberg .. **55.00**
1981 Christmas Eve In Hahnenklee . **50.00**
1982 Christmas Eve In Wasserburg . **55.00**
1983 Chapel In Oberndorf **55.00**
1984 Christmas in Ramsau **50.00**
1985 Christmas Eve in Bad Wimpfen **55.00**
1986 Christmas Eve in Gelnhaus ... **65.00**

Bing and Grondahl (Denmark)

Christmas Plates, various artists, 7" d
1895 Behind The Frozen Window . **3,600.00**
1896 New Moon Over Snow-covered Trees **1,475.00**
1897 Christmas Meal Of The Sparrows **1,100.00**
1898 Christmas Roses And Christmas Star **600.00**
1899 The Crows Enjoying Christmas **900.00**
1900 Church Bells Chiming In Christmas **800.00**
1901 The Three Wise Men From The East **485.00**
1902 Interior Of A Gothic Church .. **285.00**
1903 Happy Expectation of Children **150.00**
1904 View of Copenhagen From Frederiksberg Hill **125.00**
1905 Anxiety Of The Coming Christmas Night **130.00**
1906 Sleighing To Church On Christmas Eve **95.00**
1907 The Little Match Girl **125.00**
1908 St. Petri Church of Copenhagen **85.00**
1909 Happiness Over The Yule Tree **100.00**
1910 The Old Organist **90.00**
1911 First It Was Sung By Angels To Shepherds In The Fields **80.00**
1912 Going To Church On Christmas Eve **80.00**

Plate, Bing and Grondahl, Christmas, 1957, Christmas Candles, $155.00.

1913 Bringing Home The Yule Tree . **85.00**
1914 Royal Castle of Amalienborg, Copenhagen **75.00**
1915 Chained Dog Getting Double Meal On Christmas Eve **120.00**
1916 Christmas Prayer Of The Sparrows **85.00**
1917 Arrival Of The Christmas Boat **75.00**
1918 Fishing Boat Returning Home For Christmas **85.00**
1919 Outside The Lighted Window . **80.00**

1920 Hare In The Snow **70.00**
1921 Pigeons In The Castle Court .. **55.00**
1922 Star Of Bethlehem **60.00**
1923 Royal Hunting Castle, The Hermitage **55.00**
1924 Lighthouse In Danish Waters .. **65.00**
1925 The Child's Christmas **70.00**
1926 Churchgoers On Christmas Day **65.00**
1927 Skating Couple **110.00**
1928 Eskimo Looking At Village Church In Greenland **60.00**
1929 Fox Outside Farm On Christmas Eve **75.00**
1930 Yule Tree In Town Hall Square Of Copenhagen **85.00**
1931 Arrival Of The Christmas Train **75.00**
1932 Lifeboat At Work **90.00**
1933 The Korsor-Nyborg Ferry **70.00**
1934 Church Bell In Tower **75.00**
1935 Lillebelt Bridge Connecting Funen With Jutland **65.00**
1936 Royal Guard Outside Amalienborg Castle In Copenhagen **70.00**
1937 Arrival Of Christmas Guests .. **75.00**
1938 Lighting The Candles **110.00**
1939 Ole Lock-Eye, The Sandman .. **150.00**
1940 Delivering Christmas Letters .. **170.00**
1941 Horses Enjoying Christmas Meal In Stable **345.00**
1942 Danish Farm On Christmas Night **150.00**
1943 The Ribe Cathedral **155.00**
1944 Sorgenfri Castle **120.00**
1945 The Old Water Mill **135.00**
1946 Commemoration Cross In Honor Of Danish Sailors Who Lost Their Lives In World War II **85.00**
1947 Dybbol Mill **70.00**
1948 Watchman, Sculpture Of Town Hall, Copenhagen **80.00**
1949 Landsoldaten, 19th Century Danish Soldier **70.00**
1950 Kronborg Castle At Elsinore ... **150.00**
1951 Jens Bang, New Passenger Boat Running Between Copenhagen And Aalborg **115.00**
1952 Old Copenhagen Canals At Wintertime With Thorvaldsen Museum In Background **85.00**
1953 Royal Boat In Greenland Waters **95.00**
1954 Birthplace Of Hans Christian Andersen, With Snowman **100.00**
1955 Kalundborg Church **115.00**
1956 Christmas In Copenhagen **140.00**
1957 Christmas Candles **155.00**
1958 Santa Claus **100.00**
1959 Christmas Eve **120.00**
1960 Danish Village Church **180.00**
1961 Winter Harmony **115.00**
1962 Winter Night **80.00**
1963 The Christmas Elf **120.00**
1964 The Fir Tree And Hare **50.00**

1965 Bringing Home The Christmas Tree **65.00**
1966 Home For Christmas **50.00**
1967 Sharing The Joy Of Christmas . **48.00**
1968 Christmas In Church **45.00**
1969 Arrival Of Christmas Guests .. **30.00**
1970 Pheasants In The Snow At Christmas **20.00**
1971 Christmas At Home **20.00**
1972 Christmas In Greenland **20.00**
1973 Country Christmas **25.00**
1974 Christmas In The Village **20.00**
1975 The Old Water Mill **24.00**
1976 Christmas Welcome **25.00**
1977 Copenhagen Christmas **25.00**
1978 A Christmas Tale **30.00**
1979 White Christmas **30.00**
1980 Christmas In The Woods **42.50**
1981 Christmas Peace **50.00**
1982 The Christmas Tree **55.00**
1983 Christmas in Old Town **55.00**
1984 Christmas Letter **55.00**
1985 Christmas Eve at the Farmhouse **55.00**
1986 Silent Night, Holy Night **55.00**
1987 The Snowman's Christmas Eve **60.00**

Mother's Day Plates, Henry Thelander, artist, 6" d
1969 Dog And Puppies **400.00**
1970 Bird And Chicks **35.00**
1971 Cat And Kitten **24.00**
1972 Mare And Foal **20.00**
1973 Duck And Ducklings **20.00**
1974 Bear And Cubs **24.00**
1975 Doe And Fawns **20.00**
1976 Swan Family **22.00**
1977 Squirrel And Young **25.00**
1978 Heron **25.00**
1979 Fox And Cubs **30.00**
1980 Woodpecker And Young **35.00**
1981 Hare And Young **40.00**
1982 Lioness And Cubs **45.00**
1983 Raccoon And Young **45.00**
1984 Stork and Nestlings **40.00**
1985 Bear and Cubs **40.00**
1986 Elephant with Calf **40.00**
1987 Sheep with Lambs **42.50**

Franklin Mint (United States)

Audubon Society Birds
1972 Goldfinch **115.00**
1972 Wood Duck **110.00**
1973 Cardinal **110.00**
1973 Ruffed Grouse **120.00**
Christmas Plates, Norman Rockwell, artist, etched sterling silver, 8"
1970 Bringing Home The Tree **275.00**
1971 Under The Mistletoe **125.00**
1972 The Carolers **125.00**
1973 Trimming The Tree **100.00**
1974 Hanging The Wreath **100.00**
1975 Home For Christmas **125.00**

Goebel (Germany), see Hummel

Haviland (France)

Mother's Day (The French Collection)
1973 Breakfast	**25.00**
1974 The Wash	**30.00**
1975 In The Park	**25.00**
1976 Market	**40.00**
1977 Wash Before Dinner	**35.00**
1978 Evening At Home	**40.00**
1979 Happy Mother's Day	**30.00**
1980 Child & His Animals	**55.00**

1,001 Arabian Nights, Lillian Tellier artist
1979 Cheval Magique, Magic Horse	**60.00**
1980 Aladin et Lampe	**60.00**
1981 Scheherazade	**55.00**
1982 Sinbad the Sailor	**55.00**

The Twelve Days Of Christmas Series, Remy Hetreau, artist, 8⅜" d
1970 A Partridge In A Pear Tree, FE	**115.00**
1971 Two Turtle Doves	**40.00**
1972 Three French Hens	**35.00**
1973 Four Calling Birds	**35.00**
1974 Five Golden Rings	**30.00**
1975 Six Geese A'Laying	**30.00**
1976 Seven Swans A'Swimming	**30.00**
1977 Eight Maids A'Milking	**45.00**
1978 Nine Ladies Dancing	**35.00**
1979 Ten Lords A'Leaping	**40.00**
1980 Eleven Pipers Piping	**50.00**
1981 Twelve Drummers Drumming .	**55.00**

Plate, Haviland and Parlon, Tapestry Series, 1972, The Start of the Hunt, $70.00.

Haviland & Parlon (France)

Christmas Series, various artists, 10" d
1972 Madonna And Child, Raphael, FE	**80.00**
1973 Madonnina, Feruzzi	**95.00**
1974 Cowper Madonna And Child, Raphael	**55.00**
1975 Madonna And Child, Murillo .	**45.00**
1976 Madonna And Child, Botticelli	**50.00**
1977 Madonna And Child, Bellini ..	**40.00**
1978 Madonna And Child, Fra Filippo Lippi	**65.00**
1979 Madonna Of The Eucharist, Botticelli	**150.00**

Lady And The Unicorn Series, artist unknown, 10" d
1977 To My Only Desire, FE	**60.00**
1978 Sight	**40.00**
1979 Sound	**50.00**
1980 Touch	**110.00**
1981 Scent	**60.00**
1982 Taste	**80.00**

Tapestry Series, artist unknown, 10" d
1971 The Unicorn In Captivity	**145.00**
1972 Start Of The Hunt	**70.00**
1973 Chase Of The Unicorn	**120.00**
1974 End Of The Hunt	**120.00**
1975 The Unicorn Surrounded	**75.00**
1976 The Unicorn Is Brought To The Castle	**55.00**

Edwin M. Knowles (United States)

Americana Holidays Series, Don Spaulding, artist, 8½" d
1978 Fourth Of July, FE	**35.00**
1979 Thanksgiving	**35.00**
1980 Easter	**30.00**
1981 Valentine's Day	**25.00**
1982 Father's Day	**35.00**
1983 Christmas	**35.00**
1984 Mother's Day	**20.00**

Annie Series
1983 Annie And Sandy, FE	**25.00**
1983 Daddy Warbucks	**20.00**
1983 Annie & Grace	**19.00**
1984 Annie and the Orphans	**20.00**
1985 Tomorrow	**21.00**
1986 Annie, Lily, and Rooster	**24.00**
1987 Grand Finale	**24.00**

Gone With The Wind Series, Raymond Kursar, artist, 8½" d
1978 Scarlett, FE	**300.00**
1979 Ashley	**225.00**
1980 Melanie	**75.00**
1981 Rhett	**50.00**
1982 Mammy Lacing Scarlett	**60.00**
1983 Melanie Gives Birth	**85.00**
1984 Scarlett's Green Dress	**50.00**
1985 Rhett and Bonnie	**35.00**
1985 Scarlett and Rhett: The Finale .	**30.00**

Wizard Of Oz Series, James Auckland, artist, 8½" d
1977 Over The Rainbow, FE	**65.00**
1978 If I Only Had A Brain	**30.00**
1978 If I Only Had A Heart	**30.00**
1978 If I Were King Of The Forest ..	**30.00**
1979 Wicked Witch Of The West ..	**35.00**
1979 Follow The Yellow Brick Road .	**35.00**
1979 Wonderful Wizard Of Oz	**50.00**
1980 The Grand Finale (We're Off To See The Wizard)	**60.00**

Lalique (France)

Annual Series, lead crystal, Marie-Claude Lalique, artist, 8½" d

1965 Deux Oiseaux (Two Birds), FE	**800.00**
1966 Rose de Songerie (Dream Rose)	**215.00**
1967 Ballet de Poisson (Fish Ballet) .	**200.00**
1968 Gazelle Fantaisie (Gazelle Fantasy)	**70.00**
1969 Papillon (Butterfly)	**80.00**
1970 Paon (Peacock)	**50.00**
1971 Hibou (Owl)	**60.00**
1972 Coquillage (Shell)	**55.00**
1973 Petit Geai (Jayling)	**60.00**
1974 Sous d'Argent (Silver Pennies) .	**65.00**
1975 Due de Poisson (Fish Duet) ...	**75.00**
1976 Aigle (Eagle)	**100.00**

Lenox (United States)

Boehm Bird Series, Edward Marshall Boehm, artist, 10½" d

1970 Wood Thrush, FE	**225.00**
1971 Goldfinch	**65.00**
1972 Mountain Bluebird	**65.00**
1973 Meadowlark	**60.00**
1974 Rufous Hummingbird	**60.00**
1975 American Redstart	**50.00**
1976 Cardinal	**58.00**
1977 Robins	**55.00**
1978 Mockingbirds	**60.00**
1979 Golden-Crowned Kinglets	**65.00**
1980 Black-Throated Blue Warblers .	**75.00**
1981 Eastern Phoebes	**100.00**

Boehm Woodland Wildlife Series, Edward Marshall Boehm, artist, 10½" d

1973 Raccoons, FE	**80.00**
1974 Red Foxes	**50.00**
1975 Cottontail Rabbits	**60.00**
1976 Eastern Chipmunks	**60.00**
1977 Beaver	**60.00**
1978 Whitetail Deer	**60.00**
1979 Squirrels	**75.00**
1980 Bobcats	**90.00**
1981 Martens	**100.00**
1982 Otters	**100.00**

Llardo (Spain)

Christmas, 8" d, undisclosed artists

1971 Caroling	**30.00**
1972 Carolers	**35.00**
1973 Boy & Girl	**50.00**
1974 Carolers	**75.00**
1975 Cherubs	**60.00**
1976 Christ Child	**50.00**
1977 Nativity	**70.00**
1978 Caroling Child	**50.00**
1979 Snow Dance	**80.00**

Mother's Day, undisclosed artists

1971 Kiss of the Child	**75.00**
1972 Birds & Chicks	**30.00**

1973 Mother & Children	**35.00**
1974 Nursing Mother	**135.00**
1975 Mother & Child	**55.00**
1976 Vigil	**50.00**
1977 Mother & Daughter	**60.00**
1978 New Arrival	**55.00**
1979 Off to School	**90.00**

Reco International Corp. (United States)

Days Gone By, Sandra Kuck, artist

1983 Sunday Best	**55.00**
1983 Amy's Magic Horse	**30.00**
1984 Little Anglers	**30.00**
1984 Little Tutor	**30.00**
1984 Easter at Grandma's	**30.00**

McClelland Children's Circus Series, John McClelland, artist, 9" d

1981 Tommy The Clown, FE	**30.00**
1982 Katie The Tightrope Walker ...	**31.00**
1983 Johnny The Strongman	**31.00**
1984 Maggie The Animal Trainer ...	**29.50**

McClelland's Mother Goose Series, John McClelland, artist, 8½" d

1979 Mary, Mary, FE	**250.00**
1980 Little Boy Blue	**100.00**
1981 Little Miss Muffet	**30.00**
1982 Little Jack Horner	**30.00**
1983 Little Bo Peep	**40.00**
1984 Diddle, Diddle Dumpling ...	**30.00**
1985 Mary Had A Little Lamb	**42.00**
1986 Jack and Jill	**25.00**

Reed & Barton (United States)

Christmas Series, Damascene silver, 11" d through 1978, 8" d 1979 to present

1970 A Partridge In A Pear Tree, FE	**200.00**
1971 We Three Kings Of Orient Are	**65.00**
1972 Hark! The Herald Angels Sing	**60.00**
1973 Adoration Of The Kings	**75.00**
1974 The Adoration Of The Magi ..	**60.00**
1975 Adoration Of The Kings	**65.00**
1976 Morning Train	**60.00**
1977 Decorating The Church	**60.00**
1978 The General Store At Christmas Time	**67.00**
1979 Merry Old Santa Claus	**65.00**
1980 Gathering Christmas Greens ..	**75.00**
1981 The Shopkeeper At Christmas .	**75.00**

Rockwell, see Norman Rockwell

Rosenthal (Germany)

Christmas Plates, various artists, 8½" d

1910 Winter Peace	**550.00**
1911 The Three Wise Men	**325.00**
1912 Shooting Stars	**250.00**
1913 Christmas Lights	**235.00**
1914 Christmas Song	**350.00**

1915 Walking To Church **180.00**
1916 Christmas During War **235.00**
1917 Angel Of Peace **210.00**
1918 Peace On Earth **210.00**
1919 St. Christopher With The Christ
   Child **225.00**
1920 The Manger In Bethlehem **325.00**
1921 Christmas In The Mountains ... **200.00**
1922 Advent Branch **200.00**
1923 Children In The Winter Wood **200.00**
1924 Deer In The Woods **200.00**
1925 The Three Wise Men **200.00**
1926 Christmas In The Mountains .. **175.00**
1927 Station On The Way **200.00**
1928 Chalet Christmas **175.00**
1929 Christmas In The Alps **225.00**
1930 Group Of Deer Under The Pines **225.00**
1931 Path Of The Magi **225.00**
1932 Christ Child **195.00**
1933 Through The Night To Light .. **190.00**
1934 Christmas Peace **200.00**
1935 Christmas By The Sea **185.00**
1936 Nürnberg Angel **185.00**
1937 Berchtesgaden **195.00**
1938 Christmas In The Alps **190.00**
1939 Schneekoppe Mountain **195.00**
1940 Marien Church In Danzig **250.00**
1941 Strassburg Cathedral **250.00**
1942 Marianburg Castle **300.00**
1943 Winter Idyll **300.00**
1944 Wood Scape **275.00**
1945 Christmas Peace **400.00**
1946 Christmas In An Alpine Valley **250.00**
1947 The Dillingen Madonna **975.00**
1948 Message To The Shepherds ... **875.00**
1949 The Holy Family **185.00**
1950 Christmas In The Forest **185.00**
1951 Star Of Bethlehem **450.00**
1952 Christmas In The Alps **190.00**
1953 The Holy Light **185.00**
1954 Christmas Eve **185.00**
1955 Christmas In A Village **190.00**
1956 Christmas In The Alps **190.00**
1957 Christmas By The Sea **195.00**
1958 Christmas Eve **185.00**
1959 Midnight Mass **195.00**
1960 Christmas In Small Village **195.00**
1961 Solitary Christmas **225.00**
1962 Christmas Eve **185.00**
1963 Silent Night **185.00**
1964 Christmas Market In Nürnberg **225.00**
1965 Christmas In Munich **185.00**
1966 Christmas In Ulm **250.00**
1967 Christmas In Regensburg **185.00**
1968 Christmas In Bremen **195.00**
1969 Christmas In Rothenburg **220.00**
1970 Christmas In Cologne **165.00**
1971 Christmas In Garmisch **100.00**
1972 Christmas Celebration In Fran-
   conia **90.00**
1973 Christmas In Lubeck-Holstein . **110.00**
1974 Christmas In Wurzburg **100.00**

Bjorn Wiinblad (artist) Christmas Plates
Series
1971 Maria and Child **1,250.00**
1972 Caspar **550.00**
1973 Melchior **450.00**
1974 Balthazar **500.00**
1975 The Annunciation **200.00**
1976 Angel With Trumpet **200.00**
1977 Adoration Of The Shepherds .. **250.00**
1978 Angel With Harp **275.00**
1979 Exodus From Egypt **310.00**
1980 Angel With A Glockenspiel ... **360.00**
1981 Christ Child Visits Temple **375.00**
1982 Christening of Christ **375.00**

Plate, Royal Copenhagen, Mother's Day, 1981, Reunion, $40.00.

Royal Copenhagen

Christmas Plates, various artists, 6" d
   1908, 1909, 1910; 7" 1911 to present
1908 Madonna And Child **1,750.00**
1909 Danish Landscape **150.00**
1910 The Magi **120.00**
1911 Danish Landscape **135.00**
1912 Elderly Couple By Christmas
   Tree **120.00**
1913 Spire Of Frederik's Church, Copenhagen **125.00**
1914 Sparrows In Tree At Church Of
   The Holy Spirit, Copenhagen **100.00**
1915 Danish Landscape **150.00**
1916 Shepherd In The Field On
   Christmas Night **85.00**
1917 Tower Of Our Savior's Church,
   Copenhagen **90.00**
1918 Sheep and Shepherds **80.00**
1919 In The Park **80.00**
1920 Mary With The Child Jesus ... **75.00**
1921 Aabenraa Marketplace **75.00**
1922 Three Singing Angels **70.00**
1923 Danish Landscape **70.00**
1924 Christmas Star Over The Sea
   And Sailing Ship **100.00**
1925 Street Scene From Christian-
   shavn, Copenhagen **85.00**

1926 View of Christmas Canal, Copenhagen **75.00**
1927 Ship's Boy At The Tiller On Christmas Night **140.00**
1928 Vicar's Family On Way To Church **75.00**
1929 Grundtvig Church, Copenhagen **100.00**
1930 Fishing Boats On The Way To The Harbor **80.00**
1931 Mother And Child **90.00**
1932 Frederiksberg Gardens With Statue Of Frederik VI **90.00**
1933 The Great Belt Ferry **110.00**
1934 The Hermitage Castle **115.00**
1935 Fishing Boat Off Kronborg Castle **145.00**
1936 Roskilde Cathedral **130.00**
1937 Christmas Scene In Main Street, Copenhagen **135.00**
1938 Round Church In Osterlars On Bornholm **200.00**
1939 Expeditionary Ship In Pack-Ice Of Greenland **180.00**
1940 The Good Shepherd **300.00**
1941 Danish Village Church **250.00**
1942 Bell Tower of Old Church In Jutland **300.00**
1943 Flight Of Holy Family To Egypt **425.00**
1944 Typical Danish Winter Scene . **160.00**
1945 A Peaceful Motif **325.00**
1946 Zealand Village Church **150.00**
1947 The Good Shepherd **210.00**
1948 Nodebo Church At Christmastime **150.00**
1949 Our Lady's Cathedral, Copenhagen **165.00**
1950 Boeslunde Church, Zealand .. **175.00**
1951 Christmas Angel **300.00**
1952 Christmas In The Forest **120.00**
1953 Frederiksborg Castle **120.00**
1954 Amalienborg Palace, Copenhagen **150.00**
1955 Fano Girl **185.00**
1956 Rosenborg Castle, Copenhagen **160.00**
1957 The Good Shepherd **115.00**
1958 Sunshine Over Greenland **140.00**
1959 Christmas Night **120.00**
1960 The Stag **140.00**
1961 Training Ship Danmark **155.00**
1962 The Little Mermaid At Wintertime **200.00**
1963 Hojsager Mill **80.00**
1964 Fetching The Christmas Tree .. **75.00**
1965 Little Skaters **60.00**
1966 Blackbird At Christmastime ... **55.00**
1967 The Royal Oak **45.00**
1968 The Last Umiak **40.00**
1969 The Old Farmyard **35.00**
1970 Christmas Rose And Cat **95.00**
1971 Hare In Winter **80.00**
1972 In The Desert **85.00**

1973 Train Homeward Bound For Christmas **85.00**
1974 Winter Twilight **80.00**
1975 Queen's Palace **85.00**
1976 Danish Watermill **80.00**
1977 Immervad Bridge **75.00**
1978 Greenland Scenery **80.00**
1979 Choosing The Christmas Tree . **60.00**
1980 Bringing Home The Christmas Tree **60.00**
1981 Admiring The Christmas Tree . **55.00**
1982 Waiting For Christmas **65.00**
1983 Merry Christmas **60.00**
1984 Jingle Bells **55.00**
1985 Snowman **55.00**
1986 Wait for Me **55.00**
Mother's Day Plates, various artists, 6¼" d
1971 American Mother **125.00**
1972 Oriental Mother **60.00**
1973 Danish Mother **60.00**
1974 Greenland Mother **55.00**
1975 Bird In Nest **50.00**
1976 Mermaids **50.00**
1977 The Twins **50.00**
1978 Mother And Child **25.00**
1979 A Loving Mother **30.00**
1980 An Outing With Mother **35.00**
1981 Reunion **40.00**
1982 The Children's Hour **45.00**

Plate, Royal Doulton, Festival Children of the World, 1985, Monika, Poland, $70.00.

Royal Doulton (Great Britain)

Beswick Christmas Series, various artists, earthenware in hand-cast bas-relief, 8" sq
1972 Christmas In England, FE **40.00**
1973 Christmas In Mexico **25.00**
1974 Christmas In Bulgaria **40.00**
1975 Christmas In Norway **54.00**
1976 Christmas In Holland **45.00**
1977 Christmas In Poland **100.00**
1978 Christmas In America **45.00**

Mother And Child Series, Edna Hibel
artist, 84" d
1973 Colette And Child, FE	**450.00**
1974 Sayuri And Child	**150.00**
1975 Kristina And Child	**125.00**
1976 Marilyn And Child	**120.00**
1977 Lucia And Child	**100.00**
1978 Kathleen And Child	**95.00**

Portraits Of Innocence Series, Francisco
Masseria artist, 8" d
1980 Panchito, FE	**160.00**
1981 Adrien	**110.00**
1982 Angelica	**100.00**
1983 Juliana	**145.00**

Valentine's Day Series, artists unknown,
8¼" d
1976 Victorian Boy And Girl	**60.00**
1977 My Sweetest Friend	**40.00**
1978 If I Loved You	**40.00**
1979 My Valentine	**40.00**
1980 On A Swing	**40.00**
1981 Sweet Music	**35.00**
1982 From My Heart	**40.00**
1983 Cherub's Song	**45.00**
1984 Love In Bloom	**40.00**
1985 Accept These Flowers	**40.00**

Schmid (Japan)

Christmas, J Malfertheiner, artist
1971 St Jakob in Groden, FE	**125.00**
1972 Pipers at Alberobello	**120.00**
1973 Alpine Horn	**375.00**
1974 Young Man and Girl	**100.00**
1975 Christmas In Ireland	**90.00**
1976 Alpine Christmas	**200.00**
1977 Legend of Heligenblut	**125.00**
1978 Klockler Singers	**175.00**
1979 Moss Gatherers	**130.00**
1980 Wintry Churchgoing	**165.00**
1981 Santa Claus in Tyrol	**160.00**
1982 The Star Singers	**160.00**
1983 Unto Us A Child Is Born	**150.00**
1984 Yuletide in the Valley	**150.00**
1985 Good Morning, Good Year	**160.00**
1986 A Groeden Christmas	**75.00**
1987 Down From The Alps	**175.00**

Disney Christmas Series, undisclosed
artists, 7½" d
1973 Sleigh Ride, FE	**400.00**
1974 Decorating The Tree	**175.00**
1975 Caroling	**20.00**
1976 Building A Snowman	**35.00**
1977 Down The Chimney	**25.00**
1978 Night Before Christmas	**20.00**
1979 Santa's Surprise	**20.00**
1980 Sleigh Ride	**30.00**
1981 Happy Holidays	**18.00**
1982 Winter Games	**20.00**

Disney Mother's Day Series
1974 Flowers For Mother, FE	**80.00**

1975 Snow White And The Seven Dwarfs	**45.00**
1976 Minnie Mouse And Friends	**20.00**
1977 Pluto's Pals	**25.00**
1978 Flowers For Bambi	**20.00**
1979 Happy Feet	**25.00**
1980 Minnie's Surprise	**20.00**
1981 Playmates	**25.00**
1982 A Dream Come True	**20.00**

**Plate, Schmid, Christmas, Peanuts, 1974,
Christmas at the Fireplace, $65.00.**

Peanuts Christmas Series, Charles
Schulz, artist, 7½" d
1972 Snoopy Guides The Sleigh, FE	**90.00**
1973 Christmas Eve At The Doghouse	**120.00**
1974 Christmas Eve At The Fireplace	**65.00**
1975 Woodstock, Santa Claus	**15.00**
1976 Woodstock's Christmas	**30.00**
1977 Deck The Doghouse	**15.00**
1978 Filling The Stocking	**20.00**
1979 Christmas At Hand	**20.00**
1980 Waiting For Santa	**50.00**
1981 A Christmas Wish	**20.00**
1982 Perfect Performance	**35.00**

Peanuts Mother's Day Series, Charles
Schulz, artist, 7½" d
1972 Linus, FE	**50.00**
1973 Mom?	**45.00**
1974 Snoopy And Woodstock On Parade	**40.00**
1975 A Kiss For Lucy	**38.00**
1976 Linus And Snoopy	**35.00**
1977 Dear Mom	**30.00**
1978 Thoughts That Count	**25.00**
1979 A Special Letter	**20.00**
1980 A Tribute To Mom	**20.00**
1981 Mission For Mom	**20.00**
1982 Which Way To Mother?	**20.00**

Peanuts Valentine's Day Series, Charles
Schulz, artist, 7½" d
1977 Home Is Where The Heart Is, FE	**25.00**
1978 Heavenly Bliss	**28.00**
1979 Love Match	**20.00**
1980 From Snoopy, With Love	**24.00**
1981 Hearts-A-Flutter	**20.00**

1982 Love Patch	**18.00**

Raggedy Ann Annual Series, undisclosed artist, 7½" d

1980 The Sunshine Wagon	**65.00**
1981 The Raggedy Shuffle	**25.00**
1982 Flying High	**20.00**
1983 Winning Streak	**20.00**
1984 Rocking Rodeo	**22.50**

U. S. Historical Society (United States)

Stained Glass Cathedral

1978 Canterbury	**175.00**
1979 Flight into Egypt	**175.00**
1980 Washington Cathedral/Madonna	**160.00**
1981 The Magi	**160.00**
1982 Flight Into Egypt	**160.00**
1983 Shepherds at Bethlehem	**150.00**
1984 The Nativity	**145.00**
1985 Good Tidings of Great Joy, Boston	**125.00**
1986 The Nativity from Old St. Mary's Church, Philadelphia	**165.00**
1987 O Come, Little Children	**160.00**

Wedgwood (Great Britain)

Calendar Series

1971 Victorian Almanac, FE	**20.00**
1972 The Carousel	**15.00**
1973 Bountiful Butterfly	**14.00**
1974 Camelot	**65.00**
1975 Children's Games	**18.00**
1976 Robin	**25.00**
1977 Tonatiuh	**28.00**
1978 Samurai	**32.00**
1979 Sacred Scarab	**32.00**
1980 Safari	**40.00**
1981 Horses	**42.50**
1982 Wild West	**50.00**
1983 The Age of the Reptiles	**50.00**
1984 Dogs	**55.00**
1985 Cats	**55.00**
1986 British Birds	**50.00**
1987 Water Birds	**50.00**
1988 Sea Birds	**50.00**

Christmas Series, jasper stoneware, 8" d

1969 Windsor Castle, FE	**225.00**
1970 Christmas In Trafalgar Square .	**30.00**
1971 Piccadilly Circus, London	**40.00**
1972 St. Paul's Cathedral	**40.00**
1973 The Tower Of London	**45.00**
1974 The Houses Of Parliament	**40.00**
1975 Tower Bridge	**40.00**
1976 Hampton Court	**46.00**
1977 Westminster Abbey	**48.00**
1978 The Horse Guards	**55.00**
1979 Buckingham Palace	**55.00**
1980 St. James Palace	**70.00**
1981 Marble Arch	**75.00**
1982 Lambeth Palace	**80.00**

1983 All Souls, Langham Palace ...	**80.00**
1984 Constitution Hill	**80.00**
1985 The Tate Gallery	**80.00**
1986 The Albert Memorial	**80.00**
1987 Guildhall	**80.00**

Mothers Series, jasper stoneware, 6½" d

1971 Sportive Love, FE	**25.00**
1972 The Sewing Lesson	**20.00**
1973 The Baptism Of Achilles	**20.00**
1974 Domestic Employment	**30.00**
1975 Mother And Child	**35.00**
1976 The Spinner	**35.00**
1977 Leisure Time	**30.00**
1978 Swan And Cygnets	**35.00**
1979 Deer And Fawn	**35.00**
1980 Birds	**48.00**
1981 Mare And Foal	**50.00**
1982 Cherubs With Swing	**55.00**
1983 Cupid And Butterfly	**55.00**
1984 Musical Cupids	**55.00**
1985 Cupids and Doves	**55.00**
1986 Anemones	**55.00**
1987 Tiger Lily	**55.00**

Queen's Christmas, A Price artist

1980 Windsor Castle	**30.00**
1981 Trafalgar Square	**25.00**
1982 Piccadilly Circus	**35.00**
1983 St. Pauls	**32.50**
1984 Tower of London	**35.00**
1985 Palace of Westminster	**35.00**
1986 Tower Bridge	**35.00**

LITTLE GOLDEN BOOKS

Collecting Hints: Little Golden Books offer something for everybody. Collectors can pursue titles by specific authors or illustrators, confine the hobby to only first printings, or concentrate on television, doll, or Disney stories.

However, the goal of most collectors is to collect every title and number. Since each book was given a number, it is easy to collect and store the books numerically. Many early titles were reprinted later. All were assigned a new number in the series, especially since many had a new illustrator or freshly edited story.

Little Golden Books can still be found at yard sales and flea markets. As people who grew up in the 1940s and 1950s become more nostalgic, competition for them has increased. Good sources of books are friends, relatives, and charity book sales, especially if they have a separate children's table. Also attend doll shows and toy shows. These dealers are sources for books with paper dolls, puzzles, and cutouts. Toy dealers are also a good source for Disney, television, or cowboy titles.

Look for books with 25¢, 29¢, or no price at all on the front cover. These are the earliest books. Covers should be bright and spine paper intact. Rubbing, ink and crayon marking, or torn pages lessens the value of the book. Pencil markings are fairly easy to remove, unless extensive. Stroke gently in one direction with an art gum eraser. Do not rub back and forth.

History: Simon & Schuster published the first Little Golden Books in September, 1942. They were conceived and created by the Artists & Writers Guild, Inc., which was an arm of the Western Printing and Lithographing Company. The initial 12, forty-two page titles, priced at 25¢ each, sold over 1.5 million books within five months of publication. By the end of WWII thirty-nine million Little Golden Books were sold.

New titles were added. Most of the first thirty-six books had blue paper spines and a dust jacket. Subsequent books were issued with a gold–brown mottled spine. This mottled spine was replaced in 1950 by a shiny gold or silver foil spine.

A Disney series was begun in 1944, and Big and Giant Golden Books followed that same year. In 1949 the first Goldencraft editions were introduced. Instead of side-stapled cardboard, these books had cloth covers and were sewn so that they could hold up under school and library use. In 1958 Giant Little Golden Books were introduced, most combining three previously published titles together in one book.

1958 also marks Simon & Schuster selling Little Golden Books to Western Printing and Lithographing Company and Pocket Books. The books then appeared under the Golden Press imprint. Eventually Western bought out Pocket Books' interest in Little Golden Books. Now known as Western Publishing Company, Inc., it is the parent company of Golden Press, Inc.

In 1986 Western celebrated the one-billionth Little Golden Book by issuing special commemorative editions of some of its most popular titles, such as *Poky Little Puppy* and *Cinderella.*

Note: Prices are based on the first printing of a book in mint condition. Printing is determined by looking at the lower right-hand corner of the back page. The letter found there indicates the printing of that particular title and edition. ''A'' is the first printing and so forth. Occasionally the letter is hidden under the spine or was placed in the upper-right hand corner, so look closely. Early titles will have their printings indicated in the front of the book.

Any dust jacket, puzzles, stencils, cutouts, stamps, tissues, tape, or pages should be intact and present as issued. If not, the book suffers a drastic reduction in value—up to 80% less than the listed price. Books that are badly worn, incomplete, or badly torn are worth little. Sometimes they are useful as temporary fillers for gaps in a collection.

References: Dolores B. Jones, *Bibliography of the Little Golden Book,* Greenwood Press, 1987; Barbara Bader, *American Picture Books from Noah's Ark to the Beast Within,* Macmillan, 1976; Steve Santi, *Collecting Little Golden Books,* Books Americana, 1989.

Collectors' Club: K. Diehl, P. O. Box 5672, Baltimore, MD 21210.

Advisor: Kathie Diehl.

Activity

#A4, *Animal Paint Book,* Hans Helweg, c1955, with paints **14.00**

#A26, *Trains Stamp Book,* Kathleen N. Daly, illus E Joseph Dreany, with stamps **15.00**

#A31, *Mike and Melissa,* Jane Werner Watson, illus Adriana Mazza Saviozzi, c1959, with paper dolls **20.00**

#A34, *Little Red Riding Hood,* illus Sharon Koester, with paper dolls . **22.00**

#86, *The Color Kittens,* Margaret Wise Brown, illus Alice and Martin Provensen, c1949, with puzzle .. **30.00**

#441, *Bunny's Magic Tricks,* Janet and Alex D'Amato, illus Judy and Barry Martin, c1962, with pages that fold into tricks **5.00**

Advertising

#129, *Tex and His Toys,* Elsa Ruth Nast, illus Corinne Malvern, c1952, Texcell Cellophane Tape . **25.00**

#139, *Fun With Decals,* Elsa Ruth Nast, illus Corinne Malvern, c1952, Meyercord decals **10.00**

#399, *Doctor Dan at the Circus,* Pauline Wilkins, illus Katherine Sampson, c1960, Johnson & Johnson Band-Aids **17.00**

#550, *The Good Humor Man,* Kathleen N Daly, illus Tibor Gergely, c1964, Good Humor Ice Cream .. **6.00**

Disney

#A10, *Mickey Mouse Club Stamp Book,* Kathleen N Daly, illus Julius Svendsen, c1956, with stamps ... **20.00**

#D1, *Through the Picture Frame,* Walt Disney Studios, c1944, with dust jacket **40.00**

#D21, *Grandpa Bunny,* Jane Werner, illus Walt Disney Studios, c1951 . **14.00**

#D47, *Davy Crockett's Keelboat Race,* Irwin Shapiro, illus Mel Crawford, c1955 .... **7.50**

#D48, *Robin Hood,* Annie North Bedford, illus with scenes from the motion picture, c1955 .... **6.50**

#D50, *Jiminy Cricket Fire Fighter,* Annie North Bedford, illus Samuel Armstrong, c1956 .... **14.00**

#54, *Perri and Her Friends,* Felix Sal-

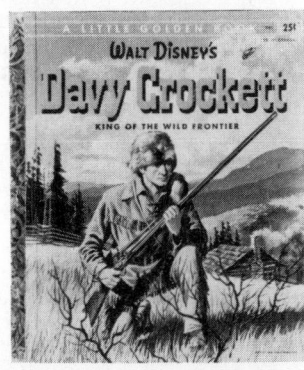

Walt Disney's Davy Crockett, King of the Wild Frontier, Irwin Shapiro, illus Walt Disney Studio, adapted by Mel Crawford/ Simon and Schuster, NY, 1955, $15.00.

ten, illus Annie North Bedford, c1956 .... 5.00

#65, *Old Yeller,* Irwin Shapiro, illus Edwin Schmidt and E Joseph Meany, c1957 .... 6.00

#75, *Manni The Donkey In The Forest World,* Emily Brown, illus Walt Disney Studios, c1959 .... 5.00

#95, *Swiss Family Robinson,* Jean Lewis, illus Paul Granger, c1961 . 5.00

General Interest

#5, *Prayers for Children,* illus Rachel Taft Dixon, c1942, with dust jacket 18.00

#13, *The Golden Book of Birds,* Hazel Lockwood, illus Feodor Rojankovsky, c1943, with dust jacket .. 20.00

#23, *The Shy Little Kitten,* Cathleen Schurr, illus Gustaf Tenggren, c1946, with dust jacket 22.00

#56, *Our Puppy,* Elsa Ruth Nast, illus Feodor Rojankovsky, c1948 ...... 10.00

#92, *I Can Fly,* Ruth Krauss, illus Mary Blair, c1950 .... 12.00

#119, *A Day at the Playground,* Miriam Schlein, illus Eloise Wilkin, c1951 .... 10.00

#144, *The Road To Oz,* Peter Archer, illus Harry McNaught, c1951 .... 22.00

#149, *Indian, Indian,* Charlotte Zolotow, illus Leonard Weisgard, c1952 .... 18.00

#159, *The Tin Woodman of Oz,* Peter Archer, illus Harry McNaught, c1952 .... 18.00

#167, *Animal Friends,* Jane Werner, illus Garth Williams, c1953 ..... 5.00

#185, *Laddie The Superdog,* William P Gottlieb, c1954 .... 5.50

#208, *Tiger's Adventure,* William P Gottlieb, c1954 .... 5.50

#210, *The Kitten Who Thought He*

Was A Mouse, Miriam Norton, illus Garth Williams, c1954 .... 9.00

#222, *The Circus ABC,* Kathryn Jackson, illus J P Miller, c1955 ...... 7.00

#227, *The Twins,* Ruth and Harold Shane, illus Eloise Wilkin, c1955 . 18.00

#229, *Houses,* Elsa Jane Werner, illus Tibor Gergely, c1955 .... 6.50

#238, *5 Pennies To Spend,* Miriam Young, illus Corinne Malvern, c1955 .... 7.50

#251, *Cars,* Kathryn Jackson, illus William J Dugan, c1956 .... 5.00

#257, *Counting Rhymes,* illus Corinne Malvern, c1947 .... 5.00

#317, *More Mother Goose Rhymes,* illus Feodor Rojakovsky, c1958 .. 10.00

#380, *Birds of All Kinds,* Walter Ferguson, c1959 .... 5.50

#388, *Our Flag,* Carl Memling, illus Stephen Cook, c1960 .... 4.50

#443, *Puff the Blue Kitten,* illus Pierre Probst, c1961 .... 8.00

#479, *Rusty Goes to School,* Pierre Probst, c1962 .... 5.00

#465, *My Little Golden Animal Book,* Elizabeth MacPherson, illus Moritz Kennel, c1962 .... 5.00

Television/Cartoons

#136, *Bugs Bunny Gets A Job,* Annie North Bedford, illus Warner Bros, c1952 .... 7.50

#150, *Rootie Kazootie Detective,* Steve Carlin, illus Mel Crawford, c1953 .... 10.00

#204, *Howdy Doody and Mr. Bluster,* Edward Kean, illus Elias Marge, c1954 .... 10.00

#223, *It's Howdy Doody Time,* Edward Kean, illus Art Seiden, c1955 12.00

#226, *Rootie Kazootie Joins the Circus,,* Steve Carlin, illus Mel Crawford, c1955 .... 11.50

#356, *Steve Canyon,* Milton Caniff, c1959 .... 5.50

#372, *Woody Woodpecker Drawing Fun for Beginners,* Carl Buettner, illus Harvey Eisenberg and Norman McGary, c1959 .... 7.50

#378, *Ruff and Ready,* Ann McGovern, illus Harvey Eisenberg and Al White, c1959 .... 6.50

#432, *Dennis The Menace Waits For Santa Claus,* Carl Memling, illus Al White, Norman McGary, Bill Lorencz, c1962 .... 7.50

#474, *Touche Turtle,* Carl Memling, illus Al White, Norman McGary, Bill Lorencz, c1962 .... 6.50

#458, *Huckleberry Hound Safety Signs,* Ann McGovern, illus Al White, c1961 .... 7.00

#476, *Little Lulu,* Gina Inoglia Weiner, illus Woody Kimbrell and Al White, c1962 .... **6.50**

#483, *Mister Ed The Talking Horse,* Barbara Shook Hazen, illus Mel Crawford, c1962 .... **9.00**

#500, *The Jetsons,* Carl Memling, illus Al White and Hawley Pratt, c1962 .... **10.00**

#502, *Wally Gator,* Tom Golberg, illus Hawley Pratt and Bill Lorencz, c1963 .... **7.00**

#556, *Peter Potamus,* Carl Memling, illus Hawley Pratt and Bill Lorencz, c1964 .... **7.50**

Western

#195, *Roy Rogers and Cowboy Toby,* Elizabeth Beecher, illus Mel Crawford, c1954 .... **10.00**

#213, *Dale Evans and the Lost Gold Mine,* Monica Hill, illus Mel Crawford, c1955 .... **8.00**

#231, *Roy Rogers and the Mountain Lion,* Ann McGovern, illus Mel Crawford, c1955 .... **9.00**

#246, *Rin Tin Tin and Rusty,* Monica Hill, illus Mel Crawford, c1955 .. **6.50**

#254, *Buffalo Bill, Jr,* Gladys Wyatt, illus Hamilton Greene, c1956 .... **5.50**

#263, *The Lone Ranger,* Steffi Fletcher, illus Joseph Dreany, c1956 .... **12.00**

#297, *The Long Ranger and Tonto,* Charles Spain Verral, illus Edwin Schmidt, c1957 .... **10.00**

#354, *Maverick,* Carl Memling, illus John Leone **7.50**

LUNCH KITS

Collecting Hints: The thermos is an intregal part of the lunch kit. The two must be present to have full value. However, there has been a tendency in recent years to remove the thermos from the lunch box and price the two separately. The wise collector will resist this trend.

Prices on lunch kits have increased significantly in the last couple of years, largely due to the publicity generated by Scott Bruce. Price speculation is rampant.

The values listed reflect realistic prices for a kit with thermos, both in near mint condition. Scratches and rust detract from a metal kit's value and lower value by more than fifty percent.

History: Lunch kits date back to the 19th century when tin boxes were used by factory workers and field hands. The modern child's lunch kit, the form most sought by today's collector, began in the 1930s. Gender, Paeschke & Frey Co. of Milwaukee, Wisconsin, issued a No. 9100

Mickey Mouse lunch kit for the 1935 Christmas trade. An oval lunch kit of a streamlined train, marked "Decoware," dates from the same period.

Television brought the decorated lunch box into a golden age. Among the leading manufacturers are: Aladdin Company; Landers, Frary and Clark; Ohio Art (successor to Hibbard, Spencer, Bartlett & Co.) of Bryan, Ohio; Thermos/King Seeley; and Universal.

References: Scott Bruce, *The Fifties and Sixties Lunch Box,* Chronicle Books, 1988; Scott Bruce, *The Official Price Guide To Lunch Box Collectibles, First Edition,* House of Collectibles, 1989.

Periodical: *Hot Boxing,* P.O. Box 87, Somerville, MA 02143.

Advisor: Bob Cereghino.

Adam-12, Aladdin Industries, Nashville, TN, 1972, $20.00.

Adco Liberty

Autry, Gene, 1950s **100.00**

Howdy Doody, 1950s, metal variety, no known metal thermos **100.00**

Aladdin

Adam 12, 1972 .... **20.00**

Annie Oakley, 1955 .... **50.00**

Batman, 1966 .... **35.00**

Battlestar Galactica, 1979 .... **15.00**

Beatles, 1966 .... **125.00**

Beverly Hillbillies, 1963 .... **65.00**

Bonanza, three varieties (1964, 1965, 1968), each **40.00**

Bond, James, 1966 .... **65.00**

Bozo, 1964 .... **30.00**

Buck Rogers, 1980 .... **15.00**

Canyon, Steve, 1959 .... **50.00**

Charlie's Angels, 1979 .... **12.00**

Corbett, Tom

1952, blue or red box **30.00**

1953, full color picture, light blue border **90.00**

Dick Tracy, 1967 .... **30.00**

Dr. Doolittle, 1968	15.00
Emergency, 1977, dome top	20.00
Fall Guy, 1982	12.00
Flying Nun, 1968	50.00
Gentle Ben, 1968	40.00
Gomer Pyle, 1966	50.00
Gunsmoke, two varieties (1959, 1962), each	35.00
Hector Heathcote, 1964	50.00
Hogan's Heroes, 1966	60.00
Hopalong Cassidy	
1952, blue or red box	25.00
1943, full color picture, black border	75.00
It's About Time, 1967	50.00
Jetson's, 1963	100.00
Land of the Giants, 1969	50.00
Laugh-In, two varieties (1969, 1970), each	30.00
Monroes, 1967	40.00
Osmonds, 1973	20.00
Paladin, 1960	65.00
Rifleman, 1961	65.00
Robin Hood	50.00
Star Trek, 1968	100.00
Tarzan, 1968	30.00
Twiggy, 1968, vinyl	50.00
Universal Movie Monsters, 1980	20.00
Voyage to the Bottom of the Sea, 1967	40.00
Waltons, 1974	15.00
Wild Bill Hickcock, 1955	40.00
Wild Wild West, 1969	40.00
Zorro, two varieties (1959, 1966), each	45.00
King Seeley (formerly American Thermos Company)	
Apples' Way, 1975	30.00
Atom Ant, 1966	40.00
Beany & Cecil, 1962, vinyl	70.00
Beatles' Yellow Submarine, 1969	125.00
Brady Bunch, 1970	40.00
Brave Eagle, 1956	60.00
Bullwinkle, 1963, vinyl	65.00
Captain Kangaroo, 1964	40.00
Cowboy in Africa, 1968	30.00
Family Affair, 1969	20.00
Fess Parker as Daniel Boone, 1965	35.00
Flipper, 1966	30.00
Get Smart	65.00
Deputy Dawg, 1962, vinyl	65.00
Green Hornet, 1967	50.00
Guns of Will Sonnet, 1968	40.00
Happy Days, 1977	15.00
Hardy Boys, 1978	15.00
Hee Haw, 1970	15.00
How the West was Won, 1979	15.00
Julia, 1969	15.00
Kung Fu, 1974	15.00
Lawman, 1961	40.00
Little House on the Prairie, 1979	15.00
Lost in Space, 1967	150.00
Man from UNCLE, 1966	50.00

Monkees, 1967, vinyl	100.00
Mork & Mindy, 1980	12.00
Mr. Merlin, 1982	10.00
Munsters, 1969	60.00
Partridge Family, 1971	15.00
Porky's Lunchwagon, 1959	40.00
Soupy Sales, 1965, vinyl	150.00
Space 1999, 1975	25.00
Trigger, 1954, no thermos	35.00
UFO, 1973	20.00
Wagon Train, 1964	40.00

MAGAZINE COVERS AND TEAR SHEETS

Collecting Hints: A good cover should show the artist's signature, have the mailing label nonexistent or in a place that does not detract from the design element, and have edges which are crisp, but not trimmed.

When framing vintage paper, use acid free mat board and tape with a water soluble glue base such as brown paper gum tape or linen tape. The tape should only be affixed to the back side of the illustration. The rule of thumb is do not do anything that cannot be easily undone.

Do not hang framed vintage paper in direct sunlight, which causes fading, or in a highly humid area (such as a bathroom or above a kitchen sink), which causes wrinkles in both the mat and art work.

History: Magazine cover design attracted some of America's leading illustrators. Maxfield Parrish, Erte, Leyendecker, and Norman Rockwell were dominate forces in the 20th century. In the mid–1930s, photographic covers gradually replaced illustrated covers. One of the leaders in the industry was *Life* magazine, which emphasized photojournalism.

Magazine covers are frequently collected by artist signed covers, subject matter, or historical events. Artist signed covers feature a commercially printed artist signature on the cover, and the artist is identified inside as "Cover by..." Most collected covers are in full color and show significant design elements. Ethnic groups, especially blacks, were often reflected in magazine covers and tear sheets. They are frequently collected as memorabilia reflecting the tempo of the times in which they were printed.

Many of America's leading artists also illustrated magazine advertising. The ads made advertising characters such as the Campbell Kids, the Dutch Girl, and Snap, Crackle and Pop world famous.

References: Patricia Kery, *Great Magazine Covers of the World*, Abbeyville Press, 1982; check local libraries for books about specific illustrators such as Parrish, Rockwell, and Jessie Wilcox Smith.

Periodical: *PCM—Paper Collector's Marketplace,* P. O. Box 127, Scandinavia, WI 54977.

Advisor: Susan Brown Nicholson.

Note: Prices of covers and complete magazines have remained stable the last few years, but prices of tear sheets have declined as more and more magazines have glutted the market. While only a short time ago magazines were thrown away when attics and garages were cleaned, now they are offered for sale. The public has been educated by the proliferation of magazine tear sheets at flea markets and mall shows. Dealers prefer to purchase complete magazines and glean their profit from selling off individual tear sheets.

As more and more magazines are destroyed for the tear sheets, complete magazines rise in value as the supply decreases. If a magazine is in mint condition, it should be left intact. Do not remove illustrations from complete magazines. Only the complete magazine can act as a tool to interpret that specific historical time period. Editorial and advertising together define the spirit of the era.

Automobile, Chrysler, Oct 1962 issue of *Saturday Evening Post,* **$2.00.**

ARTIST SIGNED

Atwell, Mable Lucie	
Pictorial Review, Nov, 1913	35.00
Others	20.00
Armstrong, Rolf	25.00
Benito, Herbert	10.00
Bevans, Torre	
Children	15.00
McCall's, 1920–1921	18.00
Pictorial Review, April, 1920	18.00
Others	12.00
Cassandre, A. M.	10.00
Christy, Howard Chandler	10.00

Coffin, Haskell	12.00
Crane, S. W.	6.00
Drayton, Grace (also Weiderseim)	
Covers	30.00
Illustrated Stories	1.00
Paper Dolls	
Large format	18.00
Small format	8.00
Tear Sheet	
Black and white	1.00
Colors	4.00
Eastman, Ruth, The Designer, Aug, 1913	10.00
Erte, Harper's Bazaar Covers	50.00
Fisher, Harrison	
Ladies Home Journal, Dec, 1913 . . .	25.00
Large format	18.00
Small format	12.00
Flagg, James Montgomery, color	6.00
Greer, Blanche, Woman's Home Companion, June, 1907	20.00
Gunn, Archie	
Truth, June 20, 1896	15.00
Others	10.00
Gutmann, Bessie Pease	25.00
Hays, Mary A., McCall's, May, 1915 .	5.00
Hoff, Guy, The Woman's Magazine, Dec, 1918	15.00
King, Hamilton, Coca Cola girl illustrator	12.00
Leyendecker	15.00
Marsh, Lucille Patterson	15.00
Mayer, My, Truth, Aug 15, 1896	25.00
McClelland, Barclay	6.00
Mucha, Alphonse	
Century	100.00
Literary Digest	40.00
O'Neill, Rose	
Illustrated articles	4.00
Kewpies Covers	
Ladies Home Journal, Dec, 1910 .	35.00
Ladies Home Journal, Dec, 1927 .	35.00
The Designer, Aug, 1911	35.00
The Pictorial Review, Jan, 1914 . .	22.00
Kewpies Stories, pages	
Large format, Woman's Home Companion, 1911–1912	12.00
Medium format, Good Housekeeping, 1916–1919	10.00
Small format, Good Housekeeping, 1914–1916	8.00
Tear Sheet	
Full page, color	6.00
Jello, black and white	3.00
Rock Island Line	4.00
Woman/Children Covers	
Metropolitan, Feb, 1900	20.00
Woman's Home Companion, Jan, 1924	20.00
Outcault, Truth, Feb 15, 1896	15.00
Parkhurst, McCall's	
Dec, 1916	15.00

March, 1918 .... **8.00**
Parrish, Maxfield
  Cover, Ladies Home Journal, Dec,
    1912 .... **60.00**
  Story illustration headlines **3.00**
  Tear Sheet, Jello **35.00**
Penfield, Edward, Harper's Weekly,
  Dec, 1898 .... **35.00**
Phillip, Coles
  Cover, McCall's, June, 1918 .... **15.00**
  Tear Sheet, Community Silver **6.00**
Ralph, Lester **6.00**
Robinson, Robert **8.00**
Rockwell, Norman
  Cover
    Prior to 1920 .... **35.00**
    Prior to 1940 .... **25.00**
    After 1940 .... **10.00**
  Tear Sheet, color **8.00**
Smith, James Calvert, McCall's, Nov,
  1921 .... **8.00**
Smith, Jessie Wilcox
  Cover
    Good Housekeeping **20.00**
    Others, large format, pre–1920 .. **25.00**
  Tear Sheet, Seven Stages of Child-
    hood **15.00**
Stanlaws, Penny **8.00**
Twelvetrees, Charles
  Covers
    Capper's Farmer, 1930s **5.00**
    Collier's, 1930s **5.00**
    Pictorial Review
      Large format, pre–1930 .... **15.00**
      Small format, pre–1930 .... **10.00**
      Suffrage, Jan, 1921 .... **25.00**
    Illustrated Stories **3.00**
Usobal, McCall's, March, 1921 ...... **8.00**
Vargas **10.00**
Wireman, H. E., Woman's Home Com-
  panion, Dec, 1915 .... **12.00**
Wood, Lawson
  Monkey images **6.00**
  Other **4.00**

BLACK MEMORABILIA

Covers feature African–American per-
  sonalities
  Armstrong, Louis **10.00**
  Clay, Cassius **7.00**
  Davis, Jr., Sammy **7.00**
  King, Martin Luther **8.00**
  Life Magazine, 1956, Slave Auction
    cover **15.00**
  Saturday Evening Post, Black images **12.00**
Stories on Black History **2.00**
Tear Sheet
  Aunt Jemima **2.00**
  Cream of Wheat
    General **10.00**
    Needlecraft Magazine **6.00**

Wyeth, N. C. **12.00**
Gold Dust Twins **8.00**

MAGAZINES

Collecting Hints: A rule of thumb for pricing general magazines without popular artist-designed covers is the more you would enjoy displaying a copy on your coffee table, the more elite the publication, and the more the advertising or editorial content relates to today's collectibles, the higher the price. *Life* magazine went into millions of homes each week, *Harper's Bazaar* and *Vogue* did not. Elite families had a greater tendency to discard last month's publication while middle–class families found the art on the *Saturday Evening Post* and *Collier's* irresistible and saved them. The greater the supply, the lower the price.

History: In the early 1700s general magazines were a major means of information for the reader. Literary magazines, such as *Harper's*, became popular in the 19th century. By 1900, the first photo-journal magazines appeared. *Life*, the prime example, was started by Henry Luce in 1932.

  Magazines created for women featured "how to" articles about cooking, sewing, decorating, and child care. Many were entirely devoted to fashion and living a fashionable life, such as *Harper's Bazaar* and *Vogue*. Men's magazines were directed at masculine skills of the time, such as hunting, fishing, and woodworking, supplemented with appropriate "girlies" titles.

References: Jack Bramble, *The Playboy Collectors Guide & Price List, 5th Edition*, Budget Enterprises, 1982; Marjorie M. and Donald L. Hinds, *Magazine Magic*, The Messenger Book Press, 1972; *Official Price Guide To Paperbacks and Magazines*, House of Collectibles, 1986.

Advisor: Susan Brown Nicholson.

Note: The prices for general magazines are retail prices. They may be considerably higher than what would be offered for an entire collection filling your basement or garage. Bulk prices for common magazines such as *Life, Collier's*, and *Saturday Evening Post* are generally from fifty cents to one dollar per issue. Dealers have to sort, protect with plastic covering, discard ones that have items clipped from the interior, or have marred covers, and make no money on those which they never sell. The end result is that a lower price is paid for magazines purchased in bulk.

Argosy **2.00**
American Boy
  Prior to 1929 .... **2.00**
  Prior to 1940 .... **1.00**
American Home **2.00**

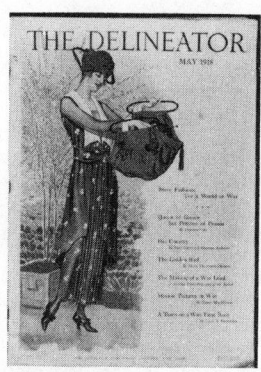

The Delineator, May, 1918, $8.00.

Arizona Highways
Prior to 1930	10.00
Prior to 1940	5.00
Prior to 1960	.50
After 1960	.25

Asia, Art Deco cover 15.00

Atlantic Monthly
1868	2.00
1911–1914	1.00
1915–1927	.75
1928–1935	.60

Better Homes and Gardens, prior to 1935 .... 1.50

Black Cat Magazine
Cover with cat's head	8.00
Cover with full figure of dressed cat	25.00

Boy's World 1.00

Business Week
Prior to 1940	.60
Prior to 1960	.40
After 1960	.10

Capper's Farmer
Prior to 1930	1.00
Twelvetrees covers	5.00

Century
1882–1893	1.50
1917–1926	1.00
Mucha covers	100.00

Child's Life, prior to 1940 .... 1.00

Coast Magazine, Seattle, 1900–1912 . 10.00

Collier's
Prior to 1910	4.00
Prior to 1920	5.00
Prior to 1935	1.00

Coronet, prior to 1950 .... 1.00

Cosmopolitan
1890–1903	1.50
Prior to 1950	1.00

Country Home .... .75

Country Life 1.00

Delineator
Large format	8.00
Small format	4.00
1918–1920	8.00
1921–1935	2.00

Designer, The
Large format	8.00
Small format	4.00
1916–1921	8.00

Ebony, 1958 .... 5.00

Esquire 2.00

Farmer's Wife, The
Mueller, Benson cover, Aug, 1925 ..	10.00
Prior to 1950	2.00
Others	1.00

Field and Stream 3.00

Flair, diecut hole in cover 4.00

Fortune
Cigar band page inside	50.00
Prior to 1935	10.00
Prior to 1940	6.00
Prior to 1950	5.00
Prior to 1960	2.00

Girl's Companion
Prior to 1940	3.00
After 1940	1.00

Godey's Lady Book, all illustrations intact
Bound, yearly	50.00
Monthly issue	8.00
1856	150.00
1861	50.00

Good Housekeeping, prior to 1955 ... 2.00

Harper's Bazaar
Erte Cover	50.00
Illustrated Covers	10.00
Photographic Covers	5.00

Harper's Monthly
1873–1896	1.50
1902–1906	3.00
1910–1917	2.50
1919–1925	2.00
1930–1935	.50

Harper's Weekly
1873–1898	8.00
Dec 1900	15.00

Hobbies, prior to 1960 .... 2.00

Holiday
Prior to 1950	1.00
Prior to 1960	.50

Hot Rod
Prior to 1960	2.00
After 1960	1.00

House and Garden
Art Deco design	6.00
Other	2.00

House Beautiful
Illustrator cover	8.00
Photographic cover	4.00

Judge
Drayton cover	30.00
Teddy Roosevelt	20.00
1898–1910	10.00
Others	5.00

Junior Home 1.00

Ladies' Home Journal
Prior to 1910	12.00

Prior to 1919	8.00
Prior to 1929	5.00
Prior to 1935	2.00
Le Rire	3.00
Le Souire	3.00
Leslie's, prior to 1920	4.00

Life
Illustrated cover, small format, 1883–1936

Artist signed covers	20.00
Other	8.00

Photographic cover, 1936–1972

Baseball Stars	15.00
Beatles	20.00
Chaplin, Charlie	10.00
Garbo, Greta	20.00
Manson, Charles	15.00
Monroe, Marilyn	25.00
Nov 23, 1936–first	50.00
Political figures	4.00
Wayne, John	10.00
World War II	8.00

Literary Digest

1920–1926	1.00
1927–1932	.75
1935+	.50
Important 20th century authors	5.00
Mucha cover	40.00

Look

Celebrities	5.00
Prior to 1950	2.00

McCall's

1919–1925	7.00
1930–1940	2.00
McClure's	2.00
Mechanics Illustrated	1.00
Modern Priscilla	1.00

National Geographic (prior to 1890, contact rare book dealer)

Coke, Santa back cov	4.00
Others	.10

Needlecraft

Prior to 1930	2.00
With Rockwell ads	4.00

Newsweek

Hitler Cover	7.00
Mae West Cover	9.00
Prior to 1950	.75
After 1950	.25
New Yorker	2.00
Outdoor Life	1.00
People's Home Journal, prior to 1920	4.00
Peterson, bound, yearly	50.00

Pictorial Review

Large format	8.00
Small format	4.00

Playboy

Volume 1, No. 1, Marilyn Monroe	2,500.00
Beatles Interview issue	30.00
Other, prior to 1960	2.00
After 1965	1.00
Popular Mechanics	1.00

Popular Science

Prior to 1930	6.00
After 1930	1.00

Puck

New York, 1898–1916	10.00
St. Louis, 1871–1873	10.00

Play Mate, April, 1943, Fern Bisel Peat cover, $4.00.

Reader's Digest

Prior to 1930	1.00
After 1930	.25

Saturday Evening Post

May 20, 1916, first Rockwell cover	150.00
Prior to 1930	8.00
After 1930	4.00
Scribner's, prior to 1920	1.50

Sports Illustrated

Swimsuit issue	4.00
Other	2.00

The Theater Magazine

Prior to 1910	5.00
Strong Art Deco covers, 1920s	8.00

Time

Prior to 1940	1.25
Prior to 1960	1.00
After 1960	.50
Town and Country, prior to 1940	5.00
Travel, prior to 1930	1.00
True	.50
Truth	8.00

T. V. Guide

Pre-national, NYC TeleVision Guide, No. 1	200.00
NYC-TeleVision Guide, 1948–1953	40.00
March 18, 1950, first Monroe cover	500.00
Feb 22, 1952, Captain Video cover	50.00

Celebrities

Bond, James	30.00
Dark Shadows	30.00
Elvis	30.00
Monkees	30.00
Savage, Doc	30.00
Superman	30.00
UNCLE	30.00

Others, early	**5.00**
After 1970	**1.00**
Vanity Fair	**4.00**
Vogue	
Illustrated cover	**10.00**
Photographic cover	**5.00**
Woman's Home Companion	
1909–1912	**9.00**
June 1907, N. C. Wyeth ad	**12.00**
Woman's World	**3.00**
Youth's Companion	**1.00**

MARBLES

Collecting Hints: Hand-made glass marbles usually command higher prices than machine-made glass, clay, or mineral marbles. There are a few notable exceptions, e.g., machine-made comic strip marbles were made for a limited time only and are highly prized by collectors. Care must be taken in purchasing this particular type since the comic figure was stenciled on the marble. A layer of glass was to be overlaid on the stencil. However, many examples exist that were not overlaid, and the stencils rub or wear off.

Some of the rarer examples of hand-made marbles are Clambroth, Lutz, Indian Swirls, Peppermint Swirls, and Sulphides. Marble values are normally determined by their type, size, and condition. Usually, the larger the marble, the more valuable it is within each type.

A marble in mint condition is unmarred and has the best possible condition with a clear surface. It may have surface abrasions from rubbing in its original package. A marble in good condition may have a few small surface dings, scratches, and slight surface cloudiness. However, the core must be easily seen, and the marble must be without large chips or fractures.

History: Marbles date back to ancient Greece, Rome, Egypt, and other early civilizations. In England, Good Friday is known as "Marbles Day" because the game was considered a respectable and quiet pastime for the hallowed day.

During the American Civil War, soldiers carried marbles and a small board to play "solitaire," a game whose object was to jump the marbles until only one is left in the center of the board.

In the last few generations, school children have identified marbles as peewees, shooters, commies, and cat's eyes.

References: Paul Baumann, *Collecting Antique Marbles*, Wallace-Homestead, 1981; Everett Grist, *Antique Marble Price Guide, Second Edition*, Collector Books, 1988; Marble Collectors Society of America, *Identification and Price Guide*, privately printed, 1989; Mark E. Randall, *Marbles As Historical Artifacts*, Marble Collectors Society; Mark E. Randall and Dennis Webb, *Greenberg's Guide to Marbles*, Greenberg Publishing Co., 1988.

Collectors' Clubs: Marble Collectors' Unlimited, 503 West Pine, Marengo, IA 52301; Marble Collectors Society of America, P. O. Box 222, Trumbull, CT 06611, publishes quarterly newsletter, *Marble Mania;* National Marble Club of America, 440 Eaton Road, Drexel Hill, PA 19026, quarterly newsletter.

Museums: Corning Museum of Glass, Corning, NY; Sandwich Glass Museum, Sandwich, MA; Smithsonian Institution, Museum of Natural History, Washington, D.C.; Wheaton Village Museum, Millville, NJ.

Advisor: Stanley A. Block.

REPRODUCTION ALERT: Comic marbles are being reproduced.

Sulphide, figure of woman, 1⅝" d, $150.00.

AGATE

A form of chalcedony quartz with banded or irregular appearance; it is usually a translucent stone found in all shades of earth colors, the most common being tones of brown with tan to white bands. Agate can be artificially dyed.

Sizes	Mint	Good
To ⅞"	15.00	6.00
1" to 1½"	50.00	15.00
1⅝" to 1⅞"	65.00	30.00

CLAMBROTH

Milk glass marbles in a solid color having many thin outer swirl lines of a different color running from pontil mark to pontil mark.

Sizes	Mint	Good
To ⅞"	125.00	45.00
1" to 1½"	400.00	100.00

CLAYS

Marbles made of clay which may or may not be colored or glazed.

Sizes	Mint	Good
To 7/8"	.10	.05
1" to 1½"	2.00	1.00
1⅝" to 1⅞"	5.00	1.00
2" and over	10.00	5.00

COMIC

Marbles manufactured by the Peltier Glass Co. 1927 to 1934 with one of twelve comic strip character faces stamped on the marble and fired so as to be permanent.

Sizes	Mint	Good
To 7/8"	50.00	20.00

END-OF-DAY

Usually composed of a solid multicolored inner surface coated with an outer covering of clear glass; also known as Cloud Marbles.

Sizes	Mint	Good
To 7/8"	30.00	15.00
1" to 1½"	200.00	60.00
1⅝" to 1⅞"	275.00	100.00
2" and over	450.00	150.00

INDIAN SWIRL

Handmade, opaque black glass marble with very colorful swirls applied next to or on top of surface.

Sizes	Mint	Good
To 7/8"	80.00	40.00
1" to 1½"	250.00	100.00

LATTICINIO CORE SWIRL

Inner part of the marble has a latticinio or lace center; usually with outer swirls of varying colors running from pontil mark to pontil mark.

Sizes	Mint	Good
To 7/8"	9.00	4.00
1" to 1½"	45.00	15.00
1⅝" to 1⅞"	90.00	35.00
2" and over	150.00	60.00

LUTZ (BANDED)

Handmade glass marbles usually with colored swirls, some of which contain copper flecks; also called Goldstone swirls. Other types of Lutz (end of day, ribbon, and opaque banded Lutz) are worth two to three times the values shown for banded Lutz.

Sizes	Mint	Good
To 7/8"	100.00	50.00
1" to 1½"	250.00	125.00
1⅝" to 1⅞"	400.00	150.00
2" & over	800.00	175.00

MACHINE-MADE GLASS

Glass marbles made by machines after World War I.

Sizes	Mint	Good
To 7/8"	.05	.02
1" to 1½"	.50	.10

MICAS

Mineral silicates occurring in thin sheet and usually reflective of silvery in appearance; handmade glass marbles of various types (usually clear colored glass) having silvery flakes inside.

Sizes	Mint	Good
To 7/8"	20.00	10.00
1" to 1½"	300.00	75.00
1⅝" to 1⅞"	400.00	250.00

OPEN CORE SWIRL

Handmade glass swirl marble with open colored bands in center of marble.

Sizes	Mint	Good
To 7/8"	9.00	4.00
1" to 1½"	45.00	15.00
1⅝" to 1⅞"	90.00	35.00
2" and over	150.00	60.00

PEPPERMINT SWIRL

Swirl glass marble resembling peppermint stick candy, usually incorporating red, white, and blue colors.

Sizes	Mint	Good
To 7/8"	80.00	40.00

POTTERY

Earthenware as distinguished on the one hand from porcelain and stoneware, and on the other hand from brick and tile.

Sizes	Mint	Good
To 7/8"	1.00	.50
1" to 1½"	10.00	4.00

SOLID CORE SWIRL

Glass marble having a solid one-color or varicolored center looking like a piece of candy with outer swirls running from pontil mark to pontil mark.

Sizes	Mint	Good
To 7/8"	15.00	6.00
1" to 1½"	50.00	25.00
1⅝" to 1⅞"	100.00	60.00
2" and over	225.00	75.00

SULPHIDES

Objects made of china clay and supersilicate of potash for inserting in marbles and a variety or other glass objects, usually three dimensional; marbles are of clear glass containing a sulphide object, usually an animal figure. Antique sulphides with numbers, human figures, or colors are worth three to five times the value shown.

Sizes	Mint	Good
1" to 1½"	100.00	60.00
1⅝" to 1⅞"	150.00	100.00
2" & over	200.00	100.00

MATCHCOVERS

Collecting Hints: Matchcovers generally had large production runs; very few are considered rare. Most collectors remove the matches, flatten the covers, and mount them in albums by category. They prefer the covers be unused.

Trading is the principal means of exchange among collectors, usually on a one for one basis. At flea markets and shows matchcovers frequently are seen marked for $1.00 to $5.00 for categories such as beer covers or pin-up art (girlies) covers. Actually these purchasers are best advised to join one of the collector clubs and get involved in swapping.

History: The book match was invented by Joshua Pusey, a Philadelphia lawyer, who also was a chemist in his spare time. In 1892 Pusey put 10 cardboard matches into a cover of plain white board. Two hundred were sold to the Mendelson Opera Company who, in turn, hand-printed messages on the front.

The first machine made matchbook was made by the Binghamton Match Company, Binghamton, New York, for the Piso Company of Warren, Pennsylvania. The only surviving cover is now owned by the Diamond Match Company.

Few covers survive from the late 1890s–1930s period. The modern craze for collecting matchcovers was started by a set of ten covers issued for the Century of Progress exhibit at the 1933 Chicago World's Fair.

The Golden Age of matchcovers was the mid-1940s through the early 1960s when the covers were a popular advertising medium. Principal manufacturers included Atlas Match, Brown and Bigelow, Crown Match, Diamond Match, Lion Match, Ohio Match and Universal Match.

The arrival of throw-away lighters, such as BIC, brought an end to the matchcover era. Manufacturing costs for a matchbook today can range from below a cent to seven or eight cents for a special die-cut cover. As a result, matchcovers no longer are an attractive "free" give-away item.

Because of this, many of the older, more desirable covers are seeing a marked increase in value. Collectors have also turned to the small pocket type boxes as a way of enhancing and building their collections.

References: Bill Retskin, *The Matchcover Collectors Resource Book and Price Guide,* published by author, 1988; H. Thomas Steele, Jim Heimann, Rod Dyer, *Close Cover Before Striking, The Golden Age of Matchbook Art,* Abbeville Press, 1987.

Periodical: *The Front Striker Bulletin,* 3417 Clayborne Avenue, Alexandria, VA 22306-1410.

Collectors' Clubs: Rathkamp Matchcover Society, 1359 Surrey Road, Vandalia, OH 43577; Trans-Canada Matchcover Club, Box 219, Caledonia, Ontario, Canada NOA-1A0. There are 33 regional clubs throughout the United States and Canada.

Advisor: Wray Martin.

Left: Foreign, London Tower, tan ground, red guards, purple borders, black and white letters, $.05; right: Restaurant, Hollywood Canteen, gray ground, red and white letters, stamped "Bestest, Joe E. Brown," on back, $.05.

SPECIAL COVERS

Apollo Flights 8-17, Cameo's, each ...	**5.00**
Dwight D. Eisenhower, 5 Star General	**15.00**

Economy Blue Print, girlies, set of 6,
1950s **45.00**
Joe Louis & Max Schmeling Champion-
ship Fight, (Giant) **18.00**
Presidential Yacht, "Patricia" **10.00**
Presidential Helicopter, "Marine One" **10.00**
Pull for Wilkie, Pullquick Match **28.00**
Racquel Welch, color photo, made in
South Africa **15.00**
Stoeckle Select Beer, Giant, Stoeckle
Brewery **6.00**
Washington Redskins, set of 20 ...... **40.00**

TOPICS

Airlines .... .25
Americana .... .05
Atlas, four color .... .05
Banks .... .02
Beer and Brewery .... .75
Best Western (Stock Design) .... .10
Best Western (Non Stock) .... .15
Bowling Alleys .... .02
Cameo's, Universal trademark .... .05
Canadian, four color .... .05
Casino's .... .05
Chinese Restaurants .... .04
Christmas .... .04
Classiques .... .40
Colleges .... .05
Contours, diecut .... .10
Conventions .... .03
Country Clubs .... .07
County Seats .... .05
Dated .... .10
Diamond Quality .... .50
Elks .... .10
Fairs .... .10
Features .... .15
Foilites, Universal trademark .... .05
Foreign .... .05
Fraternal .... .05
Full Length .... .08
Giants .... .50
Girlies, stock design .... .15
Girlies, non stock .... .40
Group One, non-advertising, old ..... .40
Group One, non-advertising, new .... .03

Note: Group One items consist of matches with no advertising. The older matchcovers were sold in tobacco stores during the 1930s and contained personalities, football, baseball and other sport figures, city scenes, and state scenes. The usual buyer bought 16 matchbooks for a dime. The new items represent matchcovers purchased from a local supermarket. These are sets (clocks, railroads, etc.) and are found in packages of fifty matchbooks for sixty cents to over a dollar.

Hillbillies .... .05
Holiday Inns, stock design .... .10
Holiday Inns, non-stock .... .15

Jewelites .... .05
Jewels .... .05
Knot Holes .... .20
Matchorama's, Universal trademark ... .08
Matchtones, Universal trademark ..... .10
Midgets .... .15
Navy Ships .... .30
Odd Strikers .... .20
Patriotic .... .05
Pearltone .... .05
Personalities 1.00
Political 1.00
Pull Quick 1.00
Radio & TV .... .05
Railroads .... .25
Rainbows, Universal trademark ...... .10
Restaurants .... .02
Savings & Loan .... .02
Service, old .... .15
Service, new .... .05
Ship Lines .... .10
Signets, Universal trademark .... .05
Small Towns .... .05
Soft Drinks .... .75
Souvenir .... .20
Sports, old 1.00
Sports, new .... .15
Ten Strikes .... .05
Transportation .... .15
Travelodges .... .05
Truck Lines .... .10
Trust Companies .... .02
VA Hospitals .... .15
Whiskey .... .30

McCOY POTTERY

Collecting Hint: Several marks were used by the McCoy Pottery Co. Take time to learn the marks and the variations. Pieces can often be dated by the mark used.

History: The J. W. McCoy Pottery Co. was established in Roseville, Ohio, in September, 1899. The early McCoy Company produced both stoneware and some art lines, including Rosewood. In October, 1911, three potteries in the Roseville area merged, creating the Brush-McCoy Pottery Co. This company continued to produce the original McCoy lines and added several new art lines. Much of the early pottery is not marked.

In 1910, Nelson McCoy and his father, J. W. McCoy, founded the Nelson McCoy Sanitary Stoneware Co. In 1925, the McCoy family sold their interest in the Brush-McCoy Pottery Co. and started to expand and improve the Nelson McCoy Company. The new company produced stoneware, earthenware specialities and artware. Most of the pottery marked McCoy was made by the Nelson McCoy Co.

Reference: Sharon and Bob Huxford, *The Collectors Encyclopedia of McCoy Pottery,* Collector Books, 1980.

REPRODUCTION ALERT: The Nelson McCoy Pottery Co. is currently producing reproductions of their original work. This may add to the confusion about this company's products and will probably affect prices.

Watering Pitcher, turtle, green, yellow eyes, mouth, and floral buds, 9½", $20.00.

Ashtray, Seagram's VO Imported Canadian Whiskey, black, gold letters ...	12.00
Bank	
Eagle, three raised stars on base, white, yellow, tan, and brown ...	15.00
Sailor, large duffle bag over shoulder	18.00
Basket, black and white, emb weave ext., double handle	18.50
Bean Pot, cov, brown glaze, emb beans and foliage	24.00
Bookends, pr, jumping horse, marked "Nu-Art"	15.00
Cache Pot, double	8.00
Candlesticks, pr, emb water lily design, blue	15.00
Centerpiece Bowl	
8¾", blue, tulips dec	6.00
10", shaped rim, finch perched in center, brown and light green glaze	50.00
Coffee Service, electric coffeepot, creamer and sugar, Porcelier Floral pattern	55.00
Cookie Jar	
Basket of Eggs	20.00
Black Stove	20.00
Bobby Baker	20.00
Cookie Bank	60.00
Frontier Family	45.00
Mammy	45.00
Monk	22.50
Oaken Bucket	15.00
Picnic Basket, 1962	35.00
Raggedy Ann	40.00
Red Apple	18.00
Sack of Cookies	25.00
Snow Bear	35.00
Spaceship	45.00

Thinking Puppy	20.00
Yosemite Sam, 1971	40.00
Creamer, Elsie the Cow	12.00
Custard Cup, vertical ridges, green ...	4.00
Decanter, Apollo Mission	25.00
Dog Food Dish, emb Scottie	12.00
Hanging Basket, stoneware, marked "Nelson McCoy," 1926	15.00
Jardiniere, raised holly dec, c1935 ...	20.00
Jug, brown, glazed top, marked "3" in blue	30.00
Mug	
Corn	35.00
Surburbia, yellow	6.50
Willow Ware, brown, c1926	10.00
Pitcher	
Chicken, c1960	9.00
Elephant, tan glaze, c1940	28.00
Water Lily, 1935	7.50
Planter	
Cat, coral glaze, green bow, c1950 .	8.75
Cradle, pink	6.50
Dog, light green, white accents	12.00
Goat, gray, red harness	7.50
Gondola, yellow	8.00
Lamb, white, blue bow	8.00
Lion, white, c1940	12.00
Rabbit, ivory	7.00
Shoe, bronzed	6.00
Sprinkling Can, white, rose decal ...	6.50
Stork, green	7.00
Swan, white, c1943	7.50
Reamer, green glaze, 8", 1948	18.00
Salt and Pepper Shakers, pr, figural, cucumber and mango, 1954	12.00
Spoon Rest	
Butterfly, dark green, 1953	12.00
Penguin, 1953	15.00
Sprinkler, turtle	15.00
Sugar Bowl, cov, emb face and scrolls, red glazed cov	5.00
Teapot	
Grecian, 1958	25.00
Sunburst Gold, 1957	20.00
Tumble Up, blue sponged dec	5.00
Vase	
6", butterfly, blue, 1940	18.00
8", bud, matte green	4.00
10", wheat, green, 1953	750

McKEE GLASS

Collecting Hint: McKee Glass was mass produced in most colors. Therefore, a collector should avoid chipped or damaged pieces.

History: The McKee Glass Company was established in 1843 in Pittsburgh, Pennsylvania. In 1852 they opened a factory to produce pressed glass. In 1888, the factory relocated in Jeannette, Pennsylvania, and began to produce many types of kitchenwares. The factory was among several located there to make Depression era wares. The factory continued until 1951 when it was sold to the Thatcher Manufacturing Co.

The McKee Glass Company produced many types of glass including glass window panes, tumblers, tablewares, Depression glass, milk glass, and bar and utility objects.

McKee named its colors Chalaine Blue, Custard, Seville Yellow, and Skokie Green. They preferred Skokie Green to jadite which was popular with other manufacturers at the time. McKee also made several patterns on these opaque colors, including dots of red, green, and black and red ships. A few items were decaled. Most of the canisters and shakers were lettered in black for the purpose they were made for.

References: Gene Florence, *Kitchen Glassware of the Depression Years, Third Edition,* , Collector Books, 1987; Lowell Innes and Jane Shadel Spillman, *M'Kee Victorian Glass*, Dover Publications, 1981.

Children's dishes, opaque white, red trim, ten pcs, $65.00.

Apple Bowl, crystal	60.00
Batter Bowl, 7½", custard	15.00
Batter Pitcher, red, metal cov, handle .	75.00
Beater Bowl, 6½", Ships, black dec . . .	7.00
Birdhouse	75.00
Bowl	
4½", Ships, spout	11.00
5", Rock Crystal, ruby	20.00
Butter Dish, cov	
Red dots, custard	40.00
Seville Yellow	65.00
Skokie Green	35.00
Butter Lid, jadite, ribbed, 1 lb	15.00
Cake Plate, 11", Rock Crystal	
Amber	30.00
Crystal	25.00
Red	50.00
Candlestick	
8½" h, Rock Crystal, ruby	65.00
10", crucifix, hexagonal base, clear .	110.00
Candy Dish, cov, Rock Crystal, crystal	40.00

Canister, cov	
Cereal, custard, 48 oz	18.00
Coffee, Skokie green	25.00
Sugar, French Ivory	18.00
Cheese Plate, 11", Rock Crystal, amber	45.00
Clock, Tambour mantel, dark amethyst	375.00
Egg Cup	
Custard, ftd	12.00
Skokie Green	8.50
Flour Shaker, Skokie Green	12.00
Jug, 8½", Rock Crystal, crystal	60.00
Measuring Cup	
Glasbake, clear, two spouts, 1 cup .	32.00
Green, three lips	15.00
Seville Yellow, two spouts	85.00
Ships	15.00
Mug, Tom & Jerry, custard, black letters	5.00
Nappy, 4½", Skokie Green	6.50
Percolator, 7½", transparent white, red	
handle	60.00
Reamer, ice blue	15.00
Refrigerator Box, ivory, blue dots	25.00
Refrigerator Dish, cov	
Red Dot, 4 x 5"	5.00
Ships	18.00
Skokie Green, 8 x 5"	14.00
Salt and Pepper Shakers, pr	
Black, arch dec	30.00
Ships	15.00
Skillet, Range-tec	8.50
Spice Jar, Roman Arch side panels, Skokie Green, black letters	15.00
Spooner, Vulcan, pink	50.00
Sugar Shaker, Seville Yellow	12.00
Teapot, Range-tec, crystal, black handle	15.00
Tray, 11", round, custard	13.00
Vase, 8¼", triangular, nude, Skokie Green	50.00
Water Bottle, Skokie Green	75.00
Whipping Machine, marked "Handyhat Whipper," Glasbake bowl, electric top	25.00

MILITARIA

Collecting Hints: Saving militaria may be one of the oldest collecting traditions. Militaria collectors tend to have their own special shows and view themselves outside the normal antiques channels. However, they haunt small indoor shows and flea markets in hopes of finding additional materials.

History: Wars always have been part of history. Until the mid-19th century, soldiers often had to fill their own needs, including weapons. Even in the 20th century a soldier's uniform and some of his gear is viewed as his personal property, even though issued by a military agency.

Conquering armed forces made a habit of acquiring souvenirs from their vanquished foes.

They brought home their own uniforms and accessories as badges of triumph and service.

References: Ray A. Bows, *Vietnam Military Lore 1959–1973,* Bows & Sons, 1988; *North South Trader's Civil War Price Guide, 4th Edition,* North South Trader, 1988; *Official Price Guide To Military Collectibles,* House of Collectibles, 1985.

Periodicals: *Military Collectors' News,* P. O. Box 702073, Tulsa, OK 74170; *North South Trader,* 724 Caroline Street, Fredericksburg, VA 22401.

Collectors' Clubs: American Society of Military Insignia Collectors, 1331 Bradley Avenue, Hummelstown, PA 17036; Association of American Uniform Collectors, 446 Berkshire Road, Elyria, OH 44035; Company of Military Historians, North Main Street, Westbrook, CT 06498; Imperial German Military Collectors Association, Box 38, Keyport, NJ 07735.

Additional Listings: See *Warman's Antiques And Their Prices* for information about firearms and swords. See also World War I and World War II, this book.

REVOLUTIONARY WAR

Document
  Bill for Common Pleas Court, partially
    printed, 4 x 6", sgd "Robert T.
    Paine," 1768 .... **275.00**
  Legal, handwritten, money being paid
    for costs of duties performed by selectmen from the estate of Joseph
    Tuttle, 7 x 5", sgd by various court
    officials, 1779 .... **75.00**
  Pay Voucher, CT, 6 x 7", Jan 17, 1783 **50.00**
Newspaper, *The Providence Gazette
  And Country Journal,* April 4, 1778 . **75.00**
Sword
  27½" single edged blade, iron semibasket hilt, double side bar, kidney
    shape guard, hand engraved
    crowned "RA" motif, British Royal
    Artillery **300.00**
  30" broad fullered single edge blade,
    Town type, brass hilt, fluted shell
    guard with hunting motif, American **150.00**

WAR OF 1812

Hat, leather, attached brass eagle, metallic rope twists, orig label **610.00**
Newspaper, *Columbian Centinel,* June
  27, 1812, proclamation of war **25.00**
Sword, 28½" sharply curved single edge
  blade, straight cross guard hilt, silver
  wire wrapped sharkskin cover back
  swept grip, light cavalry officer's saber **170.00**
Sword Belt, Civil War type dirk **140.00**

CIVIL WAR

Bayonet, rifled musket type, orig black
  leather scabbard with brass tip, brown
  leather frog stamped "Army/US/Ord.
  Dept/Sub Inspector," and "R. Nece/
  Philad," blade stamped "US" **180.00**
Blood Letter, iron blade, brass handle . **25.00**
Bowie Knife, curved blade, attached to
  hilt of artillery sword **320.00**
Bullet Mold, picket pattern bullet **40.00**
Canteen
  Leather, cantel pattern, sling **275.00**
  Tin, US model 1857, rubber coated
    sling **300.00**
Cartridge Box
  Mann's patent, straps **175.00**
  Standard .58 caliber, shoulder strap,
    tins, eagle plate and box plate ... **250.00**
  Weston **275.00**
Daguerreotype, Union, 2¾ x 3¼" **90.00**
Document
  Discharge Papers, 1st Ohio, dated
    "1863" **90.00**
  Enlistment Papers, Union, sgd **90.00**
Field Glasses, 7½", brass, made by Lemaire Fabt, Paris **100.00**
Flag, 30 x 60", 1st National pattern,
  homemade **2,500.00**
Insignia, brass
  Captain **75.00**
  General **200.00**
  Lieutenant **30.00**
Knife and Spoon, combination **25.00**
Mess Kit, bone handles, orig leather
  case **175.00**
Pike, 72" l, Confederate cavalry, iron
  blade, orig wood staff **450.00**
Revolver
  Colt Army, model 1860, plain round
    cylinder **725.00**
  Leech and Ridgon, 36 caliber, Navy
    model 1851 ....**2,000.00**
Ribbon, blue gray, Lincoln's head surrounded by "With Malice Toward
  None, With Charity For All," 1861–
  65 .... **100.00**
Saddle, Federal, officer's, brass bound
  gilded seat **750.00**
Shell Jacket, Union cavalry, buttons, lining, and inspector's marks **375.00**
Spy Glass, 16", leather wrapped, four
  sections **250.00**
Sword Belt Plate, Union, non-commissioned officer **75.00**

INDIAN WAR

Buckle, Naval officer, brass, stamped
  "Horstman, Phila" **120.00**
Insignia, hat, 3" w, cavalry, brass,
  crossed sabers **70.00**

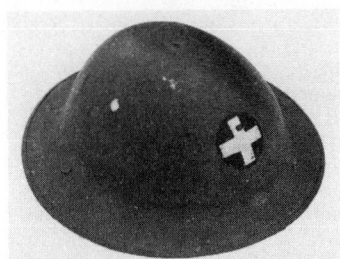

World War I, divisional helmet, American, orig liner, $48.00.

Patch, sleeve, US Military, wool, green
maltese cross, dark blue ground **25.00**
Uniform, officer **275.00**

SPANISH AMERICAN WAR

Badge, 1¾", sepia photo, yellow and
red ribbon with silver inscription "8th
Annual Department Encampment/
USWB/Reading/June 17–18, 1912,
suspended white metal cross medal . **12.00**
Buckle, marked "Anson Mills, Patent
Feb 1, 1881" **25.00**
Clothing
  Coat, enlisted man's, 1st sergeant
  stripes **150.00**
  Tunic, officer's **60.00**
  Uniform, tunic and pants, khaki **45.00**
Helmet, summer type, white, infantry
helmet plate **100.00**
Mug, 4¾" h, tankard, full color portrait
of Winfield Schley, Naval Com-
mander and hero of Santiago battle,
Columbian Art Pottery, Trenton, NJ,
1898–1900 .... **75.00**
Pinback Button, "Remember The
Maine," and battleship scene, patent
1896 .... **25.00**
Pipe, 5" l, battleship shape, "Maine"
inscription on sides, briar bowl unscrews for cleaning, June 7, 1898 patent date **125.00**
Plate, 7½" d, white metal, dark finish,
raised relief battleship, floral design
and "Maine" on edge **50.00**
Scrapbook, 12 x 15", illus of battleship
Maine, gold raised brocade border,
and title in gold with raised relief floral pattern cover, news, illus, and portrait photo clippings, 36 pgs, 1876
patent date **75.00**
Spy Glass, 16", pocket type, Naval,
brass, brown leather grip, round
holder **110.00**

VIETNAM WAR

Helmet, US tanker, fiber–glass, dark
green, intercom system on side **30.00**

Leaflet, 5 x 7", South Vietnamese Prop-
aganda, dated April, 1969 .... **5.00**
Medal
  Air Force Commendation, lapel bar
  and parade ribbon, case **25.00**
  Vietnam Service **15.00**
Trench Art, candelabra, artillery shells **40.00**
Tunic, US Army, sergeant, 5th Division
red diamonds insignia, green, gold
stripes **30.00**

MILK BOTTLES

Collecting Hints: Many factors influence the price—condition of the bottle, who is selling, the part of the country in which the sale is transacted, and the amount of desire a buyer has for the bottle. Every bottle does not have universal ap-peal. A sale of a bottle in one area does not mean that it would bring the same amount in another locale. For example, a rare Vermont pyro pint would be looked upon as only another "pint" in Texas.

A general trend indicates the growing popu-larity for pyroglaze (painted bottles) over em-bossed bottles. Pyro bottles display better at home or at shows.

History: Hervey Thatcher is recognized as the father of the glass milk bottle. By the early 1880s glass milk bottles appeared in New York and New Jersey. A. V. Whiteman had a milk bottle patent as early as 1880. Patents reveal much about early milk bottle shape and manufacture. Not all patentees were manufacturers. Many in-dividuals engaged others to produce bottles un-der their patents.

The Golden Age of the glass milk bottle is 1910 to 1950. Leading manufacturers include Lamb Glass Co. (Mt. Vernon, Ohio), Liberty Glass Co. (Sapulpa, Oklahoma), Owens-Illinois Glass Co. (Toledo, Ohio), and Thatcher Glass Co. (New York).

Milk bottles can be found in the following sizes: gill (quarter pint), half pint, 10 ounces (third quart), pint, quart, half gallon (two quart), and gallon.

Paper cartons first appeared in the early 1920s and 30s and achieved popularity after 1950. The late 1950s witnessed the arrival of the plastic bottle. A few dairies still use glass bottles today, but the era has essentially ended.

References: Don Lord, *California Milks*, pub-lished by author; John Tutton, *Udder Delight*, published by author.

Periodical: The Milk Route, 4 Ox Bow Road, Westport, CT 06880.

Museums: The Farmers Museum, Cooperstown, NY; Southwest Dairy Museum, Arlington, TX; Billings Farm Museum, Woodstock, VT.

R. M. Deger, Phoenixville, PA, emb "Pure Milk," clear, 9½", $5.00.

Alberts Dairy Inc., quart, orange, slogan "Milk for Health" **8.00**

Alta Crest Farm, Spencer, MA, quart, round, green glass, emb, cow's head on front **550.00**

Ayrhill Farms, Adams, MA, quart **7.00**

Baily and Doctor, Wilmington, DE, one half pint, emb, ... **15.00**

Ball Dairy, quart, round, clear, emb, baseball emb in slug plate **25.00**

Benewah Creamery, Spokane, WA, quart, round, clear, green pyro, Indian chief in full headdress on back **18.00**

Borden
  Experimental, never used, quart, squatty round, ruby red **1,400.00**
  Signature, quart, square, amber, white pyro, signature and picture of Gail Borden **7.50**

Bucknell University, quart, round, clear, emb **10.00**

Butler Dairy, Willimantic, CT, quart ... **12.00**

Capital Dairy, North Dartmouth, MA, quart, round, clear, emb, capital dome emb on front slug plate **12.00**

Civic Club Milk Station, Washington, Maine Seal, pint, return, crown top . **25.00**

Clover Brand Dairy Products, one half pint, round, clear, green pyro, picture of family, large milk bottle, and slogan "Follow Road to Health, Drink More Milk" **7.50**

Cream and Sweet Shop, quart, round, clear, emb **25.00**

Devine's Dairy, Norwalk, CT, quart, square, amber, white pyro **7.50**

Firestone Farms, Columbiana, OH, one half pint, round, clear, emb, Firestone emblem emb in slug plate **25.00**

Gettysburg Ice and Storage Co, Gettysburg, PA, quart, round, clear, emb . **8.00**

Hendricks, quart, square, clear, white pyro **7.50**

Honey Garden Dairy, Lebanon, NH, quart, round, clear, emb picture of beehive **20.00**

Maplewood Dairy, Fairhaven, VT & Hudson Falls, NY, quart, amber **10.00**

Noble Dairy, Baseball Milk Drink for Muscle and Strength **15.00**

Orchard Farms Dairy, Dallas, PA, quart, square, clear, red pyro, "Cop the Cream" **20.00**

Pennsylvania State University, quart, round, red pyro, tower on back **10.00**

Peoples Milk Company, Buffalo, NY, quart, round, amber, emb **50.00**

Pet Milk Company, gallon **15.00**

Rider Dairy, Danbury, CT, quart, square, clear, red pyro, cream top **8.00**

Round Hill Farms Dairy, Greenwich, CT, quart, round, clear, tin top, emb on bottom "A. V. Whitman" **40.00**

Saint Joseph's Hospital, Buckhannon, WV, one half pint, round, clear, black pyro **10.00**

Springdale Farms, Millington, NJ, quart, cream top **18.00**

Sunrise Dairy, one half pint, round, clear, red pyro, war slogan **15.00**

Taylor's Dairy, one half pint, square, amber, yellow pyro **35.00**

Thompson's Dairy, Washington, DC, quart, squatty round, clear, emb, modern top **7.50**

Universal Store Bottle, quart, round, clear, emb **3.00**

University of Connecticut, Storrs, CT, one half pint, round, clear, emb **5.00**

Weckerle Dairy, Buffalo, NY, quart, round, green, emb **300.00**

White Springs Farm Dairy, Geneva, quart, orange pyro **10.00**

MORTON POTTERIES

Collecting Hints: The potteries of Morton, Illinois, used local clay until 1940. The clay fired out to a golden ecru color which is quite easy to recognize. After 1940 southern and eastern clays were shipped to Morton. These clays fired out white. Thus, later period wares are sharply distinguished from the earlier wares.

Few pieces were marked by the potteries. Incised and raised marks for the Morton Pottery Works, the Cliftwood Art Potteries, Inc., and the Morton Pottery Company do surface at times. The Cliftwood, Midwest, Morton Pottery Company, and American Art Pottery all used paper labels in limited amounts. Some of these have survived, and collectors do find them.

Glazes from the early period, 1877–1920, usually were Rockingham types, both mottled and solid. Yellow ware also was standard during the early period. Occasionally a dark cobalt blue was produced, but this color is rare. Colorful drip glazes and solid colors came into use after 1920.

History: Pottery was produced in Morton, Illinois, for 99 years. In 1877 six Rapp brothers, who emigrated from Germany, began the first pottery, Morton Pottery Works. Over the years sons, cousins, and nephews became involved in the production of pottery. The other Morton pottery operations were spin-offs from the original pottery and brothers. When it was taken over in 1915 by second generation Rapps, Morton Pottery Works became the Morton Earthenware Company. Work at that pottery was terminated by World War I.

The Cliftwood Art Potteries, Inc., operated from 1920 to 1940. One of the original founders of the Morton Pottery Works and his four sons organized it. They sold out in 1940, and the operation continued for four more years as the Midwest Potteries, Inc. A disastrous fire brought an end to that operation in March 1944. These two potteries produced figurines, lamps, novelties and vases.

In 1922 the Morton Pottery Company, which had the longest existence of all of the Morton's potteries, was organized by the same brothers who had operated the Morton Earthenware Company. The Morton Pottery Company specialized in beer steins, kitchenwares, and novelty items for chain stores and gift shops. They also produced some of the Vincent Price National Treasures reproductions for Sears Roebuck and Company in the mid-1960s. The Morton Pottery closed in 1976, thus ending the 99 years of pottery production in Morton.

By 1947 the brothers who had operated the Cliftwood Art Potteries, Inc., came back into the pottery business. They established the short-lived American Art Potteries. The American Art Potteries made flower bowls, lamps, planters, some unusual flower frogs, and vases. Their wares were marketed by florists and gift shops. Production at American Art Potteries was halted in 1961. Of all the wares of the Morton potteries, the products of the American Art Potteries are the most elusive.

Reference: Doris and Burdell Hall, *Morton's Potteries: 99 Years,* published by author, 1982. Doris and Burdell Hall also have written a number of articles on the Morton Potteries that have appeared in the *American Clay Exchange,* (800 Murray Drive, El Cajon, CA 92020), the most recent of which is "Morton Pottery Company Wallpockets" in the January 1988 issue.

Museum: Illinois State Museum, Springfield, IL; Morton Public Library (permanent exhibit), Morton, IL.

Advisor: Doris and Burdell Hall.

MORTON POTTERY WORKS AND MORTON EARTHENWARE COMPANY, 1877–1917

Bank, 3" h, acorn shape	
Brown Rockingham glaze	20.00
Green, Acorn Stoves adv	50.00
Chamber Pot, 9' d, yellow ware, handled	50.00
Creamer, 1¾" h, miniature, brown Rockingham glaze	20.00
Dutch Jug, 6¼" h, cobalt blue, 3 pt ..	75.00
Milk Boiler, 4½" h, qt, brown Rockingham glaze	55.00
Mixing Bowl, yellow ware, waffle design base, three white slip lines, set of 3	90.00
Mug, 3¼" h, 1 pt, brown Rockingham glaze	50.00
Teapot	
American Globe, 5¼ pt, #18s, brown Rockingham glaze	50.00
Rebecca at the Well, 8½ pt, #9s, brown Rockingham glaze	65.00

Cliftwood Art Potteries, Inc., beer stein, tankard type, $30.00.

CLIFTWOOD ART POTTERIES, INC., 1920–1940

Compote	
3" h, 11" d, #228, cobalt	30.00
5" h, 8½" d, #227, chocolate drip glaze	35.00
6" h, 8" d, #229, matte white, molded candle holders on sides ..	45.00
6" h, 9" d, #226, old rose glaze ...	15.00
Figurine	
Elephant, 6 x 5", blue-gray glaze, carry boxes on sides	60.00
Lion, 6" x 3½", natural colors	35.00
Lioness, 12 x 7", green glaze	25.00
Police Dog, 8½ x 6", white	38.00
Flower Bowl, 3¾ x 7½ x 6½", tree	

trunk, chocolate drip glaze, includes
insert **40.00**
Grease Jar, cov, white, pink and green
drip glaze, matching salt and pepper,
3 pcs **35.00**
Vase
7¾", #122, bud, blue-gray drip glaze **20.00**
10", #109, six side panels, arched
top, cobalt **22.00**
13½", #111, cylinder shape, blue-
mulberry drip glaze **30.00**
Water Pitcher, 9", cov, sq top, yellow
and green drip over white glaze **50.00**

**Morton Pottery Co., cookie jar, poodle,
white ground, red dec, $25.00.**

MORTON POTTERY COMPANY,
1922–1976

Ashtray
Ovoid
Brown and green, boxer dog on
edge **20.00**
White, gold dec, horse on edge .. **18.00**
Round, hand in center, white **15.00**
Square
Dark brown, 12", cigarette snuffer
in center **16.00**
Forest green, 10", tumbler recepta-
cle in two corners **14.00**
Baking Set, five nested bowls, pastel
colors, 4 to 8" d, set **35.00**

**Midwest, Race Horse, black, raised ma-
hogany base, 7¼", $50.00**

MIDWEST POTTERIES, INC.,
1940–1944

Creamer, 5" h, cow, white, brown drip
glaze, yellow handle **18.00**
Figurine
Bluebird, 4½" h, on stump, yellow
breast **12.00**
Bluejay, 6½", on stump, natural col-
ors **15.00**
Blue Heron, 11", blue and yellow,
gold dec **35.00**
Duck, mother and three babies,
white, yellow dec, 1 pc **15.00**
Tiger, 7 x 12", natural colors **40.00**
Honey Jug, 5", gold, platinum int. **20.00**
Miniature
Figure
Hen, 2¼", white, brown dec **5.00**
Polar Bear, 1¾", white **7.00**
Rabbit, 2½", white, pink ears **6.00**
Rooster, 2¼", white, brown dec .. **5.00**
Squirrel, 2", brown **6.00**
Vase, 3¾", green-brown spray glaze,
handled **8.00**
Pitcher, 9½", duck, brown and gray
spray glaze, cattail handle **22.00**
Salt and Pepper Shaker, Scottie dog,
matte white, pr **10.00**

**Morton Pottery Co., planter, rabbit with
basket, white, pink ears, gold dec,
$18.00.**

Bank
Church, brown **22.00**
Elephant, pink **15.00**
Hen, white, red comb **20.00**
Kitten, yellow and white **18.00**
Beater Jar, 5", #143, brown Rock-
ingham, rotary beater **30.00**
Beater Pitcher, 6½", #66, yellow ware,
rotary beater **80.00**
Cookie Jar
Hen, chick finial on lid **50.00**

Poodle, white, red dec 25.00
Turkey, chick finial on lid 65.00
Figurine
John Kennedy Jr, age three, saluting,
buff and gray 25.00
Hound Dog
Paw over eye, #576 . . . .   10.00
Scratching, #583 . . . .   10.00
Sitting, #506 . . . .   10.00
Planter
Cat, cactus tail, yellow 4.00
Mother Earth Line, natural colors
Cucumber, #395 . . . .   3.00
Egg Plant, #391 . . . .   3.00
Green Pepper, #394 . . . .   3.00
Sweet Potato, #390 . . . .   3.00
Tomato, #437 . . . .   3.00
Mrs. Santa Claus, natural colors 20.00
Rabbit with basket, white, pink ears,
gold dec 18.00
Santa Claus, natural colors 25.00
Turkey, brown, red wattle 10.00
Wall Hanger
Bank, pig, pink, hanging, #671 . . . .   15.00
Planter, hanging
Owl, sitting on moon, yellow,
multicolor spray glaze 12.00
Love Birds on nest, multicolored . . .   10.00
Wishing Well, brown, #685 . . . .   12.00
Plaque, bunch-of-fruit, natural colors   20.00
String Holder, love birds on nest,
multicolored 35.00
Jewelry Holder, flower, rose and
green, blossom holds rings, leaf tip
holds watch 12.00

**American Art Pottery, planter, pheasant,
open back, natural colors, 18″ l, $25.00.**

AMERICAN ART POTTERIES,
1947–1961

Doll parts, 3″ d head, arms and legs, set   50.00
Flower Bowl
2 x 10 x 6″, six sided, rect, green,
yellow int. 6.00
3¼″, water lily shape, pink and blue
spray glaze 5.00
10″ l, S shape, yellow 8.00

Flower Frog
Frog, white, green and yellow spray
glaze 12.00
Turtle, white, green and yellow spray
glaze 12.00
Planter
Baby Shoes, pink, heart base 20.00
Hampshire Hog, black, white ribbon,
5½″ h 15.00
Pheasant, 18″ l, natural colors, open
back 25.00
Rabbit at tree base, peeking through
grass 12.00
Vase
7½″ h, shamrock shape, peach, orchid spray glaze, stemmed base . .   10.00
9½″, slender, six foil top, white, pink
int. 14.00
14″ h, ewer, lime, dark green flecks,
applied handle 16.00
Wall Pocket, 5½″, egg plant shape, pur-
ple, pale blue int. 10.00

MOVIE MEMORABILIA

Collecting Hints: Collectors tend to focus on the blockbuster hits with "Gone With The Wind" and "Casablanca" among the market leaders. The cartoon image, especially Disney material, also is very popular.

Much of the material is two dimensional. Collectors have just begun to look for three dimensional objects, although the majority of these are star and personality, rather than movie related.

The market went crazy in the mid–1970s when people sought to speculate in movie memorabilia. A self disciplining has taken place with prices falling in the 1980s. The area was compounded further by the large number of reproductions, many made in Europe, which flooded the market.

History: The golden age of movie memorabilia was the 1930s and 1940s. The star system had reached its zenith and studios spent elaborate sums promoting their major stars. Initially, movie studios and their public relation firms tightly controlled the distribution of material such as press books, scripts, preview flyers, costumes, props, etc. Copyright has expired on many of these items, and reproductions abound.

The current interest in Hollywood memorabilia can be traced to the pop art craze of the 1960s. Film festivals increased the desire for decorative film-related materials. Collecting movie posters was "hot."

Piracy always has plagued Hollywood and is responsible for the release of many items into the market. Today the home video presents new challenges to the industry.

References: Leslie Halliwell, *The Filmgoers's*

Companion, Avon, 1978; Ephraim Katz, *The Film Encyclopedia*, Perigee Books, 1979; Leonard Maltin (ed.), *TV Movies and Videos Guide*, New American Library, 1987; Anthony Slide, *A Collector's Guide To Movie Memorabilia With Prices*, Wallace-Homestead, 1983; John R. Warren, *Warren's Movie Poster Price Guide*, Overstreet Publications, 1986.

Periodicals: *Big Reel*, Route 3, P. O. Box 83, Madison, NC 27025; *Classic Images*, P. O. Box 4079, Davenport, IA 52808; *Movie Collectors' World*, P. O. Box 309, Fraser, MI 48026; *Nostalgia World*, P. O. Box 231, New Haven, CT 06473.

Collectors' Club: Studio Collectors Club, P. O. Box 1566, Apple Valley, CA 92307.

See: Cartoon Characters, Disneyana and Posters.

Mirror, advertising "Graft," Universal Pictures serial, celluloid, marked "Whitehead & Hoag, Co, Newark, NJ," $35.00.

Big Little Book, *Our Gang Adventures*, Whitman Better Little Book, 1948 .. **18.00**
Book
　Gone With The Wind
　　1936, before movie **25.00**
　　1940, movie edition, Macmillan, soft cov, color illus **35.00**
　Wings, 1924, illus, Buddy Rogers inscription **125.00**
Cookbook, *Gone With The Wind*, 5½ x 7¼", soft cover, 48 pgs, Pebeco Toothpaste premium, c1939 .... **40.00**
Cup and Saucer, 20th Century Fox Film Corp, brown and white company logo **20.00**
Film, *The King and I*, 16 mm, cinemascope, two tins with show's logo ... **450.00**
Handbill
　Men Are Not Gods, Miriam Hopkins, 6 x 9", 1930s **15.00**
　Spellbound, Gregory Peck and Ingrid Bergman, 8 x 11", 4 pgs **20.00**
Handkerchief, *Gone With The Wind*, 13" sq, Scarlet O'Hara, floral design, yellow, rose, green, black, white, and gold, black diecut foil sticker **55.00**
Ink Blotter, Our Gang, 3 x 6", brown

and white, Majestic Electric Radio adv **20.00**
Lobby Card
　Arch of Triumph, Ingrid Bergman, 11 x 14", 1947 .... **20.00**
　Billy The Kid, Buster Crabbe, 11 x 14", 1940s **10.00**
　M*A*S*H, Donald Sutherland **5.00**
　Princess and the Pirate, Bob Hope, 11 x 14", 1944 .... **15.00**
　The Burning Hills, Natalie Wood and Tab Hunter, 1956 .... **10.00**
　True Confessions, Carol Lombard, 11 x 14", 1937 .... **85.00**
Magazine
　Everyday Science and Mechanics, Feb, 1934, full color cov art and article, *The Invisible Man*, 8½ x 11½", 64 pgs **25.00**
　Private Lives of Movie Stars, 8½ x 11", Arco Publishing Co, 50 pgs, 1945 .... **20.00**
　Science and Invention Magazine, May, 1925, full color cov art and article, *The Lost World*, 8½ x 11½", 104 pgs **30.00**
Movie Script, *Maltese Falcon*, 112 pgs, 1941 .... **100.00**
Paint Set, *Tom Sawyer*, Paramount, 1931 .... **30.00**
Pinback Button, *The Phantom*, 3½", celluloid, Universal Pictures, c1960 ... **12.00**
Poster
　American Graffiti, Ron Howard, 27 x 41" **15.00**
　Annie Hall, Woody Allen, 27 x 41" . **35.00**
　Anniversary, Bette Davis, 27 x 41" .. **35.00**
　Avenging Rider, Tim Holt, 27 x 40", 1942 .... **100.00**
　Battle Circus, Humphrey Bogart, 27 x 41" **100.00**
　Beach Blanket Bingo, Frankie Avalon, 22 x 22" **20.00**
　Billy Two Hats, Gregory Peck, 27 x 41" **5.00**
　Black Fury, Paul Muni, 23 x 43", 1935 **175.00**
　Camelot, Richard Harris, 27 x 41" .. **12.50**
　Dirty Dozen, Lee Marvin, 27 x 41" . **15.00**
　Dr Zhivago, Omar Sharif, 27 x 41" . **20.00**
　Empire Strikes Back, Mark Hamill, 27 x 41" **25.00**
　Farewell to Arms, Rock Hudson, 27 x 41", 1958 .... **25.00**
　Guess Who's Coming To Dinner, Spencer Tracy, mended, 27 x 41" **15.00**
　Harlow, Carol Baker, 27 x 41" **10.00**
　Limelight, Charlie Chaplin, French, 47 x 63" **125.00**
　Shine On Harvest Moon, Ann Sheridan, 27 x 40", 1943 .... **100.00**
　Ten Commandments, 40 x 60", full color, 1956 .... **150.00**

The High and The Mighty, John
 Wayne, 27 x 41" **75.00**
The Wings of Eagles, John Wayne, 14
 x 36" **40.00**
To Have and Have Not, Humphrey
 Bogart, 22 x 28" **225.00**
Thunderball, Sean Connery, 27 x 41" **100.00**
Yearling, Gregory Peck, Jane Wyman,
 28 x 22", 1946 .... **100.00**
Press Book
 Bellboy, Jerry Lewis, 16 pgs, 1960 .. **18.00**
 Circus World, John Wayne, 14 pg .. **20.00**
 Clockwork Orange, Malcolm Mc-
  Dowell, 20 pgs **25.00**
 Girl Happy, Elvis Presley, 1965 ..... **20.00**
 Mary Poppins, Julie Andrews **10.00**
 Riding Wild, Tim McCoy, 1935, 8 pgs **65.00**
 The Caine Mutiny, Humphrey Bogart,
  18 pgs **30.00**
Press Kit
 Return of the Jedi, Mark Hamill **50.00**
 Star Trek IV, William Shatner **25.00**
Souvenir Book
 Beau Geste, Ronald Colman, William
  Powell, color scenes **50.00**
 Gone With The Wind, 1939, color . **35.00**
 Lawrence of Arabia, Peter O'Toole,
  colored photos, two foldout double
  page maps **15.00**
 Since You Went Away, 1944 Selznick
  film, 9 x 12", 20 pgs **25.00**
 The House of Rothschild, 9¼ x 12",
  1934 Darryl F Zanuck production,
  diecut opening with color portrait
  of George Arliss **30.00**
 The Sea Hawk, Milton Sills, silent ver-
  sion **50.00**
 The Song of Bernadette, 9 x 11½", 20
  pgs, 1944 religious movie, full col-
  or cov Norman Rockwell illus of
  Jennifer Jones **35.00**
 Wings, 1924, Clara Bow and Buddy
  Rogers **75.00**
Window Card
 Camelot, Richard Harris **10.00**
 High Noon, Gary Cooper, 14 x 22",
  1952 .... **75.00**
 North by Northwest, Cary Grant, 14
  x 22", 1959 .... **50.00**
 On The Waterfront, Marlon Brando,
  14 x 22", 1954 .... **125.00**
 You Only Live Twice, Sean Connery **30.00**

MOVIE PERSONALITIES

Collecting Hints: Focus on one star. Today, the four most popular stars are Humphrey Bogart, Clark Gable, Jean Harlow, and Marilyn Monroe. Many of the stars of the silent era are being overlooked by the modern collector. Nostalgia appears to be a key to the star on which a person focuses.

Remember that stars have big support staffs. Not all autograph items were or are signed by the star directly. Signatures should be checked carefully against a known original.

Many stars had fan clubs and the fans tended to hold on to the materials they assembled. The collector should be prepared to hunt and do research. A great deal of material rests in private hands.

History: The star systems and Hollywood are synonymous. The studios spent elaborate sums of money promoting their stars. Chaplin, Valentino, and Pickford gave way to Garbo and Gable.

The movie magazine was a key vehicle in the promotion. *Motion Picture, Movie Weekly, Motion Picture World,* and *Photoplay,* are just a few examples of this genre. *Photoplay* was the most sensational.

The film star had no private life and individual cults grew up around many of them. By the 1970s the star system of the 1930s and 1940s had lost its luster. The popularity of stars is much shorter lived today.

References: Leslie Halliwell, *The Filmgoer's Companion,* Avon, 1978; Ephraim Katz, *The Film Encyclopedia,* Perigee Books, 1979; Leonard Maltin (ed.), *TV Movies and Video Guide,* New American Library, 1987; Anthony Slide, *A Collector's Guide to Movie Memorabilia With Prices,* Wallace–Homestead, 1983; John R. Warren, *Warren's Movie Poster Price Guide,* Overstreet Publications, 1986.

Periodicals: *Big Reel,* Route 3, P. O. Box 83, Madison, NC 27025; *Classic Images,* P. O. Box 4077, Davenport, IA 52808; *Movie Collectors' World,* P. O. Box 309, Fraser, MI 48026; *Nostalgia World,* P. O. Box 231, New Haven, CT 06473.

Collectors' Club: Studio Collectors Club, P. O. Box 1566, Apple Valley, CA 92307.

See: Autographs, Magazines, Movie Memorabilia, and Posters.

Arden, Eve
 Coloring Book, unused, 1953 ...... **32.50**
 Paper Dolls, unused, 10½ x 12", Saal-
  field, 1953 .... **25.00**
Astaire, Fred
 Autographed Letter, 8½ x 11" RKO
  letterhead, March, 1937 .... **20.00**
 Sheet Music, *My Shining Hour* **5.00**
Blyth, Ann, coloring book, unused,
 1952 .... **35.00**
Bogart, Humphrey, sheet music, *Pas-
 sage to Marseille* **5.00**
Bushman, Francis X, magazine, Motion

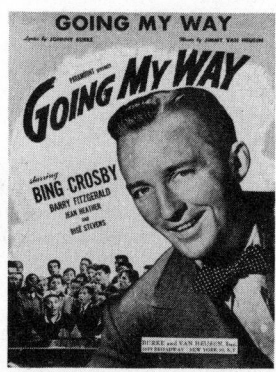

Bing Crosby, sheet music, *Going My Way,* 1944, $8.00.

Picture Classic, May, 1917, color cov portrait **35.00**
Chaney, Lon, movie book, *The Mocking Bird,* 5½ x 8", paperback, 138 pgs, 1925, MGM Movie **35.00**
Chaplin, Charlie
 Advertising, poster, Cantilever Shoes, 19 x 24½", 1927 .... **90.00**
 Bank, still, glass, figural **175.00**
 Booklet, "Charlie Chaplin In Essanay Comedies," 1915, 2¼ x 3¼" **25.00**
 Bookmark, autographed "Lila Grey Chaplin" **20.00**
 Coloring Book, "Charlie Chaplin Up In The Air," comic strip type, 10 x 17", Donohue & Co, 1917 copyright **80.00**
 Drawing Book, "Charlie Chaplin Mystery Movie Drawing Book," Chaplin on cov, 3 pgs, 2 x 3¼" .. **40.00**
 Figure, 2½ x 8", stuffed leather, full length portrait image inked in black on natural tan leather, black felt back, 1920s **65.00**
 Flasher, 2¼ x 3¼", adv for MA shoe store, naughty **25.00**
 Jewelry Box, musical, dancing plastic figure, marked "Hong Kong," 1981 **30.00**
 Magazine, Film Fun, Nov, 1918, Chaplin on cov **75.00**
 Pencil Box, 2 x 8", full figure illus .. **50.00**
Coogan, Jackie
 Clicker, metal, adv for peanut butter **20.00**
 Pencil Box, minor rust on bottom .. **12.00**
Crawford, Joan
 Sheet Music, *Sadie McKee* **5.00**
 Window Card, 10½ x 13½", cardboard, Crawford at dinner table, c1940 .... **18.00**
Crosby, Bing, game, Call Me Lucky, Parker Bros, 1954, black and white portrait on box lid and 19½" sq playing board **25.00**

Davis, Bette
 Coloring Book, 10 x 13", Merrill, 1942 .... **20.00**
 Movie Poster, *Hush, Hush Sweet Charlotte,* 27 x 41" **35.00**
 Press Book, *The Catered Affair,* 20 pgs **25.00**
 Sheet Music, *Now Voyager* **5.00**
Fairbanks, Douglas, Sr, press book, *Don Q, Son of Zorro,* 10 x 13", soft cov, "Exhibitors Campaign Book," 1925 silent film **80.00**
Flynn, Errol
 Magazine, Movie and Radio Guide, April 6, 1940, 10½ x 13½", 58 pgs **30.00**
 Movie Book
  Adventures of Robin Hood, Conklin Publishing Co, 1938, 8½ x 11", soft cover, 175 black and white glossy photos from Warner Bros movie **80.00**
  The Sea Hawk, Whitman, 1940, 8 x 11", soft cover, 64 pgs, black and white photos from Warner Bros movie **75.00**
Gable, Clark
 Magazine, Motion Picture, Feb, 1943, cov with Gable in Air Force uniform **35.00**
 Movie Poster, *The Tall Men,* 27 x 41" **50.00**
 Press Book, movie *But Not For Me,* 20 pgs **20.00**
Garland, Judy
 Movie Card, *For Me And My Gal,* MGM, 1942, 14 x 22", cardboard, full color **150.00**
 Sheet Music
  Harvey Girls **5.00**
  Trolley Song **5.00**
 Theater Program, Palace Theater, NY, 1951, Garland on cov **18.50**
Grable, Betty
 Magazine Cov, Life, 1939 .... **25.00**
 Movie Poster, *How To Be Very Popular,* 27 x 41" **20.00**
Harlow, Jean
 Book, *Jean Harlow's Life, From Cradle to Grave,* Louella Parsons **25.00**
 Dixie Cup Lid Premium, 8 x 10", color **20.00**
 Magazine Cov, Life, 1937 .... **30.00**
Hayworth, Rita, sheet music, *Cover Girl* **5.00**
Henie, Sonja
 Book, *Wings On My Feet,* 1940 .... **55.00**
 Ice Skates, orig box **100.00**
 Paper Dolls, 1930s, uncut **200.00**
 Poster, 14 x 19½", cardboard, *It's A Pleasure,* Henie skating, 1945 .... **10.00**
Hudson, Rock
 Magazine Cov, Life, 1955 .... **15.00**
 Scrapbook, 10 x 13½", color cov, unused, Whitman, 1957 .... **20.00**

Laurel & Hardy
  Movie Poster
    Four Clowns, 27 x 41" **35.00**
    Further Perils of Laurel & Hardy, 27
    x 41" **25.00**
  Salt and Pepper Shakers, ½ x 2½ x 4"
    white china tray, 4" Laurel with
    black derby, 3" Hardy with brown
    derby, Beswick, England, 3 pcs .. **100.00**
Lloyd, Harold, mechanical bank, litho
  tin, mouth opens, tongue protrudes,
  eyes roll, German, c1920, 5½" . **12,100.00**
Monroe, Marilyn
  Book
    *Gloria Jean, The Life of Marilyn
    Monroe, 1969,* dust jacket **25.00**
    Marilyn, Norman Mailer, 1973,
    270 pgs, hard cov **50.00**
  Calendar, 1953, Golden Dreams, 9 x
    11" **45.00**
  Magazine, Silver Screen, Feb, 1943,
    cov illus **35.00**
Pickford, Mary, press book, *Little Annie
  Roonie,* 10 x 13", soft cov, 1925 ... **85.00**
Rogers, Ginger, sheet music, *Suddenly
  It's Spring* **5.00**
Sinatra, Frank, sheet music, *If You Are
  But A Dream,* 1941, greentone cov, 4
  pgs, 9 x 12" **8.00**
Taylor, Elizabeth
  Jewelry, 1¼ x 4½ x 7" gray flocked
    suede display case, gold colored
    necklace, rhinestones and simu-
    lated pearls, matching earrings,
    black and white photo, c1950 ... **50.00**
  Movie Poster, *Cleopatra,* 27 x 41",
    small mend **50.00**
Three Stooges, punch out book, 7½ x
  13", Golden Press, 1962 .... **75.00**
West, Mae, magazine, Song Hits, Au-
  gust, 1935, full page photo **25.00**

MOXIE

Collecting Hints: A general rule is the older the
Moxie item, the more expensive the price. Due
to the vagaries of the Moxie Company's various
managements, some recent items have acquired
value. A large, 16 page, multicolored brochure
published in 1929 by the soon defunct Moxie
Company of America is one example. The short
lived, New Moxie venture made New Moxie bottles scarce. "The Great New Taste" debacle of
the late 1960s was not successful. Its dimpled
bottles are unknown to many Moxie collectors.

Moxie items, especially those associated with
Ted Williams, have risen dramatically in value.
Baseball collectors are constantly outbidding
Moxie collectors for the Williams' advertising
items for Moxie and for Ted's Root Beer items.

Lately, Moxie has been marketed in other soda-
pop bottles, even beer bottles. For more information write Don Wortham, 179 Orchard Drive,
Pittsburgh, PA 15235.

History: At the height of its popularity, 1920 to
1940, Moxie was distributed in approximately
36 states and even outsold Coca-Cola in many.
It became so popular that the word "moxie,"
meaning nervy, became part of the American
language.

Moxie is the oldest continuously produced soft
drink in the United States, celebrating its 100th
anniversary in 1984. It originated as Moxie Nerve
Food, a nostrum concocted by Dr. Augustin
Thompson from Union, Maine. It was first produced in Lowell, Massachusetts.

Moxie's fame is due in large part to the promotion efforts of Frank Morton Archer, an in-
trepid entrepreneur armed with charisma, wiz-
ardry, and a magnificent imagination. With a
genius for showmanship and prophesying profits
galore, Archer uncorked an advertising phenomenon by blazing a trail with eye-catching advertising vehicles and new benchmarks in una-
bashed barnstorming.

Bottle wagons were replaced by horseless carriages. Some folks called cars "Moxies," since
the first automobile they saw had MOXIE lettered
on its side. Next, Archer mounted a saddled,
dummy pony in the sidecar of a motorcycle and
put his TNT Cowboy Outfit on the road. He
followed with an even more amazing machine—
a dummy horse mounted on an automobile chassis driven from the horse's saddle.

Scarcely an event occurred in the first half of
the 20th century which Archer did not exploit
for Moxie. It was not by accident that the well
remembered Uncle Sam poster, "I Want You For
The U. S. Army," closely resembled another that
already was familiar to the public—a steely-eyed
Moxie man pointing at his viewers and commanding them to "Drink Moxie."

Moxie continues today, remaining especially
popular in the New England area. A mountain of
memorabilia surrounds the Moxie legend, much
of which its aficionados claim are superior to
Coke's both in quality and investment potential.

There are many firms which attempted to play
upon the Moxie name. During the late 1920s the
Moxie Company published a 64–page pamphlet
entitled *This Book About Substitution* which contained "A Little History of Many Big Cases."
Among the names imitative of Moxie were:
Proxie, Hoxie, Noxie, Noxie Nerve Tonic, Nox-
all, Nerv-E-Za, Non-Tox, Appetizer, Visner,
Puro, Nickletone, Neurene, Nerve Food (East India, Excelsior, Imperial, Standard), Miller, Man-
ola, Modox, Rixie, Toxie, two Canadian Moxies
and several others. Since only a limited amount
of each spurious products was produced and
many imitative bottles destroyed "whether full or

empty" by court order, those which remain are eagerly sought by collectors.

References: Q. David Bowers, *The Moxie Encyclopedia,* Vestal Press, 1985; Frank N. Potter, *The Book of Moxie,* Collector Books, 1987; Frank N. Potter, *The Moxie Mystique—The Word, The Drink, The Collectible,* published by author, 1981.

Collectors' Club: Frank N. Potter, Route 375, Box 164 Woodstock, NY 12498.

Museums: Clark's Trading Post, North Woodstock, NH; Mathews Museum of Main Heritage, Union, ME.

REPRODUCTION ALERT: Modern Moxie items are being produced and sold by Kennebec Fruit Company, 2 Main Street, Lisbon Falls, ME 04252.

Advisor: Frank N. Potter.

Ashtray	
Aluminum, emb, three notches	8.50
Ceramic, white, Moxie man, three notches	25.00
China, 5½" d, white	35.00
Balloon	1.00
Belt Buckle, bronze finish	17.50
Book	
The Moxie Menu, c1910	25.00
The TNT Cowboy, Archer, 1919	
Edition with more pages	150.00
Purple cover, 81 pgs	125.00
White cover, 81 pgs	125.00
This Book About Substitution Law, 1919	
Vol I	100.00
Vol II	75.00
Vol III, 1929	30.00
Book Cover, "Planets and the Stars" ..	5.00
Bottle	
Club size, high shoulder, paper label, 16 oz, c1928	20.00
Diet Moxie, emb neck, paper label .	15.00
Foxy Moxie, green, dumbbell shape, fox label, 1950s	50.00
Moxie	
7 oz, green tint, emb, high shoulder	6.00
10 oz, clear, dimpled, ACL "Moxie," 1960s	30.00
26 oz	
Clear, emb, high shoulder	6.00
Green tint, emb high shoulder .	7.50
Moxie Ginger Ale, paper label	25.00
Moxie Nerve Food	
Emb	10.00
Emb "COLO"	
Amber	75.00
Aqua	60.00
Emb "Lowell, Mass," clear	22.50
New Moxie, ACL, 7 oz	10.00

Pureoxia	
Clear	6.00
Green	10.00
Ted's Root Beer, 10 oz, produced by Moxie Co	10.00
Bottle Case, wood	
Moxie	
"It's Always A Pleasure"	20.00
12 bottle	20.00
24 bottle	20.00
No hand holes, c1910	25.00
No message, 24 bottle	20.00
Wheels or runners, wheelbarrows, carts, sleds	50.00
Moxie Nerve Food, twelve bottle, no hand holes	35.00
Bottle Carrying Bag, paper	
Kid Moxie, 6 bottle, 7 oz	7.00
Moxie/Pureoxia, 3 bottle, 26 oz	
Red semicircles	6.50
Vertical stripes	6.50
Bottle Hangers, paper and cardboard	
Armpit boy	10.00
Attached Moxie shoulder patch	5.00
Big Red Pen premium offer	3.00
Bottle Cap drawing, 6 for 37¢	2.00
Campfire scene, 2 bottle	25.00
Crown upper left, 10 oz bottle, king size	6.00
Tennis girl	10.00
The 3 Moxie–teers, 3 bottle, 7 oz ..	6.00
With Your Lunch, 3 bottle, 7 oz	8.00
Bottle Opener	
Moxie/Pureoxia	
Flat	5.00
Wire, straight handle	2.50
Moxieland, red, slide–out	15.00
Bottle Totes, cardboard	
2 bottle, 26 oz, red and blue	6.00
6 bottle, 7 oz, varied	5.00
8 bottle, 10 oz, expendable, "one– way bottles"	10.00
Bowl	
Cereal	20.00
Soup	25.00
Bumper Sticker	
Honk If You (heart) Moxie	1.00
I've Got Moxie, red and orange, black lettering	5.00
Try Rum'n Moxie, red and orange, black lettering	5.00
What this Country Needs Is Plenty of Moxie	2.00
Yes! We Have Moxie, orange on dark blue	7.50
Butter Dish, cov	60.00
Calendar, 1962, Old Fashion Moxie ..	5.00
Candy Box, metal	35.00
Cigar Lighter, silver	100.00
Clicker, marked "Mfg by Whitehead & Hoag Co"	50.00

Clock
- Imitation wood, horsemobile top, Roman numerals **50.00**
- Mantel, Moxie man **275.00**
- Pendulum, wall, banjo shape **500.00**
- Plastic, lighted
  - Round **17.50**
  - Square **25.00**

Clothing
- Apron **8.00**
- Cap, historic, Moxie Festivals **10.00**
- Hat, knit, (toques) **10.00**
- Mitten, pr **8.00**
- Scarf **10.00**
- Sweatshirt **18.00**
- T-shirt
  - Historic, Moxie Festivals **15.00**
  - Various **7.00**

Creamer **25.00**
Cuff Links, pr **25.00**
Cup and Saucer **20.00**
Display, fold out **23.00**
Egg Cup, large **50.00**
Fan, Eileen Percy **20.00**
Glass
- Flared top
  - Fluted base, emb "Licensed Only for Serving Moxie" **15.00**
  - Red band **12.50**
- Frosted label, syrup line **17.50**

Gravy Boat **40.00**
Ice Cream Dish, lip **20.00**
Ice Pick and Opener, "Moxie 5/ The Best Drink in the World" **44.00**
Lap Board, Moxie/Pureoxia **10.00**
Mirror, purse size, Zodiac signs **8.00**
Mug
- Ceramic **20.00**
- Emb "X" **20.00**

Napkin, boy and dog **20.00**
Novelty
- Carnival of Fun, bottle merry-go-round **10.00**
- Hitchy Koo
  - Carved head **250.00**

Jewelry, pendant, bottle cap, $15.00.

Flat head **100.00**
Pen, gold, Cross **45.00**
Pendant, SS **100.00**
Pinback Button
- Moxie man, pointing **25.00**
- Uncle Sam's hat **35.00**

Pitcher
- Large **100.00**
- Small **65.00**

Plate
- Dinner **25.00**
- Luncheon **25.00**

Platter
- Large **35.00**
- Small **25.00**

Playing Cards, Moxie man **6.50**
Portfolio, brown, imitation leather, 1920 .... **50.00**
Post Card, two children with cutouts and sign **27.50**
Poster
- Cardboard
  - Bottle, diecut **20.00**
  - Circus clown and elephant, diecut **30.00**
  - Drink Moxie, 21 x 35", squarecut, corrugated **7.50**
  - Is a Good Spring Tonic, squarecut, Public Approval Seal border ... **35.00**
  - Let's Get Acquainted, six-pack 5¢, squarecut **9.00**
  - Moxie kid with dog, diecut **40.00**
  - Moxie girl/man, two–sided, diecut **200.00**
  - Ted Williams, three dimensional, diecut, green base **135.00**
- Paper
  - Bathing beauty, white swimsuit ... **150.00**
  - Moxie League, baseball offer **20.00**
  - New England's Own Soft Drink, horsemobile **5.00**

Purse, Kid Moxie, mesh **250.00**
Record
- Moxie song
  - Gennet, sung by Arthur Fields, 10", 78 rpm, 1921 .... **50.00**
  - Vocalion, Shannon Four, 1921 ... **50.00**
- Radio Spots, Kasper–Gordon, 12", World War II **75.00**

Sauce Dish **20.00**
Serving Tray
- Copper **185.00**
- Moxie Centennial, 1984 .... **35.00**

Sign
- Braces First–Chases Thirst, squarecut **65.00**
- Drink Moxie 100%, octagonal, diecut **75.00**
- Old Moxie, New Moxie, squarecut, bottle caps **95.00**
- Pureoxia, squarecut, red oval on rectangle **75.00**
- Two-sided, left and right handed man **150.00**
- Yes! We Sell Moxie, Moxie Nerve Food, diecut, round, "X" **200.00**

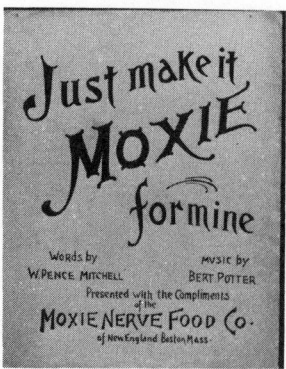

Sheet Music, *Just Make It Moxie For Mine,* **1904, $15.00.**

Sheet Music, Moxie Song, one–step,
  1921 .... **10.00**
Soup Tureen, cov **85.00**
Sugar, cov **60.00**
Tape
  Cassette, Moxie Monarch NuGrape
    Co **25.00**
  Open reel
    Mad about Moxie, jingles, 1967 . **25.00**
    Radio spots, Della Femina, 1968 . **50.00**
Tip Tray
  Girl's face **100.00**
  Violets, pre 1907 .... **225.00**
Thermometer
  It's Always a Pleasure, metal, red,
    Moxie man **75.00**
  New England's Own Soft Drink, white **7.50**
  Old Fashion, metal **20.00**
  Remember Those Days, metal, round,
    orange **20.00**
  Take Home a Case Tonight, metal,
    1920s **200.00**
  Ya Gotta Have Moxie, yellow, kid
    boxer **25.00**
Tray
  Boy's face, glass **325.00**
  Girl's face, glass **300.00**
  Our Idol, Moxie man **175.00**
Vegetable Dish, cov **75.00**
Wrist Watch, "Moxie Associate," Wal-
  tham **500.00**

MUSIC BOXES

Collecting Hints: Any figurine or box-shaped object has the potential for insertion of a music box. The following list of music boxes deals with objects in which the music box is secondary to the piece. Antique music boxes are covered in *Warman's Antiques And Their Prices.*

Collectors often tend to focus on one tune, trying to collect all the variety of ways it is used.

Others concentrate on a musical toy form, such as dolls or teddy bears. A popular item is the musical jewel box, prevalent during the 1880 to 1930 period.

History: The insertion of a small music box into toys and other products dates back to the 18th century. Initially these were limited to the children of the aristocracy; but the mass production of music boxes in the late 19th century made them available to everyone.

The music box toy enjoyed greater popularity in Europe than in America. Some of the finest examples are of European craftsmanship. After World War II there was an influx of cheap music box toys from the Far East. The popularity of the musical toy suffered as people reacted negatively to these inferior products.

Reference: *The Official Price Guide To Music Collectibles, Sixth Edition,* House of Collectibles, 1986.

Collectors' Club: Musical Box Society, International, R. D. #3, Box 205, Morgantown, IN 46160.

Museums: Bellms Car and Music of Yesterday, Sarasota, FL; Lockwood Matthews Mansion, Norwalk, CT.

Old King Cole, wood case, Swiss movement, 6¼ x 7⅜ x 2⅜", $15.00.

Ballerina, 9", bisque, glass eyes, twirls,
  cylinder in base, French **300.00**
Bank, 6¼ x 7⅜ x 2⅜", child's, wood,
  wheel, nursery rhyme characters ... **24.00**
Box
  3", round, woman on cov, ABC tune
    sheet, Swiss **75.00**
  5", wood, hand carved, floral dec
    cov, cylinder, four tunes **100.00**
  5½", cylindrical, tin litho, diamond
    dec, crank action on top **30.00**
Bride and Groom, bisque, Norman
  Rockwell Museum **95.00**
Cake Plate, revolving, metal, plays
  "Happy Birthday," c1940 .... **18.00**

Cardinal, bisque, revolving base, waltz tune **65.00**

Carousel

7¼", children, wood figures move, tune "Around the World in 80 Days" **30.00**

10", bisque unicorns, wood trim, metal base, Japan **65.00**

12", animals, Switzerland **175.00**

Cathedral, litho tin, side crank handle, Chein **50.00**

Christmas Tree Stand, revolving, Germany **75.00**

Church

4 x 6", litho tin, hand crank, Germany **140.00**

6 x 8", needlepoint, tune "Amazing Grace" **75.00**

Cigarette Box, leather, hand tooled, two tunes, Germany **50.00**

Cigarette Lighter, adv, Kitty Clover Potato Chips **25.00**

Clock, Hickory Dickory, Mattel, 1952 . **35.00**

Clown, 12", Pierrot, red suit, Gorham . **60.00**

Cradle, maple finish, doll size, windup, tune "Rock-a-bye Baby," 1930s **85.00**

Doll

11", Sammy Kaye, composition, "Swing and Sway with Sammy Kaye" **75.00**

15", Drum Major, Cecile, automated, blue uniform **100.00**

Easter Egg, litho tin, bright spring flowers, tune "Easter Parade," c1950 ... **18.00**

Elephant, 5½ x 8", plush, stuffed, gray, c1950 .... **35.00**

Jewelry Box

2½ x 3¾ x 7¾", black lacquered wood, Japanese fan design **40.00**

3¼ x 7½ x 4¼", burled walnut case, brass plaque, four round ball feet, Swiss **85.00**

Juke Box, 6", Ideola, plastic, windup, bank base **30.00**

Miniature, 1½ x 2¾", baby grand piano, sterling silver, pierced silver grill work **375.00**

Mug, 4", child's, china, nursery rhyme dec, 1930s **35.00**

Photograph Album, mirror on cov, cylinder, two tunes **185.00**

Pigs, nursery rhyme, Three Little Pigs, Jaymar **48.00**

Prom Dress, Norman Rockwell illus, Schmid **165.00**

Santa Claus, 7½", bisque, Norman Rockwell Museum **45.00**

See—A—Tune, plastic, crank, Kohner Co, 1960s **25.00**

Stein, 5", porcelain, diamond dec **35.00**

Teddy Bear

8", mohair, jointed, replaced button eyes **85.00**

10", plush, jointed **120.00**

13", mechanical, jointed **150.00**

Top, push, litho tin, Wyandotte, 1939 **35.00**

Yarn Spinner, Norman Rockwell illus, Schmid **100.00**

NAPKIN RINGS

Collecting Hints: Concentrate on napkin rings of unusual design or shape. This is one collectible which still can be used on a daily basis. However, check for the proper cleaning and care methods for the type of material you have. Many celluloid items have been ruined by storage in too dry an area or by washing in too hot water.

An engraved initial or other personalizing mark detracts, rather than adds value to a napkin ring. Many collectors and dealers have these marks removed professionally if it will not harm the ring.

History: Napkin rings enjoyed a prominent role on the American dinnertable during most of the 19th and early 20th centuries. Figural napkin rings were used in the upper class households. However, a vast majority of people used the simple napkin ring.

The shape does not mean that the decorative motif could not be elegant. Engraving, relief designs, and carving turned the simple ring into works of art. When cast metal and molded plastic became popular, shaped rings, especially for children, were introduced.

The arrival of inexpensive paper products, fast and frozen foods and a quickened pace of American society reduced American's concern for elegant daily dining. The napkin ring almost has disappeared from the dining table.

Cat, ceramic, marked "Japan," 2 x 3", $24.00.

Bisque, sailboat, yellow, 2" **60.00**

Brass, two elves, dog, dragon and leaf dec, emb **20.00**

Celluloid
Bear, figural	6.00
Grapes, emb	10.00

China, blue and pink floral dec, white
ground ... 15.00

Cloisonne
Dragon, white ground	25.00
Floral, dark blue dec, white ground	50.00

Cut Glass
Harvard Pattern	75.00
Hobstars and bow tie fans	85.00

Ivory, carved
Medallions	38.00
Openwork	20.00

Metal, lady with stick, c1942 ... 15.00
Milk Glass, Victorian, emb ... 35.00

Nippon
Floral, blue and gold, white ground	35.00
Forest and lake scene, beaded trim	75.00
Rose, gold trim, cream ground	60.00
Scenic, multicolored	55.00

Noritake
Art Deco, man	30.00
Flowers and butterfly	15.00
Rose Azalea	45.00

Papier Mache, red ... 4.00
Porcelain, owl seated on ring ... 20.00
Sabino Glass, bird, opalescent ... 40.00

Silver, plated
Barrel, Cupid on each end, Meriden	225.00
Birds and tulips, beaded base and ring, Rockford Silver Plate Co	80.00
Bulldog, Dirigo Boy	125.00
Cat, arched back	120.00
Children and goats, etched	15.00
Dog, pulling sled, emb greyhounds on sides, engraved "Sara," Meriden	165.00
Floral bouquets, Victorian, 1½"	15.00
Man, nude, running, holding torch, sq base	150.00
Oriental Fans, repousse flowers and hummingbird dec	75.00
Parrot, rect base, Rogers Mfg Co	50.00
Ring, etched dogwood branch, 1¾" w	20.00
Ring on sheet of music, violin leaning on ring, Wilcox	300.00

Silver, sterling
Art Nouveau, 1½", girl with flowing hair	25.00
Cherubs, two seated	65.00
Eagles, two	55.00
Hen, sgd "Meriden"	195.00
Koala Bear, 2 x 3", Australian	65.00
Mickey Mouse	75.00
Nursery rhyme figures	25.00
Peacock, standing	55.00
Scotty	35.00
Windham Pattern, Tiffany & Co	70.00

Souvenir
Grand Rapids, MI, scenic	10.00
Louisiana Purchase	15.00
Mt Washington, NH, 1880	18.00
St Louis World's Fair, 1904, enameled	40.00
Tin, yellow	15.00

NEW MARTINSVILLE VIKING

Collecting Hints: New Martinsville glass predating 1935 appears in a wide variety of colors. Later glass was only made in crystal, blue, ruby, and pink.

Look for cocktail, beverage, liquor, vanity, smoking and console sets. Amusing figures of barnyard and sea animals, dogs, and bears were produced. Both Rainbow Art Glass and Viking glass are handmade and have a paper label. Rainbow Art Glass pieces are beautifully colored and the animal figures are more abstract in design than New Martinsville. Viking makes plain, colored, cut and etched tableware, novelties, gift items. Viking began making black glass in 1979.

History: The New Martinsville Glass Manufacturing Company, founded in 1901, took its name from its West Virginia location. Early products were opal glass decorative ware and utilitarian items. Later productions were pressed crystal tableware with flashed-on ruby or gold decorations. In the 1920s innovative color and designs made vanity, liquor, and smoker sets popular. Dinner sets in patterns such as Radiance, Moondrops, and Dancing Girl, as well as new colors, cuttings and etchings were produced. The 40s brought black glass formed into perfume bottles, bowls with swan handles and flower bowls. In 1944 the company was sold and reorganized as the Viking Glass Company.

The Rainbow Art Glass Company, Huntington, West Virginia, was established in 1942 by Henry Manus, a Dutch immigrant. This company produced small, hand fashioned animals and decorative ware of opal, spatter, cased and crackle glass. Rainbow Art Glass also decorated for other companies. In the early 70s, Viking acquired Rainbow Art Glass Company and continued the production of the small animals.

Reference: Hazel Marie Weatherman, *Colored Glassware of the Depression Era, Book 2*, Glassworks, Inc., 1982.

Animal
Bear
Baby	40.00
Mama	200.00
Papa	225.00
Chicks, baby	20.00
Dog, 8½", orange, Viking #1316	35.00
Duck, 15", orange, Viking	50.00
Eagle, crystal	55.00
Elephant	75.00

Swan, Janice pattern, crystal, 11½ x 7½ x 8½", $32.00.

Gazelle	65.00
German Shephard	55.00
Hen	55.00
Owl, 8½", orange, Viking	100.00
Piglet, standing up	150.00
Pony, long front legs, blue	50.00
Rabbit	150.00
Rooster, large	75.00
Seal	55.00
Squirrel	35.00
Starfish	40.00
Wolfhound	65.00
Ashtray	
Fish, 4"	8.50
Skillet, 5"	12.00
Basket, 12", Janice, crystal	55.00
Bonbon, 6", Radiance, sky blue, ftd	12.00
Bookends, pr	
Cornucopia, 5¾"	45.00
Daddy Bear, 4½"	100.00
Lady's heads, crystal	255.00
Bowl, 10", Meadow Wreath, crimped	15.00
Butter Dish, cov, Radiance, crystal, SS overlay	60.00
Cake Plate, 14"	
Hostmaster, amber	24.00
Radiance, light blue	35.00
Candlesticks, pr	
Meadow Wreath	35.00
Prelude, two lite	20.00
Swan, dark green	25.00
Celery Dish, 10", Meadow Wreath	12.00
Cigarette Holder, cart shape, crystal	12.00
Console Set, Patti	50.00
Creamer and Sugar	
Eagle, crystal	20.00
Florentine	24.00
Cruet, Janice, light blue	65.00
Cup and Saucer, Hostmaster, ruby	8.50
Figure, drunk man	100.00
Fruit Bowl, 12", ftd, Janice, apricot	32.00
Goblet	
Hostmaster, 6¼", ruby	10.00
Mt Vernon, red	10.00
Prelude, etched	15.00
Ice Bowl, 5½", Hostmaster, ruby	36.00
Marmalade, cov, Janice, crystal	18.00
Mayonnaise, 3 pcs, Radiance, amber	18.00
Planter, flower cart, 5", crystal	15.00
Plate	
8½", Moondrops, amber	5.00
11", Florentine	10.00
Punch Cup, Radiance, light blue	11.00
Salad Bowl, 11", Wild Rose etching	20.00
Sherbet, Mt Vernon, cobalt	10.00
Shot Glass, Moondrops, ruby	10.00
Tumbler, Hostmaster	10.00
Vanity Set, cov box, two jars, stoppers, tray	
Geneva	50.00
Shining Star	30.00
Vase	
9", Morning Dove	35.00
12", Radiance, black, ruffled	275.00
Wine Set, decanter, six glasses	
Hostmaster, dark green	80.00
Silly Toby	75.00

NEWSPAPERS, HEADLINE EDITIONS

Collecting Hints: All newspapers must be complete with a minimal amount of chipping and cracking. The post-1880 newsprint is made of wood pulp and deteriorates quickly without proper care. Pre-1880 newsprint was composed of cotton and rag fiber and has survived much better than its wood pulp counterpart.

Front pages only of 20th century newspapers command about 60% of the value for the entire issue, since the primary use for these papers is display. Pre 20th century issues are collectible only if complete, as banner headlines were rarely used. These papers tend to run between four and eight pages.

Major city issues are preferable, although any newspaper providing a dramatic headline is collectible. Banner headlines, those extending completely across the paper, are most desirable. Also desirable are those from the city in which the event happened and command a substantial premium over the prices listed. Complete series collections carry a premium as well, such as all 20th century election reports, etc.

Twentieth century newspapers are easily stored. Issues should be placed flat in polyethylene bags, or acid free folders that are slightly larger than the paper, and kept from high humidity and direct sunlight.

Although not as commonly found, newspapers from the 17th through the 19th century are highly collectible, particularly those from the Revolutionary War, War of 1812, Civil War, and those reporting Indian and "desperado" events.

Two of the most commonly reprinted papers are the *ULSTER COUNTY GAZETTE,* of January 4, 1800, dealing with Washington's death and the *N.Y. HERALD,* of April 15, 1865, dealing with Lincoln's death. If you have either of these papers, chances are you have a reprint.

History: America's first successful newspaper was *The Boston Newsletter,* founded in 1704. The newspaper industry grew rapidly, experiencing its golden age in the early 20th century. Within the last decade many great evening papers have ceased publication, and many local papers have been purchased by the large chains.

Collecting headline edition newspapers has become popular during the last twenty years, largely because of the decorative value of the headlines. Also, individuals like to collect newspapers related to the great events which they have witnessed or which have been romanticized through the movies, television, and other media, especially those reporting events, the Old West, the gangster era.

Reference: Harold Evans, *Front Page History,* Salem House, 1984; Robert F. Karolevitz, *From Quill To Computer: The Story of America's Community Newspapers,* National Newspaper Foundation, 1985.

Advisor: Tim Hughes.

Note: The listing concentrates on newspapers of the 20th century. The date given is the date of the event itself. The newspaper coverage usually appeared the following day.

1865, April 15, Lincoln Assassinated ..	**225.00**
1885, July 23, U. S. Grant Dies	**70.00**
1886, October 28, Statue Of Liberty Dedicated	**45.00**
1898, February 15, The Maine Is Sunk	**40.00**
1900, May 11, James Jeffries Defeats Jack Corbett to Retain Heavyweight Boxing Title	**22.00**
1901, September 6, McKinley Is Shot .	**40.00**
1901, September 14, McKinley Dies ..	**35.00**
1903, December 17, Wright Bros. Fly	**220.00**
1906, April 18, San Francisco Earthquake	**40.00**
1909, September 6, Peary Discovers The North Pole	**15.00**
1912, April 15, Titanic Sunk	**170.00**
1915, May 7, Lusitania Sunk	**115.00**
1917, April 2, Wilson Calls For Declaration Of War	**38.00**
1918, November 11, Armistice Signed	**50.00**
1919, June 28, Peace Treaty Signed ..	**15.00**
1924, February 3, Woodrow Wilson Dies	**20.00**
1926, September 23, Tunney Defeats Jack Dempsey	**22.00**

1927, May 21, Lindbergh Flies The Atlantic	**35.00**
1927, September 30, Babe Ruth Hits Record 60 Home Runs In 1 Season ...	**25.00**
1929, February 14, St. Valentine's Day Massacre	**65.00**
1929, May 17, Capone Sentenced To Prison	**35.00**
1929, October 28, Stock Market Crashes	**65.00**
1929, November 29, Byrd Flies To The South Pole	**10.00**
1931, October 17, Al Capone Sentenced For 11 Years On Tax Evasion	**22.00**
1932, March 1, Lindbergh Baby Kidnapped	**18.00**
1932, November 8, Franklin D. Roosevelt Elected	**15.00**
1933, January 30, Hitler Made Chancellor Of Germany	**12.00**
1933, December 5, Prohibition Repealed	**23.00**
1934, May 23, Bonnie & Clyde Killed	**70.00**
1934, July 22, Dillinger Shot & Killed .	**35.00**
1936, December 10, King Edward VIII Renounces The Crown	**17.00**
1937, May 6, Hindenberg Crashes In Flames	**40.00**
1937, July 2, Amelia Earhart Vanishes In Round The World Flight	**14.00**
1938, March 11, Nazis Seize Austria .	**9.00**
1941, June 21, Hitler Wars On Russia	**10.00**
1941, December 7, Japan Attacks Pearl Harbor	**42.00**
1941, December 11, United States Declares War	**17.00**
World War II, any major headline	**5.00**
1943, September 8, Italy Surrenders ..	**9.00**
1944, June 5, Allied Armies Land In France	**18.00**
1944, November 7, Roosevelt Wins 4th Term	**10.00**
1945, April 12, Roosevelt Dies	**18.00**

Roosevelt Dies, The Times Herald, Newport News, VA, April 12, 1945, $18.00.

1945, May 7, War In Europe Ends	**24.00**
1945, August 6, First Atomic Bomb Dropped On Japan	**24.00**
1945, August 14, Japan Surrenders—War Over	**25.00**
1951, April 10, Truman Relieves Mc-Arthur Of His Command	**8.00**
1953, July 26, Truce Signed Ending The Korean War	**11.00**
1954, May 17, Court Bans School Segregation	**10.00**
1957, October 4, Soviets Launch Sputnik	**14.00**
1958, June 30, Alaska Joins The Union	**17.00**
1959, March 12, Hawaii Joins The Union	**18.00**
1962, February 20, John Glenn Orbits The Earth	**15.00**
1963, November 22, Kennedy Assassinated	**23.00**
1968, April 5, Martin Luther King Slain	**15.00**
1969, July 20, Man Walks On The Moon	**20.00**
1986, January 28, Challenger Explodes	**5.00**

NILOAK POTTERY

Collecting Hints: Mission ware pottery is characterized by swirling layers of browns, blues, reds and cream. Very few pieces are glazed on both the outside and inside. Usually only the interior is glazed.

History: Niloak Pottery was made near Benton, Arkansas. Charles Dean Hyten, the founder of this pottery, experimented with the native clay and tried to preserve the natural colors. By 1911 he had perfected a method that produced this effect. The result was the popular Mission ware. The wares were marked Niloak, which is Kaolin, the type of fine porcelain clay used, spelled backwards.

After a devasting fire the pottery was rebuilt and named Eagle Pottery. This factory included the space to add a novelty pottery line which was introduced in 1929. This line continued until 1934 and usually bears the name Hywood-Niloak. After 1934 the name Hywood was dropped from the mark. Mr. Hyten left the pottery in 1941. In 1946 the operation closed.

Ashtray	
Hat, figural, blue	**7.50**
Round, Mission Ware	**40.00**
Bowl, 8 x 3", chocolate brown, tan, and turquoise swirls, Mission Ware	**60.00**
Candlestick, Mission Ware	
2", brown, blue, and cream	**22.00**
12", brown, red, and cream	**65.00**
Cornucopia	
3", light pink	**5.00**

Planter, elephant on circus drum, pink and gray, 6" h, $30.00.

7", light blue	**6.50**
Creamer and Sugar, rose glaze, Hywood line	**24.00**
Figure	
Canoe, 7½", white matte	**30.00**
Frog	**20.00**
Polar Bear, white matte	**35.00**
Paperweight, rabbit, orig paper label ..	**30.00**
Pitcher	
3¼", yellow	**12.00**
7", dark green glaze	**14.00**
Planter	
Bear, 3", tan	**18.00**
Camel, 3"	**22.00**
Cannon, 3", blue	**15.00**
Deer, 8", pink and blue, matte	**30.00**
Duck, 5", pink and blue	**18.00**
Elephant, 6", white	**20.00**
Fox, 4", red	**20.00**
Frog, 4", seated on lily pad	**35.00**
Kangaroo, 5", white, brown accents	**10.00**
Log, 7", white	**15.00**
Parrot, 5", white, orange accents ...	**12.00**
Policeman and Donkey, 5", blue ...	**25.00**
Rabbit, 3", green	**12.00**
Squirrel, 6", light blue shading to tan	**25.00**
Swallow, 2", green	**8.50**
Swan, 3", light brown	**10.00**
Wishing Well, 7¼", dusty rose	**12.00**
Toothpick Holder, Mission Ware	**35.00**
Vase	
4", Mission Ware, red, cream, and brown	**36.00**
6", bud, leaf, Hywood line, blue glaze	**18.00**
7", maroon, handles	**15.00**
8"	
Aqua-green glaze, Hywood line, orig paper label	**18.00**
Gray shaded to pink ground, four flowers	**28.00**
Wall Pocket, 6", Mission Ware, brown, blue, and tan	**75.00**

NIPPON CHINA, 1891–1921

Collecting Hints: Examine each item carefully. Try not to purchase items with chips, cracks, hairlines, spiderwebs, or that have been restored. The condition of each item, in relationship to selling price, should be taken into consideration.

Also try to avoid buying sets which are incomplete. No matter what people say, you do not easily find the lid which is missing from your humidor, the cup and saucer to complete your chocolate set or the creamer to match your sugar bowl. Know what constitutes a complete set.

Beginning collectors should try to purchase only Nippon marked items. Learn the difference between the authentic marks and the reproduction marks. There are unmarked pieces from the Nippon era, but the purchase of these items should be put off until the collector has a commanding knowledge of Nippon.

History: Nippon, Japanese hand painted porcelain was made for export, between the years of 1891 and 1921.

In October 1891, the McKinley Tariff Act was passed by Congress, proclaiming that "All articles of foreign manufacture, be stamped, branded, or labeled, and all packages containing such or their imported articles, shall, respectively, be marked, stamped, branded, or labeled in legible English words, so as to indicate the country of their origin; and unless so marked, stamped, branded, or labeled they shall not be admitted to entry."

The Japanese chose to use "Nippon," which is the English equivalent of Japan, as their marking.

The McKinley Tariff Act also set rules and regulations on the marking system, stating that "all articles of foreign manufacture which are capable of being marked without injury shall be marked with the country of origin in legible English words and marking shall be nearly indelible and permanent as the nature of the article will permit." Paper labels were accepted. In the case of small articles shipped together, only the inside and outside packages were marked with the country of origin.

In 1921 the Government reversed its position and decided that: "Nippon" was no longer in compliance with the law. "After examination into the history and derivation of the word 'Nippon' and its treatment by lexicographers of recognized standing, the department is constrained to the conclusion that 'Nippon' is a Japanese word, the English equivalent of which is 'Japan', and the weight of authority does not support the earlier view that the word has become incorporated into the English language." All Japanese

items now had to be marked "Japan." thus ending the Nippon era.

Nippon marks were applied by two methods—an under the glaze decal sticker or direct imprinting.

There are over 221 recorded Nippon backstamps or marks, known to collectors today. The three most readily found and widely recognized are the "M" in Wreath, Maple Leaf and Rising Sun marks.

The majority of all marks are found in three color variations: green, blue, and magenta. The color of the mark indicates the quality of the porcelain used: green denotes first grade quality of porcelain; blue denotes second grade; and magenta denotes third grade.

References: Gene Loendorf, *Nippon Hand Painted China*, McGrew Color Graphics, 1975; Joan Van Patten, *The Collector's Encyclopedia Of Nippon Porcelain, Series One*, Collector Books, 1979; Joan Van Patten, *The Collector's Encyclopedia Of Nippon Porcelain, Series Two*, Collector Books, 1982; Joan Van Patten, *The Collector's Encyclopedia of Nippon Porcelain, Series Three*, Collector Book, 1985; *The Nippon Spotter*: A Updated and Revised Guide to Nippon Style, Patterns, Ornamentation, Techniques, Transfers, Examples, Reproductions, Chersteton, IN, privately printed.

Collectors' Clubs: Great Lakes Nippon Collectors Club, 3518 Westfield Drive, Anderson, IN 40611; International Nippon Collectors Club, P.O. Box 230, Peotone, IL 60468; Long Island Nippon Collectors Club, 3112 Clubhouse Road, Merrick, NY 11566; New England Nippon Collectors Club, 22 Mill Pond, North Andover, MA 01845.

Advisor: Kathy Wojciechowski.

REPRODUCTION ALERT: Most so called Nippon reproductions do not even resemble the Nippon era wares; but, there is a "Nippon" backstamp found on them, thus fooling many collectors and dealers.

The pattern often found and on the biggest variety of pieces is "Wildflower." These items have a bisque finish, outside edges are highlighted with gold, and pink to lavender flower blossoms are used as the decoration. All wares in this pattern are marked with a bogus hourglass in a wreath mark.

The "Green Mist" pattern items are reminiscent of Limoges pieces in shape, have a bisque finish, a light to medium green background, pink flowers, and gold trim. The mark found on these pieces is similar to the familiar Nippon rising sun mark except that the rays are connected rather than open as in the genuine mark.

The "Antique Rose" pattern is one of the newest patterns being reproduced. This can be found in a variety of shapes and bears the bogus maple leaf mark, which is almost a duplicate of the genuine mark except that it is much larger in size.

Most reproduction Nippon wares are manufactured in Japan and have a "Nippon" mark of some type under the glaze and a small paper label on the bottom saying "Made in Japan." Dealers buy wholesale from the importing firms. First, they discard the shipping boxes, then the paper label, resulting in a genuine marked "Nippon" item for the market.

Ashtray
    Round, shiny finish, geometric design
       bands **45.00**
    Triangular shape, palm trees scene,
       moriage trim, Wreath mark **85.00**
Basket
    3 x 4", floral outlined in gold, white
       background, gold handle **55.00**
    6½" l, maroon and pink roses, white
       background, gold handle **215.00**
    10" h, red and white roses, foliage,
       gold trim, Leaf mark **265.00**
    11" h, bisque, scenic, wreath mark . **225.00**
Bowl
    Blue roses and gold, open pierced
       gold handle, Wreath mark **85.00**
    Pink roses and gold, gold loop han-
       dles, 5", Rising Sun mark **65.00**
    Red roses, blown-out mold, gold
       bands, scalloped edges, unmarked **135.00**
    Roses outlined in gold, blown-out
       shape, dark green background,
       scalloped edges, Wreath mark . . . **245.00**
Cake Set, master and six small, orange
    and black flowers, TEOH mark **95.00**
Candlestick
    8½" h, roses, gray and green back-
       ground, gold beading top and bot-
       tom bands, Wreath mark **65.00**
    13" h, pale green, white lacy moriage,
       center light and dark pink roses
       medallions, sq base, unmarked, pr **450.00**
Celery Set, master and four small, yel-
    low roses, white background, TEOH
    mark **65.00**
Chocolate Set
    Floral and gold, pot, four cups and
       saucers, cobalt background, Leaf
       mark **850.00**
    Portrait medallion, pot, four cups and
       saucers, roses and gold, cobalt
       background, unmarked **650.00**
    Scenic medallion top bands, outlined
       in gold, white background, narrow
       pot, Wreath mark **375.00**
Cracker Jar
    Red and white roses, gold outline,
       gold bead centers, melon ribbed
       body, ftd, Pogoda mark **195.00**

    White flowers, gold trim, deep green
       background, Wreath mark **135.00**
Cup and Saucer
    Birds in flight scene, bisque, Rising
       Sun mark **35.00**
    Pink rose garland, green foliage,
       white background, Wreath mark . **45.00**
Doll, bisque
    4¼" h
       Child, jointed hips, stands or sits,
          blue trimmed bonnet and muff,
          incised mark **325.00**
       Policeman, incised mark **135.00**
    7", jointed arms and legs, incised
       mark **135.00**
    13", red cloth body, bisque hands and
       feet, turned head, shoulder plate,
       blue painted ribbon in hair, incised
       mark **235.00**
    22" h, ball jointed body, sleep eyes,
       open mouth, teeth, strawberry
       blonde hair, marked "FY Nippon
       #405" **475.00**
Dresser Set
    4 pcs, tray, powder box, hair receiver,
       and pin tray, pink and blue flower
       bands, green foliage, white back-
       ground, Rising Sun mark **95.00**
    8 pcs, 13" tray, hatpin holder, candle
       holder, ftd powder box, hair re-
       ceiver, two cov boxes, and pin tray,
       swans on lake, sunset on water,
       beige, Sho-Fu mark **295.00**
Dutch Shoes
    Moriage dragon, glass eyes, gray
       background, unmarked **65.00**
    Scenic, lake, trees, and house, bis-
       que, Wreath mark **175.00**
Egg Cup, double
    Pink and yellow floral bands, white
       background, 5" h **25.00**
    Pink roses top and bottom bands,
       white background, Wreath mark . **25.00**
Egg Warmer, stopper, holds four eggs,
    Rising Sun mark
    Floral band, gold and white trim . . . **125.00**
    Scenic, trees and lake **135.00**
Ewer
    9"
       Light pink to dark pink roses, gold
         branches and leaves, light green
         bisque background, Maple Leaf
         mark **450.00**
       Pink roses, white moriage, mar-
         bleized pastel background, han-
         dle bolted base, unmarked **285.00**
    10", lacy white moriage, gold trim,
       fancy spout and handle, unmarked **385.00**
Fruit Bowl, 11" w, orchids, gold outline,
    ftd, Wreath mark **165.00**
Hat Pin Holder
    Light and dark pink roses top and bot-

tom bands, gold trim, white center and background, 3½" h **55.00**

Rows of pink roses, gold outline, white background **95.00**

Swans on lake center medallion, turquoise background, Wreath mark **85.00**

Humidor

Children sitting by tree, 6½", Wreath mark **1,750.00**

Egyptian sailing ship, full sail, small sailing ships background, earth tones, 7" h, Leaf mark **375.00**

Geometric outlined panels, women carrying milk pails, woman milking cow front medallion, 6" h, 47 mark **350.00**

Hexagonal, bisque finish, black slip trailing, blue jewels, rocky island and sailboat, sailboats background, 6¾" h, Maple Leaf mark **245.00**

Scenic, black trees, lane, and house, bisque, Wreath mark **300.00**

Lemonade Set, pitcher and six mugs, TEOH mark

Bisque, purple violets, pale green background **160.00**

Dutch sailing ships and windmill ... **175.00**

Salt and Pepper Shakers, pr, matching toothpick holder, hand painted, gold tops, marked, $10.00.

Mug

4¾" h, hunt scene, moriage trim handle, Maple Leaf mark **225.00**

5½" h, moriage dragon, blue enameled eyes, gray bisque background, green M in Wreath mark **225.00**

Napkin Ring

Owl on tree stump, figural, 4" h, Wreath mark **375.00**

Windmill scene, blue background, Wreath mark **125.00**

Nappy, 5 x 5", cottage scene, beaded handle, matte finish, Wreath mark .. **25.00**

Nut Set, pedestal master and six small, colorful nuts inside bowls, moriage flowers and leaves edges, Leaf mark **185.00**

Pancake Server, 9", round, pink and

green roses, pink and green jewels, bisque finish, gold overlay design, Maple Wreath mark **325.00**

Pitcher, 7" h, moriage sea gulls, slate gray background, Maple Leaf mark . **250.00**

Plaque

10"

Arab by campfire, Art Deco rim, Wreath mark **275.00**

Countess Anna Potocka portrait, gold overlay design and beading, Maple Leaf mark **350.00**

Flying eagle, relief molded, Wreath mark **4,000.00**

Three dancing children, animals, rim, Wreath mark **350.00**

10 x 8", two Indians on horseback, sunset, bisque, Indian deco design band, Wreath mark **475.00**

10½", collie and terrier, relief molded, Wreath mark **950.00**

12", farmer sowing seeds, relief molded, Wreath mark **2,100.00**

Plate

10", center medallion portrait, gold overlay design and jewel bands, Maple Leaf mark **325.00**

11", white center, gold beaded red and pink roses bunches, gold border, Maple Leaf mark **65.00**

Potpourri, bisque, windmill, house, and lake scene, Wreath mark **95.00**

Punch Bowl

11" d, gold scenic medallions on green, gold overlay design, ftd pedestal base, 2 pcs **550.00**

12", d, man and boat scene, cobalt blue trim, cobalt and white base, gold loop handles, stand, Maple Leaf mark **300.00**

12½" d, bisque, scenic center, rose bouquets, gold and jewels dec rim, stand, Wreath mark **395.00**

Ramekin, grape bunches and leaves band, Maple Leaf mark **35.00**

Salt and Pepper Shakers, pr

Cobalt and red roses, gold overlay and beads, Maple Leaf mark **55.00**

Pastel floral top band, white background, Rising Sun mark **25.00**

Sandwich Set, 17" master tray, four 6" small plates, iris bands, Wreath mark **145.00**

Serving Tray, 11" d, gold and burgundy medallions in gold fluted rim, multicolored roses and leaves center, gold open pierced handles, Royal Kinran mark **195.00**

Shaving Mug

Pink flowers, white background, Rising Sun mark **45.00**

Red and green floral, white background, Rising Sun mark **45.00**

Smoke Set

3 pcs, 7" tray, cigar holder, and ashtray, bisque, playing card design,
deep brown and cream back-
ground, Wreath mark **185.00**

4 pcs, 11" tray, cigarette holder,
match holder, and ashtray, pastel
and sunset colored rural scene,
Wreath mark **255.00**

Spoon Holder, 7¾" w, yellow florals,
black and green leaves **35.00**

Stickpin Holder

Cobalt and gold, white background,
Wreath mark **135.00**

Multicolored roses, gold trim, 1½" h,
Wreath mark **100.00**

Tankard

12"

Forest scene, matte finish, unmarked **165.00**

Pink and white poppies, Maple Leaf
mark **265.00**

Pink and white roses, solid gold
background, Maple Leaf mark . **375.00**

14", magenta, dark blue, pink, and
green moriage design, unmarked . **585.00**

Tea Set

3 pcs, teapot, creamer, and sugar

Flying blue birds, white background, gold handles, finials,
and rims, Wreath mark **95.00**

Pink rose bunches with gold overlay design, melon rib shape, gold
handles and trim, ftd, Maple Leaf
mark **250.00**

12 pcs, teapot, creamer, sugar, and
four cups and saucers, cobalt background, gold wash, Pogoda mark . **350.00**

Tea Strainer, bisque, scenic, white underplate, Maple Leaf mark **65.00**

Urn

9½" h, white flowers outlined in gold,
turquoise background, handles,
dome lid, pedestal base, Royal
Kimran mark **425.00**

12" h, Queen Louise portrait center
medallion, turquoise background,
gold and jewels, dome lid, Maple
Leaf mark **1,200.00**

16" h, cows drinking from pond center medallion, gold overlay floral,
bolted base, gold stand-up handles,
Wreath mark **575.00**

20¾" h, scenic center, floral background, gold overlay design, Maple
Leaf mark **950.00**

Vase

6¾" h, moriage, floral with hp grapes,
ruffled top, loop handles, three
footed, Royal Moriye mark **265.00**

7" h, multicolored floral and foliage
front and back, shaded bisque

background, gold overlay collar
and base, coralene, marked "Pat-
ent Applied For" **195.00**

9" h, magenta and pink roses center
medallion with turquoise beads,
gold background, Maple Leaf mark **425.00**

10" h

Ducks on lake center medallion,
muted bisque background with
pink roses, ruffled edge, curved
gold handles, Maple Leaf mark ... **275.00**

Indian and canoe scene, Wreath mark **525.00**

11¼" h, orchids and foliage outlined
in gold, bisque to brown background, gold reticulated handles,
Maple Leaf mark **325.00**

12½" h, cobalt and swan scene, gold
overlay, Maple Leaf mark **450.00**

14" h, farmer sowing seeds, relief
molded **2,300.00**

16" h, bisque ships in harbor center
medallion, three gold pretzel ring
handles, Wreath mark **1,200.00**

Whiskey Jug

Egyptian Nile scene, bisque, gold
handle, stopper, and lip rim, 7 ½"
h, Wreath mark **425.00**

Palm trees and lake scene, raised
moriage trim **450.00**

Stag in forest, moriage trim, basketweave bottom, Wreath mark ... **450.00**

Wine Jug, 9½" h

Monk center medallion, green background, moriage trim, Maple Leaf
mark **495.00**

Moriage wheat, pale green background, Maple Leaf mark **550.00**

NORITAKE AZALEA CHINA

Collecting Hints: There are several backstamps
on the Azalea pattern of Noritake China. The
approximate dates are:

Prior to 1921:   Blue rising sun, printed "Hand
painted NIPPON"

1921–1923:   Green wreath with M, printed
"Noritake, Hand painted, Made
in Japan"

1923–1930s: Green wreath with M, printed
"Noritake, Hand painted, Made
in Japan 19322"

1925–1930s: Red wreath with M, printed
"Noritake, Hand painted, Made
in Japan 19322"

1935–1940:   Red azalea sprig, printed "Noritake Azalea Patt., Hand
painted, Japan No. 19322/
252622"

Most of the saucers and underplates do not have

a backstamp, except those stamped "Azalea 19322/252622."

Most collectors assemble sets and are not concerned with specific marks. Those concentrating on specific marks, particularly the NIPPON one, may pay more. There presently are individuals who offer replacement service.

History: The Azalea pattern of Noritake China, made of fine china, was produced first in the early 1900s. Each piece was hand painted. The individuality of each artist makes it almost impossible to find two pieces with identical painting.

In the early 1900s the Larkin Company of Buffalo, New York, sold many household items to the American public through their catalog (similar to the Sears, Roebuck catalog). In the 1924 Larkin catalog a basic, Azalea pattern, serving set was advertised. The set included the larger coffee cups with the blue rising sun backstamp.

Two forces came together in the 1920s to make the Azalea pattern of Noritake China one of the most popular household patterns in this century. First, the Larkin Company initiated their "Larkin Plan," in which housewives could sign up to become "Larkin Secretaries." Each Larkin Secretary formed a small neighborhood group of five or more women who would buy Larkin products for their homes. The Larkin Secretary earned premiums based on the volume of sales she obtained. Household items, including Azalea china, could then be purchased either for cash or premiums.

Second, many households in the 1920s could not afford a complete set of fine china in a single purchase. The Larkin Club Plan enabled them to obtain items in the Azalea pattern one or a few at a time.

Over the years, and to provide more enticements, additional pieces, such as the nut/fruit shell shaped bowl, candy jar, and child's tea set were added. Glassware, originally classified as crystal, was introduced in the 1930s but was not well received.

It became somewhat of a status symbol to "own a set of Azalea." The Azalea pattern china advertisement in the 1931 Larkin catalog claimed, "*Our Most Popular China.*"

Some Azalea pieces were advertised for sale in the Larkin catalogs for 19 consecutive years, while others were advertised for only 4 or 5 years. These latter pieces are more scarce, and more sought after by collectors, resulting in a faster appreciation in value.

The ultimate goals of most serious collectors are the child's tea set, which we believe was advertised in only two Larkin Fall catalogs, and the so-called salesmen's samples, which were never advertised for sale.

The Larkin Company ceased operations as a distributor in 1945. Due to the quality and popularity of the Azalea pattern, this beautiful china remains cherished and highly collectible.

Reference: Larkin catalogs from 1916 through 1941.

Note: The Larkin catalog numbers are given in parentheses behind each listing. If arranged numerically, you will notice gaps in the numbering. For example, numbers 41 through 53 are missing. The "Scenic" pattern, presently called "Tree in the Meadow," of Noritake China also was popular during this same time period. Many of the missing Azalea numbers were assigned to the Scenic pattern.

Plate, 7½" d, $7.50.

CHINA

Basket (193)	120.00
Bonbon Dish, 6¼" (184)	35.00
Bouillon Cup and Saucer, 5¼" (124)	15.00
Bowl	
Deep (310)	42.00
Divided (439)	225.00
Butter Chip, 3¼" (312)	65.00
Butter Tub, insert (54)	25.00
Cake Plate, 9¾" (10)	25.00
Casserole, cov	
Gold Finial (372)	400.00
Regular (16)	60.00
Celery Dish, 10" (444)	240.00
Cheese Dish, 6¼", cov (314)	85.00
Child's Set, 15 pcs (253)	1500.00
Coffeepot (182)	450.00
Compote (170)	60.00
Condiment Set, 5 pcs (14)	35.00
Creamer, (7)	15.00
Creamer and Sugar	
Gold Finial, with lid (401)	100.00
Open (123)	65.00
Cruet Bottle (190)	170.00
Cup and Saucer, (2)	14.00
Demitasse Cup and Saucer (183)	110.00
Egg Cup (120)	32.00
Grapefruit Bowl, 4½ (185)	100.00
Gravy Boat (40)	28.00
Jam Jar Set, 3 pcs (125)	115.00
Lemon Plate (121)	12.00

Mayonnaise Set, 3 pcs
Regular (3)	**25.00**
Scalloped (453)	**400.00**

Milk Jug (100) **150.00**

Mustard Jar (191) **45.00**

Plate
6¼", bread and butter (8)	**8.00**
7½", tea (4)	**7.50**
7⅝", sq (315)	**40.00**
8½", breakfast (98)	**15.00**
9¾", dinner (13)	**18.00**
10¼", grill (338)	**120.00**

Platter
10¼", (311)	**150.00**
12", (56)	**40.00**
14", (17)	**40.00**
16", (186)	**300.00**

Refreshment Set, 2 pcs (39) **35.00**

Relish
7¼", oval (194)	**45.00**
8½", oval (18)	**12.50**
10", four sections (119)	**100.00**

Salad Bowl, 10", round (12) **28.00**

Salt and Pepper Shakers, pr, 3", bulbous **18.00**

Sauce Dish, (9) **8.00**

Saucer **3.00**

Spoon Holder, 8" (189) **65.00**

Sugar, cov, (7) **15.00**

Syrup Pitcher, underplate (97) **70.00**

Teapot
Gold Finial (400)	**425.00**
Regular (15)	**75.00**

Tile, 6" (169) **30.00**

Tobacco Jar, cov (313) **500.00**

Toothpick Holder (192) **75.00**

Vase
Bulbous (452)	**900.00**
Fan, ftd, (187)	**120.00**

Vegetable Bowl, oval
9½ x 6¾", (172)	**32.00**
10½", (101)	**30.00**

GLASSWARE, HAND PAINTED

Cake Plate, 10½" (124)	**38.00**
Candlestick Holders, pr (114)	**32.00**
Cheese and Cracker Set, 2 pcs (111) ..	**50.00**
Compote, 10" (113)	**48.00**
Fruit Bowl, 8½" (11)	**40.00**
Tray, 10" (112)	**40.00**

NUTCRACKERS

Collecting Hints: The most popular modern nutcrackers are the military and civilian figures which are made in East Germany. These are collected primarily for show and not for practical use.

Nutcracker design responded to each decorating phase through the 1950s. The figural nutcrackers of the Art Deco and Art Nouveau periods are much in demand. Concentrating on 19th century models results in a display of cast iron ingenuity. These nutcrackers were largely utilitarian and meant to be used.

Several cast iron animal models have been reproduced. Signs of heavy use is one method to tell an older model.

History: Nuts keep well for long periods, up to two years, and have served as a dessert or additive to cakes, pies, bread, etc., since the colonial period. Americans most favorite nuts are walnuts, chestnuts, pecans, and almonds.

The first nutcrackers were crude hammers or a club device. The challenge was to find a cracker that would crack the shell but leave the nut intact. By the mid-19th century cast iron nutcrackers in animal shapes appeared. Usually the nut was placed in the jaw section of the animal and the tail pressed as the lever to crack the nut.

The 19th and early 20th century patent records abound with nutcracker inventions. In 1916 a lever-operated cracker which could be clamped to the table was patented as the Home Nut Cracker, St. Louis, Missouri. Perhaps one of the most durable designs was patented on January 28, 1889, and sold as the Quakenbush plated model. This hand model was plain at the top where the grip teeth were located and had twist-style handles on the lower half of each arm with the arms ending in an acorn finial.

Dog, cast iron, bronze finish, $45.00.

Bear, hand carved, wood, glass eyes, German	**100.00**
Cat, 4½", nickel covered brass	**45.00**

Dog
4⅝", cast iron, old paint	**65.00**
7¾", 3¾" h, bronze, whippet running	**75.00**
10", 5¼" h, brass	**65.00**
13", 6" h, cast iron, silver plate	**75.00**

Elephant, 10", 5" h, orig paint, c1920 . **70.00**

Gentleman, 9" h, bust, wood, hand carved **65.00**

Hand, 7⅝", holding cup, wood, hand carved **110.00**

Jester, head, brass **75.00**

Lady's Leg, 7", wood	**30.00**
Monkey, 6¾", wood, carved	**90.00**
Parrot, 5½", brass	**15.00**
Pheasant, bronze, France	**100.00**
Pliers Type	
Cast iron, Torrington	**4.00**
Silver, double	**30.00**
Steel, 5½", adjustable, c1890	**12.00**
Punch & Judy, figural, brass	**100.00**
Rabbit, head, wood, hand carved, glass	
eyes, German	**100.00**
Ram, 8½", wood, carved, glass eyes ..	**65.00**
Sailor and lady, 6¼", brass, couple	
kisses when handles squeeze together	**65.00**
Skull and Cross Bones, 6", cast iron ..	**85.00**
Squirrel	
Bronze, sitting on branch	**50.00**
Cast Iron, sitting on leaf	**45.00**
Wood, 7", eating nut, carved, twist	
and screw type	**60.00**
Table Type, Perfection Nut Cracker Co,	
Waco, TX, patented 1914, clamp and	
turn buckle	**20.00**

OCCUPIED JAPAN

Collecting Hints: Buyers should be aware that a rubber stamp can be used to mark "Occupied Japan" on the base of objects. Finger nail polish remover can be used to test a mark. An original mark will remain since it is under the glaze; fake marks will disappear. This procedure should not be used on unglazed pieces. Your eye is your best key to identifying a bad mark on an unglazed item.

Damaged pieces have little value unless the piece is extremely rare. Focus on quality pieces which are made well and nicely decorated. There are many inferior examples.

History: At the end of World War II, the Japanese economy was devastated. To secure needed hard currency, the Japanese pottery industry produced thousands of figurines and other knickknacks for export. From the beginning of American occupation until April 28, 1952, these objects were marked "Japan," "Made in Japan," "Occupied Japan," and "Made in Occupied Japan." Only pieces marked with the last two designations are of strong interest to Occupied Japan collectors. The first two marks also were used at other time periods.

The variety of products is endless—ashtrays, dinnerware, lamps, planters, souvenir items, toys, vases, etc. Initially it was the figurines which attracted the largest number of collectors; today many collectors focus on non-figurine material.

References: Gene Florence, *The Collector's Encyclopedia Of Occupied Japan Collectibles, First Series* (1976), *Second Series* (1979), and *Third Series* (1987), Collector Books.

Collectors' Club: Occupied Japan Collectors Club, 18309 Faysmith Ave., Torrance, CA 90504; O. J. Club, 29 Freeborn Street, Newport, RI 02840.

Aquarium Figure, house	**9.00**
Ashtray	
3", brown, emb elephant	**7.50**
4", floral, green	**7.00**
Ashtray Set, figural	
Elephant, 4 pcs	**5.00**
Western, boot lighter, tray, and insert	**20.00**
Bell, 3", chef holding wine bottle and	
glass	**24.00**
Butter Dish, silvered metal, glass liner	**15.00**
Candy Dish, handled, silvered metal, fi-	
ligree rim	**15.00**
Cigarette Lighter, figural	
Camera, tripod, metal	**40.00**
Horse head	**12.00**
Pistol, orig case	**18.00**
Cigarette Set, plated metal, cov box with	
Scottie dog, matching lighter	**20.00**
Coaster, set of 6, laquerware, red, gold	
scroll	**18.00**
Condiment Set, figural nodding chicken	
salt and pepper shakers, cov mustard	**45.00**
Creamer, figural	
Cow	**25.00**
Toby Jug, black hat, yellow coat,	
green vest, brown pants	**15.00**
Creamer and Sugar Set, figural, lemons,	
matching tray	**35.00**
Cup and Saucer, coralene dec, luster	
ground	**20.00**
Demitasse Cup and Saucer, hp, pastel	
sunset design, palm trees, sgd "De-	
signed by Brock of Miami," Made in	
Occupied Japan	**20.00**
Demitasse Set, 8 pcs	**40.00**
Dinnerware, Bamboo pattern, stone-	
ware type	
Cup	**3.00**
Plate, dinner	**6.00**
Platter, large	**10.00**
Salad Bowl	**4.00**
Saucer	**3.00**
Soup Bowl	**4.00**
Sugar, cov	**6.00**
Vegetable Bowl	**8.00**
Doll, 5", celluloid, movable arms, pink	
snow suit	**30.00**
Figure	
Baby, bisque, painted	**17.00**
Boy, 2½", seated on edge of brown	

and white barrel, yellow pants,
blue shirt 5.00
Colonial Couple, 6", white, gold trim   10.00
Colonial Man, 7¼", holding tricorn
hat, wine coat, light green trim,
blue knee pants with pink stripe,
ivory waistcoat, gray hair, gold trim   10.00
Cowboy, boy riding horse 95.00
Dancing Girl, 5½", blue dress, red
trim, blonde hair, gold slippers . . .   8.50
Donkey pulling cart, 4¾" l, semi-por-
celain 20.00
Dutch Girl 22.00
Frog, porcelain, dressed 40.00
Girl
2¼", seated, brown chair, holding
basket of fruit, green top, white
skirt, blue flowers, rust bonnet .   5.00
4", girl with mandolin, singing to
puppy 18.00
Lady, 4½", mandolin, blue hat 15.00
Little Fiddler, Hummel repro 25.00
Oriental Girl, kneeling, pr 15.00
Oriental Lady, 10" 13.00
Rooster, 4½ x 3", yellow, blue, and
red, pulling brown cart, blue, red,
and white wheels, green grass base   7.50
Soloist, Hummel repro 25.00
Southern Belle
3½" 7.00
4½", parasol, feather bonnet 15.00
Street Singer, Hummel repro 25.00
Well Done, Hummel repro 20.00
Woman, holding parasol, Delft 20.00
Incense Burner, woman 20.00
Kazoo, litho tin, set of 3, MIB 5.00
Lamp, 10½", colonial lady, flowers . . .   35.00
Mug
Elephant 25.00
Indian Chief 35.00
Squirrel, 5" 15.00
Nodder
Donkey, celluloid, 6 x 7½" 30.00
Man, head, cast iron, ashtray base .   30.00
Parasol, 32" d, multicolored, emb "Oc-
cupied Japan" on metal tip 50.00
Pearls, double string, orig paper label .   12.00
Perfume Bottle, 4", blue glass 15.00
Pin Cushion, metal, figural, woman's
shoe, blue fabric cushion 18.00
Planter
Boy with dog 12.00
Cat, gingham, 5¾" 22.00
Donkey 12.00
Elephant 5.00
Goose, 6" 15.00
Kitten in Basket, 3½" 12.00
Oriental, 5" 16.00
Pig, 7" 10.00
Rabbit, 6", pink 10.00
Shell, bisque, woman and angels,
7¾ x 7¾" 160.00

Plate, 9½", flowers 15.00
Powder Jar, cov, 3" d, Wedgwood style,
blue and white 15.00
Salt and Pepper Shakers, pr, figural
Chickens, yellow 10.00
Oriental Boy and Girl 18.00
Steins, matching undertray 20.00
Shelf Sitter
Black, boy with straw hat, 3" 10.00
Little Boy Blue 15.00
Stein, 6¼", handle 20.00
Tape Measure, 2½", figural, cat, cellu-
loid 20.00
Tea Set, teapot, creamer, cov sugar, cot-
tage scene, luster ground, 5 pcs 75.00

**Toothpick Holder, boot, white ground,
blue rim, brown dec, marked "PICO,
Made in Occupied Japan," 2¾" h, $10.00.**

Toothpick Holder, ceramic
Cart, 3½" l 10.00
Dog, 2¾", basket weave holder 15.00
Toy
Bear, squeeze type 18.00
Dancing Couple, wind-up, celluloid,
5" h 75.00
Dog, wind-up, celluloid, head shakes
old shoe, tail spins 40.00
Drum, tin and litho paper, wooden
sticks 15.00
Lion, wind-up, celluloid, MIB 50.00
Tricksey The Dog, wind-up, fur cov
tin, MIB 40.00
Tray, metal, hp, red, floral center, gold
trim 10.00
Vase
2½", cornucopia 8.00
4", emb tulips, orange, green, and
yellow, handle 8.50
Wall Pocket
Parrot 12.00
Violin 10.00
Wind Chimes, glass, hp, MIB 15.00

OCEAN LINER COLLECTIBLES

Collecting Hints: Don't concentrate only on ships of American registry. Many collectors favor material from only one liner or ship line. Objects associated with ships involved in disasters, such as the *Titanic*, often command higher prices.

History: Transoceanic travel falls into two distinct periods—the era of the great Clipper ships and the era of the diesel powered ocean liners. The latter craft reached their "Golden Age" in the period between 1900 and 1940.

An ocean liner was a city unto itself. Many had their own printing rooms to produce a wealth of daily memorabilia. Companies such as Cunard, Holland-America, and others encouraged passengers to acquire souvenirs with the company logo and ship name. Word-of-mouth was a principal form of advertising.

Certain ships acquired a unique mystic. The *Queen Elizabeth*, *Queen Mary*, and *United States* became symbols of elegance and style. Today the cruise ship dominates the world of the ocean liner.

Collectors' Club: Steamship Historical Society of America, Inc., 345 Blackstone Boulevard, Hall Building, Providence, RI 02906; Titanic Historical Society, P. O. Box 53, Indian Orchard, MA 01151-0053.

Ashtray
    Cunard Steamship Co, 4½", white
        bone china, clamshell shape, gold
        pin striping **10.00**
    Everett (WA) Yacht Club, brass **20.00**
    France III, French Line, cobalt blue,
        image and name in gold **18.00**
    RMS Queen Elizabeth I, Cunard Line,
        wooden ship's wheel, glass insert
        over color center photo **30.00**

Cup and Saucer, *Porsgrund*, Norway, $7.50.

Pacific Far East Steamship, china ... **25.00**
Princess, Swedish, glass **8.00**
Baggage Tag, French Line, France funnel, first class **5.00**
Belt Buckle, *Queen Elizabeth II*, Cunard Line, chrome plated solid brass, black outline of ship, name in red **14.00**
Booklet
    Anchor Line, 32 pgs, black and white photos and text, *Cameronia I* illus on cov **28.00**
    Canadian Pacific, *St Lawrence Route to Europe*, 1930, 8 x 11", 16 pgs . **24.00**
    Independence, American Export Lines, 1966 Gala Springtime Cruise, itinerary and deck plan inserts **20.00**
    Passenger Ships owned by the US Government, int. and ext. photographs of ships, 1920s **36.00**
Bridge Score Pad, French Line, CGT logo in gold on pigskin cov **28.00**
Compact, *Empress of Canada*, Canadian Pacific Line, Stratton, line flag logo, ship's name in enameled front medallion **40.00**
Cigarette Lighter, *Queen Elizabeth II*, Cunard Line, Zippo **20.00**
Cruise Book, *Scythia*, 1929 .... **30.00**
Deck Plan
    Atlantis, Chandris Line, illus **8.00**
    France III, French Line, heavy stock paper **22.00**
    SS Hamburg, 1930, fold out **35.00**
    MV Westerdam, 1950, multicolored **15.00**
Diary, passenger's *My Trip Abroad*, leather cov, 1913 .... **20.00**
Dish, *Queen Mary*, Cunard Line, ceramic, 5" l, oval, color portrait, gold edge, Staffordshire **35.00**
Excursion Announcement, *SS Cuba* ... **20.00**
Goblet, *Queen Elizabeth II*, Cunard Line, souvenir, etched image and name, mfd by Stuart Crystal, #1305 **225.00**
Menu
    Andrea Doria **15.00**
    Empress of Canada I, Canadian Pacific Line, Easter, 1924, tassels ... **16.00**
    Johnson Line **10.00**
    Lafayette French Line, 1937 .... **5.00**
    Lancastria, Cunard Line, luncheon, 1939, color sailing ship on cov .. **15.00**
    Matson Line **7.00**
    Queen Elizabeth **20.00**
Passenger List
    RMS Aquitania, full color illus of ship **50.00**
    SS Leviathan, 1924 .... **15.00**
    St Louis, American Line, eastbound trip, Feb 10, 1906 .... **35.00**
    Transylvania II, Anchor Line, June 22, 1938, eastbound **18.00**

Pennant

RMS Queen Elizabeth I, Cunard Line, 10½" l, silky, portrait, ship name and lion logo, long red tassels ... **10.00**

SS Princess Anne, 25½" l, maroon, felt, VFC logo in white, tinted white, gray, and light green cruise ship illus, c1930 .... **8.00**

Pinback Button

Carnival Cruises **3.00**

RMS Queen Elizabeth I, Cunard Line, 1¾", photo, "World's Largest Liner" at bottom **8.00**

Playing Cards, *Alaska Steamship* **15.00**

Post Card

Carconia II, Cunard Line, green, port side **5.00**

Philadelphia, American Line, color, NY Harbor scene **15.00**

President Wilson, American President Lines, color, Oriental harbor **8.00**

SS Baltic Steamship **5.00**

Print, *Titanic,* 15 x 22½", black and white, text of sinking, published by Tichnor Bro, Boston **60.00**

Program, *Cunard,* 1928 .... **7.00**

Souvenir Spoon

Cunard *White Star,* demitasse, silver plated, hallmark **18.00**

Transylvania Anchor Line, silver plated, twisted handle, blue enameled ring, flag, and crest **75.00**

Stationery

Queen Mary, Cunard Line, note paper, matching envelope, color portrait, line, and ship name, 5 x 7" . **10.00**

Sylvania, Cunard Line, beige, color portrait, line, and ship name, 5¼ x 6¾" **8.00**

Stock Certificate, Cunard Steam Ship Co, Ltd **7.50**

Tie Clasp, *Queen Mary,* Cunard Line, goldtone, red, white, and blue enameled ship **15.00**

Tin Container, *Queen Mary,* Cunard Line, Benson's Candy, McDowell illus, oct, 5 x 8 x 1¾" **24.00**

Tip Tray, American Line Ship **100.00**

View Book, Royal Mail Cabin Liners, int. views, 1924 .... **25.00**

OWL COLLECTIBLES

Collecting Hints: If you collect the "creature of the night" or the "wise old owl," any page of this book might conceivably contain an owl-related object since the owl theme can be found in hundreds of collectible categories. A sampling of these categories includes advertising trade cards, books, buttons, postcards, etc. But, don't confine yourself to these categories. Let your imagination be your guide.

Don't confine yourself just to old or antique owls. Owl figurines, owl themes on limited edition collectors' plates, and handcrafted items from modern artisans are plentiful. There are many examples available in every price range.

History: Owls have existed on earth for over sixty million years. They have been used as a decorative motif since before Christ. An owl was used with Athena on an ancient Greek coin.

Every culture has superstitions surrounding the owl. Some believe the owl represented good luck, others viewed it as an evil omen. The owl has remained a popular theme in Halloween material.

Of course, the owl's wisdom is often attached to scholarly pursuits. Expanding this theme, the National Park Service uses "Woodsey" to "Give A Hoot, Don't Pollute."

References: Allan W. Eckert and Karl E. Karalus, *The Owls Of North America,* Doubleday & Company, Inc. 1974; Faith Medlin, *Centuries Of Owls In Art And The Written Word,* Silvermine Publishers Incorporated, 1967; Heimo Mikkola, *Owls Of Europe,* Buteo Books, 1983; Jozefa Stuart, *The Magic Of Owls,* Walker Publishing Co., Inc., 1977; Krystyna Weinstein, *Owls, Owls: Fantastical Fowls,,* Buteo Books, 1985.

Periodical: *The Owl's Nest,* Howards Alphanumeric, P. O. Box 5491, Fresno, CA 93755.

Collectors' Club: Russell's Owl Collector's Club, P. O. Box 1292, Bandon, OR 97411.

Advisor: Donna L. Howard.

REPRODUCTION ALERT: Recently reproduction fruit crate labels with an owl motif have been seen at several antiques and collectibles dealers who wholesale to dealers. These labels are appearing at flea markets and in shops where they are being passed as originals.

The Westmoreland molds have been sold to several different manufacturers. The owl sitting on two books is being reissued with the original "W" still on top of the books. The three owl plate mold also was sold. As of fall 1987, no reproductions have been spotted.

The Imperial owl molds have also found new owners. Again, no reproductions have been seen, but chances are good they will appear in the near future.

Andirons, pr, 14" h overall, cast iron, copper wash, owls perched on branch, yellow glass eyes, c1920 ... **125.00**

Ashtray, 5½" w, tricorn, china, Nippon, green mark **165.00**

Bank

Brass, glass eyes **65.00**

Glass, 7", ruby **100.00**

Jar, yellow–brown glaze, black base, black int. glaze, 7" h, $12.50.

Tin, 2 x 2½", child size, owl pictured
on side **50.00**
Barometer, 11" h, carved, walnut, English **50.00**
Bell, brass, 4" h, emb feathers and features **45.00**
Book
    Lavine, Sigmund, *Wonders Of The
    Owl,* Dodd, Mead & Co, NY, 1971 **1.50**
    Mowat, Farley, *Owls In The Family,*
    Little, Brown & Co, 1961 .... **.35**
    Sparks and Soper, *Owls: Their Natural & Unnatural History,* Taplinger
    Pub., NY, 1970 .... **5.75**
Bookends, pr
    Brass, Frankart **35.00**
    Bronze, head, sgd "M Carr" **120.00**
    Van Briggle, green, matte finish .. **135.00**
Calendar Plate, owl on open book,
1912, Berlin, NE **25.00**
Calling Card Tray, 8½ x 7", quadruple
plate, emb music staff and "Should
Owl's Acquaintance Be Forgot," two
owls sitting on back of tray **85.00**
Candy Container, 4⅜" h, glass, screw
cap closure on bottom **125.00**
Clock
    Metal, 2" dial, Bentley, German **25.00**
    Wood, 6½" h, hand carved **110.00**
Cookie Jar, ceramic
    11" h, cream, one winking eye, Shawnee **50.00**
    12" h, Woodsey Owl, green hat lid . **65.00**
Decoy, 13", papier mache, two faced,
glass eyes, brown coloring, small
white area on chest **65.00**
Degenhart
    Amberina **35.00**
    Custard **35.00**
    Holly Green **20.00**
    Red Carnival **80.00**
    Vaseline **45.00**

Fairy Lamp
    Double faced figure, 3⅜" d, 4⅛" h,
    pyramid size, frosted cranberry
    glass, lavender enameled eyes,
    Clarke base **200.00**
    Painted eyes, 4" h, Clarke base **225.00**
    Three sided, bisque, owl, cat, and
    dog **250.00**
Figure
    Cybis, baby **75.00**
    Fenton, carnival glass, 3" **18.00**
    Mosser, carnival glass, 4" **20.00**
    Viking, 8½", orange **100.00**
    Westmoreland, black glass, sits on
    two books, rhinestone eyes **24.00**
Humidor, 6¾" h, octagonal, Nippon .. **375.00**
Inkwell, 8 x 4", brass, glass inset, hinged
lid, pen tray, 2" owl figure **75.00**
Jewelry, pin, blue, green, and gold
enamel, amber eyes with rhinestone
eye disks, pearl tail feathers **15.50**
Lamp, candle, 5¼", snow white china,
owl shaped shade, stump shaped
base, fitted candleholder, marked "R
S Germany" **225.00**
Letter Opener, bronze **30.00**
Mask, papier mache, c1915 .... **90.00**

Tape Measure, brass top, glass eyes, marked "Germany," 1⅜" d, $35.00.

Match Holder
    2½" h, dark green, Wetzel Glass Co **5.00**
    8" h, 3" w, metal, hanging type **18.00**
Medal
    Bronze
        American Numismatic Society,
        member's medal, 67 mm d, obv.:
        owl and oak leaves, rev.: oak sapling, designed by Frank Eliscu,
        1977 .... **25.00**
        Natural History Society of Montreal, 1¾", cast, owl with branch
        in beak **20.00**
    Metal, white, 2¼", 1890 Leeds International Exhibition, bust of Queen
    Victoria on one side **25.00**

Mustard Jar, milk glass, 5" h, screw top,
glass insert, Atterbury, cov **165.00**
Napkin Ring
  China, owl sitting on stump, Nippon **225.00**
  Silver plated, owl standing **145.00**
Owl Drug Co
  Bottle, cork top, 3½" h, 1 oz, clear,
    Oil of Sweet Almond label **4.00**
  Shot Glass, clear
    One wing **14.50**
    Two wing **13.50**
  Tin, 4¼" d, 3" h, "Theatrical Cold
    Cream," orange ground, black print **24.50**
Paperweight, cast iron, owl family, two
  babies, plus baby in papa's arms ... **35.00**
Pitcher
  China, cov, 9½", semi-vitreous, Ed-
    win M Knowles China Co **37.50**
  Glass
    Clear, ruby, owl **95.00**
    Pressed, 8" h, 6" d top, owl shape **110.00**
Plate
  Barn Owl, 1976 Wildlife, Goebel .. **38.00**
  Milk Glass
    Owl Lovers, 7½" **40.00**
    Three owl heads, 6" d, fluted open
      work edge, gold paint **65.00**
    Three owls, Westmoreland **25.00**
Quilt, cigar silks, 5¢ Owls, single-bed
  size **450.00**
Ring Tree, 3¼" d, 4" h, shallow brown
  dish, blue lining, brown and tan owl
  perched on back, marked "Doulton
  Stoneware" **325.00**
Salt and Pepper Shakers, pr, china, 3¼",
  brown and white, mortarboard hats,
  scholarly expression, horn rim glasses **6.50**
Sheet Music
  Beautiful Ohio, owl on cover **3.50**
  The Pansy and the Owl **4.50**
  The Wise Old Owl **3.50**
Slot Machine, Delicious Confection,
  Mills Novelty 5¢, SC Co, Chicago . **2,200.00**
Stein, half liter, "Bibite" on shield held
  between claws, Mettlach #2036 ... **950.00**
Thermometer, 6" h, plaster body **75.00**
Trivet, Frankoma Pottery **4.00**
Valentine, 15" l, girl and boy riding bal-
  loon, owl sitting on moon above,
  "Nobody's looking but the owl and
  the moon!" **8.00**
Vase
  7", moriage owl, two handles, blue
    maple leaf Nippon mark **230.00**
  8¼", Knifewood, Weller **150.00**
  12½", ruffled rim, two handles, 4
    feet, marked on bottom "Royal Ni-
    shiki Nippon Hand Painted" **350.00**
Watch Fob, owl, chain made of braided
  human hair **125.00**

PADEN CITY

Collecting Hints: All Paden City glass was hand-made and unmarked. The early glassware was of non-descript quality, but in the early 1930s quality improved dramatically. The cuttings were un-polished "gray cuttings," sometimes mistaken for etchings.

Paden City is noted for its colors: opal (opaque white), ebony, mulberry, Cheriglo (delicate pink), yellow, dark green (forest), crystal, amber, prim-rose (reddish-amber), blue, rose, and the ever popular red. No free-blown or opalescent glass was produced. Quantities of blanks were sold to decorating companies for gold and silver overlay and for etching.

History: Paden City Glass Manufacturing Co. was founded in 1916 in Paden City, West Virginia. David Fisher, formerly of the New Martinsville Glass Manufacturing Co., operated the company until his death in 1933 when his son, Samuel, became president. The additional financial burden placed on the company by the acquisition of American Glass Co. in 1949 forced Paden City to close in 1951.

Reference: Jerry Barnett, *Paden City The Color Company,* published by author, 1978.

Periodical: *Paden City Party Line,* 1630 Colby Ave. # 5, Los Angeles, CA 90025.

Candy Dish, amethyst, etched, dots, floral and vine dec, 6⅝" h, $55.00.

Animal
  Cottontail Rabbit
    Blue **85.00**
    Crystal **60.00**
  Pony, 11½" h **100.00**
  Rooster, 9½" **70.00**
  Squirrel on log **40.00**
Batter Set, two crystal pitchers, floral
  etching, black glass lids and tray ... **90.00**
Bowl
  6½", Caliente, yellow **5.00**

8¾", Orchid, cobalt blue **30.00**
9", Caliente, orange **12.00**
11¼", Largo, red, handles **28.00**
Cake Stand, 11", Black Forest, low foot **60.00**
Candlesticks, pr
   Caliente, orange **15.00**
   Cheriglo **28.00**
   Garrett, black **30.00**
Candy Dish, Mrs. B, three part, ruby,
   gold filigree **50.00**
Centerpiece Bowl, blue bowl, crystal
   flower frog **17.00**
Champagne, Popeye and Olive, ruby . **10.00**
Cheese and Cracker Server, Glades, co-
   balt blue **48.00**
Cocktail Shaker Set, twelve red hour
   glass shaped glasses, matching shaker **125.00**
Compote
   6½", Crow's Foot, ruby **24.00**
   7½", Ardith etching, oval **22.50**
Cordial, Cupid **30.00**
Creamer
   Crow's Foot, white milk glass **10.00**
   Cupid **20.00**
Cup and Saucer
   Caliente
      Aqua **2.00**
      Cobalt Blue **6.00**
      Orange **6.00**
   Largo, dark green **10.00**
Console Set, Gazebo etch, crystal, 3 pcs **110.00**
Cordial Decanter, Glades, red **50.00**
Cruet, #210, yellow **30.00**
Goblet, Penny Line **8.50**
Ice Tub, Nora Bird **48.00**
Mayonnaise Set, Gadroon, ruby, 3 pcs **20.00**
Pitcher, Popeye and Olive, green **30.00**
Plate
   6", Caliente, aqua **2.00**
   7½", Black Forest **50.00**
   9", Caliente
      Aqua **4.50**
      Orange **4.50**
   10", Cupid, green **15.00**
   12", Popeye and Olive, ruby **18.00**
Reamer, green, etched, two quart, 2 pcs **100.00**
Salad Bowl, 10", Caliente, orange **13.00**
Salt and Pepper Shakers, pr
   Caliente, aqua **5.00**
   Party Line, ruby **45.00**
   Penny Line
      Cobalt, flat **50.00**
      Red, ftd **65.00**
Server, Gazebo, center handle, light
   blue **35.00**
Sherbet, Peacock Reverse **25.00**
Sugar, cov
   Nora Bird, Cheriglo **35.00**
   Peacock and Wild Rose **24.00**
Tumbler
   Nora Bird **25.00**
   Party Line, 5", ftd, ruby **13.00**

Vase
   6¼", Black Forest, pink **48.00**
   8¼", Leia Bird, elliptical, green **80.00**
   10", Crow Foot, milk glass, floral dec . **66.00**
   12", California Poppy **125.00**

PADLOCKS

Collecting Hints: Collectors like to determine the age of their padlocks and identify their unmarked ones. This has also been difficult. Good reference books on old padlocks are hard to find. The best sources are old catalogs which are scarce and usually expensive. Yale & Towne Co, Miller Lock Co, E. T. Fraim Lock Co, Slaymaker Lock Co, and Eagle Lock Co are among the few manufacturers that issued catalogs. Almost all padlocks were sold by jobbers, or wholesale hardware companies to users or retailers. The jobber catalogs contain a limited variety of padlocks and give some clues on their age. A comprehensive book covering US lock companies, their padlocks, and padlock construction has not been published.

The most desirable old padlocks are cast in brass or iron. They are embossed, not stamped, with company names, logos, or decorative florals, scrolls, and figures. Other valued padlocks have odd shapes or unique construction.

Some collectors specialize in just one type of padlock (combination, logo, etc.) or a specific manufacturer. The reason is the breadth of the field and the wealth of locks made by the 200-plus manufacturers. The Eagle Lock Co., for example, made about 400 types and variations between 1880 and 1930. The most competitive collecting is in the embossed brass locks from defunct short line railroads or the very early locks from larger railroads.

Collectors will not knowingly buy padlocks if they are repaired, cracked, corrosion pitted, damaged internally, or appreciably dented. A rare lock at a greatly reduced price can be an exception. An original key increases the value of a padlock, but other keys have no value to most collectors.

Most collectors prefer American manufactured padlocks.

History: Padlocks of all shapes and sizes were made in Europe and Asia from the 1600s. The mass production of identifiable padlocks was pioneered in the United States in the mid-1800s. Almost all padlock mechanisms were adapted from earlier door and safe lock patents.

Over 200 United States padlock manufacturers have been identified. Six of the most prolific are:

   Adams & Westlake, 1857– , "Adlake" trademark started c1900, made railroad locks.
   Eagle Lock Co., 1833–1976, a general

line of padlocks from 1880, with padlock patent dates from 1867.

Mallory, Wheeler & Co., 1865–1910, partnership history started in 1834, predominate manufacturer of wrought iron lever (smokies) padlock.

Miller Lock Co. (D. K. Miller from 1870 to c1880, Miller Lock Co. to 1930), general line of padlocks.

Star Lock Works, 1836–1926, largest manufacturer of Scandinavian padlocks.

Yale & Towne Mfg. Co., 1884– , Yale Lock Mfg. Co. from 1868 to 1884, started c1840 by Linus Yale, Sr., as the "Yale Lock Shop," started making padlocks c1875.

Railroad, express, and logo locks are identified with the names of the companies that bought and used them. A series of odd and heart-shaped cast iron padlocks produced from about 1880 to 1900 with various decorative or figural embossments are called "Story Locks."

Thousands of companies had locks custom made with their names to create logo locks. Logo locks are not to be confused with locks that are embossed with the names of jobbers. This applies particularly to the round six lever push key locks. If "6–Lever" is included with the name, it is not a logo lock. Since 1827 there have been over 10,000 railroad companies in the United States, not counting trolleys and interurbans. Most of these companies used at least two types of locks; some used dozens of types.

Padlock Types: Padlocks are categorized primarily according to tradition or use: Story, Railroad, etc. The secondary listing theme is according to the type of construction. For example: if a brass lever lock is marked with a railroad name, it is called a railroad lock. Scandinavian locks have always been called "Scandinavians." "Story" locks became a common usage term in the 1970s. In the 1880s they were listed in various ways.

Reference: Franklin M. Arnall, *The Padlock Collector, Illustrations and Prices of 1,800 Padlocks of the Last 100 Years, Fifth Edition,*The Collector, 1988.

Collectors' Club: American Lock Collectors Association, 36076 Grennada, Livonia, MI 48154. Bimonthly newsletter.

Museum: Lock Museum of America, Terryville, CT.

Advisor: Franklin M. Arnall.

REPRODUCTION ALERT: Beware of brass story locks, locks from the Middle East, railroad switch locks from Taiwan, and switch lock keys from the US Midwest. Early story locks should be embossed cast iron. However, beware. There are excellent iron reproductions of the skull and crossbones story lock.

Screw key, trick, iron lever, and brass lever locks are being imported from the Middle East. The Taiwan switch locks are rougher and lighter in color than the old brass ones. The crudely cast new switch keys are obvious. The high quality counterfeits are expertly stamped with various railroad initials, tumbled to simulate wear, and aged with acid. They can be detected only by an expert.

Authentic railroad, express, and logo locks will have only one user name or set of initials. The size and shape will be like other locks that were in common use at the time, except for a few modified locks made for the US government.

All components of an old lock must have exactly the same color and finish. The front, back, or drop of an old lock can be expertly replaced with a reproduced part embossed with the name or initials of a railroad, express company, or other user.

Note: The prices shown are for padlocks in original condition and without keys.

Combination

Iowa Lock & Mfg Co, zinc alloy, 3½"	**90.00**
J.B.M.K.L., steel, 3¼" h	**5.00**
J.B. Miller Keyless Lock Co, zinc alloy, 2⅞" h	**5.00**
Junkunc Bros Mfrs, brass, round, 2¼" h	**10.00**
Junkunc Safe & Lock Co, brass, round, 1¼" h	**50.00**
Miller Keyless Lock Co, iron, emb, 3¼" h	**75.00**
No-Key, The Edwards Mfg co, brass, 2¾" h	**25.00**
Sesamee, brass, dials on bottom, 2½" h	**15.00**
Sesamee, Corbin, brass, 3" h	**3.00**
"Your Own" Keyless, brass, emb, 3⅞" h	**275.00**

Commemorative

Missouri state seal front, 1904 Exposition, brass, emb, 2" h	**75.00**
P.P.I.E., 1915 Panama Pacific Exposition, steel, emb, 3" h	**175.00**
St. Louis World's Fair, 1904, steel, brass plates, emb, USA on front, Louisiana Purchase Exposition on back, 3⅝" h	**375.00**
Corbin, emb, 2⅞" h	**4.00**
Good Luck, Barnes Man'fg Co, emb, 2" h	**40.00**

Heart Shape

3" h, various manufacturers	**10.00**
3¼" h, Browns Patent	**25.00**
Keenkutter, E C Simmons, emb, 3⅞" h	**75.00**

Brass Lever, emb "BBB," 3¼" h, $65.00.

O V B, Our Very Best, emb, 2⅞" h .	**75.00**
Rugby, emb, 2¾" h	**12.00**
Winchester, emb raised letters, 3" h	**125.00**
Yale, Y & T, rect, emb	
1¼ to 2" w	**4.00**
3" w	**70.00**

Lever Iron & Steel
Bear, emb, steel, 2⅞" h	**5.00**
Dragons, emb, steel, 2¾" h	**10.00**
Eagle, emb, steel	
2" h	**2.00**
2¾" h	**5.00**
Indian Head, emb front, steel, 3" h .	**30.00**
Pyes Patent, iron, 3½" h	**25.00**
S. Andrews, iron, 3" h	**300.00**
Yale	
2⅝" h, steel and iron	**5.00**
5" h, rect, emb, iron	**130.00**

Lever Push Key
Achilles, steel, 3⅝" h	**50.00**
Champion Six Lever, brass, emb, 2¼"	
d	**5.00**
Favorite Six Lever, brass, emb, 2¼" d	**10.00**
Romer & Co, 86, brass, 1¾" h	**20.00**
The Smith & Egge Mfg Co, brass, 3"	
h	**25.00**
Vulcan Hardware Co, brass, keyhole	
in shoulder, 4" h	**350.00**
Yale, steel case, brass caps, 2¼" h . .	**5.00**

Lever Wrought Iron (Shield, Smoke House, Smokies)
Dog, emb brass drop, 4½" h	**40.00**
M. W. & Co, brass drop and escutch-	
eons, 3½" h	**5.00**
R & E Co on brass drop, brass escutch-	
eons, 4" h	**15.00**
S & Co, brass drop, 3½" h	**5.00**

Logo
B of E, brass lever type	**10.00**
Hudson Motor Car Co, emb, Yale . .	**50.00**
I H Co, International Harvester, emb,	
2¼" d	**150.00**
Marine, Hurd	**5.00**
New York Telephone co, 1897, brass	
lever type	**30.00**
Ordnance Dept, emb, Yale	**5.00**
Phillips 66, Best	**10.00**

Pin Tumbler
Corbin, brass case	
1½ to 2" w	**2.00**
3" w	**60.00**
Ellis Lock Co, steel, 2¾" h	**20.00**
Segal, brass case	
3" h	**5.00**
3¾" h, keyhole in front	**35.00**
Unit, brass, 3" h	**35.00**
Winchester, emb, brass case	**125.00**
Yale, emb, brass case	**2.00**

Railroad, G P and Signal
I C R R, emb, brass, 2¼" d	**80.00**
Illinois Central Signal, emb, brass . .	**15.00**
K C S R Y, emb, brass, 2¼" d	**250.00**
Missouri Pacific, emb, brass	**35.00**
S. P. Co, steel	**8.00**
Santa Fe, emb, brass, v shape bottom	**110.00**
Southern Pacific, Keenkutter, emb . .	**250.00**

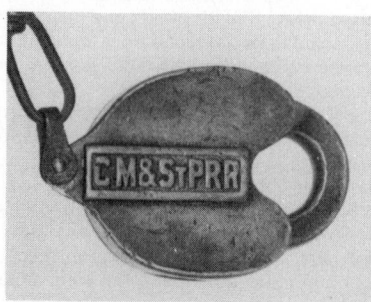

Railroad Switch Lock, CM & ST PRR, emb, $90.00.

Railroad, Switch
BA & P, emb, brass	**300.00**
CCC & ST L RY, emb, brass	**100.00**
CRI & P RR, stamped, brass	**40.00**
D & RG RR, WS, stamped, brass . . .	**75.00**
DRI & NWR, emb, brass	**400.00**
GB & W RR, stamped, brass	**30.00**
I C RR, stamped, steel	**4.00**
N & W, emb back, brass	**35.00**
NPRR, emb, brass	**100.00**
NYCS, Mon, stamped, iron	**35.00**
PRR, emb back, brass	**100.00**
STL & SF RY, stamped, brass	**40.00**
STL SW RY, Yale, stamped, steel . . .	**15.00**
STL SW Ry Co, emb, brass	**150.00**
Union Pacific CS21 Roadway &	
Bridge, emb, brass	**35.00**
U S Y of O, stamped, brass	**12.00**

Scandinavian
Dog, bull on other side, emb, brass,	
2½" h	**75.00**
J H W Climax, iron	
3½" h	**20.00**
6" h	**250.00**
999, emb, brass, 2½" h	**35.00**
Star emb bottom, iron, 2¾" h	**18.00**

Scandinavian, F. A. Hellsero, iron, 2⅝" h, $90.00.

Six Lever and Eight Lever
Corbin Iron clad Six Lever, steel	4.00
Goliath Eight Lever, steel	10.00
Quality Six Lever, Simmons, steel ..	4.00
Stilleto Six Lever, steel	12.00
Winchester Six Lever, emb, steel ...	60.00

Story, Embossed Cast Iron
Floral and scroll, shield shape	
2⅜" h	90.00
3⅝" h	150.00
Floral and eye front, floral back, The "Evil Eye" lock	500.00
Mail Box, aluminum finish	250.00
Skull and Crossbones, floral front, "NH" back	175.00

Warded
Army, US on other side, emb, round case, iron	8.00
Floral and scroll, rect case, iron or brass	10.00
Fordloc, emb, brass case	10.00
S & E, 1877, emb, iron	100.00
Safe, emb, iron, heart shape	40.00
Yale, iron case, brass panels	4.00

PAPER DOLLS

Collecting Hints: Most paper dolls are collected in uncut books, sheets, or boxed sets. Cut sets are priced at 50% of an uncut set providing all dolls, clothing, and accessories are present.

Many paper doll books have been reprinted. An identical reprint is just slightly lower in value. If the dolls have been redrawn, the price is reduced significantly.

Barbara Ferguson's *The Paper Doll* has an excellent section on the care and storage of paper dolls.

History: The origin of the paper doll rests with the jumping jacks (pantins) of Europe. By the 19th century famous dancers, opera stars, Jenny Lind, and many general subjects were available in boxed or die-cut sheet form. Raphael Tuck in England began to produce ornate dolls in series form in the 1880s.

The advertising industry turned to paper dolls to sell products. Early magazines, such as *Ladies's Home Journal, Good Housekeeping,* and *McCall's,* used paper doll inserts. Children's publications, like *Jack and Jill,* picked up the practice.

The paper doll books first appeared in the 1920s. The cardboard covered books made paper dolls available to the mass market. Leading companies were Lowe, Merrill, Saalfield, and Whitman. The 1940s saw the advent of the celebrity paper doll books. Celebrities were drawn from screen and radio, followed later by television personalities. A few comic characters, such as Brenda Starr, also made it to paper doll fame.

The growth of television in the 1950s saw a reduction in the number of paper doll books produced. The modern books are either politically or celebrity oriented.

References: Marian B. Howard, *Those Fascinating Paper Dolls: An Illustrated Handbook For Collectors,* Dover, 1981; Martha K. Krebs, *Advertising Paper Dolls: A Guide For Collectors,* two volumes, privately printed, 1975; Barbara Chaney Ferguson, *The Paper Doll: A Collector's Guide With Prices,* Wallace-Homestead, 1982; Mary Young, *A Collector's Guide To Paper Dolls: Saalfield, Lowe, and Merrill,* Collector Books, 1980; Mary Young, *A Collector's Guide To Paper Dolls, Second Series,* Collector Books, 1984.

Collectors' Club: United Federation of Doll Clubs, P. O. Box 14146, Parkville, MO 64152.

Periodicals: *Celebrity Doll Journal,* 6 Court Place, Puyallup, WA 98372; *Doll Reader,* Hobby House Press Inc, 900 Frederick St, Cumberland, MD 21502; *Midwest Paper Dolls & Toys Quarterly,* P.O. Box 131, Galesburg, KS 66740; *Paper Doll News,* P.O. Box 807, Vivian, LA 71082; Original Doll Artist Guild, Paper Doll Haven, Box 507, Sharpee, FL 32959.

Museums: Children's Museum, Indianapolis, IN; Detroit Children's Museum, Detroit, MI; Kent State University Library, Kent, OH; Museum of the City of New York, New York, NY; Newark Museum, Newark, NJ; The Margaret Woodbury Strong Museum, Rochester, NY.

Notes: Prices are based on uncut, mint, original paper dolls in book or uncut sheet form. It is not unusual for two different titles to have the same number in a single company.

BOOKS

American Colortype Co
102, Margy & Mildred, 1927	18.00
203, Corinne, 13"	30.00

Artcraft
    4330, Oliver, 4 pgs, 1968 ....   **10.00**
    5114, Nanny & Professor, 6 dolls, 4
        pgs, 1971 ....   **20.00**
    5140, Julia, 5 dolls, 4 pgs, 1971 ...   **25.00**
Avalon Industries, Teena The Teenager   **5.00**
Boucher, A Friend Paper Doll, scissors,
    1967 ....   **5.00**
Burton Playthings
    275, Your Own Quintuplets, 1935 .   **25.00**
    875, Dotty & Danny on Parade, 1935   **25.00**
    975, Sally Dimple, 1935 ....   **25.00**
Dennison Mfg
    11, Design A Doll, 1950 ....   **8.50**
    37, Dennison Dolls & Dresses **30.00**
EP Dutton, 3159, Dainty Dollies & Their
    Dresses **45.00**
Gabriel & Sons, Samuel
    D90, Betsy McCall, Biggest Paper
        Doll, 1955 ....   **20.00**
    D112, Moving Eye Dolly, Toddling
        Tom, 1920 ....   **25.00**
    D116, Pony Tail **15.00**
    D117, Carol & Her Dresses **18.00**
    D132, The Wedding Party **30.00**
    D134, Toddler Twins **25.00**
    D141, Our Happy Family, 6 dolls,
        1929 ....   **25.00**
Londy Card Corp, Big Sister, 1932 ....   **5.00**
McLoughlin
    Let's Play Paper Dolls, 1938 ....   **20.00**
    Minnie Warren, complete, orig en-
        velope **110.00**
    Real Sleeping Doll, 1939 ....   **25.00**
Merrill Publishing Co
    1560, Fairliner Paper Doll Book, 2
        dolls, 8 pgs, 1953 ....   **7.50**
    2554, Janet Leigh Cutouts & Coloring,
        2 dolls **45.00**
    3404, Gone With The Wind, c1940   **250.00**
    3480, Deanna Durbin, 1940 ....   **170.00**
    3488, Dionne Quints, 1940 ....   **235.00**
    3497, Wedding of the Paper Dolls,
        Lucille Webster artist, 10 dolls ... **85.00**
    3500, Dionne Quints - Let's Play
        House, 1949 ....   **80.00**
    4326, Baby Sandy, 1941 ....   **185.00**
Merry Mfg
    4350, Baby Merry, 1964 ....   **8.00**
    6504, Wendy Walks, 1965 ....   **10.00**
Parker Bros, Miss America Magic Doll,
    1953 ....   **18.00**
Saalfield Publishing Co
    1180, Mary's Trousseau, cut, c1918   **8.00**
    1661, Gloria Jean, 1940 ....   **165.00**
    1730, Cinderella, 4 dolls, 4 pgs **15.00**
    1787, Shirley Temple Masquerade
        Costumes, 1940 ....   **185.00**
    2725, Joan Caulfield, 2 dolls 6 pgs,
        1953 ....   **40.00**
    4311, Arlene Dahl, 5 dolls, 8 pgs,
        1953 ....   **50.00**

Saalfield, Walking Paper Doll Family,
Ruth Upham, 1934, uncut, $25.00.

Stephens Publishing Co, c1950
    135, Playtime Fashions, 1946 ......   **7.50**
    175, Patty's Party **8.00**
    176, Triplet Dolls **8.00**
    177, Glamour Models **8.00**
Treasure Books, Shari Lewis, 5 pgs ...   **32.00**
Whitman
    Our Gang, 1931, clothes uncut **55.00**
    This Is Margie, 1939 ....   **45.00**
    1173, June Allyson, 8 pgs, 1953 ...   **60.00**
    1950, Roy Rogers and Dale Evans, 2
        dolls, 1956 ....   **35.00**
    1952, Doris Day, 2 dolls, 1956 ....   **25.00**
    1954, Barbie's Boutique, 1973 .....   **7.50**
    1978, Sabrina and The Archies, 6
        dolls, 6 pgs, 1971 ....   **12.00**
    1985, Buffy, 1 doll, 6 pgs, 1969 ...   **18.50**
    1986, Daisy & Donald, 4 dolls, 4 pgs,
        Walt Disney Productions, 1978 ..   **15.00**
    2050, Pat Crowley, 2 dolls, 8 pgs,
        1955 ....   **42.00**
    2061, Gale Storm, 2 dolls, 6 pgs ...   **45.00**

FOLDER

Dean & Son, Dolly's Wardrobe, chromo
    litho, c1910 ....   **75.00**
McLoughlin Bros
    Little Folks Army Book, c1895 .....   **85.00**
    Lizzie, 1 doll, c1870 ....   **150.00**
    Paul, 1 doll, c1870 ....   **90.00**

UNCUT SHEETS

Jack & Jill, Folk Festival, Philadelphia
    Mummers, Jan, 1951, Janet Smalley
    artist **10.00**
McCall's Magazine
    Betsy McCall
        Dress n' Play, 1963 ....   **12.00**
        Fashion Shop, 1959 ....   **15.00**
    Jack & Jill at Easter, March 1921, Bar-
        bara Hale artist, 2 dolls, c1921 ..   **12.00**

Valentine's Day Boy and Girl, Feb
1921, Barbara Hale artist **15.00**
Whitman, 2101, Lucille Ball & Desi Ar-
naz, 1953 . . . .   **75.00**

PAPERBACK BOOKS

Collecting Hints: For collecting or investment
purposes, books should be in fine or better condition because many titles are common in lesser
condition as well as being less desirable. Unique
items, such as paperbacks in dust jackets or in
boxes, often are more valuable and desirable.

Most collections are assembled around one or
more unifying themes. Some common themes
are: author (Edgar Rice Burroughs, Dashiell
Hammett, Louis L'Amour, Raymond Chandler,
Zane Grey, William Irish, Cornell Woolrich,
etc.); fictional genre (mysteries, science fiction,
westerns, etc.); publisher (early Avon, Dell and
Popular Library are most popular); cover artist
(Frank Frazetta, R. C. M. Heade, Rudolph Belarski, Roy Krenkel, Vaughn Bode, etc.); and books
with uniquely appealing graphic design (Dell
mapbacks and Ace double novels).

Because quantity lots of paperbacks still turn
up, many collectors are cautious as they assemble their collections. Books in the highest condition grades remain uncommon. Many current
dealers try to charge upper level prices for books
in lesser condition, arguing that top condition is
just too scarce. This argument is not valid, just
self-serving.

History: Paperback volumes have existed since
the 15th century. Mass–market paperback books,
most popular with collectors, date from the post
1938 period. The number of mass market publishers in the 1938-50 period was much greater
than today. These books exist in a variety of
formats, from the standard size paperback and
its shorter predecessor to odd sizes like 64 page
short novels for 10¢ and 5¼" x 7½" volumes
known as digests. Some books came in a dust
jacket; some were boxed.

The "golden" period for paperback books was
from 1939 to the late 1950s, a period generally
characterized by a lurid and colorful graphic
style of cover art and title lettering not unlike that
of the pulp magazines. A lot of early paperback
publishers had been or were publishers of pulps
and merely moved their graphic style and many
of their authors to paperbacks.

References: Kenneth Davis, *Two-Bit Culture:
The Paperbacking of America,* Houghton Mifflin,
1984; Kevin Hancer, *The Paperback Price Guide,
Third Edition,* Wallace-Homestead, 1989; Piet
Schreuders, *Paperbacks USA, A Graphic History,
1939–1959,* Blue Dolphin, 1981.

Periodicals: *Paperback Market,* 5813 York Avenue, Edina, MN 55410.

Museum: University of Minnesota's Hess Collection of Popular Literature, Minneapolis, MN.

Advisor: Kevin B. Hancer.

Note: The prices given are for books in fine condition. Divide by 3 to get the price for books in
good condition; increase price by 50% for books
in near mint condition.

Sports, *Baseball Stars of 1950,* Lion Library 150, Mickey Mantle cover, $10.00.

Adventure
Anderson, Poul, *Golden Slaves,*
Avon, T-388 . . . .   **4.00**
Burroughs, Edgar Rice, *Tarzan and
the Lost Empire,* Ace, F-169 . . . . .   **4.00**
Chidsey, Donald Barr, *Panama Pas-
sage,* Perma Book, P248 . . . .   **2.00**
Fox, Gardner F., *Woman of Kali,* Gold
Medal, 438 . . . .   **4.00**
Horner, Lance, *Rogue Roman,* Gold
Medal, T1978, cov by Frazetta . . .   **3.00**
Lindsay, Phillip, *Sir Rusty Sword,* Har-
lequin, 225 . . . .   **10.00**
Raddall, Thomas, *Roger Sudden,* Har-
lequin, 141 . . . .   **9.00**
Scotland, Jay, *Traitor's Legion,* Ace,
G-532, Jay Scotland is a pseu-
donym for John Jakes **5.00**
Siegel, Jerry, *High Camp Superheroes,*
Belmont, B50-695, comic book re-
prints from the co-creator of Super-
man **4.00**
Yerby, Frank, *Captain Rebel,* Cardi-
nal, C249 . . . .   **2.00**
Biography
Cellini, Benvenuto, *The Autobiogra-
phy of Cellini,* Boni Book **4.00**
Donovan, B., *Eichman—Man of
Slaughter,* Avon, T-464 . . . .   **2.00**
Guild, Leo, *The Loves of Liberace,*
Avon, T-118 . . . .   **8.00**
Martin and Miller, *The Story of Walt
Disney,* Dell, D266 . . . .   **3.00**

Murphy, Audie, *To Hell and Back*, Perma Book, M4029 .... **2.00**

Thomas, T. T., *I, James Dean*, Popular Library, W400 .... **6.00**

Wright, W., *Life and Loves of Lana Turner*, Wisdom House, 104 ..... **2.00**

Movie, *Brigitte Bardot Story,* **Belmont L504, $20.00.**

Combat

Bartlett and Lay, *Twelve O'Clock High*, Bantam, 743 .... **4.00**

Boyington, Gregory, *Baa Baa Black Sheep*, Dell, F88 .... **2.00**

Busch, Harold, *U-Boats at War*, Ballantine, 120 .... **4.00**

Grove, Walt, *The Wings of Eagles*, Gold Medal, 649, tie-in with John Wayne movie **5.00**

Tiempo, E. K., *Cry Slaughter*, Avon, T-179 .... **2.00**

Uris, Leon, *Battle Cry*, Bantam, F1996 .... **3.00**

Erotica/Esoterica

Bingham, Carson, *The Gang Girls*, Monarch, 372 .... **10.00**

Cargo, Francis, *Perversity*, Berkley, G-33 .... **4.00**

Drago, Sinclair, *Women to Love*, Novel Library, 16 .... **6.00**

Farmer, Philip Jose, *Fire and the Night*, Regency, 118 .... **6.00**

Leem Hannah, *Yaller Gal*, Handi-Book, 84 .... **5.00**

Swados, Felice, *House of Fury*, Avon, 298 .... **20.00**

Thayer, Tiffany, *One Man Show*, Avon, 327 .... **6.00**

Van Vechten, Harold, *Nigger Heaven*, Avon, 314 .... **28.00**

Whitney, Hallan, *Backwoods Shack*,

Carnival, 943, Whitney is a pseudonym for Harry Whittington **8.00**

Woodford, Jack, *The Abortive Hussy*, Avon, 146 .... **4.00**

Horror

Avallane, Michael, *The Coffin Things*, Lancer, 74-942 .... **5.00**

Bloch, Robert, *Firebug*, Regency, 101 **8.00**

Bradbury, Ray, *The Autumn People*, Ballantine, EC, comic reprints with Frazetta cov **8.00**

Davenport, Basil (ed.), *Tales to be Told in the Dark*, Ballantine, 380 . **3.00**

Finney, Jack, *The Body Snatchers*, Dell, 42 .... **10.00**

Lovecraft, H. P., *Weird Shadow over Innmouth*, Bart House, 4 .... **25.00**

Stoker, Bram, *Dracula*, Perma Book, M4088, tie-in with Christopher Lee movie **5.00**

Humor

Addams, Charles, *Drawn and Quartered*, Pocket Books, 1964 .... **4.00**

Capp, Al, *L'il Abner*, Ballantine, 350K, tie-in with movie **4.00**

Cavanaugh and Weir, *Dell Book of Jokes*, Dell, 89 .... **24.00**

Gaines, William (ed.), *The Brothers Mad*, Ballantine, 267K **4.00**

Hatlo, Jimmy, *They'll Do It Every Time*, Avon, 366 .... **5.00**

Kurtzman, Harvey, *Help!*, Gold Medal, K1485 .... **3.00**

Links, Marty, *Bobby Sox*, Popular Library, 678 .... **3.00**

Romance, *Ex–Wife,* **Dell 277, classic mapback, $5.00.**

Mystery

Adams, Cleve, *And Sudden Death*, Prize Mystery, 5 .... **6.00**

Barry, Joe, *The Third Degree*, Prize Mystery, 12 .... **6.00**

Bliss, Tip, *The Broadway Butterfly Murders*, Checkerbook, 2 . . . .   **15.00**

Carr, J. D., *The Four False Weapons*, Berkley, G-91 . . . .   **4.00**

Carter, Nick, *Death has Green Eyes*, Vital Book, 3 . . . .   **6.00**

Hammett, Dashiell, *Hammett Homicides*, Bestseller, B81 . . . .   **10.00**

Irish, William, *Bluebeard's Seventh Wife*, Popular Library, 473 . . . .   **10.00**

Lyon, Dana, *I'll Be Glad When You're Dead*, Quick Reader, 132 . . . .   **5.00**

Woolrich, Cornell, *The Black Curtain*, Dell, 208 . . . .   **6.00**

Non-fiction

Blackstone, Harry, *Blackstone's Tricks Anyone Can Do* , Perma Book, 15   **7.50**

Disney, Walt, *Our Friend the Atom*, Dell, LB117 . . . .   **1.50**

Galus, Henry, *Unwed Mothers*, Monarch, 524, Robert Maguire cov . . .   **5.00**

Hershfield, Harry, *Book of Jokes*, Avon, 65 . . . .   **10.00**

Hynd, Alan, *We are the Public Enemies*, Gold Medal, 101 . . . .   **6.00**

Sinclair, Gordon, *Bright Path to Adventure*, Harlequin, 288 . . . .   **9.00**

Vagts, Alfred, *Hitler's Second Army*, Penguin, S214 . . . .   **3.00**

Romance

Baldwin, Faith, *Men are Such Fools*, Dell, 138 . . . .   **5.00**

Bronte, Emily, *Wuthering Heights*, Quick Reader, 122 . . . .   **8.00**

Christian, Paula, *Edge of Twilight*, Crest, 267 . . . .   **7.00**

Edmonds, Walter, *The Wedding Journey*, Dell, 10¢, 6 . . . .   **5.00**

Gaddis, Peggy, *Dr. Prescott's Secret*, Beacon, B302 . . . .   **6.00**

Howe, Cliff (ed.), *Lovers and Libertines*, Ace, D-271 . . . .   **4.00**

Kerr, Jean, *Please Don't Eat the Daisies*, Crest, s263 . . . .   **2.00**

Science Fiction

Campbell, John W., *Who Goes There?*, Dell, D-150 . . . .   **3.00**

deCamp, L. Sprague (ed.), *The Spell of Seven*, Pyramid, R-1192, Virgil Finlay cov **5.00**

Heinlein, Robert A., *Beyond this Horizon*, Signet, 1891 . . . .   **4.00**

Howard, Robert E., *Almuric*, Ace, F-305 . . . .   **6.00**

Hubbard, L. Ron, *Return to Tomorrow*, Ace, S-66 . . . .   **6.00**

Jones, Raymond, *The Deviates*, Beacon, 242 . . . .   **8.00**

Kline, Otis Adelbert, *Maza of the Moon*, Ace, F-321, Frazetta cov . .   **5.00**

Lafferty, R. A., *Space Chantey*, Ace H-56, Vaughn Bode cov **4.00**

Orwell, George, *Animal Farm*, Signet, 1289 . . . .   **5.00**

Silverberg, Robert, *Regan's Planet*, Pyramid, F-986 . . . .   **3.00**

Sports

DiMaggio, Joe, *Lucky to Be a Yankee*, Bantam, 506 . . . .   **4.00**

Jacobs, Bruce (ed.), *Baseball Stars of 1955*, Lion Library, LL12 . . . .   **5.00**

Robinson, Ray (ed.), *Baseball Stars of 1961*, Pyramid, G-605 . . . .   **2.50**

Scholz, Jackson, *Fighting Coach* Comet, 25 . . . .   **2.50**

Stern, Bill, *Bill Stern's Favorite Boxing Stories*, Pocket Books, 416 . . . . . .   **3.00**

Tully, Jim, *The Bruiser*, Bantam **2.00**

Western, *Stormy Range*, Bantam 1001, $6.00.

Western

Brackett, Leigh, *Rio Bravo*, Bantam, 1893, tie-in with John Wayne movie **8.00**

Fisher, Clay, *War Bonnet*, Ballantine, 11 . . . .   **4.00**

Grey, Zane, *Nevada*, Bantam, 3 . . . .   **3.50**

L'Amour, Louis, *Hondo*, Gold Medal, 347, tie-in with John Wayne movie   **8.00**

Lehman, Paul Evan, *Range Justice*, Star Books, 8 . . . .   **5.00**

Manfred, Frederick, *Lord Grizzly*, Cardinal, C192 . . . .   **4.00**

Old Scout, An, *Buffalo Bill's Leap for Life*, Gold Star, IL7-33, dime novel reprint **4.00**

Robertson, Frank C., *Red Rustlers*, Readers Choice Library, 24 . . . . . .   **4.00**

Sperry, Armstrong, *Wagons Westward*, Comet, 1 . . . .   **2.50**

Striker, Fran, *The Lone Ranger and the Secret of Thunder Mountain*, Bantam, 14 . . . .   **60.00**

PATRIOTIC COLLECTIBLES

Collecting Hints: Concentrate on one symbol, e.g., the eagle, flag, Statue of Liberty, Uncle Sam, etc. Remember that the symbol is not always the principal character on items. Don't miss examples with the symbol in a secondary role.

Colored material is more desirable than noncolored material. Much of the material is two dimensional, e.g., posters and signs. Seek three dimensional objects to add balance to a collection.

Much of the patriotic material focuses around our national holidays, especially the Fourth of July. Other critical holidays include Flag Day, Labor Day, Memorial Day, and Veterans' Day.

Finally, look to the foreign market. Our symbols are used abroad, both positively and negatively. One novel collection would be how Uncle Sam is portrayed on the posters and other materials from communist countries.

History: Patriotic symbols developed along with the American nation. The American eagle, among the greatest of our nation's symbols, was chosen for the American seal. As a result, the eagle has appeared on countless objects since that time.

Uncle Sam arrived on the American scene in the mid-19th century. He was firmly established by the Civil War. Uncle Sam did have female counterparts—Columbia and the Goddess of Liberty. He often appeared together with one or both of them on advertising trade cards, buttons, posters, textiles, etc.

Uncle Sam achieved his modern appearance largely through the drawings of Thomas Nast in *Harper's Weekly* and James Montgomery Flagg's famous World War I recruiting poster, "I Want You." Perhaps the leading promoter of the Uncle Sam image was the American toy industry. The American Centennial in 1876 and Bicentennial in 1976 also helped. A surge of Uncle Sam related toys occurred in the 1930s led by American Flyer's cheap version of an earlier lithographed tin, flatsided Uncle Sam bicycle string toy.

See: Flag Collectibles.

Columbia, advertising trade card, 3⅝ x 5½", titled "The President Suspender," Columbia depicted as sales clerk selling suspenders to Pres McKinley . **20.00**
Eagle
  Architectural Element, roof bird, cast iron, black **35.00**
  Bookends, 5½" l, cast white metal, worn **45.00**
  Cookie Cutter, tin, 6½" l **85.00**

Sheet Music, *Father of the Land We Love*, George M Cohan, cover artist James Montgomery Flagg, $6.00.

Figure, 6" h, pot metal, gold paint, standing **25.00**
Pinback Button
  1", National Cycle, red, white, and blue, star studded shield **25.00**
  1¼", NRA Consumer, "We Do Our Part," red, white, and blue **6.50**
  1½", Century Tire, celluloid, gold, red, white, and blue **50.00**
Tray, change, 4", Hebburn House Coal, eagle in center, holding banner, wood grain ground **42.50**
Flags and Shields
  Advertising, tray, 12" d, Jacob Metzger, American Brewing Co, Indianapolis, IN, trademark on star in center of flag **150.00**
  Automobile Set, five 4 x 5½" flags on 11" rods, 4 x 4" litho metal red, white, and blue diecut eagle shield flag holder, mounting clamp, orig 4 x 12" box, marked "Liberty Flags Sets For Automobiles, Jaymer Speciality Co," c1920 .... **25.00**
  Match Safe, 1½ x 2½", celluloid cov silvered brass, black and white bull dog standing on American flag as warships steam in background, inscribed "What We Have We'll Hold," reverse with black and white photo of Philadelphia businessman **80.00**
  Paper Dolls, Liberty Fair Dressing Doll, 7 x 13", blue and white box, Miss Liberty cardboard doll, flags on wood stick, cut, c1900 .... **45.00**
  Pin, 1 x 1¼", celluloid, diecut, red, white, and blue shield design, dark gold eagle, raised flipper inscribed "Hupmobile The Car Of The American Family On United America Tour," c1910 .... **35.00**

Pinback Button, ⅞" d

Americanism Club, red, white, and blue flag, white ground, blue letters **12.00**

Hop Ale, shows American flag and shield, c1907 .... **12.00**

Stickpin, adv, ¾ x 1", diecut, celluloid, red, white, and blue American flag on front, black and white adv text on reverse, brass stickpin, early 1900s

Artistic Pianos **10.00**

Eagle Mop Ringers and Ohio Detachable Mops **12.00**

Grande Andes Kitchen Ranges ... **12.00**

Watch Fob, 1", silvered brass, field shape, attached silvered brass horseshoe, raised eagle on front, red, white, and blue enameled name "American Badge Co," c1900 ... **25.00**

Franklin, Benjamin

Bookends, pr, cast white metal, bronzed **35.00**

Pinback Button, 1¼", Franklin Life Insurance Co, light sepia portrait bust of Franklin, sepia ground, red rim, white lettering, c1910 .... **12.00**

Liberty Bell

Bank, 4½" h, pot metal and wood, brown, marked "USA, 1947" ... **32.00**

Bread Plate, glass, Constitution signers' names, emb 1776–1876, clear **80.00**

Paperweight, 6", cast iron **50.00**

Pinback Button

¾"

General Accident Insurance, Philadelphia, blue and white, center bell, c1901 .... **10.00**

National Relief Assurance Co, Philadelphia, multicolored eagle and bell, dark blue ground, c1900 .... **12.00**

⅞", gold, red, white, and blue, Philadelphia Sesqui–Centennial, 1776–1926, small red, white, and blue flag, yellow and blue ribbon **10.00**

1¼", sepia, center bell, inscriptions "Phila 1776" and "St Louis 1904" **25.00**

Post Card

Independence Hall, Philadelphia, sepia **5.00**

Liberty Bell Trolley, insignia on front **7.50**

Sheet Music, "Liberty Bell Time To Ring Again," 1918 .... **3.50**

Tape Measure, 1¾" d, celluloid case, blue and white design, logo and inscription for Missouri and Kansas telephone company, reverse "When You Telephone, Use The Bell," cloth tape, c1900 .... **35.00**

Statue of Liberty

Advertising

Tin, Wiles Biscuits, octagonal, picture on cov **20.00**

Trade Card, Pratts Astrol Oil, night scene **18.00**

Bookmark, silk, Paris, 1878 .... **65.00**

Hat, heavy paper, "Liberty," red, white, and blue, picture of Statue, c1918 .... **20.00**

Lamp, 5½" h, dark copper finished white metal, holds small electrical bulb, wooden base, sliding base opens to hold battery, c1920 ..... **35.00**

Souvenir from Betsy Ross House, 7¼ x 4", muslin flag, cardboard card of C. H. Weisgerber painting, $25.00.

Mirror, 2½" round, tin, emb Statue of Liberty, reverse with American eagle, easel and ring, mirror inside . **65.00**

Pinback Button, 1¼", Liberty Hotel, New York City, Statue of Liberty illus, green text, white ground, c1912 .... **8.00**

Playing Cards, "606," US Playing Card Co, Cincinnati, OH, picture of Statue of Liberty and flags of nations, gold edges, complete, orig box **18.00**

Tie Slide, Boy Scout, 1¼ x 2", emb brass, detailed raised Statue, scroll banner at base, c1930 .... **20.00**

Uncle Sam

Advertising

Bank, 2¼ x 3", red, white, and blue, litho cardboard, silvered tin cap and bottom, issued by Poll Parrot Shoes **65.00**

Mirror, pocket, Watertown Times newspaper **75.00**

Puzzle, Uncle Sam's Tar Soap, Uncle Sam's National Puzzle, 4 x 4" box, 10 cards, advertising slogans, c1900 .... **30.00**

Sign

    4½" w, 8" h, "Use Jaxon Soap," Uncle Sam leaning on fence, jack knife in hand, whittling on stick, easel back **25.00**

    36 x 24", canvas, Uncle Sam selling US Paint, National Sign Co, Dayton, OH, c1910 .... **650.00**

Trade Card

    3½ x 5¼", Frank Millers Blacking, Uncle Sam type shaving with straight razor, using polished boot as mirror, eagle looking at reflection in another boot **18.00**

    3½ x 6¼", Hub Gore, Uncle Sam holding shoe, saying "Hub Gore Makers of Elastic For Shoes...It Was Honored At The World's Fair of 1893" **9.00**

Tray, Cascade Beer, San Francisco, Uncle Sam and five ethnic people **650.00**

Figure

    3 x 6 x 10", plaster, Uncle Sam, defense gun and binoculars, white paints, red stripe, blue belt, c1917 .... **35.00**

    16", plaster, Uncle Sam rolling up sleeves **30.00**

Magazine Tear Sheet, 5½ x 8½", Uncle Sam holding a "Health Bill" under his arm, looking at Cream of Wheat advertising billboard, copyright 1915 .... **20.00**

Pinback Button

    ¾", multicolored, Uncle Sam, money pouring from horn of plenty, "Federal Casualty Insurance, Detroit," c1907 .... **20.00**

    ⅞", multicolored, "Uncle Sam's Citizenship Training Corps," lieutenant rank, c1920 .... **18.00**

    1", red, white, and blue

        "Dental Health For Victory," oval, blue rim **12.00**

        "Good Teeth," Cincinnati Schools dental care program, 1930s **15.00**

    1¼"

        "Bound For Cuba," multicolored, black ground, white rim lettering, Uncle Sam with rifle and knapsack marching past sign, c1898 .... **35.00**

        "Onkel Gem Club," red, white, and blue figure, yellow ground, Nov 6, 1895 .... **30.00**

    1¾", multicolored, black inscription, "East End Improvement Society," Uncle Sam in center surrounded by firecrackers, July 4th 1920 celebration **75.00**

Post Card, multicolored **6.00**

Salt and Pepper Shakers, pr, 1½ x 2½ x 2", painted plaster, glossy white, black and red accents, red, white, and blue top hat **45.00**

Seals, "Patriotic Decorations," diecut gummed seals, each 1 x 1½", red, white, and blue, 2 x 2¼" cardboard packet, Dennison, ten of orig 25 seals, c1925 .... **15.00**

Sheet Music, "Wake Up, America!," lyrics by George Graff, Jr and music by Jack Glogau **18.00**

Stickpin, 1", diecut, white metal, tinted cherry red trousers and hat, blue coat, marching pose, c1898 . **20.00**

Watch Fob

    1¼ x 1½", brass, raised profile portrait of Uncle Sam above VFW symbol, inscribed "Dedication Uncle Sam Oakwood Cemetery," 1930s **20.00**

    1½ x 1½", silvered brass, raised portrait of Uncle Sam and IOOF Grand Lodge of NY State symbol, 1946 convention, Troy, NY **24.00**

Washington, George

    Pinback Button, 1¼", multicolored, portrait of Washington, dark red shaded to olive green ground, black inscription for Cherry Smash soft drink, c1912 .... **40.00**

    Post Card, multicolored **3.75**

    Sheet Music, "Father of the Land We Love," lyrics and music by George M Cohan, cover artist James Montgomery Flagg, 1931 .... **8.50**

    Tray, 7½ x 11", porcelain, portraits of George and Martha Washington, Mt Vernon, VA, titled "Washington's Home, Mt Vernon, VA" in center, multicolored, enhanced enameling, sq corners, gold trim, marked "Germany" **75.00**

PENS AND PENCILS

Collecting Hints: Any defects seriously affect the price downward. Defects include scratches, cracks, dents, warping, missing parts, bent levers, sprung clips, nib damage, and mechanical damage. Engraved initials or names do not detract seriously from the price.

History: The steel pen point or nib was invented by Samuel Harrison in 1780. It was not commercially produced in quantity until the 1880s when Richard Esterbrook entered the field. The holders became increasingly elaborate. Mother-of-pearl, gold, Sterling silver, and other fine materials were used to fashion holders of distinction. Many of these pens can be found intact with their velvet lined presentation cases.

Lewis Waterman invented the fountain pen in the 1880s. Three other leading pioneers in the field were Parker, Sheaffer (first lever filling action, 1913), and Wahl-Eversharp.

The mechanical pencil was patented in 1822 by Sampson Mordan. The original slide-type action developed into the spiral mechanical pencil. Wahl-Eversharp was responsible for the automatic "clic" or repeater type pencil which is used on ball points today.

The flexible nib that enabled the writer to individualize his penmanship came to an end when Reynolds introduced the ball point pen in October, 1945.

References: Glen Bowen, *Collectible Fountain Pens*, L–W Book Sales, 1986 (Revised); Cliff Lawrence, *Fountain Pens: History, Repair & Current Values, Second Edition*, Pen Fancier's Club, 1985.

Collectors' Clubs: American Pencil Collectors Society, 603 East 105th Street, Kansas City, MO 64131; Pen Fancier's Club, 1169 Overcash Drive, Dunedin, FL 33528.

Advisor: Dick Bitterman.

Combination pen and pencil, pencil turns out, pen pulls out, gold plated, point marked "E. J. Johnson & Co, New York, No. 4," 4⅞" fully extended, $48.00.

Conklin
  1903, pen, Model 30, black hard rubber **65.00**
  1918, pen, Model 20, 5⁵⁄₁₆" l, #2 Conklin point-nib, black crescent filler #20, gold clip, narrow gold band on cap, patent date May 28, 1918 stamped on clip **65.00**
  1923, pen, Model 25P, ladies filigree cap ribbon, black, crescent filler . **60.00**
  1925, desk set, black marble base, two pens, 7¾" l Endura model, side lever fill, double narrow gold color bands, marked "Patent Nov 17, 1925" on pen barrel, black-brown overlay color **120.00**

1945, pen, Cushion Point, silver-pink stripes, gold filled trim, NOZAK filler **50.00**
Dunn, 1920, pen, black, red barrel, gold plated trim **35.00**
Epenco, pen, black case, goldplated trim **20.00**
Eversharp
  1920, pencil, silverplated **18.00**
  1931, pen, lady's, Doric, Eversharp Gold Seal, green marble color, 14 carat point, twelve sided cap and barrel **95.00**
  1935, desk pen, Doric, gold seal green marble cov, lever fill, large adjustable nib **50.00**
  1936, pencil, green marbleized base, upper half gold color metal cap, first of the repeater pencil **20.00**
  1946, ball point pen, C A model, black, gold filled cap **40.00**
Laughlin, 1905, pen, silver overlay case, eyedropper filled **135.00**
Marvel, 1906, black chased hard rubber, eyedropper **70.00**
Moore
  Desk Set, gray and black marble base, black pen, 12 carat nib, side lever fill **65.00**
  Pen, rose color, fancy band around cap, warranted nib, side lever filler   **60.00**
  Ribbon Pen, lady's, black, three narrow gold bands on cap, lever filler, patent nib #2 .... **65.00**
Onoto, 1924, Ink Pencil Stylographic pen, black chased hard rubber, eyedropper **37.50**
Parker
  1915, pen, Model 48, ring top, gold filled barrel and cap, button filled   **140.00**
  1917, pen, Lucky Curve, push button filler **90.00**
  1921, ring pen, Lucky Curve, black hard rubber, gold filled trim **80.00**
  1923, pen, Duofold Senior, Flashing Black **150.00**
  1927
    Pen, No 42, gold filled metal mounted **85.00**
    Pencil, Duofold, Model 78M, ladies, fuchsia color, gold color cap and tip, originally sold for $3   **95.00**
  1929, pen and pencil set, Duofold Deluxe, black and pearl, three narrow gold color bands on cap, push button fill **450.00**
  1932
    Duofold Streamline, burgundy and black, double narrow band on cap **110.00**
    Vacumatic, gray-black, arrow clip, arrow design engraved on nib,

silver color clip and band on cap, oversized model **100.00**

1942, pen, Blue-Diamond—51, black, goldplated cap, button filled **60.00**

1944, pen, Blue-Diamond—Vacumatic, blue and black, goldplated trim, button filled **60.00**

1950, pen, Model 51, maroon, stainless steel cap, chrome plated trim, aerometric filler **30.00**

1956, pen, Model 61, first edition .. **45.00**

Pick, 1922, Exceptional pen, black chased hard rubber, gold filled trim, lever filled **60.00**

Reynolds, pen, orig ball point, Model 2 (1945–46) **65.00**

Security, 1923, pen, check protector, red hard rubber, gold filled trim **70.00**

Sheaffer

1923, pen, White Dot, green jade, goldplated trim, lever filled **80.00**

1930, pen, White Dot Lifetime, classic torpedo design cap and body, lever filler on side **95.00**

1938, pen, White Dot, pearl inlay, full size **65.00**

1940s, desk set, Triumph Lifetime, green marble base, two black snorkel design pens **85.00**

1946, pencil, Fineline 4000, novel point, platinum plating **18.00**

1948, pen, ballpoint, Strato writer, gold filled metal mounted **50.00**

1953, pen, White Dot, snorkel, black, 14 carat gold cap and band, plunger filled **35.00**

Swan (made by Mabie, Todd & Co, NY and London)

Pen, Eternal Model, black, gold filled trim, marked "44 E.T.N., Model 4," nib marked 14 carat **55.00**

Pen, hard rubber, red marbleized, lever fill, double gold band on cap, marked "Eternal" **60.00**

Pen, red ripple, band at top and bottom of cap, marked "Model 54 Eternal" on barrel, nib marked 14 carat **70.00**

Wahl

1918, pen, silver overlay case, eyedropper filled **155.00**

1919, pen, Tempoint No 305A, gold filled metal mounted, eyedropper **125.00**

1928, ribbon pen, lady's, double narrow band on cap, 14 carat #2 nib, lever fill, ... **65.00**

Wahl-Eversharp

1919, pencil, gold filled metal mounted **25.00**

1923, pencil, ring top, goldfilled case **40.00**

1924, pencil, sterling silver, engraved case **95.00**

1930, pen, gold seal, black, gold filled trim, lever filled **100.00**

Waterman

1886, pen, Model #12, mottled brown, 14 carat gold bands **110.00**

1906, Safety Pen, Model 42½V, gold filigree, retractable screw action nib, 3½" l **100.00**

1925, pen Model #71, ripple red hard rubber case, goldplated trim, wide clip, lever filled **120.00**

1936, pen, Lady Patricia, gray mottled finish, lever fill **45.00**

1944, pen, 100 Year Model, black, gold color clip, nib marked "100 Year Pen - 1944" **45.00**

1949, pen, Taperite, black, gold filled metal mounted cap, gold filled trim, lever filler **50.00**

PHOENIX BIRD CHINA

Collecting Hints: Phoenix Bird pattern has over 450 different shapes and sizes. The quality found in the execution of design, shades of blue, and shape of the ware itself also varies. All these factors must be considered in pricing. The maker's mark tends to add value; over 100 marks have been cataloged.

The more one studies Phoenix Bird china, the more one recognizes the variances. Collectors are urged to travel with a notebook in which is listed the shape, pattern, backstamp, dimensions, and conditions of the pieces owned. If the head of the phoenix is on a forward slant and its head feathers point upwards, also on somewhat of a slant, the rest of the motif will be well executed. If this is combined with a piece having an oversized border, the collector has found a "superior piece." Generally these superior pieces are marked with a flower with a "T" inside, but not always. The one rule about Phoenix Bird is that there always is an exception to the rule.

Don't buy Phoenix Bird unseen. Insist on a drawing of the piece, but most preferably a photograph. Photographs can be deceiving so ask for the dimensions as well. Xeroxing a plate is helpful for a buyer's identification of Phoenix Bird China or any of the similar Phoenix patterns.

History: The manufacture of Phoenix Bird pattern china began in the late 19th century. The ware was heavily imported into the United States during the 1920s to the 1940s. The Phoenix Bird pattern shows a bird facing back over its left wing, spots on its chest and wings that spread upward. The vast majority of the ware was of the transfer print variety. Blue and white was the dominant color. Pieces also can be found in green (celadon), but are quite rare. Coveted are the few hand painted pieces in blue which are signed with six Japanese characters on the underside and which always have the heart border.

Some of the transfer pieces also have a heart like border and are referred to as HŌ-Ō for identification. Many of these early pieces are not marked. The majority of Phoenix bird has the traditional border called the cloud and mountain (c/m) and sometimes has "Nippon" backstamped when of the 1891–1921 era.

Phoenix Bird pattern china primarily was sold through Woolworth's 5 & 10 Cent stores. It could also be ordered from the wholesale catalogs of Butler Brothers and the Charles William stores, the latter also retailing it as its New York city store. All the pieces offered were only the most basic shapes. Phoenix Bird also was carried by A. A. Vantine Co., NY, exported by Morimura Brothers, Japan.

A Phoenix Bird breakfast set could be acquired by selling a certain number of subscriptions to *Needlecraft* magazine. Ward's Grocery Catalog and A. J. Kasper Importers, Chicago, offered a Phoenix Bird cup and saucer as a premium for purchasing a particular brand of tea or coffee.

Once known as "Blue Howo Bird China," the Phoenix Bird pattern is the most sought after of several variations of the HŌ-Ō bird series. Other variations are:

Firebird-one of several less common patterns, flowing tail dragging downward; majority is hand painted, marked with six oriental characters.

Flying Dragon-all over pattern comes in blue and white as well as green and white; always has six characters underneath; bird's wings are fatter and rounder; in place of flower there is a pinwheel like design.

Flying Turkey-blue and white with heart border, head always facing forward; no spots on chest; and left wing, as one faces design, only half showing; majority is transfer printed, a larger minority than Phoenix Bird is hand painted, mark is six oriental characters.

Howo-in some cases the pattern's name is on the underside along with "Noritake," other times it is not; phoenix shows no feet, flower is more peony like.

Twin Phoenix-made by Noritake, but not always marked; pattern is only on outer-edge, rest is white; two birds face one another in pairs.

During the 1920s and 1930s an overwhelming number of potteries put their trademarks on the pieces. A majority have "Made in Japan," an M/ wreath (concave M), crossed stems with a convex "M," or a flower with a "T" inside and "Japan" underneath. The last mark shows up on some of the more uniquely shaped pieces and pieces of

highest quality. Most Japanese potteries were destroyed during the WWII, making it difficult to trace production records. The Phoenix Bird pattern was copied by an English firm, Myott & Son, in the mid-1930s. The English examples are earthenware and not porcelain as are the Japanese pieces.

References: Joan Collett Oates, *Phoenix Bird Chinaware, Book I* (1984), *Book II* (1985), *Book III* (1986), *Book 4* (1989), published by author.

Collectors' Club: Phoenix Bird Collectors of America, 5912 Kingsfield, West Bloomfield, MI 48322.

Museums: Historic Cherry Hill, Albany, NY; Huntingdon County Historical Society, Huntingdon, PA; Charles A. Lindbergh Home, Little Falls, MN; Eleanor Roosevelt's Vall-Kill Cottage, Hyde Park, NY.

Advisor: Joan Collett Oates.

REPRODUCTION ALERT. Reproduction of later shapes, with the exception of cups and saucers, have been around since 1970. The reproductions are more modern in shape, have more precise designs, more brilliant blue, have a milk-white ground and rarely are backstamped, with the exception of a covered jam jar and a butter pat dish. The reproductions generally had paper stickers on them at one time. Diagonal lines within the various designs are prevalent. The all-over design is more sparse on the post 1970 pieces and does not always reach the bottom of an item as it does on earlier Phoenix Bird; the majority of pieces do not have a backstamp.

A new type of phoenix is on the market in various forms and also is a dark blue design. It is called "T-Bird" for identification. At least one maker has been identified, Takahashi. Sometimes it is found with a group of oriental markings within a blue square.

Note: The numbering system used to identify pieces is from the four volume set of *Phoenix Bird Chinaware* by Joan Collett Oates.

Ice Cream Dish, individual, 6¾ x 4 x 1½",
$35.00.

Berry Bowl, scalloped **65.00**
Bon Bon, sq, wicker handles **45.00**
Boullion cup **12.00**
Bowl, 6" d, cereal **10.00**
Butter Dish, cov, cut-out kidney shape
   handles **65.00**
Cake Tray, cut-outs, handle **45.00**
Child's Cereal Set, teapot, creamer,
   sugar, #4 .... **65.00**
Chocolate Pot, scalloped base **100.00**
Creamer and Sugar
   #20 .... **40.00**
   #27 .... **22.00**
Cup and Saucer
   After dinner **18.00**
   Common **8.00**
   Occupied Japan **10.00**
   #5 .... **12.00**
Custard Cup, handleless **15.00**
Egg Cup, double **15.00**
Fruit Dish, 5" **6.00**
Ginger Jar, cov, post 1970 .... **18.00**
Gravy Boat, attached plate, Myott &
   Son, English **55.00**
Marmalade Jar, cov, cut-out for spoon . **45.00**
Plate
   7¼" d, dessert **8.00**
   8½" d, luncheon **15.00**
   9½" d, breakfast **25.00**
   9¾" d, dinner **40.00**
Platter, oval
   7¼" l **25.00**
   12½" l **48.00**
   14½" l **65.00**
Ramekin **18.00**
Rice Bowl, #1 .... **8.00**
Salt and Pepper Shaker, pr **22.00**
Soup Dish, 7¼" d **35.00**
Sweetmeat dish, scalloped, Imari type **45.00**
Teapot, cov **50.00**
Tile, 6" d **35.00**
Vegetable Tureen, oval **85.00**

PHOTOGRAPHIC ACCESSORIES

Collecting Hints: Photographic accessories divide into five major areas: darkroom material, camera accessories including literature, photographic studio items, objects associated with camera shops, drug stores, and other places where cameras and films were sold, and items related to major camera manufacturers. There are specialized collectors for each of these subject areas.

Most photographic accessories were used. Normal wear is accepted by the collector. Beware, if collecting chemical material! Make certain chemicals and film are stable. Early nitrate film often decomposes and is flammable.

Perhaps the most desirable items are those from the photographic studio. Neck braces and big portrait cameras are common. Backdrops, especially if painted, are very hard to find.

Many still usable camera accessories, e.g., lens, have a second value as used equipment. This value may be far above the collecting value.

History: The studio photographer dominated the photographic scene until the 1890s when the box camera, developed by George Eastman in 1888, became popular. By 1900 America had gone photography mad.

Retail outlets for cameras and supplies developed quickly. Imports, with Germany the leading supplier, were an important factor from the outset. A number of critical mergers took place among firms in the 1920s. The fiftieth anniversary of Eastman Kodak in 1930 marked its dominance of the market, especially in film and film processing. Kodak still enjoys the major market share.

Reference: James M. McKeown and Joan C. McKeown, *Price Guide To Antique and Classic Cameras, 1987–1988, Sixth Edition,* Centennial Photo Service, 1987.

Album, 35mm SLR shape, holds 24
   prints, 3¼ x 5" **5.00**
Bank
   Eastman Kodak, disc camera shape,
     black and aluminum colored plas-
     tic **3.50**
   Instamatic Camera, black plastic
     body, c1967 .... **2.00**
   Rolleicord, ceramic, Rolleicord TLR
     shape, white iridescent glaze, gold
     trim **30.00**
   Tupperware, black plastic, gray plas-
     tic knobs and lens, lettered rings
     around lens, marked "Tupper
     Toys" on front **5.00**
Catalog
   Century Cameras, 1909 .... **40.00**
   Seneca, 1912, 76 pgs, 5 x 8½" **40.00**
Close Up Attachment
   Argus, Macro Kit, copy stand, exten-
     sion tubes, two stages with ground,
     orig case and instructions **30.00**
   Eastman Kodak Close-Up Stand, Ret-
     ina I, stage **60.00**
Close Up Bellows
   Accura, assembly for Exakta **35.00**
   Kopil, folding single track, assembly
     for Exakta **10.00**
   Novoflex, universal screw mount as-
     sembly, bellows, shade, and slide
     copy attachment **65.00**
   Topcon, microscopic attachment ... **50.00**
Dark Room Developing
   Bottle, Eastman Kodak, brown,
     graphic label **15.00**

Developing Powder
Argo, tube 1.00
Eastman, spectal, four glass tubes
in orig box 7.50
Nepera Solution, Kodak, 4 oz brown
bottle, lead foil emb top, orig box,
1910 . . . .   10.00
Photo Lab Outfit, Model A, Eastman
Kodak Co, steel print box, three
trays, thermometer, graduate, tong,
developer, fixer, safelight, and in-
structions, orig box marked "A-B-C
Photo Lab Outfit, Model A" 15.00
Processing Tank
Amato, nickel 12.00
Eastman Kodak, stainless steel, 4 x
5" 40.00
Reducer and Stain Remover, Kodak,
glass tube marked "EKC" 3.50

Safelight
Aetna, No. 4, kerosene lantern, 4
x 5" glass, c1890 . . . .   20.00
Brownie Darkroom Lamp, round
plastic yellow cov, black bakelite
base 2.75
Rochester Optical Co, Universal
No. 1, kerosene 15.00

Scales, Bausch & Lomb 50.00
Sepia Toner, Defender, glass tube . .   2.00
Thermometer
Ansco, stirring rod type 5.00
Burke & James, metal 4.50
Eastman Kodak, 9", stirring rod,
wooden tube 15.00

Timer
Eastman Kodak, red key wind timer   10.00
FR Corp, interval timer, Art Deco .   4.50
Tray
Nassbaum, glass, amber, red bot-
tom 20.00
Zeiss Ikon A. G., 5 x 7", glass,
name in bottom 25.00

Exposure Meter
Ansco 10.00
Burroughs—Wellcome, photo expo-
sure calculator, handbook, and di-
ary, leather folder, c1915 . . . .   20.00
Coronet, model B 6.50
General Electric, model 213, foot
candle meter 7.50
Minolta, SR meter 40.00
Norwood Super Director, selenium .   20.00
Seiko, Auto-Leader III 12.00
Weston, model 617, 1932 . . . .   10.00
Zeiss Ikon A. G., Diaphot, selenium,
c1930 . . . .   30.00

Finder
Alpex, zoom 45.00
Graflex, flip up optical 18.00
Sandmar, zoom, 135mm 20.00

Flash
Burke & James, Ingento Flash Pan No.
1, 12" 20.00
Canon, model VT 12.50
Edison, Mazda, foil 3.75
Graflex, Graflite, reflector 3.00
Nippon Kogaku, model BC6 . . . .   7.50
Universal Camera Corp, mercury
photoflash, separate calculator
wheel 12.00
Lens
Bausch & Lomb, 150mm, brass bar-
rel, geared focusing 40.00
Burke & James, 230mm, No. 1, Ajax,
brass barrel, geared focusing 20.00
Deker & Co, convertible, 8 x 10 wide
angle rectilinear, brass barrel,
waterhouse stops 50.00
Enterprise Optical Mfg. Co, 125mm,
brass barrel, geared focusing 20.00
Gundlach, 5 x 7" wide angle, brass
barrel, rotating diaphragm, six
stops 60.00
Scientific Lens Co, 200mm/f8, brass
barrel, rotating diaphragm, five
stops 50.00
Vega, 3", stereo lens, adjustable in-
ternal diaphragm, mounting flange   300.00
Rangefinder
Eastman Kodak, pocket, clip on 20.00
Heyde, pocket 8.00
Unity, clip on style 8.50
Zeiss Ikon A. G., hand held 35.00
Tripod
Eastman Kodak Bullseye, model B,
wooden 10.00
Folmer Graflex, wooden, 1920s 18.00
Sunart Photo Co, wooden, double ex-
tension 15.00

PIG COLLECTIBLES

Collecting Hints: Bisque and porcelain pig items
from the late 19th century European potters are
most widely sought by collectors. Souvenir items
should have the decals in good shape; occasionally the gilding wears off from rubbing or washing.

History: Historically the pig has been an important food source in the rural economies of Europe
and America. It was one of the first animals imported into the American colonies. A fatted sow
was the standard gift to a rural preacher on his
birthday or holiday.

As a decorative motif the pig gained prominence with the figurines and planters made in
the late 19th century by English, German, and
Austrian potters. These "pink" porcelain pigs
with green decoration were popular souvenir or

prize items at fairs or carnivals or could be purchased at five-and-dime stores.

Many pig figurines were banks. "Piggy Bank" became a standard term for the coin bank by the early 20th century. When tourist attractions began along America's sea coasts and in the mountain areas, many of the pig designs showed up as souvenir items with the name of the area applied in gilded decal form.

The pig motif appeared on the advertising items associated with farm products and life. The era of the movie cartoon introduced "Porky Pig" and Walt Disney's "Three Little Pigs."

In the late 1970s pig collectibles caught fire again. Specialty shops selling nothing but pig related items were found in the New England area. *Time* magazine devoted a page and one-half to the pig phenomena in one of its 1981 issues.

Advisor: Mary Hamburg.

See: Cartoon Characters and Disneyana

REPRODUCTION ALERT: Reproductions of three German-style, painted bisque figurines have been spotted in the market. They are pig by outhouse, pig playing piano, and pig poking out of large purse. The porcelain is much rougher and the green is a darker shade.

Advertising
    Cork, 3", Heidsieck Dry Champagne, two pigs on front 65.00
    Mirror, 2⅛" d, Newton Collins Short Order Restaurant, St Joe, MO, yellow and orange pastel 35.00
Ashtray
    Pig artist painting, pig sketch on tablet . 85.00
    Two pigs hugging, sitting in dish, bisque, stamped "Made In Germany" . 80.00
Bank
    Gold, yellow pouch, souvenir Danville, IL 40.00
    White clay, seated, clear glaze, 3½" h 30.00
Basket, pink pig poking out of basket, orange seal 40.00
Bottle
    5" l, buff clay, white glaze with running orange 45.00
    5¼" l
        White, brown spots 30.00
        Yellowware with amber 40.00
    8¼" l, salt glaze, gray 75.00
Chocolate Mold, 2 part, tin 65.00
Cutting Board, 14 x 9½", wood, pig shape, marked "Arnold, Kent Feeds" . 10.00
Figurine
    Barber shop scene, pink pig barber with scissors in hand, pig sitting in chair, "Little bit off the top" caption, 2¾" 65.00

Figurine, high glaze, European, marked "#E1593," 7¼" l, $75.00.

Chef standing by barrel, blue hat and jacket 80.00
Jumping over green fence, black, bisque 55.00
Looking outside bassinet, 3½" 50.00
Mama Pig
    Holding piglet in blue blanket, looking at rabbit caption "Was not happy until he got it" 45.00
    Rocking two baby piglets in cradle, "Hush a bye baby Don't you cry, You'll be a sausage bye and bye" caption 80.00
    Wheeling two babies, "Wheeling his own Baby" caption, emb made in Germany 75.00
Pig and train engine, 4¼" l 75.00
Pig in case, looking through binoculars 70.00
Pig in washtub 54.00
Pig poking head out of potty, 2½" . . 48.00
Pink pig poking out of money bag, 5,000,000 on front 55.00
Pink pig sitting by green satchel, 3" . 48.00
Pink pig with wheel barrel 45.00
Standing, chalk, black and white, 27" l 350.00
Three piglets inside egg shape basin, "Triplets o fancy" caption, marked "Germany" 65.00
Three pigs sitting on trough, two orange mushrooms, 4¾" l 75.00
Three pink pigs in front of fence, two orange mushrooms, 4½" 70.00
Two pink pigs each end caboose . . . 60.00
Two pink pigs playing table tennis, "Patience" caption 90.00
Windmill, pink pig sitting, orange roof 80.00
Gravy Boat, 4", porcelain, two swinging pink pigs, English 45.00
Inkwell, pink pig sitting on green well, 3" 85.00
Jar, 2¾" h, pig along side, orange seal 38.00

Matchsafe
3" h, one pig playing piano, another playing banjo, "Home Sweet Home" caption **75.00**
4½" w, pink pig poking head through fence **60.00**

Match Safe, brass, silverplated, English, 2" l, $125.00.

Nodder, china, dressed as man and woman **55.00**
Paperweight, 2⅛" h, seated, nickel steel and brass **45.00**
Pillow, pig shape, made from quilts ... **15.00**
Pitcher, 4" h, milk, figural, brown, dressed in tie and tails **15.00**
Salt and Pepper Shakers, pr, 3", white, hp, one wearing red kerchief, other wearing blue, marked "Japan" **5.00**
Salt Dish
2½", three little pigs around water trough **50.00**
3½", two pigs along side bucket, stamped "Made in Germany" **52.00**
Sculpture, 18" l, sandstone, sgd "E Reed 1982" **425.00**
Stickpin, brass **5.50**
Toothpick Holder
2¼" h, egg, two pink pigs in front .. **50.00**
3" h, two pigs looking in water trough, stamped "Made In Germany" **55.00**
Toy, 2½", stuffed, velvet, Steiff **60.00**
Vase
Red devil's arm around pink pig, sitting on log, 7¼" h **110.00**
Two pigs poking out of large shoe, Germany **55.00**
Watch Fob, bronze, "We Save 'Em," United Serum Co, Kansas City, KS, 1912 .... **20.00**

PINBALL MACHINES

Collecting Hints: Cosmetic condition is paramount. Graphics are complex and difficult to impossible to repair. Graphics are unique to a specific model, especially backglass and playfield plastics, making replacements scarce. Prices are given for cosmetically good, 95% or more of backglass decoration present, games in good working condition.

Some wear is expected in pinballs as a sign that the game was a good one, but bare wood detracts from overall condition. Watch for signs of loose ink on the rear of the glass. Unrestorable games with good cosmetics are valuable for restoration of other games. Discount 30 to 40% of the price for a non-working game.

Add 10% if the paper items such as score card, instruction card, and schematic are present and in good condition. It is fair to suggest that regardless of mechanical condition, a game in good cosmetic condition is worth roughly twice what the same game is worth in poor cosmetic condition.

Pinball collecting is a new hobby which is still developing. It can be started inexpensively, but requires space to maintain. The tremendous diversity of models made has prevented the market from becoming well developed. There are relatively few people restoring antique pinball machines for sale. Expect to buy games in nonworking condition and learn to repair them yourself.

History: Pinball machines can trace their heritage back to the mid–1700s. However, it was not until 1931 when Gottlieb introduced "Baffle Ball" that pinball machines caught on and became a popular and commercial success. It was the Depression, and people were hungry for something novel and the opportunity to make money. Pinball machines had both. The first games were entirely mechanical, cost about twenty dollars and were produced in large numbers—25,000 to 50,000 were not uncommon.

Pinball developments include:
1932—addition of legs
1933—electric, at first using batteries
1936—addition of bumpers
1947—advent of flippers
1950—kicking rubbers
1953—score totalizers
1954—multiple players
1977—solid state electronics

The size also underwent change. The early countertops were 16 x 32 inches. Later models were free standing with the base 21 x 52 inches and the backbox 24 x 30 inches.

The total number of pinball models that have been manufactured has not yet been determined. Some suggest over 10,000 different models from 200 plus makers. After 1940 most models were produced in quantities of 500 to 2,000; occasionally, games had production figures as high as 10,000. Pinball machines have always enjoyed a high attrition rate. New models made the most money and were introduced by several of the major manufacturers at the rate of one entirely new model every three weeks during the mid-1940s and 1950s. Today the rate of new model introduction has slowed to an average of four to six new games per year.

Most operators of pinballs used the older games for spare parts to repair newer models. Earning life was less than three years in most markets. Many games were warehoused or destroyed to keep them from becoming competition for the operator's newest games; they did not want older pinball machines winding up in the wrong hands. At the very least, the coin mechanisms were removed before the game was sold. Most machines that have survived have come from home basements or from operators' storage.

Most pinballs were made in Chicago. Major manufacturers were Gottlieb, Williams, and Bally. Pinballs by D. Gottlieb & Co. are the most sought after due to generally superior play and graphics, from the 1947 to mid–1970s period especially.

Pinball art is part of the popular culture and kinetic art. The strength of the pinball playfield design carried Gottlieb as the predominant maker through the 1950s and into the 1970s. During the 1960s Gottlieb's fame grew due to the animated backglasses, intended to both amuse and attract players, which featured movable units as part of the artwork. The combination of animation and availability make the 1960s machines a key target period for collectors.

The advent of solid state games in 1977, coupled with the video game boom, dramatically changed the pinball machine market. The late electromechanical games became obsolete from a commercial point of view. Initially Bally was the predominant maker, but Williams has since attained this position. Solid state game production was high as manufacturers attempted to replace all obsolete electromechanical games. A severe dent in pinball machine production was caused by the video games of the 1980s, but collectors, who are rediscovering the silver ball, are helping the pinball machine recover some of its popularity.

References: Richard Bueschel, *Pinball I: An Illustrated Historical Guide To Pinball Machines, Volume 1,* Hoflin Publishing Ltd; Gary Flower and Bill Kurtz, *Pinball: The Lure of the Silver Ball,* published by authors; Donald Mueting and Robert Hawkins, *The Pinball Reference Guide,* Mead Co.

Periodical: *The Pinball Collectors' Quarterly,* R. D. #3, 46 Velie Road, Lagrangeville, NY 12540 has suspended publication, but back issues are available for $20.00 postpaid; *Pinball Trader,* P. O. Box 440922, Brentwood, MO 63144.

Advisors: Steve Young, Gordon Hasse, Jr., and John Fetterman.

Note: Pinballs are listed by machine name and fall into various classifications: novelty with no awards, replay which awards free games, add-a-ball which awards extra balls instead of games, and bingo where players add additional coins to increase the odds of winning bingo cards played. Some payout games were made in the mid to late 1930s which paid out coins for achieving scoring objectives. After the first add-a-ball games in 1960, many game designs were issued as both replay and add-a-ball with different game names and slight play rules modifications but similar art work.

Williams, Four Corners, 1952, $425.00.

Bally
1931, Ballyhoo, countertop	**425.00**
1933, Airway, first mechanical scoring	**300.00**
1934, Fleet, battery operated	**325.00**
1936, Bumper, electric bumpers	**300.00**
1951, Coney Island, bingo	**375.00**
1964, Mad World, captive ball	**250.00**
1968, Rock Makers, replay, unusual playfield	**275.00**
1972, Fireball, replay, spinning disc, flipper zippers	**1,400.00**
1973, Nip-It, replay, ball grapper	**300.00**
1976	
Capt Fantastic, replay, mirrored art	**750.00**
Old Chicago, deco two player	**425.00**
1980, Xenon, electronic	**325.00**

Chicago Coin
1948, Spinball, spinner action	**175.00**
1952, Big Hit, good play baseball	**300.00**
1966, Kicker, replay	**225.00**

Daval, 1934, Big Bertha, battery **300.00**

Exhibit
1939, Contact, first standard sized larger game	**325.00**
1947, Mam'selle, replay	**375.00**

Genco
1933, Jiggers, countertop	**275.00**

1941, Capt Kidd, great looking, pre-
war **325.00**
1949, Black Gold, replay **325.00**
Gottlieb
1931, Baffle Ball, countertop **425.00**
1933, Big Broadcast, mechanical
scoring **325.00**
1940, Summertime, mirrored graphics **325.00**
1945, Stage Door Canteen, first by
maker after WWII, large production **275.00**
1947, Humpty Dumpty, replay, first
flipper **750.00**
1949, K. C. Jones, replay, good art . **450.00**
1952, Happy Days, replay, tic-tac-toe
art **475.00**
1954, Jumbo, replay, first multi-player **325.00**
1958, Criss Cross, replay **400.00**
1960, Flipper, first add-a-ball **350.00**
1962, Flipper Clown, replay, ani-
mated glass **425.00**
1963, Slick Chick, replay, classic
game **525.00**
1965, Bank A Ball, replay, animated,
classic **475.00**
1966, Central Park, replay, New York
City art **475.00**
1967, Sing Along, replay, Melody
add-a-ball **325.00**
1971, Dimension, add-a-ball, target
banks 2001, replay **325.00**
1973, Jack In The Box, drop target
bank **300.00**
1975, El Dorado, replay, Gold Strike
add-a-ball **400.00**
1980, Black Hole, electronic, multi-
level **400.00**
United, 1947, Wisconsin, replay **250.00**
Williams
1946, Suspense, first by maker **375.00**
1951, Hayburners Jalopy, horses and
cars, animation **425.00**
1955, Regatta, replay **325.00**
1958, Turf Champ, replay, horserace **325.00**
1961, Metro, replay, disappearing
bumper **225.00**
1964, Soccer, replay, animated **375.00**
1967, Magic Town, add-a-ball,
Magic City, replay **300.00**
1968, Cabaret, replay, flipper post .. **300.00**
1972, Spanish Eyes, replay, DC playfield, excellent artwork **475.00**
1974, Triple Action, high scoring, fast
action **275.00**
1977, Grand Prix, replay **325.00**
1980, Firepower, electronic **400.00**

PIN-UP ART

Collecting Hints: Try to collect calendars intact.
There is a growing practice among dealers to

separate calendar pages, cut off the date information, and sell the individual sheets in hopes
of making more money. Buyers are urged not to
succumb to supporting this practice.

Concentrate on the work of one artist. Little
research has been done on the pin-up artists so
it is a wide open field. The original works of art,
whether in oils or pastels, on which calendar
sheets and magazine covers are based, have begun to appear on the market. High prices are
being asked, but the market is not yet stabilized—beware!

Pin-up material can be found in many other
collectible categories. Usually the items are referred to as "girlies" on the list. Many secondary
pin-up items are not signed, but a collector can
easily identify an artist's style.

History: Charles Dana Gibson created the first
true pin-up girl with his creation of the Gibson
Girl in the early 1900s. Other artists followed
such as Howard Chandler Christy, Coles Phillips
and Charles Sheldon. The film magazines of the
1920s, such as *Film Fun* and *Real Screen Fun,*
developed the concept further. Their front covers
featured the minimally clad beauties designed to
attract a male readership.

The 1930s featured the work of cover artists
Charles Sheldon, Cardwell Higgins and George
Petty. Sheldon did calendar art for Brown & Bigelow as well as covers. *Esquire* began in 1933;
its first Petty gatefold appeared in 1939.

The golden age of pin-up art was 1935 to
1955. The 1940s brought Alberto Vargas (the "s"
was dropped at *Esquire's* request), Gillete Elvgren, Billy DeVorss, Joyce Ballantyne and Earl
Moran into the picture. Pin-up girl art appeared
everywhere—magazine covers, blotters, souvenir items, posters, punchboards, etc. Many other
artists adopted the style.

Photographic advertising and changing American tastes ended the pin-up reign by the early
1960s.

Note: Prices have been stable for the last two
years.

Blotter, 4 x 9", "Going My Way," girl
standing in rubber raft while hitchhiking, sea plane overhead, sgd by Del
Masters, adv Laony Motor Services,
Inc., Chicago **3.00**
Calendar
1942, Esquire, Varga Girl, 8½ x 12",
plastic spiral binding, 12 pgs, horizontal format, verses by Phil Stack **65.00**
1945, Starlight, Earl Moran, full color
blonde, nude, dark green drape,
black ground **35.00**
1947, Petty, 9 x 12", spiral bound,
orig envelope, Fawcett Publications **45.00**
1948, *Esquire* Glamour Gallery, 8½ x
12" **40.00**

Magazine Tear Sheet, Esquire, February, 1940, George Petty, $12.00.

1954, Petty Girl, 8¼ x 11″, 12 pgs, vertical format, verses	**55.00**
1956, Marilyn Monroe, 8 x 14″, four full color pictures	**200.00**
1961, *Playboy* Playmate, 5½ x 6½″, desk, MIB	**45.00**
Card, 3½ x 5″, c1940, set of 3	
Earl Moran, red ground	**18.00**
Zoe Mozert, full color	**15.00**
Christmas Card, 5½ x 8″, tan, red, black, and blue, MacPherson	**22.00**
Cigarette Lighter, 1⅞″ h, black and white photos, green and red tints	**27.00**
Date Book, *Esquire* 5 x 7″, color cov, spiral binding, full color pin-up photos, copyright 1943, George Hurrell	**29.00**
Folder	
Petty Girl Revue, from Dec 1941 issue of Esquire, double sided, verses, different girl in each drawing, four 3¾ x 8½″ drawings, six 5 x 7⅝″ drawings, one 6½ x 5½″ drawing	**45.00**
Sally of Hollywood & Vine, cardboard, sliding insert changing from dress to underwear to nude	**22.00**
Hair Pin, Petty, orig 4 x 5½″ yellow, red, black, and white card, 1948, artist sgd	**20.00**
Kit, *Esquire* Magazine, 1944 Varga girl calendar, 8½ x 12″, Susan Hayward puzzle, 10 x 13″, orig 10 x 14″ envelope	**65.00**
Magazine	
Marilyn Monroe Pin-Ups, 1953, 8½ x 11″, 32 pgs, black and white and full color photos	**70.00**
Movieland Pin-Ups, Anita Ekberg, cov, 1955	**16.00**
Match Book Cover	
Petty Girl, "Its In The Bag," Martins Tavern, Chicago, late 1940s	**3.00**
Petty Girl, "Snug As A Bug," Martins Tavern, Chicago, late 1940s	**3.00**

Note Pad, 3 x 4½″, pastel, 1944 calendar on back	**6.00**
Playing Cards	
Bob Elson's Petty Pipping, 52 cards, dressed as bride	**25.00**
Vargas Girl Drawings, 53 cards, different illus, plastic coated, mfg by Creative Playing Card Co, St. Louis, green box	**150.00**
Poster	
17 x 33″, full color, woman in shorts walking wirehaired terrier, c1951, Walt Otto	**50.00**
22 x 40″, Martin Senour Paint, "If It's Worth Covering, It's Worth Martin Senour Synthol Enamel," woman removing robe to reveal sheer underwear	**100.00**
Punch Board Label, 3¾ x 8″, Elvgren, unused	**10.00**

PLANTERS PEANUTS

Collecting Hints: Planters Peanuts memorabilia is easily identified by the famous Mr. Peanut trademark. Items from the 1906 to 1916 period have the "Planters Nut And Chocolate Company" logo.

Papier mache, diecut, and ceramic pieces must be in very good condition. Cast iron and tin pieces should be free of rust and dents and have good graphics and color.

History: Amedeo Obici and Mario Peruzzi organized the Planters Nut And Chocolate Company in Wilkes-Barre, Pennsylvania, in 1906. Obici had conducted a small peanut business for several years and was known locally as the "Peanut Specialist."

Early peanut sales were the Spanish salted, red skins which sold for 10¢ per pound. Soon after Obici developed the whole, white, blanched peanut, his product became the consumer's favorite.

In 1916 a young Italian boy submitted a rough version of the now famous monocled and distinguished Mr. Peanut as an entry in a contest held by Planters to develop a trademark. A wide variety of premium and promotional items were issued shortly thereafter.

Planters eventually was purchased by Standard Brands, which itself later became a division of Nabisco.

Reference: Richard D. and Barbara Reddock, *Planters Peanuts Advertising And Collectibles,* Wallace-Homestead, 1978.

Collectors' Club: Peanut Pals, 3065 Rumsey Drive, Ann Arbor, MI 48105. *Peanut Papers* (bimonthly).

REPRODUCTION ALERT

Jar, clear, orig label, 13" h, 7½" d top, $100.00.

Ashtray, 6 x 5", emb, silver, 1906–56 .	**50.00**
Bank, 8½" h, plastic, tan, c1950	**35.00**
Book, Presidents, 7½ x 10½", 32 pgs, soft cov, multicolor and black and white illus of Presidents, 1953 copyright	**18.00**
Booklet, Peanut Pals, 3½ x 6", 24 pgs, peanut characters Percy and Peter meet Mr. Peanut at factory, 1927 copyright	**60.00**
Bookmark, diecut, cardboard, 1920–30	**20.00**
Bracelet, charm, three beige and blue Mr. Peanut figures, c1930	**12.00**
Button, 1⅛", litho, black, white, and red, marked "Vote For" top, "Mr. Peanut" center, and "The Peoples Choice" bottom	**25.00**
Coloring Book, 8¼ x 11", 32 pgs, orig letter dated June 16, 1928, Planters Nut & Chocolate Co, Wilkes-Barre, PA letterhead, and 9 x 12" envelope, six pgs neatly water colored, rest unused	**70.00**
Dish Set, 6" d serving dish, four 3" individual bowls, peanut colored design, Mr. Peanut in bottom of bowl, gold accent rim, 1940–50	**20.00**
Figure, 10", cardboard	**6.00**
Mug, pewter	**20.00**
Serving Spoon, 5¼" l, SP, Carlton, c1930	**12.00**
Shoe Polish Prize, blue 2¼" plastic figural Mr. Peanut charm, Esquire Scuff Kote, orig 2¼ x 2¼ x 5" multicolored box, c1950	**28.00**
Swizzle Stick, figural	**3.50**
Tab, 1½", metal, litho, diecut, yellow, black, and white Mr. Peanut, 1920–30	**12.00**
Toy, wind-up, 8½" h, plastic, "Mr. Peanut" inscription, marked "Made In USA," c1950	**75.00**
Whistle, plastic, red and white, chain loop, "Mr. Peanut" on hat brim, 1940–50	**10.00**

PLASTICVILLE

Collecting Hints: Collectors most prize mint condition buildings in their original box. Do not glue any pieces together. Also make certain that all pieces, including accessories, are in the box. There are many variations within each model; some models have over six color variations. Also, additional variations can be created by mixing the wrong colors together. Check carefully before buying.

Care must be exercised in storing Plasticville. Mildew will develop on the plastic if stored in a damp environment.

Collecting Plasticville is a brand new area. Prices are low. A collection can be assembled without a great outlay of money.

History: Bachmann Bros., Inc., began its operations in 1883 making handles for canes and walking sticks from hand carved ivory. In the late 1880s they switched to hair barrettes and similar ornaments and in 1912 to the manufacture of eyeglasses.

In 1949 the first train-related item was produced—a picket fence. A log cabin followed in 1950. Six to ten new buildings in O/S gauge were introduced each year. In 1955 an HO line was launched and in 1968, N gauge material. Bachmann carefully stores its dies so material can be reintroduced as demand necessitates.

Plasticville is marked either with the name or the letters "BB" on a banner within a circle. The snap together system used by Bachmann was patented and is unique to their products. All but the N gauge material is American made.

Plasticville was challenged briefly by Littletown; but, Bachmann acquired Unlimited Plastics Corp. of New York, its maker, in 1956.

References: Frank C. Hare, ed., *Plasticville "O" & "S" Scale: An Illustrated Price Guide*, published by author, 1981; *Plasticville: Market Price Guide*, April Publications, Inc., 1982.

Note: The same building was issued in as many as eight different number codes. The listing includes some, but not all of these numbers for each building and accessory.

Gas Station, #1800/149, $12.50.

Airport Administration Building, #AD-4, white sides, blue roof, 19 pcs, 1954 .... **24.00**
Apartment House, #1907, 14 pcs, 1958 **65.00**
Bank, #BK-1, blue gray sides, green roof, 9 pcs, 1955 .... **20.00**
Cathedral, #C-18, white, gray roof, 1955 .... **24.00**
Covered Bridge, #1805, 14 pcs, 1960 **10.00**
Dairy Barn, #1622, 11 pcs, red sides, gray roof, 1957 .... **10.00**
Diner, #DE-7, 5 pcs, 1952 .... **10.00**
Fire House, #FH-4, red and white, orig 6 x 7 x 2″ red, white, and blue box . **18.00**
Garden Accessories
   Bird Bath, #CB, 1 pc, 1950 .... **3.50**
   Maple Tree, #MT-2, 2 pcs, 1950 .. **.75**
   Poplar Tree Assortment, #1409, 40 pcs, 1960 .... **15.00**
   Trellis, #GT-1, 1 pc, 1950 .... **5.00**
Gas Station, #GO-3, 18 pcs, 1955 ... **18.00**
Greenhouse, #5804, 11 pcs, gray sides, white base, rows of flowers, 1959 .. **25.00**
Hospital, #HS-6, 9 pcs, 1953 .... **12.00**
House
   Bermuda Ranch, #1603, 6 pcs, 1951 **5.00**
   Bungalow, #1629, 9 pcs, 1962 .... **20.00**
   Cape Cod, #HP-9, 7 pcs, 1950 .... **5.00**
   Colonial Mansion, #1703, 8 pcs, 1957 .... **18.00**
   Log Cabin, #1985, 7 pcs, 1951 .... **7.50**
   New England Ranch, #1701, 14 pcs, 1954 .... **7.50**
Motel, #1621, 9 pcs, 1957 .... **8.00**
Police Dept, #1614, 11 pcs, gray and green, orig 6 x 7 x 2″ gray and green box **15.00**
Railroad Loading Platform, #1817, 7 pcs, 1957 .... **5.00**
Roadside Stand, #1806, 19 pcs, 1962 **20.00**
Supermarket, #1613, 7 pcs, 1953 .... **10.00**
Turnpike Interchange, #1900, 25 pcs, 1956 .... **15.00**
Water Tower, #1916, 8 pcs, 1957 .... **5.00**
Windmill, #1408, 8 pcs, 1958 ...... **25.00**

PLAYING CARDS

Collecting Hints: Always purchase complete decks in very good condition. Do research to identify the exact number of cards needed. An American straight deck has 52 cards and usually a joker; pinochle requires 48 cards; tarot decks use 78. In addition to decks, uncut sheets and single cards, if very early, are sought by collectors.

Many collectors focus on topics. Examples are politics, trains, World's Fairs, animals, airlines, advertising, etc. Most collectors of travel-souvenir cards prefer a photographic scene on the face.

The most valuable playing card decks are unusual either in respect to publisher, size, shape, or subject. Prices for decks of late 19th and 20th centuries cards remain modest.

History: The first use of playing cards dates to 12th century China. By 1400 playing cards were in use throughout Europe. French cards were known specifically for their ornate designs. The first American cards were published by Jazaniah Ford, Milton, Massachusetts, in the late 1700s. United States innovations include upper corner indexes, classic joker, standard size, and slick finish for shuffling. Bicycle Brand was introduced in 1885 by the U.S. Playing Card Company of Cincinnati.

Card designs have been drawn or printed in every conceivable size and on a variety of surfaces. Miniature playing cards appealed to children. Novelty decks came in round, crooked, and die-cut shapes. Numerous card games, beside the standard four suit deck, were created for adults and children.

References: Gene Hockman, *Encyclopedia of American Playing Cards*, several parts, privately printed, 1976 to present; Sylvia Mann, *Collecting Playing Cards*, Crown, 1966; Roger Tilley, *Playing Cards*, Octopus, London, 1973.

Periodical: *Playing Card World,* 188 Sheen Lane, East Sheen, London SW148LF England.

Collectors' Clubs: Chicago Playing Card Collectors, Inc., 1559 West Platt Blvd., Chicago, IL 60620; Playing Card Collectors Assn., Inc., 3621 Douglas Avenue, Racine, WI 53404.

Museum: Museum of U. S. Playing Card Company, Cincinnati, OH.

Note: We have organized our list by both topic and country. Although concentrating heavily on cards by American manufacturers, some foreign makers are included.

Pan American Exposition, copyright 1901, Buffalo, NY, pocket size, $35.00.

COUNTRY

Austria
Classic, Piatnik, 1955, 53 cards **18.00**
La Provence, Piatnik, 1960, 53 cards **22.00**
Belgium, Joyaux De Belgique "Sieradan
Van Belgie," Royal Belgian Coat of
Arms, 54 cards **20.00**
England
Coronation King Edward VII, 1902,
picture on back, 53 cards, orig box **80.00**
Prince of Wales National Relief Fund,
World War I, De La Rue, 1914, MIB **32.00**
France, The Parlou Sibyl, Grimaud,
1968, 3 x 4½", 52 cards **20.00**
Italy
Cucci, Maseghini, c1969, 2 x 3⅝",
40 cards complete, orig box **20.00**
World Bridge, Modiano, 1953, 54
cards **30.00**
Oriental, Fujitsu, Nintendo, Japan,
1973, 2½ x 3¹⁵⁄₁₆", orig box **30.00**
United States
A. Dougherty Triplicate Cards, #18,
1876, 53 cards, MIB **45.00**
Maxfield Parish, limited edition of
1,000 .... **15.00**
Politicards, Politicards Corp, 1971,
political people caricatures, 54
cards, MIB **25.00**

TOPIC

Advertising
American Red Cross, 1944, used ... **12.00**
General Electric Refrigerator, two 52
bridge decks, black cardboard
trays, 1930s **30.00**
Heileman's Old Style Lager Beer ... **22.00**
Parker Baltimore Whiskey Rye, single
deck, one calendar card, 1910 ... **30.00**
Prize Metal Sacks, Cincinnati, Ohio **7.00**
R C Cola, double deck, case **20.00**
Rocky Mountain Motor Co, 52 cards,
boxed **30.00**
Games and Fortune Telling
Games of Poems, boxed, 1898 ..... **25.00**
Gavitt's Stock Exchange Card Game,
instruction sheet, 1903 copyright,
W. W. Gavitt Printing and Publish-
ing Co, Topeka, Kan **20.00**
H-Bar-O, 32 cards, instructions **15.00**
Illya Kuryakin Card Game, Milton
Bradley, 1966, Metro Goldwyn
Mayer lower right corner, unused **45.00**
National Club Tourists 1881, hand-
written fortunes **20.00**
Nile Fortune Telling Cards, 1897–
1904 .... **18.00**
Souvenir
Apollo VIII, double deck, lift-off with
red borders on one, blue border on
other, plastic case **12.00**

Black Hills, Coolidge on one **25.00**
Eisenhower Collection, Washington/
Lincoln, orig box **20.00**
Gaiety, nude pinups, damaged box,
1950s **55.00**
Pittsburgh **27.00**
1977 Queens Jubilee **12.00**
Tarot
007 Game **40.00**
The New Tarot, Hurley & Horler, 2nd
edition, 1974, 2½ x 3½", 78 cards,
MIB **15.00**
Uncut Sheet, 18 x 25", B P Grimaud,
c1890, 38 cards **75.00**
Transportation
C & O Railroad, double deck, uno-
pened **35.00**
Frisco Railroad, single deck **18.00**
Furness Lines Steamship, 2 decks, day
and night scenes, boxed, late 1930 **30.00**
Long Island Railroad, 52 cards, "The
Route Of The Dashing Commuter,"
gold on dark blue background,
suede like box, 1940–50 .... **15.00**
N & W Railroad, double deck, uno-
pened **35.00**
New York Central System, two sealed
decks, "Morning Along The Hud-
son" and "Super-Van" pictured on
back, suede like box, 1960s **20.00**
Pennsylvania Railroad, double deck **70.00**
Souvenir Playing Cards/Scenes and
Descriptions Of The Denver & Rio
Grande Western And The Western
Pacific Railways inscription, 52
cards, railway tour scene, early
1900s **12.00**
US and Axis Warplanes, 52 cards, instruction card, orig red, white, and
blue box, early 1940s **15.00**
World's Fairs and Expositions
1901 Buffalo, Pan American, color
design, orig box **35.00**
1933 Chicago Century Of Progress,
1933, 52 cards, Sky Ride scene,
boxed **22.00**
1964-65, New York World's Fair, Unisphere design, unused **5.00**

POCKET KNIVES

Collecting Hints: The pocket knife collector has
to compete with other collectors such as advertising, character collectors, and period collectors.

The pocket knife with a celluloid handle and
advertising underneath dates back to the 1880s.
Celluloid handled knives are considered much
more desirable than the plastic handled models.
Collectors also tend to shy from purely souvenir
related knives.

History: Pocket knife collecting falls into two major categories. There are collectors who concentrate on the utilitarian and functional knives from firms such as Alcas, Case, Colonial, Ka-Bar, Queen, Remington, Schrade, and Winchester. The second group deals with advertising, character, and other knives, which, while meant to be used, were sold with a secondary function in mind. These knives were made by companies such as Aerial Cutlery Co., Canton Cutlery Co., Golden Rule Cutlery Co., Imperial Knife Company, and Novelty Cutlery Co.

The larger manufacturing firms also made advertising, character, and figural knives. Some knives were giveaways or sold for a small premium, but most were sold in general stores and souvenir shops.

References: James F. Parker, *The Official Price Guide To Collector Knives, Ninth Edition,* House of Collectibles, 1987; Jim Sargent, *Sargent's American Premium Guide To Pocket Knives: Identification and Values,* Books Americana, 1986; Ron Stewart and Roy Ritchie, *The Standard Knife Collector's Guide,* Collector Books, 1986.

Periodical: *Knife World,* P. O. Box 3395, Knoxville, TN 37917.

Collectors' Clubs: American Blade Collectors, P. O. Box 22007. Chattanooga, TN 37422; The National Knife Collectors Association, P. O. Box 21070, Chattanooga, TN 37421.

Museum: National Knife Museum, Chattanooga, TN.

REPRODUCTION ALERT: Advertising knives, especially Coca-Cola, have been heavily reproduced.

Note: See *Warman's Antiques And Their Prices* for a list of knife prices for major manufacturers.

Advertising, Old Reading Beer, PA, one blade, $15.00.

Advertising
Anheuser Busch, red side panels, Stanhope viewer, photograph of Busch, knife, and corkscrew	**135.00**
Cudahy Packing Co, grading and sausage knife, pearl handle	**25.00**
Dawes/Black Horse Ale & Porter, inlaid silver, green bakelite case, Canadian	**40.00**
Omega Watches, silver watch inlay .	**35.00**
Purina, three blades	**15.00**

St. Pauli Girl Beer, nickel plated . . .	**30.00**
Westinghouse Coolers, emb handle .	**30.00**

Character
Buffalo Bill, 3⅜", steel blade, plastic case, c1950	**12.00**
Davy Crockett, 3¾", single blade, hatchet bottle opener, Walt Disney	**35.00**
Lone Ranger, 3", black grip, white image of Lone Ranger and Silver, knife blade and bottle opener	**35.00**
Popeye, 3", red celluloid sides, King Features Syndicate copyright, unused	**85.00**
Tom Mix and Tony, 3", black and white celluloid, c1930	**25.00**

Figural
Baseball Bat, celluloid, Sportsman's Price, Fairmont Cutlery	**20.00**
Lady's leg, slim, bone colored handle, Buck Cutlery	**60.00**

Miscellaneous
Boy Scout, three blades, staghorn handle, inset emblem, Camillus . .	**30.00**
Commemorative, "Our Martyred Presidents," Golden Rule Cutlery Co	**150.00**
Hunting, Marbles, leather handle, marked "Woodcraft"	**150.00**
Swiss Army Knife, Victorinox, marked "Champion"	**20.00**

POLICE COLLECTIBLES

Collecting Hints: Police collectibles are primarily collected by people employed in law enforcement areas. Collectors often base their collection on badges or material from a specific locality. As a result, prices are regionalized, e.g., a California collector is more interested in California material than items from another state.

Condition is critical. Badges were worn everyday so a minimum of wear is expected.

The emphasis on police shows on television has attracted many non-law enforcement people to the field of police collectibles.

History: The first American colonists appointed someone from among their midst to maintain and enforce the laws of the land. The local sheriff was an important social and political position.

The mid-nineteenth century witnessed the development of two important trends: the growth of the professional police force in cities and the romanticizing of the western lawman. Arthur Conan Doyle's Sherlock Holmes novels popularized the modernization of police methods. Magazines, such as the *Police Gazette,* kept the public's attention focused on the sensationalism of police work.

The Gangster era of the 1920s and 30s and the arrival of the "G-Men," glamorized by Hollywood movies, kept police work in the limelight. Finally, television capitalized on the public enthusiams for police drama through shows such as Dragnet, The Untouchables, Starsky and Hutch, and Hill Street Blues.

Reference: George E. Virgines, *Police Relics,* Collector Books, 1982.

REPRODUCTION ALERT, especially police badges.

Badge, Penn Central Railroad, Sergeant, Ohio jurisdiction, brass, lacquered, $75.00.

Badge
  Boston Police, city skyline, nickel
    plated, c1880 .... 100.00
  Cambria County, Special Deputy
    Sheriff, shield shape 75.00
  El Paso Police, 111 .... 100.00
  Forest Park, IL, Chief of Police 30.00
  Grosse Point Woods, MI 90.00
  Lake Ozark, MO, Police Chief 80.00
  Overland Park, KS, Patrolman 60.00
  Silver Lake, WI 50.00
Buckle, City of New York Police Department, c1900 .... 75.00
Cabinet Card, Westerly, RI, full uniform
  policeman, town name and #3,
  photo by Schofield, Westerly 45.00
Emblem, Lieutenant, braided, gold and
  silver thread, c1800 .... 30.00
Helmet, New York City Police Department, "Riot and Patrol Helmet,"
  leather 210.00
Magazine
  The Arizona Sheriff, December 1971,
    Sheriff Bud Yancey pictured on
    front 2.00
  The Police Chief, March 1965 ..... 4.00
Night Stick, wood 6.00
Painting, 22 x 26", oil on canvas, Brooklyn Sergeant 6 .... 500.00
Patch
  Maricopa County Deputy Sheriff, star
    center 1.50

San Francisco Police, eagle 3.00
Pocket Watch, silver, engraved badge
  design with Boston Police, Matthew
  Mullen, and 16th Division, Waltham,
  1800s 510.00
Postage Stamp, Law and Order, c1968   1.00
Sheet Music, Police Parade March,
  c1917 .... 25.00
Suspenders, marked "Police," engraved
  police club on slide adjusters, pr ... 25.00
Statue, 8" h, "Old Time Policeman," ceramic, marked "George Z. Lefton" . 50.00
Toy, wind-up, 3 x 8½ x 6", policeman
  on motorcycle, tan motorcycle with
  black, white, and red wheels, policeman in red, white, and blue uniform,
  Unique Art 150.00
Uniform, pants, vest, and coat, wool,
  blue, nine brass buttons, made by
  Fred Batchelder Co, Boston 175.00

POLITICAL AND CAMPAIGN ITEMS

Collecting Hints: Items selling below $100 move frequently enough to establish firm prices. Items above that price fluctuate according to supply and demand. Many individuals now recognize the value of political items, acquiring them and holding them for future sale. As a result, modern material has a relatively low market value.

The pioneering work in the identification of political materials has been done by Theodore L. Hake, whose books are listed below. Two books have greatly assisted in the identification and cataloging of campaign materials, especially for the earlier period: Herbert R. Collins's *Threads of History* and Edmund B. Sullivan's *American Political Badges and Medalets 1789–1892.*

History: Since 1800 the American presidency always has been a contest between two or more candidates. Initially, souvenirs were issued to celebrate victories. Items issued during a campaign to show support for a candidate were actively distributed in the William Henry Harrison election of 1840.

Campaign items cover a wide variety of materials—buttons, bandannas, tokens, license plates, etc. The only limiting factor has been the promoter's imagination. The advent of television campaigning has reduced the emphasis on individual items. Modern campaigns do not seem to have the variety of materials which were issued earlier.

Modern collectors should be aware of Kennedy material. Much has been reproduced and many items were issued after his death. Knowledgeable collectors also keep in touch with Presidential libraries to find out what type of souvenir items they are offering for sale. The collector should concentrate on the items from the time of the actual campaigns.

References: Herbert R. Collins, *Threads of History,* Smithsonian Institute Press, 1979; Richard Friz, *The Official Guide To Political Memorabilia, First Edition,* House of Collectibles, 1988; Theodore L. Hake, *Encyclopedia of Political Buttons, United States, 1896–1972,* Americana & Collectibles Press, 1985; Theodore L. Hake, *Political Buttons, Book II, 1920–1976,* Americana & Collectibles Press, 1977; Theodore L. Hake, *Political Buttons, Book III, 1789–1916,* Americana & Collectibles Press, 1978; Theodore L. Hake, *1984 Revised Prices For The Encyclopedia Of Political Buttons,* Americana & Collectibles Press, 1984; Edmund B. Sullivan, *American Political Badges and Medalets, 1789–1892,* Quarterman Publications, Inc., 1981.

For information about the Americana & Collectibles Press, write to: Americana & Collectibles Press, P.O. Box 1444, York, PA 17405.

Periodical: *The Political Collector Newspaper,* 444 Lincoln Street, York, PA 17404.

Collectors' Club: American Political Items Collectors, P. O. Box 340339, San Antonio, TX 78234.

Museums: Museum of American Political Life, Hartford, CT; Smithsonian Museum, Washington, DC.

Advisor: Ted Hake.

McKinley–Hobart, mechanical dollar, Hake #216, $65.00.

William McKinley, 1896 and 1900
Glass, 4" h, portrait and slogan, 1896	20.00
Lapel Stud, ⅞" l, "McKinley-Protection '96," brass, diecut, Napoleon's hat shape	25.00
Plate, 8 x 10½", glass, oval, McKinley in center, inscribed "It Is God's Way/His Will Be Done/Born 1843-Died 1901"	35.00

Ribbon
2½ x 6", yellow, black "Sound Money Club/NPR Employees/McKinley," brass hanger and pin	25.00
3 x 7", red, white, and blue, "McKinley and Hobart," gold stamped shield and flag, brass hanger and braid tassels	30.00
Tray, aluminum, McKinley and Roosevelt sepia portraits, inscribed "Nominated Philadelphia June 1900," millinery adv on reverse	25.00

William Jennings Bryan, 1896, 1900, and 1908
Button, ⅞", black and white, silver ground, "Our Choice–Rosebery Cigar"	60.00
Jugate, 1¼", Bryan-Stevenson, black and white portraits surrounded by red, white, and blue flags, gold details	40.00
Mug, 3½" h, pressed glass, raised portrait, "The People's Money/Wm J Bryan," raised geometric pattern, flared out edge, c1896	45.00
Post Card, 3⅝ x 5½", colored, Bryan with shock of corn, "From Mr. Bryan's Fairview Farm," 1908	15.00
Watch Fob, enamel, Bryan-Kern, eagles and flags center, strap	30.00

Theodore Roosevelt, 1904 and 1912
Bandanna, 21 x 24", red and white, Roosevelt sepia portrait center, "Progressive/Roosevlet/1912/Battle Flag"	65.00
Inaugural Badge, 1905, gold letters, blue ground, celluloid bar, brass Capitol Building	50.00
Mirror, pocket, 2¼", flesh tone sepia bust portrait	65.00
Plate, 10" d, blue and white, portrait with raised edge, scenes border, "Theodore Roosevelt/26th President of the U.S.," marked "The Rowland & Marsellus Co/Staffordshire/ England"	40.00
Noisemaker, 4½" l, wood, black stenciled "Roosevelt-Fairbanks" at top, inscribed underneath "For A Rattling Good Auditor, Try Frank A. Sarstedt"	75.00
Ribbon, 2½ x 8", white fabric, blue portrait, inscription "Progressive Convention/Lincoln, Nebr/Sept 3, 1912"	40.00
Sheet Music, 7 x 11", blue on white, inscribed "Dedicated To The GOP/A Victory Is Ours/A Rousing Republican Campaign Song," 1904 copyright	15.00
Watch Fob, 1¾ x 2", brass, "Roosevelt and Fairbanks"	20.00

Alton B. Parker, 1904
  Button, 1¼", black and white portrait surrounded by Capitol dome outlined in gold, red, white, and blue star and stripe design 35.00
  Jugate, 1¼", brass, Parker and Davis, flag shield on top 35.00
  Stud, metal, bust of Parker in wreath 15.00
William Howard Taft, 1908 and 1912
  Bottle Stopper, 2½ x 3 x 3½", painted composition Taft's head, bottom cork marked "Made In Germany," c1952 .... 75.00
  Button, 1¼", black, white, and red, Taft riding GOP elephant and carrying "Big Stick," slogan "Taft From Chicago To Washington" 300.00
  Jugate, ⅞", Taft-Sherman portraits .. 20.00
  Lapel Stud, ½", gold on dark blue .. 12.00
  Mug, 5" h, figural, numbered and marked "Made In Germany," c1908 .... 75.00
  Post Card, red, white, and blue, flag motif, inscribed "For President Of USA/Wm H Taft of Ohio," inked message reverse, 1908 cancellation 15.00
  Poster, 11 x 14", sepia portrait, signature, bottom edge marked "Copyright 1908 Moffett Studio/ Chicago" 15.00
  Tip Tray, 4½" d, litho tin, jugate portraits of Taft and Sherman, rim caption "Grand Old Party/1856 To 1908," black and gold border 125.00
  Watch Fob, brass, diecut, black detailing 20.00
Woodrow Wilson, 1912 and 1916
  Button, "For President 1912 Woodrow Wilson," black and white ... 15.00
  Jugate, "Wilson and Marshall," black and white 30.00
  Pennant, 7 x 17", dark purple, felt, crimped tin support bar on edge, two brown cords for hanging, gold lettering, inscribed "Mardi Gras/ 1913 Mobile, AL," diecut paper shield with black and white picture and inscribed "March 4 Inauguration/1913 Washingt'n DC" 25.00
  Stickpin, 2¼", brass frame, black and white photo, dark blue edge 25.00
  Watch Fob, "Wilson/His Pen Mightier Than The Sword," metal, copper finish, portrait, scale with quill pen outweighing sword 20.00
Charles Evans Hughes, 1916
  Button, black and white picture surrounded by gold oval, red, white, and blue flag, and green wreath with red berries 25.00
  Jugate, Hughes and Fairbanks, black and white photo 50.00

  Watch Fob, 1½" d, celluloid, sepia, bust portrait, name below 60.00
Warren G. Harding, 1920
  Bell, "Ring For Harding and Coolidge," copper finish 20.00
  Button, "For President Warren G. Harding," brown and white portrait, dark blue rim 15.00
  Lapel Stud, metal, diecut, walking elephant with name on side 12.00
  Purse, coin, leather, silvered brass clip, President Harding between two sets of flags 35.00
James M. Cox, 1920
  Button, ⁷⁄₁₆", black and white, "Gov Cox" and slogan 30.00
  Sheet Music, "The Tie That Binds or Jimmy Is The Man For Us" 35.00
  Stamp, black and white portrait, red border, "Governor James M. Cox, Put The Ax To Tax" 30.00
Calvin Coolidge, 1924
  Bell, brass, "Ring For Coolidge" ... 15.00
  Jugate, ⅞", black and white, "For President Coolidge/Vice-President Dawes" 30.00
  Lapel Stud, metal diecut, elephant, name on side 10.00
  Mirror, 2⅛", celluloid, black and white, trigate, 1924, DE Senator and Governor 200.00
  Stickpin, brass, diecut, horseshoe design spells out name 40.00
  Thimble, aluminum, red, white, and blue band bottom edge, "Coolidge & Dawes" 15.00
John W. Davis, 1924
  Dish, 4" d, glass, incised inscription "Compliments of Hazel/Atlas Glass Co/John W. Davis Day Aug 11-24, Clarksburg, WV" 40.00
  Pin, metal, diamond shape, comet in relief, "Davis 1924" 60.00
  Poster, 22 x 16", sepia, formal portrait, 1924 .... 50.00
Herbert Hoover, 1928 and 1932
  Button, ¾", brass, "Keep Hoover/Be Safe," gold raised letters, dark blue background 25.00
  License Plate, 5 x 12", cast aluminum, diecut letters and Capitol dome, silver finish 100.00
  Pencil, 8" l, yellow, composition head on top, silver lettering, "Hoover For President 1928" 15.00
  Pin, enamel, owl, "Who Who Hoover" 20.00
  Portrait, 3½", black and white, dark blue rim, black background 100.00
Alfred E. Smith, 1928
  Button, 1", "Al Smith/A Winner For

You," gray and white cello, orig
back paper **125.00**

Jugate, 1¼", black and white portraits, dark blue background, gold
red, white, and blue design,
"Smith/Robinson" **500.00**

Lapel Stud, brass, brown derby hat
design **10.00**

License Plate, "Al Smith For President," 4½ x 12", tin, painted,
raised red letters **30.00**

Pencil, green, composition head on
top, silver lettering "Smith For President 1928" **15.00**

Pin, brass, brown derby design **8.00**

Token, 1", brass, donkey, "Al Smith
Lucky Pocket Piece/For Personal
Liberty and National Prosperity
1928" **8.00**

**Roosevelt, fan, cardboard, adv on back,
7½ x 10½", $20.00.**

Franklin D. Roosevelt, 1932, 1936,
1940, and 1944
Ashtray, 4½ × 6½ × 1", metal,
mounted 1½" bronze inaugural
medal in center, handles with
raised eagle design, stamped
"Guildcraft" and dated "Jan 20,
1941" **75.00**

Banner, 9 x 11½", cloth, red, white,
and blue, metal bar, brass loop for
hanging, inscribed "God Bless
America/Our Next President/Frank-
lin D. Roosevelt" **20.00**

Button, 1¼", "I Gotta Go And Vote
For FDR," red lettering, white background **10.00**

Inauguration Ticket, 2½ x 6", black
and white FDR and Garner portraits, yellow sunburst, marked "It
Is Suggested That The Larger Portion Of This Ticket Be Retained As
A Souvenir Of The First Inaugural
Ever To Be Held On Jan 20" **25.00**

License Plate, 3½" d, metal, red reflective background, blue and
white slogan, silver edge **35.00**

Pin, 1¼", metal, painted red, white,
and blue, gold center, cut out initials **20.00**

Portrait, color, silvered brass rect
frame **15.00**

Poster, 15 x 21", black and white
photo, Roosevelt and Garner at dining table, c1936 .... **30.00**

Ring, campaign, slivered brass, black
portrait, "Roosevelt/Garner," and
dates "1932–1940" on each side
of band **20.00**

Alfred Landon, 1936
Button, 1¾", yellow sunflower design
with brown portrait center **15.00**

Jugate, ⅞", Landon/Knox, brown,
white, and yellow, diecut brass
sunflower petal backing **25.00**

License Plate, 4" d, 5½" h, metal,
blue celluloid insert, blue and
white inscription "Landon/Knox" . **25.00**

Matchbook, red, white, blue, and yellow, lists candidates outside and inside, unused **10.00**

Pin, brass, red, white, and blue
enamel, elephant in center **15.00**

Poster, 14 x 21", red, white, and blue,
"Landon and Knox For Us," 1936 **40.00**

Tab, litho, red, white, blue, and yellow, "Landon/Knox" **10.00**

Whistle, 1", aluminum, blue enamel
band, "Landon & Knox Rep" **25.00**

Wendell L. Willkie, 1940
Ashtray, 3½" d, glass, red name, blue
slogan "Preparedness—Peace—Prosperity" **15.00**

Banner, 9 x 11½", fabric, red, white,
and blue, metal support rod, brass
hanging loop, inscribed "God Bless
America/Our Next President/Wen-
dell Willkie" **20.00**

Button
¾", blue and white, "For President
Will (key)," attached silvered
brass key **15.00**

⅞", "I'm For Willkie and McNary" **50.00**

Dice Cup, 3" h, 2½" d, leather,
"Don't Gamble, Elect Willkie," gi-
veaway from "Rome Sporting
Goods Mfg Co, Rome, NY" **10.00**

License Plate, 4 x 13½", orange, gold
letters outlined in dark blue, blue
edge **20.00**

Plaque, 9½", celluloid, black and
white portrait, dark blue background with white and red circles,
orig pink cord **100.00**

Sticker, 3½ × 6", diecut, foil, silver,

blue, and red, inscribed "Willkie/
The Hope Of America" **15.00**
Thomas E. Dewey, 1944 and 1948
Jugate, ⅞", "Dewey-Warren," black
and white, 1948 .... **30.00**
Pennant, 4½ x 12", white and ma-
roon, four felt streamers **15.00**
Tab, litho, red, white, and blue, red
eagle center, Dewey in blue banner **5.00**
Harry S. Truman, 1948
Inauguration Ticket, 2½ x 4½", red,
white, blue, and yellow, seating in-
formation front, reverse with black
and white jugate picture of Truman
and Barkley **25.00**
Program, 8 x 11", Official Inaugural
Program 1949," 72 pgs, orig mail-
ing envelope **40.00**
Ribbon, 2 x 7½", fabric, white, in-
scribed in black "President Truman
Committee," and "Stand" in red . **20.00**
Sticker, 1½ x 2¼", set of 6, red,
white, and blue, inscribed "1950/
The American Way/Register And
Vote/President Truman" **10.00**

**Pinback Button, Eisenhower–Nixon, red,
white, and blue, 3", $7.50.**

Dwight D. Eisenhower, 1952 and 1956
Button
1¼", "Dem-Ike-Crats For Eisenhower," blue picture, red, white,
and blue background **10.00**
3½", blue and white, "I Like Ike,"
Bastian Brothers **5.00**
Display Card, 13½ x 19", cardboard,
black and white photo, easel back,
c1956 .... **30.00**
License Plate, 6 x 12", metal, white,
raised black letters, "I Like IKE" .. **20.00**
Nodder, 6" h, composition, late
1950s **40.00**
Panel, 7 x 22½", fabric, white and
dark blue, inscription "Citizens For
Eisenhower" **25.00**
Pen, 5" l, brass, black and white plas-
tic, portrait, slogan "For The Love
Of Ike-Vote Republican" **25.00**

Pennant, felt, dark blue
8½ x 24", yellow image, "Your Best
Bet In 52 For A Winning Team" **15.00**
11 x 30", white, gray, and pink inscription and image, inscribed
"Second Inauguration Jan 20
1957" **25.00**
Plate, 10½" d, china, colorful Pennsylvania Dutch symbol center, inscribed "The President's First Birthday In The White House 14
October 1953," gray signature,
gray rim with two gold bands,
marked "A Limited Edition/Made
Expressly For This Occasion By
Castleton China, New Castle, Pen-
nyslvania" **30.00**

**Hat, garrison style, 1952, blue letters,
gold braiding, tan, elephant on back with
slogan "Early Times," $20.00.**

Poster, 12 x 17", black and white,
inscribed "Welcome Mr. President/
We'll See You At The Civic Auditorium Wed, Oct 17, 6 PM" **25.00**
Socks, pr, gray, red motto "I Like Ike,"
orig cardboard insert and orange
and blue paper tag **15.00**
Trivet, 4½ x 8", cast iron, painted
black, ceramic insert, inscribed
"General And Mrs. Dwight D. Eisenhower," back marked "Pilking-
ton/England," c1956 .... **12.00**
Adlai E. Stevenson, 1952 and 1956
Booklet, *A Man Named Stevenson*, 5
x 7", 16 pgs, Democratic National
Committee, 1952 .... **10.00**
Button
3", celluloid, red, white, and blue,
"Adlai-Estes" **8.00**
3½", black and white portrait, red,
white, and blue design **10.00**
4", "America Needs Stevenson,"
red, white, and blue **10.00**
License Plate, 4 x 12", metal, white
raised dark blue letters **20.00**
Record, 78 rpm, plastic, 7" sq cardboard with black and white portrait, Philadelphia AFL-CIO en-
dorsement **20.00**

Tab, 1", litho, black and white, Stevenson in block letters **1.50**

John F. Kennedy, 1960

Bank, 9" d, plastic, silver, JFK half dollar design with 1964 date, unused, 1960s **15.00**

Cigarette Lighter, 1½" d, copper finish, coin shape, inscribed "John F Kennedy 1917–1963/35th President-USA," Statue of Liberty on back **10.00**

Hat, campaign, 11 x 13 x 3½", plastic, molded, white, red, white, and blue paper band brim, inscription "Kennedy For President," oval black and white pictures left and right, black and white portrait on top **50.00**

Inaugural Invitation, 8½ x 11", engraved, emb gold inaugural seal, 4 pgs **20.00**

Keychain, brass bust of JFK, metal plate joins ring inscribed and dates of birth and death, 1917–1963 ... **12.00**

Magazine, *Life,* Jan 27, 1961, "The Kennedy Inauguration," black and white photos, 15 pgs of inauguration **8.00**

Plate

6", china, color portrait, Mrs. Kennedy seated in yellow chair, Kennedy standing behind, gold design, c1961 .... **10.00**

7½" d, china, glazed, full color portrait center President and Mrs. Kennedy, early 1960s **15.00**

Playing Cards, "Kennedy Kards," complete deck, boxed, 1963 copyright **35.00**

Salt and Pepper Shakers, pr, china, JFK in rocking chair, orig stoppers, paper labels marked "Japan" **25.00**

Tapestry, 19 x 37", woven, JFK and Capitol building, made in Belgium **15.00**

Richard M. Nixon, 1960, 1968, and 1972

Bank, 3 x 7 x 4½", mechanical, cast iron, elephant, white, red raised letters, inscribed "Vote Right/ Nixon Agnew In '72/Better The Second Time Around" **75.00**

Book, *Six Crises,* Doubleday, 1962, dj, 460 pgs, black pen signature "Richard Nixon" **75.00**

Button

1¾", red, white, and blue, "Dependability, Intergrity, Capability, Knowledge" **10.00**

3½", black and white, red, white, and blue background, "Keep Dick On The Job" **15.00**

Dart Board, 11½ x 11½", fiberboard,

silk screened design, Nixon giving "V" sign, pair of brass and yellow plastic darts, metal hanging tab .. **15.00**

Figure, 3 x 5 x 4", vinyl, elephant with Nixon head, back with black and tan world and blue blanket with "R" and "Nixon," marked "GOP," c1972 .... **15.00**

Hat, 4 x 11", paper, blue and white, slogan "Experience Counts," 1960 **8.00**

Inauguration Invitation, 8 x 11", cardboard, emb gold inaugural seal, 1973 .... **10.00**

License Plate, 6 x 12", red and blue on silver reflective background ... **15.00**

Medal, 2¾" d, Franklin Mint serial number 18151, edge marked "Solid Bronze," plastic holder ... **20.00**

Plate, 9", china, full color portrait, gold rim band, "Richard M. Nixon 37th President," c1968 .... **15.00**

Lyndon B. Johnson, 1964

Button, 6", full color portrait, red, white, and blue rim, inscribed "Inauguration Lyndon Baines Johnson Jan 20, 1965 Washington DC" ... **10.00**

Figure, 5", vinyl, wearing red, white, and blue campaign button, orig unopened cellophane package, Remco **25.00**

Hat, campaign, orange felt, red on white fabric band, "LBJ For The USA" **10.00**

Jugate, black and white photo on white, white initials on dark blue, red section center with white "National Maritime Union AFL-CIO/ Pres Joseph Curran Says All The Way" **50.00**

Wall Plaque, 9" d, celluloid, black and white portraits of LBJ and HHH **6.00**

Barry M. Goldwater, 1964

Button

3½", red, white, and blue, abstract flag design, "Save America/ Goldwater-Miller" **15.00**

6", black and white portrait, blue background, red and white curved line, three star shape designs, inscribed "Barry Goldwater 64" **10.00**

Eyeglasses, "Go Goldwater," cardboard, black on white, penciled note used at San Francisco convention **10.00**

License Plate, 4 x 12", metal, yellow, raised blue letters, "Victory In '64" slogan **10.00**

Poster, 14 x 21", red, white, and blue, "A Choice...Not An Echo" slogan **15.00**

Hubert H. Humphrey, 1968
 Button, 1¾", celluloid, orange letters,
  brown ground, "Hubie Baby" ... **4.00**
 Pencil, mechanical, black plastic and
  brass, Vice President's seal **4.00**
 Tab, 2", blue, green, red, white, and
  black, "Labor For Humphrey" ... **4.00**
 Tie Tack, brass, diecut, initials
  "HHH," 1968 .... **2.00**
George McGovern, 1972
 Button, 3", "McGovern," brown
  shaded portrait **12.00**
 Comb, plastic, blue, "McGovern-
  Shriver," smiling face **4.00**
 Shopping Bag, 15 x 17", white and
  dark blue, "President McGovern
  '72" **5.00**
 Tab, blue and white, "McGovern/
  Shriver" **2.00**
Gerald R. Ford, 1976
 Button, 2¼", multicolored "Win With
  Ford" **4.00**
 Jugate, 1", celluloid, red, white, and
  black, "Ford/For/76/with Rocky" . **4.00**
 Tab, white, President Ford '76 ..... **1.50**
James E. Carter, 1976
 Button
  3", red, white, blue, and tan, Carter
   with peanut body **5.00**
  6", black and white portraits, green
   background, red, white, and
   blue designs, inscribed "Inauguration Day Jan 20, 1977" **5.00**
  Christmas Card, 8½ x 11", watercolor
   and signature, adults and children
   look at Santa holding "Carter/Mon-
   dale/1980," sign, White House
   background **10.00**
 Jugate, 3", Carter/Mondale, black and
  white, red, white, blue, yellow,
  and brown scrolls, flag and eagle . **5.00**
 Poster, 14 x 22", green and white,
  inset with close up of Carter **2.00**
Ronald Reagan, 1980 and 1984
 Button, 2¾", red, heart shape "California Loves Reagan '76," white letters **10.00**
 Card
  Anniversary, 5 x 8", paper, red and
   white border, emb gold Presidential Seal, "Congratulations On
   Your Anniversary" and four line
   inscription, unused White House
   envelope **12.00**
  musical, 6 x 8", cellophane cov,
   gold "Reagan-Bush" on front,
   full color Reagan and Bush photo
   and quote inside, plays Star
   Spangled Banner and red lights
   glow when opened **15.00**
 Press ID, 3 x 4½", full color, laminated, metal neck chain, inscrip-

tion "Jan 20, 1981/Reagan Inau-
guration/ ABC News/Press" **15.00**

POST CARDS

Collecting Hints: Concentrate on one subject area, publisher, or illustrator. Collect cards in mint condition, when possible.

The more common the holiday, the larger the city, the more popular the tourist attraction, the easier it will be to find post cards about these subjects because of the millions of cards that still remain in these categories. The smaller runs of "real" photo post cards are the most desirable of the scenic cards. Photographic cards of families and individuals, unless they show occupations, unusual toys, dolls, or teddy bears have little value.

Stamps and cancellation marks may affect the value of cards, but rarely. Consult a philatelic guide.

Post cards fall into two main categories: view cards and topics. View cards are easiest to sell in their local geographic region. European view cards, while very interesting, are difficult to sell in America.

It must be stressed age alone does not determine price. A birthday post card from 1918 may sell for only ten cents, while a political campaign card from the 1950s may bring ten dollars. Every collectible is governed by supply and demand.

Although the most popular collecting period is 1898–1918, the increasing costs of post cards from this era have turned collectors' interest to post cards from the 1920s, 1930s, and 1940s. The main interest in the 1920–1930 period is cards with an Art Deco motif. The cards collected from the 1940s are "linens" which feature a textured "linen–like" paper surface.

Cards from the 1950–1970 period are called chromes because of their shiny surface paper. Advertising post cards from this chrome era are rapidly gaining popularity while still selling for under $3.00.

History: The golden age of post cards dates from 1898 to 1918. While there are cards printed earlier, they are collected for their postal history. Post cards prior to 1898 are called "pioneer" cards.

European publishers, especially in England and Germany, produced the vast majority of cards during the golden age. The major post card publishers are Raphael Tuck (England), Paul Finkenrath of Berlin (PFB–German), and Whitney, Detroit Publishing Co., and John Winsch (United States). However, many American publishers had their stock produced in Europe, hence, "Made in Bavaria" imprints. While some Tuck cards are high priced, many are still available in the "ten cent" boxes.

Styles changed rapidly, and manufacturers responded to every need. The linen post card which gained popularity in the 1940s was quickly replaced by the chrome cards of the post–1950 period.

References: Many of the best books are out-of-print. However, they are available through libraries. Ask your library to utilize the inter-library loan system.

Frederic and Mary Megson, *American Advertising Postcards—Set and Series: 1890–1920,* published by authors, 1985; Dorothy B. Ryan, *Picture Postcards In The United States, 1893–1918,* Clarkson N. Potter, 1982, paperback edition; Jack H. Smith, *Postcard Companion: The Collector's Reference,* Wallace-Homestead Book Company, 1989; Jane Wood, *The Collector's Guide To Post Cards,* L-W Promotions, 1984, 1987 values updated.

Periodicals: *Barr's Postcard News,* 70 S. 6th Street, Lansing, IA 52151; *Postcard Collector,* Joe Jones Publishing, P. O. Box 337, Iola, WI 54945.

Special Note: An up-to-date listing of books about and featuring post cards can be obtained from Gotham Book Mart & Gallery, Inc., 41 West 47th Street, New York, NY 10036.

Collectors' Clubs: *Barr's Postcard News* and the *Postcard Collector* publish lists of over fifty regional clubs in the United States and Canada.

Note: The following prices are for cards in excellent to mint condition—no sign of edgewear, no creases, not trimmed, no writing on the picture side of the card, no tears, and no dirt. Each defect would reduce the price given by 10%.

Advisor: Susan Brown Nicholson.

ADVERTISING

Adv on linens, large product image ...	**6.00**
Adv on chromes, large product image .	**2.00**
Automobile adv	
American prior to 1920	**20.00**
European prior to 1920	**10.00**
After 1920	**5.00**
After 1950	**1.00**
Bulova Watch, government postal back	**6.00**
Campbell Soup adv	
Horizontal format	**30.00**
Vertical format	**100.00**
Coca-Cola adv	
Duster girl in car	**450.00**
Hamilton King	**250.00**
Diner Adv, linen era	**10.00**
Do-Wah-Jack	**10.00**
DuPont Gun	
Birds	**30.00**
Dogs	**100.00**
Zeppelin	**150.00**
Elgin Watch Co	**6.00**

Formica, chrome era	**3.00**
Frog-in-the-Throat	**50.00**
Gas Station adv, linen era	**6.00**
Hotel-Motel	
Chrome	**1.00**
Early	**2.00**
Linen era	**4.00**
Livermore & Knight publishing adv ...	**10.00**
McDonald's, chrome era	**1.00**
Michelin Tire Company, featuring Michelin man	**30.00**
Parker Gun	**200.00**
Rockford Watch, calendar series	**15.00**
Seed Company adv, good images	**6.00**
Sleepy Eye Indian, flour adv, set of 9 .	**1,000.00**
Tupperware, chrome era	**3.00**
Warner Corset, Mucha	**500.00**
Waverly Cycle, Mucha	**5,000.00**
Yellow Kid Adv calendars, Outcault ..	**100.00**
Zeno gum, mechanical	**25.00**

Artist signed, Samuel Schmucker, Detroit Butterfly series, $125.00.

ARTIST SIGNED

Atwell, Mabel Lucie	
Early by Tuck	**12.00**
Regular, comic	**6.00**
Basch, Arpad, Art Nouveau	**125.00**
Bertiglia, children	**10.00**
Boileau, Philip	
By Reinthal Neuman	**15.00**
By Raphael Tuck	**100.00**
By other	**35.00**
Bompard, art dec	**10.00**
Boulanger, Maurice, cats	
Large images	**25.00**
Many in action	**12.00**
Brill, Ginks, set of 16	**10.00**
Browne, Tom	
American Baseball series, green background	**9.00**
English comic series	**3.00**

Brundage, Frances	
Children	**10.00**
Early Tuck chromolithograph	**30.00**
Brunelleschi, Art Nouveau	**200.00**
Busi, Art Deco	**8.00**
Caldecott	
Early	**8.00**
1974 reprints	**1.00**
Carmichael, comic	**3.00**
Carr, Gene, comic	**10.00**
Chiostri, Art Deco	**20.00**
Christy, Howard Chandler	**12.00**
Clapsaddle, Ellen Hattie	
Children	**15.00**
Floral, sleds, crosses	**2.00**
Halloween, mechanical	**100.00**
Suffrage	
Anti-vote, "A woman's sphere is in	
the home"	**25.00**
Pro-vote	**100.00**
Valentine, mechanical	**45.00**
Unsigned, Wolf Publishing Co	**6.00**
Corbella, Art Deco	**10.00**
Corbett, Bertha, sunbonnets	**15.00**
Curtis, E., children	**3.00**
Daniell, Eva, Art Nouveau, Tuck	**85.00**
Drayton/Weiderseim, Grace (Campbell's Kids)	**35.00**
Dwig	
Comic	**5.00**
Halloween	**15.00**
Fidler, Alice Luella, women	**6.00**
Fisher, Harrison	**12.00**
Gassaway, K., children	**6.00**
Gibson, Charles Dana, sepia	**6.00**
Golay, Mary, flowers	**1.50**
Greenaway, Kate, sgd	**350.00**
Greiner, M	
Blacks	**12.00**
Children	**5.00**
Molly and Her Teddy	**12.00**
Griggs, H. B.	**8.00**
Gunn, Archie	**3.00**
Gutmann, Bessie Pease	**10.00**
Hays, Margaret	**8.00**
Humphrey, Maud, sgd	**70.00**
Innes, John, western	**3.00**
Johnson, J., children	**4.00**
Kirchner, Raphael	
First period	**125.00**
Second period	**65.00**
Third period	**50.00**
Santa	**200.00**
Klein, Catherine	
Floral	**2.00**
Alphabet	**9.00**
Alphabet, letters X, Y, Z	**25.00**
Koehler, Mela, early	**65.00**
Kokoschka, Wiener Werkstatte	**1,500.00**
Mauzan, Art Deco	**15.00**
May, Phil, English comic series	**8.00**
McCay, Winsor, "Little Nemo"	**25.00**

Mucha, Alphonse	
Art Nouveau, months of the year	**200.00**
Slavic period, murals	**75.00**
Women, full card design	**600.00**
O'Neill, Rose	
Gross Publishing Company	**125.00**
Ice Cream adv	**100.00**
Kewpies	**35.00**
Pickings from Puck-Blacks	**100.00**
Suffrage	
Babies	**200.00**
Kewpies	**125.00**
Opper, Frederick, comic	**8.00**
Outcault	**12.00**
Parkinson, Ethel, children	**6.00**
Patella, women	**15.00**
Payne, Harry	**15.00**
Phillips, Cole, fade-away style	**25.00**
Price, Mary Evans	**5.00**
Remington, Frederic	**35.00**
Robinson, Robert	**15.00**
Rockwell, Norman	**35.00**
Russell, Charles	**9.00**
Sager, Xavier	**15.00**
Schmucker, Samuel	
Halloween greetings	**65.00**
New Years	**25.00**
Silk, any greeting	**55.00**
St. Patrick's Day greetings	**15.00**
Valentine greetings	**15.00**
Shinn, Cobb	**3.00**
Smith, Jessie Wilcox, seven different images	**15.00**
Studdy, Bonzo Dog	**12.00**
Tam, Jean, women	**20.00**
Thiele, Arthur	
Blacks	
Large faces	**25.00**
On bikes	**45.00**
Cats	
In action	**15.00**
Large heads	**20.00**
Pigs, large heads	**25.00**
Twelvetrees, Charles, comic, children	**5.00**
Underwood, Clarence	**9.00**
Upton, Florence, Golliwoggs, Tuck	**35.00**
Wain, Louis	
Cat	**45.00**
Dog	**25.00**
Frog	**35.00**
Paper doll, cat	**200.00**
Santa and cat	**100.00**
Wall, Bernhardt, sunbonnets	**15.00**
Wood, Lawson	**8.00**

EXPOSITION

Alaska-Yukon-Pacific	**10.00**
California Midwinter	**250.00**
Cotton States Exposition	**200.00**
Hudson-Fulton	**10.00**

Jamestown, mechanical, dressed bear,
    144 outfits **350.00**
Lewis and Clark **10.00**
Pan American
    Black and white **6.00**
    Color **10.00**
Portland Rose Festival **4.00**
Portola Festival
    Poster style **15.00**
    Views **3.00**
Priest of Pallas **10.00**
St. Louis, 1904
    Eggshell paper **10.00**
    Hold to light type
        General **35.00**
        Inside Inn scene **125.00**
    Silver background **10.00**
Trans-Mississippi
    Advertising **125.00**
    Officials **75.00**
World Columbian, 1893
    Officials **25.00**
    Pre-Officials, without seals **100.00**

Silk Applique **35.00**
Suits other than red **10.00**
Easter
    Animals, dressed **5.00**
    Chicks or rabbits **2.00**
    Children **4.50**
    Crosses .... **.25**
Fourth of July
    Children **5.00**
    Uncle Sam **8.00**
    Others **1.50**
Ground Hog Day
    Early, i.e. Loundsbury Publishing ... **250.00**
    After 1930 .... **20.00**

Greetings, Halloween, bright orange pumpkin, artist signed "Ellen Clapsaddle," $8.00

Halloween
    Children **3.00**
    Children, extremely colorful or artists
        sgd **8.00**
    Winsch Publishing **45.00**
Labor Day
    Lounsbury Publishing **125.00**
    Nash Publishing **95.00**
Leap Year **5.00**
Mother's Day, early **5.00**
New Year
    Bells .... **.25**
    Children or Father Time **4.00**
    Winsch Publishing, beautiful women **15.00**
St. Patrick's Day
    Children **4.50**
    No children **2.50**
Thanksgiving
    Children **3.50**
    No children .... **.50**
    Uncle Sam **4.00**
Valentines
    Children, women **4.00**
    Hearts, comic **1.00**
    Winsch Publishing, beautiful women **15.00**

Greetings, Ground Hog Day, $20.00.

GREETINGS

April Fools
    American comic **3.00**
    French litho with fish **10.00**
Birthday
    Floral .... **.10**
    Children .... **.50**
Christmas, no Santa .... **.25**
Christmas, Santa
    Artists signed **15.00**
    Black face, Coontown series **100.00**
    German, highly embossed **15.00**
    Hold to light type **100.00**
    Installment, unused **100.00**
    Kirchner **200.00**
    P.F.B. Publishing Company **20.00**
    Red Suits **8.00**

PATRIOTIC

Decoration Day	6.00
Lincoln	4.00
Patriotic Songs	3.00
Uncle Sam	8.00
Washington	4.00
World War II, linen	2.00

PHOTOGRAPHIC

Children under Christmas trees	10.00
Children with animals or toys	8.00
Christmas trees	4.00
Circus Performer, identified and close-up	15.00
Exaggerations	
Conrad Publishing, after 1935	8.00
Martin Publishing	12.00
Martin Publishing, US Coin	75.00
Main Streets	
Large cities	4.00
Unidentified towns	2.00
With trains or trollies	12.00
People	
Military with flags	5.00
Occupation, American	15.00
Portraits, instant relatives	1.00
Unusual studio backdrops	5.00
Railroad Depots	8.00
Railroad Depots, with trains	12.00
Shop Exteriors, identified	6.00
Shop Interiors, identified location	25.00

POLITICAL AND SOCIAL HISTORY

Billy Possum	15.00
Blacks	8.00
Campaign	
1900	100.00
1904	65.00
1908	35.00
Indians	8.00
Jewish, comic	8.00
McKinley's death	6.00
Prohibition	6.00
Roosevelt's African Tour	3.00
Russo-Japanese War	20.00
Suffrage	
Cargill publisher	
Number 111 only	125.00
Other numbers	12.00
Clapsaddle	50.00
General	10.00
Kewpie	125.00
Parades	10.00
Taft, cartoons	12.00
Wilson	6.00
Truman, campaign card	25.00

POSTERS

Collecting Hints: Posters are collected either for their subject and historical value, e.g. movie, railroad, minstrel, etc., or for the aesthetic appeal. Modern art historians have recognized the poster as one of the most creative art forms of our times.

Often a popular film would be re-released several times over a period of years. Most re-releases can be identified by looking at the lower right corner in the white border area. A re-release will usually be indicated with an "R" and a diagonal slash mark with the year of the newest release. Therefore, a "R/47" would indicate a 1947 issue.

History: The poster was an extremely effective and critical means of mass communication, especially in the period before 1920. Enormous quantities were produced, helped in part by the propaganda role played by posters in World War I.

Print runs of two million were not unknown. Posters were not meant to be saved. Once they served their purpose, they tended to be destroyed. The paradox of high production and low survival is one of the fascinating aspects of poster history.

The posters of the late 19th century and early 20th century represent the pinnacle of American lithography printing. The advertising posters of firms such as Strobridge or Courier are true classics. Philadelphia was one center for the poster industry.

Europe pioneered in posters with high artistic and aesthetic content. Many major artists of the 20th century designed posters. Poster art still plays a key role throughout Europe today.

References: John Barnicoat, *A Concise History of Posters*, Harry Abrams, Inc., 1976; George Theofiles, *American Posters of World War I: A Price and Collector's Guide*, Dafram House Publishers, Inc.

Advisor: George Theofiles.

REPRODUCTION ALERT: Some of the posters by A. M. Cassandre have been reproduced in France.

ADVERTISING

"Arrow Shirts With Starched Cuffs," J C Leyendecker, 21 x 11", man in smoking jacket reads book, c1916	150.00
"Be Refreshed with Healthful Delicious Doublemint Gum," Otis Shephard, 11 x 42", twins with sleek car, c1937	200.00
"Camomille Liqueur," 32 x 51", yellow bottle, blue background, c1890	225.00
"Coca-Cola-Yes," Harold Sundblum, 11 x 27", bathing beauty, 1946	150.00

World War II, 28 x 20¼", distributed by Office of Economic Stabilization, $20.00.

"Dunlopillo Mattresses," 30 x 44", blue, orange, brown, yellow, gray, and black 275.00

"Hilton–The Starched Collar For Fall–Tooke Brothers, Ltd," 11 x 21", adv for celluloid collars, autumn leaves background, c1915 .... 50.00

"Kodak," 17 x 26", monotone photo of young lady in beret, jacket, and necktie, self framed, c1920 .... 200.00

"Maxon's Polish," 14 x 20", Belgian, boot polish adv, brunette poses with horse, green, red, brown, blue, and black, c1950 .... 75.00

"Sloan's Liniment For All Mankind!," 30 x 46", red, black, green, yellow, blue, speckled white, and brown 150.00

"Tuttle's Horse Elixir," 30 x 46", black, yellow, and red 150.00

"Use Virginia Dare Double Strength Extracts," 21 x 28", smiling housewife making cookies, c1925 .... 175.00

"Welch's Wine Coolers–Wouldn't This Hit The Spot Right Now? Taste It...You'll Love It, Says Eddie Cantor," 11 x 21", 1952 .... 100.00

"Wide Angle Tillyer Lenses," Norman Rockwell, 18 x 23", window card, color, 1929 .... 165.00

AUTOMOBILES

"Mercedes Benz," 23 x 33", showroom poster, brown, blue, black, red, and yellow, white ground, futuristic racing car against ghostly logo, 1955 ..... 975.00

"Pontiac Big Six - Big Car Quality Typified by Smart, Luxurious Fisher Bodies," Hyden, 38 x 26", showroom poster, enlargement of 1929 *Saturday Evening Post* double page adv 225.00

"The New Oakland All American Six," 26 x 38", showroom poster, color en-

largement of *Saturday Evening Post* adv, 1929 .... 225.00

"The Pierce Arrow," J Sheridan, 8 x 10", placard, color 80.00

MOVIES

"Across to Singapore," 14 x 11", Ramon Navarro, color tinted scene card, 1928 .... 85.00

"Andy Hardy Comes Home," MGM, 41 x 81", Micky and Teddy Rooney, 1958 .... 80.00

"Ben Hur," MGM, 12 x 9", Ramon Navarro, Francis X Bushman, May McAvoy, 1926 .... 50.00

"Blood and Roses," Paramount, 27 x 41", Mel Ferrer, Elsa Martinelli, and Anette Vadim, 1961 .... 35.00

"Dangerous When Wet," MGM, 41 x 81", Esther Williams, Fernando Lamas, and Jack Carson, 1953 .... 65.00

"Devil Ship Pirates," Columbia, 14 x 11", Christopher Lee, set of eight color lobby cards, 1964 .... 60.00

"Flying Blind," Paramount, 27 x 41", Richard Arlen, Jean Parker, 1941 ... 50.00

"King Kong," RKO, 27 x 41", Fay Wray, Robert Armstrong, Bruce Cabot, 1936 800.00

"Manslaughter," Paramount, 27 x 41", Thomas Meighan, Morgan Litho, c1923 .... 325.00

"Now, Voyager," Warner Bros, 14 x 22", Bette Davis, Paul Henreid, 1942 ... 240.00

"Roy Rogers: On the Old Spanish Trail," Republic, 81 x 41", 1947 .... 115.00

"Sideshow," Columbia, 27 x 41", Marie Prevost, Ralph Graves, circus motif, c1923 .... 350.00

"Sunset Carson, Fighting Mustang," Yucca Pictures, 41 x 81", 1949 .... 80.00

"The Devil's Hairpin," 27 x 41", Cornel Wilde and Jean Wallace, 1957 ..... 50.00

"Tim Holt: Trail Guide," RKO, 27 x 41", 1952 .... 48.00

"Tim McCoy: Two Gun Justice," Monogram, 27 x 41", 1938 .... 62.00

"Wedding Present," Paramount, 41 x 81", Cary Grant, Joan Bennett, images inside golden wedding ring motif, 1936 .... 650.00

"Zombies of the Stratosphere," Republic Serial, 41 x 81", 1952 .... 65.00

PUBLISHING

"Donaldson Fair," 28 x 42", salesman's sample poster for 1932 Donaldson Lithographing Co 150.00

"Football & Love: A Story of the Yale–Princeton Game of '94," 12 x 12", 1895 novel by Burr W McIntosh, blue, yellow, brown, green, and black **85.00**

"Harper's, February 1896," Edward Penfield, 11 x 20", courting couple walking beside woods at dusk **200.00**

"Inland Printer, January 1897," J C Leyendecker, 10 x 17", allegory of angels blowing trumpets in heavens, rearing Pegasi **325.00**

"Lippincott's, April 1897," J J Gould, 13 x 16", finely dressed gentleman walking under umbrella with young ladies **300.00**

"Prang & Co's Holiday Publications," Louis J Rhead, 17 x 23", litho, maiden among brightly colored books and folios, holding string tied booklet, rich violet, green, deep blue, deep red, and brown, background of holly, berries, and mottled yellow, 1896 ..... **650.00**

"Romance and Tragedy of Pioneer Life," 25 x 36", broadsheet adv book, vignettes of American exploration, c1875 .... **200.00**

"The Bachelor of Arts," 13 x 17", turn of the century periodical, May, 1896 **90.00**

THEATER

"Alexander, The Man Who Knows," 41 x 81", magician wearing turban, black background, c1910 .... **250.00**

"Carter Beats The Devil," 14 x 22", Otis Litho, window card, color, 1920s .. **75.00**

"E Demas," cabaret comedian, 23 x 36", French stone litho, c1900 ..... **165.00**

"George–The Supreme Master of Magic," 20 x 27", Otis Litho, magician floating cards over approving Buddha, 1929 .... **150.00**

"Human Hearts–An Idyl of the Arkansaw Hills," 21 x 28", Miner Litho, face of young blonde haired child looks upward to sky of silhouettes of pink and red hearts, c1905 .... **165.00**

"Slaves of the Mine," 29 x 42", Enquirer Co, Cincinnati, American melodrama, c1890 .... **225.00**

"The Missouri Girl Sadie Raymond as Daisy," 28 x 42", Donaldson Litho, star in country attire, bright red background, c1905 .... **175.00**

"The Worried Husbands," 17 x 22", stone litho, blue, red, and black, c1900 .... **125.00**

"Three Penny Opera," Paul Davis, 41 x 81", two panels, 1976 .... **275.00**

TRANSPORTATION

"Aloha Hawaii," American Airlines, E. McKnight Kauffer, 27 x 41", 1953 .. **275.00**

"Along The Way of TWA - California

"Yosemite National Park," 35 x 28", deep tint color photo panorama of park, c1947 .... **125.00**

"British Railways: The Night Ferry," 25 x 40", woodcut design by A. N. Wolstenholme, sleeping cars on ferry between London and Paris **280.00**

"Las Vegas - Fly TWA," David, 25 x 40", showgirl, montage of roulette wheels, cards, etc., airliner flying in background, c1960 .... **225.00**

"Lockheed Super Constellation," KLM, 18 x 24", highly tinted photo of airliner flying over windmill and field of flowers, c1953 .... **110.00**

"Los Angeles - American Airlines," Fred Ludikens, 30 x 39", DC7 flies over LA nightscape, c1954 .... **350.00**

"Lufthansa Airlines," 25 x 39", c1955 . **150.00**

"Near East by SAS," 24 x 38", stylized imagery of camels looking up to airplane, deep purple night sky, brilliant sunset, c1955 .... **165.00**

"Red Star Line, Antwerpen–New York–Canada," 20 x 26", star behind large ship **200.00**

"Ski, The New Haven R. R.," Saucha Maurer, 28 x 42", brown, blue, red, green, and orange **245.00**

"Wheeling & Lake Erie Railroad Excursions to the Great Forepaugh and Wild West Shows," 11 x 29", illus both sides, 1889 .... **115.00**

TRAVEL

"Cambridge," Fred Taylor, 25 x 39", King's College, students walking, c1925 .... **125.00**

"Cannes," 47 x 31", spring flowers and fruits, tranquil Mediterranean coastline view **235.00**

"Denmark, The Country of The Sea," Thelander, 24 x 39", female bather, 1937 .... **200.00**

"His Hunting Ground of Yesterday National Parks," Dorothy Waugh, 28 x 39", Indian and family beside lake, c1934 .... **225.00**

"Holidays 1928," L Hockell, 25 x 41", boy and girl in 1920s seaside attire, blue, blue–green, deep green, sand, pink, orange, and red **550.00**

"Isle of Wight," Allinson, 50 x 40", rural landscape, earthy tones, c1935 .... **375.00**

"*Panama Pacific Liner* New York–California," 27 x 23", gleaming white liner going through Panama Canal, orig frame with brass plaque, c1920 **250.00**

"*S. S. Washington*," Worden Wood, 24x 30", ship in choppy water at sunset, 1933 .... **175.00**

"The *Queen of Bermuda* Entering Hamilton Harbor," Adolph Treidler, 30 x
39", silkscreened design, multicolored, 1947 .... **275.00**
"Yellowstone Park," Moran, 40 x 30",
reproduction of sweeping 1893
Moran painting, c1935 .... **375.00**

WORLD WAR I

"America's Tribute to Britain," Fred G
Cooper, 20 x 30", woodcut design .. **350.00**
"Americans All!" Howard Chandler
Christy, 28 x 40", Miss Liberty paying
honor to Honor Roll of ethnic names,
Chartex backed **225.00**
"Enlist in the Navy, Follow the Boys in
Blue for Home and Country," 29 x 21" **85.00**
"Feed a Fighter," 20 x 29", litho image
of exhausted soldier having cup of
coffee **90.00**
"Hey Fellows! Your Money Brings the
Book We Need," Sheridan, 20 x 30",
brilliant colors **80.00**
"That Liberty Shall Not Perish From the
Earth," Joseph Pennell, 20 x 30",
Chartex backed **230.00**
"The Hun - His Mark/Blot It Out," 20 x
30", bloody handprint on white
ground **50.00**
"The Road to France/The Road to Berlin," James Montgomery Flagg, 18 x
24", black and white **125.00**
"The Salvation Army Lassie, Keep Her
on the Job," 30 x 40" **120.00**

WORLD WAR II

"Bits of Careless Talk," Stevan Do-
hanos, 20 x 28", bold, brutish Nazi
hand putting pieces together to figure
out Allied secrets **145.00**
"Guard Our Shores," 25 x 38", US Army
Coast Artillery recruiting poster, dark
blue, orange, red, blue–green, and
black **175.00**
"I'm Counting On You!," 22 x 28", L
Helguera portrait of Uncle Sam, finger
to lips, bright blue background **80.00**
"Lock Up These Papers/The Enemy is
Vigilant," 22 x 28", Office of War Information, stark bold letters in red,
yellow, and black **70.00**
"Remember Dec 7th!" 28 x 40", tattered
American flag flies at half mast, grim
background of fire and smoke **185.00**
"United We Are Strong, United We Will
Win," Koerner, 20 x 28", allied can-
nons blast into fiery sky **70.00**

ELVIS PRESLEY

Collecting Hints: Official Elvis Presley items are
usually copyrighted and many are dated.

Learn to differentiate between items licensed
during Elvis's lifetime and the wealth of "fantasy"
items issued after his death. The latter are collectibles, but have nowhere near the value of the
pre–1977 material.

Also accept the fact that much of the modern
limited edition issues are purely speculative in-
vestments. It is best to buy them because you
like them and plan to live with them for an extended period of time.

History: When Elvis Presley became a rock 'n'
roll star, he became one of the first singers to
have a promotion which was aimed at teenagers.
The first Elvis merchandise appeared in 1956.
During the following years new merchandise was
added both in America and foreign countries.
After his death in 1977, a vast number of new
Elvis collectibles appeared.

References: Rosalind Cranor, *Elvis Collectibles,*
Collector Books, 1983; Jerry Osborne, *Elvis Pres-
ley Record Guide,* O'Sullivan Woodside, 1983,
Richard Peters, *Elvis, The Golden Anniversary
Tribute,* Salem House, 1984.

Museums: Jimmy Velvet's Elvis Presley Museum,
Franklin, TN; Gracelands, Memphis, TN.

Whiskey Bottle, "Yours, Elvis, '55,"
McCormick, No. 2, music box base,
1979, $75.00.

Autograph, photograph, 3¼ x 3½",
black and white, glossy, military uniform, snapshot taken in Germany,
ball-point sgd "Elvis Presley" **75.00**
Belt, metal, gold colored, intricate
mesh, two eagle head fasteners, "Russian Double Eagle" **48.50**
Book
My LIfe with Elvis, Becky Yancey,
Book Club Edition **10.00**

The Elvis Presley Story, 160 pgs, 1960, Hillman Books **35.00**

Bracelet

Charm, 1956 .... **50.00**

Dog Tag, silver link chain, tag inscribed "Presley, Elvis,/53310761/ Type O," engraved portrait and signature, orig display card, 1956 Elvis Presley Enterprises copyright .. **50.00**

Calendar, 11", sq, full color glossy, 1963, RCA **30.00**

Card, #59, color photo, biography on back, Topps Gum, late 1950s **10.00**

Decanter **35.00**

Drink Mixer, figural, guitar, 1950s **20.00**

Flasher Disc, 2¼" d, used for key chain ring, colorful, c1956 .... **15.00**

Lobby Card, 14 x 22", "Fun in Acapulco" **35.00**

Magazine

Life, April 30, 1956 .... **20.00**

Stardom Magazine, August, 1960 ... **25.00**

TV Guide, May 7, 1960, Ohio edition **45.00**

Music Box, Love Me Tender, limited edition **30.00**

Necklace, chain, heart, dated 1956 ... **45.00**

Paper doll, Elvis and Priscilla, uncut .. **40.00**

Pennant, 29" l, felt, blue, yellow design and lettering, black and white photo, white "Love, Elvis" signature, c1960 **40.00**

Pinback Button

1¾", "I Like Elvis," red and white, c1956 .... **12.00**

2½", Sept 10, 1978 fan reunion, "Always Elvis" and "V.I.P." inscriptions in red, black and white photo **12.00**

3½", 1977 Memorial, four black and white photos, red and white inscriptions top, bottom purple and white **5.00**

Postcard, 3½ x 5½", Easter Greetings, Elvis wearing gray tux, red ground, unused **35.00**

Poster

21 x 27", Girls! Girls! Girls!, color, 1960, Paramount film **5.00**

22 x 28", Wild In The Country, 1961 **30.00**

27 x 40", Live A Little, Love A Little, 1968, Metro-Goldwyn-Mayer **100.00**

Poster Book, 33 posters, 1977 .... **20.00**

Purse, clutch, 1956 .... **35.00**

Record

"A Touch Of Gold," maroon label, RCA Victor, 1959 .... **200.00**

"Double Trouble," mono, long play, photo included, RCA **25.00**

"Elvis Is Back," long play, black label, RCA Victor **100.00**

"Heartbreak Hotel," extra play, RCA Victor **20.00**

"Moody Blue, The Blue Album," jacket **20.00**

Scarf

Concert souvenir **10.00**

Neck, 8 x 38", pale blue, stitched border, printed "Sincerely Elvis Presley" signature, orig tag "100% Polyester/Made In USA" **75.00**

Sheet Music

"How do You Think I Feel?," 4 pgs, purple photo, 1954 copyright **25.00**

"Love Me," 4 pgs, brown tone close-up photo cov, 1954 .... **25.00**

"Treat Me Nice," 1957 .... **10.00**

Wallet, vinyl, tan, blue, pink, white, and flesh tone illus front cov, blue and gold stars, back 1956 Elvis Presley Enterprises copyright **150.00**

Window Card, "Viva Las Vegas" **35.00**

PULP MAGAZINES

Collecting Hints: Pulps in the finest condition are the most highly prized, but even pulps in lesser condition are collectible if priced accordingly.

Pulp collections can be limited to certain themes or as unlimited and varied as a collector's interest. Many collectors specialize in certain titles (e.g., *Weird Tales*), certain genres (science fiction and horror being the most popular), special characters (Doc Savage, The Shadow, The Spider, Wu Fang, G-8, Tarzan, etc.), or special authors (H. P. Lovecraft, Robert E. Howard, Edgar Rice Burroughs, Dashiell Hammett, etc.).

A typical collecting problem for many novice collectors is the unknowledgeable dealer who, knowingly or unknowingly, prices common issues far above any retail price that could possibly be realized from a serious collector. Much of the overpricing results because the general dealer has no experience with pulps and their actual prices among collectors. New pulp collectors are advised to find an established pulp dealer early in their collecting career to avoid overpaying for the core portion of their collection.

History: The pulp magazine was the direct descendant of the dime novel and the ancestor of the paperback book, coming into popularity in the early 20th century and lasting into the early 1950s.

The early pulps were dimensionally a little smaller than the average magazine. They derived their collective name from the fact that they were printed on cheap, pulpwood paper. Most had untrimmed edges.

Pulp magazines generally were aimed at a male audience and devoted to so-called "cheap" genres such as western, mystery, science fiction, jungle adventure, sport, air war and combat, horror, and girlie themes. "Nothing was too cheap that could not be exploited," wrote the early pulp writer Frank Gruber.

A main attraction of pulp magazines is some of the most lurid and colorful cover art ever produced. These covers were created to entice the buyer. Many are totally outrageous. The covers promised (and sometimes delivered) an interior filled with excitement, adventure, and enchantment.

Pulp magazines reached their peak of general public popularity in the 1930s, the "golden age" of this collectible in most collectors' eyes.

World War II paper shortages caused the demise of many titles and several publishers. The emergence of the popular mass market paperback a few years later finished the job. After early 1953, very few pulps existed in their original format. Those that did survive changed to a handier, digest size format.

There was a considerable renewal of interest in the pulps in the 1960s. Some of the most popular characters, e.g., Doc Savage and The Shadow, were revived and reprinted in paperback form.

References: Tony Goodstone, *The Pulps*, Chelsea House, 1980; Frank Gruber, *The Pulp Jungle*, Sherbourne Press, 1967; Kenneth Jones, *The Shudder Pulps*, FAX Collectors Editions, 1975; McKinstry and Weinberg, *The Hero Pulp Index*, Opar Press, 1971; Robert Sampson, *Yesterday's Faces: Glory Figures, Vol. 1*, Bowling Green University Press, 1983; Robert Sampson, *Yesterday's Faces: Strange Days, Vol. 2*, Bowling Green University Press, 1984.

Periodicals: *Echoes*, 504 E Morris St, Seymour, TX 76380; *Golden Perils*, 5 Milliken Mills Road, Scarboro, ME 04074; *Nemisis, Inc.*, 2438 S Highland Ave, Berwyn, IL 60402; *Pulp and Paperback Market*, 5813 York Ave, Edina, MN 55410; *Pulp Collector*, 8417 Carrollton Parkway, New Carrollton, MD 20784; *Pulp Vault*, 5451 N East River Rd, #1209, Chicago, IL 60656.

Museum: The Hess Collection of Popular Literature, University of Minnesota, Minneapolis, MN.

Advisor: Kevin B. Hancer.

Adventure
   8/1/35, contains part one of "The Feud at Single Shot" by Luke Short [NOTE: Luke's first published work]   **6.00**
   9/36, contains L Ron Hubbard story   **7.00**
Adventure Trails, 7/38, #1 .... **10.00**
All-Story, 10/12, contains "Tarzan of the Apes" by Edgar Rice Burroughs [NOTE: This is the first appearance of Tarzan and is the complete novel, not a short story version] **625.00**
All-Story Weekly
   10/21/16 .... **10.00**

12/02/16, contains part four of "Tarzan and the Jewels of Opar" by Edgar Rice Burroughs **23.00**
Amazing Stories
   8/38, contains Robert Bloch story .. **10.00**
   1/41, contains "John Carter and the Giant of Mars" by Edgar Rice Burroughs and John Coleman Burroughs **15.00**
   6/49 .... **3.00**
Argosy
   8/22/36, contains part one of "Don Peon" by Johnston McCulley **5.00**
   1/07/39, contains part one of "Synthetic Men of Mars" by Edgar Rice Burroughs **8.50**
   5/42, Gypsy Rose Lee photocover .. **8.00**
Avenger, The, 11/40 .... **9.00**
Black Mask, 9/49, contains story by Louis L'Amour **5.00**
Blue Book
   8/16 .... **12.00**
   9/16, contains part one of "The New Stories of Tarzan" by Edgar Rice Burroughs **35.00**
   8/33 .... **6.00**
   4/40, contains "Tarzan & the Champion" by Edgar Rice Burroughs ... **10.00**
Buck Jones, 11/36, #1 .... **50.00**
Capt. Combat, 4/40, #1 .... **11.00**
Capt. Future
   Winter, 1940, #1 .... **32.00**
   Fall, 1942 .... **13.00**
Comet, 12/40, #1 .... **6.00**
Detective Fiction Weekly, 8/03/40, contains story by Clayton Rawson **6.00**
Detective Novel Magazine, Spring/42 . **4.00**
Detective Short Stories, 11/42 .... **4.50**
Detective Story Magazine, 6/46 ...... **2.00**
Doc Savage
   4/36, Canadian edition **10.00**
   7/36 .... **30.00**
   4/46 .... **6.00**
Double Detective, 9/38 .... **6.00**
Exciting Sports, Winter, 1941, #1 .... **7.00**
Famous Fantastic Mysteries, 12/40 .... **3.00**
Fantastic Adventures, 8/42, contains Robert Block story **5.00**
Fantastic Novels, 9/40 .... **3.00**
Fantastic Story Quarterly, Summer, 1950 **3.00**
Fantastic Universe, 4/56, digest size, contains story by Robert E. Howard . **2.50**
Football Stories, Fall, 1937, #1 ...... **9.00**
Future Fiction, 4/41, cover by Frank Paul **3.00**
Future Science Fiction, #28, 1955, digest size, contains the Tarzan and Conan parody "Cornzan the Mighty" by L. Sprague de Camp **3.00**
Guilty Detective Story Magazine, 3/60, digest size **1.50**
Hopalong Cassidy, Winter, 1951, con-

tains "Hopalong Cassidy and the Trail to Seven Pines," by Louis L'Amour writing under the pseudonym of Tex Burns **25.00**

Ideal Love, 3/48 .... **2.00**

Imagination, 2/53, contains story by Charles Beaumont **2.00**

Jungle Stories

Winter, 1939, #1 .... **35.00**

Fall, 1946, cover by George Gross . **5.00**

Knockout Magazine, 1–2/37, #1 ..... **8.00**

Lone Ranger, 10/37 .... **25.00**

Marvel Science Stories

8/38, #1, cover by Norman Saunders **5.00**

11/40 .... **3.00**

Masked Rider, 5/45 .... **5.00**

Max Brand Western, 4/50, #1 .... **4.00**

New Western, 9/49 .... **1.50**

Operator 5, Jan-Feb/38 .... **20.00**

Other Worlds, 6/51, digest size **2.00**

Phantom Detective, 11/39 .... **8.00**

Pioneer Western, #1, 1950, contains comic book section **10.00**

Planet Stories, Summer, 1941, cover by Virgil Finlay **4.00**

Popular Western, 4/47 .... **2.00**

Red Star Mystery, 6/40, contains story by Clayton Rawson **30.00**

Saint Detective Magazine, 9/57, digest size, contains story by Fredric Brown **2.50**

Sea Novel, 11/40, #1, cover by Rudolph Belarski **8.00**

The Shadow

11/36 .... **30.00**

12/43 .... **12.00**

Sparkling Love Stories, #1, 1950, contains comic book section **10.00**

Startling Stories

11/39 .... **5.00**

Spring, 1945, Capt. Future novel by Brett Sterling **6.00**

Super Detective, 12/49 .... **3.00**

Super Science Fiction, 4/57, digest size, contains story by Harlan Ellison **2.50**

Super Science Stories

1/41 .... **3.00**

4/44 .... **3.00**

Ten Story Fantasy, #1, 1951 .... **9.00**

Thrilling Adventures

8/32, contains "Kwa of the Jungle," Paul Regard **12.00**

11/43, contains "Wings Over Brazil," Louis L'Amour and "Black Lace" by Carl Jacobi, cover by Ralph Belarski **10.00**

4/45 .... **4.50**

Thrilling Detective, 6/46 .... **4.00**

Thrilling Western, 10/48 .... **2.00**

Thrilling Wonder Stories

4/37 .... **6.00**

4/40, contains Henry Kuttner story that was basis for Ray Harryhausen film, *20 Million Miles To Earth* ... **7.00**

10/50, contains "Shadow on the Sand," John D. MacDonald **4.00**

War Stories, 2/36, #1 .... **25.00**

Weird Tales

7/35 .... **40.00**

9/43 .... **6.50**

Western Raider, 8–9/38, #1 .... **7.50**

Wonder Story Annual, #1, 1950 ..... **6.00**

PUNCHBOARDS

Collecting Hints: Punchboards which are unpunched are collectible. A punched board has little value unless it is an extremely rare design. Like most advertising items, price is determined by graphics and subject matter.

The majority of punchboards sell in the $8.00 to $30.00 range. The high end of the range is represented by boards such as Golden Gate Bridge at $85.00 and Baseball Classic at $100.00.

History: Punchboards are self-contained games of chance made of pressed paper containing holes with coded tickets inside each hole. For an agreed amount the player uses a "punch" to extract the ticket of his or her choice. Prizes are awarded to the winning ticket. Punch prices can be 1¢, 2¢, 3¢, 5¢, 10¢, 20¢, 50¢, $1.00 or more.

Not all tickets were numbered. Fruit symbols were used extensively as well as animals. Some punchboards had no printing at all, just colored tickets. Other ticket themes included dice, cards, dominoes, words, etc. One early board had Mack Sennet bathing beauties.

Punchboards come in an endless variety of styles. Names reflected the themes of the boards. Barrel of Winners, Break the Bank, Baseball, More Smokes, Lucky Lulu and Take It Off were just a few.

At first punchboards were used to award cash. As legal attempts to outlaw gambling arose, prizes were switched to candy, cigars, cigarettes, jewelry, radios, clocks, cameras, sporting goods, toys, beer, chocolate, etc.

The golden age of punchboards was the 1920s to the 1950s. Attention was focused on the keyed punchboard in the film "The Film Flam Man." This negative publicity hurt the punchboard industry.

Museum: Amusement Sales, 127 North Main, Midvale, UT 84047.

Advisor: Clark Phelps.

Big Game, fruit symbols **10.00**

Block Buster, double jackpot, cash payout, 5¢ per punch **18.00**

Charlie Ten Spots **10.00**

Delicious Cherries **10.00**

Punchboard, Professor Charley, cash value, $12.00.

Dixie Queen Cigarettes, ten color tickets	8.00
Forty Sawbucks, counter insert	25.00
Full of Tens, cash pay, 25¢ per punch	15.00
Gas with a Punch, old pump and car .	15.00
Glades Chocolates, set of 3	25.00
Hi Ho Silver, cash board, 25¢ per punch	15.00
Hit a Buck	6.00
Joe's Special Prize, cash board with name, 25¢ per punch	18.00
Knee High, cash girlie board	15.00
Musical Cigarettes	12.00
Odd Pennies Cigarettes	15.00
Pick a Cherry, cash pay, cherry seals ..	20.00
Put and Take, candy bars	10.00
Section Play, 25¢ cash board	10.00
Six Fine Prizes, fruit symbols and seals	15.00
Ten Big Sawbucks, 20¢ cash board ...	20.00
Tip Top Charley	15.00
Win a Buck	5.00
Your Pick, money seals, 10¢ per punch	30.00

PUZZLES

Collecting Hints: Choose a rationale for collecting based on your interests. Some collectors choose puzzles for their visual appeal, some for the challenge of putting them together, and others for the patterns used in cutting the puzzles. Some collectors specialize according to subject matter, e.g., advertising, maps, transportation, or comic characters. Puzzles are easiest to find in the east, where historically they were most popular.

Puzzles are often difficult to date. Collectors should be aware that some puzzles, such as Milton Bradley's Smashed Up Locomotive, were produced for decades. The most popular prints were kept in inventory or reproduced as need arose, often by several different manufacturers. Thus, the date when a puzzle was made is often years later than the date or copyright on the print or box.

Collectors should avoid puzzles whose manufacturer cannot be determined, unless the puzzle has specially attractive graphics or craftmanship.

Assembled puzzles can be displayed in frames, but should *never* be glued together. Exposure to light over long periods of time will cause fading. Dax or other plastic box frames are ideal for displays which can be changed periodically.

Puzzles remain an affordable collectible. Many old puzzles still cost less than newly manufactured puzzles of comparable size and craftsmanship. But prices are rising rapidly because of the intrinsic interest of these pieces. In addition, as game and toy prices soar, collectors are turning to the less expensive field of puzzles to build their collections. Prices have especially soared for character puzzles and top quality nineteenth century children's puzzles.

The number of collectors is growing, so that prices have risen about 50 percent in the last five years. Puzzle collecting is most established in England. Prices for European children's puzzles were well defined in 1984 when Sotheby's auctioned the dazzling Hannas collection in London.

History: John Spilsbury, a London mapmaker, made the first jigsaw puzzles in the 1760s. Spilsbury "dissected" maps and sold them as educational toys. By 1850 children's jigsaw puzzles on all subjects were being made in the United States. Prominent manufacturers of the late nineteenth century include McLoughlin Brothers, Milton Bradley, and Selchow and Righter. Although the prints on very early puzzles were hand colored, color lithography was almost universal by 1870.

The early puzzles were made from solid wood or thick cardboard, with individual pieces "hand cut" one at a time with saws. Nineteenth century puzzles had few interlocking pieces, usually only on the edges. The widespread use of plywood and better saws after World War I led to more complex puzzle designs with all the pieces interlocking. Thinner cardboard puzzles, with all the pieces stamped out at once by steel dies, were introduced around 1890. Gradually these die-cut puzzles supplanted the hand-cut puzzles.

Puzzles for adults, more than 75 pieces, are a product of the twentieth century. Their introduction in 1908 unleashed a craze lasting several years. Puzzles were even more popular in the depression years of 1932–35 when many unemployed people had time to both cut up puzzles and put them back together. This period saw the emergence of many small-scale craftspeople who cut puzzles for local markets.

Some makers, such as Par (1932–1974), specialized in high quality custom designed wood puzzles for celebrities. Few makers of the more expensive hand-cut puzzles survived after World

War II. Today there are only a handful of crafts-people still cutting puzzles in the United States. Among the post World War II die-cut puzzles, Springbok, now owned by Hallmark, is the premier domestic manufacturer.

References: Linda Hannas, *The English Jigsaw Puzzle, 1760–1890*, Wayland, 1972, out-of-print; Linda Hannas, *The Jigsaw Book*, Dial Press, 1981, out of print.

Collectors' Club: American Game Collectors Association, 4628 Barlow Drive, Bartlesville, OK 74006. Bimonthly newsletter.

Museums: Most toy and game museums include some jigsaw puzzles in their collections, puzzles were featured in the 1988 Bates College (Lewiston, ME) exhibit, "Pieces in Place: Two Hundred Years of Jigsaw Puzzles"; The Dairy Barn (P. O. Box 747, Athens, OH 45701) mounts periodic exhibits of antique and contemporary puzzles.

Advisor: Anne D. Williams.

Price Notes: Prices quoted refer to puzzles in very good condition, with the original box, and with *no* missing pieces. If pieces are missing, prices are generally 25 to 50 percent lower, although a very rare puzzle may still be well worth collecting even with missing pieces. A missing box should subtract about 25 percent from the price.

The only way to be sure of condition is to see the puzzle assembled. Unassembled puzzles should be priced cheaper, since, graphics, condition and completeness cannot be easily determined.

Twentieth century die-cut cardboard puzzles are quite inexpensive, usually in the $2.00 to $12.00 range. These puzzles are usually non descript, e.g., rustic cottages, fall foliage, fishing harbors, etc. Post World War II puzzles are abundant in flea markets and thrift stores at prices under $5.

Handcut puzzles for adults are more costly, generally $10.00 to $75.00. Price depends on subject matter, number of pieces, and quality of cut. Nineteenth century children's puzzles command the highest prices, often $50.00 to $500.00. They are still less expensive than many contemporary children's games of the same period.

Note: Dimensions listed give height first, then width.

Some European puzzles are included, since imports always have been popular in the United States. The listing also includes some other pictorial puzzles that are not strictly jigsaw puzzles. These pictorial puzzles, such as block puzzles, six-sided cube puzzles, and metamorphoses, frequently have pieces which are all the same shape.

Children's, Nineteenth Century, Mc-Loughlin, Picture Puzzle, c1980, $125.00.

CHILDREN'S PUZZLES

Nineteenth Century

Barfoot, James W., London, England, Story of the Arctic Ship Resolute, hand colored, wood puzzle, wood box, 9 x 7", c1850 .... 330.00

Milton Bradley Co, Springfield, MA
  Dissected Outline Map of the United States of America, reversible, map and US scenes, wood puzzle, wood box 8 x 9¾", c1880 ...... 95.00
  Model Ship Puzzle, box 7 x 9", c1880 150.00
  Sectional Steamer & Hose, box 5 x 7", c1880 .... 150.00

Chinnock, George, New York, NY, Centennial Puzzle Blocks, 5 wood puzzles in wood box, 11 x 22", 1876 .. 650.00

Clemens, Rev. E. J., Clayville, NY, Clemens' Silent Teacher, USA map, poster for White Sewing Machines on reverse, wood puzzle, box 7 x 9", c1885 .... 125.00

Crandall, Charles, Brooklyn, NY, wood, Expression Blocks, wood box 8 x 4", c1870 .... 250.00

Hill, S. L., Williamsburgh (Long Island), NY, Carrying Corn to the White Settlement, wood hand colored puzzle, wood box 8 x 6", c1860 .... 175.00

Horsman, E. I., New York, NY, Prize Birds, wood strip puzzle, wood box 7 x 11", c1885 .... 125.00

Lyman, Seymour, New York, The Ark Puzzle, box 7 x 10", c1880 .... 225.00

Magnus, Charles, New York, NY, The Glorious Finale of the War Dissected, hand colored, box 5 x 7", 1865 .... 300.00

McLoughlin Brothers, New York, NY
  A Peep at the Circus Picture Puzzle,
    box 12 x 10", 1887 . . . .   **450.00**
  Aunt Louisa's Cube Puzzles, Aesop's
    Fables, wood 6-sided puzzle, box
    11 x 15", with booklet, 1891 . . . .   **600.00**
  Brownie Puzzle Blocks, Palmer Cox
    designs, cardboard 6-sided puzzle,
    box 11 x 15", with booklet, 1891   **600.00**
  Criss Cross Spelling Strips, box 10 x
    9", c1880 . . . .   **90.00**
  Dissected Map of the United States,
    with world on reverse, box 10 x 7",
    1884 . . . .   **55.00**
  Home Scroll Puzzle, box 9 x 7", 1897   **125.00**
  Locomotive Picture Puzzle, box 8½ x
    11½", 1887 . . . .   **450.00**
  Picture Puzzle, The Werra (steam-
    ship), box 12 x 9", 1886 . . . .   **250.00**
  St. Nicholas Picture Puzzle, box 9 x
    13", 1890 . . . .   **350.00**
  Six Puzzle Pictures, Dame Trott and
    Her Cat, wood puzzles in wood
    box 11 x 8", c1880 . . . .   **225.00**
  Topsy Turvy Blocks, metamorphosis,
    wood box 8 x 8", c1890 . . . .   **475.00**
  Up the Heights of San Juan Scroll Puz-
    zle, box 13 x 18", 1898 . . . .   **300.00**
Novelty Game Co., New York, NY, Af-
  ter-Dinner Puzzle, box 6 x 9", c1870   **125.00**
Parker Brothers, Salem, MA
  Cut Up Locomotive, box 12 x 15",
    c18905 . . . .   **150.00**
  Darktown Fancy Ball, box 7 x 10",
    1894 . . . .   **275.00**
  Robber Kitten Picture Puzzle, two
    puzzles, box 8 x 11", c1895 . . . . .   **90.00**
Parkhurst, V.S.W., Providence, RI, met-
  amorphosis, hand colored on paper,
  c1860 . . . .   **75.00**
Selchow & Righter, New York, NY,
  Sliced Nations, box 8 x 9", 1875 . . .   **90.00**
Shaffer, Jacob, Philadelphia, PA, New
  Dissected Map of the United States,
  hand colored wood puzzle, wood
  box 7 x 8", c1865 . . . .   **85.00**
Tackabury, G.N., Canastota, NY, The
  Silent Teacher, World Map, with ad
  for White Sewing Machines on reverse, wood puzzle, wood box 8 x
  11", c1875 . . . .   **160.00**
Warne, Frederick, London & New York,
  Jack and Jill, double-sided puzzle,
  wood box 11 x 8", with book, c1890   **140.00**
Unknown Maker, English, United States
  New Double Puzzle, hand colored
  wood puzzle, wood box 7 x 9",
  c1845 . . . .   **150.00**

Twentieth Century

Army Navy Combat Picture Puzzles, set
  of 4, box 9 x 8", c1945 . . . .   **45.00**

Milton Bradley, Springfield, MA
  Four Picture Puzzles for Children, art-
    ist H. Boylston Dummer, box 10 x
    7", c1935 . . . .   **25.00**
  Cheyenne Frame Tray Puzzle, 14 x
    10", 1957 . . . .   **18.00**
  Farm Friends Puzzle Box, 3 puzzles,
    box 13 x 17", 1913–35 . . . .   **75.00**
  Funny Animal Puzzle Box, 3 puzzles,
    box 10 x 15", 1913–17 . . . .   **95.00**
  Huckleberry Hound, 4 puzzles, box
    14 x 11", 1960 . . . .   **40.00**
  Old Mother Hubbard Puzzle Box,
    No. 4212, 3 puzzles, box 9 x 13",
    1913–35 . . . .   **95.00**
  Santa Claus Puzzle Box, contains 3
    puzzles, box 9 x 13", c1920 . . . . .   **225.00**
  Three Little Kittens, reversible, box 10
    x 7", 1931 . . . .   **25.00**
  Uncle Wiggily, 3 puzzles, box 10 x
    13", 1949 . . . .   **45.00**
Cadaco-Ellis, Chicago, IL, Tableau: The
  Picture Puzzle Game, box 9 x 10",
  1941 . . . .   **35.00**

**Children's Twentieth Century, Saalfield,
Little Annie Rooney, $75.00.**

Daintee Toys, Inc, Brooklyn, NY, Red
  Riding Hood, masonite tray puzzle,
  c1940 . . . .   **15.00**
Eichhorn, Hermann, West Germany,
  Mickey Mouse Picture Cubes, wood
  suitcase-type box 6 x 7", c1980 . . . .   **15.00**
Fawcett Publications Inc., Minneapolis,
  MN, Captain Marvel Picture Puzzle:
  One Against Many, paper envelope
  10 x 7", c1941 . . . .   **25.00**
Gabriel, Samuel, Sons & Co., New
  York, NY
  Our Defenders Puzzles, set of 3, box
    12 x 16", 1940s **60.00**
  Pinky Lee, 3 Funny Picture Puzzles,
    box 12 x 9", 1955 . . . .   **20.00**
Gaston Manufacturing Co., Cincinnati,
  OH, Blondie and Dagwood Inter-

changeable Blocks, box 7 x 11",
c1950 .... **65.00**

Graphicut Corp., New York, NY, Eureko: The Great New Jig-Saw Puzzle
Game, box 10 x 13", 1942 .... **22.00**

Hammond, C.S., Brooklyn, NY, Little
Folks Picture Puzzles: Happy Hour,
set of 4, box 8 x 10", c1920 .... **32.00**

Hayter, G.J., England, Victory Farmyard
Wood Jigsaw Puzzle, box 10 x 16",
1930–70 .... **35.00**

Jaymar, New York, NY, Dick Tracy Kiddies Jigsaw Puzzle, box 8 x 10",
1950s **35.00**

Leis, George, Newark, NJ, Noah's Ark,
wood puzzle, box 12 x 17", c1945 . **32.00**

Madmar Quality Co., Utica, NY
Air Fleet Picture Puzzle, set of 3, box
10 x 8", 1930s **60.00**
Dissected Map: New York State, box
12 x 16", 1930s **25.00**

Ottmann, J. Lith. co., New York, NY,
Dissected Circus Puzzle, box 10 x
13", c1900 .... **75.00**

Parker Brothers Inc., Salem, MA
Circus Picture Puzzles, set of 3, box
8 x 11", c1925 .... **35.00**
Old Dobbin Picture Puzzles, set of 2,
box 12 x 9", c1925 .... **25.00**
United States Puzzle Map, wood, cut
on state lines, box 8 x 13", 1915–
55 .... **22.00**
Walt Disney's Mickey Mouse Comic
Picture Puzzle, set of 4, box 7 x
18", 1950s **60.00**

Platt & Munk, New York, NY, Little
Brown Bear Puzzles, set of 6, box 11
x 9", 1950 .... **30.00**

Saalfield, Akron, OH
Mother Goose, set of 3, box 12 x 10",
1943 .... **15.00**
Tom Corbett Space Cadet Puzzles, set
of 3, box 11 x 10", 1952 .... **90.00**

Selchow & Righter, New York, NY
Pandora Picture Puzzles, Bunny Rabbit Series, set of 3, box 11 x 8",
c1940 .... **60.00**
Sliced Flowers, box 9 x 10", c1920 . **25.00**

SIFO, St. Paul, MN, Little Black Sambo,
tray puzzle, masonite, 9 x 12", c1965 **12.00**

Straus, Joseph K., Brooklyn, NY, Transportation and Home Life in the US 60
Years Ago, 3 wood puzzles, box 10 x
13", c1950 .... **35.00**

Transogram Co., Inc., New York, NY,
Tony Sarg's Puzzles, box 9 x 17",
1930s **30.00**

Whitman Publishing Co., Racine, WI
Charlie McCarthy Picture Puzzles, set
of 2, box 10 x 8", 1938 .... **25.00**
Gunsmoke Frame Tray Puzzle, 15 x
11", 1958 .... **35.00**

Tarzan Big Little Book Picture Puzzles, box 11 x 8", 1938 .... **90.00**

ADULT PUZZLES

Hand Cut

Makers of individually cut adult puzzles often used hundreds of different pictures and thus did not make many copies of the same puzzle.

Parker Brothers' Pastime line included several hundred different subjects in each catalog. Pastime puzzles, which include beautifully cut figure pieces, have a base price of $30 for a 200 piece puzzle. however, those with specially appealing subjects e.g., a Maxfield Parrish print, command higher prices.

Most items listed represent base prices rather than premium prices.

Chicago World's Fair Picture Puzzle, orig box marked "A Pre-view of Chicago's Century of Progess as it will look when opened June 1, 1933," over 300 pcs, $20.00.

Art Puzzle, Lucky Fisherman, 99 pcs,
c1910 .... **15.00**

Austen, J.I., Chicago, IL, Komplikato
Duplex puzzle: Landscapes (reversible), 200 pcs, c1910 .... **30.00**

Bamberger, L. & Co., Newark, NJ, Contest Set, four 75 piece puzzles, including figures, wood box, 1932 ... **65.00**

Bouve, Marjorie, Brookline, MA, Ye Squirlijig Puzzle, Winter Sport, 99 mahogany pcs, 1911 .... **35.00**

Milton Bradley Co., Springfield, MA, Perfection Picture Puzzle: Snapshot in Holland, 150 pcs, c1910 .... **20.00**

Brewer Brothers, Cortland, NY, A Halt By The Wayside, 200 pcs including figures, 1930s **30.00**

Detroit Publishing Co., Library Picture Puzzle, Dickens Studies, 150 pcs, c1920 .... **15.00**

Eveready Specialties Mfg. Co., New York, NY, Lustre Odours & Blossoms, 150 pcs, includes figures, 1930s ... **25.00**

Fretts, Alden L., West Springfield, MA, Yankee Cut-Ups, Chorus Gentlemen, 353 pcs, includes figures, 1932 .... **35.00**

Globe Puzzle Co., Boston, MA, Song of the Lark, 200 pcs, c1910 .... **18.00**

Hayter, G.J., England, Victory Puzzle, Cunard Liner Queen Elizabeth, 175 pcs, 1950s **25.00**

Horsman, E.I., New York, NY, Confuseyu Picture Puzzle: Magnolia Blossoms, 100 pcs, c1910 .... **15.00**

Klever Kutup, Springfield, MA, The Rug Weaver, 746 pcs, c1940 .... **55.00**

Linscott, John S., Farmington, ME, Moose Fight, 200 pcs, 1930s **25.00**

Macy's Jigsaw Puzzle, New York, NY, St. Paul's, 241 pcs with figures, wood box, 1931 .... **40.00**

Madmar Quality Co., Utica, NY, Travel Set of 4 in miniature trunk, 50 pcs each, 1930s **45.00**

Nelson, Louis, Springfield and Fitchburg, MA, Old Oaken Bucket, 106 pcs including figures, 1930s **23.00**

Olney, Lee, Bath, ME, Jigleo Puzzle, A Fond Parent, 106 mahogany pcs, c1910 .... **20.00**

Par Company Ltd., New York, NY,
In High Feather, 925 mahogany pcs, includes figures, irregular edge, c1960 .... **600.00**
Nightingale's Knight, 1400 mahogany pcs, includes figures, c1950 ..... **700.00**
Paris Picture Puzzle, Forbidden Fruit, 200 pcs, c1910 .... **30.00**

Parker Brothers Inc., Salem, MA
Indian Trysting Place, 750 pcs, includes figures, 1931 .... **125.00**
Log Riders (Goodwin print), 188 pcs, includes figures, 1920 .... **40.00**
Thrill of a Lifetime, 625 pcs, includes figures, 1930 .... **100.00**

Picture Puzzle Exchange, Boston, MA, Summer Skies, 73 pcs, 1930s **15.00**

Porpine Puzzle Co., Melrose, MA, Fred's Visit to the Circus, 195 pcs, c1910 .... **35.00**

R & J Specialty Co., New York, NY, Patience Puzzle, Easter Eggs, 300 pcs, c1910 .... **40.00**

Richardson, Margaret H. (Mrs. Hayden), New York, NY, Perplexity Puzzle, The Gleaners, 406 pcs, c1910 .... **45.00**

Rowe and Emery, Waterville, ME, Happy News, 243 pcs, 1930s **30.00**

Royal Puzzlemakers, Roslindale, Indian Prayer, 165 pcs, 1930s **20.00**

Russell, Charles W., Auburn, MA, Wild Turkey Hunt, 400 pcs, includes figures, 1930s **50.00**

Ryther, H.A. Novelty Co., Millers Falls, MA, Patchwork Picture Puzzle, The Tavern, 150 pcs, includes figures, 1930s **25.00**

Salmon, J. Ltd., England, Academy, A Friendly Meal, 100 pcs, 1930s **15.00**

Shut In Society, Philadelphia, PA, Talisman, Cross Country, 100 pcs, 1930s **35.00**

Straus, Joseph K., Brooklyn, NY
Blacksmith Shop, 100 pcs, c1960 .. **10.00**
Glory That Is Autumn, 200 pcs, c1960 .... **22.00**
To The Fire, 200 pcs, 1960 .... **28.00**

Trojan Sporting Goods, Chicago, IL, Wood Masters, Old Ironsides, 100 pcs, 1930s **12.00**

U-Nit, W. Caldwell, NJ, A Quiet Game, 200 mahogany pcs, includes figures, c1960 .... **30.00**

Zeitvertreib, Waterbury, CT, The New Boarder, 141 pcs, 1908 .... **30.00**

Adult, Die Cut, Wilder Mfg Co, Movie-Land Cut-Ups, four puzzles, $125.00.

Diecut

Adult Leisure Products Corp., Locust Valley, NY, ALPSCO Star Puzzle, Bogart, 300 pcs, 1967 .... **35.00**

American Publishing Co., Dracula, 200 pcs, 1974 .... **20.00**

Milton Bradley Co., Springfield, MA

Addams Family Mystery Puzzle, 1965 **95.00**

Bonanza Jigsaw Puzzle, Expecting Trouble, 600 pcs, 1964 .... **25.00**

Chilcote Co., Cleveland, OH, Jig Time Picture Puzzle, The Mill Stream, 325 pcs, 1933 .... **4.00**

Consolidated Paper Box Co., Somerville, MA, Perfect Picture Puzzle Value-Plus Series, Orient's Magic Spell, 250 pcs, 1930s **4.00**

E-F Lith. Co., Inc., New York, NY, Mystery-Jig Puzzle with novelette, By Whose Hand?, 300 pcs, includes figures, 1933 .... **20.00**

Jaymar Specialty Co., Brooklyn, NY

Modern Fighters for Victory, Subtracting a Zero, 300 pcs, includes figures, 1942 .... **15.00**

Top Comics, featuring Dick Tracy, 1943 .... **45.00**

Walt Disney's Donald Duck, 300 pcs, includes figures, 1950s **30.00**

Jig of Jigs Maxfield Parrish Puzzle, No. 3, The Prince and Princess, 250 pcs, 1930s **75.00**

Movie Cut-Ups Co., Inc., Peabody, MA, Weekly Puzzle No. 13, Buck Jones in "White Eagle," 285 pcs, 1933 ..... **30.00**

Pearl Publishing Co., Brooklyn, NY, Mystery Puzzle of the Month No. 4, Pictures Don't Lie, 200 pcs with booklet, 1940s **12.00**

Perfect Picture Puzzle, Queen of the Rodeo, 250 pcs, c1940 .... **4.00**

Picadilly Jig Picture Puzzle, Pride of the Farm, 200 pcs, 1930s **5.00**

Pressman, J. & Co., New York, NY, Victory Picture Puzzle, Tank Busters and Jeeps on the Job, 375 pcs, includes figures, 1940s **15.00**

Saalfield Publishing Co., Akron, OH

Liberators of the World (FDR and Churchill), 500 pcs, 1940s **20.00**

Interlox Puzzle, Windjammer, 225 pcs, 1930s **3.00**

Superman Picture Puzzle, Superman Saves a Life, 500 pcs, 1940 ..... **125.00**

Salem Chemical & Supply co., Salem, MA, Witch "300" Puzzle, Tender Care, 300 pcs, 1930s **5.00**

Square Cut Puzzle Co., New York, NY, Keeper of the Flame, 520 square pcs, c1942 .... **18.00**

Transogram Co., New York, NY, Funny Pages Jigsaw Puzzle, Li'l Abner, 1938 **35.00**

Tuco Workshops, Lockport, NY, The Swing, 350 pcs, 1933 .... **6.00**

University Distributing Co., Cambridge, MA, Jig of the Week Puzzle, No. 8, Thanksgiving, 300 pcs, 1932 ...... **10.00**

Viking Manufacturing Co., Boston, MA,

Weekly Jig, Dreamy River, 160 pcs, 1933 .... **4.00**

Whitman Publishing Co., Racine, WI, Superman Jigsaw Puzzle, 150 pcs, 1966 .... **35.00**

Advertising, Standard Oil of Ohio, "A Bully Time In Spain," SOHIO Radio Jig-Saw Puzzle No. 3, die cut, cardboard, picture of Gene and Glenn on reverse, $10.00.

ADVERTISING AND NOVELTY PUZZLES

Black Cat Hosiery, diecut, 60 pcs, paper envelope, 4 x 3", c1908 .... **15.00**

Chevrolet, World's Finest 6-cylinder School Bus, diecut, 35 pcs, reversible, box 8 x 14", 1932 .... **60.00**

Clean Up and Paint Up Campaign Committee, Boston, MA, Brownie Town Picture Puzzle, 32 wood pcs, box 5 x 4", c1910 .... **20.00**

Cocomalt Puzzle, R.B. Davis Co, Hoboken, NJ, Buffalo Bill Jig-Saw Puzzle, diecut, 65 pcs, paper envelope 10 x 7", 1932 .... **20.00**

Comon Tatar Inc., Blasdell, NY, Mail-A-Puzzle postcard, Eastern DC-8, 20 pcs, 3½ x 5½", c1970 .... **3.00**

Esquire, Inc., New York, NY, Esky Gift Kit, contains Susan Hayward diecut puzzle and 1944 Varga girl calendar, paper envelope 14 x 10", 1943 .... **50.00**

Essolube, Five Star Theater, Foiled by Essolube (Dr. Seuss cartoon), paper envelope, c1940s **45.00**

Eveready flashlight Jigsaw Puzzle, Is That You Santa Claus?, diecut, 60 pcs, paper envelope 9 x 12", 1933 ..... **25.00**

Everett Piano, Cincinnati, OH, diecut advertising puzzle, box 3 x 5", c1910 **75.00**

Folger's Coffee Puzzle, diecut, cardboard canister 3½" h, c1960 .... **5.00**

Hills Brothers Coffee, San Francisco, CA, Where's the Fire?, coffeepot shape, diecut, box 4 x 6" **30.00**

Hood, C.I. & Co., Lowell, MA
  Hood Farm Puzzle Box, set of 4, die-
    cut, box 7 x 5", c1905 .... **40.00**
  Hood's Rainy Day and Balloon Puz-
    zles, reversible, diecut, box 7½ x
    5", 1891 .... **100.00**
Kolynos Co., New Haven, CT, Just Plain
  Bill, diecut, 150 pcs, paper envelope
  9 x 12" **20.00**
Lux Soap, Wayside Inn, 150 pcs, diecut,
  10 x 12", envelope, c1933 .... **8.00**
McKesson & Robbins, diecut, 11 x 13",
  1932 .... **55.00**
Miller Rubber Products, Akron, OH,
  Miller Toy Carnival, diecut, 50 pcs,
  1932 .... **35.00**
Montgomery Ward & Co., Chicago, IL,
  Merry Christmas-Circus Puzzle, die-
  cut, 15 pcs, paper envelope, c1915 **12.00**
Pacific Coast Borax Co., New York, NY,
  Hauling 20 Mule Team Borax Out of
  Death Valley, diecut with figures, pa-
  per envelope and inserts, 1933 ..... **30.00**
Parker Brothers, Salem, MA, Pastime
  Puzzle Contest Set, 8 small wood
  puzzles, box 8 x 11", 1932 .... **60.00**
Platt & Munk, New York, NY, Junior
  bank Book & Picture Puzzle, box 7 x
  9" **60.00**
Proctor & Gamble, Adventures of Pro-
  fessor Oscar Quackenbush, Chasing
  Pink Elephants, diecut, 50 pcs, en-
  velope 8 x 10", 1933 .... **15.00**
RCA Victor Co., Inc., His Master's Voice
  Jig Saw Puzzle, shows Nipper, diecut
  with figures, box 5 x 3", c1930 .... **20.00**
Rogers Novelty Card Co., Boston, MA,
  Jig-Saw Postcard, Custom House, die-
  cut, 39 pcs, c1910 .... **10.00**
Timkin Silent Automatic Oil Burner, Jig-
  Play Puzzle, diecut, 90 pcs, paper en-
  velope 5 x 7", 1930s **15.00**
Tip Top Bread (Ward's Baking Co.), Cir-
  cus Puzzle, diecut, 36 pcs, paper en-
  velope 8 x 9", 1951 .... **10.00**
Toddy, Inc., New York, NY, Treasure
  Hunt, diecut, 50 pcs, puzzle and
  game combined, 1933 .... **15.00**

RADIO CHARACTERS AND PERSONALITIES

Collecting Hints: Many items associated with radio characters and personalities were offered as
premiums. This category focuses mostly on the
non-premium items. Radio premiums have their
own separate listing elsewhere in this book.

Don't overlook the vast amount of material
related to the radio shows themselves. This can
include scripts, props, and a wealth of publicity
material. Collecting autographed photographs
was popular, and many appear on the market.
Books, especially Big Little Books and similar
types, featured many radio related characters and
stories.

Radio characters and personalities found their
way into movies and television. Serious collectors do differentiate the products which spun off
from these other two areas.

History: The radio show was a dominant force
in American life from the 1920s to the early
1950s. Amos and Andy began in 1929, The
Shadow in 1930, and Chandu the Magician in
1932. Although many of the characters were fictional, the individuals who portrayed them became public idols. A number of figures achieved
fame on their own—Eddie Cantor, Don McNeill
of The Breakfast Club, George Burns and Gracie
Allen, Arthur Godfrey, and Jack Benny.

Sponsors and manufacturers were quick to
capitalize on the fame of the radio characters
and personalities. Premiums were offered as part
of the shows themes. However, merchandising
did not stop with premiums. Many non-premium
materials such as bubble gum cards, figurines,
games, publicity photographs, dolls, etc., were
issued. Magazine advertisements often featured
radio personalities.

References: Anthony Slide, *Great Radio Personalities In Historic Photographs,* The Vestal Press,
Ltd., 1982; Tom Tumbusch, *New, Revised Illustrated Radio Premium Catalog And Price Guide,*
Tomart Publications, 1989.

See: Big Little Books, Comic Books, Radio Premiums, Super Heroes.

Jimmie Allen
  Bag, 4 x 6", cloth, white, red printing
    both sides, drawstring, reverse Cleo
    Cola logo, bottle cap and inscrip-
    tion "Listen To The Air Adventures
    of Jimmie Allen Every Broadcast For
    Bulletins About Premiums," c1934 **150.00**
  Book, *Jimmie Allen Flying Club
    Stamp Album,* 5 x 6½", red, white,
    and blue cov design, mounted
    stamps inside, 1936 .... **75.00**
  Map, 11 x 25¼", full color, printed
    letter on back, copyright 1934 ... **100.00**
  Membership Card, 2¼ x 4", "Flying
    Cadet," printed black, red stamped
    serial number, light blue airplanes
    and wing symbols design border,
    club pledge and airplane border re-
    verse, penciled signature, c1934–
    35 .... **40.00**
  Newsletter, 8½ x 11", 4 pgs, red,
    white, and green holiday design
    and signatures on front cover, black
    and white photos on back cover . **50.00**

Photo, 8½ x 10½", black and white, litho metal frame with camouflage pattern, 1934–35 .... **25.00**

Amos 'n' Andy

Figure, 4", bisque, painted, stamped "Pfeffer Porzellan, Gotha, Germany," registration marks "6495" and "9496", 1920–30, pr **300.00**

Greeting Card

Birthday, brown portraits, message includes song title "Check and Double Check," inked birthday note, Rust Craft **20.00**

Get Well, 4½ x 5½", black and white photo, Hall Brothers, 1931 copyright **30.00**

Radio Guide, photo, orig envelope . **28.00**

Jack Armstrong

Flashlight, 4½", cardboard, red, metal cap ends, c1939 .... **20.00**

Model, Tru-Flite, paper, instruction sheet, uncut parts, orig mailing envelope, 1944 copyright **75.00**

Telescope, 10½" l extended, tin, black cover paper with emb "Jack Armstrong Explorer," c1937 ..... **40.00**

Whistle Ring, gold color, Egyptian symbols, includes 3 x 4", illus code sheet, manila ring envelope, and mailing envelope, c1938 .... **100.00**

Chandu The Magician, magic trick, Galloping Coin, three metal containers, metal case, instruction sheet, orig mailing box and label **75.00**

Dick Daring, map and puzzle, combination premium, 9 x 12" map, orange, blue, and white, adventure scenes, puzzle has same scenes and color, orig 6 x 8" mailing envelope . **50.00**

Little Orphan Annie

Book, James Whitcomb Riley, *The Little Orphan Annie Book,* color illus by Ethel Betts, 1908 .... **25.00**

Photo, 8 x 10" black and white, glossy, Shirley Bell, sgd "To My Friend/Radio's Little Orphan Annie/ Shirley Bell," 1932 .... **40.00**

Lum and Abner

Almanac, family, 6 x 9", 34 pgs, orig mailing envelope, 1936 .... **50.00**

Newspaper, "Pine Edge News," 11½ x 16½", 4 pgs, black and white, Spring, 1936, orig mailing envelope **40.00**

Fibber McGee and Molly

Photo, 8¼ x 12", black and white, glossy, cast members, Fibber and Molly pictured at top, late 1930s . **25.00**

Record Album, 10¼ x 12", contains four 78 rpm records, live broadcasts, colorful Fibber design on cov, 1947 copyright **50.00**

Pinback Button, Uncle Don's Ice Cream Club, Borden's, red ground on lower half, marked "Puldin Co, Inc, NYC," 1" d, $12.00.

Charlie McCarthy

Card Game, Rummy, 1938 .... **25.00**

Game, Charlie McCarthy's Radio Party, spinner board, 21 diecut standup figures, orig envelope with instructions, Chase & Sanborn Coffee issue **50.00**

Soap, figure, 4" h, boxed, Kerk Gild, c1930–40 .... **75.00**

Spoon, silverplate **13.50**

Major Bowes, award medal, 2", gilded brass, red fabric ribbon, case **150.00**

One Man's Family

Photo Album, 7½ x 10½", 20 pgs, red, white, and blue cov, orig mailing envelope **50.00**

Scrapbook, 8 x 10", 12 pgs, features Jack Barbour, photos and news clippings, includes cover letter, 1936 copyright **40.00**

Joe Penner, valentine, 4½ x 7", diecut, mechanical, Penner holding duck on shoulder, eyeballs and mouth move back and forth, inscription "I'll Gladly Buy A Duck," 1930–40 .... **20.00**

Sgt. Preston

Game, Sgt. Preston Gets His Man, clipped from cereal box, 6 x 7" playing board, 3 x 5" perforated spinner board, mid 1950s **30.00**

Map, 7½ x 9½", full color illus, stories and territory history on back, c1955 .... **40.00**

Pedometer, 2½" d, tin, 1952–54 ... **50.00**

Poster, 16½ x 22", "Sgt. Preston Mounted Police Whistle," whistle offer from Quaker Puffed Wheat and Puffed Rice cereal, c1949–50 **200.00**

Pouch, 3½ x 4½", paper, tan, leather drawstring, orig mailing box, Quaker Cereal premium, 1955 ... **150.00**

The Shadow

Blotter, 4 x 9", cardboard, orange,

blue, and white, red silhouette, 1940s **20.00**

Figure, 7" h, china, glossy black cloak and hat, dark blue accent hat brim, 2½" d white with gold accent striping base, c1930 .... **250.00**

Game, The Shadow, 20" sq board, includes one wood token, play money, colored disks, four wood black cap dice, and shaker, boxed, Toy Creations, 1940 copyright ... **250.00**

Skippy, playing cards, 36 numbered cards, 4 x 5 x 1" box, Poll Parrot shoe sticker on lid, mid 1930s **60.00**

Speed Gibson, map, 17 x 22", green, black, and white design, includes 5½ x 7" unused record card and orig mailing envelope **150.00**

Ed Wynn, NBC Radio, promotional puzzle **25.00**

RADIO PREMIUMS

Collecting Hints: Most collections are centered around one or two specific personalities or radio programs.

History: Radio premiums are nostalgic reminders of childhood memories of radio shows. Sponsors of shows frequently used their products to promote the collection of premiums, such as saving box tops to exchange for gifts tied in with the program or personality.

References: Tom Tumbusch, *Illustrated Radio Premium Catalog and Price Guide,* Tomart Publications, 1989.

REPRODUCTION ALERT
See: Radio Characters and Personalities

Jimmie Allen
Bracelet, ID, 1935 .... **18.00**

Envelope, Lum and Abner, issued by Horlick's Malted Milk Corp, Racine, WI, post marked June 28, 1936, listing program times of NBC Blue Network, 6½ x 3⅝", $4.50.

Flight Wings, Flying Cadet, Hi-Speed, Type III, 1934 .... **8.00**
Whistle, brass, 1936–39 .... **22.00**

Amos 'n' Andy, adv puzzle, Pepsodent, 1931 .... **35.00**

Jack Armstrong
Patch, Future Champions of America, cloth, 1943 .... **15.00**
Photo, Jack on his horse Blackster, 1933 .... **10.00**
Ring, Dragon's Eye, crocodile design, green stone, 1940 .... **150.00**
Viewer, African filmstrip **30.00**

Baby Snooks, dancing puppet **25.00**

The Black Flame of the Amazon, ruler, cardboard **20.00**

Bobby Benson
Bracelet, enameled, 1932–35 ...... **25.00**
Game, Circus of Games, set of cards, booklet, 1932–35 .... **22.00**

Frank Buck
Neckerchief, "Frank Buck's Adventurers Club," 1934–38 .... **45.00**
Pinback Button, Adventure Club, 1934–38 .... **10.00**

Captain Midnight
Decoder, "Magni-Matic Code-O-Graph," 1946 .... **32.00**
Map, Chuck's Treasure Map, 1939 . **50.00**
Patch, transfer, iron-on, 1948 ...... **35.00**
Ring, Flight Commander, 1940–41 . **60.00**

Green Hornet, membership card **10.00**

Hop Harrigan, patch, "American Observation Corps," "Hop Harrigan Says Keep 'Em Flying" **15.00**

Little Orphan Annie
Bracelet, identification disc, 1934 .. **20.00**
Manual, *Radio Orphan Annie's Secret Society,* 1937 .... **30.00**
Mask, Annie, 1933 .... **30.00**
Mug, ceramic, 1932 .... **20.00**

Lone Ranger
Badge, Chief Scout, 1934–38 ...... **60.00**
Belt, Glo-in-dark, 1941 .... **30.00**
Certificate, Safety Club, 1938–40 ... **5.00**
Pinback Button, Safety Club, 1934–38 .... **15.00**
Shirt, Hi-Yo Silver design, 1941 .... **30.00**

Lum and Abner
Almanac, *1936 Family Almanac,* Horlick's Malted Milk, orig mailer **15.00**
Shaker, Horlick's Malted Milk, glass, metal cap and plunger, blue illus . **20.00**

Mandrake The Magician, pinback button, Magic Club **50.00**

Fibber McGee and Molly, spinners, Johnson's Wax, 1939, pr **45.00**

Don McNeill, Breakfast Club, yearbook, orig mailer, 1948 .... **12.00**

Tom Mix
Bandanna, checker border, 1933 ... **32.00**

Decoder Buttons, orig Ralston card, 1946 .... **75.00**
Gun and Holster, wood gun, cartridge belt, 1935 .... **75.00**
Manual, *Life of Tom Mix*, 1933 .... **38.00**
Phantom Pilot Patrol, membership badge **22.00**
Sgt. Preston
Map, "Map of Yokon Territory," color, 1955 .... **22.00**
Photo, 8½ x 11", black and white, 1949 .... **15.00**
Police Whistle, cord, 1950 .... **22.00**
The Shadow, stamp, rubber, Shadow Club **35.00**
Melvin Purvis
Badge, Junior G-Man Corps, Chief Operative, 1936 .... **8.00**
Holster, Law and Order Patrol, shoulder type, 1937 .... **15.00**
Buck Rogers
Badge, Solar Scout Member, 1935–36 **28.00**
Big Little Book, *Buck Rogers in the 25th Century*, 1933 .... **22.00**
Sky King
Signal Scope, 1947 .... **30.00**
Stamp Kit **28.00**
Superman
Belt and Buckle, 1942–50 .... **65.00**
Certificate, membership, 1938–42 .. **20.00**
Pin, Junior Defense League, 1938–42 **60.00**
Tennessee Jed, mask, paper **15.00**
Terry and the Pirates, detector ring, gold, 1943–48 .... **32.00**
Dick Tracy
Badge, Detective Club Shield **18.00**
Book, *Family Fun Book* **8.00**
Flashlight, pocket, 1939 .... **25.00**
Manual, *Secret Detective Methods & Magic Tricks*, 1939 .... **18.00**
Don Winslow
Decoder, "Golden Torpedo," 1942 . **60.00**
Membership Ring, serial number of top, 1939 .... **40.00**
Periscope, 1939 .... **45.00**
Lone Wolf, pin, Arrowhead Member, 1932 .... **10.00**

RADIOS

Collecting Hints: Radio collectors divide into three groups: those who collect because of nostalgia and those interested in history and/or acquiring radios that represent periods prior to or after World War II, and collectors of personality and figural radios. Most collectors find broadcasting, and therefore broadcast receivers, their primary interest.

The significant divisions of broadcast receivers that are represented in a small collection are:

—Crystal sets and battery powered receivers of the early 1920s
—Rectangular electric table models of the late 1920s
—Cathedrals, tombstones, and consoles of the Thirties
—Midget plastic portables and wood cabinet table models built before and after World War II
—Shaped Bakelite and other plastic cased radios
—Personality and figural radios beginning in the 1930s and extending into the 1960s.

Because the emphasis for nostalgia seems to fall on the decade of the Thirties, the cathedral style, socket powered radios, e.g., the Philco series, have become sought after items. Recently the younger set has exhibited a very strong nostalgia interest in the plastic cabinet radios built between 1945 and 1960.

The underlying force that values a radio to a traditional collector, and consequently sets the price in the market, is rarity. Very rare radios usually go directly to major collectors, seldom appearing in the general market. Wireless equipment and radios used commercially before World War I are considered rare and are not listed here.

With the newer radio collector, the controlling force is novelty with the outside appearance the primary feature. The radio must play; but, shape, color, decoration, and condition of the case far outweigh the internal workings of the set in determining desirability and consequently the price. Enclosures that represent things or figures e.g., Mickey Mouse, command premium prices.

The prices of 1920s radio sets have been stabilized by collectors' demands. Typical prices are listed. The values of Thirties' radios fall into two ranges. Cathedrals bring an average of $75 to $100 with Philco and Atwater Kent on the high end, and names like Airline and Stewart Warner on the low end. Consoles bring substantially lower prices, seldom reaching $75 except for very ornate models, such as the Victrola Hyperion or Orchestrion and the Atwater Kent Model 812.

The squarish table models of the later Thirties and the midget sets of the late 1930s and 1940s recently have attracted the attention of nostalgia buffs and new collectors. Generally their demand in the face of supply keeps their price low, holding below $50. An exception to this rule is based on decoration. Columns, figurework, and dramatic changes in texture add interest and raise the potential prices. A radio with columns outlining the dial or the speaker open can command $100. Another exception to this is the novelty radio. Treasure chest barrels, mirrored cases, and specialty items bring prices as high as $500.

The value of a radio is directly related to its condition. The critical factors are appearance and operability. The prices listed are for sets of average to good condition and based upon an electrically complete receiver that operates when powered.

Minor scratches are to be expected as is alligatoring of the surface finish. Gouges, cracks, and delaminated surfaces will cut the price by 50%. However, the penalty for a crack or broken place for plastic closures is severe. A Catalin radio with a blue case might bring $250-$400 in good condition, but with a visible crack the price drops to $30.

If parts, tubes, or components are missing or if major repairs must be made in order for the set to work, the price again must be reduced by as much as 50%. A particular radio that is unrestored, in excellent or mint condition, and playing satisfactorily can command an increase of 30 to 50% over the prices listed below.

In addition to radios, many collectors specialize in a facet of the general radio art such as loudspeakers, tubes, microphones, memorabilia, or brand names. As a result, auxiliary and related radio items are becoming collectibles along with radios themselves.

History: The art and science of radio as a communication medium is barely ninety years old. Marconi was the first to assemble and employ the transmission and reception instruments that permitted electric message-sending without the use of direct connections. The early name for radio was "Wireless," and the first application was in 1898 as a means of controlling ships. Early wireless equipment is not generally considered a collectible since its historic value makes it important for museum display.

Between 1905 and the end of World War I many technical advances, including the invention of the vacuum tube by DeForest, resulted in an extensive communication art and a very strong amateur interest in the strange new technology. The receiving equipment from that period is considered highly desirable by collectors and historians but is rarely available outside the main body of early radio and wireless collectors.

By 1920, radio technology offered the means to talk to large numbers of people simultaneously and bring music from concert halls directly into living rooms. The result was the development of a new art that changed the American way of life during the 1920s. The world became familiar in the average listener's home.

Radio receivers changed substantially in the decade of the Twenties, going from black boxes with many knobs and dials and powered from expensive and messy batteries, to styled furniture, simple to use, and operated from the house current that had become the standard source of energy for service in the home. During the Twenties radios grew more complicated and powerful as well as more ornate. Consoles appeared, loud-

speakers were incorporated into them, and sound fidelity joined distance as criteria for quality.

In the early 1930s demand changed. The large expensive console gave way to small but effective table models. The era of the "cathedral" and the "tombstone" began. By the end of the Thirties, the midget radio had become popular. Quality of sound was replaced by reduction of price and most homes had more than one radio.

Shortly after World War II the miniature tubes developed for the military were applied to domestic radios. The result was further reduction in size with a substantial improvement in quality. The advent of FM also speeded the development. Plastic technology made possible the production of attractive cases in many styles and colors.

The other development that drastically changed the radio receiver was the invention of the transistor in 1927. A whole new family of radio sets that could be carried in the shirt pocket became popular. As they became less and less expensive, their popularity grew rapidly. Consequently, they were throwaways when they stopped working. Today they are not easy to find in good condition and are quite collectible.

References: Philip Collins, *Radios: The Golden Age,* Chronic Books, 1987; Alan Douglas, *Radio Manufacturers of the 1920's, Volume I* (1980) and *Volume 2* (1989), The Vestal Press, Inc.; Robert Grinder and George Fathauer, *Radio Collector's Director and Price Guide,,* Ironwood Press, 1986; David and Betty Johnson, *Guide To Old Radios–Pointers, Pictures, and Prices,* Wallace-Homestead, 1989.

Periodicals: *Antique Radio Classified,* 9511 Sunrise Blvd., Cleveland, OH 44133; *Radio Age,* 636 Cambridge Road, Augusta, GA 30909; *Sight, Sound, Style,* P. O. Box 2224, So. Hackensack, NJ, 07606.

Collectors' Clubs: Antique Radio Club of America, 81 Steeplechase Road, Devon, PA 19333; Antique Wireless Association, 17 Sheridan Street, Auburn, NY, 13021.

Museums: Antique Wireless Museum (AWA), East Bloomfield, NY; Caperton's Radio Museum, Louisville, KY; Muchow's Historical Radio Museum, Elgin, IL; Museum of Wonderful Wireless, Minneapolis, MN; New England Museum of Wireless and Steam, East Greenwich, RI; Voice of the Twenties, Orient, NY.

A–C Electrical
    Model AC-9960, console, battery, 1929 .... **100.00**
    Model XL-30, table, battery, six tubes, two dials, 1929 .... **90.00**
    Model XL-71, table, battery, 1929 .. **135.00**
Acme Apparatus, Model S, table, battery, five tubes, single dial, 1925 ... **75.00**

Adler
  Model 10-SR, table, battery, five
    tubes, three dials, 1925 ....   **70.00**
  Model 50, console and phonograph,
    battery, five tubes, three dials, 1925   **60.00**
  Model 201, table, battery, five tubes,
    three dials, 1925 ....   **70.00**
Aerodyne, Model 2, table, battery, five
  tubes, three dials, 1925 ....   **75.00**
All American Mohawk
  Model 93, console, ten tube, one
    dial, 1929 ....   **100.00**
  Model C-6, cathedral, 1930 ....   **100.00**
  Portable, battery, loop antennae, two
    dials, 1925 ....   **135.00**
American Bosch
  Model 66 Cruiser, console, battery,
    six tubes, one dial **125.00**
  Model 360-T, tombstone, broadcast
    and shortwave bands, 1933 .....   **150.00**
  Model 460-R, console, broadcast and
    shortwave bands, 1934 ....   **110.00**
Atwater Kent
  Model 10A, breadboard type, battery,
    Model E speakers, 1923 ....   **550.00**
  Model 33, table, battery, six tubes,
    one dial, 1927 ....   **80.00**
  Model 46, table, green metal case,
    1929 ....   **115.00**
  Model 75, console, radio and phon-
    ograph, 1930 ....   **175.00**
  Model 337, tombstone, broadcast
    and shortwave bands, 1935 .....   **125.00**
  Model 944, cathedral, 1934 ....   **150.00**

**Fada, model 1001, Universal Superhel-
erodyne, wood, restored, $40.00.**

Belmont, Model 6D111, brown bakelite
  case, Art Deco **85.00**
Crosley
  Model 4-29-P, portable, battery, four
    tubes, two dials, 1926 ....   **100.00**
  Model 5-75, highboy console, bat-
    tery, five tubes, one dial, 1926 ...   **175.00**
  Model 124 Playtime Grandfather
    Clock, 1931 ....   **375.00**
Delco, car radio, "Xstr Transportable"   **35.00**

Farnsworth
  Model BK-89, console radio and
    phonograph, 1940 ....   **48.00**
  Model CT-50, bakelite case, two
    colors, 1941 ....   **195.00**
Firestone, horizontal, wood cabinet,
  push button, 1940 ....   **65.00**
Freed Eisemann
  Model NR-60 AC, table, seven tubes,
    one dial, 1927 ....   **115.00**
  Model NR-95, console, eight tubes,
    one dial, 1929 ....   **125.00**
General Electric
  Model K-52, cathedral, broadcast and
    shortwave bands, 1933 ....   **245.00**
  Model L-50, mantle, plastic, handle,
    1933 ....   **40.00**
  Model S-22, tombstone, 1931 .....   **90.00**
Grebe, syncrophase **60.00**
International, Kadette, 36, 87 ....   **35.00**
Montgomery Ward
  Model 720, table, plastic, broadcast
    and shortwave bands, twin speak-
    ers, push button, 1940 ....   **85.00**
  Model 903, console credenza, bat-
    tery, 1927 ....   **65.00**
  Model 1468, portable, battery, 1941   **20.00**
Motorola, portable, plastic **30.00**
Novelty, figural, various manufacturers,
  mint in orig box
    Blabbermouth **25.00**
    Peanut, Jimmy Carter **45.00**
    Pet Milk Can **35.00**
    Whiskey Bottle, Old Parr **45.00**
Paragon, model RD5 ....   **185.00**
Philco
  Model 20, cathedral, 1930 ....   **200.00**
  Model 37-630-X, console, broadcast
    and shortwave bands, 1935 .....   **175.00**
  Model 41-221-C, table, handle,
    broadcast and shortwave bands,
    1940 ....   **35.00**
  Model PT-91, mantle, plastic, 1941   **30.00**
RCA
  Model R-28-B, table, 1933 ....   **45.00**
  Model RE-45 Victor, console, 1929 .   **200.00**
  Model U-25, console, broadcast and
    shortwave bands, push button,
    1939 ....   **50.00**
  Radiola 62, console, highboy, nine
    tubes, one dial, 1928 ....   **225.00**
Sparks—Withington
  Model 65, table, broadcast and short-
    wave bands, 1934 ....   **50.00**
  Model 600, console, lowboy, battery,
    ten tubes, one dial, 1930 ....   **30.00**
Stromberg—Carlson
  Model 340-H, table, broadcast and
    shortwave bands, 1938 ....   **50.00**
  Model 635, table, treasure chest,
    seven tubes, one dial, 1928 .....   **150.00**
  Model 935-PL, console, radio and

phonograph, broadcast and FM
bands, push buttons, 1941 ...... **48.00**
Westinghouse
    Model WR-14, cathedral, 1931 .... **150.00**
    Model WR-101, table, broadcast and
    shortwave bands, 1935 .... **35.00**
    Model WR-308, console, broadcast
    and shortwave bands, push but-
    tons, 1940 .... **145.00**
    Model WR-676, portable, 1940 .... **20.00**
Wilcox–Gay
    Model A-33, table, teledial, 1937 .. **100.00**
    Model A-52, mantle, 1939 .... **25.00**
    Model A-93, console, 1940 .... **50.00**
Zenith
    Model 5-G-401D, portable, gray,
    handle, 1949 .... **25.00**
    Model 6-D-015, table, brown bake-
    lite case, broadcast and shortwave
    bands, 1936 .... **40.00**
    Model 10-H-573, console, broadcast
    and shortwave bands, push but-
    tons, FM, 1941 .... **185.00**

RAILROAD ITEMS

Collecting Hints: Most collectors concentrate on
one railroad as opposed to one type of object.
Railroad material always brings a higher price in
the area from which it originated. Local collectors tend to concentrate on local railroads. Material from railroads which operated for only a
short time realizes the highest prices. Nostalgia
also influences the collector.

There are many local railroad clubs. Railroad
buffs tend to have their own specialized swap
meets and exhibitions. A large one is held in
Gaithersburg, Maryland, in the fall each year.

History: It was a canal company, the Delaware
and Hudson, which used the first steam locomotive in America. The Stourbridge Lion moved
coal from the mines to the canal wharfs. Just as
America was entering its great canal era in 1825,
the railroad was gaining a foothold. William
Strickland recommended to the Commonwealth
of Pennsylvania that they not build canals, but
concentrate on the railroad. His advice went un-
heeded.

By the 1840s the railroad was established. Numerous private companies, many in business for
only a short time, were organized.

The Civil War demonstrated the effectiveness
of the railroad. Immediately following the war
the transcontinental railroad was completed, and
entrepreneurs such as Gould and Vanderbilt constructed financial empires built on railroads.
Mergers created huge systems. The golden age
of the railroad extended from the 1880s to the
1940s.

After 1950 the railroads suffered from poor

management, a bloated labor force, lack of
maintenance, and competition from other forms
of transportation. The 1970s saw the federal government enter the picture through Conrail and
Amtrak. Thousands of miles of track were aban-
doned. Many railroads failed or were merged.
Today the system still is fighting for survival.

References: Stanley L. Baker, *Railroad Collectibles: An Illustrated Value Guide, Third Edition,*
Collector Books, 1985; Phil Bollhagen, *The Pictorial Value Guide To Railroad Playing Cards,*
published by author, 1987; Arthur Dominy and
Rudolph A. Morgenfruh, *Silver At Your Service,*
published by authors, 1987; Howard Johnson,
Railroad Collectibles, L-W Promotions, 1986 revision; Richard Luckin, *Dining On Rails,* published by author, 1983, out-of-print.

Periodicals: *Key, Lock and Lantern,* P.O. Box 15,
Spencerport, NY 14559; *U. S. Rail News,* P. O.
Box 7007, Huntingdon Woods, MI 48070.

Collectors' Clubs: Railroad Enthusiasts, 456
Main Street, West Townsend, MA 01474; Rail-
roadiana Collectors Association, P. O. Box 365,
St. Ignatius, MT 59865; Railway and Locomotive
Historical Society, 3363 Riviera West Drive, Kel-
seyville, CA 95451.

Museums: Baltimore and Ohio Railroad, Baltimore, MD; Museum of Transportation, Boston,
MA; New York Museum of Transportation, Albany, NY; California State Railroad Museum,
Sacramento, CA.

**Advertising Mirror, The Travelers Insur-
ance Co, The Railroad Men's Reliance,
Hartford, CT, multicolored night scene,
2¾ x 1⅝", $65.00.**

Ashtray, Southern Railway **14.00**
Bell, steam locomotive, brass **700.00**
Blotter, Soo Line, 1920s, unused **2.00**
Book, Henry T. Williams, *Pacific Tourist
Guide Over The Continent,* NY, 1877,
300 pgs **65.00**
Booklets and Brochures
    By Way of the Canyons, Soo Line,
    booklet, 1907 .... **15.00**

California Picture Book, ATSF, illus,
1930s 5.00
Eastern Summer Trips, B & O, folder 7.50
French National Fares, turbo cov ... 6.00
Holiday Haunts Adirondacks & 1,000
Islands, folder, NYC, 1940, 63 pgs 7.00
Union Pacific RR, 1926, booklet ... 12.00
Calendar
C & O RR, 1937, Chessie 40.00
DRG & W RR, 1953 .... 20.00
Union Pacific
1966 .... 8.00
1969, Centennial 20.00
Catalog, Hibbard Spencer Bartlett & Co,
Railway and Manufacturer's Supplies,
1907, 632 pgs 50.00
China
Bouillon Cup
Wabash Banner 65.00
WP, Feather Friver, top logo, Shen-
ango 25.00
Butter Pat, Mimbreno, Syracuse
China, full backstamp 45.00
Celery Dish, Union Pacific, 10", oval,
blue and gold pattern, back-
stamped "Scannell China" 35.00
Coffee Cup, Illinois Central, Coral
pattern 12.50
Creamer
B & O Centennary 65.00
SP, Prairie Mountain, Wildflower . 25.00
Cup and Saucer
B & O, Capital 45.00
NYC, Mercury, Syracuse, back-
stamped 50.00
Southern Pacific 55.00
Demitasse Cup and Saucer
B & O, Centennial, Lamberton
China, backstamped 48.00
CMSTP & P, Traveler, Sycracuse,
backstamped 80.00
Mustard Jar, NYC, Mercury 40.00
Plate
Missouri Pacific, state flowers 250.00
NP, dinner, Yellowstone Park Line
logo, top marked, Shenango ... 125.00
NYC, dinner, Mohawk, salmon-
pink and black, top marked ... 36.00
Union Pacific, 6½", salad, Winged
Streamliner pattern, winged Art
Deco train, backstamped "Ster-
ling China" 30.00
Platter
NYC, 8¾ x 6", Hudson, green and
gold floral motif, Limoges, back-
stamp 75.00
Southern, Peach Blossom, top
marked with logo and "Southern
Serves The South," Buffalo China 100.00
Union Pacific, 8", oval, Challenger
pattern, top marked "The Chal-

lenger," backstamped Union Pa-
cific RR 35.00
Union Pacific, 15", Harriman,
blue, back stamped 125.00
Sauce Dish, NYNH & H, Indian Tree
pattern, Buffalo China, backstamp 30.00
Sherbet, PRR, Keystone, Buffalo
China 50.00
Soup Plate
B & O, Capitol, Shenango China . 75.00
New York Central, marked "Syra-
cuse China" 24.00
PRR, Purple Laurel, 6½" d, broad
lip, Sterling China 24.00
Union Pacific, 9", rimmed, Harri-
man Blue pattern, backstamped
UP Overland Route logo 40.00

Hat, Conductor, LIRR, $25.00.

Clothing and Accessories
Coat Sleeve Patch, Santa Fe, ⁵⁄₁₆ x ⅞",
silver bar 15.00
Hat, agent
Boston & Maine, gold finish,
curved top 38.00
Burlington Route 95.00
Lapel Button
Chicago North Western—Safety
First, enameled brass 12.00
Lake Shore & Michigan Southern,
mail sack shape 42.00
Tie Pin, Brotherhood Railroad Train-
men, 25 Years, 10 kt gold 12.00
Flashlight, PRR, 7½", domed glass 50.00
Forms, Documents, and Reports
Car Liquor License, NY State Rail-
road, 8 x 11", early 1960s 9.50
Car Inspector's Record, D & RGW,
Ridgway, filled in, 1928 .... 2.00
Conductor's Report, Wiscasset,
Waterville & Farmington Railway,
CO, filled in, 1920s 3.50
Engineer's Time Report Pad, 1918 .. 14.00
Freight Receipt, Utica & Black River
RR, 1873 .... 3.50

Payroll, Hartford & New Haven Railroad, 1860s **4.00**
Rules Book, C & NW, 1929, illus .. **7.00**
Seniority List, "Railroad Employees," 1923, 104 pgs, local adv **11.00**
Voucher, Union Pacific, Denver & Gulf Railway, 1890s **3.00**
Waybill
  Boston & Worcester and Western Railroads, 4½ x 15", small woodcut of old locomotive pulling two cars, filled in, 1848 .... **3.75**
  Kennebec Central, large size, filled in **4.75**
Hardware
  Baggage Check, brass, Texas Central RR, local, 1⅝ x 2", strap, Poole Bros, Chicago **35.00**
  Box Car Seal, Wiscasset, Waterville & Farmington RR, bears identification WW & F RY Co, plus serial number **5.00**
  Ticket Dater Dies
    NYC RR, White Plains, NY, fits Centennial No. 6 machine **30.00**
    NYHH & HRR Bridgeport, fits Aurora machine **35.00**
    Union Station 125th Street, fits Centennial No. 6 machine **25.00**
Lantern
  AT & SF RY, Handlan, 1928-P, red globe **80.00**
  B & LRR, brass top, bell bottom **500.00**
  B & MRR, brass top, bell bottom, red cast barrel globe **350.00**
  C & NW, red emb globe **165.00**
  Chesapeake & Ohio **55.00**
  CRR of NJ, bell bottom, star headlight **150.00**
  D & H RR, Adlake Kero, red Fresnal globe **28.00**
  DW & P, blue emb globe **500.00**
  LV RR, caboose, Lehigh Valley RR, orig chimney **100.00**
  NYC, Dietz #6, bell bottom, clear cast 6" globe **50.00**
  PRR, Keystone Casey, 1903, clear cast 5⅜" globe, cleaned to metal, keystone logo **35.00**
  Rock Island Lines, Dietz heavy iron body casting, inspector type **120.00**
  Southern, Armspear Manufacturing, clear cast 5⅜" globe **75.00**
  SP Co, Adlake Kero, red etched 3¼" globe **40.00**
  Union Pacific, Adams & Westlake, Adlake Reliable, 1913-P, clear 5⅜" globe **42.00**
  WTCO Casey, clear cast globe **150.00**
Lantern Globe, Norfolk & Western, red, tall **27.50**
Linens
  Blanket, Soo Line, wool, gray and tan squares, canted style logo in center **100.00**

Dish Towel, 18 x 16", cotton, tan, triple blue Burlington Route logos and safety slogans **7.50**
Hand Towel, 16" sq, white AT & SF RY, 1948, interwoven name on red stripe **7.00**
  UPRR, interwoven on white stripe **7.00**
Headrest Cover
  CB & Q, 15 x 18", Denver Zepher, tan ground, dome car, brown mountains **8.50**
  Seaboard Coast, 17 x 16", gold ground, interwoven green "Seaboard Coast Line Railroad" with train and palm trees **6.00**
  PRR, 15 x 18", tan ground, brown logo, electric train **10.00**
Napkin
  Burlington Route, 20" sq, linen, white, woven logo **7.00**
  C & O, linen, blue monogram ... **6.50**
  Illinois Central, 19" sq, linen, white, woven center logo **12.50**
  Rio Grande, linen, white, woven markings **10.00**
Pillowcase
  20" sq, white, ink stamped "Burlington Northern, Pillow Rental 50¢ to Destination" **6.50**
  30 x 14", white, ink stamped "Property of Pullman Co" logo . **6.50**
Tablecloth
  California Zephyr, 36 x 42", white, interwoven oval logo **15.00**
  Denver & Rio Grande, 36 x 42", white, linen, woven "Rio Grande" double markings **15.00**
  Frisco Railway, 36 x 36", white, Frisco emblem **28.00**
  Illinois Central, dining car, large woven center logo
    36 x 42", peach **20.00**
    50 x 60", gold **30.00**
  Waiter's Towel, 26 x 16", white, blue stripes, ink stamped Santa Fe logos **6.50**
Magazine, Railway Age, 1906, 64 pgs, 9 x 12" **7.50**
Matches, Union Pacific RR, carton ... **27.50**
Menu
  Amtrak, Good Morning, single card, 7 x 11" **1.50**
  Chicago & North Western Railway, 1958, luncheon, Mt Rushmore on cov, issued for "Sam Campbell Alaska Tour" **4.50**
  Lehigh Valley, Black Diamond Express, dinner, 1927, chef and train on cov **35.00**
  NYC, Thrift Grill, folder, 1955 ..... **3.50**
  Santa Fe, Super Chief, luncheon menu, folder, 1971 .... **4.00**

Union Pacific, City of Los Angeles,
domeliner, breakfast, 1971 ...... **2.50**
Milk Bottle, half pint, Missouri Pacific **15.00**
Nail File, Cotton Belt RR **7.50**
Paperweight
General American Car Co, "Modern
Milk Transportation, Refrigerated
Glass Lined Tank Car," 6 x 2 x 2½" **100.00**
Wells Fargo, 1852 .... **25.00**
Passes
Baltimore and Ohio, 1930s **3.00**
Boston and Maine, 1950s **2.00**
Cheasapeake and Ohio, 1920s **3.75**
Fort Smith & Western, 1920s **3.75**
Northern Pacific, 1940s **2.25**
Pennsylvania, 1940s **1.75**
Susquehanna & New York, 1918 ... **6.00**
Union Pacific, 1920s **3.50**
Wisconsin Central, 1910 .... **6.00**
Photograph, 23 "Railroad Maintenance
Employees," holding tools, 9 x 7" .. **25.00**
Playing Cards
Chesapeake & Ohio, Chessie and
Peake, orig box **15.00**
N & W, gold circular logo, double
deck, orig box **30.00**
Northern Pacific, logo on top,
multicolored **20.00**
Posters and Signs
Boston & Albany RR, Boston and
Worcester Division, broadside, sta-
tion time table, c1870, 16 x 28" . **20.00**
Chicago Aurora & Elgin RR, "Bad Or-
der" placard, 3½ x 8", printed on
stiff card **2.00**
New York Central, poster/handbill,
"State Fair, Syracuse, Sept 7 to Sept
12, 1931," includes fare chart from
numerous stations on upstate
branch lines, old NYC oval herald
with speeding locomotive **8.50**
Northern Pacific RR, int. of dining
car, 1889 .... **275.00**
Old Colony Line to Cottage City, Oak
Bluffs, Martha's Vineyard & Nan-
tucket, wall poster, map of line and
connections, c1880, 18 x 28" **35.00**
Western Union Telegrams, depot ext.,
hanging, two sided, white letters,
dark blue ground, porcelainized
steel, 10 x 17" **65.00**
Silver Flatware and Hollowware
ACL, bouillon spoon, Zephyr, marked
"ACL," and "Int'l" **20.00**
GM & O, dinner fork, Broadway pat-
tern, International **15.00**
Lackawanna, sugar, cov, back marked
"Lackawanna, International" **125.00**
New Haven RR
Creamer, individual size, 2 oz,
marked "Reed & Barton" **24.00**
Tray, 8", oval, deep, backstamped

"New Haven RR, International,
1936" **25.00**
New York Central
Cocktail Fork, marked "Interna-
tional Silver" **15.00**
Demitasse Spoon, marked "Inter-
national Silver" **10.00**
Ladle, small, marked "International
Silver" **15.00**
Illinois Central
Dessert Spoon **12.50**
Domed Serving Cov, 6", marked
"I.C.R.R." **30.00**
Knife **12.50**
Pencil Holder **30.00**
PRR, dinner knife, Broadway pattern,
marked "PPR" **8.50**
Santa Fe, dinner knife, Albany pattern **8.00**
Southern Pacific, soup spoon **18.00**
Switch Keys, see KEYS
Switch Lock
Adlake, Penn Central, brass **20.00**
CCC & St. Louis, steel **12.50**
Time Table
Erie, June, 1906 .... **15.00**
Lackawanna, Sept, 1952, Phoebe
Snow streamliner on front **7.50**
Niagara Falls Short Line, 1894 ..... **38.00**
Norfolk & Western, employee, 1960s **4.00**
Northern Pacific RR, 1927 .... **10.00**
Salt Lake Route, June, 1903, for trains
to fishing grounds **15.00**
Southern Pacific, July, 1915, 15 pgs **15.00**
Union Pacific, 1945 .... **10.00**

RAZORS

Collecting Hints: A major revolution has occurred in razor collecting in the 1980s. At the
beginning of the decade almost all collectors focused on the straight razor. By the late 1980s
the collecting of safety razors and their related
material as well as electric shavers has achieved
a popularity that should equal or exceed that of
the straight razor collectors by the 1990s.

Many straight razor collectors focus on the
products of a single manufacturer. Value is increased by certain names, e.g., H. Boker, Case,
M. Price, Joseph Rogers, Simmons Hardware,
Will & Finck, Winchester, and George Wosten-
holm. The ornateness of the handle and blade
pattern also influences value. The fancier the
handle or more intricately etched the blade, the
higher the price. Rarest handle materials are
pearl, stag, Sterling silver, pressed horn, and
carved ivory. Rarest blades are those with scenes
etched across the entire front.

Initially safety razor collectors are focusing on
those razors that were packaged in elaborately
lithographed tins during the 1890 to 1915 period.

Since a safety razor involves several items, i.e., razor, blades, case or tin, instructions, etc., completeness is a critical factor. Support items such as blade banks, boxes, and sharpeners also attract collectors. Many safety razors from the early period already exceed $50. As a result, new collectors are seeking safety razors from the 1920s through the 1950s because a comprehensive collection can still be assembled at a modest price.

When buying an electric shaver, make certain that it is complete and in working order. Many were sold originally with cleaning kits, most of which have been lost.

History: Razors date back several thousand years. Early man used sharpened stones. The Egyptians, Greeks, and Romans had metal razors.

Straight razors made prior to 1800 generally were crudely stamped WARRENTED or CAST STEEL with the maker's mark on the tang. Until 1870 almost all razors for the American market were manufactured in Sheffield, England. Most blades were wedge shaped; many were etched with slogans or scenes. Handles were made of natural materials—various horns, tortoise shell, bone, ivory, stag, silver and pearl. All razors were handmade.

After 1870 most straight razors were machine made with hollow ground blades and synthetic handle materials. Razors of this period usually were manufactured in Germany (Solingen) or in American cutlery factories. Hundreds of molded celluloid handle patterns were produced, such as nude women, eagles, deer, boats, windmill scenes, etc.

By 1900 the safety razor was challenging the straight razor for popularity among the shaving community. A wealth of safety razor patents were issued in the first decade of the 20th century. World War I insured the dominance of the safety razor as American troops abroad made it their preferred shaving method.

By the 1930s the first electric shavers appeared. However, electric shavers did not achieve universal acceptance until the 1950s.

References: Robert A. Doyle, *Straight Razor Collecting,* Collector Books, 1980, out-of-print; Phillip L. Krumholz, *Value Guide For Barberiana & Shaving Collectibles,* Ad Libs Publishing Co., 1988.

Collectors' Club: Safety Razor Collectors' Guild, P. O. Box 885, Crescent City, CA 95531.

Blade Bank
  2", Gem Blades, tin, book shape, gold, red, and black **7.50**
  2 x 1½ x 1", Ever-Ready, tin, treasure chest shape, orange, black, and gold **20.00**

6" h, porcelain, barber pole shape, red and white stripes, black letters **24.00**
Corn Razor
  Bandwagon, Japanese, orig cardboard box **28.00**
  Griffon, marked "Griffon Angle" ... **32.00**
  Henckels, J A, "Twin Works," Germany, rounded and shaped bone handle, plain blade, orig box, silver emb adv **48.00**
  Reliance Cutlery Co, two colored celluloid handle **75.00**
  Rogers & Sons, marked "Corn Razor," on light colored handle **20.00**
Electric Shaver, Schick, black bakelite, stamped "Model S," orig case and cord **12.00**
Razor Hone, Keen Kutter Kombination, fancy emb adv tin, yellow, green, white, and black **40.00**
Razor Strop, leather strap mounted on turned wooden spools, inscribed "Ono L Larpy," 23½" l, 19th C **110.00**

Safety, Gillette, Good Will, orig box, $15.00.

Safety Razor
  American Can Co, "The New Griffon," two part handle, interchangeable heads, tin container, patent 1901 .... **225.00**
  Bunji, Japanese, four blades **20.00**
  "Curvfit," lady's, orig instructions, orig blue and gold box **5.00**
  Devine, ivory handle, double edge, blade guard, leather cov wood case, includes "The Devine Caretaker Chicago, USA" adv sharpener **75.00**
  Ever-Ready, red and black box, cardboard blade holders **12.00**
  Gem Minute Man, metal, wall mount type, blade holder **25.00**
  Gillette, US Service Set, emb metal case, engraved "Stanley J Lane, Rochester, NY" in shield, fitted metal mirror **25.00**
  Henckels Rapide, black and gold, tin box **12.00**
  "Herbrand," Fremont, OH, orig cardboard box **10.00**
  Kampfe Bros, NY, "The Star," cylindrical tin container **275.00**
  "Kewtie Cosmetic Razor," lady's, celluloid handle and case, light blue **25.00**

"Laurel, Ladies Boudoir," orig purple tin, cardboard box, and instructions ... **25.00**

Mohican, instructions, orig "Mohican" stamped blade, orig tin **100.00**

Segal, gold plated, blades, instructions, orig box **20.00**

Shermach, lady's, underarm, MOP handle, orig pack of blades **35.00**

Stahly, wind-up type, vibrates as it shaves, orig plastic case **15.00**

"Valet," orig box, 1912 .... **20.00**

"Yankee," patent 1903, red and blue tin container, instructions on lid .. **185.00**

Straight Razor

Asco Cutlery Co, "Magnetized," imitation ivory handle, Art Nouveau floral design **32.00**

Boker, H & Co, etched "American Lines SS St. Louis" on blade, black handle **12.00**

Crown & Sword, etched "Crown & Sword Manufactory" scene blade, clear horn handle, German silver ends, dated "1873–1898" **25.00**

Garland Cutlery Co, etched "The Improved Eagle Razor" on blade, spread American eagle, black handle **15.00**

Holley Mfg Co, plain black celluloid handle **20.00**

Keen Kutter

Etched eagle on blade, emb horn handle **75.00**

"Junior," orig box **16.50**

Simmons Hardware Co, celluloid handle, twisted bamboo design, blade marked "Barber's Pet" **85.00**

Stewart & Co, tortoiseshell handle, inlaid German silver shield, semi-wedge shape blade, c1815 ...... **100.00**

Wade & Butcher, Sheffield, etched American eagle, "E. Pluribus Unum" banner, semi-wedge blade, bone handle **60.00**

Waterville Cutlery Co, CT, black celluloid handle, raised pattern of large oak leaf, scroll with acorns, blade etched "Waterville Hand Forged" **70.00**

REAMERS

Collecting Hints: Reamers seldom are found in mint condition. Cone and rim nicks are usually acceptable, but cracked pieces bring considerably less. Ceramic figurals and U. S. made glass are collected more than any other category.

Reamer collecting first became popular with the advent of the Depression Glass collector in the mid–1960s. Reamer collecting can be an endless hobby. It may be impossible to assembly one of every example made. One–of–a–kind samples do exist; they never were put into mass production.

History: Devices for getting the juice from citrus fruit have been around almost as long as the fruit itself. These devices range in materials from wood to glass and from nickel plated and Sterling silver to fine china.

Many different kinds of mechanical reamers were devised before the first glass one was pressed around 1885. Very few reamers have been designed since 1940 when frozen juice entered the market. Modern day ceramists are making clown and teapot shaped reamers.

References: Mary Walker, *Reamers—200 Years,* Muski Publishers, 1980, separate price guide; Mary Walker, *The Second Book, More Reamers—200 Years,* Muski Publishers, 1983.

Collectors' Club: National Reamer Collectors Association, Rt. #1, Box 200, Grantsburg, WI 54840.

REPRODUCTION ALERT. Reproduced reamers include:

An old 5" Imperial Glass Co. reamer, originally made in clear glass, was reproduced for Edna Barnes in dark amethyst. 1,500 were made. The reproduction is marked "IG" and "81."

Mrs. Barnes has reproduced several old 4½" Jenkins Glass Co. reamers in limited editions. The reproductions are also made in a 2¼" size. All Jenkins copies are marked with a "B" in a circle.

Note: The first book on reamers, now out–of–print, was written by Ken and Linda Ricketts in 1974. Their numbering system was continued by Mary Walker in *Reamers—200 Years*. The Ricketts–Walker numbers will be found in ( ) in our listing.

China, clown, orange base, green and orange stripe, marked "Made in Japan," Walker No. C-28, $40.00.

CHINA AND CERAMIC

Austria, 3¼" h, 2 pcs, side handle,
flower dec, gold trimmed (E-38) **80.00**
Czechoslovakia, 6" h, 2 pcs, orange
shape, white, green leaves, marked
"Erphila" (L-37) **35.00**
England
3½" h, 2 pcs, Shelley china, spatterware type dec (E-109) **85.00**
3¾" h, 2 pcs, orange shape, orange
body, green leaves (L-20) **24.00**
Germany
3¼"
Blue and white Delft type dec,(E-
66) **42.00**
White ground, yellow fruit, tan and
green trim, (E-54) **65.00**
3½" h
Scrolling flow blue dec, white
ground(E-60) **55.00**
White ground, blue, orange, lavender, and maroon flowers,
green leaves, black trim, (E-72)   **55.00**
5" d, Goebel, yellow, (E-108) **50.00**
Japanese
2¾" h, luster, duck, green head, yellow and white, orange bill, (F-12)   **45.00**
3" h, saucer type on pedestal, loop
handle, fruit dec (D-59) **40.00**
3½" h, white ground, rust leaves,
navy blue trim, (D-55) **42.00**
3¾" h, 2 pcs, strawberry shape, red,
green leaves and handle, marked
"Occupied Japan" **65.00**
4½" h, figural, clown, short, pastel
yellow, pink, green, or blue, Rising
Sun mark (C-43, C-44, C-45, C-46)   **35.00**
4¾"
Figural, seated Mexican, yellow
hat, green shirt, red pants, brown
shoes, (F-36) **85.00**
Lemon, yellow ground, white flow-
ers, green leaves, (L-40) **40.00**
5", orange, textured orange peel ext.,
yellow body, green leaves, white
int., (L-39) **48.00**
7¾" h, two piece, tan and yellow,
figural center band, (P-73) **50.00**
8½", pitcher and tumbler, blue and
white windmill dec (P-87) **48.00**
United States
Hall China, large flat, 1 pc, Chinese
red, ivory int., marked "Hall" (A-
14) **350.00**
Jiffy Juicer, 1 pc, large bowl with cone
center, elongated loop handle, ten
colors known, Pat 1938 (A-5) **60.00**
Zippy, 3¼" h, 6½" d, hand crank
cone, Wolverine Products, Detroit,
MI, several colors (A-4) **60.00**

GLASS (Measurements indicate width, not including spout and handle)

Fry Glassware, opal, fluted sides, one
pc, c1920 ....   **38.00**
Hazel Atlas, pink
Crisscross, orange size, pink, two pcs **165.00**
Tab handle, green, one pc **36.00**
Jeannette Glass Co
Crystal, Jennyware **65.00**
Delphite, Jennyware **75.00**
Light Jadite, two cup, two piece **35.00**
McKee, Sunkist
Chataline blue, name in block letters **155.00**
Light jadite, name in block letters ..   **25.00**
Tufglas, green, tab handle **75.00**

METAL (all marked with name)

Arcade #2, cast iron **65.00**
Dunlap's Improved, iron hinged, 9½" l,
(M-17) **32.00**
Ebaloy, 8¾" l, scissor type, handles
marked "Ebaloy Juicer Pat Pend" (M-
76) **12.00**
Hong Kong, 2½" h, 2 pcs, stainless
steel, flat (M-205) **8.50**
Knapp's Grapefruit Juicer, 3" h, 6½" d,
2 pcs, aluminum, hinged together at
extended handle, heavy aluminum
wire cone, wood knob crank turns
cone cov (M-86A) **18.00**
Nasco-Royal, 6" l, scissor type (M-265)   **7.50**
Sunkist Electric Juicet, 8¾" h, magic
strainer (M-192) **25.00**
Wagner Ware, 6" d, cast aluminum,
skillet shape, long rect seed dams
beneath cone, hole in handle, two
spouts (M-96) **18.00**
Williams, 9¾" l, iron, hinged, glass
insert (M-60) **32.00**

RECORDS

Collecting Hints: Collectors tend to focus on one
particular area of the music field, e.g., jazz, the
big bands, or rock 'n' roll, or on one artist. Purchase records with original dust jackets and covers whenever possible.

Also check the records carefully for scratches.
If the record cannot be played, it is worthless.

Proper storage of records is critical to maintaining their value. Keep stacks small. It is best
to store them vertically. Place acid free paper
between the albums to prevent bleeding of ink
from one cover to the next.

History: The first records were cylinders produced by Thomas Edison in 1877 and played on
a phonograph of his design. Edison received a
patent in 1878, but soon dropped the project in
order to perfect the light bulb.

Alexander Graham Bell, Edison's friend, was excited about the phonograph and developed the graphaphone which was marketed successfully by 1889. Early phonographs and graphaphones had hand cranks which wound the mechanism which keep the cylinders moving.

About 1900 Emile Berliner developed a phonograph which used a flat disc, similar to today's records. The United States Gramophone Company marketed his design in 1901. The company eventually became RCA Victor. By 1910 discs were more popular than cylinders.

The record industry continued to develop as progress was made in the preservation of sound and the increased quality of sound. The initial size of 78 rpm records was replaced by 45 rpm, then 33⅓ rpm, and finally, compact discs.

References: L. R. Docks, *1915–1965 American Premium Record Guide, Third Edition,* Books Americana, 1986; Jerry Osborne, *The Official Price Guide To Records, Eighth Edition,* House of Collectibles, 1988; Peter A. Soderbergh, *Dr. Records Original 78 RPM Price Guide,* Wallace-Homestead, 1987.

Periodicals: *Discoveries,* P. O. Box 255, Port Townsend, WA 98368; *Goldmine,* 700 E. State Street, Iola, WI 54990.

Note: Prices are for first pressings in original dust jackets or albums.

Additional Listings: Elvis Presley and Rock 'N' Roll.

Hopalong Cassidy, Square Dance Hold-Up, 78 RPM, Capitol, 1950, two record set, story, illus text, $25.00.

Big Bands
    Count Basie
        Basie Boogie, Okeh, 6330, 1941 . **4.00**
        Honeysuckle Rose, Decca, 1141, 1937 .... **7.00**
        Panassie Stomp, Decca, 2224, 1938 .... **5.00**
    Bix Beiderbecke
        Ol' Man River, Okeh, 41088, 1928 **25.00**

Royal Garden Blues, Okeh, 8544, 1927 .... **20.00**
Eubie Blake
    Cutie, Emerson, 10519, 1922 .... **8.00**
    Sweet Georgia Brown, Crown, 3197, 1931 .... **10.00**
Les Brown
    Boogie Woogie, Bluebird, 7858, 1938 .... **5.00**
    Sunday, Columbia, 36724, 1942 . **3.00**
Casa Loma Orchestra
    Smoke Rings, Decca, 1473, 1937 **5.00**
    White Jazz, Brunswick, 6092, 1931 **8.00**
Dorsey Brothers
    Have A Little Faith In Me, Banner, 0571, 1930 .... **10.00**
    The Spell of the Blues, Okeh, 41181, 1929 .... **25.00**
Benny Goodman
    Shirt Tail Stomp, Brunswick, 3975, 1928 .... **10.00**
    Wolverine Blues, Vocalion, 15656, 1928 .... **40.00**
Woody Herman
    Amen, Decca, 18346, 1942 ..... **3.00**
    Blue Downstairs/Upstairs, Decca, 2508, 1939 .... **3.00**
    Wintertime Dreams, Decca, 1056, 1936 .... **10.00**
Harry James
    Melancholy Mood, Brunswick, 8443, 1939 .... **20.00**
    Two O'Clock Jump, Brunswick, 8337, 1939 .... **7.00**
Glenn Miller
    A Blues Serenade, Columbia, 3051D, 1935 .... **30.00**
    I Got Rhythm, Brunswick, 7915, 1937 .... **8.00**
Country/Western
    Aiken Country String Band, Carolina Stompdown, Okeh, 45143 ...... **8.00**
    Allen Brothers
        Daddy Park Your Car, Vocalion, 02853 .... **15.00**
        Glorious Night Blues, Victor, 23707 .... **50.00**
        Roll Down The Line, Victor, 23551 **30.00**
    Blue Ridge Mountain Girls, She Came Rolling Down The Mountain, Champion, 16743 .... **10.00**
    Fiddlin' John Carson & His Virginia Reelers
        Arkansas Traveler, Okeh, 40108 . **10.00**
        On The Banks Of Old Tennessee, Okeh, 45488 .... **20.00**
        Times Are Not Like They Used to Be, Okeh, 45402 .... **25.00**
    Carter Family
        I'll Be Home Some Day, Bluebird, 5911 .... **5.00**
        On The Rock, Victor, 25313 ..... **25.00**

The Storms Are On The Ocean, Vo-
calion, 03160 .... **15.00**
Delmore Brothers
I'm Mississippi Bound, Bluebird,
5653 .... **10.00**
The Frozen Girl, Bluebird, 5338 . **15.00**
Georgia Yellow Hammers
Pass Around The Bottle, Victor,
20550 .... **8.00**
Peaches Down In Georgia, Victor,
23683 .... **20.00**
Hackberry Ramblers
Cajun Crawl, Bluebird, 2013 .... **12.00**
Rambling, Bluebird, 2010 .... **8.00**
Buell Kazee
East Virginia, Brunswick, 154 .... **8.00**
The Cowboy Trail, Brunswick, 481 **10.00**
Uncle Dave Macon
Carve That Possum, Vocalion,
5151 .... **30.00**
Old Dan Tucker, Vocalion, 15033 **15.00**
Thank God For Everything, Decca,
5373 .... **10.00**

Monroe Brothers
My Last Moving Day, Bluebird,
7273 .... **8.00**
Where Is My Sailor Boy?, Bluebird,
6762 .... **15.00**
George Reneau
On Top Of Old Smoky, Vocalion,
15366 .... **20.00**
Wild Bill Jones, Vocalion, 5058 .. **10.00**
Welling & McGhee
Picture From Life's Other Side,
Gennett, 7096 .... **25.00**
Ring The Bells Of Heaven, Cham-
pion, 16660 .... **15.00**
Bob Wills & His Texas Playboys
I Ain't Got Nobody, Vocalion,
03206 .... **10.00**
Mexicali Rose, Vocalion, 03086 .. **12.00**
Jazz
Louis Armstrong
Basin Street Blues, Okeh, 8690,
1928 .... **25.00**
I'm A Ding Dong Daddy, Okeh,
41442, 1930 .... **15.00**
Jazz Lips, Okeh, 8346, 1926 .... **35.00**
Cab Calloway
Jitterbug, Victor, 24592, 1934 ... **8.00**
St. Louis Blues, Brunswick, 4936,
1930 .... **5.00**
The Levee Low Down, Banner,
32221, 1931 .... **7.00**
Nat "King" Cole
Early Morning Blues, Decca, 8541,
1941 .... **4.00**
Scotchin' with the Soda, Decca,
8556, 1941 .... **4.00**
Duke Ellington
Jubilee Stomp, Okeh, 41013, 1938 **15.00**

New Orleans Low-Down, Voca-
lion, 1086, 1927 .... **75.00**
Bobby Hackett
Ain't Misbehavin', Vocalion, 4877,
1939 .... **5.00**
At The Jazz Band Ball, Vocalion,
4047, 1938 .... **5.00**
King Oliver
Black Snake Blues, Vocalion, 1112,
1927 .... **35.00**
Doctor Jazz, Vocalion, 1113, 1927 **100.00**
Jazzin' Babies' Blues, Okeh, 4975,
1923 .... **75.00**
Muggsy Spanier
Big Butter and Egg Man, Bluebird,
10417, 1939 .... **4.00**
Riverboat Shuffle, Bluebird, 10532,
1939 .... **4.00**
Thomas "Fats" Waller
Soothin' Syrup Stomp, Victor,
20470, 1927 .... **25.00**
The Minor Drag, Victor, 38050,
1929 .... **15.00**
Movie and TV Soundtracks
The Addams Family, RCA Victor,
1964 .... **25.00**
Bye Bye Birdie, Columbia, orig cast,
1960 .... **15.00**
Damn Yankees, RCA Victor, orig cast,
green cov, 1955 .... **30.00**
For Whom The Bell Tolls, Decca,
1950 .... **40.00**
King Kong, United Artists, 1976 .... **8.00**
Madame X, Decca, 1966 .... **15.00**
New York, New York, United Artists,
1977, ... **5.00**
Oklahoma, Decca, orig cast, 1953 . **40.00**
The Robe, Decca, 1953 .... **20.00**
Sayonara, RCA Victor, 1957 .... **50.00**
To Kill A Mockingbird, Ava, 1963 .. **15.00**
Wagon Train, Mercury, 1959 ...... **25.00**
Rock 'N' Roll
Boyd Bennett, Rockin' Up A Storm,
King, 4985 .... **10.00**
Chuck Berry
Let It Rock, Chess, 1747 .... **15.00**
Reeling And Rocking, Chess, 1683 **12.00**
The Coasters
Keep Rockin' With The Coasters,
Atco, 4502 .... **12.00**
One By One, Atco, 123 .... **25.00**
Fats Domino, Rolling and Rocking,
Imperial, 5180 .... **30.00**
The Everly Brothers, Bye Bye Love,
Cadence, 1315 .... **15.00**
Bill Haley, Shake, Rattle And Roll,
Decca, 5260 .... **35.00**
Jerry Lee Lewis
Great Balls Of Fire, Sun, 281 .... **15.00**
Whole Lot Of Shakin' Going On,
Sun, 267 .... **5.00**

Roy Orbison
  Lonely and Blue, Monument,
    4002, 14002 .... **25.00**
  Ooby Dooby, Sun, 242 .... **8.00**
  The Palisades, Chapel Bells, Debra,
    1003 .... **8.00**
  Surfaris, Wipe-Out, DFS, 11/12 .... **15.00**
  Teardrops, The Stars Are Out Tonight,
    Josie, 766 .... **30.00**
  Joe Turner, Boss of the Blues, Atlantic,
    1234 .... **25.00**

RED WING POTTERY

Collecting Hints: Red Wing Pottery can be found with various marks and paper labels. Some of the marks include a red wing which is stamped on, a raised "Red Wing U.S.A. #___", and an impressed "Red Wing U.S.A. #___". Paper labels were used as early as 1930. Pieces with paper labels easily lost their only mark.

Many manufacturers used the same mold patterns. Study the references to become familiar with the Red Wing forms.

History: The category of Red Wing Pottery covers several potteries which started in Red Wing, Minnesota. The first pottery, named Red Wing Stoneware Company, was started in 1868 by David Hallem. The primary product of this company was stoneware. The mark used by this company was a red wing stamped under the glaze. The Minnesota Stoneware Company was started in 1883. The North Star Stoneware Company opened a factory in the same area in 1892 and went out of business in 1896. The mark used by this company included a raised star and the words Red Wing.

The Red Wing Stoneware Company and the Minnesota Stoneware Company merged in 1892. The new company was called the Red Wing Union Stoneware Company. The new company made stoneware until 1920 when it introduced a line of pottery.

In 1936 the name of the company was changed to Red Wing Potteries Incorporated. They continued to make pottery until the 1940s. During the 1930s they introduced several lines of dinnerware. These patterns were all hand painted, very popular, and sold through department stores, Sears, and gift stamp centers. The production of dinnerware declined in the 1950s. The company began producing hotel and restaurant china in the early 1960s. The plant was closed in 1967.

References: Dan and Gail DePasquale and Larry Peterson, *Red Wing Collectibles,* Collector Books, 1985; Gary and Bonnie Tefft, *Red Wing Potters and Their Wares,* Second Edition Locust Enterprises, 1987; Lyndon C. Viel, *The Clay Giants: The Stoneware of Red Wing, Goodhue*

County, Minnesota, Book 2 (1980), *Book 3* (1987), Wallace-Homestead.

Collectors' Club: Red Wing Collectors Society, Route 3, Box 146, Monticello, MN 55362.

Compote, mauve, shaped base and standard, scalloped rim, marked "M-5008," 8⅛" d, 6¼" h, $18.00.

Ashtray, wing shape, red **25.00**
Basket, white, semi gloss **20.00**
Bean Pot, adv **85.00**
Bookends, pr, fan and scroll, green ... **15.00**
Bowl
  8", gray stoneware, blue dec, Greek
    Key border, marked "Luhman &
    Sanders, Potsville, Iowa" **65.00**
  #4, Spatterware **250.00**
Candy Dish, three part, hexagon, gray,
  semi gloss **8.50**
Cookie Jar
  Chef **55.00**
  Monk, yellow and brown **40.00**
  Rooster, green, semi gloss **28.00**
Cornucopia, burgundy, high gloss, leaf
  dec **12.00**
Crock, two gallons, birch leaf dec **40.00**
Dinnerware
  Butter Dish, cov, Bob White **25.00**
  Casserole, cov, Tampico **18.00**
  Celery Tray, Random Harvest **10.00**
  Cereal Bowl
    Damask **4.75**
    Pompeii, 6" **7.00**
    Town and Country, blue **7.50**
  Chop Plate, 12", Capistrano **15.00**
  Creamer
    Bob White **17.50**
    Iris **7.50**
  Cruet, Town and Country, chartreuse **20.00**
  Cup and Saucer
    Bob White **14.00**
    Capistrano **12.00**
    Tampico **7.00**
  Custard Cup, Fondoso, green and
    pink **15.00**

Fruit Bowl, 6"
  Capistrano **6.00**
  Lute Song **7.50**
Gravy Boat, Driftwood, blue **15.00**
Nappy, Lotus **5.00**
Plate
  6½", bread and butter
    Bob White **5.00**
    Pepe **3.00**
    Pompeii **3.00**
    Random Harvest **3.50**
  10", dinner
    Bob White **7.00**
    Lotus **5.00**
    Town and Country, blue **8.00**
  10½", dinner, Lexington Rose, **6.50**
Platter
  13", Lute Song **20.00**
  13½", Town and Country, char-
    treuse **12.50**
  15", Capistrano **15.00**
Relish, 7 x 5", Town and Country,
  blue **7.50**
Salt and Pepper Shakers, pr
  Bob White **25.00**
  Shmoo Town Country, brown **12.00**
Sauce Dish
  Lute Song **2.00**
  Town and Country, blue **7.50**
  Northern Lights **2.50**
Set, Capistrano, service for six **65.00**
Soup, cov, Lotus **7.50**
Vegetable Bowl
  Lute Song, divided **20.00**
  Town and Country, chartreuse ... **8.00**
Flower Block, Dolphin **25.00**
Jar, Kansas Druggist adv **100.00**
Jug, miniature, "Who Will Win" **135.00**
Planter
  Canoe, matte ivory, brown int. **25.00**
  Guitar, black, semi gloss **12.00**
  Puppy, aqua, semi gloss **12.00**
Refrigerator Jar, stoneware **100.00**
Teapot, yellow rooster, gold trim **65.00**
Trivet, Minnesota Centennial **60.00**
Vase
  6", fan, paneled, scroll handles, light
    green **15.00**
  8", bud, floral dec, ivory, matte **18.00**
Wall Pocket
  Bird on grapevine, gray-green **18.00**
  Gardenia, ivory, matte **20.00**

ROBOTS

Collecting Hints: The name for robots comes from markings on the robot or box and from the trade. Hence, some robots have more than one name. Do research to know exactly what robot you have. A leading auctioneer of robots is Lloyd Ralston Toys, Fairfield, Connecticut.

Condition is critical. Damaged lithographed tin is almost impossible to repair and repaint. Toys in mint condition in the original box are the most desirable. The price difference between a mint robot and one in very good condition may be as high as 200%.

Working condition is important, but not critical. Many robots never worked well, and larger robots stripped their gearing quickly. The rarer the robot, the less important is the question of working condition.

Finally, if you play with your robot, do not leave the batteries in the toy. If they leak or rust, the damage may destroy the value of the toy.

History: Atomic Robot Man, made in Japan between 1948 and 1949, is the grandfather of all robot toys. He is an all metal wind-up toy, less than 5" high and rather crudely made. Japanese robots of the early 1950s tended to be the friction or wind-up variety, patterned in brightly lithographed tin and made from recycled materials.

By the late 1950s robots had entered the battery-powered age. Limited quantities of early models were produced; parts from one model were used in later models with slight or no variations. The robot craze was enhanced by Hollywood's production of movies such as Destination Moon (1950) and Forbidden Planet (1956). Roby the Robot came from this latter movie.

Many Japanese manufacturers were small and lasted only a few years. Leading firms include Horikawa Toys, Nomura Toys, and Yonezawa Toys. Cragstan was an American importer who sold Japanese-made toys under its own label. Marx and Ideal entered the picture in the 1970s. Modern robots are being imported from China and Taiwan.

The TV program Lost in Space (1965–68) inspired copies of its robot character. However, the quality of the late 1960s toys began to suffer as more and more plastic was added; robots were redesigned to reduce sharp edges as required by the United States government.

Modern robots include R2D2 and C3PO from the Star Wars epics, Twiki from NBC's Buck Rogers, and V.I.N.CENT from Disney's "The Black Hole." Robots are firmly established in American science fiction and among collectors.

References: Robert Maline, *The Robot Book,* Push Pin Press/Harcourt Brace, 1978; Crystal and Leland Payton, *Space Toys,* Collectors Compass, 1982; Stephen J. Sansweet, *Science Fiction Toys and Models,* Vol. 1, Starlog Press, 1980.

Note: The following abbreviations are used:
  SH = Horikawa Toys
  TM = K. K. Masutoku Toy Factory
  TN = Nomura Toys
  Y = Yonezawa Toys

Tractor, Marvelous Mike, litho tin and plastic robot, rubber tractor treads, yellow body, battery operated, marked "Saunders, Aurora, IL," 1954, $225.00.

Attacking Martian, litho tin, battery operated, walks, stops, doors in chest open, firing guns emerge, flashing light and noise, marked "SH, Japan," MIB 300.00

Cragston
   10½", tin, clear plastic dome head, battery operated, walks, raises gun with flashing light and noise, antennae missing 425.00
   11", Mr Robot, tin, battery operated, bump and go action, revolving lights inside clear plastic dome ... 400.00
   11½", skirt type, tin, plastic head, battery operated, bump and go action, revolving, colored lights in dome, MIB 3,200.00

Fighting Spaceman, 11", litho tin, battery operated, walks, swings arms, blinking light in helmet, marked "SH, Japan" 300.00

Flashy Jim, 7", tin, remote control, walks, lighted eyes, marked "Ace," MIB 1,600.00

High Wheel, 10", litho tin windup, revolving plastic gears in chest, walks and sparks, marked "KO, Japan," MIB 135.00

Laughing Robot, 13", plastic, battery operated, swings arms, stretches neck, lights flash, mouth opens, laughs hysterically, marked "Waco" 250.00

Mechanic Robot 11½", tin and plastic, battery operated, bump and go action, walks and stops, gears turn, sparks, flashing lights, and noise, marked "Yonezawa, Japan" 65.00

Moon Astronaut Robot, 9", litho tin windup, walks, lifts up gun, noise, marked "Daiya, Japan," MIB 1,900.00

Moon Explorer, 7", litho tin, crank operated, walks, spinners rotate in plastic helmet, marked "KO, Japan," MIB 1,200.00

Mr Robot, Mechanical Brain Robot, 8", litho tin windup, walks, flashing light bulbs in each hand, marked "Alps," MIB 475.00

New Space Explorer, 11", litho tin, battery operated, walks, stops, doors in chest swing open, marked "SH, Japan" 100.00

Piston, 11", litho tin and plastic, battery operated, walks, pistons in chest move up and down, flashing light, noise, marked "SJM, Japan," orig box 60.00

Planet Robot, 9", litho tin windup, black, red feet and hands, walks and sparks, marked "KO, Japan," MIB .. 135.00

Radar Robot, 8", litho tin, remote control, walks, blinking light antennae, TN, MIB 3,250.00

Ratchet Robot, 8", litho tin windup, mechanic type, holds wrench on one hand, walks and sparks, TN 275.00

Robby The Robot, 8½", litho tin, remote control, walks, moving pistons in clear dome top, marked "Nomura, Japan," MIB 850.00

Swinging Baby, 6½", litho tin windup, rocks back and forth on swing, marked "Yonezawa, Japan" 200.00

Zoomer The Robot, 8", litho tin, battery operated, mechanic type, wrench in hand, walks, eyes light up, TN 475.00

ROCK 'N' ROLL

Collecting Hints: Many rock 'n' roll collections are centered around one artist. Flea markets and thrift shops are good places to look for rock 'n' roll items. Prices range according to the singer or group. The stars who have died usually command a higher price.

Glossy 8 x 10's of singers, unautographed, are generally worth $1.00.

History: Rock music can be traced back to early rhythm and blues music. It progressed and reached its golden age in the 1950s. The current nostalgia craze of the 1950s has produced some modern rock 'n' roll which is well received. Rock 'n' roll memorabilia exists in large quantities, each singer or group having many promotional pieces made.

References: L. R. Docks, *1915–1965 American Premium Record Guide, Third Edition*, Books Americana, 1986; Alison Fox, *Rock & Pop*, Boxtree Ltd. (London), 1988; Paul Grushkin, *The Art of Rock—Posters From Presley To Punk*, Abbeville Press, 1986.

Autograph, photograph
   Ray Charles, 8 x 10", black and white glossy 40.00

Fats Domino, 10 x 8", color, seated
at piano **30.00**
Cyndi Lauper, 11 x 14", black and
white glossy **85.00**
Eddie Van Halen, 8 x 10", color **50.00**
Belt Buckle, 3¾", oval, brass, Kiss in-
scription, red, amber, and silver, blue
background, 1977 copyright **15.00**
Book
I, James Dean, T. T. Thomas, Popular
Library, 1957, soft cover, 4 x 7",
128 pgs **20.00**
Rolling Stones Pixerama Foldbook, 12
glossy photos, 1964 .... **25.00**
Book Cover, Janis Joplin, 13 x 20", pa-
per, full color picture of Cheap Thrills
album, 1969 .... **10.00**
Cake Decorations, figures, drums, gui-
tars, and microphones **45.00**
Colorforms, Kiss, MIB **25.00**

**Monkees, bubble gum, box of 24 packets,
copyright 1967 Raybert Productions,
Inc., Screen Gems, Inc. trademark,
$100.00.**

Concert Program
Dave Clark Five Show, Arthur Kim-
brell Presents, 1964, English **45.00**
Manfred Man and Bill Haley and His
Comets, 1964, English **45.00**
Rolling Stones Show Concert, John
Smith Production, August 23–30,
1964 .... **100.00**
Costume, Kiss, Gene Simmons, molded
and diecut plastic mask, vinyl and
fabric costume, boxed, Collegeville
Costumes, 1978 copyright **25.00**
Figure, three from set of 5, Dave Clark
Five, 3" h, plastic, two with name tag,
mid 1960s **50.00**
Game
Kiss on Tour, MIB **55.00**
The Monkees, 17" sq board, four un-
punched figures, 7½" plastic guitar
with rubber band strings, unpunched spinner, boxed, Transogram, 1967 .... **75.00**
Guitar, Monkees, 20" h, plastic, full col-
or diecut paper label, Mattel, 1966
copyright **75.00**
Handkerchief, Paul Anka **12.00**

Hat, "Let's Twist," 8" d, 4" h, felt, red,
molded, upturned brim with scal-
loped white trim, diecut paper label,
coiled green pipe cleaner with at-
tached metal bell, "J Hats" label in-
side, c1960 .... **30.00**
Jewelry
Bracelet, Monkees, orig card **35.00**
Earrings, Ricky Nelson, clip on, black
and white photo, card marked
"Broadway   Creation/American
Styles Jewelry (sic)" **7.50**
Lobby Card, 11 x 14", Bill Haley and
His Comets, "Don't Knock The
Rock," Columbia, 1957 .... **25.00**
Lunch box, 7 x 8 x 4", Osmonds, litho
metal, thermos, unused, 1973 copy-
right **20.00**
Magazine
Life, July 14, 1972, Rolling Stones
cover article, 78 pgs **10.00**
16 Magazine, Vol. 8 #9, Feb. 1967,
features Monkees and various other
performers, 68 pgs **12.00**
Shindig, 1965, premiere issue, 1965 **15.00**
Mirror, printed black Kiss portraits design, silver background, wood frame,
late 1970s **30.00**
Pennant, Dick Clark, American Band-
stand, paper, 7½ x 12", adv **5.00**
Photograph, Ricky Nelson, photo and
autographs of family, matted, framed **150.00**
Pin, 1½", "Woodstock 69," enameled
brass, white dove on blue guitar central design, red background **30.00**
Pinback Button
Frankie Avalon-Venus, 3½", black
and white portrait, bright pink rim **20.00**
Dick Clark, 3", litho tin, black and
white photo, dark green ground .. **10.00**
Playing Cards, Monkees, 52 card deck,
black and white photos, boxed, Ed-
U-Cards, 1966 .... **25.00**
Poster, record album insert
Chicago, 22 x 33", sepia photos,
group name in shades of blue, Columbia Records, c1970 .... **12.00**
Simon & Garfunkel, 22 x 33", black
and white head photo, outline body
with full color bridge and sunset
scene, 1968 Columbia Records
copyright **15.00**
Pressbook, Don't Knock The Rock, 16
pgs, 12 x 16", red cov, 1956 .... **20.00**
Puppet, 5" h, Monkee, Mickey Dolenz,
plastic torso, movable arms, molded
vinyl head, brown curly hair, 1970
copyright **15.00**
Puzzle, jigsaw, Kiss, MIB **45.00**
Record
Paul Anka, "Diana," long play, ABC
Paramount **12.00**

Chuck Berry, "Johnny B. Goode," 78
rpm, Chess **10.00**
Chubby Checker, "The Class," 78
rpm, Parkway **45.00**
Duane Eddy, "Ring Of Fire" and
"Bobbie," 7 x 7" paper slip cover,
Jamie label, 1961 .... **12.00**
Herman's Hermits, "The End Of The
World" and "I'm Henry VIII, I Am,"
MGM label, 1965 .... **15.00**
Buddy Holly, "Words of Love," 45
rpm, Coral **18.00**
Jerry Lee Lewis, "Whole Lot of
Shakin' Going On" and "It'll Be
Me," 45 rpm, Sun label, 1956 ... **20.00**
Record Case, Dick Clark, 5 x 8 x 8",
cardboard, full color photo and sig-
nature, blue, white plastic handle,
brass closure, holds 45 rpm records **40.00**
Scrapbook, Bee Gees, 9 x 12", 34 pgs **15.00**
Sheet Music
Bob Dylan, 9 x 12", 4 pgs, "It Ain't
Me, Babe," black and white photo
front cover, 1964 copyright **15.00**
Everly Brothers, 9 x 12", 4 pgs, "So It
Always Will Be," pink tone photo
on front cover, 1963 copyright ... **10.00**
Roy Orbison, 9 x 12", 4 pgs, "Leah,"
black and white photo front cover,
Acuff-Rose Publications, Nashville,
1962 copyright **12.00**
Sunglasses, Monkees Shades **35.00**
Thermos
Bee Gees, plastic, yellow **15.00**
Monkees **55.00**
Tie Clip, Dick Clark American Band-
stand, 1¾" h, gold colored metal ... **10.00**
Viewmaster Reel, set of 3, Monkees,
Last Wheelbarrow to Pokeyville **10.00**
Watch Fob, The Band-Standers, jitter
bugging couple, music notes, marked
"Ajax Belt" **25.00**

NORMAN ROCKWELL

Collecting Hints: Learn all you can about Norman Rockwell if you plan to collect his many
artworks and illustrations. His original artworks and illustrations have been transferred onto various types of objects by clubs and manufacturers.

History: Norman Rockwell, the famous American artist, was born on February 3, 1894. His
first professional illustrations were for a children's
book, *Tell Me Why Stories*, at age 18. Next he
worked for *Boy's Life* magazine. Then he illustrated for the Boy Scouts and other magazines.
By his death in November 1978, he had painted
over 2,000 paintings.

Many of his paintings were done in oil and
reproduced as magazine covers, advertisements,

illustrations, calendars, and book sketches. Over
320 of these paintings became covers for the
Saturday Evening Post.

Norman Rockwell painted everyday people in
everyday situations with a little humor mixed in
with the sentiment. His paintings and illustrations
are well loved because of this sensitive nature.
He painted people he knew and places with
which he was familiar. New England landscapes
are found in many of his illustrations.

Because his works are so well liked, they have
been reproduced on many objects. These new
collectibles should not be confused with the original artwork and illustrations. The new collectibles, however, offer Norman Rockwell illustrations to the average pocketbook and serve to
keep his work alive.

References: Denis C. Jackson, *The Norman
Rockwell Identification and Value Guide,* pri-
vately printed, 1985; Mary Moline, *Norman
Rockwell Collectibles Value Guide, Sixth Edition,*
Green Valley World, 1988.

Museums: Corner House, Stockbridge, MA; Norman Rockwell Museum, Northbrook, IL.

Bell
Gorham
1975, Santa's Helper **45.00**
1976, Snow Sculpture **45.00**
1982, Lovers **30.00**
1983, Christmas Medley **30.00**
1985, Butter Girl **24.00**
Grossman, Dave
1975, Christmas, first edition **30.00**
1976, Ben Franklin Bicentennial . **28.00**
1979, Leapfrog **50.00**
River Shore, 1978, Garden Girl **40.00**
Figurine
Gorham
1976, Saying Grace **150.00**
1980
After the Prom **130.00**
Day In The Life Of A Boy **85.00**
Day In The Life Of A Girl **85.00**
Four Seasons, A Helping Hand,
set of 4 .... **450.00**
1982, Jolly Coachman **50.00**
1983
Antique Dealer **130.00**
Christmas Dancers **75.00**
Dave Grossman Designs, Inc.
1973, No Swimming **45.00**
1978, At The Doctors **125.00**
1980, Exasperated Nanny **125.00**
1982, Doctor and the Doll **125.00**
1983, The Graduate **32.00**
Lynell Studios
1979, Snow Queen **85.00**
1980
Artist's Daughter **65.00**
Cradle of Love **85.00**

1981, A Daily Prayer	....	**30.00**

Rockwell Museum

1978, Bedtime	....	**50.00**

1979

Baby's First Step	....	**475.00**
Bride & Groom	....	**90.00**
1980, Wrapping Christmas Presents		**120.00**
1981, Music Maker	....	**90.00**
1982, Giving Thanks	....	**160.00**
1983, Painter	....	**90.00**

Ingot

Franklin Mint

1972, Spirit of Scouting, set of 12		**275.00**
1974, Tribute to Robert Frost, set of 12	....	**285.00**

Hamilton Mint

1975

Christmas, silver	....	**40.00**
Saturday Evening Post Covers, set of 12	....	**210.00**
Santa Planning A Visit, gold plated silver	....	**45.00**
1977, Charles Dickens	....	**50.00**

Magazine

American Artist, July, 1976, Self Portrait and article	....	**15.00**
Country Gentleman, 1979, memorial issue	....	**20.00**
Saturday Evening Post, August, 1977, 250th Edition, Rockwell cov, illus, and portfolio	....	**25.00**

Magazine Cover

American

1918, November	....	**20.00**
1921, May	....	**18.00**

American Boy

1916, December	....	**30.00**
1920, April	....	**27.50**
American Legion, 1978, July	....	**5.00**

Boy's Life

1915, August	....	**50.00**
1947, February	....	**45.00**
1957, June	....	**42.50**

Colliers, 1919

March 1	....	**25.00**
April 19	....	**20.00**

Country Gentleman

1918, February 9	....	**50.00**
1920, May 8	....	**48.50**
1922, March 18	....	**45.00**

Family Circle

1967, Dec, Santa Claus	....	**10.00**
1968, December	....	**7.50**
Fisk Club News, 1917, May	....	**18.00**
Jack and Jill, 1974, December	.....	**5.00**

Literary Digest

1918, December 14	....	**30.00**
1920, September 4	....	**25.00**
1922, April 15	....	**18.00**
Look, 1964, July 14	....	**10.00**
McCall's, 1964, December	....	**12.00**

Parents

1939, January	....	**10.00**
1951, May	....	**9.00**
Red Cross, April, 1918	....	**25.00**

Saturday Evening Post

1916

June 3	....	**130.00**
October 14	....	**100.00**

1918

January 26	....	**90.00**
September 21	....	**85.00**

1920

January 17	....	**75.00**
June 19	....	**65.00**
December 4	....	**90.00**

1922

February 18	....	**85.00**
September 9	....	**50.00**

1945

March 21	....	**70.00**
August 11	....	**32.50**

1946

October 5	....	**48.00**
November 16	....	**25.00**

1950

April 29	....	**80.00**
November 18	....	**30.00**

1952

February 16	....	**30.00**
August 30	....	**40.00**

1955

March 12	....	**20.00**
August 20	....	**15.00**
1957, September 7	....	**21.50**

Magazine Cover, *Saturday Evening Post,* **June 7, 1958, $18.00.**

1960, February 13	....	**60.00**

1962

January 13	....	**12.00**
November 3	....	**10.00**
1963, Sept 12, John F Kennedy	..	**12.00**

Scouting

1934, February	....	**10.00**
1944, December	....	**12.00**

1953, October	8.50
TV Guide, 1970, May 16	5.00
Yankee, 1972, August	9.50
Paperweight, River Shore	100.00

Plate

Franklin Mint

1970, Bringing Home The Tree	330.00
1971, Under The Mistletoe	175.00
1972, The Carolers	165.00
1973, Trimming The Tree	165.00
1974, Hanging The Wreath	180.00
1975, Home For Christmas	190.00

Gorham

Boy Scout

1975, Our Heritage	60.00
1976, A Scout Is Loyal	55.00
1977, A Good Sign	35.00
1977, The Scoutmaster	60.00

1978

Campfire Story	20.00
Pointing The Way	35.00
1980, Beyond the Easel	48.00

Christmas Series

1974, Tiny Tim	65.00
1975, Good Deeds	64.00
1976, Christmas Trio	60.00
1977, Yuletide Reckoning	45.00
1978, Planning Christmas Visits	25.00
1979, Santa's Helpers	20.00
1980, Letter to Santa	25.00
1981, Santa Plans His Visit	30.00
1982, The Jolly Coachman	30.00
1983, Christmas Dancers	30.00
1984, Christmas Medley	30.00

Four Seasons, Sets of 4

1971, A Boy & His Dog	400.00
1972, Young Love	200.00
1973, Ages of Love	300.00
1974, Grandpa & Me	175.00
1975, Me & My Pal	200.00
1976, Grand Pals	200.00
1978, The Tender Years	115.00
1979, A Helping Hand	100.00
1980, Dad's Boy	130.00
1981, Old Timers	100.00
1982, Life With Father	100.00
1983, Old Buddies	115.00
1984, Traveling Salesman	115.00

Grossman Designs, Dave

Annual Series, bas-relief

1979, Leapfrog	50.00
1980, Lovers	60.00
1981, Dreams of Long Ago	60.00
1982, Doctor And The Doll	65.00

Christmas Series, bas-relief

1980, Christmas Trio, FE	80.00
1981, Santa's Good Boys	75.00
1982, Faces of Christmas	75.00

Huckleberry Finn Series

1979, The Secret	49.00
1980, Listening	40.00
1981, No Kings Nor Dukes	40.00

Tom Sawyer Series

1976, Whitewashing Fence	75.00
1977, Take Your Medicine	50.00
1978, Lost In Cave	50.00

Lynell Studios

Christmas

1979, Snow Queen	30.00
1980, Surprises For All	30.00

Mother's Day

1980, Cradle of Love	40.00
1981, Mother's Blessing	30.00
1983, Dear Mother	26.00
Special Issues Series, 1980, Poor Richard's Almanac	45.00

River Shore

1979, Spring Flowers	120.00
1980, Looking Out To Sea	110.00

1982

Grandpa's Guardian	80.00
Grandpa's Treasures	80.00
Jennie & Tina	40.00

Rockwell Museum

American Family Series

1978

Baby's First Step	80.00
Happy Birthday Dear Mother	86.00

1979

Birthday Party	30.00
First Prom	30.00
Little Mother	66.00
Mother's Little Helpers	65.00
The Student	65.00

American Family II Series

1980, New Arrival	40.00

1981

Almost Grown Up	81.00
At The Circus	96.00
Giving Thanks	96.00
Sweet Dreams	90.00
We Missed You, Dad	90.00

Rockwell Society

Christmas Series

1974, Scotty Gets His Tree	160.00
1975, Angel With Black Eye	100.00
1976, Golden Christmas	55.00
1977, Toy Shop Window	50.00
1978, Christmas Dream	50.00
1979, Somebody's Up There	30.00
1980, Scotty Plays Santa	32.00
1981, Wrapped Up In Christmas	30.00
1982, Christmas Courtship	30.00
1983, Santa on the Subway	30.00
1984, Santa in his Workshop	25.00

Heritage Series

1977, Toy Maker	260.00
1978, The Cobbler	155.00
1979, Lighthouse Keeper's Daughter	80.00
1980, Ship Builder	60.00
1981, Music Maker	30.00
1982, The Tycoon	20.00
1983, Painter	25.00

1984, Story Teller	25.00

Mother's Day Series

1976, A Mother's Love	120.00
1977, Faith	75.00
1978, Bedtime	100.00
1979, Reflections	38.00
1980, A Mother's Pride	30.00
1981, After The Party	25.00
1982, Cooking Lesson	25.00
1983, Add Two Cups	24.00
1984, Grandma's Courting Dress	25.00

Royal Devon
Christmas Series

1975, Downhill Daring	50.00
1976, The Christmas Gift	90.00
1977, The Big Moment	80.00
1978, Puppets For Christmas ...	45.00
1979, One Present Too Many ..	35.00
1980, Gramps Meets Gramps ..	35.00

Mother's Day Series

1975, Doctor And The Doll ...	85.00
1976, Puppy Love	80.00
1977, The Family	90.00
1978, Mother's Day Off	72.00
1979, Mother's Evening Out ...	35.00
1980, Mother's Treat	35.00

Sheet Music, cover illustration

Little French Mother Goodbye	35.00
Over There	25.00
Over Where The Lilies Grow	30.00

Stein

Gorham, Pensive Pals	37.50

Rockwell Museum

Braving The Storm	75.00
Fishin' Pals	75.00
For A Good Boy	95.00
Looking Out To Sea	125.00
The Music Lesson	90.00

ROSE O'NEILL

Collecting Hints: Study the dolls carefully before purchasing. Remember that composition dolls were made until the 1950s; hence, every example is not one of the early ones.

Many collectors concentrate only on Kewpie items. A specialized collection might include other O'Neill designs, such as Scootles, Ragsy, Kewpie-Gal, Kewpie-Kins and Ho-Ho.

History: Rose Cecil O'Neill (1876–1944) was a famous artist, novelist, illustrator, poet, sculptress, and creator of the Kewpie doll. O'Neill's drawing "Temptation" won her a children's art prize at the age of 14 and launched her career as an illustrator.

The Kewpie first appeared in art form in the December, 1909, issue of *Ladies Home Journal* in a piece entitled "Kewpies Christmas Frolic."

The first Kewpie doll appeared in 1913. Assisting in the design of the doll was Joseph L. Kallus. Although Geo. Borgfeldt Co. controlled the production and distribution rights to Kewpie material, Kallus continued to assist in design and manufacture through his firm, the Cameo Doll Company.

Kewpie dolls and china decorated items rapidly appeared on the market. Many were manufactured in Germany. Twenty-eight German factories made products during the peak production years. Later other manufacturers joined in the effort.

O'Neill eventually moved to south west Missouri, settling at Bonniebrook near Bear Creek. She died there in 1944. In 1947 Bonniebrook burned to the ground. Production of Kewpie items did not stop at O'Neill's death. Today Kewpie material still appears as limited edition collectibles.

References: Lois Holman, *Rose O'Neill Kewpies And Other Works,* published by author, 1983; Maude M. Horine, *Memories of Rose O'Neill,* booklet, published by author; Ralph Alan McCanse, *Titans and Kewpies,* out-of-print; Rowena Godding Ruggles, *The One Rose,* out-of-print.

Collectors' Club: International Rose O'Neill Club (IROC), P.O. Box 688, Branson, MO 65616.

Museum: Shephard of the Hills Farm and Memorial Museum, near Branson, MO.

Advisor: Lois Holman.

REPRODUCTION ALERT

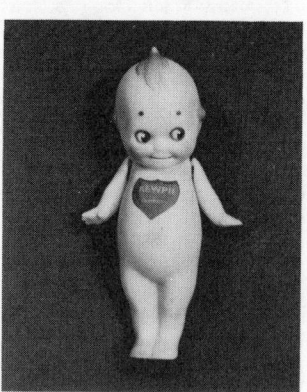

Doll, porcelain, orig Rose O'Neill copyright label on back, 4¼" h, $100.00.

Action Doll and Figurine

2", Blunderboo on sled	350.00
3¾", Sweeper, attached broom and waste can, bisque, "O'Neill" on foot and "C" mark	350.00
4", Reader, "C" mark	350.00

5", Thinker, sgd	25.00
Bell, brass	65.00

Book

Garda, dj, portrait inserts	60.00
The Goblin Woman	45.00
The Kewpies Their Book	195.00
The Master Mistress	45.00
Candleholder, 10", cast, 4½" Kewpie at base, Kewpie trademark	175.00
Candy Mold, 6", chocolate type, pewter	65.00

Carnival, plaster

Large	25.00
Small	15.00
Clock, 4⅞" h, 3½" w, rect, Jasperware, white Kewpies, flowers, and butterflies, curved top, incised mark "Rose O'Neill Wilson/Kewpie/Germany, copyrighted"	325.00
Crumb Tray, brass	30.00

Doll, Kewpie

Cameo Dolls Products, Port Allegheny, vinyl, fully jointed, orig clothes

10"	25.00
14"	60.00
16"	85.00
20"	150.00

Unidentified makers, legs together, movable arms, "O'Neill" incised bottom of foot; some still have gummed heart stickers on chest, black and white. Four different stickers used c1913, copyright sticker on back.

4"	100.00
6"	145.00
9"	375.00
10"	600.00
Feeding Dish, 10", alphabet border	150.00
Handkerchief	28.00
Ice Cream Mold, 7"	50.00

Jewelry

Charm, Ho-Ho	50.00
Hatpin, 6" l, Kewpie Kicker, Paye & Baker, Sterling Trade Kewpie mark	100.00
Ring, S, Paye & Baker, marked "P" and "B" in equal sized hearts	125.00
Letter Opener, 7", Kewpie finial, pewter	40.00
Needlepoint Panel, 8¾ x 13¾", Kewpie with rose and Kewpie in sunbonnet with heart, sage green background, Brunswick, pr	40.00
Pin Box, 2½", Kewpie with foot in air on lid, marked "Goebel"	450.00
Poster, 1973	30.00
Powder Shaker, 7", jointed arms, heart label on chest on back, French sticker label on feet	65.00
Salt and Pepper Shakers, 2½" Kewpie on ½" base, Paye & Baker, Trade Kewpie mark	250.00
Thimble, metal, marked "Kewpie"	35.00

ROSEVILLE POTTERY

Collecting Hints: Because of the availability of pieces in Roseville's later commercial ware, the prices for this type of ware are stable and unlikely to rise rapidly.

For the popular middle period patterns, which were made during the Depression and had limited production and sale, the prices are strong. Among the most popular patterns from this middle period are Blackberry, Cherry Blossom, Falline, Ferella, Jonquil, Morning Glory, Sunflower, and Windsor. The Art Deco craze has focused on Futura, especially the more angular shaped pieces.

Pinecone in blue or brown glaze continues to have a strong following as do the earlier lines of Juvenile and Donatello.

Desirable shapes include baskets, bookends, cookie jars, ewers, tea sets, and wall pockets.

Most pieces are marked. However, during the middle period paperstickers were used. These often were removed, leaving the piece unmarked.

Roseville made over one hundred and fifty different lines or patterns. Novice collectors would benefit from reading one of the several books about Roseville and viewing the offerings of dealers who specialize in art pottery. Collections generally are organized around a specific pattern or shape.

History: In the late 1880s a group of investors purchased the J. B. Owens Pottery in Roseville, Ohio, and made utilitarian stoneware items. In 1892 the firm was incorporated and joined by George F. Young who became general manager. Four generations of Youngs controlled Roseville until the early 1950s.

A series of acquisitions began: Midland Pottery of Roseville in 1898, Clark Stoneware Plant in Zanesville (formerly used by Peters and Reed), and Muskingum Stoneware (Mosaic Tile Company) in Zanesville. 1898 also saw offices move from Roseville to Zanesville.

In 1900 Roseville developed its art pottery line—Rozane. Ross Purdy designed a line to compete with Weller's Louwelsa. Rozane became a trade name to cover a large series of lines by designers such as Christian Neilson, John J. Herold, and Gazo Fudji. The art lines of hand decorated underglaze pottery were made in limited quantities after 1919.

The success of Roseville depended on its commercial lines, first developed by John J. Herald and Frederick Rhead in the first decade of the 1900s. Decorating techniques included transfers, pouncing (a method producing a pattern on the ware which could be followed), and air brush or sponging following embossed motifs. Among the lines from this early period are Dutch, Juvenile, Cameo, and Holland.

George Young retired in 1918. Frank Ferrell replaced Harry Rhead, who had replaced Frederick Rhead, as art director. Ferrell developed over 80 lines, the first being Sylvan. The economic depression of the 1930s caused Roseville to look for new product lines. Pine Cone was introduced in 1935, made for 15 years, and issued in over 75 shapes.

In the 1940s a series of high gloss glazes were tried to revive certain lines. Other changes were made to respond to the fluctuating contemporary markets. Mayfair and Wincraft date from this period. In 1952 Raymor dinnerware was produced. None of these changes brought economic success back to Roseville. In November, 1954, Roseville was bought by the Mosaic Tile Company.

References: Sharon and Bob Huxford, *The Collectors Encyclopedia of Roseville Pottery,* Collector Books, 1976; Sharon and Bob Huxford, *The Collectors Encyclopedia of Roseville Pottery, Second Series,* Collector Books, 1980.

Collectors' Club: American Art Pottery Association, P. O. Box 714, Silver Springs, MD 20901.

Note: For pieces in the middle and upper price range see *Warman's Antiques And Their Prices.*

Vase, white magnolia flowers, apricot ground, marked "446-4," 4¼" h, $40.00.

Ashtray, Silhouette, brown	20.00
Basket	
Clematis, brown	60.00
Magnolia, 10", green, marked "385-10"	85.00
Peony, 10", yellow	65.00
Pine Cone, 10", blue, marked "308-10"	195.00
Poppy, hanging, pink	45.00
Rozane, ivory, marked "I-66-2-2" . . .	70.00
Bookends, pr	
Foxglove, blue	95.00
Snowberry, pink	75.00
Zephyr, brown	80.00
Bowl	
Apple Blossom, 8", green, 328	35.00

Carnelian II, blue and purple	75.00
Corinthian, 6½"	35.00
Falline, 9", tan, handle	200.00
Magnolia, 10", blue	45.00
Monticello, blue	65.00
Panel, 5", brown	25.00
Candleholder, White Rose, green, pr . .	30.00
Candlesticks, pr	
Bleeding Heart, blue	55.00
Carnelian I, 1¾", green, tan drip . . .	23.00
Clematis, blue, marked "1158-2" . . .	28.00
Foxglove	50.00
Snowberry, brown, marked "II-143-2-1"	40.00
Console Bowl	
Ming Tree, marked "528-10"	50.00
Pine Cone	67.00
Console Set, bowl and candlesticks	
Cherry Blossom, blue	360.00
Columbine, 8" bowl, 5" candlesticks, pink	115.00
Snowberry, pink	80.00
Cornucopia	
Bittersweet	30.00
Ivory II, 8", Art Deco	40.00
Water Lily, brown	35.00
Ewer	
Bushberry, 6", blue	55.00
Columbine, 7", blue	55.00
Freesia, 6", green	35.00
Gardenia, 6", brown	32.00
Silhouette, 10", marked "717-10" . .	45.00
Snowberry, 10", blue, marked "17k-10"	65.00
Jardiniere	
Florentine, 8", brown	40.00
Poppy, 3", green	25.00
Lamp, Carnelian II, red and purple . . .	225.00
Mug, Pine Cone, 4", brown	100.00
Planter	
Artwood, gray	20.00
Silhouette, 10", white, flowers	35.00
Shelf, Iris, blue, pr	250.00
Soap Dish, Donatello	140.00
Sugar, Snowberry, pink	20.00
Teapot, Wincraft, lime	60.00
Urn, Freesia, 8", green	68.00
Vase	
Apple blossom, bud, pink	30.00
Bleeding Heart, 4", green, marked "138-4"	40.00
Bushberry, blue, double handle, marked "40-15"	150.00
Carnelian I, 8", blue and pink, handle	40.00
Cosmos, green, marked "944-4" . . .	25.00
Cremona, pink	40.00
Dahlrose, triple bud	60.00
Donatello, 4"	45.00
Ferrella, 8", orange, marked "506-8"	195.00
Foxglove, 6", blue, double open handles, marked "44-6"	45.00
Freesia, brown	40.00

Futura, 6" 165.00
Iris, blue 30.00
Ixia, 10", turquoise 45.00
Laurel 150.00
Lotus, 10", burgundy 95.00
Magnolia, brown 35.00
Mostique, 6" 35.00
Pine Cone, 8", pillow, brown, double
   handle, marked "114-8" 195.00
Rosecraft, 5", black, marked "158-5" 50.00
Snowberry, 4", blue 35.00
Thorn Apple, 6", blue 45.00
Tourmaline, 6", blue, double handle 50.00
Tuscany, 5½", pink 40.00
Water Lily, double handle, blue,
   marked "85-18" 200.00
White Rose, 6", green 35.00
Wincraft, marked "283-8" 30.00
Wall Pocket
  Carnelian I, 8", blue 65.00
  Corinthian, 9½" 110.00
  Donatello, 11½" 125.00
  Florane, handled 85.00
  Florentine, 9½, brown 75.00
  Lombardy, 8", blue glossy glaze 165.00
  Mostique, 9½" 125.00
  Snowberry, rose 72.00
  Tuscany, pink 67.00
  Vintage 110.00
  Wincraft, 5½" 70.00
  Zephyr Lily, 8", brown, marked
   "1297-8" 65.00
Water Pitcher, Raymor, brown 85.00
Window Box
  Ming Tree, 11½", blue 70.00
  Pine Cone, blue, Thorn Apple leaves 125.00

SALOON COLLECTIBLES

Collecting Hints: Collectors concentrate on materials from the pre-prohibition (1918) era, with many recreating the decor of an old time saloon in one room of their house. This material also is extremely popular with decorators. The field still is in its infancy with little information available. Many bargains can be found by the knowledgeable collector.

History: The American saloon always has been a refuge and playground for off duty males throughout history. Women and children often were forbidden to enter this masculine turf. Gambling, cursing, drinking, smoking, and fighting were the primary forms of entertainment at the saloon. Today the illusion exists that life was much more exciting in a yesteryear saloon than a modern bar.

The saloon consisted of many units—the back

bar, the front bar, and the room itself. All types of materials existed to fill needs, from bottles to spittoons.

Reference: Roger Baker, *Old West Antiques & Collectibles Illustrated Price Guide*, Chapter 5 is entitled "The Western Saloon."

BACK BAR

94", mahogany, carved, leaded windows and mirrors 8,000.00
190", wood, carved, stained glass columns, marble top, dated 1910 ..... 9,000.00

BACK BAR ITEMS

Bottle
  Cylinder
   Burke's Union Club, 8", clear 35.00
   Westminster Rye, 11", cut letters
    emb in gold 100.00
  Decanter
   Belle of Kentucky, clear, ribbed,
    gold cut letters, stopper 100.00
   Maryland Club, 8½", cut, fluted
    neck, cut stopper 45.00
   Old Canterbury Whiskey, 10", three
    rows of oval cuts around neck,
    two rows around body, gold cut
    letters 125.00
   Right and Ready Whiskey, Cort-
    wright Co, New York, fluted neck
    and base, gold letters 120.00
Cash Register, National, brass, wood
  base, two drawers 1,000.00
Mirror, 100" l, beveled 1,800.00
Whiskey Dispenser, 15½" h, glass,
  etched, "Ask for Sanderson's Whis-
  key" 475.00

Beer Tap, Neuweiler Light Lager Beer, yellow casing, black and red lettering, $12.50.

FRONT BAR AND RELATED ITEMS

Bar, 180", oak, applied carving, wood
rail **725.00**
Beer Tap Knob
  Hanleys Ale, 2¾", molded bulldog
    head **20.00**
  Stanton Lager, black ball, red, black
    and gold enamel **25.00**
Corkscrew, 3" l, brass, figural, bottle,
  "Anheuser-Busch" **45.00**
Foam Scraper Holder and Stirrer, 8 x 8",
  Bert & Harry Piel's Light Beer adv, cast
  metal **20.00**
Ice Chopper, cast steel, wood handle,
  Gilchrist **25.00**
Match Dispenser, 3¾ x 2½ x 12", metal
  and cast iron, dark blue, black base,
  "1¢ Match Dispenser" **120.00**
Shot Glass, etched, "Ruby Saloon" ... **20.00**
Statue, 10½ x 11", rearing horse, Roll-
  ing Rock Beer adv, multicolored,
  black lettering, marked "Made by Sil-
  verstri Bros. Co." **20.00**
Tobacco Dispenser, "The Good Judge
  Recommends Right-Out Chewing To-
  bacco" **150.00**
Trade Stimulator
  Kicker Catcher, 1¢, wood case, base-
    ball, win stick of gum **1,700.00**
  Pot Luck, Kalon, plunger on front
    sends three reels spinning, fruit
    symbol reels, light metal **45.00**
  Shanghai, Oriental motif, dice spin-
    ner, betting spaces, two bone dice
    under glass, operated by plunger . **110.00**
Tray, 12" d,
  Piel's Light Beer, gold and blue, green
    and red details, marked "Conco"
    on bottom **25.00**
  Straus, Gunst & Co, Full Dress Maryland
    Rye, tip, 1907 .... **100.00**

FLOOR ITEMS

Player Piano, coin-operated, rebuilt
  case, stained glass section lights up,
  includes rolls **4,000.00**
Slot Machine, Jennings Silver Chief-Bell,
  chrome front **1,250.00**
Spittoon
  6" d, 4" h, redware, small bottom,
    large mouth **50.00**
  7½" d, 4" h, pottery, brown, glazed,
    ribbed flared bowl, beaded rim,
    white mouth **75.00**
  8½" d, 5½" h, cast iron, white por-
    celain int., c1850 .... **45.00**

WALL ITEMS

Calendar, 1904, 31½ x 22½", "S.S. Patterson, Dillon, Mont, Milwaukee

Beer," Victorian lady, matted, carved
  frame **525.00**
Clock, 11 x 12", Schaefer adv, lights up
  and revolves, brown plastic case ... **35.00**
Door, pr, 60" w, beveled glass **1,500.00**
Sign
  12 x 23", "Schlitz on Tap," lights up
    red, orig manufacturers plaque ... **135.00**
  33 x 21½", Magnet/Pale Ale, reversed
    painted, mirror back, red and silver
    magnet center, "The Brewery Tad-
    caster" in gold leaf, oak frame ... **150.00**

SALT AND PEPPER SHAKERS

Collecting Hints: Collect only sets in very good condition. Make certain the set has the proper two pieces, and base if applicable. China shakers should show no signs of cracking. Original paint and decoration should be intact on all china and metal figures. All parts should be present, including the closure if important.

A collector will have to compete with collectors in other areas, e.g., advertising, animal groups, Blacks, and holiday collectibles. Many shakers will have souvenir labels which may have been added later to stock items. The form, not the label, is the important element.

Black figural shakers are rising in price. The same is true for advertising sets and comic and cartoon characters.

History: The Victorian era saw the advent of the elaborate glass and fine china salt and pepper shaker. The pioneering research work by Arthur Goodwin Peterson in books such as *Glass Salt Shakers: 1,000 Patterns* attracted collectors to this area. Figural and souvenir shakers, most dating from the mid-20th century and later, were looked down upon by this group.

This attitude is slowly changing. More and more people are collecting the figural and souvenir shakers, especially since prices are lower. Many of these patterns were made by Japanese firms and imported heavily after World War II.

Production of a form might continue for decades; hence, it is difficult to tell an early example from a modern one. This is one factor in keeping prices low.

References: Gideon Bosker, *Great Shakes: Salt and Pepper For All Tastes,* Abbeville Press, 1986; Melva Davern, *Collectors' Encyclopedia of Figural and Novelty Salt & Pepper Shakers,* Collector Books, 1985; Helene Guarnaccia, *Salt & Pepper Shakers Identification and Values,* Book I (1984) and *Book II* (1989), Collector Books; Mildred and Ralph Lechner, *The World of Salt Shakers,* Collector Books, 1976; Arthur G. Peterson, *Glass Salt Shakers,* Wallace-Homestead, 1970.

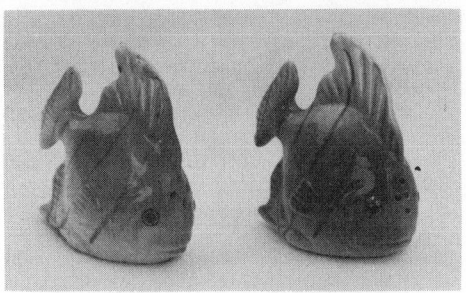

Fish, one blue, one brown, glazed ceramic, marked "Japan," 2⅝" h, $5.00.

Chalkware, Blacks, Mammy and Chef, full figure, white, black, and red ... **20.00**

China
  Amish Couple, 3½", hp, bearded man, black hat and boots, woman with white bonnet and apron **10.00**
  Bananas, 3", yellow and tan **6.50**
  Blacks
    Boys laying on bellies and reading book, marked "Japan" **15.00**
    Chef heads, one white, one black, white hats **15.00**
    Clown with seal, white hair, baggy pants, natural colors **25.00**
    Mammy and Butler, full figure, white clothes, black and pink trim **25.00**
    Mammy and Chef, full figure, Mammy holding "salt" plate, chef holding "pepper" frying pan, pink and aqua clothing, marked "Japan" **32.00**
    Porter, full figure, holding shaker suitcases, marked "Hirade, Japan" **30.00**
    Toddlers in basket, 2", hp, natural colors, marked "Japan" **30.00**

Urns, hand painted, white ground, pink flowers, green leaves, gold trim, porcelain, marked "6592," 4" h, $6.50.

Boy and Dog, multicolored, c1950 . **38.00**
Christmas Trees **20.00**
Conestoga Wagons, 3½", brown and black, white tops **8.50**
Doorway Garden, hp, house door with salt and pepper as flowers, green lawn base **15.00**
Eggs in Basket, 2¾", white "salt" egg, brown "pepper" egg, brown and beige basket **7.50**
Humpty Dumpty, seated on wall ... **24.00**
Mermaids, 3", reclining, hp, blue–green bodies, long blonde hair ... **8.50**
Mickey Mouse, glazed white china, c1940 .... **45.00**
Washing Machines, 3", hp, round tub type, wringer, white and black ... **10.00**
Watermelon Slices, 3", pink and green, brown seeds **7.50**
Depression Glass
  American Sweetheart, monax, single **100.00**
  Banded Rings, dec **40.00**
  Diana, amber **65.00**
  English Hobnail, pink **70.00**
  Florentine No. 2, crystal **35.00**
  Hazel Atlas, cobalt blue **24.00**
  Starlight, crystal **18.00**
  Waterford, crystal **5.00**
Metal
  Amish Couple, 3", cast iron, hp, bright colors **8.50**
  Dogs, sitting, painted cast metal, green, applied glass eyes **85.00**
  Grapes on branch, 3", silvered cast metal, glass grapes **10.00**
Nodder
  Fish **30.00**
  Man and Woman, marked "Souvenir of Mexico" **30.00**
Plastic
  Black, Luzianne Mammy, holding serving tray, yellow blouse, red skirt, marked "Langiappe of N. O." **12.00**
  Book Rack **8.00**
  Flower Pots **8.00**
  Hat Rack **8.00**
  Ken-L Ration, Fefi and Fido **8.00**
  Millie and Willie **8.00**
  Telephones, pink **8.00**
  Wringer Washer **9.00**
Souvenir
  Baker Hotel, hp, marked "Mineral Wells, TX" **20.00**
  Empire State Building, Statue of Liberty, silvered cast metal, marked "Souvenir of NY" **8.00**
  Flamingos, 3", hp, pink, marked "Souvenir of FL" **6.50**
  Oranges, 3", orange, green leaves, marked "Souvenir of FL" **5.00**
  Washington Monument and White

House, silvered cast metal, marked
"Souvenir of Washington, DC" .. **5.00**
World's Fair, 1939, Trylon and Peris-
phere, hp **35.00**

SANTA CLAUS

Collecting Hints: The number of Santa Claus related items is endless. Collectors are advised to
concentrate on one form (postcards, toys, etc.)
or a brief time period. New collectors will find
the hard plasic 1950s Santas easily accessible
and generally at a reasonable price.

History: The idea for Santa Claus developed from
stories about St. Nicholas, who lived about 300
AD. By the 1500s, "Father Christmas" in England, "Pere Noel" in France, and "Weihnachts-
mann" in Germany were well established.

Until the 1800s Santa Claus was pictured as a
tall, thin, stately man wearing bishop's robes and
riding a white horse. Washington Irving in *Knickerbocker's History of New York,* 1809, made him
as a stout, jolly man who wore a broad brimmed
hat and huge breeches and smoked a long pipe.
The traditional Santa Claus image came from
Clement C. Moore's poem "An Account of a Visit
from St. Nicholas" (*Troy Sentinal,* NY, 1823) and
the cartoon characterizations by Thomas Nast
which appeared in *Harper's Weekly* between
1863 and 1886.

References: E. Willis Jones, *The Santa Claus
Book,* Walker, 1976; Maggie Rogers and Peter R.
Hallinan, *The Santa Claus Picture Book: An Ap-
praisal Guide,* E. P. Dutton, Inc., 1984.

Advisor: Lissa Bryan-Smith and Dick Smith.

Additional Listings: Christmas Items.

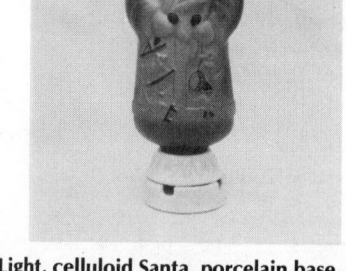

**Light, celluloid Santa, porcelain base, red
outfit, yellow highlights on front, black
highlights on toys, dark green tones on
tree, 9" h, $95.00.**

Advertising
Christmas Club Book, Carlisle De-
posit Bank and Trust Co, Carlisle,
PA, Santa looking out window on
front cov, 1934 .... **6.50**
Matchbook, 3" h, matches make San-
ta's face, Lion Match Co, NY **10.00**
Ornament, cardboard
Santa holding slate, inviting people
to join Robesonia State Bank
Christmas Club, 1932 .... **5.00**
Santa with toys, Dundee Smart
Clothes, Allentown, PA, 1941 .. **5.00**
Automata, battery operated, 9", Japan
Head turns, eyes light, waving white
star **55.00**
Pulling toys from pack **55.00**
Bank
Chalkware, Santa standing with bag
of toys, gold coat and cat, red
pants, 1950s **25.00**
Metal, 6½" h, Santa sleeping in chair,
advertising figural type for many
banks **30.00**
Candy Box, cardboard, rect
"Merry Christmas to All," Santa,
sleigh, and reindeer, string handle,
1950s **6.50**
Santa face on all sides, background
color varies, string handle, 1950s **6.50**
Santa's head in corner, dark red background, 1930s **10.00**
Candy Container
Cardboard, 8" h, round, red flocked
coat, opens at belt line, nodding
head on metal spring, West Germany, 1950s **30.00**
Composition, 5" h, composition face,
rabbit fur beard
Cardboard body, red felt coat with
removable black legs, cardboard
base, Germany, 1920–30s **150.00**
Red felt body, Santa sitting on pile
of wood logs, Germany, 1920s . **110.00**
Egg Crate Papier Mache
10" h, Santa standing, hands on
hips, red coat with white trim,
pack open on back, USA, 1940s **85.00**
10½" h, Santa climbing out of
chimney, red coat with white
trim, pack open in front, USA,
1940s **85.00**
Glass
5" h, Father Christmas, standing
Dark green, painted white beard,
metal screw on lid/base, USA **100.00**
Yellow, metal base **80.00**
5½" h, Father Christmas, red, foot
in chimney, metal base, marked
"Victory Candy Co, USA" **75.00**
6" h, Santa, standing, painted red,

white, and black, plastic head, screw on lid, 1950s, USA **65.00**

Papier Mache

4" h, Santa, rotund, standing, opening in base

Red coat, gold trim **35.00**

White coat, red trim **35.00**

4½" h, red coat, huge belly, white beard, jolly face, USA **38.00**

6" h, white coat with red trim, open pack, USA **38.00**

9" h, Santa

Standing in chimney, white coat with red and green trim, opening in base, 1920s **85.00**

Waving, large belly, white coat, red belt, red string net pack on back, opening in base, 1950s **82.00**

Plaster, 8" h, Father Christmas, molded, white mica covered long coat, black boots, white hood with chenille trim, long white beard, detailed painted face, opening in base, Germany, 1900–20s **550.00**

Plastic

4" h, soft plastic, white with black and red trim, head removes, 1960s **5.00**

5" h, rotund, red coat, standing, USA, 1950s

Green skis, pack on back is open for candy **15.00**

Holding white tennis racket **15.00**

White snowshoes, holding green tree, pack on back is open .. **15.00**

Children's Books

Dawson, Conengsby, *When Father Christmas Was Late,* Doubleday, Dorian, and Co, Garden City, NY, 1928 .... **4.50**

Johnson, Annie Fellow, *Miss Santa Claus of the Pullman,* The Century Co, NY, 1913 .... **6.50**

Moore, Clement, *The Night Before Christmas* Cuppies and Leon Co, publisher, NY, 1913 .... **15.00**

John C Winston, publisher, Philadelphia, 1942, Everett Shin, illustrator **12.00**

Page, Thomas Nelson, *A Captured Santa Claus,* Charles Scribner's & Sons, NY, 1905 .... **6.50**

Sugar, Caroline and Cyrus Leroy Baldridge, *Santa Claus Comes to America,* Alfred A Knopf, 1942 .... **10.00**

Figure

Bisque

1¼" h, red, white, and green, standing, marked "Japan," 1930s **15.00**

2½" h, red, white, and green, standing, marked "Japan," 1930s **18.00**

3½" h, red and white, USA, 1950s **20.00**

Cardboard

3" h, flat, inserted in slot in cardboard sleigh, USA, 1950s **10.00**

4" h

Flat, litho, Santa with tree, black cardboard platform, USA, 1950s **8.00**

Rolled red flocked coat, black legs, paper face, holding green tree, marked "Japan," 1930s . **22.00**

6" h, rolled red flocked coat, black legs, white celluloid face, holding white bell, marked "Japan," 1930s **30.00**

Celluloid

¾" h

Santa in red coat with pack, cardboard base, marked "Japan," 1930s **10.00**

Santa in sleigh, one deer, marked "Japan," 1930s **25.00**

3½" l, red and cream Santa in shell sleigh, one deer **28.00**

4" h, Santa standing on three books, USA **22.00**

5" h, Father Christmas, red and green, Japan **35.00**

6½" h, Santa, one hand to beard, other hand holding doll behind back, Japan **38.00**

7" l, Santa in sleigh, red, white, and green, one white deer, marked "Irwin, USA" **40.00**

12" l, red Santa, cardboard sleigh, four brown celluloid deer, Japan **48.00**

16" l, red and white Santa, red sleigh, two white deer with harness, Japan **55.00**

Chalk, 5" h, standing, red and white, pack on back, USA, 1950s **12.00**

Chenille, Japan

3" h

Green, bisque face **18.00**

Red, paper face **15.00**

4" h

Red, bisque face **18.00**

White, paper face **18.00**

Yellow, foil face **18.00**

5" h, blue, bisque face **22.00**

Composition

3½" h, Father Christmas, long red coat, Germany **30.00**

6" l, Santa, rabbit fur beard, moss cart, pulled by composition deer, Germany **200.00**

12" l, Santa, rabbit fur beard, purple felt coat, wooden sleigh, Germany **350.00**

Cotton Batting

3" h, red, black legs and arms, composition face

Cardboard airplane, Japan **75.00**

Cardboard church **45.00**
Celluloid canoe **45.00**
4" h, red, black legs and arms,
composition face, Japan **40.00**
8" h, white, black legs, white
hands, composition face, Japan **90.00**
Homemade
11" h, standing, pressed cardboard
face, cloth stuffed body, mica
cov base **75.00**
14" h, stuffed cloth body, red coat,
blue pants, stitched face, white
spun glass trim **50.00**
Papier Mache
7" h, red coat with black trim, hand
raised, standing on white base . **32.00**
10" h, red coat with white trim,
blue eyes, standing, hands on
pockets **55.00**
Plastic
3½" h, red and white, green metal
skis **15.00**
4½" h, red and white, standing in
green cart, red wheels **7.50**
9" h, red and white, waving with
interior light, 1950s **20.00**
12" h, wall hung, face with interior
light, 1950s **25.00**
24" h, red and white, interior light,
1950s **25.00**
Lantern, battery operated, metal base,
Japan, 1950s
Santa face **25.00**
Standing Santa **25.00**
Light Bulb
2½" h, milk glass, two sided face,
Japan **15.00**
3" h
Father Christmas, lacquered clear
glass, Germany **60.00**
Santa, milk glass, one leg in chimney, Japan **15.00**
Ornament, mercury glass, Germany
3" h, white coat **38.00**
4" h, face **85.00**
Perfume Bottle, 3" h, pale green blown
glass **48.00**

Post Card, emb, German, $6.50.

Post Card
"A Joyful Christmas," two children
with doll, Father Christmas in
brown coat looking over their
shoulder **5.00**
"A Merry Christmas To You," Santa
in red coat, seated in snowy forest,
basket of toys on his back, an angel
whispering in his ear, Germany,
1909 .... **10.00**
"A Very Merry Christmas," Santa in
red coat and brown pants, climbing
in chimney, 1920 .... **3.50**
"Christmas Greetings," Santa with
blue coat carrying Christmas tree
with candles and large gold cloth
bag, Germany, 1906 .... **7.50**
"Christmas Greetings," Santa with
short beard, red stocking cap, red
coat with brown fur trim, Germany,
1922 .... **6.00**
"Dear Little Santa," sketch of Santa in
workshop, Buffalo and Toronto .. **3.50**
Kindly Santa face, clutching doll and
horse in white glove, USA, 1919 . **5.00**
"Merry Xmas," Father Christmas,
head only, holding gold cane, Germany **7.00**
Souvenir Spoon, silver plate, Santa on
sleigh, "Merry Christmas" on handle,
patented 1899 .... **25.00**
Stuffed Toy, cloth
4" h, red and white plush material,
plastic face, orig chimney box,
USA **45.00**
6", terry cloth, 1950s **8.00**
Telegram, Western Union, Holiday
Greetings, Santa on top of form with
Christmas trees, dated Dec 24, 1946 **10.00**
Toy
4" h
Friction, plastic, wheels in base,
marked "Fun World, Inc, USA" **5.00**
Roly Poly, celluloid, Santa standing
on white ball **28.00**
Wind-Up
Plastic, Santa on bike, Japan ... **20.00**
Tin, Santa in sleigh, Japan **40.00**
5" h, pull toy, plastic, cloth coated
body, walks when pulled, Germany **35.00**
7"
Roly Poly, molded cardboard,
brightly painted, 1920s **450.00**
Wind-Up, red and green celluloid,
Santa in middle of carousel,
white deer around outside **45.00**

SCOUTING

Collecting Hints: Nostalgia is one of the principal
reasons for collecting scouting memorabilia; in-

dividuals often focus on the period when they were in the scouting movement. Other collectors select themes, e.g., handbooks, jamborees, writings by scout movement leaders, Eagle Scout material, etc. Jamboree ephemera is especially desirable.

Scouting scholars have produced a wealth of well researched material on the scouting movement. Many of these pamphlets are privately printed and can be located by contacting dealers specializing in scouting items.

Scout material enjoys popularity among collectors. The greatest price fluctuation occurs in modern material and as collectors define new specialized collecting areas.

Girl Scout material is about five to ten years behind Boy Scout material in respect to collecting interest. A collection can still be assembled for a modest investment. While Boy Scout uniforms have remained constant in design throughout time, the Girl Scout uniform changed almost every decade. This increases the number of desirable collectibles.

History: The Boy Scout movement began in America under the direction of William D. Boyce, inspired by a helping hand he received from one of Baden-Powell's English scouts when he was lost in a London fog in 1910. Other American boy organizations, such as the one organized by Dan Beard, were quickly brought into the Boy Scout movement. In 1916 the Boy Scouts received a charter from the United States Congress. Key leaders in the movement were Ernest Thompson-Seton, Dan Beard, W. D. Boyce, and James West.

A young illustrator, Norman Rockwell, received his first job as editor of *Boys' Life* in 1913, which began a lifelong association with the Boy Scouts.

The first international jamboree was held in England in 1920. America's first jamboree was held in 1937 in Washington, D.C. Manufacturers, quick to recognize the potential for profits, issued a wealth of Boy Scout material. Local councils and Order of the Arrow lodges have added significantly to this base, especially in the area of patches.

The Girl Scout movement began on March 12, 1912, under the direction of Juliette Gordon Low of Savannah, Georgia. The movement grew rapidly and in 1928 the Girl Scout manual suggested selling cookies as a way of raising funds. The Girl Scout movement also received wide recognition for its activities during World War II, selling over $3 million of bonds in the fourth Liberty Loan drive.

References: Mary Degenhardt and Judy Kirsch, *Girl Scout Collector's Guide,* Wallace-Homestead, 1987; William Hillcourt, *Norman Rockwell's World of Scouting,* Harry Abrams, 1977; Alburtus Hoogeveen, *Arapaho I, Council Shoul-*

der *Patches, Red & Whites, Council Patches, Jamboree Patches, Council Histories,* privately printed; Alburtus Hoogeveen, Arapaho II, *Order of the Arrow, Complete Guide To Order Of Arrow Insignia,* privately printed; J. Bryan Putman, ed., *Official Price Guide To Scouting Collectibles,* House of Collectibles, 1982; R. J. Sayers, *Identification & Value Guide To Scouting Collectibles,* Books Americana, 1984; Harry D. Thorsen, *Scouts On Stamps Of The World,* privately printed.

Privately printed pamphlets defining specialized collecting interests (contact "The Stevensons" for a price list, see Advisory Board) include: James Froehlig, *Boy Scout Fiction, Mathiews, Fitzhugh and Every Boys Library;* Kenneth Kittleberger, *Cigarette And Trade Cards Featuring Baden-Powell;* Sheldon Levy and John Adams, *United States Boy Scout (coin) Medallions;* Dr. Stephen Lomazow, *Norman Rockwell & The Boy Scouts;* D. W. Miller, *Every Boys Library Boy Scout Editions;* H. Compton Pembroke, *All Boy Scout of America Publications, 1910–1970,* 104 pgs; Max J. Silber, *Friendship Gifts;* James Stevenson, *Ernest Thompson Seton, Dan Beard, and Robert Baden-Powell;* Harry D. Thorsen, *Eagle Scout Badges;* Harry D. Thorsen, *Wood Scout Tokens.*

Collectors' Club: Scouts On Stamp Society International, 20 Cedar Lane, Cornwell, NY 12518.

Periodical: *Scout Memorabilia Magazine,* c/o The Lawrence L. Lee Scouting Museum, P. O. Box 1121, Manchester, NH 03105.

Museums: Boy Scout Museum, Murray, KY; Girl Scout National Headquarters, New York, NY; The Lawrence L. Lee Scouting Museum and Max J. Silber Scouting Library, Manchester, NH; Juliette Low National Center, 142 Bull Street, Savannah, GA; Western Scout Museum, Los Angeles; Zitelman Scout Museum, Rockford, IL.

Advisors: The Stevensons.

REPRODUCTION ALERT, especially Boy Scout jamboree patches and rare Order of the Arrow patches.

BOY SCOUTS

Book, *Golden Anniversary Book of Scouting,* 1959, 1st ed, dj, Norman Rockwell	**22.00**
Calendar, 7½ x 14", 1954, "A Scout is Reverent," Norman Rockwell	**12.00**
Handbook	
Handbook for Boys	
1st printing, 5th edition	**6.00**
5th printing, 1913, red cover	**85.00**
9th printing, 1914, Tanner	**90.00**
15th printing	**20.00**
18th printing	**50.00**

Camera, folding, Boy Scout Kodak, single lens, olive green, leather case, orig instruction booklet, $80.00.

Handbook for Patrol Leaders, 10th printing	**10.00**
Handbook for Scoutmasters	
1st edition, 1913–14	**65.00**
2nd edition	
6th printing, 1924	**25.00**
9th printing, 1926, sgd "Bunner Berg"	**30.00**
Jamborees, National	
1935, red neckerchief	**100.00**
1937, patch	**95.00**
1950, silk neckerchief	**35.00**
1953, pocket patch	**25.00**
1957, pocket patch	**18.00**
1960, picture book	**12.50**
1964, Continental currency coin	**5.00**
1969, lapel pin	**10.00**
1977, arm band, felt	**85.00**
Magazine, *Boy's Life,* 1st issue reprint, March 1, 1911	**10.00**
Manual	
Community Boy Leadership, Manual for Scout Executives, 1st ed, 1921	**20.00**
Explorer, 3/57	**6.00**
Sea Scout Manual, 6th ed, 1st printing	**15.00**
Neckerchief, Philmont, silk screened, red, gold border	**5.00**
Patch	
B. P. Jr. Leader Training, Region XI	**25.00**
BSA Aquatic Instructor, 2½"	**5.00**
Council Executive, dark red background, title	**6.00**
Eagle Scout, sq cut on green khaki, used	**40.00**
Emergency Service Explorer, red felt	**18.00**
Fiftieth Anniversary Achievement Award, 1960	**6.00**
National Camping School	**4.00**
Neighborhood Commissioner Patch	**7.50**
Patrol Flag	
Cloth, printed, Dan Beard	**7.50**
Felt, green, "Bill"	**10.00**

Pin	
Collar, National Staff, vertical, lock clasp	**40.00**
Hat, JASM, light green enamel, screw back	**40.00**
Lapel, Sea Scout Quartermaster, sterling	**45.00**
Pocketknife	
Camillus, Cub Scout, three blades, wolf rank	**10.00**
Imperial, 1st class on shield under plastic, three blades, loop	**25.00**
Ulster, Boy Scout, maroon handles	**12.00**

Sheet Music, *March of the Boy Scouts,* music by G. A. Grant–Schaefer, published by Oliver Ditson Company, cover by M. Hunter, 1913/1915, $10.00.

Sash, 25 khaki crimped merit badges	**125.00**
Whistle, BSA, brass cylindrical	**20.00**
Yearbook	
The Boy Scouts Year Book, 1926	**18.00**
The Boy Scouts Year Book of Fun in Fiction, 1938	**12.00**
The Boy Scouts Year Book of Hobbies for Fathers & Sons, 1942	**10.00**

GIRL SCOUTS

Handbook	
Brownie Scout Handbook, 8th printing	**4.00**
Girl Scout Handbook	
1st printing, new edition	**10.00**
16th printing	**3.00**
Scouting For Girls, 2nd edition, 6th printing, 1925	**6.00**
Pocketknife, Utica Featherweight, Brownie, one blade, brown stag grips	**14.00**
Ring, sterling, six sided green enamel with emblem	**20.00**
Uniform, Official Camp Fire Girl Kit, cloth leather rings, beads, orig instructions for dress, c1920	**52.00**

SEWING ITEMS

Collecting Hints: Collectors tend to favor Sterling silver items. However, don't overlook the material in metals, ivory, celluloid, plastic, and wood. Some metals were plated; the plating should be in very good condition before you buy a piece.

Advertising and souvenir items are part of sewing history. Focusing on one of these aspects will develop a fascinating collection. Another focus is on a certain instrument, with tape measures among the most common. Finally, figural items have a high value because of their strong popularity.

Most collectors concentrate on material from the Victorian era. A novice collector might look to the 20th century, especially the Art Deco and Art Nouveau periods, to build a collection.

History: Sewing was considered an essential skill of a young woman of the 19th century. The wealth of early American samplers attests to the talents of many of these young seamstresses.

During the Victorian era a vast assortment of practical as well as whimsical sewing devices appeared on the market. Among the forms were tape measures, pincushions, stilettos for punchwork, and crochet hooks. The sewing birds attached to table tops were a standard fixture in the parlor.

Many early sewing tools, e.g., needleholders, emery holders and sewing boxes, were made of wood. However, the Sterling silver tool was considered the height of elegance. Thimbles were the most popular. Sterling silver-handled items included darning eggs, stilettos, and thread holders.

In the 20th century needlecases and sewing kits were an important advertising giveaway. Plastic sewing materials are available, but they have not attracted much collector interest.

References: Pamela Clabburn, *The Needlework Dictionary,* William Morrow & Co., 1976; Joyce Clement, *The Official Price Guide To Sewing Collectibles,* House of Collectibles, 1987; Estelle Zalkin, *Zalkin's Handbook of Thimbles and Sewing Implements,* Warman Publishing Co., Inc., 1988.

Museums: Fabric Hall, Historic Deerfield, Deerfield, MA; Museum of American History, Smithsonian Institution, Washington, DC; Shelburne Museum, Shelburne, VT.

See: Thimbles.

Advertising
Guide, "Stimpson Eyelet Selector," paper, 5½" d, round, center rotates to select size of grommet, illus, c1950 .... **15.00**
Mirror, "The World's B.B. Pin Mirror, Germany," metal and leatherette . **35.00**

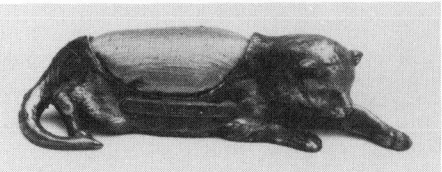

Pin Cushion, advertising, Calumet, white metal with bronze finish, pink pin cushion, marked "JB 681," 5¼" l, $125.00.

Bobbin, ivory, Chinese, Victorian, carved flowers, pr **140.00**
Book
DuBarry Patterns Book, Shortcuts to Sewing Success, 1945, 66 pgs ... **10.00**
Singer Sewing Library, four volumes, 1930, red marbleized box **35.00**
Wilcox & Gibbs Direction Book, 1900–1920, 48 pgs **22.00**
Button Hook
Bone Handle, 2½" l **13.00**
Mother of Pearl Handle, natural curvature, 6" l **38.00**
Charm, scissors, 14K gold **12.00**
Crochet Thread Holder, figural, apple, thread through stem, 4 x 3½" **23.00**
Darner
Brass, round egg **37.00**
Oak, three part, mushroom, stick, and foot form **25.00**
Wooden egg, sterling silver handle . **65.00**
Embroidery Scissors, black steel German scissors, sweet grass holder ... **25.00**
Mending Kit, bakelite, red and ivory, bakelite thimble cap, 3¾" h **20.00**
Needle Book
Adv, pastel sketch girl, flowers **4.00**
Baseball, players in action, catcher's mitt reverse **20.00**
Needle Case
Bakelite, doll shape **25.00**
Silver, ribbed, 2½" h **15.00**
Silverplate **12.00**
Wood, Russian type doll **7.50**
Pin Cushion, figural
Bird, thimble **8.00**
Doll, arms at head, 2½" **10.00**
Pyramid, wood **10.00**
Slipper, beaded leather, 5", 1920s .. **45.00**
Pin Holder
1¾", black and white, celluloid, silvered tin frame, "Keystone Boots, Colchester Rubbers," knee boot illus, name of Philadelphia store, c1880 .... **40.00**
2¼", litho tin, multicolored, slogans "The Success Spreader Fertilizes The Earth" and "Pin Your Faith To Success Spreaders," North and South America on one side, re-

versed with large lion superimposed on globe, c1900 .... **70.00**
Shoe, patterned metal **5.00**
Rug Hook, wood, cast iron, and steel, marked "Jewel," black and floral dec, dated 1886 .... **95.00**
Sewing Bird, brass, emb, orig clamp, pin cushion missing **100.00**
Sewing Box, Wheeler & Wheeler, carved lid, logo, 1920s, unused **65.00**
Sewing Kit
  Advertising
    American Red Cross, buttons and thread **20.00**
    Lydia Pinkham, metal tube **10.00**
  Celluloid case, scissors, thimble, thread **10.00**
  Chrome case, round, cushion top, thread, thimble, and thread **16.50**
  Vinyl, red, zippered, orig contents, 1950s **5.00**

Tape Measure, Yale, bulldog and football, blue and white, The Ehrman Mfg Co, Boston, MA, $30.00.

Tape Measure
  Advertising
    Angland's Glory Matches, 1½", celluloid, multicolored, match box illus **70.00**
    Colgate's Fab, 1½", celluloid, full color detergent soap box on front, text on back, c1930 ..... **30.00**
    First National Bank, Sunbury, PA, 1¼", celluloid, multicolored illus of Santa, snow capped chimney, blue star filled ground, black celluloid back with red poppy plant, c1920 .... **65.00**
    Kodak Finishing, 1¾", celluloid, blue inscription, red rim design, Minnesota photo shop illus, c1930 .... **25.00**
    Lackawanna Coal, 1½", bright orange and black, celluloid, c1930 **18.00**
    Parisian Novelty Co, 1½", blue and white, celluloid, adv text, c1920 **28.00**

Portland Cement **25.00**
Quality Drugs, 1¾", blue and white, celluloid, brass case, inscribed name of pharmacist **35.00**
RCA, ½ x 1½ x 1½", bright gold colored brass, steel spring 72" rule, black logo, engraved floral design, tape marked "Brown & Bigelow," c1930 .... **18.00**
Sears Roebuck & Co, 1¾", celluloid, fabric tape, red, white, blue, and bright yellow, "Sears, Roebuck & Co, David Bradley Plows, Cultivators, Planters," Sears guarantee in red, white, and blue text on back, c1920 .. **20.00**
Stromberg Carburetor **25.00**
White King Washing Machine Soap, 1½", blue and white celluloid, trademark picture on both sides, c1920 .... **35.00**
Figural
  Egg, enameled, figural housefly as tape end **30.00**
  Pig, wearing hat, early plastic **37.00**
Thimble Holder, sweet grass, lid and loop **22.00**
Thread Box
  Coats, wood **20.00**
  Hemingway, cardboard, litho of child, orig thread **20.00**
Thread Winder, ivory **16.50**
Valentine, 5½", fold out, boy and girl with sewing machine **10.00**

SHAWNEE POTTERY

Collecting Hints: Many Shawnee pieces came in several color variations. Some pieces also contained both painted and decal decorations. The available literature will indicate some, but not all of the variations.

Not a great deal of interest is being shown in the Shawnee art and dinnerware lines. Among the lines are Cameo, Cheria (Petit Point), Diora, and Touche (Liana). New collectors may wish to concentrate in these areas.

History: The Shawnee Pottery Co. was founded in 1937 in Zanesville, Ohio. The company acquired a 650,000 square foot plant that formerly housed the American Encaustic Tiling Company. There it produced as many as 100,000 pieces of pottery per day. In 1961 the plant closed.

Shawnee limited its chief production to kitchenware, decorative art pottery, and dinnerware. Distribution was primarily through jobbers and chain stores.

Shawnee can be marked "Shawnee," "Shawnee U.S.A.," "USA #—," "Kenwood," or with character names, e.g., "Pat. Smiley," "Pat. Winnie," etc.

Reference: Mark Supnick, *Collecting Shawnee Pottery*, L-W Books, 1989.

Advisor: Mark Supnick.

Pitcher, Corn King, 4¾" h, $18.00.

Bo Peep, pitcher, gold trim, flower decals	80.00
Bow Knot, vase, green, #819	12.00
Cherub, planter, gold trim, #536	10.00
Cockatiel, planter, #523	3.00
Cookie House	
Salt and Pepper Shakers, pr, #9	45.00
Sugar Bowl, #8	45.00
Teapot, #7	250.00
Butter Dish, cov	30.00
Cookie Jar	65.00
Cup and Saucer, set	26.00
Mixing Bowl, #6	18.00
Relish Dish, #79	20.00
Sugar Bowl	18.00
Teapot, 30 oz, #75	45.00
Vegetable Bowl	28.00
Cornucopia, vase, gold trim, #835	12.00
Daisy, creamer, marked "USA"	15.00
Doe and Fawn, planter, gold trim, #669	15.00
Flying Geese, bookends, pr, #4000	25.00
Fruit	
Casserole, #83	22.00
Cookie Jar, #84	35.00
Pitcher, #80	20.00
Salt and Pepper Shakers, pr, #82	20.00
Gazelle, figurine, black, #614	40.00
Girl with rag doll, wall pocket, #810	12.00
Giraffe, planter, #521	20.00
Little Boy Blue, pitcher, gold trim, #46	90.00
Little Chef, cookie jar	45.00
Lucky Elephant, cookie jar, gold trim and decals, marked "USA"	120.00
Mugsey	
Cookie Jar, gold trim	150.00
Salt and Pepper Shakers, pr	15.00

Puss 'N Boots	
Creamer, gold trim, #85	40.00
Salt and Pepper Shakers, pr	10.00
Sailor Boy, cookie jar	50.00
Smiley Pig	
Cookie Jar and Bank, #60	125.00
Creamer, gold trim, #86	45.00
Pitcher, gold trim, hand dec	120.00
Swan, vase, gold trim, #806	15.00
Tom Tom The Piper's Son, teapot, #44	30.00
Windmill, planter, gold trim, #715	22.00
Winnie Pig	
Cookie Jar	70.00
Salt and Pepper Shakers, pr, 5"	40.00

SHEET MUSIC

Collecting Hints: Center your collection around a theme—show tunes, songs of World War I, Sousa marches, Black material, songs of a lyricist or composer—the list is endless.

Be careful about stacking your sheets on top of one another. The ink on the covers tends to bleed. The most ideal solution is to place acid free paper between each cover and sheet.

Unfortunately, people used tape to repair tears in old sheet music. This discolors and detracts from value. Seek professional help in removing tape from rarer sheets.

During the late 1980s, mid–nineteenth century sheet music has risen rapidly in value. World War I and covers featuring Blacks currently enjoy great popularity among collectors.

History: Sheet music, especially piano scores, dates to the early 19th century. The early music contain some of the finest examples of lithography. Much of this music was bound in volumes and accompanied a young lady when she was married.

Sheet music covers chronicle the social, political, and other trends of any historical period. The golden age of the hand illustrated cover dates from 1885 to 1952. Leading artist such as James Montgomery Flagg used their talents in the sheet music area. A cover was critical to helping the song sell.

Once radio and talking pictures became popular, covers featured the stars. A song sheet might be issued in as many as six different cover versions depending on who was featured. By the 1950s piano playing no longer was popular and song sheets failed to maintain their high quality of design.

References: Debbie Dillon, *Collectors Guide To Sheet Music*, L-W Promotions, 1988; Daniel B. Priest, *American Sheet Music With Prices*, Wallace-Homestead, 1978.

Collectors' Clubs: National Sheet Music Society, 1597 Fair Park, Los Angeles, CA 90041; New

York Sheet Music Society, P. O. Box 1126, East Orange, NJ 07019; Remember That Song, 5821 North 67th Ave., Suite 103-306, Glendale, AZ 85301; The Sheet Music Exchange, P. O. Box 69, Quicksburg, VA 22847.

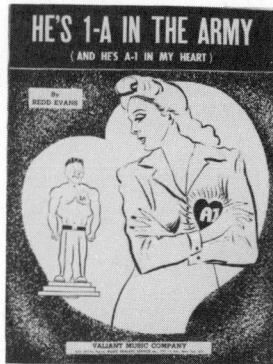

He's 1–A in the Army, music by Redd Evans, published by Valiant Music Co, blue and white cover, $4.00.

A Love Tale of Alsac Lorraine, 1928 ..	2.00
After the First of July, Allen, 1919	3.00
America Here's My Boy, Sterling/Lang, 1917	5.00
Beautiful Isle of Somewhere, Fearis, 1901	4.00
Belgian Rose, Will J. Hart, Ed Nelson, 1917	4.00
Break the News to Mother, 1897	15.00
By the Beautiful Sea, Pfeiffer, 1914 ...	6.00
By the Old Mill Where Waterlilies Grow, Morgan, 1912	2.00
Cat-Tails, Grace Drayton cov, 1927 ...	35.00
Cherie, I Love You, Rosedale Goodman, 1926	1.00
Corn Flower Waltz, Cotte Jr., 1912 ...	3.00
Cowboy Songs, 1935	3.50
Cryin' for the Moon, Conley, 1926 ...	1.00
Daddy's Prayer, Freeman, 1918	2.50
Dear Old Songs of Long Ago, D. Erwin Force, 1913	3.50
Do You Ever Dream of Me?, Goldye, 1925	1.50
Dream of Paradise, Johnston, 1902 ...	3.00
Everybody Loves a College Girl, Kerry Mills, 1911	3.00
Fascination, Powell, 1906	3.50
Fox Trail March, Zamecnik, 1917	2.00
Garden of Roses, Dempsey/Schmidt, 1909	2.50
Gee Whiz, Abe Losch, 1919	2.50
Glow Worm, Paul Lincke, 1902	4.00
Good-Bye Summer, So Long Fall, Hellow Winter, Wenrich, 1913	3.50
Gum Shoe Fox Trot, Stark, 1917	2.50
Harbor of Love, 1911	3.00

Hawaiian Twilight, Herbert Maple, 1918	2.50
He's Coming Home on the 8 O'Clock Train, Kendall, 1912	16.00
Hiawatha, Moret, 1902	5.00
Honest and Truly, Rose, 1952	.50
Hush a Bye Ma Baby, 1914	3.00
I Have a Big Jazz Band, Bowers, 1918	2.50
I Know What It Means to be Lonesome, Kendis, 1919	2.00
I Love the Ladies, 1914	3.00
Indian Summer, Herbert, 1934	3.00
I've Lost You, Howard, 1916	10.00
Jagtime Johnson's Ragtime March, Ryder, 1905	6.00
Levee Lou, Maden Edwards, 1907	4.00
Listen to the Mocking Bird, Drumheller, 1908	5.00
Little Alabama Coon, Black illus, 1893	24.00
Love Ain't Nothin' But the Blues, Alter, 1929	1.00
Lucky Moon, Stevens, 1909	3.00
Maidens Prayer, 1914	2.50
Me and My Shadow, 1927	3.50
Meet Me in St. Louis, Louis, 1904 ...	3.00
Moonbeams and Dreams of You, 1907	3.50
Mr. Ford, You've Got The Right Idea, 1916, illus of Henry Ford sailing on Ship of Peace	25.00
Mrs. Casey Jones, Newton, 1915	32.00
My Bird of Paradise, Berlin, 1915	5.00
My Wonderful Dream Girl, 1913	2.00

They'll Be Mighty Proud In Dixie Of Their Old Black Joe, music by Harry Carrol, published by Shapiro, Bernstein & Co, multicolored cover by Starmer, 1917, $10.00.

Newport Belles, Ascher, 1901	7.00
Normandy Chimes, Powell, 1913	3.00
Oh, You Beautiful Doll, 1911	5.00
Oh-Susanna, Foster, 1935	2.50
Old Rag Carpet, 1897	3.00
Over The Rainbow, whole cast on cov	25.00
Peg O' My Heart, Bryan/ Fisher, 1913	4.00

Perry's Victory March, Martin, 1913 . .	**14.00**
Prisoner's Song	**2.50**
Put on Your Old Grey Bonnet, Murphey/ Percy Wenrich, 1909	**5.00**
Rebecca of Sunnybrook Farm, Gumble, 1914	**3.50**
Rio Rita	**3.00**
Rose Petals, Wm T Pierson, 1910	**2.50**
Sail on Silvery Moon, Downs/Erdman, 1912	**3.00**
Shamrock Waltzes, 1918	**2.50**
She's Dancing Her Heart Away, Gilbert/ Kerry Mills, 1914	**4.00**
Silver Sleighbells, E T Paull, 1906	**10.00**
Sleep Little Baby of Mine, 1891	**3.00**
Snowflakes Also Christmas Chimes, 1917	**2.50**
Southern Beauty, 1904	**1.50**
Sunbonnet Sue, Cobb, 1908	**7.00**
Sweet Caroline, Claude Webber, 1904	**2.50**
Tango, Valentino cov	**4.00**
That Mellow Melody, 1912	**3.50**
The Burning of Rome, E T. Paull	**15.00**
The Chimes, Armstrong, 1912	**2.50**
The Little Red School House, Wilson, 1922	**5.00**
There's Egypt in Your Dreamy Eyes, 1917	**3.00**
Those Ragtime Melodies, Hodgkins, 1912	**6.00**
Trumpeter March, Ellis, 1924	**1.50**
Turtle Dove Polka, Franz Behr, 1900 .	**2.50**
Up in My Flying Machine, Saxby, 1910	**15.00**
Under the Mellow Arabian Moon, Nathan/Leopols, 1915	**3.50**
Vanity Fair, Stella Mathews, 1907	**2.50**
Waltz Me Around Again Willie, 1906 .	**7.50**
Way Down East Among the Shady Maple Trees, Stanford, 1900	**3.00**
Westward Ho, Wenrich, 1909	**2.50**
When a Lady Meets a Gentleman Down South, Oppenheim, 1936	**1.50**
When the Robins Sing in June, Conrad, 1908	**3.00**
Where the Red, Red Roses Grow, 1913	**3.50**
Won't You Let Me Take You Home, Doeer, 1912	**5.00**
Won't You Play a Simple Melody, 1914	**15.00**
You Can't Beat American Love, Happy O'Neil/Oliver E. Story, 1910	**3.00**
Your for Me–Me for You, Meyer, 1922	**1.50**
Your Cheatin' Heart, Williams, 1952 . .	**4.00**

SILVER FLATWARE

Collecting Hints: Focus on one pattern by one maker. Several makers used the same pattern name and a similar pattern design. Always check the backmarks carefully; several thousand patterns were manufactured. Popularity of pattern, not necessarily age, is the key to pricing.

A monogram on a piece will reduce its value substantially, at least by 50%. On Sterling, monograms occasionally can be removed. This, however, is not the case with silver plate. A worn piece of silver plate virtually has no market value.

Silver flatware sold in sets often brings less than pieces sold individually. The reason is that many buyers are looking to replace pieces or add place settings to a pattern they already own. Sterling silver sets certainly retain their value better than silver plate sets. A number of dealers specializing in replacement services have evolved in past years. Many advertise in the weekly issues of *The Antique Trader.*

Flatware marked as Alaska Silver, German Silver, Lashar Silver, and Nickel Silver is not silver plated. These materials are alloys designed to imitate silver plate.

Doris Snell's *American Silverplated Flatware Patterns* contains a section on the care and cleaning of flatware. Individuals must keep in mind that plated wares have only a very thin surface over the base metal. Once removed, it cannot be easily replaced.

Finally, there is one form of silver flatware that has value with a monogram. It is the flatware used by American railroads, for which there exists a strong market among railroad buffs.

History: The silver table service became a hallmark of elegance during the Victorian era. The homes of the wealthy had Sterling silver services made by Gorham, Kirk, Tiffany, and Towle. Silver place settings became part of a young girl's hope chest and a staple wedding gift. Sterling silver consists of 925 parts silver and 75 parts copper per 1,000 parts Sterling.

When electroplating became popular, silver plated flatware gave the common man a chance to imitate the wealthy. Silverplated flatware has a thin layer of silver plated by a chemical process, known as electrolysis, onto a base metal, usually britannia (an alloy of tin, antimony and copper) or white metal (an alloy of tin, copper and lead or bismuth). Leading silver plate manufacturers are Alvin, Gorham, International Silver Co. (a modern company which merged many older companies such as Holmes & Edwards, Rogers, etc.), Oneida, Reed & Barton, Wm. Rogers, and Wallace.

References: Fredna Harris Davis and Kenneth K. Deibel, *Silver Plated Flatware Patterns*, Bluebonnet Press, 1981; Tere Hagan, *Silverplated Flatware: An Identification & Value Guide, Third Edition,*Collector Books, 1986; *The Official Price Guide To American Silver and Silver Plate, Fifth Edition,* House of Collectibles, 1986; Dorothy T. and H. Ivan Rainwater, *American Silverplate,* Schiffer Publishing, Ltd., 1988; Doris Snell, *American Silverplated Flatware Patterns,* Wallace-Homestead, 1980.

Periodical: *The Magazine Silver,* P.O. Box 22217, Milwaukie, OR 97222.

Note: Mono – monogrammed.

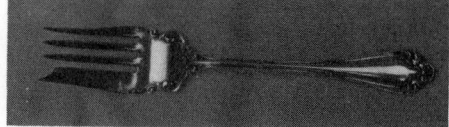

Silver plated, Astoria, cold meat fork, 1835, R Wallace, patent date 1868, $25.00.

SILVER PLATE

The patterns listed below are among the most desirable of silver plate patterns. The following general prices apply to the more common patterns which are not as eagerly collected.

Cake knife	18.00
Cold meat fork	15.00
Dinner fork	9.00
Dinner knife	9.00
Gravy ladle	14.00
Salad fork	9.00
Soup spoon	7.50
Sugar tongs	18.00
Teaspoon	7.50

Bridal Bouquet, Alvin
Butter pick	55.00
Luncheon fork, mono	25.00
Luncheon knife, mono	25.00
Teaspoon	20.00

Fortune, Oneida, 1939
Butter knife	4.25
Dinner knife	4.00
Serving spoon	4.00
Teaspoon	4.00

Moselle
Cold meat fork	35.00
Dinner fork	20.00
Dinner knife	20.00
Food pusher, mono	95.00
Gravy ladle	40.00
Salad fork	20.00
Soup spoon	27.50
Sugar tongs	38.00
Teaspoon	17.50

Orange Blossom, Alvin
Baby spoon, curved handle	45.00
Bouillon spoon	24.00
Gumbo spoon, mono	40.00
Teaspoon, P.M.	18.00
Youth fork, mono	35.00

Oxford
Cold meat fork	24.00
Dinner fork	15.00
Dinner knife	15.00

Salad Set, fork and spoon	45.00
Soup spoon	12.50
Sugar tongs	24.00
Tablespoon	18.00
Teaspoon	12.00

Remembrance, 1847 Rogers
Butter spreader, individual	9.00
Cold meat fork	20.00
Dinner fork	12.00
Dinner knife	12.00
Gravy ladle	18.00
Iced tea spoon	12.00
Salad fork	7.00
Soup spoon	12.50
Sugar tongs	24.00
Teaspoon	12.00

1776, Dominick & Haff
Bouillon spoon	28.00
Luncheon fork	24.00
Luncheon knife	24.00
Salad fork	22.00
Soup spoon	18.00
Tablespoon	35.00
Teaspoon	15.00

STERLING

Acorn, Jensen
Bottle opener	45.00
Carving set, 2 pcs	300.00
Cheese knife	40.00
Cold meat fork	265.00
Fish fork	45.00
Meat fork	125.00
Pie server	135.00
Salad fork	70.00
Salad serving set	550.00
Salt cellar	135.00
Soup spoon, oval	60.00

Adam, Frank M Whiting
Lemon fork	18.00

Bridal Rose, Alvin
Berry serving spoon	190.00
Butter, master	60.00
Cake server	135.00
Citrus spoon	35.00
Gumbo spoon	38.00
Jelly spoon	55.00
Teaspoon	55.00

Buckingham, Gorham
Luncheon fork, mono	24.00

Buttercup, Gorham
Bouillon spoon	22.00
Dessert spoon	28.00
Dinner fork	38.00
Fish slice, mono	200.00
Fruit knife	20.00
Gumbo spoon	32.00
Iced tea spoon	24.00
Luncheon fork	16.00
Luncheon knife, blunt	18.00

Pickle fork	45.00		Fairfax, Durgin	
Salad fork	25.00		Bonbon, mono	25.00
Salad serving fork, mono	90.00		Dinner fork	20.00
Soup ladle, mono	290.00		Dinner knife	20.00
Teaspoon	10.00		Flat spreader	16.00
Cambridge, Gorham			Lemon fork, mono	20.00
Beef fork	30.00		Luncheon fork	20.00
Berry fork	28.00		Luncheon knife	20.00
Bouillon spoon	10.00		Salt spoon, individual	15.00
Citrus spoon, mono	25.00		Seafood fork	17.00
Dessert spoon	25.00		Serving fork	25.00
Luncheon fork	20.00		Teaspoon	18.00
Olive spoon, long, mono	25.00		Tomato server, pierced	90.00
Pickle fork	25.00		Florentine, Alvin	
Pie server	40.00		Butter pick	65.00
Sugar sifter	78.00		Dinner fork	25.00
Sugar tongs, mono	30.00		Dinner knife	25.00
Chantilly, Gorham			Fish fork, 7", mono	55.00
Baby fork	18.00		Lemon fork, mono	30.00
Beef fork	55.00		Luncheon fork	25.00
Bonbon	28.00		Luncheon knife	25.00
Bonbon dish	65.00		Salad fork	25.00
Butter fork	25.00		Teaspoon	20.00
Cheese spreader	30.00		Frontenac, International	
Citrus spoon	25.00		Bonbon	60.00
Cold meat fork			Cake server, mono	165.00
Large	70.00		Cheese spreader, mono	45.00
Medium	55.00		Cold meat fork	155.00
Small	50.00		Demitasse spoon	25.00
Cream soup spoon	24.00		Dessert spoon	40.00
Fish fork, mono	45.00		Dinner knife	65.00
Flat spreader	17.00		Ice tongs, large	475.00
Food pusher, mono	65.00		Luncheon fork, mono	40.00
Gravy ladle	60.00		Luncheon knife, mono	35.00
Ice cream slice, mono	280.00		Master spreader, mono	65.00
Iced tea spoon	26.00		Olive fork, mono	65.00
Infant feeding spoon	30.00		Sauce ladle	65.00
Jelly spoon	25.00		Soup ladle, large, mono	525.00
Lettuce fork	55.00		Sugar shell	45.00
Luncheon fork	22.00		Sugar tongs	45.00
Mayonnaise ladle	30.00		Teaspoon, mono	16.00
Olive fork	18.00		Grande Renaissance, Reed & Barton	
Pie fork, mono	40.00		Butter knife, hollow handle	17.00
Preserve spoon	55.00		Cold meat fork, large	67.00
Salad serving set	225.00		Dinner fork	30.00
Seafood fork	16.00		Gravy ladle	50.00
Serving fork, mono	25.00		Jam server	25.00
Sugar shell	25.00		Luncheon fork	30.00
Tea strainer	100.00		Pie server	29.00
Teaspoon	50.00		Place setting	85.00
Tomato server	75.00		Place spoon	27.00
Chrysanthemum, Durgin			Salad fork	22.00
Berry serving spoon	155.00		Serving spoon	58.00
Cold meat fork	155.00		Sugar spoon	24.00
Dinner fork, mono	35.00		Teaspoon	18.00
Dinner knife, mono	35.00		Tomato server, pierced	60.00
Lettuce fork, mono	150.00		Imperial Queen, Whiting	
Luncheon fork	40.00		Berry serving spoon	60.00
Luncheon knife	40.00		Bonbon server	50.00
Master spreader, mono	50.00		Butter fork	40.00
Salad fork	18.00		Carving set, mono	65.00
Teaspoon	30.00		Cheese scoop, large, mono	120.00

Cold meat fork, mono **125.00**
Demitasse spoon, mono **21.00**
Dessert spoon, mono **38.00**
Dinner fork **45.00**
Dinner knife, mono **60.00**
Gravy ladle **70.00**
Ice cream spoon, mono **32.00**
Jelly slice, mono **100.00**
Salad serving fork, mono **100.00**
Salt spoon **15.00**
Seafood fork **22.00**
Spreader, mono **22.00**
Tablespoon **35.00**
Teaspoon, mono **45.00**
Irving, Wallace, 1899
Baked potato serving fork **31.00**
Butter fork **11.00**
Dinner fork, 7⅜", mono **30.00**
Dinner knife, 9⅝", silverplated blade **18.00**
Luncheon setting **58.00**
Sugar spoon **20.00**
Teaspoon **11.00**
Lancaster, Gorham
Beef fork
Large **35.00**
Small **25.00**
Berry serving spoon, mono **65.00**
Cake saw **225.00**
Citrus spoon **45.00**
Cocktail fork **10.00**
Cold meat fork
Large, mono **65.00**
Medium, mono **45.00**
Small **38.00**
Dessert spoon, mono **28.00**
Dinner knife **60.00**
Gumbo spoon, mono **28.00**
Luncheon fork **16.00**
Luncheon knife, mono **40.00**
Master spreader **25.00**
Napkin ring **68.00**
Oyster ladle **250.00**
Pie server **125.00**
Salad fork **65.00**
Sardine fork, mono **60.00**
Seafood fork, mono **17.00**
Serving fork, 7", gold wash, mono .. **65.00**
Spreader, mono **18.00**
Sugar tongs
Large **35.00**
Small **25.00**
Tablespoon, mono **26.00**
Teaspoon, mono **7.00**
Tomato server, mono **125.00**
Louis XV, Whiting, 1891
Berry serving spoon, small **45.00**
Bouillon ladle, mono **225.00**
Bread tray **275.00**
Cold meat fork, mono **75.00**
Cream ladle **28.00**
Crumber **150.00**
Demitasse spoon, mono **12.00**

Dinner knife, mono **45.00**
Fish fork **45.00**
Fish knife **58.00**
Fish slice, small **110.00**
Ice cream server **125.00**
Ice spoon **325.00**
Lettuce fork, mono **55.00**
Luncheon fork, mono **24.00**
Luncheon knife, mono **30.00**
Macaroni server, mono **240.00**
Master salt spoon **20.00**
Mustard ladle **45.00**
Olive spoon **25.00**
Oyster fork **35.00**
Pickle fork **24.00**
Punch ladle, mono **375.00**
Salad serving set **165.00**
Soup ladle **295.00**
Spreader, mono **20.00**
Strawberry fork **30.00**
Sugar tongs **30.00**
Tea knife **75.00**
Teaspoon **45.00**
Majestic, Alvin
Bouillon, spoon, mono **14.00**
Butter pick **65.00**
Dinner fork **40.00**
Dinner knife **40.00**
Luncheon fork, mono **25.00**
Luncheon knife, mono **25.00**
Master spreader, mono **45.00**
Teaspoon **35.00**
Marazin, Dominick & Haff, 1892
Dinner fork **25.00**
Dinner knife **25.00**
Lemon fork **28.00**
Luncheon fork **25.00**
Luncheon knife **25.00**
Salad serving set, mono **175.00**
Tablespoon, mono **38.00**
Teaspoon, mono **20.00**
Mt. Vernon, Lunt
Bouillon spoon **15.00**
Cold meat fork, mono **55.00**
Jelly spreader **27.00**
Luncheon fork **22.00**
Luncheon knife **16.00**
Serving fork **23.00**
Serving spoon **45.00**
Sugar tongs **25.00**
Tea strainer on stand, 3 pcs **135.00**
Teaspoon **13.00**
New King, Dominick & Haff
Demitasse spoon, mono **14.00**
Flat spreader, mono **16.00**
Seafood fork, mono **16.00**
Tea knife, mono **18.00**
Persian, Tiffany, 1872
Citrus spoon **45.00**
Dinner fork **60.00**
Dinner knife **58.00**
Ice cream fork **50.00**

Serving scoop	400.00
Tablespoon	65.00
Teaspoon	60.00

Repousse, Kirk

Bonbon dish, mono	90.00
Carving set	90.00
Ice tongs	225.00
Iced tea spoon	28.00
Pea spoon	275.00
Relish spoon	30.00

Violet, Wallace

Aspic slice, mono	110.00
Berry serving spoon, mono	85.00
Bonbon, mono	65.00
Bouillon spoon, mono	15.00
Cake saw, mono	100.00
Demitasse spoon, mono	15.00
Dinner fork	30.00
Dinner knife, mono	19.00
Gumbo spoon, mono	36.00
Luncheon fork, mono	22.00
Place setting	45.00
Salad fork, mono	35.00
Spreader, mono	16.00
Sugar tongs, mono	45.00
Teaspoon, mono	13.00

William & Mary, Lunt

Bouillon spoon	18.00
Butter knife, flat handle	15.00
Cream soup spoon	20.00
Lemon fork	15.00
Luncheon fork	25.00
Luncheon knife	18.00
Pickle fork	15.00
Salad fork	18.00
Serving spoon	35.00
Spoon, oval	24.00
Sugar spoon	18.00
Teaspoon	15.00

SLOT MACHINES

Collecting Hints: Check the laws in your state. Some states permit the collecting of slot machines manufactured prior to 1941, while others permit the collecting of all machines 25 years old or older provided that they are not used for gambling. A few states prohibit the ownership of any gambling machine.

A complete slot machine is one that is in working order, has no wood missing on the case, and no cracked castings. All that is needed to restore the machine is some work on appearance. Restoration costs range from $100 to over a thousand dollars. The average restoration includes plating of all castings, refinishing the cabinet, repainting the castings to the original colors, rebuilding the mechanism, tuning up the operation of the mechanism, new reel strips, and a new award card. A quality restoration will add between $400 to $800 to the value of a machine. If buying a restored machine from a dealer, a guarantee usually is given.

Most collectors stay away from foreign machines; foreign coins are hard to find. If the machine has been converted to accept American coins, it frequently may jam or not pay off the proper amount on a winner.

Condition, rarity, and desirability are all very important in determining the value of a machine. Try to find one that is in as close to new condition as possible, as "mint original" machines are bringing the same or more money than restored machines.

History: The first three-reel slot machine was invented in 1905 by Charles Fey in San Francisco. The machine was called the Liberty Bell. One of the three known survivors can be seen at the Liberty Bell Saloon, his grandson's restaurant, in Reno, Nevada.

In 1910 the classic fruit symbols were copyrighted by Mills Novelty Company. They were immediately copied by other manufacturers. The first symbols still are popular on contemporary casino machines. The wood cabinet was replaced by cast iron in 1916. By 1922 aluminum fronts were the norm for most machines. In 1928 the jackpot was added.

The 1930s innovations included more reliable and improved mechanisms with more sophisticated coin entry and advance and slug detection systems. In the 1940s drill-proof and cheat-resistant devices were added. The 1950s brought electronic lighting and electronics.

Although the goosenecks of the 1920s and 1930s often are more intricate and rarer than the models of the 1930s and 1940s, the gimmick and more beautiful machines of this later period, such as Rolatop, Treasury, Kitty or Triplex, bring more money.

References: Jerry Ayliffe, *American Premium Guide To Jukeboxes and Slot Machines,* Books Americana, 1985; Daniel R. Mead, *Loose Change Blue Book Slot Machine Price Guide, 1986-87 Edition,* published by author, 1987; Richard D. and Barbara Reddock, *Price Guide to Antique Slot Machines,* Wallace-Homestead, 1981.

Periodical: *Chicagoland Antique Advertising, Slot Machine & Jukebox Gazette* and *Coin Op Newsletter* are published by Ken Durham, 909 26th Street, N.W., Washington, DC 20037; *The Coin Slot,* 4401 Zephyr Street, Wheatridge, CO 80033; *Loose Change,,* 1515 South Commerce Street, Las Vegas, NV 89102.

Note: All machines listed are priced as if they were in "good" condition, meaning the machine is complete and working. An incomplete or nonworking machine is worth only 30% to 70% of the listed price.

Machines listed are for 5¢ and 10¢. Quarter and 50¢ machines can run several hundred dollars higher. A silver dollar machine, if you are lucky enough to find one, can add $400 to $800 to the price.

Bergerman Co, Paul E., The Chicago Ridge, 22 x 11 x 57", upright, paneled oak sides, one wheel, five choices on coin head, restored, c1897 . **3,000-3,500.00**

Buckley Bones, counter top model, payout, 1936 .... **2,000-4,000.00**

Caille
Big Six and Lone Star, combination, copper plated casing, oak cabinet, music box, 1904 ...... **24,000-30,000.00**
Detroit Floor Wheel, six way play action, 1898 .... **8,000-11,000.00**
Doughboy, plain front, coin entry on right, escalator chain drive raises coins upwards, center jackpot **500-700.00**
Silent Sphinx Bell, painted sphinx dec, 1932 .... **1,300-2,500.00**

Fey Liberty Bell, three reel, payout, 1905 .... **26,000-35,000.00**

Jennings
Ciga-Rola, combination slot and cigarette machine, cigarette pack pay out, 1937 .... **600-1,200.00**
Duchess, 20" h, three reel, mints or candy displayed behind windows flanking jackpot, orig decal, c1934 .... **1,600-2,650.00**
Electojax, electric, floor model, 1933 .... **1,200-2,400.00**
Export Chief, chrome finish, brass tiered triangle above jackpot **800-1,100.00**
Jackpot Bell, two bright blue Dutch Boys on front, 1929 ...... **900-1,800.00**
Silver Chief, chrome front with Indian head, 1937 .... **700-1,400.00**
Today Vendor Bell, four columns, Dutch boy dec on front, 1926 .... **900-1,800.00**
Victoria, three reel, two jackpots, fortune strips, c1932 .... **1,500-2,500.00**

Mills
Big Six, six numbered and color coded payoff combinations, 1904 .... **8,000-11,000.00**
Black Cherry, painted silver with black case, four applied cherries, escalator, bib award card front **850-1,100.00**
Chrome Bell, raised diamonds on both sides of front, 1939 ... **700-1,500.00**
Criss-Cross, hi-top, orig condition, working **700.00**
Dewey, floor model, ornate 6" legs, cast iron trim and six way coin head, color wheel **5,500-8,000.00**

Horsehead Bonus, escalator, horsehead above jackpot, BONUS flags nest to coin entry, pays 18 when completed **1,200-1,600.00**
Jewell Bell, high top, 1947 ... **700-1,400.00**
Lion Front, gooseneck coin entry, lion with open mouth around jackpot, 1931 .... **1,050-1,450.00**
Operator Bell, cast iron, metal sides, 1910 .... **4,000-7,000.00**

Mills, Jackpot, c1930, $2,000.00.

Poinsettia, gooseneck coin entry, flowers on lower casting, liberty bell under coin entry **800-1,100.00**
Skyscraper, gooseneck coin entry, 1933 .... **1,200-1,500.00**
War Eagle, eagle design around jackpot, escalator coin advance, coin entry on left, award card to right of reels **1,100-1,500.00**

Pace
Bantam, gooseneck, playing card design on jackpot, fortune telling reel strips, marked "Pace" under lock :.................... **850-1,150.00**
8 Star Bell, circular coin escalator, c1948 .... **600-1,200.00**
Operator's Bell, circular coin escalator, 1927 .... **1,000-2,000.00**

Watling
Brownie, counter top model, one reel, payout, 1900 .... **1,750-3,500.00**
Exchange, counter top model, one wheel, oak case, five way coin head, c1910 .... **2,000-3,000.00**
Jefferson, counter top model, 1910 .... **2,400-4,750.00**
Rol-a-top, rotary escalator, eagle above twin jackpot
Checkerboard **1,300-1,700.00**
Cherry front **1,900-2,300.00**

L. E. SMITH GLASS COMPANY

Collecting Hints: L.E. Smith glass is hand made and usually unmarked. Some older pieces bear a "C" in a circle with a tiny "S." Current glass has a paper label. The collector of older items should especially study black and Depression pieces. The Moon and Star pattern has been reproduced for many years. Smith glass of recent manufacture is found in house sales, flea markets, and gift and antique shops.

History: L. E. Smith Glass Company was founded in 1907 in Mount Pleasant, Pennsylvania, by Lewis E. Smith. Although Smith left the company shortly after establishment, it still bears his name. Early products were cooking articles and utilitarian objects such as glass percolator tops, fruit jars, sanitary sugar bowls, and reamers.

In the 20s, green, amber, canary, amethyst, and blue colors were introduced along with an extensive line of soda fountain wares. The company also made milk glass, console and dresser sets, and the always popular fish-shaped aquariums. During the 1930s, Smith became the largest producer of black glass. Popular dinner set lines were Homestead, Melba, Do-Si-Do, By Cracky, Romanesque, and Mount Pleasant.

L. E. Smith presently manufactures colored reproduction glass and interesting decorative objects. A factory outlet is available as well as factory tours. Contact the factory for specific times.

Reference: Hazel Marie Weatherman, *Colored Glassware of the Depression Era 2*, Glassbooks, Inc., 1982.

Creamer and Sugar, miniature, orange to red orange, 2" h, $10.00.

Animal
    Cat, black, reclining, marked, c1930   **20.00**
    Cow, black, reclining, marked, c1930   **18.00**
    Dog, Scottie, black, reclining, marked, c1930 .... **20.00**
    Goose, black, reclining, marked, c1930 .... **18.00**
    Horse
        Blue, rearing **35.00**

        Crystal **20.00**
        Green **38.00**
    Rooster, black, reclining, marked, c1930 .... **15.00**
    Swan, small, white opaque **15.00**
Aquarium, 10" h, 15" l, green, King-Fish, c1920 .... **250.00**
Bookends, rearing horse, 1930s, pr
    Amber, 8" h, c1940 .... **42.00**
    Crystal **30.00**
Bowl
    Amethyst, #77 .... **8.00**
    Melba green, 10½", ruffled **10.00**
Cake Plate, Do-Si-Do, handles **12.00**
Candlesticks, pr
    By Cracky, green **12.00**
    Mt Pleasant, black **15.00**
    Romanesque, pink **10.00**
Casserole, 9½" l, oval, Melba **12.00**
Compote, cov, Moon n' Star, amberina **35.00**
Cookie Jar, cov, black amethyst, floral dec **45.00**
Creamer
    Do-Si-Do **3.00**
    Homestead, pink **5.00**
    Moon n' Star, amberina **10.00**
Cruet, Moon n' Star, ruby **30.00**
Cup and Saucer
    Do-Si-Do, pink, gold trim **6.50**
    Melba, pink **4.50**
Fairy Lamp, Moon n' Star, ruby **30.00**
Fern Dish, 3 ftd, 1930s
    Greek Key
        Black **18.00**
        White, opaque **8.00**
    Kent **8.50**
Flower Block, By Cracky, 3" **3.75**
Flower Pot, 4", black, silver floral dec **8.00**
Goblet, water, Moon 'n Star, amberina **15.00**
Mayonnaise, Kent **6.00**
Mug, crystal, 12 oz **5.00**
Parfait
    Homestead **5.00**
    Soda Shop **5.00**
Planter, black amethyst, nude dancers on sides, marked "L. E. Smith" **45.00**
Plate
    6", Melba, amethyst **4.50**
    8"
        Homestead, pink **4.50**
        Mt Pleasant, pink, scalloped edge **6.00**
    9", Homestead, grill **5.00**
Rose Bowl, Mt Pleasant, cobalt, 3 ftd, rolled edges **18.00**
Salt and Pepper Shakers, pr
    Dresden, white **18.00**
    Mt Pleasant, cobalt **24.00**
Sherbet, Romanesque, black **10.00**
Slipper, 2½", Daisy and Button, amber **4.00**
Soda Glass
    Jumbo, crystal, ribbed **6.50**
    Soda Shop **6.00**

Sugar, cov
Homestead	**5.50**
Kent	**6.50**
Melba	**6.00**
Moon n' Star, amberina	**12.00**

Tray, 15 x 6", oval
Black	**12.00**
Crystal	**10.00**

Vase
6", black, silver bands	**10.00**
7", Moon n' Star, blue	**8.50**
7½", fan, Romanesque, black	**12.00**
Violet Bowl, Hobnail, white opaque ..	**7.50**
Window Box, F. W. Woolworth	**25.00**

Wine
Moon 'n Star, amberina	**12.00**
Ruby bowl, crystal stem	**5.00**

SNOWDOMES

Collecting Hints: Snowdomes are water-filled paperweights with figurines and/or panels inside a globe or dome, which are magnified by the water. The water contains loose particles (white snow, metallic or colored flecks, etc.) which swirl when the globe is turned upside down.

There are two distinctly different types of snowdomes. The first have round, leaded glass balls set on a base of ceramic, bakelite, or other plastic, wood or "marble." These are older and generally 3–4" high. The second have plastic objects, in dozens of shapes ranging from simple designs such as drums, cubes, and bottles, to elaborate figurals. Production of this second type, which average 2½" high, started in the 1950s.

Within both categories, especially the plastic, there are many sub-groups and themes which appeal to collectors, e.g., Christmas (probably the most familiar), tourist souvenirs, Biblical scenes, Disney and other cartoon characters, commercial advertisements, fairy tales, scenic railroads, famous buildings, sailing ships, geographic regions, or one-from-each-state.

There is great variety not only in the subject of the inner image of snowdomes, but in the outer shapes as well. Collectors find it challenging to find as many of the dozens of shapes as possible.

Figurals are divided into two categories: first, the entire object is a figural, such as a house, apple, a bear, or seated cartoon character with the water ball incorporated into the design at different places, and second, a plastic figurine is placed on top of the dome. Christmas figurals alone constitute a large category. At least six different figurines of a standing Santa are known, to say nothing of the dozens of elaborate designs. Other novelty features include battery-powered flashing lights which illuminate the inner scene; salt and pepper snowdomes, perpetual calendars

and banks designed in the base; and water/ring-toss games.

Many snowdomes have parts that move: a see-saw, bobbing objects attached to strings, and small objects that move back and forth on a groove in the bottom of the dome. Objects range from a ferry or bus to Elvis Presley.

The value of a particular snowdome depends on several factors, starting with the physical condition of the object itself. In dealing with glass domes it is important that the water is clear enough to see the object or is at a level which does not distort the image. Although it is possible to open and refill many of the older glass and ceramic or bakelite base styles, it is a risky procedure. Examine, also, whether the ceramic base is cracked, the condition of the label (if there is one), the condition of the figurine, and whether the paint has chipped or the colors seem faded.

The water level is not a factor in any plastic snowdome that has a plug either on the bottom of the base, or at the top of the dome. Bottle-on-its-side shapes cannot be refilled, and the domes designed by the Marx Company in the 1960s have safety plugs that cannot be removed. Safety caps on the plugs of snowdomes made for "Walt Disney Production" can be pried off with a knife point. Murky water can be drained and replaced. Clumped, dirty snow can be caught in a handkerchief, washed, and put back. While distilled water is preferred, tap water will stay clear for a year.

Of great importance is whether the front of the dome is free of streaking that obscures the scene inside. Any cracks or holes would prevent refilling with water.

While long-time collectors recognize common snowdomes, even new collectors can make an educated guess at scarcity by remembering a few key points. Snowdomes with a glass, ceramic, or bakelite, base, single figurine, and no specific label on the base were the most common. The same figurine with a decal on the base saying "Souvenir of....." is more valuable as a smaller number were sold of that figurine with that particular decal. The same figurine was used for innumerable places, hence there is often no connection between the object and the place. An incongruous match-up may have value to a particular collector, but would not necessarily affect its market value. Of greater value are those snowdomes which were obviously made for a specific place or event, where the object and the decal match, e. g., the ceramic base snowdome with a bisque Trylon and Perisphere in globe, with a decal "1939 Worlds Fair."

Plastic snowdomes are also subject to the same principle of logic, "generic" ones, without a name plaque, had the widest possible distribution.

Souvenirs of states and popular tourist attractions had a wide distribution. Since many more were made and sold their prices are lower than commemoratives or souvenirs of smaller places. SCARCITY, which can be determined by the size or popularity of a city or tourist attraction, is very important in pricing snowdomes and is a factor in the desirability of particular domes.

While mismatched figurines and decals of the glass/ceramic style should not be priced higher than logical match-ups, there are many examples of obvious mistakes in the plastic variety which are worth more than a perfect one, e. g., a dome with "Milano" printed upside down or a souvenir of a religious shrine with a "Kings Island" plaque.

The age of a plastic snowdome affects its value and can usually be determined by examining stylistic differences. It is often the style associated with a certain era that bears on its value, rather than the actual age itself. Generally, early snowdomes (50s and 60s) have greater detail and more sophisticated colors. Later snowdomes are less rich in detail and have a harsh, mass-produced appearance. Many early mass-produced snowdomes look as if they were hand-painted. Characters often have a "folk" quality to them. Most important, earlier snowdomes have much more specific detail. 1950s and 1960s state souvenirs, have many panels inside, depicting noted tourist attractions, famous citizens, and the state slogan. Later versions use only one feature. the newest mass-produced state souvenirs consist of a rainbow with a pot of gold and a glittery outline of the state's shape on a clear panel. There is no individuality.

The effects of time on snowdomes vary. A dome's physical deterioration, i. e., fading, chipping paint, even "bleaching" of the words on the plaque must be constantly evaluated by the collector. The plastic snowdomes that were introduced in the 50s, were fragile objects, easily broken, and often discarded. It is indeed a challenge to find unusual "survivors."

History: The earliest American paperweight snowdomes were leaded glass globes set on heavy black ceramic base paperweights, and were manufactured by Atlas Crystal Works of Covington, Tennessee and Trenton, New Jersey. The company started production in the 1920s, and patents were granted in the 1940s. Initially they used unpainted bisque figurines including the popular "snowbabies." Later figurines were painted and included animals and characters associated with winter or Christmas. In the late 1930s, Atlas made a series of Art Deco skyscrapers, using three-dimensional bisque statuettes with gold decals on the front of the base identifying the building: "Rockefeller Ctr., Radio City, N.Y." During World War II, they made a series of figurines featuring servicemen, generals, and equipment.

Another manufacturer in the 1930s used this same figure, and other figurines, on a brown ceramic base, which had three tiers. In addition to making such specific paperweights as one labeled "1939 World's Fair" with a bisque Trylon and Perisphere, this same manufacturer interchanged his large assortment of figurines, seemingly at random, with souvenir decals of many cities.

Glass snowdome paperweights were also manufactured in Germany, starting in the 1920s. Several German patents were granted in the late 1930s. Production stopped during the war, but resumed in the early 1950s when the Koziol firm began producing the familiar dome-shaped plastic design. The company's founder claims it was the "domed" view of a winter snow scene as seen through the arched rear view window of a VW Beetle that inspired the dome design. Koziol continues to manufacture hand-painted snowdomes, as does Walters and Prediger, another West German firm.

Snowdomes were also made in Italy, starting in the 1930s, with a distinctive design that is still used today. The base and short stand on which the glass ball sits is covered with shells and sand. The base is often scalloped. Early domes were sometimes placed on a whole, flat shell. The appropriate text was hand-written in ink on a small shell at the front of the base and matched the image on the flat rubber panel in the ball.

Bakelite bases, black at first, with thinner glass balls, were introduced in the 1940s when patents were granted to both American and Canadian manufacturers. Unlike the earlier black ceramic bases which were smooth-surfaced, the black bakelite bases were "tiered."

In the 1950s, the Driss Company, Chicago, Illinois, made four designs of popular characters—"Frosty the Snowman," "Rudolph the Red Nosed Reindeer in the Snow," "Davy Crockett," and "The Lone Ranger: The Last Round-Up"—with the decals on the base. The Davy Crockett and Lone Ranger used identical figurines, in identical poses, with different clothes and accessories. The Lone Ranger also was a ring-toss game, You looped his lasso over the calf's head. The Driss Company made many other "novelty" designs, such as an American flag with red, white, and blue "snow."

Progressive Products, of Union, New Jersey, created a variation of the classic snowdome in the 1940s and 1950s. They filled their glass ball with an oily liquid, either clear or yellow, and used a glittery "snow." They squared the base and widened it at the bottom, giving it a more angular, Art Deco look. In addition to their "generic" snowdomes with a single object inside, they made souvenirs with the name of a place written on the front of the base.

Their specialties, however, were awards and commercial advertisements. Many of the awards used a royal blue or red base with white trim around the bottom. One image could be adapted to many uses: a golden crown suspended in the liquid was used for a Winter Sports King, an ad for "Crown Termite Control," and a Baltimore newspaper. The same was true for a specific backdrop panel. There were three basic designs—an Art Deco city skyline, country landscape, and a Southwest Indian scene. A wide range of objects and images were placed inside the ball: trucks, ships, a Masonic symbol, faucet, a fishing boat used for seafood restaurants, and even a two-sided photo of a publishing house owner.

An Austrian manufacturer currently specilizes in winter and Christmas scenes. They have glass balls, either black or white plastic base, and a red "Made in Austria" sticker on top of the ball.

With the exception of the two West German manufacturers noted above, most plastic snowdomes made since their introduction in the 1950s have been "Made in Hong Kong." Copyright marks appear on a few Walt Disney Productions, King Features, and The Louis Marx Co domes. The Marx domes also have a date inscribed in Roman numerals on the bottom. The Curt S. Adler Co., New York City, holds copyrights, some granted in the U.K., for their many elaborate Christmas figurals. Adler's domes also are made in Hong Kong.

A study of plastic domes reveals bases bearing manufacturers labels from Taiwan, Japan, Canada, France, and even Florida.

Advisor: Nancy McMichael.

Advertising, left: "Crown Termite Control," 2¾" d glass ball with oily liquid, 3" w x 4" h brown bakelite base, 1950s, $35.00; right: "Jello," plastic dome, 3¾" l, 2¾" w, 2½" h, 1970s, $10.00.

Advertising
Bookbinder's Restaurant, 125 Walnut St, Philadelphia, PA, 2½" glass globe, brown, sq 2½" base, fishing boat and lobsters, early 1950s ...   **40.00**
Mountain Dew, 2¾ x 2¼ x 2", soda bottle and man on seesaw, late 1970s **12.00**
Philco, 2½" d glass ball, 5½ x 4" rect

black bakelite base, Philco logo, early 1950s **50.00**
Sears Kenmore, America's Largest Selling Washers and Dryers, 3½ x 2½ x 1", rect, one piece salt and pepper shaker, woman standing next to appliances, 1970s **17.00**
The Coolest House of all will be air-conditioned Wall to Wall by Westinghouse, 2½" glass globe, sq blue base, living room with "Cool" grid overlay, late 1950s **35.00**
Amusement Park
Cedar Point, Sandusky, OH, plastic, two dolphins on seesaw, gold printed letters on plaque on waved base, 1970s **8.00**
Coney Island, 2" d glass ball, scalloped base with sea shells, bathing beauty, 1940s **15.00**
Tivoli, 2¾ x 2¼ x 2", clown at entrance to park **7.00**
Wildworld, 2¾" plastic ball, 2⅞" red base, water slide, early 1980s **5.00**
Animal Park
Catskill Game Farm, 2¾ x 2¼ x 2", plastic dome, two elephants on slide, 1980s **4.00**
Pocono Wild Animal Farm, 2¼ x 2 x 2", plastic dome, deer and bear on seesaw, 1960s **7.00**
Bank, plastic, 2¾" d ball, red base, "Mt Vernon, VA" printed on front, house scene, 1960s **8.00**
Boat
Belle of Louisville, 2½ x 2¼ x 2", plastic dome, paddle boat, 1980s   **4.00**
Bottle
Flatside
Ambassador Bridge, Windsor, Canada, 5" l, plastic, bridge, town, and paddle boat, late 1970s ...   **7.00**
Biloxi, MS, 6" l, alligator on seesaw, 1970s **7.00**
Caverns of Luray, 5" l, cavern scene, early 1970s **6.00**
Harrisburg, PA, State Capital, 5" l, three panels, flag, state house, and memorials, late 1960s **8.00**
The Mayflower, 6" l, ship, town, and rock, 1970s **6.00**
USS Yorktown-CVIO, Patriots Point, Charleston, SC, 5" l plastic, carrier, relief 3-D helicopter and plane, 1970s **10.00**
Round, sits on stand
Blue Nose, 4½" l, 1½" d, sailing boat, 1970s **5.00**
Texas, The Lone Star State, 5¼" l, bull moves on slide, oil wells, gold cap, early 1970s **5.00**
Breweriana, Anheuser Busch, Inc., Mer-

rimac, NH, 3¾ x 2¾ x 1¾", plastic, oval, dark blue, sits on two legs, Clydesdales, wagon and brewery scene, 1970s **20.00**

Calendar, plastic, 2¾" d ball, red base with four openings where date shows, San Francisco, CA, bridge and city scene, cable car moves on slide, 1970s **4.00**

Cartoon Character

Dogpatch USA, 2⅝ x 2½ x ¾", TV shape, plastic, brown, shows Mammy and Pappy Yokum, 1960s **10.00**

Pink Panther, plastic dome, Panther skating around Inspector Clouseau, 1980s **7.00**

Popeye, figural, seated, plastic, holds water ball between hands, Olive Oyl, Sweetpea, and Wimpy in row boat that moves, King Features Syndicate, 1950s **15.00**

Character

Little Orphan Annie, 3⅝ x 2⅞ x 2¾", plastic dome, Annie and Sandy, 1970s **9.00**

Lone Ranger, round glass ball, bakelite base, green, yellow, and red, "Lone Ranger: The Last Round-Up" on decal, 1950s **25.00**

Christmas

Bell, clear, red church and pine trees, 1970s **5.00**

Boot, clear, five pine trees, red house, waving snowman, and children, holly trim, 1970s **5.00**

Chimney, red brick design, Santa's head and arms raise, Santa on sled in cube shape dome, marked "Curt S. Adler Inc, Reg Appl 961 554," 1970s **6.00**

Elf, figural, red suit, green jester collar, ball in tummy, snowman, trees, and house scene, 1960s **9.00**

Fireplace, 3½ x 3¼ x 2¼", child sleeping in pajamas in hearth, Santa in sled on seesaw in dome, marked "CSA Inc, Curt S. Adler, Inc., NY, NY 10010," 1970s **12.00**

Frosty the Snowman

Figural, 5½" h, standing black boots and top hat, removable broomstick, angel and deer in ball, 1960s **7.00**

Round, decal, yellow plastic base, marked "Frosty the Snowman, A & RS, Inc," 1950s **25.00**

Mountain, 4¾ x 4¾ x 3", frosted, textured plastic, red houses perched on ledges, three wise men leading camels to Bethlehem in dome, 1960s **12.00**

Nativity Scene, 4½ x 3¼ x 3", round dome, eight panels, three dimensional figures, late 1950s **7.00**

Rocking Horse, white horse, red runner, red fabric mane, 2¾" dome with Santa in sleigh on seesaw, marked "Curt S. Adler, Inc., NY, NY 10010," 1970s **12.00**

Rudolph the Red Nosed Reindeer, green plastic base, "Rudolph the Red Nosed Reindeer in the Snow, copyright RLM" on decal, 1950s . **20.00**

Santa

Figural, 5¾ x 3½ x 1", driving sleigh, two reindeer, rect dome with elf sitting under a mushroom, 1960s **11.00**

Pivot, plastic, round dome, holding boy and girl, yellow bag of toys, marked "MCMLXVI" and "Louis Marx" **7.00**

Sitting on reindeer, plastic, waving, cut out stars light up, round dome, 1970s **10.00**

Walking, plastic, bag of toys over shoulder, round dome, 1970s .. **3.00**

Workshop, figural, red brick design, Mr. and Mrs. Claus work at workbench, rocking horse, marked "SANTA'S WORKSHOP" on top **12.00**

Sled, 2¼ x 1¼ x 1¾", Santa, tree with candles, and reindeer, green, brown, and orange, arch dome, orange snowflake plug, beige base, marked "Made in West Germany," 1950s **12.00**

Three snowmen, slanted eyes, red plastic base, seaweed trees, marked "Made in Japan," 1960s **6.00**

Cowboy, on bucking bronco, 2¾" d, glass globe, bisque figurine, oily liquid, red bakelite base, 1950s **20.00**

Disney

Disneyland, 2¾ x 2¼ x 2", plastic dome, Tinkerbell and castle, 1970s **8.00**

Mickey Mouse, figural, plastic, 5" h, holds 2" d ball in lap, castle scene, 1960s **20.00**

The Wonderful World of Disney, 3⅝ x 2⅞ x 2¾", plastic dome, Mickey and Minnie in front of castle, multicolored snow, early 1970s .. **9.00**

Fairy Tales

Hansel and Gretel, plastic dome, green base, children, witch, and forest scene, marked "Made in Western Germany," 1980s **4.00**

Snow White and the Seven Dwarfs, 1⅞ x 2¼ x 1¼", plastic stylized dome, green flower plug, marked "Made in Western Germany," late 1950s **12.00**

Figural

Bear, walking, plastic, two bears on seesaw and "Great Smokey Mts," 1970s **8.00**

Bird, 3½" h, 2½" d plastic ball, hand holding bird seed and two birds, 4" l green wavy base, early 1980s .. **12.00**

Captain, 5¾ h, dressed in uniform with right arm raised, 2½" d ball in tummy, sailing ship, "Bar Harbor, ME," 1970s **12.00**

Church, steeple, 2¼ x 2¾ x 2½", plastic, altar, bride, and groom, marked "W Germany" on bottom, 1980s **10.00**

Figural, left: Old Salts, plastic, 5½" h, 2¾" d water ball, 1970s, $10.00; right: Mickey Mouse, 5½" h, Disneyland in 2¾" d water ball, 1970s, $10.00.

Elephant, 3¼" l, sits on plastic dome, 1970s **13.00**

Frog, 5" h, plastic, green, sitting upright, 2½" d ball in middle, frogs and grass scene, "Puerto Rico" on plaque, 1980s **9.00**

Swordfish, 4½" l, arches over dome, "Florida," early 1970s **10.00**

Tiger, 3½" , two tigers in dome, "Southwick's Wild Animal Farm, Mendon, MA," 1970s **14.00**

Flag, American, glass globe, plastic white base, red, white, and blue snow, marked "The Driss Company, Chicago, IL, Made in USA," 1950s . **30.00**

Fraternal, Masonic symbol, glass ball, oily liquid, blue bakelite base, printed on base "Mizpah Lodge, No 245, F & A.M. Harry J. Freedman W. M. 1958" **40.00**

Game, ring toss

Giraffe, plastic dome, two giraffes, hoops go over necks, decal "The Pacifier," 1970s **8.00**

Lobster, 3 x 2 x 1", plastic dome, plastic hoops, marked "Louisiana," early 1980s **5.00**

Statue of Liberty, plastic dome, hoops go over upraised arm, 1980s **4.00**

Halloween

Cat, 6½" h, figural, black, 2¾" d orange plastic ball, witch riding broomstick **12.00**

Jack 'O Lantern, black cat, 3¾" d clear glass ball, wood base **7.00**

Owl, 5½" h, figural, brown, outstretched wing, scarecrow in 2¼" ball, orange ground **12.00**

Three legs, extend upwards, glass globe, multicolored hoops, oily liquid, sq red plastic base with blue trim, marked "Atlantic City," 1950s **30.00**

Moving Parts

Balloons on string, 3½ x 2¾ x 3", monkey swings on hook, four animals in cage, "Philadelphia Zoo," 1970s **8.00**

Champagne, shot, and martini glass on strings, 3¾ x 2¾ x 2¼", naked lady, painted "The Bar is Open" bar scene backdrop, "This one is on me" plaque, "Las Vegas" on outside, 1960s **12.00**

Dice, 2⅝ x 2 x 2¼", red, float in water, blue ground, main strip in Vegas scene, 1970s **5.50**

Fish on string, green seaweed, three fish, "Ocean City, MD," 1970s .. **4.50**

Rocking Horse on glider, 3⅛ x 1¼ x 2⅝", toy soldier on his back, arched dome, black base, 1970s . **5.00**

Train, steam locomotive, moves in front of train image background, small dome, 1980s **4.00**

Trolley, Golden Gate Bridge, Chinatown background, small dome, "San Francisco," 1970s **5.00**

Wagon, horse drawn, bottle shape, moves in and out of covered barn, large dome, "New Hampshire," 1970s **7.00**

Museum

Ripley's Museum, St. Augustine, FL," "Cabin of Pennies," "Tow(sic) Headed Calf," plastic bottle, 6" l, flat sides, three plaques, three scenes, and background panel, 1960s **8.00**

Salem Witch Museum, 1692, 2¾ x 2¼ x 2", small plastic dome, house and witch on broomstick, 1970s . **7.00**

The American Museum of Natural History, Hayden Planetarium, NY," 2¾ x 2¼ x 2", plastic dome, printing on back, camera and city sky line scene, 1980s **4.00**

Nursery Rhyme

Humpty Dumpty, 2½" d glass ball,

sitting painted figurine, tiered white
plastic base, early 1980s **4.00**
Old Mother Hubbard, small plastic
dome, transparent plaque, mother,
dog, and bare cupboard, late 1960s **7.00**

Ocean Liner
Queen Mary, Long Beach, CA, plastic
dome, cut out of ship on ocean,
1970s **7.00**
SS United States, 2¾" glass globe, oily
liquid, ship in front of Art Deco skyline, blue base with red trim and
white printing, 1950s **45.00**

Regional
Arizona, 3 x 2½ x 1¼", plastic, white
base, road runner and cactus,
1970s **6.00**
Indiana, The Hoosier State, plastic
dome, Indy 500 scene, 1970s **6.00**
Georgia, The Peach State, bottle, 5"
l, flat sides, plastic, two alligators
on seesaw, tree, and mountain,
1960s **8.00**
Montana, 5" h, figural, black bear,
plastic, 2½" ball, two deer on see—
saw, state name on chest, marked
"UVC-Inc 1972" on bottom **10.00**
Virginia, small dome, state outline
and bird on branch, late 1970s .. **4.00**

Religious
Crucifixion, 3⅝ x 2⅞ x 2¾", plastic
dome, Jesus on cross, battery operated, 1960s **15.00**
Moses Crossing Red Sea, 2¾ x 2¼ x
2", plastic dome, Moses with raised
staff parting the sea, 1970s **9.00**
Nativity Scene, small plastic dome,
1980s **3.00**
The Last Supper, 2¾ x 2¼ x 2", plastic
dome, disciples at table, 1970s .. **9.00**
Roly Poly, snowman figural top, 2¾"

**Left: War Between the States, plastic
dome, 3¾" l, 2¾" w, 2½" h, 1970s, $4.00;
right: airplane, banking, painted bisque
plane, marking on wings, 2¾" d leaded
glass ball, 4" h ceramic base, 1940s,
$35.00**

dome, Santa in sled, marked "CSA
Inc. 4482 Curt S. Adler Inc, NY, NY
10010, UK Design Reg No 969 255,"
1970s **10.00**

Salt and Pepper Shakers, pr
Civil War, 3¼ x 1¼ x 2", plastic, pink
"P" with American flag, blue "S"
with Rebel flag, soldiers and cannon scene, back compartments,
1960s **14.00**
Florida's Silver Springs, 3 x 2¼ x 1",
TV shape, plastic, blue "P," pink
"S," boat on seesaw, side compartments, 1970s **12.00**
Sydney Harbor Bridge, plastic, rect,
mustard yellow, ship moves on
slide and bridge scene, 1970s **13.00**

Soap Dish, 4 x 4¼", shell shape, plastic,
blue, dome sits on back of dish,
bridge and river scene, "1000 Islands,
NY," 1970s **15.00**

Souvenir
Denmark, 2¾ x 2¼ x 2", plastic
dome, Viking ship, 1960s **7.00**
Dewey Beach, 2¾ x 2¼ x 2", plastic
dome, seagull and sea shells, 1960s **6.00**
Durban, South Africa, plastic dome,
costumed man pulling carriage,
1970s **10.00**
Empire State Building, New York, NY,
glass globe, tiered black bakelite
base, white bisque figurine, gold
decal, 1930s **35.00**
Mammoth Cave, KY, plastic dome,
cavern scene, 1960s **7.00**
Niagara Falls, 2" d ball, falls scene,
mirror base with seashells, 1930s . **25.00**
Ocean City, MD, 2¾ x 1¾", rect plastic dome with goldfish on string,
1980s **2.00**
Philadelphia, PA, plastic dome, yellow background, Liberty Bell and
two flags, early 1980s **3.00**
Ricardo di Roma, 2½" glass ball, Vatican scene, white marble tiered
base, 1930s **25.00**
Roy Rogers and Dale Evans Museum,
Victorville, CA, plastic dome, barn
scene and Trigger moves on slide,
1960s **10.00**
Scotland, 3¼ x 2¼", drum shape,
plastic, Bagpiper figure, red top,
blue bottom, gold braid criss-
crosses, 1980s **5.00**
St. Paul's Cathedral, London, 3⅝ x
2⅞ x 2¾", plastic dome, cathedral
and double decker bus move on
slide, early 1980s **5.00**
Souvenir of Mardi Gras, New Orleans, 2½" ball, painted King Rex figure, black ceramic base with gold
decal, early 1930s **50.00**

World's Fair

1939 New York World's Fair, Trylon and Perisphere bisque figurine, brown ceramic base

   With decal **50.00**

   Without decal **40.00**

1964–65 New York World's Fair

Unisphere, plastic, round ball, red sq base, perpetual calendar, "Unisphere presented by USS United States Steel, 1964 NYWF" **12.00**

Vatican Pavilion, plastic dome, two Swiss guards scene, pavilion background, "New York World's Fair" plaque **10.00**

Expo 67, Montreal, Canada, plaque, fireworks background **12.00**

1982 Worlds Fair, 3½ x 2 x 1¼", tall dome, Sunsphere **7.00**

1984 World's Fair, plastic dome, fair archway, ferry moves back and forth on groove, plaque **5.00**

World War II

Douglas MacArthur, America's Hero, glass ball, black ceramic base, bisque bust **35.00**

General Eisenhower, glass ball, black ceramic base, bisque bust, "General Dwight D. Eisenhower, Commander in Chief, Allied Invasion Forces" decal, marked "Atlas Crystal Works, Covington, TN, US Patents 231423/4/5," 1940s **50.00**

Plane, painted bisque figurine, red star on wings, tail and nose markings, glass ball, black ceramic base, marked "Atlas Crystal Works, Trenton, NJ, Patents Pending, Made in USA," 1940s **35.00**

Sailor, glass globe, saluting figure in sailor suit, black ceramic base, 1940s **30.00**

SODA BOTTLES

History: Soda bottles were made to contain soda water and soft drinks. A beverage manufacturer usually made his own bottles and sold them within a limited area. Coddball stoppers and a stopper perfected by Hutchinson were popular with early manufacturers before the advent of metal or screw top caps.

References: Paul & Karen Bates, *Commemorative Soda Bottles,* Soda Mart, 1988; Paul & Karen Bates, *Embossed Soda Bottles,* Soda Mart, 1988; Paul & Karen Bates, *Painted Label Soda Bottles,* Soda Mart, 1988; Ralph & Terry Kovel, *The Kovels' Bottle Price List, Eight Edition,* Crown Publishers, Inc, 1987; *The Official Price Guide To*

Old & New Bottles, Tenth Edition, House of Collectibles, 1986; Carlo & Dot Sellari, *The Standard Old Bottle Price Guide,* Collector Books, 1987.

Note: The books by Paul and Karen Bates are continually updated through a subscription service.

Periodical: *Antique Bottle And Glass Collector,* P. O. Box 187, East Greenville, PA 18041.

See: Coca-Cola, Moxie, and Soft Drink Collectibles.

Bon–Ton, Harold Teen Highball, Chicago, IL, printed label, 7⅞", $25.00.

Abilena Natural Cathartic Water, 10", amber **5.00**

Arter & Wilson Manuf, 7" light green applied top **16.00**

Bacon's Soda Works, 7", light green, blob top **8.00**

Belfast Ginger Ale Co, 7", round, light green, applied top **6.00**

Bryant's Root Beer, This Bottle Makes Five Gallons, 4½", amber, applied top **3.00**

Cape Arco Soda Works, Marshfield, Oregon, 7", round, light green, applied top **7.00**

Cochrane & Co, Belfast, 9¼", medium green, applied top **4.00**

Concho Bottling Works, 7½", aqua, spring stopper **15.00**

Deamer Grass Valley, 7¼", aqua, blob top **4.00**

Dennalter Bottler, Salt Lake, Utah, 7", clear **4.00**

Dr. Pepper, 12", light green, emb "L-G 723-364" **6.00**

English Soda, 8", light green, applied top **3.00**

Fizz, Southern State Siphon Bottling Co, 11" h, golden amber **12.00**

Geyser Soda Springs, 7", dark aqua, blob top **6.00**

Golden West Soda Works, 7", light green ... 10.00
Hawaiian Soda Works, 7½", aqua, emb 8.00
Hippo Size Soda Water, 10", clear, crown top ... 4.00
Italian Soda Water Manufacturing, San Francisco, 7½", dark green, applied top ... 15.00
Jackson's Napa Soda, 7¼", crown cap 4.00
Kapaa Ice & Soda Works, 8", clear, crown cap ... 4.00
Kolshorn, Chas & Bros, Savannah, GA, 8", aqua, blob top ... 15.00
Lewis Soda Bottles, Sacramento, 8½", clear ... 6.00
Los Angeles Soda Works, 8", aqua 4.00
Lubs, Henry & Co, 1885, Savannah, GA, 7½", aqua, blob top ... 10.00
Mendocin Bottling Works, A. L. Reynolds, 7", light green ... 6.00
Mission Dry Sparkling, 9¾", black 3.00
Nevada City Soda Works, E.T.R. Powell, 7", aqua, applied top ... 8.00
Ohio Bottling Works, 5½", light green, applied top ... 5.00
Orange Crush Co, Pat'd July 20, 1926, 9", light green ... 3.00
Perrier, 8½", clear, bowling pin shape, paper label ... 4.00
Phenis Nerve Beverage Co, Boston, 9½", clear, crown cap ... 3.00
Priest Natural Soda, 7½", light green .. 6.00
Rapid City Bottling Works, 8", light green, crown cap ... 4.00
Robinson, A. B., 7½", aqua, blob top . 5.00
Ross's Royal Belfast Ginger Ale, 10", green, diamond shape paper label .. 4.00
Samuel Soda Bottling Works, 9", aqua 4.00
Sandahl Beverages, 8", clear ... 4.00
Saxlehners, Hunyadi Janos Bitter Quelle, 9", olive green ... 6.00
Scott & Gilbert & Co, San Francisco, 10", brown, crown cap ... 4.00
Sequoia Soda Works, 7½", aqua ... 5.00
Seven-Up, Sparkle Springs, 7 oz, Hawaiian man label ... 12.00
Shasta Cream Soda, 8", light green, diamond shape paper label ... 4.00
Solano Soda Works, 8", aqua ... 4.00
Tahoe Soda Springs Natural Mineral Water, 7½" h, light green ... 8.00
Tolenas Soda Springs, 7½", aqua ... 6.00
Union Glass Works, 7½", dark blue, blob top ... 20.00
Uvalde Bottling Works, 7", aqua, blob top ... 8.00
Wasman, W., Atlantic City, clear ... 6.00
Williams Bros. San Jose, CA ... 20.00
Wilson's Soda Works, 8", aqua ... 4.00
XLCR Soda Works Martinez, 7¼", light green ... 5.00
Yuba Bottling Works, 8", aqua ... 4.00

SODA FOUNTAIN AND ICE CREAM COLLECTIBLES

Collecting Hints: The ice cream collector competes with collectors in many other categories—advertising, glassware, postcards, food molds, tools, etc. Material still ranges in the twenty-five cent to $200 range.

When buying a tray, the scene is the most important element. Most trays were stock items with the store or firm's name added later. Always look for items in excellent condition.

History: From the late 1880s through the end of the 1960s the local soda fountain was the social center of small town America, especially for teenagers. The soda fountain provided a center for conversation and gossip, a haven to satisfy the mid-afternoon munchies, and a source for the most current popular magazines.

Ice cream items began to appear about 1870 and extend to the present. The oldest items are the cone shaped ice cream scoops. Beginning in the 1920s, manufacturers of ice cream began to issue premiums. These items are among those most eagerly sought by collectors.

References: Paul Dickson, *The Great American Ice Cream Book*, Galahad Books, 1972; Ray Klug, *Antique Advertising Encyclopedia*, Schiffer Publishing, Ltd, 1978; Ralph Pomeroy, *The Ice Cream Connection*, Paddington Press Ltd, 1975.

Collectors' Club: The Ice Screamers, 1042 Olde Hickory Road, Lancaster, PA 17601.

Museums: Greenfield Village, Dearborn, MI; Museum of Science and Industry, Finigan's Ice Cream Parlor, Chicago, IL; Smithsonian Institution, Washington, DC.

REPRODUCTION ALERT.

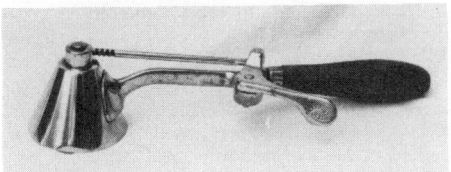

Ice Cream Scoop, Gilchrest No. 33, $125.00.

ICE CREAM

Advertising Trade Card
Lightning Blizzard Freezers, diecut, girl giving out dish of ice cream through window, mother hand cranking ice cream freezer on reverse ... 8.00

Reid's Ice Cream, "She had but one tooth! And that was for Reid's Ice Cream," old lady with one tooth .   **14.00**
Book, *Snow Ice Cream Makers Guide*, B. Heller & Co, 1911 . . . .   **10.00**
Carton, Hershey's Ice Cream, one pint, orange and blue **15.00**
Catalog, Ice Cream Maker's Formulary & Price List, Frank A. Beeler, 1910– 15 . . . .   **25.00**
Condiment Set, 7½" **25.00**
Cone Dispenser, glass, copper insert . .   **345.00**
Ice Cream Scoop Rest, Hendlers Ice Cream, brass, molded, inscription "Friendship Of Hendlers The Velvet Kind," legs, 1930–40 . . . .   **40.00**
Menu Clip, Fairmont Ice Cream, 2¾", 1930–40 . . . .   **15.00**
Milk Shaker
  Gilchrist, white **40.00**
  Hamilton Beach, green **35.00**
Mirror, 2", multicolored scene of table setting, green vase, red and yellow flowers, ice cream soda, cone shaped dish of yellow ice cream, rainbow block of ice cream, slogan in gold letters "When Looking For The Best Buy," and "Keating & Young's Ice Cream, Sandusky, OH" **75.00**
Mold, pewter
  Grape cluster **30.00**
  Indian, marked "S & Co/458" **38.00**
  Star in Circle **35.00**
Pennant, Tellings Ice Cream, felt, kids making ice cream **85.00**
Pinback Button
  ¾", Good Humor Deerslayer Scout, orange, blue, and white litho, c1930 . . . .   **18.00**
  ⅞", Artic Rainbow Ice Cream Cones, multicolored, celluloid, c1912 . . .   **20.00**
  1"
    "Ice Cream For Health," black National Dairy and Food Bureau inscription, 1930s **25.00**
    "National Ice Cream Week," blue and white, Ice Cream Review rim copyright, 1930s **15.00**
  1¼", Frosty Treat, red, white, and blue, female ice skater, red outfit, c1930 . . . .   **15.00**
Scoop
  Gilchrist #31 . . . .   **65.00**
  No-Pak, #31, 11", hole in scoop . . .   **80.00**
Sheet Music, "I Scream, You Scream, We All Scream for Ice Cream," Howard Johnson, Billy Moll, Robert King   **15.00**
Sign
  Chippewa Pride Ice Cream, tin and wood, hinged, Indian head **395.00**
  Golden Rod Ice Cream, diecut, school girl holding cone **135.00**

Ideal Ice Cream, porcelain, two sides   **155.00**
Rich Valley Ice Cream, yellow and red, 9" d, 1940s **40.00**
Syrup Dispenser, glass, brown, Middleby **650.00**
Thermometer, Abbottmaid Ice Cream, 2 x 6¼", 1920–30, orig label **35.00**
Toy
  Play Set, miniature sugar cones, soda fountain cups, straws, spoons, storefront box, Pepsi adv on back wall, MIB **45.00**
  Truck, Walgreen's Ice Cream Trailer, Marx **65.00**
Tray
  Herron's Ice Cream, rect, monogram   **55.00**
  Merringan's Ice Cream, two children eating ice cream under beach umbrella, 1925 . . . .   **300.00**
  Schuller's Ice Cream, 13 x 11", girl, ice cream cone, woman, and ice cream soda, woman eating vanilla ice cream **200.00**

Dispenser, Alka Seltzer, cast iron, chrome plated, blue paint, 13½" h, $65.00.

SODA FOUNTAIN

Book, *Spatula Soda Water Guide*, E. F. White, 160 pgs, 1915 . . . .   **75.00**
Candy Scale, Exact Weight, orig weights   **75.00**
Catalog, Tufts Soda Fountain, 1898 . . .   **45.00**
Counter Jar
  Chico's Peanuts, glass jar, tin litho lid and base **275.00**
  Nut House Peanuts, emb **275.00**
Dispenser
  Christo Ginger Ale, barrel shape, white ground, blue letters, orig pump **1,250.00**
  Dad's Old Fashioned Root Beer, barrel shape, bronze claw feet, c1920   **200.00**
  Dad's Root Beer, barrel shape, bronze claw feet **250.00**

Hires, hourglass shape, orig pump . . **1,000.00**
Hunter's Root Beer, milk glass **45.00**
Magnus Root Beer, barrel shape, co-
    balt blue band and letters **300.00**
Ward's Lemon Crush, figural, re-
    placed pump **500.00**
Door Push, Whistle Cola, picture of bot-
    tle, adjustable, 1940s **55.00**
Funnel, Lash's Bitters, copper **75.00**
Jar, Limpert's Fountain Syrup, spoon . . **80.00**
Magazine Cover, *Saturday Evening Post,*
    July 20, 1905, girl sipping soda
    through straw **10.00**
Malt Jar, Borden's
    Aluminum **30.00**
    Glass, Paneled & Fluted **85.00**
Malted Milk Container, aluminum,
    Thompsons, Borden's Horlick's **35.00**
Match Holder, Dr. Pepper, 1940s **50.00**
Measure, Birely Soda, glass **10.00**
Menu Board, 7-Up, masonite, six pack,
    1940s **35.00**
Milk Shake Mixer, white, bullet style . . **90.00**
Pinback Button, "Drink Cherry Smash,"
    ⅝", figural, cherry, gold inscription,
    orig green string stem, 1911–20 . . . . **30.00**
Postcard, Dakota Drug Co, soda foun-
    tain and man behind counter, color,
    c1915 . . . . **16.00**
Restaurant Blackboard, Dad's Root Beer   **35.00**
Sign
    Dub-L-Valu Root Beer, 11 x 18", tin,
        emb, 1930s **30.00**
    Mt. Kineo Ginger Ale, 12 x 24", tin,
        emb, 1940s **30.00**
    Nickol Cola, 12 x 30", tin, soldier and
        bottle, 1930s **35.00**
    Pepsi Cola, bottle cap, yellow back-
        ground, 15 x 15", 1950s **75.00**
    Whistle Soda, stand-up, cardboard,
        diecut, elf and bottle, 1940s **20.00**
Store Rack, Pez, 7" d, 16" h, metal rack,
    six slotted areas for holding Pez
    candy, 2 x 4" multicolored decals of
    Pez lady, c1950 . . . . **125.00**
Straw Holder
    Heisey, jar, clear **135.00**
    Pattern glass, square, no lid **200.00**
    Sani-straw, dated 1917 . . . . **135.00**
Syrup Bottle
    Cherry Red, glass, emb, shield, white
        enamel label with gold border and
        red pinstripe, black lettering and
        lines, pewter measure cap **155.00**
    Grape Cola, 11" h, glass, emb, shield
        with white enamel label, black let-
        tering and details, pewter measure
        cap **350.00**
    Grapefruit, glass, white enamel label
        with red script lettering, gold bor-
        der, plated metal measure cap,
        F.M. Williams, 1913 copyright . . . **70.00**

Syrup Dispenser
    Blossum, c1930 . . . . **200.00**
    Cherry, 10½" h **25.00**
    Coca Cola, 10½" h **60.00**
    Rootbeer **20.00**
Thermometer
    Dr. Pepper, tin, 20" h, 1960s logo . . **50.00**
    Pepsi, "Say Pepsi Please," tin, 8 x 8",
        1960s **30.00**
    Royal Crown Cola, cardboard, Santa
        Claus and bottle, 30 x 10", 1950s   **35.00**
Tin, Old Rochester Root Beer Syrup . . **28.00**

SOFT DRINK COLLECTIBLES

Collecting Hints: Coca-Cola items have dominated the field. Only recently have collectors
begun concentrating on other soft drink manufacturing companies. Soft drink collectors must
compete with collectors of advertising, bottles
and premiums for the same material.

National brands such as Canada Dry, Dr. Pepper, and Pepsi-Cola are best known. However,
regional soft drink bottling plants do exist, and
their products are fertile ground for the novice
collector.

History: Sarsaparilla, a name associated with soft
drinks, began as a medicinal product. When carbonated water was added, it became a soft drink
and was consumed for pleasure rather than medical purposes. However, sarsaparilla was only
one type of ingredient added to carbonated water
to produce soft drinks.

Each company had its special formula. Although Coca-Cola has a large market share, other
companies provided challenges in different historical periods. Moxie was followed by Hire's
which in turn gave way to Pepsi-Cola and 7-Up.

The 1950s brought soft drinks to the forefront
of everyday life. Large advertising campaigns and
promotional products produced a wealth of material. Regional bottling plants were strong and
produced local specialities such as "Birch Beer"
in eastern Pennsylvania. By 1970 most of these
local plants had closed.

Many large companies had operations outside
of the United States, which also produced a
wealth of advertising and promotional materials.
Today, the diet soda is a response to the American lifestyle of the 1980s.

Reference: Bill Vehling and Michael Hunt, *Pepsi-
Cola Collectibles*, L–W Book Sales, 1986.

Collectors' Club: Pepsi-Cola Collectors Club, P.
O. Box 1275, Covina, CA 91722.

See: Coca-Cola and Moxie.

Pinback Button, ⅞″ d, white ground, blue, red, and green letters, gold band, made by Whitehead & Hoag Co, $20.00.

Account Book, Hires Root Beer, 1892 .	**50.00**
Banner, Lime Cola, canvas	**40.00**
Beanie, Dr. Pepper, with charms	**15.00**
Blotter, Nehi Soda, 1930s	**3.00**
Bottle Carrier	
Kist Soda, cardboard	**4.00**
Royal Crown Cola, aluminum	**12.00**
Bottle Display, 7-Up, 1949	**4.50**
Bottle Opener	
Pepsi, bottle shape	**7.00**
7-Up, wall type	**30.00**
Calendar	
Dr. Pepper, 1937, Earl Moran Art, framed	**140.00**
Nu-Grape, 1941	**35.00**
Royal Crown Cola, 1966	**25.00**
Squirt, 1947	**130.00**
Clock, wall	
Hires Root Beer, plastic	**25.00**
Pepsi	**37.50**
Whistle Orange	**37.50**
Door Pull, 7-Up	**24.00**
Fan, Dr. Pepper, green and red, six pack on reverse	**50.00**
Mug	
Dad's Root Beer	**10.00**
Hires Root Beer, glass, 1940s	**10.00**
Twin Kiss Root Beer, 3″	**10.00**
Notepad, Pepsi, 2½ x 4½″, cardboard cov, red and black logo, 1914 calendar	**30.00**
Pencil, Orange Crush, mechanical	**20.00**
Pencil Clip, ⅞″ celluloid	
Orange-Crush, black and white inscription, orange ground, c1930 .	**7.50**
7-Up, black, white, and red logo ...	**5.00**
Pinback Button	
1¼″, Cherry Smash, George Washington portrait, dark red ground shaded to olive green, black inscription, c1911	**28.00**
1¾″, Dad's Root Beer, litho, bottle cap, yellow, red, blue, white, and black, c1940	**15.00**
Pitcher, Orange Crush, chrome lid	**110.00**

Playing Cards, Nu-Grape, single deck, slide out box	**22.00**
Record, Pepsi, Armed Service Man, 45 rpm	**12.00**
Sign	
B-1 Lemon Soda, 12 x 14 x 6″, light up	**20.00**
Cliquot Club Soda, 14 x 20″, stand-up, cardboard, Eskimos pulling sled	**24.00**
Dixie Springs Soda, 18 x 24″, stand-up, cardboard, 1940s	**20.00**
Dr. Pepper, tin, emb	**40.00**
Grapette, 12 x 24″, tin, emb, 1940s	**35.00**
Ma's Root Beer, 10″, cardboard	**18.00**
Nesbitt's Orange, 48 x 16″, tin, 1938	**165.00**
Norka Ginger Ale, tin, bottle, 1940s	**35.00**
Nu-Grape Soda, tin, yellow and blue, dated March 9, 1920	**125.00**
Orange Crush, 9″ round, tin	**30.00**
Pepsi, 13 x 15½″, thin steel, red, white, blue, and gray bottle cap, yellow ground, double sided, c1950	**80.00**
Squirt, 8″, cardboard, double sided, c1949	**24.00**
Thermometer, Pepsi, tin, 1950s	**25.00**
Toy	
Howel's Root Beer, 8″ h, wood, mechanical, trapeze, 5½″ jointed wood figural elf, multicolored litho trim, c1920	**40.00**
Pepsi-Cola Delivery Truck, 2½ x 7½ x 3″, white plastic body, black wood wheels, red, white, and blue Pepsi decal, three white plastic cases with 24 plastic bottles, Marx Toys, c1940	**85.00**
Tray, Hires Root Beer, 1935	**85.00**
Uniform Patch	
Dr. Pepper	
7″	**12.00**
10″, marked "Good for Life"	**22.00**
Pepsi, 7″	**10.00**
Watch Fob	
Drink Chero-Cola 5 cents	**55.00**
Hires Root Beer, 1½″, octagonal, brass, raised "Drink Hires" and boy, early 1900s	**65.00**

SOLDIERS, DIMESTORE

Collecting Hints: Soldier figures are preferred over civilian figures. The most valuable figures are the ones which had short production runs, usually because they were less popular with the youthful collectors of the period.

O'Brien and Pielin use numbering systems to identify figures in their books. Newcomers should study these books, taking note of the numerous variations in style and color.

Condition, desirability and scarcity establishe the price of a figure. Repainting or rust severely reduces the value.

Auction prices often mislead the beginning collector. While some rare figures have sold in the $150 to $300 range, most sell between $10 and $15.

History: Three dimensional lead, iron, and rubber soldier and civilian figures were produced in the United States by the millons before and after World War II. These figures were called "Dimestore Soldiers" because they were sold in "Five and Dime" stores of the era, the figures usually costing a nickel or dime. Although American toy soldiers can be traced back to the early 20th century, the golden age of the Dimestore Soldier was 1935 until 1942.

Four companies—Barclay, Manoil, Grey Iron and Auburn Rubber—mass produced the three-inch figures. Barclay and Manoil dominated the market, probably because their lead castings lent themselves to more realistic and imaginative poses than iron and rubber.

Barclay's early pre-war figures are identifiable by their separate glued-on and later clipped-on tin hats. When these are lost, the hole in the top of the head always identifies a Barclay.

The Manoil Company first produced soldiers, sailors, cowboys, and Indians. However, the younger buyers of the period strongly preferred military figures, perhaps emulating the newspaper headlines as World War II approached. Manoil's civilian figures were made in response to pacifist pressure and boycotts mounted before the war began.

Figures also were produced by such companies as All-Nu, American Alloy, American Soldier Co., Beton, Ideal, Jones, Lincoln Log, Miller, Playwood Plastics, Soljertoys, Tommy Toy, Tootsietoy, and Warren. Because of the short lived nature of these companies, numerous limited production figures command high prices, especially those of All-Nu, Jones, Tommy Toy, and Warren.

From 1942 through 1945 the wartime "scrap drives" devoured tons of the dimestore figures and the molds that produced them.

In late 1945 Barclay and Manoil introduced modernized military figures, but they never enjoyed their pre-war popularity. "Military operations" generally were phased out by the early 1950s. Similarly, the civilian figures could not compete with escalating labor costs and the competition of plastic.

References: Richard O'Brien, *Collecting Toys,* 4th Edition, Books Americana, 1985; Don Pielin, *American Dimestore Soldier Book,* privately printed, 1983.

Periodical: *Old Toy Soldier Newsletter,* 209 N. Lombard, Oak Park, IL 60302.

Advisor: Fred Wilhelm

REPRODUCTION ALERT. Some manufacturers identify the newer products; many do not.

Notes: Prices listed are for figures in original condition with at least 95% of the paint remaining. Unless otherwise noted, uniform colors are brown.

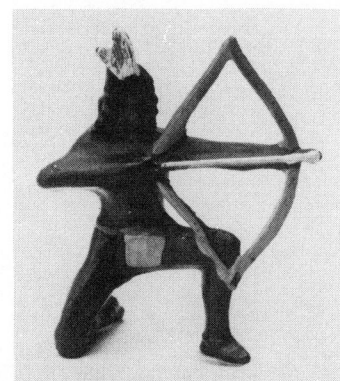

Indian, kneeling with bow and arrow, Barclay, $7.50.

CIVILIAN FIGURE

Auburn		
Baseball	....	**25.00**
Football	....	**25.00**
Barclay		
Boy Scout, signaling	....	**38.00**
Civilian Figures		
Fireman with axe	....	**11.00**
Girl skater	....	**8.00**
Mailman	....	**8.50**
Newsboy	....	**10.00**
Pirate	....	**8.00**
Policeman with raised arm	......	**8.00**
Redcap with bags	....	**8.00**
Santa Claus on skis	....	**48.00**
Woman passenger with dog	.....	**9.00**
Cowboy		
Cowboy		
Shooting pistol	....	**12.00**
Twirling lasso	....	**15.00**
Indian		
Standing, bow and arrow	......	**8.00**
Tomahawk and shield	....	**9.00**
Grey Iron		
American Family Series, 2¼" h	..	**5.00—25.00**
Pirate		
With dagger	....	**12.00**
With sword	....	**10.00**
Western		
Bandit, hands up	....	**35.00**

Cowboy
  Hold-up man **10.00**
  Standing **9.00**
Manoil
  Happy Farm Series
   Blacksmith
    Making horseshoes **20.00**
    With wheel **20.00**
   Farmer, sowing grain **15.00**

Mailman, Barclay, $8.50.

Lady
  Sweeping **18.00**
  With pie **25.00**
  Watchman with lantern **23.00**
Western
  Cowboy
   Arm raised **17.00**
   Raised pistol **14.00**
  Cowgirl, riding horse **25.00**
  Indian, with knives **18.00**

MILITARY FIGURE

Auburn Rubber
  Bugler **8.00**
  Charging with tommy gun **8.00**
  Grenade thrower **14.00**
  Machine Gunner, kneeling **11.00**
  Motorcycle with sidecar **38.00**
  Motorcyclist **22.00**
  Signalman **18.00**
  Soldier
   Kneeling with binoculars **12.00**
   Marching with rifle **7.00**
Barclay
  Post War, pot helmet
   AA Gunner, standing **16.00**
   Flag bearer **15.00**
   Machine gunner, prone **12.00**
   Officer with sword **12.00**
   Rifleman, standing **15.00**
  Pre World War II
   Ammo Carrier, tin hat **16.00**
   Anti-Aircraft gunner, standing **12.00**

Bugler, tin helmet **10.00**
Cameraman, kneeling, tin hat **18.00**
Cook in white, holding roast **8.00**
Dispatcher with dog **25.00**
Doctor in white, carrying bag **12.00**
Flag bearer, tin hat **13.00**
Machine gunner
  Kneeling **9.00**
  Standing, tin hat **10.00**
Marching with rifle, tin hat **10.00**
Marine Officer, marching with
  sword, blue uniform, tin hat ... **17.00**
Nurse in white, kneeling **11.00**
Parachutist, landing on feet **15.00**
Pilot, standing **9.00**

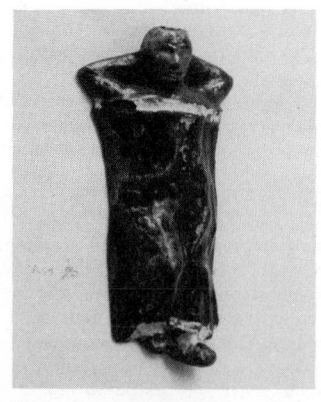

Soldier, sleeping, Barclay, 3", $15.00.

Sailor
  Carrying flag in white **16.00**
  Marching, in white **8.00**
  Signal flags, in white **15.00**
Sharpshooter
  Prone **15.00**
  Standing **11.00**
Signalman with flags **17.00**
Soldier
  Charging with rifle, gas mask .. **15.00**
  Crawling, tin hat **10.00**
  Peeling potatoes **11.00**
  Prone with binoculars **15.00**
  Releasing pigeons, tin hat **13.00**
  Running with rifle **14.00**
  Lying wounded, tin hat **9.00**
Standing
  At attention, tin hat **11.00**
  At searchlight **18.00**
Stretcher bearer **15.00**
Telephone Operator, tin hat **10.00**
Two man rocket team **18.00**
Wireless operator with antenna, tin
  hat **22.00**
Wounded
  On crutches **15.00**
  Sitting, arm in sling **12.00**

Podfoot Series, 2¾" h

Bomb Thrower	6.00
Bugler	7.00
Flag bearer	7.00
Machine gunner	
Charging	6.00
Prone	5.00
Nurse in white	18.00
Officer	6.00
Pilot, standing	6.00
Sailor	
In blue	8.00
In white	7.00
Soldier	
Charging	6.00
Marching with rifle	7.00
With bazooka	8.00

Grey Iron

Cadet Officer	9.00
Cavalryman	22.00
Colonial soldier	8.00
Doctor in white, with bag	12.00
Doughboy	
Crawling	10.00
Marching	7.00
Sentry	9.00
Signaling	14.00
With rifle, kneeling	12.00
Drum Major	13.00
Drummer	15.00
Ethiopian	
Charging, tin	32.00
Marching, tin	20.00
Flag bearer	15.00
Machine gunner	
Kneeling	8.00
Prone	11.00
Nurse in white and blue	12.00
Radio operator	30.00
Sailor	
In blue, marching	12.00
In white, marching	14.00
Wounded on crutches	24.00

Manoil

Post War

Flag bearer	20.00
Marching with rifle	16.00
Soldier	
With bazooka	20.00
With mine detector	30.00
With shell for bazooka	22.00
Tommy gunner, standing	22.00

Post War, 2½" h, marked "USA"

Aircraft spotter	25.00
Aviator, holding bomb	24.00
Flag bearer	26.00
Grenade thrower	23.00
Machine gunner, seated	16.00
Observer with binoculars	27.00
Soldier with bazooka	16.00

Pre World War II

Aviator	15.00

Aviator holding bomb	16.00
Bicycle rider	22.00
Bomb thrower, three grenades	14.00
Boxer	62.00
Cameraman with flash overhead	35.00
Cannon loader	14.00
Cooks helper with ladle	24.00
Deep sea diver, silver	16.00
Doctor in white	12.00
Fire fighter in white, "Hot Papa"	65.00
Flag bearer	18.00
Hostess in green	35.00
Machine gunner, prone	15.00
Marching	16.00
Marine, marching, dark blue	22.00
Navy gunner in white, firing deck gun	18.00
Nurse in white, carrying red liquid	16.00
Observer	
With binoculars, kneeling	12.00
With periscope	20.00
Radio operator, standing	33.00
Rifleman, standing	15.00
Sailor in white	18.00
Sharpshooter, camouflaged, prone	18.00
Signalman in white, two flags	24.00
Soldier	
At searchlight	18.00
Charging with bayonet	28.00
Gas mask and flare gun	18.00
Running with cannon	22.00
Sitting, eating	26.00
Wounded	15.00
Writing letter	38.00
Stretcher carrier with medical kit	17.00
Two man machine gun team	18.00

SOLDIERS, TOY

Collecting Hints: Consider three key factors: condition of the figures and the box, the age of the figures and the box, and the completeness of the set.

Toy soldiers were meant as playthings. However, collectors consider them an art form and pay premium prices only for excellent to mint examples. They want figures with complete paint, all moving parts, and additional parts.

The box is very important, controlling 10 to 20% of the price of a set. The style of the box is a clue to the date of the set. The same set may have been made for several decades. The older the manufacture date, the more valuable the set.

Sets have a specific number of pieces or parts. They must all be present to have full value. The number of pieces in each set, when known, is indicated in the listings below.

Beware of repainted older examples and modern reproductions. Toy soldiers still are being manufactured, both by large companies and private individuals. A contemporary collection may prove a worthwhile long-term investment, at least for the next generation.

History: The manufacture of toy soldiers began in the late 18th century by individuals such as the Hilperts of Nuremberg, Germany. The early figures were tin, pewter or composition. By the late 19th century companies in Britain (Britain, Courtenay), France (Blondel, Gerbeau and Mignot), and Switzerland (Gottschalk, Wehrli) were firmly established. Britain and Mignot dominated the market into the 20th century.

Mignot established its French stronghold by purchasing Cuperly, Blondel and Gerbeau who had united to take over Lucotte. By 1950 Mignot had 20,000 models representing soldiers from around the world.

Britain developed the hollow cast soldiers in 1893. Movable arms also were another landmark. Eventually bases were made of plastic, followed finally by the whole figure in plastic. Production ceased within the last decade.

The English toy soldier was challenged in America in the 1930 to 1950 period by the dimestore soldiers of Barclay, Manoil, and others. Nevertheless, the Britains retained a share of the market because of their high quality. The collecting of toy soldiers remains very strong in the United States.

References: Henry I. Kurtz & Burtt R. Ehrlich, *The Art Of The Toy Soldier,* Abbeville Press, 1987; Richard O'Brien, *Collecting Toy Soldiers: An Identification And Value Guide,* Books Americana, 1988; John Ruddle, *Collectors Guide To Britains Model Soldiers,* Argus Books Ltd, 1980.

Periodicals: *Old Toy Soldier Newsletter,* 209 North Lombard, Oak Park, IL 60302; *Toy Soldier Review,* 127 74th Street, North Bergen, NJ 07047.

REPRODUCTION ALERT

Britains, No. 147, African Warriors, Zulus, $125.00.

Blenheim
   B2, Coldstream Guards Colors, 1812, 2 color bearers, escort of 4 privates, orig box, 6, mint, box excellent .. **115.00**
   B37, Black Watch Pipes and Drums,

   1900, bass drummer, two tenor drums, and 2 pipes **100.00**
   B63, Royal Company of Archers Colors, 2 color bearers, escort of 4 privates, orig box, 6, mint, box excellent **90.00**
   C11, 16th Queens Lancers, 1900, mounted officer, trumpeter, and trooper **95.00**
   U. S. Naval Academy Color Guard, 4 standard bearers, escort of 2 midshipmen, orig box, 6, mint, box excellent **100.00**
Britains, sets only
   7, British Soldiers, The Royal Fusiliers, City of London Regiment ... **135.00**
   11, Black Watch Charging, fixed bayontets, 6 .... **85.00**
   12, Prince Albert's Own 11th Hussars, 5 pcs, officer, 2nd version .. **150.00**
   19, First West India Regiment, 7 pcs, 1941 .... **125.00**
   25, Soldiers To Shoot, 4 pcs, kneeling line infantry, red tunics, spiked helmets, hollow tube rifles **85.00**
   31, King's Dragons, pre war **100.00**
   35, Royal Marines Artillery, slope, full equipment **125.00**
   36, Royal Sussex Regiment, slope, mounted officer, white helmets, 1910, 7 pcs **125.00**
   44, The Queen's Bay, 2nd Dragoon Guards, 5 pcs, galloping bay horses, troopers with lances, officer on trotting horse, late 1930s **140.00**
   55, Royal Marines **100.00**

Britains, British Army, Types of the Colonial Army, $150.00.

   76, Middlesex Regiment, marching, slope, officer, 8 pcs **75.00**
   100, Empress of India's Twenty-first Lancers, 1903, box excellent **225.00**
   179, Cowboys, 5 pcs, four mounted, one on foot, lassos and rifles **100.00**
   181, Boy Scouts Display, 45 pcs, scoutmaster, 6 kneeling and standing scouts with hatchets, 8 hikers,

2 signalers, 2 pulling carts, 3 standing, trees, gate, hurdles, orig box . **750.00**

186, Mexican Rurales, slung rifles, officer, 8 pcs, 1930, orig box **265.00**

187, Arabs of the Desert on Foot, marching at slope, colorful display box, 8, very good condition **70.00**

226, West Point Cadets, winter dress, 8 pcs, orig box **90.00**

314, Coldstream Guards at Ease, officer, 8 pcs, orig box **100.00**

1426, St John Ambulance, stretcher bearers and casualty, excellent ... **115.00**

2028, Red Army Calvary, parade uniform, drawn swords, standing horses, 5, good condition **75.00**

2035, Svea Livgarde, Swedish Life Guards, marching at the slope, officer, retied in orig box, 6, mint, box good **90.00**

2092, Seaforth Highlanders, pipers, 1953, tied, box excellent **200.00**

2094, State Open Landau, drawn by 6 Windsor grays, Queen Elizabeth II and Prince Phillip, tied in orig box, 13, mint **220.00**

9127, Welsh Guards with Mounted Officer, fixed bayonets, bearskin, white plume, green slash, excellent condition **120.00**

9182, U. S. Marines Marching, officer, excellent condition **140.00**

9216, 9th Queens Royal Lancers, black uniform, standing horses, slung lance, excellent condition .. **125.00**

9406, Mounted Band of the Lifeguards, state dress, musicians on horseback, gold and maroon jackets, matched, boxed set, excellent condition **550.00**

9482, U. S. Marines Color Party, 2 flagbearers, escort at shoulder arms, dress blues, excellent condition, box excellent **235.00**

Elastolin/Lineol

Flak Gunner, blue and gray uniform, kneeling with shell, very good condition **40.00**

Medic, walking, helmet, big pack with red cross **35.00**

Nurse, attending wounded, kneeling, holds foot of soldier sitting on keg, excellent condition **40.00**

Staff Officer, pointing, field glasses, aristocratic pose **35.00**

Heyde

American Indians, orig box **425.00**

British Hospital Set, c1890 .... **425.00**

German Mounted Knights, pre-war, orig box **150.00**

Triumphal Procession, ten foot soliders with shields, four mounted, one chariot and rider, two standard bearers **475.00**

United States Infantry and Cavalry, eighteen foot soldiers, six mounted, orig box with one side panel missing **225.00**

Mignot

American Indians, on foot, orig box, multicolored label **325.00**

British Indian Army, orig box **150.00**

C. S. A. Infantry **225.00**

French Fire Department, Motor Ladder Truck, detachable ladders pompier driver, orig box, 5, mint, box excellent **225.00**

French Sailors, 1914, marching at the slope, blue uniforms, officer bugler and standard bearer, orig box, 12, mint to excellent, box excellent .. **175.00**

Mignalu Chasseur Alpine, Chasseurs D'Afrique, hollow cast, marked "Grn," **100.00**

Monaco Color Guard, summer white dress, orig box **100.00**

Sagger of the Guard, Engineer, post war **15.00**

602, Circus Display Set, 4 seated musicians, standing conductor with baton, clowns, show horses, trainer with whip and others, tied in orig box, 12, mint, box excellent **200.00**

Militia Models

Gatling Gun Team of 3rd London Rifles, Gatling gun and gunner, 2 ammunition carriers, officer holding binoculars, orig box, 5, mint, box excellent **90.00**

The Pipes and Drums of 1st Battalion Royal Irish Rangers, limited edition, pipe major and 4 pipers, 2 snare and 2 tenor drummers, drum major, orig box, 11, mint, box excellent . **125.00**

Nostalgia

1st Gurkha Light Infantry, 1800, red and blue uniforms, marching with slung rifles, officer with sword at the carry, orig box, 8, excellent, box excellent **80.00**

Kaffrarian Rifles, 1910, gray uniforms, plumed pith helmets, marching at the trail, officer with sword at the carry, orig box, 8, mint, box excellent **125.00**

Koffiefontein Defense Force, 1900, various uniformed home guardsmen marching at the trail, officer carrying riding crop, orig box, 8, mint, box excellent **90.00**

New South Wales Irish Rifles, 1900, marching at the trail, officer holding sword at the carry, orig box, 8, mint, box excellent **60.00**

S. A. E.
  1358, Royal Horse Guards, 1945,
    mounted at the halt with officer,
    orig box, 6, mint, box excellent .. **50.00**
  1761, French Cuirassiers, mounted at
    the walk, orig box, 6, mint, box
    excellent **85.00**
  3308, Mysore Lancers, charging,
    upraised swords, orig box, 6, mint,
    box excellent **80.00**

SOUVENIR AND COMMEMORATIVE ITEMS

Collecting Hints: Most collectors of souvenir and commemorative china and glass collect items from a region which is particularly interesting to them—a hometown, birthplaces or place of special interest such as a President's home. This results in regional variations in price, because a piece is more likely to be in demand in the area it represents.

History: Souvenir and commemorative china and glass date to the early fairs and carnivals when a small trinket was purchased to take back home as a gift or remembrance of the event. Other types of commemorative glass include pattern and milk glass made to celebrate a particular event. Many types of souvenir glass and china originated at the world's fairs and expositions.

During the 1900s it became popular to have souvenir plates made for churches and local events such as centennials, homecomings, etc. These plates were well received because of their local interest. Collectors search for them today because they were made in a limited number. Many show how the area changed architecturally and culturally.

Reference: Bessie M. Lindsey, *American Historical Glass,* Charles E. Tuttle, 1967.

Periodicals: *Travel Collector,* P.O. Box 475, Marion, WI 54950-0475; *Souvenir Collectors News,* Box 562, Great Barrington, MA 01230.

Book, Ohio Centennial, 1903 .... **20.00**
Bottle Opener, San Diego, 1912 ..... **20.00**
Calling Card Receiver, Philadelphia,
  1907, copper, moose, tree, lake, and
  mountains **38.00**
Cup, china, white
  St Charles Hotel, New Orleans, 2¾"
    h, 2¼" d **12.00**
  "Souvenir of the Midget's Palace,"
    Montreal, well-dressed male and
    female midgets illus, late 1800s .. **60.00**
Demitasse Cup and Saucer, Hotel Roosevelt, New Orleans **20.00**

Mug, Karlsbad, 1934, multicolored view of colonade, purple ground, gold filigree and handle, 5¾" h, $40.00.

Fan, Niagara Falls, silk **8.50**
Figure, Chinatown, NY, Chinese couple,
  3½", pr **20.00**
Hatchet, Hazelton, PA, white milk glass,
  red lettering, 6" **25.00**
Honey Pot, Belleville, KS **10.00**
Jug, miniature, Valley Springs, SD **25.00**
Match Holder, Empire State building .. **10.00**
Medallion, Souvenir of Wisconsin,
  green with gold, lacy **10.00**
Mug
  Hardwick, VT, 2⅜" h, custard glass,
    gold trim **22.00**
  New Rockford, ND, custard glass .. **30.00**
  Ottawa, IL, 3¼" h, green custard
    glass, Star and Punty pattern base,
    gold trim **28.00**
Paperweight
  Brainard, MN, lake scene, glass,
    round, 3" d **30.00**
  New Salem State Park, glass, round,
    2¾" d **30.00**
Photo Album, New Orleans, 1885 .... **10.00**
Pitcher, glass
  Bar Harbor, ME, custard glass, gold
    trim and beaded base **24.00**
  J H Morgan, 1906, Confederate Civil
    War officer, ruby stained, 4½" ... **45.00**
Plate
  Albany, Minnesota **25.00**
  Baltimore & Ohio Railroad, Harpers
    Ferry, 10½", blue, china **75.00**
  Battle Lexington Commons, 9",
    Wedgwood **45.00**
  Bridge Over Illinois River, Beardstown **10.00**
  Central High School, Duluth, Minn . **25.00**
  Copenhagen Bicentennial **30.00**
  Delaware Tercentenary Celebration
    1938, 10½", black and white,
    Spode **25.00**

Moravian Church 500th Anniversary, 1957, 10½", mulberry transfer, Home of the Choir of Unmarried Women, autographs on back **24.00**
My Old Kentucky Home, 10", cobalt, Adams **35.00**
SS Grand View Hotel - A Steamboat in the Allegheny Mountains, 10", cobalt, Adams **40.00**

Plate, Gettysburg, PA, General Meade's Headquarters, marked "F Winkle & Co, England," blue and white, 10" d, $50.00.

Trenton, NJ, State Council, 1912 ... **10.00**
Vanderbilt University, 10", rose, Jonroth **20.00**
Program, Rose Bowl Parade, 1940 .... **20.00**
Shovel, Kearney, NE, glass, 6½", gold scoop and lettering, clear handle ... **20.00**
Tape Measure, New York City, celluloid, pig **22.00**
Teapot, Morrison Hotel, Chicago **25.00**
Tip Tray, Hotel Coronado, china **8.00**
Toothpick Holder
    Glen Ullen, ND, ruby stained glass, gold **22.00**
    Horse Island, ME, Quihote pattern, custard glass, gold trim **28.00**
    Lewiston, ME, Georgia Gem pattern, custard glass, gold beads **30.00**
    Providence, Shamrock pattern, ruby stained glass **20.00**
Trowel, Acme Portland Cement, Eagle, 5½", engraved **25.00**
Tumbler, "Souvenir of Buffalo," sepia scenes **12.00**
Vase
    Opera House, What Cheer, IA, china, colored scene, 4¾" **12.00**
    Red Wing, MN, 6", custard glass, scene, c1920 .... **40.00**
Watch Fob
    Magnetic Club, NY, enameled, 1913 **25.00**
    Mormon Temple, Salt Lake City **30.00**
Whimsey, potty shape, Stratton, ME, custard glass, gold trim **22.00**

SOUVENIR & COMMEMORATIVE SPOONS

Collecting Hints: When collecting souvenir spoons be aware of several things: condition, material, subject, and any markings, dates, etc. Damaged spoons should be avoided unless they are very rare and needed to complete a collection. Some spoons have enamel crests and other decoration. This enameling should be in mint condition.

History: Souvenir spoons are mementos of special events, people, and places of interest. The peak of spoon collecting was reached in the late 1800s. During that time two important patents were issued. The first patent was issued on December 4, 1884, to Michael Gibney, a silversmith in New York who patented the first design for flatware. The other important patent was the first spoon design which commemorated a place. That patent was given to Myron H. Kinsley in 1881 for his spoon of Niagara Falls. The spoon showed the suspension bridge and was the first of many spoons to be made showing Niagara Falls.

Spoons depicting famous people soon followed with the issue of May, 1889, showing George Washington. That was followed by the issuance of a Martha Washington spoon in October of 1889. These spoons, made by M. W. Galt of Washington, D.C., were not patented, but were trademarked in 1890.

Spoon collecting is enjoying a comeback today with many new spoons being made for souvenir and commemorative purposes.

References: Dorothy T. Rainwater and Donna H. Felger, *American Spoons, Souvenir and Historical*, Everybodys Press, Inc., 1977; Dorothy T. Rainwater and Donna H. Felger, *A Collector's Guide To Spoons Around The World*, Everybodys Press, Inc., 1976.

Collectors' Club: American Spoon Collectors, 4922 State Line, Westwood Hills, KS 66205.

Note: Spoons listed below are sterling silver teaspoons unless otherwise noted.

Albuquerque, skyline cut-out handle .. **55.00**
Art Palace, 1893 Columbian Expo **65.00**
Athens, Pennsylvania, engraved high school bowl **25.00**
Baltimore, turtle handle, gold wash bowl, demitasse **20.00**
Battle Monument, Trenton, New Jersey **25.00**
Battleship maine, SP **10.00**
Ben Franklin, Philadelphia **40.00**
Bethesda Spring, Waukesha, Wisconsin **38.00**

Top: St. Louis Cathedral, New Orleans, LA, Sterling silver, fleur-de-lis handle, marked "P & B," 5½", $20.00; bottom: St. Louis Cathedral, New Orleans, LA, Sterling silver, grape cluster handle, marked "P & B," 5", $20.00.

Birmingham, Alabama, factory scenes .	30.00
Bison Hunt	60.00
Bitter Root Missoula, Montana, state scenes, reversible	20.00
Booker T. Washington	10.00
Bluffton, Indiana, engraved high school bowl	25.00
Calumet, Michigan, mining Helco Shaft #2	22.50
Celina, Illinois, engraved high school bowl	25.00
Chicago, Illinois, US Government Building, Fort Dearborn	25.00
Chief Seattle, totem pole	22.00
Cincinnati, Ohio	10.00
Cleveland, Ohio, beaded pattern handle	15.00
Columbian Expo, Chicago, 1893, Altgeld	45.00
Columbus, bust, plated	15.00
Columbus, Ohio, Lancaster pattern handle	20.00
Compliments Scott County Savings Bank, 25th Anniversary, 1883–1903, Davenport, Iowa	25.00
Cornell University, Art Nouveau woman	50.00
Cotton Expo, Atlanta, Georgia, 1895 ..	45.00
Cuba, Morro castle	40.00
Denver, Columbine handle	16.50
Detroit Skyline	60.00
Dionne Quint, Yvonne	14.00
Elgin Watch Factory	65.00
Eniwetok	20.00
Evansville, Indiana	10.00
First Presbyterian Church, Shelby, Ohio, Georgian bead handle	30.00
Fredericton, New Brunswick, spiral handle, gold wash bowl	30.00
Ft. Dearborn	20.00
Fuller, Mary, SP	20.00
Girard College, Irian Pattern handle ..	35.00
Golden Gate, San Francisco	30.00
Grant Monument, Chicago	25.00
Hamburg	110.00
Hope, Idaho	10.00

Hot Springs, Arkansas, Indian head, corn	32.00
Hotel Riverside, Cambridgeboro, Pennsylvania	25.00
Inclined Plane, Cincinnati, Ohio	25.00
Indianapolis, Soldier's & Sailor's Monument	18.00
Kansas City, Missouri Convention Hall	30.00
Lake Worth, Palm Beach, Florida	58.00
Lakewood, demitasse, Acorn pattern handle	15.00
Los Angeles, California	10.00
Louisiana Purchase Expo, 1903, plated	25.00
Madison, Wisconsin	10.00
Maryland, eagle handle	20.00
Massachusetts	12.00
McDermott Falls, Glacier National Park bowl	22.00
Meridan, Mississippi, rose floral handle	28.50
Miami, alligator figure	50.00
Michigan City, Indiana, ornate Art Nouveau handle	30.00
Miles Standish, fruit bowl	55.00
Minnehaha Falls, Minnesota, war dancing Indian	60.00
Missoula, Montana, Indian bust, corn, gold wash bowl, demitasse	20.00
Mt. Vernon	10.00
New Court House, Upper Sandusky, Ohio, picture bowl	25.00
New Park Hotel, Park City, Utah, picture bowl	25.00
New York Peace Monument, Lookout Mountain, Tennessee, picture bowl	25.00
Niagara Falls, New York, scenes, reversible handle	25.00
Notre Dame	110.00
Old Hickory, Jackson Monument	55.00
Oregon	25.00
Paul Revere	
Bunker Hill	25.00
Midnight Ride	45.00
Phil Cook, The Quaker Man	12.00
Pittsburgh, Ft. Pitt	38.00
Post Office, Bismarck, North Dakota, picture bowl	25.00
Pride of Texas, Midland, steer head, picture bowl, state handle	25.00
Quebec, open work handle	15.00
Reading, Pennsylvania, Mt. Penn Tower, demitasse	25.00
Rochester, New York	35.00
Rolex Watch	15.00
Salt Lake City, Utah, Mormon Temple handle, demitasse	22.00
San Diego, Hotel Del Coronado	58.00
San Francisco	
Cliff House, bear	65.00
Mission Dolores 1776, bear on dec handle, gold bowl	35.00
Settle Memorial Church, Owensboro,	

Kentucky, picture bowl, pattern handle **25.00**
Sioux City, Iowa, Corn Palace, 1891 .. **40.00**
Soldier's Monument, Morrisville, Vermont, picture bowl, state handle ... **25.00**
Spokane Falls, Spokane, Washington, picture bowl, state handle **25.00**
Springfield, Illinois, Abraham Lincoln . **40.00**
State Capitol, Nashville, Tennessee, picture bowl, state handle **25.00**
State Normal School, Superior, Wisconsin **25.00**
Statue of Liberty, Tiffany **60.00**
Texas, star, demitasse **15.00**
Union Station, Dayton, Ohio, picture handle, pattern handle **25.00**
Union Terminal, Dallas, Texas **12.00**
Vassar, Michigan, engraved high school bowl **25.00**
Visalia, California, state scenes, reversible handle **22.00**
Waseca, Minnesota, grape pattern **24.00**
Washington D.C., capitol **28.00**
Washington Mansion, plain bowl **20.00**
Washington's Tomb **10.00**
William McKinley **28.00**
William Penn
   Independence Hall **58.00**
   Quaker city **45.00**
Wilmington, North Carolina, floral handle, gold wash bowl, demitasse **15.00**
Windom Inst, Montivideo, Minnesota, picture bowl, pattern handle **25.00**
Yellowstone Park, etched falls bowl, bear, stag's head, and buffalo head on handle **30.00**

SPACE ADVENTURERS AND EXPLORATION

Collecting Hints: There are four distinct eras of fictional space adventurers—Buck Rogers, Flash Gordon, the radio and television characters of the late 1940s and 1950s, and the Star Trek and Star Wars phenomenon. Condition is not as major a factor in Buck Rogers material, because of its rarity, as it is in the other three groups. Beware of dealers who break apart items and sell parts separately, especially game items.

In the early 1950s a wealth of tin, battery operated, friction, and wind-up toys, not associated with a specific Space Adventurer, were marketed in the shape of robots, space ships, and space guns. They are rapidly gaining in popularity.

The "Trekies" began holding conventions in the early 1970s. They issued many fantasy items, which must not be confused with items issued during the duration of the TV show. The fantasy items are numerous and have little value beyond the initial selling price.

The American and Russian space programs produced a wealth of souvenir and related material. Beware of astronaut signed material that may contain printed or autopen signatures.

History: In January, 1929, "Buck Rogers 2429 A.D." began its comic strip run. Buck, Wilma Deering, Dr. Huer, and Killer Kane, a villain, were the creation of Phillip Francis Nowlan and John F. Dille. The heyday of Buck Rogers material was 1933 to 1937 when products such as Cream of Wheat and Cocomalt issued Buck Rogers items as premiums.

Flash Gordon followed in the mid-1930s. Buster Crabbe gave life to the character in movie serials. Books, comics, premiums,and other merchandise enhanced the image during the 1940s.

The use of rockets at the end of World War II and the beginnings of the space research program gave reality to future space travel. Television quickly capitalized on this in the early 1950s with programs such as Captain Video and Space Patrol. Many other space heroes, such as Rocky Jones, had short-lived popularity.

Star Trek enjoyed a brief television run and became a cult fad in the early 1970s. *Star Trek: The Next Generation* already has an established corp of watchers and the first collectibles are appearing. *Star Wars* (Parts IV, V, and VI) and *ET* produced a wealth of merchandise which already is collectible.

In the 1950s, real life space pioneers and explorers replaced the fictional characters as the center of the public's attention. The entire world watched on July 12, 1969, as man first walked on the moon. Although space exploration has suffered occasional setbacks, the public remains fascinated with its findings and potential.

References: Sue Cornwell and Mike Kott, *The Official Price Guide To Star Trek and Star Wars Collectibles, Second Edition,* House of Collectibles, 1986; Chris Gentry and Sally Gibson-Downs, *An Encyclopedia of Trekkie Memorabilia: Identification and Value Guide,* Books Americana, 1988; Don and Maggie Thompson, *The Official Price Guide To Science Fiction and Fantasy Collectibles, Third Edition,* House of Collectibles, 1989.

See: Robots and Space Toys.

SPACE ADVENTURERS

Johnny Apollo, game, Johnny Apollo Moon Landing Game, Marx, 10 x 16 x 1", clear hard plastic bagatelle marble game **20.00**
Buck Rogers
   Badge, Solar Scout **95.00**
   Better Little Book, *Buck Rogers And The Doom Comet,* Whitman #1178, 1935, 432 pgs, hardcover **40.00**

Buck Rogers, pencil box, red and blue figures, marked "American Lead Pencil Co, John F Dille Co," 1936, 8⅜ x 4⅞", $50.00.

Big Little Book
  Buck Rogers And The Depth Men of Jupiter, Whitman, 426 pgs, 1935 .... **75.00**
  Buck Rogers In The City Below The Sea, 1934 .... **50.00**
Card Game, "Buck Rogers In The 25th Century," 35 cards, full color illus on each, orig box, All-Fair, 1936 copyright **200.00**
Colorforms Set, diecut vinyl figures, boxed, 1979 copyright **15.00**
Crayon Box, Buck Rogers Crayon Ship, 2 x 5", cardboard, six colored pencils, c1930 .... **150.00**
Lobby Card, *The Enemy Stronghold,* Buster Crabbe, 1938 .... **180.00**
Lunch Box, 7 x 8 x 4", litho metal, 6½" h, plastic thermos **25.00**
Mask, 8 x 11", Wilma, face, paper, color **65.00**
Matchbook Cover, Popsicle adv **15.00**
Paint Book, 11 x 14", 96 pgs, Whitman, 1935 copyright **75.00**
Pencil Case, 5 x 8½ x ½", cardboard, yellow illus top and bottom, green background, brass snap fastener, American Lead Pencil Co, 1936 copyright **75.00**
Pistol, 10" l, pressed steel, instruction sheet, orig box, Daisy Mfg Co, 1946 .... **200.00**
Premium
  Badge, 1½" h, brass, diecut, Buck Rogers Solar Scouts Member, Cream of Wheat, 1934 .... **75.00**
  Big Little Book, *Buck Rogers/25th Century A.D.,* Whitman, 1938, Cocomalt **20.00**
  Holster, 5 x 10", diecut, leather, tan, incised inscription, Rogers holding gun and cloud design, Cream of Wheat, 1936 .... **100.00**
  Manual, "Buck Rogers Solar

Scouts," 5 x 7½", 16 pgs, 1936 Cream of Wheat **150.00**
  Space Rangers Kit, 1952 premium, punched **150.00**
Rocketship, "Venus Duo-Destroyer," 4¾" l, diecast metal, yellow, red trim, inscription on each side "Buck Rogers Venus Duo-Destroyer MK 24 L," boxed, 1937 copyright **125.00**
Rubber Stamp, set of 11, yellow, wood back, Wilma, Buddy, Alura, and two different Buck Rogers, c1930 .... **90.00**
Captain Video
  Decoder, 1½" d, "Capt. Video Mysto-Coder," brass, plastic wheels, lightning bolt design center **150.00**
  Gun, 2½ x 3½", "Captain Video Secret Ray Gun," includes, red plastic flashlight, secret message instructions, and glow-in-the-dark card, Power House Candy premium ... **40.00**
  Magazine, TV Star Parade, 2 page photo article, 1953 issue, Ideal Publishing Corp **15.00**
  Press Book, 12 x 18", black, white, and blue cover, newspaper headline style **80.00**
  Ring, Secret Seal Ring **40.00**
  Rocketship, 4¼" l, plastic, metallic lavender, removable cannons, inscription on tail fin, boxed, Lido Toy Co, early 1950s **50.00**
  Watch, orig card **40.00**

Tom Corbet, Space Cadet Belt, orig card, made by Yale, copyright Rockhill Productions, 13¼ x 6⅝" card, $45.00.

Tom Corbett
  Book, *Tom Corbett Space Cadet/Sabotage In Space,* Grosset & Dunlap, 5½ x 7½", hard cover, 212 pgs, dj **10.00**
  Decoder, 2½ x 4", "Tom Corbett Space Cadet Code,", black, white, and red cardboard, membership card printed on back **30.00**
  Flashlight, 7", "Space Cadet Signal Siren Flashlight," full color illus, orig box, c1952 .... **50.00**

Lunch Box, 7 x 8 x 4", litho metal, full color space scene, dark blue galaxy background, 1954 Rockhill Radio copyright **75.00**

Patch, 2 x 4", "Space Cadet," cloth, red, yellow, and blue, Kellogg's premium **25.00**

Photo, 3½ x 5½", black and white glossy, blue signature "Spaceman's Luck/Tom Corbett/Space Cadet," early 1950s **35.00**

Record, "Space Cadet Song and March," 78 rpm, 6½ x 7½" paper envelope album, full color illus on front, 1951 copyright **30.00**

School Bag, 11 x 14½", plastic, Tom on center flap, rocket designs on side, red plastic handle **25.00**

Space Rifle, plastic **150.00**

Viewmaster Reel, set of 3, orig story folder and envelope **20.00**

Flash Gordon

Bank, metal, rocket **25.00**

Better Little Book, *Flash Gordon and The Perils of Mongo*, Whitman, 1940 .... **35.00**

Big Little Book, Whitman

   Flash Gordon And The Tournaments of Mongo, 426 pgs, late 1930 .... **20.00**

   Flash Gordon In The Water World of Mongo, 424 pgs, 1937 ..... **40.00**

Book, pop-up, *Tournament Of Death*, 8 x 9¼", 20 pgs, Blue Ribbon Press and Pleasure Books, 1935 copyright **100.00**

Flash Gordon, gun, radio repeater, tin, litho, silver and red, marked "Marx, American Made," $75.00.

Coloring book, 8½ x 11", Whitman, 1952 .... **20.00**

Costume, space outfit, c1950 ...... **135.00**

Dixie Cup Lid, "Buster Crabbe Starring In the Universal Chapter Play Flash Gordon" **35.00**

Game, orig box **25.00**

Kite, 7 x 37", plastic, multicolored image, transparent ground, orig package, Roalex Co, c1950 .... **20.00**

Membership Card, 3 x 4¼", "Flash Gordon Movie Club," green, black scene and lettering, unused **500.00**

Pinback Button, 1⅛" d, black, white, and red, "Flash Gordon Club, Chicago, Herald and Examiner" **60.00**

Premium, photo, 9 x 11", color, Buster Crabbe in Flash Gordon suit, black and white film scenes on back **30.00**

Record, "City of Sea Caves," 6½" d, plastic on cardboard, 78 rpm, 1948 copyright **30.00**

Telescope, "Flash Gordon Planet Gazer," 9" l, plastic, decal portrait, orig display card with unopened plastic bubble, 1970–80 .... **10.00**

Wallet, vinyl, tan, color illus, zipper edge, unused, 1949 copyright ... **40.00**

Water Pistol, 7½" l, plastic, blue, whistle mouthpiece, inscribed on right side "Flash Gordon Water Pistol," boxed, Marx, c1950 .... **75.00**

Space Cadet, thermos, 1952 .... **25.00**

Space Patrol

Belt and Buckle, 4" buckle, brass, gold finish, rocket, decoder mounted on back, glow-in-the-dark belt, Ralston premium, early 1950s **150.00**

Dart Gun, 9½" l, plastic, red, designs on each side, US Plastic Co, early 1950s **100.00**

Drink Mixer, 8", plastic, pink rocket ship, marked on side "XY7 Rocket," orig colored carton **35.00**

Flashlight, 12" l, silvered metal body, pointed rubber red tip nose, decal inscription on fin "Official Space Patrol Rocket Lite and "Commander Buzz Corry," boxed, Ray-O-Vac Co, early 1950s **200.00**

Handbook **150.00**

Microscope, orig slides **175.00**

Paper Cup, package of 6, rocket ships, stars, and planets motif, orig cellophane with company label .. **60.00**

Puzzle, 10¼ x 14½, Terra rocketship and planetary headquarters scene, Milton Bradley, early 1950s **40.00**

Space Helmet, diecut cardboard, six sided, yellow, green, red design, black top with printed red lightning flashes **100.00**

Trading Card, 2¼ x 3½", full color "Secret Code Master" design, Ralston Cereal issue, 1950s **15.00**

Watch, silvered chrome, stainless steel back, black leather straps, "Space Patrol" inscription on dial, black numerals, US Time, early 1950s **150.00**

Star Trek
  Activity Book, 8 x 11", Whitman,
    1979 .... 8.00
  Bedsheet, 39 x 75", cotton and po-
    lyester, red, blue, yellow, black,
    and white illus, light blue back-
    ground, c1970 .... 30.00
  Book, *Star Trek–Mission To Horatius*,
    Whitman TV Adventure Book
    #1549, 1968, 210 pgs, 5 x 8" ... 12.00
  Game, "Destroy Death Star," 16 x 16"
    board with spinner disk, playing
    pieces and tokens, boxed, Kenner,
    1977 .... 15.00
  Glass, set of 4, 6" h, issued by Dr.
    Pepper, 1976 .... 50.00

Star Trek, Mr. Spock, whiskey bottle, Grenadier, 1979, $20.00.

  Model, "USS Enterprise," plastic, un-
    assembled, instruction sheet,
    boxed, AMT Corp, 1968 copyright 75.00
  Mug, 3¾" h, plastic, white, color il-
    lus, red inscription, 1975 copyright 10.00
  Paint Set, 12 x 16" canvas portrait,
    boxed, slightly used, Hasbro, 1974
    copyright 50.00
  Poster, Mr. Spock holding model of
    Enterprise, Personality Posters 18.00
  Tablecloth, 54 x 88", blue, red, yel-
    low, black, and white design, white
    background, unopened plastic
    package, 1976 copyright 15.00
  Utility Belt, phaser, tricorder, and
    communicator, Remco, 1975 .... 30.00
  View Master Reel, set of 3, 16 page
    story booklet, "The Omega Glory,"
    4½ x 4½ envelope, c1970 ...... 10.00
  Wallet, vinyl, silver, orig display card
    with unopened plastic bubble,
    1979 copyright 10.00
Star Wars
  Bubble Gum Card, Topps, Star Wars,
    Series 1, 66 cards and 11 stickers,
    1977 .... 10.00

  Children's Book, pop-up 15.00
  Clock, alarm, talking 25.00
  Cookie Jar, 13", R2D2, ceramic, MIB 50.00
  Costume, R2D2, plastic mask, vinyl
    costume, boxed, Ben Cooper, 1977
    copyright 25.00
  Figure
    AT-AT, MIB 85.00
    Bantha, MIB 15.00
  Game, Kenner, 1977, MIB 25.00
  Lunch Box 20.00
  Model Kit, unassembled, MIB
    AT-AT 10.00
    B-Wing Fighter 8.00
    C3-PO 15.00
    Darth Vader, snap together 40.00
    R2D2 .... 12.00
  Placemat, 8½ x 11", "The Empire
    Strikes Back," paper, full color,
    Burger King, 1980 copyright 5.00
  Press Kit, first movie 50.00
  Puppet, Yoda, 8" h, molded soft rub-
    ber, silver hair wisps, 1979 ...... 15.00
  Record Storybook 8.00
  Puzzle, MIB 15.00
  Telephone, Darth Vader, speaker
    phone 110.00
  Toy
    Darth Vader, Tie Fighter, MIB 28.00
    Van 5.00

SPACE EXPLORATION

Ashtray, 5½ x 5½", china, Apollo 11,
  mission insignia, marked "Johnson
  Space Center/Houston, Texas" 20.00
Autograph, envelope, inked Jack Swig-
  ert signature on back, Man on the
  Moon stamp, canceled Kennedy
  Space Center, April 11, 1970 ...... 45.00
Bank
  Freedom 7, 4½" h, plastic, silver,
    flight details listed on bottom, in-
    scription on base "Freedom 7 Cap-
    sule/Project Mercury/Redstone
    Rocket" 40.00
  John Glenn, mechanical, 10½", sil-
    vered white metal, sliding spring
    coin holder fires coin into Earth .. 70.00
Book
  First American Into Space, Robert Sil-
    verberg, Monarch Books, 142 pgs,
    1961 .... 15.00
  NASA Astronauts Biography Book,
    NASA, 1968, 8 x 10¼", soft cov . 35.00
Bottle, 10", Apollo, ceramic, beige,
  light and dark brown accents, nose
  cone with cork stopper, Thomas W.
  Sims distillery, Stanley, Ken/Dec 1969 30.00
Clock, 4 x 4½ x 2", Apollo 11, wind-
  up, animated, ivory case, red, white,
  and blue diecut, metallic blue dial,

Apollo craft illus, gold colored numerals, brass hands, marked "Lux Clock Mfg Co" **120.00**

Decanter, 8½" h, Apollo 14 Commemorative, iridescent glass, blue, raised portraits on one side, raised emblem on other side, Wheaton Ltd Edition, Great American Series, 1971 copyright **25.00**

Dish, 8" d, Apollo 11 Commemorative, iridescent glass, raised design, inscription "One Small Step," 1970s . **15.00**

First Day Cover, Moon Landing, July 20, 1969, 4¼ x 9½", black, white, and silver design, full color commemorative US postage stamp, Washington DC postmark **20.00**

Glass
Apollo 13, clear glass, 4¼" h, red, white, and blue design, set of 4 . **30.00**
Columbia Space Shuttle, 4¼" h, clear, weighted bottom, black and white facsimile of NY Times April 15, 1981, issued by Wendy's **12.00**

Gyroscope, Gemini, plastic, unopened display card, mid 1960s **25.00**

Keychain, brass, plastic insert on tag with Apollo 11 emblem on one side, other side with Lunar Module accented in black, orig box, unused card **25.00**

Letter Opener, Apollo 11, 7" l, metal gold colored, insignia on handle, grained black leather like scabbard . **25.00**

Lunch Box, astronauts, 1969, orig thermos **60.00**

Magazine
Look, Feb 2, 1960, The Lady Wants To Orbit, cov article, 6 pgs, Betty Skelton article and photos **12.00**
Time, Feb 3, 1967, Apollo tragedy, five page article and photos **8.00**

Magnet, 2 x 2¼", steel, diecut, patriotic shield, red, white, and blue accents, silvered metal insert of plaque placed on moon and Apollo 11 insignia ... **30.00**

Medal, commemorative, 1½", SS, astronaut descending from landing module onto moon, "One Small Step" inscription, plaque left on moon on reverse, acrylic case **35.00**

Model Kit, Challenger Space Shuttle, 14 x 22 x 3" box, orig clear cellophane seal, Revell, 1982 copyright **30.00**

Mug, 3" h, china, black St. Louis Globe-Democrat newspaper design of July 20, 1969 moon landing **25.00**

Pennant, 29" l, felt, red and white, blue trim, "First Man On Moon" **15.00**

Photo, 8 x 10", Apollo 16, NASA, 1972 liftoff and lunar view **12.00**

Pinback Button
1¼", New Frontier Man of The Year—Astronaut John Glenn, blue and white **30.00**
3", "Challenger 7," black and white photo, purple background **8.00**
3½", celluloid
Apollo 11, Mooning Landing, black and white astronaut photo, red, white, and blue rim **20.00**
Gemini 4, black and white portraits of McDivitt and White, red, white, and blue ground, June 3–7, 1965 walk in space mission . **25.00**
Gemini 6–7, red, white, and blue, Frank Borman and James Lovell, Dec, 1965 .... **25.00**
Glenn, John, black and white portrait, red, white, and blue rim, 1962 .... **60.00**

Plate, commemorative
Apollo 13, 7½", glass, brown and tan lunar landscape, white silhouette of astronaut on moon surface, rim inscribed "General Electric" and "United States Atomic Energy Commission," black and white NASA symbol **30.00**
Apollo 14, 7½", glass, shaded blue lunar landscape, NASA symbol, c1971 .... **25.00**
Glenn, John, 9¼", china, white, black and white illus, stylized gold edge pattern, commemorates Feb 20, 1962 flight **20.00**

Plate, commemorative, 7½", china, full color moon exploration scene, dark blue background, inscription "July 20" and "History 1969," Collector's Historic Series, Seven Seas Traders, Minneapolis, made in West Germany, registration number "875," 1969 copyright **50.00**

Press Pass, 3 x 4¼", laminated, ABC News, June 18-24, 1983, Challenger Mission, black and white photos, blue, white, and orange design **50.00**

Puzzle, Apollo 11, 1969, MIB **20.00**

Record, "America's First Man In Orbit," 33⅓ rpm, features John Glenn, orig envelope and mailing envelope **25.00**

Ruler, 12", metal, "We Want Nelson Rockefeller For President," black and red space illus, US space achievements text, 1964 .... **12.00**

Rug, 19½ x 37½", woven, full color moon landing scene, red, white, and blue stars and stripes motif border, Made in Italy, orig label **50.00**

Salt and Pepper Shakers, pr, china, 3" h, blue symbol and Columbia shuttle design, inscription "Johnson Space Center/Houston, Texas," early 1980s ... **10.00**

Spoon, 4½" l, engraved astronauts names and date, detailed design on handle, Klepa Arts, Holland

Apollo 8 .... **8.00**

Apollo 11 .... **15.00**

Tapestry, 19 x 36½", woven, colorful astronauts and moon design, black background with blue and white stars, red, white, and blue border design . **75.00**

Tie Clip, 1½", Apollo 11, brass, black accents, raised moon landing design, landing date and astronaut names on rim, orig plastic display case **30.00**

View Master Reels, set of 3, "Project Apollo," 16 page story booklet, envelope, 1964 .... **15.00**

SPACE RELATED

Book, *Victory In Space,* Otto O. Binder, 1962 copyright, 212 pgs, hard cover, 6 x 9" **15.00**

Bottle, Galaxy Syrup, emb "Space Ace," figural spaceman **35.00**

Candy Tin, 6 x 1½" d, Variety Toffee, Riley Bros, England, boy astronauts point to stars and planets, 1950s ... **60.00**

Cigarette Lighter, 6" l, rocket, silvered brass, 2" sq base, marked "Made in Occupied Japan" **30.00**

Comic Art, Dagwood Splits the Atom, premium, orig mailer **65.00**

Crayon Box, spaceship, stiff litho cardboard, enameled wood nose cone, diecut openings reveal multiplication tables **20.00**

Decanter, 3 x 14", gold colored metal, lift off nose cone for pouring, key wound musical base, inscribed "United States" in black, c1970 .... **25.00**

Figure, "Alien," 18" h, mechanical, orig box, Kenner, 1979 .... **75.00**

Flashlight, Junior Astronaut Flashlite, 4 x 8½" multicolored retail card, 3" plastic keychain flashlight, unopened, c1960 .... **18.00**

Game, Rocket Race to Saturn, 9½ x 13" board, four plastic rocket playing pcs, boxed, Lido Toy, c1950 .... **40.00**

Glass, 5" h, weighted bottom, pink illus of three spacemen, frosted white band lower edge, c1950s **15.00**

Model, Moon Survey 3-D Scenic Kit, orig plain brown sealed 12 x 23 x 3" box, Eldon, 1973 .... **75.00**

Pencil Case, 9¾", plastic, rocket shape, built-in pencil sharpener, Hasbro Toys, c1960 .... **25.00**

Sunglasses, plastic, green lenses, yellow raised rocketship on each corner, spaceman head in center, c1950 ... **30.00**

Toy

Dart Game, metal target board, litho space scenes, MIB **75.00**

Space Capsule, friction, Friendship 7 **75.00**

Top, metal, litho space scenes **20.00**

Walkie-Talkie, plastic, white, antenna, sticker with astronaut illus, 8½ x 11" display card with Armstrong on moon photo, unopened, late 1969 .... **15.00**

Whistle and Membership card, 2 x 2¼" plastic whistle, space capsule shape, white, light blue background, inscription on bottom, 2½ x 4" card, Kolonel Keds' Space Patrol, unused, Keds premium, 1950–60 .... **35.00**

SPACE TOYS

Collecting Hints: The original box is an important element in pricing, perhaps controlling 15 to 20% of the price. The artwork on the box may differ slightly from the toy inside; this is to be expected. The box also may provide the only clue to the correct name of the toy.

The early lithographed tin toys are more valuable than the later toys made of plastic. There is a great deal of speculation in modern toys, e.g., Star Wars material. Hence, the market shows great price fluctuation. Lloyd Ralston Toys, Fairfield, Connecticut, is a good barometer of the auction market.

Collect toys in very good to mint condition. Damaged and rusted lithographed tin is hard to repair. Check the battery box for damage. Don't ever leave batteries in a toy after you have played with it.

History: The Hollywood movies of the early 1950s drew attention to space travel. The launching of Sputnik and American satellites in the late 1950s and early 1960s enhanced this fascination. The advent of man in space culminating with the landing on the moon made the decade of the 1960s the golden age of space toys.

The toy industries of Japan and America responded to this interest. Lithographed tin and plastic models of astronauts, flying saucers, spacecraft and space vehicles followed quickly. Some were copies of original counterparts; most were the figments of the toy designer's imagination.

The 1970s saw a shift in emphasis from the space program and a decline in the production of science fiction-related toys. The earlier Japanese and American-made products gave way to cheaper models from China and Taiwan.

References: Crystal and Leland Payton, *Space Toys,* Collectors Compass, 1982; David Pressland, *The Art Of The Tin Toy,* Crown Publishers,

Inc., 1976; Stephen J. Sansweet, *Science Fiction Toys and Models,* Vol. 1, Starlog Press, 1980.

Note: Any rocket related toy, whether military or space, is included in this category. The following abbreviations are used:

SH = Horikawa Toys
TM = K. K. Masutoko Toy Factory
TN = Nomura Toys
Y = Yonezawa Toys

See: Robots and Space Adventurers and Explorations.

REPRODUCTION ALERT

Astronaut
  Astronaut, 7½", litho tin, wearing spacesuit, carrying gun in right hand, arms swing as he walks, marked "AN" **1,100.00**
  Mark Apollo Astronaut–Movable Spaceman, 7" white vinyl figure, jointed arms, legs, and head, orig 5 x 8 x 2" black, white, blue, and orange box, marked "Marx," 1969 **100.00**
  Mechanical Interplanetary Explorer, 8", litho tin windup, marked "AN, Japan," 1950s **275.00**
  NASA Astronaut, 12" h, plastic, battery operated, walks, rotating blades spin atop head, marked "Marx" **400.00**
  Space Man Astronaut, litho tin, remote control, space gun, wearing space suit, helmet, and oxygen tank, marked "Cragston," MIB ...**1,600.00**
Flying Saucer
  Jupiter, litho tin, built in key, clear dome, sparks, marked "K, Japan" **35.00**
  Mercury X-1 Space Saucer, 8", litho tin and plastic, battery operated, round rocket engines on back, marked "Japan," MIB **50.00**
  UFO X05, litho tin and plastic, battery operated, marked "TM, Japan," early 1960s, MIB **35.00**
  Space Patrol X–16, 8" d, 5" h, metallic green, multicolored details, battery operated, marked "Modern Toys, Japan" **100.00**
Space Dog
  6" l, litho tin, windup, runs, wiggles ears, moves mouth and eyes, marked "KO, Japan" **375.00**
  10½", Astro Dog, black and white, standing, bubble dome helmet, holding briefcase and American flag, walks, wags tail, and barks, Y, MIB **600.00**
Space Gun, electronic, marked "Remco," MIB **35.00**

Space Ship, Moon Rocket, 9" l, litho tin, battery operated, bump and go action, outside revolving astronaut, flashing colored lights, marked "MT, Japan" **100.00**
Space Station, Moon City with Space-Age Shuttle Craft, 5" l battery powered red and white spaceship Apollo, red, white, and blue stickers on each side, two large light blue spiral plastic ramps, 24" w, 15" h track, 3 x 15 x 17" multicolored box, orig instruction sheet, marked "Cragston," 1970 copyright **80.00**
Spacecraft, Rockets, and Capsules
  Atom Rocket 7 Space Ship, litho tin, battery operated, 9½" l, non fall action, flashing light, moving antennae, sound, marked "MT, Japan" . **100.00**
  Friendship 7, 4 x 5½ x 3½", litho friction, red, white, and blue capsule, red, white, and yellow astronaut, red plastic nose tip, two clear plastic windows, marked "SH, Japan" **65.00**

Capsule, Super Space Capsule, battery operated, litho, tin and plastic, stop and go circular motion, orig box, SH, Japan, $250.00

  Friendship 7–United States, 4 x 5 x 3½", litho friction, red, white, blue, and silver, tinted blue plastic window, Japanese manuf, distributed by Cragston, 1962 .... **60.00**
  Johnny Spacemobile, battery operated, blue plastic 7 x 11 x 14" control panel, marked "Topper Toys," orig 10 x 15 x 13" box, 1970 .... **80.00**
  Moon Rocket–Apollo Saturn, 4 x 4 x 21" red, white, blue, silver, and yellow tin and plastic, battery operated, two stage rocket, marked "TN, Japan" **125.00**

NASA Space Capsule, 9½" l, litho tin, battery operated, bump and go action, space noise, flashing lights and revolving antennae, marked "MT, Japan" 80.00

Pioneer 3–Stage Rocket with Launcher At Cape Canaveral, 4 x 4 x 10½", multicolored tin litho, rocket, launching pad, and gantry, orig box marked "A Kraemer Toy" 150.00

Space Craft Launching Pad, 6 x 9 x 11½", tin and plastic, crank wind, noisy siren, plastic saucer, marked "Mar Toys" 50.00

Space Satellite with Launching Station, 9 x 11½ x 4½", multicolored tin litho, orig red, white, and blue box, marked "Marx," c1950 ..... 60.00

Super Hero, 9", litho tin windup, plastic head, walks, Japan

Gaiking 75.00
Grandaezer 85.00
Great Mazinger 85.00
Ground Zero 90.00

Tank

Robo Tank Z, 10½", litho tin, battery operated, half robot, half tank, bump and go action, flashing dome light, noise, marked "TN, Japan" . 400.00

Space Patrol, 8½", litho tin, battery operated, flashing light, cockpit opens and closes, Y, MIB 175.00

Space Tank, 6" l, litho tin, battery operated, bump and go action, missing antennae, marked "SH, Japan" 150.00

Vehicle

Marvelous Mike Tractor, 13" l, litho tin, robot driver, marked "Saunders" 150.00

Mobile Space TV Unit, 10½" l, litho tin, battery operated, space tank with trailer, astronaut sitting on top operates TV camera, lights up and shows lunar landscape, marked "TN, Japan," MIB 2,300.00

Moon Car, remote control, dark blue plastic car, marked "Knickerbocker," 7 x 10 x 20" bright yellow, orange, black, and white box, orig guarantee and instructions, c1950 80.00

Moon Explorer, 4½ x 8 x 7½", tin and plastic, remote control, NASA symbols, 8½" l blue rocket shaped box, marked "Yone, Japan" 300.00

Space Race Car, 3 x 3 x 9", friction, silver, long thin metal blue and red tubes on each side, red tail section, marked "Manoman, Japan," orig box 125.00

Space Scooter, 8" l, litho tin and plastic, battery operated, bump and go action, headlight, engine noise,

boy astronaut steers, marked "MT, Japan" 90.00

Space Vehicle, 8", litho tin, battery operated, red blinking lights, floats satellite ball 115.00

STEREO VIEWERS

Collecting Hints: Condition is the key in determining price. Undamaged wooden hood models are scarce and demand a premium price in burled or bird's-eye maple. All original parts increases the value. Lots of engraving adds 20 to 30% on metal hood models. Often focusing slides and/or handles are missing. If so, deduct 75%. Lenses held in place by metal are better than shimmed in by wood.

History: The first stereo viewers, based on a design by Sir David Brewster (Brewster viewers), were made in England and France starting in 1851. They are uncommon in the United States. The Brewster viewer is a box with paired lenses at one end, a slot at the other end for inserting glass and later paper views, and a small door on top with a mirror to admit light. Brewster viewers are known with a pedestal stand, but rare. The familiar table viewer with an aluminum or wooden hood was the joint invention in 1860 of Oliver Wendell Holmes and Joseph Bates, a Boston photographer. This type of viewer also was made in a much scarcer pedestal model.

In hand viewers (Bates-Holmes models), four companies—Keystone, Griffith & Griffith, Underwood & Underwood, and H. C. White—produced viewers between 1892 and 1908 in the hundreds of thousands. Keystone View Company dominated the market after 1908.

In the mid-1850s a combination stereo viewer and picture magnifier was developed in France and eventually made in England and the United States. The instrument was called a Graphascope. It usually consisted of three pieces and folded for storage. When set up, it had two round lenses for stereo viewing, a large round magnifying lens to view cabinet photographs, and a slide, often with opaque glass, for viewing stereo glass transparencies. The height was adjustable. They were made in a variety of woods including some with inlay and carving.

A rotary or cabinet viewer was made from the late 1850s to about 1870. Becker is the best known maker. The standing floor models hold several hundred slides, the table models hold 50 to 100 (back-to-back).

From the late 1860s to 1880s there were hundreds of different viewer designs. Models had folding wires, collapsible cases (Corta-Scope), pivoting lens to view postcards (Sears' Graphascope), and telescoping card holders. The hoods also became ornate with silver, nickel, and pearl trimmed in velvets and rosewood.

Reference: Information on stereo viewers can be found in most books dealing with the history of photography. A definitive reference study is presently being prepared by the National Stereoscopic Association and should be published in the next few years.

Advisor: John S. Waldsmith.

Corte-Scope (1914), folding aluminum
    or metal, came in box with views . . **40-50.00**
Hand, common maker
    Aluminum hood, folding handle . . . **45-75.00**
    Bird's-eye maple hood, folding han-
    dle **60-90.00**
    Walnut, screw on handle, velvet
    hood **60-90.00**
    Wide hood for people who wear
    glasses, dark brown or green me-
    tal **65-95.00**
Hand, scissor device to focus, groove
    and wire device to hold card . . . **100-125.00**
Pedestal
    Foreign, French or English, nickel
    plated with velvet hood **350-450.00**
    Keystone, school and library type,
    black crinkle metal finish with
    light **75-85.00**
Sculptoscope, (Whiting) counter top
    style, penny operated **400-600.00**
Stand, Bates-Holmes, paper or wood
    hood **125-175.00**
Stereographaศope, Sears Best, lens ro-
    tates to allow viewing of photos or
    post cards **85-100.00**
Telebinocular, binocular style, black
    crinkle metal finish, excellent optics,
    came with "book" box **30-40.00**

STEREOGRAPHS

Collecting Hints: Value is determined by condition, subject, photographer (if famous), rarity, and age—prior to 1870 or after 1935. A revenue stamp on the back indicates an age of 1864–66, when a federal war tax was imposed. Litho printed cards have very little value.

Collect images that are of good grade or above, except for extremely rare images. Very good condition means some wear on the mount and a little dirt on the photo. Folds, marks on the photo, or badly worn mounts reduce values by at least 50%. Faded or light photos also reduce value.

Don't try to clean cards or straighten them. Cards were made curved to heighten the stereo effect, an improvement made in 1880.

With common cards it pays to shop around to get the best price. With rarer cards it pays to buy them when you see them since values are increasing annually. Dealers who are members of the National Stereoscopic Association are very protective of their reputation and offer a good starting point for the novice collector.

Use your public library to study thoroughly the subject matter you are collecting; it is a key element to assembling a meaningful collection.

History: Stereographs, also known as stereo views, stereo view cards, or stereoscope cards, were first issued in the United States on glass and paper in 1854. From the late 1850s through the 1930s, the stereograph was an important visual record of every major event, famous person, comic situation, and natural scene. It was the popular news and entertainment medium until replaced by movies, picture magazines, and radio.

The major early publishers were Anthony (1859–1873), Kilburn (1865–1907), Langeheim (1854–1861), and Weller (1861–1875). By the 1880–1910 period the market was controlled by large firms among which were Davis (Kilburn), Griffith & Griffith, International View Company, Keystone, Stereo Travel, Underwood & Underwood, Universal Photo Art, and H.C. White.

References: William C. Darrah, *Stereo Views, A History Of Stereographs in America And Their Collection*, published by author, 1964, out-of-print; William C. Darrah, *The World of Stereographs*, published by ahtuor, 1977, out-of-print. (Copies available from N. S. A. Book Service).

Collectors' Club: National Stereoscopic Association, Box 14801, Columbus, OH 43214. *Stereo World* (bimonthly).

Advisor: John S. Waldsmith.

Note: Prices given are for very good condition, i.e., some wear and slight soiling. For excellent condition add 25%, and for mint perfect image and mount, double the price. Reverse the process for fair, i.e., moderate soiling, some damage to mount, minor glue marks, some foxing (brown spots) and poor folded mount, very dirty and damage to tone or both images. Where applicable, a price range is given.

Alaska (Gold Rush)
    Berry, Kelley & Chadwick, miners
    working claim **18.00**
    Keystone 1530 Miners, with dogs and
    sled in camp **4.00**
Animal
    Bird, Hurst series of National History   **4-6.00**
Cat
    Keystone #2314, average cat view   **4-5.00**
    Keystone #9651, man and cat . . .   **4.00**
    Soule series, kittens & cats in play-
    ful situations **10-20.00**

Dog

Kilburn #1644, "Home Protection," dog close up **6.00**
U & U, the puppies singing school **4.00**
Universal #3231, average dog view **4-5.00**
Farm Yard, Kilburn #739, sheep and cows, 1870s **4.00**
Horses, Schreiber & Sons, Jarvis and sulky, early **18.00**
Walrus, Keystone #V21232, Bronx Zoo **3.00**
Zoo, London Stereo Company, animals in London Zoo, each **6-8.00**

Astronomy

Comet, Keystone #16645, Morehouse's **9.00**
Mars, Keystone #16767T, the planet **6.00**
Moon
Beer Bros. 1866, photo by Rutherford **15.00**
Kilburn #2630, full moon **6.00**
Soule #602, last quarter **8.00**
Observatories, pre–1800 ....**10-12.00**
Planetarium, Keystone #32688, Adler's Chicago **10.00**

Aviation

Air Mail Plane
Keystone #29446, at Cleveland .. **25.00**
Keystone #32372, Inaugural, Ford Tri-motor, air-rail serivece NY to LA, 7/2/29 .... **20.00**
Aviators, Keystone #26408t, 6 men who first circled earth **15.00**
Balloon, Anthony #4114, Prof. Lowe's flight from 6th Ave. in NYC **100.00**
Dirigibles and Zeppelins, Keystone
#17397, Los Angeles at Lakehurst **45-50.00**
#17398, The Los Angeles **45.00**
#18000, flying over German town **5.00**
#32277, Graf Zeppelin in hanger at Lakehurst, NJ **35.00**
#32740, framework of ZRS-4, Akron **50.00**
#V19216, 1918, R-34 at Mineola, from WWI set, common view .. **10.00**
Doolittle, Keystone #28031, posed by plane, 1931 .... **75.00**
General View, Keystone #32785, five biplanes fly over Chicago's Field Museum **10.00**
Lindbergh, Keystone
#28029, in plane with wife **55.00**
#30262T, next to Spirit of St. Louis **35.00**
Plane, Keystone
#18920, Michelin bomber **15.00**
#19049, Nieuport **9.00**
#V18921, twin seat fighter **9.00**
Wright Bros., Keystone #V96103, in flight at Ft. Myers **85.00**

Black

Keystone
#9506, "We done all dis a' morning," picking cotton **6.00**

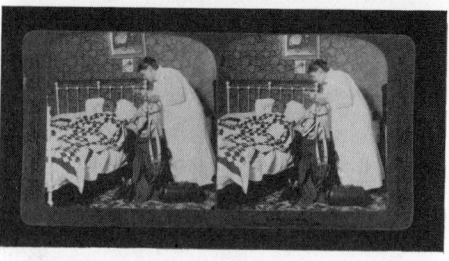

Top: Blacks, Picking Cotton on a Mississippi Plantation, Keystone View Co, #9506, copyright 1909, $6.00; bottom: Comic, Robbing the Male, Underwood & Underwood, copyright 1898, $2.50.

#10209, "One never came up," swimmers **12.00**
#10217, "One got an upper cut," fighting **10.00**
Kilburn #14317, boy and mule, typical, common **3.00**
U & U, "Cotton is King," picking .. **5.00**
U & U, "Keystone, Kilburn, Whiting, etc., cheating at cards, stealing millions, infidelity, etc **10-15.00**
Whiting
#960, "There's a watermelon smiling on the vine" **10.00**
#961, "Happiest Coon" **8.00**

Cave

Keystone
#9586, man in front of Great Oregon Caves **6.00**
#33516, int. of Crystal Springs Cave, Carlsbad **5.00**
U & U, Luray Caverns, typical **8.00**
Waldack, 1866, Mammoth Cave, early magnesium light view showing interiors **10-15.00**

Christmas

Brownies & Santa, Universal #4679 **20.00**
Children with Tree
Griffith #16833, children's Christmas dinner **17.00**
Keystone, 1895, #987, Santa in front of fireplace **15.00**
Santa coming down chimney, Keystone #11434, Santa with toys ... **20.00**
Santa with Toys, Keystone 1898, #9445, Santa loaded with toys ... **15.00**

Comics
Bicycle Bum, Graves #4551–58,
"Weary Willie," 4 card set **20.00**
Drinking
American Stereoscopic Co., 1901,
woman drinking **16.00**
Kilburn 1892, #7348, "Brown just
in from the club" **3.00**
U & U, 1897, man sneaks in after
drinking, 2 card set **8.00**
English classic (sometimes found with
London Stereoscopic Co. blind-
stamp on mount)
"Affectionate Husband," signed
"A. Silvester," tinted **15.00**
"The Anxious Mother," tinted,
shows dolls **8.00**
"The Attack," boy carves roast,
tinted **4.00**
Humor
Keystone #2346-7, before and after
marriage, set of 2 .... **7.00**
U & U, 1904, "Four queens and a
jack," 4 girls and a jackass **4.00**
Infidelity
Foolin–around, 1910, husband
fools around with his secretary,
set of 12 cards **45.00**
Keystone #12312–22, The French
Cook, set **45.00**
U & U
Sneaking–in, 1897, caught by
wife **6.00**
The French Cook, 10 card set .. **45.00**
Romance
U & U, "Going with Stream," hug-
ging couple **6.00**
Weller #353, "Unexpected," neck-
ing **4.00**
Rumors, H. C. White, 5576-5578,
quickest way to spread news: "Tell
a graph, tell a phone, tell a
woman," set **20.00**
Sentimental, American Stereo,
#2001-2012, He goes to war;
wounded; returns; reunited, etc.,
12 card set **50.00**
Wedding Set, White, #5510–19, typ-
ical, similar set made by most pub-
lishers **40.00**
Disaster
Boston Fire, 1872, Soule, ruins **8-10.00**
Chicago Fire, 1871, Lovejoy & Foster,
ruins **8-10.00**
Galveston Flood, 1900, Universal
Photo Art, ruins **10.00**
Johnstown Flood, ruins
George Barker, large orange
mounts **9.00**
U & U, Kilburn, Bonine, etc., buff
mounts **5-7.00**
Mill Creek Flood, 1874, series made

by various local Massachusetts
photographers, typical house ruins **4.00**
Portland Fire, 1866, Soule #469,
ruins **8-12.00**
St. Pierre Eruption, Kilburn #14941,
ruins **3.00**
San Francisco Earthquake
Keystone #13264, Market St **10.00**
U & U #8180, California St **12.00**
Worcester, MA, flood, 1876, Law-
rence, damage **5.00**
Doll
Graves #4362, Sunday School class **20.00**
Kilburn
#15, tired of play **15.00**
When will Santa come? **12.00**
U & U
#6922, playing doctor **15.00**
Universal Photo Art #4362, Sunday
School class **20.00**
Entertainer
Actress, J. Gurney & Son, 1870s, Mrs.
Scott or Mrs. Roland, etc. **15.00**
Dancers, Keystone #33959, Bali,
Dutch Indies **2.00**
Natives, Keystone #16423, Java,
good costumes **3.00**
James Cremer, opera, studio pose, in
costume **12.00**
Expositions and Fairs
NY Sanitary Fair, Anthony #1689-
2864, views of fountains or statues
(major exhibits are double value) . **15.00**
1872, World Peace Jubilee, Boston
Pollock, interior view **6-8.00**
1876, U.S. Close Up Centennial,
Centennial Photo Co.
Grounds and building exteri-
ors **4.00-10.00**
Corliss Engine **12.00**
Monorail **65.00**
Statue of Liberty, arm and torch .. **85.00**
1893–4, World's Columbian, Kilburn
series
Ferris wheel **7-10.00**
Most views **4-7.00**
1894, California Mid-Winter, urns
and statuary, often found tinted (for
better subject, double value) **8-12.00**
1901, Pan American, Buffalo, Kilburn
Most views **4-6.00**
President McKinley **7-9.00**
1904–5, Louisiana Purchase Exposition, St. Louis
Universal Photo Art or U & U, most
views **4-8.00**
Whiting #620, Missouri Fruit Exhibit **12.00**
1905, Lewis & Clark Centennial, Portland, Watson Fine Art #34, buildings **10.00**
1907, Jamestown Exposition, Key-

stone #14219, life saving demonstration **5.00**
1908, West Michigan State Fair, Keystone #21507 .... **8.00**
1933, Century of Progress, Chicago, Keystone #32993, Lief Ericksen Dr (unmounted smaller format Keystone views, half value) **12-20.00**

Hunting & Fishing
Bass, Ingersoll #3159, string of fish . **6.00**
Deer, Keystone #26396, hunters and kill, typical **4.00**
Halibut, Keystone #22520, commercial fishing **4.00**
Moose, Keystone #9452, 1899, typical big game kill **5.00**
Trout, Kilburn, #115, 1870, a day's catch **5.00**
Wildcat, Keystone #12264, man shoots sleeping wildcat **6.00**

Indian
Burge, J. C., Apaches bathing **75-125.00**
Continental Stereo Co., Pueblo eating bread **45-50.00**
Griffith #11873, Esquimau at St. Louis Fair **8.00**
Hayes, F. J.
#865, Crow burial ground **17-25.00**
#1742, Sioux **40-60.00**
Ingersoll #496, lithograph of Gray Eagle, typical printed view **1.00**
Jackson, Wm. H., #202, Otoe, with bow, rare **90-125.00**
Keystone
#23095, Chief Black Hawk **8.00**
#23118, Indian girl, common view **2-4.00**
#V23181, Blackfeet **8.00**
Montgomery Ward, squaws **8.00**
Soule #1312, Piute squaw **50-60.00**
U & U
Hopi or Wolpi, usually in villages **9.00**
White, H. C., #12279, pueblo .. **12.00**

Mining
Alaska Gold Rush
Keystone
#9191, men with supplies getting ready to climb the "golden stairs" at Chilkoot Pass, typical **8.00**
#21100, panning for gold **10.00**
U & U #10655, looking into glory hole **15.00**
Universal, Graves, 1902, man working a sluice, scarce **35.00**
Eastern, US (Vermont,) Anthony #474, working gold chute **50.00**
Gold Hill, Housewroth #743, city overview **70-100.00**
Hydraulic, Housewroth #799, typical water spraying **65-85.00**
Virginia City
Housewroth #713, street view .**70-100.00**

Watkins
Opera House **80-100.00**
Panorama, new series **90-125.00**
Miscellaneous
Auto
Corte-Scope set, Willys-Overland plant, Toledo, OH **200.00**
U & U, early auto in Los Angeles, 1903 ....**17-20.00**
Beach scenes, H.C. White, #476, bathers, Atlantic City **5.00**
Bicycles
Kilburn #11924, women and bike **6.00**
Thorne, big two wheeler, early 1870s **45-60.00**
Circus
U & U, Chicago **20.00**
Windsor & Whipple, Olean, NY, people with elephant **35-40.00**
Firefighting
Early 1870s, close view of pumpers **45.00**
Keystone #11684, action view of pumpers **25.00**

Top: Miscellaneous, When the frost is on the pumpkin and the fodder is in the shock, Underwood & Underwood, copyright 1904, $2.50; bottom: Ship, Christopher Columbus Flagship—The The Santa Maria, Keystone Views, #P239 P-13728, history on back, $5.00.

Glass Stereos
Foreign Scenes, usually French titles **10-20.00**
United States Scenes, Niagara Falls most common **50-75.00**
Hawaii, Keystone, #10156, hula girls **9.00**
Lighthouses
Keystone #29207, common view **3.00**
Williams, Minot Ledge Light **15-17.00**

New York City, Anthony #3938, typical busy street 12-20.00
Prisons, Pach, Sing Sing, NY, 1870s   15.00
Tinted Views
　Foreign, cleanly executed without blotchy appearance 4-6.00
　United States, cleanly executed .. 5-10.00
Tunnel, Ward #808 Hoosac Tunnel, just completed 12-15.00
Toy train, Keystone #P-21329, boy playing with Lionel trains 25.00
National Park
　Death Valley, Keystone #32666, pool   9.00
　Garden of the Gods, Thurlow, Pike's Peak 6.00
　Grand Teton, Wm. H. Jackson, #503, average, noted photographer 20.00
　Yellowstone
　　Jackson, Wm. H., #422, average   15.00
　　Keystone, U & U, etc., averge geyser view 2.00
　　Universal Photo Art, average geyser view 4.00
　Yosemite
　　Keystone #4001, Nevada Falls ...   4.00
　　Kilburn #9284, Bridal Veil Falls ..   4.00
　　Reilly, tourists at Yosemite Falls ..   10.00
　　U & U, Glacier Point 5.00
Niagara Falls
　Anthony #3731, American Falls ...   3.00
　Barker, people on ice bridge 2.00
　U & U, whirlpool rapids 1.00
　White, H. C., #7, tourists, 1903 ...   4.00
Occupational
　Blacksmith, Keystone #18206, shows many tools 4.00
　Cowboys, Keystone, #13641, Yellowstone, Montana 7.00
　Farming, Kilburn #1796, hay, 1870s   8.00
　Milkman, Keystone #P-26392, horsedrawn wagon 10.00
　Mill, U & U, linen factory, typical industrial view 2-3.00
　Store, Keystone #18209, grocery store int. 15.00
Oil
　Pennsylvania
　　Detlor&Waddell,#76,burningtanks   15.00
　　Robbins #32, Triumph Hill 15.00
　　Keystone #20352T, shooting a well   4.00
　　Robbins, #88, gas well 10.00
　　Wilt Brothers, Allegheny area 8.00
　Texas, Keystone #34864, tanks near Kilgore, common 6.00
Person, Famous
　Barton, Clara, Keystone #28002, founder of American Red Cross ..50-60.00
　Buntline, Ned, J. Gurney, portrait .. 200.00
　Burbank, Luther, Keystone #16746, with cactus 6.00

Top: Famous People, Herbert Hoover, Keystone View Co, #23028012, biography on back, $35.00; bottom: Mining, Gold Miners and Dog Team North of Arctic Circle, Alaska, Keystone Views Co, #24611530, history on back, $4.00.

Bryan, W. J., Keystone #15539, on way to hotel in NYC 30.00
Coolidge,　President,　Keystone #26303, President and Cabinet ..   25.00
Custer, General
　Lovejoy & Foster, with bear he killed 350-500.00
　Taylor #2438, with his dog in camp 500-600.00
Czar of Russia, U & U, with President of France 10.00
Edison, Thomas
　Keystone, #V28007, in lab ... 85-100.00
　U & U, in lab 100-125.00
Edison, Ford and Firestone, Keystone #18551 ....   75.00
Eisenhower, President, Keystone, at table with microphones, about 1954, rare 150-250.00
Faragutt, Admiral, Anthony, from Prominent Portrait Series 40.00
Gehrig, Lou, Keystone #32597, baseball player 200-250.00
Grant, President, Bierstadt Bros., on Mount Washington 75.00
Hayes, R. B., President, party at Hastings 100-125.00
Harding, W., President, addressing boy scouts 15-20.00
Hoover, President, Keystone #28012, close portrait 35.00
Lincoln, Abraham, Anthony, funeral, #4596 .... .50-65.00

Marconi, Keystone #V11969, radio
inventor **45.00**
McKinley, President, Keystone, Kilburn, U & U, most views **5-15.00**
Morse, Samuel, J. Gurney **200-250.00**
Queen Victoria, U & U 1897, having
breakfast **40.00**
Rogers, Will, Keystone #32796, at
1932 Chicago Democratic Convention **75.00**
Roosevelt, Franklin D., President,
Keystone #33535 .... **75.00**
Roosevelt, Theodore, President
Keystone, Kilburn, U & U, most
views **8-15.00**
U & U
At Glacier Point, Yosemite **20-30.00**
On horseback, typical view ...**12-20.00**
Ruth, Babe, Keystone #32590, baseball player **200-250.00**
Shaw, George Bernard, Keystone
#34505, on a ship **50-60.00**
Taft, President, U & U #10062, at desk **20.00**
Thomas, Lowell, Keystone #32812,
world travel expert and newsman **50.00**
Twain, Mark
Evans & Soule **350.00**
U & U #8010 or H. C. White
#13055, in bed writing **250.00**
Washington, Booker T., Keystone
#V11960, with Andrew Carnegie **50-70.00**
Young, Brigham, C. W. Carter, bust
portrait **20.00**
Photographers, views by famous
Brady, published by Anthony
1863, Tom Thumb Wedding, famous portrait **100-150.00**
#428, Captain Custer with Confederate prisoner **900.00**
#3376, Jeff Davis Mansion **50.00**
Houseworth, Thomas, San Francisco,
#150, show photo studio **100-150.00**
#429, Golden Gate **35-45.00**
Langenheim, Frederick, 1854-586,
Trenton Falls, typical view, but
scarce on glass **75-125.00**
Muybridge, Ed.
#318, The Golden Gate **80.00**
#1623, Indian scouts **250.00**
O'Sullivan, T.H., published by Anthony #826, Men's Quarters **50-60.00**
Pond, C. L., #786, Mirror Lake, Yosemite **20-25.00**
Watkins, C. E.
Panoramic, #1338, from Telegraph
Hill **45-60.00**
San Francisco street scene, e.g.,
#767, panorama from Russian
Hill **50-60.00**
Railroad
American Stereoscopic, view in Penn
Station **15.00**

Centennial Photographic Co, 1876,
locomotives on display **45.00**
Keystone
#2367, loop at Georgetown, common **5.00**
#7090, interior of Baldwin Works **8.00**
#37509, The Chief, 1930s **45.00**
Kilburn
#135, Mt Washington Cog Railway, locomotive pushing car ... **7.00**
#432, large side view of locomotive **35.00**
#779, train with engineer posed,
1870 .... **50.00**
U & U #52, train going through Pillars of Hercules, common **7.00**
Universal Photo Art #2876, Columbian Express **20.00**
Sets, in special book-like boxes
Boxer Rebellion, U & U 1901, 72
cards, rare **200.00**
Bullfight, U & U, set of 15 .... **100.00**
China, Stereo Travel, set of 100,
scarce maker, unusual subject ... **400.00**
France
Stereo Travel, set of 30, typical for
this scarce publisher, popular
country **70.00**
U & U, set of 100 .... **250.00**
Glacier Park, Forsyth, set of 30 .**125-150.00**
Greece, U & U, set of 100 .... **225.00**
India, U & U, set of 100 .... **250.00**
Italy, U & U, set of 100 .... **170.00**
Switzerland, U & U, set of 100,
guidebook and maps **200.00**
United States, U & U, set of 100,
good U. S. tour **400.00**
Wild Flowers, Keystone, 100, hand
tinted **400.00**
World Tour, Keystone
Set of 200, trip from U.S. around
world **350.00**
Set of 400 ....**450-600.00**
Set of 600, trip from U.S. around
world and back, oak cabinet **900-1,000.00**
Yellowstone, U & U, set of 30 ... **90-100.00**
Yosemite, U & U, set of 30 .....**100-125.00**
Survey and Expedition Views
Amundsen, Keystone #13327, at Antoretie Glacier, 1911 .... **6.00**
Gerlache, Keystone #13328, hunting
seals at South Pole **6.00**
Hayden, Jackson #796, people view,
typical **22-25.00**
Perry, Greenland, Keystone #13325,
ships **6.00**
Wheeler, William Bell #14, Canon
de Chelle, wall, 1873 .... **40.00**
Tissue, American Stereoscopic Co, wedding, #7, typical US subject, wedding vows **10.00**

Tissue, French (Hold to light)
Balloon, close view **60-70.00**
Diablo, 1870s, devils, skeletons, etc.,
no tears or soil **20-30.00**
Interior scene, 1870s, minor tears, but
viewable **6-8.00**
Interior scene, 1870s, nice stereo,
pin-pricked, no tears **10-20.00**
War
Boer, U & U, artillery firing, typical view **5-7.00**
Boxer Rebellion, U & U, 1901, typi-
cal view **4-7.00**
Civil War
Anthony, "War for the Union"
#3031, Dunlop Home **30.00**
#3365, Brady negative, Libby
Prison, yellow mount **25.00**
#3406, chair in which Lincoln
was shot **60.00**
Gardner, "Incidents of the War,"
#237, home of Rebel sharp-
shooter (Gettysburg) **45-50.00**
Taylor & Huntington (War Photo-
graph Co.)
#458, Conferdate fortifications .   **25.00**
#2557, pontoon boats **25.00**
#6705, powder magazine **35.00**
Russo-Japanese, U & U #4380, gen-
eral view of Port Arthur, typical
view **5.00**
Spanish American, Keystone, Kilburn,
U & U, typical view **5-12.00**
World War I, in special book-like
boxes
Set of 100 . . . .   **175.00**
Set of 200 . . . .   **300.00**
Set of 300 . . . .   **400.00**
Whaling
Freeman, J, Nantucket, beached
whales **35-50.00**
Keystone
#14768T, floating whale station,
common **6-8.00**
#V27198T, whalers cruising, com-
mon **4-6.00**
Nickerson, beached whales, rare . .**50-70.00**
Unknown maker, beached whale . .**15-25.00**

STOCK AND BOND CERTIFICATES

Collecting Hints: Some of the factors that affect
price are (1) date [with pre-1900 more popular
and pre-1850 most desirable], (2) autographs of
important persons [Vanderbilt, Rockefeller, J. P.
Morgan, Wells and Fargo, etc.], (3) number issued [most bonds have number issued in text],
and (4) attractiveness of the vignette.

Stocks and bonds are collected for a variety of
reasons, among which are the graphic illustra-

tions and the history of romantic times in America, including gold and silver mining, railroad
history, and early automobile pioneers.

History: The use of stock to raise capital and
spread the risk in a business venture dates back
to England. Several American colonies were
founded as joint venture stock companies. The
New York Stock Exchange on Wall Street in New
York City traces its roots to the late eighteenth
century.

Stock certificates with attractive vignettes date
to the beginning of the nineteenth century. As
engraving and printing techniques developed, so
did the elaborateness of the stock and bond certificates. Important engraving houses emerged
among which were the American Bank Note
Company and Rawdon, Wright & Hatch.

Reference: Bill Yatchman, *The Stock & Bond
Collectors Price Guide*, published by author,
1985.

Periodical: *Bank Note Reporter*, 700 East State
Street, Iola, WI 54990.

Collectors' Club: Bond and Share Society, 24
Broadway, New York, NY 10004.

Advisor: Ken Prag.

**Railroad, Mt Tamalpais and Muir Woods
Railway, 1914, H. S. Crocker Co, 7⅜ x
10⅛, $195.00.**

Airline, stock, Hornell Airways Inc., issued and canceled, NY, two women
and sun rising over mountains vi-
gnette, 1920s **65.00**
Automobile, stock
Cole Motor Car, 1909–25, man with
woman feeding flame vignette
Green, not sgd and sealed **25.00**
Orange, sgd, corporate seal **35.00**
Kelly-Springfield Motor Truck Co., issued and canceled, 1910–20
seated woman, anvil, and gears vignette, green or purple, American
Bank Note Company **35.00**

Willys Corporation, issued, 1921
   Brown **15.00**
   Orange **15.00**
Business, stock
  American Express Co, issued and canceled, 1860s, bulldog vignette, sgd "Henry Wells" and "William Fargo" **750.00**
  Broadway Joe's, issued and canceled, green or blue border, sports figure's restaurant **10.00**
  F. W. Woolworth Co., eagle over two hemispheres vignette, brown **4.00**
  General Foods, issued and canceled, green, brown, or orange, engraved, vignette scene on right **2.50**
  International Business Machines Corp, issued, brown **5.00**
  International Immigration & Colonization Assn., Hawaii, 1911, issued, not canceled, map vignette **100.00**
  Uncas National Bank of Norwich, 1900, green, gray and white, Indian, blacksmith, and sailing ship vignette **15.00**
  Wells Fargo Bank & Union Trust, 1940s, issued and canceled, green pony express rider vignette **25.00**
Canal, bond, Pennsylvania Canal Company, issued and canceled, 1870, canal and surrounding area vignette, two revenue stamps **125.00**
Industrial, stock
  Colorado Milling & Elevator Co., issued and canceled, gold border, company buildings vignette
   1890s **25.00**
   1920s **15.00**
  Edison Portland Cement Co, issued and canceled, engraved, rust or green, Thomas Edison vignette
   1890s **28.00**
   1900s **25.00**
  Gray Manufacturing Co, issued and canceled, orange, dial pay telephone vignette **15.00**
  Jantzen Knitting Mills, 1930s, issued and canceled, engraved, swimmer vignette, orange or green **20.00**
  Sentinel Radio Corp, issued and canceled, green or brown, goddess and two radio towers vignette **5.00**
  Waikea Mill Co., unissued, 1889, black and white sugar mill **45.00**
Mining
  Bond, Sovereign Gold Mining, issued and canceled, $5,000, Canadian, 1903, peach borders, coupon **10.00**
  Stock
   Industry Gold & Silver Mining, 1870s, unissued, fancy design, mining vignette **20.00**

Isabella Gold Mining Co., Colorado, 1890s, issued and canceled, engraved, eagle vignette **8.00**
Sheba Gold & Silver Mining, Humboldt County, Nevada, issued, not canceled, three mining vignettes, gold seal **20.00**
Sun-Hope Mining Co., Colorado, unissued, three mining vignettes **2.50**
Syndicate Mines, Inc., Nevada, unissued, brown, mining vignette, "V" cut cancel **3.50**
Railroad
  Bond
   Cairo & Norfolk RR Co., Kentucky, 1908, issued, not canceled, orange, speeding train vignette, coupons **45.00**
   New York, New Haven & Hartford, 1920, $10,000, issued and canceled, engraved, electric train vignette **48.00**
   Sacramento & Woodland RR, California, 1911, issued, not canceled, rust-brown, logo around capitol building vignette, coupons **165.00**
   Union Pacific RR, 1946, $1,000, issued and canceled, two engraved angels and company logo **15.00**
  Stock
   Cambridge Railroad Co., MA, 1880s, unissued, black and white **8.00**
   Gulf, Mobile & Ohio, issued and canceled, engraved, blue or brown, two women and diesel train vignette **3.50**
   Illinois Central, issued and canceled, engraved, orange or brown, diesel train vignette **3.50**
   Nashville & Decatur, 1880s, issued and canceled, green border, train vignette **25.00**
   Raleigh & Gaston, 1870s, issued and canceled, two vignettes ... **65.00**
Railways (Trolley)
  Bond
   Chicago & Wisconsin Valley Street Railways Co., 1912, $1,000, issued and canceled, first mortgage gold, black and white **25.00**
   New Paltz & Highland Electric RR, 1893, $500, issued and canceled, trolley car vignettes, gold seal, two pages of coupons **95.00**
   Southern Indiana, 1908, $1,000, issued and canceled, green **28.00**
  Stock
   California Street Cable RR Co., San Francisco, CA, 1884, unissued, cable car vignette **35.00**

Omaha & Council Bluffs Street Railway, 1906, issued and canceled, blue, green, or pink	20.00
Rochelle & Southern, Illinois, 1900, unissued, black and white	12.00
Rock Island & Eastern, Illinois, 1900, black and white, curved company name	15.00
Real Estate, stock, The Real Estate Association, Petaluma, CA, 1890s, issued, black and white	25.00

Utility
Bond

Columbus & Southern Ohio Electric Co., issued and canceled, blue, engraved	7.50
Consolidated Edison Co., New York, $1,000, issued and canceled, engraved, blue or purple	8.00
Long Island Lighting Co., issued an canceled, orange, engraved, woman, child, generator, and light vignette	7.50

Stock

Communications Satellite Corp., 1960s, issued and canceled, green or blue, space vignette . .	4.00
International Telephone & Telegraph, 1930s, blue, engraved, goddess and globe vignette	8.00
Maryland Telecommunications, issued and canceled, green, drawn 1957 TV and TV camera vignette	8.00
Philippine Long Distance Telephone Co., 1950s, issued and canceled, blue, engraved, woman on two globes vignette .	5.00
Tuolumne County Water Co., 1850s, issued and canceled, mining methods vignette	75.00

STUFFED TOYS

Collecting Hints: The collector tends to focus on one type of animal and collects material spanning a long time period. The company with the strongest collector following is Steiff.

Collectors stress very good to mint condition. Often stuffed toys had ribbons or clothing. All accessories must be intact to command full value.

History: The stuffed toy may have originated in Germany. Margarete Steiff GmbH of Germany began making stuffed toys for export beginning in 1880. By 1903 the teddy bear had joined Steiff's line and quickly worked its way to America. The first American teddy bears were made by the Ideal Toy Corporation. Not much is known about earlier manufacturers since com-

panies were short lived and many toys have lost their labels.

The stuffed toy has enjoyed a favorite position in the American market. Some have music boxes inserted to enhance their appeal. Carnivals used stuffed toys as prizes. Since the 1960s America has been subjected to a wealth of stuffed toys imported from Japan, Taiwan, and China. These animals often are poorly made and are not popular among serious collectors.

References: Peggy and Alan Bialosky, *The Teddy Bear Catalog*, Workman Publishing, 1984, revised edition; Shirley Conway and Jean Wilson, *Steiff Teddy Bears, Dolls, and Toys with Prices*, Wallace-Homestead, 1984; Margaret Fox Mandel, *Teddy Bears And Steiff Animals, First Series (1984) and Second Series (1987)*, Collector Books; Helen Sieverling, *3rd Teddy Bear & Friends Price Guide*, Hobby House Press, 1988; Jean Wilson, *Steiff Revised*, Wallace-Homestead, 1989.

Periodicals: *The Teddy Bear and Friends*, Hobby House Press, Inc., 900 Frederick Street, Cumberland, MD 21502; *Teddy Bear, Toy & Doll Finder*, P. O. Box H, South San Francisco, CA 94083-1508.

Collectors' Clubs: Good Bears Of The World, P. O. Box 8236, Honolulu, Hawaii 96815; Steiff Collectors Anonymous, P. O. Box 1678, Piqua, OH 45356; Teddy Bear Collectors Club, P. O. Box 601, Harbor City, CA 90710.

Note: Stuffed toys dealing with advertising, cartoon, television, and other character types will be found elsewhere in the book.

Cat, Siamese, seated, R Dankin Co, San Francisco, made in Korea, 14" l, 7" h, $10.00.

Alligator, 9½", vinyl, green and brown, glass eyes, c1950	35.00
Beaver, mohair, brown, Steiff	45.00
Boa Constrictor, plush, multicolored, felt eyes and tongue, c1958	12.00

Camel

  4½", leather, tan, single hump, straw
    saddle, c1955 .... **12.00**
  8", plush, tan, single hump, glass
    eyes, c1950 .... **65.00**

Cat

  4", Tabby, orig bell, Steiff **60.00**
  5", Snurry, sleeping **105.00**
  5¼", mohair, green plastic eyes, mov-
    able head and legs, Steiff, c1950 . **45.00**
  11" h, Diva, long white fur, sitting,
    orig Steiff tag and button **110.00**

Cow, 5½", felt, brown and white, glass
  eyes, wooden wheels **65.00**

Deer, 15", Bambi, plush, Gund, c1953 **60.00**

Dog

  4½", Scottie, cotton, plaid, embroi-
    dered features and collar, hand
    made, c1950 .... **5.00**
  6", Boxer, Steiff **75.00**
  7", Dalmatian, sitting, mohair, swivel
    head, orig collar, Steiff **75.00**
  8", plush, amber, swivel neck, over-
    sized head, milk glass and amber
    bead eyes, embroidered nose and
    mouth, stitched tail and ears, early
    20th C **75.00**
  8½", Poodle, pink, standing, glass
    eyes **18.00**
  9", Beagle, plush, glass eyes **25.00**
  10", Snoopy, black and white **15.00**
  11", Terrier, white plush, black spots,
    swivel head, white muzzle, yellow
    glass eyes, embroidered features,
    red ribbon, c1925 .... **50.00**
  12", Poodle, curly, gray, plaid coat,
    hat, and boots, c1960 .... **15.00**
  16", Huckleberry Hound **14.00**

Donkey, 11", plush, gray, brown glass
  eyes, brown yarn mane, gray tail,
  wheeled base, c1950 .... **100.00**

Duck

  4", calico, blue, yellow, and pink,
    embroidered wing and eye, hand
    made, c1950 .... **3.50**
  8", plush, standing, yellow, straw hat,
    blue suspender pants **45.00**

Elephant

  4", gray mohair, black glass eyes, red
    saddle, Steiff, c1953 .... **100.00**
  6½", standing, gray, red suspender
    pants **65.00**

Frog, 9", green velvet back, white satin
  underside, c1960 .... **12.50**

Giraffe, 42", plush, yellow, brown
  spots, brown button eyes, brown yarn
  tail, c1957 .... **20.00**

Goat, 6½", standing, white, brown felt
  horns, Steiff **50.00**

Hedgehogs, Micky & Mecky, 22", vinyl
  swivel heads, pressed mask face, tan,
  squinting eyes, smiling mouths,

bristly hair, felt bodies, sewn on
  shoes, checkered costumes, c1950,
  pr **475.00**

Hen, 7", gold and black spotted feathers, yellow plush head, felt tail, black
  button eyes, Steiff, c1949 .... **75.00**

Hippo, plush, purple, plastic eyes and
  teeth, c1962 .... **18.00**

Horse, 15", amber hopsacking, straw
  stuffing, reinforced stitching, pale yellow underbelly, amber glass eyes,
  stitched smiling mouth, applied ears,
  black fur mane, horsehair tail, velvet
  and leather saddle and harness,
  c1890 .... **85.00**

Kangaroo, 11", plush, glass eyes, two
  plastic Joeys, Steiff button in ear
  marked "Linda" **65.00**

Lamb, 9", white, fluffy, glass eyes, embroidered features, bell, flowers and
  ribbon at neck, paper label **90.00**

Llama, 11", standing, white, brown
  spots, Steiff **100.00**

Monkey

  11", mohair, jointed, felt paws and
    face, Steiff **85.00**
  36", Curious George, plush, knit yel-
    low sweater, red cap, c1975 ..... **45.00**

Mother Goose, 22", muslin, white, yellow felt feet, white cotton bonnet,
  blue floral apron, c1962 .... **30.00**

Owl, 10", Steiff **70.00**

Panda, 47", plush, black and white,
  jointed, humpback, pie shaped eyes,
  straw filled **225.00**

Parrot, 9", Lora, glass eyes, Steiff **75.00**

Pelican, 10", Piccy, glass eyes, Steiff .. **150.00**

Penguin, 10", black and white, black
  plastic wings, c1960 .... **10.00**

Pig, 6", plush, pink, pink felt cork screw
  tail, black and white felt eyes **20.00**

Rabbit

  6½", mohair, jointed, Steiff **100.00**
  12", plush, glass eyes, embroidered
    features, jointed body, paper label **70.00**
  15", felt, eating carrot, Lenci **24.00**

Raccoon, 6", Raccy, plush, glass eyes,
  Steiff **45.00**

Seal, 10", fur, black, glass eyes **85.00**

Squirrel, plush, Perri, Steiff **42.00**

Teddy Bear

  4", plush, dark brown, jointed **40.00**
  5", plush, standing, swivel head,
    "Character" label **40.00**
  6", plush, jointed, fully dressed, orig
    clothes, "Berg" label **65.00**
  9", plush, blonde, black shoe button
    eyes, shoulder hump, small tail,
    straw filled, c1905 .... **165.00**
  12", plush, amber, swivel head,
    jointed arms and legs, stitched on

ears, felt paws, functioning growler, straw filled, c1915 .... **200.00**
14"
   Knickerbocker, 1950s **26.00**
   Zotty, Hermann, platinum frosted mohair **155.00**
15", mohair, brown, black shoe button eyes, black embroidered nose, mouth, and claws, fully jointed, label "Bruin Mfg Co," c1907 ...... **250.00**
16", Molly Koala bear, gray and tan, Steiff **135.00**
17", plush, brown, tan paws, molded muzzle, Ideal Toy **50.00**
20", mohair, brown, jointed, flat face, Knickerbocker **100.00**
24", mohair, brown, glass eyes, black cloth nose, fully jointed, c1925 .. **600.00**
Tiger
   6", plush, Steiff **60.00**
   8", Tony, Esso Tiger, orange and black, felt trim **45.00**
   13", plush, Shere Khan, black-green eyes, 8" l tail, button in ear, Steiff **150.00**
Turtle, 5½", plush and felt, Steiff **40.00**
Zebra, 7", belt and white, button in ear, Steiff **75.00**

SUPER HEROES

Collecting Hints: Concentrate on a single super hero. Because Superman, Batman, and Wonder Woman are the most popular, new collectors are advised to focus on other characters or one of the modern super heroes. Nostalgia is a principal motivation for many collectors; hence, they pay prices based on sentiment rather than true market value for some items.

Comics are a fine collectible but require careful handling and storage. An attractive display requires a three dimensional object. Novice collectors are advised to concentrate on these first before acquiring too many of the flat paper material.

History: The Super Hero and comic books go hand in hand. Superman made his debut in 1939 in the first issue of *Action Comics,* six years after Jerry Siegel and Joe Shuster conceived the idea of a man who flew. A newspaper strip, radio show, and movies followed. The Superman era produced a wealth of super heroes, among them Batman, Captain Marvel, Captain Midnight, The Green Hornet, The Green Lantern, The Shadow, and Wonder Woman.

These early heroes had extraordinary strength and/or cunning and lived normal lives as private citizens. A wealth of merchandising products surround these early super heroes. Their careers were enchanced further when television chose

them as heroes for Saturday morning viewing as well as in prime time.

The Fantastic Four—Mr. Fantastic, The Human Torch, The Invisible Girl, and The Thing—introduced a new type of super hero, the mutant. Among the most famous of this later period are Captain America, Spiderman and The Hulk. Although these characters appear in comic form, the number of secondary items generated is small. Television has helped to promote a few of the characters, but the list of mutant super heroes is close to a hundred.

References: Steven H. Kimball, *Greenberg's Guide To Super Hero Toys, Volume I,* Greenberg Publishing Co., 1988; Jeff Rovin, *The Encyclopedia of Super Heroes,* Facts on File Publications, 1985.

See: Comic Books, Radio Characters, and Personalities.

Batman and Robin
   Art Kit, "Stardust Touch Of Velvet Art," two velvet pictures, supplies, unopened box, Hasbro, 1966 copyright **35.00**
   Bank, Batman, 8½" h, plastic, molded, Mego Corp, 1974 copyright **20.00**
   Card Game, playing cards with full color action scene, playing pieces, instructions inside box lid, Ideal, 1966 copyright **30.00**
   Character Mug
      Batman **12.00**
      Robin **20.00**
   Coloring Book, 8 x 11", Whitman #1002, full color covers, unused, 1967 .... **15.00**
   Figure
      Batman, 11½" h, plastic, flying position, Transogram, c1966 ..... **30.00**
      Robin, 8", plastic, movable legs and arms, synthetic outfit, Mego, 1972 copyright **40.00**
   Glass, 6½" h, full color design around side, 1966 copyright **15.00**
   Gum Pack, 2½ x 3½", yellow and black symbol with red background on wrapper, unopened, Topps, 1966 copyright **15.00**
   Helmet, plastic, blue, black mask, gold and black symbol, orig unopened display bag, Ideal, 1966 copyright **40.00**
   Lunch Box, 7 x 8 x 4", litho metal, full color action scene, 6½" h thermos with black plastic cap, 1966 copyright **50.00**
   Mask, adult, Batman, soft rubber, flexible, diecut eyes, nostrils, and mouth, c1966 .... **25.00**

Napkins, 1966, MIB
   10 x 10" **5.00**
   13⅜ x 13⅜" **8.00**
Pennant, 29" l, felt, black, full color scene, white inscription, yellow trim and streamers, 1966 copyright **15.00**
Picture, Robin, embroidered, tan burlap background, white plastic frame with silver trim, 1966 National Publications Periodicals copyright **15.00**
Pillow, 10 x 14", flannel, stuffed, red, white, blue, and black action scene, 1966 copyright **75.00**
Placemat, pr, 11 x 17", phrases and full color action illus border, Ciro Art Corp, 1966 copyright **50.00**
Puzzle, 11 x 17", action scene, 200 pcs, litho cardboard cylinder canister, American Publishing Corp, 1974 copyright **20.00**
Radio, 5½ x 6", Batman figure, diecut, carrying strap, battery-operated, orig box, made in Hong Kong, 1973 copyright **45.00**
Record, 33⅓ rpm, twelve songs including Batman theme, 12¼" sq cardboard album, Tifton label, 1966 copyright **10.00**
Slippers, child's, Batman, leather, black, white trim, name and symbol in red, c1966 .... **30.00**
Stickers, set of 5, black symbol, green and pink glo-color, unopened package, 1966 copyright **15.00**
Waste Can, 9½" h, oval, litho metal, full color picture of Batman and Robin, National Periodical Publications, 1966 copyright **30.00**
Captain America
Comic Book, Marvel Comic Vol 1 #100, April 1968 .... **10.00**
Puppet, vinyl, molded, red, white, and blue uniform, unopened display bag, Imperial Toy, 1976 copyright **12.00**
Puzzle, 11½ x 14½", full color action scene, Whitman #4531, 1966 copyright **15.00**
Ring, flasher, plastic, blue **8.00**
Toy, 5", wind-up, vinyl, walking, Marx, 1973 copyright, MIB **12.00**
Captain Marvel
Comic Book, 6½ x 8¼", "Captain Marvel Adventure," Wheaties adv and Bob Feller photo on back, 1964 copyright **30.00**
Decoder, 4" d, cardboard, diecut opening, red, white, and blue scene, Fawcett Comics, mid 1940s **75.00**
Glass, 6¼", full color picture, 1976 copyright Pepsi Super series **15.00**

Iron-on Transfer, 3¼ x 8¼ sheet, Captain Marvel flying with machine gun, red, white, and blue envelope, Fawcett Publications **50.00**
Member Card, 2¾ x 4", red, white, and blue, inked name on front, c1940 .... **25.00**
Post Card, 3¼ x 5½", magic ink, blue, red inscriptions, unused, mid 1940s **60.00**
Puzzle, 9 x 13", full color action scene, L. Miller & Sons Ltd, England issue, Fawcett publications copyright, c1940 .... **150.00**
Stationery, 7 x 8¼", full color design, unused, orig envelope, Fawcett Publications, mid 1940s **30.00**
Captain Marvel Jr.
Comic book, #6, Vs. Capt. Nazi, Fawcett Publications **20.00**
Patch, cloth, emblem **30.00**
Mary Marvel
Comics, #23, Fawcett Publications **15.00**
Picture, 8 x 10", cardboard, glows in dark, red dress, cape, yellow boots, beige background **50.00**
Watch, silvered metal, Mary in flight, gray numerals, green hands, Swiss movement, 1948 Fawcett copyright **75.00**
Captain Midnight
Better Little Book, *Captain Midnight and the Secret Squadron vs. the Terror of the Orient*, Whitman, #1458, 1942 .... **40.00**
Badge, decoder, Silver Dark, 1957 . **60.00**
Decoder, Secret Squadron, 1945 ... **75.00**
Emblem, 15th anniversary **20.00**
Handbook, Flight Commander, *Capt. Midnight Official Commission and Book of Secret Instructions*, orig mailer **200.00**
Mug, 3¼", red, decal, Ovaltine **30.00**
Record, "The Years To Remember," 33⅓ rpm, 7 x 7" paper slip case with blue and white design **15.00**
Ring, Flight Commander, 1957 ..... **45.00**
Stamp Album, complete **50.00**
Captain Zilog, pinback button, 3", litho tin, full figure, "To The Rescue" ... **5.00**
Hawkman
Comics
   #5, Zatanna **6.00**
   #18, Adam Strange **3.00**
Pinback Button, 3½" d, celluloid, full color illus, inscribed "Official Member Hawkman Super Hero Club," National Periodical, 1966 . **15.00**
Spider Man
Candy Container, Trick or Treat **15.00**
Coloring Book, large size **18.00**
Figure, 8", plastic, movable arms and

legs, stretch fabric outfit, orig unopened display card, Mego, 1979
copyright **25.00**
Pinback Button, ⅞", red, white, and
blue, Amazing Spiderman, c1975   **4.00**
Puppet, vinyl, red and blue uniform,
Imperial Toy **10.00**

Superman, wallet, leather and plastic, made in Hong Kong, copyright 1976, $25.00.

Superman
Hairbrush, boy's, wood type hand
grip, portrait decal, 1940 Superman
Inc copyright **50.00**
Children's Book, Mix and Match Storybook **12.00**
Clothing, children's underwear, Un-
deroos, sealed in orig package,
1978 ....   **25.00**
Costume, child's, shirt, trousers, and
cape, synthetic fabric, 1950s **125.00**
Game, Superman Speed Game, 13 x
16½" board, four diecut cardboard
playing figures, dice, instructions
printed on inside of box lid, Milton
Bradley, 1940s **100.00**
Glass, 5¾", light blue picture on side,
pink lettering on bottom, "Superman Uses X-Ray Vision" title, 1964
National Periodical Publications
copyright **50.00**
Hairbrush, early 1940s **45.00**
Mug, 3¼" h, white, full color, Super-
man flying over city skyline, 1971
copyright **15.00**
Pencil Box, 1 x 3¼ x 8¼", cardboard,
dark blue, brass snap, early 1940s   **50.00**
Pencil Set, set of 12, orange with blue
inscription   "Superman-Mighty
Powerful," unused, National Pencil
Co, 1955 copyright **60.00**
Pep Pin **25.00**
Puppet, 10½" h, vinyl head, fabric
body, Ideal Toy, 1965 copyright ..   **40.00**

Puzzle, 11 x 17", boxed, American
Publishing Corp, 1973 copyright .   **15.00**
Thermos, 7½" h, litho metal, red plas-
tic cap, full color scene, 1967
copyright **40.00**
Toothbrush Holder, 6½", plastic, bul-
let shape, raised Superman figure,
battery-operated toothbrush, Janex
Corp, c1974 ....   **30.00**
Valentine, 4½ x 4½", diecut, full col-
or, 1940 Superman Inc copyright .   **25.00**
Wallet, vinyl plastic, yellow, full color
picture, red int., Standard Plastic
Products, 1966 copyright **30.00**
Wonder Woman
Comic Book, #105, Wonder Wom-
an's Secret Origin, National Peri-
odical Publications **12.00**
Costume, child's **12.00**
Glass, 6½" h, full color scene, 1976
Pepsi Super Series **12.00**
Puppet, packaged, 1966 ....   **15.00**
Watch, gold colored metal case, full
color illus, blue background, black
numerals, yellow hands, black
leather like straps, unused, blue
plastic case and warranty leaflet,
Super Time Inc **150.00**

SWANKYSWIGS

Collecting Hints: Ideally select glasses whose pattern is clear and brightly colored. Rarer patterns include Carnival, Checkerboard, and Texas Centennial. Look-alike patterns from other manufacturers include the Rooster's Head, Cherry, Diamond over Triangle, and Circus pattern. The look-alike patterns date from the 1930s to the 1950s–60s.

History: Swankyswigs are decorated glass containers that were filled with Kraft Cheese Spreads. The first Swankyswigs date from the early 1930s. Production was discontinued during the last days of World War II because the paints were needed for the war effort. Production was resumed after the war ended. Several new patterns were introduced including Posy or Cornflower No. 2 (1947), Forget-Me-Not (1948), and Tulip No. 3 (1950). The last colored pattern was Bi-Centennial Tulip (1975).

In the mid-1970s, several copycat patterns emerged including: Wildlife Series (1975) and Sportsman Series (1976), most likely Canadian varieties; Rooster's Head, Cherry; Diamond over Triangle; and Circus. Kraft Cheese Spread is still available today, but in crystal-type glass.

Swankyswigs were very popular with economy minded ladies of the Depression era and used as tumblers and juice containers. They served as perfect companions to Depression glass table services and also helped to chase away the Depression blues.

The first designs were hand applied. When the popularity of Swankyswigs increased, new more and intricate machine-made patterns were introduced. Designs were test marketed. As a result of limited distribution, designs that failed are hard to identify and find.

The lack of adequate records about Swankyswigs makes it very difficult to completely identify all patterns. Since 1979, quite a few look-alikes have appeared. Although these glasses were similar, only Kraft glasses are considered Swankyswigs.

References: M. D. Fountain, *Swankyswigs, Price Guide,* privately printed, 1979; Ian Warner, *Swankyswigs, A Pattern Guide Checklist,* Depression Glass Daze, 1982.

Advisor: M. D. Fountain.

Pricing Note: If a Swankyswig retains its original label, add $4.00 to the value of the glass. Glasses with labels or original lids are scarcer than the checkerboards.

Posy pattern, Cornflower No. 2, dark blue, $2.50.

Antique (Early American antiques)
Black, coffepot and trivets	**4.25**
Brown, coal bucket and clock	**4.00**
Orange, crib and butter churn	**2.25**
Bands, black and red	**3.00**

Bi-Centennial
Green, Coin Dot design, 1975	**10.00**
Red, 1938 type tulip	**10.00**
Yellow, Coin Dot design, 1975	**10.00**
Bustlin' Betsy	**2.25**

Carnival, fired on Fiesta colors, dark blue, orange, yellow, or light yellow **8.00**
Checkerboard, green, red, and dark blue **25.00**
Daisies, red daisies on top row, white in middle, green leaves **3.00**

Dots & Circles, black, blue, green, or red **4.50**
Kiddie Cup (or Animal)
Black, pony and duck	**2.25**
Blue, pig and bear	**2.00**
Brown, deer and squirrel	**2.00**
Dark Blue, pig and bear	**2.25**
Green, kitten and bunny	**2.00**
Orange, puppy and rooster	**2.00**
Red, bird and elephant	**2.00**

Modern Flowers, dark and light blue; red or yellow
Cornflower	**3.00**
Forget-me-not	**3.00**
Jonquil, yellow, green leaves	**3.00**
Posy	**3.00**

Tulip, dark and light blue; red or yellow flowers, green leaves
No. 1, white leaves, 1937	**6.00**
No. 2, six mold bands around top, 1938	**20.00**
No. 3, four molded bands around top	**3.00**
Violets, blue flowers, green leaves	**2.00**

Sailboat, red, green, or dark blue
Racing	**20.00**
Sailing	**20.00**

Star
Black	**4.00**
Dark Blue	**4.00**
Green	**5.00**
Red	**5.50**

Texas Centennial, cowboy riding bucking horse on one side, Texas state seal on other
Black	**8.00**
Dark Blue	**9.00**
Green	**10.00**
Red	**10.00**

TARZAN COLLECTIBLES

Collecting Hints: Correct identification of first editions has long been a problem because many people confuse the copyright date with a publication date, resulting in many reprints being improperly identified as first editions (and overpriced accordingly). Reprinted books are common, gaining in value if they have the original pictorial dust jackets.

Some collectors focus only on books, movie items, or toys. Other collectors narrow their scope only to Tarzan and not Burroughs's other material. A third group wants virtually everything associated with Burroughs, including magazines that merely mention Tarzan and any material related to the actors who played Tarzan. Peripheral items usually are not worth a great deal, but may be easily saleable.

Serious collectors tend to be very knowledgeable and want items in the best condition. The market is competitive.

The imitation Tarzan items also have an established market.

History: In 1912 Edgar Rice Burroughs (1875–1950), an American author, created one of the world's most popular and enduring characters, Tarzan. Although not a great writer, Burroughs was one of the greatest literary storytellers of all time, with a seemingly limitless imagination. His stories of heroic and fantastic adventures, whether in the jungles of Africa or on faraway planets, were incredibly popular from the very beginning of his career and spawned numerous imitations throughout the years.

Burroughs inspired many fan clubs, with perhaps more fan publications devoted to him and his career than any other author.

Following his death in 1950, his books were allowed, for the most part, to disappear from bookstore shelves even though the demand was still strong. At least one book publisher who was trying to secure print rights reported that his inquiries to the Burrough estate were not even answered.

This odd situation changed in the early 1960s when a librarian in Downey, California, tried to remove Tarzan books from the library shelves because of her mistaken belief that Tarzan and Jane never were properly married. The issue caught the attention of the media. The end result was an incredible demand for Burroughs books that was satisfied by a veritable flood of new editions, authorized or not. Between 1962 and 1963 Burroughs books accounted for almost one-thirtieth of all U. S. paperback sales, a staggering achievement.

References: Lloyd Currey, *Science Fiction and Fantasy Authors/A Bibliography Of First Printings Of Their Fiction*, G. K. Hall, 1979 Kevin Hancer, *Collector's Guide To Edgar Rice Burroughs*, Crimson Cutlass, 1985; John Harwood, *The Literature of Burroughsiana*, Cazedessus, 1963; Henry Hardy Heins, *The Golden Anniversary Bibliography Of Edgar Rice Burroughs*, Donald Grant, 1964; Irwin Porges, *Edgar Rice Burroughs: The Man Who Created Tarzan*, Brigham Young University Press, 1975.

Collectors' Clubs: The Burrough Bibliophiles, P. O. Box 588, Wytheville, VA 24382; The Jungle Club, 5813 York Avenue, Edina, MN 55410.

Museum: The University of Louisville (Belknap Campus), Louisville, KY.

Advisor: Kevin Hancer.

Paperback Book, *The Son of Tarzan*, Ace F–193, $5.00.

TARZAN

Book, hardcover

At The Earth's Core, Grosset and Dunlap reprint	6.00
Carson of Venus, ERB Inc., 1948 reprint	6.00
Escape on Venus, ERB Inc., 1946, 1st edition in dust jacket	25.00
Jungle Tales of Tarzan, Grosset and Dunlap wartime reprint in dust jacket	15.00
Mad King, The, Grosset and Dunlap reprint	7.00
Son of Tarzan, The, A. L. Burt reprint	5.00
Swords of Mars, The, ERB Inc., 1948 reprint, dust jacket	25.00
Tarzan and "The Foreign Legion", EBR Inc., 1947, 1st ed in dust jacket	25.00
Tarzan of the Apes, Grosset and Dunlap reprint	5.00
Tarzan of the Apes, A. C. McClurg, 1914, lst ed, no acorn on spine	400.00
War Chief, The, Grosset and Dunlap reprint in dust jacket	30.00

Book, paperback

Chessmen of Mars, The, Ace, 1963	4.00
Princess of Mars, A, Ballantine, 1st printing, 1963	4.00
Return of Tarzan, The, Armed Services edition	45.00
Tarzan and the Lion Man, Ace, 1964	3.00
Tarzan and the Lost Empire, Dell, mapback, 1951	10.00
Tarzan and the Silver Glove, Gold Star, 1964, unauthorized title (not by Burroughs) that largely plagiarized *Tarzan and the Jewels of Opar*	9.00
Tarzan in the Forbidden City, Bantam of Los Angeles, 1940, scarce early publisher	100.00

Tarzan, Lord of the Jungle, Pinnacle (English), c1950 .... **8.00**

Tarzan of the Apes, Ballantine, 1966, 3rd printing with photo cover of TV Tarzan actor Ron Ely **3.00**

Wizard of Venus, The, Ace, 1970, 1st printing without title page illus, includes first publication of "Pirate Blood" **6.00**

Comic Book

DC, Tarzan, #211, 1973 .... **1.25**

Dell, Tarzan

#1, 1948 .... **50.00**
#28, 1950 .... **8.00**
#100 .... **4.00**

The Funnies, #43, includes John Carter of Mars, illus by John Coleman Burroughs **12.00**

Gold Key, Tarzan, #134, 1962 .... **2.00**

Jeep Comics, #23, Armed Forces giveaway with reprint of Tarzan newspaper comics **15.00**

March of Comics, #82, Tarzan issue, small comic giveaway from Sears shoe department and other shoe/variety store outlets **15.00**

Marvel, Tarzan, #3, 1977 .... **1.00**

Sparkler Comics, #26, includes reprints of Tarzan newspaper comics **10.00**

Tip Top, #16, includes reprints of Tarzan newspaper comics **12.00**

Magazine

All-Story, 10/12, contains "Tarzan of the Apes" NOTE: This is the first appearance of Tarzan and is the complete novel, not a short story version **1,000.00**

Amazing Stories

3/27, contains part two of "The Land That Time Forgot" **25.00**

1/64, contains "Skeleton Men of Jupiter" **2.50**

Argosy, 1/21/39, contains part three of "Synthetic Man of Mars" **6.00**

Blue Book, 1/30, contains part five of "Tarzan at the Earth's Core" **15.00**

Ellery Queen's Mystery Magazine, 5/64, contains "Tarzan, Jungle Detective" **2.00**

Fantastic Adventures, 11/39, contains "The Scientist's Revolt" **20.00**

Thrilling Adventures, 6/40, contains "Tarzan and the Jungle Murders" which some experts feel was written partially by Sam Mines **10.00**

Movie Material

Big Little Book, *Tarzan the Fearless*, Whitman **22.00**

Book

Swimming the American Crawl, Grosset & Dunlap, 1930s reprint,

titled "Johnny Weissmuller/How He Does It" on dust jacket **20.00**

Tarzan and the Lost Safari, Whitman, 1957, 1st ed, novelization by Frank Castle of the movie, without dust jacket as issued, Gordon Scott photo cov **10.00**

Tarzan of the Movies, Gabe Essoe, Citadel, 1968, 1st ed, dust jacket **15.00**

Lobby Card

At the Earth's Core, 1977 .... **2.00**

The New Adventures of Tarzan, 1935 .... **15.00**

Tarzan the Ape-Man, 1954, re-issue **8.00**

Paper Knife, "The New Adventures of Tarzan," movie advertising on one side, given away for 1940s re-release of the 1935 film **8.00**

Poster, one sheet size

Greystoke: The Legend of Tarzan of the Apes **12.00**

Tarzan the Ape-Man, 1932 ......**1,000.00**

Tarzan the Ape-Man, 1959 ...... **27.50**

Tarzan's Fight for Life, 1956 ..... **30.00**

Tarzan's Jungle Rebellion, 1971 .. **12.00**

Pressbook, Tarzan the Ape-Man, 1981 remake with Bo Derek **8.00**

Toys and Premiums

Better Little Book, *Tarzan the Untamed*, 1941, flip pictures **18.00**

Big Golden Book, *Tarzan*, 1964 .. **8.00**

Buckle, Belt, Gaylord's Ltd, 1970s **6.00**

Button, pinback, Signal Oil Tarzan Club, 1930s **40.00**

Button, pinback, Tarzan Radio Club—Drink More Milk, 1935 .. **50.00**

Clicker, Japanese, 1950s **8.00**

Coloring Book, *Tarzan*, Top Sellers Ltd., English, 1972 .... **10.00**

Figurine, Tarzan, Gem Clay Forming Co., 1930s, plaster statue, one of a series of statues featuring Tarzan, Jane, natives, animals, sailors, etc., unpainted

With base, labeled Tarzan **50.00**
Without base **40.00**

Knife, magic, Japanese, 1950s,

Viewmaster, single reel with brochure, Adventure of Tarzan: Tarzan Rescues Cheta, 975, $7.50.

knife blade slides back into handle **12.00**

Paper Transfer, National Trademark Co., 1940s, blue and orange iron-on transfer **8.00**

Record

Tarzan in the Eyes of the Lion, MGM Leo the Lion Series, 33rpm record album soundtrack for the first Tarzan TV episode **10.00**

Tarzan in the Valley of Talking Gorillas, Tarzan Records, 1950s, 78rpm, 3 record set in album **25.00**

Tarzan Song and Jungle Dance, Little Golden Records, 1952, pictorial sleeve **8.00**

TARZAN IMITATIONS

Book, hardcover

Chester, William L., *Hawk of the Wilderness*, Grosset & Dunlap, 1936, photoplay edition with movie photos and dust jacket featuring Herman Brix (who had just finished portraying Tarzan), orig dust jacket **20.00**

Rockwood, Roy, *Bomba the Jungle Boy*, Cupples & Leon, 1926, 1st ed, cream color binding **4.00**

Stoneham, C. T., *King of the Jungle, The Lion's Way*, Grosset & Dunlap, 1932, photoplay edition with movie photos and dust jacket featuring Buster Crabbe (who was soon to portray Tarzan), without orig dust jacket **7.50**

Book, paperback

Foster, Alan Dean, *Luana*, Ballantine, 1974, adventures of a female Tarzan **5.00**

Garron, Marco, *Azan the Ape/King Hunters*, Curtis Warren Ltd (English), 1952 .... **10.00**

Kline, Otis Adelbert, *The Planet of Peril*, Ace, 1954 .... **3.00**

Norwood, Victor, *Jacare the Untamed*, Scion Jungle Novels (English), 1952 .... **10.00**

Titan, Earl, *Anjani The Mighty*, Scion (English), 1952 .... **10.00**

Williams, Robert Moore, *Jongor of Lost Land*, Popular Library, 1970 . **4.00**

TV PERSONALITIES & MEMORABILIA

Collecting Hints: Collectors of television memorabilia fall into two categories. One is those who specialize in acquiring items from a single television series. Among these, Star Trek, Hopalong Cassidy, Howdy Doody, Roy Rogers, and Leave It To Beaver are the most popular series. The other category specializes in TV memorabilia of one type such as TV Guides, model kits, films, and cards.

There have been over 3,750 series on television since 1948. Therefore, the number of artifacts and memorabilia relating to television is large. Especially rich in TV collectibles are the early space shows and cowboy adventure series. The premiums from these types are beginning to show up at auctions and commanding high prices; they are eagerly sought by the pop culture collectors.

Systematic scheduling of television programs developed a new type of publication called TV Guide. The early guides are sought avidly. The first schedules were regional such as *TV Today* in Philadelphia, *TV Press* in Louisville, *Radio-Television Life* in Los Angeles. The first national *TV Guide* was published on April 3, 1953. Collectors enjoy these older magazines because they are often good sources for early stories about stars and their lives.

History: The late 1940s and early 1950s was the golden age of television. The first programming began in 1948. Experimentation with programming, vast expansion, and rapid growth marked the period. Prime time live drama series were very successful. Many popular stars of today first appeared on these live dramas, such as Paul Newman, Steve McQueen, Rod Steiger, Jack Lemmon, and Grace Kelly. The stars signed autographs and photographs to promote the dramas. These items, plus scripts and other types of articles have become very collectible.

After the period of live drama came to an end, the Western assault began. In 1959 there were 26 "Western" series. Many of them were movie and radio heroes adapted to life on television. The Western era continued until the early 1960s when it was replaced by the space adventure series and science fiction.

The 1970s brought the era of situation comedies, including All In The Family and M*A*S*H*. The collectibles resulting from these series are numerous. Only time can tell what values they will have.

References: Jefferson Graham, *Come On Down!!!-The TV Game Show Book*, Abbeville Press, 1988; Anthony Slide, *A Collector's Guide To TV Memorabilia*, Wallace-Homestead, 1985; Vincent Terrace, *Encyclopedia Of Television-Series, Pilots, And Specials, 1937-1973*, 3 volumes, New York, Zoetrope, 1986.

Museum: Smithsonian Institution, Washington, DC.

Captain Kangaroo, drinking cup, maroon plastic, copyright Robert Keeshan Assoc, 3½" h, $15.00.

Addams Family
  Bank, 3½ x 4½ x 3½", "The Thing," battery-operated, plastic, black, instruction sheet, boxed, 1965 copyright **150.00**
  Card Game, "Addams Family," MIB **55.00**
  Figure
    Lurch, 5¾" h, plastic, movable head, back marked "Lurch" and "The Addams Family," 1964 copyright **100.00**
    Morticia, 5" h, plastic, marked, "Morticia" and "Addams Family" on back, 1964 Filmways copyright **150.00**
  Playing Cards, 39 cards, instruction card, Milton Bradley, 1964 ...... **20.00**
  Record, 33⅓ rpm, six TV music themes, 12¼ x 12¼" cardboard slip case, RCA Victor label, 1965 copyright **25.00**
All In The Family, game, includes question and answer book, Milton Bradley, 1972 .... **15.00**
Arthur Godfrey
  Souvenir Bag, 14 x 16", paper, brown, Godfrey with CBS microphone and adv products illus, Union Bag & Paper Corp, 1940–50 **20.00**
  Ukulele, 21½" h, marbled brown plastic, ivory white front and tuning head, includes 16 page instruction and song book and automatic tuning attachment, 1950 copyright .. **75.00**
Ben Casey
  Game, 1961 .... **35.00**
  Pinback Button, 3½", white, blue lettering **15.00**
  Puzzle, 13½ x 24", Milton Bradley, 1962 copyright **25.00**
Beverly Hillbillies
  Book, punchout, 10 x 14", 6 pgs, Whitman, 1964 .... **50.00**

Coloring book, 8 x 11", Whitman, 1963 .... **15.00**
Game, 18 x 18", unused, Standard Toykraft, 1963 .... **40.00**
Thermos, 6½" h, litho metal, red plastic cap, full color scene, Aladdin, 1962–64 .... **25.00**
Toy, truck, orig characters **150.00**
Bewitched
  Activity Book, 8 x 11", 64 pgs, Treasure Books, 1965 .... **15.00**
  Card Game, Stymie, 42 cards, 20 x 22" vinyl playing sheet with full color photos, boxed, Milton Bradley, 1965 .... **25.00**
Bonanza
  Autograph, Dan Blocker, 8 x 10" black and white glossy **85.00**
  Doll Set, set of three dolls with horses **250.00**
  Double gun and holster set **150.00**
Captain Kangaroo, record, 33⅓ rpm, 17 Christmas songs, 12" cardboard album **20.00**
Car 54, coloring book, 8 x 11", 128 pgs, unused, Whitman, 1962 .... **30.00**
Charlie's Angels
  Dresser Set, comb, brush, mirror, and ornament, plastic, yellow, 8 x 11" unopened display card, Fleetwood Toys, 1977 copyright **20.00**
  Necklace, brown and white plastic beads, "Charlie's Angels" inscription bar, 7 x 10" unopened display card, Fleetwood Toys, 1977 copyright **15.00**
Combat, card game, complete deck, 6 x 7½ x 1¼" box, Milton Bradley, 1964 copyright **20.00**

Barnabas Collins Dark Shadows, game, Milton Bradley, 19 x 9½", $20.00.

Dark Shadows
  Game, Dark Shadows, MIB **75.00**
  Kit, Barnaby Collins, MIB **75.00**
  Paperback Book **1.00**
Dennis the Menace, mug, 3½", plastic, molded, painted, early 1950s **12.00**
Dr. Kildare
  Book, *Dr. Kildare Annual*, 7½ x 11",

94 pgs, comic strip stories, color photo of Richard Chamberlain on front cov **25.00**
Coloring Book, 8½ x 11", unused, Saalfield #9531, 1963 .... **15.00**
Game, 1962 .... **45.00**
Pinback Button, 3½", blue lettering, pink background, early 1960s **12.00**
Stethoscope, MIB **20.00**

Flintstones
Game, The Flintstone's Cockama-mies, Hanna Barbera Production, 1961 .... **5.00**
Night Light, Barney and Fred **25.00**
Projector, Kenner's Give A Show, bat-tery operated, 112 color slides, orig box, 1964 .... **65.00**
Target, standup, tin **20.00**
Yo Yo, Fred **8.00**

Get Smart
Poster, 21 x 24", paper, full color scene, issued by NBC-TV **40.00**
Signal ray gun, MIB **135.00**

Gilligan's Island
Coloring Book, 8 x 11", full color il-lus, unused, Whitman #1135, 1965 .... **30.00**
Photo, 8 x 10" glossy, black and white, autographed by cast mem-bers, ... **150.00**

Hogan's Heroes, thermos, dome top .. **75.00**

Howdy Doody
Bank, orig paint
Clarabell **18.00**
Bluster **15.00**
Belt, suede, embroidered Howdy face **65.00**
Clock, alarm, talking **65.00**
Face Mask, rubber, copyright Bob Smith, orig label **75.00**
Flasher Ring, cereal premium, 1950 **20.00**
Puppet, pull string, 24", MIB **45.00**
Slippers, head on slippers, 1950 ... **150.00**
Ring, cereal premium, 1950 .... **15.00**
Time Teacher Board, orig package .. **55.00**
Toy
Windup, Howdy Doody and Bob Smith at a piano **875.00**
Xylodoodle, magic piano **65.00**

I Love Lucy
Coloring Book, 8½ x 11", unused, Golden Press, 1963 .... **30.00**
Magazine, Family Circle, 8½ x 11", 112 pages, full color cov portrait, two page article and photos, 1953 **20.00**
Puppet, Little Ricky, c1950, MIB ... **60.00**

Julia, lunch box, 7 x 8½ x 4", litho metal, full color illus, lime green trim, 6½" h thermos with lime green plastic cap, unused, King-Seeley, 1969 copy-right **50.00**

Kojak, game, The Stake Out, unused, Milton Bradley, 1975 .... **25.00**

Laugh-In, waste can, 13" h, oval, litho metal, color photos on ones side, other with "Sock It to Me" slogan, 1968 copyright **40.00**

Leave It to Beaver
Coloring Book 8 x 11", full color cover illus, Whitman, 1958 ...... **30.00**
Game, "Leave It to Beaver (Money Maker)," 16¼ x 16¼", board, black and white photo of Jerry Mathers on box lid, Hasbro, 1959 .... **50.00**

Man from U.N.C.L.E.
Coloring Book, 8 x 11", The Magic Carpet Affair, 100 pgs, Watkins Strathmore Co, 1965 copyright ... **25.00**
Game, 1965 .... **45.00**

Mod Squad
Book, Assignment: The Arranger, Whitman, 5¼ x 8", 210 pgs, 1969 copyright **8.00**
Puzzle, 14 x 20", photo scene of cast characters, boxed, Milton Bradley, 1969 copyright **12.00**

Mr. Ed
Coloring Book, 8 x 11", unused, Whitman, 1963 .... **50.00**
Puppet, 11½" h, plush body, vinyl head, yarn mane, includes voice box, orig Mattel tag, 1962 copy-right **75.00**

Howdy Doody, plastic straw holder, fifty cellophane straws, orig box, 2 x 2 x 8½", $30.00.

Munsters
Bank, mechanical, tin, coffin, MIB . **100.00**
Comic Book, Gold Key #3, July 1965 **15.00**
Doll, 8½" h, Herman, vinyl plastic, movable head, arms, and legs, orig tag, Ideal Toy, 1965 .... **40.00**
Figure, 6" h, Herman, plastic, painted, 1964 copyright **40.00**
Game, Picnic **35.00**
Puzzle, tray **22.00**

My Favorite Martian, coloring book, 8½ x 11", one colored page, Golden Press, 1964 .... **25.00**

My Little Margie, newstand flyer, Gail Storm **10.00**

Palladin, game, Have Gun Will Travel, orig box, 1959 .... **55.00**

Pinky Lee, game, Pinky Lee and The Runaway Frankfurters, Lisbeth Whiting Co, 1954 copyright **50.00**

Popeye, Eraso board and magic screen set, MIB **75.00**

Presley, Elvis, TV Guide, 1961, Elvis and Frank Sinatra cov **35.00**

Rifleman, rifle **65.00**

Six Million Dollar Man
Game, 18 x 18" board, spinner, cards, and figures, boxed, Parker Brothers, 1975 .... **20.00**
Lunch Box, 7 x 8 x 4", litho metal, full color action scene, dark blue trim, 6½" plastic thermos with black cap, Aladdin, 1974 copyright **40.00**

Soupy Sales
Notebook, 3 ring, 10 x 11½", vinyl cov, black, white, and fleshtone photo on front, 1966 copyright ... **40.00**
Pinback Button, ⅞", "Charter Member/Soupy Sales Society," 1960s .. **15.00**

Untouchables, TV Guide, Elliott Ness cov **15.00**

Voyage To the Bottom of the Sea, card game, boxed, Milton Bradley, 1964 . **40.00**

Wagon Train, double gun and holster set, orig box **165.00**

Yogi Bear, lunch box and thermos **55.00**

TELEVISIONS

Collecting Hints: There are two distinct types of early television sets: mechanical and electronic. Mechanical televisions, the earliest, look nothing like their modern counterparts. Mechanical sets from the 1920s typically have a motorized 12" diameter metal disc with a "glow tube" in back and a magnifier in front. Starting in 1938 sets used picture tubes as they do today. Generally the earlier the set, the smaller the screen. The easiest way to gauge the age of a television set is by the numbers found on the channel selector. Pre-1946 television sets will tune a maximum of five stations, usually channels 1–5. In 1946 channels 7–13 were added, thus sets made between 1946 and 1948 will show channels 1–13 on the station selector.

In 1949, channel 1 was dropped, leaving all 1949 and newer sets with V.H.F. channels 2–13, as we have them today. The U.H.F. band was added in 1953, thus any set with U.H.F. capability is less than 40 years old.

Brand and model number are essential to determining a set's worth. However, physical condition of the cabinet is much more important than the operating condition of the set.

History: There are three distinct eras of early television. The first, the "mechanical" era, was from 1925–32. Sets often were known as "radiovisors," since they were visual attachments to radios. Many mechanical television sets did not have cabinets and resembled an electric fan with a round metal disk in place of the blades. These units were most prevalent in the New York City and Chicago areas.

Any complete mechanical set is valued in the several thousand dollar range. Manufacturers included Jenkins, Baird, Western Television, Insuline Corp. of America, Short-Wave and Television Corp., Daven, See-All, Rawls, Pioneer, Travler Radio & Television Corp., and others.

The second era was the pre-World War II era, which spanned 1938–1941. These were the first all-electronic sets and usually were combined with a multi-band radio in fancy cabinets. A favorite design of the era was the use of a "mirror in the lid" arrangement, whereby a mirror in the underside of a lift-lid reflected the picture tube, which was pointed straight up. No more than 2,000 sets were produced during the three years. They were concentrated in those areas with pre-war television stations: New York City, Albany/Schenectady/Troy, Philadelphia, Chicago, and Los Angeles. Depending on model and condition, these sets usually start at $1,000 and can range to $5,000 or more.

The final era of television started in 1946 with the resumption of post-war television production. Production rose rapidly. Few sets after 1949 have collectible value. There are some notable exceptions, e.g., the first "color wheel" sets [1951], the giant Dumont 30" screen sets [1953], and limited production or "oddball" sets.

Reference: Morgan E. McMahon, *A Flick of The Switch*, Vintage Radio, 1975.

Periodical: *TV Collector*, P. O. Box 188, Needham, MA 02192; *Sight, Sound, Style*, P. O. Box 2224, So. Hackensack, NJ 07606.

Caution: Do not plug in a set that has been in storage for more than 30 years without an inspection by a serviceman. Components can go bad and short-circuit, causing a fire. Many early sets had no fuses for protection.

Advisor: Arnold L. Chase.

1925–1932, MECHANICAL

Daven, kit of parts **500.00**
Insuline Corp. of America (ICA), Bakelite cabinet model **3,000.00**
See-All, open frame **1,500.00**

Short-Wave and Television Corporation,
   drum scanner **3,000.00**
Western Television Crop., "Ship's
   wheel," cabinet type **2,200.00**

1938–1941, ELECTRONIC

Andrea
   1-F-5 ....**4,000.00**
   KTE-5 ....**2,500.00**
Dumont, 180 ....**2,000.00**
General Electric
   HM-171 ....**2,500.00**
   HM-225 ....**4,000.00**
   HM-275 ....**5,000.00**
R.C.A.
   TRK-5 ....**4,000.00**
   TRK-12 ....**5,000.00**
   TRK-120 ....**3,500.00**

1946 AND LATER

CBS/Columbia, 12CC2, color wheel
   set **5,000.00**
Dumont, RA-119, 30" screen **1,000.00**
Motorola, VT-71 ....**225.00**
Philco
   Predicta, table model **225.00**
   Safari **250.00**
Pilot, TV-37, magnifier **200.00**
R.C.A.
   630TS **250.00**
   648PTK **200.00**
   8TS30 ....**100.00**
   CT-100, first RCA color set **500.00**

SHIRLEY TEMPLE

Collecting Hints: Dolls are made out of many materials—composition, cloth, chalk, papier mache, rubber, and vinyl. Composition dolls are the earliest. Shirley Temple's popularity received a renewed boost through television, resulting in a new series of Shirley Temple products being issued in the 1950s.

History: Shirley Jane Temple was born April 23, 1928, in Santa Monica, California. A movie scout discovered her at a dancing school. "Pie Covered Wagon" in 1932 was her screen test. During the 1930s she made twenty movies, earning as much as $75,000 per film.

Her mother supervised the licensing of over fifteen firms to make Shirley Temple products. These included dolls, glassware, china, jewelry, and soap. The first Shirley Temple dolls were made in 1934 by The Ideal Toy Company. They varied in height from 11 to 27 inches and were composition (pressed wood). Ideal made the first vinyl dolls in 1957.

References: John Axe, *The Encyclopedia of Ce-*

lebrity Dolls, Hobby House Press, Inc., 1983; Patricia R. Smith, *Shirley Temple Dolls And Collectibles, Series 1*, (1977) and *Series 2* (1979), Collector Books, 1977.

REPRODUCTION ALERT

Pocket Watch, $50.00.

Advertising
   Fan, teen-age Shirley with RC Cola,
     "I'll Be Seeing You" movie, ... **24.00**
   Mirror, Quaker Puffed Wheat adv,
     1937 .... **18.00**
Bank, 2" sq, celluloid, white, picture
   mounted on top, c1936 .... **75.00**
Book
   Now I Am Eight, No 1766, 1937 ... **35.00**
   Poor Little Rich Girl,, soft cover, 32
     pgs, 1936 Saalfield **30.00**
   The Shirley Temple Treasury, Random
     House, 1959, hard cover **48.00**
   Through The Day, No 1716 .... **35.00**
Bowl, cereal **40.00**
Candy Mold **25.00**
Clothing
   Coat, cashmere, label, Bambury orig,
     c1937 .... **285.00**
   Dress, child's, satin, pink, ruffled,
     blue and white tag **50.00**
Doll
   8", Heidi costume **20.00**
   12", 1957 .... **65.00**
   16", 1972, boxed **125.00**
   20", with pin, Ideal **400.00**
   25", orig clothing, pin **850.00**
Embroidery Set, tablecloth, four napkins, hoop, needle, threads, plastic
   thimble, unused, Gabriel, 1960s ... **50.00**
Figure, 8½" h, rubber, black Scottie dog
   under one arm, marked "made in
   Czechoslovakia," mid 1930s **90.00**
Game, The Little Colonel, board, diecut
   figure pieces, box with Shirley's picture, Selchow & Righter, 1935 ..... **70.00**
Jewelry
   Charm, ⅝", brass rim, cut out center,
     1930s **75.00**

Necklace, 14", brass, ⅝" cut out head
disk, 1930s **100.00**
Ring, celluloid, red, black and white
diecut head of Shirley, marked
"Made in Japan **25.00**
Movie Still, 8 x 10", *Little Miss Marker,*
Shirley on horse with Adolphe Men-
jou, Paramount Film, 1934 . . . . **20.00**
Mug **55.00**
Paper Doll
Saalfield #1765, life size, 1936 . . . . **90.00**
Uncut, 1976 . . . . **20.00**
Pinback Button, 1" d, enamel on brass,
"Sunday Referee/Shirley Temple
League," 1930s, English newspaper
issue **110.00**
Pitcher, 4½", glass, blue, white portrait
image, Wheaties offer, c1938 . . . . . . **40.00**
Pocket Mirror, 1¾", light brown on
pink, c1935 . . . . **25.00**
Postcard, 3½ x 5½", glossy sepia pic-
ture, "Captain January" scene, un-
used, 1936 . . . . **15.00**
Punchboard, Miss Charming Doll, un-
used **10.00**
Scrapbook, 11 x 15", Saalfield, 1937
copyright **25.00**
Sewing Cards, six black and white
cards, yarn, 5 x 7" box, marked
"Made by Saalfield 1936" **45.00**
Sheet Music
Good Night My Love, 1936 . . . . **18.50**
Pigskin Parade, Shirley on back **10.00**
Slipper Box, child's, 6 x 10½ x 3¼",
gray and blue design, marked "Rest-
ful," mid 1930s **75.00**
Song Album, 9 x 12", 36 pgs, words and
music, pink tinted films scenes **35.00**
Souvenir Book, 9 × 12", 32 pgs, Tour-
nament of Roses Parade, Shirley as
Grand Marshal, 1939 . . . . **22.00**
Stage, 10 x 24 x 36", cardboard, litho
red cardboard curtains, yellow cords,
early 1970s **50.00**

THIMBLES

Collecting Hints: Collectors tend to specialize in
a limited variety of thimbles, depending on what
appeals to them. Novice collectors are best advised to begin with a specialized thimble dealer
before going "bargin" hunting on their own.

Thimble collectors use the following grading
scale to determine thimble values:

Mint: Never used, perfect condition
Excellent: A slight degree of wear on the
            highest points, but in general, ex-
            cellent condition
Fair: Very worn from constant use, bent,
            or pierced by a needle

Poor: Damaged, pierced with two or
            more holes, cracked, badly bent,
            half the design worn off, or
            chipped enamel

During the 19th century and earlier a lady
would take her favorite thimble to a silversmith
to have it mended if it became pierced from
constant use. As a result, mended, 19th century
thimbles commonly are found. Collectors must
decide for themselves if they wish to add this
condition of thimble to their collection.

Thimble collecting has two specialized off-
shoots—advertising and political thimbles. Old
campaign thimbles in mint condition are rare. It
is best not to try to "touch up" the paint, as this
diminishes the value. Collectors of political items
use the term "brummagem," meaning showy but
inferior and worthless, to refer to political thimbles after 1960. They consider these later thimbles as non-official campaign items.

History: Thimbles often are thought of as common household sewing tools. Many are. However, others are miniature works of art, souvenirs
of places, people, and events, or gadgets (thimbles with expanded uses such as attached thread-
ers, cutters, or magnets).

There were many thimble manufacturers in the
United States prior to 1930. Before we became
a "throw-away" society, hand sewing was a
never ending chore for the housewife. Garments
were mended and altered. When they were beyond repair, pieces were salvaged to make a
patchwork quilt. Thimble manufacturers tried to
create a new thimble to convince the home
sewer that "one was not enough."

By the early 1930s only one manufacturer of
gold and silver thimbles remained in business in
the United States, The Simons Brothers Company
of Philadelphia, which was founded by George
Washington Simons in 1839. Simons Brothers
thimbles from the 1904 St. Louis World's Fair
and the 1893 Columbian Exposition are prized
acquisitions for any collector. The Liberty Bell
thimble, in the shape of the bell, is one of the
most novel.

Today, the company, owned by Nelson Keyser,
continues to produce silver and gold thimbles.
The Simons Brothers Company designed a special thimble for Nancy Reagan as a gift for dip-
lomats' wives who visit the White House. The
thimble has a picture of the White House and
the initials, "N.D.R."

Thimbles have been produced in a variety of
materials: gold, silver, steel, aluminum, brass,
china, glass, vegetable ivory, ivory, bone, celluloid, plastics, leather, hard rubber, and silk.
Common metal thimbles usually are bought by
the intended user, who makes sure the size is a
comfortable fit. Precious metal thimbles often
were received as gifts. Many of these do not show
signs of wear from constant use. This may result

from ill fit of the thimble or from it simply being too elegant for mundane work.

During the 20th century thimbles were used as advertising promotions. It is not unusual to find a thimble that says, "You'll Never Get Stuck Using Our Product" or a political promotion stating, "Sew It Up—Vote for John Doe for Senator."

References: Cecile Dreesmann, *A Thimble Full,* Cambium, Netherlands, 1983 (printed in Dutch and English); Helmut Greif, *Talks About Thimbles,* Fingerhutmuseum Creglingen, Germany, 1983 (English edition available from Dine-American, Wilmington, DE); Edwin F. Holmes, *A History Of Thimbles,* Cornwall Books, 1985; Eleanor Johnson, *Thimbles,* Shires Publications, England, 1982; Myrtle Lundquist, *The Book Of A Thousand Thimbles,* Wallace-Homestead, 1970; Myrtle Lundquist, *Thimble Americana,* Wallace-Homestead, 1981; Myrtle Lundquist, *Thimble Treasury,* Wallace-Homestead, 1975; John von Heille, *Thimble Collectors Encyclopedia,* Wallace-Homestead, 1986; Estelle Zalkin, *Zalkin's Handbook of Thimbles and Sewing Implements,* Warman, 1988.

Periodical: *Thimbletter,* 93 Walnut Hill Road, Newton Highlands, MA 02161.

Collectors' Club: Thimble Collectors International, P. O. Box 2311, Des Moines, IA 50310.

Advisor: Estelle Zalkin.

REPRODUCTION ALERT. Reproductions can be made by restrikes from an original die or cast from a mold made from an antique thimble. Many reproductions are sold as such and priced accordingly. Among the reproduced thimbles are a pre-revolution Russian enamel thimble and the Salem Witch thimble (the repro has no cap, and the seam is visible).

Modern, Royal Worcester, England, artist signed, $25.00 each.

THIMBLES

Corning Glass	55.00
Gadgets	
Magic Thimble, "M.T.," thread cutter	
and needle threader	15.00
Thread cutter, lip on band	15.00
Gold, 1900–40	
Plain band	75.00

Scenic band	100.00
Semi precious stones on band	200.00
Ivory	
Modern scrimshaw	20.00
Vegetable ivory	60.00
Metal, common	
Brass	
Fancy band	15.00
Cloisonne design, China	10.00
Cast Pot Metal, "For a Good Girl"	5.00
Diragold, Scandinavian gold	50.00
Silver, 1900–40	
Applied wire work, Mexico	10.00
Continental, synthetic stone cap	25.00
Cupid in high relief	100.00
Enameled	60.00
English, steel core	
DORCAS	50.00
DREEMA	125.00
DURA	125.00

Souvenir, left: Statue of Liberty, France, $35.00; right: Statue of Liberty, Simons, $15.00.

Engraved, two birds on branch	25.00
Flowers in high relief	35.00
Italian, stones on band, modern	35.00
Paneled band	30.00
Raised Design	
Bleeding Heart	25.00
Wild Rose	35.00
Scenic band	35.00
Simons, Cupid and Garlands	90.00
Souvenir	
Liberty Bell, 1976 issue	75.00
Palm Beach	75.00
Statue of Liberty, France	35.00
World's Fairs	
1892, Columbian, buildings	225.00
1904, St. Louis World's Fair	200.00
1933, Chicago World's Fair	75.00
Porcelain	
Meissen, hp, modern, Germany	125.00
Royal Worcester, hp, modern, artist	
sgd, England	25.00
Transfer print design, Modern	15.00
Scrimshaw, antique, whalebone or	
whale tooth	90.00

Thimble Holders
Glass, slipper **75.00**
Silver, round filigree **125.00**

THIMBLES, ADVERTISING

Silver and brass were the earliest materials used for advertising thimbles but were not produced in large quantities. Only 30 different silver, mostly English, and an equal number of brass thimbles have been identified.

Aluminum advertising thimbles were first produced in the early 1900s and by the 1930s became an extremely popular way to attract the attention of women. Over 2,5000 different commercial, political, charitable and other concerns distributed over one million thimbles. The type of goods being advertised was extremely diverse. Most thimbles had colored bands around the base on which the message was printed. Some thimbles, mostly of English origin, contain stone tops (and/or threader attachments). They were made with red, blue or green bands, with occasional variations in black, orange and yellow. Because of their light weight, the thimbles are frequently bent or color worn.

Plastic advertising thimbles made their appearance in the 1930s and still are being produced. The type of plastic material has changed which helps date some of the earlier ones.

The list below contains average prices. To create a range either way add or subtract $1.00 for aluminum and older plastic thimbles; $0.25 for new plastic; $2.50 for brass; and $5.00 for Sterling Silver.

Aluminum
Colored Band
Stone Top **3.00**
Threader Attachment **3.00**
No Colored Band
Inked Message **1.50**
Inscribed Message **1.50**
Brass, advertisement or inscription .. **5.50**
Plastic, old, 1930–1950
One Color **2.00**
Two colors, red top **2.00**
Sterling Silver **20.00**

THIMBLES, POLITICAL

The history of the political campaign advertising thimble begins with the amendment giving the vote to women which was ratified on August 20, 1920, just in time for the 1920 political campaign. The first Presidential campaign to use advertising thimbles was that of Warren G. Harding.

1929, "Al Smith for President" **22.50**
1936, "Roosevelt-Garner" **30.00**
1946,"Nixon for Congress. Put the
Needle in the P.A.C." **45.00**

1952 or 1956, "Lets Sew it Up for Ike
and Dick" **12.50**
1968 or 1972, "Nixon-Agnew" **4.00**
1972, President Nixon Now More
Than Ever" **9.00**

TINSEL ART

Collecting Hints: Look for those pieces which are elaborate in design and contain different colored foil. Signed pictures often are viewed as folk art and may be priced higher.

Nineteenth century material is preferred over the nondescript 20th century examples. However, Art Deco and Art Nouveau designs of quality are sought by collectors from these fields.

History: Tinsel pictures (or paintings) were both a "cottage art" and a commercial product which enjoyed popularity from the late 19th century through the 20th century. The "painting" took two forms. The first was similar to a reverse painting on glass. A design was placed on the glass and colored foil was placed behind to accent the piece. The second form consisted of a silhouette or cutting, separate from the glass, placed over a layer of crumpled foil.

The reverse painting type was highly personalized; a mother and her children could work on tinsel pictures as a family project. This handiwork often contained presentation remarks and was artist signed and dated. The silhouette type appears to be related to the Art Deco and Art Nouveau periods and may have been a form of souvenir at carnival games and the seashore. The sameness of many designs, e.g., flamingos in a swamp-like setting, denotes its commercial production.

Birds and flowers, multicolored, 10¾ x 8¾", $40.00.

Basket of flowers, multicolored, black
ground, 17¾ x 13½" **150.00**

Birds drinking from stylized fountain, trees, 23 x 27", 19th C **200.00**
Flamingos, pink, palm tree, reeds, yellow sun, black ground, 10¾ x 8¾" . **85.00**
Flower arrangement in bowl, brightly colored **30.00**
Fountain, surrounded by garland of flowers, multicolored, 15¾ x 15½" . **100.00**
Lilacs, black ground, gilt frame, 10½ x 7½", 19th C **145.00**
Motto
   "Home Sweet Home," houses and trees, reverse painted, 12¼ x 18" . **65.00**
   "The Lord Is My Shepherd," floral border, reverse painted, 12¼ x 18" **50.00**
Silhouettes, girl and boy, facing pr, framed **45.00**
Statue of Liberty, multicolored, reverse painting on glass highlights, oval wooden frame **75.00**

TOOTHPICK HOLDERS

Collecting Hints: Toothpick holders have been confused with many forms—from match holders, shot glasses, miniature spoon holders to toy table setting, mustard pots without lids, rose or violet bowls, individual open sugars, and vases. Use toothpicks to test what you have. The toothpicks should rest well in the holder with an ample extension to allow an individual toothpick to be selected easily. Match holders often are figural in nature and have a striking surface on them.

The biggest danger to the collector is a salt shaker with a ground top or a wine glass with the stem removed. Knowing the forms of salt shakers and wine glasses will avoid any confusion.

Among the forms, perhaps the silverplated figural toothpicks are least appreciated. They offer the beginner a reasonable area upon which to build an inexpensive collection.

History: Toothpick holders are small containers used to hold toothpicks. They were an important table accessory during the Victorian period.

Toothpick holders were made in a wide range of material—Art glass, colored pattern glass, colored glass novelties, milk glass, china, bisque and porcelain, crystal pressed glass, cut glass, and silverplated figurals. Makers include both American and European firms.

Toothpick holders were used as souvenir items by applying decals or transfers. The same blank may contain several different location labels.

References: William Heacock, *Encyclopedia of Victorian Colored Pattern Glass, Book I, Toothpick Holders from A to Z*, Antique Publications, 1981; William Heacock, *1000 Toothpick Hold-*

ers: A Collector's Guide, Antique Publications, 1977; William Heacock, *Rare & Unlisted Toothpick Holders*, Antique Publications, Inc., 1984.

Collectors' Club: National Toothpick Holder Collector's Society, P. O. Box 246, Red Arrow Highway, Sawyer, MI 49125.

Additional Listings: See *Warman's Antiques And Their Prices*.

Silver plated, "Take Your Pick," small standing chick, ruffled top, marked "Osborn & Co, Lancaster, PA," 2¼" h, $65.00.

Art Glass
   Amber, figural, picture frame, Greentown Glass **245.00**
   Cranberry, enamel dec **125.00**
   Custard
      Chrysanthemum Sprig, blue, gold dec **300.00**
      Souvenir, Belvedere, IL **35.00**
   Guttate, cranberry **175.00**
   Leaf Mold, cased cranberry spatter . **145.00**
   Purple Slag, figural, boot **50.00**
   Smith Bros, ribbed, opaque white, blue dot rim, pastel floral dec **125.00**
Brass
   Clown, marked "Jenning Bros" **30.00**
   Top Hat, umbrella **20.00**
China, bisque, and porcelain
   Bisque, figural
      Cat, coachman outfit, barrel **55.00**
      Dwarf, 4½" **25.00**
   Geisha Girl, 2½", blue rim **15.00**
   Majolica, figural, mouse with ear of corn **135.00**
   Nippon, hp owl sitting on a tree branch, blue night sky ground, small black beads on rim and base **110.00**
   Occupied Japan, donkey pulling cart **7.50**
   Schlegelmilch, RS Prussia, basket, roses dec **130.00**
   Top Hat, sunset hunting dog scene, green and cream ground, cobalt blue band **40.00**

Milk Glass

Barrel, metal hoops	25.00
Basketweave, Bellaire	25.00
Horseshoe and Clover	22.00
Pansy, three handles, Kemple	35.00
Scrolled Shell, goofus dec	12.00

Opalescent Glass

Beatty Rib, blue	48.00
Diamond Spearpoint, blue	125.00
Melon	48.00
Overall Hobnail, blue	28.00
Stripe, white	30.00
Windows, cranberry	45.00

Pattern Glass, Daisy and Button, amber, bucket shaped, Heacock, #211, $35.00.

Pattern Glass

Bull's Eye and Fan	12.00
Button Arches, ruby stained, souvenir, "Mother, 1947"	20.00
California, green	50.00
Colonial, Cambridge, cobalt	25.00
Continental, Heisey	42.00
Delaware, green, gold trim	90.00
Ester, clear	45.00
Feather, clear	65.00
Galloway, clear	18.00
Heart, pink opaque	60.00
Hobb's Hobnail, vaseline	20.00
Illinois, adv	27.50
Iowa, clear	22.50
King's Crown, ruby stained	38.00
Michigan	30.00
Minnesota	45.00
Paddlewheel and Star, clear	25.00
Pretty Maid	60.00
Rising Sun	35.00
Royal Oak, frosted rubina	125.00
Swinger, clear and ruby	22.00
Three Dolphins, amber	45.00
Tulip with Sawtooth	40.00
Zipper Slash	25.00

Silver Plate

Cat and bucket	65.00
Child, holding umbrella, on turtle, marked "Pairpoint"	175.00
Colonial Lady	65.00

Egg, chick emerging, feet on branch, sq base, marked "Hartford"	70.00
Rooster, 2" h, engraved "Picks"	48.00
Wood, beaver, painted features, broad tail, hollowed out trunk	5.00

TOYS

Collecting Hints: Condition is a very critical factor. Most collectors like to have examples in very fine to mint condition. The original box and any instructional sheets add to the value.

Sophisticated collectors concentrate on the tin and cast iron toys of the late 19th and early 20th centuries. However, more and more collectors are concentrating on the 1940 to 1970 period, including products from firms such as Fisher Price.

Many toys were characterizations of cartoon, radio, and television figures. A large number of collectible fields have some form of toy spinoff. The result is that the toy collector constantly is competing with the specialized collector.

History: In America the first cast iron toys began to appear shortly after the Civil War. Leading 19th century manufacturers included Hubley, Dent, Kenton, and Schoenhut. In the first decades of the 20th century Arcade, Buddy L, Marx, and Tootsietoy joined the earlier firms. The picture became complete with the addition of firms such as Built Rite, Ideal, and Fisher Price.

In Europe, Nuremberg, Germany, was the center for the toy industry from the late 18th through the mid-20th century. In England the Britain and Lesney companies challenged the German supremacy. Lesney originated the famous matchbox toys. German manufacturers were especially skilled in the areas of toy trains and stuffed toys.

References: Linda Baker, *Modern Toys, American Toys, 1930-1980,* Collector Books, 1985; Robert Carter and Eddy Rubinstein, *Yesterday's Yesteryears: Lesney "Matchbox" Models,* Haynes Publishing Group (London), 1986; Jurgen and Marianne Cieslik, *Lehmann Toys,* New Cavendish Books, 1982; Don Cranmer, *Collectors Encyclopedia, Toys–Banks,* L–W Books, 1986; Fred and Marilyn Fintel, *Yesterday's Toys With Today's Prices,* Wallace-Homestead, 1985; Edward Force, *Corgi Toys,* Schiffer Publishing Ltd., 1984; Edward Force, *Dinky Toys,* Schiffer Publishing Ltd., Edward Force, *Matchbox and Lledo Toys,* Schiffer Publishing Ltd., 1988; Edward Force, *Miniature Emergency Vehicles,* Schiffer Publishing Ltd., 1985; Richard Friz, *The Official Price Guide to Collectible Toys, 4th Edition,* House of Collectibles, 1987; Gordon Gardiner and Alistar Morris, *Illustrated Encyclopedia of Metal Toys,* Harmony House, 1984; Dale Kelley, *Collecting The Tin Toy Car, 1950-1970,* Schiffer Publishing, Ltd, 1984; T Kitahara, *Cars, Tin Toy Dreams,*

Chronicle Books, 1985; T Kitahara, *Robots, Tin Toy Dreams,* Chronicle Books, 1985; T Kitahara, *Wind-Ups, Tin Toy Dreams,* Chronicle Books, 1985; Ernest & Ida Long, *Dictionary Of Toys Sold In America,* published by author, two volumes; Albert W. McCollough, *The Complete Book Of Buddy "L" Toys: A Greenberg Guide,* I. Greenberg Publishing Co., 1982, out-of-print; Brian Moran, *Battery Toys, The Modern Automata,* Schiffer Publishing, Ltd, 1984; John J. Murray & Bruce Fox, *Fisher-Price, 1931-1963: A Historical, Rarity, Value Guide,* Books Americana, 1987; Nigel Mynheer, *Tin Toys,* Boxtree (London), 1988; Richard O'Brien, *Collecting Toys: A Collectors Indentification and Value Guide, 4th Edition,* Books Americana, 1985; Maxine A. Pinsky, *Greenberg's Guide To Marx Toys,* Greenberg Publishing Co., 1988; Nancy Schiffer, *Matchbox Toys,* Schiffer Publishing Ltd., 1983; Peter Viemeister, *Micro Cars,* Hamilton's, 1982; James Weiland and Dr. Edward Force, *Tootsie Toys, World's First Die Cast Models,* Motorbooks International, 1980; Blair Whitton, *Toys,* Alfred A.Knopf, 1984.

Periodicals: *Antique Toy World,* P. O. Box 34509, Chicago, IL 60634; *Model and Toy Collector,* 15354 Seville Road, Seville, OH 44273; *Plastic Figure & Playset Collector,* Box 1355, La Crosse, WI 54602; *Toy Collector News,* P. O. Box 451, River Forest, IL 60305; *Toy Shop,* 700 East State Street, Iola, WI 54990; *Wheel Goods Trader,* P. O. Box 435, Fraser, MI 48026; *YesterDaze Toys,* P. O. Box 57, Otisville, MI 48463.

Collectors' Clubs: American-International Matchbox, 522 Chestnut Street, Lynn, MA 01904; Antique Toy Collectors of America, Two Wall Street, New York, NY 10005; Matchbox Collectors Club, 141 West Commercial Avenue, Moonachie, NJ 07075

Museums: American Museum of Automobile Miniatures, Andover, MA; Museum of the City of New York, New York, NY; Smithsonian Institution, Washington, DC; Margaret Woodbury Strong Museum, Rochester, NY; Toy Museum of Atlanta, Atlanta, GA.

See: Automata, Cartoon Characters, Disneyana, Dolls, Games, Paper Dolls, Radio Characters, Dimestore Soldiers, Toy Soldiers, Toy Trains and many other categories.

ALPS, JAPAN, c1950.

Airplane, 7" wingspan, tin, friction, passenger, tin types, metal propellers, early 1950s	150.00
Collie, mechanical, walking, MIB	38.00
Flip Over Motorcycle, 5¼ x 5", litho tin	30.00
Old Man, nodding, litho tin windup	20.00
Pepsi Bear	65.00

Proud Peacock, 6½" l, litho tin windup, walks as tail feathers spread, orig box	150.00
Racer, 4" l, tin, friction, engine noise, open wheeled racer, marked "No. 2," bright 1950s colors, black rubber tires	45.00
Shuttling Train and Freight Yard, tin, battery operated, 7" l locomotive marked "NYC," 4" l freight car, two 5" l freight terminals, two 12" l switch track sections, two 16" l tracks, freight box, orig box, c1950	115.00
Spacecraft Apollo, 9" l, litho tin and plastic, battery operated, three litho astronauts, space noise, orange and white, MIB	90.00
Speed King Racing Boat, 4 x 7½ x 3", litho tin windup, orig box	20.00

ARCADE

The Arcade Manufacturing Company first produced toys in 1893. In 1919, the firm began to make the Yellow Cabs for the Yellow Cab Company of Chicago. The exclusive advertising rights were sold to the cab company with Arcade holding the right to make toy replicas of the cabs. This idea was popular and soon was used with Buick, Ford, etc., and McCormack and International Harvester farm equipment. The company continued until 1946 when it was sold to Rockwell Manufacturing Company of Pittsburgh.

Ambulance, 6", 1920	125.00
Automobile	
Chevy, coupe, 8"	300.00
Ford	
Model A, convertible, coupe, 4"	85.00
Model T, touring car, 6¼", rubber tires, open sides, 1920	75.00
Limousine, 12½" l, c1920	160.00
Racer, 3¾", rubber tires, c1932	30.00
Sedan, 3¾", c1940	25.00
Bus	
4" l, five windows on each side, 1920s	50.00
9 x 2½ x 2½", cast iron, Greyhound Lines, dark blue and silver, black rubber balloon tires, black and yellow Arcade decal	265.00
Catalog, 7½ x 5", *Arcade Manufacturing Co,* Fred and Jane with the Arcadian Elves, 24 pgs, 1931	85.00
Disk Harrow	15.00
Dump Truck	
8", open cab, c1920	150.00
8½", Mack, driver, c1920	125.00
11", red, c1920	225.00
12", Mack	500.00
Fire Engine	
9" l, 1930s	80.00
13½", steam boiler, removable hose reel, bell, six firemen, rubber tires, 1936	115.00

Motorcycle, 1¼ x 2 x 3″, cast iron, red, white rubber tires, marked "USA" .. **80.00**
Oil Tanker Truck, 10½″ l, American Oil Co, Mack, c1928 .... **265.00**
Steam Roller, 7½″ **70.00**
Steam Shovel, 4½″ **70.00**
Stake Truck
   7½″, Mack **225.00**
   9″, Chevy **200.00**
Taxi, 3 x 6½ x 2½″, cast iron, orange, nickel plated grille, black roof, white letters "A Century of Progress Chicago 1933," gold and blue Arcade decal, orig white tires **275.00**
Tractor
   Avery, 4¾″ l, c1920 .... **100.00**
   International Harvester, cast iron, 7″ **345.00**
   McCormack-Deering **125.00**
Wrecker, 6″ l, c1930 .... **100.00**

AUBURN RUBBER

The Auburn Rubber Company was founded in 1913 in Auburn, Indiana, as the Double Fabric Tire Corp. It began making toys in 1935 with the production of toy soldiers. Production of animals and wheeled vehicles soon followed. The toy production line was purchased in 1960 by the town of Deming, New Mexico and continued there until it ceased operation in 1968. Auburn also made wheels for other toy manufacturers.

Army Truck, 4¾″ **15.00**
Austin Race Car, 4″, cast iron **15.00**
Battleship **20.00**
Chrysler, airflow **15.00**
Fire Truck, engine, 8″ **15.00**
Lincoln Convertible, 1942 .... **15.00**
Milk Truck, 4″ **7.50**
Oldsmobile Sedan, 1938 .... **40.00**

BANDAI

Bandai Co., one of the many toy manufacturers which began production in Japan after World War II, started with tin toys and later changed to plastic and steel. Bandai Toys are found with friction action and battery operated. They are often marked "Bandai Toys, Japan." Bandai still produces toys and is a major Japanese exporter to the U. S. and other foreign countries.

Airplane, 4 x 5 x 2″, litho tin friction, red and black, yellow trim, three blade propeller, tail marked "B" and Bandai logo, black thin rubber tires, 1930s **40.00**
Cadillac, 12″, metallic bronze, MIB ... **300.00**
Chevrolet, station wagon, 8″ l, two tone green body, detailed litho tin int., 1958 .... **130.00**
Fiat 600, 6½″ l, friction, tin, green, cloth sliding sun roof, detailed litho tin int. **100.00**

Ford Ranchero Pickup, 8″ l, friction, green tin body, cream roof, black rubber tires with Ford hubcaps, 1958 .. **150.00**
Ice Cream Truck, 10″ l, litho tin and plastic, battery operated, musical, bump and go action, 1960s **112.00**
Jaguar, 8″, orig paint **70.00**
Motorcycle and Rider, 10½ x 4 x 8½″, plastic and vinyl, battery remote control, blue plastic motorcycle, silver details, yellow and brown rider, late 1960s **60.00**
Old Fashioned Ford A Convertible, 7″
   Roadster, green tin body, litho tin int., plastic running boards, MIB **45.00**
   Touring Car, cream tin body, litho tin int., black plastic running boards, MIB **50.00**
Plymouth Valiant, 8″ l, friction, blue tin body, black rubber tires **65.00**
Police Auto Cycle, 11″ h, battery operated, remote control, white tin, black tin seat and dial, rubber tips on bars and foot levers, jointed uniformed police rider, orig box **200.00**
Race Car, NSU Record Racer, 2½ x 3 x 13″, litho tin friction, streamlined, red and white, yellow and black details, sparks **75.00**
Triumph TR3, 3 x 8 x 3″, litho tin friction, dark metallic green, beige roof, red and white seats **75.00**

Buddy L, Coca-Cola Truck, with orig conveyor, c1950, $175.00.

BUDDY L

The Buddy L Toy Company was founded in 1921 by Fred Lundahl. It produced high quality, finely detailed toys. Many were large enough to ride on. Production changed from steel to lighter weight, smaller toys in the 1930s. A limited number of wooden toys were made during World War II. The firm still operates today.

Air Mail Truck, 24 x 7¾ x 8″, 1932 .. **350.00**
Airplane, orange wings, 2″ aluminum propeller, decals, c1930 .... **75.00**
Army Vehicle
   Medical Corps Truck, 20½″ l, white,

white canvas top, Medical Corps lettering, emblem on top, Buddy L bar and circle emb on doors, No. 950 .... **100.00**

Tow Truck, 9" l, plastic, tin hand winch, black rubber tires, B-Line, c1950, MIB **70.00**

Truck, artillery gun, orig decals, 1960s **40.00**

Truck and Transport, 31" l, pressed steel, canvas top, black rubber tires, c1940 .... **175.00**

Auto Wrecker, 24" l, white, red crane, electric headlights, No. 437, 1934 . **100.00**

Circus Truck, 25" l, Wild Animal Circus on Wheels, doors open, celluloid animals, red and gold trim **75.00**

Dairy Transport Truck, 26" l, Duo-Tone slant design paint, red and white, opens in back, decal **60.00**

Dump Truck, seat and handle missing, 1948 .... **100.00**

Farm Truck, Buddy L Hydraulic Farm Supplies Dumper, 6 x 21 x 5½", steel, black rubber wheels, dark green cab, black, white, and red Buddy L decals on doors, beige trailer, red and beige stickers, c1950 .... **45.00**

Fast Freight Truck, 20" l, pressed steel, white cab, orange truck, black rubber tires, c1940 .... **120.00**

Ice Truck, 26½", black front and hood, yellow cargo, natural canvas cov imprinted "Buddy L Ice Delivery," imitation ice, tongs, orig decals, 1933 . **100.00**

Machine Tommy Gun, 26", turn crank for sound, caps, 1954, MIB **245.00**

Merry Go Round Truck, one figure missing **40.00**

Oil Truck, junior line, 24" l, black, red chassis, opening doors, Firestone tires, medium green oval tank, brass knobs and caps, 1930 .... **100.00**

Pickup Truck, Ford, 1959 .... **18.00**

Rifle, paper, cracker **48.00**

Service Truck, red and white orig paint, 1953 .... **75.00**

Steam Shovel, orig red and black paint, orig decals **100.00**

Tool Box, red and black, orig decal .. **95.00**

Tow Truck, red and white **70.00**

CHEIN

The Chein Company was in business from the 1930s through the 1950s. Most of these lithographed tin toys were sold in dimestores. Chein toys are clearly marked.

Aeroswing **120.00**

Army Truck, 8½", open bed **24.00**

Chein, Lorry, litho tin and cloth, World War I, $60.00.

Cathedral, 9" h, litho tin windup, multicolored, c1930 .... **135.00**

Clown, 8" h, litho tin windup, spins parasol above nose, c1920 .... **175.00**

Drummer, 9" h, litho tin windup, blue hat and pants, red coat, c1930 ..... **175.00**

Ferris Wheel, 16 x 10 x 4", multicolored litho, six gondolas, c1930, MIB **200.00**

Grocery Truck, 6", litho tin windup ... **175.00**

Ice Truck, 9" l, litho tin, green frame, yellow tin wheels, blue and yellow body, 1930s **185.00**

Racer, 6½" l, orange and blue Indy style, yellow tin wheels, driver with 1920s style leather football helmet, 1920s . **245.00**

Roller Coaster, 19" l, 9" h, litho tin windup **275.00**

Sand Toy, tin molds, duck, frog, sifter, and shovel, orig 8 x 11" card, c1930 **35.00**

Santa Elf, 6" h, litho tin, mechanical, side to side swaying motion, c1930 . **215.00**

Taxi, litho tin windup **90.00**

CORGI

Playcraft Toys introduced Corgi miniature vehicles in 1956. This popular line soon became Corgi Toys. The first cars were made on a ¼5 to ¼8 scale. Corgi cars were the first miniature cars to have clear plastic windows. Other design features included opening doors and interiors. In 1972, the scale of ⅓6 was introduced. This scale was more durable for play but less desirable to collectors. Finally, the company added other types of cars and trucks, including character representations.

Air Sea Rescue Helicopter, #924, 1977 **7.50**

Bermuda Taxi, #430, 1962–65 ...... **40.00**

Breakdown Truck, #702, 1975–79 ... **7.50**

Corvette Sting Ray, #300, 1970–72 ... **45.00**

Elephant Cage, #607, 1961–68 ...... **32.00**

Ford, Zephyr station wagon **20.00**

Giraffe Transporter, #503, 1964–71 .. **40.00**

Hardy Boys Rolls, #805, 1970 .... **32.00**

James Bond 007, #261, MIB **45.00**

Land Rover Pickup, #406, 1957–62 ..	**24.00**
Lincoln Continental Executive Limousine, 6" l gold and black car, 3 x 4 x 8" orig unopened package, c1966 ..	**30.00**
Mercedes Benz 230 SE	**8.50**
Netherlands Helicopter	**8.00**
Oldsmobile 88, #235, 1962–66	**50.00**
Plymouth Mail Car, #443, 1963–66 ..	**35.00**
Renault Alpine, #294, 1980	**8.50**
Studebaker Golden Hawk	**45.00**
Tipping Farm Trailer, #62, 1965–71 ..	**12.00**
US Army Transporter, #1135, 1965 ..	**50.00**
Volkswagen Rally, #384, 1976–77 ...	**15.00**
Wall's Ice Cream Van, #474, 1965–68	**25.00**

FISHER PRICE

Fisher Price Toys was formed in East Aurora, New York, in 1930. The original company consisted of Irving L. Price, retired from F. W. Woolworth Co., Herman G. Fisher, who was associated with the Alderman-Fairchild Toy Co. in Churchville, New York, and Helen M. Schelle, a former toy store owner. Margaret Evans Price, wife of the company president, was the company's first artist and designer. She was formerly a writer and illustrator of children's books. The company began with sixteen designs. Herman Fisher resigned as president in 1966. In 1969 the company was acquired by the Quaker Oats Company.

Black and white rectangular logos appeared on all toys prior to 1962. The first plastic part was used after 1949.

Allie Gator, #653	**42.00**
American Airlines Flagship, #170, orig propellers	**175.00**
Bouncing Bunny Cart, #307	**40.00**
Buzzy Bee, #325	**18.00**
Cackling Hen, #120, 1958	**45.00**
Catalog, *1955 Toy Catalogue, Stull Bros Wholesale Distributors*, 4 pgs, 10 x 11", stiff blue notebook cov	**30.00**
Cow, #132	**20.00**
Dizzy Donkey	**40.00**
Donald Duck, 4 x 11 x 9", pulltoy, wood, light blue, bright red wheels, colorful paper labels, c1950	**100.00**
Fire Truck, #200	**55.00**
Hot Dog Wagon, #750	**100.00**
Humpty Dumpty, #736	**25.00**
Little Snoopy, pulltoy, 5 x 9 x 5", paper on wood, day-glow red vinyl wheels, spring tail, marked "693," 1965 copyright	**20.00**
Pinky Pig, #695	**20.00**
Playful Puppy, #626	**15.00**
Pluto, 7" l, wood jointed, blue paddle, pull strings for action	**65.00**
Pop-Up Critter, 2½ x 9½ x 7", wood, blue base, yellow, black, and red jointed Pluto figure, c1930	**40.00**

Queen Bee, #444	**15.00**
Racing Rowboat, #730	**50.00**
Seal, #694	**10.00**
Snappy Quacky	**40.00**
Tailspin Tabby, #455	**50.00**
Teddy Zilo	**45.00**
Tip Toe Turtle, #773	**20.00**
Toot Toot, #643	**25.00**
Whistling Engine, #617	**50.00**

GILBERT

The A. C. Gilbert Company was founded in 1916. Alfred Carlton Gilbert Jr was an amateur magician who began to produce magic kits under the name of Mysto Manufacturing Co. The company was located on Erector Square in New Haven, Connecticut. Alfred Carlton Gilbert III took over after his father's death. The company still produces fine quality toys and other non-toy products. It's most famous product is the Erector Set.

Action Figure, 13 x 4" orig box, 1965	
James Bond, plastic, fully jointed, tuxedo and accessories	**170.00**
Odd Job, plastic, fully, jointed, judo gear	**230.00**
Autorama Speedway Race Set, MIB ...	**70.00**
Catalog, *Erector/Gilbert Toy Catalogue*, 1952, color	**25.00**
Erector Set	
#1	**155.00**
#7½	**140.00**
Erector Set Instruction Manual, illustrated	
1915, slight cover wear	**15.00**
1954	**6.00**

HASBRO

Hasbro Industries, Inc., an American toy manufacturer, is well known for several lines. One of the most popular toys produced by this company is Mr. Potato Head. It was introduced in 1948, and is still made today, complete with a plastic potato. Another popular Hasbro line is GI Joe and all the accessories made for this series of action figures. GI Joe was introduced in 1964.

Catalog, *Hasbro*, 9 x 11", 1970, 50 pgs, eight full color pages of GI Joe	**130.00**
Digger the Dog, 13¾" l, plastic, vinyl tail and ears, orig yellow hat and leash string	**4.50**
GI Joe Accessories	
Beachhead Assault Mess Kit, MIB ..	**20.00**
Combat Mess Kit	**10.00**
Breeches Buoy, MIB	**18.00**

Foot Locker	12.00
Frogman Scuba Tank	10.00
Paratrooper, camouflage set	12.00
Survival Life Raft	10.00

GI Joe Clothing

Astronaut Suit, MIB	50.00

Dress Uniform

Air Force	90.00
Marine	90.00

Fatigue, Beachhead Assault

Pants	8.00
Shirt	10.00
Field Jacket, Combat, set	15.00
Life Vest, Sramble	10.00
Pants, Shore Patrol, MIB	30.00
Poncho, Communications	12.00

Shirt

Dress, Air Force, MIB	28.00
Work, Navy Attack	8.00

GI Joe Figure

Adventure Team, 1976, MIB	150.00
Defender, 1974, MIB	30.00
Eagle Eye, 1975, MIB	75.00
GI Nurse, 1967, orig clothes	365.00
Land Adventurer, 1970, orig clothes	75.00

Talking

Astronaut, 1969, MIB	200.00
Marine, 1967, orig clothes	120.00
Sailor, 1967, orig clothes	125.00

GI Joe Set

Air Cadet, MIB	120.00
Beachhead Assault, tent	12.00
Combat Field Pack	15.00
Combat Sand Bag Set	10.00
Communications	12.00
Demolition	20.00
Fire Fighter	35.00

Paratrooper

Helmet, MIB	18.00
Parachute Pack, MIB	40.00

GI Joe Vehicle

Army Jeep, five star, orig trailer	75.00
Desert Jeep Patrol	135.00
Military Staff Car	230.00
Navy Jet	200.00
Mr Potato Head, 1965, orig pcs and box	5.00
Scooter the Tooter, plastic, clown, flexible vinyl arms, bluebird on hat	3.50
Weebles Haunted House, plastic furniture, glow in the dark Ghost Weeble, Witch Weeble, Boy Weeble, and Girl Weeble	10.00

HUBLEY

The Hubley Manufacturing Company was founded in 1894 in Lancaster, Pennsylvania, by John Hubley. The first toys were cast iron. In 1940 cast iron was phased out and replaced with lesser metals and plastic. The production of cap pistols was increased at this time. By 1952 Hub-

ley made more cap pistols than toys. Gabriel Industries bought Hubley in 1965.

Airplane, P–38, camouflage	125.00

Cap Gun

Cowboy Jr, MIB	45.00
Dick Pistol, MIB	30.00
Flintlock, MIB	25.00
Texan Jr, MIB	45.00
Trooper Pistol, MIB	38.00

Hubley, Bell Telephone Truck, white metal, painted olive green, $45.00.

Car, MG, 2 x 2 x 6", bright red, white seats, black rubber wheels, c1950	40.00
Catalog, *Hubley 1964*, 32 pgs, 8½ x 11", full color illus	45.00
Fire Truck, hook and ladder, 3 x 3 x 9½", bright red, black plastic wheels, unpainted grill, 5" white plastic ladders, c1950	85.00
Fire Truck Set, #30, MIB	375.00
Hot Rod, Mighty Mite, MIB	15.00
Jaguar Sport Car, 7½" l, yellow diecast, green tinted plastic windshield and seats, orig box	85.00

Kiddie-Toy

Race Car

3 x 7 x 2½", metal, red body, black rubber tires, c1950	25.00
6½", diecast, red, rubber tires, marked "No. 457"	20.00
7", diecast, red and green	60.00
Roadster, MGTD, 6", dark green repaint, marked "No. 432"	12.00

Scale Model

Chevrolet Roadster, orig box, marked "Kit No. 4862"	75.00
Convertible, 2½ x 7 x 2", bright red, black rubber wheels, cast iron windshield and steering wheel, silver detailing, black, white, and green orig box, c1950	65.00
Model A Roadster, #4850, metal, MIB	45.00
Telephone Repair Truck, orig pole trailer, shovel, and crane, #482	500.00

Truck

Five Ton, 1917, yellow, red wheels	600.00
Pick Up, blue and white	15.00

IDEAL

The Ideal Toy Company was owned by Lewis David Christie. It was located in Bridgeport, Connecticut. Among the toys it produced, there were dolls, cars, and trucks, and even a line of toy soldiers produced c1920 until 1929.

Astro Base, 10 x 10 x 20" white and bright red plastic base, litho tin control plate, 5 x 9 x 7" dark blue and bright yellow space car, light blue plastic figural astronaut, orig 12 x 12 x 20" blue, white, and orange box .. **250.00**
Car, 1½ x 4½ x 1½", plastic, streamlined, red, black wheels, c1950 .... **15.00**
Ideal Fix-All Series, 1950s
  Futuristic, 16" l, blue plastic body, yellow int. **100.00**
  Pontiac, 14" l, dark pink plastic body, gray roof, black plastic tires **100.00**
Ideal Motorific Thunderbird, 1½ x 5 x 1" car, three boxes with plastic cov containing assorted pcs, adv as "The New Quick-Change Motor Toy," c1955 .... **50.00**
Knight of Darkness Figure, MIB **35.00**
Mr. Machine, 1977 .... **55.00**
Talking Police Car, MIB **125.00**
Turbo Jet Car, MIB **115.00**

LINEMAR

Airplane, 14" wingspan, 11" l, Capitol Airlines Viscount 321, four actions, c1950 .... **85.00**
Animal Truck, 2 x 2½ x 6" litho tin friction, black and red cab, silver tin cage with multicolored celluloid animals, c1950 .... **40.00**
Audrey, 4½" h, nodder, litho tin, vibrating motions as head shakes, Harvey Comics copyright, 1950s **125.00**
Bulldozer, 8", litho tin, battery operated, c1950 .... **100.00**
Chevrolet, Belair, 6" l, litho tin friction, green, cream, silver, and black, 1955 **50.00**
Drumming Soldier, 5" h, litho tin windup, MIB **140.00**
Fishing Kitty, 9", battery operated, tray, plastic fish **110.00**
Goofy Cyclist, 7", litho tin windup, cloth pants, orig box **475.00**
Greyhound Bus, 10" l, battery operated, remote control, two tone blue, black rubber tires, early 1950s style **125.00**
Hopping Squirrel, 4" h, litho tin, mechanical, c1950 .... **40.00**
Jocko Climbing Monkey **55.00**
Lady Bug, litho tin windup **75.00**
Motorcycle, 3" l, friction, red cycle, driver wearing yellow pants, green jacket, c1950 .... **55.00**

Old Jalopy, 5" l, litho tin, friction, blue, full figural driver, 1930s sayings lithoed on sides, erratic motion and noise **55.00**
Pluto, 3" l, litho tin, friction, marked "WDP," c1950 .... **100.00**
Popeye, 6½" l, litho tin windup, holds bowl of fruit and skates, 1950s **400.00**
Television Truck, litho tin, battery operated, NAR Television on side, full figure litho tin moving cameramen mounted on roof, c1950, orig box .. **400.00**
Tractor Trailer, 13" l, friction, litho tin, orange and black, silver roof, marked "Shop At Sears & Save," rear opening gate, blue tin cat, litho tin side plate "Sears Roebuck & Co," c1950 ..... **115.00**
Untouchables Playset, two friction Linemar cars, 3" metal cap gun, orig paper bags, plastic figures, wooden boxes and barrels, 14½ x 26 x 3" orig blue, white, and orange box, 1961 Desilu Productions copyright **800.00**

Marx, Mechanical Marvel Super Hero Tricycle, litho tin and plastic, orig box, $25.00.

MARX

Louis Marx founded the Marx Toy Company in 1921, stressing quality at the lowest possible price. His popular line of toys included every type of toy except dolls. The company was sold to Quaker Oats Company, who sold it in 1976 to the European company of Dunbee–Combex–Marx.

Air Borne Commando Burp Gun, 14" l, blue plastic, crank action noise, 1950s, MIB **45.00**
Airplane, 20" wing span, marked "Strato Airlines" **125.00**
Astronaut, 5" h, hard vinyl, blue, 1970 copyright **20.00**
Atomic Submarine With Light and Automatically Firing Pistols, 3 x 13½ x 4" litho tin, battery remote control, metallic gray, red and yellow details,

three red metal tail fins, orig instruction sheet and box **100.00**

Bravo, The Armored Horse, plastic horse, 17 pcs of plastic armor, pcs sealed in orig plastic bags, orig 13 x 15 x 4" full color box, 1968 copyright   **40.00**

Charlie McCarthy Benzine Buggy, windup **475.00**

Coca-Cola Truck, yellow, twelve miniature cases, #22 . . . . **500.00**

Endsville Eddie, 5" blue-green hot rod, 1964 copyright by Hawk Model Co, Inc **18.00**

Farm Combine, tin, friction, MIB **25.00**

Fort Apache Playset, twenty stiff cardboard pcs to assemble fort, 16" h cardboard tepee, orig four pg instruction folder, orig 19 x 21 x 1" white cardboard box **80.00**

Golden Pecking Goose, 9" **100.00**

Hot Rod, #23, 7½" l, litho tin friction, red, rollbar, plastic windshield, open engine, black rubber tires, litho tin int., arooga horn, 1967 . . . . **50.00**

Jaguar XKE 120, Fix-All Set, bright red plastic body, c1950 . . . . **135.00**

Jumpin' Jeep, litho tin windup, MIB . . **165.00**

Marble Game, mechanical, MIB **25.00**

Mickey Mouse, windup, whirling tail, 1950, MIB **245.00**

Motorcycle Policeman

2 x 8½ x 6", litho tin windup, large built-in key, built-in siren, silver, yellow and red cycle, bright red uniformed policeman, goggles, c1930 . . . . **165.00**

2½ x 3½ x 3", litho tin windup, sidecar, four black wood wheels, dark red cycle, blue uniformed rider, c1930 . . . . **80.00**

Nutty Mads-Waldo the Weightlifter, 6" h, chartreuse vinyl **15.00**

Old Jalopy, litho tin windup **115.00**

Pepsi-Cola Delivery Truck, 2½ x 7½ x 3", white plastic body, black wood wheels, red, white, and blue Pepsi decal, three white plastic cases with soda bottles, c1940 . . . . **75.00**

Pistol, steel, miniature, .45 caliber, Army type, orig card **12.00**

Presidents of the US, stand, MIB **65.00**

Race n' Road Set, MIB **75.00**

Ramp Walker

Donald Duck with wheelbarrow . . . **15.00**

Flintstones, Fred and Barney, plastic, 2½ x 2½", c1960 . . . . **35.00**

Rocking Horse, Hopalong Cassidy, windup **350.00**

Roy Rogers Mineral City Playset, litho tin, post office, hotel, bank, Bar M house **350.00**

Smoky Sam The Wild Fireman, 7" l,

plastic and tin, windup, yellow fireman hat, ladders attached to car, crazy car action, orig box, c1950 . . **160.00**

Tom, plastic windup, cat from Tom & Jerry **60.00**

Tractor Trailer

Marx Toyland Mack Bulldog, holds three racers **600.00**

Western Auto, red and silver, adv on side **45.00**

TV Kin

Flintstones, set of 6, MIB **65.00**

Officer Dibble, MIB **25.00**

MARUSAN TOYS

Adam 45, 3½ x 4 x 8", tin, friction, racer, red, white, and blue, three dimensional attached driver **125.00**

Atom 45 Racer, 9" l, litho tin friction, helmeted and goggled driver **335.00**

Bus, 7½ x 2 x 2½", litho tin friction, multicolored, tin front wheels, diecut windows, orig red, white, and blue box, early 1950s **235.00**

Cadillac, 5 x 12½ x 4", tin, friction, black, silver tin detailing, black, white, and red emblems, tin bumpers, c1952 . . . . **450.00**

Dump Car, 10" l, litho tin, red, black, white, and blue, blue bed, rear swing gate, c1950 . . . . **50.00**

Tugboat, 12" l, litho tin, battery operated, seven colors, engine sound, smoking action, c1950, orig box . . . **65.00**

Matchbox, Lesney Products & Co, Ltd, London, #57, Land Rover Fire Truck, diecast, red, orig package, $8.00.

MATCHBOX

Matchbox cars were first manufactured by Lesney Products, an English company founded in 1947 by Leslie Smith and Rodney Smith. Their first diecast cars were made in 1953 on a scale of 1/75. The trademark "Matchbox" was registered in 1953. In 1979 Lesney Products Corp made over 5.5 million toys a week. The company was sold to Universal International in 1982.

Airport Coach, #65E, 1978	**4.00**
Austin Metropolitan Taxi, #17C, 1960	**15.00**
Bedford 7½ Ton Tipper Truck, #38, 1961	**7.50**
Cement Truck, #19F, 1977	**7.50**
Dodge Cattle Truck, #37D, 1967	**6.50**
Fire Chief Car	**70.00**
Formula 1 Racing Car, #34D, 1971 ..	**4.00**
Hoover Truck	**8.00**
Hot Rod, #36D, 1971	**5.00**
Iron Fairy Crane, #42C, 1969	**5.00**
Lotus Super Seven, #60C, 1972	**5.00**
Mercedes Convertible, #6F, 1982	**3.00**
NASA Tracking Vehicle, #54F, 1982 ..	**7.50**
Pepsi Truck	**8.00**
Planet Scout, #59E, 1976	**4.50**
Renault STL, #21F, 1979	**12.00**
Wells Fargo Security Truck, #69E, 1979	**12.50**

MATTEL

Farmer In The Dell, litho tin, musical, 9½ x 9½ x 7", c1953	**70.00**
Moon Base Space 1999, Star Flash Computer Kit	**35.00**
Sonar Sub Hunt - A Naval Battle Game, sixteen plastic submarine tiles, eight plastic mines, two sets of crayons, orig 18 x 21 x 4" dark blue and green box, 1961 copyright	**100.00**
Spaceship, orig figure, 1968	**22.00**
Square Dancing Twins, musical, 1952	**84.00**
Whistling Train Station, tin, MIB	**35.00**

NYLINT

Coastal Unit Missile Launcher Truck, 22" l, pressed steel, three plastic missiles, steel radar antenna, four cut-out targets	**90.00**
Construction Vehicle	
Crane, orig decals, minor wear to paint, marked "Michigan"	**50.00**
Road Grader, #1400, 1953	**125.00**
Tournahopper, #1500, c1953, MIB .	**185.00**
Tournarocker, #1300, c1952, MIB .	**100.00**
Jeep, Bronco, red	**35.00**
Pick Up Truck, Ford	**35.00**

OHIO ART

The Ohio Art Company was started in 1908 by Henry S. Winzeler, in Archbold, Ohio. The company produced metal picture frames. Toy production began in 1912. In 1969, Ohio Art purchased Emenee Industries. Ohio Art is noted for colorful lithographed tin toys.

Action Andy Lawn Mower, 33", metal, motor sound, c1960	**18.00**
Barn, metal, plastic fence and animals, 1952	**25.00**
Boat, 9", litho tin, mechanical, c1960	**40.00**
Carpet Sweeper, Donald Duck, litho tin, red wood handle, 1942	**18.00**
Doll Stroller, metal, litho of teddy bears, 1958	**35.00**
Ironing Board, 20" l, metal, folding legs, 1958	**15.00**
Mickey Mouse Washing Machine, 5" d, 7½" h, full color litho tin, Mickey and Minnie washing, Pluto watching, marked "WED," c1935	**225.00**
Sand Pail, litho tin, girl feeding chickens	**28.00**
Toe-Jo	**33.00**
Tractor, 4" l, plastic	**7.50**
Watering Can, litho tin, Boy Blue and Bo Peep, sgd "Fern Bezel Peat"	**18.00**
Whirlie Bird, spinning target and pistol set, metal and plastic, c1960	**18.00**

SCHUCO

Car, 5½" l, litho tin, mechanical, coral body, striped litho tin grille with name, marked "Made in US Zone Germany," 1940s	**100.00**
Layout Accessory, gray plastic traffic intersection roadway, battery operated red and green traffic light, black and white 8 x 8 x 2" orig box marked "Schuco Varianto 3061," yellow label, c1950	**35.00**
Speedboat, plastic, windup, marked "U. S. Zone Germany, Teleco 3003 Model," orig box	**35.00**
Van, 1½ x 4½ x 1½", metal, battery operated, beige, dark blue roof, folded instruction sheet, orig box, marked "Schuco Varianto Elektro 3114," c1950	**85.00**

SUN RUBBER

The Sun Rubber Company was located in Barberton, Ohio. During the 1930s it produced a number of character dolls and Disney items in addition to a general line. It was forced to cease production during World War II because of the scarcity of rubber. Production revived after World War II and continued through the 1950s.

Car, Chrysler Airflow, 1 x 1½ x 4", dark blue, tires marked "Sunroco," c1930	**12.00**
Donald Duck and Pluto, red car	**65.00**
Porky Pig, 5" h, multicolored molded rubber, c1950, orig box	**70.00**
Race Car	
2 x 4 x 1", silver body, white rubber wheels	**20.00**

2 x 6 x 2", silver streamlined body, white rubber tires **30.00**
Sedan **15.00**
Tank **15.00**
Truck, 2 x 4½ x 1½", streamlined design, grass green paint, white rubber tires, c1930 .... **25.00**

Tootsietoy, battleship, silver, red guns, conning towers, top of smoke stacks, and command area, blue airplane, $7.50.

TOOTSIETOY

The first Tootsietoys were made in 1911, although the name was not registered until 1924, and it was not until after 1930 that the name appeared on the toys. Tootsie was an early manufacturer of prizes for Cracker Jack. Tootsie produced copies of real vehicles beginning in 1914 and continued until World War II. After the war, cars were made as toys rather than models.

Airplane Assortment, #1200, set of twelve 3½" l diecast planes, orig 13" sq plain box, c1940 .... **225.00**
Andy Gump Roadster, 1932 .... **85.00**
Austin Racer, 5" **20.00**
Bluebird I, Daytona Record Car, 1932 **20.00**
Buck Rogers Vehicle
   Battlecruiser, 5" l, diecast, red and yellow, 1937, orig box **240.00**
   Flashblast Attack Ship, 5" l, diecast, red and white, 1937, orig box ... **280.00**
   Venus Duo-Destroyer, 5" l, diecast, blue and white, 1937, orig box .. **265.00**
Cargo Van, Mack, 1933 .... **45.00**
Chevrolet Coupe, 1927 .... **50.00**
DeSota Airflow Sedan, 1935 .... **40.00**
Dodge Pickup Truck, 1950 .... **20.00**
Florist Delivery Truck, 1927 .... **80.00**
Gramam Wrecker **28.00**
Grocery Delivery Van, 1924 .... **165.00**
Horse Transporter **15.00**
Insurance Patrol, 1949 .... **15.00**
Kayo Ice Wagon, 1932 .... **80.00**
La Salle Convertible Coupe, 1936 .... **40.00**
Land and Air Set, eight green 4" l diecast combat vehicles, 13 x 9 x 2" orig color illus box, c1950 .... **165.00**
Oldsmobile, Panel Delivery Truck, 1927 .... **48.00**
Pickup Truck, Wheelie Wagon, 1972 . **25.00**

Pontiac, 1950 .... **14.00**
Rambler Station Wagon, 1960 .... **7.50**
Road Grader, 1956 .... **35.00**
Truck, three 1 x 1½ x 3" dump cars, green and black, four white tires, c1930 .... **35.00**
Twin Coach Bus, 1950 .... **18.00**
Uncle Willy Rowboat, 1932 .... **50.00**
US Mail, Mack Truck, 1931 .... **25.00**
Walt and Shand Delivery Van, 1924 .. **250.00**
Yellow Cab, sedan, 1923 .... **18.00**

UNKNOWN MAKERS

Architector Jr, building set, stone blocks, instructions, wood box **75.00**
Bilt E-Z #B, pressed steel architectural blocks **65.00**
Greyhound Bus, 3 x 11½ x 3½", litho tin, Scenicruiser, white and blue, black and white details, full color driver and hostess, multicolored orig box, Japan, c1960 .... **50.00**
Kiddie Blox, architectural wood blocks, slot and tab system, instructions, orig box **39.00**
Lincoln Logs
   Set, 3C Original Lincoln Logs, 5½" d, 18" h stiff cardboard container, metal lid, logs, four page full color design sheet, c1950 .... **50.00**
   Watch Fob, 1¾" d fiberboard fob, "I Am A Lincoln Logs Builder" on 1½" d celluloid center, c1930 .... **80.00**
Wunder Lumber, interlocking wood blocks, instructions, orig box **25.00**
Zylophone, Pressman, MIB **25.00**

WOLVERINE

The Wolverine Supply & Mfg Co was founded in 1903 and incorporated by Benjamin F Bain in 1906. The first type of tops they produced were lithographed tin sand toys. They began to make girls' housekeeping toys and action games by the 1920s. Production of toys continued and expanded in 1959 to include children's appliances, known as "Rite–Hite." The name was changed to Wolverine Toy Company in 1962. The company was originally located in Pittsburgh, PA, but relocated to Booneville, AK in 1970 after being aquired by Spang and Company.

Drum Major, 14" h, red jacket, plays drum, c1930 .... **110.00**
Kitchen Cabinet, litho tin, buff and green **60.00**
Merry Masons, 6½" w, 16" h, three masons, sand toy, c1950s **70.00**
Pinball Game, Daytona 500, 12½" l .. **15.00**
Roller Coaster, jets, mechanical **80.00**
Shoot A Loop, 1965 .... **18.00**

Sunny Andy Rabbit Chase, 9½" d, 3" h, litho tin windup, three 2" l greyhounds try to catch three 1½" l rabbits, slotted track, c1930 .... **265.00**

Zilotone, clown figure playing xylophone, c1930 .... **300.00**

WYANDOTTE

Bank, 6½", airflow gas truck, bright silver chrome body, white rubber tires, 1930s **65.00**

Cap Gun, Hopalong Cassidy, metal trigger, leather holster **650.00**

Coupe, 3 x 5 x 2½", pressed steel, dark red body, black running boards, three yellow wood wheels, one gray wheel, c1930 .... **40.00**

Davy Crockett Dart Rifle, 20" l, metal and wooden rifle, orig 21 x 3 x 1" illus box, c1950 .... **100.00**

Easter Bunny Delivery, 9" l, litho tin, Bunny on motorcycle, attached sidecar **150.00**

Express Truck **100.00**

Sand-O-Land Boat, 9" l, litho tin, red, white, blue, yellow, and black, boat on wooden wheels, Noah's ark dec, rocking motion, orig shovel and box **90.00**

Sedan, convertible, 12", missing windshield, 1940s **48.00**

Shooting Gallery **35.00**

Steam Shovel, orig orange paint **40.00**

Strato Wagon, flash **40.00**

Trapeze, orig box titled "Man on the Flying Trapeze," MIB **250.00**

Truck, Wyandotte Highway Freight, 4½ x 16 x 5", pressed steel, dark red trailer, blue and yellow cab, yellow grill, minor wear to paint, c1950 ... **40.00**

Water Pistol, red, orig decal "Thinjet," c1930, MIB **70.00**

TRAINS, TOY

Collecting Hints: Prices do fluctuate. Prices from mail order houses and stores generally are higher than those found at train swap meets. A large train swap meet is held in York, Pennsylvania each year. Condition is critical. Items in fair condition (scratched, chipped, dented, rusted or warped) and below generally have little value to the collector.

Restoration is accepted, provided it is done accurately. It does enhance the price one or two grades. Spare parts are actively traded and sold among collectors to assist in restoration efforts.

Exterior condition often is more important than operating condition. If you require a piece to operate, you should test it before you buy it.

Toy trains is a very specialized field. Collectors tend to have their own meets. A wealth of literature is available, but only from specialized book, railroad or toy train dealers. Novice collectors should read extensively before beginning to buy.

History: Railroading was an important part of many boys' childhoods, largely because of the romance associated with the railroad and the emphasis on toy trains. Almost everyone had a train layout; basements, back rooms, or attics allowed the layout to remain up year-round.

The first toy trains were cast iron and tin; the wind-up motor added movement. The golden age of toy trains was 1920–1955 when electric powered units were available, and Ives, American Flyer and Lionel were household names. Construction of the rolling stock was of high quality. The advent of plastic in the late 1950s lessened this quality considerably.

Toy trains are designated by a model scale or gauge. The most popular are HO, N, O, and S. Narrow gauge was a response to the modern capacity to miniaturize. Its popularity has lessened in the last few years.

References: John O. Bradshaw, *Greenberg's Guide To Kusan Trains*, Greenberg Publishing Co, 1987; Bruce Greenberg, (edited by Christian F. Rohlfing), *Greenberg's Guide To Lionel Trains: 1901–1942, Volume 1* (1988), *Volume 2* (1988), Greenberg Publishing Co.; Bruce Greenberg (edited by Roland La Voie and Steve Kimball), *Greenberg's Guide To Lionel Trains: 1945-1969, Volume 1* (1987), *Volume 2* (1988), Greenberg Publishing Co.; John Hubbard, *The Story of Williams Electric Trains*, Greenberg Publishing Co., 1987; Steven H. Kimball, *Greenberg's Guide To American Flyer Prewar O Gauge*, Greenberg Publishing Co., 1987; Roland La Voie, *Greenberg's Guide To Lionel-Fundimensions Trains*, Greenberg Publishing Co., 1985; Dallas J. Mallerich, III, *Greenberg's Guide to Athearn Trains*, Greenberg Publishing Co., 1987; Eric J. Matzke, *Greenberg's Guide To Marx Trains*, Greenberg Publishing Co., 1985; Al McDuffie, et. al., *Greenberg Guide to Ives Trains, 1901-1932*, Greenberg Publishing Co, 1984; John R. Ottley, *Greenberg's Guide To LGB Trains*, Greenberg Publishing Co., 1986; James Patterson and Bruce C. Greenberg, *Greenberg's Guide To American Flyer S Gauge, Third Edition*, Greenberg Publishing Co., 1988; Vincent Rosa and George J. Horan, *Greenberg Guide To HO Trains*, Greenberg Publishing Co., 1986; Robert Schleicher, *Model Railroad with L.G.B.*, Greenberg Publishing Co, 1989; Alan R. Schuweiler, *Greenberg's Guide to American Flyer, Wide Gauge*, Greenberg Publishing Co., 1989.

Collectors' Clubs: Lionel Collector's Club, P.O. Box 11851, Lexington, KY 40578; The National

Model Railroad Association, P.O. Box 2186, Indianapolis, IN 46206; The Toy Train Operating Society, Inc., 25 West Walnut Street, Suite 305, Pasadena, CA 91103; The Train Collector's Association, P.O. Box 248, Strasburg, PA 17579.

Note: All prices given are for items in very good condition, meaning that the piece shows some signs of use but all parts are present and damage from use is minor.

AMERICAN FLYER, S GAUGE

Accessories
275, Eureka Diner, 1952–53	**40.00**
566, Billboard, whistling, 1951–55 .	**18.00**
571, Truss Bridge, 1955–56	**5.00**
584, Bell Danger Signal, 1946–47 ..	**17.50**

Engines, Diesel, Electric, and Steam
Diesel and Electric
405, Silver Streak, 1952, Alco PA	**80.00**
499, New Haven, 1956–57, GE Electric	**150.00**
21551, Northern Pacific, 1958, Alco PA	**100.00**

Motorized Unit
740, Handcar	**25.00**
743, Track Maintenance Car	**24.00**

Steam Locomotive
303, 4-4-2, Atlantic, 1954–56 ...	**20.00**
316, 4-6-2, K-5, Pennsylvania, 1946	**45.00**
345, 4-6-2, Pacific, 1954	**50.00**
21084, 4-6-2, 1957	**40.00**

Rolling Stock
Box Car
623, Illinois Central, 1953	**10.00**
734, Missouri Pacific, 1954	**12.00**

Caboose
607	**8.50**
907	**17.50**
24526, 1957	**12.00**

Flat Car
609, American Flyer Lines, 1953 .	**10.00**
915, Auto Unloading Car, 1953–56	**20.00**
24516, New Haven, 1957–59 ...	**10.00**

Gondola
941, Frisco Lines, 1953–56	**7.50**
C2009, Texas & Pacific	**9.00**

Hopper and Dump Car
719, C B & Q, 1950–54	**30.00**
940, Wabash, 1953–56	**12.00**
24225, Sante Fe, 1960–65	**10.00**

Passenger Car
653, Pullman, 1946–53	**25.00**
662, Vista Dome, 1950–52	**24.00**
961, Jefferson, 1953–58	**30.00**
24773, Columbus, 1957–58	**45.00**

Tank Car
24313, Gulf, 1957–60	**20.00**
24328, Shell, 1962–66	**8.00**
24330, Baker's Chocolate, 1961–72	**25.00**

IVES

Accessories
91, Bridge, O gauge, 1912–30	**20.00**
119, Covered Platform, 1905–14 ...	**100.00**

Locomotive
17, 0-4-0, 1908	**300.00**
1118, 0-4-0, 1913–14	**265.00**
1661, 2-4-0, steam, 1932	**125.00**
3218, 0-4-0, 1917	**125.00**

Passenger Car
52, Passenger Car, 1915–25	**42.00**
130, Buffet, 1930	**75.00**
136, Observation, 1926–30	**35.00**
1813, Baggage, 1931–32	**20.00**

Rolling Stock
57, Lumber, O gauge, 1915–30	**35.00**
121, Caboose, 1929	**75.00**
198, Gravel Car, 1930	**200.00**
64158, Lehigh Valley, O gauge, 1930	**75.00**

Lionel, Silver Streak, engine #616, two passenger cars #617, and caboose #618, $500.00.

LIONEL, O GAUGE

Accessories
27, Lighting Set, 1911–23	**18.00**
64, Semaphore	**30.00**
85, Telegraph Pole	**12.00**
89, Flag Pole	**20.00**
120, Tunnel	**35.00**

Engines, Diesel, Electric and Steam
Diesel and Electric
60, Lionelville, trolley type, aluminized paper reflector, 1955-58	**175.00**
212, U. S. Marine Corps, Alco A, 1958–59	**48.00**
614, Alaska, NW-2 Switcher, 1959–60	**100.00**
706, Electric, 0-4-0, 1913–1916 .	**240.00**
3927, Lionel Lines, 1956–60	**60.00**
Handcar, 1100, Mickey Mouse, 1935–37	**600.00**

Steam Locomotives
203, 0-6-0, 1940–42 .... **325.00**
233, 0-6-0, 1940–42 .... **800.00**
665, 4-6-4, 1954–59 .... **75.00**
1062, 2-4-2, 1963–64 .... **18.00**
Rolling Stock
Boxcar
638–2361, Van Camp's Pork &
  Beans, 1962 .... **15.00**
714, 1940–42 .... **335.00**
1514, Baby Ruth **30.00**
2954, 1940–42 .... **145.00**
3356, Santa Fe Railway Express,
  1956–60 .... **35.00**
3494–275, State of Maine, 1956–
  58 .... **55.00**
6050, Lionel Savings Bank, 1961,
  coin slot **18.00**
6464-735, New Haven, 1969 .... **15.00**
6480, Explosives **4.00**
Caboose
0017, NYC, 1939–42 .... **50.00**
801, 1915–26 .... **15.00**
1007, Lionel Lines, 1948–52, SP
  Die 3 .... **1.50**
2457, Pennsylvania, semi-gloss red
  painted body, 1945–47 ...... **25.00**
2357, silver and blue **18.00**
6017, Lionel Lines, SP Dies, 1951–
  61 .... **15.00**
6119-50, D L & W, brown and
  white, 1957–59 .... **20.00**
6417-50, Lehigh Valley, 1954,
  N5C, gray **32.00**
Flatcar
1887, Flat, fence and horses, 1959 **120.00**
3330, Flat, operating submarine
  kit, 1960–61 .... **50.00**
3461, Log, dump, 1949–55 ..... **25.00**
3540, Operating Radar Car, 1959–
  60 .... **60.00**
6111, Flat, pipes, 1957 .... **2.00**
6361, Flat, timber, 1960–61,
  1964–69 .... **20.00**
6461, Transformer Car, 1949–50 . **25.00**
6650, ICBM Launcher, 1959–63 . **30.00**
6819, Flat, helicopter, 1959–60 .. **25.00**
Gondola
1717, 1933–40 .... **24.00**
2452, Pennsylvania, 1945 .... **4.50**
3444, Erie, 1957–59 .... **30.00**
4452, Pennsylvania, 1946–48 ... **48.00**
6462, NYC, red **4.50**
Hopper and Dump Car
0016, South Pacific, 1938–42 ... **60.00**
2816, 1935–42 .... **48.00**
6446-1, N&W 1954-55, "546446" **25.00**
Passenger Car
530, Observation, 1926–32 ..... **16.00**
600, Pullman, 1933–42 .... **75.00**
604, Observation, 1920–25 ..... **20.00**
605, Pullman, 1925–32 .... **65.00**

637, Coach, 1936–39 .... **55.00**
1673, Coach 1936–37 .... **18.00**
1687, Observation **145.00**
1866, West & Atlantic, Baggage,
  1959–62 .... **24.00**
2400, Maplewood, green and gray **25.00**
2401, Hillside, Pullman, 1948–49 **24.00**
2442, brown, gray trim **35.00**
2522, President Harrison, 1962–66 **60.00**
2631, Observation, 1938–42 .... **25.00**
Tank Car
0045, Shell, 1939–42 .... **50.00**
1515, 1933–37 .... **25.00**
2465, Sunoco, 1946 .... **8.00**
2955, 1940–42 .... **165.00**
6025, Gulf, 1956–57 .... **8.00**
6465, Lionel Lines, 1958–59 .... **5.00**

N GAUGE

Atlas
Locomotive, EMD E8, diesel, Santa Fe **20.00**
Rolling Stock
2204, Box Car, Great Northern .. **5.00**
2224, Reefer, Blatz Beer **2.00**
2601, Pullman, Santa Fe **7.50**
Lone Star
Locomotive
EL-65, F-7, Kansas City **15.00**
EL-68, F-7, Canadian National ... **25.00**
Rolling Stock
EL-70, Coach, British Main Line .. **3.50**
EL-77, Vista Dome, New Haven . **5.00**
EL-141, Caboose, Canadian Pacific **5.00**
Rivarossi
Locomotive, 5001A, Santa Fe, diesel **35.00**
Rolling Stock
5211D, Diner, Milwaukee Road .. **10.00**
5231H, Observation, Southern ... **8.50**
6001D, Freight, Conrail **2.50**

TRIVETS

Collecting Hints: A vast majority of the trivets
found in today's marketplace were once part of
an iron set. The triangular shape of a trivet is a
clue to this use.

Trivets can be collected by shape, material,
maker, or design. A new collector might focus
on trivets which are not cast iron, wrought iron,
or brass. There were pottery trivets, although not
much has been written about them.

A trivet that does not show signs of wear
should be suspect. Trivets were meant to be
used. Although decorative, the ornamental function always was secondary to the utilitarian function.

History: A trivet is a three-legged stand used to
support hot vessels, either in an open fireplace,

workroom, or on a table top. The trivet gained its greatest popularity in the late 19th century when it was used as a base for irons.

Cast iron trivets provide some of the finest examples of the ornate iron products of American industry. The decorative motifs are endless. Many groups commissioned souvenir trivets as mementos of outings or conventions.

By the mid-20th century the trivet was more decorative than functional. Its location moved from the table to the wall. A fancified trivet became a popular American souvenir item.

REPRODUCTION ALERT. In the 1960s reproduction wrought iron and cast iron trivets from Europe and Japan flooded the market. Many were aged to resemble the early models. Collectors and dealers are having a hard time telling early models from these modern fakes.

Cast iron, Trafford Foundry, Family Day, 1953, 4¾ x 8½, $10.00.

Brass, cast
Archer with shield, 7" l	15.00
Fox and tree, 8⅛" l	165.00
Greyhound, 9¼" l	10.00
Lattice design, 7½" l	30.00

Open work
Foliage design, 8" l	10.00
Scroll Design, iron shape, 7" l ...	30.00
Round, star flower center, 5¼" d ...	30.00
Scrolled foliage, 7" l	15.00
Star design, 8½" l	35.00

Cast Iron
Broom, 8" l, painted black	12.50
Crown, 6" l, marked "NR Streeter & Co, Groton, NY"	15.00
Eagle, color flag, GAR	80.00
Flower, ftd, five petals, ring handle .	50.00
Foliage scrolls, 9¾" l	8.00
Geometric design, green enamel, 9¼" l	15.00
Hex designs, 9¾" l	5.00

Horseshoe
5½ x 6½", "Good Luck," beaver and leaves in center	75.00
7¼" l, three figure 8's, marked "Wilton"	8.00
Jenny Lind, 10½" l	20.00
Pinwheel and compass stove, 10¾" l, painted black	30.00
Star, six pointed, rising sun, emb "The Cleveland Foundry Co"	20.00
Vintage, 7¾" l, painted black	15.00
Noritake, 5" sq, white with black stripes, yellow and purple flowers	40.00
Quimper, 9" sq, ftd, white, floral design, 19th C mark	135.00

Wrought Iron
Foliage design, 12¾" l, stylized, tooled sides, marked "A.P."	100.00
Heart, small heart handles, three drake feet, 18th C	225.00

TYPEWRITERS

Collecting Hints: Patent dates marked on frames are not accurate indicators of age since many machines were manufactured years after the patent date. The serial number is far more helpful in dating the machine.

Many machines were made by small companies. Old advertisements and catalogs can document models and approximate dates of production.

Typewriters produced after 1915 have little value. The number of typewriter collectors is small. Collectors generally know each other, swap and trade among themselves, and thus keep prices reduced.

History: The first commercially produced typewriter in America was the Sholes & Glidden, manufactured by E. Remington & Sons in 1874. This typewriter produced a row of tiny, uneven capital letters. In 1876 Remington exhibited typewriters at the United States Centennial Exposition in Philadelphia. For twenty-five cents people watched souvenir messages being typed. The machine sold for $125.00. Early typewriters remained expensive until the invention of the front striking machine.

In 1878 Remington produced the Perfected Type Writer No. 2, later named "Standard No. 2." This machine was easier to use, had a better finished product, and required fewer repairs.

By 1893 five companies joined together to form the Union Typewriter Company of America. This company produced mostly thick, squat, black office-type machines. They were blind writers, much like earlier machines, where the typist was unable to see the typed material because of the typewriter design.

John Underwood developed the first typewriter

with keys that struck the front of the platen. This 1895 invention changed the nature of the typewriter, making it much easier to use. By 1910 the typewriter had become a standard piece of office equipment. In the 1950s electric machines were developed. Cases changed from heavy black metal to bright plastic. In the 1980s, electronic machines have reached the market. They are light, have few moving parts, and have many more features than their predecessors.

References: Michael H. Adler, *The Writing Machine,* George Allen & Unwin Ltd, 1973; Wilfred A. Beeching, *Century of the Typewriters,* William Heinemann, 1974; Richard N. Current, *The Typewriter and the Men Who Made It,* University of Illinois Press, 1954; Darryl Matter, *Simplex Typewriters from the Early Twentieth Century,* Green Gate Books, 1984; Dan R. Post, *Collector's Guide to Antique Typewriters,* Post-Era Books, 1981.

Periodicals: *The Typewriter Exchange,* Box 150, Arcadia, CA 91006; *The Typewriter Trader,* 11433 Rochester Avenue, #303, Los Angeles, CA 90025.

Collectors' Clubs: Early Typewriter Collectors Association, 11433 Rochester Avenue, #303, Los Angeles, CA 90025.

Museums: Henry Ford Museum, Dearborn, MI; Milwaukee Public Museum, Milwaukee, WI; Smithsonian Institution, Washington, DC.

Blickenderfer #5, Stamford, CT, orig case, $150.00.

American Visible 100.00
Bennett Portable, last patent date 1908,
   10¾ x 4¾ x 2½" case 45.00
Blickensderfer
   No. 5, orig oak case 150.00
   No. 7, cylinder type, Stanford, CT,
     oak case 100.00
Corona, fold up model, three row keyboard, black, orig case 35.00

Fox, metal case, early 1900s 85.00
Hammond
   Multiplex, orig wood case 100.00
   Swinging sector mechanism, three row straight keyboard, inking by ribbon, oak base, bentwood cov, c1890 .... 185.00
IBM, Selectric, electric, interchangable ball type face 20.00
Keystone 75.00
Merritt, linear index mechanism, plunger type selector, double shift, inking by roller, wooden base, orig oak case, c1900, 12½" l 165.00
O'Dell, No. 4, Chicago, 1885 .... 80.00
Oliver
   No. 4, c1900 .... 35.00
   No. 5, ivory colored keys, oak baseboard, stenciled tin cov 100.00
Remington
   No. 6, orig tin cov 65.00
   Portable, 1929 .... 25.00
Shole & Glidden 275.00
Simplex, Model I, index type, red, white, and blue, orig box 45.00
Underwood, #25, orig wood case, 1929 .... 75.00

UNIVERSAL POTTERY

Collecting Hints: Not all Universal pottery carried the Universal name as part of the backstamp. Wares marked "Harmony House," "Sweet William/Sears Roebuck and Co.," and "Wheelock, Peoria" are part of the Universal production. Wheelock was a department store in Peoria, Illinois, that controlled the Cattail pattern on the Old Holland shape.

Like many pottery companies Universal had many shapes or styles of blanks, the most popular being Camwood, Old Holland, and Laurella. The same decal might be found on several different shapes.

The Cattail pattern had many accessory pieces. The 1940 and 1941 Sears catalogs listed an oval wastebasket, breakfast set, kitchen scale, linens, and bread box. Calico Fruits is another pattern with accessory pieces.

The Calico Fruits decal has not held up well over time. Collectors may have to settle for less than perfect pieces.

History: Universal Potteries of Cambridge, Ohio, was organized in 1934 by The Oxford Pottery Company. It purchased the Atlas-Globe plant properties. The Atlas-Globe operation was a merger of the Atlas China Company (formerly Crescent China Co. in 1921, Tritt in 1912 and Bradshaw in 1902) and the Globe China Company.

Even after the purchase, Universal retained the Oxford ware, made in Oxford, Ohio, as part of their dinnerware line. Another Oxford plant was used to manufacture tiles. The plant at Niles, Ohio, was dismantled.

The most popular lines of Universal were "Ballerina" and "Ballerina Mist." The company developed a detergent-resistant decal known as permacel, a key element in keeping a pattern bright. Production continued until 1960, when all plants were closed.

References: Jo Cunningham, *The Collector's Encyclopedia of American Dinnerware,* Collector Books, 1982; Betty Newbound, *The Gunshot Guide to Values of American Made China & Pottery,* Book 2, privately printed, 1983.

Periodicals: *The Daze,* 12135 North State Road, Otisville, MI 48463; *The New Glaze,* P.O. Box 4782, Birmingham, AL 35206.

Butter Dish, cov, Cattail pattern, marked "Universal Pottery, Cambridge, OH," $35.00.

Ballerina
Coaster	3.50
Coffeepot, wine	20.00
Chop Plate, 12"	5.00
Creamer	5.00
Cup and Saucer	
Dark Green	3.00
Gray	3.00
Egg Cup	10.00
Gravy Boat, gray	6.00
Plate	
9", dinner	
Dark Green	3.00
Gray	3.00
10", dinner, dark green	4.00
Salt and Pepper Shakers, pr	8.00
Sugar, cov	8.50
Tidbit Tray, two tiers, green	6.00
Tumbler	10.00

Calico Fruits
Batter Jug	24.00
Cookie Jar, cov	25.00
Creamer	4.00
Cup	6.50
Custard Cup	5.00
Plate, 10", dinner	7.50
Salt and Pepper Shakers, pr	12.00
Saucer	2.00
Spice Set, glass, tray	20.00

Cattail
Batter Pitcher, metal top	80.00
Bowl	
5"	4.00
6", tab handle	9.00
7½", cov	15.00
8¾"	12.00
Butter Dish, cov	35.00
Casserole, cov, 9½"	22.00
Coffee Percolator, electric	135.00
Creamer	8.00
Cup and Saucer	9.00
Custard Cup	10.00
Gravy Boat	20.00
Ice Tub, glass	80.00
Kitchen Scale	18.00
Pie Baker	20.00
Pie Server	22.00
Plate	
7", luncheon	5.00
9½", dinner	5.00
10", grill	12.00
Platter	
11½"	11.00
13½"	12.00
Salad Bowl, 9¾"	15.00
Salad Serving Set, fork and spoon	20.00
Soup, flat, 7¾"	10.00
Sugar, cov	10.00
Syrup, metal top	65.00
Teapot	22.00
Vegetable Bowl, oval, 10"	18.00

Iris
Bowl, 9"	10.00
Casserole, cov	15.00
Pie Baker	12.00
Plate, 10", dinner	6.50
Platter, 11"	10.00
Soup Bowl, tab handle	5.00
Stack Set, cov, 4 pcs	24.00
Tray, 11½"	10.00

Woodvine
Creamer	4.50
Cup	5.00
Gravy Boat	8.50
Jar, cov, 6"	10.00
Plate	
6", bread and butter	2.50
7", salad, sq	2.75
9", dinner	3.50
Relish	7.50
Saucer	1.75
Utility Bowl, 6", cov	15.00

VALENTINES

Collecting Hints: Valentine collectors tend to focus on cards made before 1930, with special emphasis on the nineteenth century. Cards made before 1800 are known, but most are in the hands of museums.

At present collectors tend to specialize in one type of card, e.g., transportation theme cards, lacey, honeycomb, etc. Comic sheets, Art Nouveau, and Art Deco cards are gaining in popularity. Valentine collectors now face heavy competition from other theme collectors who want valentines as supplements to their collections.

Condition of the card is more important than age in most cases. Collectors like clean cards in very good repair.

Early German mechanical cards open and close from the middle; later examples and reproductions pull down. Early mechanicals used more delicate pastel shades. Bright red is found on later cards.

Keep cards out of the light to prevent fading and brittleness. Store cards in layers in a drawer with acid free paper between them.

History: Early cards were handmade, often containing both handwritten verses and hand drawn pictures. Many cards also were hand colored and contained cutwork.

Mass production of machine made cards featuring chromolithography began after 1840. In 1847 Esther Howland of Worcester, Massachusetts, established a company to make valentines which were hand decorated with paper lace and other materials imported from England. They had a small "H" stamped in red in the top left corner. Howland's company eventually became the New England Valentine Company [N.E.V. Co.].

George C. Whitney and his brother founded a company after the Civil War which dominated the market from the 1870s through the first decades of the twentieth century. They bought out several competitors, one of which was the New England Valentine Company.

Lace paper was invented in 1834. The 1835 to 1860 period is known as the "golden age" of lacey cards.

Embossed paper was used in England after 1800. Embossed lithographs and woodcuts developed between 1825–40, with early examples being hand colored.

References: Ruth Webb Lee, *A History of Valentines, Fifth Edition,* Lee Publications, 1952; National Valentine Collectors Association, *Bulletins;* Frank Staff, *The Valentine and Its Origins,* out of print.

Collectors' Club: National Valentine Collectors Association, Box 1404, Santa Ana, CA 92702. *Newsletter* (quarterly).

Advisor: Evalene Pulati.

**Mechanical, stand up, c1910, 3⅝ x 5⅞",
$12.00.**

Art Deco, folder, 1920s	
3 x 3", heart shape	**1.50**
3 x 5", oblong, Whitney	**2.00**
5 x 7", fancy, with lace	**5.00**
6 x 9", layered, lacey	**7.50**
Art Nouveau, folder, 1900s	
3 x 5", oblong, Whitney	**3.50**
5 x 7", oblong, lacey	**7.50**
6 x 9", layered, lacey	**10.00**
Comic Sheet	
4 x 6", c1898, MCL	**6.50**
8 x 10"	
c1915, sgd "H"	**10.00**
c1920	**5.00**
8 x 14", sgd "CJH"	**15.00**
Diecut, cardboard, c1900	
4 x 4" hearts, cupids	**4.00**
Easel	
Large, couple	**7.50**
Large, hinged	**12.50**
Small, child	**5.00**
Embossed, hand made, c1865	
Folder, tiny	**7.50**
Layered	
Large, fancy, lacey	**20.00**
Small, lacey	**12.50**
Embossed, lacey, c1885	
Folder, small, simple	**5.00**
Large, real fancy	**12.50**
Layered with lace	**7.50**
German, mechanical	
Fancy, four layered	**12.50**
Large	
Auto, 1910	**50.00**
Streetcar, 1915	**75.00**
Train, 1914	**45.00**
Small, simple, pulldown	**4.00**
German, pullouts with honeycomb	
Fancy, pink umbrella	**35.00**
Large	
Pair of binoculars	**25.00**
White scale, 1914	**40.00**

Honeycomb, pullouts, 1920s

Beistle, 7", dark red	**7.50**
Car, diecut, 10", black	**15.00**
Toad Stool, light red	**5.00**

Perforated Lacy, c1850

5 x 7", Meek, hand written verse	**25.00**

8 x 10"

Double lace folder	**75.00**
Mansell, satin center	**65.00**

Small

Folder, sgd "H"	**20.00**
Meek, paste–ons	**17.50**

Standup Mantle Pieces, c1895

5 x 5"

Hand painted	**12.50**
Parchment	**7.50**
8 x 10", fancy, layered, fringed	**9.50**

Parchment

Fancy center	**15.00**
10 x 16", violin	**25.00**

VENDING MACHINES

Collecting Hints: Since individual manufacturers offered such a wide range of models, some collectors choose to specialize in a particular brand of machine. Variations are important. Certain accessories, porcelain finish, colors or special mechanical features on an otherwise common machine can add much to its value.

Original paint adds value. But numerous machines, especially peanut vendors with salt damaged paint, have been repainted. Most vendors were in service for ten to twenty years or more. Repainting normally was done by the operator as part of the repair and maintenance of his route. Repaints, recent or otherwise, if nicely done, do not necessarily lessen the value of a desirable machine. Original paint should be retained if at all possible.

Decals add much to the appearance of a vendor and often are the only means of identifying it. Original decals, again, are the most desirable. Reproductions of many popular styles have been made and are a viable alternative if originals are not available.

Some reproduction parts also are available. In some cases, entire machines have been reproduced using new glass and castings. Using one or two new parts as a means of restoring an otherwise incomplete machine is generally accepted by collectors.

Collecting vending machines is a relatively new hobby. It has increased in popularity with other advertising collectibles. New machines constantly are being discovered, thus maintaining the fascination for the collector.

History: Most of us still remember the penny gumball or peanut machine of our childhood. Many still survive on location after thirty years or more of service, due in part to the strength and simplicity of their construction.

The years 1910 to 1940 were the heyday of the most collectible style of vendor, the globe type peanut or gumball machine. Machine manufacturers invested a great deal of money throughout this period in the form of advertising and research. Many new designs were patented.

The simple rugged designs proved the most popular with the operator who had an established route of vendors as a means of making a living. Many operators made their fortunes "a penny at a time," especially during the Depression when dollars were hard to come by. Fifty years later, the same vendor that originally cost four to fifteen dollars commands a much higher price.

In addition to the globe-style variety of vendor is the cabinet-style machine. These usually incorporate a clockwork mechanism and occasionally mechanical figurines to deliver the merchandise. The earliest examples of these were produced in the 1890s.

References: Nic Costa, *Automatic Pleasures: The History of the Coin Machine,* Kevin Frances Publishing, Ltd., 1988; Bill Enes, *Silent Salesmen: An Encyclopedia of Collectible Gum, Candy & Nut Machines,* published by author, 1987; Roger Pribbenow and Jimm Lehmann, *Gumball Guide,* privately printed.

Periodical: *Coin Op Newsletter,* 909 26th Street, N. W., Washington, DC, 20037.

Ajax 5¢ Nut, commonly known as Challenger, aluminum, 1947, $175.00.

Abbey Peanut, 5¢	**95.00**
Adams' Tutti-Fruitti, gum, oak case, c1900	**650.00**
Adlee World's Best, cast iron, fancy styling	**600.00**
Advance Match Vendor	**395.00**
Advance No 11, peanut, steel construction, chrome plated front	**90.00**

Blue Anderson, 5¢, stamp **795.00**

Bluebird Bowler, gum, gumballs are played across miniature bowling alley, player can aim gumball and manually reset pins **650.00**

Chicago, peanut, nickel plated, cylinder globe, fancy and ornate, early 1900s **2,000.00**

Columbus Model A, 1¢, gum, replacement globe and padlock, restored, 1920s **265.00**

Columbus Model V, marble, tin, cylinder globe, cast iron and aluminum mechanism **500.00**

Diamond, 1¢, book matches, c1920 .. **300.00**

Double Nugget, double, polished aluminum, glass rect globes, door marked "N" and top marked "Double Nugget," 1930s **100.00**

Four-In-One, dispenses four different products, Art Deco style, swivel base, four handles and coin entries, 1930s **400.00**

Griswold, 1¢, peanut, cast iron, painted, six legged base, early 1910s **600.00**

Hance, 1¢, peanut, painted or plated finishes, early 1900s **500.00**

HiLo, cast iron, tapered cylinder globe, 1910–20 .... **500.00**

International Vending Match Machine, glass dome, c1910 .... **800.00**

Lucky Strike, 1¢, Wilson Mfg, dispenses single cigarettes, decal, c1931 ..... **795.00**

Magna Vendor, 5¢, polished aluminum, geometric styling, 14 sided faceted globe **175.00**

Mansfield Automatic Clerk, gum, etched front, clock wound mechanism, 1901 .... **325.00**

Masters Gum Machine, 1¢ **165.00**

National Self Service, 5¢, mint and gum, decal **135.00**

Northwestern 33, peanut, porcelain finish, octagonal geometric base, cylinder globe, door marked "Northwestern," 1933 .... **100.00**

Parker, 5¢, pencil, cast metal **345.00**

Penny King, gum, marked, 1930s **90.00**

Premier Baseball Card and Gumball dispenser **265.00**

Price Collar Button Vendor, 1901 ..... **575.00**

Reed's Aspirin Vendor, 10¢, graphics, orig aspirin packets **395.00**

Regal Hot Nut Vendor, glass globe, light bulb, 1930s **100.00**

Rex, gum, cast iron, cylinder globe, cross shaped knob **450.00**

Scoopy Gum Vendor, Gaylord Manufacturing, figural baker opens oven door and scoops gumball into shoot, c1920 **350.00**

Silver Comet, 1¢, dispenses gum sticks **165.00**

Superior, peanut and gumball, round base and globe, 1920–30 .... **175.00**

Yu Chu, "Jar Top," refills sold complete with new jar globe, 1930s **150.00**

Victor Baby Grand, 5¢, varnished oak sides, c1940 .... **40.00**

Victor Model V, sq base and globe, orig decal, c1940 .... **70.00**

VERNON KILNS

Collecting Hints: Vernon Kilns used 48 different marks during its period of operation. Collect examples which are in very good condition and concentrate on the specialty items rather than dinnerware.

History: During the Depression, many small potteries flourished in southern California. One of these, Poxon China, was founded in Vernon, California, in 1912. This pottery was sold to Faye G. Bennison in 1931. It was renamed Vernon Kilns and also was known as Vernon Potteries, Ltd. Under Bennison's direction, the company became a leader in the pottery industry.

The high quality and versatility of its wares made it very popular. Besides a varied dinnerware line, Vernon Kilns also produced Walt Disney figurines, advertising, political, and fraternal items. One popular line was historical and commemorative plates, which included several plate series, featuring scenes from England, California missions, and the West.

Vernon Kilns survived the Depression, fires, earthquakes, and wars. However, it could not compete with the influx of imports. In January, 1958, the factory was closed. Metlox Potteries of Manhattan Beach, California, bought the trade name and molds along with the remaining stock.

Reference: Maxine Nelson, *Versatile Vernon Kilns, An Illustrated Value Guide, Book II,* Collector Books, 1983.

Newsletter: Vernon View, P. O. Box 945, Scottsdale, AZ 85252.

Bowl
8½", Tam O'Shanter **8.00**

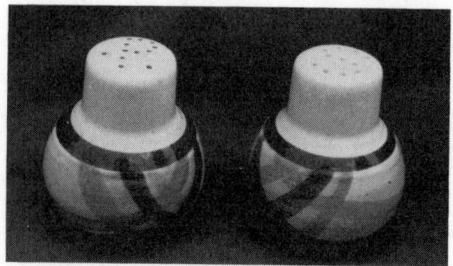

Salt and Pepper Shakers, Organdie pattern, green and yellow stripes on white ground, $8.00.

8¾", Gingham	12.00
9", Organdie	8.00
Butter Dish, cov	
Tam O'Shanter	14.00
Tampico	12.00
Casserole, cov, Tam O'Shanter, 8"	25.00
Chop Plate	
13"	
Gingham	9.00
Lei Lani	40.00
Organdie	10.00
15", Chatelaine, topaz	25.00
17", Ultra California, pink	45.00
Chowder, 6", lug handle	
Gingham	8.00
Lei Lani	20.00
Creamer	
Chintz	5.00
Organdie	4.00
Cup and Saucer	
Frontier Days	22.00
Gingham	6.00
Lei Lani	20.00
Mexicali	8.00
Organdie	5.00
Egg Cup	
Gingham	14.00
Lei Lani, double	12.00
Fruit Bowl, Yakima, WA, blue	8.00
Gravy Boat, underplate, Tampico	12.00
Pitcher	
Frontier Days, tall, streamlined	80.00
Monterey, streamlined	40.00
Plate	
6", Organdie, bread and butter	1.50
8½", Music Masters Series	
Chopin	12.00
Liszt	10.00
9", Mexicali, dinner	8.00
9¾", Organdie, dinner	4.00
10½", Lei Lani, dinner	25.00
Platter	
6½ x 10", Organdie	5.00
16", Mexicali, gold trim	30.00
Salad Bowl, Organdie, 10½"	22.00
Salt and Pepper Shakers, pr	
Gingham	10.00
Organdie	8.00
Sauce Boat	
California Heritage, green	12.00
Gingham	12.00
Serving Plate, center handle, Organdie	5.00
Souvenir Plate, 10½"	
Associated Pot and Kettle Club, 1951	15.00
Burdines, Miami, blue and white	12.00
California Missions	15.00
Chicago, IL, Marshall Field, hand tinted	4.00
Georgia Coast	10.00
Historical St Augustine	12.00
Indiana State Song	10.00
Maine	12.00

McAlester, OK	10.00
New Hampshire Aerial Tramway	12.00
Pasadena	15.00
Pennsylvania Turnpike, brown	3.00
Reno	10.00
Vicksburg, MS	8.00
Washington State Adm Day, 1889	20.00
Yakima, WA, blue	8.00
Spoon Rest, Calico	18.50
Sugar, cov	
Chintz	6.00
Organdie	6.00
Teapot, Organdie	25.00
Tidbit Server, three tiers	
Gingham	18.00
Homespun	20.00
Vegetable Bowl, cov, Organdie	25.00

VIEW-MASTER PRODUCTS

Collecting Hints: Condition is the key in determining price. In most cases, because of relative newness of this collecting category and quantities of material made, viewers and reels in mint or near new condition may still be found.

Original packaging is sought by collectors. Many viewers and reels were removed from boxes and envelopes and became subject to damage and excessive wear.

History: The first View-Master viewers and reels were made available in 1939. Invented by William Gruber, View-Master products were manufactured and sold by Sawyer's, Inc., of Portland, Oregon. The sudden growth of View-Master was cut short by World War II. Shortages of film, plastic, and paper would have crippled the operation and possibly ended the existence of View-Master had not the Army and Navy recognized the visual training potential of this product. Between 1942 and the war's end, about 100,000 viewers and 5 to 6 million reels were ordered by the military.

After the war, public demand for View-Master products soared. Production barely satisfied the needs of the original 1,000 dealer network. 1946 saw the introduction of the Model C viewer which was practically indestructible, thus making it the most common viewer found by collectors today.

In October 1966, General Aniline & Film Corporation (GAF) bought Sawyer's and revamped the View-Master line. GAF introduced new 2-D projectors and 3-D Talking View-Master.

In late 1980 GAF sold the View-Master portion of their company to a limited partnership headed by businessman Arnold Thaler. Further acquisition resulted in the purchase of Ideal Toys. Today the 3-D viewers and reels are manufactured by View-Master Ideal, Inc.

Reference: There is no book available which deals exclusively with View-Master as a whole. Much information has been collected by enthusiasts and self-published as lists.

Roger T. Nazeley's *View-Master Single Reels, Volume I,* (published by author, 1987) is a detailed listing of all known single reels.

Collectors' Club: National Stereoscopic Association, Box 14801, Columbus, OH 43214.

Advisor: John S. Waldsmith.

VIEWER

Model A, 1939, plastic, black, round front flips open	**15.00**
Model B, 1943, round front, streamlined design	**10.00**
Model C, 1946, plastic, black, reel insert on top	**1-2.00**
Model D, lighted, focuses	**35-50.00**
Various other models, plastic	**1-2.00**

PROJECTOR

S-1, metal, brown, single lens, carrying case	**45-50.00**
Stereomatic 500, 3-D, two lens, carrying case	**175-200.00**
View-Master Junior, plastic, single lens	**4-8.00**

CAMERA

Personal 3-D, custom film cutter	**125-175.00**
View-Master Mark II, film cutter, Made in Europe	**150-200.00**

REEL, SINGLE

Early hand-lettered, white reel, blue and white envelopes

84, Edison Institute Museum, Dearborn, Michigan	**9.00**
142, Zion National Park, Utah	**1.00**
256, Mt. Lassen Volcanic National Park, California	**1.50**
318, Baniff National Park, Alberta, Canada	**6.25**
345, Howe Caverns, New York	**3.00**

Gold and blue reel, hand-lettered titles, blue and white envelopes

11, Boulder Dam, Nevada	**3.00**
121, Salt Lake City, Utah, gold envelope	**11.00**
129, Yellowstone National Park, Wyoming	**1.50**
180, Phoenix, Arizona	**2.50**
245, Pikes Peak, Colorado	**2.50**
551, Guatemala City, Guatemala	**2.50**

Standard white reels, printed titles, blue and white envelopes

16, Bryce Canyon National Park, Utah, 1948	**3.00**

22, Crater Lake National Park, Oregon	**1.00**
81, Niagara Falls, New York, 1954	**1.25**
91, Oregon Caves National Monument, Oregon	**2.75**
102, Rocky Mountain National Park, Colorado	**4.00**
122, Salt Lake City, Utah, Mormon Temple and grounds	**1.00**
142, Zion National Park, Utah, 1948	**1.00**
154, Atlantic City, New Jersey, 1949	**2.00**
179, Tucson, Arizona	**3.00**
195, Beautiful Caverns of Luray, Virginia, 1946	**1.50**
203, The Black Hills of South Dakota, 1948	**2.00**
207, Sun Valley, Idaho, summer scenes	**1.00**
220, Homes of Movie Stars, Hollywood, California	**5-6.00**
248, Upper Michigan, 1949	**4.25**
256, Mount Lassen Volcanic National Park, California	**2.00**
267, Cranmore Mountain Skimobile Tramway, White Mountains, New Hampshire	**5.25**

Single Reel, 955, Hopalong Cassidy, (William Boyd) and "Topper," $2.50.

282, Santa Fe, New Mexico, 1948	**3.00**
295, St. Louis Zoological Park, Missouri, 1948	**2.50**
308, Anchorage, Alaska, 1950	**2.00**
338, Lookout Mountain, Chattanooga, Tennessee	**1.00**
360, Historic Charleston, South Carolina, 1950	**3.00**
378, Ottawa, Ontario, Canada, 1946	**1.00**
506, Pyramids of Teotihuacan and Tenayuca, Mexico, 1944	**3.50**
511, Acapulco, Mexico, 1944	**2.75**
520, Chichenitza, Mayan Ruins, Yucatan, Mexico, 1946	**12.00**
542, Cartago and the Irazu Volcano, Costa Rica, 1946	**8.00**
702, A Day at the Circus II, Ringling Bros and Barnum & Bailey, 1952	**3.50**
820, Woody Woodpecker in the Pony Express Ride, 1951	**1.00**
926, Performing Chimpanzees, St. Louis Zoo, Missouri, 1951	**2.00**

946, Roy Rogers in "The Holdup," 1953 .... **1.50**
1001, London I, England, 1948 .... **1.50**
1504, Garmisch-Partenkirchen in Winter, Baiern, Deustchland, 1958 **12.00**
1515, The Rhineland, Germany, 1954, booklet **10.00**
1531, Dinkelsbuhl, Germany, 1955 . **5.00**
1612, Naples, Italy, 1949 .... **1.25**
1622, Dolomite Mountains, Northern Italy, 1949 .... **1.00**
1640, Bologna, Italy, 1957 .... **7.25**
1952, Medieval Bruges, Belgium, 1953 .... **5.00**
2015, Making Swiss Cheese, Switzerland, 1948 .... **1.00**
2022, Pontresina, Switzerland, 1951 **5.00**
2041, Locarno-Ascona-Brissago, Switzerland, 1955 .... **11.50**
2100, Stockholm I, Sweden, 1955 .. **4.50**
2325, Vienna I, Austria, 1956 ..... **4.25**
4044, Moslem Temple Area, Jerusalem, Palestine, 1948 .... **3.75**
4050, The Arab Legion I, Transjordan, 1948 .... **2.25**
CH-8, Bible Stories, The Wise Men Find Jesus, 1947, booklet **1.00**
CH-55B, Bible Stories, The Prodigal Son (Continued), 1947, booklet .. **1.00**
DR-17, People Around the World, 1957, green lettering, demonstration reel, came with viewer, no envelope **4.25**
FT-3, Jack and the Beanstalk, 1951, booklet **2.00**
FT-9, The Ugly Duckling, 1948, booklet **4.25**
FT-50A, Alladdin and the Wonderful Lamp, Part One, 1951, booklet .. **1.00**
SAM-2, Sam Finds a Treasure (Adventures of Sam Sawyer), 1950, booklet **3.00**
SP-285, Death Valley Nat'l Monument II, California **8.00**
SP-9028, Adirondack Mountains, New York, 1950 .... **2.25**
Super Steelers, custom reel, c1975 . **17.50**

3-REEL PACKETS

Values are for complete near new packets. In most cases the 3-reel packets came with story booklets. Sawyer issues (SAW) 1953-1966, GAF issues (GAF) 1967-1981, and View-Master International, (VMI) 1981-1982.

The Coronation of Queen Elizabeth II, SAW, 405-407 .... **9.00**
Disneyland Main Street, 851 A, B, and C **4.00**
Dale Evans "Queen of the West," SAW 944 A, B, and C **25.00**

A-175, Disneyland Main Street, USA, SAW **4.00**
A-179, Disneyland, Tomorrowland, SAW **4.00**
A0331, Colorado Ski Country, GAF ... **4.50**
A-361, Grand Canyon, South Rim, Bright Angel Trail, SAW, orig cellophane wrap **8.50**

3-Reel Packet, B533, Casper the Friendly Ghost, $3.50.

A-372, Grand Canyon River Expedition, GAF **5.00**
A-440, Arkansas, SAW **3.50**
A-647, New York City at Night, GAF . **3.50**
A-671, New York World's Fair, 1964-65, General Tour, SAW **25.00**
A-856, The Old South, GAF **6.00**
A-946, Mardi Gras, New Orleans, Louisiana, SAW **4.00**
B-311, Carlo Collodi's Pinocchio, SAW **3.50**
B-342, Walt Disney's Robin Hood, GAF **3.00**
B-375, Walt Disney's Babes in Toyland, SAW, 1961 .... **5.50**
B-474, Lassie and Timmy, SAW **28.00**
B-501, Walt Disney Productions Presents The Love Bug, GAF, 1968 .... **3.50**
B-526, Mighty Mouse, SAW **4.00**
B-597, Emergency, GAF **3.50**
B-760, World's Fair, Brussels, 1958, SAW **20.00**
B-795, Old-Time Cars, GAF **8.00**
H-19, Disney World, Tomorrowland, VMI **4.00**
J-11, MASH, GAF **4.75**
J-32, Thailand, GAF **6.25**
J-79, US Spaceport, Kennedy Space Center, FL, VMI **3.50**
K-57, Star Trek, The Motion Picture, GAF, 1979 .... **11.50**
L-1, Can't Stop the Music, GAF, 1980 . **4.50**

WATCH FOBS

Collecting Hints: The most popular fobs are those relating to old machinery, either farm, construction or industrial. Advertising fobs are the next most popular group.

The back of a fob is helpful in identifying a

genuine fob from a reproduction or restrike. Genuine fobs frequently have advertising or a union trademark on the back. Some genuine fobs do have blank backs; but a blank back should be a warning to be cautious.

History: A watch fob is a useful and decorative item attached to a man's pocket watch by a strap. It assists him inremoving the watch from his pocket. Fobs became popular during the last quarter of the 19th century. Companies such as The Greenduck Co. in Chicago, Schwabb in Milwaukee, and Metal Arts in Rochester produced fobs for companies who wished to advertise their products or to commemorate an event, individual, or group.

Most fobs are made of metal and are struck from a steel die. Enamel fobs are scarce and sought after by collectors. If a fob was popular, a company would order restrikes. As a result, some fobs were issued for a period of twenty-five years or more. Watch fobs still are used today in promoting heavy industrial equipment.

Reference: John M. Kaduck, *Collecting Watch Fobs,* Wallace-Homestead, 1973.

Collectors' Club: International Watch Fob Association, Inc., 6613 Elmer Drive, Toledo, OH 43615.

REPRODUCTION ALERT

Banjo, figural, metal, MOP circle, 1⅜" l, $30.00.

Adamant Suit, Rosenthal Bros, NY, boy holding knickers, sitting on box holding extra pants **25.00**
Allis Chalmers Monarch Tractors **85.00**
American Legion, brass, diecut, Cleveland State Convention, 1946 .... **10.00**
Banigan Rubbers, brass, emb lion **24.00**
Biston's Golden Grain Coffee, brass, coffee bean shape **100.00**
Brown Gin and Liquors, 1½", brass, raised moose head, reverse "Sold by H Obernauer & Co, Pittsburgh, PA" **40.00**
Cadillac, brass, red, white, and blue enamel **80.00**
Case, J. I., oval, brass, eagle on globe center **125.00**
Chapman Drug Co, White Lion Drugs, Knoxville, silvered metal **25.00**

Davenport High School, 1904 .... **42.00**
Evening Gazette, baseball shape, score-card back, 1912 .... **75.00**
Engeman-Matthew Range, round, die-cut range **65.00**
Gold Medal Foods, 1½", white metal, ⅞" celluloid insert, black, white, and orange logo, inscribed "Gold Medal Foods," c1900s **35.00**
Green River Whiskey **30.00**
Hauser Packing Co, 1¾ x 2", white metal, raised western scene, back inscribed "Producers of Angelus Brand Hams, Bacons, and Lard" **35.00**
Huntington Pianos, dark white metal, ⅞" black, white, blue, and gold celluloid with Paderewski, inscription "Paderewski Bought One," early 1900s **35.00**
Keck Gonnerman, oval, brass **265.00**
Kellogg's Toasted Corn Flakes, cereal box shape, enameled letters **65.00**
Kelly Springfield Tires, 2", white metal, raised illus of female motorist, "Kelly Springfield Hand Made Tires" on back **45.00**
Martin-Senour Paints, 1½", silvered brass, 1" multicolored celluloid insert with hand holding dripping paint brush, text on back **40.00**
Massey-Harris Tractors **40.00**
National Rifle Association, marksman, snakeskin strap **25.00**
Northwestern Mutual Life Insurance, brass, figural, green enameled trees . **10.00**
Old Dutch Cleanser, porcelain center with Dutch lady **65.00**
Oliver, bust portrait of James Oliver in scrolled shield, emb "Oliver Gave To The World The Chilled Plow" **275.00**
Oxolin, metal, 1" celluloid inset with lady, adv on reverse **10.00**
Porter Hay Carrier, scrolled shield **140.00**
Princeton University, brass, 1908 ..... **20.00**
Quaker City Rubber Co, 1¼ x 1¾", copper colored brass over nickel, raised illus of William Penn, c1920 ...... **35.00**
Rally Day, 1½ x 1¾" white metal, ⅞" bright multicolored celluloid insert, c1920 .... **20.00**
Red Goose, red enameled goose **85.00**
Red Owl Coal, enamel, nickel over brass, oval, porcelain center with owl **85.00**
Regal Shoes, 1½", oval, copper colored brass, dress boot illus **40.00**
Republican National Convention, brass, 1920, bust of Lincoln **25.00**
Rumsey & Company, Board of Trade, Chicago, 1½ x 2", diecut, silvered brass, bull and bear cavorting, early 1900s **65.00**
Schramm Tractors **40.00**

Solarine, 1½", brass, sun on front, text on reverse, early 1900s	**30.00**
Studebaker, enameled tire design	**37.50**
Ward's Fine Cakes, white porcelain, bluebird, silvered beaded rim	**15.00**
World's Championship Rodeo Contest, Chicago	**25.00**
World's Fair, silver over brass, 1903–1904, links engraved with date of building	**125.00**
Zeno Means Good Chewing Gum, brass, high relief	**85.00**

WELLER POTTERY

Collecting Hints: Because of the availability of large numbers of pieces in Weller's commercial ware, prices are stable and unlikely to rise rapidly. Forest, Glendale, and Woodcraft are the popular patterns in the middle price range. The Novelty Line is most popular in the lower priced items.

Novice collectors are advised to look to figurals as a starting point. There are over fifty variations of frogs in the figural area. Many other animal shapes also are available.

Pieces in the middle range tend to be marked with an impressed "Weller" in block letters or a half circle ink stamp with the words "Weller Pottery." Late pieces are marked with a script "Weller" or "Weller Pottery." Many new collectors see this dated mark and incorrectly think the piece is old.

There are well over a hundred Weller patterns. New collectors should visit other collectors, talk with dealers, and look at a large range of pieces to determine which patterns they like and want to collect. It is pattern, not shape or type, by which most collections are organized.

History: In 1872 Samuel A. Weller opened a small factory in Fultonham, near Zanesville, Ohio, to produce utilitarian stoneware, such as milk pans and sewer tile. In 1882 he moved his facilities to Zanesville. In 1890 Weller built a new plant in the Putnam section of Zanesville along the tracks of the Cincinnati and Muskingum Railway. Additions followed in 1892 and 1894.

In 1894 Weller entered into an agreement with William A. Long to purchase the Lohnuda Faience Company, which had developed an art pottery line under the guidance of Laura A. Fry, formerly of Rookwood. Long left in 1895 but Weller continued to produce Lonhuda under a new name, Louwelsa. This shaded brown pottery with hand decoration under glaze was produced in over 500 different shapes. Replacing Long as art director was Charles Babcock Upjohn. He, along with Jacques Sicard, Frederick Hurten

Rhead and Gazo Fudji, developed Weller's art pottery lines.

At the end of World War I, many prestige lines were discontinued and Weller concentrated on commercial wares. Rudolph Lorber joined the staff and designed lines such as Roma, Forest and Knifewood. In 1920 Weller purchased the plant of the Zanesville Art Pottery. Weller claimed to be the largest pottery in the country.

Art pottery enjoyed a revival when the Hudson Line was introduced in the early 1920s. The 1930s saw Coopertone and Graystone Garden ware added. However, the Depression forced the closing of a Putnam plant and one on Marietta Street in Zanesville. After World War II inexpensive Japanese imports took over Weller's market. In 1947 Essex Wire Company of Detroit bought the controlling stock. Early in 1948 operations ceased.

Reference: Sharon and Bob Huxford, *The Collectors Encyclopedia of Weller Pottery,* Collector Books, 1979.

Collectors' Club: American Art Pottery Association, P. O. Box 714, Silver Springs, MD 20901.

Note: For pieces in the middle and upper price range see *Warman's Antiques And Their Prices.*

Basket, Oak Leaf, salmon and green, 9½", $65.00.

Ashtray	
Coppertone, frog seated at end	**90.00**
Roma, 2½"	**25.00**
Woodcraft, 3"	**65.00**
Basket, Melrose, 10"	**100.00**
Bowl, 5½", marbleized	**30.00**
Candlesticks, pr	
Eucid, 12½" h, orange luster	**80.00**
Lorbeck, 2" h, light lavender	**30.00**
Pumila	**45.00**
Centerpiece Bowl, Wild Rose, 7½"	**30.00**
Compote, Bonito, 4" h	**55.00**

Cornucopia
  Softone, 10", light blue **20.00**
  Wild Rose **25.00**
Ewer
  Cameo, 10", white rose, blue ground **42.00**
  Floretta, 6" **45.00**
  Panella **35.00**
  Wild Rose **42.00**
Figure
  Cactus Monkey **75.00**
  Frog, Coppertone, 2" **75.00**
  Turtle, Coppertone, 5½" **85.00**
Jardiniere
  Claywood, 8", cherries and trees ... **72.50**
  Ivory, 5" **15.00**
  Marvo, rust, 7½" **55.00**
Lamp, low relief molded peacock **135.00**
Mug
  Claywood, star shaped flowers **50.00**
  Ivory, brown accents, cream ground **35.00**
Pitcher
  Bouquet, 6", ruffled top, lavender flower, white ground, artist sgd "M" **30.00**
  Pansy, 6½" **85.00**
  Pierre, 5" **30.00**

Vase
  Baldin, red apples, green leaves, gold ground **65.00**
  Blue Drapery, 6½" **28.00**
  Bonito, 7½", ornate open handles .. **55.00**
  Cameo, 7" **20.00**
  Candis, 9", white **30.00**
  Flemish, 10" **65.00**
  Forest Line, 5½" **40.00**
  Fox Hunt Scene, white, deep blue ground, 7" **165.00**
  Glendale, 5", birds **115.00**
  Knifewood, low relief molded daisies, 7" **75.00**
  Lorbeck, 8", light lavender, Art Deco **30.00**
  Malvern **45.00**
  Oak Leaf **28.00**
  Panella, 6¾", light blue **20.00**
  Roma, 7½" **35.00**
  Tutone **35.00**
Wall Pocket
  Blue Drapery, 8" **75.00**
  Darsie, 9", turquoise **50.00**
  Flemish, 9½" **65.00**
  Panella, 8", orange **48.00**
  Wood Rose, 6", white **48.00**

Wall Pocket, Roma, 10¼", $80.00.

Planter
  Blue Drapery **42.00**
  Camel, sitting **40.00**
  Dachshund, 8½" **60.00**
  Elephant, 4", blue–green **85.00**
  Pelican, 5½", Evergreen **50.00**
  Roma, 4½", round, flower garlands . **30.00**
  Woodcraft, 11", log shape **32.00**
Plate, Zona, 10" **20.00**
Powder Box, cov, Ivoris **35.00**
Rose Bowl, Roba, 4¾", blue ground, yellow flowers, script sgd **30.00**
Teapot, Pumpkin **60.00**
Umbrella Stand, Ivory, 20" **165.00**

WESTERN AMERICANA

Collecting Hints: Western Americana is a relatively new field. The initial emphasis has been on books, prints, and paper products. The barbed wire craze of the early 1970s drew attention to three dimensional objects.

Texas material is the most sought after. All collectors tend to focus on the 19th century, rather than modern material. Within the last decade, Indian materials have moved into the level of sophisticated antique collecting.

Collectors should pick a theme or subject. The military west, exploration accounts and maps, and early photography are a few of the more popular focuses. The collecting field now has progressed to the point where there are over a half dozen dealers specializing solely in western materials.

History: From the Great Plains to the Golden West, the American west was viewed as the land of opportunity by settlers from the mid-19th century to the early 20th century. Key events caused cataclysmic changes—the 1848 Gold Rush, the opening of the Transcontinental railroad, the silver strikes in Nevada, the Indian massacres, and the Oklahoma land rush. By 1890 the west of the cowboy and cattle was dead; Indians had been relocated onto reservations.

The romance did not die. Novels, movies and television, whether through the Ponderosa or

Southfork, keep the romance of the west alive. Oil may have replaced cattle, but the legend remains.

References: Robert T. Clifton, *Barbs, Prongs, Points, Prickers & Stickers: A Complete and Illustrated Catalogue of Antique Barb Wire,* University of Oklahoma Press, 1970.

Museum: Gene Autry Western Heritage Museum, Los Angeles, CA.

Stereograph, cowboy, titled "Round–Up on the Sherman Ranch, Genesse, Kansas, USA," Keystone View Co #12475, description on back, $7.00.

Advertising
  Banner, 19½ x 29", Winchester, horse and rider center, "Headquarters for Winchester Rifles & Shotguns," fringed bottom, wooden rod **135.00**
  Charm, Bull Durham Tobacco, ⅞ x 1", diecut brass, early 1900s **7.50**
  Pinback Button
    Red Indian Cut Plug, c1898 ..... **30.00**
    Winchester, "The Topperweins Who Always Shoot Winchester Guns & Cartridges" **40.00**
  Sign
    California Gold Label Beer, bearded man and donkey in desert, self framed cardboard, sgd "Peter Hurd" **100.00**
    El Dorado Hotel Casino, reverse painted on glass, Conquistador . **75.00**
    Moccasin Agency, fierce Indian with full headdress, emb tin ... **40.00**
    Weyman Tobacco, cowboy on horse charging with gun, tobacco boxes on ground, 1890 .... **450.00**
  Token, Union Coffee adv, Buffalo Bill on back, hard rubber **50.00**
  Tray, Heptol Splits, C M Russell cowboy and bronc illus, 1904, tip size **225.00**
Autograph
  Cabinet Card, Annie Oakley, signature on small white card, matted and framed together **1,100.00**
Letter
  Fort Craig, NM Territory, historical data, 1868 .... **30.00**

Indian Territory, Pawnee movement, trader info, 1874 .... **55.00**
Badge, 1½ x 2", USA Mexican Border Service, dark finished brass links, brass center disc with soldier, reverse inscribed with Lord's Prayer, brass hanger inscribed "US Army," 1918 . **30.00**
Big Little Book
  Billy of Bar–Zero, Saalfield, 1940, written by Robert Marshall, illus by Henry Muheim **20.00**
  Bronco Bill, Whitman, 1935 Top–Line Comics, 3½ x 3½", worn cov **18.00**
  Cowboy Lingo, Whitman, 1938, written and illus by Fred Harman **24.00**
  Cowboy Malloy, Saalfield, 1940, written by Mark Millis, illus by Albert H Wick **22.00**
  Cowboy Stories, Whitman, 1933, written by Leon Morgan, illus by "Hal Arbo of the W Lazy 5 Ranch" **20.00**
Blanket
  Mexican, Qxaca area, natural and gray, eagle and snake dec **75.00**
  Navaho, Ganado, double dyed red, gray, black, and natural, diamond design, saddle size, 34 x 48, c1950 **115.00**
  Pendleton, wool, double weave, golds shading to red and green, brown ground, reverse diamond design, orig felted binding work, 60 x 80" **80.00**
Book
  Brigham, *Iowa, Its History and Its Foremost Citizens,* 1918 .... **10.00**
  Custer, Elizabeth B, *Tenting On The Plains,* 1893 .... **18.00**
  Fazzini, Lillian Davids, *Indians of America,* 1935 .... **65.00**
  Frost, John, *Frost's Pictorial History of California,* 1853, NY, illus **75.00**
  McKee, Edwin, *Grand Canyon,* 1931 **15.00**
  McKenney-Hall, *History of the Indian Tribes of North America,* Grant, 1934, 123 color plates, three volume set **115.00**
  History of Oregon, Hurst Publishing Co, 1881 .... **25.00**
Check
  Adams & Co Express Office, June 4, 1852, San Francisco, ornate script, center vignette of miners panning for gold, 4 x 8½" **50.00**
  Bank of CA, Gold Hill branch, black title and printing, 1878 .... **18.00**
  Fort Scott, Omaha, issued 1894 .... **12.00**
  Rocky Mountain National Bank, Indian and bear vignette, 1877 .... **50.00**
  Wells Fargo, San Francisco, April 7, 1879 .... **10.00**

Deed

Buffalo Gap, SD, pioneer town site, 1889 .... **18.00**

Sheriff's, AZ Territory, mine foreclosure, 1909, two pgs **20.00**

Foot Stool, horn feet, sheepskin cov, 13 x 8 x 7" **35.00**

Letterhead and Billhead, fancy title or illus of product

Burgert Saddle and Harness, Seattle, WA territory, 1889, bill for saddle repair **10.00**

Fashion Livery, AZ Territory, 1907 .. **20.00**

Fort Apache Stage Coach, Holbrook, 1904 .... **35.00**

J A Baillargeon, The Lace House, Seattle, WA territory, May 1, 1888, makers of oil cloth, corsets, embroidery, bill **12.00**

Magazine Original Art, full color, 4¼ x 7¼", titled "Maverick Brand, Hangman's Mesa," artist Robert Standley, Westport, CT, c1960 .... **40.00**

Map

Colton's North America, 13 x 16", hand colored, 1855, shows Canadian provinces, Washington, Nebraska, Kansas, Utah, and New Mexico territories **65.00**

Map of the American West, A C Black, Edinburgh, 1887, 16½ x 21½", west of Dakota-Kansas-Nebraska-Indian Territory to the Pacific Ocean **35.00**

Yosemite Valley, 8½ x 11", litho by J B Lippincott, Philadelphia, 1896, topographical **20.00**

Pinback Button

Indian Chief, ⅞", multicolored, c1890

Black Eye, Blackfeet Sioux **10.00**

Lean Wolf **10.00**

Red Cloud **12.00**

San Francisco, 2¼", multicolored, gold rim, 1922 .... **40.00**

Sir Francis Drake, 2¼", full color, floral border around portrait, issued for 350th commemoration of landing in California, c1920 .... **40.00**

South Omaha, 1¼", multicolored, bullfight illus, issued for 1901 street fair **30.00**

Post Card, 3½ x 5½", Broncho Billy, sepia portrait of G M Anderson, Essenay Film Co, London, c1910 ..... **25.00**

Poster

American Airlines–Mexico, E McKnight Kauffer artist, 30 x 40", c1947 .... **225.00**

Chicago, International Live Stock Exposition and Horse Show, window card type, 14 x 22", red, yellow, blue, black, orange, and brown .. **150.00**

Colorado, Free Homes, text promotes settlement, c1890 .... **50.00**

Grand Canyon, Oscar M Bry, 14 x 23", c1938, Sante Fe Railway adv **150.00**

Sante Fe Railway, Texas, 18 x 24", c1940, hundreds of cattle brands on brown background **110.00**

Winchester Ammunition, cowboy standing with foot on ram, rifle in hand, 1904 .... **675.00**

Your Forests–Your Fault–Your Losses, James Montgomery Flagg, 12 x 19", 1937, issued by US Forest Service, depicts forest fires **120.00**

Program

Buffalo Bill's Wild West, 7½ x 9½", 1889 performance of "Buffalo Bill's Wild West and Congress of Rough Riders of the World," illus, biographies, and stories of famous western characters **45.00**

Opera House, 1895–86 Season, Sweeney & Coombs, Houston ... **30.00**

Saddle

Colorado, hand tooled, silver conchas **1,350.00**

Kahle & Son, hand tooled, relined in wool, 1940 .... **200.00**

Vase, tapered sides, ring rim, "Texas Centennial, 1836–1936," brown, blue, and green, floral motif, brown band base and top of body, blue band on rim, glazed int., $65.00.

Stock and Bond Certificate

Atlanta Mining Co, UT territory, issued and canceled, 1878, vignette of Atlas holding silver globe **85.00**

Daly Mining Co, UT territory, issued, c1880 small mining vignette, gold lettering **35.00**

Godiva Mining Company, Utah Territory, issued for 1880, dated 1903   20.00
Pleasant Valley Land and Water, San Diego, CA, unissued, 1880, two vignettes 24.00
Toy
Johnny West–Marx Cowboy, 1½ x 3½ x 11", jointed vinyl cowboy, orig cowboy accessories 20.00
Marx Warriors of the World, hand colored plastic figure with 2 x 3 x 1" orig box
Cowboys, set of six, #2 Mike Riley, #3 Foster, #4 Mike Nichols, #5 Jack Straight, #7 Roger Dawson, and #8 Brown Bart 45.00
Indians, set of four, Little Crow, Long Bow, Slipping Bird, and Swift Bear 40.00
West of the West, Geronimo the Movable Indian and Pinto the Indian Pony, 3½ x 13 x 14½" horse, 28 accessories, orig white, tan, and brown box 35.00
Wild West Rodeo, GE, cut out, set up, 65 pcs, 1952 ....   35.00

WESTMORELAND GLASS COMPANY

Collecting Hints: The collector should become familiar with the many lines of tableware produced. English Hobnail made from the 20s to 60s is popular. Colonial designs were reproduced frequently, and accessories with dolphin pedestals are distinctive.

The trademark, an interwined "W" and "G", was imprinted on glass since 1949. After January, 1983, the full name "Westmoreland" is on all glass. Early molds were reintroduced. Numbered, signed, dated "Limited Editions" were offered.

History: The Westmoreland Glass Company was founded in October, 1899, at Grapeville, Pennsylvania. From the beginning, Westmoreland made handcrafted high quality glassware. In early years the company processed mustard, baking powder, and condiments to fill its containers. During World War I candy-filled glass novelties were popular.

Although Westmoreland is famous for its milk glass, large amounts of other glass were produced. During the 1920s, Westmoreland made reproductions and decorated wares. Color and tableware appeared in the 30s; but, as with other companies, 1935 saw the return to mainly crystal productions. In the 40s to 60s, black, ruby, and amber colors were made.

In May 1982 the factory closed. Reorganization brought a reopening in July, 1982. The Grapeville plant closed again in 1984.

Reference: Hazel Marie Weatherman, *Colored Glassware of the Depression Era, Book 2*, Glassbooks, Inc., 1982.

Collectors' Club: Westmoreland Glass Collectors Club, P. O. Box 143, North Liberty, IA 52317.

Candlestick, double, Della Robbia, pair, $55.00.

Animal Covered Dish
Duck, wavy base, milk glass 50.00
Hen on nest
Carnival glass, white 75.00
Slag, caramel, irid, 5" 45.00
Fox, milk glass 95.00
Rabbit on nest, Carnival glass, white   70.00
Appetizer, Paneled Grape, milk glass .   40.00
Ashtray, Thousand Eye, crystal 8.00
Basket
Della Robbia, colored trim 30.00
Paneled Grape, milk glass, 5" 15.00
Bonbon, Paneled Grape, milk glass, three feet 22.00
Bowl
4", cov, Beaded Grape, milk glass ..   20.00
4½", Paneled Grape, crystal 6.00
5", cov, Beaded Grape, milk glass, ftd, flared 32.50
6", Paneled Grape, milk glass 20.00
8", Old Quilt, milk glass 35.00
9", Beaded Grape, milk glass, ftd ...   35.00
12", Paneled Grape, milk glass, lipped 85.00
Butter Dish, cov, Paneled Grape, milk glass, oblong 27.00
Cake Stand, Paneled Grape, milk glass, skirted 40.00
Candlesticks, pr
Dolphin, milk glass, 9½" 70.00
Paneled Grape, milk glass, arched, two light, orig label 48.00

Candy Basket, Paneled Grape, milk
glass, split handle **20.00**
Candy Dish, cov
Beaded Grape, milk glass, 5", sq ... **18.00**
Fruits, milk glass, ftd **35.00**
Roses & Bows, stemmed, MOP **35.00**
Seashell and Dolphin, ice blue **40.00**
Candy Jar, cov
Della Robia, ftd **32.50**
Roses & Bows, milk glass, hp, green
base **18.00**
Celery
Old Quilt, milk glass **22.00**
Paneled Grape, milk glass **25.00**
Cheese Dish, Paneled Grape, milk glass **45.00**
Children's Dishes, creamer and sugar,
milk glass, orig label **18.00**
Chocolate Box, cov, Paneled Grape,
milk glass **40.00**
Cigarette Box
Paneled Grape, milk glass **35.00**
Thousand Eye, crystal, turtle shape . **35.00**
Compote
Paneled Grape, milk glass, crimped **28.00**
Thousand Eye, crystal, ruffled **18.00**
Console Bowl, Paneled Grape, milk
glass, pedestal **45.00**
Cordial, Paneled Grape, laurel green . **10.00**
Creamer and Sugar
Beaded Grape, milk glass, 3" **24.00**
Old Quilt, milk glass, individual size **25.00**
Paneled Grape, milk glass **18.00**
Cruet
English Hobnail, milk glass **25.00**
Paneled Grape, milk glass, 2 oz **18.00**
Dresser Jar, Grape **25.00**
Dresser Tray, Roses & Bows, milk glass,
hp **38.00**
Egg Cup, Chicken, milk glass, red paint **10.00**
Epergne, Paneled Grape, milk glass,
10", 2 pc **100.00**
Fairy Lamp, green mist, hp butterflies, 2
pc **30.00**
Figure, bulldog, rhinestone eyes, black,
orig label **22.00**
Fruit Bowl, Waterford, ruby **55.00**
Goblet, Paneled Grape
Laurel green **12.50**
Milk glass **15.00**
Honey Dish, cov
Beaded Grape, milk glass **20.00**
Old Quilt, milk glass **20.00**
Iced Tea, Paneled Grape, milk glass .. **14.00**
Jardiniere, Paneled Grape, milk glass . **25.00**
Jelly Box, Paneled Grape, milk glass .. **30.00**
Jug, Paneled Grape, milk glass, one pint **30.00**
Mayonnaise
English Hobnail, clear, ladle, metal
cov **15.00**
Paneled Grape, milk glass **20.00**
Mint Dish, Della Robia, clear, ftd **7.00**

Nappy, Roses & Bows, milk glass, hp,
three feet **30.00**
Perfume Bottle, Roses & Bows, milk
glass, hp **35.00**
Pitcher
Old Quilt, milk glass, 7¾" h **35.00**
Paneled Grape, milk glass, 22 oz ... **35.00**
Planter, Paneled Grape, milk glass, 8½
x 3" **25.00**
Plate
Paneled Grape, milk glass
6" **10.00**
8½" **15.00**
10½" **25.00**
Three Kittens, milk glass **25.00**
Puff Box
Paneled Grape, milk glass **30.00**
Roses & Bows, milk glass, hp **35.00**
Punch Cup, Paneled Grape, milk glass **10.00**
Rose Bowl, Paneled Grape, milk glass **25.00**
Sherbet, Rooster, milk glass **20.00**
Slipper, blue mist, hp **12.00**
Straw Jar, almond opaque glass **35.00**
Sugar, open, Old Quilt, milk glass **9.00**
Toothpick, swan, milk glass **18.00**
Torte Plate, Thousand Eye, crystal, 13" **28.00**
Tumbler
Fruits, milk glass, hp, beaded, ftd .. **10.00**
Paneled Grape, milk glass **14.00**
Vase
6", Paneled Grape, milk glass **15.00**
7", Old Quilt, milk glass, fan shape . **20.00**
9", Beaded Grape, milk glass **35.00**
11½", Paneled Grape, milk glass ... **85.00**
18", Paneled Grape, milk glass, orig
label **45.00**
Wedding Bowl, Roses & Bows, milk
glass, hp **85.00**

WHEATON COMMEMORATIVES

Collecting Hints: All issues of Wheaton Commemoratives can be obtained from the Wheaton Historical Association or Millville Art Glass. Collectors should not pay more than these factory prices. For the same reason, they should not buy a bottle in less than mint condition.

As with all modern glass and china, the resale market is yet to be tested. Currently Wheaton Commemoratives are used as attractive display pieces and serve this function well.

History: In 1967 the Wheaton Glass Company, Millville, New Jersey, a division of Wheaton Industries, began to produce commemorative decanters, flasks and bottles. The first issue was a canteen-type flask bearing the likeness of John F. Kennedy, part of a Presidential series. A miniature Presidential series also was adopted. Other series include Christmas, Great Americans, Movie Stars, Political Campaigns and Space. The Great American series features patriots, military leaders, inventors, religious and evangelistic leaders and writers.

In 1974 Wheaton Industries suspended production. The Wheaton Historical Association assumed the production of the Presidential and Christmas series from 1975 to 1982 and manufactured the bottles on a more limited basis, i.e., a maximum issue of 5,000 each. The bottles were made by hand on a semi-manual bottle making machine, rather than the automated production employed by Wheaton Industries.

Wheaton Historical Association discontinued the President and Christmas series in 1982. Future additions are being produced by Millville Art Glass Co. under a licensing arrangement.

Beginning in 1971 Wheaton Industries also manufactured a series of flasks and bottles which, while not reproductions, are similar in style to 19th century flasks and figural bottles. These were produced in milk glass, amber, ruby, blue, amethyst and green. They can be identified by "Wheaton, NJ," "Nuline," or "W" embossed on the base.

Advisor: Ed Johnson.

Note: The listing below contains factory prices, that price which a collector would have to pay purchasing the object directly from the factory. Market prices fluctuate; occasionally, bottles will be found below factory prices.

Presidential Series, John F. Kennedy, first edition, blue, 1967, $75.00.

Christmas
1971, green, unfrosted	30.00
1973, red	10.00
1975, blue	10.00
1977, green	60.00
1979, cobalt blue	55.00
1980, blue	10.00
1983, didymium	20.00
Great Americans, series consists of 17 bottles, each	10.00

Movie Stars
Clark Gable, Burley	12.00
Jean Harlow, topaz, 1972	40.00
John Wayne	12.00

Political campaign
1968, Donkey, green	10.00
1972, Elephant, amethyst	10.00

President
George Washington, frosted flint	10.00
Thomas Jefferson, red	25.00
James Monroe, topaz	80.00
John Quincy Adams, dark amber	12.00
John Tyler, dark amber	25.00
Franklin Pierce, pinetree green	20.00
Abraham Lincoln, topaz	12.00
Franklin D. Roosevelt, green	15.00
John F. Kennedy, light blue	75.00
Jimmy Carter, blue	10.00
Ronald Reagan, cobalt blue	10.00

President, miniature
Thomas Jefferson, green	6.00
W. H. Harrison, blue	5.00
Franklin Pierce, green	4.00
James Buchanan, red	5.00
Abraham Lincoln, blue	8.00
Rutherford Hayes, green	5.00
Chester Garfield, amethyst	4.00
Theodore Roosevelt, green	8.00
Harry Truman, aqua	6.00
Dwight D. Eisenhower, green	8.00
John F. Kennedy, amethyst	20.00
Richard Nixon, green	4.00

Space
Apollo 11, burnt amber	45.00
Apollo 12, red	30.00
Skylab 3	12.00

WHISKEY BOTTLES, COLLECTORS' SPECIAL EDITIONS

Collecting Hints: Beginning collectors are advised to focus on bottles of a single manufacturer or collect around a central theme, e.g., birds, trains, western, etc. Make certain to buy bottles whose finish is very good (almost no sign of wear), with no chips, and with the original labels intact.

A major collection still can be built for a modest investment, although some bottles now command over $1,000, such as the Beam Red Coat Fox. Don't overlook miniatures if you are on a restricted budget.

Finally, it is common practice to find bottles empty. In many states it is against the law to sell liquor without a license; hence, collectors tend to focus on the empty bottle.

History: The Jim Beam Distillery began the practice of issuing novelty (collectors' special edition) bottles for the 1953 Christmas trade. By the late 1960s over one hundred other distillers and wine manufacturers followed suit.

The Jim Beam Distillery remains the most prolific of the bottle issuers. Lionstone, McCormick and Ski Country are the other principal suppliers today. One dealer, Jon-Sol, Inc., has distributed his own line of collector bottles.

The "Golden Age" of the special edition bottle was the early 1970s. Interest waned in the late 1970s and early 80s as the market was saturated by companies trying to join the craze. Prices fell from record highs. Many manufacturers dropped special edition bottle production altogether.

A number of serious collectors, clubs, and dealers have brought stability to the market. Realizing that instant antiques cannot be created by demand alone, they have begun to study and classify their bottles. H. F. Montague deserves special recognition for his classification work. Most importantly, collectors have focused on those special edition bottles which show quality of workmanship and design and which have true limited editions.

References: Ralph and Terry Kovel, *The Kovels' Bottle Price List, Eighth Edition,* Crown Publishers, Inc., 1987; H. F. Montague, *Montague's Modern Bottle Identification and Price Guide,* H. F. Montague Enterprises, Inc., 1980.

Collectors' Clubs: International Association of Jim Beam Bottle & Specialties Clubs, 5120 Belmont Road, Suite D, Downers Grove, IL 60515; Michter's National Collectors Society, P.O. Box 481, Schaefferstown, PA 17088.

Museum: American Outpost, James B. Beam Distillery, Clermont, KY.

JIM BEAM

Beam Clubs and Conventions

Blue Hen Club, 1982	30.00
Cherry Hills Country Club, 1973	8.00
Conventions	
Second, Anaheim, 1972	75.00
Fifth, Sacramento, 1975	15.00
Seventh, Louisville, 1977	15.00
Ninth, Houston, 1979	70.00
Tenth, Norfolk, 1980	40.00
Thirteenth, St. Louis, 1983	50.00
Fourteenth, Hollywood, FL, 1984	45.00
Denver Club, 1970	15.00
Evergreen State Club, 9174	15.00
Five Seasons Club, 1980	12.00
Foxes	
On a Dolphin, 1980	35.00
Surfer, 1975	20.00
Gem City Club, 1983	65.00
Monterey Bay Club, 1977	15.00
Twin Bridges Club, 1971	50.00

Jim Beam, composer series, Chopin, $3.00.

Beam on Wheels	
Bobby Unser Olsonite Eagle, 1975	45.00
Cable car, 1983	65.00
Circus Wagon, 1979	35.00
Fire Engine 1867, 1978	85.00
Stutz Bearcat, yellow, 1977	40.00
Train	
Box car, 1983	55.00
Caboose, 1980	40.00
Engine, Turner, 1982	55.00
Passenger Car	50.00
Tender, coal, Grant, 1979	25.00
Volkswagen, red, 1973	35.00
Casino Series	
Cal-Neva Club, 1969	8.00
Golden Nugget, 1969	55.00
Harolds Club	
Man in Barrel #1, 1957	475.00
Silver Opal, 1957	25.00
VIP, 1967	55.00
VIP, 1971	70.00
VIP, 1975	25.00
VIP, 1979	35.00
Harvey Hotel Glass, 1969	8.00
Centennial Series, First Issued, 1960	
Alaska Purchase, 1966	8.00
Civil War, 1961	
North	30.00
South	55.00
Colorado Centennial, 1976	15.00
Hawaii, 200th, 1978	20.00
Laramie, 1968	5.00
Reidsville, 1973	8.00
San Diego, 1968	7.00
Statue of Liberty, 1975	12.00
Washington Bicentennial, 1976	18.00
Clubs and Organizations	
Bartenders' Guild, 1973	8.00
B.P.O. Does, 1971	6.00
Ducks Unlimited	
#3, 1977	65.00

#5, 1979	20.00
#7, 1981	32.00
#10, 1984	45.00
Elks National Foundation, 1978	10.00
Homebuilder's Association, 1979	25.00
National Licensed Beverage Association, 1975	8.00
Pennsylvania Dutch Club, 1974	12.00

Shriners

Indiana, 1970	8.00
Moila, 1972	35.00
Western Association, 1980	30.00
Sports Car Club, 1976	12.00
Wolverine Club, 1975	15.00

Customer Specialties

ABC Florida, 1973	15.00
Bohemian Girl, 1974	18.00
Foremost, 1956	235.00
Katz Cat, black, 1968	12.00
Ralph's Market, 1973	14.00
Ramada Inn, 1976	8.00
Richard's New Mexico, 1967	5.00

Zimmerman

Cherub, salmon, 1978	8.00
Vase, brown, 1972	18.00

Executive Series, First Issue, 1955

1955, Royal Porcelain	450.00
1957, Royal DiMonte	75.00
1958, Gray Cherub	420.00
1960, Blue Cherub	125.00
1962, Flower Basket	50.0o0
1964, Royal Gold Diamond	50.00
1966, Majestic	68.00
1969, Sovereign	12.00
1971, Fantasia	12.00
1972, Regency	12.00
1974, Twin Cherubs	15.00
1975, Reflections In Gold	15.00
1977, Golden Jubilee	18.00
1980, Titian	18.00
1983, Musical Bell	35.00

Foreign Countries

Australia

Magpie, 1978	18.00
Tigers, 1977	22.00
Germany, Pied Piper, 1974	8.00
Thailand, 1969	6.00

Glass Series, First Issue, 1952

Cocktail Shaker, Chateaux Martini, 1954	15.00
Coffee Warmer, black handle, stand, 1956	8.00

Crystal Pressed

1968, Proprietors Own	10.00
1971, blue	8.00
1974, green	6.00
Delft Rose, 1963	8.00
Humboldt County Fair, 1979	15.00
Oriental Jade, 1972	6.00
Royal Crystal, 1959	6.00
Royal Opal, 1957	8.00
Spey Royal, 1976	6.00

People Series

Charlie McCarthy, 1976	40.00
Cowboy, 1981	15.00
Hannah Dustin, 1973	30.00
John Henry, 1972	70.00
Paul Bunyan, 1970	8.00
Petroleum Man, 1971	7.00
Viking, 1973	12.00

Political Series

Ashtray, Donkey, 1956	18.00
Boxer, Elephant, 1964	18.00
Football, Donkey, 1972	8.00
Kansas City Convention Elephant, 1976	15.00
Spiro Agnew Elephant, 1970	2,200.00
Washington DC Elephant, 1972	750.00

Regal China Series

Bellringer #1, Plaid, 1970	8.00
Bonded, silver, 1975	6.00
Coffee Grinder, 1980	25.00
Green China Jug, 1965	7.00
Ivory Ashtray, 1955	25.00
Las Vegas, 1969	6.00
Musicians on Cask, 1964	6.00
New Hampshire Golden Eagle, 1971	45.00
Pony Express, 1968	8.00
Submarine-Redfin, 1970	8.00
Tobacco Festival, 1973	12.00

Sports Series

Bing Crosby, National Pro-Am

31st, 1972	30.00
33rd, 1974	32.00
37th, 1978	25.00
Fiesta Bowl, 1970	15.00

Hawaiian Open

Disk, 1975	15.00
Golf Ball, 1973	12.00
Indy 500, 1970	8.00
Kentucky Derby, 95th, pink roses, 1969	8.00
Louisiana Superdome, 1975	10.00
Mint 400, 6th, 1973	10.00
Ruidoso Downs, 1968	6.00

States Series

Alaska, 1958	65.00
Colorado, 1959	35.00
Delaware, 1972	8.00
Idaho, 1963	55.00
Montana, 1963	85.00
New Hampshire, 1968	8.00
New Mexico, 1972	15.00
South Carolina, 1970	8.00
Wyoming, 1965	58.00

Trophy Series

Bird

Duck, 1957	30.00
Eagle, 1968	15.00
Pheasant, 1960	28.00
Cat, Burmese, 1967	15.00
Dog, Poodle, gray, 1970	8.00

Fish

Crappie, 1979	15.00

Pretty Perch, 1980	**20.00**
Salmon, Coho, 1976	**12.00**
Walleye Pike, 1977	**12.00**
Horse, brown, 1967–68	**20.00**

Ezra Brooks, cable car, 1968, $12.00.

EZRA BROOKS

Animal Series
Deer, white tail, 1974	**25.00**
Hereford, 1971	**15.00**
Lion, African, 1980	**50.00**
Longhorn Steer, 1971	**18.00**
Panda, 1972	**18.00**
Tiger, Bengal, 1979	**45.00**

Automotive/Transportation Series
Corvette, 1962, Mako Shark, 1979 .	**20.00**
Ford Thunderbird, 1956, blue, 1976	**64.00**
Lincoln Continental, 1979	**35.00**
Ontario Racer, #10, 1970	**20.00**
San Francisco Cable Car, 1968	**12.00**
Train, Iron Horse, 1969	**12.00**

Bird Series
Goose, 1974	**18.00**
Owl, Scops #4, 1980	**55.00**

Heritage China Series
Liberty Bell, 1969	**8.00**
Potbelly Stove, 1968	**12.00**
Silver Dollar, black base, 1969	**8.00**
Totem Pole #2, 1973	**15.00**

Institutional Series
American Legion, Texas, 1971	**60.00**
Club Bottle #1, Distillery, 1970	**12.00**
Foremost, dancing man, 1969	**12.00**
Iowa Farmers Elevator, 1978	**35.00**
Kachina, #6, Buffalo dancer, 1977 .	**32.00**
Liquor Square, 1972	**8.00**
Wichita Centennial, 1970	**8.00**

People Series
Betsy Ross, 1975	**18.00**
Clown with balloons, 1973	**20.00**
Clown Bust	
#1, Smiley, 1979	**45.00**
#3, Pagliacci, 1979	**40.00**
Iowa Farmer, 1977	**75.00**

Max "The Hat" Zimmerman, 1976 .	**30.00**
Oliver Hardy, 1976	**18.00**
Pirate, 1971	**8.00**
Stonewall Jackson, 1974	**32.00**

Sports Series
Basketball Players, 1974	**10.00**
Bulldog-Georgia, 1971	**18.00**
Go Big Red #3, Rooter, 1972	**15.00**
Greensboro Open, Cup, 1975	**50.00**
Razorback Hog, 1979	**45.00**
Trojan, USC, 1973	**20.00**

Cabin Still, D-379 139, $30.00.

Cyrus Noble, miner, miniature, copyright 1974, Haas Bros, $18.00.

CYRUS NOBLE

Animal Series
Bear & Cubs, 1st Edition, 1978	**115.00**
Buffalo Cow & Calf, Nevada edition, 1977	**90.00**
Moose & Calf, 2nd Edition, 1977 ...	**85.00**
Mountain Sheep, 1st Edition, 1978 .	**175.00**

Carousel Series
Horse, Black Flyer, 1979	**50.00**
Pipe Organ, 1980	**45.00**

Mine Series
   Gold Miner, 1974 .... 18.00
   Mine Shaft, 1978 .... 35.00
   Music Man, 1977 .... 40.00
   Snowshoe Thompson, 1972 .... 200.00
Sea Animals
   Dolphin, 1979 .... 45.00
   Harp Seal, 1979 .... 50.00
   Sea Turtle, 1979 .... 50.00
   Tiger, 1979 .... 45.00

J. W. DANT

Field Birds, 1969
   #1, Ringnecked Pheasant 12.00
   #4, Mountain Quail 10.00
   #7, Bob White 10.00
Patrick Henry, 1969 .... 6.00

George Dickel, powder horn, $12.00.

DOUBLE SPRINGS

Bicentennial Series
   Florida 18.00
   Missouri 18.00
   New York 15.00
   Washington, D.C. 12.00
Car Series
   Buick, 1913, 1972 .... 100.00
   Mercedes Benz, 1975 .... 30.00
   Rolls Royce, 1971 .... 40.00

EARLY TIMES, 1976

Cannon Fire
   California, ... 12.00
   Delaware 25.00
Continental Congress
   Nevada 22.00
   New Mexico 28.00
Drum and Fife
   Hawaii 30.00
   Kansas 22.00
Minuteman
   Alaska 35.00

Oklahoma 25.00
Paul Revere, Wisconsin 15.00
Washington Crossing the Delaware
   Louisiana 20.00
   South Dakota 18.00

Famous Firsts, Edition No. 5, 1851 Yacht, 1970, marked "R. M. E. Orig Quidi," $35.00.

FAMOUS FIRSTS

Airplane Series
   Lockheed Transport-Jungle, 1982 ... 75.00
   Spirit of St. Louis, medium, 1972 ... 65.00
   Winnie Mae, large, 1972 .... 90.00
Animal Series
   Bears, miniature, 1981 .... 35.00
   Elephant, miniature, 1981 .... 32.00
   Hippo, baby, 1980 .... 55.00
   Rooster, Richardo, 1973 .... 18.00
Car/Transportation Series
   Balloon, 1971 .... 65.00
   Cable Car, 1973 .... 50.00
   Corvette, 1963 Stingray, white, mini-
     ature, 1979 .... 15.00
   Dino Ferrari, green, 1975 .... 18.00
   Indy Racer #11, 1971 .... 38.00
   Locomotive, 1969 .... 48.00
   Porsche Targa, 1979 .... 45.00
   Yacht America, miniature, 1978 .... 15.00
Miscellaneous
   Fireman, 1980 .... 55.00
   Geisha Dolls, set of 3, miniature,
     1978 .... 30.00
   Phonograph, 1969 .... 35.00
   Sewing Machine, 1979 .... 35.00

GRENADIER

American Revolution Series
   Eighteenth Continental, 1970 ...... 20.00
   First Pennsylvania, 1970 .... 38.00
   Third New York, 1970 .... 20.00
Bicentennial Series, 1976, 10th, 13
   types, each 15.00

Grenadier, Civil War Series, Jeb Stuart, Oct 1970, Arnart Imports, Inc., $20.00.

British Army Series
Kings African Rifle Corps, 5th, 1970	**20.00**
Sergeant Major, Coldstream Guard, 1973	**25.00**

Civil War Series
Captain, Union, 1970	**18.00**
General Robert E. Lee, ½ gallon, 1977	**145.00**
Soldier, series, miniature, 10 types, 1975, each	**18.00**

Miscellaneous
Father's Gift, 1979	**25.00**
Fire Chief, 1973	**85.00**
Jester Mirth King, 1977	**55.00**
Pancho on horse, 1977	**75.00**
San Fernando Electric Mfg. Co., 1976	**65.00**
Texas Ranger, 1977	**25.00**

Hoffman, Wildlife Series, deer, musical, $50.00.

HOFFMAN

Aesop's Fables Series, music, six types, 1978	**28.00**

Band Series, miniature
Accordion Player, 1987	**15.00**

Drummer, 1979	**18.00**

Bird Series
Canada Goose Decoy, 8 oz, 1977	**15.00**
Eagle, open wing, miniature, 1979	**20.00**
Love Birds, ½ pint, 1979	**18.00**

Cheerleaders
Dallas, 1979	**25.00**
Rams, 1980	**20.00**

Horse Series, 6 types, miniature, 1979, each	**12.00**

Mr. Lucky Series, music
Barber, 1980	**40.00**
Carolier, 1979	**45.00**
Fiddler, 1974	**26.00**
Mailman, miniature, 1976	**12.00**

Rodeo Series, 6 types, 1978, each	**30.00**
C. M. Russell Series, 6 types in 2 sets, 1976 and 1978, each	**25.00**

School Series
Kentucky Wildcats, Football, 1979	**35.00**
Mississippi Bulldogs with music, 1977	**55.00**

Wildlife Series
Doe & Fawn, 1975	**50.00**
Eagle & Fox, 1978	**35.00**
Wolf & Raccoon, 1978	**38.00**

JAPANESE FIRMS

House of Koshu
Boy with Pipe	**6.00**
Geisha, chrysanthemum, 1969	**24.00**
Maiden, 1970	**18.00**
Sake God, white, 1969	**12.00**

Kamotsuru
God #6, Bishamon (God Military), 1965	**15.00**
Treasure Tower, 1966	**18.00**

Kikukawa
Haru	**6.00**
Roosevelt, Teddy, 1970	**18.00**
Royal Couple, pr	**30.00**

LEWIS AND CLARK

Clark, miniature, 1971	**15.00**
Indian, peace pipe, 1978	**40.00**
Lewis, 1971	**85.00**

Troll Family
Grandmother Troll, 1979	**30.00**
Mrs. Troll, 1978	**28.00**

LIONSTONE

Bicentennial Series
Paul Revere, 1975	**20.00**
Valley Forge, 1975	**25.00**

Bird Series
Dove of Peace, 1977	**38.00**
Owls, 1973	**30.00**
Roadrunner, miniature, 1969	**12.00**
Robin, 1975	**32.00**

Lionstone, Old West Series, Gold Panner, 1969, $60.00.

Luxardo, basket of fruit, 1969, $25.00.

Car/Transportation Series
Corvette, 1984	**60.00**
Mercedes, miniature, 1978	**15.00**
Stutz Bearcat, miniature, 1978	**15.00**

Clown Series
#2, Sad Sam, 1978	**32.00**
#3, Say it with Music, 1978	**32.00**
#6, Lampy, 1979	**35.00**

Dog Series, miniature, 6 types in 3 sets,
1977, each	**28.00**

Firefighter Series
Fire Equipment Set, miniature, 1976	**38.00**

Fireman
#2, with child, 1974	**115.00**
#8, Fire Alarm Box, 1983	**55.00**

Old West Series
Bartender, 1969	**30.00**
Calamity Jane, 1973	**30.00**
Country Doctor, 1969	**15.00**
Dancehall Girl, 1973	**65.00**
Gambler, miniature, 1970	**12.00**
Indian, Squaw, 1973	**26.00**
Mountain Man, 1969	**15.00**
Riverboat Captain, 1969	**12.00**
Wells Fargo Man, 1969	**15.00**

Sports Series
Baseball Players, 1974	**25.00**
Hockey Players, 1974	**20.00**
Tennis Player, male, 1980	**45.00**

LUXARDO

Babylon, 1960	**18.00**
Burma Pitcher, 1960	**15.00**
Calypso Girl, 1962	**15.00**
Duck, green, 1960	**55.00**
Frog, miniature	**15.00**
Hippo, miniature	**15.00**
Medieval Palace, 1970	**8.00**
Polar Bear, miniature	**25.00**
Tower of Flowers, 1968	**20.00**

Wild Boar, miniature	**15.00**
Zodiac, 1970	**32.00**

McCORMICK

Bicentennial Series, miniature
Betsy Ross, 1976	**50.00**
John Paul Jones, 1976	**18.00**
Paul Revere, 1976	**50.00**
Spirit of '76, 1977	**25.00**

Bull Series
Black Angus, miniature, 1975	**20.00**
Charolais, 1974	**35.00**
Texas Longhorn, 1974	**35.00**

McCormick, mail car, 1970, $60.00.

Football Mascots
Arkansas Hogs	**35.00**
Drake Bulldogs, 1974	**25.00**
Indiana Hoosiers, 1974	**18.00**
Oregon Beavers, 1974	**18.00**
Texas Tech Raiders, 1972	**30.00**

Frontiersman Series, 1975
Daniel Boone	**28.00**
Kit Carson	**15.00**

Great American Series
George Washington Carver, 1977 . . .	**30.00**
Ulysses S. Grant, 1976	**28.00**
Meriwether Lewis, 1978	**35.00**
Robert E. Peary, 1977	**30.00**
Mark Twain, 1977	**32.00**

King Arthur Series, 1979
King Arthur	**45.00**
Sir Lancelot	**40.00**

Miscellaneous
Car, Packard, cream, 1980	**65.00**
McCormick Centennial, 1956	**140.00**
Woman Feeding Chickens, 1980	**45.00**

Sports Series
Air Race Pylon, 1970	**12.00**
Muhammad Ali, 1980	**50.00**
Nebraska Football Player, 1972	**25.00**

Train Series
Jupiter Engine, 1969	**24.00**
Wood Tender, 1969	**20.00**

Warrior Series, 1969
Centurion	**20.00**
Napoleon	**25.00**

Bols, music bottle, $10.00.

Michter's, King Tutankhamem Decanter, $25.00.

MICHTER'S

American Legion, Doughboy, 1979	**40.00**
Car, Fleetwood Packard, 1979	**30.00**
Jug, 1955	**55.00**
Liberty Bell, brown, 1969	**45.00**
Pennsylvania, Keystone State, 1980	**30.00**
Shrine, King Tut, white, 1978	**350.00**

MISCELLANEOUS

Aesthetic Specialties, Inc.
Bing Crosby 38th, 1978	**35.00**
Chevrolet, 1912, black, 1979	**40.00**
Kentucky Derby, 1979	**45.00**
World's Greatest Hunter, 1979	**35.00**

ALPA, Warner Bros Characters
Bugs Bunny, 1977	**8.00**
Porky Pig, 1977	**8.00**
Tweety Bird, 1978	**20.00**

Anniversary
Happy Anniversary	**25.00**
Lincoln, 1973	**15.00**
Ohio's Covered Bridges, 1974	**15.00**

Thomas Edison, 1972	**25.00**

Ballantine
Discus Thrower, 1969	**5.00**
Golf Bag, 1969	**8.00**
Mallard, 1969	**18.00**
Zebra, 1970	**15.00**

Beneagle
Barrel, thistle	**5.00**
Chess Pawn, John Knox, black, miniature	**12.00**
Loch Ness Monster wearing tam, 1960	**8.00**

Bischoff
Antique Candlestick, 1958	**24.00**
Chinese Boy, 1962	**35.00**
Grecian Vase, 1969	**15.00**
Pirate	**20.00**

Collector's Art
Bird Series, miniature
Blue Bird	**25.00**
Cardinal	**32.00**
Painted Bunting	**15.00**

Cattle Series
Black Angus, miniature, 1975	**20.00**
Texas Longhorn, 1974	**35.00**

Dog Series, miniature
Basset Hound	**25.00**
Poodle, white	**20.00**
Schnauzer	**25.00**

Garnier (France)
Alfa Romeo, 1924	**18.00**
Bouquet, 1966	**20.00**
Christmas Tree, 1956	**65.00**
Goldfinch, 1970	**15.00**
Locomotive, 1969	**15.00**
Paris Mountains	**25.00**
Robin, 1970	**12.00**
Soccer Shoe, 1962	**35.00**
Watering Can, 1958	**15.00**

Kentucky Gentleman
Confederate Soldier, 1969	**12.00**
Kentucky Gentleman	**15.00**
Pink Lady	**25.00**

Revolutionary Soldier, 1969 .... 12.00
Union Soldier, 1969 .... 12.00
W. A. Lacey
Harold's Club, 1970 .... 20.00
Log Animal
Raccoon, miniature, 1980 .... 20.00
Squirrels, 1979 .... 30.00
Tun Tavern, 1975 .... 15.00

O. B. R., Transportation Series, River Queen, 1968, $12.00.

OBR
Bus, 5th Avenue, 1971 .... 15.00
Caboose, 1973 .... 20.00
River Queen, 1968 .... 12.00
W. C. Fields, top hat, 1976 .... 15.00
Old Bardstown
Bull Dog, 1980 .... 80.00
Fighting Game Cock, pr, 750 ML ... 300.00
Stanley Steamer, 1978 .... 50.00
Old Crow
Chess Series
Bishop 12.00
Pawn 20.00
Rug 85.00
Crow, 1974 .... 15.00
Pancho Villa
Pancho Villa & Obrecon, 1976 .... 25.00
Pancho Villa on horse, 1975 .... 38.00
Potters
Clydesdale, miniature, 1978 .... 20.00
Mounty, 1980 .... 45.00
Pirate, 1973 .... 50.00
Polar Bear, 1977 .... 30.00
Rutherford
Eagle, miniature 15.00
Jug, crest, miniature, 1978 .... 8.00
Picture Frame, MacLachlan, minia-
ture 12.00

OLD COMMONWEALTH

Apothecary Series
Kentucky Peach Bowl, 1977 .... 30.00
North Carolina University, 1979 .... 30.00
Coal Miners
#1, 1975 .... 120.00
#3, with shovel, 1977 .... 40.00

#5, coal shooter, 1983 .... 45.00
Fireman Series, Modern
#1, Hero, 1982 .... 58.00
#2, Nozzleman, 1983 .... 60.00
#5, Lifesaver, 1983 .... 75.00
Miscellaneous
Boot, western, 1982 .... 48.00
Lumberjack, Old Time, 1979 ...... 20.00
Kentucky Thoroughbreds, 1977 .... 40.00
Tiger
Auburn 45.00
Missouri 45.00

OLD FITZGERALD

American Sons, 1976 .... 15.00
Blarney, Irish Toast, 1970 .... 15.00
Davidson, NC, 1972 .... 38.00
Florentine, 1961 .... 10.00
Gold Coaster, 1954 .... 15.00
Hospitality, 1958 .... 8.00
Irish Charm, 1977 .... 15.00
Monticello, 1968 .... 6.00
Rip Van Winkle, 1971 .... 35.00
Songs of Ireland, 1969 .... 15.00
Texas University, 1971 .... 18.00
West Virginia Forest Festival, 1973 ... 22.00

OLD MR. BOSTON

Assyrian Convention, 1975 .... 20.00
Bektash Temple, 1976 .... 25.00
Clown Head, 1973 .... 22.00
Concord Coach, 1976 .... 18.00
Deadwood, South Dakota, 1975 ..... 15.00
Eagle Convention, 78th Anniversary,
1973 .... 15.00
Hawk, 1975 .... 18.00
Lincoln on Horseback, 1972 .... 10.00
Molly Pitcher, 1975 .... 12.00
Nebraska, #1, gold, 1970 .... 22.00
Paul Revere, 1975 .... 15.00
Ship's Lantern, 1974 .... 18.00
Town Crier, 1976 .... 12.00

PACESETTER

Camero, Z28, yellow, 1982 .... 40.00
Corvette, 1975
Green 35.00
Light Blue, moving wheels 40.00
Tractor Series
No. 1, Big Green Machine, John
Deere, 1982 .... 90.00
No. 2, Big Green Machine, Interna-
tional Harvester, 1983 .... 65.00
Vokovich, #2, 1974 .... 30.00

SKI COUNTRY

Christmas Series
Bob Cratchit/Tiny Tim, 1977 .... 60.00

Ebenezer Scrooge, miniature, 1979 .	25.00
Mrs. Cratchit, 1978	58.00

Circus Series
Clown, bust, miniature, 1974	18.00
Elephant on Drum, 1973	45.00
Ringmaster, miniature, 1975	25.00
Tiger, 1975	45.00
Wagon, 1977	45.00

Customer Specialities
Cowboy Joe	70.00
Eagle, paperweight	185.00
Mill River Country Club, 1977	45.00
Phoenix Bird, miniature	45.00

Political
Donkey, 1976	35.00
Elephant, 1976	35.00
Submarine, miniature, 1976	30.00

Ski Country, Chukar Partridge, 1979, $40.00.

Domestic Animal Series
Bassett Hound, 1978	65.00
Labrador Dog with mallard, miniature, 1977	38.00

Indian Series
Cigar Store Indian, 1974	40.00
Dancer, Ceremonial Buffalo, 1975 ..	125.00
Look-Out Indian, miniature, 1977 ..	25.00
North American Tribe, set of 6, miniature, 1977	90.00

Waterfowl Series
Duck
Green Winged Teal, 1974	100.00
Mallard, miniature, 1973	38.00
Pelican, brown, miniature, 1976 ...	30.00
Penguin Family, 1978	50.00

Wildlife Series
Antelope, Pronghorn	70.00
Bobcat	70.00
Ferret, blackfooted, miniature	40.00
Jaguar, miniature	34.00
Koala, 1973	40.00
Mountain Lion, miniature, 1973	30.00
Otter, 1979	65.00
Polar Bear, miniature	30.00

Raccoon, 1974	60.00
Wild Turkey, 1976	200.00
Woodpecker, ivory bill, 1974	65.00

WILD TURKEY

Crystal Anniversary, 1955 ....2,000.00
Mack Truck	15.00

Series #1
1, Male, miniature, 1981	10.00
2, Female, 1972	165.00
3, On The Wing, 1973	100.00
5, With Flags, 1975	40.00
8, Strutting, 1978	48.00

Turkey Lore Series
1, 1979	45.00
2, 1980	38.00
3, 1981	45.00
4, 1982	50.00

WHISKEY PITCHERS (PUB JUGS)

Collecting Hints: Whiskey pitcher or pub jug collectors do specialize. Some concentrate on pitchers with a certain type of liquor—bourbon, scotch, rum, etc. Others deal only with figural pitchers or in pitchers associated with only one brand of liquor.

Collect pitchers that have in them the "mandatory," the statement on the proof of the liquor and its origin. Federal law requires this of all distillery-originated advertising in the United States. Pitchers without the mandatory may not be distillery-authorized.

Don't neglect foreign pub jugs. Many of these are made by fine potteries such as Royal Doulton, Royal Norfolk, Burleigh Ware, and Euroceramics. Pitchers by the Wade pottery are the most sought after by collectors.

The interest in pub jugs has fallen from the highpoint of the craze in the early 1970s. The market is stable and consists primarily of serious collectors.

History: Whiskey pitchers, more correctly pub jugs, are water pitchers with liquor advertising on them and are issued by distilleries around the world. The pub jug originated in England before the advent of modern plumbing. The pub owner kept a pitcher of water handy for the "Scotch and water" drinkers. An enterprising liquor salesman took notice of this and suggested to his firm that they provide a jug with their own name on it. The pub jugs were given by distillers to pub owners who promised to display them.

The early pub jugs were made of earthenware. Glass, porcelain, and pewter examples followed. Distilleries competed with each other to make their jugs the most attractive. Patrons quickly began asking for the pub jugs as gifts, especially the figural and more colorful ones.

By the mid-1960s the whiskey pitcher craze hit the United States. American interest stimulated the market. Britain is still the leader in pub jugs, but Italy, France, Japan, and the United States are not far behind. Almost every distiller has issued a pub jug with its name on it at one time or another. Some distillers issue a new form, color or letter pattern each year.

The typical pub jug is five to six inches in height and one of the basic colors. Older pitchers were black, brown, blue, green, or white. Today yellow, orange, and red pitchers occur. Promotional distribution of whiskey pitchers is uneven in the United States since local and state laws differ. Records on production levels of pub jugs are unknown. Collectors estimate that over 2,000 different types have been produced.

Periodical: *The Pub Jug* was issued in 1979 and 1980. It is no longer in print; issues are sought by collectors.

Captain Richard, Hennessey, $25.00.

Armagnac, XO Chabot, 4½", ceramic .	**8.00**
Bacardi Daiquiri, black, gold letters ..	**12.00**
Beefeater Gin, multicolored decal	**15.00**
Black Velvet, black, gold trim	**14.00**
Bonte Yorkshire, 3"	**5.00**
Canadian Windsor, figural, guard	**20.00**
Cutty Sark, 5⅛", yellow and black, ship decal, English	**15.00**
Four Roses	**10.00**
Jameson Irish Scotch and Water, bulbous, tan, black and red letters, Irish	**8.00**
Lionstone, figural, lion	**20.00**
Michter's Bourbon, PA Dutch symbol .	**8.00**
Nicholson's Lamplighter Distilled English Dry Gin, gray	**12.00**
Old Fitzgerald's, 6¼" h, rect, black, 24k gold detailing, red crest, "Aged in wood 8 years" in red, 1849	**8.00**
Old Grandad, sq, medallion	**10.00**

Old Weller Original 107 Proof Bourbon, 5½ x 8½", barrel shape, 24k gold trim, black lettering	**12.00**
Piper Best Scotch, Scotchman playing bagpipes, marked "Wade, England"	**12.00**
Schenley O.F.C., 7" h, oval, pale yellow, gold trim, gold, red, and black lettering	**8.00**
Seagrams	
Gin, The Perfect Martini Gin, blue top, green bottom, decal	**10.00**
7, medallion with relief 7 and crown in red, white ground	**12.00**
Tullamore Dew, white, black lettering, Made in USA, 1977	**10.00**
Wild Turkey, turkey decal	**7.00**
Wolfschmidt Genuine Vodka, Seagrams, white ground, label	**8.00**

WINE BOTTLES

Collecting Hints: Having the wine in the bottle does not add significantly to the value. The original labels are nice, but, again, add little to the bottle's value. Decoration, whether in relief or painted, is the key element. All coloration must be present to make the bottle collectible.

Interest in wine bottles has fallen during the last several years as collectors have withdrawn from this area. Most selling now takes place at collectors' clubs and through specialized publications and dealers.

History: Figural wine bottles were developed in the 1960s to help entice buyers to try foreign wines, especially those imported from Italy. The bulk of the bottles are pressed glass or ceramic figurals. Several examples are covered in leather or have a wicker basket around them.

The majority of the bottles are collected for decorative purposes with concentration on shape and color.

References: H. F. Montague, *Montague's Modern Bottle Identification And Price Guide, 2nd Edition*, privately printed, 1980.

Note: Bottles for wine and wine derivatives are included in this list. Liquor bottles are found under "Whiskey Bottles, Special Collector's Editions."

Apollo 11, stand, 1969	**15.00**
Bacchus Jug, 1963, Bacchus seated on cask	**12.00**
Bunch of Grapes, 5" h, clear, screw on lid	**4.00**
Candlestick, turned style	**8.00**
Church Steeple	**10.00**
Fish, quart, clear	**12.00**
Friar John, holding wine glass	**14.00**
Guitar, 16", amber	**12.00**

Harvest Jug, chain, grapes, and leaves	**10.00**
Horse head, Roman style, 1969	**20.00**
Lantern	**8.00**
Mandolin	**12.00**
Onion, free blown, pontil	**75.00**
Peacock, spread tail feathers	**18.00**
Pitcher	
Botticelli	**8.00**
Green striped glass, 18"	**15.00**
Murano, rose motif	**16.00**
Political, Elephant in chair, 1968	**12.00**
Queen Nefertiti, standing, miniature ..	**12.00**
Rifle, 16", green	**8.00**
Snow White and the Seven Dwarfs, miniature, 1950s, each	**70.00**
Totem Pole	**10.00**
Turtle	**8.00**
Wagon Barrel, glass barrel, frame, 1969	**20.00**
Wicker	
Chianti wine, 36" h, twisted rope neck	**15.00**
Demi-john, covered amber jug	**8.00**

WOODENWARE

Collecting Hints: Preserve the patina of your wood pieces. Don't clean and restore a wood implement to look new; the age and wear from use is what adds character and charm to the piece. Be aware that wood containers, especially buckets, may dry out, shrink and fall apart. Occasional use will prevent this problem.

History: Wood implements played an important role in the early American household and on the farmstead. Wood was used to make a wealth of utilitarian household objects from boxes to washboards, and was the principal element in most early American tools, except for cutting surfaces. Wood objects were valued and well taken care of by their owners. They were meant to last and did!

Wood survived as a key element in implements until the late 19th century. Cast and die-cast metals took over many of the household functions; aluminum and plastic absorbed the rest. Today wood survives on the farm but primarily as tool handles.

Reference: Mary Earle Gould, *Early American Wooden Ware*, Charles E. Tuttle, 1962.

Note: This category serves as a catchall for wood objects which do not fit into other categories in this book.

Apple Butter Scoop, 6½ x 15", open "D" shape handle	**220.00**
Bank, 8¼" l, mechanical, polychrome paint, Thrifty Scotchman, Norman 5500	**65.00**

Bowl	
6", round	**50.00**
9¾ x 17¼", oblong	**65.00**
Box	
Cheese, 15 x 5", round, lapped	**30.00**
Knife, 9 x 13", poplar, foliage dec, worn orig brown and green paint .	**95.00**
Salt, 6¾ x 9 x 6¼", walnut, dovetailed, hanger hole in crest	**125.00**
Seed, 25 x 8", stave construction, int. divider	**130.00**

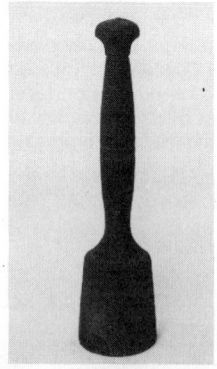

Potato Masher, turned, incised lines, knob handle, 12" h, $20.00.

Bucket	
Scrub, wringer, sgd "Eagle Mopuringer"	**20.00**
Sugar, 10" h, stave construction, impressed label on lid	**125.00**
Water, two buttonhole loops, wood pins	**145.00**
Butter Dish, cov, 4¾ x 2⅜", round, turned lines, scratched initials "M L"	**25.00**
Butter Paddle, 9½" l, maple	**45.00**
Butter Print	
Stylized floral design, 4" d	**25.00**
Swan, 3¾" d, turned handle	**125.00**
Tulip design, 4" d, dark finish	**200.00**
Candlesticks, pr, 9" h, turned, dark finish	**20.00**
Chalice, 5", walnut, turned	**45.00**
Cheese Drainer, slanted sides, slat bottom	**120.00**
Clothes Hanger, 17¾" l, turned wood .	**50.00**
Clothes Rack, 37" h, pine, expandable	**35.00**
Coffee Grinder, 12", iron handles	**45.00**
Coat Rack, ten pegs	**20.00**
Compote, 6¼", turned, orig dark finish	**50.00**
Cookie Board, 4 x 7", carved, urn of fruit	**25.00**
Cranberry Scoop, 19" w, maple and pine, black stenciled "F.L. Huckingham Mfg, Plymouth, Mass," branded "E.W.L."	**200.00**

Cutting Board
    6½ x 8", oval with flowers and two
    hearts design, inscription "Donne
    Paramitie" **175.00**
    21 x 18 x ¾", maple, horse head
    shape, early 20th C **65.00**
Dipper, 17½" l, crooked handle, dark
    finish **115.00**
Doughnut Cutter, knob handle **85.00**
Drying Tray
    Herb, 17¼ x 17½", wire nail con-
    struction **45.00**
    Tobacco, 26 x 39", gray **75.00**
Funnel, maple **140.00**
Food Mold, 3½ x 8½", cut turtle design,
    handle **50.00**
Furkin, 8½ x 10 ½", stave construction,
    brass and iron bands, handle **100.00**
Grain Measure, 6 x 8½" d, round, orig
    sage green paint **30.00**
Inkwell, 2¾ x 4½" d, turned, brown
    graining, gold stencil detail, glass in-
    sert and cork stopper, orig red wool
    bottom label, S. Silliman & Co, Ches-
    ter, CT **90.00**
Keg, rum, stave construction, metal
    bands **80.00**
Kraut Cutter, 11¾ x 1¼" **25.00**
Ladle, 14" l, hand made, c1860 ...... **38.00**
Lemon Squeezer **35.00**
Measure, 9¼ x 13½", bentwood, han-
    dle **100.00**
Nutmeg Grater, 7½" l, brass trim **135.00**
Paddle, 7¾", flat blade **10.00**
Pie Peel, short handle **85.00**
Pipe Box, 18½" h, oak, dark finish ... **170.00**
Plate, 7¼ x 7¾", patina **250.00**
Potato Masher, leather strap for hanging **15.00**
Rake, 71" l, hickory, red **200.00**
Rolling Pin, 18¾" l, curly maple **80.00**
Rope Bed Tightener **25.00**
Salt Bowl, cherry **30.00**
Sander, 2 ½", boxwood **45.00**
Scoop, 12¼" l, maple, curved handle . **90.00**
Shoe Sole Pattern, 11", marked "9AAA,
    MA Whinney Last Co, Brockton,
    Mass" **15.00**
Soap Mold, 2½ x 10", three parts, scal-
    loped circle and block design **30.00**
Sock Stretcher
    Adult **30.00**
    Child's, hand made **24.00**
Spoon, 6¾" **30.00**
Storage Box, 10¼" d, bentwood, round,
    compass star design on lid, brown pa-
    tina, impressed label "R. LR. Ansdel,
    Rindge, NH" **100.00**
Toddy Stick, birch **15.00**
Towel Rack, 24½ x 32¼", pine, turned
    posts, feet, and bars, worn finish ... **75.00**
Trencher, 9 x 9½", oval, turned detail . **145.00**

Wash Board, double faced, tusk tenon
    mortising, cut nails **50.00**

WORLD WAR I COLLECTIBLES

Collecting Hints: Most veterans of World War I have died, so nostalgia does not play as large a part in this collecting area as it does for World War II. Also, America's involvement was much more limited both in time and personnel. Equipment was not as sophisticated and patches to differentiate units were not used until the end of the war.

Reenactment groups have been organized; several mock encounters have been staged on the European battlefields.

Try to obtain as much information as you can about the source of the material you buy. Many uniform and equipment pieces were prewar models and some forms lasted into the peace time army. Purists want equipment that was "over there."

History: The assassination of Archduke Ferdinand of Austria in 1914 set in motion a series of internal conflicts within Europe that eventually led to full-scale war. After initial German successes, the war evolved into a series of trench engagements. In 1917 America entered the war. After a series of military defeats, Germany and its allies surrendered on November 11, 1918.

Periodicals: *Military Collectors News,* P. O. Box 702073, Tulsa, OK 74170.

Collectors' Clubs: American Society of Military Insignia Collectors, 1331 Bradley Avenue, Hummelstown, PA 17036; Association of American Military Uniform Collectors, 446 Berkshire Road, Elyria, OH 44035.

See: Newspapers (Headline Editions), Posters, Sheet Music, Dimestore Soldiers, etc.

Silk, white, black, maroon border, 15 x 15", 16½ x 16½" frame, $35.00.

Badge
  "American Red Cross-Military Wel-
    fare," cap, enamel **12.00**
  Tank Corps, British cap, 8th Churka   **15.00**
  Ward Service Ship Building, bronze   **18.00**
Bayonet, orig case **15.00**
Belt, web **8.00**
Belt and Buckle, "Hate Belt," button
  and cap insignias around belt, Ger-
  man, Wurttenburg **95.00**
Canteen, Army **10.00**
Certificate, 9½ x 12½", Liberty Loan,
  multicolored **25.00**
Cigarette Lighter, trench, German **30.00**
Coat, US Army **75.00**
Flip Book, 2 x 2½ x¼", soldier, sailor
  and Uncle Sam presenting the colors,
  pledge of Allegiance, Liberty Bond
  promotion, 1917 copyright **25.00**
Gas Mask, carrying can, shoulder strap,
  canister attached to bottom, German   **40.00**
Handkerchief, 11" sq, "Remember Me,"
  soldier and girl in center, red, white,
  and blue edge **12.00**
Handkerchief Holder, 10 x 11", padded
  fabric, green, red, white, and blue
  bow, diagonal pocket across one cor-
  ner, window banner flap with "Greet-
  ing/US Medical Corps" inscription
  and insignia **15.00**
Helmet
  German, leather, spiked **225.00**
  US, 3rd Army insignia **45.00**
Jacket, Sergeant's **40.00**
Leggings, motorcycle, leather **30.00**
Medal
  Iron Cross **25.00**
  Service, "San Francisco to Her War-
    rior Sons, 1919", SS **50.00**
Victory, five bars, orig box **25.00**
Periscope, wood, used in trenches **40.00**
Picture Frame, iron, emb dec, dated
  1917 ....   **35.00**
Pillow cover, 16 x 17½", full color
  printed soldier portrait surrounded by
  flags and American eagle, gold letter-
  ing "Forget Me Not," full color Miss
  Liberty holding stone table reads
  "World War Service" **35.00**
Pin
  ¾ x 1⅜", Rainbow Division 166/
    1917; almond shape, 10k gold,
    openwork, two crossed rifles in
    center **35.00**
  1", Victory Loan, bond seller, 1919 .   **15.00**
Plaque, 20 x 14½", bronze, Democracy
  and Patriotism poems **40.00**
Pocket Mirror, 2¾", oval, "Leaders of
  the World War For Democracy,"
  world leaders and flags **25.00**
Poster
  "Clear the Way," sailors on deck,

ship, gun, furled flag, and Miss
  America in background, Christy
  Liberty Loan **110.00**
"I Am Telling You," red, white, and
  blue, Uncle Sam with hands on
  hips illus, black lettering, James
  Montgomery Flagg **30.00**
"Lend the Way They Fight, Buy Bonds
  to Your Utmost," full color action
  scene, red and black lettering,
  green border **40.00**
"US Marines/First To Fight in France
  For Freedom," 30 x 40", multicol-
  ored, marines charging **125.00**
Print, 156th Field Artillery, Col. Miller
  Commanding Camp Sheridan, AL,
  Nov 22, 1917, 52" l **87.50**
Ribbon, 2 x 5", "Welcome Home 26th
  Division" **12.00**
Stickpin, porcelain, wounded German
  soldier, 1914–1918 ....   **25.00**
Sword, cipher on handle, folding clam-
  shell guard, blackened, fittings, Im-
  perial **125.00**
Tobacco Jar, cov, 6½", ceramic, brown
  glaze, General Pershing **125.00**
Toy
  Machine gun, wood and tin, maga-
    zine on top holds wood bullets,
    turn crank to fire **50.00**
  War camp, miniature, dated 1917 ..   **45.00**
Uniform, US Army, Engineer, coat, belt,
  pants, cap, canvas leggings, wool
  puttees, and leather gaiters, canteen   **200.00**
Watch Fob, flag on pole, USA, beaded,
  blue **20.00**
Wings, German fliers, set of 24 ......   **240.00**
Yardlong, framed, USS Sibenoy Arriving
  At US Naval Base, Aug 8, 1919 ....   **125.00**

WORLD WAR II COLLECTIBLES

Collecting Hints: World War II material still is
plentiful. Collectors should specialize either in
actual military equipment or material issued for
children and adults on the home front. Many
collectors narrow the topic further by focusing
on one form, e.g., manuals, patches, sheet music, toys, etc.

Uniforms and cloth material should be stored
and cleaned carefully. Remember that World War
II items are now forty-five or more years old; the
cloth may not hold up in a modern washing
machine.

The more personal information about an object
you can obtain the better. Whenever possible
identify the military unit and theater of operation.
Collectors tend to favor materials related to the

United States. The principal foreign collectible is Nazi items.

History: Although America's formal involvement in World War II lasted from 1941 to 1945, World War II collectors focus on the 1936 to 1948 period. The early dates cover America's response to the German military activities in Europe and Japan's invasion of Korea and China. The later period covers the time of American military occupation in Europe and Japan.

Besides equipping and supplying American Armed Forces abroad, the U. S. government and industry produced a wealth of material to prepare America for possible invasion and to bolster American morale. Any collectible field active during World War II should be checked for related material.

Periodicals: *Military Collectors News,* P. O. Box 702073, Tulsa, OK 74170.

Collectors' Clubs: American Society of Military Insignia Collectors, 1331 Bradley Avenue, Hummelstown, PA 17036; Association of American Military Uniform Collectors, 446 Berkshire Road, Elyria, OH 44035.

Advisor: Dick Bitterman.

See: Bubble Gum Cards, Cracker Jack, Newspapers (Headline Editions), Posters, Sheet Music, Dimestore Soldiers, Toys, etc.

Sheet Music, *Any Bonds Today,* by Irving Berlin, copyright by Henry Morgenthau Jr, Sec'y of Treasury, theme song of the National Defense Savings Program, $8.00.

Arm Band, Civilian Defense Air Raid Warden, 4" w, white, 3½" blue circle, red and white diagonal stripes within a triangle	6.00
Atlas	
Global Atlas of World At War, Mathews-Northup, 1944	7.50

Liberty World Atlas, Pictorial History of World War II, Hammond, cutout globe assembly	10.00
1942 War Atlas, Pure Oil	7.50
Badge, Infantry, German	25.00
Beanie, felt, multicolored, "Remember Pearl Harbor–Keep Em Flying"	22.00
Binoculars, Army, M-17, field type, 7½" l, olive drab, 7 x 50 power, clear, fixed optics	85.00
Book, *World War II in Headlines and Pictures,* Philadelphia, "Evening Bulletin," 10½ x 14", softbound, 1956	32.00
Booklet, US Navy 150th Anniversary	6.00
Bottle Stopper, 4", three dimensional head of General MacArthur	40.00
Bracelet, AAF P-47, Sweetheart, gilt metal body, side view of P-47, gilt wrist chain	14.00
Cap, AAF Officer's "50–Mission," crash cap, small gilded eagle, front and back straps, soft bill, gaberdine, marked "Flighter by Bancroft, O.D."	75.00
Card Game, "Navy Aircraft Squadron Insignia," 4 x 5 x 1" box	20.00
Drinking Glass, silk screen design, 4⅝" h, 2⅝" d, "Remember Pearl Harbor–Dec. 7, 1941," multicolored	22.00
Envelope, Iwo Jima flag, raising, 8/29/45, artist G F Hadley	15.00
Factory I D Badge, Mullins Mfg Co, Salem, OH, #1630, worker shown as 5'7" tall	12.00
Flight Suit, Army Air Force, Type A-4, olive drab gaberdine, matching belt, zipper front, size 38	65.00
Gas Mask, Japanese, head straps, attached canister	40.00
Helmet, MI, olive drab sand finish, olive drab chin strap, orig liner, thin mesh helmet net	120.00
Jacket, A-2 Army Air Force, leather, cowhide, light brown, name tag, size 42	450.00
Letter Opener, brass, rifle diecut, "Compliments of Dreifus & Co"	25.00
Magazine, "Sea Power," 1945	6.50
Manual	
Bureau of Aeronautics, Navy Department, Washington, D C, June 1943, *Recognition Pictorial Manual,* contains silhouettes and technical information on Allied and Axis aircraft, 6 x 10", 80 pgs, black and white	35.00
German pilot's aircraft recognition manual, pocket size, shows British, German and Italian aircraft silhouettes and specifications, 1941	45.00
Map, silk, AAF rayon escape map, Holland, Belgium, France, and Germany, 1944, orig carrying case, mint	35.00

Paper Airplane, Crestcraft Co, Chicago, copyright 1943, 11 x 14", multicolored pgs showing four different planes, Brewster Buffalo, Model F2A2, Curtiss Warhawk P-40, Flying Fortress B-19, Lockheed Lightning P-38 .... **25.00**

Paperweight, 2½ x 4 x 3", wood, syroco, three military men riding in jeep scene **24.00**

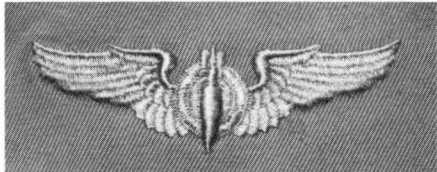

Patch, AAF, cloth, bombardier wings, embroidered silver and gray, tan cotton, unused, $10.00.

Patch
  Bombardier Wings, embroidered silver gray on tan cotton **10.00**
  Pilot's Wings, leather, AAF, emb, standard design, flying jacket attachment type **25.00**
  Squadron Jacket, Navy Fighter Squadron 33, 5" d, black and white border, winged demon head **30.00**

Pencil holder, 3½", plastic, red, white, and blue, "Victory," back lumber yard adv **10.00**

Pin, ¾", stamped brass, "Remember Pearl Harbor," small simulated pearl in center **10.00**

Postcard
  Boeing Flying Fortress, one of series of 10, details about plane on back **5.00**
  Curtiss Hawk P-40, one of series of 10, details about plane on back .. **5.00**
  Seabees, dated June 15, 1943 ...... **6.00**

Poster
  20 x 28½", American flag, "Give It Your Best," full color, unsigned .. **55.00**
  22 × 28, Sailor looking out port hole, "This Man May Die If You Talk Too Much," full color, artist sgd "Sarra" **65.00**
  25 x 38", B-17 with American flag waving overhead, "Keep Em Flying - Do Your Part," full color, artist sgd "D. V. Smith & A. Dorne" **200.00**

Shovel, fox hole type **8.00**

Sign, Dunhill Service Lighter, 5¼ x 7", cardboard **10.00**

Sweater, sleeveless, olive drab, "V" neck **18.00**

Tank, miniature, copper colored metal, 3" l, green felt bottom **20.00**

Toy Airplane, Hubley
  P-38, 12¾" wing span, 9" l body, silver color, red pilot cockpit and undercarriage, twin fuselage **30.00**
  P-40, die cast, 8¼" wing span, 7¾" l body, yellow wings, orange balance and propeller, rubber wheels **35.00**

Wall Plaque, "Victory-Liberty," "God Bless those In Our Service," 9", red, white, blue, and gold, octagonal cardboard, 1943 .... **6.00**

Weapon, knife
  Camillus USN Mark S Sheath Knife, black finish blade, light scabbard wear, USN and name marked on guard, gray web belt loop, gray fiber scabbard **35.00**
  Cattaraugus 225Q Fighting Knife, mint condition blade, dark leather grips, leather scabbard **125.00**

Window Banner, "Welcome Home," 8 x 12", red, white, and blue, cloth brown eagle, gold fringe **7.00**

WORLD'S FAIRS AND EXPOSITIONS

Collecting Hints: Familiarize yourself with the main buildings and features of the early World's Fairs and Expositions. Many of the choicest china and textiles pictured an identified building, assuming the buyer was aware of the significance. Many exposition buildings remained standing long after the fair was over, and souvenirs proliferated. Prices almost always are higher in the city or area where an exposition was held.

There have been hundreds of local fairs, state fairs, etc., in the last hundred years. These events generally produced items of little value except to local collectors.

History: The Great Exhibition of 1851 in London marked the beginning of the World's Fair and Exposition movement. The fairs generally feature exhibitions from nations around the world displaying the best of their industrial and scientific achievements.

Many important technological advances have been introduced at world's fairs. Examples include the airplane, telephone, and electric light. The ice cream cone, hot dog, and iced tea were products of vendors at fairs. Art movements often were closely connected to fairs with the Paris Exhibition of 1900 generally considered to have assembled the best of the works of the Art Nouveau artists.

References: Carl Abbott, *The Great Extravaganza: Portland and the Lewis and Clark Exposition*, Oregon Historical Society, 1981; S. Applebaum, *The New York World's Fair 1939–40,*

Dover Pub., 1977; Kurt Krueger, *Meet Me In St. Louis—The Exonumia of the 1904 World's Fair,* Krause Publications, 1979; Howard Rossen and John Kaduck, *Columbia World's Fair Collectibles,* Wallace-Homestead, 1976, revised price list 1982.

Periodical: *World's Fair,* P. O. Box 339, Corte Madera, CA 94925.

Collectors' Clubs: Expo Collectors & Historians Organization (ECHO), 1436 Killarney Avenue, Los Angeles, CA 90065; World's Fair Collectors' Society, Inc., P. O. Box 20806, Sarasota, FL 33583.

Philadelphia, 1876, locket, Independence Hall, Memorial Hall, oval, copper with plated tin, 1½ x 1¼", $30.00.

1876, PHILADELPHIA, Centennial Exposition
Bandanna, 19 x 25", black, white, and red Memorial Hall Art Gallery illus and patriotic eagle, red and white star border 90.00
Cuff Links, 1⅛", tortoise shell, silver Art Gallery scene and title, pr 100.00
Liberty Bell, brass, wood handle, inscribed "Proclaim Liberty" and 1776 and 1876 .... 75.00
Locket Pill Case, 1½", oval, silvered brass, raised relief Independence Hall and 1776 date on one side, other Memorial Hall and 1876 date, chain loops on end 75.00
1893, CHICAGO, The Columbian Exposition
Atlas 30.00
Chamberstick, metal, corn cob pipe shape 95.00
Glass, ruby flashed 25.00
Matchsafe 50.00
Paperweight
Ferris wheel 90.00
Ten medallion coin stack, 1" h, 1¼" d, brass, raised Columbus por-

trait top and inscription "Christopher Columbus/1492–Chicago, USA–1892" 50.00
Pass, day 8.00
Rose Bowl, 11½", acid etched rose bouquet, raised base 135.00
Spoon, 4", SP, Machinery Hall bowl 18.00
Souvenir Book, 5½ x 9", 36 pgs, issued by Lion Coffee of Woolson Spice Co 15.00
Tumbler, acid etched 25.00
1898, OMAHA, Trans–Mississippi Exposition
Button, 1½", sepia photo of ride, "Omaha 1898" inscription
Giant See Saw 60.00
Shooting The Shoots 50.00
Napkin Ring, engraved 8.00
1901, BUFFALO, Pan American Exposition
Demitasse Spoon, McKinley Tower . 24.00
Letter Opener, brass, figural, buffalo 35.00
Matchsafe, 1½ x 2½", brass, silvered, ladies with outstretched arms serve as Niagara Falls crest on ones side, Manufacturers and Liberal Arts Building on other, hinged lid 60.00
Notepad Holder, aluminum, emb, spine clamp, buffalo, floral design and inscription "Souvenir Pan-American Exposition 1901" on cov 20.00
Pan, 2¼" l, tin, litho, diecut, red, white, and blue, lard pail center, "Pan-American Exposition 1901" inscription 25.00
Stickpin, ¾" l, metal, black, buffalo 15.00
Tape Measure, 1¾", theme symbol on one side, steer head on other 25.00
Tray, brass, handled 58.00
1904 ST. LOUIS, Louisiana Purchase Exposition
Button, 1¼", lady holding trumpet, brass rim, attached ribbon with "Dedication Exposition/St. Louis, Mo" inscription, dated 1903 ..... 40.00
Cuff Links, ¾" h, brass, blue and white enameling, inscribed "Louisiana Purchase Exposition 1904," pr 35.00
Demitasse Spoon 14.00
Fob, brass, raised relief Louisiana Purchase symbol, Palace Of Arts, and Palace of Mines design 60.00
Handkerchief, 15 x 15", linen, white, embroidered Art Gallery illus one corner, other with "From Joyce" embroidered script 40.00
Matchsafe, striker and cigar cutter .. 55.00
Photo, New Jersey Building, attached blue fabric ribbon 30.00
Pin, ⅝", brass, emb, Louisiana flag . 15.00
Pocket Knife, emb 38.00

Postcard, hold to light type, Administration Building illus, inscription "Official Souvenir World's Fair—St. Louis 1904," unused 20.00
Stereocard 2.50
Tip Tray, humorous 50.00
Zither 235.00

1905, PORTLAND, Lewis & Clark Centennial
Needle Holder, 3¾" h, wood, blue enamel, silvered brass neck and cap, gold and black "Souvenir" label 90.00
Stickpin, brass, cello diecut flag with explorers and Miss Liberty sighting Pacific, blue border Boston Piano Co reverse 75.00

1907, JAMESTOWN
Fob, 1½ x 1¾", silvered brass 40.00
Photograph Book, 9 x 12" 25.00
Pin, 1¼ x 1¾", brass, red, white, and blue enameled hanger bar, Main Auditorium 20.00

1909, SEATTLE, Alaska-Yukon-Pacific Exposition
Button, 1¼", Indian woman flying over city, holding yellow flag, yellow on dark blue rim inscribed "City Of Seattle/AYPE/1909/Washington" 75.00
Fob, 1½" d, brass, three Art Nouveau style ladies design, red rim "Alaska–Yukon–Pacific Exposition—Seattle 1909" 100.00
Jewelry Set, Space Needle 45.00
Spoon, SS 65.00

1915, SAN FRANCISCO, Panama–Pacific International Exposition
Coin Purse, 2½ x 3½", suede leather, green, silvered brass hinged snap . 25.00
Fob, 1½", silvered brass, diecut, inscribed "Completion Of The Panama Canal 1915," title and date .. 50.00
Razor Strop, double 22.00
Souvenir Book 30.00

1933-34, CHICAGO, Century of Progress
Bank, American Can Co 15.00
Box, emb 7.50
Bracelet, brass, exhibits 18.00
Cigarette Lighter, brass, printed symbol on one side with black accents 25.00
Clothing Brush, 8" l, china pajamas doll figural handle with Sky Ride and Fort Dearborn decal, boxed, marked "9092" German made ... 50.00
Doll, 13", Czechoslovakia, ethnic costume 35.00
Keg, ceramic, oak stand 35.00
Lamp, desk, enamel, white, glossy cardboard shade with black design

edge, "1833–1933" inscription on base 100.00
Mug 45.00
Night Light 60.00
Photo Reel, orig box 30.00
Piano Scarf 48.00
Pocket Mirror, oval 35.00
Poker Chip, 1½", cardboard, pressed, blue on white 15.00
Stationery, 12 sheets and envelopes, black and white etching on left corner, unused 25.00
Thermometer, 2½ x 2½", octagonal shape, silver and blue dial symbol and "Chicago 1934," brass rim, black metal back and hanging ... 50.00
Tie Clasp 15.00
Token, wooden nickel, 1⁵⁄₁₆", Indian in feathered headdress on one side, symbol design on reverse, inscriptions "A Century Of Progress" 1833, and 1933 .... 15.00
Tray, 4¾" d, brass, emb, raised detailed exhibit buildings 25.00

New York, 1939, pencil, oversized, $20.00.

1939 NEW YORK, New York World's Fair
Admission Ticket 6.00
Ashtray, 3¼" d, metal plated, raised Trylon and Perisphere design, Egyptian motif on base edge 20.00
Bandanna, 19 x 20", printed design, blue, yellow, green, and white, red background 40.00
Bank, 3½" h, "Libby's Treasure Ship," juice can design, fair scenes around sides, inscription and date 60.00
Blotter Pad, 3 x 6", cardboard, orange, gold inscription, Administration Building 35.00
Bracelet, brass, Trylon, Perisphere, and nine exhibit buildings, spring clasp catch 30.00
Cane, oak, spring action, map 100.00
Certificate, 7½ x 11", white, black lettering, gray background designs, inked recipients name and printed signatures 75.00
Cigarette Box, photo 15.00
Coaster, 3" d, glass, imprinted Trylon

and Perisphere, and Dutch exhibit, "Made in Holland" **25.00**

Compact, 2 x 2¼", brass, blue and orange enamel, design lid **30.00**

Cookie Tin, 10" d, litho, orange, black, and white lid scene, "Packed For R. H. Macy & Co, Inc. New York" rim edge **40.00**

Glass, 5" h, applied yellow design, Textile Building, bottom green band with name and date **20.00**

Guide book, 5¼ x 8", soft cov, 256 pgs, first edition, Expositions Publications, Inc. **30.00**

Handkerchief, 12 x 13", New York City map in green, lavender, and black, white background, Trylon and Perisphere and "New York/The Wonder City/New York World's Fair, 1939" inscription on lower corner **40.00**

Key Chain, enameled **15.00**

Letter Opener, 1½ x 4", molded Trylon and Perisphere design, General Electric and symbol **20.00**

Matchbook, unused **3.00**

Matchbook Holder, 1½ x 2", brass, hinged lid, Trylon and Perisphere, George Washington bust and 150th anniversary inauguration text on bottom **60.00**

Mirror, blue Trylon/Perisphere silhouette and inscription, Pittsburgh Plate Glass Co Exhibit, box **30.00**

Nut Cup Set, Planters Peanut, 4 pcs **15.00**

Paperweight, 2¾ x 4¼", glass, clear, Maritime Building **30.00**

Pillow Cover, 17 x 17", orange and blue Trylon/Perisphere design **40.00**

Pin, 1⅛ x 2¼", metal, diecut, painted, Trylon and Perisphere accented with rhinestones blue accents, green base **50.00**

Pipe Rest, syroco wood, hewed log, Trylon and Perisphere symbol on end **40.00**

Pocket Knife, 3¼" l, metal, marbleized yellow plastic sides, orange and blue Trylon and Perisphere, orange inscription, Imperial **50.00**

Puzzle, 10 x 11½", cardboard, aerial view, Sloan's Liniment and company name in margin, orig box .. **25.00**

Ring, metal, raised Marine and Transport Building, adjustable, "New York 19" inscription on one band, other "39 World's Fair" **25.00**

Salt and Pepper Shakers, pr, metal, silver finish, Trylon and Perisphere shape, NYWF copyright **50.00**

Snowdome, 3" d glass, white bisque Trylon and Perisphere, 5¾" black

plastic ashtray base with orange and blue decal **40.00**

Table Knife, emb theme building ... **20.00**

Tray, 11½ x 17½", tin, litho, orange, blue and white design **40.00**

1962, SEATTLE, Century 21 Exposition

Cigarette Lighter, 9¼", chromed metal, tower shape, "Seattle USA/ Space Needle" inscription on base, unused **55.00**

Doll, 7½" h, plastic, jointed arms, white fabric gown, blue inscription on yellow sash, 9" h, plastic bell shape case with inscribed decal "Official Miss Seattle World's Fair; Seattle–1962" and fair symbol **25.00**

Pin, 1 x 2⅛", plastic, diecut, silver paint, rhinestone accents, Space Needle tower **30.00**

Plate, 10½", china, fairgrounds, green, yellow, and blue accents, white background, turquoise edge with silver stripe accent **20.00**

Pocket Knife, 3" l, metal, plastic inserts, Space Needle on one side, year and title on other, made by Colonial **15.00**

View Master Reels, titles "Space Needle By Night," "Monorail and Fairgrounds," "Space Needle By Day," "Architectural Wonders," and "Amazing Exhibits," set of 5 . **15.00**

1964, NEW YORK, New York World's Fair

Ashtray, 5 x 7½", china, blue Unisphere, yellow and brown skyline, dark brown edges, raised gold letter inscription **15.00**

Bank, 6" h, Unisphere, plastic, orig box **35.00**

Button, 1¾", orange and white on one half, other blue and white, Unisphere and "Peace Through Understanding" in black **15.00**

Charm, 1⅛", aluminum, Unisphere, metallic blue and orange accents, rim inscription **12.00**

Figure, 3" d, Unisphere, plastic, silvered metallic, black base inscribed in gold, diecut cardboard display **50.00**

Guide Book, 5 x 8", 312 pgs, Time-Life Books, ... **15.00**

Key Chain Tag, 1¼", brass, emb, Unisphere, text description on reverse with United States Steel Corp logo, 1961 copyright **10.00**

Plate, 10", china, white, seven fair attractions, gold floral design rim . **12.00**

Pocketknife, 2¼" l, orange and blue design on sides **10.00**

Nodder, 3½" d, Unisphere, dark blue

composition base, 1961 copyright, Made in Japan sticker **25.00**
Plate **25.00**
Postcard **12.00**
Puzzle, 10 x 14", frame tray, grounds scene illus, titled "Scene 1, New York World's Fair," Milton Bradley, 1964 copyright, orig wrapper **15.00**
Ring, flasher type, plastic, blue, image changes from Souvenir Of The New York World's Fair to Unisphere at night **10.00**
Tray, 8 x 11", litho, Unisphere and Avenue Of Flags, eggshell white rim, gold inscription **15.00**
Wall Plaque, 9", oval, plaster, raised Unisphere in center, blue accents, hanging cord **25.00**
1967, MONTREAL, Montreal Expo
Stickpin, ½", brass, diecut, maple leaf, cherry red enamel **10.00**
Tab, 1½", tin, litho, blue and white, US Pavilion, compliments of Avis car rental on reverse **12.00**
1976, PHILADELPHIA, Bicentennial
Charm, 1¼", metal, emb, fife and drum trio on one side, Statue of Liberty and 200 years of transportation on other **8.00**
Medal, 1½", brass, emb, raised Liberty Bell on one side, covered wagon family and Clinton, OK bank name on other **5.00**

WRIGHT, RUSSEL

Collecting Hints: Russel Wright worked for many different companies in addition to creating material under his own label, American Way. Wright's contracts with firms often called for the redesign of pieces which did not produce or sell well. As a result, several lines have the same item in more than one shape.

Wright was totally involved in design. Most collectors focus on his dinnerware; however, he also designed glassware, plastic items, textiles, furniture, and metal objects. Bleached and blonde furniture were part of his contributions. His early work in spun aluminum often is overlooked as is his later work in plastic for the Northern Industrial Chemical Company.

History: Russel Wright was an American industrial engineer with a design passion for domestic efficiency through simple lines. His streamlined influence is found in all aspects of living. Wright and his wife, Mary Small Einstein, wrote *A Guide To Easier Living* to explain the concepts.

Russel Wright was born in 1904 in Lebanon, Ohio. His first jobs included set designer and stage manager under the direction of Norman Bel Geddes. He later used this theatrical flair for his industrial designs, stressing simple clean lines. Some of his earliest designs were executed in polished spun aluminum. These pieces, designed in the mid-1930s, included trays, vases, teapots, and other items. Wright received awards from the Museum of Modern Art in 1950 and 1953. His designs garnered many other awards.

Among the companies for which Russel Wright did design work are Chase Brass and Copper, General Electric, Imperial Glass, National Silver Co., Shenango, and Steubenville Pottery Company. In 1983 a major exhibition of Wright's designs was held at the Hudson River Museum in Yonkers, New York, and at the Smithsonian's Renwick Gallery in Washington, D.C.

References: Ann Kerr, *Russel Wright And His Dinnerware: A Descriptive Price Guide*, privately printed, 1981; Ann Kerr, *The Steubenville Saga*, privately printed, 1979, out-of-print.

Creamer, American Modern, $7.50.

AMERICAN MODERN

Made by the Steubenville Pottery Company, 1939–59. Initially this pattern was issued in Seafoam Blue, Coral, Chartreuse Curry, Granite Gray, White and Bean Brown, also issued in Black Chutney, Cedar Green, Cantaloupe, and Glacier Blue. The Ideal Toy Co made a set of miniature dishes, which were distributed by Sears, Roebuck.

Ashtray or coaster **10.00**
Baker, 10¾" **15.00**
Celery, Black Chutney **17.50**
Children's Dishes, tumbler
Chartreuse Curry **35.00**
Coral **40.00**
Creamer, Chartreuse Curry **20.00**
Fruit Bowl, lug handle
Cedar Green **6.00**
Granite Gray **7.50**
Cup and Saucer, Granite Gray **5.00**
Gravy Boat, Granite Gray **10.00**
Pitcher, water, Chartreuse Curry **22.00**
Plate
6", bread and butter, Seafoam Blue . **3.00**

8¼", salad, Coral	**5.00**
10", dinner, Granite Gray	**6.00**
Salad Bowl, Cantaloupe	**24.00**
Salt and Pepper, pr	
Coral	**9.00**
Glacier Blue	**9.00**
Soup, lug handle, Granite Gray	**7.50**
Sugar, cov	
Chartreuse Curry	**20.00**
Granite Gray	**6.00**
Vegetable Bowl, Black Chutney	**14.00**

IROQUOIS

Made by the Iroquois China Co and Garrison Products, 1946–60s. Initially it was issued in Ice Blue, Forest Green, Avocado Yellow, Lemon Yellow, Nutmeg Brown, and Sugar White. Also issued in Lettuce Green, Charcoal, Ripe Apricot, Pink Sherbet, Parsley Green, Cantaloupe, Oyster Gray, Aqua, Brick Red, and Grayed-Blue. A patterned line was offered in 1959.

Bowl	
5"	
Avocado Yellow	**4.00**
Charcoal	**5.00**
5½"	
Avocado Yellow	**4.50**
Charcoal	**5.50**
Parsley Green	**4.50**
10", Ice Blue	**16.00**
Butter, cov, Avocado Yellow	**50.00**
Carafe, Sugar White	**40.00**
Casserole, cov, Nutmeg Brown, 2 qt ..	**20.00**
Cereal Bowl, Sugar White	**4.50**
Creamer and Sugar, stacking, Sugar White	**15.00**
Cup and Saucer	
Avocado Yellow	**5.00**
Brick Red	**10.00**

Pink Sherbet	**5.00**
Sugar White	**5.00**
Gumbo, Ice Blue	**12.00**
Mug, Nutmeg Brown	**15.00**
Plate	
7", luncheon	
Brick Red	**7.00**
Lemon Yellow	**3.00**
Lettuce Green	**3.00**
Pink Sherbet	**3.00**
Turquoise	**7.00**
9", dinner	
Avocado Yellow	**4.00**
Lettuce Green	**4.00**
Sugar White	**4.00**
10", dinner	
Brick Red	**10.00**
Turquoise	**10.00**
Platter	
13", Ice Blue	**10.00**
14", Avocado Yellow	**14.00**
Salt and Pepper Shakers, pr, stacking	
Ice Blue	**12.00**
Sugar White	**15.00**
Vegetable Bowl	
Avocado Yellow	**18.00**
Sugar White	**15.00**

WHITE CLOVER

Made by Harker China, 1951–55. Initially it was issued in Meadow Green, Coral Sand, Golden Spree, and Charcoal.

Cereal Bowl	**5.00**
Clock, General Electric	**60.00**
Cup	**6.00**
Pitcher, cov	**25.00**
Plate, 10" dinner	**8.00**
Saucer	**3.00**

PHOTO CREDITS

We wish to thank those who permitted us to photograph objects in their possession. Unfortunately, we are unable to identify the sources for all of our photographs; nevertheless, we are deeply appreciative to all who contributed to this and past editions, and to the editions of *Warman's Antiques and Their Prices.*

Arizona: Phoenix, Jim and Nancy Schaut, Don Stewart. **Arkansas**: Fairfield Bay, Doris and Burdell Hall. **California**: Carlsbad, Dan Golden; Leucadia, Fred L. Wilhelm; Moor Park, Tony and Jackie Anello; Claremont, Franklin Arnall; Oceanside, Lois Misiewicz; Sacramento, David Stone; San Francisco, Butterfields, Ken Prag; Santa Ana, Evalene Pulati; Redlands, Barbara Shaeffer; Woodlake, Lorie Cairns. **Connecticut**: New Canaan, Mildred Fishman; Stamford, Donal Markey, Donna Schilero; West Hartford, Arnold Chase; Westport, Tom Gallagher; Woodbury, Daria of Woodbury. **Delaware**: Lewes, The Price's, Sea Gert Antiques. **Florida**: Cape Coral, The Calico Cat, Elizabeth Clancey, The Collector's Den, Lois Nordlund, Lois Antiques, Sandra Martz, Country Closet Antiques; Clearwater Beach, Bill Wheeler, The Oar House; Ft. Myers, Ft. Myers Antique Mall, Mina Tinsley, Things Unlimited; Hollywood, Cynthia and Joseph Klein; Miami, Jack Seiderman; Miami Beach, Estelle Zalkin; Orlando, Peg Harrison, Harrison's Antiques. **Georgia**: Atlanta, Walter Glenn, Geode Ltd., Jim Marin, Art Deco Atlanta. **Illinois**: Arlington Heights, T. Johnson; Chicago, Dick and Bindy Bitterman, Eureka! Antiques and Collectibles; Danville, Mary Hamburg; Lislie, Susan Brown Nicholson; Mapleton, White's Antiques and Furniture Finishing; Monmouth, David and Betty Hallam; Northbrook, Al and Susan Bagdade, Norman Rockwell Museum; Peotone, Kathy Wojciechowski. **Iowa**: Spencer, Paul and Paula Brenner; Spirit Lake, Gaylord and Margaret Franken. **Kansas**: Witchita, M. D. Fountain. **Maine**: Kennebunk, Richard W. Oliver Auction & Art Gallery; Lewiston, Anne Williams; Oxford, Oxford Common; Topsham, Allan and Helen Smith, The Country House. **Maryland**: Baltimore, Kathie Diehl; Laurel, Ken Cohen, Julie Rich; Temple Hills, John Rosenberg. **Massachusetts**: Cambridge, Stan Tillotson; Hyannis Port, Richard A. Bourne, Inc.; Somerville, Richard W. Massiglia; Winchester, Lorry and Bruce Hanes, Dad's Follies; Worcester, Ralph R. Saarinen.

Michigan: Monroe, Herb and Joyce Krueger, Mostly Majolica; Utica, Virgil Rogers and David Graves, Avant-Garde; Warren, Marilyn Dipboye; West Bloomfield, Joan Collett Oates. **Minnesota**: Edina, Kevin Hancer. **Missouri**: Sedalia, Crystal and Leyland Payton; Springfield, Jo Cunningham. **New Hampshire**: Peterborough, Lee and Rally Dennis; Salem, Bea and Bill Laycock, B & B Antiques & Collectibles. **New Jersey**: Bellmawr, Angie Ricciaardi Antiques; Demarest, Mimi Rudnick, The Salt Lady Antiques; Hackensack, Roz Albert; Madison, Don Fiore, The Toy Man; Magnolia, Carol Pollock, Custom Covers; Montclair, Susan Morse; Moorestown, Cindy and James Townes, Ladybug's Cupboard; Morris Plains, Elyce Litts; New Egypt, Red Barn Antiques; Old Bridge, Sue Theurich, Respectable Collectables; Paterson, Edward W. Leach; Short Hills, Cynthia Klein, Joseph Klein, C. J. K. Kollectibles; Stewartsville, Marcia and Bob Weissman, Neat Olde Things; Toms River, Shelley, Norman and Phyllis Galinkin; West Orange, Barbara and Melvin Alpern; Woodcliff Lake, Joan Raines Antiques. **New York**: Auburn, Lower Lake Collectibles; Carmel, Bob Cahn, The Primitive Man; Elmsford, Gerald and Carol Newman; Fishkill, Robert A. Doyle; Livingston, Langes Steinworld; Malverne, Roselyn Gerson; New Platz, Charlotte and Larry Settle; New York, John High; Queens, Flamingoes; Valley Stream, Craig Dinner; Webster, Richard and Joan Randles, From The Cutter's Wheel; Woodstock, Frank N. Potter. **North Carolina**: Chapel Hill, Alda Horner, Whitehall Shop. **Ohio**: Akron, Betty Franks; Beachwood, Rita Orons; Canton, Lewis Bettinger; Cincinnati, Connie Rogers; Newton Falls, Bob and Kathy Wujcik; Novelty, Peggy Bialosky; Urbana, Parker's Antiques; Worthington, Betty Powell.

Pennsylvania: Adamstown, Dottie Freeman and Allan Teal; Allentown, The Borgmans, Wanamaker R.R. Depot Antiques, LeFevre's Antiques, Jim Lo Antiques, Phyllis and Alvin Kahn, The Pen Man's Antiques, Arlene Rabin, Edna Stauffer, Today & Yesterday; Bath, Roy Repsher; Bethlehem, Doris M. Squyres; Cabot, Clair Bargerstock; Coatesville, Chet Ramsay Antiques; Cogan Station, Roan Bros. Auction Gallery; Coopersburg, Bob Greenbaum, Neil and Clodogh Wotring; Danville, Lissa L. Bryan-Smith, Richard Smith, Holiday Antiques; Eagleville, Tyler's Antiques; Easton, Harold Mellor, Coach and Four Antiques; Elkins Park, Rose Sill, The Window Sill; Elysburg, John Fetterman; Emmaus, Anna M. Benner; Glen Rock, Ron Lieberman; Johnstown, Precious Metals Co; Lampeter, James S. Maxwell, Jr.; Leola, R. C. Lauchnor's Collectables; Lewisburg, John Selsam; Lititz, Doug Flynn and Al Bolton, Holloway House; Montgomeryville, Clarence and Betty Maier, Burmese Cruet; Montoursville, M. Jeanne Foust, Jeanne's Glass House; New Freedom, George Theofiles, Miscellaneous Man; New Hope, Debby Bogdan, Ferry Hill, Ted and Linda Freed; Northampton, David and Sue Irons, Irons Antiques; Oley, Mrs. Lena Eyrich; Orefield, Gloria Burkos, Gloria's Collectibles; Philadelphia, Shelly Hoffman, Ed Kelberg, Marcy Kula, Ed Volkrecht, Ed's Antiques, Inc., Murray and Selma Petersons; Pittsburgh, Regis and Mary Ferson, Edward Grzybowski; Pottsville, George and Tedi Hahn, Doorway To Glass; Quakertown, Doris Castellon, Brick House Antiques, Mary Webber, Webber's Antiques; Schnecksville, David Koch; Whitehall, Herb and Nancy Hallman, The Churn Antiques; Wilkes-Barre, Al Sallitt Antiques, Golden Webb Antiques; Williamsport, Michael Rath; Yardley, Ellie Archer; York, Lookenbill's Antiques.

South Dakota: Huron, Joan Hull. **Tennessee**: Elaine J. Luartes, Athena Antiques. **Texas**: Dallas, Ted Birbilis; Euless, The Stevensons; Ft. Worth, Gary L. Miller and K. M. Scotty Mitchell. **Utah**: Midvale, Clark Phelps. **Vermont**: Cavendish, Henry and Doris Sigourney, Sigourney's Antiques. **Virginia**: Arlington, Carolyn Smith; Crozet, Betty L. Loba, Rose Valley Antiques; Hopewell, Carolyn R. Morris, Yestermorrow's Collectibles and More; Portsmouth, Whitney Le Compte; Radford, Roy M. Collins. **Washington, D. C.**: Nancy McMichael. **Wisconsin**: Kaukauna, Ferill J. Rice. **Canada, Ontario**: Hamilton, Wray Martin.

INDEX

Year After Year Collectors Ask: "What does Warman's say?"

Warman's Antiques and Their Prices

For more than 40 years, *Warman's Antiques and Their Prices* has been the most useful price guide you can buy. It gives you the "critical edge" for buying and selling at flea markets, antique shows and auctions, and puts you on a par with the professionals.

- 50,000 items priced, with detailed descriptions
- Hundreds of American Pattern Glass designs
- 1,000 photographs, illustrations and factory marks
- Fully indexed for quick reference
- Published annually . . . always current

Warman's English & Continental Pottery & Porcelain
by Susan and Al Bagdade

A price and reference guide to the entire field. 200 makers, 1,000s of items, 600 + photos and factory marks, plus histories, references and collecting hints.   Paperback

Zalkin's Handbook of Thimbles & Sewing Implements
by Estelle Zalkin

A colorful new treasury of information covering 1,400 objects, 780 photographs and current prices. Useful histories and backgrounds on everything from thimbles and chatelaines to scissors and workboxes.   Hardcover

ALL NEW FOR 1989!

Wallace-Homestead Price Guide to American Country Antiques, Ninth Edition
by Don and Carol Raycraft

Country antiques gain in value with each passing year, and the Raycrafts' popular price guide is the collector's bible in this volatile field. The all-new ninth edition features 800 photographs of the best buys in furniture, pottery, decoys, kitchen and hearth utensils, and more. For the first time, it includes an in-depth section on how to buy country antiques at shows, antiques malls, and flea markets.Accurate, up-to-date prices and advice from a variety of experts are hallmarks of this bestselling series: here, collectors can study the authentic article and learn what its price is now in shops nationwide.   ANNUAL BEST SELLER! Paperback

Guide to Old Radios: Pointers, Pictures, and Prices
by David and Betty Johnson

Descriptions and price ranges for approximately 3300 radios. The history of radio, both the broadcast medium and the instrument itself. Speakers and cabinets, from the earliest days.   Paperback

American Clocks and Clockmakers
by Robert W. and Harriett Swedberg

Over 350 clocks available to today's collector are shown and described, with prices. Pricing guidelines and smart buying; a patent date chart; an invention chronology; list of leading American clockmakers; and a glossary of horological terms. Paperback

Wallace-Homestead Price Guide to Baskets, Second Edition
by Frances Johnson

A thorough revision and expansion, this edition provides historical background for hundreds of basket types, photographs to aid identification, construction and materials information, and detailed and accurate listings. The arrangement is alphabetical. Baskets included range from Indian to twentieth-century imports. All items are priced.

Frances Johnson has created more than a price guide. Readers will learn a great deal about how baskets have been made over the years; they will find this book a marvelous aid to developing their skills at identification. The author is well-known for Wallace-Homestead's *Antiques from the Country Kitchen.*   Paperback

Food and Drink Containers and Their Prices
by Al Bergevin

Classic examples of advertising memorabilia. Includes coffee and spice containers, food-stuff tins, boxes.   Paperback

Contemporary Fast-Food and Drinking Glass Collectibles
by Mark E. Chase and Michael Kelly

A generously illustrated, concise guide to thousands of collectible glasses. Geographic distribution, copyright data, realistic prices, and exact reproduction of wording.   Paperback

Steiff Toys Revisited
by Jean Wilson

Jean Wilson and Shirley Conway's *Steiff Teddy Bears, Dolls, and Toys With Prices,* published by Wallace-Homestead in 1984, is the foremost resource book currently available on Steiff collectibles. Since its publication Jean Wilson has assembled a wealth of new information about Steiff toys sold privately and at auctions and antiques shows, located many catalogs that were previously unpublished, traced the latest production offerings, established additional contacts with major collectors throughout the world, and published a Steiff newsletter. Jean shares the results of her efforts in *Steiff Toys Revisited.* With all this new information and accurate up-to-date prices, *Steiff Toys Revisited* is destined to become the new classic.   Paperback

Wallace-Homestead Price Guide to Plastic Collectibles
by Lyndi Stewart McNulty

Hundreds of illustrations and detailed descriptions. Plastics in advertising, appliances, toys, and timepieces.   Paperback

QUANT. TITLE	PRICE
_____ Warman's Antiques and Their Prices, 24th Ed. (W560-6)	$13.95
_____ Warman's English & Continental Pottery & Porcelain (W011-6)	$18.95
_____ Zalkin's Handbook of Thimbles & Sewing Implements (W014-0)	$24.95
_____ Wallace-Homestead Price Guide to American Country Antiques, Ninth Edition (W524-X)	$14.95
_____ Guide to Old Radios: Pointers, Pictures, and Prices (W518-5)	$16.95
_____ American Clocks and Clockmakers (W525-8)	$16.95
_____ Food and Drink Containers and Their Prices (W511-8)	$16.95
_____ Contemporary Fast-Food and Drinking Glass Collectibles (W517-7)	$16.95
_____ Wallace-Homestead Price Guide to Baskets, Second Edition (W542-8)	$16.95
_____ Steiff Toys Revisited (W538-X)	$18.95
_____ Wallace-Homestead Price Guide to Plastic Collectibles (W494-4)	$17.95

Method of payment—please check one:

_____ I have enclosed a check or money order made payable to Wallace-Homestead Book Company. Please include $2.00 for postage and handling for the first book, plus $ .50 for each additional book.

_____ Bill my MasterCard _____ Bill my VISA

Credit card # _____

Expiration date _____ Signature _____

Or call toll free 1-800-345-1214.

Ship to: _____

Name _____

Address _____

City _____ State _____ Zip _____

Telephone # _____

Wallace-Homestead Book Company
One Chilton Way, Radnor, Pennsylvania 19089